NARESH K. MALHOTRA

DAVID F. BIRKS

PETER WILLS

MARKETING RESEARCH

AN APPLIED APPROACH

FOURTH EDITION

PEARSON

Harlow, England • London • New York • Boston • San Francisco • Toronto • Sydney • Auckland • Singapore • Hong Kong
Tokyo • Seoul • Taipei • New Delhi • Cape Town • São Paulo • Mexico City • Madrid • Amsterdam • Munich • Paris • Milan

Pearson Education Limited
Edinburgh Gate
Harlow
Essex CM20 2JE
England

and Associated Companies throughout the world

Visit us on the World Wide Web at:
www.pearson.com/uk

Original 6th edition entitled *Marketing Research: An Applied Orientation* published by Prentice Hall, Inc.,
a Pearson Education company
Copyright © 2010 Prentice Hall Inc.

This edition published by Pearson Education Limited 2012

ISBN 978-0-273-72585-5

British Library Cataloguing-in-Publication Data
A catalogue record for this book is available from the British Library

Library of Congress Cataloging-in-Publication Data
A catalog record for this book is available from the Library of Congress

10 9 8 7 6
16

Typeset in 10/12pt Minion by 30
Printed and bound by Rotolito Lombarda, Italy

Brief contents

Contents

Supporting resources

Visit **www.pearsoned.co.uk/malhotra_euro** to find valuable online resources

Companion Website for students
- Annotated links to relevant sites on the web
- Online glossary
- Flashcards to test your knowledge of key terms and definitions
- Foreword by the managing director of *Sports Marketing Surveys*, who has provided many of the case studies throughout the book.

For instructors
- Complete, downloadable Instructor's Manual
- PowerPoint slides that can be downloaded and used for presentations

Also: The Companion Website provides the following features:
- Online help and support to assist with website usage and troubleshooting

For more information please contact your local Pearson Education sales representative or visit **www.pearsoned.co.uk/malhotra_euro**

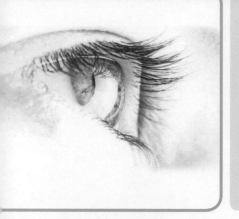

Preface

To the memory of Maria Birks

Marketing research opportunities

Working as a marketing researcher can be intellectually stimulating, creative and rewarding in so many ways. Stimulation, creativity and rewards are afforded by the opportunities in an industry and a discipline that continues to undergo huge changes. These opportunities may be seen as threats; there are many challenges inherent in huge change. Decision-makers that use marketing research are demanding greater value for their investment in research, a much quicker turnaround of research projects and more insight and integration of any information collected. The growth of social media has enabled decision-makers to learn characteristics of the nature, behaviour and motives of consumers in entirely new ways. This has opened up even more competition to marketing research, to add to competition from the suppliers of competitive intelligence, management consultants, customer database analysts, customer relationship management advisors, web analysts and DIY research. In addition, participants are clearly aware of the value of their knowledge and the time they give to researchers. Participants engage in social media activities in engaging and fun ways. They use mobile devices to communicate with and share experiences with family, friends and brands. Participants are more sceptical of the motives and value of surveys. They expect to be engaged and rewarded for their participation and to see studies conducted by responsible researchers of integrity. These challenges represent great opportunities for the researchers who develop and use their skills to fully embrace and engage with the changes occurring in today's business world.

Coping with technological and digital developments represent one of the most challenging skill developments. Marketing researchers must be able to cope with the mass of digital developments that are changing the manner in which established research methods are conducted and are creating new methods. Digital developments are fundamentally shaping how researchers plan, gather, analyse and interpret information. Researchers must be aware of the challenges faced by the array of managerial and design- based decision-makers who trust sound marketing research. They must be able to empathise with the people they aim to question and observe, and to treat them with care and respect. Creative researchers that rise to the emerging challenges can have a genuine impact at the board level of organisations and on the strategic direction of a company. Their future offers many stimulating ventures and great rewards.

Understanding the emerging marketing research challenges, developing creativity, finding the confidence to conduct research and to discover insight in findings may seem difficult with so many options to consider. This is where we believe *Marketing Research, An Applied Approach, 4th European Edition* can help. Founded on the enormously successful USA editions and the 1st, 2nd and 3rd European editions, this text aims to be comprehensive, authoritative and applied. This edition includes a greater array of European and international examples, practices and illustrations. It portrays a balance of qualitative and quantitative approaches to conducting research that allows the creative support of decision-makers. It will guide the reader through the challenges faced in conducting marketing research of the highest quality. This is achieved through an appropriate blend of scholarship with a highly applied and managerial orientation.

The 4th edition

The book is written for use at both the undergraduate and postgraduate levels. The coverage is comprehensive and the depth and breadth of topics are well suited to both levels. The material is presented in a manner that is easy to read and understand. There are numerous diagrams, tables and examples to help explain and illustrate the basic concepts. If a chapter does not cover a particular topic in sufficient depth, there are numerous references to follow a line of enquiry. The web addresses presented throughout allow for further illustration of ideas and in many instances, demonstration versions of software. The companion website presents a *Marketing Research Software* section, links to the book's companion Marketing Research agency – IMF Sports Marketing Surveys, more European cases, exercises and web links. We have retained the most desirable features of the previous USA and European editions. Changes have been made to improve the clarity of explanations, with many new examples and updated references.

The introduction of a new author, Peter Wills, to this edition has been fundamental in portraying just how important technological, digital and social media research developments are for researchers and how they are impacting upon the nature and scope of marketing research. All chapters have benefited from more up-to-date references and, where appropriate, more relevant examples that reflect the European and international focus. There has been more use of Conference papers from the European Society of Opinion and Marketing Research (ESOMAR) and the Market Research Society (MRS). These Conference papers reflect the thinking and practice of some of the most well regarded marketing research practitioners from across the globe.

The fourth edition contains major revisions that include:

1. *Updating.* New and updated material starts with Chapter 1 and continues throughout the text.
2. *A new chapter.* A new Chapter 25, 'Structural Equation Modeling and Path Analysis', completes our coverage of popular data analysis techniques. It explains structural equation modeling and path analysis from an intuitive perspective and presents the techniques in a simple and easy to understand manner, retaining the text's applied and managerial orientation.
3. *New material.* New and developing research methods and techniques are described and illustrated throughout the text. Technology and digital developments are driving many of these changes. Many of the changes are encapsulated at the end of each chapter, (except the quantitative data analysis chapters)

with a section entitled 'Digital developments in marketing research'. One of the major impacts of digital developments has been the growth of social media research techniques. Descriptions and examples of these techniques are presented throughout the text.

4. *New and updated examples.* New examples in the form of 'Real Research' and 'IMF Sports Marketing Surveys' are presented.
5. *New video cases.* Each chapter, except the quantitative data analysis chapters, is followed by a question related to a video case. The video cases are drawn from Pearson's video library and can be used to debate a great number of marketing research challenges.
6. *Added emphasis on SAS.* Relevant Chapters contain a special section on SAS Learning Edition, along with another on SPSS Windows, that illustrate the relevant programs and the steps required to run them.
7. *New SPSS and SAS Computerised Demonstration Movies.* We have created computerised demonstration films illustrating step-by-step instructions for running each data analysis procedure – SPSS and SAS – available for downloading from the website for this book.
8. *SPSS and SAS step-by-step instructions.* Each quantitative data analysis chapter contains separate step-by-step SPSS and SAS instructions for conducting the data analysis presented in the book using SPSS as well as SAS. These are available at the text website for downloading.
9. *SNAP and NVivo demonstrations.* On the text's website, we describe and illustrate the use of Snap Survey Software. Snap enables you to design and analyse web, paper, kiosk, email, phone, PDA and Tablet questionnaires. The demonstration version of Snap comes with a Getting Started Guide with training videos. We also describe and illustrate the use of NVivo qualitative data analysis software. NVivo enables you to: organise qualitative data and your thoughts; develop and refine ideas giving meaning and theoretical propositions of what is 'seen' in qualitative data; share and report findings. The website link takes you to a full working version of NVivo that you can use for a period of three months. NVivo comes with an Animated Tutorial and a series of case studies.
10. *Updated references.* Each chapter contains many references dated 2010 or later. Of course the classic references have been retained.

Integrated Learning Package

If you take advantage of the following special features, you should find this textbook engaging, thought provoking and even fun.

1. *Balanced orientation.* We have blended scholarship with a highly applied and managerial orientation showing how researchers apply concepts and techniques and how managers use their findings to improve marketing practice. In each chapter, we discuss real marketing research challenges to support a great breadth of marketing decisions.

2. *Real-life examples.* Real-life examples (Real Research) describe the kind of marketing research that companies use to address specific managerial problems and how they implement research to great effect.

3. *Hands-on approach.* You will find more real-life scenarios and exercises in every chapter. The end of chapter exercises challenge you to research online, role play as a researcher and a marketing manager. You can tackle real-life marketing situations in which you assume the role of a consultant and recommend research and marketing management decisions.

4. *International focus.* Every chapter has a section entitled 'International Marketing Research' (except the quantitative data analysis chapters). As digital developments are breaking down many cultural and communication barriers, many of the examples used throughout each chapter address international research challenges.

5. *Ethics focus.* Ethical issues are pervasive in marketing research. The development and implementation of research codes of practice gives integrity to the marketing research profession and distinguishes the practice from many other forms of data gathering. Every chapter has a section entitled 'Ethics in Marketing Research' (except the quantitative data analysis chapters). Additional examples that address ethical issues are presented throughout the text.

6. *Digital development focus.* We will show you how online research activities have impacted upon the thinking, planning and practice of marketing research. Technological and digital developments are continually shaping the nature and value of research practice. Every chapter has a section entitled 'Digital Developments in Marketing Research' (except the quantitative data analysis chapters). Additional examples that address technological and digital developments and their impact upon research practice are presented throughout the text.

7. *Contemporary focus.* We apply marketing research to current challenges such as customer value, experiential marketing, satisfaction, loyalty, customer equity, brand equity and management, innovation, entrepreneurship, relationship marketing, creativity and design, and socially responsible marketing throughout the text.

8. *Statistical software.* We illustrate data analysis procedures with emphasis upon SPSS and SAS. Separate SPSS Windows and SAS Learning Edition sections in the relevant chapters discuss the programs and the steps you need to run them. On our website we also describe and illustrate the use of Snap survey software and NVivo qualitative data analysis software.

9. *Running cases based on the work of IFM Sports Marketing Surveys.* Cases are presented throughout the text from the portfolio of projects undertaken by IFM Sports Marketing Surveys. This research agency specialises in providing market insight and strategic consultancy within the sports, sponsorship, leisure and tourism industries. They are an independent research agency with full service capability. With offices on every continent, IFM Sports Marketing Surveys have extensive in-house capability for multi-country studies.

10. *Companion website.* The companion website has been updated to reflect the changes in this edition. There are new European case studies with discussion points and questions to tackle. All the referenced websites on the text are described with notes of key features to look for on a particular site.

11. *Instructors manual.* The instructor's manual is very closely tied to the text, but is not prescriptive in how the material should be handled in the classroom. The manual offers teaching suggestions, answers to all end-of-chapter questions, Professional Perspective discussion points, and case study exercises. The manual includes PowerPoint slides, incorporating all the new figures and tables.

12. *Photography.* With the growth of social media, consumers are expressing characteristics of their behaviour, attitudes and emotions through the use of photographs. Marketing research students benefit enormously from a development of visual awareness, both in engaging with research participants and with research users, especially in the visualisation of data. To support a visual awareness, we see the photographs in this text as a means to encapsulate the essence of marketing research and its challenges. Some of the images in this edition have a serious intent, linking a particular image to concepts and aiding the recall of a concept. Others are there to lighten the sometimes-difficult technical passages. In their own right, each image has many technical and artistic merits.

Acknowledgements

Many people have been most generous in helping to write the four European editions.

In developing the critical approach I take in marketing research practice and writing, I must thank my Consumer Behaviour teacher and PhD supervisor, John

Southan of the University of Salford. My friend and former work colleague, the late Kevin Fogarty, retains a special distinction for his humour, creativity and for shaping many of the values I hold dear.

In putting together the IFM Sports Marketing Surveys cases, Erica Greer helped me immensely in gaining access to material generated in some of her most compelling research projects. She worked with great patience, humour and diligence to get just the right material I was looking for. In working through the Digital Developments in Marketing Research, colleagues and associates of Association for Survey Computing (ASC) have been of great help. In particular, I have had excellent support and advice from ASC member Tim Macer, Honorary Research Fellow at the University of Winchester. In evaluating the emergent skills and development of future researchers I have had excellent support from Danny Wain, Honorary Knowledge Exchange Fellow at the University of Winchester. For his critique, insight and excellent feedback I am most grateful to Dr Johan van Rekom of the Erasmus University, Rotterdam.

To Rachel Gear at Pearson Education with whom I planned and delivered this edition, I have so much for which to thank you. I have really enjoyed our working relationship and your totally positive outlook. Sharing our stories of family holidays and trips to the glorious North Devon coast helped me in so many ways. Rachel introduced and managed relationships with an array of excellent Pearson colleagues; the team support has been great. Her guidance and vision have been superb, I could not have asked for more.

At Pearson Education the book has come together with the help of Tim Parker, Desk Editor; Kelly Miller who designed the cover; Kevin Ancient who helped with the internal design; and Emma Violet, Editorial Assistant. I would also like to thank Paul Silk and George White who introduced and tutored me in the use of the Pearson Online Database (POD). POD is a rich resource of visuals; I enjoyed learning how to use this database and especially working with the amazing images that were available to me

Last but by no means least, to be able to find the time and space to write; the love, support and understanding of your family is vital. Since the 3rd edition, I have lost my beautiful mother. The love and values of Maria Birks are always with me. To my partner Helen, enormous thanks and love for all that you give to me and to my beautiful son Jesse, who with Helen brings me so much laughter, inspiration and light.

David F. Birks

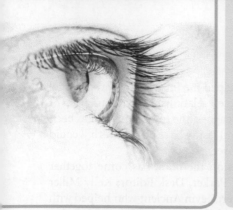

Guided tour

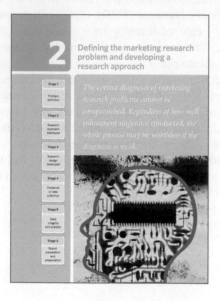

Stage flowcharts show how the chapter fits into the six stages of the marketing research process.

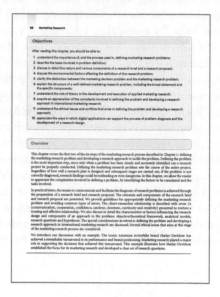

Objectives at the beginning of each chapter outline what you should expect to learn from the chapter.

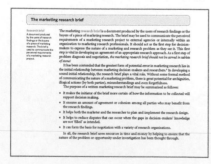

Margin definitions highlight the key terms in the text. A **Glossary** of these terms is provided at the end of the book and on the website at **www.pearsoned. co.uk/malhotra_euro**

Focus on IFM Sports Marketing surveys is a set of sports marketing case studies that run throughout the text, including material on the Moving motor show and the BAFTAs.

The **Real Research** boxes provide an invaluable insight into how marketing research theory is applied to a number of businesses.

International marketing research shows how different aspects of the marketing research process fit into an international context.

Ethics in Marketing Research focuses on the ethical practice of the marketing research and the dilemmas that researchers face.

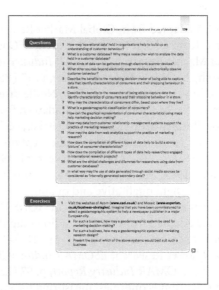

Test yourself at the end of each chapter with a set of **Questions.**

Exercises help you to apply what you have learnt, by testing your understanding in a practical context.

Digital applications in marketing research illustrate the impact of technology and the Internet on marketing research.

Publisher's acknowledgements

We are grateful to the following for permission to reproduce copyright material:

Figures

Figure 6.2 from Changing the culture of a hospital: from hierarchy to network, *Public Administration*, 78(3), 487 (Bate, S.P. 2000); Figures on page 924, page 925 from Snap Surveys.

Screenshots

Screenshot on page 315 from Khan, R., Managing Director, Cobalt Sky; Screenshot on page 915 from E-Tabs

Tables

Table 1.2 adapted from Global Market Research, *ESOMAR Industry Report*, pp. 92–3 (ESOMAR 2010); Table 1.3 adapted from Global Market Research, *ESOMAR Industry Report*, p. 6 (ESOMAR 2010); Table 1.4 adapted from Global Market Research, *ESOMAR Industry Report*, p. 16 (ESOMAR 2010); Table 1.5 adapted from Global Market Research, *ESOMAR Industry Report*, p. 17 (ESOMAR 2010); Table on page 44 adapted from From consumer connection to consumer insight: a Nestle case study, *ESOMAR Consumer Insights Conference, Milan*, May (Blachowska, M. 2007); Table 4.1 adapted from Brownlie, D., 'Environmental scanning' in *The Marketing Book*, 3rd ed., Butterworth-Heinemann (Baker, M.J. 1994) p. 158, ISBN: 978-0-7506-2022-2; Table 6.1 from Divided by a common language: diversity and deception in the world of global marketing, *Journal of the Market Research Society*, 38(2), p. 105, April (Goodyear, M. 1996); Table 6.2 from Jill Collis and Roger Hussey, *Business Research* published 1997, Macmillan Business, reproduced with permission of Palgrave Macmillan; Table 6.3 adapted from Research design: qualitative and quantitative approaches by CRESWELL, JOHN W. Copyright 1994 Reproduced with permission of SAGE PUBLICATIONS INC BOOKS in the format Textbook via Copyright Clearance Center. Table 7.2 adapted from Online audio group discussions, a comparison with face to face methods, *International Journal of Market Research*, 51(2), pp. 219–41 (Cheng, C.C., Krumwiede, D. and Sheu, C. 2009); Table 10.5 from Global Market Research, *ESOMAR Industry Report*, p. 102 (ESOMAR 2010); Table 10.6 from Global Market Research, *ESOMAR Industry Report*, p. 97 (ESOMAR 2010); Table on page 493 adapted from Women in the world's Muslim economies: measuring the effectiveness of empowerment, *ESOMAR Annual Congress, Berlin*, September (Feld, K. 2007); Table 26.2 adapted from *Globalpark Annual Market Research Software Survey 2010*, Seventh annual survey, meaning ltd (Macer, T. and Wilson, S. 2011).

Text

Epigraph on page 151 from The research industry needs to embrace radical change in order to thrive and survive in the digital era, *Annual Conference* (Woodnutt, T. and Owen, R. 2010), Market Research Society; Example on pages 572–3 from How was it for you?, *Research*, July, pp. 8–9 (Park, C. 2000), Fieldwork Supplement, Originally published in *Research* magazine – www.research-live.com. Republished with permission.

Photos

1, 400, 460 Digital Vision. Steve Rawlings; 11, 37, 46, 174, 325, 491, 584, 597, 918 Photodisc; 23 Nick White. Image Source; 28, 117, 219, 267, 497, 576, 965, 979 Photodisc. Photolink; 41, 64, 75, 151, 156, 162, 182, 199, 232, 246, 276, 285, 293, 373, 407, 449, 506, 577, 589, 636, 649, 664, 728, 744, 749, 778, 793, 801, 821, 829, 846, 863, 886, 951 Imagestate. John Foxx Collection; 84, 616 Pearson Education Ltd. Jules Selmes; 98 Photodisc. Cole Publishing Group. Ernie Friedlander; 106, 663 Photodisc. Getty Images; 113, 369, 737, 959 Digital Stock; 135 Philip Parkhouse; 137 Photodisc. Ryan McVay; 185 Photodisc. Buccina Studios; 213 Photodisc. Cartesia; 253 Ian Cartwright. Imagestate; 270 Photodisc. Cole Publishing Group. Patricia Brabant; 288 H. Wiesenhofer. Photolink. Photodisc; 310, 338, 802 Image Source; 355 Digital Vision. Rod Steele; 361 Comstock Images. Alamy; 376 Digital Vision. Rob van Petten; 413, 438, 528, 554, 633, 904 Photodisc. Steve Cole; 433 Photodisc. Lawrence M. Sawyer; 466, 476 Digital Vision; 518 Photodisc. Steve Mason; 540 Dex Image. Yoshio Sawargai. Alamy; 545 BananaStock; 562 Photodisc. Photolink. Jack Star; 570 James Hardy. PhotoAlto. Getty Images; 601 Pearson Education Ltd. Lord and Leverett; 687, 854 Photodisc. Siede Preis Photography; 695 Jack Hollingsworth. Photos.com. Jupiterimages; 703 Photodisc. Nancy R. Cohen; 722 Photodisc. Geostock; 758 Stockdisc. Getty Images; 772 Jupiter Images. Brand X. Alamy; 792 Rob Judges. Pearson Education Ltd; 815 Photodisc. Daisuke Morita; 835 Photodisc. Photolink. C. Sherburn; 864 Photodisc. John A. Rizzo; 877 Photodisc. Lawrence Lawry; 900 Digital Vision. Getty Images; 930 PhotosIndia.com LLC. Alamy; 947 Stockbyte; 953 Photodisc. Duncan Smith; 965 Photodisc. Photolink; 975 Photodisc. Nick Rowe.

In some instances we have been unable to trace the owners of copyright material, and we would appreciate any information that would enable us to do so.

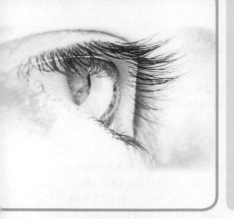

About the authors

Dr Naresh K. Malhotra is Regents' Professor, DuPree College of Management, Georgia Institute of Technology. He is listed in *Marquis Who's Who in America*, 51st Edition (1997), 52nd Edition (1998), 53rd Edition (1999), and in the *National Registry of Who's Who* (1999).

In an article by Wheatley and Wilson (1987 AMA Educators' Proceedings), Professor Malhotra was ranked number one in the country based on articles published in the *Journal of Marketing Research* from 1980 to 1985. He also holds the all-time record for the most publications in the *Journal of Health Care Marketing*. He is ranked number one based on publications in the *Journal of the Academy of Marketing Science* (JAMS) from its inception through volume 23, 1995. He is also number one based on publications in JAMS from 1986 to 1995. He is listed as one of the best researchers in marketing in John Fraedrich, 'The best researchers in marketing', Marketing Educator (Summer 1997), p. 5.

He has published more than 75 papers in major refereed journals including the *Journal of Marketing Research, Journal of Consumer Research, Marketing Science, Journal of Marketing, Journal of Academy of Marketing Science, Journal of Retailing, Journal of Health Care Marketing*, and leading journals in statistics, management science and psychology. In addition, he has also published numerous refereed articles in the proceedings of major national and international conferences. Several articles have received research awards.

He was Chairman, Academy of Marketing Science Foundation, 1996–1998, and was President, Academy of Marketing Science, 1994–1996, and Chairman of the Board of Governors from 1990 to 1992. He is a Distinguished Fellow of the Academy and Fellow of the Decision Sciences Institute. He serves as an Associate Editor of *Decision Sciences Journal* and has served as Section Editor, Health Care Marketing Abstracts, *Journal of Health Care Marketing*. Also, he serves on the Editorial Boards of eight journals.

His book entitled *Marketing Research: An Applied Orientation*, Sixth Edition, was published by Prentice Hall, Inc in 2010. An International Edition and an Australian Edition of his book have also been published, along with a Spanish translation. The book has received widespread adoption at both the graduate and undergraduate levels with more than 100 schools using it in the USA.

Dr Malhotra has consulted for business, non-profit and government organisations in the USA and abroad and has served as an expert witness in legal and regulatory proceedings. He is the winner of numerous awards and honours for research, teaching and service to the profession.

Dr Malhotra is a member and Deacon, First Baptist Church of Atlanta. He lives in the Atlanta area with his wife, Veena, and children, Ruth and Paul.

Dr David Frederick Birks is a Professor in Marketing at Winchester Business School, the University of Winchester, England. He teaches quantitative and qualitative marketing research and is leading developments across the University in digital marketing research. David moved to Winchester Business School after a period of four years working at Winchester School of Art, the University of Southampton. With the growth and impact of social media research upon marketing research thinking and practice, the School of Art played a major role in his thoughts on emerging data capture, analysis and presentation techniques in marketing research. David has lectured at the School of Management at the University of Southampton where he designed and was Programme Director for their MSc in Marketing Analytics. He has also lectured at the Universities of Bath, Strathclyde and Salford. In the School of

Management at the University of Bath he was the Director of Studies for their Executive MBAs in Malaysia and China, and their Postgraduate Research Programme. David's publications have covered the fields of Housing, Statistics, Marketing and Information Systems. In the field of Information Systems he has co-edited a 2012 special edition on the use of Grounded Theory in Information Systems Research, for the European Journal of Information Systems. In 2011 David co- chaired and edited the Association of Survey Computing's (ASC) 6th International Conference, 'Shifting the Boundaries of Research', at the University of Bristol. He is an active committee member of the ASC, being committed to their agenda of sharing best thinking and practice in the use of technology in research.

 **Peter Wills** is the Chairman of Snap Surveys and Honorary Knowledge Exchange Fellow at the University of Winchester. He brings his distinguished expert knowledge of technology within the marketing research industry to this new edition. Peter founded Snap Surveys in 1981 to develop software products for desktop computers. Snap Surveys were the first company to create a desktop-based system for analysing surveys. From this point he led the expansion of their product line into areas such as web based surveys, scanning, and multimode data capture, along with additional services to provide outsourced data processing services, consultancy and training. Peter set up a US operation in 1995 to support North and South American Snap Survey users. He now oversees a staff of 70 in the UK and the US, with a client base of 30,000 users in both the public and private sector across the globe. Peter was responsible in 1992 for proposing an industry standard for the interchange of survey information between competing software products. This initiative has flourished and continues to operate as triple-s www.triple-s.org. He is the Chairman of the Association for Survey Computing, the world's leading society for the advancement of knowledge in software and technology for research surveys and statistics.

1 Introduction to marketing research

Stage 1

Problem definition

Stage 2

Research approach developed

Stage 3

Research design developed

Stage 4

Fieldwork or data collection

Stage 5

Data integrity and analysis

Stage 6

Report preparation and presentation

Researchers support decision-makers by collecting, analysing and interpreting information needed to identify and solve marketing problems.

Objectives

After reading this chapter, you should be able to:

1 understand the nature and scope of marketing research and its role in supporting the design and implementation of successful marketing decisions;

2 describe a conceptual framework for conducting marketing research as well as the steps of the marketing research process;

3 distinguish between problem identification and problem-solving marketing research;

4 appreciate the impact that the Research 2.0 movement is having on the nature of the marketing research industry;

5 appreciate the relative values and importance of marketing research in regions and countries throughout the world;

6 understand the types and roles of research suppliers, including internal and external, full-service and limited-service suppliers;

7 understand why some marketers may be sceptical of the value of marketing research;

8 appreciate the demands for researchers to supplement their technical research skills with managerial skills;

9 appreciate the complexities involved in international marketing research;

10 understand the basis of ethical aspects of marketing research and the responsibilities that marketing research stakeholders have to themselves, each other and to the research project;

11 appreciate how digital developments are shaping the manner in which marketing research is planned and conducted.

Overview

Marketing research comprises one of the most important and fascinating facets of marketing. In this chapter, we describe the nature and scope of marketing research, emphasising its role of supporting marketing decision making, and provide several real-life examples to illustrate the basic concepts of marketing research. We give a formal definition of marketing research and show how this links to a six-stage description of the marketing research process. This description is extended to illustrate many of the interconnected activities in the marketing research process. We then subdivide marketing research into two areas: problem identification and problem-solving research. The extent and growth rates of marketing research expenditure throughout the world are then presented, followed by an overview of marketing research suppliers and services.

The marketing research industry is going through a huge change process. Much of this change derives from technological developments that are affecting how consumers engage with brands. The emergence and growth of Web 2.0 and subsequent technological developments to Web 3.0 have resulted in many authors and practitioners arguing that fundamental questions need to be asked of traditional notions of marketing research. These arguments and the emergence of the concept of Research 2.0 will be presented. There are many successful marketing decisions that have been founded upon sound marketing research; however, marketing research does not replace decision making. Justifying investment in marketing research is evaluated along with the challenges facing marketing research as an industry. These challenges and the demands upon the marketing research industry are creating new ways for researchers to design and produce research that are actionable and relevant to marketing decision-makers. To capitalise upon these opportunities, the skills required of contemporary researchers are evaluated. Many individual examples will be presented to illustrate the managerial challenges of making marketing research actionable and relevant. Beyond these individual examples we showcase the exciting work of IFM Sports Marketing Surveys. This independent marketing research agency has specialised in the sponsorship and sports industry over the past 25 years. The sports industry and many sponsorship deals are often multi-country in their reach and activity, and to meet these challenges IFM Sports Marketing Surveys has the capability of working and reporting on a worldwide basis, in over 200 countries, for events such as the Olympic Games and the Football World Cup. Work from many projects conducted by IFM Sports Marketing Surveys will be used as running examples throughout this book.

The topic of international marketing research is introduced. International marketing research will be discussed systematically in subsequent chapters and will be tackled in a dedicated chapter. The ethical aspects of marketing research and the responsibilities that marketing research stakeholders have to themselves, to each other and to the research project are presented and developed in more detail throughout the text. Finally, a general introduction to the impact of digital applications in marketing practices upon marketing research thinking and practice is made. Specific issues and examples relating to the impact of digital applications will be integrated throughout each chapter with key notes summarised at the end of each chapter.

What does marketing research encompass?

The term 'marketing research' is broad in meaning and application. This breadth will be explored and illustrated throughout this chapter. What will become apparent is that it is related to supporting marketing decision making in many traditional and new digital manners. The following example illustrates a contemporary marketing research approach adopted by easyJet and the applications supported by this approach.

Real research | Co-creating the future – the easyJet community[1]

easyJet was one of the first airlines to embrace the opportunity of the Internet when it sold its first seat online in April 1998. easyJet established a research function in 2006 using an array of traditional research methods to generate consumer insight. As a relatively new and limited research function, easyJet faced a great breadth of research requirements working on a very tight budget; it conducted a significant amount of research via email and used databases to conduct a limited number of consumer panels; and it wished to supplement its traditional research methods with a properly conducted online research community. To make this community effective, easyJet wanted a community that was: properly managed, active, with non-participating members quickly replaced; an open channel of communication so that members felt involved and would have an ongoing dialogue; able to dovetail with other more traditional research methods; moderated to ensure the development of conversations that would provide an enhanced level of understanding; used to support and fit with the key approaches of its existing research programme; and in ultimately moving towards 'co-creating the future', it clearly saw this as an innovative way to stay ahead of their competition. The easyJet Community was launched in 2008 and consists of 2,000 active participants who had flown with it in the previous 12 months. New discussion topics were introduced each week, with members receiving an email inviting them to take part in a specific discussion and/or survey. All of those taking part in the community were entered into a monthly prize draw with the chance to win a free pair of return flights to an easyJet destination. Some of the types of research covered with example topic areas included: advertising and brand communications; brand strategy; concept testing and development; customer experience and service delivery; network development; customer understanding; and the website. As well as the breadth of research objectives met by the community, a main benefit for easyJet was the ability to provide findings more quickly than traditional approaches.

The use of a variety of techniques is vital to support a variety of key marketing decisions. The following two examples from Philips and Orange demonstrate something of the breadth of marketing research techniques, applications and the use of digital technology. They further illustrate how integral well-designed and crafted marketing research can be to sound decision making.

Real research | **From dream to purchase**[2]

Products like FTVs (Flat Televisions, LCD + plasma), MP3s, PCs, mobile phones, PlayStation, Xbox, Wii, TiVo, iPod with Tunes, the BlackBerry, digital cable box, iPhone, Bluray have completely transformed consumer experiences. In order to respond to these experiences, most technology companies have changed, particularly in their product development processes. There is now much more involvement of the consumer in design innovation and new product development. Despite this involvement, Philips believed that it was still missing consumer understanding of consumer behaviour in store and what consumers' needs are in the purchase process of digital products. To rectify this, Philips conducted shopper insight studies in several European countries and the USA. The research approach took account of three differentiated and interconnected stages in the shopping–buying process: Philips concluded that copying traditional fast-moving consumer goods (FMCG) research approaches did not work and new models needed to be developed. In strong cooperation with retailers, Philips was able to experiment with a new way of conducting shopper research. Philips wanted to learn about the end user, shopper and browser/buyer, and about their shopping and buying process. It decided to conduct focus groups to learn about the end users and to understand their needs and perceptions of different retailers. For the shopping and buying process it interviewed consumers on the shop floor in front of product displays. Retailers had to provide permission to recruit consumers for focus groups in front of displays and for the interviews on the shop floor. Philips felt it had to catch consumers at the right moment, in store, in front of a display, considering or buying a product. Before actually buying digital products, Philips learned that consumers go through a process which they called 'defining the need stage'. Surprisingly every consumer in Europe and the USA went more or less through the same clear sequence of consideration process. Looking at the purchase process, Philips learned that for most consumers it was quite a long process. Word of mouth was extremely important and the role of the children was underestimated by manufacturers and retailers.

Real research | **When time is of the essence**[3]

Decision-makers cannot afford to wait weeks for the results of a survey, especially in areas such as advertising and public relations – 'immediate' responses may be needed. This is something that mobile research is extremely good at doing. In a study conducted by The 3rd Degree (**www.the3rddegree.co.uk**) and Ipsos MORI (**www.ipsos-mori.com**) for Orange, a questionnaire was issued to a panel of 1,000 business decision-makers just minutes after the Chancellor of the Exchequer's (the UK's finance minister's) budget speech at lunchtime. In just three hours, sufficient responses had been received to report on. The vast majority of responses arrived in the first hour and a great many arrived almost instantaneously. Such an approach can work well in achieving the following:

1 To reach key business decision-makers, a tough target group of busy people, many of whom will be in meetings or out and about over the course of a day, without access to the Internet or office phone.

2 To react almost instantly to a major event. In this case a key political one but it could just as easily be in response to a major advertising campaign or a competitor's campaign.

In this case, the study fulfilled the objectives with regard to reach, speed, quality and cost. The data gathered from this were in the press by the evening and were widely followed up by major news titles the next morning and over to the Sunday newspapers.

These examples illustrate only a few of the methods used to conduct marketing research, which may range from highly structured surveys with large samples to open-ended, in-depth interviews with small samples; from the collection and analysis of readily available data to the generation of 'new' quantitative and qualitative data; from personal face-to-face interactions to remote observations and interactions with consumers via the Internet; from small local studies to large global studies. This book will introduce you to the full complement of marketing research techniques and challenges. These examples also illustrate the crucial role played by marketing research in designing and implementing successful marketing plans.[4] This book will also introduce you to a broad range of marketing applications supported by marketing research.

The role of marketing research can be better understood in light of a basic marketing paradigm depicted in Figure 1.1. The emphasis in marketing, as illustrated in the Philips example above, is on understanding customer experiences and the delivery of satisfaction. To understand customer experiences and to implement marketing strategies and plans aimed at delivering satisfying experiences, marketing managers need information about customers, competitors and other forces in the marketplace. In recent years, many factors have increased the need for more accurate and timely information. As firms have become national and international in scope, the need for information on larger and more distant markets has increased. As consumers have become more affluent, discerning and sophisticated, marketing managers need better information on how they will respond with new products and other new experiences. As competition has become more intense, managers need information on the effectiveness of their

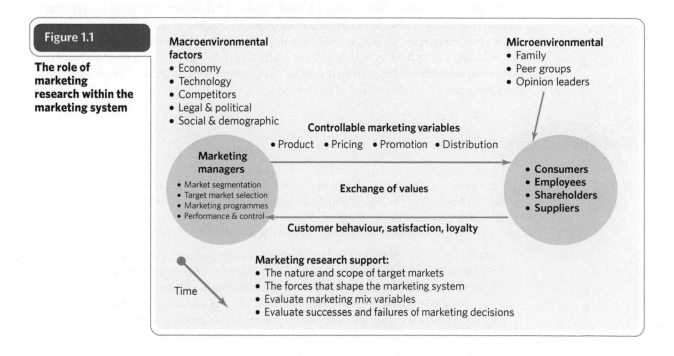

Figure 1.1

The role of marketing research within the marketing system

marketing tools. As the environment is changing more rapidly, marketing managers need more timely information to cope with the impact of changes.[5]

Marketers make decisions about what they see as potential opportunities and problems, i.e. a process of identifying issues. They go on to devise the most effective ways to realise these opportunities and overcome problems they have identified. They do this based on a 'vision' of the distinct characteristics of the target markets and customer groups. From this 'vision' they develop, implement and control marketing programmes. This 'vision' of markets and subsequent marketing decisions may be complicated by the interactive effects of an array of environmental forces that shape the nature and scope of target markets. These forces also affect the marketers' ability to deliver experiences that will satisfy their chosen target markets. Within this framework of decision making, marketing research helps the marketing manager link the marketing variables with their environment and customer groups. It helps remove some of the uncertainty by providing relevant information about marketing variables, environment and consumers.

The role of the researcher in supporting the marketing decision-maker can therefore be summarised as helping to:

- describe the nature and scope of customer groups;
- understand the nature of forces that shape customer groups;
- understand the nature of forces that shape the marketer's ability to satisfy targeted customer groups;
- test individual and interactive variables that shape consumer experiences;
- monitor and reflect upon past successes and failures in marketing decisions.

Traditionally, researchers were responsible for designing and crafting research of great integrity and providing relevant information support, while marketing decisions were made by the managers. The clarity and distinction of these roles are blurring somewhat. Researchers are becoming more aware of decision making; conversely, marketing managers are becoming more aware of research and the use of an eclectic array of data sources that can support their decision making. This trend can be attributed to better training of marketing managers and advances in technology; we will discuss this in more detail towards the end of this chapter. There has also been a shift in the nature and scope of marketing research, where increasingly marketing research is being undertaken not only on an ongoing basis, but sometimes even on a 'real-time' basis rather than perhaps a traditional notion of research being in response to specific marketing problems or opportunities on an ad hoc basis.[6] Major shifts are occurring in the marketing research industry that are impacting upon the perceived nature and value of marketing research.[7] The nature of these shifts and their impact upon new approaches to marketing research will be addressed later in this chapter. The current and developing role of marketing research is recognised in its definition.

Definition of marketing research

The European Society for Opinion and Marketing Research (ESOMAR) bases its view of marketing research in the 2004 definition approved by the American Marketing Association. For the purpose of this book, which emphasises the need for information of the highest integrity in the support of decision making, marketing research is defined as follows:

> *Marketing research is the function that links the consumer, customer, and public to the marketer through information—information used to identify and define marketing opportunities and problems; generate, refine, and evaluate marketing actions; monitor marketing performance; and improve understanding of marketing as a process. Marketing research specifies the information required to address these issues, designs the*

Marketing research
Marketing research is the function that links the consumer, customer, and public to the marketer through information — information used to identify and define marketing opportunities and problems; generate, refine, and evaluate marketing actions; monitor marketing performance; and improve understanding of marketing as a process. Marketing research specifies the information required to address these issues, designs the method for collecting information, manages and implements the data collection process, analyzes the results, and communicates the findings and their implications. (American Marketing Association)

Market research
Market research is the systematic gathering and interpretation of information about individuals or organisations using the statistical and analytical methods and techniques of the applied social sciences to gain insight or support decision making. The identity of participants[8] will not be revealed to the user of the information without explicit consent and no sales approach will be made to them as a direct result of their having provided information. (ESOMAR)

method for collecting information, manages and implements the data collection process, analyzes the results, and communicates the findings and their implications.

Several aspects of this definition are noteworthy. It stresses the role of 'linking' the marketer to the consumer, customer and public to help improve the whole process of marketing decision making. It also sets out the challenges faced by marketing decision-makers and thus where research support can help them make better decisions and/or decisions with lower risks.

There can be some confusion with the distinctions between marketing research and market research. These distinctions can be important as, in general, many research practitioners across Europe see their industry in a slightly different way to the USA. ESOMAR defines market research as follows:

> *Market research is the systematic gathering and interpretation of information about individuals or organisations using the statistical and analytical methods and techniques of the applied social sciences to gain insight or support decision making. The identity of participants will not be revealed to the user of the information without explicit consent and no sales approach will be made to them as a direct result of their having provided information.*

This definition still sees a focus upon the consumer to support decision making but does not explicitly refer to the broader context in which this works. It is worth noting the ethical dimension of this definition, i.e. in the protection of the identity of individuals who participate in research. This point will be developed more at the end of this chapter and developed further in every chapter. The final point of note is the use of the word 'insight'. For many years, many marketing and market research professionals and functions have been termed or associated with 'consumer insight' as illustrated by the following example from Diageo. There has been much debate about what consumer insight means and how this may give a 'richer' understanding of consumers compared with traditional notions of market research. At the heart of this debate is a clear recognition that the links to consumers and support given to marketing decision-makers are being delivered by a much broader and diverse array of techniques and sources.

At the core of the definitions of marketing and market research is an understanding of the consumer and what shapes consumers. Regardless of whether a research professional is defined as a 'marketing researcher', 'market researcher' or a 'consumer insight manager', the focus upon consumers is paramount. However, the role and expectations of the marketing researcher can be argued to have the widest scope of practice. The expectations and demands of such a scope will be addressed later in this chapter, but for now we will use and adopt the broader definition of marketing research. Focusing upon 'marketing research' helps to

| **Real research** | **What consumer insight means to Diageo[9]** |

Diageo's (**www.diageo.com**) strong belief is that in order to be a world class company, it all starts with the consumer: 'knowing them, understanding them, understanding their motivations, understanding what drives them, and subsequently utilising this information to better serve consumers'. 'Consumer Insight' is at the heart what they see makes them a world class company. Consumer insight as defined by Diageo is: 'A penetrating discovery about consumer motivations, applied to unlock growth':

Penetrating – same data, but much deeper understanding.
Discovery – ah-ha! eureka!
Motivations – understand the why?
Applied – leveraged for their brands.
Growth – organic from brand strategies based on deep consumer understanding.

encapsulate the profession of managing the process of measuring and understanding consumers in order to better support marketing decision making, a profession that strives for the highest levels of integrity in applying sound research methods in an ethical manner. It is recognised that marketing research can now include understanding the macro business operating environment, monitoring market trends, conducting competitive analyses, answering business questions, identifying business opportunities and assessing potential risks.[10] More analytics, insights and future outlooks are demanded from business leaders to help them better understand their customers, the marketplace and the overall business environment. Researchers have to adapt and respond to these demands.

One of the major qualities of the American Marketing Association's definition of marketing research is its encapsulation of the marketing research process. The process is founded upon an understanding of the marketing decision(s) needing support. From this understanding, research aims and objectives are defined. To fulfil defined aims and objectives, an approach to conducting the research is established. Next, relevant information sources are identified and a range of data collection methods are evaluated for their appropriateness, forming a research design. The data are collected using the most appropriate method(s); they are analysed and interpreted, and inferences are drawn. Finally, the findings, implications and recommendations are provided in a format that allows the information to be used for marketing decision making and to be acted upon directly.

Marketing research process
A set of six steps which define the tasks to be accomplished in conducting a marketing research study. These include problem definition, developing an approach to the problem, research design formulation, fieldwork, data preparation and analysis, and report generation and presentation.

In order to attain the highest integrity, marketing research should aim to be objective. It should attempt to provide accurate information in an impartial manner. Although research is always influenced by the researcher's research philosophy, it should be free from personal or political biases of the researcher or decision-makers. Research motivated by personal or political gain involves a breach of professional standards. Such research is deliberately biased to result in predetermined findings. The motto of every researcher should be 'Find it and tell it like it is.' Second, it is worth noting the term 'total field of information'. This recognises that marketing decisions are not exclusively supported by marketing research. There are other means of information support for marketers from management consultants, raw data providers such as call centres, direct marketing, database marketing telebusinesses and social media.[11] These alternative forms of support are now competing with a 'traditional' view of marketing research. The methods of these competitors may not be administered with the same scientific rigour and/or ethical standards applied in the marketing research industry. Nonetheless, many marketing decision-makers are increasingly using these other sources which collectively are changing the nature of skills demanded in researchers.

The marketing research process

The marketing research process consists of six broad stages. Each of these stages is developed in more detail in subsequent chapters; thus, the discussion here is brief. The process illustrated in Figure 1.2 is of the marketing research seen in simple stages. Figure 1.3 takes the process a stage further to show the many iterations and connections between stages. This section will explain the stages and illustrate the connections between the stages.

Step 1: Problem definition. The logical starting point in wishing to support the decision-maker is trying to understand the nature of the marketing problem that requires research support. Marketing decision problems are not simple 'givens', as will be discussed in Chapter 2. The symptoms and causes of a problem are not in reality as neatly presented as they may be in a case study, such as those found in marketing textbooks. In Figure 1.3, the first three stages show the iterations between *environmental context of the problem*, *marketing decision problem* and *marketing research problem*. Understanding the environmental context of the problem has distinct stages that will be discussed in Chapter 2. It involves discussion with decision-makers, in-depth interviews with industry experts, and the collection and analysis

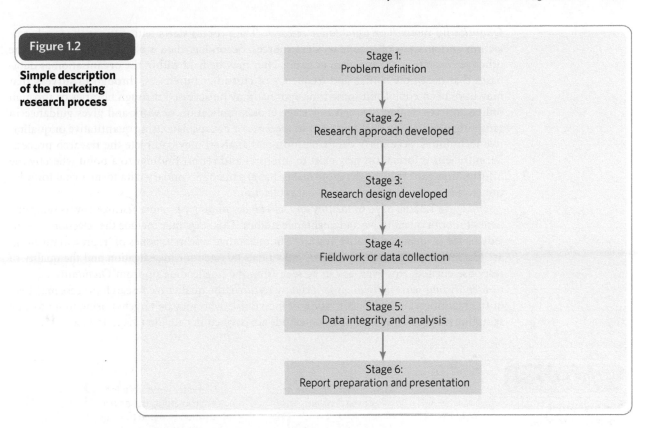

Figure 1.2

Simple description of the marketing research process

of readily available published information (from both inside and outside the firm). Once the problem has been precisely defined, the researcher can move on to designing and conducting the research process with confidence.

Step 2: Development of an approach to the problem. The development of an approach to the problem involves identifying factors that influence research design. A key element of this step involves the selection, adaptation and development of an appropriate theoretical framework to underpin a research design. Understanding the interrelated characteristics of the nature of target participants, the issues to be elicited from them and the context in which this will happen rely upon 'sound' theory. 'Sound' theory helps the researcher to decide 'what should be measured or understood' and 'how best to encapsulate and communicate the measurements or understandings'. In deciding what should be either measured or encapsulated, the researcher also develops a broad appreciation of how the data collected will be analysed. The issues involved in developing an approach are tackled in more detail in Chapter 2.

Step 3: Research design developed. A research design is a framework or blueprint for conducting a marketing research project. It details the procedures necessary for obtaining the required information. Its purpose is to establish a study design that will either test the hypotheses of interest or determine possible answers to set research questions, and ultimately provide the information needed for decision making. Conducting any exploratory techniques, precisely defining variables to be measured and designing appropriate scales to measure variables can also be part of the research design. The issue of how the data should be obtained from the participants (e.g. by conducting a survey or an experiment) must be addressed. These steps are discussed in detail in Chapters 3 to 13.

Step 4: Fieldwork or data collection. In Figure 1.2, this stage could be simplified to 'collecting the required data'. In Figure 1.3, a whole array of relationships between stages of data collection is shown, starting at *Secondary data collection and analysis* through to

Quantitative research or *Qualitative research*. The process starts with a more thorough collection and analysis of secondary data sources. Secondary data are data collected for some other purpose than the problem at hand. They may be held within the organisation as databases that detail the nature and frequency of customer purchases, through to surveys that may have been completed some time ago that may be accessed through libraries or through online sources. Going through this stage avoids replication of work and gives guidance in sampling plans and in deciding what to measure or encapsulate using quantitative or qualitative techniques. Secondary data collection and analysis may complete the research process, i.e. sufficient information may exist to interpret and report findings to a point whereby the information gaps that the decision-maker has are filled. Secondary data form a vital foundation and essential focus to primary data collection.

In Figure 1.3, the stage of *Identify and select individuals for primary research* covers sampling issues for both quantitative and qualitative studies. This stage may include the selection of individuals for in-depth qualitative research. In qualitative research, issues of 'representativeness' are less important than the quality of individuals targeted for investigation and the quality of response elicited. However, as can be seen from the line leading up from *Qualitative research* to *Identify and select individuals for primary research*, the qualitative research process may help in the identification and classification of individuals who may be targeted using more formal sampling methods. These sampling methods are covered in detail in Chapters 14 and 15.

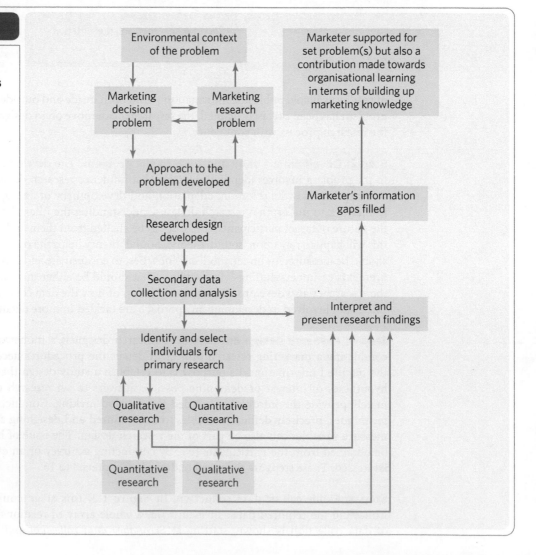

Figure 1.3

The marketing research process, detailing iterations between stages

Beyond the issues of identifying and selecting individuals, the options available for primary data collection vary considerably. A stage of *Qualitative research* alone may be sufficient to support the decision-maker, as indeed could a stage of *Quantitative research*. The following example illustrates the use of qualitative observation to support marketing decision making. This example mirrors one of the research techniques used by UBS, helping it to build up a 'picture' of target consumers. In their own right, qualitative techniques do not necessarily have to be followed by a survey or quantitative work to confirm the observations. In-depth interviewing will be described and evaluated Chapter 8.

Real research | **Storytelling with international millionaires**[12]

UBS (**www.ubs.com**) is one of the world's largest managers of private wealth assets and so has a rich knowledge of both the financial markets and high net worth individuals. In 2002, UBS operated under its current brand name for the first time (after the merger of the Swiss Bank Corporation, the Union Bank of Switzerland and later Paine Webber). It had become a global powerhouse in financial services, but nobody knew about it. The challenge it had was to establish a single brand with relevance and meaning to: high net worth individuals with investable assets of $1 million or more and business audiences including corporate executives, asset management buyers, intermediaries and institutional investors. After an exhaustive global brand and market audit, a new brand positioning was needed to represent this new 'ideal' financial services firm. UBS commissioned Spring (**www.springresearch.co.uk**) to conduct 90 in-depth interviews in the UK, Germany, Brazil, China and the USA. In each country Spring talked to 10 high net worth individuals (with investable assets of $1 million or more, or equivalent), five senior executives within large corporations and institutions (with primary responsibility for the selection of financial services firms) and three UBS Client Advisors (who interact with high net worth individuals on a daily basis), as it wanted to understand both sides of the relationship. Four key ways to maintain differentiation emerged from the research that were instrumental in where UBS developed its advertising and marketing strategies.

A research problem may require a stage of qualitative and quantitative research to run concurrently, perhaps measuring and encapsulating different characteristics of the problem under investigation. Alternatively, a stage of qualitative research could be used to precede a stage of quantitative research. For example, a series of focus groups may help to generate a series of statements or expectations that are subsequently tested out in a survey to a representative sample. Conversely, a survey may be conducted and, upon analysis, there may be clear statistically significant differences between two distinct target markets. A series of qualitative in-depth interviews may follow to allow a more full exploration and understanding of the reasons for the differences between the two groups.

Step 5: Data integrity and analysis. Data preparation includes the editing, coding, transcription and verification of data. In Figure 1.3, this stage is not drawn out as a distinct stage in its own right, but is seen as integral to the stages of *Secondary data collection and analysis* through to *Quantitative research* or *Qualitative research*. The process of data integrity and analysis is essentially the same for both quantitative and qualitative techniques, for data collected from both secondary and primary sources. Considerations of data analysis do not occur after data have been collected; such considerations are an integral part of the development of an approach, the development of a research design and the implementation of individual quantitative or qualitative methods. If the data to be collected are qualitative, the analysis process can occur as the data are being collected, well before all observations or interviews have been completed. An integral part of qualitative data preparation and analysis requires researchers to reflect upon their own learning and the ways they may interpret what they see and hear. These issues will be developed in Chapters 6 to 9.

If the data to be analysed are quantitative, each questionnaire or observation form is inspected or edited and, if necessary, corrected to ensure the integrity of data. The data from questionnaires are loaded, transcribed or keypunched into a chosen data analysis package. Verification ensures that the data from the original questionnaires have been accurately transcribed, whereas data analysis gives meaning to the data that have been collected. Univariate techniques are used for analysing data when there is a single measurement of each element or unit in the sample; if there are several measurements of each element, each variable is analysed in isolation (see Chapter 18). On the other hand, multivariate techniques are used for analysing data when there are two or more measurements of each element and the variables are analysed simultaneously (see Chapters 18 to 25).

Step 6: Report preparation and presentation. The entire project should be documented in a written report that addresses the specific research questions identified, describes the approach, research design, data collection and data analysis procedures adopted, and presents the results and major findings. Research findings should be presented in a comprehensible format so that they can be readily used in the decision-making process. In addition, an oral presentation to management should be made using tables, figures and graphs to enhance clarity and impact. This process is encapsulated in Figure 1.3 with the reminder that the marketer's information gaps are filled and that the marketer is supported for the set problem, but also a contribution is made towards organisational learning in terms of building up marketing knowledge (see Chapter 26).

A classification of marketing research

The ESOMAR definition encapsulates two key reasons for undertaking marketing research: (1) to identify opportunities and problems; and (2) to generate and refine marketing actions. This distinction serves as a basis for classifying marketing research into problem identification research and problem-solving research, as shown in Figure 1.4. Linking this classification to the basic marketing paradigm in Figure 1.1, problem identification research can be linked to the description of the nature and scope of customer groups, understanding the nature of forces that shape customer groups, and understanding the nature of forces that shape the marketer's ability to satisfy targeted customer groups. Problem-solving research can be linked to test individual and interactive marketing mix variables that create consumer experiences, and to monitor and reflect upon past successes and failures in marketing decisions.

Problem identification research
Research undertaken to help identify problems that are not necessarily apparent on the surface, yet exist or are likely to arise in the future.

Problem identification research is undertaken to help identify problems that are, perhaps, not apparent on the surface and yet exist or are likely to arise in the future. Examples of problem identification research include market potential, market share, brand or company image, market characteristics, sales analysis, short-range forecasting, long-range forecasting and business trends research. Research of this type provides information about the marketing environment and helps diagnose a problem. For example, a declining market potential indicates that the firm is likely to have a problem achieving its growth targets. Similarly, a problem exists if the market potential is increasing but the firm is losing market share. The recognition of economic, social or cultural trends, such as changes in consumer behaviour, may point to underlying problems or opportunities.

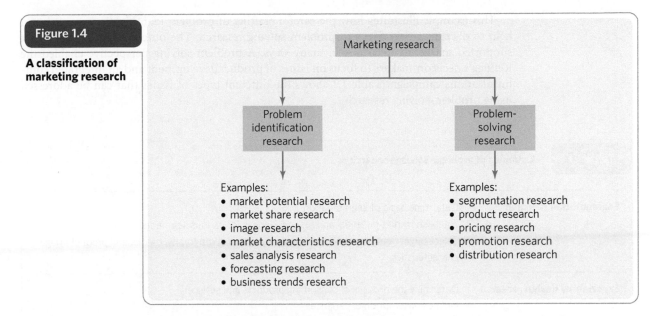

Figure 1.4
A classification of marketing research

Problem-solving research

Research undertaken to help solve specific marketing problems.

Once a problem or opportunity has been identified, problem-solving research may be undertaken to help develop a solution. The findings of problem-solving research are used to support decisions that tackle specific marketing problems. Problem-solving research linked to problem identification research is illustrated by the following example of developing a new cereal at Kellogg's.

Real research

Crunchy Nut Red adds colour to Kellogg's sales[13]

Kellogg's (**www.kelloggs.com**), marketing its products in more than 180 countries as of 2009, experienced a slump in the market and faced the challenge of reviving low cereal sales. Through problem identification research, Kellogg's was able to identify the problem, and through problem-solving research, develop several solutions to increase cereal sales. Kellogg's performed several tasks to identify the problem. Researchers spoke to decision-makers within the company, interviewed industry experts, conducted analysis of available data, performed some qualitative research, and surveyed consumers about their perceptions and preferences for cereals. Several important issues or problems were identified by this research. Current products were being targeted to children, bagels and muffins were winning for favoured breakfast foods, and high prices were turning consumers to generic brands. Other information also came to light during the research. Adults wanted quick foods that required very little or no preparation. Collectively, these issues helped Kellogg's identify the problem. The company was not being creative in introducing new products to meet the needs of the adult market. After defining the problem, Kellogg's went to work on solutions. It developed and tested several new flavours of cereals based upon the results of survey interviews with adult consumers. Based on the results, Kellogg's introduced new flavours that were more suited to the adult palate but were not the tasteless varieties of the past. For example, in 2008 it introduced Kellogg's Nutri-Grain Cereal Bar Blackberry. The new cereal bar was supported by an advertising campaign and major in-store promotions. Through creative problem identification research followed by problem-solving research, Kellogg's not only saw an increase in sales, but also increased consumption of cereal at times other than breakfast.

This example illustrates how the careful crafting of problem identification research can help to develop a clear focus to problem-solving research. The outcome was research that supported marketing decisions in many ways. A problem-solving perspective enabled the Kellogg's decision-makers to focus on issues of product development and an integrated communications campaign. Table 1.1 shows the different types of issues that can be addressed using problem-solving research.

Table 1.1	**Examples of problem-solving research**
Segmentation research	Determine basis of segmentation Establish market potential and responsiveness for various segments Select target markets and create lifestyle profiles: demography, media, and product image characteristics
Experiential design research	Determine the process of consuming products and services Online consumption experiences Social media engagement Sensory tests
Product research	Determine optimal product design Test concept Package tests Product modification Brand positioning and repositioning Test marketing
Pricing research	Importance of price in brand selection Pricing policies Product line pricing Price elasticity of demand Initiating and responding to price changes
Promotions research	Optimal promotional budget Optimal promotion mix Copy decisions Creative advertising testing Evaluation of advertising effectiveness
Distribution research	Attitudes of channel members Intensity of wholesale and retail coverage Channel margins Retail and wholesale locations

Problem identification research and problem-solving research can go hand in hand as seen in the Kellogg's case, and a given marketing research project may combine both types of research.

The global marketing research industry

Huge changes in the marketing research industry have been developing for a number of years. In order to appreciate the nature and impact of these changes, we turn our attention to the relative rates of demand for marketing research and industry growth rates across the globe. To monitor rates of expenditure and growth, we evaluate the annual ESOMAR Global Market Research Industry Study (**www.esomar.nl**), with summaries and commentary from the magazine *Research World*.

The figures presented in forthcoming tables are estimates of all the work conducted within individual countries, by research agencies. Not included in the data is marketing research undertaken by non-profit research institutes, governments, universities or advertising agencies using their own resources. The data also do not include the internal supply of marketing research, i.e. the costs of a marketing research function located within a firm. In addition, not included are costs incurred by the more sophisticated users of marketing research who integrate the data and analyses of their operational databases to understand customers and support marketing decision making. Though these estimates are static, may quickly go out of date and only tell part of the story of supporting marketing decision making, they are a vital means to illustrate developments in the marketing research industry.

The total global expenditure on marketing research in 2009 amounted to €28.9 billion.[14] Where this money was spent is illustrated in Table 1.2 which lists the top 20 countries with the highest marketing research spend per capita. Though it is clear to see that the USA as a country spent the most on marketing research, on a per capita basis a different story emerges. Six European countries spent more than the USA, with the UK spending €36.80 on marketing

Table 1.2	Top 20 countries with highest marketing research spend per capita, 2009[15]		
Country	**Turnover (€m)**	**Population (million)**	**Spend per capita (€ per capita)**
1 UK	2,339	62	36.8
2 France	1,935	63	30.1
3 Sweden	261	9	27.6
4 Germany	2,086	82	24.7
5 Norway	102	5	20.4
6 Denmark	112	6	19.8
7 USA	6,161	307	19.5
8 Switzerland	145	7	19.3
9 Australia	415	22	18.4
10 Finland	94	5	17.0
11 Netherlands	263	16	15.5
12 Ireland	68	4	14.9
13 Belgium	148	11	13.3
14 Austria	112	8	13.1
15 Canada	454	34	13.1
16 New Zealand	53	4	12.0
17 Spain	473	46	10.0
18 Japan	1274	128	9.7
19 Italy	545	60	8.9
20 Hong Kong	63	7	8.9

research for every citizen, with France second at €30.10 and Sweden at €27.60. The top 20 are dominated by countries with mature marketing research industries and with relatively high price levels for their research services.

Table 1.3 lists the regional and total global shares of marketing research expenditure and the growth rates in these regions between 2008 and 2009. Global marking research turnover fell to €20.8 billion in 2009, representing a decline of 3.7% and 4.6% after adjustment for inflation. This was the first decline since ESOMAR began measuring the industry in 1988, but in line with expectations given the global economic downturn in this period.

When set in a global context, Table 1.3 shows that, between 2009 and 2010, across all global regions the marketing research industry contracted. However, looking back five years to 2005, it is clear to see that there has been significant growth in marketing research expenditure across all regions. Within Europe, for the first time in a number of years, the mature research markets of the EU15[16] (where almost 90% of the region's turnover is generated) outperformed the emerging markets of Europe. The Asia-Pacific marketing research sector experienced the slowest declines globally. Performances in the region in 2009 were varied, with economies such as Japan and Australia experiencing large declines while emerging markets such as China and India performed well. China and South Korea posted growth rates for 2010. Though the Middle East and African region is the smallest global one, there were economies where growth was experienced. East African industry was the fastest growing in the region, driven by overall economic growth, particularly in telecoms, services and finance sectors. There was also an increased focus among global brands towards developing economies in the region and in Africa in particular.[17] Examples of marketing research conducted in these emerging and fast-growing economies will be used throughout the text in the sections of International Marketing Research.

Marketing research in Europe still has many great prospects as illustrated by the long-term growth rates throughout Europe and in developing economies across the globe. ESOMAR forecasts a global growth rate of 3% for 2010 which it describes as 'a happy return to growth, but lower than the level experienced before the downturn'.[18] Obviously with 2009 showing negative growth rates, many commentators hope that this may be attributed to a global economic downturn. The impact of low growth rates and recession within economies can certainly explain part of the decline in growth rates. More troubling for the marketing research industry could be a switch in spending patterns by companies that commission marketing research, from 'traditional' sources to just about any alternative source of information that could apply insight they can apply and believe in.[19] The result of the decline in the industry and shift to alternative sources of insight has generated a greater competitive intensity between marketing research suppliers, exacerbating the demand for a broader mix of managerial and technical skills from researchers.

How marketing research expenditure is spent on different research methods is illustrated in Table 1.4. Quantitative research methods account for 80% of global research spend, with quali-

Table 1.3	Turnover, growth rates and market share per region, 2005–2009[20]			
Region	Turnover 2005 (€m)	Turnover 2009 (€m)	Real growth rate 2008–2009 (adjusted for inflation) (%)	Share of global market, 2009 (%)
Europe	8,397	9,575	–5.9	46
North America	5,980	6,615	–3.5	32
Asia-Pacific	2,401	3,226	–2.2	15
Latin America	733	1,070	–4.6	5
Middle East and Africa	254	354	–10.2	2
Total world	17,776	20,840	–4.6	100

tative accounting for 13%. The remaining 7% includes desk and secondary research. This table makes distinctions between different forms of online research, for instance highlighting online qualitative research, where there are many examples of companies specialising in online focus groups, in-depth interviews and ethnography. These examples will be discussed in Chapters 6 to 9. Online quantitative research increased from a share of 20% of expenditure in 2008 to 22% in 2009. Telephone and postal techniques both declined by 1% in the same period. Online research and online traffic/audience measurement will be discussed in more detail in Chapters 3, 4 and 10. Table 1.5 illustrates which countries spend the most on online research methods as a percentage of their total spend; 22 countries spent 10% or more on online research. Bulgaria emerges as the country with the highest percentage of online research, taking over from Canada, despite Canada having an increase from 35% in 2008 to 39% in 2009. Finland had the highest percentage increase of 11% in this period to take it to a level of 33%.

The bases for the estimates in Tables 1.2 to 1.5 emerge from external marketing research suppliers or agencies. External suppliers are outside firms hired to supply marketing research data. These external suppliers collectively comprise the 'marketing research industry'. They

External suppliers
Outside marketing research companies hired to supply marketing research services.

Table 1.4 — Spend by research method for 2009[21]

Spend by research method	Spend (%)	Spend 2009 (€m)
Online quantitative	22	4,585
Telephone	17	3,543
Automated digital/electronic	16	3,334
Face to face	13	2,709
Postal	4	834
Online traffic/audience	1	208
Other quantitative	7	1,459
Group discussions	9	1,876
In-depth interviews	2	417
Online qualitative	1	208
Other qualitative	1	208
Other	7	1,459

Table 1.5 — Top 10 countries with highest online research spend as a percentage of total spend 2009[22]

Spend by research method	Spend (%)
Bulgaria	43
Canada	39
Japan	36
New Zealand	36
Finland	33
Netherlands	30
Germany	29
Australia	28
Sweden	27
UK	26

Full-service suppliers
Companies that offer the full range of marketing research activities.

Syndicated services
Companies that collect and sell common pools of data designed to serve information needs shared by a number of clients.

Customised services
Companies that tailor research procedures to best meet the needs of each client.

Online services
Companies which specialise in the use of the Internet to collect, analyse and distribute marketing research information.

Market research reports and advisory services
Companies which provide off-the-shelf reports as well as data and briefs on a range of markets, consumer types and issues.

range from small (one or a few persons) operations to very large global corporations. Further details and analyses of external suppliers and the top 25 global marketing research companies can be found on the website that accompanies this book. We now examine the nature of services that may be supplied by external suppliers. As illustrated in Figure 1.5, external suppliers can be classified as full-service or limited-service suppliers.

Full-service suppliers offer the entire range of marketing research services: for example, defining a problem, developing a research design, conducting focus group interviews, designing questionnaires, sampling, collecting, analysing and interpreting data, and presenting reports. They may also address the marketing implications of the information they present, i.e. have the management skills to interpret and communicate the impact of their research findings at the highest levels. They may also manage customer database analyses, being able to integrate the management and analyses databases with the management and analyses of conventional marketing research techniques.

The services provided by these suppliers can be further broken down into syndicated services, standardised services and customised services (see Figure 1.5). Examples of these companies include Kantar (**www.kantar.com**) and Synovate (**www.synovate.com**).

Syndicated services collect information of known commercial value that they provide to multiple clients on a subscription basis. Surveys, diary panels, scanners and audits are the main means by which these data are collected. Examples of these companies include Nielsen (**www.nielsen.com**) and GfK (**www.gfk.com**).

Customised services offer a variety of marketing research services specifically designed to suit a client's particular needs. Each marketing research project is treated uniquely. Examples of these companies include TNS (**www.tnsglobal.com**) and Research International (**www.research-int.com**).

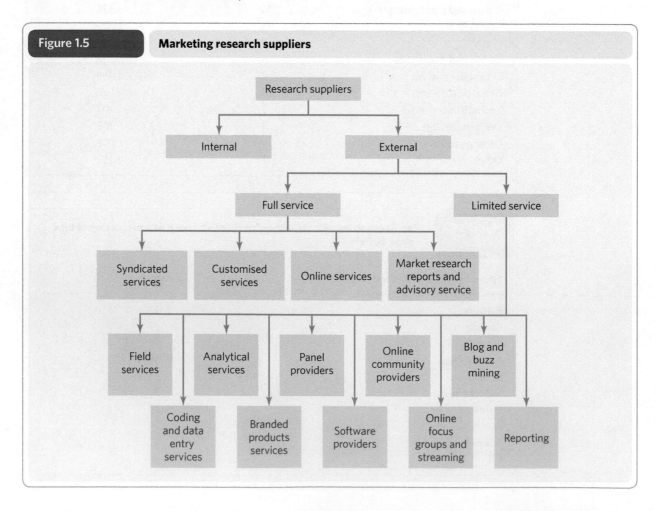

| Figure 1.5 | **Marketing research suppliers** |

Online services offer a combination or variety of secondary data and intelligence gathering, survey or qualitative interviewing, social media engagement and the analysis and publication of research findings, exclusively online. Examples of these companies include YouGov (**www.yougov.com**) and OnePoll (**www.onepoll.com**).

Market research reports and advisory services provide off-the-shelf reports as well as data and briefs on a range of markets, consumer types and issues; as such they are thought of as part of the broader information market and not necessarily part of the traditional marketing research industry. Examples of these companies include Euromonitor (**www.euromonitor.com**) and Mintel (**www.mintel.com**).

Limited-service suppliers specialise in one or a few phases of a marketing research project. Services offered by such suppliers are classified as field services, coding and data entry, analytical services, branded products, viewing facilities, panel providers, software providers, web analytics, online community providers, online focus groups and streaming, blog and buzz mining, and reporting.[23]

Field services collect data through postal, face-to-face interviews, telephone interviews and the Internet. Firms that specialise in interviewing are called field service organisations. These organisations may range from small proprietary companies that operate locally to large multinationals. Some organisations maintain extensive interviewing facilities across the country for interviewing shoppers. Many offer qualitative data collection services such as focus group interviewing (discussed in detail in Chapter 7). Examples of these companies include GMI (Global Market Insite) (**www.gmi-mr.com**) and Indiefield (**www.indiefield.co.uk**).

Coding and data entry services include editing completed questionnaires, developing a coding scheme and transcribing the data for input into a computer. Examples of these companies include Eurodata Computer Services Limited (**www.data-entry-service.co.uk**) and The Analysis Solution (**www.plus4.co.uk/analysis_solution**).

Analytical services include designing and pretesting questionnaires, determining the best means of collecting data, and designing sampling plans, as well as other aspects of the research design. Some complex marketing research projects require knowledge of sophisticated procedures, including specialised experimental designs (discussed in Chapter 10) and analytical techniques such as conjoint analysis and multidimensional scaling (discussed in Chapter 24). This kind of expertise can be obtained from firms and consultants specialising in analytical services. Examples of these companies include Cobalt Sky Ltd (**www.cobalt-sky.com**) and Digitab (**www.digitab.uk.com**).

Branded marketing research products and services are specialised data collection and analysis procedures developed to address specific types of marketing research problems. These procedures may be patented, given brand names, and marketed like any other branded product. Examples of these companies include Comparisat® at FDS (**www.fds.co.uk/about_comparisat.asp**) and Millward Brown's Optimor (**www.millwardbrown.com/mboptimor**).

Panel providers offer researchers the opportunity to access consumer, b2b and specialist panels of participants alongside scripting and hosting surveys. Examples of these companies include e-Rewards (**www.e-rewards.co.uk**) and Toluna (**www.toluna.com**).

Software providers offer software packages that create platforms to script, host and analyse surveys, or Software as a Service (SaaS) options. Examples of these companies include Confirmit (**www.confirmit.com**) and SNAP (**www.snapsurveys.com**).

Online community providers build online research communities where researchers can employ a wide variety of quantitative and qualitative techniques to connect to consumers. Examples of these companies include Communispace (**www.communispace.com**) and FreshMinds (**www.freshminds.co.uk**).

Online focus groups and streaming provide platforms for running online focus groups and streaming the results. Examples of these companies include ActiveGroup (**www.activegroup.net**) and FocusVision (**www.focusvision.com**).

Blog and buzz mining provide the means to observe, track or initiate views in research communities, social networks and anywhere else that people post comments, visuals, music and other forms of art on the Internet. Examples of these companies include Nielsen's Buzzmetrics (**www.nielsen.com**) and SimplyZesty (**www.simplyzesty.com**).

Reporting
Offers research companies
reporting solutions that seek
to engage clients in oral and
electronic presentations
beyond conventional reporting
methods such as hard-copy
reports and PowerPoint.

Reporting offers research companies reporting solutions that seek to engage clients in oral and electronic presentations beyond conventional reporting methods such as hard-copy reports and PowerPoint. They utilize specialist art and graphic design services to create static data presentation formats and data dashboards that can be interrogated. Examples of these companies include E-Tabs (**www.e-tabs.org**) and Wordle (**www.wordle.net**).

Justifying the investment in marketing research

The 2010 ESOMAR Global Market Research report highlights many of the pressures that the marketing research industry is facing. One of the key weaknesses the report highlights is how the value of good marketing research is communicated.[24] This is not a recent phenomenon, it is a challenge that the marketing research industry has faced from its inception. It is a challenge that has become more prevalent in recent times:

> *the price of consumer data is trending downwards and parts of market research are becoming commoditised. This is in part driven by aggressive procurement processes, growing expectations for demonstrable return on investment and increasing macro-economic pressure. 'consumer data' is now more abundant and automated.*[25]

Return on investment in marketing research spend is and will continue to be a factor that all practising researchers will need to address.

It must be recognised that if decision-makers use researchers, even if the best theories and practice of the marketing research process are followed 'to the letter', there is no guarantee that a marketing decision supported by research will be successful. The act of decision making and conducting marketing research are distinctive activities and there are examples where the vital link between these activities has resulted in failure. If decision-makers have gaps in their knowledge, if they perceive risk and uncertainty in their decision making and cannot find support at hand within their organisation, they can gain support from marketing research. However, many decision-makers can recount cases where the use of marketing research has resulted in failure or where decisions based upon gut feeling or intuition have proved to be successful. Such cases present a challenge to researchers, especially in light of the competition faced by the industry from alternative data sources.[26] Reflecting upon such cases should remind researchers to maintain a focus of offering real and valuable support to decision-makers. Understanding what real and valuable support means should underpin the whole array of creative data collection and analysis procedures available to the researcher. The following example starts this reflection process with a case that is very close to home!

Real research | What's this marketing research then, Dave?

James Birks founded and successfully ran a kiln construction company for over 40 years. He designed, built and maintained kilns for some of the most demanding porcelain and ceramics manufacturers worldwide, including Wedgwood, Royal Doulton and Spode. At retirement age he sold his company as a going concern – a very wealthy man. James was presented with a copy of the first edition of this text by his nephew, David Birks. He was very pleased with the present but was intrigued by the title and asked 'What's this marketing research then, Dave?' He certainly had a clear idea of what marketing meant to his business and what was involved in being a successful marketer in his industry, but the notion of researching marketing activities and spending money on research was alien to him.

The intriguing aspect of this question is that James Birks had run a successful business on an international basis for over 40 years without the need to be aware of or to use marketing research. Had he used marketing research, could he have been even more successful, or would it have been a wasted investment? Could he have been practising marketing research 'activities' in a very informal manner to support marketing decisions? In his business-to-business marketing situation, he knew his customers and competitors well, and knew what shaped their demands. He understood the networks and relationships within those networks that were vital to the running and development of his business. This knowledge he acquired on a day-to-day basis, nurturing a curiosity about opportunities and how to realise them – without resorting to support from formal ad hoc marketing research. The example of James Birks shows that decision-makers do not rely solely upon marketing research and in certain circumstances can survive and perform well without it.

Another view to reflect upon is the damning comment from Anita Roddick of The Body Shop, who said that 'market research is like looking in the rear view mirror of a speeding car'.[27] This may be a valid point if one sees the relationship of marketing and marketing research from the perspective illustrated by the respected research practitioner, Wendy Gordon:[28]

> *Traditional marketers delegate responsibility to the processes of marketing research. They believe that you can ask people what they want and need in the future and then deliver it to them. It is a fallacy. Marketing research removes people from experiencing reality, where the signs of change bubble up in unexpected places. Sitting in comfort behind a one-way mirror, listening to a debrief from researchers describing the world 'out there' or reading statistical reports on markets and the 'aggregate consumer' is not real, it is sanitised and second-hand.*

Given the above criticisms, it is a fair point to acknowledge that there are cases where the use of marketing research has resulted in poor decision making or even failure. Ultimately, this examination should lead to a stronger justification of what ensures strong and valuable marketing research support. It may be a painful path to tread but this journey has to be made!

There are two areas of misconception of the role of marketing research that are still relevant today:[29]

Marketing research does not make decisions. The role of marketing research is not to make decisions. Rather, research replaces hunches, impressions or a total lack of knowledge with information that can be trusted.

Marketing research does not guarantee success. Research, at best, can improve the odds of making a correct decision. Anyone who expects to eliminate the possibility of failure by doing research is both unrealistic and likely to be disappointed. The real value of research can be seen over a long period where increasing the percentage of good decisions should be manifested in improved bottom-line performance and in the occasional revelation that arises from research.

The last point shows the long-term benefits of conducting marketing research, i.e. that the results of a study may help decision-makers with an immediate problem, but by building their knowledge they can also have long-term benefits.

The following example illustrates how marketing research could be used in new product development. In this case, the designer and entrepreneur chose to ignore the findings, and ultimately achieved immense levels of success. This is not always the case, as many different designers embrace marketing research techniques to support their design thinking and practice to great effect.

Doing a Dyson[30]

Just 23 months after its launch in the UK, the Dyson bagless vacuum cleaner became the country's best seller, overtaking sales of Hoover, Electrolux, Panasonic, Miele and all other vacuum cleaners. The Dyson clear bin was given a resounding thumbs-down in marketing research. People said they did not like the dirt being visible in the bin in case their neighbours saw how much dirt had been picked up in their homes. Some retailers said they would not want to have dust on display in demonstration machines. Yet, the dust was there because they began using Dyson display machines to clean their shops. Dyson felt compelled to launch its vacuum cleaner with a clear bin, believing that it was important to see when it was full. Moreover, what better way was there to show stockists, sales staff and customers proof of its increased efficiency than to see the dirt being collected? How would consumers react to a new vacuum cleaner with totally radical styling, revolutionary internal engineering and a price tag almost twice that of the current brand leader? The response proved immediately that innovative products do sell, even at a premium price. However, marketing research did not point to this product having the potential to be a success. James Dyson argued that 'marketing research will only tell you what has happened. No research can tell you what is going to happen.' This is a theme that James Dyson has reiterated over the years. In an interview in 2006, giving tips to would-be inventors and entrepreneurs, he said:

> you can't go out and do marketing research to try and solve these problems about what to do next because usually, or very often, you're doing the opposite of what marketing research would tell you. You can't base a new project two years ahead on current market trends and what users are thinking at the moment. That sounds very arrogant. But it isn't arrogance. You can't go and ask your customers to be your inventors. That's your job.

Out of the array of research and information support approaches, there is no one guaranteed approach, research design or technique that can create the perfect means to support decision-makers. If decision-makers complain that research is misleading or is only telling them what they already know, the researcher may argue that the fault lies with managers who pose the wrong questions or problem in the first place. If one takes the narrow view that the decision-maker poses the questions and the researcher finds the answers, there may be some validity in such an argument. It does not hold if one considers that the decision-maker and the researcher have a joint commitment to solve problems. In this joint commitment they have quite distinct but complementary creative skills that they can bring together to understand what problem they should be researching, how they conduct the research and how they interpret their findings.

Can researchers survive in an age of increasing competition from other information providers? Can they cope with the threats of growth of in-house research, new entrants to the industry that adopt new technologies and techniques, especially in the use of social media? Can the industry fend off the challenge from the armies of consultants and avoid research being seen as a commodity?[32] To achieve this, the industry has to offer marketers' insights that have integrity and can be trusted rather than just 'robust' data collection and analysis. Such insights should lead to fresh perspectives to business problems and/or a competitively advantaged solution.[33] The researcher's input must be seen to benefit the bottom line. Initiatives that bring marketers and researchers closer together are needed, initiatives that educate buyers that marketing research has as much if not more to offer than much more expensive consultancy firms.[34]

The future – Research 2.0 and the nature of skills demanded of researchers

Millions of people are actively engaging in online discussions, giving their opinions, meeting new people, showing their activities, preferences, uses and attitudes, talking about brands, services, music and films. The marketing research industry has been criticised for being slow to recognise that these engagements are having a significant impact upon the nature, value and integrity of their work. In marketing research, the 'first Internet' was used as a digital extension of activities that could be done offline, taking the survey from face to face, then to telephone (with computer-assisted telephone interviewing (CATI)) and then online with web surveys. It has been argued that 'the survey' has not really embraced the breadth and richness of digital developments, with many surveys conducted online being originally designed to be administered by interviewers face to face.[35] There are examples that include multimedia such as video, audio or pictures, but in essence it is a survey. These attempts to engage participants are in response to evidence that shows completion rates of surveys are dropping as participants grow tired of lengthy arduous surveys.[36] However, it seems to ignore a social media revolution where people are now expressing their opinions and feelings in far more sophisticated and complex ways. The following example illustrates how Philips is developing new marketing research techniques. It illustrates how social media are being used to supplement and integrate with techniques that have been described as 'traditional marketing research'.

Real research   ### Philips' online community[37]

For companies such as Philips, traditional marketing research methods such as surveys, focus groups and in-depth interviews play an important role in product development and marketing. For a company that is eager to discover new avanues of innovation, research methods whose horizons are typically short term and a narrowly defined scope, this is not ideal, especially in the 'fuzzy front end' phase of product development. Philips viewed many of its existing research methods as better suited to the latter stages of concept and product development. To 'retrofit' traditional research to deliver more forward-looking, unexpected insights would be prohibitively expensive and time consuming. Traditional research methods simply are not effective or efficient for gathering and assimilating exploratory feedback, which is often more open-ended and prone to evolutionary changes as consumers adopt new technology and interact with new brands and one another. Gaining 'longitudinal insights' from consumers would be logistically challenging and expensive with traditional research methods. Philips approached this challenge by continuously experimenting with and incorporating new research methods. The new methods helped it bring a new level of consumer insight, but it also brought its own limitations. Ethnographic research proved to be time consuming, expensive and limited in the number of participants Philips could include. It envisioned that an online community would complement the company's existing research initiatives by providing a new, effective tool for uncovering critical insights, including unforeseen and unmet needs. Beyond assisting new product development, the community would provide an outlet for other marketing research needs, such as validation of concepts, naming research and studying brand associations.

The Philips example illustrates the use of emerging research techniques that can dovetail with traditional marketing research techniques or in some cases be a replacement. The term used in the industry to describe the development of social-media-based research techniques is Research 2.0 or NewMR. Research 2.0 has grown out of the development of Web 2.0. a term first coined by O'Reilly Media (**www.oreilly.com**) in 2004 to describe two interrelated phenomena. The first phenomenon was the growth in websites where users could contribute content to the website, often referred to as user-generated content, or simply UGC. Examples of these types of services included photo sharing sites such as Flickr, video uploaded sites such as YouTube, collaborative projects based on wikis (such as Wikipedia), social networks such as MySpace and Facebook, and blogging. The second phenomenon that was embraced under the term Web 2.0 was the creation of a wide range of tools that made using the Web much easier and more rewarding. These tools included such things as AJAX (Asynchronous Java-Script and XML), PHP and MySQL. With Web 2.0 the users were creating content and shaping their experiences and the services they got. During 2004 and 2005, as the term Web 2.0 became increasingly established, people began to apply the 2.0 label to a wider range of activities, including law, architecture and even government. In the world of marketing research, the term Research 2.0 came into being in 2006, to reflect a shift away from the old 'command and control' paradigm of marketing research towards a more collaborative approach. The core of Research 2.0 was to move away from an assumption that the brand (decision-makers) and the researcher knew everything, towards a tripartite discussion between the brand, the researcher and the customer. The term 'Research 2.0' divides techniques into two broad categories, namely passive or active. Passive techniques are based on measuring the conversations that are happening on the Web, e.g. by using blog mining. The following example of RTL Netherlands illustrates the use of a passive Research 2.0 technique.

Real research	**Stop asking questions and start listening**[38]

RTL Netherlands and its innovative research agency Insites Consulting (**www.insites.eu**) illustrated the power of buzz mining in the Dutch version of the *X Factor*. Because the *X Factor* lasts for several weeks, from auditions, to boot camp, to the knockout rounds, the show was particularly suitable for an iterative research process. In this case, the iterative research used searching and web scraping online conversations during the show. During the project, over 70,000 comments were captured from a variety of Dutch language online communities. In a version of online ethnography or discourse analysis, Insites Consulting analysed what people were saying about the show, its contestants, the songs and the way the show was shaping. RTL Netherlands was able to use this information to make week-by-week alterations to the show and the acccompanying website to make the show 'sharper' and increase the interest of the audience. The show was broadcast on Fridays, so the agency did its web scraping on Mondays, reporting back to RTL on Wednesdays, which allowed the information to impact upon the show on Friday.

The earliest forms of Research 2.0 tended to be passive techniques based around blogs. Active techniques are now the most significant area of interest and commercial activity primarily in the area of online research communities. Online research communities have become well established in the USA and Western Europe.[39] The example of easyJet earlier in this chapter illustrated the use of online research communities. A key target group that engages well with online research communities is 18 to 24 year olds or the 'youth market'. Traditional research techniques, such as focus groups and one-to-one interviews, while they still relate to younger audiences, do not apply as readily as collaborative techniques, aligned more to conversation and empowering participants than to seeking specific responses. In isolation, face-to-face research with young people tends to deliver patchy results.[40] The combination of web and electronic media use and proficiency by youth audiences has forced marketing research to evolve and embrace mixed methodologies. By engaging with younger audiences in 'youth-friendly' media, the quality and range of insight returned has risen. In contexts that are familiar, interactive but not physically engaging, younger audiences come alive. On the Web, the need for social acceptance is less intense and discussion flows more freely. When presented with a task (as opposed to a question) online, youth involvement can become more spontaneous and enthused. Introducing a project or problem-solving approach helps youth research recruits feel empowered and that their opinions are being listened to. Further, enabling younger participants to express themselves in pictures and multimedia, as they would to their friends, delivers a rich research experience that cannot be replicated offline.[41] If young audiences are researched using familiar tools and media, they accept responsibility to share their voice, to address research objectives seriously and to make a positive contribution.

Many commentators are arguing that the marketing research industry cannot afford to ignore how consumers are engaging and being empowered by their use of the Web. Given the importance and significance of Research 2.0 upon the marketing research industry, descriptions and examples of techniques will be presented throughout this book. There are also a wide range of issues that Research 2.0 creates, but the most fundamental ones are:[42]

1 *Trust.* Ensuring that research buyers understand the basis of the advice they are given. Decision-makers have been assured for over 70 years that the research is 'true' because it is based on a scientific approach to knowledge development, thus it will take a while for the new messages to be widely understood.

2 *Theoretical base.* At the moment most of the Research 2.0 techniques are being used in a theoretical vacuum, thus researchers need to address this and rebuild a body of knowledge and theory that supports the techniques being used.

3 *Ethical base.* There are new privacy, security and safety issues. Social media have changed the rules on how 'findable' somebody is. This has enormous implications for privacy and safety. For example, including a literal quote from an online forum in a report is essentially the same thing as naming the individual, since a search on the quote will usually return information about the person making it. The discussion about 'what is in the public domain' and what can be used when, where, and how has barely started and will develop rapidly over the next few years.

Again these issues will be described, illustrated and debated throughout this book. With the downturn in growth in the marketing research industry as presented by ESOMAR in its 2010 Global Market Research report, the challenges of justifying investment in marketing research and the challenges presented by Research 2.0 and beyond, a pessimistic view could be taken of what the future holds for marketing research. The corollary of these events can also be seen in that the future of the marketing research industry is laden with great opportunities and it is in this spirit that we also wish to portray the subject. There are many new challenges, techniques and debates to be developed in marketing research. There are many commercial and scholarly opportunities but these will demand a different set of skills, thinking and outlook compared with the researcher of the past.

The following example illustrates the demands on researchers that were articulated before the emergence of Research 2.0. These demands are still relevant and should be read while reflecting upon the new demands created by Research 2.0.

What do clients want from research?[43]

Richard Henchoz, Director Marketing Planning Services with responsibility for marketing research for Africa and the Middle East and Duty Free at Phillip Morris International, expects that clients increasingly want and ask for actionable insights from researchers – the kind of insights that include an answer to the question: 'What would you do if you were in my place?' Henchoz believes researchers must be able to provide this kind of strategic information. Richard, a Swiss national based at Phillip Morris International's headquarters in Lausanne, put into perspective concerns about the loss of relevance of the research function:

I have been in research for about 20 years now and the call for more creativity has been going on for a long time. In the 1980s, when working as a researcher for Proctor & Gamble, I already aspired to move on from just executing research projects to a role in which I could be more creative, by making concrete recommendations to decision-makers. To me, it seemed an almost natural inclination for a researcher. And yes, clients will indeed require far more creativity and business intelligence from providers and international researchers. We are definitely working towards this goal at Phillip Morris.

The emerging generation of researchers will be expected to continue to master the skill of borrowing and adapting tried and tested theories and techniques from the social sciences. The challenges of writing engaging questionnaires, observing consumers, consumer experiences and the context of their consumption, deciding what constitutes a meaningful sample, and making sense of data will still have to be met. Increasingly, marketing decision-makers demand a far more integrated approach to analysing often contradictory and imperfect sources of evidence; there is a mounting need for the capacity to work in an eclectic and holistic way with qualitative and quantitative data. Increasingly, researchers will have to analyse multiple and often imperfect datasets. In terms of engaging with decision-makers, the future researcher will be more than a project manager developing methods, coordinating fieldwork, analysing research material and finally producing engaging reports. The future researcher will be more of a creative consultant, working together with designer colleagues to produce videos or interactive presentations but also skilled him- or herself in visualising results with the help of design software or interactive applications. Research will become more encompassing, holistic and multi-faceted.[44] To achieve all of this, researchers will need new holistic analytic frameworks to be able to make sense of the data and to present this to decision-makers in a coherent, confident and effective manner.[45]

The marketing research industry has great opportunities to add value to research. Researchers can move up the value chain to offer more advice and insight, thus improving their stature and ultimately their profitability. They can help decision-makers to make sense of a variety of data sources rather than walking away from a project when the research is complete.[46] Moving towards a business model that is driven by researchers offering actionable consumer insight means that researchers and the marketing research industry of the future will be required to:[47]

● *Think conceptually* – by developing 'conceptual' thinkers, i.e. researchers who feel comfortable working with higher order business concepts and talking the language of senior decision-makers. These individuals must understand the relationship between information and key business concepts. They must go beyond their technical and skill-based knowledge and offer strategic and tactical advice for business advantage based on detailed consumer and market knowledge.

- *Communicate in the way that those who commission research think* – by knowing how to communicate in the way senior people think, i.e. researchers presenting findings as a compelling narrative, not as disparate blocks of information.

- *Interpret findings in terms of the whole picture* – by thinking holistically about 'evidence', i.e. researchers with the skills to work in a 'holistic' way with all available customer evidence, recognising the need to interpret often imperfect marketing information. They must draw knowledge from a host of different sources including qualitative and quantitative techniques, a variety of forms of observation, customer relationship management systems, financial and customer profile information. These individuals will have to draw heavily upon the use of analytical models that represent the way customers think and behave.

- *Integrate findings with others that support marketing decision-makers* – by working in a multi-disciplinary way with related marketing services companies, with researchers working alongside branding and design and other marketing specialisms to gain a wider market understanding. This makes sure that everything is tailored to business solutions and is not just the result of rigid prescriptive research designs. This bottom-up, multi-disciplinary approach provides flexibility and differentiates 'strategic marketing intelligence' from the 'top-down' approach of full-blown management consultants. This will also mean the cultivating of a more creative environment with a more 'hands-off' management style rather than a prescriptive techniques-driven approach.

Finally, in a note of optimism, it is worth reflecting upon the views of three new graduates arguing what makes marketing research a great career choice. They worked for the research company Synovate (**www.synovate.com**) and were presenting their views to professional researchers at the Annual Conference of the Market Research Society:[48]

1 *Variety.* This can apply to the kind of work and the projects one experiences, the sectors one can specialise in, the people and the teams one will work with depending on the project. Then, the actual day-to-day work is varied (be it data analysis one day, fieldwork the next, charting, etc.). Ad hoc research also has the benefit of offering a variety of projects that can last from a few weeks up to a year or more.

2 *Career progression.* Marketing research has many clearly defined roles across the industry. Not only is there clear career progression within a company, but there is also the option to move client side (or vice versa), do international research, relocate to another country (a key selling point for a global business), specialise in a particular sector or even move to other roles such as brand consulting.

3 *Responsibility.* Compared with other industries, marketing research can offer a large amount of responsibility from an early stage of a person's career. Where graduates in some industries may still be doing photocopying and other mundane administrative tasks, those working in marketing research may be at a stage where they are managing large international projects.

4 *Intellectual eclecticism.* Marketing research is open to graduates from all disciplines; all subject disciplines are applicable as there are a variety of roles and the nature of work can demand skills from all subject areas.

5 *Working environment.* Marketing research has some of the most intelligent, interesting, fun and inspiring people, and that makes it a great place in which to work and develop. The culture (particularly agency side) is relaxed and friendly with a mix of personalities and characters. It is not until you actually work in marketing research that you realise this.

Supporting decision-makers in sports marketing

Focus on   ## IFM Sports Marketing Surveys

Quality research for management action

In most forthcoming chapters, examples will be presented based upon projects conducted by the marketing research agency **IFM Sports Marketing Surveys**. The best examples from this company in the third edition will be incorporated into this edition, but new projects have been selected to illustrate how marketing research is managed in practice. Elements of these commercially sensitive projects will be chosen to show how the company managed the challenges of conducting successful actionable marketing research. IFM Sports Marketing Surveys (**www.sportsmarketingsurveys. com**) is a full-service independent marketing research agency that has specialised in the sponsorship and

sports industry over the past 25 years. The sports industry and much sponsorship is often multi-country in reach and activity. IFM Sports Marketing Surveys has responded to this by having the capability to work and report on a worldwide basis in over 200 countries for events such as the Olympic Games, Formula One and the football World Cup. The agency's offices are in Surrey in the UK and Karlsruhe in Germany, with global offices in: **Europe** – Belgium, France, Greece, Ireland, Italy, Turkey; **Africa and the Middle East** – South Africa, United Arab Emirates; **The Americas** – Brazil, Canada, USA; **Australasia and Asia** – Australia, China, Japan, Malaysia, South Korea.

IFM Sports Marketing Surveys provides specialist consultancy and commercial advice on all aspects of sport, sponsorship and leisure research. Its expertise includes the following areas: **advisory and consultancy services; economic, legacy, tourism and environmental impact studies; event research; audience audit and validation; bespoke research studies; naming, title and property rights valuations; sponsorship evaluation and return on investment analysis; bidding and hosting evaluation; compliance monitoring.**

International marketing research

With the spread of marketing and research skills has come a noticeable decline in a 'national research culture'. There was a time when each country had a stubbornly distinctive approach to research, making it extremely difficult to get a consistent research design across markets. Most managers and researchers are aware now that there are different and equally legitimate ways to approach research problems and that no one school of thought has absolute authority for all types of problem. This greater flexibility has made multi-country coordinated projects much more feasible though not easier, as they represent intellectually, logistically and diplomatically the most demanding of problems.

Conducting international marketing research is much more complex than conducting domestic marketing research. International marketing research will be discussed and illustrated in individual chapters as individual techniques are developed and in greater detail in Chapter 26. The marketing, government, legal, economic, structural, socio-cultural and informational environments prevailing in target international markets, and the characteristics of target consumers that are being studied, influence the manner in which the marketing research process should be performed. Examples of these environmental factors and their impact on the marketing research process are illustrated in detail in subsequent chapters. The following example illustrates some of the challenges faced by researchers in a global context.

Real research	A world of chicken flavours[49]

A study was conducted to support the development of 'new chicken flavours', sponsored by flavour consultants Givaudan (**www.givaudan.com**) and delivered by QualiData (**www.qualidataresearch.com**). With the cooperation of local research agencies, the study was conducted within multiple regions in eight countries: USA, Mexico, Colombia, Brazil, France, Spain, China and Indonesia. A critical idea underlying the study was that the experience of flavour was more than just sensory; it was also deeply cultural. To fulfil the study's objectives, the researchers devised a research design based on ethnographic methods, across the regions explored. In each case, they accompanied shoppers as they purchased chickens and other ingredients used in the creation of various dishes. This took them to local markets, shops and supermarkets where they often discussed chicken production methods with vendors. They then went home with the consumers to observe in painstaking detail how dishes were prepared and then served to their households. At mealtimes, they paid attention to other foods and beverages prepared alongside chicken, how dishes were served with respect to household hierarchies and how leftovers were saved and stored for future usage. At every step, they considered the impact of the process upon flavour creation and discussed flavour with all household members. A critical element in the study was the selection of appropriate participants. The key family cook they were seeking was someone who regularly prepared meals consistent with local cooking styles and used fresh ingredients. Their participants were typically, but not exclusively, female. These cooks did not need to use cookbooks but confidently relied instead upon sensory cues, memory and intuition while preparing meals. The most challenging aspects of this project were the large-scale logistics involved in an eight-country project and the emerging knowledge integration and use of that knowledge. The global presentation of the study's findings was a major feat of logistics. It had sites in Singapore, China, Mexico, Brazil, USA and several European cities scheduled on a six-hour conference call and Web-based slide presentation. The first hour was a summary presentation starting at 7.00 a.m., the best time to obtain attendance from every country. This was followed by more detailed presentations of countries rolling from Indonesia, to China, European countries, and finally Mexico, Colombia, Brazil, and the USA. Part of knowledge integration was creating insight and innovation by weaving the ethnography results into the other sources of consumer insight that were ongoing and related to chicken flavour. This would include the use of consumer surveys, product testing and other forms of insight generation which varied by country and by the key issues in the local markets. As a consequence, the process of extracting, integrating and utilising the information from this project fell out over a period of about a year, as other related projects were completed.

Ethics in marketing research

Marketing research often involves contact with the participants and the wider public, usually by way of data collection, dissemination of the research findings, and marketing activities such as advertising campaigns based on these findings. Thus, there is the potential to abuse or misuse marketing research by taking advantage of these people. If participants feel that they or their views are being abused or misrepresented, they either will not take part in future studies or may do so without honesty or full engagement in the issues being researched. They may also lobby politicians to protect them from what they see as intrusions into their privacy and liberties. In short, unethical research practices can severely impair the quality of the research process, undermine the validity of research findings and ultimately inflict serious damage upon the body of professional researchers. If participants cannot distinguish between genuine marketing research and unethical telemarketing or direct marketing where surveys are used to gain access to participants to deliver a sales pitch or to generate sales, there can be severe repercussions for the marketing research industry through legislation designed to protect the privacy of citizens. The marketing research industry in Europe and the USA has got to a point where it has had to defend the quality of its practices.

ESOMAR distinguishes marketing research from other competitive forms of data gathering, primarily through the issue of the anonymity of participants. It stresses that in marketing research the identity of the provider of information is not disclosed. It makes a clear distinction between marketing research and database marketing where the names and addresses of the people contacted are to be used for individual selling, promotional, fundraising or other non-research purposes. The distinction between marketing research and the database as a research tool is ultimately not so clear. There is a growing amount of support given to marketing decision-makers from database analyses and Research 2.0 activities that are not 'participant specific'. It is possible to perform database analyses with the same level of professional standards as is applied in the marketing research industry but social media research techniques are not so clear. ESOMAR has eight principles that encapsulate the scientific aim and character of marketing research as well as its special responsibility towards participants, clients and the public.

The eight principles that have now been incorporated into the ESOMAR code of conduct are:[50]

1 Researchers will conform to all relevant national and international laws.
2 Researchers will behave ethically and will not do anything which might damage the reputation of marketing research.
3 Researchers will take special care when carrying out research among children and other vulnerable groups of the population.
4 Participants' cooperation is voluntary and must be based on adequate, and not misleading, information about the general purpose and nature of the project when their agreement to participate is being obtained and all such statements must be honoured.
5 The rights of participants as private individuals will be respected by researchers and they will not be harmed or disadvantaged as the result of cooperating in a marketing research project.
6 Researchers will never allow personal data they collect in a marketing research project to be used for any purpose other than marketing research.
7 Researchers will ensure that projects and activities are designed, carried out, reported and documented accurately, transparently, objectively and to appropriate quality.
8 Researchers will conform to the accepted principles of fair competition.

The basic principles of the ESOMAR code of conduct and the full array of ESOMAR codes of conduct can be viewed at: **http://www.esomar.org/index.php/codes-guidelines.html**

The use of online interactions and Web 2.0 has shown that people are far more willing to self-disclose and to trade information about themselves.[51] Mike Cooke, Global Director: Online Development, at GfK NOP (**www.gfknop.com**) summed up the question of 'what happens to the principles of knowledge and control when it comes to consumer data on the internet?' as follows: 'If we can collect vast amounts of data passively without the individual being aware of the data trail they are leaving, does that give researchers the right to use it for other purposes?' Some researchers would answer with a resounding 'yes', and see chat rooms, forums and blogs as the ideal setting to conduct unbiased ethnography by 'lurking' at the sites of interest without announcing their presence.

One view within the research community seems to be that postings and blogs are 'published material'. However, bloggers and networkers might not see it in the same way. Teenagers often rue what they have written when they realise employers and university admissions tutors are able to view their 'published' outpourings.[52] These dilemmas have yet to be resolved within the marketing research industry, but it has been argued that in order to abide by the spirit of the marketing research Code of Conduct, researchers should be able to answer in the affirmative to the following questions: 'Are my research intentions transparent? Has the participant given informed consent? Can I verify the age of my participant? Can I verify that I have parental permission of under-16s?'[53]

There are many instances where database analyses generated from store data, loyalty card and web analytics can add clarity and focus to marketing research activities. Given the huge impact that such analyses are having upon marketing decision making, these issues will be developed more fully in Chapter 5. Research 2.0 and its emergent marketing research techniques are creating many ethical dilemmas for researchers. It is vital that these are addressed and so each chapter in this book will examine social responsibility and ethical issues connected to the chapter heading. Digital developments present ethical challenges that are impacting upon marketing research practices. The following example encapsulates the challenges with a strong metaphor.

| Real research | **Does anonymity matter?**[54] |

What if we were to create research methods where anonymity did not matter? Where clients could ask straight questions of customers on customer databases or customer websites, and get straight answers back from them? John Griffiths (**www.planningaboveandbeyond.com**) offers the view:

> *I am reminded of my induction into digital telephony over 20 years ago, where a technologist explained that by going digital, telephone companies had found a way to put voices and computer data into packets that they could send down a wire. Once they had made this jump, the challenge was to find ways to send data faster. Now thousands of people use the same wire at the same time to pass voice and data to each other in both directions in real time. While telephone stayed analogue we needed an operator to make a physical connection between two telephones, and while the two parties were using that single piece of wire no other information could be passed down that wire. That is where marketing research is stuck now. The analogue way to get trustworthy information from a participant is to set up a separate circuit isolated from everything else. Which makes it clunky, costly, slow and methodologically suspect. But what if client companies find that they can indeed get usable customer data without analogue circuitry? Supposing in a flurry of e-communications as a customer sends off for a new car brochure, they browse websites, watch ads on YouTube and Google Video and answer pop-up questionnaires before and after? Suppose car companies find ways for customers to browse information systems in the showroom to choose their cars and then integrate research capture. They could be gathering research data at the same time as selling. Unthinkable? Why ever not? This is called duplex information flow. All digital devices have had it for years, but marketing research hasn't. Playing 'peekaboo' with identity is a poor way to protect an industry as established as marketing research. If the industry does not find a way around the anonymity issue, we may be like the rest of analogue technology and find ourselves consigned to history. The client can talk directly to customers and prospects and they willingly talk back, even initiating an exchange. So, what was your role again?*

Digital applications in marketing research

As online applications of marketing research were first used, there was no real consensus within the industry of how things would develop. Many predicted that online methods would ultimately replace all other methods of data collection, while others argued that it would just add another means to measure, understand or observe participants.[55] Tables 1.4 and 1.5 illustrated how important online research now is to the marketing research industry. With the advent of Research 2.0, it is now clear that online methods are impacting upon the nature, methods and standards applied in marketing research in ways that could not have been predicted at the advent of the new millennium. Advances in technology have been fuelled by the growth of Internet and mobile penetration and advances in the sophistication of online platforms and mobile devices. These advances are opening up new consumers to measure and observe and are creating opportunities to improve methods and ways of engaging participants, clients and talent to the marketing research industry. Social media developments are creating opportunities to reach and observe participants in novel ways, changing the dynamics of research to a more collaborative process. The rise in social media has also shown researchers how open participants can be with their thoughts, opinions and data. There are a number of pioneering individuals and 'new wave' research agencies that are inspiring advances in thinking and application in marketing research. These newer agencies are creating a healthy competitive environment, stimulating the development of innovative products and services.[56] The following example illustrates how digital applications in marketing research are engaging with participants in new ways and creating the opportunities that will shape the future of the industry.

Given the importance of digital developments to the marketing research process and industry, key issues and debates in this subject will be addressed and illustrated. Throughout this book we show how the stages of the marketing research process are facilitated by online developments and other emerging technologies and software.

| Real research | **Lean Cuisine eCollage**[57] |

BuzzBack Market Research (**www.buzzback.com**) has developed an eCollage tool. This transforms traditional collage making into a game-like exercise in self-expression, where consumers use intuitive online functionality and a familiar drag and drop feature to reveal their innermost beliefs, characteristics and attitudes. The creativity remains, but the visually rich and interactive eCollage records image selection, swapping, sequence and placement. The underpinning technology captures all the data, as placement of each image on the online canvas is a measurable transaction. These data can be overlaid with consumers' other survey data, including follow-up questions about their eCollage. In an engagement with Lean Cuisine, BuzzBack wanted to understand how consumers perceive a competitor brand: Healthy Choice. BuzzBack compared the reactions to a word-based request, 'Describe how you feel about Healthy Choice frozen dinners and entrees' versus an eCollage and text request, 'Create a collage that shows how you feel about Healthy Choice frozen dinners and entrees.' The text-based word count averaged 18 words, while the eCollage-based word count averaged 40 words; there was a much richer emotional response to the visual stimulation of eCollage. Consumers' emotional response was expressed by a storytelling language, packed with metaphors, which provided Lean Cuisine with the keys to unlock the optimal way of talking to its consumers in its own language.

Summary

Marketing research provides support to marketing decision-makers by helping to describe the nature and scope of customer groups, understand the nature of forces that shape the needs of customer groups and the marketer's ability to satisfy those groups, test individual and interactive controllable marketing variables, and monitor and reflect upon past successes and failures in marketing decisions. The overall purpose of marketing research is to assess information needs and provide the relevant information in a systematic and objective manner to improve marketing decision making. The marketing research process consists of six broad steps that must be followed creatively and systematically. The process involves problem definition, research approach development, research design formulation, fieldwork or data collection, data integrity and analysis, and report preparation and presentation. Within these six broad steps are many iterations and routes that can be taken, reflecting the reality of marketing research in practice. Marketing research may be classified into problem identification research and problem-solving research. In general terms, problem identification uncovers the potential that may be exploited in markets, problem solving uncovers the means to realise that potential.

The major developed economies, especially in Europe and the USA, are the biggest users of marketing research on a per capita and total expenditure basis. In 2010, ESOMAR recorded a fall in the growth of global marketing research spend. This was the first such fall since their first study in 1988. Commentators have debated whether this fall can be attributed solely to the global economic downturn. Alternative explanations have focused upon the development in social media usage that has been termed Research 2.0. New ways of engaging and collaborating with consumers are being generated that challenge many of the principles upon which 'traditional marketing research' has been built.

Marketing research may be conducted internally (by internal suppliers) or may be purchased from external suppliers. Full-service suppliers provide the entire range of marketing research services, from problem definition to report preparation and presentation. They may also manage customer database analyses and social media research, being able to integrate the management and analyses databases with the management and analyses of conventional marketing research techniques. Limited-service suppliers specialise in one or a few phases of the marketing research project.

Marketing research is not a panacea for all marketing problems. There are examples where marketing research has not adequately supported decision-makers. Many of the problems that arise from poor marketing research derive from poor communications between decision-makers and researchers. In order to resolve these problems, there are growing demands upon the marketing research industry to produce research findings that are more actionable and relevant to marketing decision-makers. As well as having the technical skills to conduct research in a professional and ethical manner, researchers are increasingly expected to have the ability to interpret their findings in a manner that is relevant to decision-makers.

International marketing research can be much more complex than domestic research because the researcher must consider the environments prevailing in the international markets being researched. Research is founded upon the willing cooperation of the public and of business organisations. Ethical marketing research practices nurture that cooperation, allowing a more professional approach and more accurate research information. There are many competitive threats to the marketing research industry that have been exacerbated by the development of social media interactions. However, there are many great opportunities for researchers as afforded by social media interactions and digital developments. New types of participant can be reached across global markets, with new forms of engagement that may be integrated with more traditional forms of marketing research.

Questions

1 Describe the purpose of marketing research.

2 What decisions are made by marketing managers? How does marketing research help in supporting these decisions?

3 What do you see as the major challenges for researchers that emerge from the ESOMAR definition of marketing research?

4 What problems are associated with using consumer databases in marketing research?

5 How may the sound practice of problem identification research enhance the sound practice of problem-solving research?

6 What challenges exist in trying to quantify the size and growth of the marketing research industry on a global basis?

7 Explain one way to classify marketing research suppliers and services.

8 Describe the steps in the simple marketing research process.

9 Explain why there may be the need for iterations between stages of the marketing research process.

10 What arguments can be used by sceptics of marketing research?

11 What management skills are increasingly being demanded from researchers?

12 What arguments would you use to defend investment in marketing research?

13 What factors fuel the growth of international marketing research?

14 Discuss the ethical issues in marketing research that relate to (a) the client, (b) the supplier, and (c) the participant.

15 Summarise the nature of threats and opportunities that social media offer the researcher.

Exercises

1 Visit the website of Taylor Nelson Sofres, **www.tns-global.com**. Examine the nature of the Research Services and the Business Solutions it offers. How do you see these fitting together and what is the impact of this fit upon the career opportunities the company advertises?

2 Visit the website of the Market Research Society, **www.mrs.org.uk**. Work through the array of publications and support it gives to its members. Specifically examine and register for **www.research-live.com** and examine the published code of conduct. Compare the MRS code of conduct with that available on the ESOMAR website, **www.esomar.org**. Are there any differences in their respective approaches to maintaining professional standards in the marketing research industry?

3 Visit the website **www.trendwatching.com** and register for trend watching. Critically evaluate the worth of trend watching for the researcher.

4 From national or international newspapers, track down stories of successful entrepreneurial ventures. Evaluate the extent to which marketing research is attributed to their success and/or an awareness of their market(s).

5   In a small group discuss the following issues: 'What is the ideal educational background for someone seeking a career in marketing research?' and 'Is it possible to enforce ethical standards within the marketing research industry?'

Video case exercise: Burke Inc.

Burke describes marketing research as 'an important and dynamic component of modern business'. How are other means of supporting the marketing decision-maker affecting the importance and dynamism of marketing research?

Notes

1   Dekkers, S. and Lawrence, G., 'easyJet community – using online communities to co-create the future', ESOMAR Panel Research, Dublin (October 2008).

2   van Veen, Y., 'From dream to purchase: shopping and purchase behaviour in consumer digital products', ESOMAR Retail and Shopper, London (March 2009).

3   Macer, T., 'Technology futures: perspectives on how technology will transform the market research of tomorrow', Market Research Society Conference (2009).

4   For the strategic role of marketing research, see Methner, T. and Frank, D., 'Welcome to the house of research: achieving new insights and better brand knowledge through courageous ways of collaboration in what is usually a competitive environment', ESOMAR, Congress Odyssey, Athens (September 2010); Bakken, D.G., 'Riding the value shift in market research: only the paranoid survive', ESOMAR, Congress Odyssey, Athens (September 2010); Kaufmann, R. and Wakenhut, G., 'Crossing the frontier – the fusion of research, consulting and creativity', ESOMAR, Annual Congress, Montreal (September 2008).

5   For relationships between information processing, marketing decisions and performance, see Roberts, D. and Adams, R., 'Agenda development for marketing research: the user's voice', *International Journal of Market Research* 52 (3) (2010), 339–363.

6   Dexter, A. and Page, A., 'The business of insight: the price of everything, and the value of nothing?; Market Research Society Annual Conference (2008).

7   Briggs, R., 'The collective brain: why market research will be overrun by the software power houses, and what you can do to compete', ESOMAR, Congress Odyssey, Athens (September 2010).

8   The use of the term 'participant' demonstrates a greater respect to those who mostly give their views and time for free. Embracing this attitude, the term 'participant' rather than 'respondent' or 'informant' is used throughout this chapter and the remainder of the book.

9   Renkema, R. and Zwikker, C., 'Development of a new brand concept', ESOMAR Consumer Insights Conference (March 2003).

10   Kung, A. and Tse, G., 'The evolving role of in-house market research professionals: from "reactive" to "proactive"', ESOMAR, Asia Pacific, Beijing (April 2009).

11   Casteleyn, J., Mottart, A. and Rutten, K., 'How to use Facebook in your market research', *International Journal of Market Research* 51 (4) (2009).

12   Hamburger, S. and Lawry, P., 'Storytelling with international millionaires – a creative approach to research', ESOMAR Annual Congress, Montreal (September 2008).

13   Boal, K., 'Kellogg rolls out new cereal and snacking options', *Bakery & Snacks* (12 February, 2007); Anon., 'Kellogg's Crunchy Nuts gets ready for adult breakfast', *Grocer* 224 (7524) (6 October, 2001), 53 and **www.kelloggs.com**.

14   ESOMAR, 'Global Market Research', ESOMAR Industry Report (2010), 3.

15   ESOMAR, 'Global Market Research', ESOMAR Industry Report (2010), 92–93.

16   The 15 EU member countries in 2003.

17   ESOMAR, 'Global Market Research', ESOMAR Industry Report (2010), 7–11.

18   ESOMAR, 'Global Market Research', ESOMAR Industry Report (2010), 19.

19   ESOMAR, 'Global Market Research', ESOMAR Industry Report (2010), 3.

20   ESOMAR, 'Global Market Research', ESOMAR Industry Report (2010), 6.

21   ESOMAR, 'Global Market Research', ESOMAR Industry Report (2010), 16.

22   ESOMAR, 'Global Market Research', ESOMAR Industry Report (2010), 17.

23   ESOMAR, 'Global Market Research', ESOMAR Industry Report (2010), 28.

24   ESOMAR, 'Global Market Research', ESOMAR Industry Report (2010), 44.

25   Woodnutt, T. and Owen, R., 'The research industry needs to embrace radical change in order to thrive and survive in the digital era', Market Research Society, Annual Conference (2010).

26 ESOMAR, 'Global Market Research', ESOMAR Industry Report (2010), 48.

27 Lury, G., 'Market research cannot cover for the "vision thing"', *Marketing* (9 November 2000), 34.

28 Gordon, W., 'Be creative to innovate', *Research* (January 2000), 23.

29 Lehmann, D.R., *Market Research and Analysis*, 3rd edn (Homewood, IL: Irwin, 1994), 14.

30 Kearon, J., 'The paradox of success – learning to love failure as pioneers of market research', ESOMAR Annual Congress (September 2008); Muranka, T. and Rootes, N., *Doing a Dyson* (Dyson Appliances, 1996), 22; Mesure, S., 'A day in the life of James Dyson', *Independent* (27 May 2006), 55.

32 ESOMAR, 'Global Market Research', ESOMAR Industry Report (2010), 48.

33 Srivatsa, A., Puri, A. and Raj, S., 'The case of the elusive insight: lessons from the greatest researcher of them all', Consumer Insights Conference, Milan (May 2005).

34 Chelliah, J. and Davis, D., 'But do you like your (expensive management) consultant?', *Journal of Business Strategy* 31 (2) (2010), 34–42; Keegan, S., '"Emergent inquiry": a practitioner's reflections on the development of qualitative research', *Qualitative Market Research: An International Journal* 12 (2) (2009), 234–248; Florin, D., Callen, B., Pratzel, M. and Kropp, J., 'Harnessing the power of consumer insight', *Journal of Product & Brand Management* 16 (2) (2007), 76–81.

35 Meller, D., 'Social media and market research in Latin America', ESOMAR, Latin America, Cartagena (May 2010).

36 ESOMAR, 'Global Market Research', ESOMAR Industry Report (2010), 48.

37 Dierikx, R. and Lynch, A., 'Fuelling Philips' innovation engine – continuous ideas and feedback from users', ESOMAR Annual Congress, Montreal (September 2008).

38 Poynter, R., 'Stop asking questions and start listening', *Admap Magazine* (July/August 2010).

39 Poynter, R., Cierpicki, S., Cape, P., Lewis, A. and Vieira, S., 'What does research 2.0 mean to consumers in Asia Pacific?', ESOMAR, Asia Pacific, Beijing (April 2009).

40 Antilli, L. and Vishney, A., 'Digital media and technology in youth audience research', *Admap Magazine* Issue 498 (October 2008).

41 Kaufmann, R. and Wakenhut, G., 'Crossing the frontier – the fusion of research, consulting and creativity', ESOMAR Annual Conference, Montreal (September 2008).

42 Poynter, R., 'A taxonomy of new MR', Market Research Society, Annual Conference (2010).

43 Havermnans, J., 'What do clients want from research?', *Research World* (March 2005), 10.

44 Kaufmann, R. and Wakenhut, G., 'Crossing the frontier – the fusion of research, consulting and creativity', ESOMAR Annual Conference, Montreal (September 2008).

45 Nagle, C., Williams, H. and Hickey, K., 'Research alchemy: combining creativity and rigour with a sprinkling of sugar', ESOMAR, Annual Congress, Berlin (September 2007); Van Hamersveld, M. and Smith, D., 'From data collection to decision support (2)', *Research World* (November 2003), 18.

46 ESOMAR, 'Global Market Research', ESOMAR Industry Report (2010), 46.

47 Gordon, W., Ratcliff, M., Wynberg, R., Edwards, P., Helyar, R., Simmons, S., Fryer, S., Taylor, R. and O'Brien, Y., 'The future of research', *Admap* July/August (2010), 18–23; Van Hamersveld, M. and Smith, D., 'From data collection to decision support (3)', *Research World* (December 2003), 20.

48 Radbourne, V., Boneham, D. and Muttiallu, J., '"When I grow I want to be…": attracting, developing and retaining graduate talent', Market Research Society, Annual Conference (2008).

49 Mariampolski, H., 'A world of chicken flavours – using ethnography in multi-country studies', ESOMAR, Annual Congress, Montreal (September 2008).

50 Havermans, J., 'New international MR practice in 8 principles', *Research World* (May 2004), 20–21.

51 Griffiths, J., 'Viewpoint – MR confidential: anonymity in market research', *International Journal of Market Research* 50 (6) (2008), 717.

52 Cooke, M., 'The new world of Web 2.0 research (Guest editorial)', *International Journal of Market Research* 50 (5) (2008), 570–572.

53 Nairn, A., 'Conference notes – research ethics in the virtual world', *International Journal of Market Research* 51 (2) (2009), 276–278.

54 Griffiths, J., 'Viewpoint – MR confidential: anonymity in market research', *International Journal of Market Research*, 50 (6) (2008), 717–718.

55 Tarran, B., 'Worldwide global', *Research* (November 2005), 27.

56 ESOMAR, 'Global Market Research', ESOMAR Industry Report (2010), 42–46.

57 Oxley, M. and Light, B., 'Research 2.0: engage or give up the ghost?' Market Research Society, Annual Conference (2010).

2

Defining the marketing research problem and developing a research approach

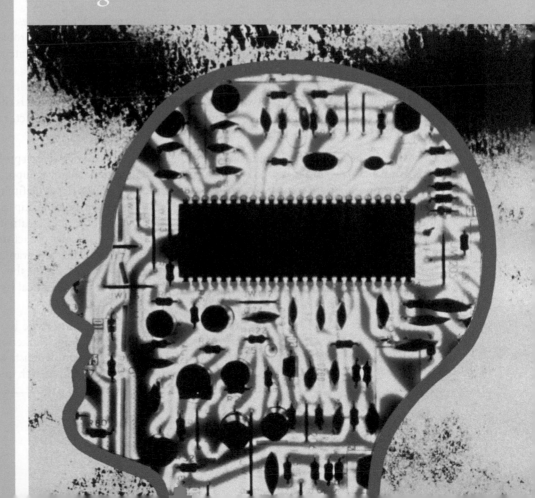

Stage 1

Problem definition

Stage 2

Research approach developed

Stage 3

Research design developed

Stage 4

Fieldwork or data collection

Stage 5

Data integrity and analysis

Stage 6

Report preparation and presentation

The correct diagnosis of marketing research problems cannot be compromised. Regardless of how well subsequent stages are conducted, the whole process may be worthless if the diagnosis is weak.

Objectives

After reading this chapter, you should be able to:

1 understand the importance of, and the process used in, defining marketing research problems;

2 describe the tasks involved in problem definition;

3 discuss in detail the nature and various components of a research brief and a research proposal;

4 discuss the environmental factors affecting the definition of the research problem;

5 clarify the distinction between the marketing decision problem and the marketing research problem;

6 explain the structure of a well-defined marketing research problem, including the broad statement and the specific components;

7 understand the role of theory in the development and execution of applied marketing research;

8 acquire an appreciation of the complexity involved in defining the problem and developing a research approach in international marketing research;

9 understand the ethical issues and conflicts that arise in defining the problem and developing a research approach;

10 appreciate the ways in which digital applications can support the process of problem diagnosis and the development of a research design.

Overview

This chapter covers the first two of the six steps of the marketing research process described in Chapter 1: defining the marketing research problem and developing a research approach to tackle the problem. Defining the problem is the most important step, since only when a problem has been clearly and accurately identified can a research project be properly conducted. Defining the marketing research problem sets the course of the entire project. Regardless of how well a research plan is designed and subsequent stages are carried out, if the problem is not correctly diagnosed, research findings could be misleading or even dangerous. In this chapter, we allow the reader to appreciate the complexities involved in defining a problem, by identifying the factors to be considered and the tasks involved.

In practical terms, the means to communicate and facilitate the diagnosis of research problems is achieved through the preparation of a research brief and research proposal. The rationale and components of the research brief and research proposal are presented. We provide guidelines for appropriately defining the marketing research problem and avoiding common types of errors. The client–researcher relationship is described with seven Cs (communication, cooperation, confidence, candour, closeness, continuity and creativity) presented to nurture a trusting and effective relationship. We also discuss in detail the characteristics or factors influencing the research design and components of an approach to the problem: objective/theoretical framework, analytical models, research questions and hypotheses. The special considerations involved in defining the problem and developing a research approach in international marketing research are discussed. Several ethical issues that arise at this stage of the marketing research process are considered.

We introduce our discussion with an example. The iconic American motorbike brand Harley-Davidson has achieved a remarkable turnaround in its performance and brand positioning. Marketing research played a major role in supporting the decisions that achieved this turnaround. This example illustrates how Harley-Davidson established the focus for its marketing research and developed a clear set of research questions.

| Real research | **Marketing an American icon**[1] |

The motorcycle manufacturer Harley-Davidson (**www.harleydavidson.com**) made such an important comeback in the early 2000s that there was a long waiting list to get a bike. In 2007, Harley-Davidson's revenues exceeded €4 billion with a market share of about 50% in the heavyweight bike category. Although distributors urged Harley-Davidson to build more motorcycles, the company was sceptical about investing in new production facilities.

The years of declining sales taught top management to be more risk averse than risk prone. Harley-Davidson was now performing well again, and investing in new facilities meant taking risks. Would the demand follow in the long term or would customers stop wanting Harleys when the next fashion came along? The decrease in motorcycles' quality linked to Harley's fast growth had given the company all its bad years. Top management were afraid that the decision to invest was too early. On the other hand, investing would help Harley-Davidson expand and possibly become the clear market leader in the heavyweight segment. Discussions with industry experts indicated that brand loyalty was a major factor influencing the sales and repeat sales of motorcycles. Secondary data revealed that the vast majority of motorcycle owners also owned other vehicles. Forecasts predicted an increase in consumer spending on entertainment and recreation up to the year 2015. Focus groups with motorcycle owners further indicated that motorcycles were not used primarily as a means of basic transportation but as a means of recreation.

This process and the findings that emerged helped define the management decision problem and the marketing research problem. The management decision problem was: should Harley-Davidson invest to produce more motorcycles? The marketing research problem was to determine whether customers would be loyal buyers of Harley-Davidson in the long term. Specifically, the research had to address the following questions:

1 Who are the customers? What are their demographic and psychographic characteristics?
2 Can different types of customers be distinguished? Is it possible to segment the market in a meaningful way?
3 How do customers feel about their Harleys? Are all customers motivated by the same appeal?
4 Are customers loyal to Harley-Davidson? What is the extent of brand loyalty?

One of the Research Questions (RQs) examined and its associated hypotheses were:

RQ: Can the motorcycle buyers be segmented based on psychographic characteristics?
H1: There are distinct segments of motorcycle buyers.
H2: Each segment is motivated to own a Harley for a different reason.
H3: Brand loyalty is high among Harley-Davidson customers in all segments.

This research was guided by the theory that brand loyalty is the result of brand beliefs, attitudes, affect and experience with the brand. Both qualitative and quantitative research were subsequently conducted. First, focus groups of current owners, would-be owners and owners of other brands were conducted to understand their feelings about Harley-Davidson. Then 16,000 questionnaires were posted to customers to determine their psychological, sociological and demographic profiles and their perceptions of Harley-Davidson.

Key findings included the following. Seven categories of customers could be distinguished: (1) the adventure-loving traditionalist; (2) the sensitive pragmatist; (3) the stylish status seeker; (4) the laid-back camper; (5) the classy capitalist; (6) the cool-headed loner; and (7) the cocky misfit. Thus H1 was supported.

All customers, however, had the same desire to own a Harley: it was a symbol of independence, freedom and power. This uniformity across segments was suprising, contradicting H2.

All customers were long-term loyal customers of Harley-Davidson, supporting H3.

Based on these findings, the decision was taken to invest and in this way to increase the number of Harley's built in the future.

Importance of defining the problem

Problem definition
A broad statement of the general problem and identification of the specific components of the marketing research problem.

Although each step in a marketing research project is important, problem definition is the most important step. As mentioned in Chapter 1, for the purpose of marketing research, problems and opportunities are treated interchangeably. Problem definition involves stating the general problem and identifying the specific components of the marketing research problem. Only when the marketing research problem has been clearly defined can research be designed and conducted properly:

> *Of all the tasks in a marketing research project, none is more vital to the ultimate fulfilment of a client's needs than an accurate and adequate definition of the research problem. All the effort, time, and money spent from this point on will be wasted if the problem is misunderstood and ill-defined.*[2]

An analogy to this is the medical doctor prescribing treatment after a cursory examination of a patient – the medicine may be even more dangerous than the condition it is supposed to cure! The truly serious mistakes are made not as a result of wrong answers but because of asking the wrong questions. This point is worth remembering because inadequate problem definition is a leading cause of failure of marketing research projects. Further, better communication and more involvement in problem definition are the most frequently mentioned ways of improving the usefulness of research.

The importance of clearly identifying and defining the research problem cannot be overstated. The foundation of defining a research problem is the communication that develops between marketing decision-makers and researchers. In some form or another, marketing decision-makers must communicate what they see as being the problems they face and what research support they need. This communication usually comes in the form of a research brief. The researcher responds to the research brief with a research proposal, which encapsulates the researcher's vision of a practical solution to the set research problem. The following example illustrates that a research brief may not always be particularly well thought out. The researcher is expected to develop the brief into a research proposal and in doing so has a vital role to play in the diagnosis of research problems.

Real research   **How to bait the interview hook for those top 1,000 big fish**[3]

The groans from researchers when another brief arrives asking for 100 or 200 interviews with chief executive officers (CEOs) or equivalents within the Times Top 1000 companies typify the attitude generated by business-to-business marketers' constant demand to reach this audience. When the research brief arrives, it is certainly worth examining whether, practically, what is requested can actually be done. The research proposal developed must reflect the practicalities of questioning managers who are constantly bombarded with requests to respond to research questions. The number of interviews,

the timescale, the nature of questions and the structure of the sample all need to be taken into account.
For example, is it really worth undertaking just 200
interviews within any single European country? If we
were limited to one per organisation, we would be
interviewing to strike rates of between 1 in 2.5 and
1 in 5. If the research targets companies throughout Europe, individual countries such as the UK and
France may have few large companies compared
with the USA, while Italy has a small number of very
large companies and a great many smaller ones. In
actually reaching the target audience, a number of
issues need to be taken into account. International
business-to-business research with senior business

audiences brings with it not only the particular difficulties of reaching them but also the
need to understand both country and cultural issues that impact on the research. Telephone interviews (even if possible) are considered inappropriate in many Far East and
Middle East markets, especially South Korea and Japan. In Singapore and Hong Kong, the
telephone is fine, provided the interviews are not too long (over 15 minutes).

The marketing research brief

Research brief
A document produced
by the users of research
findings or the buyers
of a piece of marketing
research. The brief is
used to communicate the
perceived requirements
of a marketing research
project.

The marketing research brief is a document produced by the users of research findings or the
buyers of a piece of marketing research. The brief may be used to communicate the perceived
requirements of a marketing research project to external agencies or internally within an
organisation to marketing research professionals. It should act as the first step for decision-
makers to express the nature of a marketing and research problem as they see it. This first
step is vital in developing an agreement of an appropriate research approach. As a first step of
problem diagnosis and negotiation, *the marketing research brief should not be carved in tablets
of stone!*

It has been contended that the greatest form of potential error in marketing research lies in
the initial relationship between marketing decision-makers and researchers.[4] In developing a
sound initial relationship, the research brief plays a vital role. Without some formal method
of communicating the nature of a marketing problem, there is great potential for ambiguities,
illogical actions (by both parties), misunderstandings and even forgetfulness.

The purpose of a written marketing research brief may be summarised as follows:

- It makes the initiator of the brief more certain of how the information to be collected will
  support decision making.
- It ensures an amount of agreement or cohesion among all parties who may benefit from
  the research findings.
- It helps both the marketer and the researcher to plan and implement the research design.
- It helps to reduce disputes that can occur when the gaps in decision-makers' knowledge
  are not 'filled' as intended.
- It can form the basis for negotiation with a variety of research organisations.

In all, the research brief saves resources in time and money by helping to ensure that the
nature of the problem or opportunity under investigation has been thought through.

Components of the marketing research brief

The rationale for a marketing research brief may seem logical, but actually generating a brief from marketing decision-makers can be extremely difficult. These difficulties will be tackled later in this chapter. If a decision-maker has a very clear idea of the nature of decision support needed *and* can define the research objectives that will create such support *and* define the research design that will fulfil the research objectives, then the decision-maker can write a research brief that is highly structured. A structured brief created in these conditions would basically be a tender document, allowing a number of research suppliers to pitch for business on a like-for-like basis. Not all marketing decision-makers have such clarity of the marketing research support they need. Even if they do, by sticking to highly structured and prescriptive marketing research briefs, they can underutilise the experience and creativity of researchers. This is illustrated by the following quote, based upon the experiences of a researcher who has seen many research problems misdiagnosed:

> *When a client calls for a meeting on a research brief, quite often the tendency is for a methodology meeting: 'I'd like to have a product test done on three new flavours that we have developed'. Off goes the researcher, conducts the test, identifies the winning flavour, the client launches it and finds to their dismay that it fails dismally. Why? It turns out the flavours were developed to try and revitalise an ageing product category and brand. In the product test, the familiar flavours orange and lemon won over the more exotic flavour to boost the category image. Had the researcher been allowed to look beyond the brief and ask one simple question on why the flavours were being made, it may have led to a clearer brief which in turn would have led to a research design which was more appropriately designed to cull out the real insight, which was that the consumers were bored and something rather more than flavour extensions were needed to revitalise the category.[5]*

The following format for a research brief helps to make the most of the experience and creativity of both the marketing decision-maker and the researcher and has clear advantages for both parties. First, it does not demand that decision-makers have a great deal of technical knowledge about research. Their focus can remain upon the gaps in their knowledge, the nature of support they need, not the technicalities of how data are to be collected and analysed. Second, it allows the researchers the opportunity to demonstrate their creative abilities and awareness of the latest research and analysis techniques. Using their experiences from problems faced by other decision-makers, perhaps from a great variety of contexts and industries, researchers have the possibility of examining the marketing and research problem from many different perspectives. They can create, develop and adapt a research design to the research problem that supports the marketing decision-maker within clear time and cost parameters (Figure 2.1):

1 *Background information.* The background serves to put research objectives into context, helping the researcher to understand why certain research objectives are being pursued. Decision-makers would detail what they see as being the main events that have caused or contributed to the problem under study. Such a background gives a framework for the researcher to investigate other potential events, contributory factors or causes.

2 *Objectives.* The first part of this section would detail which marketing decisions are to be completed once the research has been undertaken. This requires decision-makers to explain what they see as the focus of the decisions they plan to make. They then go on to explain what gap(s) they see in their knowledge. Those gaps create the focus to planned research activities and set the research objectives. The formulation of the marketing objectives can encompass two areas: organisational objectives and personal objectives of the decision-maker. For a research project to be successful, it must serve the objectives of the organisation and of the decision-maker. For the researcher, this may not be explicit or obvious to discern. It may take some time working with a decision-maker or a particular organisation to see potential conflicts in organisational and personal objectives. The problem faced by researchers is that decision-makers may not formulate marketing objectives clearly. Rather,

it is likely that objectives tend to be stated in terms that have no operational significance, such as 'to improve corporate image'. Ultimately this does not matter, as this 'first-step' brief offers the opportunity for the researcher to draw out and develop a much clearer vision of marketing and research objectives. Drawing out and developing decision-makers' perspectives of objectives, even if they have no operational significance, helps the process of developing a common understanding of what the decision-maker is trying to achieve.

3 *Target to research.* Any marketing research project will measure, understand or observe a target group of individuals. These may be distinct groups of consumers, channel members such as retailers or competitors, or company employees. In this section, details of the characteristics of the target group(s) can help in many research design decisions. These cover areas of identification, gaining access to conduct research, understanding which techniques are appropriate to measure or understand these individuals, and the best environment or context in which to conduct research.

4 *Who is to use the findings?* This section would outline brief details of the decision-makers who will use the research findings. For example, certain decision-makers may be entrepreneurial and introspective, looking for short-term tactical advantages. Presenting research findings that make tactical advantages apparent would be the best way to communicate to such managers. Managers with a background and training in statistics may expect results to be analysed and presented in a particular manner to have any credibility. Other managers, e.g. those responsible for many product and/or communications design decisions, may not have such training or may even be distrustful of statistical analyses and seek a more qualitative interpretation. These issues have an impact upon the nature and extent of analysis conducted upon the data collected and the style and format in which research findings will be presented.

5 *Constraints.* The main limitation to researchers carrying out what they may perceive as being the correct way to research a problem is the time and money that decision-makers can afford. Proposing a large-scale project that would cost €200,000 when only €50,000 has been budgeted obviously will not meet management approval. In many instances, the scope of the marketing research problem may have to be reduced to accommodate budget constraints. With knowledge of time and cost constraints, the researcher can develop a research design to suit these needs. The researcher may also demonstrate other courses of action that could demand greater amounts of money or time, but could have clear benefits that the marketer may be unaware of. Other constraints, such as those imposed

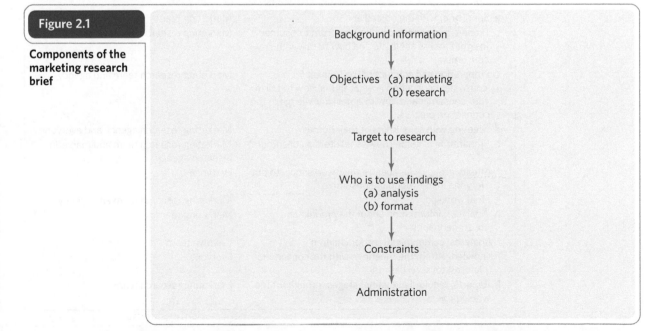

Figure 2.1

Components of the marketing research brief

Background information
↓
Objectives   (a) marketing
                   (b) research
↓
Target to research
↓
Who is to use findings
(a) analysis
(b) format
↓
Constraints
↓
Administration

by the client firm's personnel, organisational structure and culture, or decision-making styles, should be identified to determine the scope of the research project. Yet, constraints should not be allowed to diminish the value of the research to the decision-maker or to compromise the integrity of the research process. In instances where the resources are too limited to allow a project of sufficient quality, the firm should be advised not to undertake formal marketing research. In the following example, researcher Malgorzata Blachowska of Nestlé in Poland describes how she helped to develop a research brief that facilitated creative input from researchers, marketers and their communications agency.

6   *Administrative considerations.* These would lay out administrative details in completing the research project. Examples could be the expected delivery of interim reports, contacts in an organisation that may be able to help supply further information, or reference to sources of materials and individuals that are needed to complete the research successfully.

Real research | **Can marketing research support effective communication ideas for children?[6]**

The marketing team of the Ice Cream Division of Nestlé in Poland wished to brief its creative agency. It turned to the marketing research team to see what support it could give to develop strong communications with the target market of children. The researchers seized the opportunity to be part of the process of advertising development, rather than simply delivering data or consumer test results. They decided to try a new way of cross-functional team cooperation to the challenge, which started with the preparation of a research brief. Their short brief described:

1   Clear and straightforward project objectives, including details of the target group they would be addressing. In this particular case the research objective was to *reconstruct consumer insights, which help to build the most relevant and effective communication for children in the ice cream category in Poland.* The core target group was children aged 6 to 11 years old.
2   Details of participant characteristics.
3   A detailed plan of the project:

What?	Who is responsible?
a Short brief with the objective	Marketing team
b Prepare and conduct the training from Consumer Insight Process at Nestlé and how to talk with consumers.	Marketing research team
c Preparation and conduct of the training for 'consumer connection' – what this is, how to talk to your consumer and how to obtain knowledge in the connection process.	Marketing research team and agency
d Meeting with consumers at their homes	Marketing research agency and everyone
e Preparation of guide (how to talk to the consumers)	Marketing research team and marketing research agency
f Affinity groups – just before their workshop – to put everyone in the 'mood of consumers'	Everyone
g Final workshop	Marketing research team and agency
h Analyses: information about the product and consumer habits	Marketing team
i Analyses: communications for children	Creative team
j Knowledge from the meetings with the consumers (pictures, toys, verbatims)	Everyone
k Reports; required at distinct stages throughout the whole project	Marketing research team

Three of the best ideas were tested in the research study; one was chosen, filmed and aired. The outcome was a success for the new business in Poland (Nestlé was a relatively new brand which did not really exist in consumers' minds as it had taken over the Scholler brand). The marketing team increased awareness of the Nestlé brand and the BluMis brand (hero of the Nestlé children's ice creams in Poland); the team sold much more than the operational plan and began building the image of the brands. This is an example of an action research approach which will be discussed in more detail in Chapter 6.

With a formal marketing research brief and perhaps preliminary discussion with the organisation that is to commission the research, the researcher has the necessary material to develop a research proposal. In many instances, however, the researcher does not enjoy the luxury of a written research brief.[7] The marketing decision-maker may outline ideas in an oral manner, perhaps on an informal basis. This can happen if the decision-maker is not aware of the personal benefits of producing a written research brief as detailed above. Decision-makers may see the brief as a time-consuming process that really is the job of the researcher. If researchers are faced with an oral brief, they can use the proposed brief outline above as a guideline to the issues they should elicit in informal discussions in order to develop an effective proposal.

The marketing research proposal

Research proposal
The official layout of the planned marketing research activity.

In response to a research brief, the researcher will develop a research plan (covered in detail in Chapter 3) and will develop a research proposal to communicate this plan. The marketing research proposal contains the essence of the project and, in its final format, can serve as a contract between the researcher and decision-makers.[8] The research proposal covers all phases of the marketing research process. It allows the researcher to present an interpretation of the problems faced by management and to be creative in developing a research solution that will effectively support decision-makers. Although the format of a research proposal may vary considerably, most proposals address all the steps of the marketing research process and contain the elements shown in Figure 2.2:

1 *Executive summary.* The proposal should begin with a summary of the major points from each of the other sections, presenting an overview of the entire proposal.

2 *Background.* The researcher would be expected to have researched and developed ideas beyond those presented in the brief 'background'. Other potential causes of the problems faced or alternative interpretations of the factors that shape the background in an environmental context should be presented. The extent of developmental work on the background to a research project will depend mostly upon how much past work researchers have done for the decision-makers. In projects where researchers and decision-makers are working together for the first time, much exploratory work may be undertaken by the researcher to understand an industry, organisation, decision-makers, planned campaigns, etc. After a number of projects, much of this may be understood and not need restating. The following example from a proposal to BAFTA illustrates how IFM Sports Marketing Surveys presents a relatively short but well-focused background. The two companies have worked together before and are building upon their shared knowledge and their shared language.

3 *Problem definition.* Again, if necessary, the researcher may go beyond the problem definition presented in the brief. If the researcher sees potential to add value for the marketer through alternative diagnoses of the problem presented in the brief, then these should be shown. If the researcher sees a problem in the brief that is ambiguous or unattainable, other alternative diagnoses should be presented. From this section, the marketer's gaps in knowledge should be apparent.

Figure 2.2

Components of the marketing research proposal

Executive summary
↓
Background
↓
Problem definition
↓
Research objectives
↓
Research design
↓
Fieldwork/data collection
↓
Data analysis
↓
Reporting
↓
Cost & timetable
↓
Research organisation & researchers
↓
Appendices
↓
Agreement

Focus on   IFM Sports Marketing Surveys

BAFTA – British Academy Film Awards Rights

Research proposal
Background

The British Academy of Film and Television Arts (BAFTA) supports, promotes and develops the art forms of the moving image; film, television and video games. BAFTA ensures that the very best creative work can be accessed and appreciated by the British public and hosts the annual Orange British Academy Film Awards.

In 2009, BAFTA commissioned S:COMM (a subsidiary of IFM Sports Marketing Surveys) to carry out an evaluation of the media delivery of the title sponsorship of the British Academy Film Awards. The basis of this work identified the requirement for a more comprehensive review of the media coverage generated by the event, and a full rights valuation assessment of the title partner rights package.

The rights valuation model will provide a fair market value for the sponsorship, including media data and taking into account:

- A full audit of the rights and benefits available as part of the sponsorship package, including naming rights and access to content granted by BAFTA.
- An assessment of the value of association with the property driven by intangible benefits relating to the sponsorship, such as the prestige associated with the BAFTA name.

The ultimate aim of the rights valuation is to help BAFTA to develop their sponsorship partner package, and negotiate more effectively with independent assessment.

4 *Research objectives.* These may be presented in the form of clear hypotheses that may be tested. They may also cover broader areas in terms of 'research questions' that are to be explored rather than formally measured in a conclusive manner.

5 *Research design.* The research design to be adopted, classified in broad terms as exploratory, descriptive or causal, should be specified. Beyond such a broad classification should be details of the individual techniques that will be adopted and how they will unfold and connect to each other. This means that the reader will clearly see methods of collecting the desired data, justification for these methods, and a sampling plan to include details of sample size(s). This applies to both quantitative and qualitative approaches. The following example from IFM Sports Marketing Surveys' BAFTA project is a descriptive research design. This summarises the stages, but note that each stage is developed in more detail in the actual proposal. Of particular note is how the stages work concurrently to form a proprietary model to value sponsorship rights.

Focus on	**IFM Sports Marketing Surveys**

BAFTA – British Academy Film Awards Rights

Research design
1 Media evaluation
S:COMM will work closely with BAFTA's Public Relation's agency Freud Communications (**www.freud.com**) to ensure that the major media stories over the period of the British Academy Film Awards are collected. Freud's work will largely revolve around collecting UK national media coverage. S:COMM will supplement Freud's tracking with the following monitoring and evaluation:

a Television
  - BBC coverage of the event – live and highlights plus any after show coverage.
  - UK national and regional news coverage of the event.
b Print
  - Regional UK press coverage during the months of January and February 2010.
c Online
  - UK websites during the months of January and February.
d Radio
  - UK national and regional coverage at peak listening times from 21 January to 26 February 2010.

As part of the above programme S:COMM will evaluate the 'missed sponsor exposure opportunities', i.e. when Orange is not referenced alongside British Academy Film Awards.

2 Consumer research

S:COMM proposes conducting 500 UK nationally representative face-to-face interviews. Topic areas will include:

- **BAFTA specific**: Image of BAFTA, image of film awards, opinions and attitudes to BAFTA, awareness of BAFTA's role.
- **Sponsorship**: Awareness of sponsorship, source of awareness – TV, websites, word of mouth, impact of sponsorship – image, favourability, brand preference, consideration.
- **Profiles**: Age, gender, socio-economic grades, following of British Academy Film Awards.

3 Other data collection

This will focus around the collation of other rights including:

- Level of hospitality and ticketing.
- Online visits/unique users to specific branded web pages.
- Film promoter advertising.
- BAFTA event advertising – media and outdoor.

Any existing secondary data that are available in-house at BAFTA or S:COMM will be used to build the intangible elements of the rights valuation. S:COMM will work closely with BAFTA in getting this data from the appropriate sources within the company.

6 *Fieldwork/data collection.* The proposal should discuss how the data will be collected and who will collect them. If the fieldwork is to be subcontracted to another supplier, this should be stated. Control mechanisms to ensure the quality of data collected should be described.

7 *Data analysis.* This should describe the kind of data analysis that will be conducted, e.g. content analysis, simple cross-tabulations, univariate analysis or multivariate analysis. If software packages are to be used in these analyses, they should be specified, as they will be indicative of the potential analyses that can be conducted. There should be further description of the extent to which the results will be interpreted in light of the set marketing objectives, beyond the specified analysis techniques.

8 *Reporting.* The proposal should specify the nature of any intermediate reports to be presented, what will be the form of the final report, and whether an oral presentation of the results will be made.

9 *Cost and timetable.* The cost of the project and a time schedule, broken down by phases, should be presented. A critical path method chart might be included. In large projects, a payment schedule is also worked out in advance.

10 *Research organisation and key researchers working on the project.* When an organisation is working with researchers for the first time, some idea of past research projects and clients should be displayed. This can help the marketer to trust the researchers in problem diagnosis, research design and implementation (e.g. how credible the researchers may be seen to be by the individuals they are to research and how this may affect participant openness and honesty), and interpretation of the findings.

11 *Appendices.* Any statistical or other information of interest to only a few people should be contained in appendices.

12 *Agreement.* All parties concerned with fulfilling the research plan should sign and date their agreement to the proposal.

Preparing a research proposal has several advantages. It ensures that the researcher and management agree about the nature of the project, and it helps sell the project to a wider array of decision-makers who may contribute to and benefit from the research findings. As preparation of the proposal entails planning, it helps the researcher conceptualise and execute the marketing research project. The following example illustrates a Coca-Cola European brand tracking study that required a major overhaul. This situation resulted in 400 research proposals being generated by marketing research agencies in 32 countries. Imagine the research, quality and creativity that went into the proposal that won the contract, not offering the cheapest option to Coca-Cola.

| Real research | **Coca-Cola's Beverage Brand Barometer[9]** |

Coca-Cola's Knowledge & Insights (K&I) marketing research team established a multi-country task force to consolidate its disparate brand trackers into a common framework to better understand consumers across the globe. The K&I task force launched the Beverage Brand Barometer (B3), feeling that having a consistent format would quickly pay its way. Coca-Cola's K&I team reduced its global yearly research spend by 10%, while improving the quality of its insights. Two years after the launch, in the midst of a global economic and financial crisis, another Coca-Cola research task force was established, this time in Europe. Its aim was to review the brand tracker's performance, and to validate consumer feedback on the experience of completing the B3 study in different European markets. The results of the review were conclusive: the B3 survey was too complex, extremely long and repetitive. This generated serious concerns over the quality of the data. In addition, structural changes within Coca-Cola Europe resulted in an increased need to benchmark, consolidate and cluster data across markets. With budget pressures and a tracking tool not delivering on business needs because of quality issues, the need for a shakeup was clear. In order to allow Coca-Cola Europe to improve its study, the B3 Global Council revisited the B3 core structure and significantly reduced all global mandatory sections, giving the Europe team the flexibility it needed. Because the study stretched across 32 European markets, consolidating all European B3 services with one marketing research supplier was identified as the best strategic and most feasible option. Working with a single partner on the revamped B3 across Europe would provide a new perspective while allowing for productivity gains. The new study would improve quality by shortening the questionnaire, but it had also to generate savings for each individual market, while increasing the research supplier's share of business. Five global agencies were briefed to put forward proposals for each individual market, as well as a potential pan-European package. However, the Coca-Cola project team also reviewed the local agency route to ensure fair local pricing, thus resulting in more than 400 proposals to be reviewed (i.e. five to seven agencies per market providing up to two proposals across 32 markets). Finally, Kantar (**www.kantar.com**) was chosen as the single strategic partner for Europe. Within Kantar, Millward Brown (**www.millwardbrown.com**) took the lead with TNS (**www.tnsglobal.com**) playing a supporting role. Kantar was already well integrated into the Coca-Cola Company business via advertising testing and other tracking initiatives, and it presented a viable business case not only for the European central team but also for each individual market.

The process of defining the problem and developing a research approach

By formally developing and exchanging a marketing research brief and research proposal, the marketing decision-maker and the researcher utilise their distinctive skills. They ensure that the marketing problem and research problems have been correctly defined and an appropriate research approach is developed. The research brief and the research proposal are the formal documents that ensure each party is clear about the nature and scope of the research task. These documents allow decision-makers and researchers formally to present their perspective of the task in hand. The nature of negotiations between decision-makers and researchers may occur between a sponsoring client organisation, e.g. Coca-Cola, and a research agency, e.g. Kantar. It could also happen within an organisation, i.e. there may be an in-house marketing research team. In successfully diagnosing a marketing decision and marketing research problem, the access to, and the understanding of, decision-makers by researchers can make a major difference. There are many positive reasons for using marketing research agencies but it is worth noting that there has been a growth in the use of in-house marketing research, sometimes described in a derogatory manner of DIY (Do-It-Yourself) research.[10] Where marketing research is practised without a full appreciation of the skills and creativity needed or the limitations of particular techniques, much damage can be done. The growth in relatively cheap proprietary software to support DIY research has exacerbated concerns about the quality of some in-house marketing research. However, much in-house research is conducted by well-qualified researchers, many of whom have worked at the best marketing research agencies. Such researchers can help diagnose research problems well and then outsource specific elements of data gathering and analysis to the many different types of research organisation that were detailed in Chapter 1. The following two examples illustrate how two major organisations have adopted 'DIY research'.

Real research   **Do-it-yourself research in Finland[11]**

Like the country's high-tech industries, research in Finland is expected to be increasingly driven by Internet and software developments. One consequence, warns Research International's (**www.research-int.fi**) Managing Director Jukka Tolvanen, is that 'many customers gather information themselves'. Juha Aalto, Managing Director of Taloustutkimus (**www.taloustutkimus.fi/in_english/**), goes further: 'the increase in do-it-yourself research has been fast and furious'. At MTV, Research Manager Taina Mecklin has changing needs in an increasingly diffuse media industry. Although generally satisfied with services, she warns 'we already have the tools to conduct many projects ourselves. Agencies should think about how they can help us instead of wanting to keep the whole process to themselves.' Public broadcaster YLE (**www.yle.fi/fbc**) also boasts its own research expertise. However, Head of Audience Research Erja Ruohomaa explains that she buys fieldwork to gain a 'better understanding of the significance our programming for all Finns'.

Real research   **DIY research at Readers Digest[12]**

Spurred on by technological, mostly Web-based IT advancements, 'do-it-yourself' or DIY market research is growing. Not only does the online marketing of global brands cross international borders, but, most of all, Web-based marketing research can be cost effective and fast. Additionally, as part of the growing importance of business intelligence departments and improved data management, it offers companies the bonus of keeping their information as close to the source as possible. One company where the DIY approach has played an integral role for a number of years is Readers Digest (**www.readersdigest.co.uk**). Apart from being a worldwide publisher of books, music and the magazine of the same name, Readers Digest also offers financial services. It supports all these products with a substantial amount of in-house research. This covers all the international markets in which Reader's Digest operates. Additionally, the company executes an annual European Trusted Brands survey in 14 European countries for its advertisers. Gavin Murray, Strategy Director, explains:

> *rather than being approached by a third party, our readership appreciates direct contact. We are in the unique position of being able to communicate directly with our customers and most of these customers are happy to participate in surveys sent out by us.*

Whether marketing research is conducted by research agencies, in-house or a combination of these, the diagnosis and articulation of what should be researched is vital. The following section details the process that needs to be undertaken in order to produce research proposal documents. The detail of defining the nature of problems and developing an appropriate research approach to the point of creating a research design is shown in Figure 2.3. Bear in mind, at this point, the challenges of gaining access to and understanding the demands of decision-makers in this process.

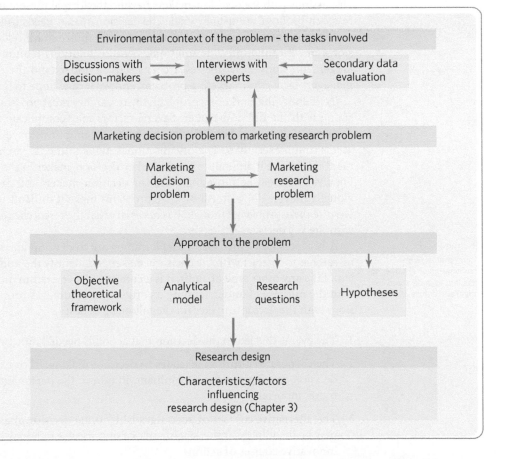

Figure 2.3

The process of defining the problem and developing an approach

Environmental context of the problem – the tasks involved

Discussions with decision-makers ⟶ Interviews with experts ⟵ Secondary data evaluation

Marketing decision problem to marketing research problem

Marketing decision problem ⟶ Marketing research problem

Approach to the problem

Objective theoretical framework | Analytical model | Research questions | Hypotheses

Research design

Characteristics/factors influencing research design (Chapter 3)

The tasks involved in problem definition consist of discussions with decision-makers, qualitative interviews with industry experts and other knowledgeable individuals, and analysis of readily available secondary data. These tasks help the researcher to understand the background of the problem by analysing the environmental context. Certain essential environmental factors bearing on the problem should be evaluated. An understanding of the environmental context facilitates the identification of the marketing decision problem. Then, the marketing decision problem is translated into a marketing research problem. Based on the definition of the marketing research problem, an approach to the problem is established and an appropriate research design is developed. The components of the approach may consist of an objective/theoretical framework, analytical models, research questions and hypotheses. Further explanation of the problem definition process begins with a discussion of the tasks involved.

Environmental context of the problem

The tasks involved in understanding the environmental context of the marketing and research problem can include discussions with decision-makers, qualitative interviews with industry experts, and secondary data collection and analysis. The purposes of these tasks are to develop an understanding of forces that may affect the nature of decision-makers' problems and related research problems.

Discussions with decision-makers

Discussions with the decision-makers beyond the formal presentation of a research brief and research proposal are usually vital. The decision-maker needs to understand the capabilities and limitations of research.[13] Research provides information relevant to management decisions, but it cannot provide solutions, because solutions require managerial creativity and judgement. Conversely, the researcher needs to understand the nature of the decision that managers face – the marketing problem, and what they hope to learn from the research.

To identify the marketing problem, the researcher must possess considerable skill in interacting with the decision-maker. Several factors may complicate this interaction. Access to decision-makers may be difficult, and some organisations have complicated protocols for access to top executives. The organisational status of the researcher or the research department may make it difficult to reach the key decision-maker in the early stages of the project. Finally, there may be more than one key decision-maker, and meeting collectively or individually may be difficult. All of these problems make it difficult to develop a research brief. Despite these problems, though, it is necessary that the researcher attempts to interact directly with the key decision-makers.[14]

Problem audit
A comprehensive examination of a marketing problem to understand its origin and nature.

A problem audit provides a useful framework to develop ideas from a brief, allowing the researcher to interact with the decision-maker and identify the underlying causes of the problem. Like any other type of audit, it is a comprehensive examination of a marketing problem with the purpose of understanding its origin and nature.[15] A problem audit involves discussions with the decision-maker on the following issues:

1 The events that led to the decision that action is needed, or a brief history of the problem.

2 The corporate culture as it relates to decision making.[16] For example, in some firms, the decision-making process is dominant; in others, the personality of the decision-maker is more important.

3 The alternative courses of action available to the decision-maker. The set of alternatives may be incomplete at this stage, and exploratory research may be needed to identify more innovative courses of action.

4   The criteria that will be used to evaluate the alternative courses of action. For example, new product offerings might be evaluated based on sales, market share, profitability, or return on investment.

5   What the decision-maker perceives to be gaps in their knowledge.

6   The manner in which the decision-maker will use each item of information in making the decision.

It may be necessary to perform a problem audit, because the decision-maker may have only a vague idea of what the problem is. For example, the decision-maker may know that the firm is losing market share but may not know why; decision-makers may tend to focus on symptoms rather than on causes. An inability to meet sales forecasts, a loss of market share and a decline in profits are all symptoms. The researcher should treat the underlying causes, not merely address the symptoms. For example, loss of market share may be caused by much better advertising campaigns by the competition, inadequate distribution of the company's products, or any number of other factors. Only when the underlying causes are identified can the problem be successfully addressed.

A problem audit, which involves extensive interaction between the decision-maker and the researcher, can greatly facilitate problem definition by determining the underlying causes. The interaction between the researcher and the decision-maker is facilitated when one or more people in the client organisation serve to liaise and form a team with the researcher. To be fruitful, the interaction between the decision-maker and the researcher can be characterised by the following:

1   *Communication.* A free exchange of ideas between the decision-maker and the researcher is essential.

2   *Cooperation.* Marketing research is a team project in which both parties (decision-maker and researcher) must cooperate, from problem diagnosis through to the interpretation and presentation of findings.

3   *Confidence.* Mutual trust of each other's distinct skills and contribution should underlie the interaction between the decision-maker and the researcher.

4   *Candour.* There should not be any hidden agendas, and an attitude of openness should prevail.

5   *Closeness.* An understanding of each other's problems should result in a closeness that should characterise the relationship between the decision-maker and the researcher.

6   *Continuity.* The decision-maker and the researcher must interact continually rather than sporadically.

7   *Creativity.* The interaction between the decision-maker and the researcher should be creative rather than formulaic. Though the research process may be laid out in 'easy-to-follow' steps, in reality great amounts of creativity are needed at every stage.

Interviews with industry experts

In addition to discussions with decision-makers, qualitative interviews with industry experts, individuals knowledgeable about the firm and the industry, can help in diagnosing the nature of the marketing and research problem.[17] These experts may be found both inside and outside an organisation commissioning the research. Typically, expert information is obtained by unstructured interviews. It is helpful, however, to prepare a list of topics to be covered during the interview. The order in which these topics are covered and the questions to ask should not be predetermined. Instead, they should be decided as the interview progresses, which allows greater flexibility in capturing the insights of the experts (see Chapter 8 for full details of in-depth interviewing techniques). The list of topics to cover and the type of expert sought should evolve as the researcher becomes more attuned to the nature of the marketing problem. The purpose of interviewing experts is to explore ideas, make new connections between ideas, and create new perspectives in defining the marketing research problem. If the technique works well by identifying an appropriate individual with the qualities to give insight upon a particular topic, and an amount of trust and rapport is developed, the potential to generate and test ideas can be immense. Experts may have other contacts that the researcher may not be aware of or may not be able to get access to. They may also have secondary data which, again, the researcher may not be aware of or have access to. Unfortunately, two potential difficulties may arise when seeking advice from experts:

1   Some individuals who claim to be knowledgeable and are eager to participate may not really possess expertise.

2   It may be difficult to locate and obtain help from experts who are outside the commissioning organisation, i.e. access to these individuals may be problematic.

For these reasons, interviews with experts are more useful in conducting marketing research for industrial firms and for products of a technical nature, where it is relatively easy to identify and approach the experts. This method is also helpful in situations where little information is available from other sources, as in the case of radically new products and markets. For example, in a marketing research study of Indian high net worth consumers, much work went into the environmental context of the problem. Understanding the characteristics of such a complex and fragmented group of wealthy consumers demanded an understanding of significant cultural changes in India. As well a critical evaluation of relevant theories and secondary data, interviews with experts helped enormously with the challenge of developing a research approach and research design. Identifying credible experts on India came from an immersion in good theories and secondary data. Identifying them was just the first challenge, gaining access to them and/or their network of contacts was the major test.

Real research   The changing Indian consumer[18]

Modernisation theories propose that the central challenge for developing economies is to manage the transition from traditional to modern societies. In the 18 years since liberalisation, urban Indian society has become consumerist in its orientation. As a result of the political, social and economic changes of the past six decades, urban India today can be described as a modern society with strong traditional roots. The modern values and ideas that have made inroads into Indian society and culture include money, power, equality, democracy, individuality, pleasure and indulgence, celebrity and glamour, enterprise, experimentation and technology. Many of these represent 'rational' and 'self-expressive' values, as defined in modernisation theories. At the same time, there are several core values that retain their imprint on Indian society. These include hierarchy, primacy of family, importance of religion, belief in the supernatural, importance of relationships, mutual duty, alignment to the group, male superiority and scarcity consciousness. These core values have founded the Indian cultural unconscious for thousands of years. Today, it results in a constant churn and intersection of traditional and modern to create new blends, amalgams and trends that are uniquely Indian. Culture experts have commented about this fundamental aspect of Indian society in different ways. Professor Rapaille, a French–American culture guru, author of the recent bestseller, *The Culture Code*,[19] has studied the cultures of India, China and America. He says:

India has a different cultural code to China. The collective unconscious of India has a way to integrate the outside world without losing their soul. A culture which was able to get rid of the British, the Moguls, the Persians, the Arabs, and so on, could survive anything. We will not have, in India, a phase of self-destruction like the Chinese Cultural Revolution, but more of a slow practical way of using the incredible commerce ability of the Indians to their advantage without destroying their culture.

Professor Sudhir Kakar, India's foremost psychoanalyst and social commentator, writing in *The Inner World*,[20] says:

its aim dramatizes a cultural ideal of the whole society, namely, a receptive absorption rather than an active alteration and opposition.

He also talks of the Elastic Indian – the eclectic Hindu who absorbs all manner of new religious practices such as reiki, pranic healing, Buddhist meditation, alongside traditional Hindu practices. These expert views point to the 'and-ness' of the Indian world-view, where the aim of the cultural unconscious is to find the 'and' answer to potentially conflicting values and ideas. Indians employ a variety of strategies to achieve 'and-ness': blend, balance, manipulate, conceal or negotiate and, when all other options fail, co-exist.

Initial secondary data analyses

Secondary data
Data collected for some purpose other than the problem at hand.

Primary data
Data originated by the researcher specifically to address the research problem.

Secondary data collection and analysis will be addressed in detail in Chapters 4 and 5. Here it can be seen in a broad context to include data generated within organisations, externally generated data and business intelligence. A brief introduction here will demonstrate the worth of secondary data at the stage of problem diagnosis. Secondary data are data collected for some purpose other than the problem at hand. Primary data, on the other hand, are originated by the researcher for the specific purpose of addressing the research problem. Secondary data include data generated within an organisation, including customer databases, information made available by business and government sources, commercial marketing research firms and the vast resources available online. Secondary data are an economical and quick source of background information. Analysis of available secondary data is an essential step in the problem definition process: primary data should not be collected until the available secondary data have been fully analysed. Past information, forecasts and commentary on trends with respect to sales, market share, profitability, technology, population, demographics and lifestyle can help the researcher to understand the underlying marketing research problem. Where appropriate, this kind of analysis should be carried out at the industry and organisation levels. For example, if an organisation's sales have decreased but industry sales have increased, the problems will be very different than if the industry sales have also decreased. In the former case, the problems are likely to be specific to the firm. Past information and forecasts can be vital in uncovering potential opportunities and problems.

Marketing decision problem and marketing research problem

The **marketing decision problem** asks what the decision-maker needs to do, whereas the **marketing research problem** asks what information is needed and how it can best be obtained.[21] The marketing decision problem is action oriented. It is concerned with the possible actions the decision-maker can take. How should the loss of market share be arrested?

Should the market be segmented differently? Should a new product be introduced? Should the promotional budget be increased?

In contrast, the marketing research problem is information oriented. It involves determining what information is needed and how that information can be obtained effectively and efficiently. Consider, for example, the loss of market share for a particular product line. The decision-maker's problem is how to recover this loss. Alternative courses of action can include modifying existing products, introducing new products, changing other elements in the marketing mix and segmenting the market. Suppose that the decision-maker and the researcher believe that the problem is caused by inappropriate segmentation of the market and want research to provide information on this issue; the research problem would then become the identification and evaluation of an alternative basis for segmenting the market. Note that this process requires much interaction, in the sense that both parties critically evaluate, develop and defend each other's ideas to clarify the nature of decision and research problems, and to ensure there is a clear and logical connection between them. The following example further illustrates the distinction between the marketing decision problem and the marketing research problem. It also illustrates the interactive nature of identifying the marketing decision problem and the research problem, each one unfolding and informing the understanding of the other.

The following example and Table 2.1 further distinguish between the marketing decision problem and the marketing research problem.

Real research	**Defining the problem**

Bank X: We are experiencing a loss of market share in France in corporate banking.

Researcher: Is it just France?

Bank X: No, but as we conduct the majority of our business there, the loss is causing us the greatest amount of concern.

Researcher: Why do you think you are losing market share?

Bank X: We wish we knew!

Researcher: How are your competitors coping?

Bank X: We suspect that other French banks are also suffering, and the multinational banks are capturing market share.

Researcher: How do your customers feel about the quality of services you deliver?

Bank X: We recently attained our ISO 9000 for service quality, which we are proud of!

Researcher: But how does your service delivery compare with your competitors?

After a series of discussions with key decision-makers, analysis of secondary data and business intelligence sources within the bank and from other sources, the problem was identified as follows:

- *Marketing decision problem*. To improve the the relationship experience with clients both in face-to-face and online relationships in order to arrest the decline in market share of Bank X.
- *Marketing research problem*. To determine the relative strengths and weaknesses in terms of relationship experiences of Bank X, vis-à-vis other major domestic and international competitors in France. This would be done with respect to factors that influence a company in its choice of a bank to handle its transactions.

Table 2.1	Marketing decision problems versus the marketing research problem

Marketing decision problem	Marketing research problem
Evaluates what the decision-maker needs to do	Evaluates what information is needed to support the identified marketing decision
Action oriented	Information oriented
Focuses upon symptoms	Focuses on the underlying causes .

The following examples further distinguish between the marketing decision problem and the marketing research problem:

Which product line extension should we invest in?	To determine consumer perceptions of the qualities and fit to existing products of a selection of product line extensions
Should we invest in celebrity X to endorse our brand in Europe?	To determine consumer perceptions of the qualities and fit to a brand of a selection of celebrities
Should we reposition our brand with an emphasis upon raising prices?	To determine the price elasticity of demand and impact on sales and profits of various levels of price changes

Conceptual map
A way to link the broad statement of the marketing decision problem to the marketing research problem.

While distinct, the marketing decision problem has to be closely linked to the marketing research problem. A good way to link the broad statement of the marketing decision problem with the marketing research problem is through the use of a conceptual map (Figures 2.4 and 2.5). A conceptual map involves the following three components:

Figure 2.4	A conceptual map for problem definition (DM = decision-maker)

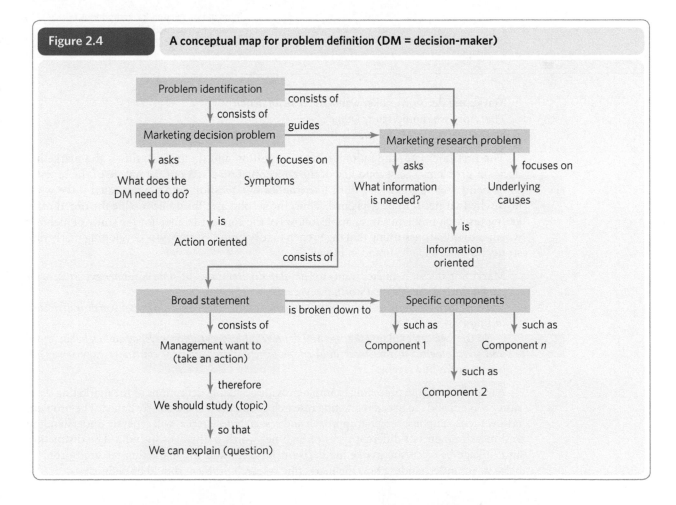

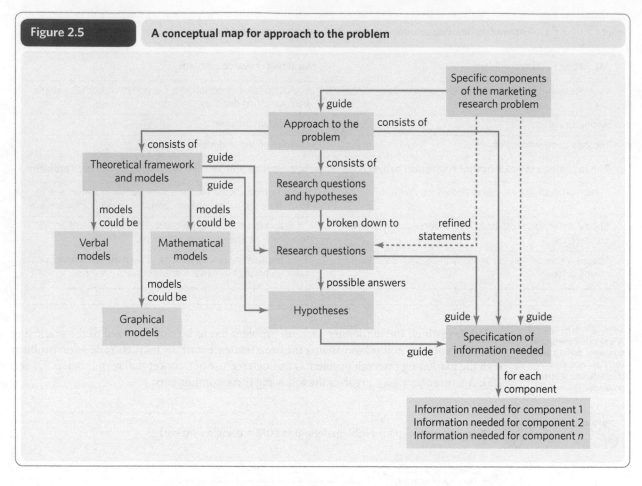

Figure 2.5   **A conceptual map for approach to the problem**

Marketing decision-maker wants to (*take an action*)
Therefore we should study (*topic*)
So that we can explain (*question*)

The first line states the rationale for the question and the project; this is the marketing decision problem. The second line of the conceptual map sets out the nature of the broader topic being investigated. The third line implies the question being investigated – the who/how/why that needs to be explained. Thus, the second and third lines define the broad marketing research problem. An example follows of the conceptual map for the study of high net worth individuals, assuming that the French luxury brand Hermès was developing marketing strategies to develop its brand in India:

Marketing decision-maker wants to (*develop differentiated in-store customer experiences for particular types of high net worth individuals*)
Therefore we should study (*ways to segment different types of high net worth individuals in India*)
So that we can explain (*the essential demographic, geographic, psychographic, behavioural and psychological factors that could shape differentiated in-store consumer experiences for luxury goods and services*)

As can be seen, the preceding example provides valuable definitions of the marketing decision problem and the broad marketing research problems that are closely linked. The problem is now focused upon a research approach and research design that will generate understanding and measurements of different types of high net worth individuals in India. The distinction and linkage between the marketing decision problem and the marketing research problem helps us in understanding how the marketing research problem should be defined.

Defining the marketing research problem

The general rule to be followed in defining the research problem is that the definition should:

- allow the researcher to obtain all the information needed to address the marketing decision problem;
- guide the researcher in maintaining focus and proceeding with the project in a consistent manner.

Researchers make two common errors in problem definition. The first arises when the research problem is defined too broadly. A broad definition does not provide clear guidelines for the subsequent steps involved in the project. Some examples of excessively broad marketing research problem definitions are: developing a marketing strategy for a brand, improving the competitive position of the firm, or improving the company's image. These are not specific enough to suggest an approach to the problem or a research design.

The second type of error is just the opposite: the marketing research problem is defined too narrowly. A narrow focus may preclude consideration of some courses of action, particularly those that are innovative and not obvious. It may also prevent the researcher from addressing important components of the marketing decision problem. For example, in a project conducted for a consumer products firm, the marketing problem was how to respond to a price cut initiated by a competitor. The alternative courses of action initially identified by the firm's research staff were to:

- decrease the price of the firm's brand to match the competitor's price cut;
- maintain price but increase advertising heavily; or
- decrease the price somewhat, without matching the competitor's price, and moderately increase advertising.

None of these alternatives seemed promising. When outside marketing research experts were brought in, the problem was redefined as improving the market share and profitability of the product line. Qualitative research indicated that in blind tests consumers could not differentiate products offered under different brand names. Furthermore, consumers relied on price as an indicator of product quality. These findings led to a creative alternative: increase the price of the existing brand and introduce two new brands – one priced to match the competitor and the other priced to undercut it. This strategy was implemented, leading to an increase in market share and profitability.

The likelihood of committing either error of problem definition can be reduced by stating the marketing research problem in broad, general terms and identifying its specific components (see Figure 2.6). The broad statement of the problem provides perspective and acts as a safeguard against committing the second type of error. The specific components of the problem focus on the key aspects and provide clear guidelines on how to proceed further, and act as a safeguard against committing the first type of error. Decisions requiring research support linked to fitting marketing research problem definitions are provided in the following example.

Broad statement of the problem
The initial statement of the marketing research problem that provides an appropriate perspective on the problem.

Specific components of the problem
The second part of the marketing research problem definition that focuses on the key aspect of the problem and provides clear guidelines on how to proceed further.

Figure 2.6

Proper definition of the marketing research problem

Marketing research problem

Broad statement

Specific components

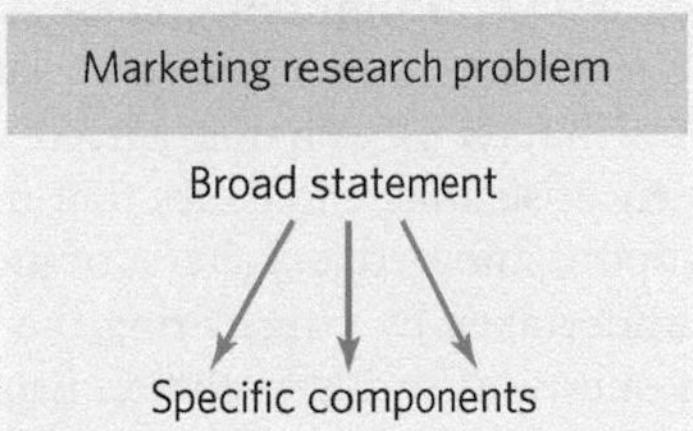

Nokia – Connecting people through relevance[22]

In 2009 Nokia launched Project Relevance, a new research programme aimed at securing relevance for the brand within the upper end of the smartphone marketplace. Project Relevance demonstrated Nokia's desire to continue placing consumer focused 'solutions' right at the front of their operations. North America was chosen as the lead market for this work as this was where the most advanced web and mobile web usage patterns were developing. A 'solution' was defined as the combination of device, software, business planning, design and marketing, different aspects of the innovation process that should be pulled together from the start in order to provide an optimal experience for the consumer. The business was aware that innovation should start with observing what people are doing, understanding their experiences, and then increasing the value of those practices through creating what is relevant and evolving it into fully formed solutions. The question was – how? The business recognised that this was a challenging brief and it was convinced that a new insight and innovation approach was needed to ensure the strategic vision and developed solutions would be consumer driven, and that the outputs of the programme would be delivered as quickly as possible. With this in mind, Face (**www.faceresearch.org**) was briefed to help Nokia (**www.nokia.com**) define what 'relevance' meant for leading-edge smartphone users. Nokia also had to create a number of consumer-driven cross-platform propositions that would allow it to leapfrog into the position of delivering the most relevant global solutions. On the basis of this brief, marketing research problems were articulated as follows:

- Define the value of 'relevance' and what this meant to consumers.
- Uncover the 'hacks' (secret codes) that consumers were employing to make their mobile experience more 'relevant'.
- Co-create with consumers the user experience and design for a future generation of Nokia 'solutions' that delivered on the value of 'relevance'.

Components of the research approach

Paradigm
A set of assumptions consisting of agreed-upon knowledge, criteria of judgement, problem fields and ways to consider them.

Once the marketing decision-maker and researcher have clarified the decision problem and established the research problem they face, it has to be decided how to approach the research problem. The research problem may be very clear in the sense that there are strong established theories of what should be measured and how to conduct the measurements. Conversely, the research problem may lack theoretical foundation, with the researcher trying to cope with a broad set of issues that have not been sufficiently researched beforehand and unable to trust existing theories. How the researcher perceives the research problem affects the paradigm they will adopt in either an implicit or explicit manner. The researcher's adopted paradigm is built upon a set of assumptions. These assumptions consist of 'agreed upon' knowledge, criteria of judgement, problem fields and ways to consider them[23] (these factors will be developed further in Chapter 6). What is 'agreed-upon' refers to how strong the theories are in defining and encapsulating the issues that make up a research problem.[24] Bringing together the 'agreed-upon' knowledge, criteria of judgement, problem fields and ways to consider them can be undertaken by considering the objective/theoretical framework, analytical models, research questions and hypotheses. Each of these components is discussed in the following sections. Collectively they may be considered to be the 'approach' that a researcher will take.

Objective/theoretical framework

Theory
A conceptual scheme based on foundational statements, or axioms, that are assumed to be true.

Objective evidence
Perceived to be unbiased evidence, supported by empirical findings.

In general, researchers should aim to base their investigations upon objective evidence, supported by theory. A theory is a conceptual scheme based on foundational statements called axioms that are assumed to be true. Objective evidence is gathered by compiling relevant findings from secondary sources. Likewise, an appropriate theory to guide the research might be identified by reviewing academic literature contained in books, journals and monographs. The researchers should rely on theory to help them to measure or understand the variables they are investigating. Academic sources of new developments to measure, understand and analyse consumers should be constantly evaluated; the following example illustrates why.

Real research | **Using faces: measuring emotional engagement: FaceTrace™[25]**

The research company BrainJuicer (**www.brainjuicer.com**) tested a number of adverts that had won awards from the Institute of Practitioners in Advertising, and had therefore been shown to deliver against their business objectives. Alongside these, BrainJuicer tested a set of adverts from each of the same categories, with what might commonly be termed as having the same kind of advertising objective (i.e. direct message, relaunch, brand building). An experiment was conducted online, and each advert was tested with 150 participants. The emotional scale BrainJuicer developed stated how many viewers felt each emotion, having viewed the adverts, and also the intensity with which they felt any emotion. A review of methods used to measure emotion led the company to the conclusion that it needed to develop a self-report technique (it needed to be easy to administer and user-friendly) that overcame some of the criticisms of self-report, one that identified the emotion felt without the need for a great deal of cognitive processing on the part of the participant.

The company turned to the work of Paul Ekman,[26] a respected psychologist, who puts a case for a set of seven basic emotions, *happiness, surprise, sadness, fear, anger, contempt and disgust*, all of which are universally conveyed by and recognisable in the face. Ekman's research on reading emotion in people's faces had two important implications:

1 It gave BrainJuicer a framework for understanding which emotions they should be looking to capture.
2 It provided a means of accessing what participants feel, with minimal cognitive processing on their part.
3 Ekman's research findings served as BrainJuicer's theoretical framework for measuring emotional response. They were fundamental in helping to set out important new findings for the measurement of emotion in advertising.

Researchers should also rely on theory to determine which variables should be investigated. Past research on theory development and testing can provide important guidelines on determining dependent variables (variables that depend on the values of other variables) and independent variables (variables whose values affect the values of other variables). Furthermore, theoretical considerations provide information on how the variables should be operationalised and measured, as well as how the research design and sample should be selected. A theory also serves as a foundation on which the researcher can organise and interpret the findings: 'nothing is so practical as a good theory'.[27] Conversely, by neglecting theory, researchers increase the likelihood that they will fail to understand the data obtained or be unable to interpret and integrate the findings of the project with findings obtained by others. The role of theory in the various phases of an applied marketing research project is summarised in Table 2.2.

Applying a theory to a marketing research problem requires creativity on the part of the researcher. A theory may not specify adequately how its abstract constructs (variables) can be embodied in a real-world phenomenon. Researchers must therefore take the best of what they believe to be the most novel theories to represent and encapsulate consumer thinking and behaviour. It is also vital for researchers to recognise that theories are incomplete; they deal with only a subset of variables that exist in the real world. Hence, the researcher must also identify and examine other variables that have yet to be published as theories. This may involve the researcher developing 'grounded theory',[28] which will be explained and developed in Chapter 6.

Table 2.2	The role of theory in applied marketing research
Research task	**Role of theory**
Conceptualising and identifying key variables	Provides a conceptual foundation and understanding of the basic processes underlying the problem situation. These processes will suggest key dependent and independent variables
Operationalising key variables	Provides guidance for the practical means to measure or encapsulate the concepts or key variables identified
Selecting a research design	Causal or associative relationships suggested by the theory may indicate whether a causal, descriptive or exploratory research design should be adopted (see Chapter 3)
Selecting a sample	Helps in defining the nature of a population, characteristics that may be used to stratify populations or to validate samples (see Chapter 14)
Analysing and interpreting data	The theoretical framework and the models, research questions and hypotheses based on it guide the selection of a data analysis strategy and the interpretation of results (see Chapter 17)
Integrating findings	The findings obtained in the research project can be interpreted in the light of previous research and integrated with the existing body of knowledge

Analytical model

Analytical model
An explicit specification of a set of variables and their interrelationships designed to represent some real system or process in whole or in part.

Verbal models
Analytical models that provide a written representation of the relationships between variables. variables, usually in equation form.

An analytical model is a set of variables and their interrelationships designed to represent, in whole or in part, some real system or process. Models can have many different forms. The most common are verbal, graphical and mathematical structures. In verbal models, the variables and their relationships are stated in prose form. Such models may be mere restatements of the main tenets of a theory. Graphical models are visual. They are used to isolate variables and to suggest directions of relationships but are not designed to provide numerical results. They are logical, preliminary steps to developing mathematical models.[29] Mathematical models explicitly specify the relationships among variables, usually in equation form.[30] These models can be used as guides for formulating the research design and have the advantage of being amenable to manipulation.[31] The different models are illustrated in the context of the proprietary sponsorship model used by IFM Sports Marketing Surveys.

Graphical models
Analytical models that provide a visual picture of the relationships between variables.

Mathematical models
Analytical models that explicitly describe the relationships between variables, usually in equation form.

As can be seen from this example, the verbal, graphical and mathematical models depict the same phenomenon or theoretical framework in different ways. The phenomenon of 'sponsorship impact', stated verbally, is represented for clarity through a figure (graphical model) and is put in equation form (mathematical model) for ease of statistical estimation and testing. Graphical models are particularly helpful in clarifying the concept or approach to the problem.

The verbal, graphical and mathematical models complement each other and help the researcher identify relevant research questions and hypotheses.

Focus on	**IFM Sports Marketing Surveys**

After the initial decision has been taken to use sponsorship as a marketing tool, it is vital to ensure that the most appropriate sponsorship is selected. It is also essential from both the rights holder's and sponsor's point of view to have an independent assessment of the value of a sponsorship. To this end, IFM Sports Marketing Surveys has its own sponsorship selection, valuation and evaluation (in terms of impact and exposure) model in partnership with IEG (International Events Group, **www.sponsorship.com**).

Model building

Verbal model

Marketing management wish to include an investment in sponsorship as part of the portfolio of integrated marketing communications. They wish to understand the impact of their sponsorship investment. They start by deciding what key objectives should be fulfilled through a sponsorship relationship. They then select a sector (sports, arts, culture, environment, broadcast) and the type of property (event, team, performance, individual, programme). Once the sector and property have been selected, they set specific objectives that can be developed to help to set realistic targets and a set of metrics as a means to measure success.

Graphical model

Communications objectives

↓

Role of sponsorship in integrated marketing communications – impact

↓

Sponsorship sector

↓

Sponsorship property

↓

Revised objectives and success metrics

Mathematical model

$$y = a_0 + \sum_{i=1}^{n} a_i x_i$$

where
y = sponsorship impact
a_0, a_i = model parameters to be estimated statistically
x_i = sponsorship requirement factors

Research questions

Research questions
Refined statements of the
specific components of the
problem.

Research questions are refined statements of the components of the problem. Although the components of the problem define the problem in specific terms, further detail may be needed to develop an approach. Each component of the problem may have to be broken down into subcomponents or research questions. Research questions ask what specific information is required with respect to the problem components. If the research questions are answered by the research, then the information obtained should aid the decision-maker. The formulation of the research questions should be guided not only by the problem definition, but also by the theoretical framework and the analytical model adopted. For a given problem component, there are likely to be several research questions.

Focus on | **IFM Sports Marketing Surveys**

The Moving Motor Show, Goodwood 2010

Research questions

The Moving Motor Show was a new initiative for Goodwood's 2010 Festival of Speed. The initiative was introduced as a response to the enthusiasm and demand from vehicle manufacturers and motorists alike for an annual motor show that would enable car buyers to see and experi-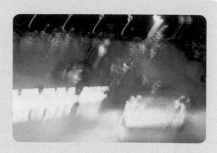
ence the latest models, and give companies the opportunity to showcase their products.

To measure the success of this initiative, the following key research questions were addressed:

- What are the levels of interest in motorsport, motoring and the automotive industry?
- What are the reasons for attending the Moving Motor Show?
- What are the positives and negatives of the event experience?
- What are the attitudes towards facilities and event organisation?
- What is the image of the event?
- What is the image of Goodwood as a motorsport venue?
- Does attending the event have an influence on future car buying?
- What is the attendee profile?
- Where have the attendees travelled from; how did they get there; and who did they come with?

These research questions were then further refined by precisely defining the variables and determining how they could be turned into specific questions, i.e. operationalised. To illustrate, in wishing to measure the reasons for attending the Moving Motor Show the following question was posed:

Why did you choose to attend this event? Please tick your top three reasons for attending this event?

The most popular response was 'Love of Cars' (68%) followed by 'Complimentary ticket' (33%) and 'I enjoy coming to Goodwood' (30%). Those under the age of 35 were most likely to cite their love of cars as the reason behind attending the Moving Motor Show (87%).

Hypothesis

Hypothesis
An unproven statement or proposition about a factor or phenomenon that is of interest to a researcher.

A **hypothesis** is an unproven statement or proposition about a factor or phenomenon that is of interest to the researcher. For example, it may be a tentative statement about relationships between two or more variables as stipulated by the theoretical framework or the analytical model. Often, a hypothesis is a possible answer to the research question.[32] Hypotheses go beyond research questions because they are statements of relationships or propositions rather than merely questions to which answers are sought. Research questions are interrogative; hypotheses are declarative and can be tested empirically (see Chapter 18). An important role of a hypothesis is to suggest variables to be included in the research design.[33] The relationship between the marketing research problem, research questions and hypotheses, along with the influence of the objective/theoretical framework and analytical models, are described in Figure 2.7 and illustrated by the following example from IFM Sports Marketing Surveys.[34]

Hypotheses are an important part of the approach to a research problem. When stated in operational terms, as H_1 and H_2 in the IFM Sports Marketing Surveys example, they provide guidelines on what, and how, data are to be collected and analysed. When operational hypotheses are stated using symbolic notation, they are commonly referred to as statistical hypotheses.

Figure 2.7

Development of research questions and hypotheses

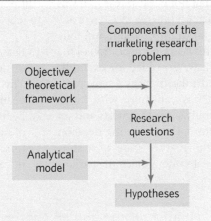

Focus on | **IFM Sports Marketing Surveys**

The Moving Motor Show, Goodwood 2010

Hypotheses

The following hypotheses were formulated in relation to the research question on the reasons for attending the Moving Motor Show:

H_1: *Male attendees have a greater propensity to attend the show for their love of cars.*

H_2: *Female attendees have a greater propensity to attend the show if they are given a complimentary ticket.*

These hypotheses guide the research by ensuring that variables which affect relationships are included in the research design. The connection between questions that form hypotheses and the appropriate analyses needed are thought out clearly before the research plan and questionnaire are designed.

It is important to note that not all research questions can be developed into hypotheses that can be tested. Certain research questions may be exploratory in nature, with the researcher having no preconceived notions of possible answers to the research questions, nor the ability to produce statements of relationships or propositions. If the researcher is faced with such a situation, it does not mean that the investigation will not be as valid as one where hypotheses are clearly established. It means that the researcher may have to adopt a different approach or paradigm to establish its validity.

International marketing research

The precise definition of the marketing research problem is more difficult in international marketing research than in domestic marketing research. Unfamiliarity with the environmental factors of the country where the research is being conducted can greatly increase the difficulty of understanding the problem's environmental context and uncovering its causes.

As the Heinz example illustrates, many international marketing efforts fail not because research was not conducted, but because the relevant environmental factors were not taken into account and fully appreciated. Generally, this leads to a definition of the problem that is too narrow. Consider, for example, the consumption of soft drinks. In many Asian countries such as India, water is consumed with meals and soft drinks are generally served to guests and on special occasions. Therefore, the marketing decision problem of increasing the market share of a soft-drink brand would translate into a different marketing research problem in India as compared with many European countries. Understanding these differences may not be so obvious at the point of diagnosing decision and research problems. A major problem for researchers is that their perception of problems may be reflected through their own social and cultural development. Before defining the problem, researchers should reflect upon their unconscious reference to cultural values. The following steps help researchers to reflect upon their own cultural values:[35]

1. Define the marketing research problem in terms of domestic environmental and cultural factors. This involves an identification of relevant European traits, economics, values, needs or habits.
2. Define the marketing research problem in terms of target market environmental and cultural factors. Make no judgements. This involves an identification of the related traits, economics, values,

Real research   Heinz Ketchup couldn't catch up in Brazil[36]

In 2009, Heinz was selling products in over 200 countries and sales were over €10 billion. Despite good records of global sales, the H.J. Heinz Company failed in Brazil, a market that seemed to be South America's biggest and most promising market. Heinz entered a joint venture with Citrosuco Paulista, a giant orange juice exporter, because of the future possibility of buying the profitable company. Yet the sales of its products, including ketchup, did not take off. Where was the problem? A problem audit revealed that the company lacked a strong local distribution system. Heinz lost control of the distribution because it worked on consignment. Distribution could not reach 25% penetration. The other related problem was that Heinz concentrated on neighbourhood shops because this strategy was successful in Mexico. The problem audit, however, revealed that 75% of the grocery shopping in São Paulo is done in supermarkets and not the smaller shops. Although Mexico and Brazil may appear to have similar cultural and demographic characteristics, consumer behaviour can vary greatly. A closer and intensive look at the Brazilian food distribution system and the behaviour of consumers could have averted this failure.

needs or habits in the proposed market culture. This task requires input from researchers familiar with the target market environment.

3. Examine the differences between steps 1 and 2. The unconscious reference to cultural values can be seen to account for these differences.

4. Redefine the problem without the social/cultural influence and address it for the target market situation. If the differences in step 3 are significant, the impact of the social/cultural influences should be carefully considered.

While the above steps may seem at face value to be straightforward, note the words 'unconscious reference' in step 3. They mean that the researchers need to reflect upon their own values and attitudes, the factors that may bias the way they perceive things and what they observe. As these factors may be 'unconscious', this reflection and introspection may take some time to realise. These issues will be more fully developed in Chapter 9.

While developing theoretical frameworks, models, research questions and hypotheses, remember that differences in the environmental factors, espe-cially the socio-cultural environment, may lead to differences in the formation of perceptions, atti-tudes, preferences and choice behaviour. For exam-ple, orientation towards time varies considerably across cultures. In many parts of Asia, Latin America and the Middle East, people tend not to be as time conscious as many Westerners. This influences their perceptions of and preferences for convenience foods such as frozen foods and prepared dinners. In devel-oping an approach to the problem, the researchers should consider the equivalence of consumption and purchase behaviour and the underlying factors that influence them. This is critical to the identification of the correct research questions, hypotheses and char-acteristics/factors that influence the research design.

The following example reveals how the use of how more in-depth secondary data and business intelli-gence gathering and analysis (including exploring blogs and postings through social media sources) could have helped to reveal social/cultural charac-teristics of the Japanese. Focus groups would have allowed the correct identification of research ques-tions, leading to a more successful product launch.

Real research   **Surf Superconcentrate faces a super washout in Japan**[37]

Unilever attempted to break into the Japanese detergent market with Surf Super-concentrate. It initially achieved 14.5% of the market share during test marketing but fell to a shocking 2.8% when the product was introduced nationally. Where did Unilever go wrong? Surf was designed to have a distinctive pre-measured packet as in teabag-like sachets, joined in pairs because convenience was an important attribute to Japanese consumers. It also had a 'fresh smell' appeal. Japanese consumers, however, noticed that the detergent did not dissolve in the wash, partly because of weather conditions and because of the popularity of low-agitation washing machines. Surf was not designed to work in the new wash-ing machines. Unilever also found that the 'fresh smell' positioning of new Surf had little relevance since many consumers hang their washing out in the fresh air. The research approach was certainly not without flaw, as Unilever failed to identify critical attributes that are relevant in the Japanese detergent market. Fur-thermore, it identified factors such as 'fresh smell' that had no relevance in the Japanese context. Appropriate secondary data and business intelligence gather-ing and analysis and even some exploratory qualitative research from the target market could have revealed the correct characteristics or factors leading to a suit-able research design. Despite having to withdraw from the Japanese market, Surf continued to perform well in several markets including India. Surf launched in India in 1952 and, by 2009, it was the third biggest selling product in the washing detergent market behind Unilever's Persil and Procter & Gamble's Ariel.

Ethics in marketing research

Ethical situations arising from the process of problem definition and developing an approach are likely to occur between the researcher and the client. As explained earlier, identifying the correct marketing research problem is crucial to the success of the project. This process can, however, be compromised by the personal agendas of the researcher or the decision-maker. For example, the researcher, after performing the tasks involved in problem definition and analysing the environmental context of the problem, realises that the correct marketing research problem may be defined in a way that makes primary research unnecessary. This would reduce the cost of the project and the research firm's profit margin substantially. Does the researcher define the problem correctly, fabricate a research problem that involves primary data collection, or refuse to proceed with this project in lieu of those more profitable? The researcher is faced with an ethical dilemma, as in the following example.

Such ethical situations would be satisfactorily resolved if the client–researcher relationship developed with both the client and the researcher adhering to the seven Cs discussed earlier: communication, cooperation, confidence, candour, closeness, continuity and creativity. This would provide a relationship of mutual trust that would check any unethical tendencies.

Real research   Taste (profits) or image (ethics)?[38]

A marketing research firm was hired by a soft drinks company to conduct taste tests to determine why its newly introduced soft drink brand had not captured the expected market share. The researcher, after following the process outlined in this chapter, determined that the problem was not one of taste but of image and product positioning. The client, however, had already defined the problem as a taste problem and not as the broader, market-share problem. The researcher had to weigh the relatively high profit margin of taste test research against the less lucrative survey research needed to answer questions pertaining to soft drink image. What should the research firm have done? Should it have simply conducted the research the client wanted rather than the research it felt the client needed? The 2010 Market Research Society Code of Conduct[39] specifically addresses 'Designing and setting up a research project'. It states that:

> *Members must not knowingly take advantage, without permission, of the unpublished work of another research practitioner that is the property of that other research practitioner.* **Comment***: This means, where applicable, that Members must not knowingly carry out or commission work based on proposals prepared by a research practitioner in another organisation unless permission has been obtained.*
>
> *All written or oral assurances made by any Member involved in commissioning or conducting projects must be factually correct and honoured by the Member.*
>
> *Members must take reasonable steps to design research to the specification agreed with the Client.*
>
> *Members must take reasonable steps to design research that meets the quality standards agreed with the Client.*
>
> *Members must take reasonable steps to ensure that the rights and responsibilities of themselves and Clients are governed by a written contract and/or internal commissioning contract.*
>
> *Members must not disclose the identity of Clients or any confidential information about Clients without the Clients' permission unless there is a legal obligation to do so.*

Ethical situations affecting the researcher and the client may also arise in developing an approach to the problem. When researchers conduct studies for different clients in related industries (e.g. banking and financial services) or in similar research areas (e.g. customer satisfaction) they may be tempted to cut corners in theoretical framework and model development. Take an example where a grocery chain client has on its board of directors the chairman of a bank. The bank had recently conducted customer satisfaction research using a client-specific model, and the bank-affiliated board member has access to this research. The researcher feels that a customer satisfaction model for the bank could be easily adapted to work for the grocery chain. The client feels that it would not be a good business decision to have access to this information and not use it. Is it ethical for the client and researcher to obtain and use this model developed for another company by another research firm? There is an underlying trust between the researcher and the client that the research firm is honour bound not to reuse client-specific models or findings for other projects.

The client also has an ethical responsibility not to solicit proposals merely to gain the expertise of the research firms without pay. It is unethical for a client to solicit proposals from a few research firms, then adopt one or a combination of the approaches suggested in them, and conduct the project in-house. The client must respect the rights of a firm by realising that an unpaid proposal belongs to the research firm that generated it. However, if the client firm pays for the development of the proposal, it has a right to use the information contained in it.

Digital applications in marketing research

The development of social media has opened up great opportunities for marketing decision-makers and researchers to listen to consumers. By listening, they can hear and see the words, language, emotions, images, stories, poetry and music that consumers use. These expressions are not necessarily about brands, products, services or consumption experiences; they can be about any aspect of their lives. There are numerous approaches to 'listening' ranging from one-to-one private dialogue to open global forums through blogging (accumulating group discussions) and twitter (mini personal broadcasts with selected exchange). Such virtual communities, or 'digital destinations' where people interact and create meaningful dialogues with one another, afford many opportunities to marketers and researchers by providing 'up-to-minute assessments of consumers' collective pulse'.[40] The nature and value of 'listening' are illustrated in the example overleaf.

'Listening to consumers' is not a new concept. In the 1930s and 1940s Mass Observation (**www. massobs.org.uk**) made significant advances in research techniques and concepts designed to 'listen in' to conversations between individuals in public places.[41] Listening to consumers now occurs in the context of digital developments that allow a global platform for consumers to connect, share and engage in personal discourse of their true feelings about brands, their meanings, the intersection between brands and their own lifestyles – in short, their 'lived experiences'.[42] Marketing decision-makers can use the knowledge they glean from social media to support the process of problem diagnosis and the development of research design. There may be specific marketing research problems and questions that can be answered through social media sources, but this is not guaranteed. It is more likely that through listening to consumers via social media sources, a richer environmental context of a problem, a greater understanding of a marketing decision problem and a marketing research problem can all be developed. A much clearer focus on which consumers should be questioned or observed, and what issues they should be questioned about, can be justified. Listening to consumers utilising the speed and power of social media methods opens up great opportunities and prospects for researchers.

The BMW 'wow' factor[41]

Jess Cusumano has spent much of his entire BMW career 'listening', long before digital conversations were the norm. Cusumano, BMW's North America's Internet Communications Manager, started with the company's call centre, 'a place where you could listen in for free, it was a great resource'. The sales representatives knew what was going on with consumers long before anyone online. In the early 2000s, he continued, 'a switch flipped; instead of being scared of the internet, BMW, as a brand, knew that it had to leverage the internet'. Initial forays were largely partnerships aimed at 'discovering what we could do with the data'. Today, BMW – the car, the motorcycle, the Mini and the Rolls Royce – monitors millions of blogs, message boards and social networking sites. As part of that effort, it makes a strong effort to keep in touch with customers by responding with answers as soon as a customer posts a question. 'It's a wow factor', Cusumano explained:

> We take a close look at 5,000 or 6,000 posts and answer them. If there's a technical question, we might post a page from the manual. Or, if someone is dissatisfied, we'll tell them that we've heard their concern and that we'll follow up. It works to our advantage in three ways: it's unsolicited advice to drivers, it's a new resource for enthusiasts, and it's a way to continue earning the trust of current and future customers. And people are freaked out that we're interacting. They can't believe it. Yes, we're a corporation. But we're also a peer.

How has the blogosphere affected consumer perception? In four years to 2008, the number of brand-related posts has increased from slightly more than 200,000 to more than 800,000.

Summary

Defining the marketing research problem is the most important step in a research project. Problem definition is a difficult step, because frequently decision-makers have not determined the actual problem or only have a vague notion about it. The researcher's role is to help decision-makers identify and define their marketing research problem.

The formal ways in which decision-makers and researchers communicate their perspectives on a research problem and how to solve it are through the development of a research brief and a research proposal. To develop these documents fully, researchers should be proactive in arranging discussions with key decision-makers, which should include a problem audit whenever possible. They should also conduct, where necessary, interviews with relevant experts, and secondary data collection and analyses. These tasks should lead to an understanding of the environmental context of the problem.

Analysis of the environmental context should assist in the identification of the marketing decision problem, which should then be translated into a marketing research problem. The marketing decision asks what the decision-maker needs to do, whereas the marketing research problem asks what information is needed and how it can be obtained effectively and efficiently. The researcher should avoid defining the marketing research problem either too broadly or too narrowly. An appropriate way of defining the marketing research problem is to make a broad statement of the problem and then identify its specific components.

Developing an approach to the problem is the second step in the marketing research process. The components of an approach may consist of an objective/theoretical framework, analytical models, research questions and hypotheses. It is necessary that the approach developed be based upon objective evidence or empirical evidence and be grounded in theory as far as it is appropriate. The relevant variables and their inter-relationships may be neatly summarised in an analytical model. The most common kinds of model structures are verbal, graphical and mathematical. The research questions are refined statements of the specific components of the problem that ask what specific information is required with respect to the problem components. Research questions may be further refined into hypotheses. Finally, given the problem definition, research questions and hypotheses should be used to create a method either to measure or elicit an understanding of target participants.

When defining the problem in international marketing research, researchers must be aware of the impact of their own cultural values when evaluating the environmental impact upon the nature of a problem. Likewise, when developing an approach, the differences in the environment prevailing in the domestic market and international markets should be carefully considered. Several ethical issues that have an impact on the client and the researcher can arise at this stage but can be resolved by adhering to the seven Cs: communication, cooperation, confidence, candour, closeness, continuity and creativity.

The development of digital social media has opened up great opportunities for marketing decision-makers and researchers to listen to consumers. It is likely that through listening to consumers via social media sources, a richer environmental context of a problem, together with a greater understanding of a marketing decision problem and a marketing research problem, can all be developed.

Questions

1 What is the nature of the first step in conducting a marketing research project?
2 Why is it vital to define the marketing research problem correctly?
3 What is the role of the researcher in the problem definition process?
4 What are the components of a marketing research brief?
5 What are the components of a marketing research proposal?
6 How may a researcher be creative in interpreting a research brief and developing a research proposal?
7 What is the significance of the 'background' section of a research brief and research proposal?
8 Describe some of the reasons why management are often not clear about the 'real' problem they face.
9 What interrelated events occur in the environmental context of a research problem?
10 What are some differences between a marketing decision problem and a marketing research problem?
11 Describe the factors that may affect the approach to a research problem.
12 What is the role of theory in the development of a research approach?
13 What are the most common forms of analytical models?
14 What are the differences between research questions and hypotheses?
15 Is it necessary for every research project to have a set of hypotheses? Why or why not?

Exercises

1   Imagine that you are the Marketing Director of KLM Airlines.

   a   Make a list of potential marketing objectives whose fulfilment could improve the performance of KLM.

   b   Select what you feel would be the most important marketing objective. Develop a set of marketing research objectives that you consider would support the decisions needed to fulfil that marketing objective.

2   You are a consultant to the Ford Premier Automotive Group, working on a project for Aston Martin.

   a   Use online databases to compile a list of articles related to the Ford Premier Automotive Group, Aston Martin and the global high-performance luxury car market in the past year.

   b   Visit the Aston Martin and Ferrari websites and evaluate the extent of competitive information available at each.

   c   Based upon the information collected from 2a and 2b, write a report on the environmental context surrounding Aston Martin.

3   In a small group discuss the following issues: 'Is it feasible that marketing decision-makers may not conceive of or be able to express the nature of decision support they need? What are the implications of such a possibility in the development of research proposals?' And 'From where may theory emerge to ground applied marketing research and what may be the relative worth of the source of theories used by researchers?'

4   Visit **www.innocentdrinks.co.uk** and **www.ft.com** and gather relevant information about the marketing challenges of Innocent Smoothies. As a brand manager for Innocent Smoothies you are concerned about improving the performance of your brand. Identify possible factors that you feel may shape the future performance of the brand. Write a brief report of 1,000 words that sets out Innocent's marketing challenges and concludes with your views of factors that could shape their future performance.

5   Visit **www.fabindia.com**. In particular, look at the sections that describe the philosophy behind this business. Gather online secondary data and business intelligence from online sources, especially your library's online databases. If Fabindia were to develop its brand further in selected European countries, what would the key challenges be? Write a brief report of 1,000 words that sets out Fabindia's challenges, identify five experts who may have a view of capitalising upon these challenges, and give brief details of why these individuals may be seen as experts.

Video case exercise: Burke Inc.

Burke describes how, beyond just collecting marketing research data, it helps to diagnose problems. Burke describes how it engages with clients to help define the marketing research problem to be studied. What barriers may prevent Burke being able to engage with clients in the way it describes the process?

Notes

1. Corporate Design Foundation, 'Harley-Davidson: marketing an American icon', **www.cdf.org/issue_journal/harley-davidson_marketing_,an_american_icon.html**, accessed 2 November 2010; Alva, M., 'Hog maker gets (financial) motor running', *Investor's Business Daily* (28 January, 2002).

2. 'Marketing profs knowledge exchange: money spent, marketing research, decision-making', **www.marketingprofs.com/ea/qst_question.asp?qstID=11527**, accessed 4 November 2010; Sheth, J.N. and Sisodia, R.S., 'Marketing productivity: issues and analysis', *Journal of Business Research* 55 (5) (May 2002), A9; Butler, P., 'Marketing problem: from analysis to decision', *Marketing Intelligence & Planning* 12 (2) (1994), 4–12.

3. Ingledew, S., 'How to bait the interview hook for those Top 1000 big fish', *ResearchPlus* (October 1996), 4.

4. John, C.F., 'From Iliad to Odyssey: the Odyssey of our profession', ESOMAR Congress Odyssey, Athens (September 2010); Greenhalgh, C., 'How should we initiate effective research?', The Market Research Society Conference (1983).

5. Srivatsa, A., Puri, A. and Raj, S., 'The case of the elusive insight: lessons from the greatest researcher of them all', ESOMAR Consumer Insights Conference, Milan (May 2007).

6. Blachowska, M., 'From consumer connection to consumer insight: a Nestlé case study', ESOMAR Consumer Insights Conference, Milan (May 2007).

7. Methner, T. and Frank, D., 'Welcome to the house of research: achieving new insights and better brand knowledge through courageous ways of collaboration in what is usually a competitive environment', ESOMAR Congress Odyssey, Athens (September 2010).

8. Pagani, P., Raubik, P. and May, J., 'Coca-Cola Europe and the philosopher's stone: crafting a rare win-win-win situation', ESOMAR, Congress Odyssey, Athens (September 2010).

9. Pagani, P., Raubik, P. and May, J., 'Coca-Cola Europe and the philosopher's stone: crafting a rare win-win-win situation', ESOMAR, Congress Odyssey, Athens (September 2010).

10. ESOMAR, 'Global Market Research', ESOMAR Industry Report (2010), 48.

11. Heeg, R., 'Do-it-yourself', *Research World* (December 2005), 25.

12. Heeg, R., 'DIY', *Research World* (February 2006), 15.

13. Cooke, M. and Buckley, N., 'Web 2.0, social networks and the future of market research', *International Journal of Market Research* 50 (2) (2008), 267–292; Marshall, G.W., 'Selection decision making by sales managers and human resource managers: decision impact, decision frame and time of valuation', *Journal of Personal Selling and Sales Management* (Winter 2001), 19–28.

14. Anon., 'How to decide who should get what data', *HR Focus* (May 2001), 7; Cronin, M.J., 'Using the web to push key data to decision makers', *Fortune* 36 (6) (29 September 1997), 254.

15. Copernicus Marketing Consulting, 'Auditing a marketing program', **www.copernicusmarketing.com/univers/audit.shtml**, accessed 10 November 2010; Reid, M., 'IMC-performance relationship', *International Journal of Advertising* 22 (2) (2003), 227–248; Morgan, N.A., 'Marketing productivity, marketing audits, and systems for marketing performance assessment: integrating multiple perspectives', *Journal of Business Research* 55 (5) (May 2002), 363; Merrilyn, A.T., 'Quick marketing audit', *Law Practice Management* 23 (6) (September 1997), 18, 63; Berry, L.L., Conant, J.S. and Parasuraman, A., 'A framework for conducting a services marketing audit', *Journal of the Academy of Marketing Science* 19 (Summer 1991), 255–258; Ackoff, R.L., *Scientific Method* (New York: Wiley, 1961), 71; Ackoff, R.L., *The Art of Problem Solving* (New York: Wiley, 1978).

16. Balmer, J.M.T., 'Corporate marketing: apocalypse, advent and epiphany', *Management Decision* 47 (4), (2009), 544–572; Charan, R., 'Conquering a culture of indecision', *Harvard Business Review* (April 2001), 74; , Nwachukwu, S.L.S. and Vitell, S.J. Jr, 'The influence of corporate culture on managerial ethical judgments', *Journal of Business Ethics* 16 (8) (June 1997), 757–776.

17. Grisham, T., 'The Delphi technique: a method for testing complex and multifaceted topics', *International Journal of Managing Projects in Business* 2 (1) (2009), 112–130; Malo, K., 'Corporate strategy requires market research', *Marketing News* 36 (2) (21 January 2001), 14; Winett, R., 'Guerilla marketing research outsmarts the competition', *Marketing News* 29 (1) (January 1995), 33.

18. Shivakumar , H., '"And-ness"': the key to the changing Indian consumer', *Admap* 479 (January 2007), 38–40.

19. Rapaille, C., *The Culture Code: An Ingenious Way to Understand Why People Around the World Buy and Live as They Do* (Portland, OR: Broadway Books, 2007).

20. Kakar, S., *The Inner World: A Psycho-analytical Study of Hindu Childhood and Society* (Oxford: Oxford University Press, 2008).

21. Ganeshasundaram, R. and Henley, N., 'The prevalence and usefulness of market research: an empirical investigation into "background" versus "decision" research', *International Journal of Market Research* 48 (5) (2006), 525–550; Roe, M. and Vervoot, J., 'A market research training simulation – bringing market research closer to decision-makers', ESOMAR, Innovate! Conference, Paris (February 2005); Gordon, A., 'Linking marketing decisions with consumer decision making: closing the gap between feelings and behaviour', ESOMAR, Annual Congress, Lisbon (September 2004).

22. D'Orazio, F., Garland, E. and Crawford, T., 'Designing relevance: how open and agile research methodologies can help complex organizations respond to change and stay relevant', ESOMAR, Online Research, Berlin (October 2010).

23. Potter, G., *The Philosophy of Social Science: New Perspectives* (Harlow: Pearson, 2000), 242.

24. Saren, M. and Pels, J., 'A comment on paradox and middle-range theory: universality, synthesis and

supplement', *Journal of Business & Industrial Marketing* 23 (2) (2008), 105–107.

25. Wood, O., 'Using faces: measuring emotional engagement for early stage creative', ESOMAR, Annual Congress, Berlin (September 2007).

26. Ekman, P., *Emotions Revealed, Understanding Faces and Feelings* (London: Phoenix 2003).

27. Nyilasy, G. and Reid, L.N., 'The academician-practitioner gap in advertising', *International Journal of Advertising* 26 (4) (2007), 425–445; Lilien, G.L., 'Bridging the marketing theory', *Journal of Business Research* 55 (2) (February 2002), 111; Hunt, S.D., 'For reason and realism in marketing', *Journal of Marketing* 56 (April 1992), 89–102.

28. Goulding, C. and Saren, M., 'Immersion, emergence and reflexivity: grounded theory and aesthetic consumption', *International Journal of Culture, Tourism and Hospitality Research* 4 (1) (2010), 70–82.

29. For an illustration of a graphical model, see Nauckhoff, F., Asberg, P. and Hemmingsson, C., 'Managing media planning and brand positioning across media platforms', ESOMAR, Worldwide Media Measurement, Stockholm (May 2009).

30. For an illustration of a mathematical model based on it, see Suher, J. and Sorenson, H., 'The power of Atlas: why in-store shopping behavior matters', *Journal of Advertising Research* 50 (1) (2010), 21–29.

31. Patwardhan, P. and Ramaprasad, J., 'Rational integrative model of online consumer decision-making', *Journal of Interactive Advertising* 6 (1) (Fall 2005), 2–13; Malhotra, N.K. and Wu, L., 'Decision models and descriptive models: complementary roles', *Marketing Research* 13 (4) (December 2001), 43–44.

32. For an example of hypothesis formulation, see Bian, X. and Moutinho, L., 'The role of brand image, product involvement, and knowledge in explaining consumer purchase behaviour of counterfeits: direct and indirect effects', *European Journal of Marketing* 45 (1/2) (2010), 191–216.

33. For an example of model development and hypothesis formulation, see Heath, R.G., Nairn, A.C. and Bottomley, P.A., 'How effective is creativity? Emotive content in TV advertising does not increase attention', *Journal of Advertising Research* 49 (4) (December 2009), 450–463.

34. The integrated role of theory, models, research questions and hypotheses in marketing research can be seen in Nygaard, A. and Dahlstrom, R., 'Role stress and effectiveness in horizontal alliances', *Journal of Marketing* 66 (April 2002), 61–82; Nunes, J.C., 'A cognitive model of people's usage estimations', *Journal of Marketing Research* 37 (4) (November 2000), 397–409.

35. Sekhon, Y.K. and Szmigin, I., 'The bi cultural value system: undertaking research amongst ethnic audiences', *International Journal of Market Research* 51 (6) (2009), 751–771; Douglas, S.P. and Craig, C.S., *International Marketing Research* (Englewood Cliffs, NJ: Prentice Hall, 1983).

36. Verhaeghe, A., de Wulf, K., Schillewaert, N. and De Boeck, F., 'Beyond benchmarking – concept performance across countries', ESOMAR, Innovate! Conference, Copenhagen (June 2008); Reyes, S., 'Heinz builds on EZ squirt success with adult skewing kick'rs line', *Brandweek* 43 (3) (21 January 2002), 4; Judann, D., 'Why Heinz went sour in Brazil', *Advertising Age* (5 December 1988).

37. Anon., 'Unilever (Household and domestic)', *Euromonitor Profiles* (July 2010); Singh, S., 'Unilever picks global brand director for Surf', *Marketing Week* (7 March 2002), 7; Kilbum, D., 'Unilever struggles with Surf in Japan', *Advertising Age* (6 May 1991).

38. Brans, J.P., 'Ethics and decisions', *European Journal of Operations Research* 136 (2) (16 January 2002), 340; Laczniak, G.R. and Murphy, P.E., *Ethical Marketing Decisions: The Higher Road* (Boston, MA: Allyn & Bacon, 1993), 64.

39. Market Research Society, 'Code of Conduct' (April 2010).

40. Kozinets, R.V., 'Click to connect: netnography and tribal advertising', *Journal of Advertising Research* 46 (3) (2006), 279–288.

41. Passingham, J. and Blyth, B., 'A small rock holds back a great wave: unleashing our potential', ESOMAR, Congress Odyssey, Athens (September 2010).

42. Jayanti, R.K., 'A netnographic exploration: listening to online consumer conversations', *Journal of Advertising Research* 50 (2) (2010), 181–196.

43. Precourt, G., 'Listen up: how access to digital media is transforming consumer research', *Warc Exclusive* (September 2008).

3

Research design

There are a huge array of alternative research designs that can satisfy research objectives. The key is to create a design that enhances the value of the information obtained, while reducing the cost of obtaining it.

Objectives

After reading this chapter, you should be able to:

1 define research design, classify various research designs, and explain the differences between exploratory and conclusive research designs;

2 compare and contrast the basic research designs: exploratory, descriptive and causal;

3 understand how participants or the subjects of research design affect research design choices;

4 describe the major sources of errors in a research design, including random sampling error and the various sources of non-sampling error;

5 explain research design formulation in international marketing research;

6 understand the ethical issues and conflicts that arise in formulating a research design;

7 appreciate how digital developments can create opportunities for researchers to be creative in crafting research designs.

Overview

Chapter 2 discussed how to define a marketing research problem and develop a suitable approach. These first two steps are critical to the success of the whole marketing research project. Once they have been completed, attention should be devoted to designing the formal research project by formulating a detailed research design (as a reminder, see Figure 2.3).

This chapter defines and classifies research designs. We examine the nature of research design from the perspectives of decision-makers and participants. Two major types of research design are then discussed: exploratory and conclusive. We further classify conclusive research designs as descriptive or causal and discuss both types in detail. The differences between the two types of descriptive designs are then considered (cross-sectional and longitudinal) and sources of errors are identified. The special considerations involved in formulating research designs in international marketing research are discussed. Several ethical issues that arise at this stage of the marketing research process are considered. The chapter concludes by examining how digital developments can help in the crafting of creative research design. A better appreciation of the concepts presented in this chapter can be gained by first considering the following example, which illustrates the use of a number of interrelated techniques to build a research design.

Real research   **Getting to know you**[1]

Building a relationship with consumers is a challenge facing all organisations, but particularly so in the case of 'emergent drinkers', those of legal drinking age up to 25. Allied Domecq Spirits and Wines (**www.allieddomecq.com**) recognised the danger of being distanced from this crucial group, particularly across geographical markets. Allied Domecq worked with Pegram Walters International (**www.aegisplc.com**) on a project that went far beyond an exploration of the current usage and attitudes towards spirits. The objectives of the project encompassed an exploration of the target groups' personal values, their feelings about their lives, their universe, their hopes and dreams. There were three stages to the research design. In the first stage the researchers conducted one-hour in-depth interviews. There were three clear objectives for this stage: to understand personal viewpoints on marketing and lifestyle issues; to clarify and/or narrow down topics for subsequent exploration; and to recruit appropriate 'information gatherers'. From this stage, hypotheses were formulated on issues such as how participants saw themselves and their future, their relationships, self-discovery and opting in or out of the system. In the second stage, from 20 in-depth interviews, 10 participants were retained as 'information gatherers'. 'Leading-edge' bars were rented out and 50 adult emergent drinkers were invited to participate in workshops. Given a task guideline, the information gatherers led discussions. As an additional record, the workshops were video recorded. The participants felt comfortable within their peer group and, in the more natural bar environment, fed back real, relevant and honest information. The third stage occurred on the night following the workshops. Focus groups were used, made up of the 'information gatherers'. They discussed what happened in the workshops and their interpretation of what it actually meant. In order to ensure that the information remained topical, useful and easily accessible, it was felt important to create a vehicle for an ongoing communication and dialogue with the target market. To achieve this, a high-impact 'magazine' was created to bring the research to life after the presentation of findings. This was referred to as a magazine and not a research report to reflect the lifestyle of the consumer group in question: it contained images, layouts and fonts typically associated with the generation.

The above example illustrates a very creative and useful exploratory research design. As a research design it worked well in that it achieved a balance of the needs and expectations of marketing decision-makers and participants. Decision-makers helped to set clear research objectives based upon the gaps in their knowledge of the target market. Participants related well to the questions and issues posed to them, in a context and environment in which they felt comfortable. An understanding of the fundamentals of research design, its components and the trade-offs between the parties involved in crafting an effective research design enabled the researchers to formulate the most appropriate design for the problem at hand.

Research design definition

Research design
A framework or plan for conducting the marketing research project. It specifies the details of the procedures necessary for obtaining the information needed to structure or solve marketing research problems.

A research design is a framework or plan for conducting a marketing research project. It details the procedures necessary for obtaining the information needed to structure or solve marketing research problems. Although a broad approach to the problem has already been developed, the research design specifies the details, the practical aspects of implementing that approach. A research design lays the foundation for conducting the project. A good research design will ensure that the marketing research project is conducted effectively and efficiently. Typically, a research design involves the following components or tasks, which will be discussed in detail in various chapters:

1 Define the information needed (Chapter 2).

2 Decide whether the overall design is to be exploratory, descriptive or causal (Chapter 3).

3 Design the sequence of techniques of understanding and/or measurement (Chapters 4 to 12).

4 Construct and pretest an appropriate form for data collection or questionnaire (Chapters 7, 8 and 13).

5 Specify the qualitative and/or quantitative sampling process and sample size (Chapters 6, 14 and 15).

6 Develop a plan of qualitative and/or quantitative data analysis (Chapters 9 and 17).

In formulating a research design, the researcher has to balance the perspectives of marketing decision-makers and target participants. From their education and experience, marketing decision-makers may have certain techniques that they believe to be the most effective and in which they subsequently have more confidence. There is no problem with this, providing the technique is the best means to measure or understand the issue under investigation, from the perspective of participants. In the example at the start of this chapter, decision-makers had confidence in the qualitative techniques and the data generated. The techniques worked well with the participants, drawing out a rich picture of participant behaviour, lifestyle and aspirations. However, should the decision-makers feel that survey techniques were the most effective, giving them the most confidence to support their decisions, the researchers may face a dilemma. If they use survey techniques they may find that participants may have a different relationship with interviewers, do not reflect in the same manner and ultimately do not reveal so much. Thus, research design involves the researchers developing an understanding of the type of data decision-makers have confidence in, plus an understanding of how participants may respond to different techniques. The first part of this balancing act involves understanding research design from the decision-makers' perspective; the second part involves understanding the participants' perspective.

Research design from the decision-makers' perspective

Marketing decision-makers seek support from researchers that is of practical relevance to the decisions they face. To give practical support, decision-makers expect information that is:

- *Accurate*, i.e. the most valid representation of the phenomena under investigation, that has come from the most reliable or consistent form of measurement or understanding, that is sufficiently sensitive to the important differences in individuals being measured or understood. Combining these three criteria refers to the degree to which information may be deemed as 'accurate'.

- *Current*, i.e. as up to date as possible. This is particularly important where consumer attitudes, lifestyle or behaviour change rapidly, perhaps due to rapid technological changes or new product offerings in a highly competitive market.

- *Sufficient*, i.e. the completeness or clarity of a 'picture' that reflects the characteristics of the marketing problem the decision-makers face.

- *Available*, i.e. that access to the relevant information can be made when a decision is imminent. This is particularly important where competitive activity forces the decision-makers into making a rapid response.

- *Relevant*, i.e. that the support given 'makes sense' to decision-makers. In a very general sense, decision-makers may criticise qualitative research approaches and techniques for being biased and unrepresentative, and conversely quantitative approaches and techniques for lacking depth and a contextual perspective. Whichever approach or techniques are adopted, decision-makers should be aware of their benefits, limitations and even alternatives. With this awareness they can use the findings with confidence to build upon their existing experiences and knowledge.

Generating information that fulfils all the above characteristics is extremely difficult, if not impossible to achieve in marketing research. The evaluation of sources of error, presented later in this chapter, and the restrictions of budget and timescales mean that this list represents 'ideals'. Realistically, trade-offs must be made among the above characteristics. Within the first characteristic of accuracy there are further trade-offs which are primarily caused by what the researcher is attempting to measure or understand:[2]

1 The subject of investigation is usually human.

2 The process of measuring or observing humans may cause them to change.

3 It is difficult to assess the effect of extraneous variables in marketing experiments and thus their applications are limited.

Given the complexity of the subjects under study, the context or environment in which measurements are taken, and the skills required to perform and interpret measurements, it is difficult (if not impossible) to gain completely objective and accurate measurements.[3] Of all the potential trade-offs, if one were to remove *relevance* then the whole rationale of supporting the marketing decision-maker would be removed. Therefore this characteristic can never be compromised.

Relevance embraces, inter alia, the ability to plan and forecast from research findings, to be able to distinguish real differences in consumer traits, and to know that characteristics are representative of groups of individuals. With relevant information such as this, the decision-maker can build up a stronger understanding or awareness of markets and the forces that shape them. In building up this understanding, the decision-maker cannot turn to a single technique or even body of techniques that may be deemed 'ideal' in ensuring that information is relevant.[4] In different types of decision-making scenarios, different techniques will offer the best support for that decision-maker. Establishing the best form of support is the essence of research design.

A fundamental starting point in deciding an appropriate design is viewing the process from the point of view of the potential subject or participant of a marketing research study.

Research design from the participants' perspective

The potential participants in any marketing research investigation play a vital role in deciding which research design will actually work in practice. A subject of study may be complex and need time for participants to reflect upon and put words to the questions posed. Certain methods are more likely to build up a rapport and trust, in these circumstances putting the participants in the right frame of mind and getting them to respond in a full and honest manner. Figure 3.1 is a framework that serves to remind how participants may be accessed, and what kinds of response may be generated.[5]

In Figure 3.1 the box under the heading 'Layers of response from respondents' represents how participants may react to questions posed to them. In the first layer of 'Spontaneous, Reasoned, Conventional' are questions that participants can express a view about quickly, and that are simple for them to reflect upon, relating to common everyday occurrences that are at the forefront of their minds. In such circumstances, simple structured questioning (or self-reporting) in a standardised manner is possible. Further, the same procedure can be conducted in a consistent manner to a whole array of 'types' of participant such as age groups, social class and intellectual levels. For example, if questions were posed on which newspapers someone reads, it is a reasonable assumption that participants would be aware of the newspaper title(s), these title(s) can be communicated and the topic of newspaper readership is not a sensitive issue. In these circumstances, where answers to questions on reading habits are relatively easy to access and respond to, highly structured questionnaires are appropriate. Clearly, in such situations, quantitative techniques are applicable that allow very detailed descriptions or experiments to be conducted. The following example illustrates the use of a structured online survey that allowed detailed descriptions and attitudinal measurements of visitors to an exclusive event.

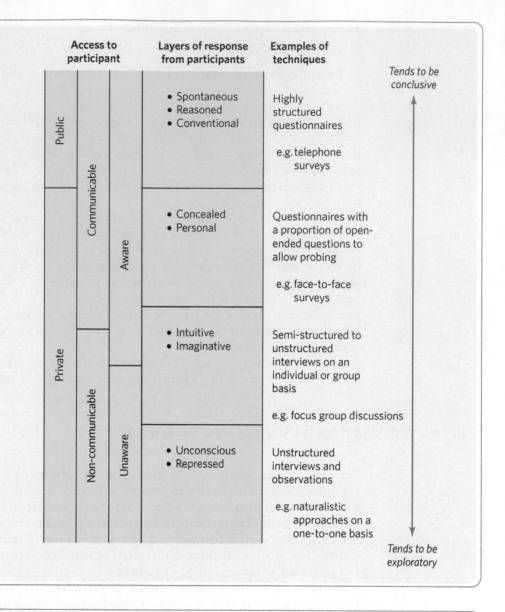

Figure 3.1

Responses to interviewing

Focus on

IFM Sports Marketing Surveys

The Moving Motor Show: Goodwood

Online survey

Held within the spectacular grounds of Goodwood Park, the exclusive 2010 Moving Motor Show (**www.goodwood.co.uk/festival-of-speed**) was an important addition to the Festival of Speed. The show enabled a limited number of motoring enthusiasts and new car buyers to see the very latest models up close for the first time in the UK, and, in some cases, also climb aboard and experience the vehicles first-hand, strictly at the invitation of the attending vehicle manufacturers. Following the show, IFM Sports Marketing Surveys contacted visitors using its ticketing database as a sampling frame. Event attendees were invited to complete an online questionnaire. The nature of questions posed in this survey addressed attitudinal, behavioural and demographic questions. These questions did not demand in-depth reflection on the part of participants; their responses could be articulated with ease in a concise survey that took five minutes to complete. As most attendees to the event were passionate about Goodwood and cars, their engagement with the subject was high, resulting in 777 completed questionnaires. The show succeeded in attracting new visitors to Goodwood: 26% of visitors had never been to any event prior to this visit. Encouragingly, 37% of visitors had nothing negative to say about their visit to Goodwood; however, 27% disliked the walk from the car park to the event.

Progressing down Figure 3.1, at the second level are questions that are more personal and more sensitive. There are two characteristics that can turn otherwise mundane topics into sensitive ones.[6] The first involves any private, sacred or stressful aspect of a participant's life. The second is the real or perceived stigma associated with specific thoughts or actions. A great amount of business-to-business research can be added to these in terms of commercially sensitive information. Again, structured questionnaires can measure the relevant issues but an amount of rapport may be needed to induce participants to trust the interviewer and reveal their 'more personal' attitudes and behaviour. Where the presence of the interviewer causes discomfort or bias, the method of audio/computer-assisted/self-interviewing may be used[7] or, far more frequently, the anonymity of online research methods can facilitate more honest and open responses.[8] Such techniques combine the higher response rates of personal interviews with the privacy of self-administered questionnaires. The following example illustrates how the condom manufacturer Durex managed to research a sensitive topic.

Real research | ## Minimising unease, embarrassment or reluctance in disclosing intimate personal information[9]

Durex (**www.durex.com**) wishes to support each individual's right to enjoy a healthy and rewarding sex life. The challenge for Durex, in this vision, is to develop a brand platform that encompasses sexual well-being (and, through this, the promise of an enhanced and better sex experience), without eroding its safe sex and barrier protection. To fulfil its overall business objective of providing insights to support the commercial vision for the brand, marketing research was needed to address a number of discrete research objectives. These ranged from understanding sexual well-being and how it fits into people's lives, through exploring the sexual activities they take part in, to future trends. It was also critical to ensure that within the overarching aim, the needs of individual stakeholder audiences were met through a robust and reliable research design. The stakeholder audiences included internal business teams and divisions, sexual well-being and health experts, clinicians, politicians, opinion formers and teachers. Openness to talking about sex can vary greatly, not only from individual to individual, but from one culture to another. So a key challenge for the research was to ensure that unease, embarrassment or reluctance in disclosing intimate personal information was minimised. For those who would choose to participate in the survey, their concerns were in participant willingness to answer more specific, detailed and sensitive questions (e.g. on sexual activities or dysfunctions). In designing the survey, these issues needed to be front of mind and every effort made to minimise their potential impact on response rates, data quality and ultimately on costs and feasibility. The duty of care to participants in the survey was at the centre of the thinking throughout questionnaire design and the respective codes of conduct in each of the 26 countries covered in the research were rigorously followed. The focus of the approach was the idea of 'Treating others as we expect to be treated.' So, it was extremely important to be open and honest about the nature of the survey from the very beginning. The introduction advised participants of the sensitive nature of the questions and it also stressed that researchers were not in any way intending to cause any offence. Participants were consequently able to make an informed choice as to their participation. A funnel approach to questionnaire design was adopted with the less sensitive questions placed at the beginning of the questionnaire to build trust, so that participants felt comfortable being asked the more sensitive questions later on. Throughout the survey participants were given the option to decline to answer, or suspend, to ensure they did not feel pressured into answering questions they did not feel comfortable with. After careful consideration of the strengths and limitations associated with each mode of data collection available in a researcher's toolkit, an online approach was singled out as the best one for this survey. This approach presented a number of key advantages over other methods for the following reasons:

- The sensitive topic area required an approach that allowed for honesty and openness.
- Removing any interviewer influence or bias was also considered key to data quality.
- The need for global coverage.
- Reach/cost ratio: an online approach was the most cost-effective way of obtaining global reach.

However, an online approach was not feasible in Nigeria, principally due to low penetration levels of the telephone and Internet. Instead, a face-to-face self-completion approach was adopted in this country.

At the third level are questions that require participants to be creative. For example, if participants were to be asked about their attitudes and behaviour towards eating yogurt, this could be done in a very structured manner. Questions could be set to determine when it was eaten, favourite flavours and brands, where it was bought, how much was spent, etc. The same can be said of alcohol consumption, though this could well be a sensitive issue for many participants. Now imagine a new product idea that mixes yogurt and alcohol. What combinations of alcohol and yogurt would work, and what types of consumer would be attracted to them? Would they be a dessert liqueur such as Baileys Irish Cream or frozen yogurt to compete with the Häagen-Dazs luxury ice creams? Would champagne, advocaat, whisky or beer be the best alcoholic ingredient? Should any fruits be added? Individually? Forest fruits? Tropical fruits? How would the product be packaged? What name would best suit it? What price level would it sell at? On what occasions would it be consumed?

Answering these questions demands a great amount of creativity and imagination. It demands that participants reflect upon ideas, can play with ideas and words, and dig deep to draw out ideas in a relaxed manner. Structured questionnaires cannot do this; such a scenario would work best with the use of focus groups. One of the major participant access challenges faced at this level relates to how participants articulate their views and feelings, especially their emotional states related to brands. The following example illustrates how research participants can be helped to articulate what they may feel about sensations and brands.

Real research	**What the nose knows**[10]

Thomas Inglesant is the European Market Research Director of the fragrances and flavours company Givaudan (**www.givaudan.com**). The task of his team is to help brands match household products like floor cleaners with scents that appeal to consumers. One of the main activities of his team is the broad pursuit of an understanding of consumers, covering their attitudes and usage habits as they relate to different products. This work is growing with group discussions, one-to-one interviews and in-home ethnography as commonly used tools. Thomas notes: 'the negative side is there are no numbers so you cannot do statistics with the results, but the positive is that it is more to do with the "why", rather than the "what" and the "how much"'. One of the problems with asking consumers about different scents is that they tend not to have many words to be able to describe either a smell, or why they do or don't like it. Words like 'clean' and 'fresh' are used almost universally by people describing a whole range of scents they like. In case words fail them, consumers can be shown pictures to help them associate scents with certain moods, colours or scenes. Researchers draw on a bank of about 100 pictures, everything from food and flowers to mountain views and people pulling different facial expressions – to help discussions along. In some instances consumers are given a bank of descriptive words and asked to choose which best describe the fragrance they are given.

At the fourth level may be questions that participants may not be able to conceptualise, never mind be able and willing to express what they feel about particular views and feelings. Consumers may absorb masses of marketing related stimuli, react to them and 'intend' to behave without really knowing why or even being aware of the true drivers of their intentions or behaviour.[11] An example may be trying to understand the childhood influences of family and friends on an individual's perception and loyalty to brands that the individual may purchase perhaps on a habitual basis, an example being washing-up liquid. Another example may be understanding the image consumers have of themselves and an image they wish to portray by spending €20,000 on a Rolex wristwatch. Participants do not normally have to think through such issues or articulate reasons for buying expensive luxury or fashion brands, until a researcher comes along!

> There is an implicit assumption in research that people carry attitudes around in their head that determine their buying behaviour. Most of the time, we don't give much thought to the burger we've eaten or even the flight we've made. Our natural inclination is to be polite and cooperative. If a researcher asks us to give an opinion we will do our best to formulate one on the spot.[12]

In circumstances where the researcher is digging deep into topics that participants do not normally think about or articulate, polite responses to questions may be very misleading. The characteristics of the individual participant may determine what is the best way to probe and elicit appropriate responses. Nothing is standardised or consistent in these circumstances, the researchers having to shape the questions, probes and observations as they see fit in each interview or observation situation. The following example illustrates the challenges faced by researchers and research participants in thinking and articulating their emotional relationships to brands.

Real research   **Winning people's hearts[13]**

There are plenty of brands that that give consumers satisfaction, and then there are brands like Apple (**www.apple.com**) and Godiva (**www.godiva.com**) that have something extra. This intangible something is what Marc Gobé, CEO of Desgrippes Gobé Group (**www.dga.com**), calls 'emotional branding' and he says it is what makes consumers fall in love with a brand:

This magnetism can be manufactured and there's a big role for research in coming up with the right chemistry to create it. Nike is a good example of an emotional brand. It made sportswear accessible to non-sports people with a brand story that inspired not just success but energy and determination.

Marc says that it is important to evaluate visual codes and emotional stimuli associed with brands and their competitors, to determine how consumers experience brands on a sensory level. What he does not do is ask consumers to describe their own feelings about brands and visual stimuli, recalling famous brands like Absolut and Red Bull that have flopped in focus groups:

It is very difficult to ask consumers, particularly in that kind of environment that is not conducive to imagination, about what they feel. I think consumers are not honest all the time and we are limited by the words that we use to express the emotions we have. It is very difficult to truly understand what it is that consumers really will accept in their lives, particularly when it comes to innovation.

As well as understanding how participants may react to particular issues, researchers should also understand how the context or environment may affect participants. The following examples illustrate why 'context' is so important when thinking about where participants are questioned and/or observed. The first example sets out ideas to experiment with different contexts in which to conduct qualitative interviews. The second example questions the context in which focus groups are conducted and the possible impact of context upon participant engagement, reflection and honesty.

Real research | **Taxis, vans and subways: capturing insights while commuting[14]**

The Mexican research company In/situm (**www. insitum.com**) has been experimenting with new ways to conduct qualitative research by reaching consumers in their own context instead of making them move to a local facility and participate in a study.

The company tried three approaches:

1 Designing and implementing a research taxi in which participants are taken to their destination while they participate in an interview conducted by the researcher–driver.
2 Moderating focus group sessions inside a private van in which passengers participate while they travel from a suburb to the city centre.
3 Conducting shadowings (observations and interviews) with subway passengers during their home–work commute.

The three approaches had mixed results and opportunities for improvement with clear logistical challenges. However, they all successfully developed new insights of consumers who were happy to discuss issues and be observed in contexts that they felt 'comfortable' in.

Real research	**Real-time global research – a qual revolution[15]**

In 2007, a leading UK high-street bank set ICD Research (**www.icd-research.com**), nqual (**www.nqual.com**), and The iD Factor (**www.theidfactor.com**) a simple challenge: to prove that an online focus group (e-group) would match the findings from traditional qualitative research. The objectives of the project were centred on a new credit card proposition. Consumer interest and adoption were required as well as suggested improvements. In setting up the e-group they used existing profiled data within The iD Factor financial panel. Participants were selected based on their consideration to switch credit card providers within the next 12 months. A recruitment email validated this pre-existing consideration, with the invitation to attend the sessions. The client was invited to attend a showcase session and, in total, 12 client observers accepted from the Innovation team, credit card team and equivalent teams in both Ireland and the USA. While the main moderator was based in London, a secondary moderator, based in Australia, was also present. At 7.55 p.m., a total of nine participants were active within the session, with an additional 18 observers across five companies/subsidiaries and three continents watching. In the context of this project, nqual's Managing Director Jamie Hamilton commented on the environmental aspects of running focus groups online:

For people with no experience of e-groups, 'online research environment' conjures an image of participants magically zipping down cables to meet in some cold, abstract, virtual space. This is a misrepresentation, in the same way as two friends chatting on a mobile are two electromagnetic waves bouncing off a satellite. The experience for the user is simply one of connection with the person that they wish to speak to. The e-group environment is actually wherever you choose to be sitting when you attend: the board room, a hotel in the Bahamas with a glass of Moet, or in your study, slippers on, drinking Horlicks. 'Online' is just the interface between you and the other participants, and the tools by which you interact with them. You don't go to an e-group, it comes to you, in your home or office, the computer is just the medium. An offline group involves a single, formal, and unfamiliar, environment; online there can be as many informal and familiar environments as there are attendees. Disclosing personal thoughts, feelings and information in front of a group in alien surroundings is always going to feel uncomfortable and risky. What if the others won't be as open? What if nobody understands or agrees? How will they judge me? That participants withhold or modify their input on delicate subjects may not be perceptible to even the most gifted moderator, let alone under their control. This, in turn, can lead to important decisions being made on the basis of unreliable findings, without anyone realising anything is amiss. Online participants, on the other hand, are perfectly at ease talking about deeply personal matters freely, and frankly. Whether it is the natural habitat, the anonymity, or detachment from threat of physical confrontation or judgment, something about e-groups facilitates a dramatic lowering of barriers. Evidence of this has been unequivocal for us, and for the client, revelatory. E-groups on sensitive issues – such as personal finance and saving plans for children – consistently gain insight which is conspicuously different from, and more trustworthy than, their offline equivalents.

As a further example, return to the first level of Figure 3.1, where participants may be more relaxed and feel in control if they can answer the set questions about their newspaper reading habits online rather than on the street. In the example at the start of this chapter that explored the hopes and dreams of 'emergent drinkers', techniques were used at the third and fourth levels of Figure 3.1. The context of the interviews was in 'leading-edge bars'. This context could have helped the target participants to relax, to develop a better rapport with interviewers and other participants, and to think more about the issues and express their feelings more clearly. If the interviews were conducted online, the same levels of relaxation and rapport might not work so well. If the interviews were targeted at older participants, they would have felt very self-conscious in 'leading-edge bars', which might restrict their responses. Researchers therefore must understand the characteristics of participants, how they react to particular issues and how they react in different contexts or environments. These factors are illustrated in Figure 3.2, which acts as a reminder of the understanding of participants that researchers must develop, in order to choose and apply the best research technique.

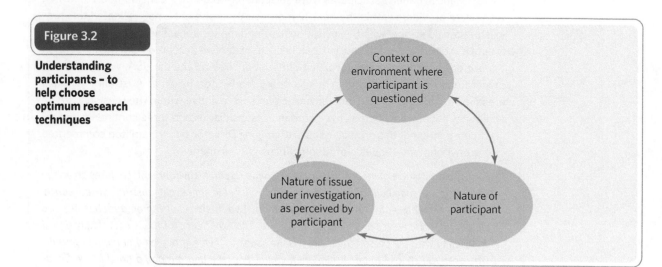

Figure 3.2

Understanding participants – to help choose optimum research techniques

Research design classification

Exploratory research
A research design characterised by a flexible and evolving approach to understand marketing phenomena that are inherently difficult to measure.

Conclusive research
A research design characterised by the measurement of clearly defined marketing phenomena.

Research designs may be broadly classified as exploratory or conclusive (see Figure 3.3). The differences between exploratory research and conclusive research are summarised in Table 3.1.

The primary objective of exploratory research is to provide insights into and an understanding of marketing phenomena.[16] It is used in instances where the subject of the study cannot be measured in a quantitative manner or where the process of measurement cannot realistically represent particular qualities. For example, if a researcher was trying to understand what 'atmosphere' meant in a restaurant, exploratory research may help to establish all the appropriate variables and how they connect together. What role did music play? What type of music? How loud? What types of furniture? What colours and textures? What types of lighting? What architectural features? This list could go on to consider what 'atmosphere' may mean in the context of a restaurant experience for particular types of consumer. 'Atmosphere' may not be measurable from the participant's perspective. From the perspective of the creative director in an advertising agency, quantitative measurements of the individual components of 'atmosphere' may not create the holistic feel of a restaurant in a manner the creative director can relate to.

Exploratory research may also be used in cases where the problem must be defined more precisely, relevant courses of action identified, or additional insights gained before going on to confirm findings using a conclusive design. The following example of researching computer games players illustrates the connection between exploratory and conclusive designs.

Figure 3.3

A classification of marketing research designs

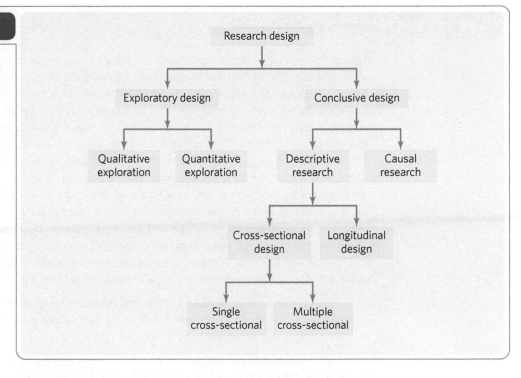

Table 3.1	Differences between exploratory and conclusive research

	Exploratory	Conclusive
Objectives	To provide insights and understanding of the nature of marketing phenomena	To test specific hypotheses and examine relationships
	To understand	To measure
Characteristics	Information needed may be loosely defined	Information needed is clearly defined
	Research process is flexible, unstructured and may evolve	Research process is formal and structured
	Samples are small	Sample is large and aims to be representative
	Data analysis can be qualitative or quantitative	Data analysis is quantitative
Findings/results	Can be used in their own right	Can be used in their own right
	May feed into conclusive research	May feed into exploratory research
	May illuminate specific conclusive findings	May set a context to exploratory findings
Methods	Expert surveys	Surveys
	Pilot surveys	Secondary data
	Secondary data	Databases
	Qualitative interviews	Panels
	Unstructured observations	Structured observations
	Quantitative exploratory multivariate methods	Experiments

Greedy Gamers[17]

Future Publishing (**www.futureplc.com**), a leading computer games magazine publisher, wanted to identify the role that the specialist games press plays within the gaming community. In particular, it was interested in the extent to which games magazines can both influence the decision-making process for games purchases and generate positive word-of-mouth recommendations. Future asked Continental Research (**www.continentalresearch.com**) to conduct the research. Qualitative research was initially conducted with active gamers. It quickly became clear that gaming was a very competitive activity for some, and it was therefore important to understand the difference between reported gaming activity and success, and reality. For example, there was talk of dusk-til-dawn gaming sessions; of the 'friend' who could complete four games within one day; and the teenager whose mum had to write him a sick note because his thumbs ached and his vision went blurry after a heavy gaming session! The key role of the qualitative research in all of this was to identify different gaming typologies in terms of not only their gaming activity, but also their communication role in the gaming fraternity.

For example: **Greedy Gamers** *eat and breathe gaming (some of them quite literally, as they would eat while playing a game one-handed). For them, it was a key topic of conversation with everyone that they came into contact with.*

Once different typologies had been identified, Continental was able to hypothesise about the likelihood of communication between different types of gamers. For the quantitative research stage of the project, Continental spoke to a representative sample of active gamers aged between 10 and 35. Continental's Grapevine matrix analysis tool enabled it to use the typologies in its questionnaire. The matrix identified the extent to which readers of the gaming press (whether exposed to adverts, reviews, previews or demo discs) were transmitting knowledge to other gamers. The research findings gave publishers and editors a greater insight into their readers and core target market. It was also of great use to advertising sales, providing a better understanding of how advertising within Future's magazines works.

In this example, the information needed was loosely defined at an exploratory stage, using research questions rather than specific hypotheses or actual measurements. The research process that was initially adopted can be characterised as flexible, loosely structured and, in some circumstances, evolutionary in nature.

In an example of a flexible, loosely structured and evolutionary approach, consider conducting personal interviews with industry experts. The sample, selected to generate maximum insight, is small and non-representative. However, the emphasis in the sampling procedure is focused upon 'quality' individuals who are willing to open up, use their imagination, be creative and reveal perhaps sensitive thoughts and behaviour. 'Quality' also may emerge from their level of expertise; for example, there may only be a small population of chief executives of airline companies in Europe. If a small sample of, say, six chief executives from the largest and fastest developing airlines allowed access to a researcher and revealed their attitudes and behaviour, insights might be gained that no conclusive study could achieve. By being flexible in the issues to discuss, loosely structured in how probes and additional issues emerge, and evolutionary in the nature of who to talk to and the best context in which to gain their confidence and get them to express what they really feel, an exploratory design can be very beneficial.

There is an exception to exploratory designs being built around qualitative techniques. There are examples of quantitative findings being used for exploratory purposes. For example, within a survey that examines specific research questions and hypotheses lies the opportunity to examine additional connections between questions that had not been initially considered. Simple correlations through to multivariate techniques that explore potential connections between questions may be conducted; this process is known as data mining. In essence, data mining searches for significant connections or patterns in a dataset that a researcher or decision-maker may be unaware of.

To summarise, exploratory research is meaningful in any situation where the researcher does not have enough understanding to proceed with the research project. Exploratory research is characterised by flexibility and versatility with respect to the methods, because formal research protocols and procedures are not employed. It rarely involves structured questionnaires, large samples and probability sampling plans. Rather, researchers are alert to new ideas and insights as they proceed. Once a new idea or insight is discovered, they may redirect their exploration in that direction. That new direction is pursued until its possibilities are exhausted or another direction is found. For this reason, the focus of the investigation may shift constantly as new insights are discovered. Thus, the creativity and ingenuity of the researcher play a major role in exploratory research. Exploratory research can be used for any of the purposes listed in Table 3.2.

Table 3.2	A summary of the uses of exploratory research designs

1 To obtain some background information where absolutely nothing is known about the problem area

2 To define problem areas fully and to formulate hypotheses for further investigation and/or quantification

3 To identify and explore concepts in the development of new product or forms of marketing communications

4 During a preliminary screening process such as in new product development, in order to reduce a large number of possible projects to a smaller number of probable ones

5 To identify relevant or salient behaviour patterns, beliefs, opinions, attitudes, motivations, etc., and to develop structures of these constructs

6 To develop an understanding of the structure of beliefs and attitudes in order to aid the interpretation of data structures in multivariate data analyses

7 To explore the reasons that lie behind the statistical differences between groups that may emerge from secondary data or surveys

8 To explore sensitive or personally embarrassing issues from the participants' and/or the interviewer's perspective

9 To explore issues that participants may hold deeply, that are difficult for them to rationalise and that they may find difficult to articulate

10 To 'data-mine' or explore quantitative data to reveal hitherto unknown connections between different measured variables

The objective of conclusive research is to describe specific phenomena, to test specific hypotheses and to examine specific relationships. This requires that the information needed is clearly specified.[18] Conclusive research is typically more formal and structured than exploratory research. It is based on large, representative samples, and the data obtained are subjected to quantitative analysis. Conclusive research can be used for any of the purposes listed in Table 3.3.

As shown in Figure 3.3, conclusive research designs may be either descriptive or causal, and descriptive research designs may be either cross-sectional or longitudinal. Each of these classifications is discussed further, beginning with descriptive research.

Table 3.3	A summary of the uses of conclusive research designs

1   To describe the characteristics of relevant groups, such as consumers, salespeople, organisations, or target market
2   To estimate the percentage in a specified population exhibiting a certain form of behaviour
3   To count the frequency of events, especially in the patterns of consumer behaviour
4   To measure marketing phenomena to represent larger populations or target markets
5   To be able to integrate findings from different sources in a consistent manner, especially in the use of marketing information systems and decision support systems
6   To determine the perceptions of product or service characteristics
7   To compare findings over time that allow changes in the phenomena to be measured
8   To measure marketing phenomena in a consistent and universal manner
9   To determine the degree to which marketing variables are associated
10   To make specific predictions

Descriptive research

Descriptive research
A type of conclusive research that has as its major objective the description of something, usually market characteristics or functions.

As the name implies, the major objective of descriptive research is to describe something, usually market characteristics or functions.[19] A major difference between exploratory and descriptive research is that descriptive research is characterised by the prior formulation of specific research questions and hypotheses. Thus, the information needed is clearly defined. As a result, descriptive research is preplanned and structured. It is typically based on large representative samples. The following example illustrates the use of descriptive research in study that determines the interest in and perceptions of horse racing at Goodwood.

Focus on	**IFM Sports Marketing Surveys**

Racing for Change: Goodwood 2010

Descriptive research

Renowned as one of the most finest flat horse racing courses in the world, Goodwood (**www.goodwood.co.uk/horse-racing**) is one of the world's greatest venues for entertaining in international sport. From its tentative launch as a flat horse racing course for local officers by the third Duke of Richmond in 1802, to its programme of events, fixtures, weddings and entertaining, Goodwood is also one of the UK's great estates and historic homes. In an effort to broaden the appeal of horse racing in the UK, visitors were given the opportunity to experience a day at the races free of charge. Goodwood was one of nine racecourses taking part in the 'Racing for Change' initiative and it had a requirement to measure the following:

- Horse racing interest and racing attendance.
- Reasons for attending the 'Racing for Change' event.
- Positives and negatives of the event experience?
- Attitudes towards facilities and event organisation?

- Image of the event?

- Image of Goodwood as a horse racing venue?

- Whether attendees were more educated about horse racing as a result of their attendance.

- Attendee profile?

- Where the attendees have travelled from; how they got there; and who they came with?

Following the 'Racing for Change' event, Goodwood Racecourse used its database of event attendees as a sampling frame and, through IFM Sports Marketing Surveys, invited them to complete an online questionnaire: 1,305 questionnaires were completed out of a sample of 7,000 attendees, a 19% response rate.

'Racing for Change' succeeded in widening the appeal of horse racing beyond its core audience: 17% of visitors had never been to any horse racing event prior to their day at Goodwood. The event was particularly attractive to younger age groups: 31% of under 35s were attending a racing event for the first time.

A descriptive research design specifies the methods for selecting the sources of information and for collecting data from those sources.

Examples of descriptive studies in marketing research are as follows:

- Market studies describing the size of the market, buying power of the consumers, availability of distributors, and consumer profiles.

- Market-share studies determining the proportion of total sales received by a company and its competitors.

- Sales analysis studies describing sales by geographic region, product line, type of account and size of account.

- Image studies determining consumer perceptions of the firm and its products.

- Product usage studies describing consumption patterns.

- Distribution studies determining traffic flow patterns and the number and location of distributors.

- Pricing studies describing the range and frequency of price changes and probable consumer response to proposed price changes.

- Advertising studies describing media consumption habits and audience profiles for specific TV programmes and magazines.

These examples demonstrate the range and diversity of descriptive research studies. Descriptive research can be further classified into cross-sectional and longitudinal research (Figure 3.3).

Cross-sectional designs

Cross-sectional design
A type of research design involving the collection of information from any given sample of population elements only once.

Single cross-sectional design
A cross-sectional design in which one sample of participants is drawn from the target population and information is obtained from this sample once.

Multiple cross-sectional design
A cross-sectional design in which there are two or more samples of participants, and information from each sample is obtained only once.

The cross-sectional study is the most frequently used descriptive design in marketing research. Cross-sectional designs involve the collection of information from any given sample of population elements only once. They may be either single cross-sectional or multiple cross-sectional (Figure 3.3). In single cross-sectional designs, only one sample of participants is drawn from the target population, and information is obtained from this sample only once. These designs are also called sample survey research designs. In multiple cross-sectional designs, there are two or more samples of participants, and information from each sample is obtained only once. Often, information from different samples is obtained at different times. The following examples illustrate single and multiple cross-sectional designs respectively.

Real research   **Television motivations[20]**

Much marketing research is directed at understanding the 'drivers' of consumer behaviour. In a study commissioned by Corning Display Technologies (**www.corning.com**), the motivations for choosing a new TV were measured. An online survey of 2,500 respondents in China, France, Germany, Japan, the UK and USA was administered. Qualitative research grounded in motivational theory underpinned the survey. The qualitative research suggested a number of consumer concerns and interests that might have an impact on TV preferences, especially across the countries being studied. This knowledge was used to develop a list of concerns and interests that could encompass selection and use of a TV set. The survey included a discrete choice exercise to measure preferences for different types of TV sets, such as traditional picture tube TVs, plasma and liquid digital display (LCD) flat-panel TVs, and rear projection TVs. The survey also contained a list of TV viewing occasions and activities, and participants were asked to indicate the frequency of each occasion for their households. Participants selected three viewing activities or occasions that would be most important to their choice of a TV set. To be part of the survey, participants had to indicate a likelihood of purchasing in the next four years either a TV set with a diagonal screen size of at least 76 cm or an LCD TV of any size.

Real research   **Life cycle, objective and subjective living standards and life satisfaction – multiple cross-sectional design[21]**

Centrum Badania Opinii Spotecznej (CBOS) (**www.cbos.pl**) is a major Polish polling centre, a non-governmental foundation, whose main goal is to conduct a monthly survey of public opinion on all important current problems and events. The centre wished to build a composite measure of living conditions, based upon household material wealth and life satisfaction. In order to do this it conducted seven surveys in Poland between 1992 and 2004. Through 2003 the surveys were conducted on stratified probability random samples of Polish addresses. The data from all surveys are weighted to assure their representativeness in respect of the main socio-demographic characteristics of the population. Satisfaction with various aspects of life was also investigated many times during the 1992–2004 period. However, only once, in September 1999, was it included in the same survey together with the questions on household possessions. Effective sample sizes were 1,788 in 1992, 1,222 in 1994, 1,177 in 1996, 1,167 in 1998, 1,092 in 1999, 1,060 in 2002, 1,057 in 2004 and 1,022 in 2004.

The survey devoted to measuring motivations of TV purchases, a single cross-sectional design, involved only one group of participants who provided information only once. On the other hand, the Polish study involved eight different samples, each measured only once, with the measures generally obtained two years apart. Hence, the latter study illustrates a multiple cross-sectional design. A type of multiple cross-sectional design of special interest is cohort analysis.

Cohort analysis consists of a series of surveys conducted at appropriate time intervals, where the cohort serves as the basic unit of analysis. A cohort is a group of participants who experience the same event within the same time interval.[22] For example, a birth (or age) cohort is a group of people who were born during the same time interval, such as 1951–1960. The term 'cohort analysis' refers to any study in which there are measures of some characteristics of one or more cohorts at two or more points in time.

Cohort analysis
A multiple cross-sectional design consisting of surveys conducted at appropriate time intervals. The cohort refers to the group of participants who experience the same event within the same interval.

It is unlikely that any of the individuals studied at time 1 will also be in the sample at time 2. For example, the age cohort of people between 8 and 19 years was selected, and their soft drink consumption was examined every 10 years for 30 years. In other words, every 10 years a different sample of participants was drawn from the population of those who were then between 8 and 19 years old. This sample was drawn independently of any previous sample drawn in this study from the population of people aged 8 to 19 years. Obviously, people who were selected once were unlikely to be included again in the same age cohort (8 to 19 years), as these people would be much older at the time of subsequent sampling. This study showed that this cohort had increased consumption of soft drinks over time. Similar findings were obtained for other age cohorts (20–29, 30–39, 40–49 and 50+). Further, the consumption of each cohort did not decrease as the cohort aged. These results are presented in Table 3.4 in which the consumption of the various age cohorts over time can be determined by reading down the diagonal. These findings contradict the common belief that the consumption of soft drinks will decline with the greying of Western economies. This common but erroneous belief has been based on single cross-sectional studies. Note that if any column of Table 3.4 is viewed in isolation (as a single cross-sectional study) the consumption of soft drinks declines with age, thus fostering the erroneous belief.[23]

Table 3.4	Consumption of soft drinks by various age cohorts (percentage consuming on a typical day)				
Age	**1950**	**1960**	**1970**	**1980**	
8–19	53	63	73	81	
20–29	45	61	76	76	C8
30–39	34	47	68	71	C7
40–49	23	41	59	68	C6
50+	18	29	50	52	C5
		C1	C2	C3	C4

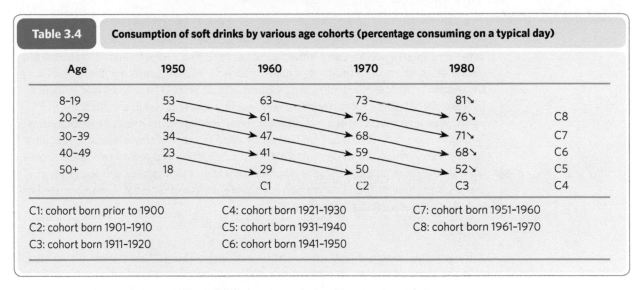

C1: cohort born prior to 1900   C4: cohort born 1921–1930   C7: cohort born 1951–1960
C2: cohort born 1901–1910   C5: cohort born 1931–1940   C8: cohort born 1961–1970
C3: cohort born 1911–1920   C6: cohort born 1941–1950

Cohort analysis can also be used to predict changes in voter opinions during a political campaign. Well-known researchers such as YouGov (**www.yougov.com**), or Ipsos MORI (**www.ipsos-mori.com**), who specialise in political opinion research, periodically question cohorts of voters (people with similar voting patterns during a given interval) about their voting preferences to predict election results. Thus, cohort analysis is an important cross-sectional design as illustrated in the following example which builds on the previous example of the Polish polling centre CBOS.

Real research	**Life cycle, objective and subjective living standards and life satisfaction – cohort analysis[24]**

Cohort analysis of the household material wealth and life satisfaction in Poland allowed joint examination of the impacts of age, time and period of being born. It can be said that though age-related differences were similar in each survey, between-survey differences suggested that material wealth was rapidly growing in time. This growth was evidently faster in young groups than in older ones, so the youth benefited the most from the changes. In addition, accumulated wealth was evidently much smaller in older age groups. That may bring an inexperienced researcher to a completely false conclusion that after a short period of acquiring wealth, people get rid of it rather than accumulate it in time. Thus, cohort analysis can be indispensable in properly examining the changes in wealth during the span of life.

Longitudinal design
A type of research design involving a fixed sample of population elements measured repeatedly. The sample remains the same over time, thus providing a series of pictures that, when viewed together, vividly illustrate the situation and the changes that are taking place.

Longitudinal designs

The other type of descriptive design is longitudinal design. In a longitudinal design, a fixed sample (or samples) of population elements is measured repeatedly as in the following example at Philips.

Real research   **True Loyalty[25]**

True Loyalty is a large-scale joint research project developed by Philips (**www.philips.com**) and Interview NSS (**www.interview-nss.com**). The project aims to measure the actual sales effect of consumers' experiences with Philips Consumer Electronics and Domestic Appliances/Personal Care products and services. The project was influenced by the work of Frederick Reichheld[26] who introduced the term 'Net Promotor Score (NPS)' which was a widely accepted indicator for many leading companies. Other than most findings reported on the NPS, True Loyalty decided to set up a single-souce longitudinal survey. Customers from whom it had obtained satisfaction and recommendation scores via ongoing research projects were recontacted 9 to 18 months later and both their purchases and those of friends and colleagues were assessed. The database consisted of over 25,000 recontacted customers.

A longitudinal design differs from a cross-sectional design in that the sample or samples remain the same over time. In other words, the same people are studied over time. In contrast to the typical cross-sectional design, which gives a snapshot of the variables of interest at a single point in time, a longitudinal study provides a series of 'pictures'. These 'pictures' give an in-depth view of the situation and the changes that take place over time. For example, the question 'How did the Danish people rate the performance of Prime Minister Lars Løkke Rasmussen immediately after the 2009 United Nations Climate Conference?' (**www.en.cop15.dk**) would be addressed using a cross-sectional design. A longitudinal design, however, would be used to address the question 'How did the Danish people change their view of Rasmussen's performance during his term of office?'

Panel
A sample of participants who have agreed to provide information at specified intervals over an extended period.

Access panel
A general 'pool' of individuals or households who have agreed to be available for surveys of widely varying types and topics.

Often, the term 'panel' is used in conjunction with the term 'longitudinal design'. A panel consists of a sample of participants, generally households, who have agreed to provide general or specific information at set intervals over an extended period. The emphasis of the panel is on measuring facts, e.g. who in the household bought what, where they bought it, when, and other aspects of their behaviour. Panels are really only established when observations or measurements over an extended period are meaningful. The observations are usually gathered through questionnaires such as purchase diaries or increasingly through social media methods. Panels are maintained by syndicated firms such as TNS (**www.tnsglobal.com**) and panel members are compensated for their participation with gifts, coupons, information or cash.[27]

Access panels are made up of a 'pool' of individuals or households who have agreed to be available for surveys of widely varying types and topics.[28] They are used to provide information for ad hoc decisions rather than for longitudinal studies, a typical use being for new product testing. A pre-recruited panel that is willing to participate makes it easier to set up the test and conduct interviews after the test. Access panels are also used to test concepts, advertising and pricing decisions.

Online consumer access panels are becoming increasingly prevalent in marketing research.[29] The growth in use of access panels has partly been in response to the challenges of rising rates of non-response or refusal to take part in surveys. The growth of online surveys and the need for electronic addresses of willing participants have also favoured the use of access panels. Given this growth and prevalence, we will further address access panels in Chapters 4, 10 and 14. The following example illustrates how access panels have been used in the telecommunications industry.

Real research | **Online panels for telecommunications[30]**

Jason Buchanan, Chief Development Director of Research Now (**www.researchnow. com**), argues that online panels provide a ready-made, pre-profiled set of participants. These can be specifically recruited to meet a range of complex sample targets and quotas, which are often in demand in the telecommunications industry. 'Online participants tend to be highly representative of some of the key target groups of interest to telecoms companies and suppliers', says Jason:

Panels can be very useful for targeting users of particular mobile phone networks, pre-paid or contract users, or users of particular mobile services and customers of specific competitors. It is quick and cost effective to screen for something very specific, such as ownership of a certain phone, rather than trying to call up or find the right people on the street.

There are important considerations when using online panels for telecommunications research, given the fast-moving nature of the industry. 'Taking into account when the panel was screened is particularly important for the telecommunications sector', says Jason:

The industry moves forward at such a fast pace that samples can easily be left behind. Frequency of internet usage is a classic example; what people were doing 12 or even 6 months ago will be different to what they are doing now. In a fast-moving research sector it is important to keep up to date with the latest gadgets, technologies and service offerings and to keep the panel updated with these.

Relative and disadvantages of longitudinal and cross-sectional advantages designs

The relative advantages and disadvantages of longitudinal versus cross-sectional designs are summarised in Table 3.5. A major advantage of longitudinal design over cross-sectional design is the ability to detect change as a result of repeated measurement of the same variables on the same sample.

Tables 3.6 and 3.7 demonstrate how cross-sectional data can mislead researchers about changes over time. The cross-sectional data reported in Table 3.6 reveal that the purchases of Brands A, B and C remain the same in periods 1 and 2. In each survey, 20% of the participants purchase Brand A, 30% Brand B and 50% Brand C. The longitudinal data presented in Table 3.7 show that substantial change, in the form of brand switching, occurred in the study period. For example, only 50% (100/200) of the participants who purchased Brand A in period 1 also purchased it in period 2. The corresponding repeat purchase figures for Brands B and C are, respectively, 33.3% (100/300) and 55% (275/500). Hence, during this interval Brand C experienced the greatest loyalty and Brand B the least. Table 3.7 provides valuable information on brand loyalty and brand switching (such a table is called a turnover table or a brand-switching matrix).[31]

Longitudinal data enable researchers to examine changes in the behaviour of individual units and to link behavioural changes to marketing variables, such as changes in advertising, packaging, pricing and distribution. Since the same units are measured repeatedly, variations caused by changes in the sample are eliminated and even small variations become apparent. Another advantage of panels is that relatively large amounts of data can be collected. Because panel members are usually compensated for their participation, they are willing to participate in lengthy and demanding interviews. Yet another advantage is that panel data can be more accurate than cross-sectional data. A typical cross-sectional survey requires the participant to recall past purchases and behaviour; these data can be inaccurate because of memory lapses. Panel data, which might involve continuous recording of purchases in a diary, place

Table 3.5	Relative advantages and disadvantages of longitudinal and cross-sectional designs		
Evaluation criteria	**Cross-sectional design**	**Longitudinal design**
Detecting change	–	+
Large amount of data collection	–	+
Accuracy	–	+
Representative sampling	+	–
Response bias	+	–

Note: + indicates a relative advantage over the other design, whereas – indicates a relative disadvantage.

Table 3.6	Cross-sectional data may not show change	
	Time period	
Brand purchased	**Period 1 survey**	**Period 2 survey**
Total surveyed	1,000	1,000
Brand A	200	200
Brand B	300	300
Brand C	500	500

Table 3.7	Longitudinal data may show substantial change			
	Brand purchased in period 2			
Brand purchased in period 1	**Brand A**	**Brand B**	**Brand C**	**Total**
Total surveyed	200	300	500	1,000
Brand A	100	50	50	200
Brand B	25	100	175	300
Brand C	75	150	275	500

less reliance on the participant's memory. A comparison of panel and cross-sectional survey estimates of retail sales indicates that panel data give more accurate estimates.[32]

The main disadvantage of panels is that they may not be representative. Non-representativeness may arise because of the following:

1 *Refusal to cooperate.* Many individuals or households do not wish to be bothered with the panel operation and refuse to participate. Consumer panels requiring members to keep a record of purchases have a cooperation rate of 60% or less.

2 *Dropout.* Panel members who agree to participate may subsequently drop out because they move away or lose interest. Dropout rates can be as high as 20% per year.[33]

3 *Payment.* Payment may cause certain types of people to be attracted, making the group unrepresentative of the population.

4 *Professional participants.* Most concerns about representativeness arise from the claim that research panels generate 'professional' participants. 'Panel conditioning' is the term used to describe the effect of participants who engage with a number of surveys over time and on a regular basis. Their self-reported attitudes and behaviours can be shaped by what they feel is the type of response expected of them.[34]

Another disadvantage of panels is response bias. New panel members are often biased in their initial responses. They tend to increase the behaviour being measured, such as food purchasing. This bias decreases as the participant overcomes the novelty of being on the panel, so it can be reduced by initially excluding the data of new members. Bias also results from boredom, fatigue and incomplete diary entries.[35] The following example from the marketing research agency Taylor Nelson Sofres (TNS) illustrates how it copes with potential panel bias.

Real research   ## Rubbish in, rubbish out[36]

Arno Hummerston, Head of Interactive Solutions Worldwide at TNS Interactive, notes that companies like TNS spend a lot of money on recruiting participants to online panels: 'If you start with rubbish you end up with rubbish.' As part of the ESOMAR Project Team on online panels, TNS has been looking at how to define a well-recruited panel. For TNS, a panel is recruited from multiple sources with the panellist's details verified. Arno argues that care must be taken to account for the differences between the type of people who take part in online panels and those who do not, to ensure that the panel is truly representative. TNS deals with this issue by running parallel studies to make sure that online panellists are responding in the same way online as they would offline. If a bias is found, the results are calibrated to account for it. In this respect, he argues, online is no different from any other form of research.

Causal research

Causal research
A type of conclusive research where the major objective is to obtain evidence regarding cause-and-effect (causal) relationships.

Causal research is used to obtain evidence of cause-and-effect (causal) relationships. Marketing managers continually make decisions based on assumed causal relationships. These assumptions may not be justifiable, and the validity of the causal relationships should be examined via formal research.[37] For example, the common assumption that a decrease in price will lead to increased sales and market share does not hold in certain competitive environments. Causal research is appropriate for the following purposes:

1   To understand which variables are the cause (independent variables) and which variables are the effect (dependent variables) of marketing phenomena.

2   To determine the nature of the relationship between the causal variables and the effect to be predicted.

3   To test hypotheses.

Like descriptive research, causal research requires a planned and structured design. Although descriptive research can determine the degree of association between variables, it is not appropriate for examining causal relationships. Such an examination requires a causal design, in which the causal or independent variables are manipulated in a relatively controlled environment. Such an environment is one in which the other variables that may affect the dependent variable are controlled or checked as much as possible. The effect of this manipulation on one or more dependent variables is then measured to infer causality. The main method of causal research is experimentation.[38]

Due to the complexity and importance of this subject, Chapter 11 has been devoted to causal research designs.

Relationships between exploratory, descriptive and causal research

We have described exploratory, descriptive and causal research as major classifications of research designs, but the distinctions among these classifications are not absolute. A given marketing research project may involve more than one type of research design and thus serve several purposes as illustrated in the following example.

Real research | ## Italians and Americans face each other at dinner[39]

The ways in which we select, prepare and consume foods are tied to the habits and customs that define a people in their place and time. The foods that are valued and enjoyed are linked to circumstances of availability, tradition, self-image and cultural transference. In research commissioned by Barilla Alimentare (**www.barillagroup.com**), Hy Mariampolski and Sharon Wolf (**www.qualidataresearch.com**) studied ideas about the 'Italian-ness' influence on foods eaten in the USA alongside a contrasting study of attitudes toward American foods eaten in Italy conducted by Luigi Toiati (**www.focusresearch.it**). Italian food in the USA, whilst being seen as an essential part of American cuisine, has been losing

its previous cachet. Competing against other cuisines, particularly Asian and Mexican meals, Italian foods have been riddled with unhelpful ideas emanating from popular cultural stereotypes: that Italian meals consist of enormous quantities of pasta heavily sauced with cheese and meaty red tomato purée. These myths tend to reduce Italian foods as downscale and inappropriate for low-carbohydrate diets. Italy too has its own complex mythology regarding the USA and its cuisine: that it consists of heaping portions of food that are mediocre at best, over processed, lacking tradition, fattening and eaten too hastily. The general conclusion is that 'America is a country worth visiting, but where it's not worth eating'. In the Italian mind, overweight Americans stuff themselves with anonymous, monotonous food, simply eating for eating's sake with no regard for taste! The researchers wanted to help reverse these disparaging stereotypes. Digging deeply into the meaning of 'authenticity' and seeking positive and constructive aspects of the national mythologies helped to secure consumer insights that promoted consumption of Italian brands in the USA and American foods in Italy. The methods used in this study of food culture were: **semiotic analysis** of media images to gain insights into the ideas communicated about Italy and the USA in popular culture; **in-depth interviews** with experts and influential consumers; **ethnographic** home visits to see how ideas about the foods of each culture were expressed in meal preparation; **focus group discussions** to explore emerging ideas; and descriptive **face-to-face street interviews**.

Which combination of research designs to employ depends on the nature of the problem. We offer the following general guidelines for choosing research designs.

1 When little is known about the problem situation, it is desirable to begin with exploratory research. Exploratory research is appropriate for the following:

   a When the nature of the topic under study cannot be measured in a structured, quantifiable manner.

   b When the problem needs to be defined more precisely.

   c When alternative courses of action need to be identified.

   d When research questions or hypotheses need to be developed.

   e When key variables need to be isolated and classified as dependent or independent.

2 Exploratory research may be an initial step in a research design. It may be followed by descriptive or causal research. For example, hypotheses developed via exploratory research can be statistically tested using descriptive or causal research.

3 It is not necessary to begin every research design with exploratory research. It depends on the precision with which the problem has been defined and the researcher's degree of certainty about the approach to the problem. A research design could well begin with descriptive or causal research. To illustrate, a consumer satisfaction survey that is conducted annually need not begin with or include an exploratory phase.

4 Although exploratory research is generally the initial step, it need not be. Exploratory research may follow descriptive or causal research. For example, descriptive or causal research results in findings that are hard for managers to interpret. Exploratory research may provide more insights to help understand these findings.

The relationships between exploratory, descriptive and causal research are further illustrated by the following example.

How great insight led to Panadol's most successful advertising campaign[40]

Panadol's (**www.panadol.com**) 'Absolute Confidence' advertising campaign ran for four years in Australia. Midway through the campaign, Panadol was the victim of extortion threats and a recall. During the recall customers started shopping around and trying different painkillers. Then Panadol's key competitor Herron (**www.herron.com.au**) launched a new advertising campaign which saw its market share grow to the point that it was close to taking the market leadership position. Panadol responded with another advertising campaign but did not regain its former market share. Research was needed to deternine how the Panadol brand could establish a more emotional connection with consumers.

Led by the marketing research company Leading Edge (**www.theleadingedge.com. au**), qualitative research (in-depth interviews and 'mini-group' discussions) was used at the start of the project. This was used to understand consumers' needs, motivations and values, their attitudes to health and medications, their perceptions of the brand and how they use painkillers. Research was carried out into trends in society and health care, along with interviews with opinion leaders in the health care profession. These were used to help explain the consumer findings and predict what behaviours and attitudes might become more or less important in the future. A quantitative phase involved 400 online interviews. A multi-disciplinary team was involved in conducting the research. The client, GlaxoSmithKline, conducted about one-third of the in-depth interviews. Weekly meetings and an online bulletin board were used to share learning and ideas along the way.

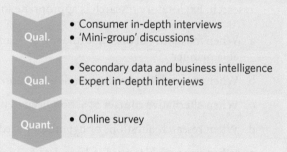

- Consumer in-depth interviews
- 'Mini-group' discussions

- Secondary data and business intelligence
- Expert in-depth interviews

- Online survey

The research identified that when consumers are looking for a paracetamol pain-relief product, they feel an emotional connection to one brand over another. Consumers were also more actively seeking their own pain solutions and brand differentiation would help them make a decision. The research suggested aligning the Panadol brand with a 'modern approach to pain relief', which involved building an 'active partnership' with consumers. An advertising campaign was built upon this research and achieved excellent ratings for appeal, brand differentiation, credibility and brand relevance.

Examples of multi-method research designs can be criticised for taking too long to undertake, being too expensive and perhaps applying too many techniques that do not offer sufficient additional understanding. Such criticism cannot really be addressed without knowing the value that decision-makers may get from this decision support (not just at the end but at the many stages of research as it unfolds), compared with how much they would have to pay for it. Decision-makers can receive interim reports and feed back their ideas to give more focus to the issues and types of participant in subsequent stages. The example also illustrates that researchers can be very creative in their choice of techniques that combine to make up a research design.

Potential sources of error in research designs

Several potential sources of error can affect a research design. A good research design attempts to control the various sources of error. Although these errors are discussed in detail in subsequent chapters, it is pertinent at this stage to give brief descriptions.

Where the focus of a study is a quantitative measurement, the total error is the variation between the true mean value in the population of the variable of interest and the observed mean value obtained in the marketing research project. For example, the annual average income of a target population may be €85,650, as determined from census information via tax returns, but a marketing research project estimates it at €62,580 based upon a sample survey. As shown in Figure 3.4, the total error (in the above case €23,070) is composed of random sampling error and non-sampling error.

Total error
The variation between the true mean value in the population of the variable of interest and the observed mean value obtained in the marketing research project.

Random sampling error
The error arising because the particular sample selected is an imperfect representation of the population of interest. It may be defined as the variation between the true mean value for the sample and the true mean value of the population.

Non-sampling error
An error that can be attributed to sources other than sampling and that can be random or non-random.

Random sampling error

Random sampling error occurs because the particular sample selected is an imperfect representation of the population of interest. Random sampling error is the variation between the true mean value for the population and the true mean value for the original sample. Random sampling error is discussed further in Chapters 14 and 15.

Non-sampling error

Non-sampling errors can be attributed to sources other than sampling, and may be random or non-random. They result from a variety of reasons, including errors in problem definition, approach, scales, questionnaire design, interviewing methods, and data preparation and analysis. Non-sampling errors consist of non-response errors and response errors.

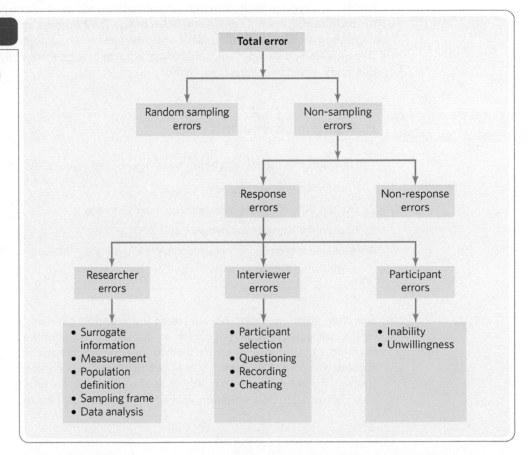

Figure 3.4

Potential sources of error in research designs

Non-response error

A type of non-sampling error that occurs when some of the participants included in the sample do not respond. This error may be defined as the variation between the true mean value of the variable in the original sample and the true mean value in the net sample.

Response error

A type of non-sampling error arising from participants who do respond but who give inaccurate answers or whose answers are mis-recorded or mis-analysed. It may be defined as a variation between the true mean value of the variable in the net sample and the observed mean value obtained in the market research project.

A non-response error arises when some of the participants included in the sample simply do not respond. The primary causes of non-response are refusals and not-at-homes (see Chapter 15). Non-response will cause the net or resulting sample to be different in size or composition from the original sample. Non-response error is defined as the variation between the true mean value of the variable in the original sample and the true mean value in the net sample.

Response error arises when participants give inaccurate answers or their answers are mis-recorded or mis-analysed. Response error is defined as the variation between the true mean value of the variable in the net sample and the observed mean value obtained in the marketing research project. Response error is determined not only by the non-response percentage, but also by the difference between participants and those who failed to cooperate, for whatever reason, as response errors can be made by researchers, interviewers or participants.[41] A central question in evaluating response error is whether those who participated in a survey differ from those who did not take part, in characteristics relevant to the content of the survey.[42]

Errors made by the researcher include surrogate information, measurement, population definition, sampling frame and data analysis errors:

- *Surrogate information error* may be defined as the variation between the information needed for the marketing research problem and the information sought by the researcher. For example, instead of obtaining information on consumer choice of a new brand (needed for the marketing research problem), the researcher obtains information on consumer preferences because the choice process cannot be easily observed.

- *Measurement error* may be defined as the variation between the information sought and information generated by the measurement process employed by the researcher. While seeking to measure consumer preferences, the researcher employs a scale that measures perceptions rather than preferences.

- *Population definition error* may be defined as the variation between the actual population relevant to the problem at hand and the population as defined by the researcher. The problem of appropriately defining the population may be far from trivial, as illustrated by the following example of affluent households. Their number and characteristics varied depending on the definition, underscoring the need to avoid population definition error. Depending upon the way the population of affluent households was defined, the results of this study would have varied markedly.

Real research   **How affluent is affluent?**

The population of the affluent households was defined in four different ways in a study:

1   Households with an income of €80,000 or more.

2   The top 20% of households, as measured by income.

3   Households with net worth over €450,000.

4   Households with discretionary income to spend being 30% higher than that of comparable households.

- *Sampling frame error* may be defined as the variation between the population defined by the researcher and the population as implied by the sampling frame (list) used. For example, the telephone directory used to generate a list of telephone numbers does not accurately represent the population of potential landline consumers due to unlisted, disconnected and new numbers in service. It also misses out the great number of consumers who choose not to have landlines, exclusively using mobile phones.

- *Data analysis error* encompasses errors that occur while raw data from questionnaires are transformed into research findings. For example, an inappropriate statistical procedure is used, resulting in incorrect interpretation and findings.

Response errors made by the interviewer include participant selection, questioning, recording and cheating errors:

- *Participant selection error* occurs when interviewers select participants other than those specified by the sampling design or in a manner inconsistent with the sampling design.

- *Questioning error* denotes errors made in asking questions of the participants or in not probing, when more information is needed. For example, while asking questions an interviewer does not use the exact wording or prompts as set out in the questionnaire.

- *Recording error* arises due to errors in hearing, interpreting and recording the answers given by the participants. For example, a participant indicates a neutral response (undecided) but the interviewer misinterprets that to mean a positive response (would buy the new brand).

- *Cheating error* arises when the interviewer fabricates answers to a part or the whole of the interview. For example, an interviewer does not ask the sensitive questions related to a participant's debt but later fills in the answers based on personal assessment.

Response errors made by the participant comprise errors of inability and unwillingness:

- *Inability error* results from the participant's inability to provide accurate answers. Participants may provide inaccurate answers because of unfamiliarity, fatigue, boredom, question format, question content or because the topic is buried deep in the participant's mind. An example of inability error is where a participant cannot recall the brand of toothpaste he or she purchased four weeks ago.

- *Unwillingness error* arises from the participant's unwillingness to provide accurate information. Participants may intentionally misreport their answers because of a desire to provide socially acceptable answers, because they cannot see the relevance of the survey and/or a question posed, to avoid embarrassment, to please the interviewer.[43] For example, to impress the interviewer, a participant intentionally says that he or she reads *The Economist* magazine.

These sources of error are discussed in more detail in subsequent chapters; what is important here is that there are many sources of error. In formulating a research design, the researcher should attempt to minimise the total error, not just a particular source. This admonition is warranted by the general tendency among naïve researchers to control sampling error by using large samples. Increasing the sample size does decrease sampling error, but it may also increase non-sampling error, e.g. by increasing interviewer errors. Non-sampling error is likely to be more problematic than sampling error. Sampling error can be calculated, whereas many forms of non-sampling error defy estimation. Moreover, non-sampling error has been found to be the major contributor to total error, whereas random sampling error is relatively small in magnitude. The point is that researchers must not lose sight of the impact of total error upon the integrity of their research design and the findings they present. A particular type of error is important only in that it contributes to total error.

Sometimes, researchers deliberately increase a particular type of error to decrease the total error by reducing other errors. For example, suppose that a mail survey is being conducted to determine consumer preferences in purchasing shoes from a chain of specialist shoe shops. A large sample size has been selected to reduce sampling error. A response rate of 30% may be expected. Given the limited budget for the project, the selection of a large sample size does not allow for follow-up mailings. Past experience, however, indicates that the response rate could be increased to 45% with one follow-up mailing and to 55% with two follow-up mailings. Given the subject of the survey, non-participants are likely to differ from participants in many features. Therefore it may be wise to reduce the sample size to make money available for follow-up mailings. While decreasing the sample size will increase random sampling error, the two follow-up mailings will more than offset this loss by decreasing non-response error.[44]

International marketing research

When conducting international marketing research, it is important to realise that, given environmental differences, the research design appropriate for one country may not be suitable in another. Consider the problem of determining household attitudes towards major appliances in the Netherlands and Saudi Arabia. While conducting exploratory research in the Netherlands, it may be appropriate to conduct focus groups jointly with male and female heads of households. It would be inappropriate to conduct such focus groups in Saudi Arabia, however. Given the traditional culture, wives may be unlikely to participate freely in the presence of their husbands. It would be more useful to conduct one-on-one in-depth interviews with both male and female heads of households being included in the sample. An understanding of cultural influences can affect the choice and application of individual research techniques. The following example illustrates cultural differences in international research and how this may impact upon what may be seen as a sensitive issue.

Real research	### Sanitary napkins: building the idea of intimacy[45]

What is a sanitary napkin? It is a female 'protection pad' whose functional value is based on its absorption capacity, its maximum thinness and its anatomical adaptability. Saul Feldman of FOCOS Latinoamerica (**www.focoslatin.com.ar**) has conducted qualitative research throughout Latin America for a number of product categories that include the sensitive nature of buying and using sanitary napkins. Using focus groups, ethnographic interviews, creative workshops and semiotic analysis of advertisements, Saul has built up a strong understanding of cultural differences in the region. Far from having the same meanings in every culture, there were differences from one society to another as evidenced in his work in Colombia (Bogotá), Costa Rica (San José) and Argentina. In Columbia, more rigid and traditional in terms of gender roles, women felt the need to look the same in 'those days' without breakdowns and trying obsessively to hide their condition. In Costa Rica, the period was accepted from the standpoint that there was no difference with men, as something 'natural' and therefore not prone to giving themselves permits. In Argentina, tolerance of 'those days' was greater and it was allowed to be different; to search for pleasure, permits and treats. One aspect studied was the organisation of the product on supermarket shelves, and the way in which women 'navigated' to buy them. Saul wanted to understand how they managed to pick what they wanted in a category with a lot of different varieties, but also with small packs, full of 'objective' information, with multiple details, lots of descriptions and little differentiation among them. In Columbia, with fast, effective and determined attitudes at the shelves (a public place for something so intimate), such products should not be shown. Costa Rica showed the opposite; women took more time to observe, find new products, choose what was best, it was just another purchase. Argentinians demanded more feminine rhetoric for presentations and moved around shelves with apparent certainty as if they already knew what they wanted to find, with the idea that having to choose was superfluous. Sanitary napkins are a product category where culture can be approached directly as an intrinsic component, necessary to understand the category, establish insights and release new products.

In many countries, particularly developing countries, consumer panels have not been developed, making it difficult to conduct descriptive longitudinal research. The development of panels using social media research techniques may overcome this problem. In many countries the marketing support infrastructure – that is, retailing, wholesaling, advertising and promotional infrastructure – is lacking, making it infeasible to implement a causal design involving a field experiment. In formulating a research design, considerable effort is required to ensure the equivalence and comparability of secondary and primary data obtained from different countries. In the context of collecting primary data, qualitative research, survey methods, scaling techniques, questionnaire design and sampling considerations are particularly important. These topics are discussed in more detail in subsequent chapters.

Ethics in marketing research

During the research design stage, not only are the concerns of the researcher and the client involved, but the rights of the participants also must be respected. Although normally there is no direct contact between the participants and the other stakeholders (client and researcher) during the research design phase, this is the stage when decisions with ethical ramifications, such as using hidden video- or audiotape recorders, are made. Responsibilities to research participants must not be overlooked. The researcher should design the study so as not to violate the participants' rights to safety, rights to privacy, or rights to choose. Furthermore, the client must not abuse its power to jeopardise the anonymity of the participants. These concerns are exacerbated with developments in social media that create new privacy, security and safety issues. Social media have changed the rules on how 'findable' somebody is. This has enormous implications for privacy and safety. This point is illustrated in the following example.

Real research | Real name attribution[46]

The open, connected and 'always available' nature of the resources accessible through social media invites new questions in terms of market research ethics and the protection of consumer privacy. Traditional marketing research has already been adapted for the Web, where interview techniques and focus groups have been modified to take place within Internet forums and community groups. There are many more revealing and more risky sources of rich and real-time consumer data. But social media are useful only if anchored in real identities and lives. An example of this can be found on www.Amazon.com, which encourages the use of names, or as the company puts it:[47]

> A Real Name attribution is a signature based on the name entered by the author as the cardholder name on his or her credit card, i.e. the author represents this name as his/her identity in the 'real world'. An author willing to sign his or her real-world name on content posted on Amazon.com is essentially saying 'With my real-world identity, I stand by what I have written here.'

In other words, the traditional marketing research 'tool' of a person with a clipboard asking 'real' people questions in the street may be supplanted by new mediated ways of collecting data from 'real' people and 'real' actions across social media. For example, the posting of video content on YouTube may also be shared and simultaneously cross-posted to corresponding social network sites such as Facebook. Thus the individual is ever traceable to others. We have already seen how Web 2.0 resources heralded by the 'Wisdom of Crowds', 'collective intelligence' and 'participatory culture' have helped to capture this synchronisation of shared information.[48]

Research ethics may also be applied to the fundamental question of the type of research design which should be adopted (i.e. descriptive or causal, cross-sectional or longitudinal). For example, when studying brand switching in toothpaste purchases, a longitudinal design is the only actual way to assess changes in an individual participant's brand choice. A research firm that has not conducted many longitudinal studies may try to justify the use of a cross-sectional design. Is this ethical? Researchers must ensure that the research design utilised will provide the information needed to address the marketing research problem that has been identified. The client should have the integrity not to misrepresent the project and should describe the constraints under which the researcher must operate and not make unreasonable demands. Longitudinal research takes time. Descriptive research might require interviewing customers. If time is an issue, or if customer contact has to be restricted, the client should make these constraints known at the start of the project. The client buying services from a marketing research firm should not take undue advantage of it to ask for unreasonable concessions or discounts for a current project by making false promises of future research contracts, as illustrated in the following example.

As well as its general code of conduct, ESOMAR produces a series of guidelines that are specific to particular research techniques (Internet research), types of participant (children) and types of industry (pharmaceutical). To see how ESOMAR guides the ethical practices of the marketing research industry in Europe, and how marketing research associations in individual countries throughout the world guide the ethical practices of domestic marketing research, visit **www.esomar.org**.

Real research   ## Big Brother or Big Bully?[49]

Ethical dilemmas may arise due to the strong desire of marketing research firms to become suppliers to large organisations which invest heavily in marketing research projects. Many companies in financial services, airlines, beverages and automobiles, for example, have enormous marketing budgets and regularly employ external marketing research firms. Large clients can manipulate the price for a current project or demand unreasonable concessions in the research design (e.g. the examination of additional variables, more focus groups, a larger or more targeted sample for the survey, or additional data analyses) by implying that there is the potential for the marketing research firms to become a regular supplier. This may be considered just business, but it becomes unethical when there is no intention to follow up with a larger study or to use the research firm in the future.

Digital applications in marketing research

Online research methods including social media research techniques are delivering more opportunities to researchers to be creative in crafting research designs. These opportunities are not just traditional research techniques that can be facilitated online, but entirely new techniques. Digital applications are enabling marketing research techniques to be more engaging, making the process of questioning, debate and sharing views more fun. Examples of this creativity can be seen in the two main classifications of research design.

Exploratory research

If an exploratory research design is to be utilised, discussion groups, chat rooms, blogs or newsgroups can be used to discuss a particular topic to great depth. Files can be exchanged that can include moving images and sounds, allowing questions and probes to be built around this material. Formal online focus groups may be conducted with experts or individuals representing target groups, all on a global basis if needed. Digital applications can help to gain access to individuals that previously could not be accessed, or if they could be accessed it would be at great cost or take much time. They can also facilitate accessing individuals in contexts where they feel comfortable to engage in research. The following example illustrates how the mobile phone can be used to access notoriously difficult research participants.

Real research	**Mobile in the qualitative space – digital ethnography in India**[50]

Anjali Puri, Executive Director at TNS Qualitative Research, Shopping Consulting and Digital Media (**www.tnsglobal.com/global/alm/india**), believes that mobile phones have added richness to ethnographic studies. Youth marketers and telecommunications companies were the first to take to incorporating the mobile into traditional ethnographic studies. The approach was to recruit a panel of participants and send them messages to share what they were doing, who they were with, what they were eating, and to share pictures of their surroundings, abruptly at different times of the day. Says Anjali:

> *The proliferation of smart mobile phones with urban youth has made it far more efficient to conduct digital ethnographic studies. You can collect a week's worth of data at a fraction of the costs of capturing the participant's lives through videocams. But perhaps the biggest advantage of the mobile phone is that it is far less intrusive in the participants' lives and therefore the data one can collect is a lot more spontaneous and relatively bias free. And, of course, it is possible to capture snapshots of their lives anytime anywhere.*

TNS has also used mobile phone logs in a rural ethnography study. The data bias arising from an urban (mostly female) researcher fitting in with the rural opinion leaders is fairly acute. It can be a cost-intensive exercise to conduct rural ethnographic studies as the 'warm-up' period is much longer. In one study, after establishing initial contact with participants, the research relied on the collection of information from opinion leaders in a village by mobile phone contact (in this case, largely voice and camera applications) conducted over a longer period of time. The mobile logs were found to be equally candid and rich in data as the information collected through personal contacts.

Conclusive research

In Chapter 1, in examining the patterns of global marketing research spend, ESOMAR created a distinct category named 'automated digital/electronic' which covered online traffic/audience measurements and digital/electronic research including retail audits. In 2009, this category accounted for 16% of all marketing research spend. If the spending on online quantitative research (which is the highest category spend, standing at 22%) is added, then 38% of all marketing research expenditure was applied to conclusive online quantitative research and automated digital/electronic methods.[51] Conclusive online quantitative research has grown year on year in both expenditure terms and as a proportion of all marketing research spend. It is expected that this will grow, not just in its own right, but also in integrated forms that allow other techniques to be applied. The following example illustrates this form of integration where a series of conclusive online surveys were supported by participants photographing the context in which they were experiencing the World Cup.

World Cup 2010 – redefining 'multimodal' research to understand audience engagement[52]

The 2010 FIFA World Cup in South Africa showcased athletic prowess, compelling stories of players and teams, national pride and many unexpected moments The event bridged nations, languages, cultures and passions. The Nielsen Life360 project (**www.nielsen.com**) was a new research approach to measure the effects of the World Cup via three multimedia screens: TV, Internet and mobile devices. The project was built upon a set of clear objectives: capture the 'day in the life' behaviour of sample participants and their interactions with the World Cup anytime, anywhere they occurred. The Nielsen researchers equipped a panel of 420 South African adults (ages 16+ years) with Web-enabled BlackBerry devices running the Techneos SODA (**www.techneos.com**) mobile research application in four main tournament cities: Johannesburg, Pretoria, Durban and Cape Town. Each participant carried the mobile phone for the full four and a half weeks of the tournament and completed a series of prompted surveys that asked them to share 'in the moment' behaviour, moods and location, plus retrospective media usage along with photos. Surveys were delivered five times daily in a choice of languages: Afrikaans, English, Tswana and Zulu. Question formats included multiple-choice, open-ended responses and extended to brand awareness and select daily expenditures. For games watched, details such as platform, channel and participating teams could be recorded. Data from the sample were weighted for age, gender, language and economic status in proportion to South Africa's total population and reported on a daily, weekly and full-round basis via a proprietary online dashboard. In all, 61,000 data records and more than 54,000 images were collected during the month-long tournament. The method delivered abundant rich data garnered from multiple screens, platforms, countries and demographics supplanted by a plethora of photos shared by participants. Its key capacity for capturing on-the-ground and 'in the moment' engagement with the tournament delivered new insights and previously unattainable figures. One immediate benefit of the complex research undertaking identified a core advantage: being able to measure 'out-of-home' enabled a new capacity to engage and understand the experiences of the fans across Johannesburg, Pretoria, Durban and Cape Town watching TV at work, friends' homes, entertainment facilities and at fan parks.

Summary

A research design is a framework or plan for conducting a marketing research project. It specifies the details of how a project should be conducted in order to fulfil set research objectives. The challenge faced by researchers in developing a research design is that they need to balance an understanding of research design from the decision-makers' perspective with an understanding of potential participants' reactions to issues researched using different techniques, applied in differing contexts. Research designs may be broadly classified as exploratory or conclusive. The primary purpose of exploratory research is to develop understanding and provide insights. Conclusive research is conducted to measure and describe phenomena, test specific hypotheses and examine specific relationships. Conclusive research may be either descriptive or causal. The findings from both exploratory and conclusive research can be used as input into marketing decision making.

The major objective of descriptive research is to describe market characteristics or functions. Descriptive research can be classified into cross-sectional and longitudinal research. Cross-sectional designs involve the collection of information from a sample of population elements at a single point in time. These designs can be further classified as single cross-sectional or multiple cross-sectional designs. In contrast, in longitudinal designs repeated measurements are taken on a fixed sample. Causal research is designed for the primary purpose of obtaining evidence about cause-and-effect (causal) relationships. Many research designs combine techniques that can be classified as exploratory, descriptive and causal. In cases where there is an array of interrelating techniques, the researcher should examine the ultimate aim of an investigation, and decide what encapsulates the overall research design, i.e. a desire to explore, describe or experiment.

A research design consists of six components and errors can be associated with any of these components. The total error is composed of random sampling error and non-sampling error. Non-sampling error consists of non-response and response errors. Response error encompasses errors made by researchers, interviewers and participants. In formulating a research design when conducting international marketing research, considerable effort is required to ensure the equivalence and comparability of secondary and primary data obtained from different countries. In terms of ethical issues, the researchers must ensure that the research design used will provide the information sought and that the information sought is the information needed by the client. The client should have the integrity not to misrepresent the project and should describe the situation within which the researcher must operate and must not make unreasonable demands. In creating a research design, every precaution should be taken to ensure the participants' right to safety, right to privacy, or right to choose. With the rise in social media research methods, protecting the privacy of participants has become a more arduous task for researchers. Online research methods including social media research techniques are delivering more opportunities for researchers to be creative in crafting research designs. These opportunities are not just traditional research techniques that can be facilitated online, but entirely new techniques.

Questions

1. Define research design in your own words.
2. What expectations do marketing decision-makers have of research designs?
3. How does the subject of a study as seen by potential research participants affect research design?
4. How does formulating a research design differ from developing an approach to a problem?
5. Differentiate between exploratory and conclusive research.
6. What are the major purposes for which exploratory research is conducted?
7. Describe how quantitative techniques may be used in exploratory research.
8. What are the major purposes for which descriptive research is conducted?
9. Discuss the advantages and disadvantages of access panels.
10. Compare and contrast cross-sectional and longitudinal designs.
11. Describe cohort analysis. Why is it of special interest?
12. What is a causal research design? What is its purpose?
13. What is the relationship between exploratory, descriptive and causal research?
14. What potential sources of error can affect a research design?
15. Why is it important to minimise total error rather than any particular source of error?

Exercises

1   Imagine that you are the researcher appointed by BMW and that you have been hired to conduct a study of its corporate image.

   a   Discuss the potential issues that may affect your choice of context in which to interview female executives that buy the 7-series cars.

   b   Discuss the potential issues that may affect your choice of context in which to interview teenagers whose parent(s) own a BMW.

2   Visit the website of the Market Research Society. Browse through its Research Buyer's Guide (**www.rbg.org.uk**) to get a feel for the nature of industries and marketing issues that may be supported by exploratory studies. Find the agency Brainjuicer and examine the work of this research company (**www.brainjuicer.com**). In what manner(s) does this agency link exploratory designs to conclusive designs?

3   Visit **www.ingdirect.co.uk** (look for the site in your home country) and search online using your library's online databases to gather information of consumers' attitudes towards online banking. ING Direct would like to determine consumers' attitudes towards online banking and hope to repeat this project annually. What type of research design would you recommend and why? As the CEO of ING Direct, how would you use information about consumers' attitudes towards online banking in improving the competitiveness of your bank?

4   Visit the website of the research organisation JD Power and Associates (**www.jdpower.com**). Work through its corporate site and choose a study that it has conducted. What research design was used for this study and what potential error issues could emerge given the nature of what it was investigating?

5   In a small group discuss the following issues: 'There are many potential sources of error in a research project. It is impossible to control all of them. Hence, all marketing research contains errors and we cannot be confident of the findings.' And 'If a research budget is limited, small sample sizes through exploratory studies are the best solution.'

Video case exercise: Nike

Innovation is a core value of the Nike brand. What factors may demand an innovative research design for challenges such as measuring or understanding the brand values of Nike?

Notes

1. Perkins, H. and Carney, P., 'In touch with the spirit world', ESOMAR, Consumer Insights Conference, Madrid (April 2003); Acreman, S. and Pegram, B., 'Getting to know you', *Research* (November 1999), 36–41.

2. Branthwaite, A. and Patterson, S., 'The vitality of qualitative research in the era of blogs and tweeting: an anatomy of contemporary research methods', ESOMAR, Qualitative, Barcelona (November 2010); Tait, B., 'How "marketing science" undermines brands', *Admap* (October, 2004), 46–48.

3. Hunt, S., 'Objectivity in marketing theory and research', *Journal of Marketing* 57 (April 1993), 71–91.

4. Roberts, D. and Adams, R., 'Agenda development for marketing research: the user's voice', *International Journal of Market Research* 52 (3) (2010), 329–352.

5. Cooper, P., 'In search of excellence: the evolution and future of qualitative research', ESOMAR, Annual Congress, Berlin (September 2007); figure adapted from Cooper, P. and Branthwaite, A., 'Qualitative technology –

new perspectives on measurement and meaning through qualitative research', Market Research Society Conference, 2nd Pre-conference Workshop, 1979.

6. Examples of research conducted on sensitive topics include: Kouznetsov, A. and Dass, M., 'Does size matter? A qualitative study into areas of corruption where a firm's size influences prospects for distributors of foreign-made goods in Russia', *Baltic Journal of Management* 5 (1) (2010), 51–67; Vasconcelos, A.F., 'Intuition, prayer, and managerial decision-making processes: a religion-based framework', *Management Decision* 47 (6), (2009), 930–949; Yap, M.H.T. and Ineson, E.M., 'HIV-infected employees in the Asian hospitality industry', *Journal of Service Management* 20 (5) (2009), 503–520.

7. Chambers, K., 'Lies, damn lies and sensitive topics', *Imprints* (July 2004), 6.

8. Brüggen, E. and Willems, P., 'A critical comparison of offline focus groups, online focus groups and e-Delphi', *International Journal of Market Research* 51 (3) (2009), 363–381.

9. Murray, D. and Manuel, L., 'Coming together…', Market Research Society, Annual Conference (2008).

10. Bowman, J. 'What the nose knows', *Research News* (May 2007), 32–33.

11. Heath, R. and Feldwick, P., 'Fifty years using the wrong model of advertising', *International Journal of Market Research* 50 (1) (2008), 29–59; Gordon, W., 'Consumer decision making', *Admap* (October 2004), 74.

12. Clegg, A. 'What do you really think?', *Marketing Week* (25 November 2004), 39.

13. Bowman, J., 'Winning people's hearts', *Research World* (January 2008) 13–14.

14. Arnal, L. and Holquin, R., 'Taxis, vans and subways: capturing insights while commuting', ESOMAR Qualitative Research, Paris (November 2007).

15. Hamilton, J. and Dixon, P., 'Real-time global research – a qual revolution', Market Research Society, Annual Conference (2009).

16. Yaman, H.R. and Shaw, R.N., 'Marketing research and small travel agents: an exploratory study', *Journal of Vacation Marketing* 8 (2) (2002), 127–140; Halman, I.M., 'Evaluating effectiveness of project start-ups: an exploratory study', *International Journal of Project Management* 20 (January 2002), 81.

17. Beaumont, J. and Horton, L., 'They got game', *Research* (May 2005), 36–37.

18. Kover, A.J., Carlson, L. and Ford, J., 'Comments – the quant-qual debate: where are we in advertising?', *International Journal of Advertising* 27 (4) (2008), 659–669; Creswell, J.W., *Research Design: Qualitative, quantitative, and mixed method approaches*, 2nd edn (Thousand Oaks, CA: Sage, 2002); Lee, H., Lindquist, J.D. and Acito, F., 'Managers' evaluation of research design and its impact on the use of research: an experimental approach', *Journal of Business Research* 39 (3) (July 1997), 231–240; Wilson, R.D., 'Research design: qualitative and quantitative approaches', *Journal of Marketing Research* 33 (2) (May 1996), 252–255.

19. For examples of descriptive research, see Lindstrand, A. and Lindbergh, J., 'SMEs' dependency on banks during international expansion', *International Journal of Bank Marketing*, 29 (1) (2010), 65–83; Robinson, W.Y., 'Is the

first to market the first to fail?', *Journal of Marketing Research* 39 (1) (February 2002), 120–128; Song, S.M. and Perry, M.E., 'The determinants of Japanese new product success', *Journal of Marketing Research* 34 (February 1997), 64–76.

20. Bakken, D., 'Renewing the original bonds – let's put psychology back into market research (and marketing!)', ESOMAR Annual Congress, London (September 2006).

21. Zagórski, K., 'Life cycle, objective and subjective living standards and life satisfaction: new indexes building and applications, Poland, 1992–2004', ESOMAR, Public Sector Research, Berlin (May 2004).

22. Yang, K. and Jolly, L.D., 'Age cohort analysis in adoption of mobile data services: gen Xers versus baby boomers', *Journal of Consumer Marketing* 25 (5) (2008), 272–280; Creswell, J., *Research Design: Qualitative, quantitative and mixed method approaches*, 2nd edn (Thousand Oaks, CA: Sage, 2002); Misra, R. and Panigrahi, B., 'Changes in attitudes toward women: a cohort analysis', *International Journal of Sociology & Social Policy* 15 (6) (1995), 1–20; Glenn, N.D., *Cohort Analysis* (Beverly Hills, CA: Sage, 1981).

23. Gayen, K., McQuaid, R. and Raeside, R., 'Social networks, age cohorts and employment', *International Journal of Sociology and Social Policy* 30 (5/6) (2010), 219–238; Rentz, J.O., Reynolds, F.D. and Stout, R.G., 'Analyzing changing consumption patterns with cohort analysis', *Journal of Marketing Research* 20 (February 1983), 12–20; see also Rentz, J.O. and Reynolds, F.D., 'Forecasting the effects of an aging population on product consumption: an age-period-cohort framework', *Journal of Marketing Research* (August 1991), 355–360.

24. Zagórski, K., 'Life cycle, objective and subjective living standards and life satisfaction: new indexes building and applications, Poland, 1992–2004', ESOMAR, Public Sector Research, Berlin (May 2004).

25. Otker, T. and van Leeuwen, H., 'WOM', *Research World* (September 2006), 36.

26. Reichheld, F.F., *The Loyalty Effect: The Hidden Force Behind Growth, Profits, and Lasting Value* (Boston, MA: Harvard Business School Press, 2001).

27. For example, see Tinson, J., Nancarrow, C. and Brace, I., 'Purchase decision making and the increasing significance of family types', *Journal of Consumer Marketing* 25 (1) (2008), 45–56; Elrod, T. and Keane, M.P., 'A factor-analytic probit model for representing the market structure in panel data', *Journal of Marketing Research* 32 (February 1995), 1–16.

28. De Wulf, K., Friedman, M. and Borggreve, B., 'Pavlov revisited – comparing panel conditioning and quality between panel methods', ESOMAR, Panel Research, Dublin (October 2008); Michaelsen, F., 'A quick ABC of panels', *Research World* (February 2005), 27.

29. de Jong, K., 'CSI Berlin: the strange case of the death of panels', ESOMAR, Online Research, Berlin (October 2010).

30. Blackadder, J., 'Growth in telecommunications research', *Research News* (June 2006), 15.

31. Table 3.7 can also be viewed as a transition matrix. It depicts the brand-buying changes from period to period. Knowing the proportion of consumers who switch allows for early prediction of the ultimate success of a new product or change in market strategy.

32. Rindfleisch, A., Malter, A.J., Ganesan, S. and Moorman, C., 'Cross-sectional versus longitudinal survey research: concepts, findings and guidelines', *Journal of Marketing Research* 45 (3) (June 2008), 261–279; de Vaus, D., *Research Design*, 4 vols (Thousand Oaks, CA: Sage, 2005); Brannas, K., 'A new approach to modelling and forecasting monthly guest nights in hotels', *International Journal of Forecasting* 18 (1) (January–March 2002), 19; Coupe, R.T. and Onudu, N.M., 'Evaluating the impact of CASE: an empirical comparison of retrospective and cross-sectional survey approaches', *European Journal of Information Systems* 6 (1) (March 1997), 15–24.

33. Brewer, J., *Foundations of MultiMethod Research* (Thousand Oaks, CA: Sage, 2005); Taris, T.W., *A primer in longitudinal data analysis* (Thousand Oaks, CA: Sage, 2001); Van Den Berg, D.G., Lindeboom, M. and Ridder, G., 'Attribution in longitudinal panel data and the empirical analysis of dynamic labour market behaviour', *Journal of Applied Econometrics* 9 (4) (October–December 1994), 421–435; Winer, R.S., 'Attrition bias in econometric models estimated with panel data', *Journal of Marketing Research* 20 (May 1983), 177–186.

34. De Wulf, K. and Berteloot, S., 'Challenging conventional wisdom', *Research World* (January 2008), 44.

35. Pearson, C. and Kateley, V., 'Why are we trying to create new communities for market research purposes? A case study comparing learnings from an existing community vs. a research panel', ESOMAR, Online Research, Berlin (October 2010); Lee, J.K.H., Sudir, K. and Steckel, J.H., 'A multiple ideal point model: capturing multiple preference effects from within an ideal point framework', *Journal of Marketing Research* 39 (1) (February 2002), 73–86; Maytas, L. and Sevestre, P. (eds), *The Econometrics of Panel Data: A Handbook of the Theory with Applications* (Norwell, MA: Kluwer Academic, 1996).

36. Murphy, D., 'More efficiency and integration of data', *Research World* (February 2005), 29.

37. Huertas-Garcia, R. and Consolación-Segura, C., 'Using statistical design experiment methodologies to identify customers' needs', *International Journal of Market Research* 51 (1) (2009), 115–136; Hulland, J., Ho, Y. and Lam, S., 'Use of causal models in marketing research: a review', *International Journal of Research in Marketing* 13 (2) (April 1996), 181–197; see also Cox, K.K. and Enis, B.M., *Experimentation for Marketing Decisions* (Scranton, PA: International Textbook, 1969), 5.

38. Ryals, L. and Wilson, H., 'Experimental methods in market research: from information to insight', *International Journal of Market Research* 47 (4) (2005), 345–364; Winer, R.S., 'Experimentation in the 21st century: the importance of external validity', *Journal of the Academy of Marketing Science* (Summer 1999), 349–358.

39. Mariampolski, H., Wolf, S. and Luigi, T., 'Americans and Italians face each other at dinner', *Research World* (January 2006), 32–33.

40. Mills, A., 'Competitive advantage', Research Effectiveness Awards, *Research News* (November 2006), III.

41. Poynter, R., 'A taxonomy of new MR', Market Research Society, Annual Conference (2010); Lee, E., 'Are consumer survey results distorted? Systematic impact of behavioural frequency and duration on survey response errors', *Journal of Marketing Research* (February 2000), 125–133; Dutka, S. and Frankel, L.R., 'Measuring response error', *Journal of Advertising Research* 37 (1) (January/February 1997), 33–39.

42. van Meurs, L., van Ossenbruggen, R. and Nekkers, L., 'Do rotten apples spoil the whole barrel? Exploring quality issues in panel data', ESOMAR, Panel Research, Orlando (October 2007); Loosveldt, G., Carton, A. and Billiet, J., 'Assessment of survey data quality: a pragmatic approach focused on interviewer tasks', *International Journal of Market Research* 46 (1) (2004), 68.

43. Blyth, B., 'Mixed mode: the only "fitness" regime?', *International Journal of Market Research* 50 (2) (2008), 241–266; Brooks, D.V., 'A hands on approach to response rates', *Imprints* (October 2003), 24.

44. Manfreda, K.L., Bosnjak, M., Berzelak, J., Haas, I. and Vehovar, V., 'Web surveys versus other survey modes: a meta-analysis comparing response rates', *International Journal of Market Research* 50 (1) (2008), 79–104; Sinha, P., 'Determination of reliability of estimations obtained with survey research: a method of simulation', *International Journal of Market Research* 42 (3) (Summer 2000), 311–318; Rollere, M.R., 'Control is elusive in research design', *Marketing News* 31 (19) (15 September 1997), 17; Corlett, T., 'Sampling errors in practice', *Journal of the Market Research Society* 38 (4) (April 1997), 307–318.

45. Feldman, S., 'Building market paradoxes – cross cultural experiences in different categories', ESOMAR Latin America Conference, Mexico City (May 2008).

46. Hardey, M., 'Conference notes – the social context of online market research: an introduction to the sociability of social media', *International Journal of Market Research* 51 (4) (2008), 562–564.

47. Amazon.com, **www.amazon.com/gp/help/customer/ display.html?ie=UTF8&nodeId=14279641**, accessed November 2010.

48. Shirky, C., *Here comes everybody: The power of organizing without organizations* (New York: Penguin, 2008).

49. Herndon, N.C. Jr, 'An investigation of moral values and the ethical content of the corporate culture: Taiwanese versus US sales people', *Journal of Business Ethics* 30 (1) (March 2001), 73–85.

50. Chakraborty, M. and Arora, S., 'Billion dollar baby: leveraging mobile technology for research applications in India', ESOMAR Asia Pacific, Kuala Lumpur (April 2010).

51. ESOMAR, 'Global Market Research', ESOMAR Industry Report (2010), 16.

52. Benezra, K., Conry, S. and Singh, S., '3 screen measurement: soccer World Cup 2010 – redefining "multi-modal" research to understand audience engagement', ESOMAR, Congress Odyssey, Athens (September 2010).

4 Secondary data collection and analysis

| Stage 1 |
| Problem definition |

| Stage 2 |
| Research approach developed |

| Stage 3 |
| Research design developed |

| Stage 4 |
| Fieldwork or data collection |

| Stage 5 |
| Data integrity and analysis |

| Stage 6 |
| Report preparation and presentation |

The act of sourcing, evaluating and analysing secondary data can realise great insights for decision-makers. It is also vital to successful problem diagnosis, sample planning and collection of primary data.

Objectives

After reading this chapter, you should be able to:

1 define the nature and scope of secondary data and distinguish secondary data from marketing intelligence and primary data;

2 analyse the advantages and disadvantages of secondary data and their uses in the various steps of the marketing research process;

3 evaluate secondary data using the criteria of specifications, error, currency, objectives, nature and dependability;

4 describe in detail the different sources of secondary data, focusing upon external sources in the form of published materials and syndicated services;

5 discuss in detail the syndicated sources of secondary data, including household and consumer data obtained via surveys, purchase and media panels, and scanner services, as well as institutional data related to retailers and industrial or service firms;

6 explain the need to use multiple sources of secondary data and describe single-source data;

7 understand the challenges of using secondary data in international marketing research;

8 explain the ethical issues involved in the use of externally generated secondary data;

9 understand the researchers' challenges in coping with the burgeoning amount of externally generated secondary data;

10 appreciate how social media research techniques are integrating with traditional forms of research and how this integration may impact upon what may be defined as secondary data.

Overview

The collection and analysis of secondary data help to define the marketing research problem and develop an approach. In addition, before collecting primary data, the researcher should locate and analyse relevant secondary data. Thus, secondary data should be an essential component of a successful research design. Secondary data can help in sample designs and in the details of primary research methods. In some projects, research may be largely confined to the analysis of secondary data because some marketing problems may be resolved using only secondary data.

This chapter discusses the distinction between primary data, secondary data and marketing intelligence. The advantages and disadvantages of secondary data are considered, and criteria for evaluating secondary data are presented, along with a classification of secondary data. Internal secondary data are described and major sources of external secondary data, such as published materials, online and offline databases, and syndicated services, are also discussed. Using secondary data in international marketing research is discussed. Several ethical issues that arise in the use of secondary data are identified. The impact of the growth and development of secondary data sources on the Web will be evaluated.

To begin with, we present an example that illustrates how secondary data were used in a research design for the Virgin brand.

Real research	**A 21st century approach to brand development[1]**

As a leading global brand, Virgin has created more than 200 companies in 29 different countries. Virgin brands are independent businesses, empowered to run themselves but united by Virgin's brand values of being fun, innovative, challenging and offering great service and value for the customer. The lack of management layers and bureaucracy creates an optimum 'start-up' atmosphere backed up by the support of a wider 'family' of brands operating as a community to support and challenge each other. As such, the Virgin brand can mean many things to many different people. Virgin had an intuitive feel for what this was but lacked any firm evidence of the Virgin brands supporting each other. Measuring the equity of the Virgin brand required a customised approach to assess the impact of the brand at both industry and Virgin group level. Virgin needed a research solution that would move beyond a 'recap' of the brand health and provide a roadmap to increase consumer engagement, support new category entry and, ultimately, generate a tangible return for the business. With the opportunity of a new phase of research, Virgin wanted to throw away the rule book, creating a programme of brand evaluation that would help Virgin 'join the dots' across its family of brands and harness the voice of the consumer in a more intuitive way. The research had to balance the need for ongoing tracking and global benchmarking research while delivering an increased understanding of the consumer. A new phase of research always generates debate and in an organisation like Virgin there was no shortage of ideas for moving things forward, shaking things up and challenging the status quo. A balance was required to ensure the great ideas and insights from previous work were not ignored. It was extremely important to move this phase of research forward without throwing away the ideas and insights that the brand team and wider research users had been using effectively. There were three key phases: (1) reviewing historical research (both in terms of past reports and in an engagement in the 'stories' that surround past research); (2) evaluating internal and external secondary data sources; and (3) in-depth interviews with Virgin executives and executives from supporting agencies. Searching for past research and secondary data beyond the Virgin brand team to agency partners presented further resources to explore. They worked through Mullen's (a full-service integrated advertising agency, www.mullen.com) internal resources which in turn provided access to Simmons (**www.simmonssurvey.com**) psychographic profiling and media databases. Utilising secondary data was a critical step in creating not simply a brand research review, but a dynamic brand research 'resource' that could provide more versatile elements of brand research that could be used directly to target Virgin customers.

Defining primary data, secondary data and marketing intelligence

Primary data
Data originated by the researcher specifically to address the research problem.

Secondary data
Data collected for some purpose other than the problem at hand.

Primary data are data originated by a researcher for the specific purpose of addressing the problem at hand. They are individually tailored for the decision-makers of organisations that pay for well-focused and exclusive support. Compared with readily available data from a variety of sources, this exclusivity can mean higher costs and a longer time frame in collecting and analysing the data.

Secondary data are data that have already been collected for purposes other than the problem at hand. At face value, this definition seems straightforward, especially when contrasted to the definition of primary data. However, many researchers confuse the term, or quite rightly see some overlap with marketing intelligence.

Marketing intelligence
Qualified observations of
events and developments
in the marketing
environment.

Marketing intelligence can be defined as 'qualified observations of events and developments in the marketing environment'. The use of the word 'observations' is presented in a wide sense to include a variety of types of data, broadly concerned with 'environmental scanning'.[2] In essence, though, marketing intelligence is based upon data that in many instances have been collected for purposes other than the problem at hand. To clarify this overlap in definitions, Table 4.1 compares secondary data with marketing intelligence through a variety of characteristics.

Table 4.1	A comparison of secondary data and marketing intelligence[3]	
Characteristic	**Secondary data**	**Marketing intelligence**
Structure	Specifications and research design tend to be apparent	Can be poorly structured; no universal conventions of reporting
Availability	Tend to have regular updates	Irregular availability
Sources	Generated in-house and from organisations with research prowess	Generated in-house and from unofficial sources, especially through social media
Data type	Tend to be quantitative; many issues need qualitative interpretation	Tends to be qualitative; many issues difficult to validate and quantify
Source credibility	Tend to be from reputable and trustworthy research sources	Questionable credibility; can be generated from a broad spectrum of researchers and authors
Terms of reference	Tend to have clear definitions of what is being measured	Ambiguous definitions; difficult to compare over different studies
Analysis	Mostly conventional quantitative techniques	Opinion based, interpretative
Ethics	In-company data gathering may be covered by Data Protection Acts; externally generated data may be covered by research codes of conduct, e.g. ESOMAR	Some techniques may be seen as industrial espionage – though there is an ethical code produced by the Society of Competitive Intelligence Professionals

Note in these comparisons the repeated use of the word 'tend'. The boundaries between the two are not absolutely rigid. Consider the following example, based upon an article published in the journal *Admap*. The authors may have collected, analysed and presented quantitative data including 'buzz scores' from social media sources to support the qualitative interpretation of the future developments of a market. The data used and presented may come from credible sources and be correctly analysed, but what about the choice of data to support their argument? Other sources of data that may contradict this view may be ignored.

Buzz score
Is based on the total
number of people
searching for specific
subjects on web search
engines.

The small amount of data presented on buzz scores can be seen as a secondary data source and interpreted in its own right by another researcher. The interpretation and argument of the authors can be seen as intelligence and have some credibility. In its entirety, such an article has elements of both secondary data and marketing intelligence, and it may be impossible to pull them apart as mutually exclusive components.

As will become apparent in this chapter, there are clear criteria for evaluating the accuracy of secondary data, which tend to be of a quantitative nature. Marketing intelligence is more difficult to evaluate but this does not mean that it has less value to decision-makers or researchers. Certain marketing phenomena cannot be formally measured: researchers may not be able to gain access to conduct research, or the rapid unfolding of events means that it

Green actions offer consumer value and environmental benefit[4]

Before 2008, green marketing was all about creating a new language; 'fairtrade', 'organic' and 'ethical' brands were worn as a badge that reflected your lifestyle choices. We have seen the introduction of a generation of ecologically friendly and/or ethically sound brands such as the Toyota Prius, Wholefoods, Green & Black's, The Body Shop, Green People and the Co-operative Bank. Looking ahead, green consumers are looking for 'green plus value'. Now it is all about making clever choices that demonstrate you are a savvy consumer who can both find a bargain and do your bit for the environment. The benefit of this is that green now has the potential to be adopted more widely, rather than as a niche interest. Starbucks has recently received some very

bad press on a green-related issue. It has been labelled as wasteful by the UK media because of its practice of constantly running water into a dipper-well to wash utensils. This undoes any good work it has done in its green marketing, such as a commitment to coffee-growing communities and recycling programmes. What is more, it is already having an impact on brand health measures. 'Buzz' for the brand dropped to −13%; this dip may increase as time progresses. More importantly, however, is that the brand's index (overall general brand health) scores have also seen a decline since the announcement. Starbucks already had a negative buzz score before the announcement, but the announcement caused the brand to see its score hit new lows.

is impracticable to conduct timely research. The following example illustrates the importance and challenges of gathering intelligence, especially in a complex and rapidly changing business environment.

Gathering marketing intelligence in China[5]

The very nature of marketing intelligence gathering means that much of what researchers discover is often new and surprising. This is particularly true of intelligence gathering in China, where the rapid changes in the commercial landscape mean changes to commercial structures and processes, and projections, happen very quickly; an industry report can be out of date within six months. Some of the challenges that are faced in gathering marketing intelligence in China include the following:

• Protecting information is part of the culture, as is a reluctance to be the one blamed for losing information. There is little incentive for a typical purchasing or operations manager or government employee to provide information to an external party. There is potential risk associated in passing on information and since marketing research is relatively new in China, interviewers have to be more reassuring about how 'normal' the process is in order to facilitate meetings, interviews and informative responses.

- Research participants can be from social and educational backgrounds ranging from First to Third World, but all can be working in the same district. This phenomenon is particularly apparent in the '1st-tier cities', as Beijing, Shanghai and Guangzhou are collectively known. There is a complex convergence of those with money and international experience, those with money but no international experience, and those with very little money and no experience outside one small area of the country. When this diverse combination occurs within one family, it causes specific challenges to researchers. In marketing intelligence gathering, the progression from very low knowledge and awareness of international influences on an industry to full awareness happens very fast.

- Fragmented industries and a vast country with hundreds of local marketplaces abound. Extracting comment on the nature of one industry across the country is unrealistic and so it is for the researcher to merge the jigsaw pieces from across the country to build a national picture. A senior manager in a company in Zhejiang will often assume automatically that we are speaking only about the Zhejiang province when posed questions about the development of the industry in the coming five years.

Many major organisations invest huge amounts in the hardware and software needed for a systematic approach to gathering intelligence, some even engaging in the use of 'shadow teams'. A shadow team is a small cross-functional boundary-spanning group that learns everything about a competitive unit. A competitive unit can be a competitor, product line, supply chain or prospective partner in a strategic alliance. The objective of a shadow team is to learn everything possible about its target through published data, personnel and network connection, and organisation knowledge or hearsay. It brings together knowledge from across an organisation, so that it can think, reason and react like the competitive unit.[6] Competitive intelligence will be discussed in more detail in the context of business-to-business marketing research in Chapter 27.

Such widespread use of intelligence in major organisations means it has a role to play in supporting decision-makers, but it has many limitations, which are apparent in Table 4.1. In the development of better founded information support, credible support can come from the creative collection and evaluation of secondary data. This requires researchers to connect and validate different data sources, ultimately leading to decision-maker support in its own right and support of more focused primary data collection. As this chapter and Chapter 5 unfold, examples of different types of secondary data will emerge and the applications of secondary data will become apparent.

Shadow team
A small cross-functional boundary-spanning group that learns everything about a competitive unit.

Advantages and uses of secondary data

Secondary data offer several advantages over primary data. Secondary data are easily accessible, relatively inexpensive and quickly obtained. Some secondary data sources can be accessed free of charge, but many sources do charge fees to reflect the investment made to gather, analyse and present accurate information. Nonetheless, with the availability of freely available data (of variable quality and integrity) there are arguments that government-sourced secondary data should be freely available, as argued in the following example.

Free our data[7]

Marketers make extensive use of information that is collected by government. In recent years the pressure has mounted for public data to be more freely available in order to stimulate innovation. Many businesses rely on accurate secondary data to make better business decisions, especially in targeting new markets. In doing this, they can draw on an array of government datasets and surveys. These data have the particular advantage of having a consistent national coverage, being relatively unbiased and created to high research standards. Government suppliers include:

- *Office for National Statistics – especially for the Census and large-sample surveys*
- *Post Office – the Postcode Address File*
- *Ordnance Survey – Grid references, map background and boundaries*
- *Land Registry – house prices*
- *Companies House – details of businesses.*

It has been argued that as public information is collected largely at taxpayers' expense, the barriers to its widespread use should be removed wherever possible. Users will have better information, a step towards the 'perfect knowledge' assumed in economists' views of perfect markets.

Some secondary data, such as those provided by the National Censuses, are available on topics where it would not be feasible for a firm to collect primary data. Although it is rare for secondary data to provide all the answers to a non-routine research problem, such data can be useful in a variety of ways.[8] Secondary data can help to:

1 Diagnose the research problem.

2 Develop an approach to the problem.

3 Develop a sampling plan.

4 Formulate an appropriate research design (e.g. by identifying the key variables to measure or understand).

5 Answer certain research questions and test some hypotheses.

6 Interpret primary data with more insight.

7 Validate qualitative research findings.

Given these advantages and uses of secondary data, we state the following general rule:

> *Examination of available secondary data is a prerequisite to the collection of primary data. Start with secondary data. Proceed to primary data only when the secondary data sources have been exhausted or yield marginal returns.*

The rich dividends obtained by following this rule are illustrated in the example at the start of this chapter. It shows that the collection and analysis of even one relevant secondary data source can provide valuable insights. The decision-maker and researcher can use the ideas generated in secondary data as a very strong foundation to primary data design and collection. However, the researcher should be cautious in using secondary data, because they have some limitations and disadvantages.

Disadvantages of secondary data

Because secondary data have been collected for purposes other than the problem at hand, their usefulness to the current problem may be limited in several important ways, including relevance and accuracy. The objectives, nature and methods used to collect the secondary data may not be appropriate to the present situation. Also, secondary data may be lacking in accuracy or may not be completely current or dependable. Before using secondary data, it is important to evaluate them according to a series of factors. These factors are discussed in more detail in the following section.

Criteria for evaluating secondary data

The quality of secondary data should be routinely evaluated, using the criteria presented in Table 4.2 and the discussion in the following sections.

Table 4.2	Criteria for evaluating secondary data	
Criteria	**Issues**	**Remarks**
Specifications and research design	• Data collection method • Response rate • Population definition • Sampling method • Sample size • Questionnaire design • Fieldwork • Data analysis	Data should be reliable, valid and generalisable to the problem at hand
Error and accuracy	Examine errors in: • Approach • Research design • Sampling • Data collection • Data analysis • Reporting	Assess accuracy by comparing data from different sources
Currency	Time lag between collection and publication. Frequency of updates	Census data are periodically updated by syndicated firms
Objective	Why the data were collected	The objective will determine the relevance of data
Nature	• Definition of key variables • Units of measurement • Categories used • Relationships examined	Reconfigure the data to increase their usefulness, if possible
Dependability	Source: • Expertise • Credibility • Reputation • Trustworthiness	Preference should be afforded to an original rather than an acquired source

Specifications: research design and how the data were collected

The specifications of the research design used to collect the data should be critically examined to identify possible sources of bias. Such design considerations include size and nature of the sample, response rate and quality, questionnaire design and administration, procedures used for fieldwork, and data analysis and reporting procedures. These checks provide information on the reliability and validity (concepts developed in Chapter 13) of the data and help determine whether they can be generalised to the problem at hand. The reliability and validity can be further ascertained by an examination of the error, currency, objectives, nature and dependability associated with the secondary data.

Error: accuracy of the data

The researcher must determine whether the data are accurate enough for the purposes of the present study. Secondary data can have a number of sources of error or inaccuracy, including errors in the approach, research design, sampling, data collection, analysis and reporting stages of the project. Moreover, it is difficult to evaluate the accuracy of secondary data because the researcher did not participate in the research. One approach is to find multiple sources of data if possible and compare them using standard statistical procedures.

Real research	Measuring media internet[9]

Gone are the days of the Internet being a collection of static web pages. Now it extends across almost every platform and is intertwined with nearly every medium. TV, radio and mobile are now directly connected with the Internet. Such is the change that the terms 'TV' and 'radio' are fast becoming redundant, in exchange for the terms 'video' and 'audio', as the English language evolves to keep up. The fragmentation of media has created more niche audiences than ever before; they are constantly dividing, sub-dividing and regrouping in many different forms at different levels on a national, even global scale. Publishers and broadcasters are now media companies with a mixed content offering. The effects of the fragmentation of media and emergence of Web 2.0, among other things, have made it increasingly challenging for sample-based research to measure these fragmented audiences accurately. For instance, there might be 1,000 people a month who are regularly visiting a blog on gardening. These people have distinct interests and needs, and may well be a very valuable audience; however, in countries with populations of millions, these people are simply not being picked up. Over the past two years nearly all the national newspaper brands have committed to publishing their monthly web traffic figures to industry-agreed standards. Publishers report their online traffic through ABCe (**www.abc.org.uk**; *ABC is owned by the media industry and ABCe independently verifies* and reports on media performance, providing trusted traffic and related data across a *broad range of digital platforms*). These industry-agreed standards are a step forward, as greater transparency will better inform advertisers and media agencies in their decisions when allocating advertising budgets. However, Web 2.0 and the natural development of the Internet have brought a host of new opportunities and challenges for measuring the Internet in the shape of blogs, video, audio, RSS feeds, podcasts, and so the list goes on. The TV, radio and mobile industry sectors are making positive steps to establish industry-backed measurement standards to help quantify online audiences. Broadcasters have been swift to make moves to measure video delivered over the Internet. Major broadcasters have come together to form the BMWG (Broadband Measurement Working Group) to develop a common approach for measuring online video content to deliver accountability to rights holders. Broadcasters clearly feel that video over the Internet has reached a point where a reliable measurement tool is needed. This is particularly important for commercial broadcasters, who are investing a great deal in developing a variety of video-on-demand services and will need to generate revenue from video advertising to sustain their businesses. The Internet is a global medium and so the international implications cannot be ignored. In fact, global measurement structures are helpful. The International Federation of Audit Bureaux of Circulation (IFABC) (**www.ifabc.org**) draws together ABCe's sister organisations across the globe to implement constructive international measurement initiatives.

As the above example indicates, the accuracy of secondary data can vary: What is being measured? What rules apply to those measurements? What happens if there are rapid changes in what is being measured? With different researchers potentially measuring the 'same' phenomena, data obtained from different sources may not agree. In these cases, the researcher should verify the accuracy of secondary data by conducting pilot studies or by other exploratory work that verifies the analytical framework used to arrive at certain figures. Often, by judicious questioning of those involved in compiling the figures, this can be done without much expense or effort.

Currency: when the data were collected

Secondary data may not be current and the time lag between data collection and publication may be long, as is the case with much census data which may take up to two years from collection to publication. Moreover, the data may not be updated frequently enough for the purpose of the problem at hand. Decision-makers require current data; therefore, the value of secondary data is diminished as they become dated. For instance, although the Census of Population data are comprehensive, they may not be applicable to major cities in which the population has changed rapidly during the last two years.

Objective: the purpose for which the data were collected

Data are invariably collected with some objective in mind, and a fundamental question to ask is why the data were collected in the first place. The objective for collecting data will ultimately determine the purpose for which that information is relevant and useful. Data collected with a specific objective in mind may not be appropriate in another situation. Working with our opening example, suppose that the magazine *Inside Flyer* (**www.insideflyer.com**) conducted a survey where the sample was made up of 'frequent flyers'. The objective of the study could be 'to uncover the airline characteristics consumers consider most important'. Virgin, however, may wish to target 'business-class' flyers and 'to uncover perceptions related to trade-offs made in customer service–price–safety'. Even though there may be identical questions used in both surveys, the target participants may be different, the rationale for the study presented to participants will be different, and ultimately the 'state of mind' that participants may be in when they come to comparable questions will be different. The *Inside Flyer* survey would be conducted for entirely different objectives from those Virgin has for its study. The findings from the *Inside Flyer* survey may not directly support decision making at Virgin, though they may help to define who Virgin should talk to and what questions it should put to them.

Nature: the content of the data

The nature, or content, of the data should be examined with special attention to the definition of key variables, the units of measurement, the categories used and the relationships examined. If the key variables have not been defined or are defined in a manner inconsistent with the researcher's definition, then the usefulness of the data is limited. Consider, for example, secondary data on consumer preferences for TV programmes. To use this information, it is important to know how preference for programmes was defined. Was it defined in terms of the programme watched most often, the one considered most needed, most enjoyable, most informative, or the programme of greatest service to the community?

Likewise, secondary data may be measured in units that may not be appropriate for the current problem. For example, income may be measured by individual, family, household or spending unit and could be gross or net after taxes and deductions. Income may be classified into categories that are different from research needs. If the researcher is interested in high-income consumers with gross annual household incomes of over €120,000, secondary data with income categories of less than €20,000, €20,001–€50,000, €50,001–€75,000 and more than €75,000 will not be of much use. Determining the measurement of variables such as income may be a complex task, requiring the wording of the definition of income to be precise. Finally, the relationships examined should be taken into account in evaluating the nature of data. If, for example, actual behaviour is of interest, then data inferring behaviour from self-reported attitudinal information may have limited usefulness. Sometimes it is possible to reconfigure the available data – for example, to convert the units of measurement – so that the resulting data are more useful to the problem at hand.

Dependability: how dependable are the data?

An overall indication of the dependability of data may be obtained by examining the expertise, credibility, reputation and trustworthiness of the source. This information can be obtained by checking with others who have used the information provided by the source. Data published to promote sales, to advance specific interests, or to carry on propaganda should be viewed with suspicion. The same may be said of data published anonymously or in a form that attempts to hide the details of the data collection research design and process. It is also pertinent to examine whether the secondary data came from an original source, one that generated the data, or an acquired source, one that procured the data from an original source and published them in a different context. Generally, secondary data should be secured from an original rather than an acquired source. There are at least two reasons for this rule: first, an original source is the one that specifies the details of the data collection research design; and, second, an original source is likely to be more accurate and complete than a surrogate source.

Classification of secondary data

Internal data
Data available within the organisation for whom the research is being conducted.

Figure 4.1 presents a classification of secondary data. Secondary data may be classified as either internal or external. Internal data are those generated within the organisation for which the research is being conducted. An example of this source of data for any marketing decision-maker and researcher is the corporate revenue ledger at individual transaction level. Analyses of who is buying and the different ways that these customers may be classified or segmented, what they bought, how frequently and the monetary value of their purchases, can give a basic level of understanding customer buying behaviour. With a number of years of transaction data, the lifestages of customer segments can be better understood and how customers have reacted to an array of marketing activities. One of the main problems that researchers face with accessing and analysing transaction data is 'corporate territorialism', i.e. the attitude that each department should only be concerned with the operational data it needs for the business to run on a day-to-day basis.[10] Given the growth and significance of this element of marketing decision support, secondary data generated from internal sources will be examined in more detail in Chapter 5.

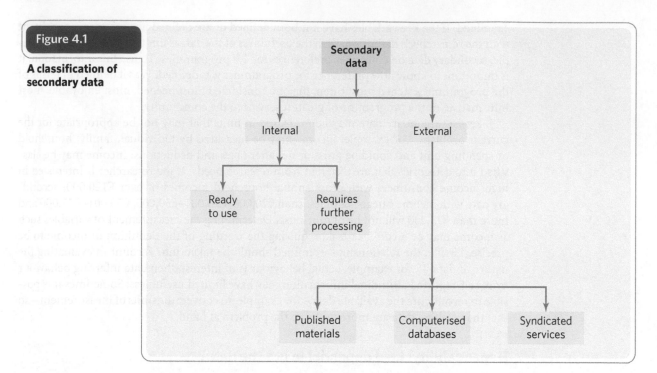

Figure 4.1

A classification of secondary data

External data

Data that originate outside the organisation.

External data, on the other hand, are those generated by sources outside the organisation. These data may exist in the form of published material, online databases, or information made available by syndicated services. Externally generated secondary data may be more difficult to access, more expensive and more difficult to evaluate for accuracy, in comparison with internal secondary data. These factors mean that, before collecting external secondary data, it is vital to gather, analyse and interpret any readily available internal secondary data and intelligence.

Published external secondary sources

Sources of published external secondary data include local authorities, regional and national governments, the EU, non-profit organisations (e.g. Chambers of Commerce), trade associations and professional organisations, commercial publishers, investment brokerage firms and professional marketing research firms.[11] In fact, such a quantity of data is available that the researcher can be overwhelmed. Therefore, it is important to classify published sources (see Figure 4.2). Published external sources may be broadly classified as general business data or government data. General business sources comprise guides, directories, indexes and statistical data. Government sources may be broadly categorised as census data and other publications. These data types are discussed further with specific sources used as examples.

General business sources

Businesses publish a lot of information in the form of books, periodicals, journals, newspapers, magazines, reports and trade literature. This information can be located in hard copy and electronically by using guides, directories and indexes. Sources are also available to identify statistical data.

Guides Guides are an excellent source of standard or recurring information. A guide may help identify other important sources of directories, trade associations and trade publications. Guides

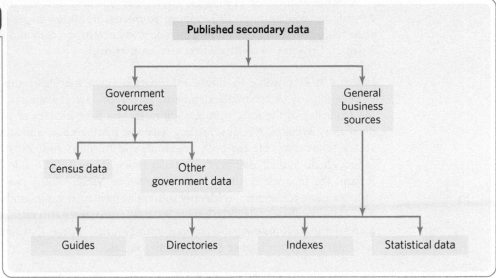

Figure 4.2

A classification of published secondary sources

are one of the first sources a researcher should consult when commencing research. Libraries, whether these be public, at universities, or businesses will have a guide to classify the resources they hold. Within library holdings will be databases such as WARC (**www.warc.com**) which compiles industry-based data and commentary to support marketers, communications and research professionals. Commercial guides can be used to assist decision-makers or researchers to uncover current issues and sources regarding individual industries or countries. An example of one of these would be the Datamonitor guides (search for 'guides' on **www.datamonitor. com**). Another example is the @BRINT guide to business technology management and knowledge management sites with editorial comments (**www.brint.com**).

Directories Directories are helpful for identifying individuals or organisations that collect specific data. Examples of directories used by researchers are the Hollis directories that support the industries of sponsorship and public relations (**www.hollis-sponsorship.com; www.hollis-pr.com**).

Real research | **Hollis-PR.com**

For more than 40 years Hollis has been the public relations world's major information provider, publishing the market-leading directories such as *Hollis UK PR Annual, Hollis Europe* and *Hollis-PR*.

Hollis-PR.com is a gateway to PR information requirements. It has a search engine that enables researchers to:

- Find a PR consultancy – to find the ideal agency partner.
- Source an in-house PR contact – through subscription – access to 7,788 in-house PR contacts.
- Locate a specialist service – a free supplier search to locate specialist support.
- Search for a UK media contact – through subscription – access to a UK media database for newspapers, magazines and broadcast media.

Another example is Europages, a reference business directory in Europe that classifies 23 million companies in 35 European countries, in 26 languages (**www.europages.com**). Other directories worth exploring include **www.bizeurope.com** and ESOMAR's *Directory of Research Organisations* (**http://directory.esomar.org**).

Indexes It is possible to locate information on a particular topic in several different publications by using an index and abstracts. Indexes and abstracts, therefore, can increase the efficiency of the search process. Libraries will have indexes or A–Z lists of e-resources, databases, websites, e-books, reading lists and bibliographic software. Several indexes and abstracts are available for both academic and business sources. Examples of newspaper indexes include the *Financial Times Index* (**www.ft.com**), *Le Monde Index* (**www.le-monde. fr**) and the Japanese Business News online, *The Nikkei Weekly* (**www.nikkei.co.jp**). These indexes allow researchers to identify sources of particular topics, industries and individuals. The Gale database, formerly known as Infotrac (**www.gale.cengage.com**), pulls together many of the leading newspaper, magazine and journal sources that allow researchers to access secondary data, intelligence and literature sources.

Non-governmental statistical data Business research often involves compiling statistical data reflecting market or industry factors. A historic perspective of industry participation and growth rates can provide a context for market-share analysis. Market statistics related to population demographics, purchasing levels, TV viewership and product usage are some of the types of non-governmental statistics available from secondary sources. As well as any published commentary presented in these resources, further statistical analyses and graphical manipulations can be performed on these data to draw important insights. Examples of non-governmental statistical data include trade associations such as the Swedish Tourism Trade Association (**www.sverigeturism.se**). The Swedish Information 'Smorgasbord' is a large single source of information in English on Sweden, Swedish provinces, nature, culture, lifestyle, society and industry. Other examples include Euromonitor (**www.euromonitor. com**), which publishes monthly market research journals covering a great breadth of industries and countries across the world. Keynote (**www.keynote.co.uk**) produces reports focusing on European markets, built upon a combination of primary data collection and other secondary data sources.

The United Nations provides an example of an organisation with a Statistics Division that provides a wide range of statistical outputs on a global basis (**http://unstats.un.org**). The Statistics Division produces printed publications of statistics and statistical methods in the fields of international merchandise trade, national accounts, demography and population, social indicators, gender, industry, energy, environment, human settlements and disability. The Statistics Division also produces general statistical compendiums including the *Statistical Yearbook* and *World Statistics Pocketbook*.

Government sources

European governments and the EU also produce large amounts of secondary data. Each European country has its own statistical office which produces lists of the publications available (and the costs involved). Examples of national statistical offices include the Centraal Bureau voor de Statistiek Nederlands (**www.cbs.nl**), Danmarks Statistik (**www.dst.dk**), the Federal Statistical Office of Germany (**www.destatis.de**), the French Institut National de la Statistique et des Études Economiques (**www.insee.fr**) and the British Office for National Statistics (**www.statistics.gov.uk**). All of these links allow you to examine quickly the array of publications that they produce. Their publications may be divided into census data and other publications.

Census data Most European countries produce either catalogues or newsletters that describe the array of census publications available and the plans for any forthcoming census. In the UK, for example, **www.ons.gov.uk/ons/guide-method/census/2011/index.html** contains the latest information about the 2011 Census in England and Wales. Census Marketing in Britain can supply unpublished data from the 1961, 1971, 1981, 1991, 2001 Censuses in the form of Small Area Statistics (SAS). SAS are available for standard census areas within England and Wales, such as counties, local government districts, London boroughs, wards, civil parishes and enumeration districts. Maps can also be purchased to complement the data.

Census data can be kept in electronic format, allowing them to be analysed and presented in a variety of formats at a detailed geographical level. Given the long periods between the National Censuses and the amount of change that can occur in these periods, other data sources are used to maintain an up-to-date picture of specific regions.

Other government publications In addition to the censuses, national statistical offices collect and publish a great deal of statistical data. As well as general population censuses, national statistical offices produce an array of nationally relevant statistics. The value of these may lie in evaluating and describing markets, operating environments and the challenges and opportunities these hold. The British Office for National Statistics covers areas that include: agriculture and environment; children, education and skills; crime and justice; the economy; government; health and social care; the labour market; people and places; the population; travel and transport. Business and energy statistics may be viewed at **www.statistics.gov.uk/hub/business-energy/**.

Examples of reports from the British Office for National Statistics include *Social Trends*, drawing together social and economic data from a wide range of government departments and other organisations. This report provides a comprehensive guide to British society today, and how it has been changing.

Real research

UK citizens rate health care relatively highly compared with the rest of the EU

An established reference source, *Social Trends*, draws together social and economic data from a wide range of government departments and other organisations; it paints a broad picture of British society today, and how it has been changing. There are 13 chapters each focusing on a different social policy area, described in tables, figures and text: population, households and families, education and training, labour market, income and wealth, expenditure, health, social protection, crime and justice, housing, environment, transport, lifestyles and social participation. The zip file provides links to Excel spreadsheets which contain the data for each table, figure and map. An example of the output is encapsulated in the following extract from *Social Trends News Release*:

Date: 11 November 2010 *Coverage:* United Kingdom *Theme:* Social and Welfare

UK men born in 2007 could expect to live 1.6 years longer than the 'average man' in the EU-27, according to a report published today by the Office for National Statistics. However, women could expect to live 0.3 years less than the EU-27 average for females. The International comparisons chapter of Social Trends also shows that in 2007 life expectancy for UK women stood at 81.9 years at birth (82.2 for EU-27) compared with 77.7 years for men (76.1 for EU-27).

In the EU, statistics and opinion polls are published by the Statistical Office of the European Community in a series called Eurostat (**http://europa.eu; http://europa.eu/documentation/ statistics-polls**). Tables normally contain figures for individual member states of the EU plus totals for all countries. Eurostat divides its publications into themes, which are:

- General and regional statistics
- Economy and finance
- Population and social conditions
- Industry trade and services
- Agriculture and fisheries
- External trade
- Transport
- Environment and energy
- Science and technology.

It also produces general titles which include the *Eurostat Regional Yearbook, The EU in the world – A statistical portrait, Europe in figures – Eurostat yearbook, Key figures on European Business*.

To examine any of the national statistics offices in Europe and Global Regions, visit the excellent Central Statistics Office Ireland website **www.cso.ie/links** and follow the country links. There are also links to many other important organisations with relevant statistics such as the European Central Bank (**www.ecb.int**) and the International Monetary Fund (**www. imf.org**).

Databases

A major category of secondary data is available in the form of browsable online databases.[12] From the 1980s to date, the number of databases, as well as the vendors providing these services, have grown enormously. Browsable online databases offer a number of advantages over printed data, including:[13]

1 The data can be current, up to date and even 'live'.

2 The search process is more comprehensive, quicker and simpler. Online vendors can provide ready access to hundreds of databases. Moreover, this information can be accessed instantaneously, and the search process is simplified as the vendors provide uniform search protocols and commands for accessing the database.

3 The cost of accessing these is relatively low, because of the accuracy of searching for the right data, and the speed of location and transfer of data.

4 It is convenient to access these data using many forms of working online, including mobile devices.

Although online database information can be helpful, it is not necessarily free. It is vital to consider what costs are incurred in generating, presenting and updating quality and dependable information databases. The number of database vendors and the breadth of subjects covered can be vast and confusing, especially at the commencement of a project. Thus a classification of online databases is helpful.

Classification of online databases

Online databases may be classified as bibliographic, numeric, full text, directory or special-purpose databases as shown in Figure 4.3.

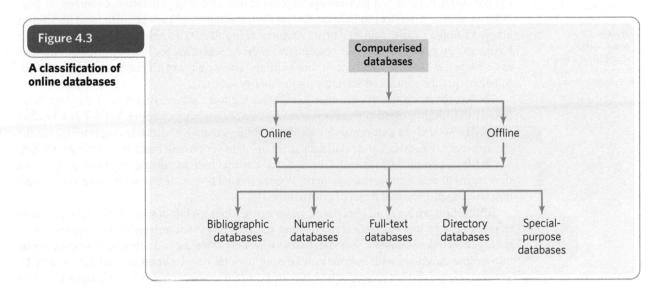

Figure 4.3

A classification of online databases

Bibliographic databases are composed of citations to articles in journals, magazines, newspapers, marketing research studies, technical reports, government documents and the like.[14] They often provide summaries or abstracts of the material cited. The IMRI database is a good example of this. It includes over 50,000 abstracts of Market Research Reports & Sources (including journals, databases, audits, published surveys, etc.). This is a comprehensive directory of Marketing Research Agencies, Publishers and Associations in over 100 countries. Besides country listings, agencies appear in regions (e.g. Asia), specialist fields (e.g. Quantitative) and market sectors (e.g. Healthcare and Pharmaceutical). The IMRI database is hosted on Datastar, Thompson/Dialog's collection of information databases (**www.dialog.com**).

Numeric databases contain numerical and statistical information. For example, some numeric databases provide time series data about the economy and specific industries. The earlier examples of census-based numeric databases using data over a series of censuses provide an example of a numeric database. The Experian MOSAIC database is a good example of a numeric database (**www.experian.co.uk/business-strategies**). Experian data include business and consumer demographics and classifications, mapping, economic forecasts and statistics, local area data, and retail and business information. This numeric database is delivered in a range of formats, including databases, reports and products such as Experian's Mosaic consumer classification.

Full-text databases contain the complete text of the source documents held in the database. They usually have the ability to conduct advanced searches for topics, authors, phrases, words and interconnections between these. Examples include Emerald Insight (**www.emeraldinsight.com**) and the Gale Newspaper Database (**www.gale.cengage.com**). Emerald is an independent publisher of global research with an impact in business, society, public policy and education. Its database provides access to more than 68,000 articles, some dating back as far as 1898. It has backfiles of over 120 business and management titles in one unified platform and access to 217 business and management e-journals. The Gale Newspaper Database indexes and provides full-text articles for example in the UK from the *Financial Times*,

Online databases
Databases that can be accessed, searched and analysed via the Internet.

Bibliographic databases
Databases composed of citations to articles in journals, magazines, newspapers, marketing research studies, technical reports, government documents, and the like. They often provide summaries or abstracts of the material cited.

Numeric databases
Databases containing numerical and statistical information that may be important sources of secondary data.

Full-text databases
Databases that contain the complete text of secondary source documents comprising the database.

the *Guardian*, the *Independent*, the *Independent on Sunday*, the *Observer*, *The Times* and *The Sunday Times*. The Gale database is a global resource so is worth accessing for any specific country or region. The *Gale Directory of Databases* is published every six months. Volume 1 covers online databases and Volume 2 covers CD-ROMs and other offline databases.

Directory databases
Databases that provide information on individuals, organisations and services.

Special-purpose databases
Databases that contain information of a specific nature, e.g. data on a specialised industry.

Directory databases provide information on individuals, organisations and services. European Directories (**www.europeandirectories.com**) is an example of a directory database. European Directories is a pan-European local search and lead generation company. It provides local search services to help customers find, evaluate and connect with local businesses across multiple media including print, online and mobile. It can help advertisers ensure they have a strong presence wherever consumers might be searching for local businesses. Another example is the Directory of Open Access Journals (**www.doaj.org**). This directory covers free, full-text, quality-controlled scientific and scholarly journals.

Finally, there are special-purpose databases. A good example of a special-purpose database is the fashion trend forecasting service WGSN (**www.wgsn.com**). WGSN is a leading online trend-analysis and research service providing creative and marketing intelligence for the apparel, style, design and retail industries. Its data support all business functions, including design, production, manufacturing, purchasing, merchandising, marketing, product development and general management. WGSN has a 12-year archive with more than 5 million images and 650,000 pages of information.

In addition, virtually all libraries of major universities maintain special-purpose databases of research activities that reflect the distinct specialisms of that university. Beyond the internally generated, special-purpose databases, university libraries and reference libraries maintain online databases with instructions relating to what may be accessed and how it may be accessed. Another library source worth examining for online sources is the European Commission's 'Libraries' site (**http://europa.eu**). The site, which is multilingual, is distributed by the EUROPA server, the portal site of the EU. It provides up-to-date coverage of European affairs and essential information on European integration. Users can access websites of each of the EU institutions.

Syndicated sources of secondary data

Syndicated sources (services)
Information services offered by marketing research organisations that provide information from a common database to different firms that subscribe to their services.

In addition to published data or data available in the form of online databases, syndicated sources constitute the other major source of external secondary data. Syndicated sources, also referred to as syndicated services, are companies that collect and sell common pools of data designed to serve information needs shared by a number of clients. These data are not collected with a focus on a specific marketing problem, but the data and reports supplied to client companies can be personalised to fit specific needs. For example, reports could be organised based on the clients' sales territories or product lines. Using syndicated services is frequently less expensive than commissioning tailored primary data collection. Figure 4.4 presents a classification of syndicated sources. Syndicated sources can be classified based on the unit of measurement (households and consumers or institutions). Household and consumer data may be obtained from surveys, purchase and media panels, or electronic scanner services. Information obtained through surveys consists of values and lifestyles, advertising evaluation, or general information related to preferences, purchase, consumption and other aspects of behaviour. Diary panels can focus upon information on purchases or media consumption as illustrated in the following example.

Electronic scanner services might provide scanner data only, scanner data linked to panels, or scanner data linked to panels and (cable) TV. When institutions are the unit of measurement, the data may be obtained from retailers, wholesalers or industrial firms. An overview of the various syndicated sources is given in Table 4.3. Each of these sources will be discussed.

Figure 4.4

A classification of syndicated services

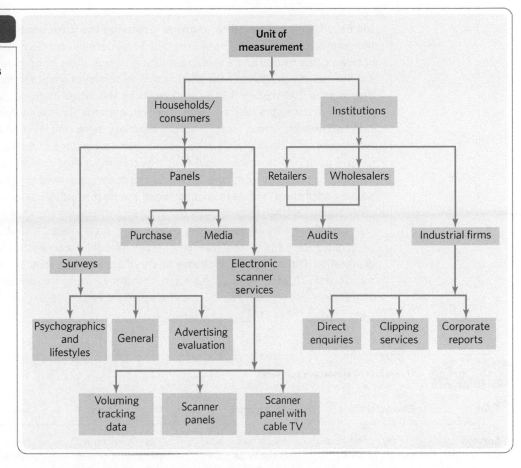

Making the news[15]

In a technology-enabled world, where online news aggregation is common, Mobile Internet is a reality, and social networking is mainstream, how do people consume news? A Taylor Nelson Sofres (TNS) (**www.tnsglobal.com**) syndicated study, researched news consumption by addressing the intersections between the platforms (conventional platforms, from newspapers and TV to radio and news websites, as well as word-of-mouth channels), news brands, content and news consumers that constitute the news world. The study delivered to multiple clients a detailed understanding of the role and place of news in the lives of consumers. It provided evidence of the complex nature of news gathering, revealing how a news story first sparks interest, to where further information is sourced, both online and offline, to flesh out a story, through to the impact each platform and brand has on conveying facts, forming opinion and encouraging the sharing of opinion with others – thus extending the lifecycle of the story and starting the news cycle afresh. The study relied on an innovative qualitative methodology, inspired by ethnography and made possible by technology, which allowed the observation and probing of research participants in any product category. Over the course of 10 days participants recorded all their contact with news, noting what they consumed, what stories attracted them and why, the platforms and brands they used, and how they followed up and passed on the news. They were able to post links, photos, videos and comments throughout the day. TNS monitored their journeys, observing the participants' routines and their thoughts and feelings as the news unfolded. This intensive process produced a rich record of news consumption and a valuable multimedia repository of information to review. In a follow-up stage TNS met the participants in person in small groups, to talk through their diaries and explore themes thrown up by the online journeys; what caught their attention and why; the role of news in their lives, patterns of consumption and the relationship between platforms. Using mapping exercises, personification and other projective techniques, participants were asked about their perceptions of media brands and their relative positions, as well as about their expectation for the future of news consumption. Most participants were extremely engaged and committed, were compliant, doing all that was asked of them, and were unconstrained by the method. Some posted very personal contributions and had to be reminded that their contributions would be seen by others. As expected, there were also some poor contributors; some missed their daily updates, failed to upload photos and videos, were short on detail in their diary entries and provided little explanation. Participants could choose to say what they want about themselves as no one could check. TNS's research did have a mechanism for accountability, because the participants knew they would meet TNS face to face at the end of the diary period.

Table 4.3	Overview of syndicated services			
Type	**Characteristics**	**Advantages**	**Disadvantages**	**Uses**
Surveys	Surveys conducted at regular intervals	Most flexible way of obtaining data; information on underlying motives	Interviewer errors; participant errors; response rate challenges	Market segmentation, advertising theme selection and advertising effectiveness
Purchase panels	Households provide specific information regularly over an extended period of time; participants asked to record specific behaviour as it occurs	Recorded purchase behaviour can be linked to the demographic/psychographic characteristics	Lack of representativeness; response bias; maturation	Forecasting sales, market share and trends; establishing consumer profiles, brand loyalty and switching; evaluating test markets, advertising and distribution
Media panels	Electronic devices automatically recording behaviour, supplemented by a diary	Same as purchase panels	Same as purchase panels	Establishing advertising; selecting media programme or air time; establishing viewer profiles
Scanner volume tracking data	Household purchases recorded through electronic scanners in supermarkets	Data reflect actual purchases; timely data, less expensive	Data may not be representative; errors in recording purchases; difficult to link purchases to elements of marketing mix other than price	Price tracking, modelling effectiveness of in-store promotions

Table 4.3	*Continued*			
Type	**Characteristics**	**Advantages**	**Disadvantages**	**Uses**
Scanner panels with cable TV	Scanner panels of households that subscribe to cable TV	Data reflect actual purchases; sample control; ability to link panel data to household characteristics	Data may not be representative; quality of data limited	Promotional mix analyses, copy testing, new product testing, positioning
Audit services	Verification of product movement by examining physical records or performing inventory analysis	Relatively precise information at retail and wholesale levels	Coverage may be incomplete; matching of data on competitive activity may be difficult	Measurement of consumer sales and market share; competitive activity; analysing distribution patterns; tracking of new products
Industrial product syndicated services	Data banks on industrial establishments created through direct enquiries of companies, clipping services and corporate reports	Important source of information in industrial firms; particularly useful in initial phases of research projects	Data can be lacking in terms of content, quantity and quality, i.e. this equates more with business and competitor intelligence services	Determining market potential by geographical area, defining sales territories, allocating advertising budget

Syndicated data from households

Surveys

Surveys
Interviews with a large number of participants using a questionnaire.

Omnibus survey
A distinctive form of survey that serves the needs of a syndicate group. The omnibus survey targets particular types of participants such as those in specific locations, e.g. Luxembourg residents, or customers of particular types of product, e.g. business air travellers. With that target group of participants, a core set of questions can be asked with other questions added as syndicate members wish.

Many marketing research companies offer syndicated services by conducting surveys and omnibus surveys. As with any survey, the process involves interviews with a large number of participants using a pre-designed questionnaire. Survey design and the relative advantages and disadvantages of different survey types will be discussed in detail in Chapter 10. The distinction made here is that rather than designing a survey for the specific needs of a client company, the syndicated survey is designed for a number of client companies. The needs of sometimes quite a disparate array of client companies can be met by a syndicated survey. The key benefits of the syndicated survey lie in combining the resources of a number of clients to craft a survey of high quality and the economies of scale this may bring to individual clients. The downside may be that all the information needs of an individual client may be met, and additional primary data may need to be collected. One of the most prolific forms of syndicated survey is the omnibus survey. The distinction of the omnibus survey compared with ad hoc surveys is that they target particular types of participants such as those in certain geographical locations, e.g. Luxembourg residents, or consumers of particular types of products, e.g. business air travellers. The following example illustrates just one of many omnibus surveys conducted by Ipsos MORI (**www.ipsos-mori.com**).

Real research   **Clients speak their minds about UK advertising agencies[16]**

Marketers rarely miss an opportunity to tell advertising agencies what they think of them. So there were few refusals to participate in a study of clients' views on the UK communications industry. Conducted on behalf of the Institute of Practitioners in Advertising (**www.ipa.co.uk**), a section of Ipsos MORI's (**www.ipsos-mori.com**) ongoing omnibus survey, *Captains of Industry*, asked a key question: '*Were advertising and communications agencies good at supplying advice on intangible asset creation?*' The sample comprised 99 boardroom executives selected from a universe that included (1) the UK's top 500 companies by market capitalisation; (2) the top 500 by turnover; and (3) the top 100 by capital employed. In answer to that key question, 64% replied 'Yes – they did consider advertising and communications agencies as good at supplying advice on intangible asset creation.' Other perceptions of advertising and communications agencies included: '26% indicated that advertising and communications agencies were good at supplying advice on organic growth creation whilst 37% indicated that they were poor at this'. Among those participants that make use of advertising and communications agencies (84), 55% rated the quality of management at the main marketing and communications agency they used as above average. In response to the survey, IPA President Moray Maclennan commented:

The IPA and its members lead the way in championing effectiveness, which made it doubly appropriate to measure progress in our boardroom agenda. The data threw down a challenge to the industry regarding its reputation for generating organic growth.

With a defined target group of participants, a core set of questions can be asked with other questions added as syndicate members wish. Other syndicate members can 'jump on the omnibus' and buy the answers to all the questionnaire responses or to specific questions of their choice. Surveys and omnibus surveys may be broadly classified based on their content as psychographics and lifestyles, advertising evaluation, or general surveys.

Psychographics
Quantified profiles of individuals based upon lifestyle characteristics.

Lifestyles
Distinctive patterns of living described by the activities people engage in, the interests they have, and the opinions they hold of themselves and the world around them.

Psychographics and lifestyles Psychographics refers to the psychological profiles of individuals and to psychologically based measures of lifestyle. Lifestyles refers to the distinctive modes of living of a society or some of its segments. Together, these measures are generally referred to as activities, interests and opinions.[17] Companies may wish to buy syndicated data that describe the lifestyles of consumers as this can help them to understand further the characteristics of their existing and especially potential customers. A good example of a marketing research agency that works upon the measurement and marketing applications of lifestyles can be found at the Natural Marketing Institute (**www.nmisolutions.com**).

Advertising evaluation The purpose of using surveys to evaluate advertising is to assess the effectiveness of advertising that may be delivered through print, broadcast, online, outdoors and social media.[18] A good example of a marketing research agency specialising in advertising evaluation is Harvey Research (**http://harveyresearch.co.uk**). Evaluation of effectiveness is critical to all forms of advertising. Companies that communicate to target consumers wish to understand the impact of their advertisements and thus the return on their advertising investment. Companies that sell advertising space and services wish to demonstrate that their medium will have the best impact on particular consumers.[19] The sums involved in planning, creating and delivering effective advertising mean that research has long played a part in supporting advertising decisions, and surveys continue to play a major role in that evaluation process. The subject of advertising research has a long history and very large literature base with strong academic and practitioner viewpoints.[20] A few examples may illustrate the complexity and value of advertising research. TV advertisements can be evaluated using either the recruited audience method or the in-home viewing method. In the former method, participants are recruited and brought to a central viewing facility, such as a theatre or mobile viewing laboratory. The participants view the advertisements and provide data regarding their knowledge, attitudes and preferences related to the product being advertised and the advertisement itself. In the in-home viewing method, participants evaluate advertisements at home in their normal viewing environment. New advertisements can be pretested at the network level or in local markets distributed via DVDs. A survey of viewers is then conducted to assess the effectiveness of the advertisements.

One of the main contemporary challenges in measuring the impact of advertising is in isolating a specific medium, as illustrated in the following example. This example shows that creative research designs can be used to isolate and measure the impact of a single communications medium.

Real research	**It can be measured**[21]

Radio Ad Effectiveness Lab (RAEL, **www.radioadlab.org**) was founded in 2001 and is dedicated to providing research about how radio advertising works. One of its first studies was dedicated to the return on investment (ROI) on radio advertising. With the help of Millward Brown (**www.millwardbrown.com**) and Information Resources Symphony (IRI **www.symphonyiri.com**) and four adventurous advertisers, RAEL created a 'real-world' test. RAEL used IRI's BehaviorScan Targetable TV test market capabilities to control the delivery of TV advertisements household by household, while simultaneously using test and control markets to deliver or not deliver radio advertising. This involved a six-month test of actual advertising campaigns for multiple advertisers. RAEL created four matching test cells: one with no local radio or national TV advertising; one with only the national TV ads; one with only an equivalent weight of local radio advertising; and one with equivalent weights of both national TV and local radio advertising. Alongside the survey data collected, RAEL also had corresponding scanner shopping data from IRI for four national advertisers. At the end of the six-month period, RAEL looked at the cell-by-cell details for each advertiser. On a sales lift basis, the radio campaigns for the four advertisers acquitted themselves very well. The radio campaigns were linked to a statistically significant sales lift of 4.1%. Meanwhile, TV with a much higher spend level accounted for 7.5% in additional sales. When advertising costs were considered, radio delivered 49% better ROI than the corresponding (and similar weights of) national TV advertising.

General surveys Syndicated surveys are also conducted for a variety of other purposes, including examination of purchase and consumption behaviour. Because a variety of data can be obtained, survey data have numerous uses. They can be used for market segmentation, as with psychographic and lifestyle data, and for establishing consumer profiles. Surveys are also useful for determining product image, measurement and positioning, and conducting price perception analysis. The following example from IFM Sports Marketing Surveys illustrates the nature and value of a general survey designed to support brands associated with tennis.

Focus on   **IFM Sports Marketing Surveys**

International Sports Event Survey

Online survey

This online survey was targeted at individuals aged between 16 and 65. It was adminis-tered to 300 participants in each of the following countries: Australia, China, France, Ger-many, Hong Kong, India, Ireland, Italy, Poland, Russia, Singapore, Spain, the UK and the USA. Fieldwork was conducted shortly after a number of major summer sporting events including: the Beijing Olympic Games; the enthralling tennis rivalry between Roger Fed-erer and Rafael Nadal peaking at the Wimbledon Final; and golf's premier Ryder Cup. The survey was designed to create an in-depth analysis of: sports sponsorship includ-ing: corporate social responsibility, sports following, sports lifestyle and leisure time, and sports event interest. The survey findings would be of interest to sports brands engaged in sponsorship, events, TV programming, clothing and equipment, to name but a few of the potential beneficiaries.

Purchase and media panels

About a fifth of all research budgets is spent on panels in their various formats, among the largest investors in this format in Europe being Switzerland at 38%, Germany at 34% and the Netherlands at 31%.[22] Panels were discussed in Chapter 3 in the context of longitudinal research designs. Panels are samples of participants who provide specified information at regular intervals over an extended period of time. These participants may be organisations, households or individuals, although household panels are most common. The distinguishing feature of panels is that the participants record specific behaviours as they occur. Previously, behaviour was recorded in a handwritten diary, and the diary returned to the research organi-sation every one to four weeks. Panel diaries have been gradually replaced by electronic dia-ries and blog diaries.[23] Now, most panels are online and consumption and media behaviour is recorded electronically, either entered online by the participants or recorded automatically by electronic devices.

Media panels
A data gathering technique composed of samples of participants whose TV viewing behaviour is automatically recorded by electronic devices, supplementing the purchase information recorded in a diary or blog.

In media panels, electronic devices automatically record viewing behaviour, thus supple-menting a diary. Media panels yield information helpful for establishing advertising rates by radio and TV networks, selecting appropriate programming, and profiling viewer or lis-tener subgroups. Advertisers, media planners and buyers find panel information particularly useful. Another media vehicle that competes heavily for advertising budgets is the Internet. The following example illustrates how TNS use media panels to understand the likelihood of viewers responding to advertisements.

Real research   **Targeting ad responders[24]**

The Skyview panel, conceived and developed by BSkyB (**www.sky.com**) and TNS (**www.tnsglobal.com**), comprises 33,000 Sky households, from which detailed second-by-second TV viewing data covering all TV channels is collected via a set-top box. Of these homes, 6,000 are also members of Worldpanel, the service operated by TNS which pro-vides details on each household's purchasing of grocery products on a continuous basis. Sky Media (**www.skymedia.co.uk**) is the media sales arm of BSkyB and it wanted to use data from Worldpanel to identify which households are the most responsive to advertising. Having identified these 'high responders', Sky Media could then go on to examine their viewing patterns and thus find ways in which advertising could be more effectively targeted at the most responsive buyers through the better use of timing advertisements throughout the day, channels and specific programmes. Worldpanel data reveal when each household made a purchase of a product category and  whether the advertised brand or another brand was bought. It was possible to count the number of times the advertised brand was bought when the household was exposed to the brand's advertising. Sky Media built upon this relationship to help predict the likelihood of someone responding to an advertisement. To investigate this Sky Media studied 33 brands across three categories: breakfast cereals, shampoo and yogurts. In each case it identified the 'ad responders'. For each panellist it added a description of their demographics, together with their scores on 137 attitudinal statements and their propensity to view TV. On average, 13% of panellists were classified as 'ad responders'. Those with the highest propensity to be ad responders were people who liked advertising, were heavy consumers of commercial TV and had two or more people in the household. By contrast, the least responsive were those who claimed not to like advertising, were living on their own and working full time.

Purchase panels
A data gathering technique in which participants record their purchases, either online, or in a diary or blog.

Purchase panels provide information useful for forecasting sales, estimating market shares, assessing brand loyalty and brand-switching behaviour, establishing profiles of specific user groups, measuring promotional effectiveness and conducting controlled store tests.

Compared with sample surveys (see Chapter 10), panels offer certain distinct advantages.[25] Panels can provide longitudinal data (data can be obtained from the same participants repeatedly). They enable specific types of consumer to be targeted for study, relatively quicker than generating a bespoke sample. People who are willing to serve on panels may be more motivated to engage in a particular study and thus provide more and higher quality data than one-off sample participants. In purchase panels, information is recorded at the time of purchase, eliminating recall errors.[26] If information is recorded by electronic devices, it is generally more accurate as it eliminates recall errors.

The disadvantages of panels include lack of representativeness, maturation and response biases.[27] This problem is further compounded by refusal to respond and attrition of panel members. Over time, maturation sets in, and the panel members should be replaced. Response biases may occur, since simply being on the panel may alter behaviour. There has been much debate on the challenges of creating representative and/or probability-based samples, with some researchers claiming that panels are an unsustainable research method.[28] Due to the seriousness of this latter claim, the 'scientific rigour' of panels is further explored in Chapters 14 and 15. In spite of these disadvantages, purchase panels are extensively used in marketing research and the following example illustrates how they can effectively support decision-makers.

Real research

SCI INTAGE – A Japanese nationwide retail panel survey[29]

In 1960, a time when Japan was fast developing into a consumer market, Marketing Intelligence Corporation (MiC), the forerunner of INTAGE Inc., was established as Japan's first true comprehensive marketing research organisation. The fledgling firm's first businesses were SDI (nationwide drug-store panel research) and custom research. In 1964 the company launched SCI, a nationwide household consumer panel research (**www.intage.co.jp/english**). SCI was based upon a sample of 12,008 two- or more member households. Data from this study were extensively used by Japanese retailers and the following example shows how SCI supported decision-makers. One-day-only sales and short-term discount promotions were often run by Japanese retailers. Such price changes entailed costly operational and stock control complexities. Why did they change prices at short intervals despite the drawbacks? The situation had its basis in the unique characteristics of the purchasing behaviour of Japan's consumers. According to SCI data on housewife purchasing behaviour, even when shopping for perishable foods is excluded, housewives shopped at supermarkets 2.5 times per week. Japanese housewives on average shopped at 4.7 supermarkets and 13.3 stores across all SCI channels during the course of a year. What these data revealed was that Japan's consumers shopped every few days and at different stores rather than always shopping at the same stores. For this reason, retailers wanted to offer novel experiences to attract customers to their stores on as many shopping occasions as possible. They did not wish to continue discounting of a single product for a full week, but rather to rotate products frequently to be discounted for short periods of time.

Electronic scanner services

The following example illustrates the nature and value of electronic scanner services as undertaken by A.C. Nielsen, Worldwide Consumer Panel Services (**http://uk.nielsen.com**). A.C. Nielsen's Panel Services operates in 27 countries, based on consumer purchase information from over 210,000 households. Another major global research company worth examining with expertise in panel services and electronic scanning is Kantar (**www.kantarworldpanel.com**).

Real research

A.C. Nielsen Worldwide Consumer Panel Services

A.C. Nielsen Homescan was launched in 1989, the first continuous consumer panel in Europe to use in-home bar code scanners to collect data. The panel is regionally and demographically balanced to represent the household population and captures consumer package goods purchases brought back into the home, including variable weight and non-bar-coded fresh products. Each household provides daily information on its purchases of consumer goods for in-home use. Collected on a continuous basis, it is possible to measure the ongoing changes and interactions of households' purchasing behaviour across all grocery and fresh food products. Homescan incorporates both descriptive and diagnostic information. Consumer panel data provide information on purchaser attributes, purchase behaviour, market penetration, share of category requirements, brand loyalty, brand switching and parallel consumption plus a wide range of other powerful analytics. The database provides insights into why consumers behave the way they do. Subscribers can get answers to questions specific to their brand such as: How many households purchased a product on a trial basis? Did they return later to purchase again? What did buyers purchase before a marketing campaign, what did they purchase subsequently? Where did buyers of a brand come from? What else do buyers purchase? Where else do buyers shop? How store loyal are shoppers? What is the demographic composition of buyers? How do lifestyles and attitudes impact upon purchasing behaviour?

Although information provided by surveys and purchase and media panels is useful, electronic scanner services have continued to deliver great value to decision-makers. The role of scanned data as a foundation to developing sophisticated consumer databases is developed further in Chapter 5. In this chapter we examine scanned data as a distinct source of syndicated data. **Scanner data** reflect some of the latest technological developments in the marketing research industry. They are collected by passing merchandise over a laser scanner that optically reads the bar-coded description (UPC, or Universal Product Code) printed on the merchandise. This code is then linked to the current price held on the computer and used to prepare a sales slip. Information printed on the sales slip includes descriptions as well as prices of all items purchased. Checkout scanners have revolutionised packaged goods marketing research.

Three types of scanner data are available: **volume tracking data**, **scanner panels** and **scanner panels with cable TV**. Volume tracking data provide information on purchases by brand, size, price and flavour or formulation, based on sales data collected from the checkout scanner. This information is collected nationally from a sample of supermarkets (rather than individual supermarkets tracking their customers' purchases using loyalty cards) with electronic scanners. In scanner panels, each household member is given an ID card. Panel members present their ID card at the checkout counter each time they shop. The checker scans their ID and each item of that customer's order. The information is stored by day of week and time of day.

Scanner panels with cable TV combine panels with new technologies growing out of the cable TV industry. Households on these panels subscribe to one of the cable or TV systems in their market. By means of a cable TV 'split', the researcher targets different advertisements into the homes of the panel members. For example, half the households may see test advertisement A during the 6 p.m. newscast while the other half see test advertisement B. These panels allow researchers to conduct fairly controlled experiments in a relatively natural environment. It is possible to combine store-level scanner data with scanner panel data to do integrated analyses of consumer behaviour. This was illustrated earlier with the earlier *Real Research* example of the Skyview panel developed by BSkyB and TNS. The following example illustrates how panel and scanning organisations like Nielsen are striving to make this work.

Scanner data
Data obtained by passing merchandise over a laser scanner that reads the UPC from the packages.

Volume tracking data
Scanner data that provide information on purchases by brand, size, price and flavour or formulation.

Scanner panels
Scanner data where panel members are identified by an ID card, allowing information about each panel member's purchases to be stored with respect to the individual shopper.

Scanner panels with cable TV
The combination of a scanner panel with manipulations of the advertising that is being broadcast by cable TV companies.

Real research	**From fragmentation to integration**[30]

Paul Donato is Executive Vice President and Chief Research Officer for The Nielsen Company (**www.nielsen.com**). His responsibilities include integrating all research functions within The Nielsen Company, overseeing the development and evaluation of all research, and serving as Nielsen's research liaison to clients and industry associations. In describing Nielsen's drive to integrate more of their data he illustrated this through NielsenConnect:

The concept of Connect is based on the fact that there are limits to how much you can ask any one person within a survey. That makes a strong case for integrating various databases with our people-meter panel **http://www.agbnielsen.net**. *We do this via a hub, where we take homes from the people-meter panel and for two years collect other media usage data from these homes. To start with, we put a Niesen/NetRatings meter in these panel house-*

holds, but in the long term we may also measure other media. One of our visions is to measure internet usage in as many TV people-meter homes as we can. We have done some tests and we know that people react to internet measurement differently and we estimate that realistically only 30–40% of people-meter households will sign up for internet measurement as well. Our plan is to grow the number of TV panel households to around 37,000, which should yield approximately 12–13000 TV plus online panel homes onto which the balance of the 130,000-strong Nielsen//NetRatings panel. Importantly, for internet measurement advertisers they will benefit from the large 130,000 sample, which enables them to evaluate smaller, more specialist sites.

Scanner data are useful for a variety of purposes.[31] National volume tracking data can be used for tracking sales, prices and distribution, for modelling and for analysing early warning signals. Scanner panels with cable TV can be used for testing new products, repositioning products, analysing promotional mixes and making advertising decisions, including budget, copy and media, and pricing. These panels provide researchers with a unique controlled environment for the manipulation of marketing variables. The following example gives an example of this using GfK's BEHAVIORSCAN (**www.gfk.com/group/services/instruments_and_services**).

Real research   ## GfK BEHAVIOURSCAN

GfK BEHAVIORSCAN tests advertising spots in a random sample of the test households. Because of the capability to split these into test and control groups, a range of different budgets or campaigns can be tested and compared. The comparability of test and control groups is achieved by 'matching', a mathematical optimisation program. Comparability is based on socio-demographic factors, purchasing behaviour in the category and, as far as the product is established, on the test product. GfK BEHAVIORSCAN can test the entire marketing mix of a product in a real environment controlled by members of the GfK team to produce results at the level of a complete household panel. It can help answer important questions such as: How many trial buyers do I gain? How satisfied are the customers? Which product variants and which packet size sell best? How do TV advertisements work? How profitable is the invested advertisement budget? How profitable are campaigns, mail shots, vouchers and in-home samples? What market share will I achieve with my new product? Which competitor does it attack and who will lose out?

Scanner data have an obvious advantage over surveys and panels: they reflect purchasing behaviour that is not subject to interviewing, recording, memory or expert biases. The record of purchases obtained by scanners is complete and unbiased by price sensitivity, because the panellist is not required to be particularly conscious of price levels and changes. Another advantage is that in-store variables such as pricing, promotions and displays are part of the dataset. The data are also likely to be current and can be obtained quickly. Finally, scanner panels with cable TV provide a highly controlled testing environment.

A major weakness of scanner data can be a lack of representativeness. National volume tracking data may not be projectable onto the total population. Not all purchases are scanned in the manner of large supermarkets. Many types of retail and wholesale outlets, which consumers may physically or virtually shop at, may well be excluded. Scanner data provide product and media behavioural and sales information, they do not provide information on underlying attitudes and preferences and the reasons for specific choices.

Syndicated data from institutions

Retail audits

As Figure 4.4 shows, syndicated data are available from retailers as well as industrial firms. A retail audit is a regular survey that monitors sales of products via a sample of retail outlets. Retail audit data allow decision-makers to analyse their product structure, pricing and distribution policy, and their position in relation to their competition. (See the example of the work of German marketing research company GfK at **www.gfk.com/group/services/instruments-and_services** which conducts retail and wholesale audits in the following sectors: consumer electronics, IT and office equipment, telecommunications, domestic appliances, photographic equipment, DIY/gardening products and entertainment hardware/software.)

Audit
A data collection process derived from physical records or performing inventory analysis. Data are collected personally by the researcher, or by representatives of the researcher, and are based on counts usually of physical objects rather than people.

The most popular means of obtaining data from retailers is an audit, a formal examination and verification of product movement carried out by examining physical records or analysing inventory. Retailers who participate in the audit receive basic reports and cash payments from the audit service, but the main beneficiary is the brand owner who wishes to monitor the sales of the brand through many retail outlets. Audit data focus on the products or services sold through the outlets or the characteristics of the outlets themselves. The following example illustrates how a Nielsen audit helped Unilever to understand the nature of its marketing problem and once it had worked through a solution, to measure the impact of its actions.

Real research

Comfort Fabric Conditioner – Comfort challenges the 'rules' and wins big in South-East Asia[32]

Global FMCG marketers know that the major growth markets of South-East Asia (SEA) have already become some of the most valuable to their brands, and the region has been targeted to make up for slow growth in mature Western markets and contribute an ever-increasing share of global growth targets. In 2006, Nielsen's retail audit revealed that Unilever's top global fabric conditioner brand, Comfort, was stagnating in the region. Comfort had long been market leader in the key markets of Vietnam, with 57.1% share versus its nearest competitor at 35.4%, and Indonesia (where the brand is known as 'Molto'), at 58.0% share versus its nearest competitor at 35.8%. Based on these data, Comfort developed an advertising campaign 'Andy and Lily's Clothworld' aimed at creating brand differentiation and perceived value in what was seen as a commoditised market. This became one of the most effective campaigns in the region and in just three years boosted brand health – increasing brand preference and loyalty by over a third, and increasing annual sales growth to 40% in just the first year. Nielsen's retail audit revealed that Comfort's share of the category rose from 58% to 67% and generated incremental sales of €142 million over the campaign period. As the Comfort brand grew stronger, the business took off. The audit also revealed that its regional market share grew to a record 65.8% in 2009, compared with 57.4% in 2006, a 14.6% increase. In both Vietnam and Indonesia Comfort substantially increased the gap between itself and the nearest challengers.

The uses of retail audit data include: (1) determining the size of the total market and the distribution of sales by type of outlet, region or city; (2) assessing brand shares and competitive activity; (3) identifying shelf space allocation and inventory problems; (4) analysing distribution problems; (5) developing sales potentials and forecasts; and (6) developing and monitoring promotional allocations based on sales volume. Thus, audit data can be particularly helpful in understanding and developing the environmental context should further stages of research need to be administered.

Audits provide relatively accurate information on the movement of many different products. Furthermore, this information can be broken down by a number of important variables, such as brand, type of outlet and size of market. Audits may have limited coverage; not all categories of particular products or brands are necessarily included. In addition, audit information may not be timely or current, particularly compared with scanner data. At one time, there could be a two-month gap between the completion of the audit cycle and the publication of reports. Another disadvantage is that, unlike scanner data, audit data cannot be linked to consumer characteristics. In fact, there may even be a problem in relating audit data to advertising expenditures and other marketing efforts. Some of these limitations are overcome in online audit panels. GfK Retail and Technology (**www.gfkrt.com**) performs online tracking in over 80 countries and covers markets such as tourism, optics and fashion. The following example illustrates the nature and value of its work for fashion brands.

Real research	**GfK FashionLife**

GfK FashionLife offers market figures and the fast, fact-based delivery of detailed information to allow companies to steer their performance accordingly. The power to benchmark products and markets allows fashion companies to maintain a firm grip on insights by channel. Reporting includes information on sales volume, sales value and average prices, and forms the basis for a continuous service for both retailers and suppliers within the fashion industry. Reports are available from top-level aggregation down to single-product level and are customisable according to individual client needs. Delivery is on a monthly or weekly basis. Fashion products tracked by GfK FashionLife include: watches, luggage, jewellery, clothing and shoes, leisure, home textiles. GfK pitches the benefits of its online retail audit for fashion businesses as: fast weekly data directly from retailers; high levels of granularity in reporting; a basis for decisions on product assortments and ranges; a platform for understanding performance against competitors and the impact price has on market share; additional information to help target advertising and promotional activities; help in maximising stock efficiency.

Industry services

These provide syndicated data about industrial firms, businesses and other institutions. Examples of these include Datamonitor, Bureau Van Dijk and Dun and Bradstreet. The Datamonitor Group (**www.datamonitor.com**) is a provider of global business information, delivering data, analysis and opinion across the automotive, consumer packaged goods, energy and sustainability, financial services, logistics, pharmaceutical and health care, retail, sourcing, technology and telecoms industries. It supports over 6,000 of the world's leading companies in strategic and operational decision making. Its market intelligence products and services are delivered online. Bureau Van Dijk (**www.bvdinfo.com**) provides a range of company information products that are co-published with many renowned information providers. Its product range includes databases of company information and marketing intelligence for individual countries, regions and the world. Its global database, Orbis, combines information from around 100 sources and covers nearly 65 million companies. It also provides e-publishing solutions, based on open and flexible platforms, and offer features such as search, secure delivery, e-commerce, rendering systems and hosting. Clients include publishers of books, scientific, technical and medical journals, news, directories and reference guides. Dun and Bradstreet (**www.dnb.com** but also look for specific countries, e.g. Netherlands, **http://dbnetherlands.dnb.com**) has a global commercial database that contains more than 151 million business records. Through the D&B Worldwide Network clients gain access to perhaps the world's largest global commercial business information database. D&B has global data coverage on business records in over 190 countries. To help ensure the accuracy and completeness of its information, D&B uses sophisticated data collection tools and updates the database over 1.5 million times a day.

Information provided by industrial services is useful for sales management decisions, including identifying potential target markets, defining territories and measuring market potential by geographical areas. It can also support communications decisions such as targeting prospects, allocating communications budgets, selecting media and measuring communications effectiveness. Given the rich competitive intelligence available, these sources of information are also useful for segmentation and positioning decisions. Industry services represent an important contextual source of support in defining the environmental context for management decisions and any subsequent bespoke marketing research. They are particularly valuable for researchers who aim to measure and understand the networks and relationships of industrial firms (to be addressed in more detail in Chapter 27).

International marketing research

A wide variety of secondary data are available for international marketing research.[33] As in the case of domestic research, the problem is not a lack of data but the potential overabundance of information. The international researcher has to work through an array of potential sources to find accurate, up-to-date and relevant information. Evaluation of secondary data is even more critical for international than for domestic projects. Different sources report different values for a given statistic, such as the GDP, because of differences in the way the unit is defined. Measurement units may not be equivalent across countries. In France, for example, some workers are still paid a 13-monthly salary each year as an automatic bonus, resulting in a measurement construct that is different from those in other countries.[34] The accuracy of secondary data may also vary from country to country. Data from highly industrialised countries in Europe are likely to be more accurate than those from developing nations. Business and income statistics are affected by the taxation structure and the extent of tax evasion. Population censuses may vary in frequency and year in which the data are collected. In most developed economies,

their census is conducted every 10 years. In China there was a 29-year gap between the censuses of 1953 and 1982 but China has now developed a system of also conducting a census every 10 years. This situation, however, is changing quickly, as many countries are considering replacing their population censuses with an amalgamation of different data sources that they already collect for all manner of services they deliver, e.g. national insurance, health, education, pensions.

One of the more significant developments in international research relates to how research companies in fast-growing economies are using advanced technological solutions. For example, one of the staple methods in traditional syndicated research has been the consumer diary. Encouraging participants fully to engage in and complete their diaries has always been a challenge. In the following example, the diary is completed as a blog and is enhanced with images, allowing participants to express their feelings in novel and enjoyable ways. Though this example delivered information support to an individual client, the approach could be used to great effect in syndicated research.

Real research | Chinese real estate product development[35]

Vanke (**www.vanke.com**), founded in 1984, is one of the leading real estate developers in China. Vanke used to be designer oriented with its product developing process. What it hoped would make its properties stand out was its designers' capabilities in design. Vanke felt that targeting potential customers after the product had been shaped posed a substantial risk. Therefore, Vanke selected Horizon Research to cooperate in exploring a customer-oriented development model in residential properties. The Horizon and Vanke research team started its research by observing the 'high-powered, high-stress' young generation. The team started the project by understanding the needs of designers, rather than consumers. Designers typically were frustrated that marketing research findings do not communicate to them in ways that they find useful. What is useful to designers are not direct questions, such as how large should an apartment be, how many bathrooms or bedrooms, but how people are going to live in the apartment, what furniture and decorations they are going to use, how they relate themselves to each space and what they dream for the apartment. In order to visualise such needs, 40 young people in Beijing, Shanghai and Guangzhou were asked to keep diaries in the following format:

- To write two blogs on the topics of 'ideal life' and 'ideal home'.
- To take photographs of their favourite surroundings and products, and provide brief comments on each photograph.

Following the diary, the most enjoyable environment for participants was chosen to conduct a relaxed in-depth interview to learn of their ideal choice and preferences from their blogs and photos. The researchers took photos and conducted interviews while visiting the participant's current home; this helped them to understand the participants' lives and unmet needs. The participants' needs were translated into the language that designers could understand for a more precise concept generation process. The concepts based on this research were adopted and localised in many cities, and finally became homes, sold with more competitive advantage. This project not only demonstrated a customer-oriented product development process, but also helped Vanke to form a customer-oriented design culture. Horizon continued to work with Vanke on a series of product development projects such as 'Little Kid Family' and 'Active Adult'.

Ethics in marketing research

Possible ethical dilemmas exist when using internal or external secondary data. The ethical challenges presented by the use of internal secondary data will be discussed in Chapter 5 but some generic ethical issues that relate to secondary data include:

- The unnecessary and expensive collection of primary data when the problem can be addressed based on secondary data alone.
- Cutting corners through the use of only secondary data when primary data are needed.
- The use of secondary data and intelligence that have been gathered through morally questionable means.
- Compromising the anonymity of participant details.

As was discussed in Chapter 2, the unnecessary collection of expensive primary data when the research problem can be addressed using only secondary data is unethical. In this case, the researcher is using a more expensive method that is less appropriate. Similarly, the exclusive reliance on secondary data when the research problem requires primary data collec-

tion could raise ethical concerns. This is particularly true if the researcher is charging a fixed fee for the project and the research design was not specified in advance. Here again, the researcher's profit goes up, but at the expense of the client. The researcher is ethically obliged to ensure the relevance and usefulness of secondary data to the problem at hand. The secondary data should be evaluated by the criteria discussed earlier in this chapter. Only data judged to be appropriate should be used.

Finally, the ethical issues related to the growth of digital measurement of consumers in creating secondary data have to be considered. A lot of attention has been focused on the array of digital measurement tools and how much secondary data are collected, analysed and reported online. Relatively less consideration has been given to people's acceptance of these devices and processes. The challenge that researchers face is overcoming the perception and in many case the practices that digital measurement poses as a privacy threat.[36]

Digital applications in marketing research

As we have illustrated throughout this chapter, secondary data and marketing intelligence can be obtained from an ever-increasing number of vendors. More newspapers, magazines and journals can be accessed online with excellent indexing facilities to locate particular subjects, companies and individuals. Government data for the European Community and for individual countries through to regional and city councils can be accessed online. The sources and quantity of data have grown, but this should be clearly distinguished from the quality of data. Being able to evaluate the quality of secondary data and marketing intelligence is vital in understanding what may be used to support specific decisions and/or the design and implementation of further primary data collection and analyses.

It is not only the quantity and quality of data that should concern the researcher, but also how Internet developments have shaped the expectations of decision-makers. More analytics, insights and future outlooks are demanded from decision-makers to help them better understand their customers, the marketplace and the overall business environment. Researchers can be expected to help understand the macro business operating environment, monitor market trends, conduct competitive analyses, answer business questions, identify business opportunities and assess potential risks.[37] Given this wider job scope, gathering and validating good secondary data and marketing intelligence is seen as a vital skill for researchers. Conducting quality desk research, gathering syndicated reports, news clippings, key performance indicators and customer behaviour data, and being able to integrate and interpret these sources are vital to actionable marketing research. Researchers may have to see themselves as 'data curators' or aggregators of data, integrating disparate types of data with our more traditional lines of enquiry and making strategic sense of it for decision-makers.[38]

Another major impact of digital applications is how they are used by consumers and how their experiences are shaping their engagement with marketing research and the research process. This engagement is becoming more apparent with consumers for whom the Internet is not 'new'; it has always been a part of their life and their being. For younger marketing research participants, traditional marketing research techniques, such as surveys, interviews and focus groups, can be relevant. These techniques, however, may not apply as readily as new, more collaborative techniques, aligned more to conversation, listening and empowerment than to seeking specific responses. The combination of web and electronic media use and proficiency by youth participants is forcing marketing research to evolve and embrace mixed methodologies including a breadth of social media techniques. On the Web, the need for social acceptance is less intense and discussion can flow more freely. When presented with a task (as opposed to a question) online, youth involvement becomes spontaneous and enthused. Introducing a project or problem-solving approach helps youth participants to feel empowered and that their opinions are being listened to. Further, enabling younger participants to express themselves in pictures and multimedia,[39] as they would to their friends, delivers a rich research experience that cannot be replicated offline. With the evolution of online social media techniques, blended research programmes, long a mainstay of quality research initiatives, are now more cost effective, more accurate and adaptable.[40] The following example illustrates how these challenges can be addressed primarily through online and digital approaches to completing consumer diaries, again a mainstay of syndicated research. The research topic is highly sensitive but is presented to participants in a most relevant and engaging manner.

One of the principal changes in approach to marketing research through social media is that of 'listening' to consumers, rather than questioning in a controlled manner. An emerging practice of 'listening' online enables researchers to observe naturally occurring conversations between consumers about products, brands and companies. It has been argued that 'listening' to conversations captures the context and emotions of consumers better than traditional methods in marketing research.[41] The SENSOA example below presents a means to think of traditional 'questioning' techniques as a complement to 'listening'. If researchers are expected to 'listen' to consumers as a complement to more traditional forms of conducting research, this raises the question of what types of data 'listening' constitutes? Social media 'listening techniques' question what may be seen in the future as 'secondary data' and 'marketing intelligence'. This question will be further developed in Chapter 5 as we explore the similarly burgeoning nature of internally generated sources of secondary data and marketing intelligence.

SENSOA – All about sex[42]

SENSOA (**www.sensoa.be**) is a Flemish expert organisation on sexual health and HIV issues. Its website was old (over five years), had a low level of dynamism, hardly any interaction and, most of all, did not build further on the insight of how young people deal with sex and relationships. SENSOA worked with Boondoggle (**www.boondoggle.eu**), a full-service communication agency with offices in Leuven and Amsterdam, to build a new website. Together with the concept for its new website, Boondoggle also created a new name 'all about sex' (**www.allaboutsex.be**). Building on the view that a lack of information is the main problem for young people, it created the site and communication around asking questions. The 'all about sex' site was intended to become the source of information for all young people wanting information about sex. Boondoggle promoted the site with a campaign based on a viral movie and embedded the site in existing social networks (a brand page on **www.netlog.be**, the biggest community site in Belgium, and a fan page on Facebook) and made the video available on video sharing platforms like YouTube. Boondoggle launched the campaign with a press conference that resulted in radio, TV and newspaper coverage. Boondoggle partnered with InSites Consulting (**www.insites.eu**) to set up an impact measurement model for the campaign. InSites Consulting completed a broad and in-depth study that aimed to develop a method to track conversations using its 'Conversations KPIs' (Key Performance Indicators) and to formulate guidelines for designing impactful conversations. The study used an innovative online diary in which 800 Belgians (representative of the Belgian population between 15 and 55 years old) reported all brand or product-related conversations in a structured manner for four consecutive weeks. Several findings were translated into actionable guidelines for word-of-mouth marketing. One of the main results showed the importance of facilitating questions as a way to create influence, rather than stimulating spontaneous (and often intrusive) evangelist actions. By stimulating website visitors to ask the right questions and matching this with well-informed answers, the impact of conversations can be increased up to 75% opinion change.

Summary

In contrast to primary data, which originate with the researcher for the specific purpose of the problem at hand, secondary data and marketing intelligence are data originally collected for other purposes. Secondary data can be obtained quickly and are relatively inexpensive though not free, especially for accurate, high-quality data. Secondary data have limitations, and should be carefully evaluated to determine their appropriateness for the problem at hand. The evaluation criteria consist of specifications, error, currency, objectivity, nature and dependability.

A wealth of information exists in the organisation for which the research is being conducted. This information constitutes internal secondary data. External data are generated by sources outside the organisation. These data exist in the form of published (printed) material, online and offline databases, or information made available by syndicated services. Published external sources may be broadly classified as general business data or government data. General business sources comprise guides, directories, indexes and statistical data. Government sources may be broadly categorised as census data and other data. Online databases may be online or offline. Both online and offline databases may be further classified as bibliographic, numeric, full text, directory or specialised databases.

Syndicated sources are companies that collect and sell common pools of data designed to serve a number of clients. Syndicated sources can be classified based on the unit of measurement (households and consumers or institutions). Household and consumer data may be obtained via surveys, purchase or media panels, or electronic scanner services. When institutions are the unit of measurement, the data may be obtained from retailers or industrial units. It is desirable to combine information obtained from different secondary sources.

Several specialised sources of secondary data are useful for conducting international marketing research. The evaluation of secondary data becomes even more critical, however, because the usefulness and accuracy of these data can vary widely. Ethical dilemmas that can arise include the unnecessary collection of primary data, the use of only secondary data when primary data are needed, the use of secondary data that are not applicable, and the use of secondary data that have been gathered through morally questionable means. The growth of online sources of externally generated secondary data has exerted demands upon researchers to be able to access, integrate and interpret these data. The emergence of social media research techniques has generated not only new research techniques, but also new forms of data that could raise questions about what constitutes 'secondary data' and 'marketing intelligence'.

Questions

1 What are the differences between primary data, secondary data and marketing intelligence?

2 What are the relative advantages and disadvantages of secondary data?

3 At what stages of the marketing research process can secondary data be used?

4 Why is it important to locate and analyse secondary data before progressing to primary data?

5 How may secondary data be used to validate qualitative research findings?

6 What is the difference between internal and external secondary data?

7 How can intranets help in the location and dissemination of secondary data?

8 By what criteria may secondary data be evaluated?

9 What criteria would you look for when examining the design and specifications of secondary data? Why is it important to examine these criteria?

10 To what extent should you use a secondary data source if you cannot see any explicit objectives attached to that research?

11 If you had two sources of secondary data for a project, the first being dependable but out of date, the second not dependable but up to date, which would you prefer?

12 Evaluate the desirability of using multiple sources of secondary data and intelligence.

13 List and describe the main types of syndicated sources of secondary data.

14 Explain what an online panel is, giving examples of different types of panel. What are the advantages and disadvantages of online panels?

15 What is an audit? Describe the uses, advantages and disadvantages of audits.

Exercises

1 Select an industry of your choice. Using secondary sources, obtain industry sales figures and the sales of the major firms in that industry for the past year. Estimate the market shares of each major firm. From another source where this work may have already been completed, e.g. Mintel, compare and contrast the estimates:

   a To what extent do they agree?

   b If there are differences in the estimates, what may account for these differences?

2 Select an industry of your choice. Write a report on the potential growth in that industry and the *factors* that are driving that growth. Use both secondary data and intelligence sources to build your case.

3 Using your library's online databases, search through secondary data sources to gather data on the use of celebrities in the promotion of fashion brands. You are conducting a marketing research project to determine the effectiveness of celebrity endorsements in Louis Vuitton Moet Hennessy (**www.lvmh.com**). What secondary data sources have you found to be the most useful? As a Marketing Director at LVMH, how would you use secondary data that describe celebrity endorsement investments to determine whether you should continue to use celebrities in LVMH advertising campaigns?

4 Visit the Central Statistics Office Ireland website (**www.cso.ie/links/**) and follow a link to the national statistics office in a country of your choice. Write a report about the secondary data available from this office that would be useful to a national housing developer for the purpose of formulating its marketing strategy

5 In a small group discuss the following issues: 'What are the significance and limitations of government census data for researchers?' and 'Given the growing array of alternative data sources that describe characteristics of individuals and households in a country, would it be a disaster for researchers if formal government censuses were scrapped?'

Video case exercise: Acme whistles

Acme wish to conduct in-depth interviews with b2b buyers who purchase (or could purchase) its whistles for sports-related applications. Given it growing international presence, Acme would like to reach out to participants across the globe. How would you use secondary data and intelligence to target the right participants to interview?

Notes

1. Peters, J., Appleby, M. and LaRue, S., 'Virgin USA – a 21st century approach to brand development', ESOMAR, Annual Congress, Montreal (September 2008).

2. Fleisher, C.S., 'Using open source data in developing competitive and marketing intelligence', *European Journal of Marketing* 42 (7/8) (2008), 852–866; Rothberg, H.N. and Erickson, G.S., *From knowledge to intelligence: creating competitive advantage in the next economy* (Burlington, MA: Butterworth–Heinemann, 2005); Aguilar, F.J., *Scanning the Business Environment* (London: Macmillan, 1967).

3. Adapted from Brownlie, D., 'Environmental scanning', in Baker, M.J., *The Marketing Book*, 3rd edn (Oxford: Butterworth–Heinemann), 158.

4. Sampson, A. and Guard, K., 'Green actions offer consumer value and environmental benefit', *Admap*, Issue 500 (December 2008), 22–25.

5. Mitchelson, L., 'Gathering business intelligence in China – the ups and downs', *Admap Magazine, China supplement* (February 2008).

6. Neves, M.A., 'Strategic marketing plans and collaborative networks', *Marketing Intelligence & Planning* 25 (2) (2007), 175–192; Rothberg, H.N. and Erickson, G.S., *From knowledge to intelligence: creating competitive advantage in the next economy* (Burlington, MA: Butterworth–Heinemann, 2005), 21.

7. Dugmore, K., 'Viewpoint: public information – now it's time to make it freely available', *International Journal of Market Research* 49 (2) (2007), 153–154.

8. For applications of secondary data, see Allen, L. and Spencer, N., 'Managing knowledge, maximising returns – revolutions in business information management', ESOMAR,Congress, Montreux (September 2009); Houston, M.B., 'Assessing the validity of secondary data proxies for marketing constructs', *Journal of Business Research* 57 (2) (2004), 154–161; Kotabe, M., 'Using Euromonitor database in international marketing research', *Journal of the Academy of Marketing Science* 30 (2) (Spring 2002), 172.

9. Foan, R., 'Measuring media internet', *Admap* Issue 496 (2008), 28–31.

10. Piercy, N.F., 'Evolution of strategic sales organizations in business-to-business marketing', *Journal of Business & Industrial Marketing* 25 (5) (2010), 349–359; Lawson, J., 'Buying behaviour', *Database Marketing* (October 2004), 35–38.

11. Allen, L. and Green, C., 'Connecting insight with the organisation: knowledge management online', *Market Research Society, Annual Conference* (2006); Fries, J.R., 'Library support for industrial marketing research', *Industrial Marketing Management* 11 (February 1982), 47–51.

12. Tasgal, A., 'Inspiring insight through trends', Market Research Society, Annual Conference (2009).

13. Jackson, M., Gider, A., Feather, C., Smith, K., Fry, A., Brooks-Kieffer, J., Vidas, C.D. and Nelson, R., 'Electronic Resources & Libraries, 2nd Annual Conference 2007', *Library Hi Tech News* 24 (4) (2007), 4–17.

14. Saw, G., Lui, W.W. and Yu, F., '2010: a library odyssey', *Library Management* 29 (1/2) (2008), 51–66 ; Tenopir, C., 'Links and bibliographic databases', *Library Journal* 126 (4) (1 March 2001), 34–35.

15. Vir, J., Simpson, I. and Brown, K., 'Making the news', Market Research Society, Annual Conference (2009).

16. Anon., 'Clients speak their minds about UK ad agencies', *WARC News* 1 February (2008).

17. Lekakos, G., 'It's personal: extracting lifestyle indicators in digital television advertising', *Journal of Advertising Research* 49 (4) (December 2009), 404–418.

18. Bennett, G., Ross, M., Uyenco, B. and Willerer, T., 'Lifestyles of the ad averse: a proposal for an advertising evaluation framework', ESOMAR, Worldwide Multi Media Measurement (WM3), Dublin (June 2007).

19. Hu, Y., Lodish, L.M., Krieger, A.M. and Hayati, B., 'An update of real-world TV advertising tests', *Journal of Advertising Research* 49 (2) (June 2009), 201–206.

20. Nyilasy, G. and Reid, L.N., 'The academician-practitioner gap in advertising', *International Journal of Advertising* 26 (4) (2007), 425–445.

21. Peacock, J. and Bennett, M., 'It can be measured', *Research World* (September 2005), 70–71.

22. ESOMAR, 'Global Market Research', ESOMAR Industry Report (2010), 104.

23. Bryant, J.A. and Christensen, L., 'I want MySpace! Helping an industry innovator (re)innovate', ESOMAR, Online Research, Berlin (October 2010).

24. Roberts, A. and Bristowe, L., 'Targeting ad responders', *Admap Magazine* Issue 486 (September 2007).

25. Comley, P., 'Panel management and panel quality issues – understanding the online panellist', ESOMAR, Conference on Panel Research, Budapest (April 2005); Eunkyu, L., Hu, M.Y. and Toh, R.S., 'Are consumer survey results distorted? Systematic impact of behavioural frequency and duration on survey response errors', *Journal of Marketing Research* 37 (1) (February 2000), 125–133.

26. Clancy, K.J., 'Brand confusion', *Harvard Business Review* 80 (3) (March 2002), 22; Sudman, S., *On the Accuracy of Recording of Consumer Panels II, Learning Manual* (New York: Neal-Schumen, 1981).

27. Sassinot-Uny, L. and Gadeib, A., 'Panel satisfaction index. Quality target for online access panels owners?' ESOMAR, Panel Research, Orlando (October 2007).

28. de Jong, K., 'CSI Berlin: the strange case of the death of panels', ESOMAR, Online Research, Berlin (October 2010).

29. Kondo, T., 'Creating a win-win relationship by maximizing both manufacturer sales and retailer profits', ESOMAR, Asia Pacific Conference, Tokyo (March 2005).

30. Mareck, M., 'From fragmentation to integration', *Research World* (September 2007), 48–50.

31. Examples of scanner data applications include González-Benito, O., Martínez-Ruiz, M.P. and Mollá-Descals, A., 'Latent segmentation using store-level scanner data',

Journal of Product & Brand Management 17 (1) (2008), 37–47; Lemon, K.W. and Nowlis, S.M., 'Developing synergies between promotions and brands in different price-quality tiers', *Journal of Marketing Research* 39 (2) (May 2002), 171–185; Chintagunta, P.K., 'Investigating category pricing behaviour at a retail chain', *Journal of Marketing Research* 39 (2) (May 2002), 141–154.

32. Wiesser, B., Brenikov, D. and Soliman, A., 'Comfort Fabric Conditioner – Comfort challenges the "rules" and wins big in South-East Asia', Institute of Practitioners in Advertising, Silver, IPA Effectiveness Awards (2010).

33. Imms, M., 'So, what are we talking about? What the 50th anniversary collection of conference papers tell us about market research in the UK today', Market Research Society, Annual Conference (2007).

34. Chisnall, P.M., 'Marketing research: state of the art perspectives', *Journal of the Market Research Society* 44 (1) (1st Quarter 2002), 122–125.

35. Zhang, G.J., Tan, M.O. and Minghui, Z., 'Market research: the pathway from consumer needs to final products', ESOMAR Asia Pacific, Kuala Lumpur (April 2010).

36. Kachhi, D. and Link, M.W., 'Too much information: does the Internet dig too deep? *Journal of Advertising Research* 49 (1) (March 2009), 74–81.

37. Kung, A., and Tse, G., 'The evolving role of in-house market research professionals: from "reactive" to "proactive"', ESOMAR Asia Pacific, Beijing (April 2009).

38. Woodnutt, T. and Owen, R., 'The research industry needs to embrace radical change in order to thrive and survive in the digital era', Market Research Society, Annual Conference (2010).

39. Kaufmann, R. and Wakenhut, G., 'Crossing the frontier – the fusion of research, consulting and creativity', ESOMAR Annual Conference, Montreal (September 2008).

40. Antilli, L. and Vishney, A., 'Digital media and technology in youth audience research', *Admap Magazine*, Issue 498 (October 2008).

41. Wiesenfeld, D., Bush, K. and Sikdar, R., 'The value of listening: heeding the call of the snuggie', *Journal of Advertising Research* 50 (1) (2010), 16–20.

42. Anon., 'SENSOA – all about sex', WARC Word of Mouth Marketing Awards (2008).

5

Internal secondary data and the use of databases

Stage 1

Problem definition

Stage 2

Research approach developed

Stage 3

Research design developed

Stage 4

Fieldwork or data collection

Stage 5

Data integrity and analysis

Stage 6

Report preparation and presentation

The research industry needs to evolve in order to weather the digital storm of change that threatens to engulf it.[1]

Objectives

After reading this chapter, you should be able to:

1 describe the nature and purpose of researchers utilising internal sources of secondary data;

2 appreciate how different types of company databases have developed into powerful means to understand customer behaviour;

3 understand how geodemographic information systems can help in integrating and displaying customer data;

4 understand how customer relationship systems can capture and model customer data and thus support marketing research;

5 understand how web analytics can capture and model customer data and thus support marketing research;

6 appreciate how different sources of customer data and marketing research can build up behavioural and attitudinal profiles of target markets;

7 appreciate the challenges of international data capture issues;

8 understand the ethical problems of having individual consumer data held on databases;

9 appreciate how different technological developments have increased the breadth of internally generated secondary data.

Overview

Marketing research as a function does not support marketing decision making in isolation. It is seen by many industry commentators as a component of strategic marketing intelligence. Huge information technology and system advances have been made in recent years that have fundamentally changed the way that marketing decisions are supported. These changes have shaped the expectations of decision-makers in terms of what they see as information they can rely on to help them make timely and effective decisions. As well as giving direct support to the marketer, new technology and systems advances can improve the quality of marketing research planning, implementation, analyses and interpretation.

This chapter describes how internal secondary data and databases have developed to make major impacts upon how decision-makers are supported. The data collected and analysed through database marketing can be seen as internally generated secondary data sources. As with all good secondary data sources, they have a major impact upon the conduct and direction of primary data collection, analyses and interpretation. There are also many quality and ethical issues that the marketing research industry is facing that relate to utilising internally generated customer data and the use of databases.

We introduce the chapter with examples of the use of databases, how they can directly support decision making, but also support the implementation of marketing research. Databases generated within companies or bought in from specialist sources are primarily viewed as a tool to generate direct sales and target promotion activities. However, internally generated customer databases are a secondary data source of immense value to researchers. Technological developments in the collection, analysis and presentation of internally generated secondary data present great opportunities to researchers. They also create conflicts with the core premise of participant anonymity in marketing research.

The first example illustrates how a customer database in the form of a customer relationship system (CRM) was used to support the development of online surveys. The second example illustrates how a customer database was interrogated and enhanced with the use of geodemographic data in order to develop more refined descriptions of customer segments and to model behaviour.

| Real research | **Creation of a pan-European online customer panel for Nintendo[2]** |

Nintendo wished to develop a platform to integrate online customer surveys with data stored in its CRM system. Globalpark (**www.globalpark.com**) worked in close cooperation with Nintendo to develop a workflow that networked its existing CRM system with Globalpark survey software. As a result, almost 1 million registered Nintendo customers could be managed and surveyed with its EFS (Enterprise Feedback System) Panel. An interface in the EFS Panel made it possible to extract samples from the customer database according to specific criteria such as socio-demographic features. The master data could be used to identify suitable participants for a specific survey. Collected data from the survey was then fed back into the integrated system. The entire survey process, from the development of the survey, the recruitment of participants from the Nintendo CRM system and the invitation via e-mail, to field control and the delivery of rewards at the end of the survey, could be coordinated using the EFS Panel. This process allowed Nintendo to conduct online product tests, customer satisfaction analyses, communications campaigns and ad hoc marketing research projects.

| Real research | **Geodemographics at Boden[3]** |

Boden (**www.boden.co.uk**) is renowned for catalogue-based retailing of high-quality women's, men's and children's clothing. Starting in 1991, Johnnie Boden delivered his first catalogue with only eight menswear pieces, Boden now sends out over 20 million catalogues per annum, and 500 employees jointly share responsibility for shipping more than 4,000 orders per day. In early 2001 Boden identified a requirement to gain better insight into its growing customer base and purchased smartFOCUS (**www.smartfocus. com**) Intelligent Marketing Analysis solutions. This enabled better customer segmentation with an increase in specific customer cells for targeting from 20 to 80 individual segments. Boden used the smartFOCUS analysis and visualisation, data mining and campaign planning solutions to enhance its understanding of the 2.2 million people on its database. 'Propensity to buy' information discovered through smartFOCUS indicated that the womenswear range was delivering faster growth than other ranges; specifically, menswear buyers had a higher lapse rate and were more likely to buy every other year. This type of customer knowledge helped Boden plan more accurately and to forecast more effectively. Its purchase of MOSAIC geodemographic data (**www.experian.co.uk/business-strategies**) to enhance the Boden customer view enabled even more sophisticated segmentation analyses. Boden improved response rates by profiling profitable customers and identifying groups of prospects with similar profiles for specifically targeted marketing promotions. In addition, improved product transaction history enabled models to be built ensuring that customer retention was maximised. The awareness and usage of this technology within Boden was also developing with even the clothing designers requesting profile information on customers to create a better picture of their target audience. Designers wanted to ensure that more of their products met customer expectations.

There is no doubt that the database analyses in the opening examples acted (or could act) as an excellent foundation for marketing research design in deciding who to research and what issues to focus upon. These examples may be seen as anathema to traditional researchers as they could be linked to direct marketing practices and the sanctity of research participant anonymity. However, decision-makers are confidently and increasingly using a breadth of information sources such as these examples, and researchers cannot ignore this. The growth and impact of these sources mean that an examination of the opportunities and challenges inherent in internally generated secondary data is vital; the practice of marketing research cannot be independent or 'siloed'.[4] There are arguments that the perceived value of 'traditional research' and methods based upon reported attitudes and behaviour are eroding. A key factor in this erosion is that 'consumer data' are now more abundant and automated. For example, web analytics provides masses of behavioural data on what consumers are looking for, what they do on a website, how they got there and critically whether they did what was wanted of them (e.g. buying a product). This behavioural data can carry more weight with decision-makers since what someone actually does could be considered more reliable than what they say, think, feel or plan to do. Similarly, online feedback and internally managed customer relationship management surveys are providing customer insight without necessarily involving marketing research in order to gather it.[5] Some of the challenges and opportunities generated by the growth of internally generated data are encapsulated in the views of three leading research practitioners in the following example.

Real research	**The enlightened researcher**[6]

Colin Shearer, of SPSS (**www.ibm.com/software/analytics/spss**):

I think in the future we will see a reassessment of where marketing research and related disciplines sit within an organisation. Historically, marketing research has been kept separate from things like CRM and marketing. There is a move to use the same techniques used to conduct surveys to collect feedback information from customers and act on it. The term that has been coined for this is 'Enterprise Feedback Management'. It uses the same tools and techniques as marketing research, but in a different way, so it needs to be reconciled with traditional marketing research as supplied by agencies.

Jim Spaeth, of the New York agency Sequent Partners (**www.sequentpartners.com**):

I think marketing research will continue to evolve. The 'digitalisation' of almost everything, and the creation of continuous data streams, not for research but to run the business will continue to change the nature of data collection from ad hoc to continuous. Analytic techniques will be validated through their empirical relationship with important business outcomes, all measured through the same enterprise data stream. Our emphasis will continue to move from data collection to data analysis and onto business decision support.

Clare Bruce, CEO of the Consumer Insight Agency Nunwood (**www.nunwood.com**):

There has been a stampede to use web technologies to collect data more quickly. We are using it to analyse data and devolve insight into our clients' organisations. We also collect data online, but all our research and development from the technology point of view has been focused on enabling clients to disseminate insight more quickly and effectively. Our market analytics division takes the data and provides clients with a more in-depth, more strategic view on how the data can help, and more and more they are being asked to undertake implementation programmes so clients don't just want answers to the questions, and insight, which is another layer on the raw data: they actually want us to tell them how to use it and guide their implementation.

The views in the above example illustrate not only the impact of new technologies and systems upon marketing research, but also the expectations of decision-makers of what marketing research should do to support them. The phenomenal growth in internally generated secondary data and the means to analyse, interpret and action these data have brought about much reflection and consternation within the marketing research industry as discussed in Chapter 1. The nature, value and challenges of internally generated secondary data have been hotly debated over recent years but this is not a new phenomenon. To reflect upon the roots of such debates it is worth examining what internal secondary data are.

Internal secondary data

Internal secondary data
Data held within an organisation for some purpose other than a research problem at hand.

Operational data
Data generated about an organisation's customers, through day-to-day transactions.

Chapter 4 described the nature, purpose and value of secondary data to researchers. A vital source of secondary data comes from within organisations that commission marketing research, namely internal secondary data. These data are generally seen as being drawn from operational data, i.e. data that represent the daily activities, transactions and enquiries of a business.

Daily transactions may be held in different departments such as sales, accounts or human resources and stored in different manners. The use of operational data has presented opportunities to researchers for as long as businesses have been recording their daily transactions. Even in the days of transactions being recorded manually, it has been invaluable for researchers to track down different sources of data and analyse them. The value of such data at all stages of the marketing research process means that locating and analysing internal sources of secondary data should be the starting point in any research project. The main reasons are that they are invaluable in defining the nature of a marketing decision problem and in defining who should be questioned or observed and the nature of questions and observations to be directed at these individuals. These reasons are fundamental to the quality, action orientation and perceived value of marketing research. In addition, as these data have already been collected, there are no additional data collection costs, there should be fewer access problems (though individual managers may make access difficult for personal or political reasons) and the quality of the data should be easier to establish (in comparison with externally generated data).

Most organisations have a wealth of in-house information even if they are not marketing or customer focused, so some data may be readily available. For example, imagine a shoe manufacturer that has traditionally sold shoes to retailers e.g. Grenson (**www.grenson. co.uk**). It creates invoices for all its sales to these business accounts. Its accounts department handles this process and maintains the data that it generates. Yet, there exists much consumer behaviour data in these invoices. They could be analysed by:

- What products do customers buy?
- Which customers buy the most products?
- Which customers repeat purchases?
- Which customers are more active when there are special offers?
- Where are these customers located?
- Which customers are the most loyal?
- Which customers are the most profitable?
- Seasonal patterns of purchasing behaviour by product types and customer types.

Grenson has also developed e-business capabilities, with a website that enables it to sell its shoes directly to consumers. In such an instance Grenson would have the ability (perhaps for the first time if it has not previously invested in marketing research) to understand the above characteristics of the final consumers of its products, rather than characteristics of the retailer intermediaries. Beyond transactional data, there may also be data that relate to promotional activities such as spending on advertising, trade fairs, sponsorship deals or personal selling. It is not unusual for large organisations to have a multiplicity of different data sources, e.g. sales orders, customer relationship management, assets, stock, distribution, advertising, marketing and accounting. Each of these operational data systems may have its own databases but there is no guarantee that these systems and databases are linked.[7] Thus the researcher may be faced with many discrete and/or integrated internal data sources from which characteristics of customers, their past behaviour and potential behaviour may be discerned. The norm for many companies is to integrate formally data about their customers and invest in developing and maintaining a customer database.

The customer database can be used to design and deliver marketing activities and strategies, and the response from these activities is fed back to improve and update it. Databases support techniques such as segmentation analysis, which at one time were developed from data gathered from relatively small samples collected at considerable expense. With a customer database, insights can be developed from larger samples obtained at almost no marginal cost as the data usually were gathered in the course of normal business operations.[8] A major development in how customer insight may be generated is through the use of store or loyalty cards. Such an example of a customer database is illustrated in the following example.

Customer database
A database that details characteristics of customers and prospects that can include names and addresses, geographic, demographic and buying behaviour data.

Real research

Consumer Zoom: the French experience on loyalty card data[9]

More than nine French households in ten hold at least one loyalty card from a hypermarket or supermarket brand name, and more than one in two participate in at least two programmes. Major retailers have information on several million clients with a detail by product (European Article Number – EAN-13 bar codes are product identification numbers) and this for each till receipt. The development of store loyalty programmes has enabled researchers to follow and analyse consumer behaviour at the point of sale. After several years dedicated to client recruitment and optimisation of their programmes, FMCG retailers are now reviewing the use of the huge databases generated by loyalty programmes. This information is first used to analyse purchases of store loyalty card holders, then to describe behavioural characteristics of these customers. An additional method of analysis now exists, thanks to the size of the fast-moving consumer goods stores' (FMCG) customer databases: the analysis of consumer behaviour on product categories and consumer reaction before marketing stimuli displayed by manufacturers and retailers. Marketing-Scan (**www.marketingscan.fr**) developed a Consumer Zoom approach through a partnership built with two French retailers, including the Auchan store (**www.auchan.fr**). One level of analysis performed by Consumer Zoom was the study of purchase habits by product category. Retailers as well as manufacturers are interested in this approach, as it is possible to find brand growth opportunities by analysing customers' purchase habits. The Auchan Consumer Zoom tool is built from a representative sample of 600,000 store loyalty card holders.

The essence of the Auchan Consumer Zoom example is that the scanned data of products sold in Auchan stores are linked to known customers: the system links customer identification to product usage. Any promotional offers, competitive activity, new product offerings, discounts, where to locate a new store, to name but a few marketing activities, can be analysed and related to classifications of customer. This example also illustrates one of the most prolific devices designed to capture customer behaviour data, i.e. the storecard or loyalty card.

Loyalty card
At face value, a sales promotion device used by supermarkets, pharmacists, department stores, petrol stations and even whole shopping centres and towns to encourage repeat purchases. For the researcher, the loyalty card is a device that can link customer characteristics to actual product purchases.

The loyalty card is the device that supermarkets, pharmacists, department stores, petrol stations and even whole shopping centres and towns have developed in order to link customer characteristics to actual product purchases.

The loyalty card may be offered to customers as they make a purchase in a store. Basic customer data can be gathered as customers normally complete an application form which may include their name and address, demographic details, household details, media usage and even some lifestyle characteristics. Once customers use their loyalty cards, the products they have purchased are scanned and a link can be made through the 'swiped' card to their characteristics that can then be related to the scanned data of their product purchases. In return, the customers earn 'points' for their total spend and may earn additional points for buying particular products.

From the researchers' perspective, many benefits also accrue from the internally generated secondary data from a loyalty card and product scanning system. The following list summarises the benefits to the researcher:

1 *Profiles of customers can be built up.* The types of individual who are being attracted to a store, particular types of products and responses to different types of promotion can be monitored. The returns and contributions made by particular types of customer can be measured. Profiles of the 'ideal' customer type can be built up, and plans developed to attract potential customers based upon these profiles.

2 *One big laboratory.* Experimental methods will be described in Chapter 11, but, in essence, the monitoring of customers, markets and interrelated marketing mix activities allows for many causal inferences to be established. For example, what is the effect, and upon whom, of raising the price of Häagen-Dazs ice cream by 10%? What is the effect of inserting a cutout coupon to give a discount on after-sun lotion, placed in *Cosmopolitan* magazine?

3 *Refining the marketing process.* With time series of responses to planned marketing activities, statistical models of consumer response can be built with associated probabilities of a particular outcome. Likewise, models of the consumers over their lifetimes can be built. Again, statistical models can be built with associated probabilities of particular types of product being bought at different stages of a consumer's life.

4 *Developing a clear understanding of 'gaps' in the knowledge of consumers.* The scanner and loyalty card electronically observe behaviour but do not encapsulate attitudinal data. The nature and levels of satisfaction, what is perceived as good-quality service, or what image is associated with a particular brand, are examples of attitudinal data. The use of the database helps to identify target populations to measure and the attitudinal data that need to be collected. In all, there can be a much greater clarity in the nature of primary marketing research that tackles attitudinal issues.

5 *Linking behavioural and attitudinal data.* If attitudinal data are elicited from consumers, the data gathered can be analysed in their own right. It is possible, however, to link the gathered data back to the behavioural data in the database. The term 'fusing' the data from different sources is used. The key to fusing lies in identifying individual participants so that one large dataset is built up. The notion of fusing together databases and survey data from different sources is at the heart of building a strong understanding of both the behaviour and motivation of consumers.

The iterative knowledge gained from consumer interactions mean that new targeted offerings can be formulated, and the nature of the customers' response can be recorded. Researchers and decision-makers can model and learn much about customers' behaviour from transaction data. They should also be able to see the gaps in their knowledge of the current and potential customers. The awareness of these gaps in knowledge can be the foundation of well-designed and actionable marketing research. In the development of good research designs, the customer database can be seen as a vital resource to the researcher when conducting internal secondary data searches. The idea of accessing a customer database represents a clear opportunity for researchers, but such a resource may not be singular and can be integrated with many other databases and systems. There are a whole array of different means to capture electronically customer transaction behaviour and even potential customers through their search for information to buy services and products. Some indication of their nature and impact is highlighted in the following example.

| Real research | # The BIMRMEMM threat to marketing research[10] |

BIMRMEMM is based upon three acronyms: BI, MRM and EMM. They may represent the largest long-term business model change for marketing research. BI (Business Intelligence) is a large multi-billion-dollar market category comprising systems that provide data warehouses and graphical user interfaces to access complex corporate data and insights from that data. BI companies have recently experienced a large wave of consolidation, with few large independent players remaining. These systems grew out of financial analysis systems, and deal well with large volumes of data and fact finding within the volumes of information. MRM stands for Marketing Resource Management. MRM is the software that handles marketing budgeting and planning. EMM, Enterprise Marketing Management, defines a category of software used by marketing organisations to manage their end-to-end process from gathering and analysing customer data across websites and other channels, to planning, budgeting and managing the creative production process, to executing targeted customer communications, to measuring results and effectiveness. EMM is a superset of other marketing software categories such as web analytics, campaign management, marketing resource management, marketing dashboards, lead management, event-driven marketing, customer relationship marketing (CRM), sales management and predictive modelling.

It is beyond the scope of this chapter to describe and evaluate the array of technologies, e-business methodologies and touchpoints with consumers as illustrated above. Many of these systems and technologies can be integrated and so pulling apart all these touchpoints with consumers represents a major task. We will, therefore, just concentrate on three major subject areas where internally generated data can be integrated with marketing research to produce greater consumer and marketing insights. A summary of how these can be integrated with marketing research will then be presented to illustrate the power of measuring and understanding consumers in different and integrated manners. The three areas are geodemographic data analyses, customer relationship management systems and web analytics.

Geodemographic data analyses

Geodemographic information system (GIS)
At a base level, a GIS is a business tool that matches geographic information with demographic information. This match allows subsequent data analyses to be presented on maps.

Insight gleaned from databases as illustrated in the preceding section can emerge from the linking of different data sources from operational data that relate to customers. The ability to create those links and to display analyses graphically has long been achieved with the use of a geodemographic information system (GIS). At a base level, a GIS is a business tool that matches geographic information with demographic information, allowing analyses to be presented on thematic maps. This base can be built upon with data from customer databases, databases from other sources and survey data. The combined data again can be presented on maps and in conventional statistical tables. Though the creation of geodemographic information systems comes from a variety of externally generated data sources, they have been instrumental in empowering decision-makers to make sense of their internally generated secondary

Thematic maps
Maps that solve marketing problems. They combine geography with demographic information and a company's sales data or other proprietary information.

data, namely customer databases. The earliest forms of GISs were developed in the early 1980s and were immediately a great success – not only their ability to integrate a disparate array of data sources, but also their ability to display analyses in a very clear and engaging manner.

The geographic dimension of where consumers live is vital as a base to the system. Growing up and living in different geographical locations can have an effect upon what consumers buy and the nature of their lifestyles. Look at the huge diversity of consumers around Europe! It is easy to see differences in consumers and their spending habits, between countries and regions within countries, between cities and towns and even areas within a town, and between different sides of a street. Differences can be seen between geographical locations that affect the lifestyle of residents, the array of products and services they buy, their ability to buy different types of products and services, and their hopes, fears and aspirations. The founding premise of a GIS is that the type of property a consumer lives in says much about the consumer's lifestyle and consumption patterns. For example, consumers living in small one-bedroom flats over shops in a city centre will tend to have very different lifestyles and consumption patterns from those living in large detached rural properties. Consumers in different property types have different propensities or probabilities of buying particular goods and services and of undertaking activities that make up their lifestyle. They also have different propensities to use and be exposed to different types of media.

From a marketing decision-making perspective, geography can be pivotal in strategic thinking. Knowing where one's consumers are located affects the means and costs of distribution. For example, should a new retail outlet be built and if so in which city and then in which part of that city? Which customers will have to pass our competitors in order to get to us? What features and facilities should the outlet have? The location of consumers also affects the means to communicate with them. Are consumers dispersed over a wide area or tightly clustered together? Do they read the same type of newspaper or magazine? Do they watch the same TV programmes or films at the cinema? Do they prefer to spend more time on Facebook or YouTube? The following example of the charity Sense Scotland shows how the organisation used geodemographic analyses to generate a greater depth of understanding their donors.

Real research	**Connecting to the 'Captains of Industry' – Sense Scotland**

Sense Scotland (**www.sensescotland.org.uk**) is a significant service-providing organisation that is engaged in policy development for children and adults with complex support needs because of deafblindness or sensory impairment, learning disability or physical disability. As part of an ongoing process of profiling and analysing its donor database, Sense Scotland commissioned CCR Data (**www.ccr.co.uk**) to find out about the types of donors who had previously been asked to convert from a home money box to a direct debit payment for donations. CCR analysed Sense Scotland's donor database using Experian's Mosaic Scotland consumer classification. This allowed CCR to assess Sense Scotland's previous performance with individual donor segments and its performance related to Mosaic Scotland groups. For example, Mosaic Scotland Type A01 'Captains of Industry' made up 6.67% of the donors who had been asked to convert. This type of consumer, the wealthiest in Scotland, made up only 1.92% of the population, which revealed that the original method of targeting donors had worked well. Further analysis showed that each person who had converted from the 'Captains of Industry' group had given 22% more than the average donor in regular gifts. Using Sense Scotland's donor database and Mosaic data, CCR was able to refine further the process of analysing donor profiles and behaviour prediction. Following this analysis, Sense Scotland made the decision to develop a completely new form of profiling the donors on its database.

One of the major factors that have seen decision-makers engage with geodemographics are the maps and other graphical devices used to present data analyses. Such data analyses can be used to portray a huge variety of consumer characteristics and essential differences between target consumers. A map can identify all properties in a country (or even countries), all roads, shopping centres and major facilities in towns and cities. Data related to where consumers live and shop can be easily portrayed on these maps. The data typically originate from a number of internal and external sources and have the common feature of being able to relate to a specific postcode or zip code. Examples of such a system are those produced by CACI (**www.caci.co.uk**) and Experian Mosaic (**www.experian.co.uk/business-strategies**). The CACI system has been well established in the UK for many years, giving detailed analyses of specific locations and specific industry types such as telecommunications, retailing and finance. Experian Mosaic is also well established in the UK but has also developed systems specifically tailored for a number of countries throughout the world. The sources and details of data available in each of the above countries differ, as does the legislation that determines what can be stored and analysed on databases. Typically for each country, statistics can be gathered and used to develop individual GISs based upon census data, postal address files, electoral registers, consumer credit data, directories of company directors, mail order purchase records, car registrations and data on access to retail outlets.

From the data collected, the purpose is to classify consumers on a geodemographic basis. Experian defines a geodemographic classification as follows:

Geodemographic classification

This groups consumers together based on the types of neighbourhood in which they live. If sets of neighbourhoods are similar across a wide range of demographic measures, they may also offer similar potential across most products, brands, services and media.

> *Geodemographic classification groups consumers together based on the types of neighbourhood in which they live. If a set of neighbourhoods are similar across a wide range of demographic measures, they will also offer similar potential across most products, brands, services and media.*

With the variables chosen for a particular country, i.e. the types of data that are available to build a GIS, cluster analyses are performed (Chapter 23 details the nature and purpose of cluster analysis). These analyses help to create consumer classifications, based upon the types of property the consumers live in and the propensity of consumers to have certain lifestyles and behave in particular manners. The analyses ensure that each of the descriptions used is reasonably homogeneous in terms of demographic measurements and consumer behaviour. As well as being able to discriminate and describe distinctive groups of consumers, the analyses produce 'pictures' of consumers that are meaningful to marketing decision-makers.

Experian has also produced 'Mosaic Global' (**www.experian.co.uk/business-strategies/ mosaic-global**) as a consistent segmentation system that covers over 380 million of the world's households. It is based on the proposition that the world's cities share common patterns of residential segregation. Each country has its ghettos of Metropolitan Strugglers, suburbs of Career and Family, and communities of Sophisticated Singles. In terms of their values and lifestyles, each type of neighbourhood can display strong similarities in whichever country it is found. Using local data from 25 countries and clustering methods, Experian has identified 10 distinct types of residential neighbourhood, each with a distinctive set of values, motivations and consumer preferences, which can be found in each of the countries. Mosaic Global uses the data from the national Mosaic classification systems for the following countries: Australia, Austria, Belgium, Canada, Czech Republic, Denmark, Finland, France, Germany, Greece, Hong Kong, Israel, Italy, Japan, Ireland, the Netherlands, New Zealand, Norway, Romania, Singapore, Spain, Sweden, Switzerland, the UK and the USA.

The resulting analyses have produced a classification of 10 main consumer types. The examples opposite describe characteristics of the Mosaic Global group labelled as *Sophisticated Singles*.

With a GIS, it is possible to pinpoint where the *Sophisticated Singles* are in any of the countries analysed, whether they are clustered in particular regions or cities, or whether they are dispersed. If one were to dig deeper within each country, there would be clear differences in the proportions of these groups between cities and regions. From these classifications and the data that can be added from other internal databases, models of behaviour can be developed for consumers in markets across the world. The profile of customers that a company has can

Example	Sophisticated Singles

Sophisticated Singles contains young people, mostly single and well educated, who positively enjoy the variety and stimulation afforded by life in large cities. Typically international in their outlook and with a rich network of personal contacts, they are quick to explore and adopt new social and political attitudes and are important agents of innovation, in terms of both lifestyles and the adoption of consumer products. Most are at the stage of their lives when the development of 'human' capital, i.e. skills, contacts, knowledge, continues to take precedence over the maximisation of their incomes or indeed the accumulation of financial assets. Much of their income is spent on 'experiences', such as entertainment, eating out, travel, books and magazines, rather than on equipment. They exhibit a variety of household arrangements and typically marry and have children later in their lives. Such people gravitate towards the smarter downtown areas of major cities where they spend short periods of time living in small, rented apartments.

be compared with national, regional or city profiles. Data that are captured on customer databases can be mapped out. For example, ING Bank NV can map out which customers have responded to an offer to take out a personal loan at a discounted rate, as well as building up a profile of those who respond. In addition to customer behaviour from an organisation's customer database being added to the GIS, survey data can also be added. The key that would link the survey to the customer database may be either a named customer or a postcode. The following examples illustrates how geodemographic data from both Experian Mosaic and CACI have been integrated with marketing research techniques. In the first example, Experian's Mosaic was used to create more valid and reliable sampling frames for international surveys and more detailed analyses of target markets. In the second example, CACI's GIS was used after stages of qualitative interviewing and telephone interviewing were conducted.

Real research	Research Now and Mosaic

Research Now (**www.researchnow.com**) specialise in managing access panels across the globe and international online fieldwork for both business-to-consumer and business-to-business relationships. It has combined the details of its 2 million panel members with Experian's multi-country analysis (**www.experian.co.uk/business-strategies**). Mosaic classifies 1 billion consumers across 25 countries, covering Europe, the Americas and Asia-Pacific. The partnership enables international researchers to improve the design of their surveys through detailed sample definitions and selection, being able to monitor and manage sample quotas during fieldwork. With more detailed profiles of consumers available through this link, individual clients can have specific market segment specifications applied to their study which can be applied to survey findings in data analyses and tables.

Real research	Segmentation of the baby milk market[11]

The formula milk market has an unusual feature in that the vast majority of women will have given negligible thought to the product prior to becoming pregnant, and because of the intent and encouragement to breastfeed, relatively little even during their pregnancy. When the time comes to buy the product, mothers are confronted with a bewildering choice of brands, milk types, pack and product formats and sizes. Somehow, they have

to make a decision on what is best for their baby and for themselves. SMA (**www.smanutrition. co.uk**) wanted to ensure that they were providing products, formats and communications which were in tune with mothers' complex needs. SMA established that a segmentation study was needed and thus established a cross-functional team of marketing, marketing research and sales personnel from SMA, researchers from Leapfrog (**www.leap-frogresearch.co.uk**) and management consultants. The first phase was to conduct qualitative research to deepen the understanding of mothers and their attitudes and behaviour, particularly in respect of feeding patterns and choices. Leapfrog ran 38 paired in-depth interviews across the UK and Ireland that including first-time and subsequent mothers. The qualitative research produced a wealth of data on mothers, their influences and decision processes and also theories on market segmentation which needed quantitative validation and refinement. The second phase was to conduct telephone interviews of first-time pregnant women, first-time mothers and subsequent mothers. A key factor in the choice of telephone interviewing was the need for a very wide geographical dispersion so as to enable subsequent geodemographic modelling. The sampling frame used to contact participants was built from four sources: a commercial mailing list, the customer base of a leading retailer, callers to the SMA careline and the SMA Mums' Network. The telephone interviews covered full details of feeding behaviour and the influences on every decision made (e.g. the switch from a first milk to a milk for a hungrier bottle-fed baby). In addition there was extensive attitudinal information which formed the basis of developing segmentation. The development of a national set of segments was the first step towards realising the individual needs of the customer base at a level of detail never previously achieved. The starting point was to identify each segment down to postcode sector level. CACI (**www. caci.co.uk**) was commissioned to undertake this exercise, using its geodemographic tool ACORN. The task was achieved by matching key attributes in CACI lifestyle segments to those identified in the SMA customer segmentation exercise, resulting in SMA being able to identify the type of mother residing at each postcode sector level. The next step was to share the segmentation analyses and descriptions with the entire SMA division at a specially organised conference. A video was specifically created in order to bring each of the defined segments to life. The process helped to validate the accuracy of the segments based upon the salesperson's knowledge of different localities. The customer segmentation work provided SMA with strong evidence to help design its customer relationship (CRM) programme. The whole project also helped management consultants design a model for SMA, allowing the business to understand the core dynamics of the feeding experience by key stages in babies' development. This was the first time that SMA's market share data was based upon the number of customers (penetration figures) using infant formula, rather than volume and value sales. SMA experienced record levels of women joining their CRM programme and has seen more first-time bottle-feeding mothers than ever using the SMA brand, as measured by TNS (**www.tnsglobal.com**).

In this example, the organisation did not previously have a clear means to measure and understand its existing or potential customers. There was a distinct role and integration of qualitative and quantitative research that helped it to characterise its target markets. Geodemographic analyses helped the organisation to refine its profiles of target markets and get a sense of the potential markets and with its research data, to understand what would be needed to turn prospective customers into actual customers. Having used geodemographics in this study, SMA can subsequently map out and form graphical representations of customers' behaviour, their attitudes and their levels of satisfaction; there is much that could be achieved in representing characteristics of how SMA customers relate to its brand. Of note also in this example is how the data and analyses of customers were used as a foundation for the CRM programme. We continue by examining the nature and impact of (CRM) tools that have emerged from the database marketing and geodemographics industries. Remember that the customer data generated in the following evaluation of CRM systems can be mapped out using GISs.

Customer relationship management

Customer relationship management
The processes involved in the identification of profitable customers and/or customer groups and the cultivation of relationships with these customers. The aim of such processes is to build customer loyalty, raise retention rates and therefore increase profitability.

The foundation of customer relationship management (CRM) is to analyse and target the right people with the 'right offers', aiming to understand profitability trends at the individual customer level, to know who to target, why and with what.[12] Marketing decision-makers continue to realise the benefits of analysing customer data held within operational databases within their organisations. This realisation and the technological developments in collecting, analysing and presenting insight in customer generated data have developed into the concept and practice of CRM. CRM definitions can vary but in essence the concept can be seen as:

> *The processes involved in the identification of profitable customers and/or customer groups and the cultivation of relationships with these customers. The aim of such processes is to build customer loyalty, raise retention rates and therefore increase profitability.*[13]

The growth of CRM has emerged from the use and subsequent integration of various direct marketing channels (direct mail, telemarketing) and the rise of e-business, e-communication and the increasing use of the Internet as a conduit for customer care and sales.[14] In the same manner that consumer insights generated from social media sources have impacted upon the practice of traditional marketing research, CRM practitioners are integrating social media data with internally generated customer data.[15] The main challenge of implementing CRM is to integrate customer data from the post, telephone, personal visits, e-business and social media into a central database so that it holds all transactions and contacts with each customer (and indeed browsing, potential customers) allied with the ability to update the data constantly and to access them immediately whenever necessary.[16] The principles of CRM are straightforward: organisations gather accurate data about their customers and prospects from all the sources that contact or engage with them. They analyse and sometimes model these data to generate insight into the behaviour of different customers. They can then formulate marketing strategies and offerings that differentiate between customer segments, sometimes differentiating down to the individual customer level. Greater resources can be focused on higher value or higher prospect customers. Every opportunity is used to amass additional data about each customer to personalise offerings and build a closer relationship[17] and indeed to build stronger models of customer behaviour. The following example illustrates how the fashion retailer Debenhams has used customer data generated through its storecard and CRM system to help model and predict customer behaviour.

Real research   **Customer analytics are in style at Debenhams**[18]

As one of the most successful fashion retailers in the UK, Debenhams (**www.debenhams.com**) has to create the best possible customer experience and needs to understand what its customers want from its 139 stores. Understanding customer shopping habits can be seen as crucial for any retailer and identifying trends early can be critical to success. Debenham's team of analysts was responsible for researching and evaluating all aspects of the customer relationships, including analysing customer buying habits as well as marketing campaigns and activity around new store openings. Debenhams used SPSS's Predictive Analytics (**www-01.ibm.com/software/analytics/spss**) to support three areas of the analytics team's work: (1) supporting planning and decision making within buying and merchandising; (2) supporting marketing and CRM activity; (3) analysing potential new stores. Using the software, the analytics team could look at which special offers were generating the most sales, as well as identifying 'cross-sell' opportunities; for example, if a customer buys a new shirt, which tie was the customer most likely to buy to go with it? The team also applied analytics to understand why some lines were selling better than others. The SPSS tool has also played a crucial role in the lifecycle of new store openings, from strategy to actual openings. This included preparing the initial business case, evaluating the optimum mix of product lines to carry, through to evaluating marketing campaigns for the new store.

The use of the term 'CRM' has grown rapidly over past years and now encompasses many functions associated with superior customer service and management, relationship building and electronic shopping. CRM often includes sales force and front office applications that assist in customer interaction, addition of customer and product information, and sometimes have the ability to integrate with other operational systems, including finance, inventory and ERP (Enterprise Resource Planning) to develop a full e-business or Web-based system.[19] There is no doubting the value and impact of CRM systems in generating customer insight, but for researchers the means by which data are generated on individual customers can generate conflicts with the fundamentals of their code of practice. The ESOMAR International Code on Market and Social Research states in its 'Basic Principles':[20]

> Market research shall be clearly distinguished and separated from non-research activities including any commercial activity directed at individual participants (e.g. advertising, sales promotion, direct marketing, direct selling etc.).

Participant anonymity has been a hallmark of bone fide marketing research for as long as it has been professionally practised. However, in its Global Market Research Report of 2010, ESOMAR recognised that one of the biggest threats to the industry lies in the alternative data sources that decision-makers use, which clearly includes customer insight generated from CRM data:

> As CRM databases improve, a growing amount of data collection needs to be non-anonymous and linked to customer databases – at the moment marketing research is not well placed to contribute to that process.[21]

The dilemmas faced by researchers, who recognise the value of customer insight generated through CRM systems, are presented in the following example.

Real research	**Playing the Egg game**[22]

The online bank Egg (**www.egg.com**) was launched in 1997 and offered a full range of financial services including credit cards, savings, insurances, mortgages and loans to over 3 million customers. Its customers needed to be online in order to buy products and access its services. Therefore Egg was able to deal with all of its customers online through its website and by email using a call centre to service certain aspects of its products. One of Egg's strategic aims was to help customers achieve the outcomes they wanted in their life using financial services products to do that. However, consumers often made choices about such products without sufficient knowledge of whether the products purchased were the most suitable for them. Egg's strategy, '*To transform how our customers feel about life by enabling them to progress what they want through making informed choices about their money*', has integrated insight generated from customer interviews at key moments in customers' relationship with the bank. Achieving a high level of emotional engagement with customers (e.g. their hopes, fears and aspirations) was a central part of this strategy. Confirmit's Enterprise Feedback Management (EFM) (**www.confirmit.com**) was used to help in this engagement through the measurement of customer experiences. Through this system, surveys delivered by Egg were pre-populated with data from its CRM systems. During calls to the contact centre, customers were asked to quantify their experience of the call, their attitudes to Egg and their financial situation. To personailse the contact, surveys and email invitations included relevant information including the name of the agent, the data and time of the call and the subject under discussion. Responses that indicated dissatisfaction generated an alert to the call centre leading to a follow-up call to resolve the issue with the customer. Online surveys included open-text responses to give customers the chance to tell their side of the story. These were incorporated into the alerts and reports to management. Customers' comments prompted analyses within insight workshops in which management and team members participated. These were monitored by the quality team and through waves of customer insight feedback. This programme was successful because online surveys were used as a proactive relationship management tool and, since it began, Egg has seen higher savings and provisions for bad and doubtful debts, and a significant rise in the total value of acounts.

In this example, the researchers at Egg who designed their online surveys faced a clear dilemma. If a customer was surveyed and expressed a problem with service delivery or any other aspect of his or her account, how would the researchers cope with the personal details of the 'participant'? Would they pass the problem as expressed by their dissatisfied customer onto others in the organisation to resolve the issue as quickly as possible or aggregate the details of this problem in an anonymous manner with other survey responses as may be deemed consistent with ESOMAR's Code of Conduct? Egg decided that it simply had to respond to the individual requests and complaints of the customers. It recognised that the survey and the individual response to the survey were totally integrated into the customers' experience of the bank. With the support of consultants and software Egg managed to cope in servicing the individual needs of its customers. It was also able to cope quickly with the huge number of open-ended responses to survey questions and form aggregated responses to see if patterns were emerging in the nature of problems that customers were experiencing. The following example explains how Egg achieved this.

| Real research | **Cracking the code: what customers say, in their own words**[23] |

An important part of achieving an emotional engagement with customers was not only through carrying out extensive experience and event-based surveys online, but, crucially, in how Egg was able to respond to these both in aggregate and at an individual level, when a customer was experiencing a difficulty and had expressed this in a survey response. The research team at Egg had developed an *alerts system* whereby the team responded to customers who had expressed dissatisfaction through low scores in rating-scale questions; this was triggered from a closed-survey question. The next step was to interpret and categorise the emotions expressed in the thousands of verbatim comments that Egg received and ultimately generate alerts from the open-ended verbatim in the same way as had been implemented successfully for closed-survey questions. Open-ended questions remain a perennial feature of most quantitative surveys, yet extracting the meaning and value from them is usually the weakest link in the research process. The move to online research has exacerbated the problem, as participants tend to be more generous and expansive in their responses. At the same time, online research raises the expectation of near-instant reporting and actioning of all the results, which had been impossible to achieve where verbatim response data are involved. An important challenge of online research was thus analysing the large quantities of verbatim text returned by participants in answer to open-ended questions, so as to allow prompt response both at an individual level and at an aggregate level. The sheer volume of responses received had made any systematic analysis of them impossible. In partnership with meaning ltd (**www.meaning.uk.com**), a research technology consultancy, Egg commissioned the Institute for the Science and Technology of Information of the Italian National Council of Research (ISTI-CNR). meaning ltd and ISTI-CNR built a novel software solution for the automatic analysis of the many thousands of verbatim comments collected through event and customer experience surveys conducted online. Unlike other automated or computer-assisted software, the system developed for Egg was novel in that it applied machine learning to the problem of analysing and classifying verbatim texts from open-ended questions. Since the software was implemented at Egg, dramatic savings in cost and time have been demonstrated, making comprehensive and highly systematic analysis of many thousands of verbatim responses cost effective.

The challenge faced by Egg is becoming common in many organisations, especially those that engage with their customers online. Their CRM data helped Egg create a more meaningful online survey that could be more personal, relevant and better focused for participants. The survey responses fed into the CRM system that ultimately helped to deliver more satisfying experiences for their customers. Researchers may argue that the research experience and the brand experience should be kept far apart. However, almost any interaction consumers have within a branded context will influence their perceptions of that brand and if the research part of that experience is dull and turgid but, more importantly, they cannot see that their efforts will bring any personal benefits, then that will reflect back on the brand in a negative manner. Consumers do not tend to separate their worlds into neat little boxes; a survey on the back of a coupon from a retailer that asks them to text their opinion to a number for a survey is a brand touchpoint. The survey that follows is not suddenly seen as disconnected from the retail experience. Consumers do not tend to think: 'I just had a lovely brand experience and now I am going to enter a marketing research experience that is a separate phase of my life and I will now disassociate it from the earlier brand experience'. There are still many situations when a more neutral experience is needed that does not tie marketing research to the brand, but research where the experience is boring and has no personal benefits reflects badly on the brand experience of the consumer.[24] These views are fundamental to the design of survey and questionnaire experiences and will be further developed in Chapters 10 and 13. As in the Egg example, a key element of CRM systems is the customer data generated from website interactions.

Web analytics

There are very few organisations today that do not have their own website. The functionality of organisation websites can vary enormously from a simple display of characteristics of that organisation (a basic digital brochure), through to a range of e-business models where consumers may buy products. As well as selling products or services, websites may be designed to encourage consumers to visit retail outlets, share their views and interact with the organisation or other consumers in a variety of manners. Organisations can use their websites to facilitate a whole array of consumer experiences that may enhance their brand equity, as well as more obviously making sales. For many organisations, their website offers a great opportunity to 'reach over' retailers (who may traditionally hold much end consumer data) and communicate directly with final consumers, and, more importantly from a researcher's perspective, learn about their customers. Reaching out to final customers and building knowledge of them are illustrated in the following example.

Real research   **P&G to consolidate database for 360-degree consumer insights[25]**

In 2010, Procter & Gamble claimed it would have a new vision in place. For three years it had been exploring and mining data on its 120 brands which were analysed individually through its own brand web platforms. P&G did not have aggregated data on individuals who bought across its brands and its new vision was to achieve this, generating what it saw as a 360-degree view of each customer's interaction with P&G. Everything it collects it sees as 'one-to-one' marketing and so anything it can identify about customer behaviour will go into one big database. The goal of P&G's centralised customer information centre was driven by behavioural data online that allowed insight into individual preferences. P&G see that it will be able to perform better targeting, a better understanding of consumer behaviour, especially how that behaviour relates to its channels. With these data, P&G will clearly identify which consumers it should target, and not spend beyond that boundary. P&G plans to cross-sell, upsell and portfolio-sell, which it sees as relationship selling with some of its most important prime prospects.

As in the P&G example, many organisations see the great opportunities afforded to them in measuring and understanding how existing and prospective customers interact with their websites. This knowledge not only helps the organisations to improve the design and offerings of their website, it can help them to function better as competitive organisations. The process of measuring and understanding the interaction with, and impact of, a website can

Web analytics
The process of collection, measurement and analysis of user activity on a website to understand and help achieve the intended objective of that website.

be broadly termed web analytics. This can be seen as the process of collection, measurement and analysis of user activity on a website to understand and help achieve the intended objective of that website. As well as focusing upon their own customers, organisations may also include activities such as competitor web analysis, which is the practice of assessing and analysing strengths and weaknesses of competing websites. In the context of internally generated secondary data, web analytics can enable researchers and decision-makers to build upon existing customer data. Handled correctly, researchers can undertake behavioural analyses of customers that with good base data can enhance known demographic, geographic and other behavioural characteristics. As well as developing profiles of customers, analyses can be performed to gauge how existing and potential customers respond to different stimuli (advertising, marketing and customer service).

Web analytics can make it possible to track every page viewed, every element 'moused over', every menu dropped down, every key pressed, every video watched. Tracking techniques can collect the most complete picture of what a visitor does on a site, even capturing data entered into a form that the visitor chooses not to submit.[26] When linked to other databases within an organisation or integrated with a GIS or CRM system, this form of electronic observation can measure and model customers in ways that marketing research techniques may find impossible to replicate. In the tracking and analysis of web interactions, knowledge of customers can be created. Figure 5.1 summarises this process starting from individual website clicks being captured, through to an understanding of how visitors (which includes potential customers that turn into customers – or not) are browsing a website. Once actual shopping takes place via the website, further customer details and their behaviour can be recorded and modelled. This figure highlights the important distinction between 'browsing' and 'shopping' behaviour and what insight can be developed as a potential customer moves to become an actual customer.

Figure 5.1

Building consumer profiles from website events

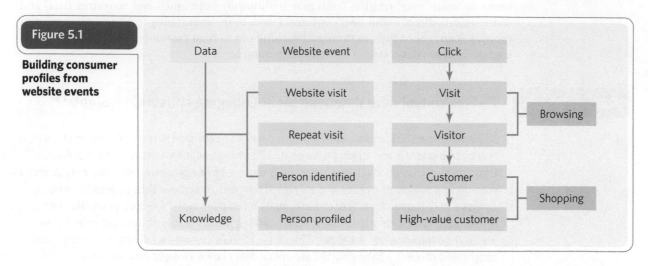

The value of measuring and understanding browsing and actual purchasing behaviour is illustrated in the following example. Holiday and travel industries have seen major competitive changes and pressures through consumers being able to organise and buy products and services directly from websites. This example shows how Thomson Holidays have realised the benefits of these changes through capturing customer behaviour from its website.

Real research | ## Thomson Holidays: Behavioural Conversion Programme[27]

The holiday industry is hugely competitive, with tough challenges facing major operators in an industry where customer loyalty is hard won. Using enquirer tracking, email and web analytics, Thomson Holidays (**www.tuitravelplc.com**) developed its Engagement Warehouse which captured on- and offline pre-purchase behaviour on millions of customers and prospects. It combined historical transactions, live web and email click, search and select behaviour, retail store visits, and enquirer touchpoints to help it understand how customers and prospects acted before making a purchase. This was a strategic investment in a technical capability that allowed Thomson to know when its prospects were actively thinking about and planning holidays, what products they were considering and when they wanted to go. Thomson could identify individuals who were currently in the market, seek out those who want to go away at different times, to different places, with or without children, to 5-star hotels or budget products. It was a sophisticated data structure, with proprietary software, triggered web services, email and web content integration, delivering strategic and competitive advantage through eCRM services in a highly commoditised and price-sensitive market. The Engagement Warehouse extended Thomsons's understanding of customers' pre-purchase journey and was at the heart of a well-defined data strategy engaging all Thomson contacts, historical transactions, email engagement and web analytics. It revealed previously untapped analytical trends, tactical and strategic opportunities.

A huge array of web analytics products exist that range from the free version of Google Analytics (**www.google.com/analytics**) to a full enterprise-level implementation, including Web 2.0 analytics from companies like Omniture (**www.omniture.com**) and iJento (**www.ijento.com**). In a full-enterprise system, the integration of web-user data is included with other customer data sources. This is illustrated in Figure 5.2 where potential sources of customer touchpoints with an organisation are brought together to create enhanced customer profiles and models of their behaviour. This figure illustrates how a 'visitor' can connect with an organisation in a range of ways. Certain customers may choose to connect to and shop with an organisation in one way; others may use a range of methods to browse, plan, experience and finally make a purchase. Each of these connections may be deemed a visit. The use of a visitor profile database is illustrated in the following example of Europe's largest retailer, Tesco. The example shows how Tesco has used data from the loyalty card, plus web analytics data, to build customer profiles and targeted offerings. It also shows how Tesco builds and integrates smarketing research.

Figure 5.2

Visitor profile database

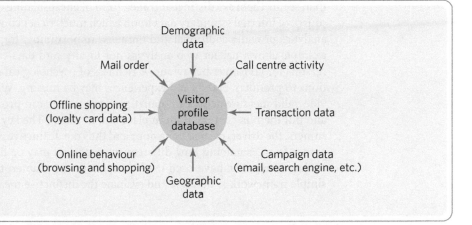

Real research

Tesco: integrating research and analytics[28]

The UK supermarket giant Tesco (**www.tesco.com**) first introduced its Clubcard in 1995, and now has an estimated 16 million members, equating to around three-quarters of the total number of people who shop at Tesco in the UK each week. Every purchase made in its stores delivers 45 separate pieces of information to the company, based around factors ranging from price to whether a customer has opted for an own-label or branded product, and a 'basic' or more unusual item. Tesco customers are sorted into a variety of different demographic profiles, such as whether they have children or pets, or whether they appear to make complex or simple meals. Dunnhumby (**www.dunnhumby.com**), the marketing firm that pioneered the Clubcard platform, and which is now owned by Tesco, assesses 100 transactions a second, or around 6 million shopping trips a day. Tesco also has a major online shopping facility, allowing it to identify and profile consumers that shop online and/or in-store. iJento (**www.iJento.com**) manages Tesco's web analytics, helping to coordinate its web 'Visitor Behaviour Information System'. The information that is generated through its databases helps Tesco decide which goods to stock, where promotional activity could boost sales, and even when it could expand its store brand range. Tesco has integrated its market research and analytics capability. In order to understand 'why' consumers are behaving in the way it has identified, Tesco can target specific customers, pre-populate the survey with known customer data, tailor questions that are specific to the behaviour of that customer and offer a reward that is meaningful to the customer. Tesco estimates that 16% of its margin is attributable to the knowledge it gets from its customer database. That makes the database a $3.2 billion asset. Alongside offering Tesco an insight into the behaviour of its customers, major FMCG firms such as Coca-Cola, Nestlé and Unilever pay to access these data.

Web analytics can reveal what consumers do online and how they respond to different pieces of digital communications. What consumers do online and what it physically means to be 'online' are changing dramatically. As with the marketing research and CRM industries, web analytics providers are seeking to understand and incorporate the impacts of Web 2.0 (and beyond).[29] The growth of social media interactions is adding richness and complexity to web analytics, providing decision-makers with not only masses of behavioural data on consumers, but also some attitudinal and emotional data. The wealth of data can carry more weight with decision-makers, as the capturing of what consumers actually do could be considered more reliable than what consumers say they think, feel or will do in response to survey questions. In a world where customer touchpoints and brand engagement are being constantly captured, the marketing research industry must take full advantage of these digital tools rather than seeing them as a distinct and alien form of encapsulating consumer behaviour. If seen as a source of internal secondary data upon which much richer consumer insights can be built, web analytics provides additional and immense opportunities for the researcher. As in the Tesco example above, neither web analytics nor loyalty card data can totally reveal the underlying reasons for consumer behaviour. A richness of psychological reasoning and emotive connections to products, brands and experiences may be missing. With the established skills to provide valid measurements of populations, researchers can provide datasets that bridge others and put them in context, both in place and in time.[30] The key to gaining rich insights of consumers, the drivers of their behaviour and thus the distinctive role and power of the researcher, comes from examining how different types of data may be linked and integrated. Examples of data integration have been used throughout the chapter; the following section presents a simple framework to describe and evaluate the distinctive means to encapsulate consumers.

Linking different types of data

The SMA, Egg and Tesco examples in the three sections above illustrate how different types of data can be linked to form more richer and powerful analyses of existing and potential customer characteristics. The following example takes these examples further by illustrating how Nestlé has made organisational changes that have delivered a stronger understanding of the nature, dynamics and influences upon its customers.

Real research	**Boosting consumer excellence at Nestlé[31]**

When Denyse Drummond-Dunn joined Nestlé in 2004, the company's sources of consumer information were fragmented. She set out to bring together three departments where consumer information was available: consumer services; consumer insights; and consumer relationship management. This integration of the three departments came after a major change in the way Nestlé developed consumer insights. The company built consumer insights on four different sources of information. A first source was market data, such as sales or media data. Second, it used information derived from consumer 'Safaris', e.g. during consumer events organised by Nestlé or during 'consumer experience sessions'. A third source was information developed through marketing research, both quantitative and qualitative. The fourth source consisted of data about the wider environment the company operates in, such as socio-economic trends or competitive activity data. 'Integrating information from different sources is not new', Denyse pointed out:

> *What is unique at Nestlé is that we not only integrate information from different sources, but also ensure that the ensuing consumer insights are actually applied when we take decisions. This is done in all business units and countries we operate in.*

These examples support what may be seen as one of the primary functions of supporting marketing decision-makers, i.e. helping them to build a clear vision of the nature and dynamics of their target markets. Traditionally this would be seen as performing segmentation analyses and using these analyses to define and select target markets. It is not intended to work through the theory, practice or implementation of segmentation or target marketing. However, it is worth examining how different data sources can be linked and integrated to make segmentation and targeting work more effectively. Figure 5.3 sets out five basic methods of segmenting markets. Individually, each of these methods delivers different levels of insight to decision-makers. They also demand that different types of data be captured, with differing challenges in that capturing process. The figure is somewhat deceiving in that it may imply that the process of building stronger profiles of consumers is a linear process and that once one level is complete, one moves on to the next. The reality is that consumers may be constantly changing and the building up of profiles of consumers is an iterative process and may never be complete. The examples in this chapter reveal that consumer data can be constantly updated to represent who the consumers are, where they are located, what they 'do' and why they behave in that manner (and indeed could behave).

Figure 5.3 gives examples of where data may be obtained from, to help build up profiles of customers and markets. In the example of 'psychographics' or lifestyle measurements, data may be generated from CRM databases, web analytics or surveys. In the case of CRM data and web analytics, the purchasing or even browsing of particular types of products can indicate characteristics of a lifestyle. In a more direct manner, questions in a survey or qualitative study can help to build a profile of lifestyle behaviour. In its own right, 'lifestyle' can be a valid means of segmenting a market, perhaps positioning products and services to consumers who aspire to a particular lifestyle. However, being able to combine demographic measurements, broader behavioural characteristics and a knowledge of where these consumers live helps to build a 'picture' of consumers that facilitates strong marketing decision-making support. Figure 5.3 indicates that as one moves from the demographic through to psychological characteristics the measurement and capturing process can become more difficult. Putting aside the differences in techniques to capture 'demography', 'behaviour' or 'psychology', what is being captured becomes more difficult as one moves towards psychological variables. If one considers psychological variables that are vital to marketing which could be captured, examples such as satisfaction, loyalty, trust and quality are not as easy to capture as questions such as gender, age or where one lives. Chapter 12 will explore the concept of measurement in more depth, but at this stage consider what 'satisfaction' actually means, and then the problems of measuring that concept in a valid and consistent manner.

Conversely, as the measurements become more difficult to conduct, they add more to the 'picture' of consumer and market profiles. To say that a market is primarily female, aged

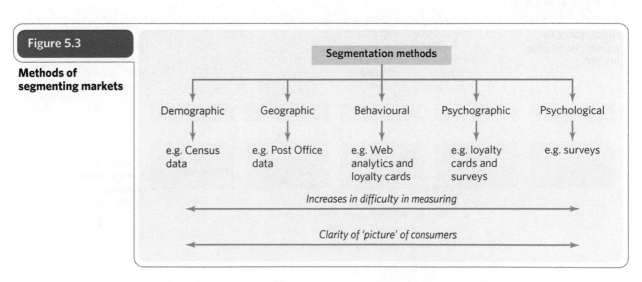

Figure 5.3

Methods of segmenting markets

between 25 and 40, and lives in a detached property with a mortgage starts to build a very basic 'picture' of target consumers. To add details of their media behaviour, the array of products and services they buy, characteristics of their lifestyle and even something of their dreams and aspirations in life can help to build up a rich and, for decision-makers, a much more powerful 'picture' of target consumers. Examining the variety of data sources that can be used in an interrelated manner to build market profiles, it is clear to see distinct contributions from externally generated secondary data founded in GISs, transactional scanned data, loyalty card data, customer data in CRM systems, web analytics data, the use of traditional survey work and indeed other forms of quantitative and qualitative marketing research. The challenges in integrating these sources together can be summarised as:

1   *Data challenges.* To source, gather, validate, store, integrate, feed, model, analyse and interpret internal and externally generated quantitative and qualitative data.

2   *Information systems challenges.* To manage this array of data, develop and support emergent marketing knowledge in an organisation.

3   *Marketing challenges.* To keep abreast of the nature and dynamism of what should be an organisation's target markets and performance in those markets.

There is a clear interdependence among the different data sources and, as in the Nestlé example, with the will and means to integrate these sources, much more powerful consumer insights can be generated. The main approaches to generating consumer insight can be summarised as in Figure 5.4. Though each of the four segments is presented as a distinct approach, and there are organisations that deliver these distinct specialisations, there is much overlap in how they work.

This overlap is especially prevalent in the development and use of social media research as introduced in Chapter 1 and as discussed and illustrated in most chapters of this book. Experts in CRM, web analytics, business intelligence as well as marketing research see the development of their discipline tightly interwoven to developments in social media research. This social media research has the potential to add many psychological characteristics of consumers, and as such has much to add to the other three approaches laid out in Figure 5.4. The explosion of data generated through social media and Internet developments could well lead to far more integration between these approaches. This explosion and its impact are described in the following example, from 'Using math marketing to increase your return on investment' by Dimitri Maex (Head of Global Data Practice, Ogilvy & Mather Worldwide, **www.ogilvy.com**).

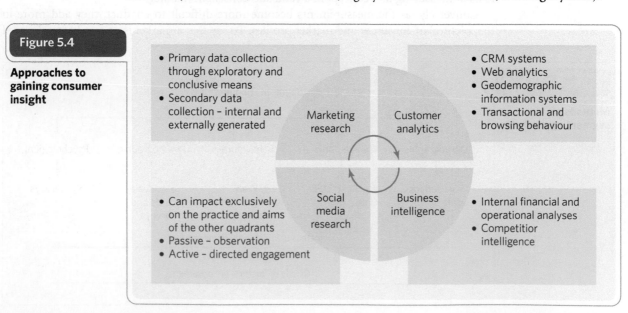

Figure 5.4

Approaches to gaining consumer insight

- Primary data collection through exploratory and conclusive means
- Secondary data collection – internal and externally generated

Marketing research

Customer analytics

- CRM systems
- Web analytics
- Geodemographic information systems
- Transactional and browsing behaviour

- Can impact exclusively on the practice and aims of the other quadrants
- Passive – observation
- Active – directed engagement

Social media research

Business intelligence

- Internal financial and operational analyses
- Competitior intelligence

| Real research | **Moving beyond the traditional single customer view[32]** |

Research data is the raw material for marketing, and the volumes gathered every day are staggering. Imagine for a moment that you had a database that held every word ever spoken by a human being, every utterance from the dawn of language on to the babble you hear around you right now. That's a damn big database, right? You would need twenty databases of that size to hold the data that will exist by the end of next year. And the amount of data we spool out skyrockets every year! Not all of this data can be used by companies to improve their marketing efforts. After all, much of it is junk, but quite a bit of it can be helpful. Companies that adapt to the new scales of available data will thrive. Adapting organisations will adopt a single enterprise view of their business, not to replace the traditional single customer view but to augment it. This will allow them to access huge volumes of data, producing intricate analytics and targeted messaging that has both mass economies of scale and single-customer precision. Companies that adapt to the new scales of available data will thrive. Those that do not, well, no one said that evolution was kind.

This view of the impact of continuing digitisation of everyday life means that ever more individual-level data about consumer behaviour will be available for marketers to respond to.[33] Marketing research, like any of the other approaches in Figure 5.4, has to recognise that it contributes part of a wider understanding required to formulate effective and successful business and marketing strategies. Relying on marketing research as a sole data source or arguing that it is the most valid data source could lead to a very one-dimensional view of consumers and the worlds they live in. Researchers need to recognise that marketing research has a distinctive role to play in a single-enterprise view of a business, adding value and distinction through being able to:

1   Focus upon existing and potential customers.

2   Use quantitative and qualitative approaches to tap into a rich array of consumer attitudes, emotions and aspirations.

3   Tap into a rich array of sensory and experiential characteristics of consumers.

4   Draw on a well-established and robust theoretical base in measuring and understanding consumers.

5   Draw on a well-established and robust theoretical base in being 'representative' and generalising populations.

6   Demonstrate social responsibility through a long-established, proactive and open code of conduct.

'Old-style' researchers who may conduct studies to meet specific objectives and just deliver the results of the research are becoming rare. Even if researchers were to see the nature and scope of their work in this narrow sense, they would be designing and delivering relatively weak research by not tapping into the array of internally generated secondary data that are at their disposal. In order to utilise internal secondary data, researchers need to equip themselves with more information-gathering skills and techniques than they have been traditionally trained to do.[34] In order to thrive, researchers need to become 'data curators' by embracing and integrating new information sources. *We must ensure that we are the 'aggregators' not just the aggregated.*[35]

International marketing research

Linking the array of databases that may be held within organisations with survey data and/or other forms of quantitative and qualitative data has transformed international marketing research. Within individual companies, customers may be analysed from CRM systems and web analytics data within individual countries, showing different patterns of behaviour between different regions or cities and relating that behaviour to their marketing activities. When a company operates across borders, country differences become just another geographical variable. In deciding to operate or develop in a particular country, companies may buy a geodemographic information system (should one be developed for that country). A GIS may be used as a foundation to add to their internally generated secondary data. However, international marketers face a dilemma in choosing between 'consistency' and 'richness of detail'. It is possible to create GISs to individual countries across the globe based upon the data sources available within that country, its data protection laws and how current and accurate those data sources are. Such systems work extremely well if one's marketing activities are based within that country. The problem arises when, as an international marketer, one wishes to have consumer classifications that are consistent across borders. Mosaic Global is one of many solutions to this problem. Performing analyses within countries can be most fruitful, provided a base GIS has been established. Problems start where there is no base GIS. In many countries there are great problems in tracking down and combining data sources that can be relied upon. Further, even if reliable data can be located, legislation may make the use of certain data types illegal. In many developing countries, the data needed to build a GIS are sparse. With the data that are available, much experimentation is needed to enable valid classifications that reflect consumer types that are useful to marketers and researchers.

Researchers now have access to powerful tools and techniques enabling them to: engage consumers via social media tools; listen to audiences by mining social media; reach an increasingly sought-after, younger generation of consumers through social media, and be able to do this across international markets. With the advent of Twitter and social networks including Facebook, user-generated content (UGC) is becoming increasingly accessible and intertwined with the daily lives of consumers across the globe. Consequently, the way researchers can tap into consumer views online has changed enormously. Social media research is not a fad, but a fundamental shift in the way researchers can communicate and gather information. Thanks to the exceptionally rapid growth of social media, the Internet offers limitless opportunities for researchers to connect with vast populations of diverse people who are spending more of their free time online every day. Blogs, communities and

various Web 2.0 mechanisms are empowering the transformation of marketing research into an engaging and iterative process. Combining tools like these into the research mix enables researchers to gather more in-depth insights in real time while observing consumers in their natural habitat and enhancing the innovation process.[36] Many of these developments and their impacts upon the conduct of international marketing research will be described and illustrated throughout the book. In the context of evaluating internally generated secondary data, it is worth considering, for example, the extent to which the content of a company's Facebook page would constitute a valuable resource for the researcher. Such a resource is illustrated in the following example.

Real research	**Coca-Cola's bold offensive[37]**

In addition to the traditional media strategies (TV, radio, print, in-store) that have been a hallmark of Coca-Cola's communications strategies over many years, the company has invested heavily in social media and mobile campaigns. One example of this was its Expedition 206 integrated campaign (**www.Expedition 206.com**). This was billed as a quest to find the secret to a happy life in all 206 countries where Coca-Cola products are sold. The campaign featured three consumers turned 'ambassadors' interacting with people they met on a 365-day trip around the world. The trio, selected from a list of candidates via a worldwide online vote, posted photos and videos on **Expedition206.com**, writing blog entries, and sending Twitter updates about their 275,000-mile trip. Coca-Cola products served as tools for starting conversations with people the trio did not know, and talking about things that bring happiness and purpose into their lives. Website visitors could track how many miles the ambassadors had travelled and the countries they had visited and could sign up to receive updates on their cell phone or another mobile device. As of the first quarter of 2010, the site had 350 million members. In 2008, a Facebook page devoted to Coke sprang up, with no involvement from Coca-Cola. The page built up about 1 million followers, but because it was not officially authorised by Coca-Cola it was removed. Given such a loyal following, Coca-Cola established an official Facebook page that now has over 5 million fans. Expedition 206 and the company's realisation of the impact and potential of Facebook are changing perspectives about marketing at the company. The notion of experiential marketing forming an intersection with social and community marketing is increasingly where Coca Cola wants to see their brand. They would argue that they have formed a partnership with consumers who have become some of their best content drivers.

Ethics in marketing research

From the emergence of marketing research as a discipline, researchers have been confronted by ethical challenges related to the use of customer data. Research Associations such as ESOMAR have been very clear in their codes of conduct to draw a distinction between direct marketing activities (e.g. using customer data in CRM systems) and bone fide marketing research. With the growth of social networking, blogging, online communities and Web 2.0 technologies, protecting the anonymity of research participants has become far more problematic. Protecting participant privacy and client confidentiality has never been as challenging for researchers as it is now.[38] Technological advances in computing power, mobile devices and storage media carry many benefits, but they too add risk that must be mitigated. The risks posed by online and social media research include identity theft, harassment, defamation of character and maintaining client confidentiality. ESOMAR has formulated basic principles to help researchers working with the latest developments in online and social research, where the possibilities created by new technologies are running ahead of formal regulation. The principles are as follows: treat participants with respect; aim to create a relationship based on trust, respect and reciprocity which will lead to a good experience for people who participate in online research; tell people what you are doing and obtain informed consent from research subjects; avoid practices which might cause concern if explained clearly to participants or legislators; activities which use marketing research methodologies but which are not intended solely for research purposes must be clearly differentiated from non-research activities; remember that online research is global; the industry will be required to conform to the rules in the most restrictive nations, not the most permissive.[39]

Earlier in the chapter we illustrated the dilemma faced by the online bank Egg in designing online surveys using data and knowledge gained from its CRM systems. The example showed that with due care it can be possible to combine marketing research ethics and databases generated through CRM systems and web analytics, though there would be many who baulk at such approaches. Given the phenomenal growth and power of CRM, web analytics and other operational databases used in marketing and the support they offer to decision makers, they are here to stay. They can be seen as competing with marketing research approaches to deliver what may be seen as more relevant and better value consumer insights, or they can be seen as complementary. With well-planned traditional marketing research integrated with database analyses, the strategic power of consumer and market analyses can be phenomenal. If marketers abuse their knowledge of consumers, they stand to do great harm to their brands and corporate image. Consumers are now more aware of how valuable knowledge of their behaviour is and how it is used by marketers.[40] They are willing to trade this knowledge for specific rewards and mutual respect. Decision-makers and researchers should be aware of the rewards and respect expected of consumers and the dangers of abusing the knowledge that is imparted to them.

Digital applications in marketing research

At the start of the 1990s, this chapter would not have existed in a marketing research textbook. The idea of conducting internal secondary data searches and analyses would have merited a paragraph or two as part of the process of developing primary data collection. The amount of data available to the researcher and the time taken to utilise that data might have militated against heavy investments in internal secondary data searches and analyses. Since then, internal secondary data driven by a plethora of operational databases have grown enormously. As presented in an earlier example, Enterprise Marketing Management (EMM) defines a category of software used by consumer-oriented organisations. EMM is used to manage an end-to-end process of gathering and analysing customer data across websites and other channels, to plan, budget and manage the creative production process, to execute targeted customer communications, to measure results and effectiveness. It is a superset of other marketing software categories such as web analytics, campaign management, marketing resource management, marketing dashboards, lead management, event-driven marketing, customer relationship management (CRM), sales management and predictive modelling. This chapter could not cover the nature and integration of such systems but has provided examples (and will continue to provide examples throughout the book) of how these systems integrate with and effect excellent marketing research. What should be clear from the growth and array of systems and digital applications that encompass EMM is that the evaluation of internal secondary data cannot be ignored by researchers. Examples chosen to illustrate why such systems cannot be ignored can quickly become outdated, not only over the shelf life of a textbook but even in the time taken to produce a book. However, the following two examples illustrate major digital applications that should continue to impact upon how researchers should continue to engage with customer data. The first example focuses on web analytics. It illustrates how a company with a global presence and a large portfolio of brands has used Google Analytics to understand and communicate characteristics of its customers. The second example focuses on mobile technologies. It illustrates how an online publisher has used 'mobile research' to understand characteristics of the users of its 'apps'. With a juxtaposition of knowledge it has of its website users, its mobile surveys of iPhone and iPad users have given it a much stronger profile of the nature and behaviour of its customers.

Real research | **Diageo uses Google Analytics to empower its global brand managers**

Diageo is a leading global producer of alcoholic beverages with some of the world's best-known brands such as Guinness, Johnnie Walker, Smirnoff and Baileys and with annual revenues of €14,500 million. For a company of Diageo's size, the logistics of delivering accurate analytics across hundreds of websites in over 20 countries was a daunting task. Marketing and brand managers required instant access to their website's analytics reports in their native language. Though Google hosts and manages the server and hardware infrastructure for the entire Google Analytics platform, Diageo worked with a specialist agency to deploy Google Analytics across its global brands and to train its marketing teams. ConversionWorks (**www.conversionworks.co.uk**), a Google Analytics Certified Partner, worked with each brand's web design agency. ConversionWorks quickly found that Diageo's needs were very different from those of smaller organisations that have marketing teams centralised in one location: with potentially thousands of marketing executives spread around the globe, their challenge was to bring the data to the brand managers and not have them chasing after it. Using the Google Application Programming Interface, Diageo was able to show the latest reports and data directly on their intranet dashboards. Data was automatically extracted from each Google Analytics account and shown each time executives logged into the intranet.

Real research | **Mobile surveys at TOMORROW FOCUS Media**[41]

TOMORROW FOCUS Media (**www.tomorrow-focus.de**) is one of Germany's leading Internet marketing providers. Its portfolio includes FOCUS online and HOLIDAYCHECK as well as partner portals CHIP Online, FAZ.net and FREUNDIN.de. It knew that 350,000 people had downloaded its iPhone app and were keeping abreast of the news (350,000 downloads). However, it did not have any hard facts about the users of its app, e.g. how many were male or female or how old they were. It was already conducting 'traditional' online surveys but in order to measure and understand customer characteristics of its apps, it decided to conduct surveys on iPhones and iPads. Working with GlobalPark (**www.globalpark.com**), it selected 1,930 users of the iPhone app and included a small advertisement within the news content, asking them to participate in a survey. Of these, 152 completed the whole questionnaire. TOMORROW FOCUS was able to start building up a profile of its app users and to update this periodically by running additional surveys. The project highlighted that it was possible to survey hard-to-reach consumers via iPhones. TOMORROW FOCUS discovered that a very high percentage of its app users had a high salary and tended to be younger than the users of its website; most were also male. In its newer iPad app survey, it discovered that the app was used mainly in the evenings and at weekends for leisure purposes. The users of the iPad were also predominantly male and with a very high income.

Summary

The overall tone of this chapter has been to demonstrate that internally generated secondary data offer great opportunities not only for decision-makers but also for researchers. As with all good secondary data sources, they have a major impact upon the design, focus and value of primary data collection, analyses and interpretation.

Databases, including customer operational data, geodemographic data, CRM data, web analytics and survey data, are radically changing how marketing decision making is supported. There is much debate as to whether the use of databases is compatible with traditional techniques of marketing research. With the junk mail connotations of databases and compromises of participant anonymity, many researchers may seek to keep the marketing database at arm's length. However, handled with the professional acumen that researchers have displayed for many years, the database presents great opportunities for the researcher. In Europe, many of the leading marketing research agencies and research functions within companies have embraced the marketing database as an essential component of their need to deliver powerful customer insight.

For the researcher, databases help to build profiles of consumers, linked to the products, communications and distribution methods those consumers favour. Databases present opportunities to experiment in 'one big laboratory', build models of consumer behaviour, develop an understanding of the gaps in knowledge of consumers and make links between behavioural and attitudinal data. Much of the data that offer these benefits capture customer buying and even browsing behaviour. The use of the 'loyalty card' is one example. Different types of data, including scanner, loyalty card, CRM, web analytics and survey data, may be combined and displayed using geodemographic information systems (GISs). Using base geographic and demographic data, characteristics of existing and potential customers can be analysed and mapped out.

Disparate database and marketing research sources can be integrated to create powerful consumer insights. As well as what may be seen as traditional forms of marketing research, methods of customer transaction analysis and business intelligence can be mutually supportive and integrated. Social media research methods can add further insights to these forms of gaining consumer insight. There are distinctive forms of expertise and organisations that support these individual approaches. Researchers can see these approaches and the skills required to implement them as a competitive threat. Alternatively, marketing research can embrace these approaches as an opportunity and be proactive in seeking the means to deliver superior consumer insight. The challenges in integrating these approaches lie in characteristics of the data they generate, information systems that portray emergent knowledge in an organisation and marketing challenges of what should be an organisation's target markets and its performance in those markets.

The growth and development of internally generated secondary data has created many opportunities for international researchers. GISs, CRM systems and web analytics enable stronger measures and understanding of the distinctive characteristics of consumers in, within and across different countries and regions. The ethics of using databases provokes much debate in the marketing research industry. As many research practitioners grow more accustomed to using databases, marketing research guidelines and codes of practice are being developed to reflect the good practices that exist in many companies. These codes of practice are being constantly updated to reflect technological developments and the changing expectations of consumers, decision-makers and researchers. The growth and development of social media and online research has been driven by major digital advances. Developments in social media research, especially in mobile Internet usage, will shape many of the challenges and opportunities that researchers face.

Questions

1 How may 'operational data' held in organisations help to build up an understanding of customer behaviour?

2 What is a customer database? Why may a researcher wish to analyse the data held in a customer database?

3 What kinds of data can be gathered through electronic scanner devices?

4 What other sources beyond electronic scanner devices electronically observe customer behaviour?

5 Describe the benefits to the marketing decision-maker of being able to capture data that identify characteristics of consumers and their shopping behaviour in a store.

6 Describe the benefits to the researcher of being able to capture data that identify characteristics of consumers and their shopping behaviour in a store.

7 Why may the characteristics of consumers differ, based upon where they live?

8 What is a geodemographic classification of consumers?

9 How can the graphical representation of consumer characteristics using maps help marketing decision making?

10 How may data from customer relationship management systems support the practice of marketing research?

11 How may the data from web analytics support the practice of marketing research?

12 How does the compilation of different types of data help to build a strong 'picture' of consumer characteristics?

13 How does the compilation of different types of data help researchers engaged in international research projects?

14 What are the ethical challenges and dilemmas for researchers using data from customer databases?

15 In what way may the use of data generated through social media sources be considered as 'internally generated secondary data'?

Exercises

1 Visit the websites of Acorn (**www.caci.co.uk**) and Mosaic (**www.experian.co.uk/business-strategies**). Imagine that you have been commissioned to select a geodemographic system to help a newspaper publisher in a major European city.

a For such a business, how may a geodemographic system be used for marketing decision making?

b For such a business, how may a geodemographic system aid marketing research design?

c Present the case of which of the above systems would best suit such a business.

2   Call in at a supermarket or store that operates a reward or loyalty card scheme that requires you to apply for membership. Pick up an application form and examine the nature of questions you are expected to answer.

   a   What marketing research use can be made of the data collected from this application form?

   b   Evaluate the design of this form and make recommendations on how the nature of questions could be improved.

3   You are a marketing manager for Carlsberg beer. One of your major customers is a supermarket that uses a loyalty card scheme to observe its customers electronically.

   a   What would this supermarket know about beer buying behaviour through its scheme?

   b   If it would not share this with you, evaluate any marketing research, web analytics and social media research techniques that you think could generate the same knowledge.

4   Visit the SPSS website **www.ibm.com/software/analytics/spss** and evaluate its 'predictive analytics' products. Write a report on how marketing research may feed into and/or feed from predictive analytics for key decisions that may be planned by either a bank or major retailer.

5   In a small group discuss the following issues: 'What ethical problems exist with the use of marketing databases for researchers?' and 'If, on ethical grounds, researchers refused to utilise the benefits of marketing databases, what inherent weaknesses may exist in their research designs?'

Video case exercise: Subaru

How could Subaru's survey analyses and internal and external secondary data collection help it to profile and target female drivers?

Notes

1. Woodnutt, T. and Owen, R., 'The research industry needs to embrace radical change in order to thrive and survive in the digital era', Market Research Society, Annual Conference (2010).

2. Havermans, J., 'Knowing everything a customer wants', *Research World* (January 2006), 18–19.

3. **www.smartfocus.com**, accessed 14 January 2011.

4. Berelowitz, M., 'Ready for Enterprise 2.0?', *Market Leader* 3 (June 2009), 48–51.

5. Woodnutt, T. and Owen, R., 'The research industry needs to embrace radical change in order to thrive and survive in the digital era', Market Research Society, Annual Conference (2010).

6. Murphy, D. 'The enlightened researcher', *Research World* (December 2006), 18–20.

7. Macer, T., 'Conference notes – making technology decisions in combining attitudinal and behavioural data', *International Journal of Market Research* 51 4 (2009), 543–546.

8. Bakken, D.G., 'Riding the value shift in market research: only the paranoid survive', ESOMAR Best Paper Overall, Congress Odyssey, Athens (September 2010).

9. Jolly, M. and Battais, L., 'Loyalty card databases, revolutionary analysis in shopping behaviour', ESOMAR Retail Conference, Valencia (February 2007).

10. Briggs, R., 'The collective brain: why market research will be over-run by the software powerhouses, and what you can do to compete', ESOMAR Congress Odyssey, Athens (September 2010).

11. Hindmarch, J., Wells, C. and Price, F., '"It's as vital as the air that they breathe". The development of a segmentation

of the baby milk market by SMA Nutrician and Leapfrog Research & Planning', Market Research Society, Annual Conference (2005).

12. Noble, Y., 'Personalisation, relevance and consistency in database marketing', *Admap* 497 (September 2008).

13. Oktar, S., 'Integrating decision making and marketing intelligence', ESOMAR, Technovate Conference, Cannes (January 2003).

14. Greenberg, P., 'The impact of CRM 2.0 on customer insight', *Journal of Business & Industrial Marketing* 25 (6) (2010), 410–419; Evans, M., Nancarrow, C., Tapp, A. and Stone, M., 'Future marketers: future curriculum; future shock?', *Journal of Marketing Management* 18 (5–6) (2002), 579–596.

15. Greenberg, P., 'The impact of CRM 2.0 on customer insight', *Journal of Business & Industrial Marketing* 25 (6) (2010), 410–419.

16. Dawe, A., 'Integration is the thing', *The Times – Special Edition e-CRM* (11 April 2001), 2–3.

17. Sumner-Smith, D., 'Getting to know clients lifts profits', *The Sunday Times* (26 September 1999), 17.

18. Havermans, J., 'Knowing everything a customer wants', *Research World* (January 2006), 18–19.

19. Fletcher, K., 'Consumer power and privacy', *International Journal of Advertising* 22 (2) (2003), 249–271.

20. ICC/ESOMAR International Code on Market and Social Research (December 2007), 4.

21. ESOMAR, 'Global Market Research', ESOMAR Industry Report (2010), 48–49.

22. Jennick, J. and Schwartz, G., 'Playing the Egg game', *Research World* (December 2006), 36–37.

23. Macer, T., Pearson, P. and Sebastiani, F., 'Cracking the code: what customers say, in their own words', Market Research Society: Annual Conference (2007).

24. Kung, A., Wong, J. and Fai, K., 'Marrying CRM analytics with research insights to formulate the best in class customer loyalty strategy', ESOMAR: Congress Odyssey, Athens (September 2010).

25. Precourt, G., 'P&G to consolidate database for 360-degree consumer insights', *WARC Exclusive* (September 2009).

26. Sterne, J., 'Web analytics and the march toward better measurement', *Marketing NPV* 4 (3) (2007), 18–19.

27. Anon., 'TUI UK: engagement warehouse & behavioural conversion programme', Direct Marketing Association – UK: Gold Award (2010).

28. Maex, D., 'Learning to read the river: using math marketing to increase your return on investment', WPP Atticus Awards: Highly Commended (2009); Anon., 'Tesco uses loyalty scheme to drive growth', *WARC News* (7 October 2009); Rawlinson, R., 'Beyond brand management – the anatomy of the 21st century marketing professional', *Market Leader* 34 (Autumn 2006).

29. Harbert, T., 'One giant leap for analytics?', *ANA Magazine* (February 2008).

30. Passingham, J. and Blyth, B., 'A small rock holds back a great wave: unleashing our potential', ESOMAR: Congress Odyssey, Athens (September 2010).

31. Havermans, J., 'Boosting consumer excellence', *Research World* (April 2006) 28–29.

32. Maex, D., 'Learning to read the river: using math marketing to increase your return on investment', WPP Atticus Awards: Highly Commended (2009).

33. Hayward, M., 'Conference notes – Connecting the dots: joined-up insight finally becomes possible', *International Journal of Market Research* 51 (2) (2009).

34. Page, A. and Lai, S., 'Understanding your competitors: completing the marketing intelligence jigsaw', ESOMAR Asia Pacific Conference, Tokyo (March 2005).

35. Woodnutt, T. and Owen, R., 'The research industry needs to embrace radical change in order to thrive and survive in the digital era', Market Research Society, Annual Conference (2010).

36. Case, S., 'How social media is democratizing research', ESOMAR: Congress Odyssey Athens (September 2010).

37. Wilkinson, T., 'Coca-Cola's bold offensive', *ANA Magazine* (April 2010).

38. Stark, D., 'From social engineering to social networking – privacy issues when conducting research in the web 2.0 world', ESOMAR: Congress, Montreaux (September 2009).

39. Phillips, A., 'IJMR Research Methods Forum: "Start listening, stop asking" – Researchers snooping and spies – the legal and ethical challenges facing observational research', *International Journal of Marketing Research* 52 (2) (2010), 275–281.

40. Nancarrow, C., Tinson, J. and Brace, I., 'Consumer savvy and intergenerational effects', *International Journal of Market Research* 50 (6) (2008), 731–755.

41. Wilke, A., 'Mobile surveys win new business for TOMORROW FOCUS Media', GlobalPark Case Study (2011).

6

Qualitative research: its nature and approaches

Stage 1

Problem definition

Stage 2

Research approach developed

Stage 3

Research design developed

Stage 4

Fieldwork or data collection

Stage 5

Data integrity and analysis

Stage 6

Report preparation and presentation

Qualitative research helps the marketer to understand the richness, depth and complexity of consumers.

Objectives

After reading this chapter, you should be able to:

1 explain the difference between qualitative and quantitative research in terms of the objectives, sampling, data collection and analysis, and outcomes;

2 describe why qualitative research is used in marketing research;

3 understand the basic philosophical stances that underpin qualitative research;

4 understand the nature and application of ethnographic approaches;

5 understand how qualitative researchers develop knowledge through a grounded theory approach;

6 explain the potential of action research to qualitative researchers;

7 discuss the considerations involved in collecting and analysing qualitative data collected from international markets;

8 understand the ethical issues involved in collecting and analysing qualitative data;

9 describe how developments in social media research have changed established qualitative research techniques and added new techniques.

Overview

Qualitative research forms a major role in supporting marketing decision making, primarily as an exploratory design but also as a descriptive design. Researchers may undertake qualitative research to help define a research problem, to support quantitative, descriptive or causal research designs, or as a design in its own right. Qualitative research is often used to generate hypotheses and identify variables that should be included in quantitative approaches. It may be used after or in conjunction with quantitative approaches where illumination of statistical findings is needed. In some cases qualitative research designs are adopted in isolation, after secondary data sources have been thoroughly evaluated or even in an iterative process with secondary data sources.

In this chapter, we discuss the differences between qualitative and quantitative research and the role of each in marketing research. We present reasons for adopting a qualitative approach to marketing research (Stage 2 of the marketing research process). These reasons are developed by examining the basic philosophical stances that underpin qualitative research. The concept of ethnographic techniques is presented, with illustrations of how such techniques support marketing decision-makers. The concept of grounded theory is presented, illustrating its roots, the steps involved and the dilemmas for researchers in attempting to be objective and sensitive to the expressions of participants. Action research is an approach to conducting research that has been adopted in a wide variety of social and management research settings. Action research is developing in marketing research, especially in areas such as product, communications and brand design. The concept of co-creation in design through action research offers great potential for consumers, decision-makers and researchers alike. The roots of action research are presented, together with the iterative stages involved and the concept of action research teams. The considerations involved in conducting qualitative research when researching international markets are discussed, especially in contrasting approaches between the USA and Europe. Several ethical issues that arise in qualitative research are identified. Technological developments and the emergence of social media research techniques are changing the manner in which traditional qualitative research techniques are conducted. In addition, a whole array of new qualitative research techniques have become possible through social media developments. Examples of these changes and new techniques will be presented, along with the challenges and opportunities these present.

We begin by evaluating the nature of qualitative research with the use of three examples. Given the nature of its products and competitive environment, the first example illustrates how Weihenstephan has used qualitative research in the development of an online research community. The second example illustrates how LG Electronics uses qualitative techniques to support design decisions. Note in this example how LG uses different techniques to capture characteristics of consumers that they may be totally unaware of. In the third example, IFM Sports Marketing Surveys uses qualitative brainstorming techniques and focus groups as part of a research design to support the development of rugby league. These examples illustrate the rich insights into the underlying behaviour of consumers that can be obtained by using qualitative techniques.

Real research	## The Weihenstephan online research community[1]

Weihenstephan is a German dairy company belonging to the international Mueller Dairy Group (**www.muellergroup.com**). As a premium brand it faced major challenges in the German dairy market which was characterised by very strong private label brands. It faced numerous strong national brands with intense promotional activities in high-volume categories like fruit yogurts, flavoured milk drinks and desserts. This category was affected by very important and influential topics for consumers, e.g. sustainability, fair treatment of farmers and GMO-free products (Genetically Modified Organisms). Weihenstephan recognised that social media were profoundly changing the basics of interpersonal communication, but it also saw several new challenges for researchers arising from this 'web evolution': discussion groups developed without being previously sampled; answers were given to questions that had not yet been asked; well-constructed interviews were replaced by dynamic social interaction in virtual communities. In planning its response to the challenges and opportunities to social media research, Weihenstephan felt it could establish two types of research community: (1) by expanding an already existing open consumer-oriented website (**www.weihenstephan-erleben.de**) into a branded open-source community; and (2) setting up a dedicated, closed online research community. It saw the development of co-creation processes in these communities providing the advantages of combining the classical focus group concept with the benefits of Web 2.0. Both types of community could have the same functionalities and features (e.g. creating user profiles, establishing different forums, including quantitative research elements like voting). Weihenstephan chose the second option, the closed online research community, establishing one place for conducting all qualitative and quantitative marketing research. Qualitative–exploratory questions were investigated within the community. The company targeted around 100–150 participants representing various regions in Germany (equally spilt in urban areas of Munich, Stuttgart, Cologne, Berlin and Hamburg). Its community is working and several key projects have been discussed including: new concept and product ideas in existing subcategories, possible line extensions, general attitudes and habits in possible new sub categories for the brand.

Real research   **Living with your customers[2]**

When designing domestic appliances, the German branch of Korean-based LG Electronics needed a way to find out what people need from its kitchen equipment, washers and vacuum cleaners. The answer was to use ethnographic research with a combination of video diaries and long in-depth interviews so that they could understand its customers through sharing their experiences. The company combined the two methods because one drawback of filming participants was that they might behave atypically, being aware that they were in a test situation. There can also be verbal or subconscious non-verbal communication with the camera operator. The company therefore used the two methods to apply what it saw as 'non-presence while being present' in different households and countries. The projects were directed to find out how European consumers used electrical appliances, their workflow in the kitchen, how they go about doing their laundry, and their habits in wet and dry floor cleaning. The company believed that habitual non-conscious behaviour should be researched in an authentic environment with a minimum of external factors, so it worked at participants' homes, usually for a period of five to eight days. It carried out research focusing on the kitchen (10 households each in Hamburg, London and Paris), laundry (10 households each in Hamburg, Budapest, Stockholm, Madrid and London) and vacuum cleaning (15 households in Paris, Budapest, Madrid and London). To observe kitchen behaviour, it installed cameras focused on major appliances for a week for the video diaries. For the laundry study, it installed fixed cameras with a motion detector to observe behaviour with the washing machine and dryer. If these appliances were in the bathroom or toilet, where no one wanted to be filmed, participants could switch the camera on themselves whenever they used the appliances. The company adjusted the technical equipment and location of video cameras according to different individuals and households so it could observe how people sorted clothes, dealt with stains, dried their laundry and did the ironing.

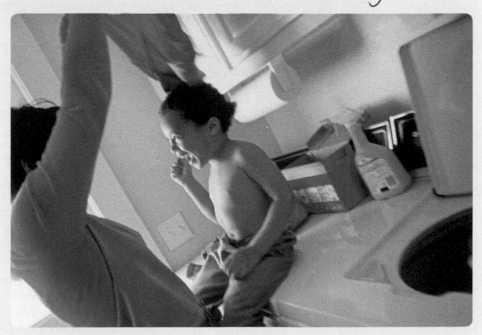

IFM Sports Marketing Surveys

Rugby league study

Sports Marketing Surveys was commissioned by the Rugby Football League (the governing body of rugby league in the UK) to:

- gain an understanding of the target audience for rugby league;
- investigate the core values of rugby league;
- verify the core values and quantify the new branding concepts.

The figure below sets out the research design adopted for the project, setting out the research objectives, the qualitative and quantitative techniques used, and how each stage feeds the development of subsequent stages.

Rugby league study – research design

Stage 1: GAIN AN UNDERSTANDING OF THE TARGET AUDIENCE FOR RUGBY LEAGUE

Sporting insights: Online specialist sports fan research tool using a pool of rugby league fans and links to Rugby Football League websites

BRAINSTORM/WORKSHOP 1
Construct initial draft definition statements and unique sales propositions for the sport, use as a basis for Stage 2 discussion guide and stimulus materials

Stage 2: INVESTIGATE THE CORE VALUES OF RUGBY LEAGUE

Focus/discussion groups: Gain insight into views, attitudes and aspirations for the sport, evaluate and validate values/definition statement, identify representative images of the sport. Stimulus constructed from Stage 1 results

BRAINSTORM/WORKSHOP 2
The basis for a final definition statement for the sport. Develop the unique sales propositions for the sport, identify/validate the brand hierarchy and understanding barriers for entry. Develop creative brief to complete brand image changes.

Stage 3: QUANTIFY THE CORE VALUES AND NEW BRANDING CONCEPTS

Face-to-face interviews – Test reactions amongst a wider quantitative audience, representing the rugby league target market
Sporting insights – Test on 1,000 general sports fans and 500 rugby leagues fans through online survey

In qualitative research, research agencies and companies are continually looking to find better ways to understand consumers' thought processes and motivations. This has led to a wealth of research approaches, including techniques borrowed from anthropology, ethnography, sociology and psychology. For example, Philips has a specialist team of researchers, including ethnographers, anthropologists and psychologists.

As Marco Bevolo, Design Director at Philips Design, says[3]

> *At Philips Design, we have created research tools to enable ethnographic insights to be delivered into the creative process in a truly actionable way. We aim to push the agenda of research from the side of future studies, people research and their lively embodiment into advanced design.*

Primary data: qualitative versus quantitative research

As explained in Chapter 4, primary data are originated by the researcher for the specific purpose of addressing the problem at hand. Primary data may be qualitative or quantitative in nature, as shown in Figure 6.1.

Qualitative research
An unstructured, primarily exploratory design based on small samples, intended to provide depth, insight and understanding.

Quantitative research
Research techniques that seek to quantify data and, typically, apply some form of measurement and statistical analysis.

Dogmatic positions are often taken in favour of either qualitative research or quantitative research by researchers and decision-makers alike. The positions are founded upon which approach is perceived to give the most accurate measurements and understanding of consumers. The extreme stances on this issue mirror each other. Many quantitative researchers are apt to dismiss qualitative studies completely as giving no valid findings, indeed as being little better than journalistic accounts. They assert that qualitative researchers ignore representative sampling, with their findings based on a single case or only a few cases. Equally adamant are some qualitative researchers who firmly reject statistical and other quantitative methods as yielding shallow or completely misleading information. They believe that to understand cultural values and consumer behaviour, especially in its full contextual richness, requires interviewing or intensive field observation. Qualitative techniques they see as being the only methods of data collection sensitive enough to capture the nuances of consumer attitudes, motives and behaviour.[4]

There are great differences between the quantitative and qualitative approaches to studying and understanding consumers. The arguments between qualitative and quantitative researchers about their relative strengths and weaknesses are of real practical value. The nature of marketing decision making encompasses a vast array of problems and types of decision-maker. This means that seeking a singular and uniform approach to supporting decision-makers by focusing on one approach is futile. This should have become apparent when evaluating the huge array of data sources that can generate consumer insight, as discussed in Chapter 5. Defending qualitative approaches for a particular marketing research problem through the positive benefits it bestows and explaining the negative alternatives of a quantitative approach is healthy, and vice versa. Business and marketing decision-makers have always used both approaches and will continue to need both.[5]

The distinction between qualitative and quantitative research can be in the context of research designs as discussed in Chapter 3. There is a close parallel in the distinctions between 'exploratory and conclusive research' and 'qualitative and quantitative research'. There is a parallel, but the terms are not identical. There are circumstances where qualitative research can be used to present detailed descriptions that cannot be measured in a quantifiable manner: for example, in describing characteristics and styles of music that may be used in an advertising campaign or in describing the interplay of how families go through the process of choosing, planning and buying a holiday.[6]

Conversely, there may be circumstances where quantitative measurements are used conclusively to answer specific hypotheses or research questions using descriptive or experimental techniques. Beyond answering specific hypotheses or research questions, there may be sufficient data to allow data mining or an exploration of relationships between individual measurements to take place.

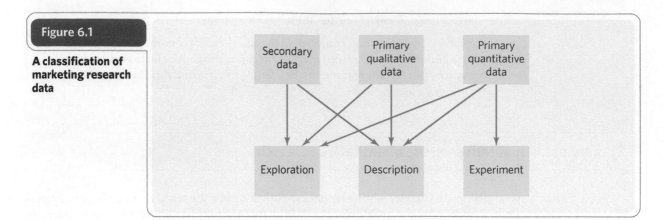

Figure 6.1

A classification of marketing research data

The nature of qualitative research

The nature of qualitative research

Qualitative research encompasses a variety of methods that can be applied in a flexible manner, to enable participants to reflect upon and express their views or to observe their behaviour. It seeks to encapsulate the behaviour, experiences and feelings of participants in their own terms and context; for example, when conducting research on children, an informal and child-friendly atmosphere is vital, considering features such as the decoration of the room with appropriately themed posters.[7] Qualitative research is based on at least two intellectual traditions.[8] The first and perhaps most important is the set of ideas and associated methods from the broad area of in-depth psychology and motivational research.[9] This movement was concerned with the less conscious aspects of the human psyche. It led to a development of methods to gain access to individuals' subconscious and/or unconscious levels. So, while individuals may present a superficial explanation of events to themselves or to others, these methods sought to dig deeper and penetrate the superficial. The second tradition is the set of ideas and associated methods from sociology, social psychology and social anthropology, and the disciplines of ethnography, linguistics and semiology. The emphases here are upon holistic understanding of the world-view of people. The researcher is expected to 'enter' the hearts and minds of those they are researching, to develop an empathy with their experiences and feelings. Both traditions have a concern with developing means of communication between the researcher and those being researched. There can be much interaction between the two broad traditions, which in pragmatic terms allows a wide and rich array of techniques and interpretations of collected data.

Qualitative research is a significant contributor to the marketing research industry, accounting for substantial expenditure (around 13% of all spending on marketing research methods).[10] If one considers the growth and development of social media research, much of which is qualitative in nature, it is clear to see that this form of research is growing and of major impact upon decision making. In commercial terms, it is a global industry that generates revenues over €1 billion annually. However, it is not just a matter of business value. Qualitative thinking has had a profound effect upon marketing, strategic and design thinking and the marketing research industry as a whole.

Rationale for using qualitative research

It is not always possible, or desirable, to use structured quantitative techniques to obtain information from participants or to observe them. Thus, there are several reasons to use qualitative techniques. These reasons, either individually or in any combination, explain why certain researchers adopt a particular approach (Stage 2 of the marketing research process) to how they conduct research, analyse data and interpret their findings:

1 *Preferences and/or experience of the researcher.* Some researchers are more oriented and temperamentally suited to do this type of work. Just as some researchers enjoy the challenge of using statistical techniques, there are researchers who enjoy the challenges of qualitative techniques and the interpretation of diverse types of data. Such researchers have been trained in particular disciplines (e.g. anthropology) and philosophies (e.g. hermeneutics) that traditionally make use of qualitative research designs and techniques.

2 *Preferences and/or experience of the research user.* Some decision-makers are more oriented to receiving support in a qualitative manner. This orientation could come from their training but it could also be due to the type of marketing decisions they have to take. Decision-makers working in a creative environment of product design, advertising copy or the development of brand 'personalities', for example, may have a greater preference for data that will feed such design and visually based decisions. In the following example, consider how decision-makers would get to understand and cope with the frustrations felt by consumers. Consider also the implications for a brand if designers and marketers do not fully understand the consumer behaviour that was presented in a visual manner.

Real research | **I once sat with a women who was ironing for 5 hours[11]**

Microsoft's chief design anthropologist Anne Kirah set out what she believed was one of her most successful research projects. She watched 40 ordinary, randomly chosen American families try to set up and use an early version of Windows XP. Not one of them managed to do it. After many hours of frustration, most ended up furious with Microsoft, and the video she took of these families made a big impact at Microsoft. The first assumption from management was that something was wrong with the people she had chosen, among them a couple in their seventies. What management realised was that, on the contrary, there was something wrong with the way they had been testing software until then: volunteers who had completed the task in laboratory conditions were all tech enthusiasts and therefore not at all representative of the population. Anne says:

> *I am an observer; that is what an ethnographer is. It is not taking a list of questions you would otherwise ask online and sitting in someone's kitchen, ask the same thing. I go to people's homes when they wake up and leave when they go to bed; I go with them. If they are changing a baby's nappy, I watch them do it. I once sat with a women who was ironing for five hours. I do not go into homes to study computers. I do not give a damn whether they have a computer or not. If you really want to know what makes people tick, and their motivations and aspirations, that is where innovation comes from. Do not ask them questions, listen to them.*

---

3 *Sensitive information.* Participants may be unwilling to answer or to give truthful answers to certain questions that invade their privacy, embarrass them, or have a negative impact on their ego or status. Questions that relate to sanitary products and contraception are examples of personally sensitive issues. In business-to-business marketing research, questions that relate to corporate performance and plans are examples of commercially sensitive issues. Techniques that build up an amount of rapport and trust, that allow gentle probing in a manner that suits individual participants, can help researchers get close to participants, and may allow sensitive data to be elicited.

4 *Subconscious feelings.* Participants may be unable to provide accurate answers to questions that tap their subconscious. The values, emotional drives and motivations residing at the subconscious level are disguised from the outer world by rationalisation and other ego defences. For example, a person may have purchased an expensive sports car to overcome

feelings of inferiority. But if asked 'Why did you purchase this sports car?' that person may say 'I got a great deal', 'My old car was falling apart', or 'I need to impress my customers and clients'. The participants do not have to put words to their deeper emotional drives until researchers approach them! In tapping into those deeper emotional drives, qualitative research can take a path that evolves and is right for the participant.

5   *Complex phenomena.* The nature of what participants are expected to describe may be difficult to capture with structured questions. For example, participants may know what brands of wine they enjoy, what types of music they prefer or what images they regard as being prestigious. They may not be able to clearly explain why they have these feelings or where these feelings are coming from.

The following example illustrates a qualitative research challenge that tapped into and revealed characteristics of sensitive information, subconscious feelings and complex phenomena. The use of visual ethnography for MTV proved to be highly engaging and relevant for the participants.

Real research | **Visual ethnography at MTV[12]**

MTV Networks (**www.mtvne.com**) wanted to understand identity construction among young people. Instead of using a traditional ethnographical approach, it used an alternative approach that combined principles from visual ethnography, netnography and Research 2.0. Using pictures for observing individuals in their environment is at the core of visual ethnography. In the early days of visual ethnography, pictures were mainly taken by the observer. A new approach has shifted control towards participants who take their own (self-relevant) pictures. In line with this new approach, MTV gave full control to the participants. The user-generated ethnography took place in two phases. First, participants got the general instruction to take pictures of all aspects of their lives that *they* believed that we should know about in order to get a better understanding of who they were and to get a sense of their daily lives. Next, at several times they received 'special tasks'. These tasks were created to make sure that they collected enough 'relevant observations' in order to help answer the research questions. When creating the special tasks, it was important not to mention the topic of the study directly. Instead each participant was asked to photograph the context where their identity manifests itself. A special role was assigned to clothes and peers. Clothes are one of the main product categories that teenagers use to express their identity. Participants were therefore asked to take pictures of clothes that they wear on several different types of occasions: clothes that they wear at home as a reflection of their personal identity; clothes that represent their social identity; clothes that give insights into their aspirational identity; clothes that they do not want to wear. A similar reasoning was applied for peers, asking participants to take pictures of the friends and people they find important (social identity), others with whom they are not friends but would like to be friends (aspirational identity), adolescents who they would not like to be friends with (non-group) and others that are different than themselves but still socially acceptable. This last group was included to get a more detailed view on all social groups. To get a better understanding of personal identity, participants were also invited to take pictures of objects that were typical of themselves. Finally, participants were asked to take pictures of the place where they could really be themselves.

---

6   *The holistic dimension.* The object of taking a holistic outlook in qualitative research is to gain a comprehensive and complete picture of the whole context in which the phenomena of interest occur. It is an attempt to describe and understand as much as possible about the whole situation of interest. Each scene exists within a multi-layered and interrelated context

and it may require multiple methods to ensure the researcher covers all angles. This orientation helps the researcher discover the interrelationships among the various components of the phenomenon under study. In evaluating different forms of consumer behaviour, the researcher seeks to understand the relationship of different contextual environments upon that behaviour. Setting behaviour into context involves placing observations, experiences and interpretations into a larger perspective.[13] An example of this may be of measuring satisfaction with a meal in a restaurant. A questionnaire can break down components of the experience in the restaurant and quantify the extent of satisfaction with these. But what effect did the 'atmosphere' have upon the experience? What role did the type of music, the colour and style of furniture, aromas coming from the kitchen, other people in the restaurant, the mood when entering the restaurant, feelings of relaxation or tension as the meal went on, contribute to the feeling of atmosphere? Building up an understanding of the interrelationship of the context of consumption allows the qualitative researcher to build up this holistic view. This can be done through qualitative observation and interviewing.

7 *Developing new theory.* This is perhaps the most contentious reason for conducting qualitative research. Chapter 11 details how causal research design through experiments helps to generate theory. Qualitative researchers may argue that there are severe limitations in conducting experiments on consumers and that quantitative approaches are limited to elaborating or extending existing theory. The development of 'new' theory through a qualitative approach is called 'grounded theory', which will be addressed later.

8 *Interpretation.* Qualitative techniques often constitute an important final step in research designs. Large-scale surveys and audits often fail to clarify the underlying reasons for a set of findings. Using qualitative techniques can help to elaborate and explain underlying reasons in quantitative findings.[14]

Philosophy and qualitative research[15]

Positivist perspectives

Theory
A conceptual scheme based on foundational statements, or axioms, that are assumed to be true.

Operationalised
The derivation of measurable characteristics to encapsulate marketing phenomena, e.g. the concept of 'customer loyalty' can be operationalised through measurements such as the frequency of repeat purchases or the number of years that a business relationship has existed.

Empiricism
A theory of knowledge. A broad category of the philosophy of science that locates the source of all knowledge in experience.

Positivism
A philosophy of language and logic consistent with an empiricist philosophy of science.

In Chapter 2 we discussed the vital role that theory plays in marketing research. Researchers rely on theory to determine which variables should be investigated, how variables should be operationalised and measured, and how the research design and sample should be selected. Theory also serves as a foundation on which the researcher can organise and interpret findings. Good marketing research is founded upon theory and contributes to the development of theory to improve the powers of explanation, prediction and understanding in marketing decision-makers.[16]

The dominant perspective of developing new theory in marketing research has been one of empiricism and more specifically positivism. The central belief of a positivist position is a view that the study of consumers and marketing phenomena should be 'scientific' in the manner of the natural sciences. Researchers of this persuasion adopt a framework for investigation akin to the natural scientist. For many, this is considered to be both desirable and possible. A fundamental belief shared by positivists is the view that the social and natural worlds 'conform to certain fixed and unalterable laws in an endless chain of causation'.[17] The main purpose of a scientific approach to marketing research is to establish causal laws that enable the prediction and explanation of marketing phenomena. To establish these laws, a scientific approach must have, as a minimum, reliable information or 'facts'. The emphasis on facts leads to a focus upon objectivity, rigour and measurement.

As an overall research approach (using the description of a paradigm or research approach as developed in Chapter 2) qualitative research does not rely upon measurement or the establishment of 'facts' and so does not fit with a positivist perspective. However, if qualitative research is just seen as a series of techniques, they can be used to develop an understanding of the nature of a research problem, and to develop and pilot questionnaires. In other words, the positivist perspective of qualitative research is to see it as a set of techniques, applied as preliminary stages to more 'rigorous' techniques that measure, i.e. surveys and questionnaires. This use of qualitative techniques is fine but can have many limitations. Conducting in-depth interviews, focus groups or ethnographic techniques can help enormously in understanding the language and logic of consumers. In turn, this understanding of a language and logic can strengthen and focus the design of surveys and questionnaires. However, using qualitative techniques just to develop quantitative techniques represents a narrow perspective of their rich, creative and exploratory powers. As an illustration, we will examine how different perspectives of the nature and value of qualitative research can impact upon how a technique may be conducted, in this case focus group discussions.

The term 'focus group discussion' is commonly used across all continents, yet it subsumes different ways of applying the technique. There are two main schools of thought that underpin the technique which may be termed 'cognitive' and 'conative'. The American, Japanese and European illustrations used simplify much of the variations that occur and develop within these states. The examples serve to illustrate the origins, thinking and focus that can be adopted in running focus groups:

1   *Cognitive.* American and Japanese researchers generally follow this tradition, which largely follows a format and interviewing style as used in quantitative studies. 'American-style groups' is shorthand in Europe for large groups (10 participants on average), a structured procedure and a strong element of external validation. Within the cognitive approach, the analysis or articulation has been worked on before, and so the interviews are largely meant to confirm or expand on known issues. The following example presents a caricature of the Japanese style of focus group to illustrate a *cognitive* underpinning.

Real research | ## Japanese focus groups[18]

The aspiration in using the focus group in Japan is to replicate the often stimulating, rich and thought-provoking experience (for clients) that one often finds in the West. Yet, many of the practices and reflexes in use in the West are at odds with the need at the heart of Japanese research orthodoxy to reduce the bias in the focus group. For instance, the moderator has been discouraged from explaining too much about the concept of the focus group, what marketing research does and what the study at hand is trying to achieve. Sharing such information has been considered contamination of the participants and introducing a bias. For the moderator to show human warmth beyond the strictly polite has likewise been considered a biasing approach. Free expression of opinion and having an opinion is a value in Western culture whereas in Japan it is not. Non-Japanese clients are inevitably frustrated with the failure to achieve a group that engage in an open discussion with the sharing of deep thoughts and opposing statements: people there do not usually and openly express an opinion on things and people. As part of the quantitative heritage of qualitative research in Japan and the consequent obsession with avoiding bias, the focus group room has been synthetic, grey and devoid of emotion and 'homeyness' in an attempt to reach a neutral bias-free setting. Japanese research has introduced boardrooms and office chairs into rooms with no windows and artificial light on grey walls. Is it a surprise that it is hard for participants to talk about their daily lives and personal matters? The successful application of home-visit and ethnography research in Japan demonstrates that in relaxed and humanised conditions, consumers can talk more openly about their inner needs and private thoughts. We believe that a room with a relaxing décor, music in the background, dimmed lights and even alcohol can help the participant engage in the group situation and offer deeper insight. What this means is that it is important to create a more at-home atmosphere.

2 *Conative.* European researchers generally follow this tradition. This style assumes a different starting point, one that emphasises exploration, with analysis taking place during and after the group. There is less structure to the questions, with group members being encouraged to take their own paths of discussion, make their own connections and let the whole process evolve.

Table 6.1 summarises the differences between the American (cognitive) and European (conative) approaches to conducting focus groups. Note the longer duration of the European approach to allow the exploration to develop. To maintain the interest and motivation of participants for this time period, the interview experience must be engaging, stimulating and enjoyable. International marketers have always been aware that qualitative research as it developed in the USA and Europe involves quite different practices, stemming from different premises and yielding different results. American-style qualitative research started from the same evaluative premise as quantitative research but on a smaller scale. This made it cheaper, quicker and useful for checking out the less critical decisions. European-style qualitative research started from the opposite premise to quantitative research: it was developmental, exploratory and creative rather than evaluative. It was used as a tool of understanding, to get underneath consumer motivation.[19]

The American style uses a detailed discussion guide which follows a logical sequence and is usually strictly adhered to. The interviewing technique involves closed questions and straight answers. This type of research is used primarily to inform about behaviour and to confirm hypotheses already derived from other sources. For this reason, clients who have attended

Table 6.1	The two schools of thought about 'focus group discussions'[20]	
Characteristics	**Cognitive**	**Conative**
Purpose	Demonstration	Exploration
Sample size	10–12	6–8
Duration	1.5 hours	1.5 to 6 hours
Interviewing	Logical sequence	Opportunistic
Questions	Closed	Open
Techniques	Straight question, questionnaires, hand shows, counting	Probing, facilitation, projectives, describing
Response required	Give answers	Debate issues
Interviewer	Moderator	Researcher
Observer's role	To get proof	To understand
Transcripts	Rarely necessary	Usually full
Analysis	On the spot	Time consuming
Focus of time	Preplanning	Post-fieldwork
Accusations against other style	'Formless'	'Over-controlling'
Suited for	Testing or proving ideas	Meaning or understanding
Output	To be confirmed in quantitative studies	Can be used in its own right to support decision-makers

groups often feel they do not need any further analysis; the group interaction supplies the answers. Transcripts are rarely necessary and reports are often summarised or even done away with altogether.

The European style is used primarily to gain new insight; it also works from a discussion guide, but in a less structured way. The interviewing technique is opportunistic and probing. Projective techniques are introduced to help researchers understand underlying motivations and attitudes. Because the purpose is 'understanding', which requires a creative synthesis of (sometimes unconscious) consumer needs and brand benefits, analysis is time consuming and usually involves full transcripts.

In the above descriptions of American and European traditions of applying qualitative techniques, it is clear to see that the American perspective is positivist, i.e. aims to deliver a 'factual' impression of consumers. The facts may be established, but they may not be enough; they may not provide the richness or depth of understanding that certain marketing decision-makers demand. So, although a positivist perspective has a role to play in developing explanations, predictions and understanding of consumers and marketing phenomena, it has its limitations and critics. In a seminal paper that reviews the evolution and future of qualitative research, the eminent qualitative practitioner Peter Cooper encapsulated the power of focus groups, viewed in a non-positivist manner. He argued that they have delivered and continue to deliver understanding and anticipation of consumers, opening up factors driving choice, adapting to and predicting the changing power and influence of consumers:

> *Forming groups has given us primates our evolutionary competitive edge. They enable us to learn, solve problems, communicate, share experiences, and understand others. Around the flickering campfire we swapped stories, developed relationships, built up togetherness, groomed one another, resolved conflicts, played games, adopted roles, deceived, told falsehoods, and invented spirits and gods. There is a compulsion about groups that we all share. One explanation is that in the contemporary world where campfires no longer exist and there is reduced opportunity for real social interaction, joining in groups is yearned for. But focus groups are not kinship groups. True, participants are paid to come, but most are made up of people who do not know one another, and are largely drawn from wider circles that happen to have some behaviour in common. We know them as types not as people. This is where their everlasting fascination lies. Participants are often deliberately strangers, 'virtual' people, who then disappear. We know that people posture, exaggerate, deceive, but we can step into their shoes for a fleeting few hours.*[21]

The dominance of positivist philosophy in marketing research has been and is being challenged by other philosophical perspectives, taken and adapted from disciplines such as anthropology and sociology. These perspectives have helped researchers to develop richer explanations and predictions and especially an understanding and a meaning as seen through the eyes of consumers.

Interpretivist perspectives

In general, there are considered to be two main research paradigms that are used by marketing researchers.[22] These are the positivist paradigm and the interpretivist paradigm (though these are by no means the only research paradigms that may be adopted by researchers).[23] Table 6.2 presents alternative names that may be used to describe these paradigms.

While it may be easier to think of these as quite clear, distinct and mutually exclusive perspectives of developing valid and useful marketing knowledge, the reality is somewhat different. There is a huge array of versions of these paradigms, presented by philosophers, researchers and users of research findings. These versions change depending upon the assumptions of researchers and the context and subjects of their study, i.e. the ultimate nature of the research problem. It has long been argued that both positivist and interpretivist paradigms are valid in conducting marketing research and help to shape the nature of techniques that researchers apply.[24]

Table 6.2	Alternative paradigm names[25]
Positivist	**Interpretivist**
Quantitative	Qualitative
Objectivist	Subjectivist
Scientific	Humanistic
Experimentalist	Phenomenological
Traditionalist	Revolutionist

In order to develop an understanding of what an interpretivist paradigm means, Table 6.3 presents characteristic features of the two paradigms.

Comparison of positivist and interpretivist perspectives

The paradigms can be compared through a series of issues. The descriptions of these issues do not imply that any particular paradigm is stronger than the other. In each issue there are relative advantages and disadvantages specific to any research question under investigation. The issues are dealt with in the following subsections.

Reality. The positivist supposes that reality is 'out there' to be captured. It thus becomes a matter of finding the most effective and objective means possible to draw together information about this reality. The interpretivist stresses the dynamic, participant-constructed and evolving nature of reality, recognising that there may be a wide array of interpretations of realities or social acts.

Table 6.3	Paradigm features[26]	
Issue	**Positivist**	**Interpretivist**
Reality	Objective and singular	Subjective and multiple
Researcher–participant	Independent of each other	Interacting with each other
Values	Value free = unbiased	Value laden = biased
Researcher language	Formal and impersonal	Informal and personal
Theory and research design	Simple determinist	Freedom of will
	Cause and effect	Multiple influences
	Static research design	Evolving design
	Context free	Context bound
	Laboratory	Field/ethnography
	Prediction and control	Understanding and insight
	Reliability and validity	Perceptive decision making
	Representative surveys	Theoretical sampling
	Experimental design	Case studies
	Deductive	Inductive

Researcher–participant. The positivist sees the participant as an 'object' to be measured in a reliable or consistent manner. The interpretivist may see participants as 'peers' or even 'companions', seeking the right context and means of observing and questioning to suit individual participants. Such a view of participants requires the development of rapport, an amount of interaction and evolution of method as the researcher learns of the best means to gain access and elicit information.

Values. The positivist seeks to set aside his or her own personal values. The positivist's measurements of participants are being guided by established theoretical propositions. The task for the positivist is to remove any potential bias. The interpretivist recognises that their own values affect how they observe, question, probe and interpret. The task for interpretivists is to reflect upon and realise the nature of their values and how these impact upon how they observe, question and interpret.

Researcher language. In seeking a consistent and unbiased means to measure, the positivist uses a language in questioning that is uniformly recognised. This uniformity may emerge from existing theory (to allow comparability of findings) and/or from the positivist's vision of what may be relevant to the target group of participants. Ultimately, the positivist imposes a language and logic upon target participants in a reliable or consistent manner. The interpretivist seeks to draw out the language and logic of target participants. The language used may differ between participants and develop in different ways as the interpretivist learns more about a topic and the nature of participants.

Causality

Causality applies when the occurrence of X increases the probability of the occurrence of Y.

Extraneous variables

Variables other than dependent and independent variables which may influence the results of an experiment.

Determinism

A doctrine espousing that everything that happens is determined by a necessary chain of causation.

Target population

The collection of elements or objects that possess the information sought by the researcher and about which inferences are made.

Reliability

The extent to which a scale produces consistent results if repeated measurements are made on the characteristic.

Validity

The extent to which a measurement represents characteristics that exist in the phenomenon under investigation.

Case study

A detailed study based upon the observation of the intrinsic details of individuals, groups of individuals and organisations.

Theory and research design. In the development of theory, the positivist seeks to establish causality (to be discussed in detail in Chapter 11) through experimental methods. Seeking causality helps the positivist to explain phenomena and hopefully predict the recurrence of what has been observed in other contexts. There are many extraneous variables that may confound the outcome of experiments, hence the positivist will seek to control these variables and the environment in which an experiment takes place. The ultimate control in an experiment takes place in a laboratory situation. In establishing causality through experiments, questions of causality usually go hand in hand with questions of determinism, i.e. if everything that happens has a cause, then we live in a determinist universe.

The positivist will go to great pains to diagnose the nature of a research problem and establish an explicit and set research design to investigate the problem. A fundamental element of the positivist's research design is the desire to generalise findings to a target population. Most targeted populations are so large that measurements of them can only be managed through representative sample surveys. The positivists use theory to develop the consistent and unbiased measurements they seek. They have established rules and tests of the reliability and validity of their measurements and continually seek to develop more reliable and valid measurements.

In the development of theory, the interpretivist seeks to understand the nature of multiple influences of marketing phenomena through case studies. The search for multiple influences means focusing upon the intrinsic details of individual cases and the differences between different classes of case. This helps the interpretivist to describe phenomena and hopefully gain new and creative insights to understand ultimately the nature of consumer behaviour in its fullest sense. The consumers that interpretivists focus upon, live, consume and relate to products and services in a huge array of contexts, hence the interpretivist will seek to understand the nature and effect of these contexts on the chosen cases. The contexts in which consumers live and consume constitute the field in which interpretivists immerse themselves to conduct their investigations. In understanding the nature and effect of context upon consumers, the interpretivist does not consider that *everything* that happens has a cause and that we live in a determinist universe. There is a recognition and respect for the notion of free will.

The interpretivist will go to great pains to learn from each step of the research process and adapt the research design as their learning develops. The interpretivist seeks to diagnose the nature of a research problem but recognises that a set research design may be restrictive and

Evolving research design
A research design where particular research techniques are chosen as the researcher develops an understanding of the issues and participants.

Theoretical sampling
Data gathering driven by concepts derived from evolving theory and based on the concept of 'making comparisons'.

so usually adopts an evolving research design. A fundamental element of the interpretivist's research design is the desire to generalise findings to different contexts, such as other types of consumer. However, rather than seeking to study large samples to generalise to target populations, the interpretivist uses theoretical sampling. This means that the data gathering process for interpretivists is driven by concepts derived from evolving theory, based on the notion of seeking out different situations and learning from the comparisons that can be made. The purpose is to go to places, people or events that will maximise opportunities to discover variations among concepts. Interpretivists use theory initially to help guide which cases they should focus upon, the issues they should observe and the context of their investigation. As their research design evolves they seek to develop new theory and do not wish to be 'blinkered' or too focused on existing ideas. They seek multiple explanations of the phenomena they observe and create what they see as the most valid relationship of concepts and, ultimately, theory. Interpretivists seek to evaluate the strength of the theory they develop. The strongest means of evaluating the strength of interpretivist theory lies in the results of decision making that is based on the theory. Interpretivists continually seek to evaluate the worth of the theories they develop. A principal output of research generated by an interpretivist perspective should therefore be findings that are accessible and intended for use. If they are found to be meaningful by decision-makers and employed successfully by them, this may constitute further evidence of the theory's validity. If employed and found lacking, questions will have to be asked of the theory, about its comprehensibility and comprehensiveness and about its interpretation. If it is not used, the theory may be loaded with validity but have little value.

Summarising the broad perspectives of positivism and interpretivism

Deduction
A form of reasoning in which a conclusion is validly inferred from some premises, and must be true if those premises are true.

Induction
A form of reasoning that usually involves the inference that an instance or repeated combination of events may be universally generalised.

The positivist seeks to establish the legitimacy of his or her approach through deduction. In a deductive approach, the following process unfolds:

- An area of enquiry is identified, set in the context of well-developed theory, which is seen as vital to guide researchers, ensuring that they are not naïve in their approach and do not 'reinvent the wheel'.

- The issues to focus an enquiry upon emerge from the established theoretical framework.

- Specific variables are identified that the researchers deem should be measured, i.e. hypotheses are set.

- An 'instrument' to measure specific variables is developed.

- 'Participants' give answers to set and specific questions with a consistent language and logic.

- The responses to the set questions are analysed in terms of a prior established theoretical framework.

- The researchers test theory according to whether their hypotheses are accepted or rejected. From testing theory in a new context, they seek to develop existing theory incrementally.

Such a process means that positivists reach conclusions based upon agreed and measurable 'facts'. The building and establishment of 'facts' forms the premises of deductive arguments. Deductive reasoning starts from general principles from which the deduction is to be made, and proceeds to a conclusion by way of some statement linking the particular case in question.

A deductive approach has a well-established role for existing theory: it informs the development of hypotheses, the choice of variables and the resultant measures.[27] Whereas the deductive approach starts with theory expressed in the form of hypotheses, which are then tested, an inductive approach avoids this, arguing that it may prematurely close off possible areas of enquiry.[28]

The interpretivist seeks to establish the legitimacy of their approach through induction. In an inductive approach, the following process unfolds:

- An area of enquiry is identified, but with limited or no theoretical framework. Theoretical frameworks are seen as restrictive, narrowing the researcher's perspective, and an inhibitor to creativity.

- The issues to focus an enquiry upon are either observed or elicited from participants in particular contexts.

- Participants are aided to explain the nature of issues in a particular context.

- Broad themes are identified for discussion, with observation, probing and in-depth questioning to elaborate the nature of these themes.

- The researchers develop their theory by searching for the occurrence and interconnection of phenomena. They seek to develop a model based upon their observed combination of events. Such a process means that interpretivists reach conclusions without 'complete evidence'.

With the intense scrutiny of individuals in specific contexts that typify an interpretivist approach, tackling large 'representative' samples is generally impossible. Thus, the validity of the interpretivist approach is based upon 'fair samples'. Interpretivists should not seek only to reinforce their own prejudice or bias, seizing upon issues that are agreeable to them and ignoring those that are inconvenient. If they are to argue reasonably they should counteract this tendency by searching for conflicting evidence.[29] Their resultant theory should be subject to constant review and revision.

Ethnographic research

It is clear that an interpretive approach does not set out to test hypotheses but to explore the nature and interrelationships of marketing phenomena. The focus of investigation is a detailed examination of a small number of cases rather than a large sample. The data collected are analysed through an explicit interpretation of the meanings and functions of consumer actions. The product of these analyses takes the form of verbal descriptions and explanations (sometimes supported by visuals or other forms of art), with quantification and statistical analysis playing a subordinate role. These characteristics are the hallmark of a research approach that has developed and been applied to marketing problems over many years in Europe and increasingly so across the globe. This research approach is one of ethnographic research.

Ethnography

A research approach based upon the observation of the customs, habits and differences between people in everyday situations.

Ethnography as a general term includes observation and interviewing and is sometimes referred to as participant observation. It is, however, used in the more specific case of a method which requires a researcher to spend a large amount of time observing a particular group of people, by sharing their way of life.[30] Ethnography is the art and science of describing a group or culture. The description may be of a small tribal group in an exotic land or a toy factory in Poland. The task is much like the one taken on by the investigative reporter, who interviews relevant people, reviews records, takes photographs, weighs the credibility of one person's opinions against another's, looks for ties to special interests and organisations, and writes the story for a concerned public and for professional colleagues. A key difference between the investigative reporter and the ethnographer, however, is that whereas the journalist seeks out the unusual, the murder, the plane crash, or the bank robbery, the ethnographer writes about the routine daily lives of people. The more predictable patterns of human thought and behaviour are the focus of enquiry.[31]

The origins of ethnography are in the work of nineteenth-century anthropologists who travelled to observe different pre-industrial cultures. An example in a more contemporary context could be the study of death rituals in Borneo, conducted over a period of two years by the anthropologist Peter Metcalf.[32] Today, 'ethnography' encompasses a much broader range of work, from studies of groups in one's own culture, through experimental writing, to political interventions. Moreover, ethnographers today do not always 'observe', at least not directly. They may work with cultural artefacts such as written texts, or study recordings of interactions they did not observe at first hand,[33] or even, as in the following example, the observations of teenagers as viewed through photographs taken on their mobile phones.

Chocolate or mobile?[34]

Ayobamidele Gnädig and Oliver Schieleit are project directors at the German qualitative research agency H.T.P. Concept (**www.htp-concept.de**). They asked teenagers to photo-blog their snacking habits with their mobile phones and saw that many of these were 'boredom-relief' moments where they were waiting for trains, buses or friends who were late for an appointment. When they spent time with them, a whole day or just an afternoon, they saw this moment crop up time and again. They also believe they witnessed a change in that these moments were increasingly being filled

differently than maybe five or ten years ago. Instead of quickly buying a Mars bar at the nearby kiosk, a young teen was just as likely to spend time waiting for a bus in writing text messages to friends. This meant that in some contexts, the text message had become 'top of the mind' over the chocolate bar. Through understanding by observing and not by probing the dynamics, H.T.P. Concept offered a first step for chocolate brands to develop new ideas, communications and distribution concepts to address this opportunity.

Ethnography cannot reasonably be classified as just another single method or technique.[35] In essence, it is a research discipline based upon culture as an organising concept and a mix of both observational and interviewing tactics to record behavioural dynamics. Above all, ethnography relies upon entering participants' natural life worlds, at home, while shopping, at leisure and in the workplace. The researcher essentially becomes a naïve visitor in that world by engaging participants during realistic product usage situations in the course of daily life. Whether called on-site, observational, naturalistic or contextual research, ethnographic methods allow marketers to delve into actual situations in which products are used, services are received and benefits are conferred. Ethnography takes place not in laboratories but in the real world. Consequently, clients and practitioners benefit from a more holistic and better nuanced view of consumer satisfactions, frustrations and limitations than in any other research method.[36]

Researchers apply ethnographic methods in natural retail or other commercial environments in order to fully appreciate the nature of consumer experiences. There are several objectives that lie behind these studies, one of which is oriented towards a detailed ecological analysis of sales behaviour. In other words, consumer interactions with all of the elements that comprise retail store environments: lighting, smells, signage, display of goods, the location, size and orientation of shelving. Observing how these may impact upon the consumers' experience and their ultimate buying behaviour can be of great value to designers and marketers. The ethnographer's role is to decode the meaning and impact of these ecological elements. Often, these studies utilise time-lapse photography as a tool for behavioural observation and data collection over extensive periods of time and can avoid actual interaction with consumers.

Ethnographic research achieves this immersion with consumers through the following aims:

- *Seeing through the eyes of others.* Viewing events, actions, norms and values from the perspective of the people being studied.

- *Description.* Built up in many written and visual forms to provide clues and pointers to the layers of 'reality' experienced by consumers.

- *Contextualism.* Attending to mundane detail to help understand what is going on in a particular context. Whatever the sphere in which the data are being collected, events can be best understood when they are situated in the wider social and historical context.

- *Process.* Viewing social life as involving an interlocking series of events.

- *Avoiding early use of theories and concepts.* Rejecting premature attempts to impose theories and concepts which may exhibit a poor fit with participants' perspectives. This will be developed further in this chapter when we examine grounded theory.

- *Flexible research designs.* Ethnographers' adherence to viewing social phenomena through the eyes of their participants or subjects has led to a wariness regarding the imposition of prior and possibly inappropriate frames of reference on the people they study. This leads to a preference for an open and unstructured research design which increases the possibility of coming across unexpected issues.

The following example displays characteristics of all the above aims and introduces new developments in ethnography as applied in marketing research.

Real research | **Netnography at Nivea**[37]

Nivea is the best-known brand of the multinational corporation Beiersdorf based in Hamburg, Germany. In order to integrate the voice of consumers beyond traditional marketing research techniques like concept tests or focus groups, the Nivea Body Care Division instituted a holistic co-creation process that included the application of netnography. They used this approach to start new-product development, helping R&D to immerse and orientate itself in the consumers' world. The goal was to draw a landscape of needs, wishes, concerns, consumer language and potential product solutions by users, which were explicitly and implicitly expressed in online communities and social media. They started with a broad search of more than 200 online communities, forums and blogs in three languages, screening all kinds of 'consumer tribes' that have emerged online. The most relevant and insightful communities and forums on cosmetics, health, lifestyle, fashion, sports and do-it-yourself were observed and analysed, examples being **beauty24. de**, **bubhub.com.au**, **badgerandblade.com**, **glamour.de** or **undershirtguy.com**. To follow this search, threads of consumer conversations were analysed using qualitative data software. In the field of deodorants, the consumer dialogue revealed that users speak about a number of issues revolving around the buying, application and effectiveness of deodorants in their own language and with a distinct classification. In order to overcome issues consumers also resorted to self-made remedies or diverted substances from their intended use. Certain needs, concerns or suggestions for product improvements repeatedly occurred in consumers' online conversations. Those 'gold nuggets', i.e. fresh, relevant, inspiring and enduring findings, were then aggregated to consumer insights. For example, one consumer insight introduced Nivea to do-it-yourself solutions which were exchanged between users online. Those self-made remedies were systematically structured, depicted and supported by a coding report of consumer statements. The consumer insights helped Beiersdorf to develop a deep understanding of consumers, the language they use and what truly bothers them. Applying the netnography method Beiersdorf was able to identify trends in the field of body care and obtain innovative product and marketing ideas. In the final step of the netnography, product designers joined the research team and helped to interpret and translate the consumer insights into initial products.

Netnography
An adaptation of ethnography that analyses the free behaviour of individuals in online environments.

Co-creation
The practice of developing new designs including products or marketing communications through collaboration with consumers.

This example introduces the method of netnography, an adaptation of ethnography that analyses the free behaviour of individuals in online environments.[38] Observing online communities can be much faster, simpler and less expensive than traditional ethnography. It is also unelicited, so more natural and unobtrusive than surveys and interviews. Netnography can refer to the passive process of following conversations and interactions on the Net at the individual level; this was the approach taken by Nivea. It can also involve a more active engagement with consumers on the net directing questions, or becoming a participant observer in a community.[39] Passive or active netnography approaches create privacy, security and safety challenges for researchers. Social media have changed the rules on how 'findable' somebody is. This has enormous implications for privacy and safety. Debates about what is 'in the public domain', and what can be used when, where and how, will impact enormously upon the development of codes of conduct for researchers.

Irrespective of ethical challenges they may bring, the use of ethnographic approaches has rapidly developed in marketing research. The Nivea example illustrates a very creative and engaging use of netnography as part of a co-creation process. Co-creation is the practice of developing new designs including products or marketing communications through collaboration with consumers. In the early 2000s, large advertisers including Nike established successful co-creation projects. The Danish toy company Lego was another advocate of co-creation, with a project beginning in 2004 signing up 'master-builders' to help design products. Initially, only four people were invited to join; the following year 10 collaborators joined followed by 100 from 10,000 consumers who applied.[40] Enthusiasm for what Lego was doing spread to the blogosphere and to social networks, with a host of unofficial websites set up by fans, suggesting further innovations to the firm.[41]

One of the key features of all the descriptions and illustrations of forms of ethnography is the context in which the consumer is behaving. The researcher observes people experiencing, taking in and reacting to communications, product and services, retail experience, all behaving naturally in the set context. For example, in the context of shoppers this does not just mean the retail outlet they visit. The processes of choosing and buying products, of using products or giving them as gifts, of reflecting upon and planning subsequent purchases, are all affected by contextual factors. Context operates on several levels, including the immediate physical and situational surroundings of consumers, as well as language, character, culture and history. Each of these levels can provide a basis for the meaning and significance attached to the roles and behaviour of consumption:

> *Can we divorce the ways we buy, use and talk about products from the cultural and linguistic context within which economic transitions occur? The answer is an emphatic NO.*[42]

The ethnographer may observe the consumer acting and reacting in the context of consumption. The ethnographer may see a shopper spending time reading the labels on cat food, showing different brands to their partner, engaged in deep conversation, pondering, getting frustrated and putting tins back on the shelf. The ethnographer may see the same shopper more purposefully putting an expensive bottle of cognac into a shopping trolley without any discussion and seemingly with no emotional attachment to the product. The ethnographer may want to know what is going on. How may the consumer explain their attitudes and motivations behind this behaviour? This is where the interplay of observation and interviewing helps to build such a rich picture of consumers. In questioning the shopper in the above example, responses of 'we think that Rémy Martin is the best' or 'we always argue about which are the prettiest cat food labels' would not be enough. The stories and contexts of how these assertions came to be would be explored. The ethnographer does not tend to take simple explanations for activities that in many circumstances may be habitual to consumers. Ethnographic practice takes a highly critical attitude towards expressed language. It challenges our accepted words at face value, searching instead for the meanings and values that lie beneath the surface. In interviewing situations, typically this involves looking for gaps between expressed and non-verbal communication elements. For example, if actual practices and facial and physical gestures are inconsistent with a participant's expressed attitudes towards the expensive cognac, we are challenged to discover both the reality behind the given answer and the reasons for the 'deception'.

Ethnographic research is also effective as a tool for learning situationally and culturally grounded language, the appropriate words for everyday things as spoken by various age or ethnic groups. Copywriters and strategic thinkers are always pressed to talk about products and brands in evocative and original ways. Ethnography helps act as both a discovery and an evaluation tool.[43] To summarise, ethnographic approaches are useful when the marketing research objectives call for:[44]

1 *High-intensity situations.* To study high-intensity situations, such as a sales encounter, meal preparation and service, or communication between persons holding different levels of authority.

2 *Behavioural processes.* To conduct precise analyses of behavioural processes, e.g. radio listening behaviour, home computer purchasing decisions or home cleaning behaviour.

3 *Memory inadequate.* To address situations where the participant's memory or reflection would not be adequate. Observational methods can stand alone or can complement interviewing as a memory jog.

4 *Shame or reluctance.* To work with participants who are likely to be ashamed or reluctant to reveal actual practices to a group of peers. If they were diabetic, for example, participants may be reluctant to reveal that they have a refrigerator full of sweet snacks, something that an ethnographic observer would be able to see without confronting the subject.

In these applications, the ethnographer is expected to analyse critically the situations observed. The critique or analysis can be guided by theory but in essence the researcher develops a curiosity, thinks in an abstract manner and at times steps back to reflect and see how emerging ideas connect. By reacting to the events and participants as they face them, to draw out what they see as important, ethnographers have the ability to create new explanations and understandings of consumers. This ability to develop a new vision, to a large extent unrestricted by existing theory, is the essence of a grounded theory approach, which is explained and illustrated in the next section. Before we evaluate the nature and application of grounded theory, it is worth examining one final example of an ethnographic study that embraces the idea of 'listening'.

Listening

Listening involves the evaluation of naturally occurring conversations, behaviours and signals. This information that is elicited may or may not be guided, but it brings the voice of consumers' lives to brand.

Listening involves the evaluation of naturally occurring conversations, behaviours and signals. The information that is elicited may or may not be guided, but it brings the voice of consumers' lives to brand. Every day, millions of consumers talk about all aspects of their lives online. This wealth of naturally occurring consumer expression offers the opportunity to understand consumers on their terms, using their language and logic. Due to the Internet, high-speed access and the 'conversational webs' of blogs, forums, social networks, Twitter, communities and wikis, people are talking with one another about their problems, experiences, likes and dislikes, life in general, and their feelings and experiences of brands. By tuning in to relevant conversations (i.e. by listening), it is argued that more can be learned about consumer attitudes and needs than through traditional 'questioning' methods alone. Advocates of listening approaches would argue that researchers have interacted with 'participants' on their terms: *they* ask the questions they want to ask, the way *they* want to ask them, when *they* want to ask them. This can be seen as intrusive and out of step with the lives of consumers and is not conducive to developing a thorough, context-laden understanding of consumer opinions and needs.[45] By listening, researchers may be able to learn more about consumers and prospects by understanding the natural, rich, unfiltered word of mouth around products and service experiences. This approach is illustrated in the following example.

The essentials of listening at Hennessy Cognac[46]

Hennessy (**www.hennessy.com**), the leading cognac brand, discovered a rising trend in links made between its company website and BlackPlanet.com, the largest social network for African-Americans. Digging deeper, Hennessy learned that numbers of BlackPlanet members linked their personal pages to Hennessy's site. Some went further, decorating their pages with borrowed images of Hennessy brands. By listening to signals embedded in linking behaviour, Hennessy had stumbled upon a passionate market it was not aware of. Interested to learn more about these consumers, Hennessy then studied a random sample of BlackPlanet member web pages to understand their themes and use of brand imagery. Hennessy also commissioned an online survey with research partner CRM Metrix (**www.crmmetrix.com**) to profile audience attitudes, usage and influence. Hennessy discovered that visions of the Hennessy brand expressed in the member pages 'were not necessarily ours, but this does not make them any less valid'. Research showed that 'the brand belongs as much to its consumers as to its managers . . . We must listen without prejudice.' Stated another way, this was a shining illustration of customer 'co-creation' and extraordinary brand engagement. The survey data described 8 of 10 of these individuals as 'high-value' consumers, with a strong influence on the alcohol choices of people around them. About half the participants were opinion leaders, a higher-than-usual percentage. Recognising the inherent and potential long-term value in BlackPlanet members, Hennessy then sought to learn what would improve the site and make it more interesting and enjoyable. Hennessy went further than just tweaking the site; it asked for and listened to suggestions about 'what would make your experience of drinking Hennessy cognacs more enjoyable?' Realising that BlackPlanet members enjoyed drinking socially and mixing Hennessy into drinks, it added recipes highlighting cognac as an ingredient and offered Hennessy-branded e-invitations for parties. Five years after the initial round of responses, the Hennessy site showed the brand's ongoing commitment to listening and evolving the relationship and experience. In 2009, Hennessy's 'Artistry' initiative sponsored musicians and music tours, streamed music and showcased artists. Hennessy also added a social networking component by creating presences on Facebook and YouTube.

Grounded theory

Grounded theory
A qualitative approach to generating theory through the systematic and simultaneous process of data collection and analysis.

The tradition of grounded theory was developed by Glaser and Strauss in the late 1950s and published in their seminal work in 1967.[47] At that time, qualitative research was viewed more as impressionistic or anecdotal, little more than 'soft science' or journalism.[48] It was generally believed that the objective of sociology should be to produce scientific theory, and to test this meant using quantitative methods.[49] Qualitative research was seen to have a place, but only to the extent to which it developed questions which could then be verified using quantitative techniques. Glaser and Strauss accepted that the study of people should be scientific, in the way understood by quantitative researchers. This meant that it should seek to produce theoretical propositions that were testable and verifiable, produced by a clear set of replicable procedures. Glaser and Strauss defined theory as follows:

> theory in sociology is a strategy for handling data in research, providing modes of conceptualization for describing and explaining. The theory should provide clear enough categories and hypotheses so that crucial ones can be verified in present and future research; they must be clear enough to be readily operationalized in quantitative studies when these are appropriate.[50]

The focus upon developing theory was made explicit in response to criticisms of ethnographic studies that present lengthy extracts from interviews or field observations. Strauss sought to reinforce his view of the importance of theory, illustrated by the following quote:

> *much that passes for analysis is relatively low level description. Many quite esteemed and excellent monographs use a great deal of data, quotes or field note selections. The procedure is very useful when the behavior being studied is relatively foreign to the experiences of most readers or when the factual assertions being made would be under considerable contest by skeptical and otherwise relatively well-informed readers. Most of these monographs are descriptively dense, but alas theoretically thin. If you look at their indexes, there are almost no new concepts listed, ones that have emerged in the course of research.*[51]

In contrast to the perhaps casual manner in which some ethnographers may be criticised for attempts at developing theory, the grounded theorist follows a set of systematic procedures for collecting and analysing data. This systematic procedure is used to encourage researchers to use their intellectual imagination and creativity to develop new theories, to suggest methods for doing so, to offer criteria to evaluate the worth of discovered theory, and to propose an alternative rhetoric of justification.[52] The most distinctive feature of grounded theory is its commitment to 'discovery' through direct contact with the social phenomena under study, coupled with a rejection of a priori theorising. This feature does not mean that researchers should embark on their studies without any general guidance provided by some sort of theoretical understanding. It would be nigh on impossible for a researcher to shut out the ideas in the literature surrounding a particular subject. However, Glaser and Strauss argued that preconceived theories should be rejected as they obstruct the development of new theories by coming between researchers and the subjects of their study. In other words, the strict adherence to developing new theory built upon an analytical framework of existing theory can result in 'narrow-minded' researchers who do not explore a much wider range of explanations and possibilities. With the rejection of a priori theorising and a commitment to imaginative and creative discovery comes a conception of knowledge as emergent. This knowledge is created by researchers in the context of investigative practices that afford them intimate contact with the subjects and phenomena under study.[53]

The following example illustrates the use of grounded theory in the development of theory related to how advertising works. The study was conducted by a senior marketing research professional and a professor of advertising. The example is then followed by a description of the process involved in developing theory through a grounded theory process.[54]

Real research | **Agency practitioners' meta-theories of advertising**[55]

What do advertising agency practitioners think about how advertising works? This study's basic aim was to understand practitioners' thinking about the work of advertising in their own terms. As there was little substantive research of this perspective, a grounded theory approach to qualitative research was used. Semi-structured, in-depth interviews were used as the key field method; these allowed the discovery of participant-determined points of view. Preliminary preparations for data collection started well before actual interviewing. Informal interviews were conducted with qualitative–ethnographic experts. Email and phone conversations were exchanged about the feasibility of the project, opinions about method and tips for effective interviewing were exchanged. Based on the insights gained in these preparations and from the relevant literature, an initial interview guide was developed. This was built around three questions: (1) what the content of practitioners' knowledge is; (2) how practitioners know what they know;

and (3) how they use this knowledge in everyday practice. The interview guide used both opening 'grand tour' questions as well as more specific probes. Twenty-eight participants were interviewed until theoretical saturation was achieved (i.e. concepts were identified and linked to other concepts until no new information was obtained). Three occupational groups were interviewed: account managers, account planners and creative directors. Interviews lasted from 45 to 90 minutes. Most took place in the participants' offices. Practitioners were encouraged to talk freely but were also probed using academic theories in the early stages of the interviews for comparative purposes. Extensive field notes were composed immediately following the interviews. These reflections helped refine ways of asking questions and with the development of emerging concepts. The field notes were entered into the NVivo (**www.qsrinternational.com**) qualitative data analysis software. The findings, presented in a manuscript format, were checked with participants. They agreed that the content accurately reflected their thoughts. This study was the first attempt to get at agency practitioners' fundamental presuppositions about advertising knowledge in a thoroughly holistic and theoretically informed way.

Attempting to gain an objective viewpoint

As will be discussed in detail in Chapter 9, much of the thinking and application of qualitative data analysis is inextricably linked to the collection of data. For the grounded theorist, data collection and analysis occur in alternating sequences. Analysis begins with the first interview and observation, which leads to the next interview or observation, followed by more analysis, more interviews or fieldwork, and so on. It is the analysis that drives the data collection. Therefore there is a constant interplay between the researcher and the research act. Because this interplay requires immersion in the data, by the end of the enquiry the researcher is shaped by the data, just as the data are shaped by the researcher. The problem that arises during this mutual shaping process is how one can become immersed in the data and maintain a balance between objectivity and sensitivity. It could be argued that objectivity is necessary to arrive at an impartial and accurate interpretation of events. Sensitivity is required to perceive the subtle nuances and meanings of data and to recognise the connections between concepts. Both objectivity and sensitivity are necessary in making sense of data and creating insight. Objectivity enables the researcher to have confidence that the findings are a reasonable, impartial representation of a problem under investigation, whereas sensitivity enables creativity and the discovery of new theory from data.[56]

During the analytic process, grounded researchers attempt to set aside their knowledge and experience to form new interpretations about phenomena. Yet, in their everyday lives, they rely on knowledge and experience to provide the means for helping them to understand the world in which they live and to find solutions to problems encountered. Most researchers have learned that a state of objectivity is impossible and that in every piece of research, quantitative or qualitative, there is an element of subjectivity. What is important is to recognise that subjectivity is an issue and that researchers should take appropriate measures to minimise its intrusion into their investigations and analyses. Being objective means a constant drive for transparency in the actions, decisions and conclusions taken in relation to data.

Qualitative researchers should have an openness, a willingness to listen and to 'give voice' to participants, in whatever manner they wish to express themselves. This is particularly important given the array of forms of expression that are possible through social media. Good qualitative research means hearing what others have to say, seeing what others do and representing these as accurately as possible. It means developing an understanding of those they are researching, while recognising that their understanding is often based on the values, culture, training and experiences that they bring from all aspects of their lives; these can be quite different from those of their participants.[57] As well as being open to participants, qualitative researchers should reflect upon what makes them, as observers, 'see' and 'listen' in particular ways. This usually means that, while working on a particular project, the researcher keeps a diary or journal. This diary is used to make notes about the conditions of interviews and observations, of what worked well and what did not, of what questions the researcher would have liked to ask but did not think of at the time. As the researcher reads through the diary in the analysis process, the entries become part of the narrative explored, and reveal to the researcher and to others the way the researcher has developed their 'seeing' and 'listening'. Again, research diaries will be covered in more detail in examining qualitative data analysis in Chapter 9.

Developing a sensitivity to the meanings in data

Having sensitivity means having insight into, and being able to give meaning to, the events and happenings in data. It means being able to see beneath the obvious to discover the new. This quality of the researcher occurs as they work with data, making comparisons, asking questions, and going out and collecting more data. Through these alternating processes of data collection and analysis, meanings that are often elusive at first later become clearer. Immersion in the data leads to those sudden insights.[58] Insights do not just occur haphazardly; rather, they happen to prepared minds during interplay with the data. Whether we want to admit it or not, we cannot completely divorce ourselves from who we are and what we know. The theories that we carry around in our heads inform our research in multiple ways, even if we use them quite unselfconsciously.[59]

Ultimately, a grounded theory approach is expected to generate findings that are meaningful to decision-makers and appropriate to the tasks they face. Ethnographic techniques are well suited to being driven by a grounded research approach. As with other interpretivist forms of research, if it is found meaningful by decision-makers and employed successfully by them, there is further evidence of the theory's validity. Another qualitative approach that is absolutely meaningful to decision-makers in that its primary focus is to deliver actionable results is called action research.

Action research

Background

Action research
A team research process, facilitated by a professional researcher(s), linking with decision-makers and other stakeholders who together wish to improve particular situations.

The social psychologist Kurt Lewin had an interest in social change and specifically in questions of how to conceptualise and promote social change. Lewin is generally thought to be the person who coined the term 'action research' and gave it meanings that are applicable today.[60] In **action research**, Lewin envisaged a process whereby one could construct a social experiment with the aim of achieving a certain goal.[61] The classic case of the origins of action research comes from the early days of the Second World War. The case revolved around a problem that essentially was a traditional marketing research challenge. Lewin was commissioned by the US authorities in their quest to use tripe as part of the regular daily diet of American families.[62] The research question was: 'To what extent could American housewives be encouraged to use tripe rather than beef for family dinners?' Choice cuts of beef were scarce at this time and were destined primarily for the fighting troops.

Lewin's approach to this research question was to conduct a study in which he trained a limited number of housewives in the art of cooking tripe for dinner. He then surveyed how this training had an effect on their daily cooking habits in their own families. In this case, action research was synonymous with a 'natural experiment', meaning that the researchers in a real-life context invited participants into an experimental activity. This research approach was very much within the bounds of conventional applied social science with its patterns of authoritarian control, but it was aimed at producing a specific, desired social outcome.

The above example can be clearly seen from a marketing perspective. It is easy to see a sample survey measuring attitudes to beef, to tripe, to feeding the family and to feelings of patriotism. From a survey, one can imagine advertisements extolling the virtues of tripe, how tasty and versatile it is. But would the campaign work? Lewin's approach was not just to understand the housewives' attitudes but to engage them in the investigation and the solution: to *change* attitudes and behaviour.

Lewin is credited with coining a couple of important slogans within action research that hold resonance with the many action researchers that practise today. The first is 'nothing is as practical as a good theory' and the second is 'the best way to try to understand something is to change it'. In action research it is believed that the way to 'prove' a theory is to show how it provides an in-depth and thorough understanding of social structures, understanding gained through planned attempts to invoke change in particular directions. The appropriate changes are in the proof. Lewin's work was a fundamental building block of what today is called action research. He set the stage for knowledge production based on solving real-life problems. From the outset, he created a new role for researchers and redefined criteria for judging the quality of the enquiry process. Lewin shifted the researcher's role from being a distant observer to involvement in concrete problem solving. The quality criteria he developed for judging a theory to be good focused on its ability to support practical problem solving in real-life situations.[63]

From Lewin's work has developed a rich and thriving group of researchers who have developed and applied his ideas throughout the world. In management research, the study of organisational change with the understanding and empowerment of different managers and workers has utilised action research to great effect. There has been comparatively little application of action research in marketing research, though that is changing. Researchers and marketing decision-makers alike are learning of the nature of action research, the means of implementing it and the benefits it can bestow. In an era where marketers, designers (of brands, products, communications and a whole array of consumer experiences) and consumers in co-creation projects are working more closely together, action research holds many rich possibilities.

Approach

The term 'action research' includes a whole range of approaches and practices, each grounded in different traditions, in different philosophical and psychological assumptions, sometimes pursuing different political commitments. Sometimes it is used to describe a positivist approach in a 'field' context, or where there is a trade-off between the theoretical interests of researchers and the practical interests of organisation members. Sometimes it is used to describe relatively uncritical consultancy based on information gathering and feedback.[64] It is beyond the scope of this text to develop these different traditions, so the following describes an approach that is grounded in the Lewin foundations of the approach, and, like his work, is applicable to marketing.

Action research is a team research process, facilitated by one or more professional researchers linking with decision-makers and other stakeholders such as customers who together wish to change or improve particular situations. Together, the researcher and decision-makers or stakeholders define the problems to be examined, generate relevant knowledge about the problems, learn and execute research techniques, take actions, and interpret the results of actions based on what they have learned.[65] There are many iterations of problem definition, generating knowledge, taking action and learning from those actions. The whole process of iteration evolves in a direction that is agreed by the team.

Action researchers accept no a priori limits on the kinds of research techniques they use. Surveys, secondary data analyses, interviews, focus groups, ethnographies and life histories are all acceptable, if the reason for deploying them has been agreed by the action research collaborators and if they are used in a way that does not oppress participants.

Action research is composed of a balance of three elements. If any one of the three is absent, then the process is not action research:

1   *Research.* Research based on any quantitative or qualitative techniques, or combination of them, generates data, and in the analyses and interpretation of the data there is shared knowledge.

2   *Participation.* Action research involves trained researchers who serve as facilitators and 'teachers' to team members. As these individuals set their action research agenda, they generate the knowledge necessary to transform the situation and put the results to work. Action research is a participatory process in which everyone involved takes some responsibility.

3   *Action.* Action research aims to alter the initial situation of the organisation in the direction of a more self-managed and more rewarding state for all parties.

An example of an action research team in marketing terms could include:

● *Researchers.* Trained in a variety of qualitative and quantitative research techniques, and with experience of diagnosing marketing and research problems.

● *Strategic marketing managers.* Decision-makers who work at a strategic level in the organisation and have worked with researchers, as well as those who have no experience of negotiating with researchers.

● *Operational marketing managers.* Decision-makers who have to implement marketing activities. These may be the individuals who meet customers on a day-to-day basis and who really feel the impact and success of marketing ideas.

● *Advertising agency representatives.* Agents who have worked with strategic decision-makers. They may have been involved in the development of communication campaigns to generate responses from target groups of consumers.

● *Customers.* Existing customers who may be loyal and have had many years of experience of the company (initiating and funding the action research), its products and perhaps even its personnel.

● *Target customers.* Potential customers who may be brand switchers or even loyal customers to competitive companies.

Figure 6.2[66] illustrates how action research may be applied. This model of action research is taken from the subject area of the management of change, which is relevant to many of the

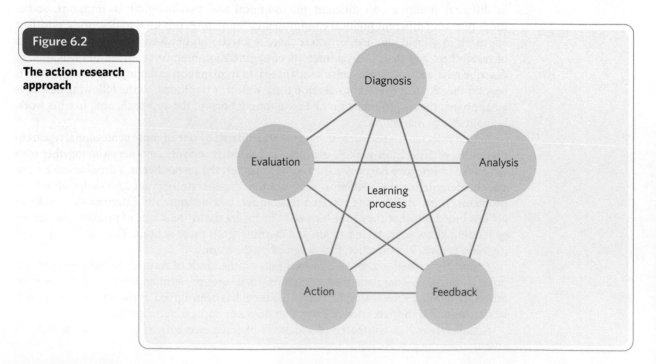

Figure 6.2

The action research approach

problems faced by marketing decision-makers. The process aims to create a learning community in a team such as that above. The team develops an understanding of issues to the extent that it makes sound judgements and takes effective action to implement the changes it wishes to make.

The process in Figure 6.2 can be described as follows:

- *Diagnosis.* The present state of affairs would be set out, including the perceived barriers to change and an initial broad statement of desired direction for the organisation. Diagnosis would include documenting the change process and all data gathering activities such as secondary data gathering, surveys, interviews or observations.

- *Analysis.* An initial interpretation of data gathered would be made. From this the issues to be tackled would be identified. Summary findings and the development of a framework, with set tasks for team members in subsequent data gathering, would be drawn up.

- *Feedback.* Data analyses would be fed back for examination and discussion in the team. 'Ownership' of the diagnosis would be developed to formulate a commitment to action.

- *Action.* Individual courses of action and the development of broader strategies would be formulated.

- *Evaluation.* There would be an ongoing review of methods and outcomes. The effectiveness of any action would be evaluated against agreed criteria and critical success factors.

All of these stages are interrelated, so there is no definitive path that the team would take. In subsequent iterations of activities, the team could move around the stages in any order that suits its needs.

The process is illustrated in the following example where action research was used in the development process of a new product. The detail of the case is limited, but there is sufficient to see action research being successfully practised in a manner that brings together a team with diverse forms of thinking and expertise.

Real research | **The dissolution of the demarcation lines between clients, researchers and consumers[67]**

To obtain an optimum number of results usable for the development process of a new product, a joint research approach was chosen by Deutsche Telekom Laboratories (**www.laboratories.telekom.com**). The idea was to combine 'the best of three worlds' by forming one team of researchers experienced in the field of consumer segmentation and qualitative research methods (members of Sinus Sociovision, **www.sinus-institut. de**) and one team of experts in the field of consumer behaviour and needs (members of Deutsche Telekom Laboratories and Berlin University of Technology). In addition, five experts from the field of innovation development with a background in psychology, speech recognition and engineering were invited to join the research preparations and to provide a broader view on the technology landscape. The task of the researchers was to formulate an approach by which the everyday life of information and communications technology (ICT) users could be explored. For Deutsche Telekom Laboratories the most important issue was to find out about ICT rituals and the situations in which ICT was used. Issues like 'fears' and 'barriers' were also of interest, especially for the development of appropriate applications and services in the future. In order to attain these results, the researchers had to dive deep into the world of the Deutsche Telekom Laboratories and to learn about their ideas, problems, attitudes, and cognitive structures, decision-making processes and organisational structures. Via meetings and workshops prior to the project/ study, research experts were enabled to think like the developers and Deutsche Telekom Laboratories specialists. A first round of interviewing was applied, and additional rounds of expert interviews were conducted to understand the client. They installed feedback loops in order to discuss changes in the team during the research process and to include possible new issues in the interviews or observations. Among the researchers, a continuous learning process was observable since many participants developed their own ideas about how they integrate ICT into their everyday lives. The findings from this research were summarised in an additional feedback loop in order to coach the ICT specialists working for the client.

International marketing research

The benefits of qualitative research should be clear at this stage. Researchers can develop a deep understanding of consumer experiences and the drivers of their behaviour and aspirations. Capturing the rich context of product, media and shopping behaviour and the manner in which consumers express themselves can support many marketing, branding and design decisions. As well as supporting decisions directly, well-crafted qualitative research can help to plan effective and actionable quantitative research. Such a richness and depth of understanding of consumers can be paramount in international marketing. Understanding the nuances of language, gestures, symbols and the rich array of expressions in different cultures can be of huge importance in successful international marketing. Understanding cultures and how they shape and are shaped by consumers brings many challenges to the qualitative researcher; the main three challenges are briefly described. The first challenge lies in implementing research techniques that in Western cultures may be logical and possible to administer. At one time international qualitative marketing research equated to flying expensive Western focus group moderators around the world. Now, qualitative marketing research needs to become more adaptive to local cultures, with far more emphasis on training local researchers to adapt and develop techniques that are relevant to participants. The challenge to many international companies was and is to achieve balance between 'local' and 'global', or 'glocal' as it came to be called.[68] The second challenge lies in interpreting

what is being expressed by participants.[69] For example, focus groups or ethnographic techniques can be designed with a sound philosophical, theoretical and ethical basis. They can be adapted in how they are delivered for local cultures. However, analysing the data and drawing out the insights can represent a major challenge. It is not just a matter of building a set of transcripts and simply translating them. As noted earlier in the chapter, much analysis occurs in an evolutionary manner as necessary changes to questions and probes become apparent. The quality of communications among researchers can be vital in drawing out the subtleties that can deliver valuable consumer insights. The final challenge lies in the new 'competitors' to traditional forms of qualitative research. The uses of qualitative data generated through chat rooms, bulletin boards and other forms of social media are all functions of technological developments. Qualitative moderators often now become part of the 'e-communities' they study, blurring the differences between marketing and research. Posted dialogues around a theme, or a brand, can now be content analysed. Consumers leave a trail of communications, website hits and blogs, that can be followed and 'sniffed' for interests, attitudes and unfulfilled needs.[70] Technological developments and how consumers engage with that technology are shaping what qualitative research means and how it can best engage in international communities. The benefits and challenges of qualitative research in an international setting are illustrated in the following example.

| Real research | The middle class in China and India[71] |

In India, the large middle class is the bastion of popular opinion, culture and consumption. As the middle class in China becomes a growing force, and companies look to develop in both countries, they are keen to find out how the characteristics from one market can be transposed to the other. Ogilvy and Mather (**www.ogilvy.com**) set out to unearth the cultural and social roots that determined life and consumption choices in the two countries. The deeply immersive nature of video ethnography posed a challenge in terms of sample size. Sample sizes are relatively small, which meant that the participants and their location must be carefully selected. While being conscious of the stereotypical 'Bangalore is India' and 'Shanghai is China', these two cities did not necessarily represent the larger middle class, which was spread across the country. In order to strike a balance between tradition and modernity, Ogilvy and Mather looked at cities that were very old and yet were embracing the new wave of economic and social activity. To capture the essence of the evolving Indian and Chinese society and yet not lose the flavour of tradition, Ogiloy and Mather chose Pune in India and Nanjing in China. Pune and Nanjing are at the cusp of tradition and modernity. Neither city is out and out a commercial centre and yet both demonstrate the co-existence of modernity and traditional local culture. The researchers spent two days prior to the video shoot with participant families. On one hand, this was to make the families feel comfortable about the camera's presence; on the other hand, it was aimed at priming the researchers with the families' ways of living and to make the enquiry more tailored to their lives. As the research developed, the researchers modified their techniques to serve the research requirements better. Instead of leaving the camera as a passive recording device in the household, the researchers brought in interactivity at the end of the second day of shooting the families. They did this by discussing the key observations from the footage with different family members. This was done to validate the observations and to clarify any unexplained activities that were found relevant, by focusing on the *why* of families' behaviour. Families were filmed over a weekend and a weekday. This was aimed at ensuring that the researchers got an account of the household routine across both a working day and a holiday. The Chinese participants did not feel embarrassed about acknowledging the role of advertising and media in their purchase decisions. The researchers would rarely get to hear this in any interaction with an Indian: 'We bought this brand because we liked the advertisement.' Indians always prefered to point out the logical reasons for the purchase decision (even if emotional reasons are the drivers for purchase).

Ethics in marketing research

Qualitative researchers have an ethical responsibility to the participants with whom they engage and to their clients or decision-makers they are supporting. The researchers have a duty to ensure that the intentions of their research are transparent, that participants engage in activities on a voluntary basis and that they have sufficient knowledge and understanding of what may be involved in a project to make this decision. The best researchers ensure that transparency, informed consent, knowledge and control are paramount in all research regardless of medium.[72] However, as some of the examples illustrate in this chapter, accessing the rich array of qualitative data available through Internet developments presents ethical challenges that researchers have yet to resolve clearly. One major qualitative technique that has benefited from Internet and social media developments is ethnography. A number of ethical challenges relate to ethnography in electronic community research. These surround the protection of participants, the means of collecting research data and the reporting of results.[73] These challenges address the implications of attempting to be transparent, gaining informed consent and delivering knowledge and control to participants. The challenges are summarised, based on the work of US and UK academics, Neil Hair and Moira Clark.

Challenge 1: Preventing harm or wrongdoing to participants, and preserving their dignity

What is harm, physical and psychological, in an electronic context? The answer will often be dependent on the nature of the community. What is dignity in the specific electronic community? This is particularly difficult to answer given the research that identifies people often playing out alternative personalities in electronic environments, perhaps within the same community. Who defines what is right and wrong in research terms within the community? Community members? The researcher? The owners of the community's technical infrastructure or the sponsors of the research?

Challenge 2: Preserving the confidentiality, anonymity and privacy of participants

While the ethical principles of confidentiality, anonymity and privacy are well known in marketing research, these issues present a number of unique challenges in virtual environments. Throughout the field of electronic community research there has been a tendency to consider community postings as 'public'. Ensuring privacy through name changes, pseudonyms, offering participants access to materials held on them are also well-cited steps in ensuring ethical practice. However, the nature of the Internet continues to exacerbate potential issues of privacy. An increasing ability with the sophistication of search engines such as Google makes it possible for readers to search for quotes taken verbatim from community postings.

Challenge 3: Avoiding deception and remaining honest

A major issue is one of whether research should be conducted covertly or overtly with the researcher as a participant and community member. Issues here surround the impact the researcher will have on that which is being researched. Clearly, acting as a member of the community will have some impact upon it. To be involved may be to damage, pollute and alter. A further challenge to researchers is being honest and open about the aims of a project while maintaining participants' agreed involvement and preserving their trust. One means of maintaining honesty and avoiding deception is through the challenge of ensuring informed consent.

Challenge 4: Ensuring informed consent

Traditionally ethnographers would seek the written permission of every participant in their research. That may extend itself to the entire community. This is clearly not always possible in electronic communities that may have tens of thousands of participants, and given the transient nature of community membership. Ethnographic research often lacks a predetermined definition of the study's aims, favouring highly exploratory and inductive research processes. This poses the question: to what extent can researchers ever offer a comprehensive view of the study? Doing so ignores the organic and participative nature of qualitative research. Ensuring informed consent in its own right is not sufficient, especially given the interconnectedness of these challenges.

Challenge 5: Maintaining transparency, avoiding misrepresentation and ensuring reciprocity through the reporting of results

Ethnographies have in the past tended towards larger monologues that capture the essence of the culture they purport to examine; in this way they claim transparency. Researchers have the challenge that 50 pages of script are unlikely to impress decision-makers. A challenge exists for researchers trying to capture sufficient depth and richness without the length normally associated with ethnographies, and this can lead to ethical lapses. One way of meeting this challenge is by publishing details of the steps taken. This is traditionally done by returning results to participants and the wider community for assessment.

Challenge 6: The challenge of diversity

In summary, the above challenges are perhaps eclipsed by one final issue for the virtual ethnographer and that is the diverse nature of online communities and the technology they use. What counts as ethical research in one community will clearly differ from the next. Exploring a sports community versus a community of social support will involve differing degrees of challenge. While the nature and diversity of electronic communities make it difficult to be prescriptive, the answers to these complex situations and considerations are perhaps best served in ethical relativism. With a relativistic approach comes the need to open up the decision-making process of researchers to the external scrutiny of other stakeholders.

Qualitative research is dependent on participant cooperation and trust. Researchers rely on participants' cooperation in order to tap into an in-depth understanding of consumers. But the non-directive and open-ended nature of qualitative questioning and observation techniques means that researchers also rely on participants being positively engaged by the process, willing and eager to apply their minds, and happy to reveal their behaviour, thoughts and aspirations.[74]

Digital applications in marketing research

The Internet presents huge opportunities for the qualitative researcher: online versions of focus groups, semi-structured or in-depth interviews, ethnography applied to virtual communities and the collection of documents, images and other forms of expression in chat rooms and bulletin boards. Applying traditional techniques as well as developing new techniques using the Internet presents a whole array of advantages and challenges.[75] These may be summarised as follows.

Advantages

- *Extending access to participants.* Provided that potential participants have access to the technology, researchers can cross time and space barriers. They can reach a much wider geographical span of participants, and also populations that are normally hard to reach, especially through the use of mobile technologies.

- *Sensitive subjects.* For some participants the sensitivity of the subject being studied may mean that they would not discuss it in a face-to-face manner. The anonymity and distance can help to draw out open and honest views from such participants.

- *Targeted interest groups.* A variety of online formats, such as chat rooms, mailing lists and conferences, focus on specific topics, drawing together geographically dispersed participants who may share interests, experiences or expertise.

- *Cost and time savings.* Issues such as the time and travelling expenses of researchers, the hire of venues and the costs of producing transcripts can make face-to-face interviewing an expensive option for many researchers, especially if they are using qualitative approaches for the first time. The Internet dramatically reduces or eliminates many of these costs and thus makes qualitative approaches more accessible to a wider array of companies and decision-makers.

- *Handling transcripts.* As interviews or observations are built up through dialogue on the Internet, many of the potential biases or mistakes that occur through audio recordings can be eliminated.

Challenges

- *Computer literacy for the researcher.* Applying qualitative research on the Internet means that some degree of technical expertise is required of the researcher. The extent of expertise depends upon which techniques are being used. For example, moderators of focus groups online will have to learn about the capabilities of the chosen software for running a focus group. They will also have to learn about the specific skills in making the group experience work well online, perhaps by participating in online research conferences or gaining exposure to alternative discussion practices online.

- *Making contact and recruitment.* Establishing contact online requires a mutual exchange of contact details. There is an array of techniques that can encourage potential participants to engage in a research project, but in essence the researcher has to develop rapport and trust to gain access to and draw the most out of participants.

- *Interactive skills online.* Even if the researcher develops skills online, it must be remembered that participants use their technology with varying degrees of expertise – from the naïve through to the most sophisticated and cutting-edge user.

- *Losing access.* A key challenge for online studies is to sustain electronic connection with participants for the whole period of the qualitative research process. This is a reminder that, unlike a survey which may be a short, one-off contact with a participant, qualitative techniques may unfold and evolve over time and involve returning to participants as issues develop and theory emerges.

The issues above lay out the broad advantages and challenges of the Internet and digital developments for the qualitative researcher. As we develop more detailed descriptions and evaluations of qualitative techniques in Chapters 7 to 9, we will examine these points in more detail as there are many rapid innovations occurring to support qualitative researchers.

Summary

Qualitative and quantitative research should be viewed as complementary. Unfortunately, many researchers and decision-makers do not see this, taking dogmatic positions in favour of either qualitative or quantitative research. The defence of qualitative approaches for a particular marketing research problem, through the positive benefits it bestows and through explaining the negative alternatives of a quantitative approach, should be seen as healthy, as should the defence of quantitative approaches. Decision-makers use both approaches and will continue to need both.

Qualitative and quantitative approaches to marketing research are underpinned by two broad philosophical schools, namely positivism and interpretivism. The central belief of a positivist position is a view that the study of consumers and marketing phenomena should be 'scientific' in the manner of the natural sciences. Researchers of this persuasion adopt a framework for investigation akin to that of the natural scientist. The interpretivist researcher does not set out to test hypotheses in the manner of the positivist researcher. Their aim is primarily to explore and understand the nature and interrelationships of marketing phenomena. The focus of investigation is a detailed examination of a small number of cases rather than a large sample. The data collected are analysed through an explicit interpretation of the meanings and functions of consumer actions. The product of these analyses takes the form of verbal descriptions and explanations, with quantification and statistical analysis playing a subordinate role.

In examining qualitative approaches, ethnography as a general term includes observation and interviewing and is growing in use through the use of social media observations and interactions. Ethnography is used to describe a range of methods which require researchers to spend a large amount of time observing a particular group of people, by sharing or immersing themselves in their way of life. The ethnographer is expected to analyse critically the situations observed. The critique and the analysis can be guided by theory but in essence the researcher develops a curiosity, thinks in an abstract manner and at times steps back to reflect and see how emerging ideas connect. By reacting to the events, narrative, images and other forms of participants and by drawing out what they see as important, ethnographers have the ability to create new explanations and understandings of consumers.

Some ethnographers may be criticised in their attempts at developing theory. In response, the grounded theorist follows a set of systematic procedures for collecting and analysing data. A distinctive feature of a grounded theory approach is that the collection of data and their analysis take place simultaneously, with the aim of developing general concepts, to organise data and integrate these into a more general, formal set of categories.

Ethnographic techniques and a grounded theory approach can be applied in an action research framework. Action research is a team research process, facilitated by one or more professional researchers, linking with decision-makers and other stakeholders who together wish to improve particular situations. Together, the researcher and decision-makers or stakeholders define the problems to be examined, generate relevant knowledge about the problems, learn and execute research techniques, take actions, and interpret the results of actions based on what they have learned. There are many iterations of problem definition, generating knowledge, taking action and learning from those actions. The whole process of iteration evolves in a direction that is agreed by the team.

International qualitative research can reveal the cultural nuances of consumer behaviour, aspirations and forms of expression. Such nuances can deliver great opportunities to marketers working in international markets, or indeed in domestic markets where there may be diverse multicultural communities. The challenges in realising these opportunities lie in implementing techniques in other cultures that have been developed, tried and tested in advanced Western economies, in interpreting the language and other forms of expression not only when all the data have been gathered, but as a research project unfolds, and in how new digital developments are changing how techniques such as focus groups and ethnography are managed and how new techniques are used.

When conducting qualitative research, the researcher and the client must respect participants. This should include protecting the anonymity of participants, honouring all statements and promises used to ensure participation, and conducting research in a way not to embarrass or harm the participants. With the emergence of techniques that use social media such as ethnography using electronic communities, maintaining an ethical relationship with participants is becoming far more challenging.

The Internet and digital developments present huge opportunities for the qualitative researcher. Online versions of traditional forms of qualitative research such as focus groups, semi-structured or in-depth interviews, and ethnographic techniques have been developed to great effect. New qualitative techniques have been developed that add further consumer insights. These developments have the potential to present research to participants as meaningful and enjoyable engagements.

Questions

1   What criticisms do qualitative researchers make of the approaches adopted by quantitative researchers, and vice versa?

2   Why is it not always possible or desirable to use quantitative marketing research techniques?

3   Evaluate the differences between a European and an American approach to qualitative research.

4   Describe the characteristics of positivist and interpretivist researchers.

5   In what ways may the positivist and the interpretivist view potential research participants?

6   What role does theory play in the approaches adopted by positivist and interpretivist researchers?

7   What does ethnographic research aim to achieve in the study of consumers?

8   What is netnography? What additional consumer insights can netnography deliver?

9   Why may marketing decision-makers wish to understand the context of consumption?

10 Describe and illustrate two research techniques that may be utilised in ethnographic research.

11 What stages are involved in the application of a grounded theory approach?

12 Is it possible for researchers to be objective?

13 What does 'listening' mean for the qualitative researcher? How may researchers 'listen' to consumers?

14 Describe the key elements to be balanced in the application of action research.

15 What do you see as the key advantages and challenges of conducting qualitative research online?

Exercises

1   An advertising agency has selected three pieces of music that it could use in a new advertising campaign. It has come to you as a researcher to help in making the case for selecting the right piece of music for the campaign. What would be the case for using qualitative techniques for this task?

2   Would a 12-year-old schoolchild who has not been exposed to any academic theories about 'service delivery quality' be more creative and open-minded, and thus better suited to conduct a grounded theory approach, compared with a 22-year-old business studies graduate? Would your view change in any way if the study were about a game or toy that was specifically targeted at 12 year olds?

3   You are a brand manager for Lynx deodorant. You wish to invest in an ethnographic study (that could include netnography techniques) of young men. Ask another student to play the role of marketing director. What case would you make to the marketing director about the value of investing in an ethnographic study?

4   In the above case of an ethnographic study of young men for Lynx deodorant, what would you feel to be appropriate contexts or circumstances to conduct this work?

5   In a small group discuss the following issues: 'Quantitative research is more important than qualitative research because it generates conclusive findings' and 'Qualitative research should always be followed by quantitative research to confirm the qualitative findings.'

Video case exercise: Wild Planet

What does ethnographic research mean for Wild Planet? How does it conduct ethnographic techniques? What challenges does it face in conducting these techniques?

Notes

1. Methner, T. and Frank, D., 'Welcome to the house of research: achieving new insights and better brand knowledge through courageous ways of collaboration in what is usually a competitive environment', ESOMAR: Congress Odyssey, Athens (September 2010).

2. You, J.S. and Kaltenback, E., 'Living with your customers', *Research World* (November 2005), 40.

3. Murphy, D., 'Feeding inspiration', *Research World* (April 2006), 14–15.

4. Ford, J., Carlson, L. and Kover, A.J., 'Comments – the quant-qual debate: where are we in advertising?', *International Journal of Advertising* 27 (4) (2008), 659–669; Alioto, M.F. and Gillespie, D., 'The complex customer: applying qualitative methods in automotive NPD', ESOMAR Qualitative Research, Athens (October 2006).

5. Cooper, P., 'We've come a long way', *Research World* (November 2007), 8–11; Cooper, P., 'Consumer understanding, change and qualitative research', *Journal of the Market Research Society* 41 (1) (January 1999), 3.

6. Bowman, J., 'Sounding off', *Research World* (July/August 2006), 36–37.

7. Kenway, J., 'Keep on moving', *Research* (November 2005), 36.

8. Cooper, P., 'In search of excellence: the evolution and future of qualitative research', ESOMAR Annual Congress, Berlin (September 2007).

9. Sykes, W., 'Validity and reliability in qualitative market research: a review of the literature', *Journal of the Market Research Society* 32 (3) (1990), 289; De Groot, G., 'Qualitative research: deeply dangerous or just plain dotty?', *European Research* 14 (3) (1986), 136–141.

10. ESOMAR, 'Global Market Research', ESOMAR Industry Report (2010), 16.

11. Bowman, J., 'Real people for real data', *Research World* (January 2007), 40.

12. Verhaeghe, A., den Bergh, J.V. and Colin, V., 'Me, myself and I: studying youngsters' identity by combining visual ethnography & netnography', ESOMAR Qualitative Research, Istanbul (November 2008).

13. Truong, Y., 'Personal aspirations and the consumption of luxury goods', *International Journal of Market Research* 52 (5) (2010), 655–673.

14. Branthwaite, A. and Patterson S., 'The vitality of qualitative research in the era of blogs and tweeting: an anatomy of contemporary research methods', ESOMAR, Qualitative, Barcelona (November 2010).

15. It is recognised that this topic is treated in a superficial manner and is really a basic introduction to the key ideas. Students who are interested in developing these ideas further should see Harrison, R.L. and Reilly, T.M., 'Mixed methods designs in marketing research', *Qualitative Market Research: An International Journal* 14 (1) (2011), 7–26; Rod, M., 'Marketing: philosophy of science and "epistobabble warfare"', *Qualitative Market Research: An International Journal* 12 (2) (2009), 120–129; Heath, R. and Feldwick, P., 'Fifty years using the wrong model of advertising', *International Journal of Market Research* 50 (1) (2008), 29–59; Silverman, D., *Interpreting Qualitative Data: Methods for Analysing Talk, Text and Interaction* (London: Sage, 2006), 9.

16. Hunt, S.D., *Modern Marketing Theory* (Cincinnati, OH: South Western Publishing, 1991); Hunt, S., *Marketing Theory: The Philosophy of Marketing Science* (Homewood, IL: Irwin, 1983), 2.

17. Tasgal, A., '"All because …": from command and control to cascades and contexts', Market Research Society, Annual Conference (2005).

18. Djourvo, D., 'A global method, a local approach: how the Japanese group can gain focus', ESOMAR Asia Pacific Conference, Singapore (April 2008).

19. Cooper, P., 'The evolution of qualitative research: from imperialism to synthesis', ESOMAR, Qualitative Research Singapore (1997); Broadbent, K., 'When East meets West, quite what does "qualitative" mean?', *ResearchPlus* (March 1997), 14.

20. Goodyear, M., 'Divided by a common language: diversity and deception in the world of global marketing', *Journal of the Market Research Society* 38 (2) (April 1996), 105.

21. Cooper, P., 'In search of excellence: the evolution and future of qualitative research', ESOMAR Annual Congress, Berlin (September 2007).

22. Hussey, J. and Hussey, R., *Business Research* (Basingstoke: Macmillan Business, 1997).

23. For a comprehensive review of the philosophy of social sciences, see Jarvie, I.C. and Zamora-Bonilla, J. (eds), *The SAGE Handbook of the Philosophy of Social Sciences* (London: Sage, 2011); in addition see Nicolai, A. and Seidl, D., 'That's relevant! Different forms of practical relevance in management science', *Organization Studies* 31 (9–10) (2010), 1257–1285; Healy, M. and Perry, C., 'Comprehensive criteria to judge validity and reliability of qualitative research within the realism paradigm', *Qualitative Market Research: An International Journal* 3 (3) (2000), 118–126.

24. Channon, C., 'What do we know about how research works?', *Journal of the Market Research Society* 24 (4) (1982), 305–315.

25. Hussey, J. and Hussey, R., *Business Research* (Basingstoke: Macmillan Business, 1997).

26. Creswell, J.W., *Research Design: Qualitative and Quantitative Approaches* (Thousand Oaks, CA: Sage, 1994).

27. Hamlin, R.P., 'Forum – small business market research: examining the human factor', *International Journal of Market Research* 49 (5) (2007), 551–571; Ali, H. and Birley, S., 'Integrating deductive and inductive approaches in a study of new ventures and customer perceived risk', *Qualitative Market Research: An International Journal* 2 (2) (1999), 103–110.

28. Bryman, A., *Quantity and Quality in Social Research* (London: Unwin Hyman, 1988).

29. Magee, B., *Fontana Modern Masters – Popper* (London: Fontana, 2010); St Aubyn, G., *The Art of Argument* (London: Christophers, 1956), 61–75.

30. Angrosino, M., *Doing Ethnographic and Observational Research* (London: Sage, 2007); Travers, M., *Qualitative Research through Case Studies* (London: Sage, 2001), 4.

31. Schensul, J.J., *Designing and Conducting Ethnographic Research: An Introduction*, 2nd edn (Lanham, MD: AltaMira Press, 2010); Fetterman, D.M., *Ethnography: Step by step* (Thousand Oaks, CA: Sage, 1998), 1.

32. Metcalf, P., *A Borneo Journey into Death: Berawan Eschatology from its Rituals* (Kuala Lumpur: Abdul Majeed, 1991).

33. Silverman, D., *Interpreting Qualitative Data: Methods for Analysing Talk, Text and Interaction*, 2nd edn (London: Sage, 2001), 45.

34. Gnädig, A. and Schieleit, O., 'The death of depth: skimming the surface', *Research World* (January 2006) , 44–45.

35. Stewart, A., *The Ethnographer's Method* (Thousand Oaks, CA: Sage, 1998), 5.

36. Mariampolski, H., 'The power of ethnography', *Journal of the Market Research Society* 41 (1) (January 1999), 79.

37. Bilgram, V., Bartl, M. and Biel, S., 'Successful consumer co-creation: the case of Nivea Body Care', Market Research Society, Annual Conference (2010).

38. Kozinets, R.V., 'Click to connect: netnography and tribal advertising', *Journal of Advertising Research* 46 (3) (2006) 279–288.

39. Poynter, R., 'A taxonomy of new MR', Market Research Society: Annual Conference (2010).

40. **http://johnbell.typepad.com/weblog/2006/09/3_ways_lego_lea.html**, accessed 8 February 2011.

41. Anon., 'Co-creation', *WARC Exclusive* (November 2010).

42. Mariampolski, H., 'The power of ethnography', *Journal of the Market Research Society* 41 (1) (January 1999), 82.

43. Ibid., p. 81.

44. Mariampolski, H., *Qualitative Marketing Research: A comprehensive guide* (Thousand Oaks, CA: Sage, 2001), 52.

45. Wiesenfeld, D., Bush, K. and Sikdar, R., 'The value of listening: heeding the call of the snuggie', *Journal of Advertising Research* 50 (1) (2010), 16–20.

46. Rappaport, S.D., 'Putting listening to work: the essentials of listening', *Journal of Advertising Research* 50 (1) (2010), 30–41.

47. Glaser, B. and Strauss, A., *The Discovery of Grounded Theory* (Chicago: Aldine, 1967).

48. Blumer, H., 'Sociological analysis and the variable', in Blumer, H., *Symbolic Interactionism: Perspective and Method* (Berkeley, CA: University of California Press, 1969), 127–139.

49. Travers, M., *Qualitative Research through Case Studies* (London: Sage, 2001).

50. Glaser, B. and Strauss, A., *The Discovery of Grounded Theory* (Chicago: Aldine, 1967), 3.

51. Strauss, A., Fagerhaugh, S., Suczek, B. and Wiener, C., *The Social Organisation of Medical Work* (Chicago: University of Chicago Press, 1985).

52. Locke, K., *Grounded theory in management research* (London: Sage, 2001), 33.

53. Ibid., p. 34.

54. This outline summarises a quite detailed procedure. For a definitive practical guideline to performing grounded theory see Corbin, J. and Strauss, A., *Basics of qualitative research: Techniques and procedures for developing grounded theory* (Thousand Oaks, CA: Sage, 2008); Goulding, C., *Grounded Theory: A practical guide for management, business and market researchers* (London: Sage, 2002); Strauss, A. and Corbin, J.M., *Basics of Qualitative Research: Techniques and Procedures for Developing Grounded Theory*, 2nd edn (London: Sage, 1998).

55. Nyilasy, G. and Reid, L.N., 'Agency practitioners' meta-theories of advertising', *International Journal of Advertising* 28 (4) (2009), 639–668.

56. Strauss, A. and Corbin, J.M., *Basics of Qualitative Research: Techniques and Procedures for Developing Grounded Theory*, 2nd edn (London: Sage, 1998), 53.

57. Bresler, L., 'Ethical issues in qualitative research methodology', *Bulletin of the Council for Research in Music Education* 126 (1995), 29–41; Cheek, J., 'Taking a view: qualitative research as representation', *Qualitative Health Research* 6 (1996), 492–505.

58. Strauss, A. and Corbin, J.M., *Basics of Qualitative Research: Techniques and Procedures for Developing Grounded Theory*, 2nd edn (London: Sage, 1998), 46–47.

59. Sandelowski, M., 'Theory unmasked: the uses and guises of theory in qualitative research', *Research in Nursing and Health* 16 (1993), 213–218.

60. Greenwood, D.J. and Levin, M., *Introduction to Action Research: Social Research for Social Change* (Thousand Oaks, CA: Sage, 1998), 17.

61. Lewin, K., 'Forces behind food habits and methods of change', *Bulletin of the National Research Council* 108 (1943), 35–65.

62. Tripe – the first and second divisions of cow stomachs, but could also be sheep or goats.

63. Greenwood, D.J. and Levin, M., *Introduction to Action Research: Social Research for Social Change* (Thousand Oaks, CA: Sage, 1998), 19.

64. Reason, P. and Bradbury, H., *Handbook of Action Research* (London: Sage, 2002), xxiv.

65. Greenwood, D.J. and Levin, M., *Introduction to Action Research: Social Research for Social Change* (Thousand Oaks, CA: Sage, 1998), 4.

66. Bate, S.P., 'Changing the culture of a hospital: from hierarchy to network', *Public Administration* 78 (3) (2000), 487.

67. Dörflinger, T., Gutknecht, S., Klär, K. and Tabino, O., 'Digital divorce or digital love affair – understanding consumer needs by breaking down frontiers', ESOMAR Annual Congress, Montreal (September 2008)

68. Cooper, P., 'In search of excellence: the evolution and future of qualitative research', ESOMAR: Annual Congress, Berlin (September 2007).

69. Totman, P., 'Arbiters of meaning: the hidden role of the interpreter in international qualitative research', ESOMAR: Qualitative, Barcelona (November 2010).

70. Cooper, P., 'In search of excellence: the evolution and future of qualitative research', ESOMAR: Annual Congress, Berlin (September 2007).

71. Sinha, K. and Ramachandra, P., 'Real environments: video ethnography for true understanding', ESOMAR Asia Pacific Conference, Singapore (April 2008).

72. Nairn, A., 'Protection or participation? Getting research ethics right for children in the digital age', ESOMAR: Congress, Montreux (September 2009).

73. Hair, N. and Clark, M., 'The ethical dilemmas and challenges of ethnographic research in electronic communities', *International Journal of Market Research* 49 (6) (2007), 781–800.

74. Murphy, D., 'Fishing by the Net', *Marketing* (22 August 1996), 25.

75. Mann, C. and Stewart, F., *Internet Communication and Qualitative Research: A Handbook for Researching Online* (London: Sage, 2000), 17–38.

7 Qualitative research: focus group discussions

Stage 1
Problem definition

Stage 2
Research approach developed

Stage 3
Research design developed

Stage 4
Fieldwork or data collection

Stage 5
Data integrity and analysis

Stage 6
Report preparation and presentation

The best moderators of focus groups are those that create a spirit of spontaneity and a passion for the issues under discussion.

Objectives

After reading this chapter, you should be able to:

1 understand why the focus group is defined as a direct qualitative research technique;
2 describe focus groups in detail, with an emphasis on planning and conducting focus groups;
3 evaluate the advantages, disadvantages and applications of focus groups;
4 describe alternative ways of conducting qualitative research in group settings;
5 discuss the considerations involved in conducting qualitative research in an international setting, extending the contrast between European and American traditions of running focus groups;
6 understand the ethical issues involved in conducting focus groups;
7 appreciate how digital developments are extending the scope and application of group research in the use of marketing research online communities.

Overview

In this chapter, we start by presenting a means of classifying qualitative research techniques and we examine the implications of such classification. The characteristics of the focus group are presented along with their advantages and disadvantages. The manner in which focus groups should be planned and conducted is then presented. Running successful focus groups depends upon the skills of a moderator, i.e. the person who manages the group, and the ensuing discussion. We present the qualities needed in moderators to get the most out of focus group discussions. There are variations on the main theme of running a focus group; these are described as well as other qualitative group activities. Some of the misconceptions of focus groups are examined, with a reminder of the qualities that make group techniques work well. In Chapter 6 we contrasted the purpose and different ways of running focus groups in the USA and in Europe; this contrast is developed and illustrated further in examining international marketing research issues. Several ethical issues that arise in running focus groups are identified. Running focus groups online (or the e-group) is well established. The relative advantages and disadvantages of these groups compared with 'offline' or face-to-face groups are evaluated. There are also many new group-based techniques that are emerging through social media research. These techniques and their applications will be evaluated.

The following examples illustrate how using focus groups helps researchers and decision-makers to understand the issues faced by consumers. The three examples represent major variations of the focus group in terms of a traditional focus group, an online focus groups and an online bulletin board. In all the examples, the issues being researched are expressed in consumers' own words and sometimes in ways that words cannot convey. The examples also illustrate that researchers and decision-makers may think that they know of all the issues they should be questioning, but once an exploration starts, participants can reveal new issues that they perceive to be of more importance, and these issues can drive very innovative marketing decisions.

Real research

Chinese views of chicken tastes[1]

How is it possible to encapsulate flavour experiences and enable improved flavour innovations for Chinese consumers? The producer of flavours and fragrances, Givaudan (**www.givaudan.com**), sponsored a study that was executed by Labbrand (**www.labbrand.com**). Out of the five senses, taste may be considered the most abstract, and therefore the most difficult to describe. In China there was a huge amount of information that could be considered in flavour creation for roast chicken. There were more than 30 variations of cooking methods for chicken, the most famous being 'roast' and 'fry' and with very specific flavour characteristics like the 'Gong Bao Ji Ding' or the Beggar's chicken. Before discussing flavours with consumers, preliminary research was conducted on the variety of dishes, flavours and brands to understand cultural references. This research helped in the planning of focus groups directed at Chinese consumers to understand their flavour experiences. From the discussions of over 12 groups held in different Chinese cities, three categorical distinctions were apparent when a food experience was described: **Emotions and sensations** 'generous'; 'smoky' (general and conceptual, not linked to a specific context); **Practical experience** 'at McDonald's'; 'with friends', 'at a picnic' (when, where, with whom, how); **rules, etiquette and common beliefs** 'eating the bones clean makes me feel I am full'; 'white meat with friends can be embarrassing because it can get stuck between the teeth'. One issue faced when conducting research on taste experience, expectations and needs was that participants mixed these three dimensions of discourse. An additional complexity was that flavour experience is multidimensional. To describe a certain flavour, the participant may give a description in terms of **taste** (sweet, sour, bitter, salty and savoury – the basic tastes) and in term of **smells** (fresh, burned, smoked, fruity) and/or **texture**. Because describing flavours was so complex, the role and expertise of the focus group moderator was crucial. The group setting was also crucial so that participants could build on each other's responses to arrive at more complete descriptions.

Real research

City Hunter e-group[2]

City Hunter was a Japanese anime in 13 episodes (**www.animenewsnetwork.com**). The main character of the TV programme had different experiences with women in which conquest and seduction both featured. After being aired on cable TV for two months, increasing the audience was considered by moving City Hunter to an Argentinian broadcast network. The brand also wanted to evaluate the possibility of airing the programme in other countries in the region. To achieve these aims, DatosClaros (**www.datosclaros.com**) was asked to assess these possibilities. Online focus groups (e-groups) were used to: determine the strongest points of interest and the level of understanding that viewers had in relation to the series; assess whether some of the scenes in the story would be considered shocking and how viewers interpreted them; assess views on the format, contents, characters, type of animation and the plot of the series. E-groups allowed for several people to discuss issues at the same time, all connected remotely and coordinated by a moderator. In the main window, discussions took place and in an adjacent window a stimulus was shown: in this case, images of the characters/logos and videos with clips of two episodes used for the study. Participants entered their opinions and answers as the main themes included in the moderator's guide were presented. In general terms, this approach meant that: results were presented in much shorter time frames as the transcript of the discussions could be saved and analysed as soon as the discussion finished; multimedia stimuli could be included; the client had the chance to 'watch' the study as it took place, no matter where the client was; and the client could also send the moderator comments via a private chat. Considering the client's particular requirements, the approach offered additional advantages: it allowed an uninhibited, unstructured contact, avoiding inaccuracies that could be caused by the physical presence of other participants or the moderator; it addressed issues that could be considered 'taboo' or difficult to discuss face to face, since participants connected in the context of their own familiar personal locations; it allowed viewers from widely dispersed geographical locations to participate; it was a novel, attractive research method for participants that provided additional engagement and motivation for them, especially for younger viewers.

Real research   ## How does Philips execute its online bulletin boards?[3]

Online bulletin boards at Philips have used several studies at critical time points in the corporate strategic planning process. Initial studies differed in their particular aims, and in the sub-audiences targeted, but they generally took the following form. For a reasonable fee, senior influencers including executives, journalists, senior physicians, senior hospital administrators, urban planners and lighting designers agreed to join an online discussion. They logged on at their own convenience for a minimum specified number of minutes per day, over a period of two or three days. In 2010, three separate influencer panels were recruited to participate in a series of six one- or two-day online bulletin board sessions. Individuals were not always able to participate in all six sessions, but on average at least 75% participated each time. (Rare) panel dropouts were replaced with new members. Logging in and out whenever convenient to them, panel members interacted across multiple time zones and/or countries that shared a common language. Since Philips is a global company with worldwide reach, influencers were recognised across a wide range of geographies. Allowing senior individuals to interact with their transatlantic peers was engaging for participants as well as valuable in yielding cross-cultural insight. The issue of audience heterogeneity was addressed by running several online bulletin boards concurrently, with the different sub-audiences each interacting at peer group level while discussing a mixture of topics, some that were common across all audiences and others that are specific to the sub-audience concerned. The flexible format enabled ongoing discussion guide development throughout a given fielding period, and incorporated a wide variety of visual aids and modes of enquiry. The studies for Philips included pre-seeded discussion, questionnaire rating scales, and evaluation of print ads, multimedia clips and websites in development.

Classifying qualitative research techniques

Direct approach
A type of qualitative research in which the purposes of the project are disclosed to the participant or are obvious given the nature of the interview.

A classification of qualitative research techniques is presented in Figure 7.1.

These techniques are classified as either direct or indirect, based on whether the true purpose of the project is known to the participants. A direct approach is not disguised. The purpose of the project is disclosed to the participants or is otherwise obvious to them from the questions asked. Focus groups and in-depth interviews are the major direct techniques. Even though the purpose of the project is disclosed, the extent to which the purpose of the

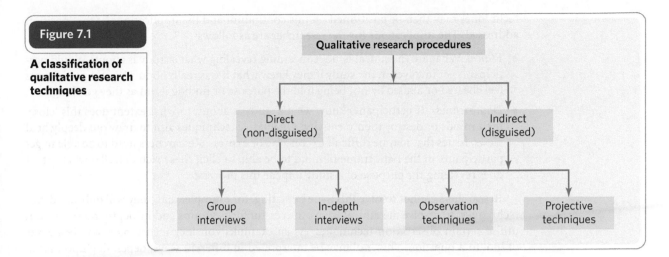

Figure 7.1

A classification of qualitative research techniques

research is revealed at the start of a focus group or in-depth group may vary. Suppose that the researcher wanted to understand how participants felt about the Prada brand, what their views were of Prada advertising campaigns, the style and quality of Prada clothes, how 'cool' the brand was, the importance of its being an Italian company – to name but a few issues that could be tackled. Rather than stating these objectives or even that the study was for Prada right at the start, the researcher may initially hide these issues. If revealed at the start, participants might focus straight onto these issues and not the surrounding contextual issues that may reveal the 'relative' impact of the Prada brand. Thus the researcher may initially reveal that the discussion is going to be about 'what clothes mean to you'. The researcher may explore what participants feel to be good and poor examples of clothing advertisements and why – what types of clothing and accessories do participants see as stylish, how important is it to wear stylish clothes, how important is it to wear 'cool' clothes? – drawing out examples of brands to illustrate these views. Italy as a country could be explored in terms of characteristics of Italians or Italian design and style. If participants bring up Prada in the discussion, the researcher can then focus upon specific questions about the brand, contrast it with other brands and clearly see which subjects generated positive or negative views of Prada. Participants may deduce that the study is being conducted for Prada as the discussion proceeds, which may be apparent by the end of the discussion, or the researcher may clarify this point and explain why it was not revealed at the beginning.[4]

In using focus groups or in-depth interviews, the researcher employs a direct approach but has control over how much 'directness' to reveal at the start of the discussion. The researcher must consider what 'frame of mind' participants should be in at the start of the discussion, as too narrow or set a focus at the start can impede the thought processes and creativity of the participants and the success of the discussion.

Indirect approach

A type of qualitative research in which the purposes of the project are disguised from the participants.

In contrast, research that takes an indirect approach totally disguises the purpose of the project. In an indirect approach, the researcher wants participants to behave as naturally as possible without any impediment of research purposes. In observation or ethnographic techniques, consumers may be seen shopping, choosing products, using products, interacting with other people and objects, hopefully in a natural environment and a natural manner. The 'participants' may not know that they are being observed or, if they do and have agreed to be observed, may not really know why. The purpose of using projective techniques (presented in Chapter 8) is to discover underlying motivations, beliefs, attitudes or feelings regarding consumer behaviour. The techniques allow indirect questioning to allow participants to discover novel ways to think about and express their feelings, where direct questioning would fail.

Figure 7.1 presents a useful way to remember which qualitative techniques tend towards directness and indirectness. Another way of thinking about these issues would be to visualise a continuum with 'totally direct' at one extreme and 'totally indirect' at the other. Qualitative techniques may then be positioned on this continuum and the implications of that position addressed. The implications for the researcher are as follows:

- *Ethical.* What are the ethical issues concerning revealing what a study is about? Would participants get involved in the study if they knew what it was really about? Would participants feel cheated or abused by not being told the purpose or finding it out as they go along?

- *Data richness.* If participants know what a study is about, to what extent does this 'close' their minds or destroy their creativity? Qualitative techniques aim to draw out deeply held views, issues that may be difficult to conceive or express. Researchers need to be able to get participants in the right frame of mind to be able to elicit these rich data. To what extent does revealing the purpose of a study impede this process?

Researchers cannot resolve this issue by stating, for example, that 'they will only use direct techniques' to resolve the ethical issues. Successful focus groups and in-depth interviews can utilise certain observation techniques. As an example, consider recording a simple answer of 'no' to a question. This 'no' may be interpreted in different ways, depending upon facial expressions ('was the participant smiling?'), the tone of the participant's voice ('was it sharp and direct?'), the participants' posture and body language ('were they hunched and hiding their faces?'), or their positioning and reactions to others around them ('were they seeking support from others of the same view, by gestures directed towards those participants?'). The researcher can use and manipulate scenarios to observe participants as a means of interpreting the answers they give to questions. The same can be said of projective techniques, all of which can be used to great effect in focus groups and in-depth interviews.[5]

The researcher ultimately has to work out the extent of directness or indirectness of the chosen qualitative techniques and address the ethical and data richness issues before setting out the detail of how to administer the qualitative techniques. These issues may be unique in each investigation, depending upon the nature of participants being studied and the questions they face. In practice, the qualitative researcher may resolve the best means to administer a technique by experimenting and adapting; these issues are tackled later in this chapter.

Focus group discussion

Focus group
A discussion conducted by a trained moderator among a small group of participants in an unstructured and natural manner.

Moderator
An individual who conducts a focus group interview, by setting the purpose of the interview, questioning, probing and handling the process of discussion.

A focus group is a discussion conducted by a trained moderator in a non-structured and natural manner with a small group of participants. A moderator leads and develops the discussion. The main purpose of focus groups is to gain insights by creating a forum where participants feel sufficiently comfortable and relaxed. In such a forum, it is hoped that participants can reflect and portray their feelings and behaviour, at their pace and using their language, means of expression and logic. It has been argued that the single most compelling purpose of the focus group is to bridge social and cultural differences between researchers and their target participants.[6] The value of the technique and its role in bridging social and cultural differences lie in discovering unexpected findings, often obtained from a free-flowing discussion that is respectful and not condescending to participants.[7] Focus groups are the most important qualitative marketing research procedure accounting for 9% of all global marketing research expenditure in 2010.[8] They are used extensively in new product development, advertising development and image studies. They are so popular that many marketing research practitioners consider this technique synonymous with qualitative research.[9] Given their importance and popularity, we describe the salient characteristics of focus groups in detail.[10]

Characteristics

The major characteristics of a focus group are summarised in Table 7.1.

One of the main characteristics and key benefits lies in the amount of creative discussion and other activities that may be generated. Group members have the time to reflect upon the

Table 7.1	Characteristics of focus groups
Key benefit	Group members 'feed' off each other and creatively reveal ideas that the researcher may not have thought of or dared to tackle
Key drawback	Group members may feel intimidated or shy and may not reveal anything of significance
Group size	6-10
Group composition	Homogeneous, participants pre-screened by questionnaire or through known characteristics
Physical setting	Relaxed, informal atmosphere, 'comfortable' from the perspective of the participants
Stimulating discussion	Use of storyboards, mood boards, products, advertisements, films, music, websites, brochures
Time duration	1.5 to 6 hours
Recording	Use of audiocassettes, videotapes and notes from observations
Moderator	Observational, interpersonal and communication skills

discussion and range of stimuli that may be presented to them. The stimuli may come from other group members and/or from the moderator. Using their intuition and imagination, group members can explain how they feel or behave, in words or other forms of expression that they are comfortable with and using logic that is meaningful to them. The key drawback lies in how intimidating the group scenario may be to certain individuals. Many individuals may be self-conscious in expressing their ideas, feeling they may be ridiculed by others, or they may be shy and unable to express themselves freely in a group. A focus group is generally made up of 6 to 10 members. Groups of fewer than six are unlikely to generate the momentum and group dynamics necessary for a successful session. Likewise, groups of more than 10 may be too crowded and may not be conducive to a cohesive and natural discussion.[11] Large groups have a tendency to splinter into subgroups as group members compete to get their views across.

A focus group generally should be homogeneous in terms of demographic and socio-economic characteristics. Commonality among group members avoids interactions and conflicts among group members on side issues.[12] An amount of conflict may draw out issues or get participants to rationalise and defend their views in a number of ways; it can also mean that the discussion does not get stale with everybody agreeing with each other and setting a scenario where genuine disagreement gets stifled. However, major conflicts should and can be avoided by the careful selection of participants. Thus, for many topics, a women's group should not combine married homemakers with small children, young unmarried working women and elderly divorced or widowed women, because their lifestyles may be substantially different. Participants should be carefully screened to meet stated criteria. These criteria are set by the researcher to ensure that participants have had adequate experience with the object or issue being discussed. The most fundamental basis screening of participants is through demographic classification. Common demographic characteristics for determining group composition are: gender, race or ethnicity, age, household location, education level, occupation, income and marital status or family composition. Selecting participants using these characteristics can help increase compatibility but does not guarantee it; their backgrounds should be carefully balanced with their experiences.[13] Participants who have already taken part in numerous focus groups should not be included. These so-called professional participants are atypical, and their participation leads to serious validity problems.[14]

The physical setting for the focus group is also important. A relaxed, informal atmosphere helps group members to forget they are being questioned and observed. What is meant by a relaxed, informal atmosphere may change depending upon the type of participant and the subject being tackled. Examples of what 'relaxed and informal' means can include the home of a friend within a particular community, a works canteen, a village hall, a room in a leisure centre, a meeting room in a hotel or a purpose-built discussion group room. The poor acoustics and hard seats of a works canteen may not seem relaxed and informal. To group participants, however, it may be the place where they are happy to talk and willing to open up to a moderator. An example of this could be using part of a furniture store to discuss issues around house decoration, furnishings and cleaning or maintaining the home. Such a setting may set a very strong frame of reference to start the focus group and provide lots of stimuli. This example does not mean that all research needs to be conducted *in situ*, but that the technique can be designed to allow the findings from the real and the research environments to inform the overall recommendations.[15] Light refreshments should be served before the session and made available throughout; these become part of the context of relaxation. The nature of these refreshments largely depends upon how long the discussion lasts, the nature of tasks faced by the participants and the ethical viewpoint of the researcher.

Although a focus group may last from one to six hours, a duration of one and a half to two hours is typical. When a focus group lasts up to six hours, participants may be performing a series of projective techniques such as building 'mood boards' or 'role playing'.

The following example shows how mood boards were used in the IFM Sports Marketing Surveys project on rugby league. The photographs represent one of four mood boards that were used to great effect in eliciting the core values of rugby league. Imagine how the discussion may flow around these images as participants reflect upon the images and the connotations they see. In a relaxed, engaging and fun context, participants could take their time to focus on the passions, feelings and stereotypes associated with the sport and the match-day experience.

Focus on	**IFM Sports Marketing Surveys**

Rugby league study

In the focus groups four mood boards were presented to participants. The themes presented on the mood boards encapsulated **impact**, **athletic**, **north** and **entertainment**. These were built following the findings that emerged from an online survey and a brainstorming workshop. The aim of the mood boards was to ascertain:

- Was there an overall theme?
- What were the pictures about?
- What relevance did they have to rugby league?
- What did they say about rugby league?
- What word or phrase would sum up the board?

Avid male fans described these images as:

- **Demolition**, power, damage, aggression, impact.
- **Wildlife programme**, locking horns like a scrum.
- **Car crash**, implies permanent damage.

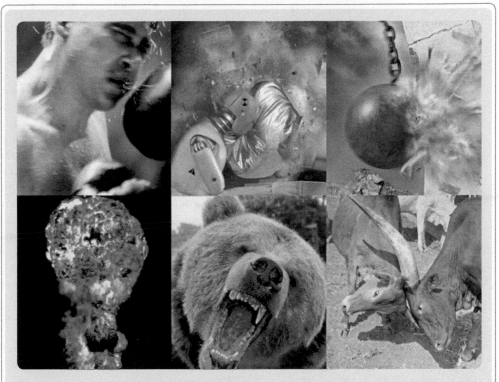

They did not want to see the sport portrayed like this – not what it's all about, it's not representing the game, aggressive in a negative manner. While it was not the main theme of the game, the image had contextual applications. The hardness and contact of the sport is an important variable, but not the core factor of the sport.

Avid female fans described these images as:

- *Negative aggression*, injury, violence, pain.
- *Distasteful face*, not appealing to children, dummy suggests fatality.
- *More like football*, does not say anything about rugby league.

They saw rugby league as far more colourful than these images. They recognised that appropriate pictures must capture the toughness and determined aggression of the sport. It is combative and compelling, but not violent and threatening.

Participants can also be given additional stimuli to discuss such as advertising storyboards and products (existing, new, competitors) to handle and examine. A focus group that lasts for up to six hours will invariably require a break for a meal, but in all circumstances a flow of drinks and snacks should be made available, noting special dietary requirements, e.g. vegan food and drinks. The opportunities and problems that occur by serving alcoholic drinks in focus groups will be discussed in the 'Ethics in marketing research' section later in this chapter.

The lengthy period of discussion in a focus group is needed to establish rapport with the participants, to get them to relax and be in the right frame of mind, and to explore in depth their beliefs, feelings, ideas, attitudes and insights regarding the topics of concern. Focus group discussions are invariably recorded, mostly using audiotape but often on video, for subsequent replay, transcription and analysis. Video recording has the advantage of capturing facial expressions and body movements, but it can increase the costs significantly. Frequently, where focus groups are conducted in purpose-built studios, decision-makers as 'clients' observe the session from an adjacent room using a two-way mirror or through video transmission. However, the existence of the mirror can impact upon everyone's perceptions of what is happening in the discussion. The idea of invisible and unknown people sitting on the other side of the glass can be daunting and inhibiting to participants. Who are they? Why are they there? What are they doing? What are they going to think of me? Participants may not divulge private thoughts, confess to indulgent practices or generally open up if they feel intimidated by the interview process.[16] The 'City Hunter e-group' and 'Philips' examples at the start of this chapter illustrated how clients or decision-makers are able to observe and even influence the development of group discussions. This issue will be developed in this chapter when we compare the relative advantages and disadvantages of face-to-face discussions and e-groups.

In the physical setting of the focus group, care must be taken with both audio and video recording of participants. A judgement must be made of how comfortable participants are with being recorded and what effects recorders have on how much they relax and honestly portray how they feel. Many moderators can give rich examples of how the most interesting points to emerge from a focus group occur when recorders are switched off at the end of the discussion. This happens when a group of participants have really become involved in the subject of discussion and have enjoyed talking to their fellow participants. Even when the moderator has finished the discussion, some participants carry on discussing the issues between themselves as they put their coats on, leave the room and even perhaps as they walk to their cars. Moderators can hear issues discussed in this informal manner that they wish had been tackled with the full group.

The moderator plays a vital role in the success of a focus group. The moderator must establish rapport with the participants and keep the discussion flowing, including the **probing** of participants to elicit insights. Typically, probing differs from questioning in that the probes and the nature of probing are more spontaneous, and involve comments such as:[17]

Probing
A motivational technique used when asking questions to induce the participants to enlarge on, clarify or explain their answers.

- Would you explain further?
- Can you give me an example of what you mean?
- Would you say more?
- Is there anything else?
- Please describe what you mean.
- I don't understand.
- Tell me more about that.
- How does that work?

Sometimes the moderator may put a probe question to the whole group such as:

- Who else has something?
- What about the rest of you?
- I see people nodding their heads; tell me about it.
- We want to hear all the different points of view. Who else has something that might be a bit different?

It is seen as good practice to probe early in the discussion in order to communicate the importance of precision or a developed explanation, and to use probes sparingly in later discussion.

In addition, the moderator may have a central role in the analysis and interpretation of the data. Therefore, the moderator should possess skill, experience, knowledge of the discussion topic, and an understanding of the nature of group dynamics.

Advantages and disadvantages of focus groups

Focus groups offer several advantages over other data collection techniques. These may be summarised by the 10 Ss:[18]

1 *Synergy.* Putting a group of people together will produce a wider range of information, insight and ideas than will individual responses secured privately.

2 *Snowballing.* A bandwagon effect often operates in a group discussion in that one person's comment triggers a chain reaction from the other participants. This process facilitates a very creative process where new ideas can be developed, justified and critically examined.

3 *Stimulation.* Usually after a brief introductory period, the participants want to express their ideas and expose their feelings as the general level of excitement over the topic increases in the group.

4 *Security.* Because the participants' feelings may be similar to those of other group members, they feel comfortable and are therefore willing to 'open up' and reveal thoughts where they may have been reluctant if they were on their own.

5 *Spontaneity.* Because participants are not required to answer specific questions, their responses can be spontaneous and unconventional and should therefore provide an accurate idea of their views.

6 *Serendipity.* Ideas are more likely to arise unexpectedly in a group than in an individual interview. There may be issues that the moderator had not thought of. The dynamics of the group can allow these issues to develop and be discussed. Group members, to great effect, may clearly and forcibly ask questions that the moderator may be reluctant to ask.

7 *Specialisation.* Because a number of participants are involved simultaneously, the use of a highly trained, but expensive, interviewer is justified.

8 *Scientific scrutiny.* The group discussion allows close scrutiny of the data collection process in that observers can witness the session and it can be recorded for later analysis. Many individuals can be involved in the validation and interpretation of the collected data, and the whole process can be very transparent.

9 *Structure.* The group discussion allows for flexibility in the topics covered and the depth with which they are treated. The structure can match the logical structure of issues from the participants' perspective as well as the language and expressions they are comfortable with.

10 *Speed.* Since a number of individuals are being interviewed at the same time, data collection and analysis can proceed relatively quickly. This advantage has become even more pronounced with the development of e-groups.

Disadvantages of focus groups may be summarised by the five Ms:

1 *Misjudgement.* Focus group results can be more easily misjudged than the results of other data collection techniques. As discussed in Chapter 6, as a qualitative technique, focus groups can evolve through a line of questioning and probing. The specific direction of questioning and the ultimate interpretation of findings can be susceptible to the bias of the moderator and other researchers working on a project.

2 *Moderation.* As well as being great fun to moderate, focus groups can be difficult to moderate. Much depends upon the 'chemistry' of the group in terms of how group members get on with each other and draw ideas and explanations from each other. Even moderators with many years of experience may not connect with particular groups of participants or topics and can get into difficulty with group members who disrupt the discussion. The quality of the results depends upon how well the discussion is managed and ultimately on the skills of the moderator.

3 *Messiness.* The unstructured nature of the responses makes coding, analysis and interpretation difficult in comparison with the much more structured approach of quantitative techniques. Focus group data tend to be messy and need either strong theoretical support or the discipline of a grounded theory approach to ensure that decision-makers can rely upon the analyses and interpretations.

4 *Misrepresentation.* Focus group results concentrate on evaluating distinct target groups, describing them and contrasting them to other groups or types of participant. Trying to generalise to much wider groups, in the same manner as with a quantitative survey based on a representative sample, can be very misleading.

5 *Meeting.* There are many problems in getting potential participants to agree to take part in a focus group discussion. Even when they have agreed to participate, there are problems in getting focus group participants together at the same time. Running online e-groups has helped to resolve these problems to a great extent and is one of the main factors in the growth of this approach. For some participants a 'virtual meeting' is still not a solution. An example is in conducting business research with managers as participants. Given the amount of travel and tight schedules that many managers have, getting them together at the same time is very difficult. With many managers reluctant to reveal their company's behaviour and plans in front of other managers, one can see that the focus group may be very difficult to administer in getting managers to meet up and discuss issues.

Planning and conducting focus groups

The procedure for planning and conducting focus groups is described in Figure 7.2.

Planning begins with an examination of the marketing research problem(s) and objectives. In most instances, the problem has been defined by this stage, but it is vital to ensure that the whole process is founded upon a clear awareness of the gaps in the knowledge of marketing decision-makers. Given the problem definition, the objectives of using focus groups should be clarified. There should be a clear understanding of what information can be elicited and what the limitations of the technique are.

Figure 7.2

Procedure for planning and conducting focus groups

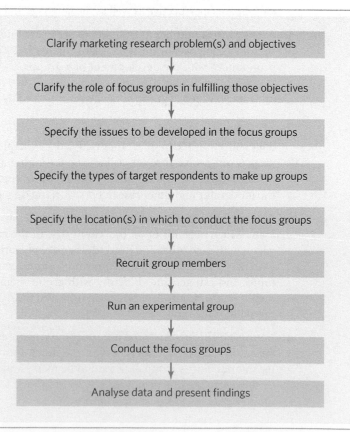

Topic guide

A list of topics, questions and probes that are used by a moderator to help manage a focus group discussion.

The next step is to develop a list of issues, or topic guide, that are to be tackled in the focus groups. This list may be a series of specific questions but is more likely to be a set of broad issues that can be developed into questions or probes as the focus group actually takes place. Specific questions may be of help to the moderator who feels that a consistent set of points needs to be presented to different groups in order to allow clear comparisons to be made. Specific questions also act as a 'prop' when the discussion is failing; indeed some group participants may initially feel that their role is to react to specific questions. However, treating the whole discussion as a means to present set questions may stifle the creativity and spontaneity that are the hallmarks of successful focus groups. The moderator should open the discussion with a general *introductory question* to make participants comfortable with the subject and the purpose of the research. This question should encourage conversation and interaction among the participants. It should not be threatening, it may even question in the third person, i.e. not asking participants what they do or think, and as such it may not be critical to the analysis, though there can be much revealed at this point. The discussion moves on to one or two *transition questions*, which move the discussion towards the key questions and issues. Transition questions help participants to envision the topic in a broader scope. Through these questions, participants become more aware of their fellow participants. Transition questions can ask participants to go into more depth about their experiences and uses of a product, making the connection between the participant and the topic under investigation.[19] The moderator can then move on to the *key questions* developing specific questions, issues and probes that can advance as the moderator tunes into the dynamics of the group. There may be additional, new issues that develop and, indeed, issues that group members do not see as being appropriate, and these can be discussed. The emphasis should be upon an evolution and learning process rather than administering a consistent set of questions.

The types of group members to take part in the discussions are then specified. From this specification, a questionnaire to screen potential participants is prepared. Typical information obtained from the questionnaire includes product familiarity and knowledge, usage behaviour, attitudes towards and participation in focus groups, and standard demographic characteristics. With the types of participants specified, consideration must be taken of what would make them relaxed and comfortable, balanced in both a physical and psychological sense.

Having decided on the location of the focus groups, the actual recruitment of group members progresses. This is one of the most difficult tasks, as potential group members may be sceptical of what may happen at the group, sometimes fearing that they are exposing themselves to a hard-sell campaign of time-share holidays or home improvements! If individuals have attended a focus group beforehand, the process of recruitment is easier, but getting the right types of participant together at the right place and time can prove difficult. With the screening questionnaire, recruitment may take place on a face-to-face basis through street interviews or through database details by phone or email. One traditional approach is to give the specification of group members to an individual in whose home the discussions are to take place. That individual then recruits participants who fit that specification from the local community. The advantage of this approach is the individual's ability to persuade participants that the process is a bona fide research process and is going to be rewarding in many ways; ultimately the individual makes sure that potential participants actually attend. The big disadvantage is ensuring that those recruited match the screening questionnaire requirements. Whichever method of recruiting participants is used, even when individuals have said that they will participate in the group, a follow-up is necessary to remind and motivate group members.

Group participants have to be rewarded for their attendance. Usually they enjoy the experience immensely once they are there, but that does not ensure that they attend in the first place. Attendance can be rewarded with cash, a donation to charity or a gift. The following example illustrates the difficulties involved in recruitment and a researcher's creative solution to the problem.

So how do you upstage a Ferrari owner?[20]

Researching a high net worth, socially active audience is difficult at the best of times. The target can be opinionated, demanding, often resistant to research and almost impossible to reach. So, when we got the brief to conduct focus groups among Ferrari, Porsche, top Mercedes and other exotic sports car owners, we were tempted to panic. We knew we could find them, but how could we persuade them to participate? We realised the one thing that would link our target, who were also defined as keen drivers, not just poseurs, was their love of cars and desire to know the latest news about new models (and to try them out if possible). That's why we decided

to offer the carrot of a drive around a race and proving track and the opportunity to meet the design and management team at our famous sports car maker. If anything might motivate people who clearly already had sufficient money to indulge a very expensive taste, it should be this package. It worked like a dream, and we had great success getting the right people to come and, more importantly, to participate.

Experimental group
An initial focus group, run to test the setting of the interview, the opening question, the topic guide and the mix of participants that make up the group.

The first focus group to be run should be seen as an experimental group. All aspects of running the group should be evaluated. Were the group members relaxed and comfortable in the chosen location, i.e. did the context work as intended? How did they react to the audio recorder, video or two-way mirror, i.e. at what point did they seem to relax and forget that they were being recorded? What types of member interacted well or not, and what issues helped or hindered interaction? How did the introductory and transition questions work in opening up and developing the discussion? How did the topic guide work; were there issues missing or issues that individuals would not tackle? How comfortable was the moderator handling the topics; did they have to interject to liven the discussion? How much did the moderator have to know about the subject to have credibility with the participants? With reflection on these issues, any necessary alterations can be made to the way that the remaining focus groups are administered. There may be very useful information that emerges from the experimental group that can be included in the main analysis. However, if the group does not work well, the information gleaned may be of little use, but the lessons learnt are invaluable in running the remaining groups.

Finally, the focus groups can be actually run. The question arises here of how many groups should be run. Beyond the first experimental group, the number of groups needed can vary. The extent to which comparisons are sought in analyses can determine how many groups are needed. Seeking comparisons means recruiting participants with different backgrounds or experiences. If there are a great variety of types of individual that make up a target market, then many homogeneous groups may be needed to reflect the variety of types, e.g. a group of 18–25-year-old single-male car owners compared with groups of women or groups of older males, married men or non-car owners. The definition of these distinct target groups to question is entirely bound by the nature of the research problem.

A confounding factor in the definition of these groups is the extent to which different types of participant will mix together in a single group. In an experimental focus group that explored attitudes and behaviour related to sports activities in the English city of Bath, distinct target groups of participants did not work well together. Older participants who participated in more 'gentle' sports activities did not particularly appreciate, listen to or respect the views of younger participants. In addition, there was a gender split in that male participants showed very little respect for the views of female participants. The older male participants were particularly patronising to younger females. As a result it was decided to run groups that separated younger and older participants and males and females. This meant an increase in the total number of focus groups conducted but also meant that the remaining focus groups worked well and that the views of distinct target groups were clearly presented.

If target participants are geographically widespread, then many groups may be needed to represent this diversity. The following example of an A.C. Nielsen hypermarket study illustrates the comparisons made in focus group analyses. The important markets the study concentrated upon were Russia, Hungary, Poland and the Czech Republic and so focus groups would be needed to represent each country. Further analyses of two distinct target groups were also needed. Thus, a minimum of two groups per country, i.e. eight groups plus an experimental group, would be needed, which would be doubled if it were subsequently felt to be important to run exclusively male and female groups.

| Real research | **Hypermarkets in Eastern Europe and Russia**[21] |

International retailers have pounced upon the opportunity to dominate grocery retailing in Central Eastern Europe and Russia. With inefficiencies in many local retailing networks, this has created enormous changes in the way that people shop. Never before have shoppers had such choice in store numbers, formats and product assortment. To better understand these changes, A.C. Nielsen conducted eight focus group discussions with housewives aged 25–40 years in Moscow, Warsaw, Prague and Budapest. Participants who were active shoppers, visiting at least three retail outlets every month, provided further insights through self-completion questionnaires. Hungarians were the most enthusiastic about hypermarkets, which they might visit up to twice a week, compared with the fortnightly trip for Czechs. Russians were more budget minded and preferred no-frills discount retailers. Shoppers in Poland were the most satisfied with hypermarkets.

Another factor to be considered in determining the number of focus groups to conduct relates to whether the researcher is using focus groups as part of a grounded theory approach. With such an approach (as described in Chapter 6 and further developed in Chapter 9) theoretical sampling is adopted whereby further examples or instances are sought that may contradict the nature of the emerging grounded theory. The complexity of the developing grounded theory and the extent to which the qualitative researcher makes sense of the issues being explored will ultimately determine the number of discussions needed. This can be contrasted to focus groups conducted from a positivist perspective, focusing upon generating an understanding of issues to be confirmed in a subsequent survey. In the latter scenario, the researcher may not need to continue to search for more contradictory perspectives. Whichever paradigm underpins the application of focus groups, resources permitting, one should conduct additional discussion groups until the moderator can anticipate what will be said. The last sentence is a reminder of the final factor determining the number of discussions – the time and money afforded by the client.

In summary, the number of focus groups that should be conducted on a single subject depends on the following factors:

- The extent to which comparisons between different types of participants are sought.
- The types of participant to be targeted and how well they interact in a discussion.
- The geographic spread of participants.
- The paradigm that underpins the planning, administration and analysis of the focus group.
- The time and budget available.

Another dimension of running the groups, beyond the actual number of groups, is the nature of stimuli that the moderator chooses to input. At certain times, examples of particular products or brands may be introduced for participants to examine, to taste, touch, smell or sample if the nature of the product permits. Advertising material such as brochures, posters or even video recordings of TV or cinema adverts can be shown and a response generated. One of the most frequently used forms of stimuli is the mood board.

The 'mood board' is really the creation of a collage (though in some discussions, pre-prepared collages are given to participants as illustrated on page 226).[22] Focus group participants are given a pile of magazines and asked to snip words and pictures from them. The direction they are given is to select images and words that they think represent characteristics of a brand, a consumer type or lifestyle, or whatever issue the researcher wishes to be illustrated in this manner. The resultant collage can then be used to stimulate discussion and to help draw together ideas and connect them. Creative marketing decision-makers in copywriting or advertisement development may develop many ideas directly from the collages or mood boards as illustrated in the following examples.

Mood board
A collage created in a focus group setting. Focus group participants are asked to snip words and pictures from magazines that they see as representing the values a particular brand is perceived to have. In some circumstances, collages can also be made up from audio-and videotapes.

Real research | **Y bother with insurance**[23]

Suncorp (**www.suncorp.com.au**) wished to launch a new under-25 'Family Discount' insurance offer. In order to make this work, Suncorp wanted to engage with parents and their children simultaneously. A team of young researchers was recruited to have frank discussions with the youth market. Suncorp wanted to know what their relationship with their parents was like. Suncorp wanted to see if there was any common ground between them and their parents they could use, and what issues it should avoid. Focus groups using mood board exercises produced surprising results: Generation Y were not 'trapped' at home, they 'share' with their parents, the more liberal of whom have no objection to boy/girlfriends staying over. Parties within reason. No curfews. It could be seen in their fashions: the boho chic of Gen Y girls was not too different from their baby boomer mothers' youthful fashions. They talked of wardrobe sharing and recycling. The fundamental values of the two generations were far more aligned than the angry Generation X and their parents, or the baby boomers and their depression-era parents. While this understanding may seem fairly obvious to anyone actually living this situation, very little of this was obvious in marketers' approaches to Generation Y.

Real research | **Becoming a brand**[24]

The Turkish white goods company Arçelik (**www.arcelik.com.tr**) commissioned focus group research to ask consumers how they perceived Arçelik at present and how they would like to see the brand in the future. The findings were revealing. Some of the clip-art visuals used by the consumers in their collages to depict Arçelik included: Traditional family. A bit aged. Military. Hamamizade Ishak Efendi (an historical music composer). Old TV sets. Managers in black and white photos. Black and white photos of past Miss Turkey winners. The British Royal Family. An old lady with back pain. A wooden bridge. A classical painting. Old shots from Turkish TV authority broadcasts. Turkish carpets . . . . The same groups said they would like to see Arçelik in the future as: 'Smiling. Smiling youngsters. Young women. Motor sports. Cute babies. Luxury cars. Happy families. Family values. Portable shelves. Astronauts. Computers.'

The mood board has two main functions:

1 *Reference point.* The moderator can use the mood board to reflect upon the discussion, in which case issues can emerge that were not so apparent in the heat of a discussion.

2 *Enabling device.* The mood board gets participants to loosen up and talk more freely. The focus group is not to get participants to talk rationally but to display what 'feels right' to them. The collage can help to express feelings they may not be able to put into words, or enable those words to have more clarity. This can happen by questioning what is included in a mood board as well as what is omitted.[25]

The mood board and the creation of collages can develop beyond two-dimensional images. Given the growth of social media, individuals have become far more adept at expressing their personalities, their likes and dislikes through music and videos. The growth and engagement with sources such as Facebook, YouTube and SecondLife demonstrates an array of ways that consumers wish to express themselves and the skills they have developed to form expressions.[26] As a result, there are many examples of participants producing video and audio collages in both group and individual settings.

The final stage in planning and conducting focus groups involves the analysis of data. Chapter 9 discusses qualitative data analysis in more detail. However, at this point there are two essential points to note:

1 *Evolving analysis.* Focus groups can change and develop in terms of the issues discussed and the stimuli used to draw out views from participants. The changes are made as the moderator generates and develops new ideas as each focus group progresses. The moderator makes observations and notes to help as the discussion progresses and also for when it is over. The moderator may also interact with the client as the discussion progresses and/or when individual groups are completed. These observations and notes are part of the total analysis in that they decide which issues to probe, which issues to drop and the form of summarising issues that may be presented to groups at certain stages of the discussion.

2 *Not just the narrative.* If the discussion is recorded then transcripts can be produced which can be analysed with proprietary software. These transcripts form a major part of the analysis procedure but the accumulation and reflection upon observations and notes forms a key part of the analysis.

The moderator

Throughout this chapter we have referred to the moderator as an individual who conducts a focus group discussion, by setting the purpose of the discussion, questioning, probing and handling the process of discussion. This individual may also be the researcher handling the project. More likely it will be someone who specialises in the technique, or, given the number of groups to run and the time allowed to complete them, a number of specialist moderators will be employed. Whoever is to undertake the task of 'moderating' will require the following qualities:[27]

- *Kindness with firmness.* The moderator must quickly develop an empathy with group members. From this the moderator should show kindness to make participants feel welcome, combined with a firmness to stop particular individuals taking over the discussion.

- *Permissiveness.* The moderator must be permissive, allowing the flow of discussion to develop as the group sees fit. However, the moderator must be alert to signs that the group's cordiality or purpose is disintegrating.

- *Involvement.* The moderator must encourage and stimulate intense personal involvement. In certain circumstances, this may mean becoming involved in the actual discussion itself. This can happen if a tendency for 'group speak' emerges. 'Group speak' happens when little debate or creativity in ideas develops, as particular individuals may not wish to be seen as going against a perceived group norm.

- *Incomplete understanding.* The moderator must encourage participants to be more specific about generalised comments by exhibiting a feigned naïvety or incomplete understanding.

- *Encouragement.* The moderator must encourage unresponsive members to participate.

- *Flexibility.* The moderator must be able to improvise and alter the planned outline amid the distractions of the group process.

- *Sensitivity.* The moderator must be sensitive enough to guide the group discussion at an intellectual as well as emotional level. The moderator must also be attuned to mood changes and issues that fire up enthusiastic responses or conversely cause the discussion to dry up. Sensitivity can also encompass the subtle nuances in the manner that they are viewed by participants, e.g. their dress, speech and manner; language and forms of expression used by participants; cultural references and context of these references as expressed in the discussion.

- *Observation.* As the group progresses, notes must be made of ideas or questions to come back to, interpretations of particular silences or bouts of laughter, and how group members are interacting with each other. These observations help the group discussion to progress well and the interpretation of the discussion to have greater meaning.

Other variations of focus groups

Many developments have occurred in the format of group discussions. An illustration of one development was set out in the Philips example at the start of the chapter in the use of bulletin boards for group discussions. As with the Philips example, most developments have been facilitated by the growth of online technologies and will be discussed later in this chapter. However, in examining how moderators may adapt and change their role in order to engage and elicit more from participants, it is worth examining several variations of the standard focus group procedure. These include:

- *Two-way focus group.* This allows one target group to listen to and learn from a related group. In one application, physicians viewed a focus group of arthritis patients discussing the treatment they desired. A focus group of these physicians was then held to determine their reactions.

- *Dual-moderator group.* This is a focus group discussion conducted by two moderators. One moderator is responsible for the smooth flow of the session, and the other ensures that specific issues are discussed.

- *Duelling-moderator group.* Here also there are two moderators, but they deliberately take opposite positions on the issues to be discussed. This allows the researcher to explore both sides of controversial issues. It also encourages participants who may support a particular perspective to express their views without fear that they will be 'attacked' by the rest of the group.

- *Participant–moderator group.* In this type of focus group, the moderator asks selected participants to play the role of moderator temporarily to improve group dynamics.

- *Client–participant group.* Client personnel are identified and made part of the discussion group. Their primary role is to offer clarifications that will make the group process more effective.

- *Mini group.* These groups consist of a moderator and only four or five participants. They are used when the issues of interest require more extensive probing than is possible in the standard group of 6–10.
- *Telephone focus groups.* These are conducted using a telephone conferencing system with the same number of participants as conventional focus groups, but typically within a narrower time frame, no more than an hour. These can work well in gaining access to widely dispersed experts in a range of professions or specialists. They would not be cost effective with 'average' consumers, except perhaps in cases where follow-up from survey participants is desired.[28]

Other types of qualitative group discussions

Brainstorming

Traditional brainstorming has been used for several decades, especially in the context of management or marketing issues.[29] Whether formal or informal, the process is the same: think of as many ideas as you can and say them out loud; leave the evaluation until later; build on and combine others' ideas; be as imaginative as possible, the wilder the ideas the better. The group moderator seeks to nurture an atmosphere of creativity, tapping into the intuition of participants, generating novel ideas and connections between ideas. When it works well, ideas flow freely from an interplay that may never have occurred if the group had not brainstormed together.

Two problems plague traditional brainstorming: production blocking and evaluation apprehension:

- *Production blocking* occurs when a group member has an idea, but someone else is talking. When it is his or her turn, the group member has forgotten the idea, or thinks it is redundant or not that good. If the group is large or dominated by talkative people, such members lose interest and do not say what they think.
- *Evaluation apprehension* occurs when participants become anxious about what others think of their thoughts. Ideas may be censored, as there is a fear of being labelled as odd. When participants feel this apprehension, they do not produce as many new and potentially useful ideas but keep them to themselves and therefore defeat the purpose of brainstorming.

As with traditional focus groups, online developments have generated a large variety of new approaches to brainstorming and generating ideas. These can include the use of research communities, Twitter and games.[30] The following example illustrates a comparison of traditional versus online approaches to brainstorming.

Real research	**BrainJuicer online brainstorming**[31]

The research agency BrainJuicer (**www.brainjuicer.com**) has created a four-stage approach to online brainstorming: (1) identify 'creative consumers' via an online creativity test; (2) brief 50 creative consumers online to create 500 new ideas for a certain product/category and collect the new ideas digitally; (3) categorise the output, select the most promising 50 ideas from the total; (4) after this the client team focuses on what it is good at: harvesting, articulating sound and appealing concepts. Harvesting can be done in a joint workshop to create commitment to the ideas. Using this process BrainJuicer was asked to generate new product ideas for Unilever Deodorants, both for men (e.g. Axe) and for women (e.g. Rexona). Halfway through the process it was decided to feed the ideas from the creative consumers into a brainstorming workshop and then invite some of them to participate in the workshop. After the workshop a total of 40 ideas, 21 originally from Unilever resources (generated using traditional brainstorming techniques) and 19 originally from the BrainJuicer process were selected by Unilever to be evaluated head to head in BrainJuicer's screening tool, the Predictive Market™. The Predictive Market uses a large diverse crowd to decide on ideas with the most potential in the marketplace. Participants get virtual shares in all ideas tested. They need to maximise their own wealth by selecting one idea that they think will be a big failure in the market and one idea that they feel will be most successful in the market. For each idea they assessed how often it had been selected 'to sell' and how often it had been selected 'to double shares in'. Among the deodorant ideas for men, the two winning ideas were inspired by the BrainJuicer process. Five out of six 'question marks' (often polarising ideas with niche potential) were inspired by the process. From the Unilever Deodorant results it was clear that the traditional brainstorming approach was less successful in generating fresh potent ideas than the group of creative consumers working individually online.

Misconceptions about focus groups

There has been much debate about the use and value of focus group discussions. Much of the debate has been misinformed through the development of myths and misconceptions built around the technique. Misconceptions about focus groups have emerged from assumptions made by researchers or the users of focus group findings or even journalists. Their assumptions may have been useful at one time, in a particular context, or when tackling a certain subject. The assumptions may well apply to specific contexts but may not be applicable to focus groups in general. Working through the misconceptions can help researchers make decisions about when and how to use focus groups, and even whether they should be using them at all.[32] The misconceptions about focus groups can be summarised by the five Es:

1 *Economical – they are low cost and quick.* The idea that focus groups are low cost and quick has emerged through comparison with other research methods. In comparison with survey research, focus groups and especially e-groups may be conducted with a smaller budget and more quickly. This is not a fair comparison given the sample sizes that the techniques work with and the type of data they generate. In comparison with other qualitative methods, focus groups are often more expensive than observation and individual interviewing, primarily due to more expensive recruiting methods. The biggest resource involved in the technique, however, is that of the researcher in the careful planning, execution and analysis of focus groups. The analysis of the data generated can be 'cheap and quick' if it is a case of decision-makers taking away their own conclusions from focus groups they have observed. Analysis can be far more expensive and time consuming if the careful planning and execution is followed up by the assembly of data, reflective diaries and memos and the full immersion into those data of the researcher as detailed in Chapter 9.

2 *Experts – they require professional moderators.* The qualities of a good moderator were detailed above. A professional moderator with experience of tackling different subjects, questioning and probing different types of participant and working in a variety of contexts undoubtedly has much to offer any project. However, in many instances it is not the amount of experience that matters most in moderating. Sometimes a less experienced moderator who has more contact with the issues under question, more contact with the participants, and is perhaps more comfortable in the interview location, can elicit better

data. This is especially true when working with distinctive ethnic, linguistic or cultural groups. For example, an undergraduate student working on a project for a leading deodorant brand was about to enter the room to conduct a focus group. Looking at the 18–20 year olds before he entered the room, he realised that he was wearing the 'wrong' logo. With a quick change of his shirt, he continued with the discussion to great effect. Upon reflection, he revealed that the logo he was wearing and indeed the colour of his sweatshirt would have said things about him to the group that would have affected his credibility with the assembled participants. He felt that he would not have been able to engage with the group and get it to reveal so much in his original clothing. His acute sensitivity to this cultural nuance made this focus group particularly effective; an older and more experienced moderator may not have picked this up. The best moderators are not necessarily those with the most experience. It is the individual that can best engage with, listen to and draw out the best of target participants.

3　*Easily upset – they do not work for sensitive topics.* Focus groups are regularly used in projects related to sexual behaviour, substance abuse and stressful life events, which have marketing or other social implications. This misconception is based upon what may be deemed as socially acceptable in conversations, perhaps around the dinner table. However, focus groups present an atypical setting for discussion. The moderator is encouraging everyone in the group to share values and experiences that they all have an interest in. There may be little consequence to what they say, especially if they are meeting with strangers whom they may never meet again. Handled with caution, the moderator can encourage participants to reveal things they would normally keep to themselves. Researchers and moderators working with sensitive issues must make plans to encourage appropriate self-disclosures, and to cope with disclosures that go beyond the boundaries of the project. These plans go beyond the wording of the questions and probes, into the atmosphere the researchers wish to create at the discussion, the nature of the location being particularly important here.

4　*Endorsement – they must be validated by other research methods.* This is part of the general misconception that all qualitative techniques play a preliminary role that prepares the way for a conclusive technique. Focus groups can serve a useful role as the first stage of developing questionnaires or experiments, but that is not their sole purpose. Focus groups can illuminate and indeed help to validate many of the statistical findings that emerge from surveys, e.g. helping to understand and describe findings from factor and cluster analyses. They can be used in isolation to produce the kind of in-depth understanding of an issue that no other technique can provide: for example, if the use of a particular celebrity in an advertisement can generate a series of emotional responses that could impact upon the brand values – and those values are compounded by the particular use of music and who is playing that music. To uncover what is happening to the viewers and how their values may have changed, the focus group may well be the most efficient and effective technique, of all qualitative or quantitative options.

5　*Exposure – they reveal how consumers will behave.* Focus groups, in-depth interviews and surveys all depend upon verbal reporting. They depend upon a belief in what participants say about how they intend to behave. In many circumstances, even when it comes down to it, the most sincere participants can change their minds. In focus groups, participants may talk about their likely behaviour in many hypothetical scenarios, moderators can watch other participants nod their heads in agreement and the evidence is compelling. It must be recognised that the data generated are attitudinal, and trying to predict behaviour from attitudes is most problematic. The rise in customer databases and ethnographic methods has helped researchers to predict consumer behaviour and validate the findings of focus groups and surveys.

The focus group, like every research technique, is never foolproof or perfect. To get the most from focus groups, the following thinking should be encouraged.[33] First, the quality of moderating is crucial to the success of the discussion. The quality of the findings is directly related to the talents, preparation and attentiveness of the moderator. Second, teamwork is vital. As well as star moderators, there must be quality recruiters, note-takers, analysts and reporters. Third, this team has always something to learn from the participants. For a short period of time, the participants open their lives and share their experiences, preferences and beliefs. The most destructive thing a researcher can do in a focus group is to display arrogance, condescension or superiority. It is much better to sit back and let participants tell you everything you wanted to know, and more! Finally, there are many ways to conduct successful focus groups. Given the nature of the topic under investigation and the nature of the target participants, there are many options to choose for the best context and approach to draw out the best from participants. Focus groups vary enormously in how they are planned, administered and analysed, from the very structured interview in a studio bristling with technology, through to a passionate dialogue conducted globally online, to a riotous exchange on a tropical beach. Experimentation with new ways of conducting focus groups should be positively encouraged rather than being bound by the thought that there is one ideal way to conduct them.

Online focus groups – e-groups

Throughout the chapter we have referred to and illustrated the use and value of online focus groups or 'e-groups'. The fundamental principles of why focus groups are conducted, their management and the data analysis challenges are similar between traditional focus groups and e-groups. However, the approaches have distinctive strengths and weaknesses which are worth exploring. Before examining their relative strengths and weaknesses it is worth considering a general description of online focus groups. There is no one generic format for an e-group. As with traditional focus groups, there are many variations and adaptations in e-groups, and their adaptation and use in Marketing Research Online Communities (MROCs) will be explored later in the chapter. To get some sense of the nature, variation and applications of e-groups, look at the work of the following two leading specialists: VisionsLive (**www.visionslive.com**) and nqual (**www.nqual.com**).

As in the case of traditional focus groups, e-group participation is by invitation only. The participants are pre-recruited and generally come from lists of individuals who have expressed an interest in particular products, services or issues. An example of such a list could be the use of access panels (detailed in Chapter 4), such as (**www.researchnow.com**). A screening questionnaire can be administered online to qualify participants, even if access panel members have already been profiled. Those who qualify are invited to participate in the e-group and given clear benefits and a reward for their participation. They receive a time, a URL, a room name and a password via email. Before the e-group begins, participants receive information about the discussion that covers such things as how to express emotions when typing. Electronic emotion indicators are produced using keyboard characters and are standard in their use on the Internet. Obvious examples include :-) and :-(for happy and sad faces. The emotions are usually inserted in the text at the point at which the emotion is felt. Emotions can also be expressed using a different font or colour. There are a wide range of emotions to choose from expressed such as: I'm frowning, I'm laughing to myself, I'm embarrassed, I'm mad now, I'm responding passionately now. These are then followed by responses. Participants can also preview information about the discussion topic by visiting a given website and reading information or downloading and viewing visuals such as TV advertisements. Then, just before the e-group begins, participants visit a website where they log on and get some last-minute instructions.

When it is time for the discussion, participants move into a Web-based chat room. In the chat room, the moderator and participants type to each other in real time. The general practice is for moderators always to pose their questions in capital letters and participants use upper and lower case. Participants are asked always to start their response with the question or issue number, so the moderator can quickly tie the response to the proper question. This makes it fast and easy to transcribe an e-group discussion. A raw transcript is available as soon as the discussion is completed and a formatted transcript can be available within 48 hours (the form of data used depends upon whether the transcript is to be input into qualitative analysis software and is to be built up as the groups progress, and/or is to be read by the client). The whole process of conducting the discussions and uploading transcripts for analysis is much faster than traditional focus groups.

New forms of e-groups continue to emerge. For example, online bulletin boards such as the Philips example outlined at the start, involve the moderator and participants over an extended period of time, from a few days to a few weeks. Questions and challenges can be slowly fed out over time, allowing the researcher to reflect upon responses that have been received and adapt subsequent questions. Participants can reflect in more depth and respond at their own convenience. Participants may also be given tasks such as collecting and posting visuals and music or offering web links to illustrate ideas and issues. Such an approach can enable an in-depth discussion among 25 or more participants. The extended time period allows participants to react to and build upon each other's ideas in a way that is often not possible during a traditional focus group that lasts even up to six hours. The following example illustrates a demonstration of how e-groups could work for a design challenge faced by a bank. Of particular note is the value of input and observations made by the client, a topic discussed earlier in the chapter.

Real research	**E-group vs. traditional focus group experiment**[34]

A leading high-street bank set iCD Research (**www.icd-research.com**), nqual (**www.nqual.com**) and The ID Factor (**www.theidfactor.com**) a challenge: to demonstrate that an e-group would match the findings from traditional qualitative research. The objectives of the project were centred on a new credit card proposition. To demonstrate the capabilities, a two stage e-group was proposed to be conducted at 8 p.m. on a Tuesday and Wednesday night. Utilising existing data within The iD Factor financial panel, participants were selected on their consideration to switch credit card providers within the next 12 months. A recruitment email validated this consideration, with the invitation to attend the night sessions. This information, as well as a demographic and attitudinal profile of each participant, was sent to the client prior to the session. A main moderator was based in London, and a secondary moderator, based in Australia, was also present. At 7.55 p.m., a total of nine participants were active within the session, with an additional 18 observers across five companies/subsidiaries and three continents watching. The approach adopted within **e-group 1** was consistent with an offline topic guide but adopted techniques that could be integrated into e-groups without risking participant focus or the trust in the moderation. The structure of the session followed what might be considered a 'traditional' qualitative format, including evaluation of a proposition as well as the incorporation of participant-suggested improvements. The use of client observers and a second moderator allowed the client proposition to be adapted 'live' based on initial and user-generated comments and 'built' by the second moderator, uploaded into the session and evaluated. Client participation was crucial as it allowed participant-generated queries to be addressed and answered correctly as well as assisting the moderator in steering the conversation in a way that could deliver against the set objectives. At 10 p.m. nqual delivered the discussion transcript to iCD Australia moderators. The Melbourne office was then able to take their observations, transcript and start the analysis process at 9 a.m. Australian EST. By 8 a.m. UK time the following morning, a summary report with proposition and stimulus recommended changes was delivered to the UK team, who by 9 a.m. had delivered a report to the client and worked with the client to make changes for **e-group 2**. A fresh, but matched demographic and behavioural sample of participants was recruited for the second e-group. This followed a similar structure to e-group 1, with the revised stimulus and proposition. With the Australian office co-moderating and observing again, summary and analysis was again conducted overnight, which included quantitative recommendations. In response to this an online survey was launched on the Friday, completed by the Sunday and fed back on the Monday. The combined qualitative and quantitative project was commissioned, recruited, delivered within a seven-day period. When comparing the trial of e-groups with the previously commissioned research, the key themes, initial feedback and suggested user improvements were completely consistent for both approaches. Nevertheless, the client viewed the online approach more positively, because it was faster, and was able to refine the proposition in real time and actively contribute to the session.

Advantages of e-groups

Participants from all over the country or even the world can take part, and with mobile technology advances they can physically be anywhere that they are comfortable. Likewise the client or decision-maker can observe and comment on the discussion from anywhere. Geographical constraints are removed and time constraints can be lessened. Unlike traditional groups, there is the opportunity to contact participants again at a later date, to revisit issues, or introduce them to modifications in material presented in the original focus group. The Internet and the use of profiled consumers via access panels enable the researcher to reach segments that are usually hard to interview: doctors, lawyers, professionals, working mothers and others who are leading busy lives and not interested in taking part in traditional focus groups.

Moderators may also be able to carry on side conversations with individual participants, probing deeper into interesting areas. Participants may be less inhibited in their responses and can be more likely to express their thoughts fully, especially if they have the facility to reflect and upload images, music or other forms of expression. Many e-groups go well past their allotted time as so many responses are expressed as participants become engaged in the discussion. Finally, as there is no travel, videorecording or facilities to arrange, the cost is much lower than traditional groups. Firms are able to keep costs between one-fifth and one-half the cost of traditional groups.[35]

Disadvantages of e-groups

Only individuals who have access to and know how to use a computer (fixed or mobile) can participate in e-groups. The global growth and access to computers means that many types of individual can be accessed, but there remain significant numbers and types that cannot. Since the name of a participant is often private, actually verifying who the participant is and thus whether they fit a target profile is difficult. To overcome this limitation, other traditional methods such as telephone calls are used for the recruitment and verification of participants. This is an area where the use of a well-managed access panel can help in ensuring the profile of a participant is correct for a particular study. Body language, facial expressions, silences and the tone of voice cannot be observed and electronic emotions cannot capture as full a breadth of emotion as videorecording. Another factor that must be considered is the general lack of control over the participant's environment and potential exposure to distracting external stimuli. Since e-groups could potentially have participants scattered all over the world, researchers and moderators have no idea what else participants may be doing during the discussion. This has to be balanced against the comfort that may be felt by the e-group participants in being able to conduct the discussion in a context where they feel comfortable. Only audio and visual stimuli can be tested. Products cannot be touched (e.g. clothing) or smelled (e.g. perfumes). It may be more difficult to get clients or decision-makers involved in e-groups as they can be in observing traditional groups. It is hard to replicate the compelling views of consumers, expressing themselves in an uninhibited manner, on what they feel about a product or service. Table 7.2 presents a summary comparison of e-groups and traditional focus groups.[36]

Table 7.2	Online versus traditional focus groups	
Characteristic	**E-groups**	**Traditional focus groups**
Group size	4 to 8 participants	6 to 10 participants
Group composition	Anywhere in the world	Drawn from a targeted location
Time duration	1 to 1.5 hours – though can last over a week as participants are given tasks and come back to the discussion	1.5 to 6 hours
Physical setting	Researcher has little control – but the participants can be in a place that is comfortable to them, especially with the use of mobile technology	Under the control of the researcher
Participant identity	In some circumstances can be difficult to verify	Can be easily verified
Participant attentiveness	Participants can engage in other tasks – not seen by the moderator	Attentiveness can be monitored
Participant recruitment	Easier. Can be recruited online, by email, by access panel, or by traditional means	Recruited by traditional means (telephone, mail, mail panel)
Group dynamics	Limited	Synergistic, snowballing (bandwagon effect)
Openness of participants	Participants can be candid – may be more open with identities hidden to some extent	Participants can be candid as they build up trust of each other Difficult with sensitive topics
Non-verbal communication	Body language and facial expressions cannot be observed Some emotions can be expressed	Easy to observe body language and facial expressions Expression of emotions easier to monitor
Use of physical stimuli	Limited to those that can be displayed online – unless specific engagement tasks given to participants	A variety of stimuli (products, advertising, demonstrations) can be used
Transcripts	Available immediately	Time consuming and expensive to obtain
Observers' communication with moderator	Observers can communicate with the moderator on a split screen	Observers can send messages to the moderator from behind two-way mirrors
Unique moderator skills	Software familiarity, awareness of chat-room slang	Observational

Table 7.2	Continued	
Characteristic	**E-groups**	**Traditional focus groups**
Turnaround time	Can be set up and completed in a few days	Takes many days to organise, administer and analyse
Client travel costs	None	Can be expensive
Client involvement	Limited	High
Basic focus group cost	Much less expensive	More expensive due to facility rental, refreshments, video/audio taping, and transcript preparation

International marketing research

There are many researchers who have criticised the focus group as a technique, yet it still remains the most widely used qualitative technique. The focus group can be argued to be the most efficient approach for time and money to gather a range of views and managing creative challenges, especially when decision-makers need to be present to challenge and shape these views. The development of e-groups makes the time and money arguments much stronger. Focus groups have always been challenging in exploring both the individual versus group response and managing any bias from individual dominance/group opinion leader issues.[37] Focus groups, however, remain at the core of understanding consumers as social and cultural beings and it is this factor that makes their application in international marketing so important. In an international setting, the basic foundation of focus groups is to explore, confirm and assess key customer-driven trends. This foundation is fundamental to the successful development and marketing of products and services across many cultures. Focus groups can clearly support decision-makers in their understanding of the social and cultural context of consumer behaviour. They can support an in-depth understanding of the nature of consumers and the factors that shape their behaviour and relationships to brands. The following example illustrates how focus groups can be used for in-depth cross-cultural studies where participants faced creative challenges based upon their sensory experiences.

Real research   Globalisation put to the test[38]

In a study of global brand management, focus groups were conducted in Hamburg (Germany) and Shanghai (China). The aims of this cross-cultural study were: understanding consumers' perception of brands in today's world of globalisation; importance of the country of origin in the perception of brands; evaluation of Chinese brands and products entering the German market on the basis of the assessment of Chinese white and red wine. In order to emphasise cultural influence factors, a category was chosen that was extremely sensitive to the local culture and habits: beverages. In eight focus groups held in China and Hamburg, consumers conducted sorting exercises and projective techniques to express their views and feelings about brands in today's world and discussed a possible effect of the globalisation trend: the acceptance of 'exotic' products, such as Chinese Chardonnay and Cabernet Sauvignon. These products were tested by German wine drinkers accustomed to Riesling and Grauburgunder. German wine entering the Chinese market was tested by Chinese wine drinkers. Each focus group lasted approximately 2.5 hours and consisted of between six and eight participants. Besides the common recruitment criteria (e.g. excluding people with a marketing, research or gastronomic background, decision-makers regarding the relevant product in the household), the participants were screened according to the following *profile*: **Age** (two groups with younger consumers aged between 20 and 35 years and two groups with older consumers aged between 40 and 55 years in each country); **Gender** (approximately 50% males and 50% females per group); **Income level** (only China) and education level; **Awareness** of international brands and had purchased some brands within the past two months (mix of presumably global/fusion/local brands that were relevant in the market); **Familiarity** with (grape) wine and consumption at least one to two times per month; **Attitude** towards globalisation according to statement battery (two groups with pro-consumers and two groups with anti-globalisation consumers in each country).

The value of focus groups in international marketing may be debated.[39] For the researcher, the main issue is one of making the focus group work in different cultural settings. This does not mean imposing a Western (either American or European) model of conducting the focus group, but in developing an understanding of a culture in order to adapt the technique. This may mean that indigenous researchers are not just trained in managing, delivering and analysing focus groups. Their knowledge must be respected and prized in developing creative and effective focus groups in their cultures. For example, Western researchers observing participants in Japanese focus groups may miss much of the dynamics of the group or what may be articulated though body language and facial expressions. It is almost impossible to learn to interpret Japanese non-verbal communication in a short space of time. Even for native speakers a tilt of the head can mean 'not really' but also 'it's OK'. It is best to ensure that native Japanese speakers interpret these. Examples of other misleading non-verbal behaviours can be: a smile and a laugh can often be a sign of anxiety or nervousness;

Japanese people avoiding eye contact to be polite; businessmen closing their eyes during meetings as a sign of concentration and not tiredness! In a focus group in Japan, participants may wait until they fully comprehend each point before speaking. They will not lose face by misunderstanding an implication in front of others. There will also be extensive introductions to allow people to comprehend fully the relevant relationships.[40] In this example, one could argue that any focus group study of Japanese consumers should be left firmly in the hands of Japanese researchers. The challenge comes in cross-cultural research where comparisons are sought. The researcher needs to know that any similarities or differences that are observed between cultures cannot be solely attributed to differences in techniques. There is a large array of published examples of applying focus groups in different cultural settings. As the use of e-groups and online bulletin boards grows, especially in international contexts, the lessons from such examples are invaluable to researchers. Further lessons and examples will be more fully developed in Chapter 26.

Ethics in marketing research

A number of ethical issues related to running focus groups have emerged in this chapter. The focus group can be a direct qualitative research technique where the purpose of the discussion is made clear to participants before it starts. However, the focus group can incorporate observational and projective techniques that introduce elements of indirectness, i.e. elements or all of the purpose of the discussion being hidden from participants. This is where researchers face a real ethical dilemma. If they fully reveal the purpose of their study, would this put off potential participants whose views are important to the success of the study? Even if they do manage to recruit potential participants, the researchers have to consider how they may feel when the real purpose of the study becomes apparent through the nature of the discussion or by the moderator revealing all at the end. The nature of the dilemma faced by researchers is that by revealing too much at the start of the study they may compromise the quality of their discussion. A full revelation may not be conducive to participants reflecting, making new connections and expressing themselves about issues that may be deeply held, difficult to conceive and express.

Researchers should take all reasonable precautions to ensure that participants are in no way adversely affected or embarrassed as a result of the focus group. What is meant by an adverse effect and embarrassment will largely depend upon the issues being explored and how they are perceived by target participants. Some participants may find personal hygiene issues very embarrassing to talk about in a group scenario, but not financial issues. Other individuals may be very frank about their sexual behaviour, while others would be shocked at the notion of talking about sex with a group of strangers. The researchers must get to know how the issues they wish to explore are perceived by their target participants by examining the literature, secondary data and the use of experimental focus groups.

Another major ethical problem that is research issue and participant specific is the use of alcoholic drinks during focus groups. For certain groups of participants, relaxing and socialising in a comfortable context, drinking wine or beer is very natural. Researchers with experience of running many focus groups would argue that serving alcoholic drinks can help to reduce tension in certain participants and give them the confidence to express their particular

viewpoint. Other researchers would argue that this is unethical practice, that in effect the researcher is 'drugging' the participants. Whatever the researcher decides is right for the type of participants, the issues they are questioning them about and the context in which the discussion takes place, there are practical problems involved with serving alcohol. Controlling the flow of alcohol and how much is given to certain participants may take attention away from the discussion. If control is not exerted, particular participants may get out of hand and disrupt or even destroy the discussion. Researchers could be accused of not taking reasonable precautions to ensure that participants are in no way adversely affected or embarrassed as a result of the focus group, should the use of alcohol be abused by certain participants. In no circumstances should researchers use audio or video recording or two-way mirrors in focus groups without gaining the consent of participants. It must be made clear to participants that recording or observation equipment is to be used and why it needs to be used. Participants must then be free to decline any offer to take part in a discussion.

Finally, researchers have always found that running traditional focus groups with children as participants has many distinct challenges, some of which are described in the following example.

| Real research | Becoming a brand[41] |

Young focus group participants are different creatures from adults, and this calls for some adaptations to the way researchers approach their work. Young people can be deeply self-conscious and lack confidence in revealing and articulating their views in front of others. A forum that seeks to source this information from them can therefore be an uncomfortable one. If they are involved in focus groups, it is like asking them to attend an event that can look like a school scenario. If it is not differentiated, this can result in an uncooperative or unmanageable group, as giggles take over and the moderator loses control. Generating comfort, and thus confidence, is crucial. It is worth adding a question to the recruitment screening about their possible 'subcultural' or 'tribal' leanings. With little else to use in self-definition, these visual distinctions can be all-important. Sworn enemies on the local high street, emo/indie/goth kids and 'townie' or 'hoodie' youths do not make easy group partners. In a group setting, girls tend to open up and share together fairly quickly. Boys need more time because their group dynamics are based on clear-cut roles. It can be worth asking them to arrive 30 minutes early and leave them to play games together or complete a task before the group kicks off. This will give them time to form some sense of group structure. Alternatively, start the group with some smaller team tasks before bringing them back together to talk as a whole. Where possible, it is worth trying to work with young people's existing friendship groups. As well as providing a young person with security and familiarity, it offers a much more authentic understanding of brand adoption behaviours. By working with a set of friends, it can be possible to see how deliberations and decisions are played out and negotiated. What brought them to group consensus? What, or who, was the all-important lever in that consideration process?

Many of the challenges of physically managing traditional focus groups have been overcome with e-groups. Children can be more comfortable and engaged in the use of online discussions. This, however, brings major ethical challenges for the researcher in understanding who is actually contributing to a discussion, what the child's characteristics are and what the impact of the discussion may be upon that child. Research companies such as Dubit (**www.dubitlimited.com**) use e-groups which allow children to air/share their views in ways that children may have not been able to do before. Speaking through an avatar they have found that children are often much more comfortable than they would be in a face-to-face focus group where concerns about confidence and appearance are much more acute. E-groups may be a natural location for youth research and marketing but many ethical challenges emerge from this development. ESOMAR has codes of practice that address the challenges of researching children but the emergence of new online techniques presents ethical challenges that have yet to be fully debated and addressed in a manner that gives clear guidance to researchers.[42]

Digital applications in marketing research

The development of Web 2.0 functionality with examples such as forums, blogs, texting, photo and video galleries, chat rooms, have underpinned the development of Marketing Research Online Communities (MROCs). An MROC is an invited group of consumers with a common focus on a particular brand. This group is brought together online to develop conversations and to react to set quantitative and qualitative tasks. The information from MROCs can help in the development of new ideas in products, advertising, service concepts and positioning concepts. They can help to identify problems and opportunities, helping clients to understand better the perceptions and motivations of their customers and even potential customers. MROCs are growing in popularity and in terms of their application. One of the main reasons for this could be the relative costs.[43] The following example illustrates the relative costs of running an MROC compared with traditional focus groups.

As with the focus groups, MROCs are developed around a group of people but now invited to participate in a primarily online environment established to address either one or a series of research objectives. This could be over a fixed period or may be running in perpetuity. In marketing research terms, MROCs tend to be qualitative in nature but they may also feature surveys or other quantitative techniques. They can vary in size from tens to tens of thousands of people. A fundamental difference to the focus group is that MROCs tend to feature a more long-term brand engagement. They actively seek to invite participants to be part of the brand development. Often the ultimate aim of an MROC is to develop the relationship with participants to a stage where they become 'critical friends' to the brand, offering continuing honest feedback. MROCs are moderated asking questions, posting discussions, probing answers. As with the focus group, the MROC is run by a moderator. The characteristics and skills of MROC combine those required in both traditional focus groups and e-groups. The moderator has a role in policing, providing technical support and answering other queries. Moderation is challenging in many ways; the content must be clear and concise, broad to encourage debate, specific so as not to be ambiguous, but not leading. The number of questions in any one topic can be limited. Moderators need to be sensitive to misunderstanding from participants, clarify meaning or context of questions. By understanding the specific online behaviour of the target audience a moderator can make the question interesting to the participants and remain in tune with the client's objectives. The moderator becomes an interpreter in the widest sense of the word. Moderators must understand their community and preferably

Marketing Research Online Community
An invited group of consumers with a common focus on a particular brand. This group is brought together online to develop conversations and to react to set quantitative and qualitative tasks.

Real research   ## Penny for your thoughts?[44]

A typical online research community will have around 3–400 members. The cost of running a community equates to the cost of running two focus groups per month. In order to get a real return on investment, client companies do a lot more than two focus groups' worth of activities each month. In a typical community, members are engaged in between three and five activities, requiring around 45 minutes of their time each week. They are compensated by small gifts or cash payments, but no one is going to get rich by taking part in a community. Jim Figura, Vice President of Consumer Insights & Research at Colgate-Palmolive (**www.colgate.com**), argues that members contribute to online communities because they feel valued. They get a great sense of contributing and the community is an excellent way of dealing with small issues that previously would not have got a lot of research attention. He tells his community: 'You are our professional consultants and we value your input.'

show similar behaviours to those they are talking to in the community. They need to understand 'the way things work' online. It is important for a moderator to be culturally sensitive and in a position to understand and acknowledge that social norms and simple points of reference are different both between and sometimes within countries. Community moderators also have to create the right conditions for content generation and dissemination. This aim can be achieved by: promoting conditions for an open exchange of ideas and information; creating time and space for dialogue exchange; supporting innovative thinking. Moderation can also be aided by those within the community. By seeking out the more engaged participants, they can be asked to become quasi-researchers, interacting with others on the site to help draw out further thoughts. Indeed, they can become reporters on the community as a whole, adding a whole other layer of interpretation to the work. Often people are happy that their contribution has been acknowledged by a brand/moderator/community they have a good relationship with.[45] As such, MROCs can be developed following action research principles and become a powerful means of co-creation for marketers, designers and researchers. MROCs are not a direct replacement for traditional focus groups or e-groups. The development of MROCs, in both practice and theory, and the benefits they deliver to decision-makers will shape the future development and application of focus groups.

Summary

In direct qualitative methods, participants are able to discern the true purpose of the research, whereas indirect methods disguise the purpose of the research to some extent. Focus groups can be a completely direct qualitative method, though by the use of observational and projective techniques elements of indirectness can be introduced. In deciding how 'direct' a focus group should be, researchers have to face ethical issues and questions related to the richness of data that they can draw from participants. Focus group discussions are the most widely used qualitative research method.

Focus groups are conducted by a moderator in a relaxed and informal manner with a small group of participants. The moderator leads and develops the discussion. In a focus group, participants can portray their feelings and behaviour, using their own language and logic. The value of the technique lies in the unexpected findings that emerge when participants are allowed to express what they really feel, especially as different sensory experiences are explored. An experimental focus group should always be run at the start of any series of discussions. The researcher needs to understand how comfortable target participants feel in the chosen location for discussion, how the opening question works, the topic guide, the probes, the mix of participants and the refreshments, including any alcoholic drinks. In a nutshell, one could argue that one should continue running focus groups until nothing new is learned from target participants. This perspective oversimplifies how diverse and spread out different participants may be and how well they mix together in a group situation. The time and budget available will also mean that a cut-off point has to be drawn and the strongest analysis and interpretation has to be made at that point. Online technical and technique developments have seen the e-group emerge as a means to engage with geographically dispersed participants. Such engagement can be conducted in a speedier and cheaper manner than traditional focus groups. Traditional focus groups allow for richer observations of participants and more creative sensory experiences to be evaluated. There is no one absolute correct method to administer a focus group; the researchers should understand the factors that will make the technique work for their particular research problem and the type of participants they have to work with.

Researchers face challenges in planning, administrating and analysing focus groups when set in international contexts. It is vital that researchers do not impose their norms of running focus groups in different cultures but learn from indigenous researchers. This learning is vital in making cross-cultural comparisons. A key element of ensuring that the focus group works well lies in the ethical issues of how much is revealed to participants before they get involved and during the discussion. Getting participants to relax and be open may involve the use of alcoholic drinks which for many researchers creates no problems but for some creates ethical and practical problems. With the growth of e-groups, the ethical challenge of understanding who is actually engaged in a discussion is paramount. This is particularly relevant in researching children where ESOMAR guidelines have to keep up with emerging technologies and practices. Social media developments have resulted in the emergence and growth of Marketing Research Online Communities (MROCs). These communities are being adopted by many brands to engage with their existing and potential customers. E-groups can be conducted in the context of MROCs, but the development of communities as a potentially richer and cheaper data source will impact upon decision-makers' views of the use and value of focus groups.

Questions

1 Why may researchers not wish to fully reveal the purpose of a focus group discussion with participants before it starts?

2 What are the key benefits and drawbacks of conducting focus group discussions?

3 What are the difficulties in conducting focus groups with managers or professionals?

4 What determines the questions, issues and probes used in a focus group?

5 Evaluate the purpose of running an experimental focus group discussion.

6 What does a 'comfortable setting' mean in the context of running a focus group?

7 To what extent can a moderator achieve an 'objective detachment' from a focus group discussion?

8 Why is the focus group moderator so important to the success of a focus group discussion?

9 What are the relative advantages and disadvantages of being able to observe covertly a focus group discussion?

10 What can the researcher do to make potential participants want to take part in a focus group?

11 What determines the number of focus groups that should be undertaken in any research project?

12 Describe the purpose and benefits of using stimulus material in a focus group.

13 What is an e-group? What are the distinct advantages and disadvantages of running e-groups compared with traditional focus groups?

14 Describe the opportunities and difficulties that may occur if alcoholic drinks are served during focus group discussions.

15 What is a Marketing Research Online Community (MROC)? How can an MROC be viewed as a group-based qualitative research technique?

Exercises

1   Following the methods outlined in this chapter, develop a plan for conducting a focus group study to determine consumers' attitudes towards organic foods. Specify the objectives for the groups, write a screening questionnaire, list potential props or physical stimuli that you could use in the discussion and develop a moderator's outline.

2   Your campus sports centre is trying to recruit more members from the local non-student community. In achieving this aim, evaluate the marketing decisions that could be supported by focus groups, either as a technique in its own right or as validated with other techniques.

3   You are a brand manager for Johnny Walker whiskies. You wish to invest in an e-group study of whisky buyers and drinkers. Explain how you would identify and recruit such participants from across the globe. What incentive(s) would you offer potential participants?

4   Visit the website of the Association of Qualitative Research Practitioners (**www.aqr.org.uk**). Examine the reports and views of contributing practitioners and write a report on what you feel are the latest developments and/or exciting opportunities in the use of focus groups.

5   In a small group discuss the following issues: 'The dress, appearance and speech of the moderator create biases in group discussions that cannot be evaluated' and 'Mood boards created in focus groups are more useful to marketing decision-makers compared with a formal written analysis of the discussions'.

Video case exercise: Nike

For Nike, how could focus groups have helped in the development of the 'Presto' new product line?

Notes

1.   Djurovic, V. and Depeux, V., 'Semiotics of taste: application in China for international (and local) food and flavor industries', ESOMAR: Qualitative, Barcelona (November 2010).

2.   Kahane, S. and Itzcovich, M., 'Naked truth – online focus groups: getting to the bottom of the consumer's mind', ESOMAR: Online Research, Berlin (October 2010).

3.   Mesure, P., McGouran, O. and Feehan, M., 'Using online bulletin boards to develop high value corporate strategy', ESOMAR: Congress Odyssey, Athens (September 2010).

4.   To understand more of how a luxury brand may be researched using qualitative techniques, see Healy, M.J., Beverland, H.O. and Sands, S., 'Understanding retail experiences – the case for ethnography', *International Journal of Market Research* 49 (6) (2007), 751–778.

5.   For an excellent discussion on the problems of interpreting 'silence' in interviews, see Prasad, S., 'Listening to the sounds of silence', ESOMAR: Asia Pacific, Kuala Lumpur (April 2010).

6.   Ewing, T., 'Confessions of a moderator: how web communities fail and how marketers can stop that happening', Market Research Society: Annual Conference

(2008); Morgan, D.L., 'Focus group interviewing', in Gubrium, J.F. and Holstein, J.A. (eds), *Handbook of Interview Research: Context and Method* (Thousand Oaks, CA: Sage, 2002), 141–159.

7.   Morrison, D.E., 'Focus group research: a misunderstood history', ESOMAR, Qualitative Research, Venice (November 2003); Morgan, D.L. and Krueger, R.A., 'When to use focus groups and why', in Morgan, D.L. (ed.), *Successful focus groups: Advancing the state of the art* (Newbury Park, CA: Sage, 1993), 3–19.

8.   ESOMAR, 'Global Market Research', ESOMAR Industry Report (2010), 16.

9.   Bloor, M., Frankland, J., Thomas, M. and Robson, K., *Focus Groups in Social Research* (Thousand Oaks, CA: Sage, 2001).

10.   Kreuger, R.A. and Casey, M.A., *Focus Groups: A practical guide for applied research*, 3rd edn (Thousand Oaks, CA: Sage, 2000); Drayton, J. and Tynan, C., 'Conducting focus groups – a guide for first-time users', *Marketing Intelligence and Planning* 6 (1) (1988), 5–9.

11.   For more discussion, see Dexter, A. and Ngoc Hieu An, B., 'From Bricolage to Pho – Vietnam as a model for global influences and assimilations at meal times', ESOMAR, Asia

Pacific, Beijing (April 2009); Andrews, M. and Langmaid, R., 'Theory and practice in the large group', Market Research Society, Annual Conference (2003); Morgan, D.L., *Planning focus groups* (Thousand Oaks, CA: Sage, 1998), 71–76.

12. Forrest, C., 'Research with a laugh track', *Marketing News* 36 (5) (4 March 2002), 48; Mazella, G.F., 'Show-and-tell focus groups reveal core bloomer values', *Marketing News* 31 (12) (9 June 1997), H8.

13. Morgan, D.L., *Planning focus groups* (Thousand Oaks, CA: Sage, 1998), 71–76.

14. MacDougall, C., 'Planning and recruiting the sample for focus groups and in-depth interviews', *Qualitative Health Research* 11 (1) (January 2001), 117–126; Kahn, H., 'A professional opinion', *American Demographics* (Tools Supplement) (October 1996), 14–19.

15. Gordon, W., 'New life for group discussions', *ResearchPlus* (July 1993), 1.

16. Baskin, M., 'Observing groups', *WARC Best Practice* (November 2010).

17. McPhee, N., 'Is there a future for "real" qualitative market research interviewing in the digital age?', ESOMAR, Congress Odyssey, Athens (September 2010); Krueger, R.A., *Moderating focus groups* (Thousand Oaks, CA: Sage, 1998), 30.

18. Stokes, D. and Bergin, R., 'Methodology or "methodolatry"? An evaluation of focus groups and depth interviews', *Qualitative Market Research: An International Journal* 9 (1) (2006), 26–37; Goldsmith, R.E., 'The focus group research handbook', *The Services Industries Journal* 20 (3) (July 2000), 214–215; Greenbaum, T.L., *The Handbook for Focus Group Research* (Newbury Park, CA: Sage, 1997).

19. Krueger, R.A., *Developing questions for focus groups* (Thousand Oaks, CA: Sage, 1998), 25.

20. Ellis, R., 'So how do you upstage a Ferrari owner?', *ResearchPlus* (November 1994), 10.

21. Ghosh, S., 'Hypermarkets lead to new shopping habits', *Research World* (November 2004), 32–33.

22. Toiati, L., 'How do you call collages in Asia?', ESOMAR, Asia Pacific Conference, Singapore (December 2002), 1–20.

23. Jowell, C. and Barber, A., 'Suncorp – "Family Discount" campaign: Y bother with insurance?', Account Planning Group (Australia), Finalist, Creative Planning Awards (2006).

24. Vardar, N., 'Arçelik: From "a passion for manufacturing" towards "becoming a brand"', Turkish Foundation of Advertising: 'Turk Markalari-2', Turkish Foundation of Advertising Publications (2008).

25. Croft, M., 'Art of the matter', *Marketing Week* (9 October 1997), 71.

26. Jalboukh, T. and Chaudhry, A., 'Reality YOUTH research – the Arabian YOU (TH) Tube!' ESOMAR: Consumer Insights, Dubai (February 2009).

27. Sharma, A. and Pugh, G., 'Serpents with tails in their mouths: a reflexive look at qualitative research', ESOMAR: Qualitative Research, Paris (November 2007); Katcher, B.L., 'Getting answers from the focus group', *Folio: The Magazine for Magazine Management* (Special Sourcebook Issue for 1997 Supplement) 25 (18) (1997), 222; and an adaptation from Chase, D.A., 'The intensive group interviewing in marketing', *MRA Viewpoints* (1973).

28. Mariampolski, H., *Qualitative Marketing Research: A comprehensive guide* (Thousand Oaks, CA: Sage, 2001), 47.

29. Gallupe, R.B. and Cooper, W.H., 'Brainstorming electronically', *Sloan Management Review* 35 (1) (Fall 1993), 27.

30. Cierpicki, S., Davis, C., Eddy, C., Lorch, J., Phillips, K., Poynter, R., York, S. and Zuo, B., 'From clipboards to online research communities: a cross-cultural review of respondents' perceptions', ESOMAR, Congress Odyssey, Athens (September 2010); Poynter, R., Vieira, S., Alexander-Head, D., Coulter, A., Zuo, B. and Gao, A., 'Will Twitter change the way that market researchers communicate?', ESOMAR, Asia Pacific, Kuala Lumpur (April 2010); Verbrugge, J., Geels, A., Verbiest, S. and Fletcher, A., 'Gaming 0.0 – a research game as an innovative "offline" research tool', ESOMAR, Congress, Montreux (September 2009).

31. Johnston, C., 'Getting over the courtesy bias', *Research World* (July 2007), 29.

32. McCracken, G. and Morgan, D.L., *The Long Interview + Focus Groups as Qualitative Research* (Thousand Oaks, CA: Sage, 2009).

33. Morgan, D.L., *The focus group guidebook* (Thousand Oaks, CA: Sage, 1998), 52–54.

34. Hamilton, J. and Dixon, P., 'Real-time global research – a qual revolution', Market Research Society: Annual Conference (2009).

35. Reid, D.J. and Reid, F.J., 'Online focus groups', *International Journal of Market Research* 47 (2) (2005), 131–162; O'Connor, H. and Madge, C., 'Focus groups in cyberspace: using the internet for qualitative research', *Qualitative Market Research* 6 (2) (2003), 133–143; Kozinets, R.V., 'The field behind the screen: using netnography for marketing research online communities', *Journal of Marketing Research* 39 (1) (February 2002), 61–72.

36. Cheng, C.C., Krumwiede, D. and Sheu, C., 'Online audio group discussions: a comparison with face-to-face methods', *International Journal of Market Research* 51 (2) (2009), 219–241; Brüggen, E. and Willems, P., 'A critical comparison of offline focus groups, online focus groups and e-Delphi', *International Journal of Market Research* 51 (3) (2009), 363–381.

37. Dexter, A. and Gillespie, D., 'From Bricolage to Pho – Vietnam as a model for global influences and assimilations at meal times', ESOMAR, Asia Pacific, Beijing (April 2009).

38. Rademacher, U., Lee, D. and Ma, Y., 'Local jewels and global heroes: the fusion model of global brand management', ESOMAR, Annual Congress, Berlin (September 2007).

39. Alioto, M.F. and Gillespie, D., 'The complex customer: applying qualitative methods in automotive NPD', ESOMAR, Qualitative Research, Athens (October 2006).

40. Cantle, N., 'Research insights into Japanese culture', *Admap* 480 (February 2007), 35–37.

41. Macdonald, N., 'Unlocking response from young people', *Admap* 504 (April 2009), 12–13.

42. Nairn, A., 'Protection or participation? Getting research ethics right for children in the digital age', ESOMAR, Congress, Montreux (September 2009).

43. Poynter, R., 'Are communities an answer to the economic recession?' ESOMAR, Congress, Montreux, (September 2009).

44. Johnston, C., 'Getting over the courtesy bias', *Research World* (July 2007), 29.

45. Child, P., Fleming, K., Shaw, R. and Skilbeck, T., 'Vive la différence: understanding, embracing and evolving MROCs globally', ESOMAR, Congress Odyssey, Athens (September 2010).

8 Qualitative research: in-depth interviewing and projective techniques

Stage 1

Problem definition

Stage 2

Research approach developed

Stage 3

Research design developed

Stage 4

Fieldwork or data collection

Stage 5

Data integrity and analysis

Stage 6

Report preparation and presentation

With no social pressure to conform to group responses, participants can be questioned in depth in a context that allows them to really express how they feel.

Objectives

After reading this chapter, you should be able to:

1 understand why the in-depth interview is defined as a direct qualitative research technique and observation and projective techniques are defined as indirect techniques;

2 describe in-depth interview techniques in detail, citing their advantages, disadvantages and applications;

3 explain how theory may be used to create structure to questioning and analysis in in-depth interviewing by reference to the laddering technique and the repertory grid technique;

4 describe projective techniques in detail and compare association, completion, construction and expressive techniques;

5 understand the context of interviewing and language problems that should be considered by international qualitative researchers;

6 understand the ethical dilemmas faced by qualitative research practitioners;

7 appreciate how digital developments are shaping the manner in which in-depth interviews and projective techniques are managed.

Overview

Having discussed qualitative research in terms of its nature and approach, and evaluated focus groups as the main body of marketing research techniques, we now move on to describe and evaluate other qualitative techniques.

We start by describing and evaluating what is meant by an in-depth interview and the procedure of in-depth interviewing. The role of the in-depth interviewer is described and the advantages and disadvantages of the technique are summarised. In the process of conducting in-depth interviews, the techniques of 'laddering' and 'repertory grid' can be applied to help to structure the elicitation and analysis process. Laddering and repertory grid techniques will be described and illustrated. The indirect qualitative association, completion, construction and expressive projective techniques are described and illustrated. The applications of these techniques are detailed, followed by an evaluation of their advantages and disadvantages. This is developed into an overall summary of the relative strengths and weaknesses of qualitative techniques under the headings of 'focus groups', 'in-depth interviews', 'projective techniques' and 'ethnographic techniques'.

The following example illustrates a subject that for many individuals would be difficult to articulate: how fragrances appeal to them and their fragrance experiences. The subject requires a qualitative technique to generate data of a kind that will support creative product design, packaging and advertising decisions. The subject matter, however, is ideal for the application of in-depth interviews and projective techniques where time can be spent building trust and rapport between the interviewer and participant. In-depth interviews allow participants talking about fragrances the time and space to express ideas about everyday events that normally they just get on with and do not have to explain or rationalise to anyone!

Real research

In-depth interviews and fragrances[1]

Christian Dior and the research agency Repères (www.reperes.net) developed a research approach that tested consumer reactions to new fragrances and the context in which they are used. This work was particularly aimed at supporting decisions made in the launch of new fragrances. The researchers' exploration was built upon the use of metaphors and an individual qualitative approach through in-depth interviews. They felt there were limitations in how consumers could talk about fragrances and so chose metaphors as a way of describing an object using words other than those that consumers may usually employ. A library of images was built that encompassed the broadest array possible of meanings and feelings. Why in-depth interviews? The researchers felt that individual interviews enabled them to go beyond initial reactions and explore the emotional unconscious. This enabled them to explore the whole emotional and imaginary chain underlying the perception of a fragrance. They felt that group discussions would never go as far into perceptions because participants could be restricted in their emotional reactions by the perceptions of other participants. One-to-one in-depth interviews allowed them to analyse the perceptions of different participants, identifying issues common to all (or to a particular target) vs. those specific to the characteristics of each participant. Participants were recruited with a specifically designed recruitment questionnaire that ensured that all had a minimum level of creativity and were able to articulate their thoughts. The room and the moderator were prepared to be as neutral as possible and ensure that a certain level of sensory deprivation was in place so that the fragrance under study was the 'star' of the experience. The moderator avoided wearing perfume so as not to 'pollute' the air. The participants, however, were not asked to attend unscented. This was because this would not be true to life. If the participants wore a specific scent on a daily basis they may not feel comfortable being deprived of this olfactory enhancement. They were asked to place the tested fragrance on their skin as they were needed to 'claim ownership' of the fragrance. It was key to let the fragrance 'live' and develop on the participant.

In-depth interviews

The meaning of 'in-depth'

In-depth interview
An unstructured, direct, personal interview in which a single participant is probed by an experienced interviewer to uncover underlying motivations, beliefs, attitudes and feelings on a topic.

An in-depth interview is an unstructured, direct, personal interview in which a single participant is probed by an experienced interviewer to uncover underlying motivations, beliefs, attitudes and feelings on a topic.[2] It is a qualitative interview and as such is based upon conversation, with the emphasis on researchers asking questions and listening, and participants answering.[3] The purpose of most qualitative interviews is to derive meaning through interpretations, not necessarily 'facts' from participant talk. The emphasis should be upon a full interaction to understand the meaning of the participant's experiences and life worlds.[4] In order to tap into these experiences and life worlds, in-depth interviewing involves a certain style of social and interpersonal interaction. In order to be effective and useful, in-depth interviews develop and build upon intimacy; in this respect, they resemble the forms of talking one finds among close friends. They can resemble friendship, and may even lead to long-term friendship. They are also very different from the nature of talking one finds between friends, mainly because the interviewer seeks to use the information obtained in the interaction for some other purpose.[5] As the name implies, in-depth interviewing seeks 'deep' information and understanding. The word 'deep' has four meanings in this context.[6] These meanings will be illustrated with a scenario of a researcher trying to understand the eBay (**www.eBay.com**) shopping experience:

1   *Everyday events.* Deep understandings are held by the participants in some everyday activity, event or place. The interviewer seeks to achieve the same deep level of knowledge or understanding as the participants. For example, if the interviewer has never used eBay to buy or sell goods and this experience is what is being investigated, in-depth interviewing can be used as a way to learn the meanings of participants' actions. In this respect, the participant acts as a kind of teacher and the interviewer a student, one interested in learning the ropes.

2   *Context.* Deep understandings go beyond common-sense explanations of some cultural form, activity, event, place or artefact. In-depth interviewing aims to explore contextual boundaries to uncover what is usually hidden from ordinary view and to penetrate the more reflexive understandings about the nature of that experience. In an eBay investigation, the interviewer can explore the meanings of different shopping experiences, the thrill of 'winning' a deal and the 'joy' of owning a particular artefact, the 'disappointment' felt when a beautiful pair of shoes that look perfect on the screen are slightly shoddy when they arrive, to name but a few contextual boundaries.

3   *Multi-faceted.* Deep understandings allow multiple views and perspectives on and meanings of some activity, event, place or cultural object. The researcher may wish to explore the many perspectives of eBay buyers and sellers, family members who 'enjoy' or 'suffer' eBay transactions in their household, executives who manage eBay, eBay competitors, high-street retailers, again to name but a few facets of the total experience.

4   *Interviewer reflection.* Deep understandings can help to reveal the interviewer's common-sense assumptions, practices, ways of talking and self-interests. This issue will be developed in Chapter 9. In this example, however, if the interviewer traditionally buys goods from the high street, wanting to examine the goods before buying, or has not conducted an Internet transaction, what will the interviewer 'see' or 'hear' in a particular in-depth interview? This situation mirrors children–parent relationships. Children do not learn what their parents tell them, but what they are prepared and ready to hear. The same holds for in-depth interviewers: researchers do not necessarily 'hear' what their informants tell them, but only what their own intellectual, social, cultural and ethical development has prepared them to hear.

Going deep into the minds of consumers is a learning process. Researchers make mistakes; they sometimes say the wrong things or upset participants in some way. They learn that their race, age, gender, social class, appearance or voice makes one kind of difference with some participants and another kind of difference with other informants.[7] The lesson from this is that there is no 'ideal' means to conduct the in-depth interview. Researchers learn from their experiences, discovering strengths and playing to them, realising weaknesses and understanding how to compensate for them. In this spirit of experimentation and learning we present a procedure that encapsulates how a researcher may approach the in-depth interview.

Procedure

To illustrate the technique, a scenario is set whereby the researcher is interviewing the marketing director of a soap brand that has successfully sponsored a major athletics event. The sponsorship has resulted in many industry awards, increased sales and better employee–employer relations. The researcher wishes to understand why the soap manufacturer became involved in the sponsorship and how it achieved such success.

The in-depth interview with this busy executive may take from 30 minutes to well over an hour. It may occur on a one-off basis or it may unfold over a number of meetings as more understanding is developed. Once the interviewer has gained access to the marketing director (which can be very problematic; why should they give up valuable time and share commercial knowledge?), the interviewer should begin by explaining the purpose of the interview, showing what both will get out of taking part in the interview and explaining what the process will be like. Beyond the introduction the interviewer may ask the marketing director a general introductory question such as 'what impacts have the industry awards had upon your business?' The interviewer would be expected to have done their homework to know what the awards were, what they were awarded for and who the brand was competing against. This is a very positive feature of the sponsorship experience, and it would be hoped to boost the ego of the marketing director and encourage them to talk freely about the different impacts of the awards. The impact of sponsorship could be upon existing and potential new customers, employees and suppliers. The discussion could then flow into any of these areas. After asking the initial question, the interviewer uses an unstructured format, guided by a topic guide as a reminder of important subject areas to cover. The subsequent direction of the interview is determined by the participant's initial reply, the interviewer's probes for elaboration and the participant's answers.

As with the focus group topic guide and the moderator managing that guide, spontaneity ensures that the process is creative and meaningful to the participant. Suppose that the participant replies to the initial question by saying:

> The award for the 'best use of sponsorship' in the launch of a new product gave us the most satisfaction. It has made us review how we execute all of our new product launches and integrate our different marketing agencies, our employees and supply chains.

The interviewer might then pose a question such as 'was it the award that initiated the review or would you have done that anyway?' If the answer is not very revealing, e.g. 'we may have', the interviewer may ask a probing question, such as 'what did the award tell you about how you worked as a team?' This question could open up a whole series of issues such as 'trust', 'relationship development' or 'technical support', to name a few. Such an exchange of questions and answers could emerge from a heading of 'Integrating sponsorship with other marketing communications' on the topic guide. The interviewer will keep an eye on the topic guide to ensure that all the important issues are tackled, but the specific wording of the questions and the order in which they are asked is influenced by the participant's replies.

Probing is of critical importance in obtaining meaningful responses and uncovering hidden issues. Probing can be done by asking general questions such as 'why do you say that?', 'that's interesting, can you tell me more?' or 'would you like to add anything else?'[8] Probing can search for general issues but also be more specific, an example in the above scenario being 'what does good teamwork mean to you?' One of the main success factors of specific probing is that the researcher understands something about the nature of the subject being researched. This means the researcher appreciates the significance of particular revelations, understands the language (even technical language and jargon in certain areas, like the soap industry) and has credibility with the participant that encourages them to open up to the interviewer.

The interviewer must be alert to the issues to go through but also the issues that the participant is willing to talk about, and must listen carefully to and observe which issues fire enthusiasm in the participant. The questions and probes the interviewer puts to participants should follow the interest and logic of the participants, making them feel motivated to respond in a manner that suits them. As with a focus group discussion, the participants should feel comfortable and relaxed, which could mean holding the interview in their office, their home, a bar, a sports club. There have even been experiments using a 'research taxi' in which participants are taken to their destination while they participate in an interview conducted by the researcher–driver and shadowings (observations and interviews) with subway passengers during their home–work commute.[9] In these examples any context in which participants feel at ease can result in a willingness to be more reflective, honest and open. Answering in a manner that suits the participant helps to make the interview more comfortable and relaxed. For a great amount of business research, the in-depth interview is the best way to gain access and to talk to managers. Much of the interviewing takes place in their office at a time that is convenient to them. Researchers can also observe characteristics of the manager in their office environment that can be of help in their analyses. Examples of this could be levels of formality in the workplace, reports and books that the manager has for reference, the manager's use of technology, or the tidiness of the workplace. In the example above where a manager has received a sponsorship award, it could be how that and other awards are displayed, photographs from advertisements, displays of new products. These observations would be entirely based upon the purpose of the study, but the context of the office can be of help to the manager and the researcher. In order to make the above process work, the interviewer should:

1   Do their utmost to develop an empathy with the participant.

2   Make sure the participant is relaxed and comfortable.

3   Be personable to encourage and motivate participants.

4   Note issues that interest the participant and develop questions around these issues.

5   Not be happy to accept brief 'yes' or 'no' answers.

6   Note where participants have not explained clearly enough issues that need probing.

In marketing research that focuses upon managers or professionals as illustrated above, the context of the in-depth interview helps to set the frame of mind of the participant. The context should also help the participant and interviewer to relax, engendering an atmosphere to explore and develop issues that they feel to be relevant. The following arguments help to focus on the issues faced by the interviewer coping with managers and professionals, trying to find the right context to allow these participants to express how they really feel.[10] The in-depth interview helps to overcome:

1   *Hectic schedules.* The best participants tend also to be the busiest and most successful people. They can make time for an interview, but are rarely able to spare the much greater time needed for them to come to a group discussion at some location away from their office. So groups exclude the best participants.

2   *Heterogeneity.* Whereas mothers evaluating nappy advertisements, or beer drinkers the latest lager, have only their personal preferences to consider, it is very different for executives evaluating copiers, airline advertisements or computer software. This is because their reactions are complicated by the type of job they do and who they work for. The group discussion is dependent on the group's composition being fairly homogeneous; the job backgrounds of business people make them too varied to be entirely comfortable in a group.

3   *Live context.* A lot of information comes from seeing the participant at their desk, which is missed in a group discussion. Work schedules pinned to the wall, the working atmosphere, artefacts placed on the desk, family photographs, the way coffee is served, all help to fill out the picture.

4   *Interviewer reflection.* Groups do not allow the researcher enough thinking time. Two groups, each taking an hour and a half over successive evenings, do not even begin to compare with two or three full days of non-stop interviewing. Individual interviews give much more scope for experimentation. If one way does not work, it is only one participant, not a whole group that is affected.

The following example illustrates the types of professionals or experts that may be targeted to participate in individual in-depth interviews.

Real research   ## Connecting with experts[11]

Unilever's Axe men's range of toiletries was inspired by an unconventional approach to consumer research. The research approach started with in-depth interviews with a group of individuals identified as experts in 'understanding men' and what drives them. The experts included a professor of evolutionary psychology, sex psychologists, adult film directors, a 'burlesque' dancer, a game developer and a senior writer on *Loaded* magazine. They were all interviewed in their own working environments, either by Unilever's Consumer Insight Manager or using researchers from the international qualitative and youth research company Firefish (**www.firefish.ltd.uk**).

Another major application of in-depth interviews where the context of the interview plays a major part is in the interviewing of children.[12] Researchers into children and teenagers spend considerable time working out the best research approach. Debates proliferate on the most appropriate research designs and interviewing techniques: in-depth interviews versus group, mini groups versus standard groups, friendship pairs versus stranger groups, association projective techniques versus expressive ones, and of digital media-based techniques.[13] These debates make researchers focus on the implications of how research is conducted and which technique provides the best results. One vital element is often overlooked, and that is the issue of context: in other words, the need to ensure that the situation in which children are interviewed is relevant to the research needs.

Like adults, children have multi-faceted personalities. The same teenager can be sullen at home, obstructive in the classroom, but the life and soul of the peer group. The essential difference between children and adults, however, is the extent to which different aspects of the persona can be accessed on one occasion and in one situation, the research setting. Adults have insight into the different roles and behaviour, which they adopt in different contexts, and can project other aspects of themselves which they bring into the research situation. Children and young teenagers, on the other hand, react to the moment and thus project only one aspect of themselves. They lack the maturity, experience and self-knowledge to draw on other parts of themselves and therefore find it almost impossible to know, let alone admit or explore, how they might behave in another circumstance.[14]

The above evaluation of the importance of context also shows that question formulation, the very heart of marketing research, can be more important in interviewing children than when dealing with adults. A straightforward 'what do you think about X?' may throw children into confusion. A formulation such as 'if you were to call your friends about this, what would you tell them?' would be more likely to produce illuminating responses. An innovative approach to interviewing children is illustrated in the following example.

Real research   ## Quantifying the emotional aspects of advertising[15]

In order to understand how to 'talk' to children we need to find ways to connect to them, and hence explore what it is like to be a 10 year old. The way Optimisa (**www.optimisaresearch.com**) goes about researching children taps into the very areas where they are not adults. It is about how we as adults adapt to who they are, finding a way to engage with every child, and building a bridge to help us reach their world. A good starting point is often an awareness of the skills they have developed in school, using these as the building blocks for the technique. So, rather than asking a child a direct question, which more often than not will result in a long blank look, we can ask children to draw a picture, or select a photograph, or even write a story that simply relates to the question we are trying to ask. Children react well to this approach and find the prop easy to talk around, often giving the researchers more than they hoped for.

On a project for Cartoon Network, a child depicted in a picture one of the pressures of the fierce consumer society we live in. The picture was about exclusion and showed a group of boys; outside the group, another boy was crying. On closer inspection it was not the boy crying that told the story, but why he was doing so. A Nike tick was distinctly missing from his trainers.

Friendship pair
A technique used to interview children as two friends or classmates together.

An effective technique when working with children is the use of friendship pairs – interviewing two friends or classmates together. This helps to cut out lying because children are not alone with strangers and because if one tells a lie, the other tells on that one. The ingrained honesty of children arguably makes them easier to research than adults, who of course are far more accomplished exponents of deception.

Advantages and challenges of in-depth interviews

In-depth interviews have the following advantages. They can:

- Uncover a greater depth of insights than focus groups. This can happen through concentrating and developing an issue with the individual. In the group scenario, interesting and knowledgeable individuals cannot be solely concentrated upon.

- Attribute the responses directly to the participant, unlike focus groups where it is often difficult to determine which participant made a particular response.

- Result in a free exchange of information that may not be possible in focus groups because there is no social pressure to conform to group response. This makes them ideally suited to sensitive issues, especially commercially sensitive issues.

- Be easier to arrange than the focus group as there are not so many individuals to coordinate and the interviewer can travel to the participant.

The following are not necessarily disadvantages, but really the challenges that researchers face when using this valuable technique:

- The lack of structure makes the results susceptible to the interviewer's influence, and the quality and completeness of the results depend heavily on the interviewer's skills. As with all qualitative techniques, the interviewer needs to develop an awareness of the factors that make them 'see' in a particular way.

- The length of the interview, combined with high costs, means that the number of in-depth interviews in a project tends to be few. If few in-depth interviews can be managed, the researcher should focus upon the quality of the whole research experience. 'Quality' in this context means the qualities that the participant possesses in terms of richness of experience and how relevant the experiences are to the study; the quality of drawing out and getting participants to express themselves clearly and honestly; and the quality of analysis in terms of interpretation of individual participants and individual issues evaluated across all the interviews conducted.

- The data obtained can be difficult to analyse and interpret. Many responses may not be taken at face value; there can be many hidden messages and interpretations in how participants express themselves. The researcher needs a strong theoretical awareness to make sense of the data or the technical means to develop theory if using a grounded theory approach. As well as the transcripts of the interview, additional observations add to the richness and multi-faceted analyses and potential interpretations.

The use of the laddering technique in the next example illustrates how a theoretical awareness can help to develop structure, elicit or draw more out of participants and help to make sense of the data they generate. It is an illustration of how the three challenges outlined above can be overcome. Balance what may be seen as the advantages and disadvantages of in-depth interviews in evaluating this example. Implementing the following discussion guide would be challenging but would also generate many unique consumer insights. It illustrates that the in-depth interview is not a fixed and formulaic approach. This builds upon the Christian Dior example at the start of this chapter. The use of 'laddering techniques' will be further explained and illustrated in the next section.

Real research | **Christian Dior In-depth Interview Discussion Guide[16]**

The in-depth interview approach developed by Christian Dior and the research company Repères broadly followed these stages allied to a laddering technique:

1 Gather initial sensations, emotions that come up instantly after a first sniff:
   a Evocations and imagery were explored:
      (i) Association, imaginary place/scene, Chinese portrait, a photofit of the fragrance.

2 Gather new sensations a few minutes after the first sniff once the fragrance had developed and then re-evaluate the different sensations mentioned to obtain:
   a A detailed description of each sensation (e.g. if sensation of warmth, is it warmth from a chimney fire, from the noon sun, from a duvet, human warmth) and where it operates (on the body, on the mood, on the nerves, on the mind/state of mind).
   b The source of this sensation: what note, what scent (if concrete description possible) or what 'sort' of odour (if analogous description) produced this sensation.

3 Analyse the olfactory journey or construction of the fragrance, its mechanism (it goes from what sensation/effect to what sensation?).

4 Identify the resulting personality of the fragrance: descriptors, values, objectives/mission/role of the juice, image, distinctive specificity.
   a The projected target: what is the likely female (male) profile for the fragrance?

5 Image assessment using visual stimuli (varied photos from the picture library: different colours, shapes, materials, places, characters, scenes from life) to expose hidden or unconscious perceptions:
   a First, ask for a justified choice of six photos, each one representative of a perceived aspect or dimension of the fragrance.
   b Then force associations as the moderator selects six photos at random and not chosen at the beginning by the participant, asking what matches/does not match the fragrance under study.

6 Then close up with a critical assessment of the potential and risks/limitations of the fragrance.

The laddering technique

The in-depth interview can be driven by a topic guide, made up of just a few topics covering a very broad range of issues. From these few topics, the nature of questions, the order of questions and the nature of probes can be driven by the interviewer's perception of what will draw the best out of participants. Alternatively, an in-depth interview can be semi-structured where parts of the interview use consistent and highly structured questions, with set response categories, interspersed with open-ended questions involving probes that again suit the nature of the participant. There are other variations on the technique that can help the interviewer and participant to apply useful structure to issues that can be very 'messy' and unstructured. One of the most popular techniques to apply structure is called laddering. Laddering requires interviewers to be trained in specific probing techniques in order to develop a meaningful 'mental map' of the consumer's view towards a particular product. The ultimate goal is to combine mental maps of consumers who are similar, which lead to the reasons why consumers purchase particular products.

Laddering
A technique for conducting in-depth interviews in which a line of questioning proceeds from product characteristics to user characteristics.

The laddering technique is made up of a linking or ladder of elements that represent the link between products and the consumer's perception process. It enables an understanding of how consumers translate product attributes, through personal meanings associated with them.[17] Theories of consumer behaviour act as a foundation to this approach, based on the contention that consumption acts produce consequences for the consumer. Consumers learn to associate these consequences to specific product attributes. These associations are reinforced through consumers' buying behaviour and, as a result, they learn to choose products that have certain attributes in order to obtain the consequences they desire. There are two features of this theory that the researcher using the laddering technique will focus upon:

1 *Motivation.* The laddering technique focuses upon generating insight into the motives behind the consumption of certain products. It represents a more contemporary approach to classical motivation research.[18] The technique aims to stimulate participants to reflect upon their buying behaviour in a way unconnected from their usual behaviour.

2 *Cognitive structure.* This feature is also a development of theory, in this case means–end–chain (MEC), developed by Gutman.[19] MEC starts from a point of consumer motivation. It contends that motivation leading towards a form of behaviour is derived from the connection between tangible product attributes and more abstract cognitive structures that involve the physical and emotional consequences derived from these attributes. At a more abstract level, the consequences lead to values held by the consumer.

The laddering technique is therefore designed to identify and follow the chain of

$$\text{attributes} \rightarrow \text{consequences} \rightarrow \text{values (A–C–V)}$$

The in-depth interview using the laddering technique is based on comparisons of the consumer's choice alternatives. These can include, for example, different products used for the same purpose, such as an electric toothbrush and a conventional toothbrush, and/or varieties in a product line such as full-fat and skimmed milk, and/or product brands such as Heineken and Amstel beer, and/or kinds of packaging such as wine in bottles and in cartons. Other elements that can affect consumer choices can be added to the above list. In making the comparisons, the interviewer poses a question that hopes to encourage the participants to put aside their established rationale and reflect upon their consumption behaviour, in ways that they would not normally do. In other words, questions are posed that make participants think about consumption from other points of view to try to release participants from fixed attitudes, perceptions and values. The interviewer's role is to build up a rapport with participants and get them to relax and feel comfortable to respond with whatever comes to mind. The interview revolves around three basic questions based on the A–C–V chain. The questions posed would be:

1 *Values.* How important is this for you? (e.g. health)

2 *Consequences.* What does this difference mean? (e.g. not fattening)

3 *Attributes.* What is different about these alternatives? (e.g. low calories)

From the attribute of 'low calories' in comparing different product varieties in a product line such as full-fat and skimmed milk, a further and negative consequence of 'watery taste' could be elicited, followed by the values of 'unnatural'. The interviewer aims to build a great repertoire of chains through these levels spontaneously, choosing the right comparisons to draw out the next link in the chain. The resulting responses are analysed to establish possible categories of attributes, consequences and values. The categories are then organised according to the qualitative comments made between the relationship of an attribute, its consequence and value. The result is an association matrix that graphically displays the categories and the connections that have emerged.

Laddering requires an interviewer with experience of in-depth interviewing, with a realisation of what will relax participants and get them in a frame of mind to 'play' with the associations sought. The interviewer needs to appreciate the theoretical foundations of the technique,[20] not only to help determine what should be elicited from participants, but also to help generate sound and meaningful analyses. Laddering sets out to unravel 'how consumers translate product attributes, through personal meanings associated with them' to provide a motivational and cognitive structure to purchase decisions in a given market. In essence, the technique looks at a brand in terms of the attributes that make it different from other brands, the consequences of this for the individual (what does the difference mean?), and the value the difference has (how important is it?).[21] The following example illustrates the consumer insights and marketing implications that emerged through the use of laddering.

Real research | **Climbing the ladder to PlayStation2 success[22]**

The laddering technique was used to determine consumer attitudes and purchasing motivations towards the Sony PlayStation2 (**www.scea.com**). The key laddering insights for this product included:

- My friends come over and we spend an evening working together through a game or playing against each other.
- Challenging games require more critical thinking and decision making. It feels more like a puzzle than a game.
- Some games are suited to adults only, so I don't feel like I'm playing a 'children's' game, but taking part in a high-quality gaming experience.

The marketing implications that emerged from these insights include:

- Set up kiosks in large cities to attract adults.
- Advertise through programmes such as *Friends* with Joey and Chandler playing games on a PlayStation2.
- Target magazines such as *Wired* and *Sports Illustrated* with more mature advertisements.

The insights generated helped to develop further research at Sony and helped with creative marketing decisions in all aspects of designing products, distribution, pricing and promotions.

The repertory grid technique

Another widely used technique that applies structure to qualitative in-depth interviewing is the repertory grid technique (RGT). This technique was originally developed by George Kelly in 1955[23] to explore the meanings that people attach to the world around them, which they find particularly hard to articulate. As with the laddering technique, there is a theoretical underpinning, personal construct psychology.[24] The repertory grid technique is rooted in a grounded theory perspective. The categories used in the findings emerge from the data rather than being introduced by the researchers. It is a technique that grounds the data in the culture of the participants, if they choose both the elements and the constructs, and it is clearly useful where there is a need to explore the personal worlds of participants. The repertory grid has gained status in management research because of its distinctive strengths. It helps researchers to explore the unarticulated concepts and constructs that underlie people's responses to the world. Moreover, it is a technique that may reduce the problem of interviewer bias in in-depth interviews. A particular strength of the repertory grid technique is that it can help to access the underlying realities in situations where the cultural or people issues are particularly strong, and where participants might otherwise feel constrained to try to answer in the way they think they should, as opposed to how they really think.[25] There are a number of variations of the technique and arguments about whether it should be implemented and analysed in a positivist or interpretivist manner,[26] but in essence the stages involved in the repertory grid technique are:[27]

1. Element selection
2. Construct elicitation
3. Element comparisons
4. Data analysis.

Element selection. The elements selected will depend upon the nature of consumer behaviour that the interviewer wishes to examine. In a study that wished to understand *broad-based patterns of consumer behaviour*[28] the elements chosen included 30 generic products and services such as newspapers, holidays, chocolate bars, eggs, alcoholic drinks, shoes, toothpaste, savings accounts, restaurant meals and shampoo. In another study that wished to understand *the process of effective new product development*[29] the elements chosen included 30 successful new products and services such as Slim Fast, Pull Ups, Loed Tea, Ultraglide, Baby Jogger, Gourmet Coffee, Zantac, Paragliders, MTV and Carmen Soft. These elements should be chosen by the participants, not just chosen and presented by the interviewer. There should be some homogeneity in the elements in the sense that the participant sees the elements relating to and representative of the behaviour being studied.

Construct elicitation. Having selected elements that the participant believes to encapsulate the behaviour being studied, the interviewer now seeks to understand what connects them together. The first stage of this involves the interviewer selecting three of the chosen elements at random and then presenting to the participant small cards with a summary of these elements. The participant is then asked to describe how they see two of the three to be alike and how the third may be different. The researcher selects different 'triads' to the point where all the elements have been contrasted or the participant cannot describe further 'similarities' or 'differences'. Construct elicitation therefore draws out the participant's perspective of the important features that encapsulate a particular form of consumer behaviour.

Element comparisons. The constructs elicited from participants are now turned into bipolar descriptions in a manner similar to the semantic differential scale described and illustrated in Chapter 12. For example, suppose that in a study of *the process of effective new product development*, three elements were compared: MTV, Gourmet Coffee and Paragliders. The participant may say that MTV and Gourmet Coffee are alike in that there are many similar competitive products that they can be compared with, whereas Paragliders is different in that there are few competitive 'personal' means to fly long distances. Whether this is factually correct or whether the interviewer agrees with this is immaterial; it is how the participant sees it that is important. Such a belief could be turned into a bipolar scale as illustrated below:

| No other products like this in the market | 1 | 2 | 3 | 4 | 5 | 6 | 7 | Lots of competitive products |

Other scales would be constructed to cover the ways that participants compared the chosen elements, i.e. the constructs elicited would be turned into a series of bipolar scales. Participants would then be expected to evaluate all the original elements using these scales. If they felt that Gourmet Coffee has many competitors they could tick a line at the (6) or (7) point. So, if there were 30 elements that encapsulate the behaviour under study and 20 constructs elicited to evaluate these elements, a total of 30 × 20 or 600 ratings would need to be performed.

Data analysis. A grid can be assembled for each participant to represent in the above example the 30 × 20 ratings. Again, an illustration of this comes from a small extract of *the process of effective new product development* study. The following represents an extract of the total response from one participant:

Construct	MTV	Gourmet Coffee	Paragliders
Market newness	6	6	2
Company newness	3	7	1
Technology newness	2	4	6

With a number of these completed grids, factor analysis (Chapter 22) can be performed to discover the important underlying factors or dimensions that encapsulate a particular form of behaviour.[30] The analysis can continue by performing cluster analysis (Chapter 23) to explore patterns of similarity or dissimilarity in different types of participant, i.e. to discover and describe groups of participants who may view particular forms of behaviour in similar ways.

The above process can take a great deal of time to select the elements, to elicit the means to compare the elements and to evaluate them. It requires an amount of rapport between the interviewer and the participant and patience in working through the stages. All of the stages may not be completed in one interview. It may require the interviewer to return to the participant to develop the next stage, especially in transferring the elicited elements to bipolar descriptions to allow all the elements to be evaluated.

The Zaltman metaphor elicitation technique

Another technique that creates a 'mental map' of the consumer's view towards a particular product is the Zaltman metaphor elicitation technique (ZMET). It is a qualitative in-depth technique that is used by companies such as Procter & Gamble, AT&T, Kodak, Ford and General Motors. It was developed at the Harvard Business School by Professor Jerry Zaltman and is patented in the USA. In a ZMET study, before coming in for an in-depth interview, participants are asked to gather pictures that reflect their thoughts and feelings about an advertisement and brand.[31] Anderson Analytics (**www.andersonanalytics.com**) uses cartoon pictures as a stimulus toolbox to generate stories.[32] The technique uses images and metaphors to reveal how consumers think and feel about brands, issues or other research topics. It does not ask consumers 'what they think about the things researchers think about'. Instead, it lets participants' own frames of reference shape the in-depth interview, without losing sight of the research aims. The technique, its application and the power of visual metaphors are illustrated in the following examples.

Real research	Diving for pearls[33]

ZMET allows the participant to define the frame of reference for an interview. The use of metaphor is extremely effective in revealing submerged thoughts and feelings and specifically in allowing access to the emotional domain. Participants are given a question a few days before their actual interview, and asked to source (non-literal) images reflecting their feelings. For example, in a study of looking at how people choose which financial products to buy and which suppliers to use, one participant brought in a picture of two dogs, a fully grown Saint Bernard towering over a tiny Chihuahua, to express his feeling of being intimidated by large companies. This period of reflection brings tacit knowledge to the surface. At an in-depth interview, participants explain the significance of each image and how it relates to the question. Probing for clarification, cause and consequence reveals the meaning behind each idea and the connections between ideas. The results reveal the consumers' mindset: the issues most salient to them and the thoughts and feelings they attach to each issue. In ZMET, the main ideas are coded and mapped by Metaphoria, proprietary software that shows the links between them. The result is a consensus map of 'the mind of the market'. Although product performance remains central to this map, the process also allows highly emotional outcomes, such as confidence, joy, fear and alienation to emerge.

Real research	Using metaphor[34]

Metaphors seem to express emotions more vividly than literal language because they evoke an emotional response directly. Memories that have emotional significance seem to have the greatest resonance; metaphors that link directly to emotions are the most powerful. The scales we use to measure consumer views of brands and brand communications are language based and literal, not visual or metaphorical. Participants need to consider their response before answering, but by consideration they get further away from emotions. The emotion may still be present but it becomes blended with thinking and is more prone to post-rationalisation. The Conquest Metaphorix (**www.metaphorixuk.com**) approach incorporates visual metaphorical scales based on primary metaphors linked with emotional states, such as love, affection and intimacy, which have particular relevance to brand engagement. These online scales use a range of engaging visual devices to represent metaphors associated with different emotional states, using visual depictions of (for example) proximity/closeness and warmth.

ZMET aims to understand the images and associations that underpin both spoken and tacit thoughts and feelings through the elicitation of both rational and emotional thinking. The process especially allows the emotional aspects of products and their use to become apparent. The resultant analysis creates a graphical visualisation of the 'mind of the market'. This visualisation creates a link between consumer perceptions and those involved in creative activities of product design and marketing communications. Such an approach accelerates the creative process and helps design and advertising agencies to add more emotional value to their work.

Applications of in-depth interviews

Applying in-depth interviews, with high or low levels of structure, with a strong theoretical foundation such as laddering, the repertory grid technique or ZMET, or with the desire to generate grounded theory, presents challenges but also many rewards. There are many marketing decisions that can be made with support from researchers using the broad array of techniques under the heading of 'in-depth interviews'. The following summarises the applications:[35]

1 Interviews with professional people (e.g. finance directors using banking services).

2 Interviews with children (e.g. attitudes towards a theme park).

3 Interviews with elite individuals (e.g. wealthy individuals involved in large philanthropic ventures).

4 Detailed probing of the participant (e.g. new product development for cars).

5 Discussion of confidential, sensitive or embarrassing topics (e.g. personal hygiene issues).

6 Situations where strong social norms exist and where the participant may be easily swayed by group response (e.g. attitudes of university students towards sports).

7 Detailed understanding of habitual or tacit behaviour (e.g. the 'rituals' an individual may go through when preparing to get ready for an evening out).

8 Detailed understanding of complicated behaviour (e.g. the purchase of fashion or 'high-status' goods).

9 Interviews with competitors who are unlikely to reveal the information in a group setting (e.g. travel agents' perceptions of airline travel packages).

10 Situations where the product consumption experience is sensory in nature, affecting mood states and emotions (e.g. perfumes, bath soap).

In the application of in-depth interviews, the researcher can use other techniques to help maintain the interest of participants, to make the experience more enjoyable for the participants and the researcher alike, and ultimately to draw out the true feelings of participants. A set of techniques that help to achieve all this, and that have been applied with great success over many years, is the body of indirect techniques called 'projective techniques'.

Projective techniques

Projective technique
An unstructured and indirect form of questioning that encourages participants to project their underlying motivations, beliefs, attitudes or feelings regarding the issues of concern.

Projective techniques are a category of exercises designed to provoke imagination and creativity that can be used in in-depth interviews. Projective techniques are subject-oriented, non-verbal and indirect self-reporting techniques that have the ability to capture responses from participants in a less structured and more imaginative way than direct questioning. They get beyond the rational replies participants often make in interview situations, encouraging them to project their underlying motivations, beliefs, attitudes or feelings regarding the issues of concern.[36] They are useful techniques for drawing out emotional values, exploring issues in a non-linear manner or for bypassing participants' rational controls. They also help participants to verbalise unframed, subconscious, low-salience or low-involvement attitudes.[37] Viewed as 'face-saving' techniques, projection provides participants with the facility to project their thoughts and feelings onto another person or object (e.g. via completion tests). Fundamentally projective techniques can enable research participants to express feelings and thoughts they would otherwise find difficult to articulate.[38] In projective techniques, participants are asked to interpret the behaviour of others rather than to describe their own behaviour. In interpreting the behaviour of others, it is contended that participants indirectly project their own motivations, beliefs, attitudes or feelings onto the situation. Thus, the participants' attitudes are uncovered by analysing their responses to scenarios that are deliberately unstructured, vague and ambiguous. The more ambiguous the situation, the more participants project their emotions, needs, motives, attitudes and values, as demonstrated by work in clinical psychology on which projective techniques are based.[39]

The following example illustrates a use of projective techniques, as part of the process of pretesting advertisements.

Real research   **Pretesting mould-breaking advertisements[40]**

In an environment where consumers value originality, communications that really 'break the mould' offer advertisers rewards in terms of increased relevance. In a study for Sony, TNS (**www.tnsglobal.com**) felt that qualitative projective questioning techniques could be used alongside quantitative pretesting techniques on mould-breaking advertisements. TNS felt that projective techniques could help participants reveal how mould-breaking advertisements work at a deeper, emotional level. Its NeedScope™ technique used photo-sets representing different personality types. The Sony Bravia Television (**www.sony.co.uk/BRAVIA**) *'Paint'* commercial was chosen to apply the technique. The exploding 'paint-fest' set on a Glasgow council estate was an unexpected way to advertise a new TV. There were no lists of features, no voice-over describing the benefits, no happy family sitting around their new TV, and not even a glamorous tropical location. Sony's website stated:

When you're introducing the next generation of television, you want to make an impact – but that doesn't mean you have to be predictable. To announce the arrival of the new Bravia LCD and SXRD range, we want to get across a simple message – that the colour you will see on these screens will be like no other.

For a clear majority of participants, the brand represented a carefree, lively, bold personality. In terms of brand image, the strongest attributes were 'vibrant colour', 'lively', 'outgoing', 'dynamic' and 'cool/trendy' – very much where the Sony Bravia communication strategy wanted to be. The results from projective questioning were examined holistically with the results from other questions on likeability, recall and branding. Given the recognised importance of emotions in brand communications and engagement, projective techniques have a lot to offer in pretesting advertisements.

Association technique
A type of projective technique in which participants are presented with a stimulus and are asked to respond with the first thing that comes to mind.

Word association
A projective technique in which participants are presented with a list of words, one at a time. After each word, they are asked to give the first word that comes to mind.

As in psychology, these projective techniques are classified as association, completion, construction and expressive. Each of these classifications is discussed below.[41]

Association techniques

In **association techniques**, an individual is presented with a stimulus and asked to respond with the first thing that comes to mind. Word association is the best known of these techniques. In **word association**, participants are presented with a list of words, one at a time, and encouraged to respond without deliberation to each with the first word that comes to mind. The words of interest, called test words, are interspersed throughout the list, which also contains some neutral, or filler, words to disguise the purpose of the study. For example, in the IFM Sports Marketing Surveys – Racetrack Project, individual Formula One teams may be examined with test words such as competitive, dangerous, inspirational, elitist, sexy. The participant's response to each word is recorded verbatim and responses are timed so that participants who hesitate or reason out (defined as taking longer than three seconds to reply) can be identified. The interviewer, not the participant, records the responses.

The underlying assumption of this technique is that association allows participants to reveal their inner feelings about the topic of interest. Responses are analysed by calculating:

1 The frequency with which any word is given as a response.

2 The amount of time that elapses before a response is given.

3 The number of participants who do not respond at all to a test word within a reasonable period.

Those who do not respond at all are judged to have an emotional involvement so high that it blocks a response. It is often possible to classify the associations as favourable, unfavourable or neutral. An individual's pattern of responses and the details of the response are used to determine the person's underlying attitudes or feelings on the topic of interest, as shown in the following example.

Real research   **Dealing with dirt**[42]

Word association was used to study womens' attitudes towards detergents. Below is a list of stimulus words used and the responses of two women of similar age and household status. The sets of responses are quite different, suggesting that the women differ in personality and in their attitudes towards housekeeping. Ms M's associations suggest that she is resigned to dirt. She sees dirt as inevitable and does not do much about it. She does not do hard cleaning, nor does she get much pleasure from her family. Ms C sees dirt too, but is energetic, factual-minded and less emotional. She is actively ready to combat dirt, and she uses soap and water as her weapons.

Stimulus	Ms M	Ms C
Washday	Everyday	Ironing
Fresh	And sweet	Clean
Pure	Air	Soiled
Scrub	Does not; husband does	Clean
Filth	This neighbourhood	Dirt
Bubbles	Bath	Soap and water
Family	Squabbles	Children
Towels	Dirty	Wash

These findings suggest that the market for detergents could be segmented based on attitudes. Firms (such as Procter & Gamble) that market several different brands of washing powders and detergents could benefit from positioning different brands for different attitudinal segments.

There are several variations to the standard word association procedure illustrated here. Participants may be asked to give the first two, three or four words that come to mind rather than only the first word. This technique can also be used in controlled tests, as contrasted with free association. In controlled tests, participants might be asked 'what Formula One teams come to mind first when I mention "boring"?' More detailed information can be obtained from completion techniques, which are a natural extension of association techniques.

Completion techniques

Completion technique
A projective technique that requires participants to complete an incomplete stimulus situation.

Sentence completion
A projective technique in which participants are presented with a number of incomplete sentences and are asked to complete them.

Story completion
A projective technique in which participants are provided with part of a story and are required to give the conclusion in their own words.

In completion techniques, participants are asked to complete an incomplete stimulus situation. Common completion techniques in marketing research are sentence completion and story completion.[43]

Sentence completion is similar to word association. Participants are given incomplete sentences and are asked to complete them. Generally, they are asked to use the first word or phrase that comes to mind, as illustrated in the context of the IFM Sports Marketing Surveys – Racetrack Project.*

This example illustrates one advantage of sentence completion over word association: participants can be provided with a more directed stimulus. Sentence completion may provide more information about the subjects' feelings than word association. Sentence completion is not as disguised as word association, however, and many participants may be able to guess the purpose of the study. A variation of sentence completion is paragraph completion, in which the participant completes a paragraph beginning with the stimulus phrase. A further expanded version of sentence completion and paragraph completion is story completion.

In story completion, participants are given part of a story, enough to direct attention to a particular topic but not to hint at the ending. They are required to give the conclusion in their own words, as in the following example.

Focus on	**IFM Sports Marketing Surveys**

Racetrack Project

Sentence completion

A Formula One fan that supports a team rather than a driver is _____
_____

A sponsor who selects drivers based on how competitive they are is _____
_____

The Ferrari team is most preferred by _____
_____

When I think of watching Formula One on television, I _____
_____

* The Racetrack Project did not use projective techniques. The examples presented illustrate how they could have been applied.

Focus on	IMF Sports Marketing Surveys

Racetrack Project

Story completion

> The marketing director of a mobile phone company had championed the sponsorship of a Formula One team for 10 years. A new chief executive has been appointed and he believes that the sponsorship is just an excuse for senior executives to party at the company's expense. He wants to see a measurable impact in terms of sales for any sponsorship activity. The marketing director has tried to defend the Formula One sponsorship in terms of corporate image development in being associated with the sport. She has also pointed out the impact of hospitality events upon major clients and other stakeholders that are important to her company. She has tried to get the new chief executive to attend the Monaco Grand Prix, but is having great difficulty.

What should the marketing director do? _____

_____

Why? _____

_____

The participants' completion of this story could reveal characteristics of successful sponsorship that may not be measurable. It could examine why, after such a lengthy relationship, the mobile phone company should explore other sponsorship activities. The relationship between the marketing director and the chief executive could be explored as could many directions and facets of the sponsor relationship.

Construction techniques

Construction technique
A projective technique in which participants are required to construct a response in the form of a story, dialogue or description.

Picture response technique
A projective technique in which participants are shown a picture and are asked to tell a story describing it.

Cartoon tests
Cartoon characters are shown in a specific situation related to the problem. Participants are asked to indicate the dialogue that one cartoon character might make in response to the comment(s) of another character.

Construction techniques are closely related to completion techniques. Construction techniques require the participants to construct a response in the form of a story, dialogue or description. In a construction technique, the researcher provides less initial structure to the participants than in a completion technique. The two main construction techniques are picture response techniques and cartoon tests.

The roots of picture response techniques can be traced to the thematic apperception test (TAT), which consists of a series of pictures of ordinary as well as unusual events. In some of these pictures, the persons or objects are clearly depicted, while in others they are relatively vague. The participant is asked to tell stories about these pictures. The participant's interpretation of the pictures gives indications of that individual's personality. For example, an individual may be characterised as impulsive, creative, unimaginative, and so on. The term 'thematic apperception test' is used because themes are elicited based on the subject's perceptual interpretation (apperception) of pictures.

In cartoon tests, cartoon characters are shown in a specific situation related to the problem. Participants are asked to indicate what one cartoon character might say in response to the comments of another character. The responses indicate the participants' feelings, beliefs and attitudes towards the situation. Cartoon tests are simpler to administer and analyse than picture response techniques.

Expressive techniques

In expressive techniques, participants are presented with a verbal or visual situation and asked to relate the feelings and attitudes of other people to the situation. The participants express not their own feelings or attitudes, but those of others. The main expressive techniques are role playing, the third-person technique and personification.

In role playing, participants are asked to play the role or to assume the behaviour of someone else. Participants are asked to speak as though they were someone else, such as another household member with whom they would share a decision or an authority figure. For example, 'Bernard, you are a 15-year-old boy; Eva, you play Bernard's mother; George, you play Bernard's father. Imagine you are at home deciding which summer holiday you would like this year as a family.' The discussion that emerges is likely to reveal unspoken objections as well as those of overcoming resistance to features of the holiday, locations and ways of travelling there that may be favoured by Bernard but not his parents, or even his mother and not by the two males. The researcher assumes that the participants will project their own feelings into the role.[44]

In the third-person technique, participants are presented with a verbal or visual situation and are asked to relate the beliefs and attitudes of a third person rather than directly expressing personal beliefs and attitudes. This third person may be a friend, a neighbour, a colleague, or any person that the researcher chooses. Again, the researcher assumes that the participants will reveal personal beliefs and attitudes while describing the reactions of a third party. Asking an individual to respond in the third person reduces the social pressure to give an acceptable answer.

In the personification technique, participants imagine that the brand is a person and then describe characteristics of that person, e.g. their lifestyle, status, demographics, home(s). They can build up layers of this description using words and images from a variety of sources. These descriptions help to uncover and develop the perceived nature of a brand's personality. The following example shows why the brand personality is of importance to the marketer and how an understanding of personality may be used in advertising.

Real research | **Coors – Coors Light**[45]

Brand personality

The most common definition states that brand personality is 'the set of human characteristics associated with a brand'. Consumers find it natural to imbue brands with personality characteristics, such as 'honest', 'cheerful', 'charming' or 'tough'. Moreover, the personality traits associated with a brand, such as those associated with an individual, tend to be relatively enduring and distinct.[46] Coors Light was a brand at a crossroads. Since its launch in 1984 it had become the best selling light beer in Canada. In 2002 a superficial analysis of Coors Light would reveal a strong brand. It was growing in share and volume and had carved out a strong position. This came from the brand's history. It had capitalised on lifestyle trends like health, fitness and lower calorific intake. Creatively, it had leveraged its Rocky Mountain heritage to communicate a healthy, active, fun lifestyle. However, Coors Light loyal drinkers were getting older and they were lighter drinkers. At one time a young man in a focus group said that he had tried the beer 'once with an uncle at a funeral' – ouch! Coors Light was not relevant to their lifestyle. Coors wished to develop a new brand personality that would drive all elements of marketing and business strategy. For a brand to become a leader Coors did not believe it should mimic the attitude and personality of its target drinkers. It needed to develop a brand personality and a voice that 'earned a right to be a part of the party'. Coors' qualitative research projected 'young adult oriented brands' generally falling into two camps. There were 'skateboarding monkey' brands which inserted themselves into a scenario and tried to earn consumer affinity through proximity; these brands usually ended up looking as if they were wearing their younger brother's clothes, and young adults were able to see through this approach. Then there were brands that became a part of the culture they were looking to infiltrate. They weren't just using the words. They understood their meaning and believed in the core values of the target group. These brands earned a lasting and enduring affinity.

Brand personality can also be uncovered using role playing.[47] In a group discussion scenario, participants may be asked to play out the personality of a brand. In the Coors example, the setting could be a sports bar after work on a Friday evening, with individuals acting out what they see as the personas of the brands Coors, Guinness, Becks, Stella Artois and Heineken. What the individuals as a brand do, what they say, how they interact with each other in the bar, all allow an expression of personality that straight questioning may not reveal. Video recording of the event, played back to the group, acts as a means to discuss and elicit further meaning of a brand's personality, highlighting any positive and negative associations of the brand.

Advantages and disadvantages of projective techniques

The major advantage of projective techniques is that they may elicit responses that participants would be unwilling or unable to give if they knew the purpose of the study. At times, in direct questioning, the participant may intentionally or unintentionally misunderstand, misinterpret or mislead the researcher. Personal accounts can be more self-conscious and self-justifying than the actions themselves, because they represent the way an individual would like to be judged.[48] This is one of the values of projective techniques which frame the actions as those of 'someone else'. Projective techniques can increase the validity of responses by disguising the purpose. This is particularly true when the issues to be addressed are personal, sensitive or subject to strong social norms. Projective techniques are also helpful when underlying motivations, beliefs and attitudes are operating at a subconscious level.[49]

Projective techniques suffer from many of the disadvantages of unstructured direct techniques, but to a greater extent. These techniques generally require personal interviews with individuals who are experienced interviewers and interpreters; hence they tend to be expensive. Furthermore, as in all qualitative techniques, there can be a risk of interpretation bias. With the exception of word association, all are open-ended techniques, making the analysis and interpretation more problematic.

Some projective techniques such as role playing require participants to engage in what may seem to be unusual behaviour. Certain participants may not have the self-confidence or the ability to express themselves fully with these techniques. In role playing, for example, the skills of acting may make some participants more articulate at expressing their feelings compared with others. The same may be said of techniques where pictures and cartoons are put together and interpreted, in that distinctive skills may make certain participants more adept and comfortable in expressing themselves. To counter this, one could argue that there is a great amount of skill required in articulating ideas and feelings in an open-ended in-depth interview. One could point to fiction writers or poets who are able to encapsulate particular feelings most clearly and succinctly, which again is enormously skilful.

With such skill requirements, the disadvantage of the technique lies in the nature of the participants who agree to participate, and how characteristic they may be of distinct target markets.

Applications of projective techniques

Projective techniques are used less frequently than unstructured direct methods (focus groups and in-depth interviews). A possible exception may be word association, which is commonly used to test brand names and occasionally to measure attitudes about particular products, brands, packages or advertisements. As the examples have shown, projective techniques can be used in a variety of situations.[50] The usefulness of these techniques is enhanced when the following guidelines are observed. Projective techniques should be used:

1   Because the required information cannot be accurately obtained by direct questioning.

2   In an exploratory manner to elicit issues that participants find difficult to conceive and express.

3   To engage participants in the subject, by having fun in expressing themselves in interesting and novel ways.

Comparison between qualitative techniques

To summarise comparisons between qualitative techniques, Table 8.1 gives a relative comparison of focus groups, in-depth interviews, projective techniques and ethnographic approaches (qualitative observation).

The nature of qualitative research is such that, within the broad categories above, there are numerous variations of the techniques with distinct strengths and weaknesses in eliciting and representing consumer feelings. Really, it is not possible to say that one technique is better or worse than the other. Faced with a given problem, it would seem to be the case of deciding which technique is the most appropriate to represent or understand consumers.[51] What may

Table 8.1	**A comparison of focus groups, in-depth interviews, projective techniques and ethnographic techniques**			
Criteria	Focus groups	In-depth interviews	Projective techniques	Ethnographic techniques
Degree of structure	Can vary from highly to loosely structured	Can vary from highly to loosely structured	Tends to be loosely structured	Loosely structured though can have a framework to guide observation
Probing of individual participants	Low	High	Medium	None when used in isolation and in a covert manner
Moderator bias	Medium	Relatively high	Low to high	None when used in isolation and in a covert manner
Uncovering subconscious information	Low	Medium to high	High	High
Discovering innovative information	High	Medium	Low	Medium
Obtaining sensitive information	Low	Medium	High	High
Involving unusual behaviour or questioning	No	To a limited extent	Yes	Perhaps on the part of the observer

affect this choice is the confidence that marketing decision-makers may have in particular techniques. Thus, for example, any number of arguments may be made for the use of a projective technique as being the best way to tackle a sensitive issue indirectly. If the marketer who has to use the research findings does not believe it to be a trustworthy technique, then other, perhaps less appropriate, techniques may have to be used.

International marketing research

One of the major contributors to the success of in-depth interviews and projective techniques is getting the context of questioning right. The context of questioning can have two key components. The first component is the actual location, such as an office, hotel room, bar or even the back of a taxi. Given the issues that are to be tackled and the characteristics of the target participants, the location plays a significant role in helping the participant to relax and feel comfortable about responding in a manner that the interviewer is looking for. For some participants, e.g. a young graduate manager, being questioned about issues relating to 'night life and entertainment', talking in a noisy environment, perhaps outside a venue where smokers gather, may be far more natural than talking in a 'business suite' at a hotel. The same participants being questioned about cleaning their homes may be far more comfortable in a quiet 'home' environment, though perhaps not their own home. The interviewer has to work out what location will work best for the target participants and the issues that will be discussed. The interviewer has to appreciate that this location may change between different participants and may also change as they discover what effect location has on getting the most out of participants.

The second component of the context of questioning is the protocol of conducting the interview. The protocol can include the clothes the interviewer wears, the manner in which the interviewer greets participants, introduces the interview, conducts the interview and terminates it. This means that, even if an interviewer is technically adept at questioning, the interviewer may still not get the most out of participants. For example, an interviewer who dresses formally when the participants see themselves 'off duty' may result in an interview that is tense and lacking in spontaneity.

There are no firm rules about the balance of participant characteristics, related to issues to be questioned and the context of questioning. The interviewer has to be aware of the balance, and make adjustments when learning what works well in drawing out a quality response. Much of what works in a particular context is culturally bound. There can be striking differences between countries in how comfortable participants may feel talking about issues in their home, for example. There can be striking differences in the protocol of clothing, greeting people, questioning in a direct manner and giving 'gifts' as a reward for taking part in an interview. The problem of 'context' was paramount in the following example. This example illustrates a case in which in-depth interviews helped to probe in detail the views of professionals, which given the detail of banking relationships could be deemed as highly complex and sensitive.

In the example, each interview had the same interviewer who ensured a degree of consistency in the approach. This required the interviewer to visit 20 countries in order to conduct the 60 interviews. This interviewer had to have a strong awareness of the technical issues of banking and banking information systems in order to be seen as credible by the participants, to be able to question and probe, and to appreciate the relevance of the responses elicited. The interviewer had to be aware of the context of interviewing in each of the target countries in order to get the most out of participants. The first component of context, the actual location for the interviews, was consistent throughout each country. The interviews were held in the offices of the finance directors of Europe's largest companies, who made up the participants. This was an environment where the participants are naturally used to thinking and talking about the issues under question. It was also an environment where they could talk uninterrupted; the participant was in control of the interview space and could relax. The second component of context, i.e. the protocol of the interview, was where the interviewer needed local support. Most of the technical language and terms used in banking were 'American'. Many finance directors speak English, but some did not, and even if they did, at times they needed to express a view in their native tongue. To understand the protocol and language issues, the interviewer was supported by another interviewer in each country, drawn from indigenous business schools.

This interviewer helped to explain the protocol of individual countries, the peculiarities of greeting participants, posing questions in particular ways and closing an interview. These interviewers could help with the translation of questions and responses and ultimately in interpreting the findings. Using one main interviewer allowed a full understanding of the interplay between the participant, the issues and the context of interview. Using a fellow interviewer in individual countries allowed for the subtle charac-teristics of protocol and language to be incorporated into the whole process.

Understanding the interplay of participant, issue and context is vital to the success of in-depth inter-viewing and projective techniques. Working in alien cultures in international markets makes this under-standing more difficult. Investing in the time and means to develop this understanding ensures that the interviewer generates quality information, getting to reflect really what international participants feel.

Real research | **Why are you going to make more use of electronic banking?**

A syndicated study of banking in Europe was conducted by a consor-tium of banks from Finland, France, Germany, Ireland, Norway, Spain, the UK and the USA. These banks formed a steering committee that helped shape the research design, which was primarily a postal survey followed by in-depth interviews. Each bank had different information requirements to support its marketing strategies, which meant that there was a big demand for a wide array of ques-tions to be asked. There was much debate about which questions should be tackled and, given the detail of information sought, whether these would be best achieved through a structured questionnaire or with in-depth interviews. For example, the questionnaire asked companies what future changes they planned. An example of a response to this question was 'to make greater use of electronic banking'. Statistical analyses could reveal the the types of participant (e.g. util-ity companies) who were to make greater use of electronic banking. However, the questionnaire could not question *why* they were going to make more use of electronic banking. When around 50% of the responses to the postal survey were received, an interim report was presented to the steering committee. The issues that they deemed the most important to probe formed a topic guide for in-depth interviews. With the completed questionnaires, profiles of the participants could be analysed and those with behaviour relevant to the issues that needed to be explored in depth could be contacted. For example, 'sophisticated' users of cash management services could be profiled. These 'sophisticated' users were then contacted and invited to take part in an in-depth interview. Around 60 in-depth interviews were conducted, with a minimum of two interviews in any one country.

Ethics in marketing research

The essence of qualitative research is that consumers are examined in great depth. They may be questioned and probed about subjects they hardly reflect upon on a day-to-day basis, never mind talk to strangers about. Great care must be taken not to upset or disturb participants through such intensive questioning. In survey work, reassuring participants that their responses will be confidential can work if there is a demonstrable link between their responses to questions and a means of aggregating all of the findings, making the individual response 'hidden'. In qualitative research, the process is far more intimate and the link between the response and the participant is far more difficult to break.

At the end of the second point above comes the reason why the marketing research industry is so concerned about how qualitative research participants are handled. More consumers are being questioned in both domestic and business scenarios. If they are to 'open up' and reveal deeply held feelings, perhaps in front of a group of strangers, or if they are to take part in projective techniques that they may see as being unorthodox, they have to be reassured about how the data captured will be used. As well as the ethical questions of potentially damaging participants come the problems of participants either not willing to take part or, if they do, being very guarded with their responses.

Ethical questions also arise when videorecording sessions with participants. Some of the pertinent questions involve how to tell participants and when clients should be allowed access. When videorecording participants, regardless of whether or not they were aware of the camera during the meeting, at the end of the meeting they should be asked to sign a written declaration conveying their permission to use the recording. This declaration should disclose the full purpose of the video, including who will be able to view it. If any participant refuses, the tape should be either destroyed or edited to omit that participant's identity and comments completely. The researcher should be sensitive to the comfort level of the participants, and respect for the participants should warrant restraint. When a participant

| Real research | **Just how 'anonymous' is a quali participant?**[52] |

'Confidentiality' in qualitative research is a different concept from confidentiality as applied to survey work. In survey work the emphasis is upon anonymity, i.e. the identity of individual participants should not be revealed. This creates two problems for qualitative research:

1 Anonymity cannot be promised in qualitative research, especially in the light of current practices where it is increasingly common for clients and others to come to groups, listen to audio, watch video and other primary data. This issue further demands consideration of the question: 'Where does the identity reside?' In a name, a face, the voice, perhaps even a turn of phrase? It is of course also pertinent to ask: 'Do participants actually care if their identity is revealed?'

2 In quantitative research, participant identity is generally unimportant. The very essence of sampling theory is that a sufficiently large and randomly chosen sample will represent the views, behaviour or attitudes of any known population as a whole. As such, the identity of any one individual is irrelevant to quantitative findings. In sharp contrast, in qualitative research the relationship between the specific individuals and their views is at the heart of analysis and interpretation. You cannot reach qualitative findings without having 'revealed' the individual as part of the research process. Therefore, confidentiality through anonymity is a methodologically untenable concept wherever anyone other than the interviewer is privy to any part of the research process. Yet at the same time, more clients attend groups and more groups take place in viewing facilities.

feels uncomfortable and does not wish to go on, the researcher should not aggressively probe or confront any further. It has also been suggested that participants should be allowed to reflect on all they have said at the end of the interview and should be given the opportunity to ask questions. This may help return the participants to their pre-interview emotional state.

Digital applications in marketing research

The following example illustrates the use of digital applications to gain access to and build rapport with a very specialised group of research participants. It presents one solution to the problem of participants feeling engaged with a research technique and the topic of research. That engagement resulted in high-quality in-depth responses.

Real research

Understanding the media habits of government elites[53]

Hall & Partners (**www.hall-and-partners.com**) uses digital technologies to make research more insightful and timely using techniques like bulletin boards, blog journals, personal videos and collages. The company believes that to get close to consumers it has to develop rapport. To achieve this, it 'comes clean' with participants about what it is trying to find out and asks for their help. This approach has yielded some of the richest insights. In one example, a client wanted to understand the media habits of 'government elites', a small group of powerful people who influence government policy. Having conducted media diaries via bulletin boards with other target participants, Hall & Partners was unsure whether this would work with people with such hectic and demanding schedules. So, after recruiting them, it started sending them emails to establish a personal connection between them and a researcher who would eventually meet them. The response was beyond their expectations. They responded in much greater and much more personal depth through an email dialogue than they might have done under pressure to complete and return an 'old-fashioned' diary, even if the diary had been online.

The Internet has opened up many possibilities to researchers who wish to use in-depth interviews and projective techniques. Through the use of email, and increasingly so through social network sites, researchers can reach and engage participants from all over the world. To be able to track down and engage with specific individuals with the desired qualities for a particular study, without the time and cost implications of travelling, presents significant benefits for the researcher.

Being able to track down and talk to participants, i.e. gaining access to qualitative participants, is vital, but the quality of the discussion with these participants should be considered.[54] In the case of in-depth interviews, a full dialogue can develop between an interviewer and participant, either in real time or in non-real time, i.e. a series of emails or input into proprietary qualitative interview software over a period of time. The discussion, questions and probes can be tailored to specific participants, allowing them time to reflect upon the issues and express their views in their own manner. The interviewer can present stimuli in terms of tasks, images or audio recordings that may help to elicit more from the participants. It is possible to use webcams to observe participants and for participants to view interviewers, provided of course that both parties have this technology.

However, even with the use of webcams, much of the non-verbal communication that makes in-depth interviews work is lost. Subtle changes in facial expression and body language may be missed. These non-verbal forms of communication are important in developing a rapport between interviewer and participant and are vital in the development of dialogue and the analysis of data. The limitation of visual interaction can make projective techniques difficult to implement. For certain projective techniques such as the array of completion and construction techniques, the anonymity afforded by the distance between interviewer and participant can be a positive feature. Some participants may find the presence of an interviewer inhibiting when they are trying to think of and present a story completion. Where participants feel inhibited, working through a response in their own space and time may be the ideal context in which to tackle particular issues.

In evaluating the worth of the Internet in in-depth interviewing and projective techniques we can return to the example in the 'International marketing research' box. Meeting participants face to face allowed a great richness of dialogue and understanding to be built up. There was no question about how successful the interviews were in understanding why participants behaved in particular ways. However, consider the travel and other costs involved. Consider the time involved in conducting the interviews and just typing up the transcripts of the interviews. Compare the cost and timing requirements of meeting face to face in an international setting with a dialogue by email. The process could have been conducted online much more quickly and cheaply. The dilemma faced is whether the participants would have allowed such a dialogue in the first place and how much they would open up and develop a dialogue. The final example illustrates how such an in-depth interview process can work online, engaging participants in role playing, detailed probing and an array of creative tasks.

| Real research | **MTV Seeding Lab[55]** |

MTV Italy needed to analyse its News programme in terms of format, content, style and execution. In order to conduct this study, it recruited participants who were viewers of MTV and aware of MTV News but were also familiar and extremely comfortable with the Internet. Forty participants were recruited to meet criteria based on: viewing intensity of the MTV channel; awareness of MTV scheduling and number of programmes viewed regularly vs. occasionally; relation with and satisfaction with MTV News; and aged between 18 and 28 years old. MTV wanted to build a relationship and engagement with the participants so it asked them to role-play, asking them to produce content for MTV News as if they were broadcasters. As is the case with traditional qualitative interviews, in order to establish a closer bond with participants, the researchers spent time online: introducing themselves, explaining that they would be managing the relationships with participants; they would administer any stimuli and handle email communications; and would manage the process in a manner consistent with Web 2.0 engagement, i.e. fostering respect through a peer-to-peer approach. MTV learnt that probing and prompting was the most important part allowing it to investigate specific topics and statements in greater depth and to interpret all the shades of views. Throughout the two-week discussion, a great variety of stimulus material was used and a number of questioning techniques were put in place. The challenge consisted in gathering responses and information from different points of view, to give everyone the possibility to express themselves using the communication style they felt most in tune with and to keep high levels of attention and curiosity. Every day at a given time, a new stimulus task would be posted or a new discussion forum opened that would be available online for all the participants throughout the duration of the community; this helped in creating some sort of routine everybody got used to. From time to time deadlines to send in feedbacks were set (for instance, when it was all about creativity tasks); at other times participants were able to express themselves in a free manner.

Summary

The qualitative techniques of in-depth interviewing allow researchers to focus upon individuals with the qualities they deem to be important to their research objectives. With a 'quality individual' the researcher can question and probe to great depth and elicit a quality understanding of that individual's behaviour or feelings. The technique is well suited to tackling commercially and personally sensitive issues. It is also well suited to interviewing children. There are many types of interview that can be applied under the term 'in-depth interview'. They can range from the very open and unstructured to semi-structured exchanges. The application of structure in an in-depth interview can be founded on a theoretical underpinning of how individuals should be questioned and probed. Three relevant and widely used examples of interviews using a theoretical underpinning are laddering, repertory grid techniques and the Zaltman metaphor elicitation technique (ZMET). Laddering seeks to reveal chains of attributes, consequences and values that participants associate with products. The repertory grid seeks to elicit the underlying elements and the connection of those elements, related to a particular form of consumer behaviour. ZMET seeks to understand the images and associations that underpin both spoken and tacit thoughts and feelings through the elicitation of both rational and emotional thinking.

Indirect projective techniques aim to project the participant's motivations, beliefs, attitudes and feelings onto ambiguous situations. Projective techniques may be classified as association (word association), completion (sentence completion, story completion), construction (picture response, cartoon tests) and expressive (role playing, third-person personification) techniques. Projective techniques are particularly useful when participants are unwilling or unable to provide the required information by direct methods.

The qualitative researcher needs to develop an understanding of the interplay between characteristics of the target participants, the issues they will be questioned about and the context in which they will be questioned. The context can be broken down into the physical location of the interview and the protocol of starting, running and terminating the interview. Building up this understanding is vital to the success of conducting in-depth interviews and projective techniques in international markets.

The marketing research industry is concerned about how qualitative research participants are handled in interviews and observations. More consumers are being questioned in both domestic and business scenarios. If they are to 'open up' and reveal deeply held feelings, perhaps in front of a group of strangers, or if they are to take part in projective techniques that they may see as being unorthodox, they have to be reassured of how the data captured will be used.

The Internet has opened up many possibilities to conduct in-depth interviews and use projective techniques on a global basis. A rich dialogue and engagement between an interviewer and a participant can be developed and recorded with much lower cost and time demands when compared with meeting face to face. The loss of subtle eye contact and body language may be a price to pay for the savings afforded by online research.

Questions

1 What is an in-depth interview? Summarise the process of administering an in-depth interview.

2 What are the major advantages of in-depth interviews?

3 What are the requirements of the researcher undertaking in-depth interviews? Why are these requirements particularly important when conducting interviews with managers?

4 Why may a structure be applied to the in-depth interview in the form of laddering or the repertory grid technique?

5 Describe the process of administering the repertory grid technique.

6 Evaluate the context and timing requirements that you think would be needed to make the repertory grid technique work.

7 Choose any particular application of an in-depth interview and present a case for why you think the technique may work much better than a focus group.

8 What are projective techniques? In what circumstances should projective techniques be used?

9 Describe the word association technique. Give an example of a situation in which this technique is especially useful.

10 Describe the story completion technique. Give an example of the type of participant and the context in which such a technique would work.

11 Describe the criteria by which researchers may evaluate the relative worth of qualitative techniques.

12 Why is the context of questioning particularly important when conducting in-depth interviews in international marketing research?

13 Why may in-depth interviews or projective techniques upset or disturb participants?

14 Describe a projective technique that you feel would work particularly well online – without the use of webcams.

15 What limitations are there to conducting in-depth interviews online, compared with meeting participants face to face?

Exercises

1 Could an in-depth interview about the phenomenon of online casinos be conducted online? Present a case for how you would conduct such interviews and set out what you see as the advantages and disadvantages of this approach.

2 Baileys Irish Cream wishes to understand something of the nuances of serving and enjoying its drink. Develop a cartoon test for this purpose.

3 A cosmetics firm would like to increase its penetration of the student market through a new range of organic and 'ethical' products. Conduct two experimental in-depth interviews with a male and female student. Write a report setting out plans for any subsequent form of in-depth interviews and associated techniques, showing how the experimental interviews have impacted upon these plans.

4 Jeffery West shoes (**www.jeffery-west.co.uk**) wishes to develop an understanding of its brand personality. Design a role-playing scenario that will help to achieve this aim. Who would you invite to the sessions? Where would you run the sessions? What roles would you ask the participants to play?

5 In a small group discuss the following issues: 'Are there any dangers (for researchers and participants) in conducting in-depth studies on issues that participants hardly reflect upon on a day-to-day basis?' and 'Projective techniques cannot work well with shy and introverted participants.'

Video case exercise: Acme Whistles

Acme wishes to conduct in-depth interviews with b2b buyers who purchase (or could purchase) its whistles for sports-related applications. How would you recommend Acme conducts such interviews with participants spread across the globe? Create a topic guide that would help you to question participants about their purchasing behaviour. How could you use these interviews to support the development of new products?

Notes

1. Rédier, E. and McClure, S., 'Let the product talk', ESOMAR, Fragrance Conference, Paris (November 2007).

2. Supphellen, M., 'Understanding core brand equity: guidelines for in-depth elicitation of brand associations', *International Journal of Market Research* 42 (3) (2000), 319–342; Harris, L.M., 'Expanding horizons', *Marketing Research: A Magazine of Management and Application* 8 (2) (Summer 1996), 12.

3. Kvale, S., *Interviews: An introduction to qualitative research interviewing* (Thousand Oaks, CA: Sage, 1996); Rubin, H.J. and Rubin, I.S., *Qualitative Interviewing: The art of hearing data* (Thousand Oaks, CA: Sage, 1995).

4. Warren, C.A.B., 'Qualitative interviewing', in Gubrium, J.F. and Holstein, J.A. (eds), *Handbook of Interview Research: Context and method* (Thousand Oaks, CA: Sage, 2002), 83–101.

5. Johnson, J.M., 'In-depth Interviewing', in Gubrium, J.F. and Holstein, J.A. (eds), *Handbook of Interview Research: Context and method* (Thousand Oaks, CA: Sage, 2002), 104.

6. Ibid., pp. 106–107.

7. Schwalbe, M.L. and Wolkomir, M., 'Interviewing men', in Gubrium, J.F. and Holstein, J.A. (eds), *Handbook of Interview Research: Context and method* (Thousand Oaks, CA: Sage, 2002), 203–220.

8. Schnee, R.K., 'Uncovering consumers' deepest feelings using psychologically probing qualitative research techniques', Advertising Research Foundation Workshops, Consumer Insights Workshop (October 2000); 'Looking for a deeper meaning', *Marketing* (Market Research Top 75 Supplement) (17 July 1997), 16–17.

9. Arnal, L. and Holguin, R., 'Taxis, vans and subways: capturing insights while commuting', ESOMAR, Qualitative Research, Paris (November 2007).

10. Bloom, N., 'In-depth research? A bit controversial!', *ResearchPlus* (June 1993), 12.

11. Bowman, J., 'When everything Clicks into place', *Research World* (December 2006), 31.

12. Baxter, S., 'It's not kids' play! Reflecting on the child-orientated research experience', *International Journal of Market Research* 53 (1) (2011), 63–74.

13. Clarke, B., Goodchild, M. and Harrison, A., 'The digital world of children and young adolescents: children's emotional engagement with digital media', ESOMAR, Congress Odyssey, Athens (September 2010).

14. Parke, A., 'When not to rely on the young imagination', *ResearchPlus* (March 1997), 14.

15. Milling, A., 'Don't supersize me', *Research* (November 2005), 38–39.

16. Rédier, E. and McClure, S., 'Let the product talk', ESOMAR, Fragrance Conference, Paris (November 2007).

17. Bakken, D.G. and Breglio, V.J., 'Cultural differences in consumer decision-making – Asian consumers, western research methods: what we've learned', ESOMAR, Asia Pacific Conference, Tokyo (March 2005); De Andrade Marseilles Reis, A.H.M., 'Laddering: an efficient tool for the formation of product positioning strategies and ways of communication', The Dynamics of Change in Latin America, ESOMAR Conference, Rio de Janeiro (1997).

18. Dichter, E., *The Strategy of Desire* (New York: Doubleday, 1960).

19. Reynolds, T., Gutman, J. and Craddock, A., 'The MECCAS framework to advertising strategy', *Brand Management Models* (2006), 230–231; Gutman, J., 'Laddering: extending the repertory grid methodology to construct attribute-consequence-value hierarchies', in Heath, D.C. (ed.), *Personal Values and Consumer Psychology* (Lanham, MD: Lexington Books, 1984).

20. For example, Grunert, G.K. and Grunert, S.C., 'Measuring subjective meaning structures by the laddering method: theoretical considerations and methodological problems', *International Journal of Research in Marketing* 12 (1995) 209–225.

21. Best Practice, 'Understanding motivation', *Admap* 446 (January 2004), 13.

22. Guth, R.A., 'PlayStation2 helps Sony beat forecasts', *Wall Street Journal* (28 January 2002), A12; Wasink, B., 'New techniques to generate key marketing insights', *Marketing Research* (Summer 2000), 28–36.

23. Kelly, G.A., *The Psychology of Personal Constructs* (New York: Norton, 1955).

24. Kelly, G.A., *A Theory of Personality: The Psychology of Personality* (New York: Norton, 1969).

25. Rogers, B. and Ryals, L., 'Using the repertory grid to access the underlying realities in key account relationships', *International Journal of Market Research* 49 (5) (2007), 595–612.

26. Marsden, D. and Littler, D., 'Exploring consumer product construct systems with the repertory grid technique', *Qualitative Market Research: An International Journal* 3 (3) (2000), 127–144.

27. Slater, A., 'Understanding individual membership at heritage sites', *International Journal of Culture, Tourism and Hospitality Research* 4 (1) (2010), 44–56.

28. Van Raaij, W.F. and Verhallen, T.M.M., 'Domain specific market segmentation', *European Journal of Marketing* 28 (10) (1994), 49–66.

29. Jin, Z.Q., Birks, D.F. and Targett, D., 'The context and process of effective NPD: a typology', *International Journal of Innovation Management* 1 (3) (September 1997), 275–298.

30. McDonald, H., 'Understanding the antecedents to public interest and engagement with heritage', *European Journal of Marketing* 45 (5) (2011), 780–804; Fransella, F. and Bannister, D., *Manual for Repertory Grid Technique* (London: Academic Press, 1977).

31. Micu, A.C. and Plummer, J.T., 'Measurable emotions: how television ads really work – patterns of reactions to commercials can demonstrate advertising effectiveness', *Journal of Advertising Research* 50 (2) (2010), 137–153.

32. Schindlbeck, T., 'Unlocking consumer's hearts and minds', *ResearchWorld* (January 2008), 29.

33. Wornell, T., 'Diving for pearls', *Research* (April 2005), 39.

34. Penn, D., 'In search of the buy button', *Research World* (January 2008), 10.

35. Sharma, A. and Pugh, G., 'Serpents with tails in their mouths: a reflexive look at qualitative research', ESOMAR, Qualitative Research, Paris (November 2007); Sokolow, H., 'In-depth interviews increasing in importance', *Marketing News* (13 September 1985), 26.

36. Branthwaite, A., 'Investigating the power of imagery in marketing communication: evidence-based techniques'. *Qualitative Market Research: An International Journal* 5 (3) (2002), 164–171; Chandler, J. and Owen, M., *Developing brands with qualitative market research* (Thousand Oaks, CA: Sage, 2002) 86–100; Best, K., 'Something old is something new in qualitative research', *Marketing News* 29 (18) (28 August 1995), 14.

37. Mariampolski, H., *Qualitative Marketing Research: A comprehensive guide* (Thousand Oaks, Sage, 2001), 206.

38. Boddy, C., 'Projective techniques in market research – valueless subjectivity or insightful reality?', *International Journal of Market Research* 47 (3) (2005), 239–254.

39. Zaichowsky, J.L., 'The why of consumption: contemporary perspectives and consumer motives, goals, and desires', *Academy of Marketing Science* 30 (2) (Spring 2002), 179; Levy, S.J., 'Interpreting consumer mythology: structural approach to consumer behaviour focuses on story telling', *Marketing Management* 2 (4) (1994), 4–9.

40. Burden, S., 'Case study: pre-testing mould breaking ads', *Admap Magazine*, 485 (July/August 2007), 48–49.

41. Catterall, M., 'Using projective techniques in education research', *British Educational Research Journal* 26 (2) (April 2000), 245–256; Kennedy, M.M., 'So how'm I doing?', *Across the Board* 34 (6) (June 1997), 53–54; Lindzey, G., 'On the classification of projective techniques', *Psychological Bulletin* (1959), 158–168.

42. Byron, E., 'How P&G led also ran to sweet smell of success', *Wall Street Journal* (4 September, 2007), B2; Walsh, K., 'Soaps and detergents', *Chemical Week* 164 (3) (23 January 2002), 24–26; 'Interpretation is the essence of projective research techniques', *Marketing News* (28 September 1984), 20.

43. Grimes, A. and Kitchen, P., 'Researching mere exposure effects to advertising – theoretical foundations and methodological implications', *International Journal of Market Research* 49 (2) (2007), 191–219.

44. Clarke, B., 'If this child were a car, what sort of car would it be? The global child: using appropriate projective techniques to view the world through their eyes', ESOMAR, Qualitative Research, Cannes (November 2004); Suprenant, C., Churchill, G.A. and Kinnear, T.C. (eds), 'Can role playing be substituted for actual consumption?', *Advances in Consumer Research* (Provo, UT: Association for Consumer Research, 1984), 122–126.

45. Anon., 'Coors – Coors Light', Institute of Communication Agencies, Silver, Canadian Advertising Success Stories (2007).

46. Maehle, N. and Supphellen, M., 'In search of the sources of brand personality', *International Journal of Market Research* 53 (1) (2011), 95–114.

47. Strachan, J. and Pavie-Latour, V., 'Forum – food for thought: shouldn't we actually target food advertising more towards kids and not less?', *International Journal of Market Research* 50 (1) (2008), 13–27.

48. Branthwaite, A. and Patterson, S., 'The vitality of qualitative research in the era of blogs and tweeting: an anatomy of contemporary research methods', ESOMAR, Qualitative, Barcelona (November 2010).

49. McPhee, N. and Chrystal, G., 'Who's eaten my porridge? Discovering brand image differences', ESOMAR, Healthcare Conference, Rome (February 2008); Gill, J., and Johnson, P., *Research Methods for Managers*, 3rd edn (Thousand Oaks, CA: Sage, 2002); Varki, S., Cooil, B. and Rust, R.T., 'Modeling fuzzy data in qualitative marketing research', *Journal of Marketing Research* 37 (4) (November 2000), 480–489.

50. For more on projective techniques, see Burden, S., 'Emotional...but does it sell?', *Admap* 496 (July/August

2008), 41–42; Clarke, B., 'If this child were a car, what sort of car would it be? The global child: using appropriate projective techniques to view the world through their eyes', ESOMAR, Qualitative Research, Cannes (November 2004); Valentine, V. and Evans, M., 'The dark side of the onion: rethinking the meaning of "rational" and "emotional" responses', *Journal of the Market Research Society* 35 (April 1993), 125–144.

51. Branthwaite, A. and Cooper, P., 'A new role for projective techniques', ESOMAR, Qualitative Research, Budapest (October 2001), 236–263.

52. Imms, M., 'Just how "anonymous" is a quali participant?', *Research* (April 1997), 20.

53. Heeg, R., 'The changing face of advertising research', *Research World* (March 2007), 41.

54. Schillewaert, N., De Ruyck, T. and Verhaeghe, A., 'Connected research' – how market research can get the most out of semantic web waves', *International Journal of Market Research* 51 (1) (2009), 11–27; Pincott, G. and Branthwaite, A., 'Nothing new under the sun?', *International Journal of Market Research* 42 (2) (2000), 137–155.

55. Paterlini, C. and Sbarbaro, S., 'MTV Seeding Lab: a cutting edge on-line qualitative approach', ESOMAR, Innovate, Barcelona (November 2010).

Qualitative research: data analysis

Stage 1

Problem definition

Stage 2

Research approach developed

Stage 3

Research design developed

Stage 4

Fieldwork or data collection

Stage 5

Data integrity and analysis

Stage 6

Report preparation and presentation

Qualitative analysis involves the process of making sense of data that are not expressed in numbers.

Objectives

After reading this chapter, you should be able to:

1 understand the importance of qualitative researchers being able to reflect upon and understand the social and cultural values that shape the way they gather and interpret qualitative data;

2 describe the stages involved in analysing qualitative data;

3 describe the array of data types that qualify as qualitative data;

4 explain the nature and role of coding in the stage of reducing qualitative data;

5 appreciate the benefits of being able to display the meaning and structure that qualitative researchers see in their data;

6 understand why qualitative data analysis pervades the whole process of data gathering and why the stages of analysis are iterative;

7 appreciate the nature and roles of grounded theory, content analysis and semiotics in qualitative data analysis;

8 understand the ethical implications of the ways that qualitative researchers interpret data;

9 appreciate the strengths and weaknesses of analysing data using qualitative analysis software.

Overview

The application of qualitative techniques is not necessarily a predefined and structured process. In the majority of instances, qualitative researchers modify their direction as they learn what and who they should focus their attention upon. Data gathering techniques, the nature of participants and the issues explored can change and evolve as a project develops. This chapter starts by examining how researchers reflect upon what happens to the way they perceive and observe as these changes unfold. It discusses how these reflections form a key source of qualitative data to complement the narrative generated from interviews and observations.

The stages involved in a generic process of analysing qualitative data are outlined and described. The first stage of the process involves assembling qualitative data in their rich and varying formats. The second stage progresses to reducing the data, i.e. selecting, classifying and connecting data that researchers believe to be of the greatest significance. A key element of this stage is the concept of coding. The third stage involves the display of data, i.e. using graphical means to display the meaning and structure that researchers see in the data they have collected. Manual and electronic means of displaying data are discussed. The final stage involves verifying the data. Researchers aim to generate the most valid interpretation of the data they collect, which may be supported by existing theories or through the concept of theoretical sampling. Though these stages seem quite distinct, the reality is that they are iterative and totally interdependent upon each other; the stages unfold in 'waves' to produce an ultimate interpretation that should be of great value to decision-makers. Three alternative perspectives on analysing qualitative data are presented. First, the purpose and concept of grounded theory are discussed, with the stages involved in building theory. Second, content analysis is presented, a much simpler approach to analysing qualitative data, which is sometimes viewed as a quantitative technique. Third, the purpose and concept on semiotics are presented. This approach adopts the view that consumers should be viewed as products of culture, constructed and largely determined by the popular culture within which they live. It allows for the integrated analysis of cues that emerge from text, pictures and sounds.

The social and cultural values of qualitative researchers affect how they gather and analyse data. Understanding the social and cultural norms of participants in international environments is discussed. The social and cultural values of researchers affect their interpretation of qualitative data, and the ethical implications of not reflecting upon these values are addressed.

The digital applications in the stages of qualitative data collection and analyses are described. There are many distinct advantages to the use of qualitative data analysis software, but many researchers contend that it should be a 'hands-on' process that cannot be mechanised. The arguments from both of these perspectives are presented. To be able to cope with the great amount of data generated from qualitative techniques, a great variety of software packages are available. Examples of analysis software are briefly described followed by website addresses that allow demonstration versions of the software to be downloaded and explored. NVivo, the qualitative data analysis package specifically designed for researchers, is presented. This is the software package that is available with this text as a full-working version, for use over 90 days.

The qualitative researcher

Self-reflection of social and cultural values

In Chapter 2, when discussing the diagnosis of research problems, we stated:

> *A major problem for researchers is that their perception of problems may be reflected through their own social and cultural development. Before defining the problem, researchers should reflect upon their unconscious reference to cultural values … The unconscious reference to cultural values can be seen to account for these differences.*

This implies that researchers need to reflect upon their own values and attitudes, the factors that may bias the way they perceive and what they observe. This reflection is just as important in the analysis of qualitative data as it is in the diagnosis of research problems. To illustrate why researchers need to reflect upon what may bias the way they perceive and what they observe, we start this chapter with an example from the world of literature and the treatment of narrative. The example is a précis of an English translation of a Japanese novel; the example could be taken from any novel.

Real research   ## South of the Border, West of the Sun[1]

This novel tells the story of an only child, Hajime, growing up in the suburbs of postwar Japan. His childhood sweetheart and sole companion in childhood was Shimamoto, also an only child. As children they spent long afternoons listening to her father's record collection. When Hajime's family moved away, the childhood sweethearts lost touch. The story moves to Hajime in his thirties. After a decade of drifting he has found happiness with his loving wife and two daughters, and success in running a jazz bar. Then Shimamoto reappears. She is beautiful, intense, enveloped in mystery. Hajime is catapulted into the past, putting at risk all he has at the present.

Imagine that you had been asked to read this novel, but before you read it you were expected to prepare by reading a description of conditions in postwar Japan. From that you might appreciate the significance of a record collection of 15 albums, and how privileged a family may be to own a record player and to have this collection. Imagine someone else being asked to prepare by reading a biography of the author. From that you might appreciate the social and economic conditions of his upbringing, the literature, music and education that he enjoyed. Preparing to read the novel in these two ways may mean that a reader sees very different things in the story. The reader may interpret passages differently, have a different emotional attachment with the conditions and behaviour of the characters, and appreciate the effect of quite subtle events upon the characters.

Put aside any prior reading and imagine a female reader enjoying the book. She may empathise with the main female character Shimamoto and understand her attitudes, values and behaviour in the way that male readers may not be able to comprehend. In the story, Shimamoto suffered from polio as a child, which made her drag her left leg. Imagine a reader who has had to cope with a disability and who may appreciate how as a child one copes with the teasing of young children. The two main characters were 'only children'; imagine a reader who was an only child and who can recall how he or she would view large families and appreciate the joys, disappointments and array of emotions of being an only child. The list could go on of the different perspectives of the story that may be seen. The reader, with their inherent values and attitudes, may perceive many different things happening in the story. The reader does not normally reflect upon their unconscious values and attitudes, but just enjoys the story. In talking to others about the story, the reader might be surprised about how others see it. In watching the film version of the book, the reader might be shocked at the different images the film director presents, images that are very different from the one that resides in the reader's head. Now consider whether there is one ultimate interpretation of the novel, one ultimate 'truth'. It is very difficult to conceive that there is one ultimate interpretation. One may question why anyone would want to achieve such a thing; surely the enjoyment of literature is the ability to have multiple interpretations and 'truths' of a novel.[2]

Narrative for the qualitative researcher

What is the link from the interpretation of a novel to qualitative data analysis in marketing research? Quite simply, the qualitative researcher builds up a narrative and creates a story of the consumers whom decision-makers wish to understand. Imagine yourself as a qualitative researcher, supporting decision-makers who wish to develop advertisements for an expensive ride-on lawnmower. The key target market they wish to understand is 'wealthy men, over the age of 60, who own a home(s) with at least 1 hectare of garden'. The decisions they face may include the understanding of:

1 What gardening and cutting grass mean to target consumers.

2 How they feel about the experience of buying and using a lawnmower.

3 What relative values (tangible and intangible) are inherent in different brands of lawnmower.

4 What satisfaction they get from the completed job of mowing a large lawn.

5 The nature and qualities of celebrities they admire (who may be used to endorse and use the product in an advertisement).

These questions may be tackled through the use of focus groups. Imagine yourself running these groups. What could you bring to the groups if you have personally gone through the experience of buying an expensive ride-on lawnmower and have gardening and lawn-mowing experiences? You may have an empathy with the participants in the same manner as the 'only child' reading of the experiences and emotions of an only child in a story. From this empathy, you may be able to question, probe and interpret the participants' answers really well, drawing an enormous amount from them. Without those experiences you may have to devise ways to 'step into the shoes' of the participants. You may look to the attitudes, values

and behaviour of your parents, grandparents or friends for a start, looking for reference points that you are comfortable with, that make sense to you. As you go through a pilot or experimental focus group, you may be surprised by certain participants talking about their lawnmowers as 'friends', giving them pet names and devoting lavish care and attention upon them. Getting an insight into this may mean looking at cases from past research projects or literature from analogous situations such as descriptions of men forming a 'bond' with their cars.

The direction that qualitative researchers take in building up their understanding and ultimately their narrative is shaped by two factors. The first factor is the *theoretical understanding* of the researchers as they collect and analyse the data. This theoretical understanding can be viewed from two perspectives. The first is the use of theory published in secondary data, intelligence and literature. The use of theory from these sources may help the researchers to understand what they should focus their attention upon, in their questioning, probing, observations and interpretations. The second is the use of theory from a grounded theory perspective. The researchers may see limitations in existing theory that do not match the observations they are making. These limitations help the researchers to form the focus of their questioning, probing, observations and interpretations.

The second factor that shapes the direction that the researchers take is a *marketing understanding*. In the case of understanding the wealthy male lawnmower owner, the researchers need to understand what marketing decision-makers are going to do with the story they create. The researchers need to appreciate the decisions faced in creating an advertisement, building a communications campaign or perhaps changing features of the product. Reference to theoretical and marketing understanding in researchers helps them to present the most valid interpretation of their story to decision-makers. Unlike writing a novel, where the author is happy for the readers to take their own 'truth', researchers are seeking an ultimate interpretation and validity in their story. Achieving a valid interpretation enables the researchers to convey to decision-makers a vision or picture of a target market that they can quickly 'step into'. Marketing decision-makers, for example, may wish to include a passage of music in an advertisement that the target market has an emotional attachment to, which they find positive and uplifting. With a rich picture or vision of this target market they may be able to choose the right piece of music. The decision-makers' cultural and social development may mean that the piece of music is meaningless to them, but you as a researcher have given them the confidence and enabled them to step into the world of the target market. The following example illustrates how qualitative research, based upon blogging via mobile devices, helped the Knorr brand to understand the characteristics, behaviour and views of a very distinctive target market.

| Real research | **Tokyo Girls Collection metrics**[3] |

In Japan, Knorr wished to develop a new Soup Pasta to target the primary gourmets of noodle cuisine: younger, female consumers. The hardest question Knorr faced was how to develop a Soup Pasta that fitted the target segment's taste preferences. To generate and commercialise the product successfully, the company needed frank and honest opinions from young, female consumers during the idea generation, idea screening, concept development, product design and detailed engineering phases. In order to do this, Knorr decided to tie its new product development project to the Tokyo Girls Collection (TGC). The TGC was a twice-annual celebration of 'all things cute', organised by **Girlswalker. com** magazine to showcase the season's fashionable streetwear. The fashion event included such attractions as live performances by renowned artists, a charity auction, and the final stage selection and presentation of the TGC Contest. The fashion show used only amateur models known as 'Dokusha moderu' (in English, 'reader models'), chosen from trendsetting girls' magazines, such as *Vivi* or *Ray*. The TGC exemplified a grassroots movement that has become so huge in Japan that it has rendered the traditional fashion houses anachronistic. Many previous TGC tie-up campaigns have proven very successful, because young female consumers tended to spread the word about their favourite brands. Knorr's new product development project was announced at the TGC venue, with star TGC models assigned as official new Soup Pasta development project members. Knorr launched a mobile site on the mobile **Girlswalker.com** site, where TGC project members described the product development process in their blogs. Knorr's blogging project to support its new Soup Pasta development was an ideal way for it to generate such openness. The TGC served as a critical mental and symbolic venue for the virtual discussions.

The researcher's learning as qualitative data

Qualitative researchers have to reflect upon their own social and cultural development, their own attitudes and values to see how these have shaped the narrative and how they shape their interpretation of the narrative. The researchers should recognise their own limitations and the need to develop and learn; in the cases above, this means learning about wealthy men and their relationship with lawnmowers or Japanese girls and their relationships with soup and fashion. Ultimately they wish to present the most valid story that they see, to have examined the story from many perspectives, to have immersed themselves in the world of their target markets. The following example illustrates the research impact of not recognising one's own biases and social/cultural conditioning.

Real research	**We see our own beliefs reflected in research**[4]

Different advertising agencies cherish different beliefs about what will work and what will not work in an advertisement. Take for instance 'influencing lifestyle' (such as: drive less, drink less, stop smoking, don't drink and drive). In this field, there are at least two different schools. One school promotes the 'confrontation' strategy: show the negative effects of behaviour as extremely as possible: show cancerous lungs in an anti-smoking campaign, show the remorseful victims of smoking-related diseases. Another school feels that such an approach does not really work, because the consumers will actively shut their system off from this kind of information, countering it with arguments such as 'I have to die anyway' or 'I never have a problem drinking and driving'. This school claims that you can better focus on a more positive approach or an approach that avoids showing negative consequences. Both schools will be able to find proof for their ideas, and both will tend to open up to reality supporting their ideas, avoiding evidence that goes against their views. In conducting research, both schools will find their views supported by consumers, one asking for 'extreme examples', the other claiming to be immune to such an approach and asking for a more positive approach. From the observations of Dutch researchers Jochum Stienstra (**www.ferro-mco.nl**) and Wim van der Noort (**http://english.minaz. nl**) in viewing focus group discussions: the participant that gives 'the right answer' is embraced: '*You see, I knew it, scaring them off doesn't work.*' Two participants later, another communication manager or researcher will hear proof of the opposite opinion: '*This is exactly what I mean. They are asking for extreme emotions, otherwise they won't listen.*' They contend that research that tries to find the right communication approach involves a danger: you might end up finding what you already thought was right, or – even worse – you might find an internal quarrel aggravated since both schools will find their standpoint proved. This means that research as we know it cannot help us out, cannot transfer the problem from the realms of belief to the realms of 'proof'.

If you are reading a novel, you may not be inclined to make notes as your reading progresses. You may not make notes of other books to read that may help you to understand the condition of particular characters, or to understand the environment in which they behave. You may not wish to write down the way that you change and learn as you read through the story. A reflection of your unconscious social and cultural values as revealed through your interpretation of the novel may be the last thing you want to do.

As a qualitative researcher you need to do all the above as you build and interpret your story of target consumers. A notebook or diary should be on hand to note new question areas or probes you wish to tackle, and to reflect upon how they have worked. As interviews unfold and you feel your own development and understanding progress, a note of these feelings should be made. As you seek out specific secondary data, intelligence or theory to develop your understanding, you should note why. If you see limitations in existing theories or ideas, you should note why. As an understanding of how decision-makers can use the observations that are being made, these should be recorded. Included in these notes should be feelings of failure to ask the right question or probe, emotional states should be noted, of feeling up or down, sad or angry, or nervous.[5] Ultimately the story that emerges in your own notebook should be a revelation of your own social and cultural values. There should be an explicit desire to develop this self-awareness and understand how it has shaped the direction of an investigation and the ultimate story that emerges.

The creation and development of the researcher's notebook is a major part of the narrative that is vital to the successful interpretation of questions and observations of consumers. The key lesson that emerges from the creation and development of the researcher's notebook is that qualitative data analysis is an ongoing process through all stages of data collection, not just when the data have been collected:

> *Analysis is a pervasive activity throughout the life of a research project. Analysis is not simply one of the later stages of research, to be followed by an equally separate phase of 'writing up results'.*[6]

The evolution of questions and probes, deciding who should be targeted for questions and observations and even deciding the context for questioning or observing, means that analysis takes place as data are being gathered.

The process of qualitative data analysis

We go through four perspectives of analysing qualitative data starting with a generic process. Many of the terms used here differ from those linked to specific types of software or to researchers who follow a particular theoretical approach derived from a specific discipline. The generic process outlined is designed to give an understanding of what is involved in qualitative data analysis and how the stages link and interact. The four stages of the generic process are outlined in Figure 9.1. The concept of coding is introduced in this section, a vital concept to understand in all approaches to analysing qualitative data. The second perspective presented is the concept of grounded theory. The third perspective is the process of content analysis. The fourth is the discipline of semiotics.

Data assembly

Data assembly
The gathering of data from a variety of disparate sources.

Data assembly means the gathering of data from a variety of sources. These would include:

1 Notes taken during or after interviewing or observations.

2 Reflections of researchers, moderators or observers involved in the data collection process.

3 Theoretical support – from secondary data, intelligence or literature sources.

Chapter 9

Figure 9.1

Stages of qualitative data analysis

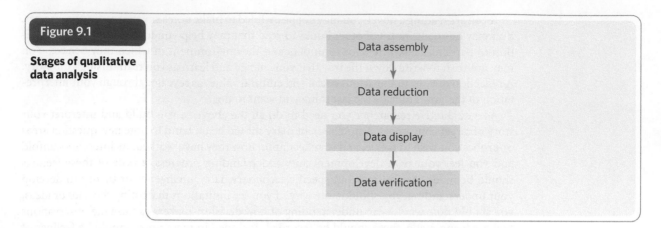

4   Documents produced by or sourced from participants.

5   Photographs, drawings, diagrams, i.e. still visual images.

6   Audiotape recordings and transcripts of those recordings.

7   Video recordings.

8   Records made by participants such as mood boards or collages.

Field notes

A log or diary of observations, events and reflections made by a researcher as a study is planned, implemented and analysed.

As discussed in the previous section, the researcher should get into the habit of maintaining a notebook, diary or **field notes**. As a qualitative investigation evolves in terms of the issues to explore and the participants to target, the researcher goes through a learning process. This learning process means that the researcher may see things differently as interviews or observations progress. Keeping field notes aids the researcher's memory when it comes to the formal process of data analysis and helps enormously in categorising and interpreting collected data. It ultimately helps to generate a 'deeper and more general sense of what is happening'.

In order to make a 'deeper and more general sense of what is happening', it is suggested[7] that researchers keep four separate sets of notes in order to systematise the process and thus improve their reliability:

1   Short notes made at the time of observation or interview.

2   Expanded notes made as soon as possible after each session of interviews or observations.

3   A fieldwork journal to record problems and ideas that arise during each stage of fieldwork.

4   A provisional running record of analysis and interpretation.

Data assembly also includes deciding lines of enquiry which should be developed and those that should be dropped. Given that qualitative research is primarily exploratory in nature, questions and probes are not fixed. As an interview or observation takes place, the researcher learns more about an issue and can develop a new question or probe and decide that a question, initially thought to be vital, is no longer relevant. There may be issues that can be compared over a series of interviews or observations, but the whole data collection and data assembly can evolve. Keeping notes is vital as memory alone is fallible, unreliable and potentially biased. Being able to recall, for example, the hesitation in replying to a question displayed by a focus group participant may upon reflection be seen as someone evading the issue. After all the group discussions have been completed and the same question has been posed to others, the interpretation may change to the individual being embarrassed about an issue, primarily through becoming aware of their own ignorance. The researchers' notes help them to recall how they were feeling at the point of setting the question, and recall the situation in other groups that gives meaning to a pause that shows up as a quiet spot in an audio or video recording. The notes may also help the researcher appreciate what is happening when laughter occurs by participants in qualitative techniques. The first example below illustrates the importance of humour in devising a strategy to develop a brand. It shows the dilemma facing the researcher in interpreting the meaning of laughter. In this example, the researcher, Chris Forrest, suggests that the humour in an advert can be sensed through the 'relative energy in the room'. If this is the case, group dynamics, the pitch and intensity of laughter, or even the sly smile that masks a feeling that something is incredibly funny, would need to be recorded in the researcher's notes, to set a vital context to the narrative of any discussion. The same challenges are faced in the second example which deals with the nature of silence in an interview; what does a particular silence mean? The researcher's notes at the time of the silence may hold vital clues to what is being felt by participants but not expressed.

Real research   ## Funny business, serious money[8]

Humour is something that can communicate a strategy very powerfully, but is not a solution in its own right. There are pitfalls in understanding humour in the research process, with the focus group seen as a poor place to find out if an advertisement is funny. In groups people laugh to show they fit in, to please the moderator or other participants, or simply because laughter can be contagious. In short, laughter (or its absence) is an unreliable piece of evidence. However, Chris Forrest, from the research agency The Nursery (**www.the-nursery.net**), argues that the focus group can detect what is funny and what is not:

> *A really strong script will have a group in stitches, participants will even insist it is an ad that has to be made. Naturally one cannot always hope to be researching a knock-out script, and in these cases its useful to have more than one script.*

Then, Chris says:

> *It is possible to benchmark a group's reaction. Even when a group isn't laughing a lot, you can tell from the relative energy in the room which one they respond to the best.*

Real research   ## Listening to the sounds of silence[9]

> *My in-depth interview went really badly! It was full of long silences ... my participants just would not open up!!*

This is a cry from researchers who believe that discussions that are not full of verbal give and take have not 'got going'. Many fail to understand that the silence received in response to the question asked may have told the researchers what they needed to know. The way people communicate is deeply linked with the culture, values and norms of a society. If one understands the reason for the silence, one can end up with a far stronger set of findings and interpretations. The following is based on the reflections of over 200 focus group discussions and 100 in-depth interviews conducted in different parts of India by Shobha Prasad (**www.drshti.com**). Silence in India could be based on the social structure between castes. For example, a study conducted in rural Rajasthan among

▶

young men ran into severe issues arising from mingling of castes within the focus group. There were demarcated places where castes were allowed to mingle and communicate; they would talk to each other outdoors but not indoors. It was only when some of the participants were taken out of the group that others opened up to voice their opinions. Language block was occasionally encountered where sessions were conducted in Hindi and participants had differing levels of comfort with the language. In some sessions more educated participants would express themselves in English, creating a sense of inequality in the group. Those who were less educated would then become quiet unless the researcher directly addressed them and tried to draw them back into the discussion. Indians rarely contained strong emotions in silence; they tended to let these feelings out through words. Therefore silence resulting from the two extremes; extreme positive and extreme negative emotion were rare and if they occurred were short-lived. 'Extreme delight' was very rarely silent. Extreme negativity tended to result in a short silence which very often just 'broke itself'. The body language accompanying strong negative emotions was very obvious: a closed expression, folded arms, rigid body and refusal to make eye contact. In some cases participants would whisper among themselves. The slightest direct probe was usually adequate to get a verbalisation of these thoughts. The more common causes for silence among both women and men was incomprehension, confusion and feelings of inadequacy, and a lack of confidence. These reasons generally came to light as the session went on, when at some point in response to a probe, participants would admit to have been confused or bewildered.

Unfortunately, the recording and use of field notes or a diary is limited in many qualitative marketing research projects. This may be due to the contents of such notes which could include photographs and other non-verbal data sources. These are unavoidably 'subjective', being what the researcher has chosen to notice. They are developmental, representing the learning and self-reflection that the researcher goes through. The subjective choices are reasoned choices, where issues are deliberately included or excluded. Understanding the reasons for those choices, recognising the learning and self-development that can emerge from these notes, can add so much more depth and greater insight into qualitative data. By developing self-awareness, qualitative researchers can take a more balanced view of the data they collect as they realise many of their own biases and hidden agendas.

Beyond taking notes or keeping a diary, many qualitative techniques make extensive use of material of a semi- or non-verbal nature, generated through participant tasks such as the use of projective techniques (as described in Chapter 8). These materials can include drawings, lists, stories, clay models or structures, and collages of photographs, video footage and music. The commonly held view is that it is not these materials that should be analysed but the meanings attached to them by the participants who produced them.[10] These meanings as narrative will have been captured as part of the recorded discussion or are in the notes of the researcher.[11] The materials themselves would normally be available during analysis, enabling the possibility to notice useful features such as consistencies and differences between participants. They can also be useful in communicating and illustrating findings. Other qualitative researchers go further, taking the view that it is legitimate to 'read' these materials in the absence of the participants who produced them. They would argue that significant and valid meaning can be extracted from them provided they have a strong theoretical basis to drawing their conclusions and meanings.

This relationship between participants' discourse and non-verbal materials mirrors the debate in using photography in ethnographic studies (a common occurrence in qualitative marketing research where participants are given disposable or digital cameras to capture stills or moving images of their experiences). Many significant anthropological ethnographies dating from the mid-1920s onwards include photographs relating to the fieldwork. The question that faces anthropologists relates to why photographs may be used in analysis and the relationship, if any, between the photograph and the written text. It is difficult to generalise, but it seems to be the case that photographs have been included in ethnographic reports more for evidential than analytic purposes. The photographs serve essentially presentational and illustrative purposes rather than providing a focus for a more sustained analysis of the visual dimensions of culture.[12] Such perspectives are radically changing as more visual ethnographic techniques gain prominence in qualitative marketing research as illustrated in the following example.[13]

Real research	**Participant photography in visual ethnography[14]**

Visual ethnography is an anthropological approach that incorporates visuality throughout the research process. In a project designed to investigate the consumption of households, an exploratory, initial investigation was designed to expose the various ways that household shoppers engaged with the consumption spaces that they visited. A key aim was to have the householders focus on their shopping in as natural a way as possible and record this so that it could be discussed during an in-depth interview. A researcher following participants on shopping trips was deemed to be quite intrusive in that having a stranger along could affect the usual flow of the experience, no matter how much rapport was developed. It was important, however, to try to capture everyday practice as accurately as possible in order to bring to the investigation the real ways in which shoppers engaged with the process of consumption. The research process asked participants to keep a shopping log of all household expenditure over a period of two weeks. This was a straightforward procedure of putting all their receipts into a plastic wallet provided and noting any expenses without a receipt on a notepad. After the fortnight had elapsed they were interviewed using the receipts as prompts and following several themes derived from the literature. Another important element was the addition of a disposable camera. Researchers met with the shoppers and explained their part in the data gathering process. This initial contact established a rapport before the interview proper, but it continued by explaining the research process and covering ethical issues. In addition, participants were issued with a disposable flash camera and asked to take photographs of anything interesting connected to their shopping. Prior to the in-depth interviews, the photographs were collected and added to the receipts and notes to facilitate probing and the development of issues.

The key feature of the use of photography and visuals is the subtlety of characteristics or events that can be captured and portrayed where words alone may be deficient. This feature has an impact for qualitative researchers for two reasons. The first can be seen from the perspective of qualitative technique participants. Certain participants may not be able to express what they feel about a product, service, advertisement, brand or any design element of their experiences solely using words. They may, however, be able to use visual cues from sources like photographs to represent their feelings. The second can be seen from the perspective of decision-makers who use qualitative research findings. Certain marketing decision-makers working in visually creative fields such as advertising, product and package design, and branding, work better with visual data compared with words or statistics. They may understand the impact of how consumers feel and will react to their designs through very subtle interpretations of visual data. Given the importance of visual data to this type of decision-maker, we explore the concept of semiotics later in this chapter.

Data reduction

Data reduction involves handling the data. This process involves organising and structuring the data. It means having to throw some data away! Imagine a series of 10 focus group discussions and the amount of data that could be collected. There are the memories and notes of the moderator and any other observers who took part, there are the transcripts of what was actually said in interviews, and there may be contributions from participants in the form of mood boards. The transcripts are a vital and for most studies *the* primary data source in qualitative data analysis and much care should be taken in transcribing them. Transferring the dialogue from tape or digital devices can be tortuous as recordings are notoriously 'unclear'. Imagine a focus group in full swing: not every participant takes their turn to speak without talking over other participants, and then they may not speak clearly and loudly enough. As a result it can take a great deal of time to work out what participants actually said and how the questions, responses and ideas connect together. In producing transcripts, it is much better for the researchers to work through the recordings and piece together the components using their notes and memory of events. This is very time consuming, so many researchers use typists to transcribe their recordings of interviews, arguing that their time is better spent reading through and editing transcripts produced in this manner. The use of online software for in-depth interviews and focus groups means that this time-consuming task is eliminated as the transcript is built up as the interview progresses.

The researchers with their transcripts, notes and other supporting material have to decide what is relevant in all these data. Reducing the data involves a process of coding data, which means breaking down the data into discrete chunks and attaching a reference to those chunks of data. Coding is a vital part of coping with qualitative data analysis and, given this importance, the process is discussed in some detail.

Coding data. Researchers need to be able to organise, manage and retrieve the most meaningful bits of qualitative data that they collect. This is normally done by assigning 'labels' or codes to the data, based upon what the researcher sees as a meaningful categorisation. What happens is that the researcher condenses the great mass of data from a study into analysable units by creating categories from the data.[15] This process is termed the coding of data. Coding is the process of bringing together participants' responses and other data sources into categories that form similar ideas, concepts, themes, or steps or stages in process. Coding can also enable the categorisation of names, evidence or time sequences. Any hesitations, emotional states or levels of humour can be coded. Indeed, anything that is felt to be revealing in the data can be coded. Data such as a simple response to a question can be coded in many different ways, or placed into many different categories; there is no expectation of mutual exclusivity and data can be recoded as often as is thought necessary.[16]

An illustration of coding is presented using the data presented in Table 9.1. This table presents the verbatim responses from an open-ended question in a self-completion survey targeted at 12 to 14 year olds. The question asked participants what facilities they would like in a planned new community centre. Though the technique used was quantitative, the survey generated qualitative data and in its much shortened format demonstrates the process that qualitative researchers must go through.

In categorising the responses, the researcher could create codes of '**swimming pool**' or '**disco**' and count the times that these were literally expressed. Alternatively, the researcher could code on the basis of '**sports activities**' or '**recreational activities**' and group together activities such as 'swimming, basketball and snooker' for sports and 'computers, television, discos and tuck shop' for recreational activities. The researcher could code '**indoor activities**' and '**outdoor activities**', or activities that would need supervision and those that would need no supervision. There are many ways that the researcher can categorise the data, it is their choice. Consider how the researcher may cope with the requests for a 'computer room' and 'computers'. Could these be combined under one heading of '**computing**' or would this lose the meaning of having a devoted space, away from other activities that could be noisy

Table 9.1	Teenager requests for facilities at a planned community centre	

Requested feature of new community centre	Gender
Skate park, death slide, basketball courts, swimming pool	Male
Computer room	Male
Stuff for all ages	Male
Swimming pool	Male
Computers, snooker room	Male
A space for computers, tuck shop	Male
Music, television, up-to-date magazines, pool tables	Female
Music, discos	Female
Swimming pool	Female
Music, pool/snooker, discos	Female
What people will enjoy	Female
All the things people enjoy	Female

and distracting? Consider also how the researcher would cope with the requests for 'stuff for all ages', 'what people will enjoy' and 'all the things people enjoy'. It may seem obvious that a new leisure centre needs to develop facilities that people enjoy and that these may be discarded, but there may be a hint in the first statement of 'stuff for all ages' that may link to the word 'people' used in the two other statements. If the researcher interprets the statements in this way, a category of 'activities to draw in all ages' could be created; these responses may be seen as tapping into a notion of a leisure centre that is welcoming and not exclusive.

Table 9.2 presents a small selection of the verbatim responses from the same open-ended question in a self-completion survey, this time targeted at adults.

The interesting feature in comparing the statements from the adults with those from the teenagers is how they express themselves in more detail and how they thought beyond specific facilities that make up the leisure centre. These statements were unprompted, so one can imagine how much richer the explanations and justifications would be with an in-depth interview or a focus group. Again, there are many ways that the researcher can categorise the

Table 9.2	Adult requests for facilities at a planned community centre

Requested feature of new community centre	Gender
Regard for residents living nearby, special car parking area to avoid streets nearby being jammed	Male
New centre would soon bring the wrong sort of people; it could form a centre for thugs and crime	Male
Strict rules so as to inconvenience local people living close by as little as possible, e.g. noise	Male
Run and organised well to run functions at affordable prices with dress rules for the lounge and bar	Male
Membership should be given on signature of applicants to a strict set of rules	Male
Emphasis on youth on the estate and run in a way to encourage rather than regiment them	Male
Supervised youth activities, daytime crèche, dance floor, serve coffee/soft drinks for youths	Female
Should be very welcoming and developed for all kinds of people	Female
Active participation by those using the facilities which should give opportunities for the young	Female
To make a safe place for all people of all ages to enjoy	Female
Exterior should be modern. Inside decorated tastefully with nice seats and tables, plenty of hall space	Female
Youth club with a youth leader. Luncheon club for older groups and gentle keep-fit for the elderly	Female

data, perhaps even more than with the teenagers. Categorising these adult statements is not as straightforward as for the teenagers. The researcher could draw out the words 'youth' or 'rules' and set these as categories. The researcher could pull out named 'facilities' such as 'dance floor' and 'nice seats and tables' or 'activities' such as 'youth club' and 'luncheon club'. What becomes apparent in reading through the statements (especially with the full set of responses) are implied problems related to issues of parking, the types of people that are attracted or could be attracted, and how 'regimented' or not the centre should be. These are categories or patterns that may be apparent to a researcher, though not explicitly expressed. There may be words expressed that make up the categories, but the words broken down and taken in isolation may lose their impact, if they are just counted.

Table 9.2 illustrates that categorisation into the component words may mean that the contextual material that gives these words meaning can be lost. From the above example, coding can be thought of as a means to:

1   *Retrieve data*, i.e. from the whole mass of data, particular words or statements can be searched for and retrieved to examine the 'fit' with other words or statements.

2   *Organise the data*, i.e. words or statements can be reordered, put alongside each other and similarities and differences evaluated.

3   *Interpret data*, i.e. as words or statements are retrieved and organised in different ways, interpretations of the similarities and differences can be made.

Coding is a process that enables the researchers to identify what they see as meaningful and to set the stage to draw conclusions and interpret meaning. Codes are essentially labels to assign meaning to the data compiled during a study.

In broad terms the coding process involves the following stages:

1   *Set up a broad group of coding categories.* These would emerge from an initial reading of the gathered data and the intended purpose of the study. For example, these may be the themes that structured a number of focus group interviews or in-depth interviews.

2   *Work through the data to uncover 'chunks' of data that may be put into brackets or underlined or highlighted.* Codes are usually attached to 'chunks' of varying size, i.e. words, phrases, sentences, paragraphs, an extended story, an image, indeed any component of the collected data, connected or unconnected to a specific context.[17] Sometimes a single sentence or paragraph might be coded into several categories. For example, one paragraph where participants are overtly discussing parking problems at a community centre may also be discussing issues of 'mobility' or 'independence'. Once the start and end of a chunk to be coded is established, a name or number is assigned to it.

3   *Review the descriptions given to the codes.* Working through the data, it may be clear that important themes emerging from the data do not fit into the preset categories or that one theme blurs into two or more separate concepts. At this point new categories have to be set to fit the data. With new categories, the data must then be reviewed and recoded where appropriate. This stage therefore is one of immersion in the data and refining the nature of categories as more meaning is uncovered in the data.

4   *Examine differences between types of participant.* This could be simple demographic comparisons, e.g. to see if there are differences between men and women in how they view independence. The comparisons could be between types of participant that emerge from other codes, e.g. lifestyle aspirations may emerge from the data with groups emerging that may be labelled 'sophisticated minimalists' and 'spiritual warriors'. Comparisons of the behaviour between these emerging groups can be made. Through these comparisons, new insights may emerge about the assigned codes and the descriptors applied to them. New insights may also emerge about the way that participants are described and categorised,

combining knowledge of their demographic, geographic, behavioural, psychographic and psychological characteristics. The following IFM Sports Marketing Surveys example on rugby league illustrates how it classified focus group participants to perform the analyses.

5 *Develop models of interconnectivity among the coded categories.* This involves basic graphical modelling to explain a sequence of events or a process that the data describe. It could show how categories relate to each other, how participants may be alike or differ and how different contexts impact upon the categories and participants. Again, new insights may emerge about the meaning seen in the data, and the coding process may be further refined.

6 *Iterate between the code descriptions and the developing model.* This stage is again one of immersion in the data, with continual refining of the nature of categories and the structural relationship of those categories. These iterations continue until the researchers have what they believe to be the most valid meaning that they see in the data.

Focus on   **IFM Sports Marketing Surveys**

Rugby league study

In the rugby league study, IFM Sports Marketing Surveys analysed its focus group findings based upon gender, behavioural and attitudinal characteristics. The analysis focused upon four distinctive groups that it labelled and described as:

Male Avid Rugby League Fans – whose interest in the game ranged from 7 to 65 years, following and experience, averaging over 30 years. Most of them were brought up with the game encapsulated by *'first match inside mother's stomach!'*, *'since I was a student'*, *'Granddad used to play, I used to play'*. They all attended matches with their family: *'go with my daughter'*, *'the wife, she's madder about it than me!'*, *'the whole family – my aunts, uncles, cousins . . . everyone!'*

Female Family Rugby League Fans – whose interest in the game ranged from half to 'all' of their lives, initiated by *'dad made us watch it when we were small'*, *'thought it would be good for my son, and social for me'*, *'kids got tickets from school'*. They all attended matches with their family from a single parent with her son, through to attending with a husband after all the children had grown up and moved on.

Male Occasional Rugby League Fans – whose interest in the game was part of an overall 'sports interest'. Around half also played other sports but 'armchair involvement' was popular: *'mad about all sports!'*, *'sports freak all my life'*, *'play golf, badminton, swim, go to football with friends, rugby league finals sometimes'*. They were all family men with children ranging from toddler age to young adults, but more likely to attend games with friends and colleagues (albeit usually football).

Male General Sports Fans – whose interest in the game was part of an overall *'sports interest'*, were *'non-rejectors'* of rugby league but were predominantly avid football supporters: *'watch anything with a ball!'*, *'like all sports'*, *'watch all sports, but selectively!'* They were all family men with two or three children, who were most likely to watch live football games outside their family unit or *'prefer to watch in the pub where there are no distractions'*.

The approach described above can be completed manually or a range of software solutions can be used. The relative advantages and disadvantages of manual or electronic approaches to analysing qualitative data, and especially the iterative process of coding and modelling, are presented later in the chapter. The point to consider at this stage is that the immersion in the data to draw out meaning is not formulaic, especially as one considers the different types of qualitative data that can be included in analyses. Reducing qualitative data to the essence of meaning as seen by the researchers is a highly creative and subjective process. Given the time that may be allocated to this process, coding can be observed from two perspectives. First, if there is relatively little time for the researchers to immerse themselves in the data, it can be thought of as a means to simplify or reduce the mass of data. If an initial broad group of coding categories is kept and their number is relatively small, then the data can be 'stripped down' to a simple general form. This coding approach can be compared directly with simple forms of content analysis.[18] Second, if more time can be afforded, it can be thought of as a means to expand, transform and reconceptualise data, opening up more diverse ideas and analytical possibilities. The general analytical approach is to open up the categories in order to interrogate them further, to try to identify and speculate about further features. Coding here is about going beyond the data, thinking creatively with the data, asking the data questions, and generating theories and frameworks.[19]

Coding is a major process involved in data reduction. The process forces the researchers to focus upon what they believe to be the most valid meaning held in the data. In order to develop that meaning further, the researchers need to communicate their vision to others, to evaluate their interpretations of the data and to reflect upon their own vision. The stage of data display is the means by which researchers communicate their vision of meaning in the data.

Data display

Data display

Involves summarising and presenting the structure that is seen in collected qualitative data.

Data display is an organised, compressed assembly of information that permits conclusion drawing and action.[20] The most frequent form of display for qualitative data in the past has been *extended text*. Such an approach is cumbersome, dispersed and sequential, poorly structured and extremely bulky. The qualitative researcher can resolve these problems with the use of matrices, graphs, charts, networks or 'word clouds'. All are designed to assemble information into an immediately accessible, compact form so that the analyst can see what is happening and either draw justified conclusions or move on to the next step of analysis the displays suggests may be useful. The creation and use of displays is not an end output of analysis, it is an integral part of the analytic process. For example, designing a matrix as a display involves decisions on what should be displayed in the rows and columns, and deciding what qualitative data, in which form, should be entered in the cells.

Data display also allows a 'public' view of how the researcher has made connections between the different 'data chunks'. Even if others may not have made the same connections and interpret the data in exactly the same manner, the logic of connections should be clear. The display may be in a graphical format, with boxes summarising issues that have emerged and connecting arrows showing the interconnection between issues. Verbatim quotes can be used to illustrate the issues or the interconnections. Pictures, drawings, music or advertisements can also be used to illustrate issues or interconnections. The overall structure allows the decision-maker who is to use the analysis to see the general meaning in the collected data. The illustration of issues or interconnections brings that meaning to life.

One of the simplest means to display data is through the use of a spreadsheet. This can be built up and displayed in a manual or electronic format. Table 9.3 presents an example of how a spreadsheet may be set out. This spreadsheet is a sample of all the interviews that may be conducted and the number of issues that may be tackled. The example relates to a bus and tram operator who wishes to understand the attitudes and behaviour of 18 to 25 year olds related to using public transport. In the columns, details of each interview are presented, and in the final column, notes are made of observations between interviews with a focus on each issue. In the rows, the issues that were discussed in the interviews are presented. These issues may be generated from the topic guide used and/or from the notes of the researchers related to what they see as the emerging issues. The final row details notes of the dynamics of the group, explaining why particular exchanges may be interpreted in a particular way. The

Table 9.3	**Spreadsheet data display of focus group discourse**				
Interviews?	Group 1: 18–25-year-old male car drivers	Group 2: 18–25-year-old female car drivers	Group 3: 18–25-year-old male bus and tram users	Group 4: 18–25-year-old tram users	Notes on the similarities and differences between groups on issues?
Evening travel	Verbatim discourse taken from the interview that relates to this issue				
Commuting					
Freedom					
Friends					
Notes on the dynamics of individual groups?					

analyst cuts and pastes extracts from the transcripts into the relevant cells. With the spreadsheet built up of the reordered transcripts (each focus group may tackle the issues in a different order and with different emphases), comparisons can be made across the columns on particular issues, looking for similarities and differences. Connections between issues can be mapped out with the use of arrows to show the flow of dialogue. The responses from types of participants such as 'city-dwellers' or 'suburb-dwellers' can be colour coded in order to compare similarities or differences. Different notes, images or any other supplementary material can be pasted onto the spreadsheet to help in the interpretation; all the assembled data can be displayed, or more probably a reduced and coded set of data can be displayed.

Such a spreadsheet can be built up manually using large sheets of paper from, for example, flip charts, divided into a grid, and the evidence such as chunks of the transcript physically pasted in. This could even be tacked to a large wall allowing the researcher to stand back, reflect, move things about, and add data. The big advantage of this approach is being able to visualise the whole body of data and to move around the data to 'play' with ideas and connections. This works particularly well when there is more than one person working on the analysis and they are drawing ideas and questions out of each other as they relate to the data. The disadvantage is that editing, moving data around and recategorising data can become very cumbersome and messy. This is where electronic means of displaying the data work well. With electronic means, images and notes can be scanned in and added to the transcripts. Changes can be made very easily and quickly in moving data around, recategorising and incorporating new material. Different versions can be easily stored to allow an evaluation of how the thought processes of the researcher have developed. The disadvantage of the approach is that, when attempting to view the data in their entirety, the entire dataset is there but in effect is viewed through a 'window' with a limited field of vision. The 'window' can be readily moved about but the overall perspective is limited.

Another simple means to display data is through the use of a qualitative cross-tabulation. Table 9.4 presents an example of how a cross-tabulation may be set out. Again, the example relates to a bus and tram operator who wishes to understand the attitudes and behaviour of 18 to 25 year olds related to using public transport. The table shows a sample of categories that have been built around issue of 'evening travel'. As the analyst works through the transcripts and codes distinct chunks of data, and with knowledge of who expressed a particular view that is embodied in that chunk, that relationship can be displayed. The table shows that the analyst has established codes to represent views of 'expense', 'personal attacks' 'spontaneity' and 'style'. With a simple classification of participants, in this case by gender, the analyst can display differences in the number of incidences that a specific code emerges. The large differences between males and females in how they brought up the issues 'expense' and 'personal attacks' can help the analyst to explore the data further, or indeed collect more data to understand what is creating such divergent attitudes and behaviour. Again, different notes, images or any other supplementary material can be pasted onto the cross-tabulation to help in the interpretation.

Table 9.4	Cross-tabulation of emerging categories related to evening travel by gender	
Evening travel	**Gender**	
	Male	**Female**
Expense	16	2
Personal attacks	8	24
Spontaneity	5	5
Style	3	5

The other major means of displaying data is to use flow charts. Figure 9.2 displays a very basic structure of the issues or major categories and subcategories related to how 18–25 year olds view the use of public transport after an evening out.

Visualising the data in this matter can allow the researchers to dip back into the transcripts and their notes to seek alternative ways of connecting evidence and justifying connections. This means that this form of graphic can play a vital role in data reduction and coding, i.e. in making sense of the data, as well as in portraying a final interpretation of the data. Most proprietary qualitative analysis software packages allow data structures to be displayed as in Figure 9.2 but with far more sophisticated features to display structure, differences and supporting evidence. A simple illustration of this in Figure 9.2 is the 'M/F' label attached to categories, used to display behavioural tendencies of male or female participants. With a proprietary qualitative analysis package, quite distinctive structures for participant types may be mapped, with the ability to tap into supporting evidence in actual categories or in the links between categories.[21] Once researchers have displayed what they see as the meaning in the data, they need to demonstrate the credibility of their vision. This involves data verification.

Data verification

Data verification
Involves seeking alternative explanations of the interpretations of qualitative data, through other data sources.

Data verification involves seeking alternative explanations through other data sources and theories. From the start of data collection, qualitative researchers are beginning to decide the meaning of their observations, and noticing regularities, patterns, explanations, possible configurations, causal flows and propositions. The researcher should form these meanings 'lightly' maintaining openness and scepticism, developing conclusions that are embryonic and vague at first, then increasingly explicit and grounded. Final conclusions may not appear until data collection is over, depending upon the volume of data collected in all their forms, the coding, storage and retrieval methods used, and the resource constraints placed upon researchers. When final conclusions have been drawn, researchers need to demonstrate that they have presented a valid meaning of the data that they have collected. They need to show that the structure or meaning they see is not just a reflection of their own views. This is

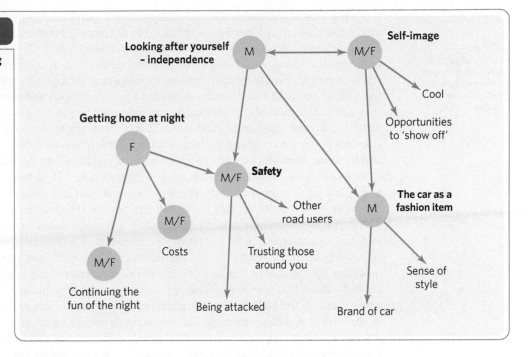

Figure 9.2

Flow chart depicting how 18–25-year-olds view public transport

where the concept of theoretical understanding as discussed at the start of this chapter can help. It is also where the use of the researchers' field notes proves to be invaluable. The use of theory from secondary data, intelligence and the literature can help to guide what may be reasonably expected as a meaning. Other means to verify the data can be through seeking 'similar' research findings and explanations taken from different contexts, different time frames and different researchers.[22] Though the findings from these different scenarios will not be the same, there can be categories that give qualitative researchers the confidence that they are representing a valid view of their participants. This process is illustrated in the following example.

Real research   ## Ethnographic interpretations[23]

Ethnography generally emphasises deep understanding though a focus on small numbers of participants and getting to know their lifestyles intimately. Interpretations become more robust when researchers openly draw upon information from other sources. As well as using more traditional marketing research sources such as focus groups or surveys, other methods can be integrated. To understand what kind of products and services might resonate effectively with Generation Y consumers, researchers from IDEO (**www. ideo.com**) went as deep as they could with individuals, interviewing and observing them in different contexts. They talked to experts: parents, teachers, youth programme leaders and therapists. They held classes at universities made up of students from this generation and collaborated with them to study their own cohort. They engaged individuals who were willing to make mini-documentary videos of their own lives. Combining insight from these various sources and experiences, they were able to reach a deeper understanding around complex areas like identity. They could see how identity played out through their behaviours in co-opting brands, sampling from pop culture, borrowing from other continents, cultures and time periods. By triangulating methods, their understanding became more nuanced and ultimately more useful as a foundation for relevant innovation.

Two forms of validation have been suggested as particularly appropriate to the logic of qualitative research.[24] The first is termed 'triangulation', a term derived from navigation, where different bearings give the correct position of an object. Triangulation is a process that facilitates the validation of data through cross-verification from more than two sources. In research terms, comparing different kinds of data (e.g. dialogue and photographs, quantitative and qualitative) and different methods (e.g. observations and interviews) allows reflection upon the extent of corroboration, and what may be the causes of any differences.[25] The second is termed 'participant validation'. This involves taking one's findings back to the participants under study. Where the feedback from participants on emergent conclusions is verified by them, there can be more confidence in the validity of the findings.

The concept of validity will be examined in more detail in Chapter 12.[26] At this stage it is worth noting that the qualitative researchers should not just present an interpretation and then seek validation or verification of that perspective. The search for verification is a quest that permeates the whole research process. At face value, data assembly, reduction, display and verification appear to be quite distinct and consecutive stages of data analysis. The reality is that they are iterative and totally interdependent upon each other. As researchers assemble new data, they should be thinking of means to validate their views, asking questions of different individuals in different ways and recording these thoughts in their field notes. As data are being reduced and coded, the researchers seek different possible explanations and evidence to support categorising, naming and connecting views in a particular manner. Researchers should question their interpretations of words and gestures and their own ways of seeing. This questioning process adds to the verification. The use of data display is a means to communicate to others the meaning and structure that researchers 'see' in qualitative data. The display allows others to understand that vision, to question and evaluate it. The exposure and critique of the vision by other researchers and decision-makers further verify the data. Ultimately, such critique can direct the researchers to further data assembly, reduction and display; the stages may unfold in 'waves' to produce an ultimate interpretation of great value to decision-makers.

Triangulation
A process that facilitates the validation of data through cross-verification from more than two sources.

Grounded theory

In 1967 Glaser and Strauss published the seminal work *The discovery of grounded theory*.[27] It was their formal description of the approach to handling and interpreting qualitative data that they had developed in the 1960s in a participant observation study of hospital staff's care and management of dying patients.[28] The method they developed was labelled grounded theory to reflect the source of the developed theory which is ultimately grounded in the behaviour, words and action of those under study.[29] The essence of their beliefs was:[30]

Grounded theory
A qualitative approach to generating theory through the systematic and simultaneous process of data collection and analysis.

- The need to conduct field research if one wants to understand what is going on.
- The importance of theory grounded in 'reality'.
- The nature of field experiences for participants and researcher as something that continually evolves.
- The active role of persons in shaping the worlds they live in through the process of symbolic interaction.
- An emphasis on change and process and the variability and complexity of life.
- The interrelationship between meaning in the perception of participants and their action.

The application of grounded theory means that the researcher develops conclusions that are grounded in the 'data'. Grounded theory is meant to be transparent; in other words, for any given conclusion or theory that comes out of the analysis, anyone should be able to reference the theory back to the text, see the steps the researchers have taken to arrive at their conclusions, and follow the development of the theory in a step-by-step way, leaving little or no room for subjectivity, preconception and prejudice.[31] Grounded theory researchers collect data and analyse them simultaneously right from the initial phases of research. They would argue that in the initial stages of research it is not possible to exactly know what the most significant social and social psychological processes are in particular settings. Research could be guided by existing theories which may help to predict processes, but they would argue that such guidance may constrain their observations, forcing them to observe a particular setting from a narrow perspective. So they start with broad areas of interest and form preliminary interviewing questions to open up many areas that could hold relevance. They explore and examine participants' views and then further develop questions around those views, seeking out participants whose experiences address the emerging issues. This sequence is repeated several times during a research project, which means that researchers are kept 'close' to their data. Grounded theory gives researchers tools to analyse data that are concurrent with obtaining additional focused data that inform, extend and refine emerging analytical themes. This means that interviews become more focused with a tight fit between the collected data and the data analysis. With grounded theory, the researcher works in the actual environments in which the actions take place, in order to relate participants perspectives to the environments through which they emerge (such as ethnographers sharing the homes of families to observe how they use and listen to the radio).[32] The style of grounded theory adapts well to capturing the contextual complexities in which action unfolds, enabling researchers to understand better the interrelationships of context and action. It is especially useful where existing theories fail to explain observed phenomena, enabling researchers to challenge existing accepted views and think beyond conventional paradigms.[33]

Essentially the approach is most commonly used to:

1 Generate new theory where little is already known.

2 Provide a fresh perspective on existing knowledge, i.e. to supplement existing theories.

3 Challenge existing theories. Researchers may challenge or disagree with existing theories for two reasons. The first is based upon the substantive representation of what the theory explains, e.g. of how children respond to certain forms of advertising. The second may be based upon how the theory was created, i.e. the research approach, techniques or forms of analysis.

The grounded theory approach to analysing data

Grounded theory provides researchers with guidelines for analysing data at several points in the research process, not simply at an end point or 'analysis stage'. It involves the following four stages:[34]

Coding data in grounded theory
A form of shorthand that distils events and meanings without losing their essential properties.

1 Coding data. Grounded theory coding is at least a two-step process. It starts with an initial or open coding process, which forces the researchers to begin making broad analytical decisions about the data they are collecting. It moves on to more selective or focused coding in which the researchers use the most frequently appearing initial codes to synthesise and conceptualise large amounts of data. In essence, coding is a form of shorthand that distils events and meanings without losing their essential properties. During the coding process, researchers work through their collected data on a line-by-line basis, use 'active' terms or descriptors to define what is happening in the data, and ultimately follow leads in the initial coding through further data gathering. Throughout the process of coding in grounded theory, the researchers should regularly address the data, as they are built up and in their entirety, with the following list of questions. Attempting to answer these facilitates the questioning of how codes are defined, connected and subsumed into broader categories:[35]

a *What?* What is it about here? Which phenomenon is mentioned?

b *Who?* Which persons are involved? What roles do they play? How do they interact?

c *How?* Which aspects of the phenomenon are mentioned (or not mentioned)?

d *When? How long? Where?* Time, course, location?

e *How much? How strong?* Aspects of intensity.

f *Why?* Which reasons are given or can be reconstructed?

g *What for?* With what intention, to what purpose?

h *By which?* Means, tactics and strategies for reaching that goal.

Memo writing
Loosely written notes through to fully formed analytical arguments which are added to the original data and interpretations.

2 Memo writing. Memo writing links coding to the writing of a first draft of the analysis. This stage helps researchers to: define the properties of the categories that they have created, specify conditions under which each category has developed, note the impact of each category and the interrelationships with other categories. Memos can be loosely written notes to fully formed analytical arguments which are added to the original data and interpretations. The process of memo writing helps the researcher to achieve the following:[36]

a Stop and think about what is emerging from the data.

b Generate ideas to explore through other means of collecting data.

c Reflect upon gaps and missed opportunities in earlier interviews and observations.

d Reflect upon the meanings and impact of personal field notes.

e Treat coded data as distinct categories to analyse.

f Clarify categories, through their definitions, properties, distinctive elements, consequences and interconnectivity with other categories.

g Make explicit and constant comparisons of data with data, category with category, concept with concept.

Theoretical sampling
Data gathering driven by concepts derived from evolving theory and based on the concept of 'making comparisons'.

3 Theoretical sampling. This concept was introduced in Chapter 6 in our discussion of the differences between a positivist and interpretivist approach to research. This type of sampling is not designed to represent a chosen population, but to develop theory by seeking out new data. The process of gathering more data is driven by the challenges in building categories and concepts that are derived from evolving theory. It is based on the notion of seeking out different situations and learning from the comparisons that can be made. Theoretical sampling helps researchers to construct and discard hypotheses and theoretical explanations of the data they are immersed in. Its purpose is to encourage researchers to go to places, people or events that will maximise their opportunities to discover variations among concepts. By generating more focused data to fill in any gaps in emerging categories and concepts, the whole process of theory building becomes more precise, explanatory and predictive. The process of theoretical sampling helps the researcher to achieve the following:[37]

Integrating analysis
Creating an order and connectivity that is seen to be emerging from memos.

a Define gaps within and between emerging categories that their coding suggests.

b Discover variation within these categories.

c Develop the validity of categories and their interconnections.

d Seek out and gather more focused and rich data.

e Seek out and gather other theoretical frameworks that may help to explain what is emerging in the data.

4 Integrating analysis. Producing more focused and well-developed memos as the analysis proceeds should enable researchers to produce theory that is clear and well validated.

Researchers should aim to integrate the memos they have crafted in order to reflect the theoretical direction of their analysis or stages of a process. They have to create the order (how do the ideas fit together?) and the connectivity (what order makes the most sense?) that they see emerging from their memos. The process of integrating the analysis helps the researchers to achieve the following:

a   Sort the memos, usually done by the titles of categories.

b   Map out a number of ways to order the memos.

c   Choose an order that works for the analysis and whoever is going to use and benefit from the emergent theory.

d   Create clear links between categories.

When ordering memos, researchers should consider whether a particular order reflects or challenges the logic of the experiences of participants and their target audiences of decision-makers. A balance needs to be made between both parties, which may mean collapsing categories for clarity and ease of reading.

Limitations of grounded theory

Grounded theory has been criticised for its failure to acknowledge implicit theories which guide researchers in the early stages of their work. Grounded theory researchers argue that such guidance may constrain their observations, forcing them to question and observe a particular setting from a narrow perspective. The downside of claiming to have such an approach is that it may be extremely difficult to ignore theories that may be embedded into researchers' ways of thinking. It may also be counterproductive to ignore relevant theories (used with a healthy dose of scepticism) that could be useful in creating focus in gathering and interpreting data. Another major criticism of grounded theory is that the process can degenerate into a fairly empty building of categories, with a great abundance of description, especially when aided by data analysis software.[38]

Content analysis

Content analysis
The objective, systematic and quantitative description of the manifest content of a communication.

In qualitative research, **content analysis** is one of the classical procedures for analysing textual material, forms of communication and images rather than behaviour or physical objects. The focus of the analysis may range from the narrative or images held in brochures or advertising copy, to dialogues held in interview data. Primarily the objective of content analysis is to 'reduce' the data, to simplify by summarising and structuring the data according to rules derived from existing theory. In effect, even though a researcher may be working with qualitative data, content analysis should be classified as a quantitative technique based upon classifying and 'counting'. Content analysis is seen by many as an 'objective', systematic and quantitative description of the manifest content of a communication.[39] The term 'content analysis' is set to include observation as well as analytic activity. The unit of analysis may be words (different words or types of words in the message), characters (individuals or objects), themes (propositions), space and time measures (length or duration of the message) or topics (subject of the message). Analytical categories for classifying the units are developed, and the communication is broken down according to prescribed rules. Marketing research applications involve observing and analysing the content or message of advertisements, newspaper articles, TV and radio programmes and the like. The following example illustrates an application and process of content analysis that was visually based.

Food advertising to children[40]

Content analysis was used to provide descriptive statistics of incidence and a thematic analysis of messages contained in a sample of food advertisements in Australia during children's TV programming. Three weeks' data were collected (Monday to Friday on Channel 10 from 7 to 8.30 a.m. and Saturday on Channel 7 from 7 to 9 a.m.) from the two Perth commercial TV channels with morning children's programming. The data were then independently coded by two researchers using a highly detailed coding instrument that provided an exhaustive list of predetermined options to increase inter-coder reliability. Pilot testing was carried out on a selection of advertisements that were not included in the final sample. Each advertisement was viewed first in its entirety without undertaking any coding, then all spoken and written text was transcribed onto the coding form and a summary of the story and events generated. The advertisement was then viewed several times to capture the information required on the coding instrument. Next, the results were compared across the two coders' output. There was almost complete agreement, with just a few discrepancies related to the food groups to which certain packaged foods belonged. These discrepancies were resolved after investigation of the products' ingredients, resulting in complete coder agreement. After the frequencies were tabulated for each code, the ad descriptions and summaries were analysed qualitatively to develop themes relating to the advertisement content. This involved constant iterations between the data and emerging themes to ensure soundness of fit. The 28.5 hours of children's TV programming sampled contained 950 advertisements. This equated to more than 33 advertisements per hour of TV viewed. These included 212 advertisements for food products and represented 30 discrete advertising campaigns. Several of the 30 campaigns were repeated many times, often appearing twice in the same break. When categorised into the National Health and Medical Research Council's food groups, the foods advertised to children were diametrically opposed to the foods recommended for children.

Content analysis has several virtues.[41] First of all, it is a standardised technique that permits the processing of large amounts of data covering long time spans. It is an unobtrusive research method, avoiding the problems of researcher effects on the data that are inherent in interpretative research methods such as in-depth interviewing.

Limitations of content analysis

Content analysis has its shortcomings; the most serious involve the issues of manifest content, data fragmentation and quantification. For qualitative researchers, these set limits on the usefulness of the method for the analysis of visual representations:[42]

1 *Manifest content*. A crucial requirement to the success of content analysis is that the established categories of analysis are sufficiently precise to enable different coders to arrive at the same results when the same body of material (e.g. advertising copy) is examined. Thus, manifest content refers to what may be seen to be manifestly apparent in the established categories of any communication. This means that in coding the meanings in any communication a clearly defined category system must plainly state the characteristics of content, there can be no implicit or hidden meanings from the coding operation. For some analysts,[43] the insistence upon coding only manifest content is too restrictive. The essence of their argument is that excessive emphasis on a standardised approach can result in reliability being attained at the expense of validity. The significance of the message may lie more in its context than in its manifest content.

2   *Data fragmentation.* By virtue of the constraint of focusing upon manifest content, the tendency is to break up communications into their elements, and it is solely the presence, absence or frequency of these elements that is deemed relevant to the investigation. This categorisation isolates those elements of the communication determined by the researcher's analytical framework or theory. This process de-contextualises the message in a communication, a process described as losing the phenomenon, or failing to respect the original right of the data.[44]

3   *Quantification.* It has been argued that content analysis is essentially a quantitative research technique and that applying qualitative considerations in the technique risks its objectivity and its systematic nature. The strength of the technique lies in allowing the selection and rational organisation of categories to condense the substantive meanings of a communication, with an aim to testing assumptions or hypotheses. If the aim of a study were to count frequencies in order to test hypotheses about communications, then the technique has much to offer. In this case it could be argued that the requirements of objectivity and a systematic approach should be the prime aim of the content analyst, and that the issue of manifest content be treated on a case-by-case basis. When examining individual cases and contexts, the presence or absence of a 'theme' may be measured, but not the frequency with which it occurs in the communication. What the essence is of that 'theme' takes the method into the realms of qualitative research.[45]

Semiotics

Semiotics
The study of signs in the context of consumer experience.

We have described a range of different qualitative techniques and approaches that primarily focus on the participants or the consumers, questioning and observing them in a direct or indirect manner. Semiotics takes a different approach in that consumers are not viewed as independent, self-determining agents, making their own choices. Rather, consumers are viewed as products of culture, constructed and largely determined by the popular culture within which they live. Consumer needs and aspirations are seen as not being the result of freely made choices of the individual, but a reflection of the surrounding cultural discourses. Semiotics therefore moves the researcher's focus towards the cultural context of the consumer, including both popular culture and the marketing context.[46] Semiotics combines knowledge and research techniques from across a spectrum of disciplines, including linguistics, psychology, anthropology, cultural studies and the visual arts. It analyses data such as paintings and photography that some other qualitative research methods do not tackle so well.[47] It is based on a detailed analysis of language and images which untangle how meaning is conveyed as well as what that meaning is. A semiotic approach can be integrated with qualitative techniques that may generate much visual data, such as ethnography. This link is illustrated in the following example.

| Real research | **Pushing the glamour button**[48] |

Unilever wished to grow the Rexona deodorant brand (**www.rexona.com**) in Russia. To generate consumer insight for its brand development, Unilever undertook a qualitative research approach, using ethnography and semiotics within a creative workshop environment. The semiotics input gave it useful ways of thinking around issues and an inspiration for future communications. Uncovering some of the essential codes that underpinned Russian attitudes around identity, femininity and social status, semiotic methods led to a deeper understanding of deodorant consumers. The most influential aspect of Russian culture identified by semiotics was around the issue of femininity. Unilever noted that 'Prada was the new Pravda'. That glamour was the new one-party ideology of modern Russian culture. Qualitative research had already identified Russian women's ambivalent attitudes towards the affluent glamour of the Moscow elite. In Unilever's semiotic work they expanded on this contradictory state of admiration, jealousy, aspiration and loathing. It seemed that the 'glamour button' was the right one to push. While most Russian women, as elsewhere in the world, cannot afford to buy into the high-fashion world of Gucci and Prada, it was felt that the use of deodorant could provide a valuable displacement activity around glamour. On the one hand, 'regular' women could appreciate the notion that the richest, most glamourous Muscovites could be let down by their body odour. On a more positive note, the representation of glamour with a degree of accessibilty offered women a chance to 'buy into' the fame and beauty without having to spend three months' wages on a handbag.

Semiotic researchers aim to develop a richer and more holistic understanding of consumers by unearthing the cultural frameworks that underpin their behaviour. This can work across diverse global markets, supporting the design of brands and all the creative output that shapes brands in different cultures.[49] In approaching a research problem, a conventional qualitative researcher might ask, 'Why does Frank buy Pot Noodle?' The semiotic researcher would be more likely to ask, 'How does consumer culture give meaning to Pot Noodle, and what are these meanings?' The semiotic researcher might argue that if we can answer these questions, we will be able to make a good guess not just at why Frank buys it, but also why anyone buys it. This is because behavioural meanings are constructed within popular culture, and consumers are influenced and constrained by this cultural context. An understanding of the broader cultural context is something that semiotic analysis is uniquely well placed to provide, because it focuses on the culture and not just on the consumer.[50]

Examples of how semiotics can help marketing decision-makers are:[51]

- Mapping out a new market or a whole field of cultural activity.
- Seeing opportunities to position new brands.
- Analysing how different aspects of marketing communications work together, and the means to create synergies across different media.
- Evaluating in-store developments and harmonising the different aspects of marketing communications.
- Diagnosing problems with brand or marketing communications.
- Providing models and guidelines for successful brand communications, indicating the key signifiers within the relevant context.
- Understanding the process of encoding and decoding more precisely, to minimise the potential for misunderstanding between the marketer and the consumer.

As can be seen from the above list, semiotics can play a major role in the development of a wide array of marketing communications. In terms of conducting a qualitative analysis of marketing communications, the approach goes into far more depth in comparison with content analysis. Semioticians investigate the subtext of communication. They begin with the brand, combing through the cultural connotations of advertising imagery and language, the colour, shape and forms of corporate identity, where the brand is distributed and how it is displayed. Then they look outwards to the consumer's world, hunting for shifts in cultural meaning – how concepts such as masculinity, heroism or indulgence have changed over time and how they might be reinterpreted.[52] To illustrate this point, the following questions may be set by a researcher examining the advertising of a particular brand, looking at the past, the potential and the competition. The questions would be directed at the text, sounds and images of the advertisements, the wide breadth of qualitative data:[53]

- What are the major signifiers (i.e. the material signs – what it is)?
- What signifieds (i.e. the conceptual sign – what it means) might they be creating and to whom?
- How do the advertisements work on a symbolic/metaphorical and on a product/metonymical (literal) level?
- How do the form and content of the advertisement work together?
- What codes (i.e. bundles of signs) do the advertisements use?
- How does the advertisement measure up to the brand's historical codes and those of its competitors?
- How do the advertisements work in relation to the brand's history and its futures?
- Is the advertisement using a dominant (everyday, mainstream), emergent (leading edge, culturally dynamic) or residual (old fashioned, lacking in energy) set of codes or are residual codes being applied in an emergent way?
- What kinds of discourse or discourses are apparent, e.g. postmodernism, feminism, spirituality?

This set of questions and processes will illuminate the advertising material under development. They will help the researcher to understand more completely the material that viewers will be evaluating. However, this may not be readily achievable using a single researcher. To maximise the potential of semiotics, an action research approach (described in Chapter 6) may offer the best results. This would involve taking a more facilitative and involving approach; sharing the actual techniques and questions of semiotic analysis with researchers and decision-makers working together towards the co-creation of knowledge. This would be more open and interactive. Semiotics specialists would be vital to the process, but as facilitators and mentors in a workshop style of joint working, helping clients identify and understand the way forward themselves. A more involving approach also provides the tools to recode, enabling the client to move from insight to the successful implementation of new strategy in any of the applications above.[54]

Limitations of semiotics

Although it is able to analyse a great breadth of interrelated qualitative data, there are four core criticisms of semiotics:[55]

1 *Reliability.* The main criticism of semiotics lies in how reliable or replicable it is.[56] Although an individual analyst's interpretation may be very insightful and could be a valid representation of cultural influences upon the consumer, there is little guarantee that another analyst would come to the same conclusion about the relevant codes or structures.

2 *Qualitative dataset.* In practice it can be hard to assemble the relevant data to analyse, given that there is usually no discourse or discussion as may be assembled with a series of focus groups or in-depth interviews.

3 *Logic of interpretation.* It is not usually clear how the analyst has arrived at an interpretation. It must be accepted that there is no unique way to interpret text or other types of qualitative data. On this score, Derrida[57] makes the point that no single interpretation can

ever claim to be the final one.[58] In the case of semiotics, in many instances an interpretation seems to rely upon a shared knowledge of a cultural background and intuition, which may be valid but extremely difficult to validate. This is where an action research approach can help, where the team of researchers and marketing decision-makers share and 'own' the interpretation.

4 *Consumer theory.* The position of the consumer can be unclear in semiotic analysis. In principle, the consumer is seen as passive, determined by culture and unable to break out of their contextual frame.[59] Many consumer theorists would disagree with this view, giving the consumer a more active role in interpreting, accepting or resisting the brand's semiotically encoded meanings.

International marketing research

If one were to take the very naïve view of qualitative data analysis being to feed data into an analysis package, and to wait for processed data to emerge, then international analysis would focus purely upon issues of language and translation. Such a perspective of qualitative analysis would ignore the context and process of collecting data and the role that these factors play in interpreting the meaning that emerges from interviews and observations. As discussed at the start of this chapter, qualitative researchers need an acute awareness of how they 'see' – which affects the way they pose questions and interpret answers.

Consumers in any country use their social and cultural frames of reference to interpret questions posed to them by qualitative researchers and to present a response. Likewise, qualitative researchers use their social and cultural frames to present questions and interpret answers. If the researcher and the participant share the same or similar social and cultural frames of reference, the analysis and interpretation of the data can be relatively straightforward. If the qualitative researcher goes into an international market, there is the potential for big differences in social and cultural frames between the researcher and the researched. The qualitative researcher needs to

develop an understanding of the social and cultural frames of the types of participant in an international market. At the same time, qualitative researchers must have a strong awareness of their own social and cultural frames. Only when qualitative researchers have examined both perspectives can they start to interpret consumer responses.

The process is summarised by leading qualitative researchers Virginia Valentine and Malcolm Evans as:[60]

Consumers give a 'coded' version of the social and cultural relationship with products and brands that drive their 'feelings'. Because language (and language systems) are the medium of culture, the rules of language become the rules of the code. Qualitative research then becomes a matter of working with the code through understanding the rules of language.

Thus, simple literal translations of transcripts of interviews from international markets entered into a qualitative data analysis package are doomed to failure. The following example examines some of the challenges faced in translating and interpreting Japanese culture.

Real research   Research insights into Japanese culture[61]

International researcher Neil Cantle offers the following views of the challenges involved in interpreting Japanese culture. He sees Japanese as a very ambiguous language and this ambiguity, *'Aimai sa'*, is celebrated. Meaning is often implied or understood contextually. Even the simplest of words can be ambiguous. There is even no direct translation for 'yes' or 'no'. The word *'Hai'*, usually understood to mean 'yes' in the West, actually just means 'I have heard you' and a refusal or negative statement is usually implied. Omitting parts of a sentence can also heighten this feeling of ambiguity. In Japanese, the subject, verb and tense do not have to be explicitly stated. Meaning is often interpreted in terms of context and tone. Not finishing sentences and understanding incomplete sentences is an art form to be embraced and practised. Interpreting meaning plays an important part in conversation, and spoken Japanese can be a tricky business even for native speakers. From a research perspective this means that it is very important to find an experienced bilingual and bicultural researcher able not only to interpret what is being said, but also to communicate that back to you. It is often remarked that the Japanese do not give much away in body language, facial expressions or gestures, but many Japanese say the same thing about the Westerners. It is almost impossible to learn to interpret Japanese non-verbal communication in a short space of time. Even for native speakers a tilt of the head can mean 'not really' but also 'it's OK'. It is best to ensure a native Japanese speaker interprets this for you.

Understanding the rules of language and understanding oneself are vital for the qualitative researcher to interpret interviews and observations. As the rules of language, with the social and cultural forces that shape those rules, become more alien to the researcher in international markets, the task of analysis and meaningful interpretation becomes more difficult.

Ethics in marketing research

It is interesting to note that within the ESOMAR code of conduct, little reference is made to what is deemed the ethical practice of data analysis, be that quantitative or qualitative. This is understandable, as the chief concern for the marketing research industry is how participants are handled, i.e. the process of eliciting data from them. Care must be taken to ensure that the precious resource of participants is not misled or manipulated. However, with the emergence of social media research techniques, the ability to gather characteristics and views of consumers from multiple sources has generated new ethical challenges. The following example illustrates how multiple qualitative data sources can be utilised and the differing attitudes to these sources.

Real research   Sitting in the chair of King Canute[62]

The use of Internet content in marketing research is abundant and growing. The use of websites, blog postings, microblogs such as Twitter, photography sites such as Flickr, video sites such as YouTube, social platforms such as Facebook, MySpace, Yahoo and MSN, are generating huge qualitative datasets. These are made even more valuable by the use of data aggregators such as FriendFeed (**www.friendfeed.com**). It is possible to tie these separate platforms together and monitor the same person using any or all of these websites. The tools for monitoring and analysing these are also many and varied, from cookies which are locked to the individual machine, to content searches to pick up every incidence of a particular word used in the last 24 hours, to keyword searches which use the keyword tags that blog posters put on their postings so that they can be found more easily. None of these require the permission of the person who has posted the data and there is no sense in which online anonymity can be guaranteed. Many decision-makers and researchers talk about online content as public, accessible for anybody to use in whatever way they think fit. The analysis of Internet content is usually carried out without the codes of conduct, disciplines and strictures familiar to research practitioners. The industry of mining Internet content bears little resemblance to a marketing research paradigm that gathers samples, validates them and asks participants questions in tried and tested manners. In analysing this difference between an emerging and established research industry, John Griffiths (**www.planningaboveandbeyond.com**) speculates that by 2020 research will be more in the hands of clients or decision-makers who will be doing it themselves. Companies will be researching their stakeholders continually without needing constantly to recruit, requalify and validate them. Researchers will still be involved but as analysts and insight specialists who 'tune the data' and add value to it. A current and similar approach is used by Tribe Research (**www.triberesearch.com. au**) in Australia who considers a company's entire range of stakeholders – clients, suppliers and employees – as needing to have a voice in the decision-making process. Tribe Research developed Tribal Tool-Kit which, while survey based, has been developed also to use broader applications to analyse outputs of website pages, text and Tweets; or ask people from these spaces and client databases to provide feedback. What is radical about Tribe Research's approach is that it has treated all stakeholders as effectively an internal audience inside the company perimeter.

With quantitative data, as will be seen in Chapters 18 to 24, there are many established and consistent procedures of analysis. With qualitative data, even though there exists a broad framework to manage analysis procedures, there does not exist a body of consistent and established procedures of analysis. The difficulty in establishing consistent procedures lies primarily in the great diversity of data that can be included in the analysis procedure. Go back to the 'Data assembly' subsection and the example above to see the types and nature of qualitative data and it is easy to see why this is so. Combining the researcher's notes, transcripts of interviews, pictures, audio and video recordings and mood boards does not lead to a structured process. It is a messy process that owes much to individual patience, creativity and vision.

In searching for support of ethical practice to cope with such a 'messy process', there is one area of support that comes from the Code of Conduct of the Market Research Society in the UK. In its section 'Analysis and reporting of findings', Rules B.56 to 58 state:[63]

B.56 Members must ensure that reports and presentations clearly distinguish between facts and interpretation.

B.57 Members must ensure that when interpreting data they make clear which data they are using to support their interpretation.

B.58 Members must ensure that qualitative reports and presentations accurately reflect the findings of the project in addition to the interpretations and conclusions.

The key element of these rules is that the researcher should be explicit about their interpretation of the data collected. This takes us back to the start when we discussed the self-reflection of the social and cultural values of researchers. If qualitative researchers fail or cannot be bothered to reflect upon their own values and cultural norms, their interpretation of qualitative data may be extremely biased. It therefore follows that, for the most valid as well as the most ethical interpretation of qualitative data, researchers must continually reflect and test the extent and effect of their social and cultural values.

Digital applications in marketing research

A major problem for the qualitative researcher is the sheer volume of data that may be collected. One simple solution to encapsulate and display the narrative of qualitative research is the use of a word cloud. This approach counts the number of times a particular word is used in any document or numbers of documents. This does not analyse the data, but presents an image that can be powerful in sparking debate and sharing ideas in subsequent analysis. The process can draw data together from a great array of sources and create a graphical representation of word counts with great speed. The following example presents an example of the use of a word cloud.

Real research	WordCloud Generator

WordCloud Generator from Cobalt Sky (**www.cobalt-sky.com**) allows researchers to view verbatim responses in a word cloud, indicating the number of occurrences of each word, with the ability to drill down to the underlying source comments. WordCloud Generator allows researchers to: specify minimum occurrences of words for inclusion; specify minimum word lengths; define dictionaries of words to discard; count of verbatims containing a word regardless of number of occurrences; customise the colours used in the output. The word cloud is generated as an HTML page which is self-contained and can be distributed to other users. WordCloud Generator is multi-language and will handle input from a variety of sources; currently the tool reads directly from Excel files and is available as a plug-in to SPSS's Desktop Reporter. The following example is a simple illustration based upon the frequency of words used in newspaper reporting of the 2010 World Cup. Word clouds can analyse data from literature and secondary data sources, responses to open-ended questions and interview transcripts.

Google World Cup 2010 Summary

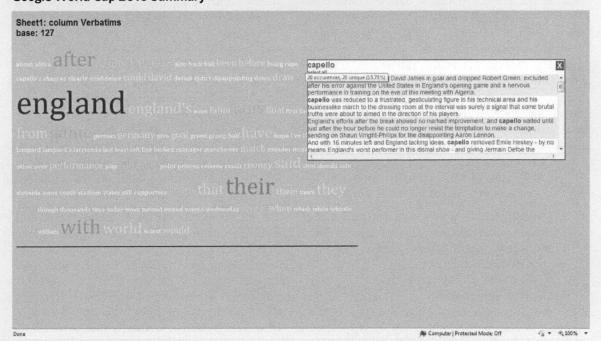

World Cup Summary 2010 – Sent to Wordle

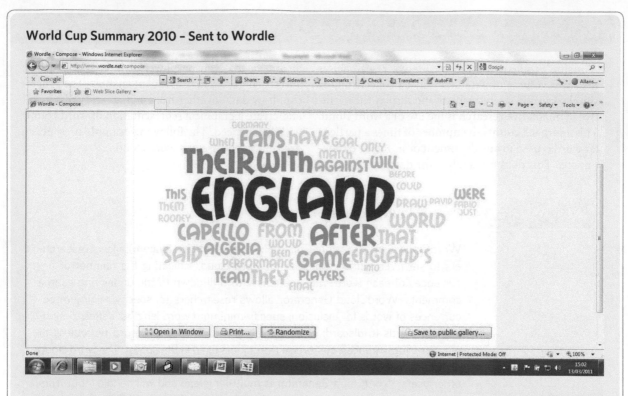

Qualitative data analysis goes beyond the words in interview transcripts. In an attempt to 'step into the shoes' of target consumers, a whole array of questions, probes, observations, answers and personal notes have to be analysed. As with quantitative data analyses, it is possible to complete qualitative analyses without the aid of a computer. With quantitative analysis, it would be a rare occurrence to analyse data without a computer. With qualitative analysis it is not so rare; many researchers still believe in a 'hands-on' immersion in the rich data they have collected. Using the computer should provide speed, memory, ease of data access and the ability to transform and manipulate data in many ways. Overall it should allow a much more efficient and ultimately effective process, as the researcher's effort may be focused upon generating the most effective support for decision-makers as quickly as possible rather than upon laborious administrative tasks. The following list summarises qualitative research activities that may be supported by the use of computers:

1 *Field notes.* Making notes before, during and after interviews and observations. Writing and editing these notes if needed as part of a data display to justify a particular interpretation.
2 *Transcripts.* Building up transcripts to represent the discourse in interviews.
3 *Coding.* Attaching keywords to chunks of data or text.

4 *Storage, search and retrieval.* Keeping data in an organised manner, so that relevant segments of data or text can be located, pulled out and evaluated.
5 *Connection.* Linking relevant data segments with each other.
6 *Memos.* Writing up reflective comments that can be 'pasted' onto relevant codes and connections.
7 *Data display.* Placing selected or reduced data in a condensed and organised format using a spreadsheet matrix or network. The display can be part of the development of the analysis or in the final vision produced by the researcher.
8 *Drawing conclusions and verification.* Aiding the researcher to interpret the data display and to test or confirm findings.
9 *Theory building.* Developing systematic and conceptually coherent explanations of findings that are meaningful to marketing decision-makers.
10 *Reporting.* Presenting interim and final reports of the findings in a written and oral manner.

Many of these tasks can be performed with readily available word-processing, spreadsheet and presentation packages. Many researchers may be very comfortable using such packages to gather and record data and to present findings. What may be new to many researchers is the use of proprietary software to help with the technical integration of data assembly, reduction, display and verification. Improvements in the functions and power of software that copes with this technical integration occur at a rapid pace. To see examples of different qualitative data analysis packages, download demos and cases and evaluate how applicable they may be to a particular qualitative technique. Visit the following websites:

Qualitative data analysis software	Website
NVivo and XSight	**www.qsrinternational.com**
Atlas.ti	**www.atlasti.com**
C-I-SAID	**www.code-a-text.co.uk**

We present an NVivo software demonstration that can be downloaded from the website for this book. The following example illustrates why Progressive Sports Technologies (www.progressivesports.co.uk) use NVivo and the qualitative techniques that are supported by this software. We recommend that you visit the QSR website to evaluate descriptions of applications and cases of NVivo applications. You can then choose when you wish to start working with your NVivo demo. Remember that this demo has the full suite of NVivo features and that, once it is installed, you will be able to use it for a period of 90 days.

Real research	**Taking sporting equipment to a new standard[66]**

Progressive Sports Technologies Ltd is a UK based sports innovation consultancy that specialises in the research and design of cutting edge fitness equipment for major global sports brands like Nike, Reebok and Speedo. In a research project on elite sporting products they used NVivo to conduct qualitative data analysis. The sport and fitness sector is a highly competitive industry where athletes and participants search for the latest training advancements in order to gain improved results. Whether training at an elite level or working out for general health and fitness, sporting participants demand goods and services that will better help them achieve their goals. The biggest challenge for sporting manufacturers is working out exactly what elite athletes want from their equipment. Understanding what this elite group wants is more difficult than it sounds. Athletes who are at the top of their game and striving for the smallest improvement in results may not necessarily be able to articulate where they want changes made. Traditionally, sporting equipment designers have first created prototypes of new products and then asked athletes for their feedback, in order to fine tune the equipment. At Progressive, they've turned this process on its head by opening up direct communication channels between their designers and the elite athletes via a new perception study. In Progressive's perception study, detailed interviews were conducted with 25 elite athletes across two countries. By providing the athletes with four distinct products within the same category, such as four very different pairs of running shoes, each participant was asked to describe their perceptions towards the different products in great detail. All interviews were recorded, transcribed and entered into NVivo. The software was used to group all keywords and themes that the athletes were describing. Numerous athletes were tested on multiple days, in different venues and countries. The software was used as an archive of all the testing carried out. The data files had in the order of 50,000 words relating to the athletes' product perceptions. The software was seen as a huge time saver and allowed Progressive to organise the work in a clear and logical manner. The time saved was huge, the process definitely halved the sorting and evaluation time. In addition, the audiovisual capabilities available in NVivo allowed Progressive to import all files under one umbrella, including sound and movie files for future studies.

Qualitative data analysis packages do not automate the analysis process, nor is that their purpose. The process of coding, as described in the data verification section, depends upon the interpretations made by the researcher. The overall description, model or theory that emerges from the analysis also depends upon interpretations made by the researcher. No analysis package can perform such interpretations. Qualitative data analysis is not formulaic; it requires an approach that gives quick feedback to the researcher on the results of emergent questions. This involves an iterative cycle of reflection and innovation, which means total interaction between the researcher and the computer. So, rather than seeing analysis as an automated process, the purpose of software is to aid the researcher to analyse data in a systematic and thorough manner. The researcher seeks patterns, meanings and interconnections in the qualitative data. This can be conducted manually, but by using software the researcher can manipulate the data far more efficiently to help see patterns, meanings and interconnections and ultimately to develop theory. In summary, software packages offer the qualitative researcher the following advantages.

Advantages of computer-assisted qualitative data analysis

1 *Speed.* The speed at which programs can carry out sorting procedures on large volumes of data is fast. This gives the researcher more time to think about the meaning of data, enabling rapid feedback of the results of particular analytic ideas so that new ones can be formulated. Analysis becomes more devoted to creative and intellectual tasks, less immersed in routine.

2 *Rigour.* Rigour adds to the trust placed in research findings. In this context it means counting the number of times things occur as well as demonstrating that negative incidences have been located rather than selecting anecdotes that support a particular interpretation.

3 *Team.* In collaborative research projects where researchers need to agree on the meaning of codes, a check can easily be made of whether team members are interpreting segments in the same way. This is particularly useful as coding moves from the more descriptive and mundane codes to ones that reflect broader theoretical concerns. Researchers can pass coded interviews between them, and compare the results.

4 *Sampling.* It is easy to keep track of who *has* been interviewed, compared with the intentions of who *should* be interviewed. Beyond the sampling of individuals is the concept of theoretical sampling, i.e. the inclusion of events that corroborate or con-

tradict developing theory. As researchers have more time to spend on creative and intellectual tasks, they can develop stronger descriptions and theories and strengthen the validity of their views by ensuring they have sampled sufficient incidences.[64]

It must be reinforced that software packages cannot interpret and find meaning in qualitative data. The programs do facilitate, and in some cases automate, the identification and coding of text. But there is sometimes a false assumption that identification and coding are simple and unproblematic, and critical evaluation and scrutiny of coded segments and code counts are not needed. By facilitating quick analyses which focus on quantitative category relationships, the software may discourage more time-consuming, in-depth interpretations. Thus while the programs are intended as a means of allowing the researcher to stay close to the data, their misuse can have the unintended result of distancing the researcher from the data. As discussed earlier, many decision-makers who use qualitative marketing research do not question how analysis is completed, or indeed why it should be completed. The following arguments illustrate the nature of their concerns.[65]

Disadvantages of computer-assisted qualitative data analysis

1 *Mechanistic data analysis.* The computer cannot replace the creative process expected of the qualitative researcher. The researcher can evaluate the interrelated play on particular words, the tone of voice or the gestures of a particular participant. The sensitivity towards these relationships and connections can be lost in a mechanistic search for statements.

2 *Loss of the overview.* The researcher may be seduced into concentrating on the detail of individual chunks of data and assigning codes to the data. This focus may detract from the overall context that is so vital to identify and name chunks of data. Making sense of codes can be greatly facilitated by an ability to visualise the data in their entirety.

3 *Obsession with volume.* Given the ability to manipulate large amounts of data, there may be a push to increase the number of interviews. This may be counterproductive in that the emphasis should be on the interrelated qualities of:

a individual participants

b the data capture process.

4 *Exclusion of non-text data.* As noted earlier, qualitative 'text' can include notes, observations, pictures and music that make up the total 'picture' or

holistic representation of individuals. Many programs can only cope with the narrative of questions and answers recorded in transcripts (though rapid developments have been made to overcome this shortcoming). The following example illustrates how 'non-text data' can impact upon the holistic representation of individuals. This example is also relevant when thinking of data captured when conducting qualitative research in a face-to-face context compared with online media.

Qualitative analysis software developers have recognised the above limitations and have gone to great pains to overcome them. One of the trade-offs faced by software developers in overcoming these limitations is the user-friendliness of their programs compared with the sophistication of being able to manipulate and represent the structure that may lie in multifarious data. As qualitative researchers use and learn how to generate the most from the software, user-friendliness may take a lesser though not ignored role. Experienced qualitative researchers can demand more sophistication to match the realities of coping with qualitative data. For the novice qualitative researcher the packages may seem daunting, but this problem is analogous to an initial exposure to sophisticated survey design packages such as SNAP or statistical packages such as SPSS. In all cases researchers need to appreciate how the software may serve them and work through the examples and cases, to experiment and to build up their knowledge and confidence.

Real research	Measuring facial expressions[66]

There is a strong connection between how decisions are made by the brain and how emotions are made on the face. Facial muscles have a direct connection to the brain, revealing involuntary emotions expressed in a fifth of a second, too quickly for the person to be aware of them and often too rapidly to detect without the aid of video analysis. It follows that fleeting involuntary emotions are a window into the decisive moment when the 'emotional brain' is at work. How far we can predict how the emotional brain will decide, on the basis of the unconsciously expressed emotions, is an open question. Dr John Habershon of Momentum Research (**www.momentumresearch.co.uk**) sought to clarify this by running a small-scale test on press advertising for the bank Lloyds TSB. The advertisement contained seven benefits of being with the bank, ranging from 24-hour telephone banking to the fact that the bank had more branches than any other in the UK. The question was, which of these statements impressed participants and had the potential to move to action, and which were merely nice-to-have features? During the course of the interview, each of the six partcipants was shown the individual benefits on a board as if they were read out. They were asked not to comment and their facial expressions were captured on video. The process was repeated, and this time, the participants were invited to express their views. The non-verbal responses were analysed using a visual coding system comprising 10 expressions signifying engagement, ranging from the angle of the head, through to the gaze and the movement of the mouth. It was apparent when a participant paid attention, listened, looked and showed approval of a proposition. Six signs of lack of engagement were used, ranging from a lack of focus on the proposition, to small signs of displeasure in the brow and mouth. The results of the test were clear. Three of the benefits engaged the participants, provoking an immediate emotional response. Their verbal responses broadly reflected approval, but with a less defined difference between the 'nice-to-have' benefits and those with emotional power. The future of this technique could see many computerised applications, ranging from the pleasure of car driving to controlling video games. The Fraunhofer Institute in Germany (**www.fraunhofer.de/en**) is working on technology to capture responses to outdoor poster advertising.

Summary

Qualitative researchers should reflect upon how their social and cultural values affect the way they perceive and observe target participants. These reflections should be built up as field notes as the whole process of data gathering develops and evolves. These notes form a key source of qualitative data to complement the broad array of qualitative data generated from interviews and observations. To successfully draw together a valid interpretation, qualitative data analysis must be set in the context of a theoretical understanding of the issue being researched and an understanding of the marketing decision-makers' use of the findings.

The first stage of the process of analysing qualitative data involves assembling data in their rich and varying formats. The second stage involves reducing the data, i.e. selecting, classifying and connecting data that are believed to be of the greatest significance. A key element of this stage is the concept of coding. The third stage involves displaying data, i.e. using graphical means to display the meaning and structure that a researcher sees in the data collected. The final stage involves verifying the data. The researcher aims to generate the most valid interpretation of these data, which may be supported by existing theories or through the concept of theoretical sampling. The stages of analysis seem quite distinct but in reality they are totally dependent upon each other.

Three of the most commonly used approaches to analysing qualitative marketing research lie in grounded theory, content analysis and semiotics. Grounded theory is an approach that develops theory which is ultimately grounded in the behaviour, words and action of those under study. Content analysis is used to 'reduce' qualitative data, to simplify them by summarising and structuring the data according to rules derived from existing theory. Semiotics combines research techniques from across a spectrum of disciplines, including linguistics, psychology, anthropology, cultural studies and the visual arts. It helps to analyse visual data that some other qualitative research methods do not tackle so well.

The qualitative researcher needs to develop an understanding of the social and cultural frames of target participants in international markets. At the same time, qualitative researchers must have a strong awareness of their own social and cultural frames. Only when they have examined both perspectives can they effectively interpret consumer responses. There are ethical implications of the extent to which researchers seek the valid interpretations they can make of the qualitative data they have gathered. With the explosion of qualitative data afforded by social media exchanges, the researcher faces new ethical challenges. Consumers may be more open and expressive through social media sources, which can be of great benefit to researchers, but protecting their anonymity represents a great challenge. To be able to cope with the great amount of data generated from qualitative techniques, a great variety of software packages are available. Used correctly, they can facilitate a speedy and rigorous exploration of qualitative data, allowing teams of researchers to perform creative and incisive analyses and interpretations. The main concern with the use of qualitative data analysis packages lies in the potential for them to be mechanistic and to encourage yet more interviews to be completed, sacrificing the quality of data capture.

Questions

1 How may the social and cultural background of researchers affect the way they:
   a gather qualitative data?
   b interpret the whole array of qualitative data they have gathered?

2 What is the significance of a qualitative researcher having a theoretical and marketing understanding of the subject they are researching?

3 Why should a qualitative researcher maintain a field notebook?

4 What should be recorded in a field notebook?

5 What may be classified as 'data' when assembling data as part of the data analysis process?

6 What does the word 'coding' mean in the context of qualitative data analysis? What problems do you see associated with the process of coding?

7 What are the advantages and disadvantages of handing over recordings of qualitative interviews to a typist who has taken no part in the interviews?

8 Evaluate the purpose of displaying qualitative data.

9 What advantages and disadvantages do you see in displaying qualitative data in a spreadsheet format?

10 Evaluate 'when' the stage of data verification should occur.

11 How may theoretical sampling aid the process of verification?

12 How may different types of software help in the whole process of qualitative data gathering and analysis?

13 Evaluate the main concerns that exist with the use of software in qualitative data analysis.

14 Why is the researcher's understanding of their social and cultural values particularly important in international marketing research?

15 Why does the interpretation of qualitative findings have ethical implications?

Exercises

1 You have been given the task of conducting a series of in-depth interviews about luxury cruises targeted at women of 50 years of age and over. What preparatory work could you do to understand the characteristics of this subject, the target group and how the target group relates to the subject?

2 You have just started to work for a major qualitative marketing research agency. The CEO notes that her researchers use a great variety of methods to keep field notes, ranging from scrappy notes taken at interviews to detailed diaries. You have been given the task of designing a format of field notes that will incorporate 'short notes made at the time of observation or interview', 'expanded notes made as soon as possible after each session of interviews or observations', 'a fieldwork journal to record problems and ideas that arise during each stage of fieldwork', and 'a provisional running record of analysis and interpretation'. Present the design and the case you would make to other researchers to use your format.

3   You have conducted a series of focus groups with 18 to 21 year olds about travelling home from evening events. As you complete each group, you ask participants to photograph significant events of their journeys home for the forthcoming weekend using their mobile phones. What would you do with the images that they send to you?

4   An ethnographic study is planned of young men using Lynx deodorant. Compare the relative merits of the qualitative data analysis packages ATLAS.ti (**www.atlasti.com**) and NVivo (**www.qsrinternational.com**) in terms of coping with the types of data that will be generated and the interpretations that will be performed.

5   In a small group discuss the following issues: 'Quantitative techniques of analysis and data display have no role to play in qualitative data analysis' and 'Theoretical sampling could never work in commercial marketing research given that it creates an open-ended agenda of issues to explore and participants to pursue.'

Video case exercise: Wild Planet

To what extent do you feel the gender of qualitative researchers has an impact upon how they interpret the differences between boys and girls playing with Wild Planet toys?

Notes

1. Murakami, H., *South of the Border, West of the Sun* (London: Harvill, 1999).

2. Interpreting narrative, i.e. the nature and scope of analysing literature, is a major subject area in its own right. For a simple introduction to the field, see Barry, P., *An introduction to literary and cultural theory* 3rd edn (Manchester: Manchester University Press, 2009).

3. Okazaki , S., 'Mobile finds girls' taste: Knorr's new product development', *Journal of Interactive Advertising* 9 (2) (Spring 2009), 32–39.

4. Stienstra, J. and van der Noort, W., 'Loser, hero or human being – are you ready for emergent truth?', ESOMAR, Best Methodology, Annual Congress, Montreal (September 2008).

5. For an example of the use of field notes in a qualitative study, see Drenten, J., Okleshen Peters, C. and Boyd Thomas, J., 'An exploratory investigation of the dramatic play of preschool children within a grocery store shopping context', *International Journal of Retail & Distribution Management* 36 (10) (2009), 831–855; Rubin, H.J. and Rubin, I.S., *Qualitative Interviewing: The art of hearing data* (Thousand Oaks, CA: Sage, 1995), 120.

6. Coffey, A. and Atkinson, P., *Making Sense of Qualitative Data: Complementary Research Strategies* (Thousand Oaks, CA: Sage, 1996), 10–11.

7. Spradley, J.P., *The Ethnographic Interview* (New York: Holt, Rinehart & Winston, 1979).

8. Southgate, N., 'Funny business, serious money', *Research* (March 2004), 28–30.

9. Prasad, S., 'Listening to the sounds of silence', ESOMAR, Asia Pacific, Kuala Lumpur (April 2010).

10. Snowden, D. and Stienstra, J., 'Stop asking questions: understanding how consumers make sense of it all', ESOMAR, Annual Congress, Berlin (September 2007); Ereaut, G., *Analysis and Interpretation in Qualitative Market Research* (London: Sage, 2002), 63.

11. Gordon, W. and Langmaid, R., *Qualitative Market Research: A practitioner's and buyer's guide* (Aldershot: Gower, 1988).

12. Ball, M.S. and Smith, G.W.H., *Analyzing visual data* (Newbury Park, CA: Sage, 1992), 9.

13. Verhaeghe, A., Van den Bergh, J. and Colin, V., 'Me myself and I: studying youngsters' identity by combining visual ethnography and netnography', ESOMAR, Qualitative Research, Istanbul (November 2008).

14. Brace-Govan, J., 'Participant photography in visual ethnography', *International Journal of Market Research* 49 (6) (2007), 735–750.

15. Coffey, A. and Atkinson, P., *Making Sense of Qualitative Data* (Thousand Oaks, CA: Sage, 1996), 26.

16. Rubin, H.J. and Rubin, I.S., *Qualitative Interviewing: The art of hearing data* (Thousand Oaks, CA: Sage, 1995), 238.

17. Hubermann, A.M. and Miles, M.B., 'Data management and analysis methods', in Denzin, N.K. and Lincoln, Y.S. (eds), *Handbook of Qualitative Research* (Thousand Oaks, CA: Sage, 1994), 428–444.

18. Weltzer-Ward, L., 'Content analysis coding schemes for online asynchronous discussion', *Campus-Wide Information Systems* 28 (1) (2011), 56–74; Roberts, M. and Pettigrew, S., 'A thematic content analysis of children's food advertising', *International Journal of Advertising* 26 (3) (2007), 357–367; Krippendorf, K., *Content Analysis: An Introduction to its Methodology* (Beverly Hills, CA: Sage, 1980).

19. Coffey, A. and Atkinson, P., *Making Sense of Qualitative Data: Complementary Research Strategies* (Thousand Oaks, CA: Sage, 1996), 29–30.

20. Miles, M.B. and Huberman, A.M., *Qualitative Data Analysis: An expanded sourcebook*, 2nd edn (Thousand Oaks, CA: Sage, 1994), 11.

21. This is a very basic overview of the different means to display qualitative data. For a fuller discussion, the following is recommended: Huberman, M. and Miles, M.B., *The Qualitative Researcher's Companion: Classic and Contemporary Readings* (Thousand Oaks, CA: Sage, 2002); and especially the five chapters devoted to data display in Miles, M.B. and Huberman, A.M., *Qualitative Data Analysis: An expanded sourcebook*, 2nd edn (Thousand Oaks, CA: Sage, 1994), 90–244.

22. This process is known as triangulation. For a fuller description of this topic, set in the context of researcher bias, see Schillewaert, N., De Ruyck, T. and Verhaeghe, A., 'Connected research – how market research can get the most out of semantic web waves', *International Journal of Market Research* 51 (1) (2009), 11–27; Griseri, P., *Management Knowledge: A Critical View* (Basingstoke: Palgrave, 2002), 60–78.

23. Fulton Suri, J. and Gibbs Howard, S., 'Going deeper, seeing further: enhancing ethnographic interpretations to reveal more meaningful opportunities for design', *Journal of Advertising Research* 46 (3) (September 2006), 246–250.

24. Silverman, D., *Doing Qualitative Research*, 3rd edn (London: Sage, 2009), 292–310.

25. Patton, M.Q., *Qualitative research and evaluation methods*, 3rd edn (Newbury Park, CA: Sage), 2002.

26. For a fuller explanation of validity in qualitative research, see Barnham, C., 'Qualis? The qualitative understanding of essence', *International Journal of Market Research* 52 (6) (2010), 757–773; Kirk, J. and Miller, M.L., *Reliability and Validity in Qualitative Research* (Newbury Park, CA: Sage, 1986).

27. Glaser, B.G. and Strauss, A.L., *The discovery of grounded theory* (Chicago: Aldine, 1967).

28. Locke, K., *Grounded theory in management research* (London: Sage, 2001), 1.

29. Goulding, C., *Grounded Theory: A practical guide for management, business and market researchers* (London: Sage, 2002), 40.

30. Glaser, B.G., *Basics of Grounded Theory Analysis: Emergence v Forcing* (Mill Valley, CA: Sociology Press, 1992), 16.

31. Tottman, P., 'The Rashoman effect: exploring the meaning of qualitative research analysis', Market Research Society, Annual Conference (2010).

32. Baszanger, I., 'The work sites of an American interactionist: Anselm L. Strauss, 1917–1996', *Symbolic Interaction* 21 (4) (1998), 353–378.

33. Bryant, A. and Charmaz, K., 'Grounded theory in historical perspective: an epistemological account', in Bryant, A. and Charmaz, K. (eds), *Handbook of Qualitative Research* (Thousand Oaks, CA: Sage, 2007), 32–57.

34. Charmaz, K., 'Qualitative interviewing and grounded theory analysis', in Gubrium, J.F. and Holstein, J.A., *Handbook of Interview Research* (Thousand Oaks, CA: Sage, 2002), 683–690.

35. Böhm, A., Legewie, H. and Muhr, T., *Kursus Textinterpretation: Grounded Theory* (Berlin: Technische Universität, Bericht aus dem IfP Atlas, 1992), 92–93, MS.

36. Adapted from Charmaz, K., 'Qualitative interviewing and grounded theory analysis', in Gubrium, J.F. and Holstein, J.A., *Handbook of Interview Research* (Thousand Oaks, CA: Sage, 2002), 687.

37. Ibid., p. 689.

38. Silverman, D., *Interpreting Qualitative Data: Methods for analysing text, talk and interaction*, 2nd edn (London: Sage, 2001), 71.

39. Allan, D., 'A content analysis of music placement in prime-time television advertising', *Journal of Advertising Research* 48 (3) (September 2008), 404–417; Neundorf, A.N., *The Content Analysis Guidebook* (Thousand Oaks, CA: Sage, 2002); Wang, C.L., 'A content analysis of connectedness vs separateness themes used in US and PRC print advertisements', *International Marketing Review* 18 (2) (2001), 145.

40. Roberts, M. and Pettigrew, S., 'A thematic content analysis of children's food advertising', *International Journal of Advertising* 26 (3) (2007), 357–367.

41. Voorveld, H., Neijens, P. and Smit, E., 'The interactive authority of brand web sites: a new tool provides new insights', *Journal of Advertising Research* 50 (3) (2010), 292–304; Ball, M.S. and Smith, G.W.H., *Analyzing visual data* (Thousand Oaks, CA: Sage, 1992), 15.

42. Bang, H.-K., Raymond, M.A., Taylor, C.R. and Moon, Y.S., 'A comparison of service quality dimensions conveyed in advertisements for service providers in the USA and Korea: a content analysis', *International Marketing Review* 22 (3) (2005), 309–326.

43. Glassner, B. and Corzine, J., 'Library research as fieldwork: a strategy for qualitative content analysis', *Sociology and Social Research* 66 (1982), 305–319.

44. Waksler, F., 'Studying children: phenomenological insights', *Human Studies* 9 (1986), 71–82.

45. Berelson, B., *Content analysis in communication research* (New York: Free Press, 1952).

46. Desai, P., *Methods beyond interviewing in qualitative market research* (London: Sage, 2002), 84.

47. Lawes, R., 'The research gallery', *Research* (October 2003), 23.

48. Rowland, G. and Jaroslav, C., 'Pushing the glamour button', *Research World* (February 2008), 46–47.

49. Valentine, V., 'Unlocking cultural codes', *ResearchWorld* (October 2006), 15.

50. Gadsby, N., 'Enchantment: using semiotics to understand the magic of branding', Market Research Society, Annual Conference (2010); Desai, P., *Methods beyond interviewing in qualitative market research* (London: Sage, 2002), 85.

51. Adapted from the Semiotics Solutions website **www. semioticsolutions.com**, in Desai, P., *Methods beyond interviewing in qualitative market research* (London: Sage, 2002), 85.

52. Maggio-Muller, K. and Evans, M., 'Culture, communications and business: the power of advanced semiotics', Market Research Society, Annual Conference (2006); Clegg, A., 'Just a sign of the times?', *Marketing Week* (19 August 2004), 36.

53. Wardle, J., *Developing advertising with qualitative research* (London: Sage, 2002), 53.

54. Valentine, V., 'Semiotics, what now, my love?', Market Research Society, Annual Conference (2007); Clatworthy, T. and Flanagan, C., 'White light white heat', *Research* (December 2003), 41.

55. Arning, C., 'Viewpoint – semiotics: a winning formula?', *International Journal of Market Research* 51 (3) (2009), 289–291.

56. Slater, D., 'Analysing cultural objects: content analysis and semiotics', in Seale, C. (ed.), *Researching society and culture* (London: Sage, 2002), 233–244.

57. Derrida, J., *Positions*, A. Bass (trans.) (Chicago: Chicago University Press, 1981).

58. Lawes, R., 'Futurology through semiotics', Market Research Society, Annual Conference (2009); O'Shaughnessy, J. and Holbrook, M.B., 'The linguistic turn in marketing research', *Journal of the Market Research Society* 30 (3) (April 1988), 210.

59. Desai, P., *Methods beyond interviewing in qualitative market research* (London: Sage, 2002), 97.

60. Valentine, V. and Evans, M., 'The dark side of the onion: rethinking the meanings of "rational" and "emotional" responses', *Journal of the Market Research Society* 35 (2) (April 1993), 127.

61. Cantle, N., 'Research insights into Japanese culture', *Admap* 480 (February 2007), 35–37.

62. Griffiths, J., 'Content analytics and the future of market research: the Cloud of Knowing Project', Market Research Society, Annual Conference (2010).

63. 'Code of Conduct', Market Research Society (April 2010), 20.

64. Schmidt, M., 'Quantification of transcripts from depth interviews, open ended responses and focus groups: challenges, accomplishments, new applications and perspectives for market research', *International Journal of Market Research* 52 (4) (2010), 483–509.

65. Ishmael, G. and Thomas, J.W., 'Worth a thousand words', *Journal of Advertising Research* 46 (3) (September 2006), 274–278; Packenham, L., 'Can qual research benefit from data-analysis software?', *Admap* 462 (June 2005), 48–49; Dembrowski, S. and Hanmer-Lloyd, S., 'Computer applications – a new road to qualitative data analysis?', *European Journal of Marketing* 29 (11) (November 1995), 50; Wolfe, R.A., Gephart, R.P. and Johnson, T.E., 'Computer-facilitated qualitative data analysis: potential contributions to management research', *Journal of Management* 19 (3) (Fall 1993), 637.

66. **www.qsrinternational.com/solutions_case-studies-detail.aspx?view-153** Accessed 14 Feb 2012

67. Habershon, J., 'Measuring facial expressions', *Admap* (January 2010), 19.

10 Survey and quantitative observation techniques

Stage 1

Problem definition

Stage 2

Research approach developed

Stage 3

Research design developed

Stage 4

Fieldwork or data collection

Stage 5

Data integrity and analysis

Stage 6

Report preparation and presentation

Know exactly what you want to measure – and then select a survey or observation technique that creates cooperative participants, willing to think and be honest.

Objectives

After reading this chapter, you should be able to:

1 discuss and classify survey techniques available to researchers, and describe various survey techniques;

2 identify the criteria for evaluating survey techniques, compare the different techniques and evaluate which is the best for a particular research project;

3 explain and classify the different quantitative observation techniques;

4 identify the criteria for evaluating observation techniques, compare the different techniques and evaluate which are suited for a particular research project;

5 describe the relative advantages and disadvantages of observation techniques and compare them with survey techniques;

6 discuss the considerations involved in implementing surveys and observation techniques in an international setting;

7 understand the ethical issues involved in conducting survey and observational research;

8 appreciate how digital developments are shaping the manner in which surveys and quantitative observation techniques are managed and applied.

Overview

In this chapter, we focus on the major techniques employed in descriptive research designs: surveys and quantitative observation. As explained in Chapter 3, descriptive research has as its prime objective the description of something, usually consumer or market characteristics. Survey and quantitative observation techniques are vital techniques in descriptive research designs. Survey techniques may be classified by mode of administration as online, telephone surveys, face-to-face and postal surveys. We describe each of these techniques and present a comparative evaluation of all survey techniques. Then we consider the major observational techniques: personal observation including mystery shopping research, electronic observation and trace analysis. The relative advantages and disadvantages of observation over survey techniques and the considerations involved in conducting survey and observation research when researching international markets are also discussed. Several ethical issues that arise in survey research and observation techniques are identified. Many digital developments are shaping how surveys are designed and delivered in manners that are more engaging for participants. Digital developments are also shaping how and what may be observed of consumers.

To begin our discussion, we present two example of how digital developments are shaping the practice of survey and observation design. The first example illustrates how researchers designed and implemented an Internet survey via mobile phone. The second example illustrates advances in outdoor communications and a means to measure the impact of individuals observing billboards and posters.

Real research | **Location-specific mobile research**[1]

Adidas Japan wanted to gauge the performance of an advertising campaign targeted at football fans. The company's particular need was to assess whether the Tokyo-based campaign had succeeded in generating awareness outside the capital, via television coverage. In order to do this, the company decided to conduct a mobile survey at an international football match played in the city of Sendai. Fans were invited to participate via flyers handed to them as they entered the stadium. The flyers explained how to enter the survey with details of a prize draw and the chance of winning shirts signed by star players. The flyers generated a 29% hit rate on the survey home page and a 33% completion rate among fans visiting the site. For Adidas Japan this meant 333 completed questionnaires based upon the distribution of 3,500 flyers at the game. The survey took on average eight minutes to complete. This was a reflection that, at 18 questions, the questionnaire was rather long for a mobile survey. One of the strengths of this method was that participants were able to complete the survey at a time of their own choosing, but while the event was still fresh in their minds. Very few fans completed the survey during the game itself; the majority completed after the game while travelling home.

Real research | **The great outdoors goes digital**[2]

Many outdoor poster and billboard locations have been converted to digital screens by JCDecaux (**www.jcdecaux.co.uk**) and Clear Channel (**www.clearchannel.com**). Advertisers are able to utilise the flexibility of the screens to show different copy at different times of the day and make live changes throughout a campaign. This flexibility allows smaller advertisers to rent space for a limited time, in effect hiring screen time. This also means that the medium competes with TV advertisements. Added to this ability to digitise outdoor advertisements is the increased ability to measure their impact. In Canada, scientists have developed Eyebox2 whereby infrared technology assesses how many passers-by turn to look at a display (and for how long). The data from these observations can be linked to point-of-sale data in stores to give even more powerful insights into the impact of a billboard.

Survey methods

Survey method
A structured questionnaire administered to a sample of a target population, designed to elicit specific information from participants.

Structured data collection
Use of a formal questionnaire that presents questions in a prearranged order.

The survey method of obtaining information is based upon the use of structured questionnaires administered to a sample of a target population. Participants may be asked a variety of questions regarding their behaviour, intentions, attitudes, awareness, motivations, and demographic and lifestyle characteristics. These questions may be asked verbally, in writing or via a computer (including mobile devices), and the responses may be obtained in any of these forms. 'Structured' here refers to the degree of standardisation imposed on the data collection process. In structured data collection, a formal questionnaire is prepared and the questions are asked in a prearranged order; thus, the process is also direct. Whether research is classified as direct or indirect is based on whether the true purpose is known to the participants. As explained in Chapter 7, a direct approach is undisguised in that the purpose of the project is disclosed to the participants or is otherwise obvious to them from the questions asked.

The structured direct survey, the most popular data collection method, involves administering a questionnaire. In a typical questionnaire, most questions are fixed-response alternative questions that require the participant to select from a predetermined set of responses. Consider, for example, the following question, designed to measure a dimension of students' attitudes towards the way they are assessed in marketing research classes:

	Strongly agree	*Agree*	*Neutral*	*Disagree*	*Strongly disagree*
I prefer written examinations compared with continual assessment	☐	☐	☐	☐	☐

The survey method has several advantages. First, the questionnaire is simple to administer. Second, the data obtained are consistent because the responses are limited to the alternatives stated. The use of fixed-response questions reduces the variability in the results that may be caused by differences in interviewers. Finally, coding, analysis and interpretation of data are relatively simple.[3]

The disadvantages are that participants may be unable or unwilling to provide the desired information. For example, consider questions about motivational factors. Participants may not be consciously aware of their motives for choosing specific brands or shopping at particular stores. Therefore, they may be unable to provide accurate answers to questions about their motives. Participants may be unwilling to respond if the information requested is sensitive or personal. In addition, structured questions and fixed-response alternative questions may result in loss of validity for certain types of data such as beliefs and feelings. Finally, wording questions in a consistent manner to all potential survey participants is not easy (see Chapter 13 on questionnaire design). In other words, the survey imposes the language and logic of the researcher on the questionnaire participants. Given this core characteristic of survey techniques, great care must be taken to ensure that the language and logic used in questionnaires are meaningful and valid to potential participants. Despite the above disadvantages, the survey approach is by far the most common method of primary data collection in marketing research, representing around 72% of all marketing research spending.[4] The following example illustrates how one company has realised the benefits of applying different survey methods. The International Data Group primarily focuses upon the use of online surveys to connect to and engage with the readers of its magazines.

Fixed-response alternative questions
Questions that require participants to choose from a set of predetermined answers.

Real research   **Online market research optimises online publications[5]**

The International Data Group (IDG) (**www.idg.com**) is one of the world's leading providers of IT media, IT research, and specialist conferences and exhibitions for the IT industry. The publishing group has more than 300 newspaper and magazine titles in 85 countries with more than 100 million readers. It also operates more than 400 websites, including a number of Web-only titles. The digitisation of media content has changed the nature of market conditions in the publishing industry. The trend towards declining circulations for print titles has also had an impact on IDG's original core business. Besides magazine titles, the group now offers its customers wide-ranging Internet publications, including a number of titles that are only available online. It also organises trade fairs, specialist congresses and seminars for the IT sector. The changed business model has also altered the conditions for the media company's market research team, which can now easily reach the IT industry's target groups online. IDG's marketing research team has changed from paper and telephone-based surveys to online survey methods. The surveys are also now being used for an ever-wider range of applications. For example, readers are questioned on an ongoing basis about their satisfaction with editorial content, their preferences and their requirements. The surveys deliver vital insights into the demographic struc-ture of the readership, which is fundamentally important to advertising customers. IDG also offers its advertising customers online surveys into the impact of advertisements. In these surveys, readers indicate which advertisements they remember and what they think of them. This can enable the success of individual advertisements and advertising campaigns to be measured and assessed. Another vital source of feedback is IT experts, who provide IDG with information on the latest trends. All of the processes involved are managed using the Web-based interface from GlobalPark's Enterprise Feedback Suite (**www.globalpark.co.uk**).

Access to survey participants may be conducted through two routes (see Figure 10.1). The first is via traditional approaches to building sampling frames, i.e. through personal contact, directories and databases. These will be discussed in more detail in Chapters 14 and 15. The second is via the access panel. Access panels were described in Chapter 3 but, in short, spe-cialist companies (such as ResearchNow, **www.researchnow.com**) manage large panels of individuals who have agreed to take part in surveys that are relevant to their backgrounds, location and/or interests. Access panels primarily work for online surveys and have been instrumental in the rapid growth of online surveys. However, it is possible to use the details of panel members to allow other methods of survey to be conducted.

Survey questionnaires may be administered in four major modes: (1) online surveys; (2) telephone surveys; (3) face-to-face surveys; and (4) postal surveys. Online surveys can be

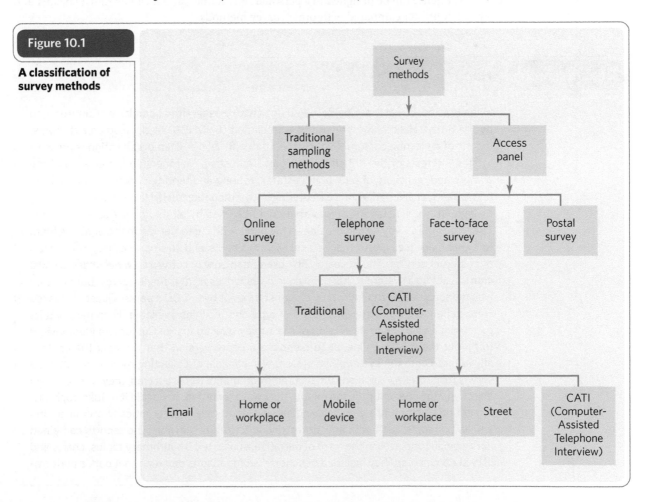

Figure 10.1

A classification of survey methods

conducted via the Internet on devices in home and offices. The use of mobile devices in administering surveys could be classified as a telephone survey. While many mobile devices are indeed telephones, viewing them solely as a means to conduct a telephone survey misses much of their potential. Mobile devices enable consumers to access audio and video, while communicating via text, email, social media and web browsing. Globally there are more smartphones in circulation that have great power and functionality and are able to cope with an array of research engagements.[6] We thus classify mobile devices as a form of online survey. Telephone surveys may be further classified as traditional telephone survey and computer-assisted telephone interviews (CATIs). Face-to-face surveys may be conducted in the home or workplace, as street surveys, or as computer-assisted personal interviews (CAPIs). The final major method, postal surveys, takes the form of the traditional hard copy, self-completion survey administered through the post. We now describe each method.

Online surveys

Online surveys can be conducted on devices in homes or the workplace, or administered on mobile devices. They constitute around 22% of the worldwide total spend on research methods. Examples of countries with low and high spending on this technique range from Greece at 1% to Finland at 33%.[7] As a proportion of global spend on marketing research techniques, the use of online surveys has grown consistently over many years, and continues to do so. The following example illustrates why the online survey continues to grow in popularity. The survey experience can be designed in a personalised manner, and it can be much cheaper and faster to administer compared with other survey methods.

Real research | Happy campers

Hugh Inwood, Director at The Research Box (**www.researchbox.co.uk**), was approached by the British Holiday & Home Parks Association (BH&HPA) to develop an automated means of collecting customer satisfaction data. BH&HPA is an organisation representing the interests of the British holiday parks industry. Membership is made up of the owners and managers of park home estates, touring and tenting parks, caravan holiday home parks, chalet parks and self-catering accommodation. BH&HPA wanted to develop a single-visitor satisfaction survey that could be used by all its holiday park members. The aim of the survey was to provide all the parks with customer feedback, enabling them to benchmark their performance against other parks and to improve their own levels of customer service. The Research Box used Snap survey software (**www.snapsurveys. com**) to set up a system to host and collect responses from a single survey, but one that was personalised to the individual circumstances at over 2,000 parks. Questions asked were dependent on the accommodation type and facilities available. Each park had its own unique web link to its version of the survey questionnaire. Customers were invited to fill out the survey online, or to complete a paper version that the park then manually entered onto the system. The system was capable of collecting more than 100,000 survey responses a year. If any unfavourable comments were received, they were emailed directly to the relevant park the minute they were recorded, to enable it to take appropriate action. Each month, personalised survey reports were automatically produced and emailed direct to each park and stored online for future viewing. The reports contained park-specific analyses in the form of narrative, supported by summary tables, charts and lists of comments. They included benchmark comparisons between that park's performance and other similar parks, and that park's performance for the current month versus the equivalent period last year. The accumulated response data from all parks and for all periods are also available for analysis by The Research Box on behalf of BH&HPA. These analyses are used to identify industry trends and to act as supporting material for business or political case building. Over 275 parks have adopted the system and are actively using it to research their customers' attitudes.

Email surveys

We begin with email surveys as they can be seen as the forerunner to the massive development of online surveys. Text-based email surveys can be convenient for participants because they require no facilities or expertise beyond those that they use in their day-to-day email communications. They can be conducted online at home, in the workplace or on mobile devices. To conduct an email survey, a list of email addresses is first obtained. The survey is written within the body of the email message which is then sent out over the Internet. Email surveys use pure text (ASCII) to represent questionnaires and can be received and responded to by anyone with an email address. Participants type the answers to either closed-ended or open-ended questions at designated places, and click 'reply'. Responses are then data entered and tabulated in the manner of a postal survey or imported with software that interprets the emailed responses and reads the answers directly into a format compatible with the requirements of an analysis package. Email surveys have several limitations, primarily being that they can appear dry and uninteresting.[8] Given the advantages of other online survey methods, the popularity of the email survey is waning. The problems of the email survey for certain types of participant are illustrated in the following example.

Real research   ### Send an email? Err . . . sorry, you seem to have mistaken me for a sad old geezer[9]

Email is in steady decline as younger people switch to social networking, texting and instant messaging. According to the marketing research company comScore (**www.comscore.com**), millions of Britons have abandoned email services, led by the under 25s. Younger users say that email still has its uses receiving their favourite newsletters or when writing formal messages to strangers. As a result, many have taken to more personal forms of communication. The likes of Facebook and instant messaging systems ensure that people only ever get contacted by people whom they have already accepted as friends. A similar trend is developing worldwide and is likely to continue. 'It's an evolution', said Ian Angell, a Professor of Information Systems at the London School of Economics. 'This is how faxes have more or less disappeared.'

Given the technical limitations of most email systems, questionnaires cannot utilise programmed skip patterns, logic checks or randomisation. The limited intelligence of ASCII text cannot keep a participant from, say, choosing both 'yes' and 'no' to a question where only one response is meaningful. Skipping instructions (e.g. 'If the answer to Question 5 is yes, go to Question 9') must appear explicitly, just as on paper, as there is no automated routing. These factors can reduce the quality of data from an email survey and can require much post-survey data cleaning.[10] There are also problems in locating accurate and current email address lists and, even if these can be located, given spam protection software, there is no guarantee that an email will reach intended participants.

Online surveys using fixed and mobile devices

Early versions of Internet surveys were labelled as CAWI (Computer-Assisted Web Interviews) to follow previous acronyms within the research industry of CATIs (Computer-Assisted Telephone Interviews) and CAPIs (Computer-Assisted Personal Interviews). The far simpler term 'online' is used for all Internet surveys hosted on a website. Participants may be recruited online from potential participant databases maintained by either a research agency or a panel management company, or they can be recruited by conventional techniques (telephone, face-to-face or postal). Frequently, participants are not recruited, but those who happen to be visiting a website on which the survey is posted (or other popular websites) are invited to participate in the survey. Either all or every nth web visitor is allowed to participate. Web surveys offer several advantages over email surveys. It is usual to construct buttons, checkboxes and data entry fields that prevent participants from selecting more than one response where only one is intended, or from otherwise typing where no response is required. Skip patterns can be programmed and performed automatically as in CATI or CAPI. It is possible to validate responses as they are entered. Additional survey stimuli such as graphical images, animations and links to other web pages may be integrated into or around the survey. For a good example of creative and engaging sources of flash animation that can be integrated into online surveys, examine the options designed by Annik Systems at **www.surveyflash-tools.com**. The visual layout and care taken in designing additional stimuli can do much for participant engagement. This can contribute to a higher quality experience for participants, encouraging a more committed response.

Researchers are also conducting online surveys using mobile devices. The smartphone and tablet offer many possibilities as tools that are in nearly every pocket or purse, providing both portability and immediacy for anytime, anywhere data collection. These devices represent the next generation for online communication, just as notebook computers replaced desktop computers as they became smaller, lighter and more powerful.[11] There is much potential for researchers to reach and engage with participants who may be difficult to access via other forms of survey, though there remain many challenges. There is a wide variety of mobile devices, from more than a dozen major manufacturers, in a variety of models. It is reported that there are over 1,600 different models of smartphones and new models are brought to market frequently. Screen sizes, resolution, processing power, memory and input modalities vary widely, even between devices from the same manufacturer. Operating systems and application programming environments are also very different.[12] Regardless of the technical challenges, there are a growing number of survey applications using mobile devices as illustrated in the following example.

IP Deutchsland: Wireless Application Protocol offers[13]

Mobile operators and advertising companies are interested in discovering which user groups can be reached with WAP offers and how they respond to mobile forms of advertising. The media marketing company IP Deutschland (**www.ip-deutschland.de**) conducted a study for its advertising customer Sony Ericsson, in which the cell phone was used for a quantitative ad hoc survey of mobile portal visitors. EFS Mobile Extension from Globalpark (**www.globalpark.co.uk**) was used as the technical platform for the survey. The survey was conducted during a WAP portal relaunch for the private TV broadcaster RTL (**http://mobile.rtl.de**). The relaunch also marked the start of a cross-media advertising campaign of the cell phone manufacturer Sony Ericsson. In addition to communication activities in other types of media, a banner ad was displayed in the cell phone portal. A second banner ad was integrated to trigger participation in the survey. As an incentive, IP Deutschland entered all survey participants into a prize draw to win the game 'RTL

Racer'. Participants had to click on a web link, which took them directly to the survey. To evaluate the overall impact of the promotion, IP Deutschland conducted a survey at both the start and end of the advertising campaign. In total, 282 people participated in the two mobile surveys. The results of the surveys showed that the target group currently using RTL's Mobile Internet services was very attractive to advertising companies. On average, mobile portal visitors had a higher level of education than other online users in Germany.

The following lists summarise the advantages and disadvantages of online surveys.[14]

Advantages

- *Speed*. Compared with other survey methods, especially when conducting international research, the time taken to conduct a survey can be reduced to a matter of days rather than weeks. Even if one includes the time taken to contact participants, to establish their willingness to take part in a survey, for them to reply, for the survey to be sent, for it to be completed and then emailed back (the procedure adopted to reduce the perception of 'junk' email), such a survey can be completed relatively quickly. The only other method that could match its speed would be the telephone survey.

- *Cost*. Once the electronic questionnaire is designed, it is almost as easy to mail it to 10,000 people as to 10, since there are no printing, stationery and postage costs. Preparing data for analyses needs less manual intervention and can be also much cheaper.

- *Quality of response*. A range of design features can be used to make the survey more appealing and interesting. Graphics can be used to create visual and moving forms of scaling to maintain the interest of participants, but also to put them in a frame of mind that elicits more from them. The following example illustrates how Sony views this advantage.

Real research | **'Surveytainment'[15]**

Many of the methods Sony implemented in its online surveys included what it referred to as 'surveytainment'. This encapsulated a way of making surveys more emotional, engaging and fun for participants. Surveytainment used eye-catching question types and technology, including Windows-driven graphic capabilities, audio and video clips, drag and drop rankings and collaborative tools. For example, by using a 'whiteboard' application participants could show Sony what made an attractive cover by rearranging and altering the images provided. Although more complex, it was also possible for participants to upload their own images or text. The key to making 'surveytainment' effective was in ensuring that the techniques increased participant understanding. For example, the more imagery on a screen, the less likely a participant may read any long question text, relying on inference versus the written word. Sony believed that the ideas behind 'surveytainment' had a unique importance in the music/entertainment industry as it introduced sound and imagery into questions that would otherwise be static or require participants to rely on recall. Before the aid of the Web and digital recordings, song and video testing with large samples was limited and financially impractical. But no longer are tests based upon focus group responses to a CD on a stereo system; there can be thousands of active music enthusiasts, experiencing and responding to a song or video in their natural music listening habitat: online, and in their home, offices or anywhere!

- *Interviewer bias removed.* The method maintains the key advantage of postal surveys in being able to present a consistent form of measurement.

- *Data quality.* Logic and validity checks can be built in, thus allowing the development of more personalised questionnaire designs. In areas where open-ended or 'other – please state' responses are required, the participant types in answers ready for analysis.

- *Contacting certain target groups.* Many participants may be reluctant to complete surveys by traditional methods such as postal and face-to-face surveys. Much of this reluctance can be attributed to the context of where the survey is administered and how comfortable participants are in these contexts. With the online survey, the participants are largely in control of the context and can respond in circumstances that they feel comfortable with. In addition, with the growth of access panels where participants sign up to take part in research projects, very precise definitions of participant types can be devised.

Disadvantages

- *Sampling frames.* There are a growing number of access panels that provide means to access particular types of participant. However, there are still major questions surrounding their representativeness and the motivations of panel members.[16] Email directories exist beyond access panels but there can be questions about their currency, accuracy and means of classifying different types of target participant. Another sampling issue is that participants who are recruited through browsing or clicking through banner ads or sources such as Facebook are self-selecting and the researcher does not know whether those who choose to take part are really representative of a target population. Being able to generalise findings to a particular population becomes difficult with a self-selecting sample.

- *Access to the Web.* Though access to the Internet has grown enormously, and continues to grow in even remote and poor communities across the globe, the penetration of households and businesses is still highly variable within countries and across countries. Much depends upon the characteristics of the types of participant that are being targeted for a survey. Even if they do have access to the Internet, do they have access to the means to engage with the survey in the manner intended by the questionnaire designer?

- *Technical problems.* Depending upon the hardware and software that participants use, the questionnaire may 'work' or not, as was intended by the designer; this is particularly true with online surveys. Unlike the general homogeneity of the computer browsers used, virtually no uniform standards exist for the often individually adapted software on mobile devices. Processing power and storage capacity vary more sharply among mobile devices and more restraint is needed in the graphic design of mobile online surveys.[17]

Telephone surveys

As stated earlier, telephone surveys may be categorised as traditional or computer-assisted. They constitute around 17% of the worldwide total spend on research methods. Examples of countries with low and high spending on this technique range from Japan at 3% to Switzerland at 46%.[18] As a proportion of global spend on marketing research techniques, telephone surveys are in decline.

Traditional telephone surveys

Traditional telephone surveys involve phoning a sample of participants and asking them a series of questions, using a paper questionnaire to record the responses. From a central location, a wide geographical area can be covered, including international markets. Given that telephone interviewers cannot give participants any visual prompts, they have to write down answers to any open-ended questions and may have to flick through the questionnaire to find appropriate questions for a particular participant (filtering). These surveys tend to be short in duration and have questions with few options as possible answers. Today, this approach is rarely used in commercial marketing research, the more common approach being CATI.

Computer-assisted telephone interviews (CATIs)

CATI uses a computerised questionnaire administered to participants over the telephone with a questionnaire on a networked computer or a PC. The interviewer sits in front of a terminal and wears a small headset. The terminal replaces a paper questionnaire, and the headset substitutes for a telephone. Upon command, the computer dials the telephone number to be called. When contact is made, the interviewer reads questions posed on the screen and records the participant's answers directly to the computer, ready for immediate analysis. The main benefit of CATI is the speed of collecting data and analyses. Speed is of the essence in subjects where participant attitudes and behaviour can change quickly, an example being the 'latest' toys that parents may wish to buy for their children. One of the most widespread uses of CATI is for political opinion polls.

With CATI, the computer systematically guides the interviewer. Only one question at a time appears on the screen. The computer checks the responses for appropriateness and consistency. It uses the responses as they are obtained to personalise the questionnaire. Data collection flows naturally and smoothly. Interviewing time is reduced, data quality is enhanced, and the laborious steps in the data collection process, coding questionnaires and entering data into the computer, are eliminated. Because the responses are entered directly into the computer, interim and update reports on data collection or results can be provided almost instantaneously. The following example shows how CATI was used to support decisions in a critical advertising campaign.

Real research | **Go safe – it's the last gift you can give this Christmas**[19]

In 2008 there was alarm caused by a sudden upsurge in road deaths in Northern Ireland. A creative, strategic, media and psychology team from the advertising agency LyleBailie International (**www.lylebailie.com**) met urgently to review the developments. The team knew from research that serious increases in reported aberrant behaviour could have the effect of normalising the dangerous and the abnormal, conditioning road users into a resigned fatalism about road 'accidents'. This could worsen the prospects for December, already identified as the killer month for road deaths. The team agreed to construct an urgent December advertising campaign, on top of the booked anti-drink-drive TV campaign. The campaign was branded with the theme 'Go safe – it's the last gift you can give this Christmas'. This idea personalised the consequences and the sense of individual responsibility needed to change behaviour. To monitor this campaign, LyleBailie commissioned Millward Brown Ulster (**www.millwardbrownulster.com**) on behalf of the Department of the Environment's Road Safety Division, to conduct an independent awareness and influence telephone survey on the campaign among 500 adults. Of the 1,699 calls made to potential participants, 817 of them agreed to complete an interview, and 61.2% (500) were aware of the advertisement and completed the questionnaire. One outcome of the study was that the majority of the media spend was allocated to radio which was used to reach various 'at-risk' audiences as they travelled in their car. Key danger times of day and days of the week were targeted with upweights of media activity. Station planning was successfully optimised to reach young adults.

The biggest drawback of CATI lies in participants' willingness to be interviewed by telephone. In a 2003 study of participant cooperation by the Council for Marketing and Opinion Research (CMOR) in the USA, only 7% of participants called were willing to answer questions. Across Europe there are several developments that impact upon telephone usage: the percentage of households equipped with a fixed phone is dropping, while the percentage of households equipped with mobile phone access is rising. Additionally, the percentage of mobile-only households is increasing, while the percentage of households that have only fixed-phone access is decreasing. In countries such as Finland, Italy, Portugal, Belgium and Slovenia, fixed-phone coverage has already been overtaken by mobile phone coverage and there seems to be an unequivocal tendency to a widespread generalisation of the phenomenon to other countries.[20]

There are many factors that make it very difficult to conduct telephone surveys. At times, the technique may be confused in the minds of participants with cold-call selling techniques. To overcome this problem requires interviewers who are trained to reassure participants and to make the interviewing experience worthwhile. In most businesses, phone calls are screened; how else could managers avoid calls from companies and individuals they do not want to talk to? Many businesses have set up formal procedures to minimise unnecessary calls to management. This is a hurdle that well-trained interviewers are taught to circumvent. Experienced interviewers can 'run the gauntlet' of three or four screenings and still secure an interview without in any way upsetting the interviewee.[21]

Face-to-face surveys

Face-to-face surveying methods may be categorised as home, workplace, street or computer-assisted. They constitute around 13% of the worldwide total spend on research methods. Examples of countries with low and high spending on this technique range from Sweden at 5% to Turkey at 50%.[22] Most cases of high proportions of marketing research spend on face-to-face surveys can be found in developing economies. As a proportion of global spend on marketing research techniques, face-to-face surveys are in decline, one of the main reasons being the costs involved, as illustrated in the following example.

Real research   **European Social Survey[23]**

The European Social Survey (ESS) (**www.europeansocialsurvey.org**) is an attitude survey time series carried out in over 30 countries across Europe. The survey began in 2001 and fieldwork is carried out from September to December every two years. The questionnaire consists of two parts: a core section that is repeated every round, and two rotating modules that are repeated less frequently. The core modules include subjects such as media consumption, political and social trust, religious identification and socio-demographic background data, while the rotating modules each cover a substantive topic in more detail. Rotating modules so far have covered topics such as well-being, work–life balance, ageing, welfare attitudes, immigration and citizenship. To help ensure equivalence of outputs, the hour-long survey interview is conducted face to face in all countries. This mode was initially chosen not only because it tends to get the highest response rates and is the only mode that offers complete coverage in all countries, but also because the ESS questionnaire is particularly well suited to face-to-face interviews. In particular, it involves a long interview, many showcards and some complex routing. It is, however, becoming clear that using face-to-face interviewing as the sole mode of data collection might now need to be reconsidered in view of its rising cost and diminishing response rates. In addition, different countries have different experiences and expertise as well as different penetration of data collection modes, which means they may be better equipped to use a different mode.

Home or workplace surveys

In face-to-face home or workplace surveys, participants are interviewed face-to-face in their 'personal space'. The interviewer's task is to contact the participants, ask the questions and record the responses. In recent years, the use of face-to-face home and workplace surveys has declined due to their high cost. However, there are many situations where they are used because of the reassurances of quality of the interview process, the comfort of the context felt by certain participants and the nature of the questions that are being administered. The following example illustrates such a case where it was paramount to use a face-to-face home survey.

Real research	**PARC: 360-degree view of the consumer**[24]

The Pan Arab Research Centre (PARC) (**www.arablandemographics.com**) conducts an ongoing, comprehensive study of the Arab Republic of Egypt. The scope of the survey covers product and brand usage, media exposure, lifestyle and attitudes, daily activities, shopping behaviour and leisure activities. Fieldwork is conducted across different seasons of the year and consisted of approximately 5,000 interviews. Two different methods are used to question participants: first, a home interview is used to collect demographics and data related to media exposure (including magazines, newspapers, radio, TV and Internet). Second, at the end of the interview, fieldworkers leave behind a self-completion questionnaire covering personal and household usage of more than 400 product categories and services and 5,000 brands, as well as attitude and lifestyle statements. A wide range of techniques have been used to elicit the full cooperation of participants. Listed households were informed by mail that they would be contacted by an interviewer. Up to six separate attempts were made to contact difficult-to-reach participants. Households presenting language barriers were reassigned to specifically qualified interviewers, as were refusals and other unusual cases.

As well as using face-to-face surveys for ad hoc studies, they are also widely used by syndicated firms for omnibus surveys, as illustrated in the following example.

Real research	**Millward Brown Ulster omnibus survey**[25]

The omnibus survey is a cost-effective means of measuring and tracking consumer awareness, behaviour and attitudes. Each omnibus survey incorporates a range of topics. The costs for each survey are directly shared between clients in proportion to the number of questions each decides to include. However, the questions included and the ensuing results are exclusive to each client, with each section treated completely confidentially. The Ulster omnibus survey is based upon a nationally and regionally representative sample of 1,000 adults aged 16 or over, in Northern Ireland. It is conducted twice monthly by personal surveys conducted in-home. The omnibus survey delivers extensive background information on the participants and their household. This covers standard demographics of gender, age, socio-economic group, ethnicity, working status, marital status, household size, presence and age of children in the household, religion, mobility and tenure, through to issues such as Internet access. All of this information is available, either for targeting questions or for cross-analysis to determine any significant differences in responses by segments. Applications of the Ulster omnibus survey include:

- *Advertising*. The majority of Northern Ireland's high-profile advertising campaigns have used this omnibus to benchmark attitudes pre-campaign and track them post-campaign to measure advertising effectiveness.

- *Charities.* The methodology has been used by many charities to measure awareness, behaviour and attitudes towards specific organisations, their messages and donation giving.
- *Health.* Changing attitudes and behaviour in the area of personal health and activity have been routinely assessed using the omnibus survey. Some aspects of behaviours that have been monitored include issues such as smoking, drinking, healthy eating, recreational drug use and physical activity.

Face-to-face surveys are used extensively in business-to-business research for participant subjects who cannot be effectively interviewed by telephone or post. Managers being interviewed have the comfort and security of their office and can control the timing and pace of the interview. For the researcher, the big benefit of meeting managers in their office is the ability to build up a rapport, probe and gain the full attention of the manager.

Street surveys

For street surveys, participants are intercepted while they are shopping in city centres or shopping centres. They may be questioned there and then in the street or taken to a specific test facility. In the testing of new product formulations, test facilities are ideal to allow participants the time and context to sample and evaluate products. The technique can also be used to test merchandising ideas, advertisements and other forms of marketing communications. The big advantage of the street survey is that it is more efficient for the participant to come to the interviewer than for the interviewer to go to the participant.[26]

Computer-assisted personal interviews (CAPIs)

In CAPI, a computer partially replaces the interviewer. There are several user-friendly software packages that design easy-to-use surveys with help screens and understandable instructions. The use of colour, graphical images and on- and off-screen stimuli can all contribute to making the interview process both interesting and stimulating. This method has been classified as a face-to-face survey technique because an interviewer is usually present to guide the participant as needed. CAPI has been used to collect data at test facilities from street surveys, product clinics, conferences and trade shows. It can be used in a kiosk format at locations such as museums or heritage sites to conduct visitor surveys. It may also be used for home or workplace surveys. The following example illustrates an application of CAPI where many visual aspects of football sponsorship could be displayed for questioning.

| Real research | ## Brands fall short of their goal[27] |

Major consumer brands use a plethora of sports sponsorship platforms, from players to stadiums, to communicate with a global consumer market and gain international exposure and recognition. Sporting events are an effective vehicle to gain access to a swathe of potential customers yet, according to the CAPI study conducted by TNS Sport, young people and children have a greater awareness than adults of those brands that sponsor leading football clubs. Its research among people who watch football on TV revealed that spontaneous recall of brands by adults (aged over 16) across a range of sponsors was generally less than that of children (aged 10–19).

A major development for marketers, especially in financial services, has been the use of customer satisfaction surveys to guide strategic and operational decisions. With traditional survey techniques, the interviewer may have to carry a huge questionnaire to cope with questions that measure attitudes to a range of banks and a range of services taken from those banks. With CAPI, when a particular bank is chosen, particular questions may be filtered out, and choosing a particular service from that bank can filter out further questions. Questions specific to the participant may then be asked, in all making the interview process far more efficient.

Postal surveys

Postal surveys constitute around 4% of the worldwide total spend on research methods. Examples of countries with low and high spending on this technique range from Greece at 1% to Sweden at 15%.[28] As a proportion of global spend on marketing research techniques, postal methods are in decline.

In the postal survey, questionnaires are mailed to preselected potential participants. A typical mailed package consists of the outgoing envelope, cover letter, questionnaire, return envelope and possibly an incentive. The participants complete and return the questionnaires. There is no verbal interaction between the researcher and the participant in the survey process.[29] There may be an initial contact with potential participants, to establish the correct person to send the questionnaire to, and to motivate them before they receive the survey. Before data collection can begin, a sampling frame needs to be compiled so that potential participants can be identified. Therefore, an initial task is to obtain a valid mailing list. Mailing lists can be compiled from telephone directories, customer databases or association membership databases, or can be purchased from publication subscription lists or commercial mailing list companies[30] Regardless of its source, a mailing list should be current and closely related to the population of interest. (Chapters 13 and 14 will detail the full questionnaire design and sampling implications of this approach.) With an understanding of characteristics of target participants and what will motivate them to respond honestly, as fully and as quickly as possible, the researcher must also make decisions about the various elements of the postal survey package (see Table 10.1).

Table 10.1	Some decisions related to the postal survey package
Outgoing envelope	Method of addressing; envelope size; colour; postage
Covering letter	Personalisation; sponsorship; type of appeal; signature
Questionnaire	Size, length and content; colour and layout; format and reproduction; participant anonymity
Instructions	As part of covering letter; a separate sheet; alongside individual questions
Return envelope	Whether to include one; type of envelope; postage
Incentives	Feedback of findings; monetary vs. non-monetary; prepaid vs. promised amount

A comparative evaluation of survey methods

Not all survey techniques are appropriate in a given situation. Therefore, the researcher should conduct a comparative evaluation to determine which techniques are appropriate. Table 10.2 compares the different survey techniques through a range of criteria. For any particular research project, the relative importance attached to these criteria will vary. These factors may be broadly classified as task, situational and participant factors. Task factors relate to tasks that have to be performed to collect the data and to the topic of the survey. These factors consist of flexibility of data collection, diversity of questions, use of physical stimuli, sample control, quantity of data, and response rate. The situational factors comprise control of the data collection environment, control of field force, potential for interviewer bias, potential to probe participants, potential to build rapport, speed and cost. The participant factors relate to perceived participant anonymity, social desirability, obtaining sensitive information, low incidence rate and participant control. We discuss in detail an evaluation of the different survey methods on each of these factors.

Task factors

The demand that the survey task places upon participants and the data collection process influences the survey method that should be used.

Flexibility of data collection

The flexibility of data collection is determined primarily by the extent to which the participant can interact with the interviewer and the survey questionnaire. The face-to-face survey, whether conducted as a home, workplace or street survey, affords a very high form flexibility of data collection. Because the participant and the interviewer meet face to face, the interviewer can administer complex questionnaires, explain and clarify difficult questions, and even use unstructured techniques.

By contrast, the traditional telephone survey allows only moderate flexibility because it is more difficult to use unstructured techniques, ask complex questions, or obtain in-depth answers to open-ended questions over the telephone. CATI and CAPI and online surveys allow somewhat greater flexibility because the researcher can use various question formats, can personalise the questionnaire and can handle complex skip or filter patterns (directions for skipping questions in the questionnaire based on the subject's responses). One benefit of the online survey is the ease with which a survey may be modified. For example, early data returns may suggest additional questions that should be asked. Changing or adding questions as the need becomes apparent would be almost impossible with a postal survey, possible but difficult with face-to-face or telephone surveys, but achievable in a matter of minutes with some online surveys.

Diversity of questions

The diversity of questions that can be asked in a survey depends on the degree of interaction that the participant has with the interviewer and the questionnaire, as well as the participant's ability actually to see the questions. A variety of questions can be asked in a face-to-face survey because the participant can see the questionnaire and the interviewer is present to clarify ambiguities. Thus home and office surveys, street interviews and CAPI allow for diversity. In online surveys, multimedia capabilities can be utilised and so the ability to ask a diverse set of questions is moderate to high, despite the absence of an interviewer. In postal surveys and email surveys, less diversity is possible. In traditional telephone surveys and CATI, the participant cannot see the questions while answering, and this limits the diversity of questions. For example, in a telephone survey or CATI, it would be very difficult to ask participants to rank 15 TV programmes in terms of preference.

Table 10.2	A comparative evaluation of survey techniques						
	Email	Online	Telephone CATI	Home and workplace	Street surveys	CAPI	Postal
Flexibility of data collection	*	****	****	*****	*****	****	*
Diversity of questions	***	****	*	*****	*****	*****	***
Use of physical stimuli	*	***	*	****	*****	*****	***
Sample control	*	**	****	****	****	***	*
Quantity of data	***	****	**	***	***	***	**
Response rate	*	**	***	*****	****	*****	*
Control of data collection environment	*	*	***	****	*****	*****	*
Control of field force	*****	*****	***	*	***	***	*****
Potential for interviewer bias	None	None	***	*****	*****	*	None
Potential to probe participants	*	*	*	*****	***	***	*
Potential to build rapport	*	*	***	*****	****	****	*
Speed	*****	*****	*****	****	***	****	*
Low cost	*****	*****	***	*	**	**	****
Perceived participant anonymity	***	*****	***	*	*	*	*****
Social desirability	*****	*****	***	**	*	****	*****
Obtaining sensitive information	***	***	*	*****	*	***	***
Low incidence rate	***	*****	*****	*	*	*	***
Participant control	*****	****	**	*	*	*	*****

(key: low = *, moderate to low = **, moderate = ***, moderate to high = ****, high = *****)

Use of physical stimuli

Often it is helpful or necessary to use physical stimuli such as products, product prototypes, commercials or promotional displays during an interview. For the most basic example, a taste test involves tasting a product and answering questions that evaluate the taste. In other cases, photographs, maps or other audio-visual cues are helpful. In these cases, face-to-face surveys conducted at central locations (guided through street surveys and CAPI) are preferable to home surveys. In the central location, many intricate visual stimuli can be set up prior to the actual interview. Postal surveys are moderate on this dimension, because sometimes it is possible to mail the facilitating aids or even product samples. Online surveys are also moderately suitable, because the questionnaires can include multimedia elements such as prototype web pages and advertisements. The use of physical stimuli is limited in traditional telephone surveys and CATIs, as well as in email surveys (depending upon the participant's ability to open attachments).

Sample control

Sample control
The ability of the survey mode to reach the units specified in the sample effectively and efficiently.

Sampling frame
A representation of the elements of the target population that consists of a list or set of directions for identifying the target population.

Sample control is the ability of the survey mode to reach participants specified in the sample effectively and efficiently.[31] At least in principle, home and workplace face-to-face surveys offer the best sample control. It is possible to control which sampling units or participants are interviewed, who is interviewed, the degree of participation of other members of the household, and many other aspects of data collection. In practice, to achieve a high degree of control, the researcher has to overcome several problems. It is difficult to find participants at home during the day because many people work outside the home. Also, for safety reasons, interviewers are reluctant to venture into certain neighbourhoods and people have become cautious of responding to strangers at their door. Street surveys allow only a moderate degree of sample control. Although the interviewer has control over which participants to intercept, the choice is limited to individuals who are walking down a street or through a shopping centre, and frequent shoppers have a greater probability of being included. Also, potential participants can intentionally avoid or initiate contact with the interviewer. Compared with street surveys, CAPI offers slightly better control, as sampling quotas can be set and participants randomised automatically.

Moderate to high sampling control can be achieved with traditional telephone surveys and CATIs. Telephones offer access to geographically dispersed participants and hard-to-reach areas. These procedures depend upon a sampling frame, a list of population units with their telephone numbers.[32] The sampling frames normally used are telephone directories, but telephone directories are limited in that:

(1) not everyone has a phone or even a 'conventional' phone, while some individuals have several phone numbers partly due to the growing use of mobile phones with rapidly changing numbers;[33] (2) the growth in number portability which allows people to transfer their landline telephone number to a mobile phone and to move to any geographical area of the country;[34] (3) some individuals have unlisted phones or are ex-directory and directories do not reflect new phones in service or recently disconnected phones; and (4) some individuals no longer use landlines, relying solely using their mobile phone exclusively.

Online and postal surveys require a list of addresses of individuals or households eligible for inclusion in the sample. This requirement has underpinned the growth of access panels across the globe. These surveys can reach geographically dispersed participants and hard-to-reach areas. Without the use of access panels, mailing lists are sometimes unavailable, outdated or incomplete, especially for electronic addresses. Another factor outside the researcher's control is whether the questionnaire is answered and who answers it. Some subjects refuse to respond because of lack of interest or motivation; others cannot respond because they are illiterate.[35] Given these reasons, the degree of sample control in online and postal surveys without the use of access panels tends to be low.[36]

The use of access panels provides moderate to high control over the sample. They can provide samples matched to national census statistics on key demographic variables. It is also possible to identify specific user groups within a panel and to direct the survey to households with specific characteristics. Specific members of households in the panel can be questioned. Finally, low-incidence groups, groups that occur infrequently in the population, can be reached with panels, but there is a question of the extent to which a panel can be considered representative of an entire population.

Not all populations are candidates for online survey research. Although participants can be screened to meet qualifying criteria and quotas imposed, the ability to meet quotas is limited by the number and characteristics of participants who may visit a website. However, there are some exceptions to this broad statement. For example, computer product purchasers and users of Internet services are ideal populations. Business and professional users of Internet services are also an excellent population to reach with online surveys. Sample control is low to moderate for online surveys, while email surveys suffer from many of the limitations of postal surveys and thus offer low sample control.

Quantity of data

Home and workplace face-to-face surveys allow the researcher to collect relatively large amounts of data. The social relationship between the interviewer and the participant, as well as the home or office environment, can motivate the participant to spend more time in the interview. Less effort is required of the participant in a face-to-face survey than in a telephone or postal survey. The interviewer records answers to open-ended questions and provides visual aids to help with lengthy and complex scales. Some face-to-face surveys last for as long as 75 minutes. In contrast to home and workplace surveys, street surveys and CAPIs provide only moderate amounts of data. Because these surveys are conducted in shopping centres and other central locations, a participant's time is more limited. Typically, the interview time is 20 minutes or less.

Postal surveys also yield moderate amounts of data. Fairly long questionnaires can be used because short questionnaires do not necessarily generate higher response rates than long ones. The same is true for email and online surveys, although online is a better medium in this respect.

Traditional telephone surveys, CATIs and surveys conducted using mobile devices result in limited quantities of data. They tend to be shorter than other surveys because participants can easily terminate the telephone conversation or engagement at their own discretion. These interviews commonly last about 15 minutes and could be shorter in the case of mobile devices. Longer interviews may be conducted when the subject matter and the questioning tasks set are of interest to the participants.[37]

Response rate

Response rate
The percentage of the total attempted interviews that are completed.

Survey **response rate** is broadly defined as the percentage of the total attempted interviews that are completed. Face-to-face, home and workplace, street and CAPI surveys yield the highest response rates (typically between 60 and 80%), though this is not generalisable to all countries as illustrated in the next example.

Telephone surveys, traditional and CATI, yield response rates between 40 and 60%. These modes also suffer from not-at-homes or no-answers. In a study involving qualitative interviews and a census of all Australian telephone market research providers it was reported that about half of all placed telephone calls go unanswered; refusals can outnumber interviews by up to six to one. Three call-backs per survey were built into the research design in most companies but surprisingly, in some cases, there were none, despite research that shows that call-backs can increase response rates by up to 76%.[38]

Real research | **Where participants are particularly reluctant to give their opinions[39]**

Non-response is a common problem in most countries, but Germany had a particularly bad reputation when it came to 'closed doors'. A manager, responsible for supplier management at a domestic products company, worked with most global agencies in Germany for quantitative research. For products in baby care, for example, it proved very cumbersome to find out German opinion: 'Door to door was virtually impossible, due also to the fact that there are a lot of apartment blocks. Telephone research was very difficult too, Germans were very careful before answering.' John Attfield of RMM Marketing Research International worked in England before his 11-year stint in Germany. The differences in response he observed were dramatic. He took extra care in designing questionnaires, for instance:

One cannot approach Germans with the same introductory texts as in, for instance, the US. In the US the assumption is made that the participant was going to enjoy the survey. But in Germany people thought it was a pain.

Non-response bias
Bias caused when actual participants differ from those who refuse to participate.

Critical request
The target behaviour being researched.

Postal surveys have the poorest response rate. In a postal survey of randomly selected participants, without any pre- or post-mailing contact, response rates can be less than 15%. Such low response rates can lead to serious bias (non-response bias). This is because whether a person responds to a postal survey is related to how well the benefits of taking part in the survey are meaningful to the person and are clearly communicated to them. The magnitude of non-response bias increases as the response rate decreases.

Online surveys can have very poor response rates, much depending upon how comprehensive and current the sampling frame is. With a well-constructed sampling frame that is relevant to the survey topic, online survey response rates can be relatively high. This challenge is where the access panel has helped to improve online response rates. With a good relationship between panel participants and the panel owner, and well-chosen incentives to take part in online surveys, response rates can be greatly improved.

A comprehensive though dated review of the literature covering 497 response rates in 93 journal articles found weighted average response rates of 81.7%, 72.3% and 47.3% for, respectively, face-to-face, telephone and postal surveys.[40] However, response rates have decreased in recent times and are seen as a major threat to the marketing research industry.[41] The same review also found that response rates increase with the following:

- Either prepaid or promised monetary incentives.
- An increase in the amount of monetary incentive.
- Non-monetary premiums and rewards (pens, pencils, books).
- Preliminary notification.
- Foot-in-the door techniques. These are multiple-request strategies. The first request is relatively small, and all or most people agree to comply. The small request is followed by a larger request, called the critical request, which is actually the target behaviour being researched.
- Personalisation.
- Follow-up letters.

A further discussion of improving response rates is given in Chapter 15.

Situational factors

In any practical situation, the researcher has to balance the need to collect accurate and high-quality data with the budget and time constraints. The situational factors that are important include control of the data collection environment, control of field force, potential for interviewer bias, potential to probe participants, potential to build rapport, speed and cost.

Control of the data collection environment

The context in which a questionnaire is completed can affect the way that a participant answers questions. An example of this would be the amount of distraction from other people around, noise and temperature. The degree of control a researcher has over the context or environment in which the participant answers the questionnaire differentiates the various survey modes. Face-to-face surveys conducted at central locations (from street surveys and CAPIs) offer the greatest degree of environmental control. For example, the researcher can set up a special facility for demonstrating a product upon which a survey is based. Home and workplace face-to-face surveys offer moderate to high control because the interviewer is present. Traditional telephone surveys and CATIs offer moderate control. The interviewer cannot see the environment in which the interview is being conducted, but can sense the background conditions and encourage the participant to be attentive and involved. In postal surveys, email and online surveys, the researcher has little or no control over the environment. In the case of mobile online surveys, the questionnaire can be completed anywhere with the result that there is little or no consistency in the context in which the survey is completed. However, this ability for the participant to have control over the context may be instrumental in their fully engaging in the survey.

Control of field force

Field force

Both the actual interviewers and the supervisors involved in data collection.

The field force consists of interviewers and supervisors involved in data collection. Because they require no such personnel, postal surveys, email and online surveys eliminate field force problems. Traditional telephone surveys, CATIs, street surveys and CAPIs all offer moderate degrees of control because the interviews are conducted at a central location, making supervision relatively simple. Home and workplace face-to-face surveys are problematic in this respect. Because many interviewers work in many different locations, continual supervision is impractical.[42]

Potential for interviewer bias

An interviewer can bias the results of a survey by the manner in which the interviewer:

- Selects participants (e.g. interviewing a male aged 34 when required to interview a male aged between 36 and 45).
- Asks research questions (omitting questions).
- Poses questions in another way when participants do not understand the question as presented on the questionnaire.
- Probes (e.g. by offering examples to encourage participants).
- Records answers (recording an answer incorrectly or incompletely).

The extent of the interviewer's role determines the potential for bias.[43] Home, workplace and street face-to-face surveys are highly susceptible to interviewer bias. Traditional telephone surveys and CATIs are less susceptible, although the potential is still there: for example, with inflection and tone of voice, interviewers can convey their own attitudes and thereby suggest answers. CAPIs have a low potential for bias. Postal surveys, email and online surveys are free of it.

Potential to probe participants

Although the interviewer has the potential to create bias in the responses elicited from participants, it is balanced somewhat by the amount of probing that can be done. For example, a survey may ask participants which brands of beer they have seen advertised on TV over the past month. A list of brands could be presented to participants and they could simply look at the list and call out the names. What may be important in the survey is what brands they could remember. There may be a first response, of a brand that could be remembered unaided. A simple probe such as 'any others?' or 'any involving sports personalities?' could be recorded as a second response.

Much deeper prompts and probes can be conducted, within limits. The intention is not to turn the structured interview into a qualitative interview but, for example, some of the reasons why a participant has chosen a brand may be revealed. Home, workplace and street face-to-face surveys have great potential for probing participants. Traditional telephone surveys and CATIs can also probe but not to the same extent as being face to face. CAPIs have limited potential to probe, though particular routines can be built into a survey to ask for further details. Postal surveys, email and online surveys have very limited means to probe participants.

Potential to build rapport

Another counter to the bias in the responses elicited from participants by face-to-face surveys is the amount of rapport that can be built up with participants. Rapport may be vital to communicate why the survey is being conducted, with a corresponding rationale for the participant to spend time answering the questions. Beyond motivating participants to take part in a survey is the need for the participant to answer truthfully, to reflect upon the questions properly and not to rush through the questionnaire. Building up a good rapport with participants can be vital to gain a full and honest response to a survey.

Home, workplace and street face-to-face surveys have great potential to build up rapport with participants. Traditional telephone surveys and CATIs can also develop rapport but not to the same extent as being face to face. CAPI has limited potential to build up rapport through particular graphics and messages that can be built into a survey. Postal surveys, email and online surveys have very limited means to build up a rapport with participants. This challenge is where the access panel has helped to improve the online experience. With a good relationship between panel participants and the panel owner, and well-chosen incentives to take part in online surveys, rapport can be developed.

Speed

First, there is the speed with which a questionnaire can be created, distributed to participants and the data returned. Because printing, mailing and data keying delays are eliminated, data can be in hand within hours of writing an online or telephone questionnaire. Data are obtained in electronic form, so statistical analysis software can be programmed to process standard questionnaires and return statistical summaries and charts automatically. Thus, online surveys can be an extremely fast method of obtaining data from a large number of participants. The email survey is also fast, although slower than the online survey, since more time is needed to compile an email list and data entry is also required.

Traditional telephone surveys and CATIs are also fast means of obtaining information. When a central telephone facility is used, several hundred telephone interviews can be done per day. Data for even large national surveys can be collected in a matter of days or even within a day. Next in speed are street and CAPI surveys that reach potential participants in central locations. Home face-to-face surveys are slower because there is dead time between interviews while the interviewer travels to the next participant. To expedite data collection, interviews can be conducted in different markets or regions simultaneously. Postal surveys are typically the slowest. It usually takes several weeks to receive completed questionnaires; follow-up mailings to boost response rates take even longer.

Low cost

For large samples, the cost of online surveys is the lowest. Printing, mailing, keying and interviewer costs are eliminated, and the incremental costs per participant are typically low, so studies with large numbers of participants can be done at substantial savings compared with postal, telephone or face-to-face surveys. Face-to-face surveys tend to be the most expensive mode of data collection per completed response, whereas postal surveys tend to be the least expensive. In general, the cost increases from online to email, postal, traditional telephone, CATI, CAPI, street and finally face-to-face home and workplace surveys. This is a reflection of the progressively larger field staff and greater supervision and control. Relative costs, however, depend on the subject of enquiry and the procedures adopted.[44]

Participant factors

Since surveys are generally targeted at specific participant groups, participant characteristics have to be considered when selecting a survey method. The participant factors that are important include perceived participant anonymity, social desirability, obtaining sensitive information, low incidence rate and participant control.

Perceived participant anonymity

Perceived participant anonymity

The participants' perceptions that their identities will not be discerned by the interviewer or researcher.

Social desirability

The tendency of participants to give answers that may not be accurate but may be desirable from a social standpoint.

Perceived participant anonymity refers to the participants' perceptions that their identities will not be discerned by the interviewer or the researcher. Perceived anonymity of the participant is high in postal surveys and online surveys because there is no contact with an interviewer while responding. It is low in face-to-face surveys (home, street and CAPI) due to face-to-face contact with the interviewer. Traditional telephone surveys and CATIs fall in the middle. It is also moderate with email; while there is no contact with the interviewer, participants know that their names can be located on the return email.

Social desirability

Social desirability is the tendency of participants to give answers that they feel to be acceptable in front of others, including interviewers. When participants are questioned face to face by an interviewer, they may give an answer that they feel to be 'acceptable' rather than how they really feel or behave. Because postal and online surveys do not involve any social interaction between the interviewer and participant, they are least susceptible to social desirability. Traditional telephone surveys and CATIs are moderately good at handling socially desirable responses, as there is an amount of anonymity afforded by not meeting face to face. The weakest techniques are face-to-face surveys, though in the case of home and workplace surveys, the chance to build up a rapport with participants may nurture them to reveal how they really feel.[45] The best techniques to avoid participants distorting their views are those where face-to-face contact is avoided; this is the case in postal surveys.

Obtaining sensitive information

Sensitive information may mean an issue that is personally sensitive, such as the way in which a participant may be classified or the use of hygiene products. What may be deemed 'sensitive' varies enormously between different types of participant. For some participants, asking questions about the type and amount of household cleaning products may be seen as revealing characteristics of their personal cleanliness; they see it as a sensitive issue and would need a lot of reassurance before revealing the truth. Many classification questions in a survey, such as the participant's age, gender, educational or income level, can also be seen as highly sensitive. In business research, characteristics of an organisation's activities may be seen as commercially sensitive.

In some situations, the interviewer plays a very important role in explaining to participants why they are being asked such a question and that their views will be handled in a confidential and proper manner. Home and workplace surveys allow the time and context to build up such explanations and reassure participants. Interviews conducted in this way may be seen as the best means to handle certain sensitive topics. For some issues, participants may not wish to face any interviewer and would like to complete the survey alone. CAPI can be set up so that the interviewer introduces the participant to a terminal and then leaves the participant to get on with the on-screen interview.[46] Postal and online surveys can be seen as moderately successful in handling sensitive questions. Their success depends upon how well the purpose of sensitive questions is introduced. Handled correctly, participants can take their time to answer questions without any embarrassing contact. For telephone and street surveys, the interviewer can reassure the participant about the questions being asked, but may not have the time and context really to relax participants and overcome any embarrassment.

Perceived anonymity, social desirability and obtaining sensitive information are interrelated criteria. With some exceptions, social desirability is the mirror image of perceived anonymity. When perceived anonymity is high, social desirability is low and vice versa. With some exceptions, obtaining sensitive information is directly related to perceptions of anonymity. Participants are more willing to give sensitive information when they perceive that their responses will be anonymous.

Low incidence rate

Incidence rate
Incidence rate refers to the rate of occurrence or the percentage of persons eligible to participate in a study.

Incidence rate refers to the rate of occurrence or the percentage of persons eligible to participate in the study. As will be discussed in more detail in Chapter 15, incidence rate determines how many contacts need to be screened for a given sample size requirement. There are times when the researcher is faced with a situation where the incidence rate of survey participants is low. This is generally the case when the 'population' represents a niche or a highly targeted market. Suppose a study was focused upon buyers of new sports cars, specifically to measure and understand the characteristics of consumers who aspire to own and could afford a new Audi R8.[47] The incidence of such potential consumers in the wider population would be very low. A lot of wasted effort would be exerted if the 'general population' were to be sampled for a survey. In such cases, a survey method should be selected that can locate qualified participants efficiently and minimise waste. The access panel, which can profile potential participants in some detail, offers great benefits in understanding incidence. The telephone survey can be very effective as a method of screening potential participants to determine eligibility; all it takes is a phone call. Face-to-face methods are all inefficient because the interviewer has to make personal contact with potential participants. Postal surveys and email are moderate in terms of efficiency as they are relatively low cost and can be used to contact a large number of potential participants so the desired sample size of qualified participants is obtained. Online, however, is very good in this respect as screening questions can be used to weed out ineligible participants quickly and efficiently.

Participant control

Methods that allow participant control over the interviewing process can solicit greater cooperation and engagement. Two aspects of control are particularly important to participants. The first is control over when to answer the survey, and the flexibility to answer it in parts at different times and even via different modes. The second aspect of control pertains to the ability of the participants to regulate the rate or pace at which they answer the survey. Postal surveys and email are the best in giving this control to participants. Some control is lost in online surveys because in random pop-up surveys participants do not have the flexibility of answering at a later time. However, online surveys can be designed to allow participants to come back and complete them. The pace of telephone surveys is regulated by the interviewer and although the telephone call can be rescheduled, the participant must commit to a specific time. With face-to-face methods, the pace is regulated by the interviewer and generally the interview cannot be rescheduled. The main exception in face-to-face methods may lie with workplace surveys, as accessing business participants may be driven by their timetables.

Other survey methods

We have covered the basic survey methods. Other survey methods are also used, which are variations of these basic methods. The more popular of these other methods are described in Table 10.3.

Table 10.3	Additional survey methods	
Method	**Advantages/disadvantages**	**Comment**
Completely automated telephone survey (CATS)	Same as CATI	Useful for short, in-bound surveys initiated by participant
Central location interview	Same as street survey	Examples include new product tests, advertising tests, trade shows, conferences
Kiosk-based computer interview	Same as CAPI	Useful in museum, heritage and exhibition sites
Drop-off survey	Same as postal survey, except higher cost and higher response rate	Useful for local market surveys

Mixed-mode surveys

As is evident from Table 10.2 and the preceding discussion, no survey method is superior in all situations. Depending on such factors as information requirements, budgetary constraints (time and money) and participant characteristics, none, one, two or even all techniques may be appropriate.[48] Remember that the various data collection modes are not mutually exclusive, but can be employed in a complementary fashion to build on each other's strengths and compensate for each other's weaknesses. The researcher can employ these techniques in combination and develop creative twists within each technique. With the growth in the use of email and the Internet as a means of communication, online methods have become the most feasible and popular means of conducting surveys. Where online methods are not appropriate for particular types of participant, a choice can be made by individual participants to select the survey method that they prefer. Most survey analysis packages that include the function of questionnaire design have the ability to formulate the questionnaire into all survey method formats. Mixed-mode designs are increasingly being used for multi-country studies. Depending on the mix of countries being surveyed, face-to-face, CATI or online methods may be employed, with online being the preferred choice for the USA and a growing number of other countries with relatively high Internet penetration. Single-mode within-country and mixed-mode between-country methods may be the most common mixed-mode designs in marketing research.[49] Mixed-mode research offers one of the most serious ways to tackle falling response rates. The key features of making mixed-mode research work are:[50]

- Common questions across all modes.
- Different templates applied to different modes to ensure that each looks appropriate.
- Mode-specific text alternatives in addition to support for foreign language translations.
- A single database for all survey data, updated in real time.
- The ability to determine the mode of initial contact from the sample.
- Easy switching of any interview from one mode to another.
- Automatic concealment of any interviewer-recorded data when switching a self-completion mode.

- Management tools that allow progress to be viewed across all modes and identify separate modes.
- Support for mode-specific questions or question types.

Care should be exercised when using different methods in the same domestic marketing research project. The method used may affect the response obtained and hence the responses obtained by different methods may not be comparable.

Observation techniques

Quantitative observation
The recording and counting of behavioural patterns of people, objects and events in a systematic manner to obtain information about the phenomenon of interest.

Mystery shopper
An observer visiting providers of goods and services as if they were really a customer, and recording characteristics of the service delivery.

Structured observation
Observation where the researcher clearly defines the behaviours to be observed and the techniques by which they will be measured.

Unstructured observation
Observation that involves a researcher monitoring all relevant phenomena, without specifying the details in advance.

Ethnography
A research approach based upon the observation of the customs, habits and differences between people in everyday situations.

Quantitative observation techniques are extensively used in descriptive research. Observation involves recording the behavioural patterns of people, objects and events in a systematic manner to obtain information about the phenomenon of interest. The observer does not question or communicate with the people being observed unless he or she takes the role of a mystery shopper. Information may be recorded as the events occur or from records of past events. Observational techniques may be structured or unstructured, disguised or undisguised. Furthermore, observation may be conducted in a natural or a contrived environment.[51]

Structured versus unstructured observation

For structured observation, the researcher specifies in detail what is to be observed and how the measurements are to be recorded, such as when an auditor performs a stock or inventory analysis in a store. This reduces the potential for observer bias and enhances the reliability of the data. Structured observation is appropriate when the phenomena under study can be clearly defined and counted. For example, suppose that the researcher wished to measure the ratio of visitors to buyers in a store. The reason for such observations could be to understand the amount of browsing that occurs in a store. The researcher could observe and count the number of individuals who enter the store and the number who make a purchase. Counting people who enter a shop could be a manual observation, and could have a rule that the store visitors are counted 'if they actually look at any of the products on display'. Counting the number of transactions through the till may be a simpler electronic observation. With these two counts the researcher could simply calculate the required ratio. Structured observation is suitable for use in conclusive research.

In unstructured observation the observer monitors all aspects of the phenomenon that seem relevant to the problem at hand, such as observing children playing with new toys and trying to understand what activities they enjoy the most. This form of observation can be used when a research problem has yet to be formulated precisely and when flexibility is needed in observation to identify essential components of the problem and to develop hypotheses. Unstructured observation is most appropriate for exploratory research and as such was discussed in detail in Chapter 6 under the heading of ethnography. Ethnographic techniques require a researcher to spend a large amount of time observing a particular group of people, by sharing their way of life.[52]

Disguised versus undisguised observation

In disguised observation, the participants are unaware that they are being observed. Disguise enables participants to behave naturally because people tend to behave differently when they know they are being observed. Disguise may be accomplished by using two-way mirrors, hidden cameras or inconspicuous electronic devices. Observers may be disguised as shoppers, sales assistants or other appropriate roles. One of the most widespread techniques of observation is through the use of mystery shoppers as illustrated in the following example.

Real research	**Mystery shopping uncovers age discrimination**[53]

Help the Aged and Age Concern are two well-known charities that fight for the rights of all older people in society. The two charities came together to fund research to investigate evidence of discrimination in the markets for motor and travel insurance, as experienced by older people. A solid evidence base was required that demonstrated in depth the behaviour, successes, challenges and frustrations that older customers faced. Evidence was provided by combining a comprehensive study based upon in-depth interviews, group discussions and an innovative mystery shopping exercise. The latter involved recruiting a sample of those aged 65 to 85 and a control sample aged 30 to 49. Participants made real-life insurance quote requests through different channels, and gave interviews before and after the event. The study delivered substantial evidence of age discrimination, both in terms of offering services at all and in the pricing of insurance. Quotations from the shopping team provided powerful illustrations. They also uncovered age-related concerns about Internet-only access to some products, and in the way suppliers talk to customers. Wide-ranging recommendations were published, aimed at the insurance industry and government.

Typically a mystery shopper would go into a bank, for example, note practical things such as the number of counter positions open, the number of people queuing, or the availability of specific leaflets, and then ask a number of specific questions. The mystery shopper takes the role of the ordinary 'man or woman in the street', behaves just as a normal customer would, asks the same sorts of questions a customer would, leaves, and fills in a questionnaire detailing the various components observed in the visit. Mystery shopping differs from conventional survey research in that it aims to collect facts rather than perceptions. Conventional customer service research is all about customer perceptions. Mystery shopping, on the other hand, aims to be as objective as possible and to record as accurately as possible what actually happened in encounters such as the following.[54]

Personal visits

- How long were you in the queue?
- How many tills were open?
- Did the counter clerk apologise if you were kept waiting?
- What form of greeting or farewell was given?

Telephone calls

- How many rings were there before the phone was answered?
- Did the person who answered the phone go on to answer all your questions?
- Were you asked a password?
- How many times during the conversation was your name used?

A major development in disguised and undisguised observation lies in social media research techniques. The terms used to represent disguised and undisguised may be replaced with the terms 'passive' and 'active' respectively.[55] Passive observation through social media incorporates a variety of blog and buzz mining techniques. These include searching the Internet for conversations from blogs to Twitter, from social networks to comments on news stories, gathering information about brands and social issues. Active observation through social media can include participant blogs. Participants are recruited to engage in blogs using social media. Researchers set the context and may ask some questions, but the process is mostly participant driven.[56]

In undisguised or passive observation, participants are aware that they are under observation. Participants may be aware of the situation either by being told that an observer is in their presence or by its being obvious that someone is recording their behaviour. Researchers disagree on how much effect the presence of an observer has on behaviour. One viewpoint is that the observer effect is minor and short-lived. The other position is that the observer can seriously bias the behaviour patterns.[57] There are ethical considerations to disguised versus undisguised observations that will be tackled at the end of this chapter.

Natural versus contrived observation

Natural observation
Observing behaviour as it takes place in the environment.

Contrived observation
Observing behaviour in an artificial environment.

Natural observation involves observing behaviour as it takes place in the environment. For example, one could observe the behaviour of participants eating a new menu option in a pizza restaurant. In **contrived observation**, participants' behaviour is observed in an artificial environment, such as a test kitchen.

The advantage of natural observation is that the observed phenomenon will more accurately reflect the true phenomenon, as the behaviour occurs in a context that feels natural to the participant. The disadvantages are the cost of waiting for the phenomenon to occur and the difficulty of measuring the phenomenon in a natural setting.

Observation techniques classified by mode of administration

As shown in Figure 10.2, observation techniques may be classified by mode of administration as personal observation, electronic observation and trace analysis.

Personal observation

Personal observation
An observational research strategy in which human observers record the phenomenon being observed as it occurs.

Electronic observation
An observational research strategy in which electronic devices, rather than human observers, record the phenomenon being observed.

In **personal observation**, a researcher observes actual behaviour as it occurs. The observer does not attempt to control or manipulate the phenomenon being observed but merely records what takes place. For example, a researcher might record the time, day and number of shoppers who enter a shop and observe where those shoppers 'flow' once they are in the shop. This information could aid in designing a store's layout and determining the location of individual departments, shelf locations and merchandise displays.

Electronic observation

In **electronic observation**, electronic devices rather than human observers record the phenomenon being observed. The devices may or may not require the participants' direct participation. They are used for continuously recording ongoing behaviour for later analysis.

Figure 10.2

A classification of observation methods

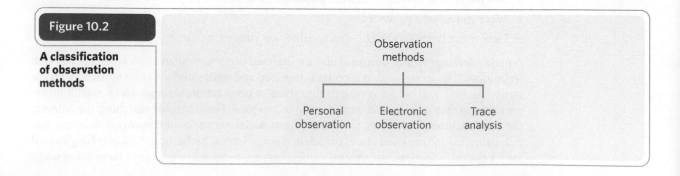

Of the electronic devices that do not require participants' direct participation, the A.C. Nielsen audimeter is best known. The audimeter is attached to a TV set to record continually the channel to which a set is tuned. Another way to monitor viewers is through the people meter. People meters attempt to measure not only the channels to which a set is tuned, but also who is watching.[58] In recent years, there has much interest in collecting and analysing television set-top box (STB) data. As TV moves from analogue to digital signals, digital STBs are increasingly common in homes. Where these are attached to some sort of return path (as is the case in many homes subscribing to cable or satellite TV services), these data can be aggregated and licensed to companies wishing to measure TV viewership. Advances in distributed computing make it feasible to analyse these data on a huge scale. Whereas previous TV measurement relied on panels consisting of thousands of households, data can now be collected and analysed for millions of households. This holds the promise of providing accurate measurement for much (and perhaps all) of the niche TV content that eludes current panel-based methods in many countries.[59]

Chapter 5 detailed and evaluated an array of electronic observation techniques including purchasing and browsing behaviour through web analytics. The chapter also detailed the observation of in-store purchasing behaviour through the use of the bar codes on products. The use of optical scanners can determine which products have been sold. With a link to a 'loyalty card', electronic observation links the whole array of purchases made by a consumer to the actual identity of that consumer. In this example, electronic observation does not require direct involvement of the participants.

In contrast to the Internet, there are many electronic observation devices that do require participant involvement. These electronic devices may be classified into five groups: (1) eye tracking monitors, (2) pupilometers, (3) psycho-galvanometers, (4) voice pitch analysers and (5) devices measuring response latency. Eye tracking equipment – such as oculometers, eye cameras or eye view minuters – records the gaze movements of the eye. These devices can be used to determine how a participant reads an advertisement or views a TV commercial and for how long the participant looks at various parts of the stimulus as illustrated in the following example. Such information is directly relevant to assessing advertising effectiveness.

Eye tracking equipment
Instruments that record the gaze movements of the eye.

Real research

Through the shopper's eyes[60]

Mobile eye tracking allows the researcher to see exactly what the shoppers see as they go about their shopping. 'Magic glasses' contain two video cameras, one pointing outwards to record the field of vision and one pointing at the shoppers' eye to measure exactly where it focuses. The eye positions are overlaid onto the field of vision so the researcher can pinpoint exactly what each shopper looks at and for how long. Jigsaw (**www.jigsawresearch.com.au**) in partnership with Access Testing (**www.accesstesting.com.au**) completed a study using mobile eye tracking for Colgate Palmolive. Shoppers were recruited to meet up with researchers in a store. Following questions on their attitudes to shopping, participants were set up with the 'magic glasses' and their shopping trolley. After being sent off alone for a warm-up task, the participant was sent off to complete the research task: making a purchase based on his or her current or most recent purchase needs. Once the task was complete, the video footage was immediately replayed to the shoppers so they could talk through the process. The researchers could see the real-life purchase process through the shoppers' eyes and follow it up with discussion around why they had behaved as they did. The researchers saw shoppers get lost, pick up the wrong products, spend minutes agonising over which special offer to buy. They even saw them talking and singing to themselves (the glasses also have a microphone) and eyeing up fellow shoppers. Researchers could see what participants actually did compared with what they said they would do.

Neuromarketing
The application of
neuroscience in marketing,
primarily to measure
emotions through brain
imaging.

Neuromarketing is concerned with the direct measurement of the brain's conscious and unconscious responses to marketing stimuli. Typically this involves the measurement of a participant's brain activity through quantitative electroencephalography (qEEG). This measurement is of electrical activity at specific sites across the surface of the brain through sensors affixed to the participant's scalp. Through knowledge of brain function, insight into the mental activity associated with a particular stimulus or study condition can be determined.[61] An example of neuromarketing is illustrated in the following example.

Real research	How a female robot grew sales for Philips[62]

A radical new international campaign for a Philips shaver swapped 'persuasive' product messages for a female robot and doubled market share in just six months. The Philips MSS combined the best of 'wet' (blade) and 'dry' (electric) shaving; it also had a built-in Nivea lotion dispenser, which moisturised and protected the face during shaving. The MSS product was good, but set against powerful competition this was not enough. By 2007, something needed to change for Philips. The MSS share of electric shaving was now down to just 6% (a mere 1% share of all shaving), and was declining fast. Philips' first instinct was to tackle the problem through product innovation: could it make the MSS better in some way? Philips quickly realised that this was not right or necessary. Nor did just telling men about the product seem enough. The previous advertising had done that and share kept on declining. Research indicated the problem lay in a different place, in the emotional associations young men had with electric shaving. However good the product was, electric shaving (and thus MSS) just was not cool. Philips had to create new emotional associations around electric shaving. In exploratory research, young men were brutally dismissive about what they saw as patronising and sexist shaving advertising clichés. They hated breathless Hollywood blockbuster voice-overs, the soaring soundtracks, the swooshes over close-ups of gleaming metal. The creative communications team came up with the concept of 'skin technology'. It sounded futuristic, hybrid, almost a new breed. Enter the 'Fembot': a sexy female robot shaving accomplice. Enigmatic and beguiling, she was a sensual dramatisation of MSS technology and Nivea care. The campaign line summarised the promise of this new shaving experience: 'Feel Different'. The launch TV ad had no overt product details, no message and no voice-over. To slow, haunting instrumental music, the ad showed a man entering a futuristic bathroom. The Fembot slowly and meticulously laid out towels and prepared the shower, before helping him to shave with the moisturising shaver. This was a totally different sort of shaver ad, more akin to a pop promotion than an ad. The ad focused on conveying emotions, not facts. The Fembot idea got a fantastic response in pretesting; the campaign was much more effective than previous MSS advertising. How did it work so well? To help answer this, Philips turned to neuroscience. Monitoring brain activity while men watched the ad showed two scenes in particular were critical to its success. In the shower scene, men showed very high levels of activity in brain regions linked to 'emotional intensity'. Of all 700 ads ever tested by the research company, this ad was in the top 1%. Then, at the end, they showed very high scores for 'personal relevance' (top 1% again), as they 'got' the ad. Both scenes generated very strong scores for pleasure and liking (top 3% of all ads ever tested). But most importantly, both scenes prompted *extremely* high levels of activity in the brain areas associated with long-term memory encoding. This mattered because long-term memory encoding was known to be the best predictor of behavioural intent and future sales effects. It did not need to communicate the fine product details – those could be found out online if needed. But it did boost sales, in both the short and the long term. It seems that the TV ad worked *because* of the lack of rational messaging, not in spite of it.

Psycho-galvanometer
An instrument that measures a participant's galvanic skin response.

Galvanic skin response
Changes in the electrical resistance of the skin that relate to a participant's affective state.

Voice pitch analysis
Measurement of emotional reactions through changes in a participant's voice.

Response latency
The amount of time it takes to respond to a question.

Trace analysis
An approach in which data collection is based on physical traces, or evidence, of past behaviour.

Cookie technology
An identification code stored in the web surfer's browser that identifies a particular user.

The **psycho-galvanometer** measures **galvanic skin response** (GSR) or changes in the electrical resistance of the skin.[63] The participant is fitted with small electrodes that monitor electrical resistance and is shown stimuli such as advertisements, packages and slogans. The theory behind this device is that physiological changes such as increased perspiration accompany emotional reactions. Excitement leads to increased perspiration, which increases the electrical resistance of the skin. From the strength of the response, the researcher infers the participant's interest level and attitudes towards the stimuli.

Voice pitch analysis measures emotional reactions through changes in the participant's voice. Changes in the relative vibration frequency of the human voice that accompany emotional reaction are measured with audio-adapted computer equipment.[64]

Response latency is the time a participant takes before answering a question. It is used as a measure of the relative preference for various alternatives.[65] Response time is thought to be directly related to uncertainty. Therefore, the longer a participant takes to choose between two alternatives, the closer the alternatives are in terms of preference. On the other hand, if the participant makes a quick decision, one alternative is clearly preferred. With the increased popularity of computer-assisted data collection, response latency can be recorded accurately and without the participant's awareness. Use of eye tracking monitors, neuromarketing, psycho-galvanometers and voice pitch analysers assumes that physiological reactions are associated with specific cognitive and affective responses. This has yet to be clearly demonstrated. Furthermore, calibration of these devices to measure physiological arousal is difficult, and they are expensive to use. Another limitation is that participants are placed in an artificial environment and know that they are being observed.

Trace analysis

An observation method that can be inexpensive if used creatively is **trace analysis**. In trace analysis, data collection is based on physical traces, or evidence, of past behaviour. These traces may be left by the participants intentionally or unintentionally. Several innovative applications of trace analysis have been made in marketing research:

- The selective erosion of tiles in a museum indexed by the replacement rate was used to determine the relative popularity of exhibits.

- The number of different fingerprints on a page was used to gauge the readership of various advertisements in a magazine.

- The position of the radio dials in cars brought in for service was used to estimate share of listening audience of various radio stations. Advertisers used the estimates to decide on which stations to advertise.

- The age and condition of cars in a car park were used to assess the affluence of customers.

- The magazines people donated to charity were used to determine people's favourite magazines.

- Internet visitors leave traces that can be analysed to examine browsing and usage behaviour through **cookie technology**.

The following example briefly outlines the use of cookies, which basically underpin much of the web analytics that were described in Chapter 5.

| Real research | **Have a cookie**[66] |

The cookie is an identification code stored in the web surfer's browser that identifies a particular user. Companies and individuals that host websites use cookies to observe behavioural characteristics of visitors. Cookies follow the traveller through the website and record the pages accessed by the visitor and the number of minutes spent on each page. The name, address, phone number and access site can be collected by the cookie and saved into a database if the visitor enters any information. During a follow-up visit, the cookie accesses this information and has the ability to repeat it to the visitor. In essence, the cookie collects data on the user during every visit to the site. Expedia (**www.expedia.com**) uses cookies to collect information about site traffic. The information helps marketing personnel at the travel site to collect demographics on the reader. Also, the company can monitor 'hits' on particular topics and gain valuable feedback on user interest. Data collection is based upon visitor behaviour. This disguised technique enables Expedia to monitor use patterns and to eliminate socially acceptable response bias. Information collected in this manner has been used to modify editorial content and format to make the website more appealing and useful to visitors.

A comparative evaluation of the observation techniques

A comparative evaluation of the observation techniques is given in Table 10.4. The different observation techniques are evaluated in terms of the degree of structure, degree of disguise, ability to observe in a natural setting, observation bias, measurement and analysis bias, and additional general factors.

Structure relates to the specification of what is to be observed and how the measurements are to be recorded. As can be seen from Table 10.4, personal observation is low, and trace analysis is medium on the degree of structure. Electronic observation can vary widely from low to high, depending on the techniques used. Techniques such as optical scanners are very structured in that the characteristics to be measured – for example, characteristics of items purchased and scanned in supermarket checkouts – are precisely defined. In contrast, electronic techniques, such as the use of hidden cameras to observe children at play with toys, tend to be unstructured.

Table 10.4	**A comparative evaluation of observation techniques**		
Criteria	**Personal observation**	**Electronic observation**	**Trace analysis**
Degree of structure	*	* to *****	***
Degree of disguise	***	****	*****
Natural setting	*****	****	*
Observation bias	*****	*	***
Analysis bias	*****	**	***
General remarks	Most flexible	Can be intrusive	Limited traces available

(key: low = *, moderate to low = **, moderate = ***, moderate to high = ****, high = *****)

Personal observation offers a medium degree of disguise because there are limitations on the extent to which the observer can be disguised as a shopper, sales assistant or employee. Trace analysis offers a high degree of disguise because the data are collected 'after the fact': that is, after the phenomenon to be observed has taken place. Some electronic observations such as hidden cameras offer excellent disguise, whereas others, such as the use of eye tracking equipment, are very difficult to disguise.

The ability to observe in a natural setting is low in trace analysis because the observation takes place after the behaviour has occurred. Personal observation and audits are excellent on this score because human observers can observe people or objects in a variety of natural settings. Electronic observation techniques vary from low (e.g. use of eye tracking equipment) to high (e.g. use of turnstiles).

Observation bias is low in the case of electronic observation because a human observer is not involved. Observation bias is medium for trace analysis. In this technique, human observers are involved and the characteristics to be observed are not very well defined. The observers typically do not interact with human participants during the observation process, thus lessening the degree of bias. It is high for personal observation due to the use of human observers who interact with the phenomenon being observed.

Trace analysis has a medium degree of data analysis bias as the definition of variables is not very precise. Electronic observation techniques can have a low (e.g. scanner data) to medium (e.g. hidden camera) degree of analysis bias. Unlike personal observation, the bias in electronic observation is limited to the medium level due to improved measurement and classification, because the phenomenon to be observed can be recorded continuously using electronic devices.

In addition, personal observation is the most flexible, because human observers can observe a wide variety of phenomena in a wide variety of settings. Some electronic observation techniques, such as the use of eye tracking equipment, can be very intrusive, leading to artificiality and bias. Audits using human auditors tend to be expensive. As mentioned earlier, trace analysis is a method that is limited to where consumers actually leave 'traces'. This occurs infrequently and very creative approaches are needed to capture these traces.

Evaluating the criteria presented in Table 10.4 helps to identify the most appropriate observation technique, given the phenomena to be observed, the nature of participants being observed and the context in which the observation occurs. To strengthen the choice of a particular observation technique, it is also helpful to compare the relative advantages and disadvantages of observation versus survey techniques.

Advantages and disadvantages of observation techniques

Other than the use of scanner data, few marketing research projects rely solely on observational techniques to obtain primary data.[67] This implies that observational techniques have some major disadvantages compared with survey techniques. Yet these techniques offer some advantages that make their use in conjunction with survey techniques quite fruitful.

Relative advantages of observation techniques

The greatest advantage of observational techniques is that they permit measurement of actual behaviour rather than reports of intended or preferred behaviour. There is no reporting bias, and potential bias caused by the interviewer and the interviewing process is eliminated or reduced. Certain types of data can be collected only by observation. These include behaviour patterns which the participant is unaware of or unable to communicate. For example, information on babies' and toddlers' toy preferences is best obtained by observing babies at play, because they are unable to express themselves adequately. Moreover, if the observed phenomenon occurs frequently or is of short duration, observational techniques may cost less and be faster than survey techniques.

Relative disadvantages of observation techniques

The biggest disadvantage of observation is that the reasons for the observed behaviour may be difficult to determine because little is known about the underlying motives, beliefs, attitudes and preferences. For example, people observed buying a brand of cereal may or may not like it themselves; they may be purchasing that brand for someone else in the household. Another limitation of observation is the extent to which researchers are prepared to evaluate the extent of their own bias, and how this can affect what they observe (this was discussed in Chapter 9). In addition, observational data can be time consuming and expensive to collect. It is also difficult to observe certain forms of behaviour such as personal activities that occur in the privacy of the consumer's home. Finally, in some cases such as in the use of hidden cameras, the use of observational techniques may border on being or may actually be unethical. It can be argued that individuals being observed should be made aware of the situation, but this may cause them to behave in a contrived manner.

International marketing research

The selection of appropriate survey and observation techniques is more challenging in an international context given the breadth of environmental factors that can shape choices. Given the differences in the economic, structural, informational, technological and socio-cultural environment, the feasibility and popularity of the different survey techniques vary widely. Table 10.5 provides an illustration of proportions of marketing research spend in different countries across the globe in 2009. Though there are few major differences in spend between quantitative and qualitative methods, it is clear that quantitative methods dominate spending. Within quantitative method spending there are major differences between countries. The USA spent 15% on postal, telephone and face-to-face methods and 63% on online and digital methods. By contrast South Africa spent 60% and 30% in the same respective methods. There are many reasons for such differences that will be developed further in Chapter 26. For illustration purposes for just one factor, Table 10.6 provides a breakdown of the different types of client in the

Table 10.5	A comparative evaluation of spend by research method[68]								
Country	Online	Online traffic/ audience	Postal	Telephone	Face-to-face	Automated digital	Other quantitative	Total quantitative	Total qualitative
Bolivia	3	0	0	15	60	2	0	80	20
Finland	33	3	14	22	9	7	4	92	7
Greece	1	0	1	19	34	28	5	88	11
Iran	0	0	0	13	55	0	15	83	17
Japan	36	0	11	3	12	0	21	83	15
Nigeria	2	0	0	2	62	2	0	68	31
Poland	2	1	2	12	43	9	9	78	20
Russia	5	1	1	20	30	15	3	75	22
South Africa	1	24	0	12	48	5	0	90	9
USA	22	1	2	12	1	40	8	86	14

Note: Totals may not equal 100% due to rounding up or down.

Table 10.6	A comparative evaluation of spend by client type[69]									
Country	Manufacturing	Business to business	Wholesale and retail	Financial services	Utilities	Public sector	Media	Advertising agencies	Research institutes	Other
Bolivia	45	5	5	10	15	10	10	0	0	0
Finland	31	10	12	5	5	6	23	4	3	1
Greece	45	1	3	6	7	3	12	6	12	5
Iran	78	0	0	0	18	0	4	0	0	0
Japan	37	2	3	1	4	5	10	17	13	8
Nigeria	42	2	1	8	18	12	8	3	2	4
Poland	51	1	4	7	10	9	9	4	4	1
Russia	53	4	5	6	11	4	9	4	3	1
South Africa	58	1	5	9	8	2	5	1	0	11
USA	44	4	5	4	2	8	28	2	1	2

Note: Totals may not equal 100% due to rounding up or down.

same countries. There are many economic, structural and technological factors that underpin these differences. These tables emphasise that it is unlikely that a single data collection approach will be effective in multi-country research.

Selection of survey methods

No survey method can be deemed to be superior. Though this chapter has demonstrated how much more popular and dominant online surveys are in a global sense, this does not necessarily mean that they are 'superior'. Each individual survey method has its own distinct advantages and disadvantages that the researcher must evaluate. But if the researcher is designing a survey that is to work in different geographical locations, the additional challenges and opportunities inherent to the selected locations must also be evaluated. Table 10.7 presents a comparative evaluation of the major modes of collecting quantitative data in the context of international marketing research. In this table, the survey techniques are discussed only under the broad headings of online, telephone, face-to-face and postal surveys. The use of CATI, CAPI, online and access panels depends heavily on the state of technological development in the country. Likewise, the use of street interviewing is contingent upon the dominance of shopping centres in the retailing environment.

Table 10.7	A comparative evaluation of survey techniques for international marketing research			
Criteria	Online	Telephone	Face-to-face	Postal
High sample control	–	+	+	–
Difficulty in locating participants at home	+	+	–	+
Inaccessibility of homes	+	+	–	+
Unavailability of a large pool of trained interviewers	+	+	–	+
Large population in rural areas	–	–	+	–
Unavailability of maps	+	+	–	+
Unavailability of current telephone directories	+	–	+	–
Unavailability of mailing lists	+	+	+	–
Low penetration of telephones	–	–	+	+
Lack of an efficient postal system	+	+	+	–
Low level of literacy	–	–	+	–
Face-to-face communication culture	–	–	+	–
Poor access to computers and the Internet	–	+	+	+

Note: A plus denotes an advantage, and a minus denotes a disadvantage.

Ethics in marketing research

Participant anonymity was discussed in the context of qualitative research in Chapter 8. It was argued then that large samples could 'hide' the specific answers of individual participants. This is true to some extent but participants may still be identifiable. It is up to the researcher to protect a participant's identity and not disclose it to anyone outside the research organisation, including the client. The client is not entitled to see the names and contact details of participants. The only instance where participants' identity can be revealed to the client is when participants are notified in advance and their consent is obtained prior to administering the survey. Even in such situations, the researcher should have the assurance that the participants' trust will be kept by the client and their identities will not be used in a sales effort or misused in other ways.

Special care must be taken to ensure that any record which contains a reference to the identity of a participant is securely and confidentially stored during any period before such reference is separated from that record and/or destroyed. Ethical lapses in this respect by unscrupulous researchers and marketers have resulted in a serious backlash for marketing research. The result has contributed to a consistent fall in the levels of response rate, to all forms of survey method. This reinforces the message that considering the needs of survey participants makes sound research sense as well as being ethically sound. Dubious practices may generate a response for a single survey but may create long-term damage to the marketing research industry.

Another issue facing the marketing research industry is image, as the public may not distinguish between telephone research and telemarketing. This identity crisis is exacerbated by the action of some firms to commit 'sugging' and 'frugging', industry terms for selling or fundraising under the guise of a survey. The overall effect of these activities has given a poor image in particular to telephone research, raising the cost and making it difficult for researchers to obtain full and representative samples.

Although concerns for the participants' psychological well-being are mild in survey data collection when compared with either qualitative or experimental research, researchers should not place participants in stressful situations. Disclaimers such as 'there are no correct responses; we are only interested in your opinion' can relieve much of the stress inherent in a survey. In many face-to-face survey situations, participants are given a 'thank you booklet' at the end of the interview. As well as saying a genuine 'thank you' for taking part in a survey, the booklet briefly sets out the purpose and benefits of bona fide marketing research. The use of the 'thank you booklet' helps to educate potential participants to distinguish between genuine, professionally conducted marketing research and 'research' conducted as a front for generating sales leads.

Observation of people's behaviour without their consent is often done because informing the participants may alter their behaviour.[70] But this can compromise the privacy of the participants. One guideline is that people should not be observed for research in situations where they would not expect to be observed by the public. Therefore, public places like a shopping centre or a grocery aisle may be fair game. These are places where people observe other people routinely. However, notices should be posted in these areas stating that they are under observation by researchers.

With the growth of mystery shopping, where the essence of the technique is that service deliverers cannot spot the observer, the debate over what is ethical practice has intensified. If potential participants perceive marketing research as a means to generate sales and 'snoop' on service delivery practices, then the goodwill needed to generate full and honest responses will wither. ESOMAR has specific guidelines to help with issues in mystery shopping, which can be seen at **www.esomar.com**.

Sugging
The use of marketing research to deliberately disguise a sales effort.
Frugging
The use of marketing research to deliberately disguise fundraising activities.

Digital applications in marketing research

The Internet has become the predominant means to conduct surveys and observe consumers. Though there are many countries that have yet to reach the levels of adoption seen in most developed economies, the growth in online methods is a global phenomenon. While online surveys may be the most prevalent technique, the marketing research industry still battles with decreasing participant engagement and the ability to access hard-to-reach targets including youth and multicultural participants. The challenge to engage and reward survey participants can be tackled with digital developments in marketing research. In the 2010 ESOMAR Global Market Research Report, advances in technology were seen as a major opportunity to be grasped:

> *The most exciting opportunities for the industry seem to stem from developments in technology, opening up new end markets to measure, creating opportunities to improve methodologies and engaging respondents [sic] and new talent. The transformation has been fuelled by strong growth in internet and mobile penetration and advances in the sophistication of mobile devices and online platforms.*[71]

Examples of improving engagement include the concept of offering virtual currency for survey participation. But more important, by offering interesting, entertaining and diverse surveys with no requirement to divulge contact information, participants are further encouraged to engage in surveys and to provide accurate information, on their terms. Affinity networks and communities enable researchers to target low-incidence groups that many traditional access panels have a hard time reaching.[72] The following example illustrates how digital developments are making an engaging experience for participants while capturing data that previously may have been most tortuous and expensive. It shows how imagery and music can be part of the motivation for participating in a survey, allied to a notion that a participant's view is important in shaping the creative destiny of an organisation.

Real research　Warner Music's customer panel[73]

Warner Music Group (WMG) worked with Globalpark (**www.globalpark.co.uk**) to form an advisory panel with more than 10,000 customers who agreed to share their opinions, observations and buying behaviour. The online community, including the surveys, website and incentives management, ran on Globalpark's Enterprise Feedback Suite (EFS). WMG needed a representative sounding board of music fans in order to stay on top of industry trends, determine how to best promote artists, and retain fan loyalty. One of the main ways that WMG relied on the panel was in judging new artists. With existing musicians, WMG had a good understanding of who bought its work, so it was not too difficult to decide how to promote them and how much money to spend on advertising. However, with new artists, this was not the case. In the past, WMG would make an educated guess based on genre or personality of the artist, and past artist experience. Alternatively, WMG might have employed a research agency to conduct an ad hoc study. Now, WMG can quickly and cost-effectively do 'more research with less'. The way this works is that WMG places songs by new artists on the panel website, either as video or sound files, and then announces their availability to the community. Those who listen to the songs are invited to take part in a survey. Participants were generally keen to engage in the WMG surveys and they were rewarded with points which could be exchanged for goods or entries into prize draws. The recruiting of new members was boosted by advertising campaigns involving participants who were already active and by encouraging word-of-mouth referral. The quality of the panel was assured through built-in features that identified suspicious or irrelevant participants and removed them from the results. By collecting basic participant data (e.g. socio-demographic characteristics) specific groups were available as target-oriented samples for individual surveys. The software supported times series analyses by combining all participants' response data generated from different online surveys, to track changes over time. WMG had a direct channel to monitor music trends and buying behaviours. It also had a critical audience at the ready to test new artists and marketing platforms before investing in costly campaigns. This helped it to grow new artists, improve campaign effectiveness and optimise returns on expenditure, steering the company's decision-making processes.

There are a growing number of survey applications that are being designed to advance the experience of interviews using mobile devices. There are compelling reasons why researchers see great advantages in the use of mobile devices for marketing research. Entire generations across the globe are being raised to send text messages, surf the Web, conduct transactions, and engage in many ways with family, friends and business associates, all with just a few touches on their mobile devices. These devices represent the next generation for online communication, just as notebook computers replaced desktop computers as they became smaller, lighter and more powerful. However, country to country, the percentage of participants with suitable devices that enable the more data-rich forms of survey engagement varies widely. What does not vary is how the mobile device enables researchers to access participants who in the past may have been well out of their reach. In the USA for example, teens, young men and ethnic populations are among the heaviest users of mobile devices. They are also the hardest to reach via the Web or landline phones for survey purposes. Every demographic group is well represented among

mobile device users, perhaps better than the representation today found among those with landlines and broadband web access at home. The portability and accessibility of the mobile device provides for the ability to make research even more increasingly actionable and closely integrated with marketing campaigns by moving the survey research closer to the point of consumer buying activities. The combined immediacy and portability provided by mobile devices extends the advantages of electronic interviewing to specific challenges confronting researchers today.[74]

In order to see applications of survey software design, to read case material and in some instances to download demo versions, visit the websites of the following companies: Askia (**www.askia.com**), Confirmit (**www.confirmit.com**), GlobalPark (**www.globalpark.com**) and Snap Surveys (**www.snapsurveys.com**). This is not an exhaustive list, but one that will give examples of questionnaire design and survey design whether it is delivered online, telephone, face-to-face, postal or multimode surveys. These sources will also illustrate forms of statistical analyses and reporting.

Summary

The two basic means of obtaining primary quantitative data in descriptive research are through survey and observation techniques. Survey involves the direct questioning of participants, while observation entails recording participant behaviour or the behaviour of service deliverers.

Surveys involve the administration of a questionnaire and may be classified, based on the method or mode of administration, as (1) online surveys, (2) email surveys, (3) traditional telephone surveys, (4) computer-assisted telephone interviews (CATIs), (5) home or workplace face-to-face surveys, (6) street surveys, (7) computer-assisted personal interviews (CAPIs), (8) traditional postal surveys. Of these techniques, CATIs, CAPIs and in particular online surveys have grown enormously in their use in developed Western economies. Each method has some general advantages and disadvantages. Although these data collection techniques are usually thought of as distinct and 'competitive', they should not be considered to be mutually exclusive in much the same manner as using quantitative and qualitative techniques should not be considered to be mutually exclusive. It is possible to employ them productively in mixed-mode approaches, especially in conducting surveys across cultures.

Quantitative observational techniques may be classified as structured or unstructured, disguised or undisguised, and natural or contrived. The major techniques are personal observation (including mystery shopping), electronic observation (including some active and passive social media research techniques), and trace analysis. Compared with surveys, the relative advantages of observational techniques are that they permit measurement of actual behaviour, there is no reporting bias and there is less potential for interviewer bias. Also, certain types of data can best, or only, be obtained by observation. The relative disadvantages of observation are that very little can be inferred about motives, beliefs, attitudes and preferences, there is a potential for observer bias, most techniques are time consuming and expensive, it is difficult to observe some forms of behaviour, and questions of ethical techniques of observation are far more contentious. Observation is rarely used as the sole method of obtaining primary data, but it can be usefully employed in conjunction with other marketing research techniques to corroborate, validate and enrich analyses and interpretations.

Each individual survey method has its own distinct advantages and disadvantages that the researcher must evaluate. But if the researcher is designing a survey that is to work in different geographical locations, the additional challenges and opportunities inherent to their selected locations must also be evaluated. Participants' anonymity should be protected, and their names should not be turned over to clients. People should not be observed without consent for research in situations where they would not expect to be observed by the public. Digital developments in marketing research have fundamentally changed the way that researchers engage with participants, design questionnaires, collect survey data and analyse them. These developments continue with the use of mobile devices to conduct surveys and quantitative observations.

Questions

1 Given that survey researchers may impose their language and logic upon potential participants, what do you see as being the advantages and disadvantages of conducting surveys?

2 Discuss the dilemma faced by the survey designer who wishes to develop a survey that is not prone to interviewer bias but also sees that interviewer rapport with participants is vital to the success of the survey.

3 Evaluate the reasons why response rates to surveys are declining.

4 Why do interviewers need to probe participants in surveys? What distinguishes survey probing from probing conducted in qualitative interviews?

5 What are the relevant factors for evaluating which survey method is best suited to a particular research project?

6 What are the distinct advantages of conducting a survey using CAPI technology compared with a traditional postal survey?

7 What are the key advantages of conducting online surveys? Evaluate the potential that this technique holds for the future.

8 How would you classify mystery shopping as an observation technique? Why would you classify it in this way?

9 How may electronic observation techniques be used in supermarkets?

10 Explain, using examples, where trace analysis may be used.

11 Describe the criteria by which you would evaluate the relative benefits of different observation techniques.

12 What is the difference between qualitative and quantitative observation?

13 Describe the relative advantages and disadvantages of observation.

14 Describe a marketing research problem in which both survey and observation techniques could be used for obtaining the information needed.

15 What do you see as being the main ethical problems of mystery shopping?

Exercises

1 The manager of your college/university school/ department has been asked to review which survey method would be the most effective for a study of undergraduate experiences and attitudes at the end of each academic year. She has come to you to help her make the case. Which method would be best and why would it be the best?

2 Visit the YouGov organisation's website at **www.yougov.com**. Which survey methods have been used by YouGov in some of the recent surveys posted on this site? Given YouGov's specialist studies and target participants, describe any limitations that you see in the survey methods it uses.

3 Locate an online survey, print off the pages and examine the content carefully. What would be the relative advantages of administering the same survey via a street survey? What would a street interviewer need to make this survey effective in a street situation?

4 You have been hired by the campus bookstore to observe covertly students making purchasing decisions while shopping. Spend 30 minutes making these observations and write a report that covers:

a How you feel students make their purchasing decisions for books and any other goods available in the shop.

b What you feel to be the benefits, limitations and challenges of this approach.

5 In a small group discuss the following issues: 'Telling consumers that they are being observed destroys what you are trying to observe. It is much better to see consumers behaving naturally, even if this requires the use of hidden cameras.' And 'Given the decline in response and cooperation rates to surveys, it would be much better for marketers to invest in quantitative observation techniques and forget conducting surveys.'

Video case exercise: Subaru

What technique(s) would you recommend to conduct surveys with Subaru buyers? Why?

Notes

1. Till, A., 'Right here…Right now…', *Research World* (December 2006), 44–45.

2. Heeg, R., 'The great outdoors goes digital', *Research World* (March 2008), 19.

3. Surveys are commonly used in marketing research. See, for example, Rindfleisch, A., Malter, A.J., Ganesan, S. and Moorman, C., 'Cross-sectional versus longitudinal survey research: concepts, findings and guidelines', *Journal of Marketing Research* 45 (3) (June 2008), 261–279; Malhotra, N. and McCort, D., 'A cross-cultural comparison of behavioural intention models: theoretical consideration and an empirical investigation', *International Marketing Review* 18 (3) (2001), 235–269.

4. ESOMAR, 'Global Market Research', ESOMAR Industry Report (2010), 16.

5. EFS Survey, 'IDG Business Media uses online market research to optimize its print and online publications', *GlobalPark Case Study* (2011), **www.globalpark.co.uk**, accessed 23 March 2011.

6. Cohen, E. and Jacobs, P., 'How mobile is changing the sociology, psychology and the entertainment/work environment', ESOMAR, WM3, Berlin (October 2010).

7. ESOMAR, 'Global Market Research', ESOMAR Industry Report (2010), 102–103.

8. St-Laurent, N., Mathieu, A. and Coderre, F., 'Comparison of the quality of qualitative data obtained through telephone, postal and email surveys', *International Journal of Market Research* 46 (3) (2004), 349–357; Mann, C. and Stewart, F., *Internet Communication and Qualitative*

Research: A Handbook for Researching Online (London: Sage, 2000), 67.

9. Ahmed, M., 'Send an e-mail? Err … sorry, you seem to have mistaken me for a sad old geezer', *The Times* (24 December 2010), 19.

10. Schwartz, M., 'Postal and email "Combos" gain favor with marketers', *B to B* 87 (2) (11 February 2002), 25; Stevens, J. and Chisholm, J., 'An integrated approach: technology firm conducts worldwide satisfaction research survey via email, Internet', *Quirk's Marketing Research Review* 11 (8) (October 1997), 12–13, 64–65.

11. Lavine, S., 'Mobile interviewing – the next frontier of data collection', ESOMAR, Online Research, Chicago (October 2009).

12. Zahariev, M., Ferneyhough, C. and Ryan, C., 'Best practices in mobile research', ESOMAR, Online Research, Chicago (October 2009).

13. EFS Survey, 'IP Deutschland: study on the user structure of mobile portals via a cell phone survey', *GlobalPark Case Study* (2011) **www.globalpark.co.uk**, accessed 23 March 2011.

14. Gorman, J.W., 'An opposing view of online surveying', *Marketing News* (24 April 2000); Johnston, A., 'Welcome to the wired world', *Research* (November 1999), 22–25; Comley, P., 'Will working the web provide a net gain?', *Research* (December 1996), 16.

15. Goon, E., 'Friends or foes? The Internet versus the music industry', *GlobalPark Case Study* (2010), **www.globalpark. co.uk**, accessed 23 March 2011.

16. Poynter, R., 'Online research: stop asking questions and start listening', *Admap* July/August 2010), 32–34.

17 Hellwig, J.O. and Wirth, T., 'Panel based mobile online research – why mobile online questionnaires contribute to improve data quality?' ESOMAR, Panel Research, Dublin (October 2008).

18. ESOMAR, 'Global Market Research', ESOMAR Industry Report (2010), 102–103.

19. Lyle, D., Bailie, J.A., Rooney, F., Martin, D., Lyle, R. and Ludlow, V., 'Road safety – how a short sharp burst can reduce deaths', Institute of Practitioners in Advertising, IPA Effectiveness Awards (2009).

20. Vicente, P., Reis, E. and Santos, M., 'Using mobile phones for survey research: a comparison with fixed phones', *International Journal of Market Research* 51 (5) (2009), 613–634.

21. Heeg, R., 'MR will be a fundamental tool in our country', *Research World* (May 2004), 6–7.

22. ESOMAR, 'Global Market Research', ESOMAR Industry Report (2010), 102–103.

23. Eva, G. and Jowell, R., 'Conference notes – prospects for mixed-mode data collection in cross-national surveys', *International Journal of Market Research* 51 (2) (2009), 267–269.

24. Smith, A., Brown, L. and Garner, S., 'Charities and the not-for-profit sector', *Admap* 495 (June 2008), 38–40.

25. **www.millwardbrownulster.com/omnibus.html**, accessed 25 March 2011.

26. Folkman Curasi, C., 'A critical exploration of face-to-face interviewing vs. computer mediated interviewing', *International Journal of Market Research* 43 (3) (2001), 361–375; Bush, A.J. and Hair, J.E. Jr, 'An assessment of the mall-intercept as a data collection method', *Journal of Marketing Research* (May 1985), 158–167.

27. Rines, S., 'Brands fall short of their goal', *Marketing Week* (16 June 16 2005), 32–33.

28. ESOMAR, 'Global Market Research', ESOMAR Industry Report (2010), 102–103.

29. Manfreda, K.L., Bosnjak, M., Berzelak, J., Haas, I. and Vehovar, V., 'Web surveys versus other survey modes: a meta analysis comparing response rates', *International Journal of Market Research* 50 (1) (2008), 79–104; Borque, L., *How to conduct self-administered and mail survey*, 2nd edn (Thousand Oaks, CA: Sage, 2002); Brossard, H.L., 'Information sources used by an organisation during a complex decision process: an exploratory study', *Industrial Marketing Management* 27 (1) (January 1998), 41–50.

30. Schmid, J., 'Assigning value to your customer list', *Catalog Age* 18 (5) (April 2001), 69; Alan, C.B. and Tse, A.C.B., 'Comparing response rate, response speed and response quality of two methods of sending questionnaires: e-mail vs. mail', *International Journal of Market Research* 40 (4) (1998), 353–361; Yoegei, R., 'List marketers head to cyberspace', *Target Marketing* 20 (8) (August 1997), 54–55.

31. Anolli, L., Villani, D. and Riva, G., 'Personality of people using chat: an on-line research', *CyberPsychology & Behavior* 8 (1) (February 2005), 89–95; Thompson, S.K.,

Sampling (New York: Wiley, 2002); Childers, T.L. and Skinner, S.J., 'Theoretical and empirical issues in the identification of survey participants', *Journal of the Market Research Society* 27 (January 1985), 39–53.

32. Rao, J.N.K. and Lohr, S., 'Estimation in multiple-frame surveys', *Journal of the American Statistical Association* 101 (475) (September 2006), 1019–1030; Murphy, G.B., 'The effects of organizational sampling frame selection', *Journal of Business Venturing* 17 (3) (May 2002), 237; Smith, W., Mitchell, P., Attebo, K. and Leeder, S., 'Selection bias from sampling frames: telephone directory and electoral rolls compared to door-to-door population census: results from the Blue Mountain eye study', *Australian & New Zealand Journal of Public Health* 21 (2) (April 1997), 127–133.

33. Heeg, R., 'Every study in Belgium is an international study', *Research World* (February 2004), 8–9.

34. Tarran, B., 'Worldwide USA', *Research* (July 2005), 26–27.

35. Printz, J. and Maltby, D., 'Beyond personalisation: when handwriting makes a difference', *Fund Raising Management* 28 (3) (May 1997), 16–19; Conant, J.S., Smart, D.T. and Walker, B.J., 'Mail survey facilitation techniques: an assessment and proposal regarding reporting practices', *Journal of the Market Research Society* 32 (October 1990), 569–580.

36. Erdogan, B.Z., 'Increasing mail survey response rates from an industrial population: a cost effectiveness analysis of four follow-up techniques', *Industrial Marketing Management* 31 (1) (January 2002), 65; Edmonston, J., 'Why response rates are declining', *Advertising Age's Business Marketing* 82 (8) (September 1997), 12; Hubbard, R. and Little, E.L., 'Promised contributions to charity and mail survey responses: replications with extension', *Public Opinion Quarterly* 52 (Summer 1988), 223–230; Erdos, P.L. and Ferber, R. (eds), 'Data collection methods: mail surveys', *Handbook of Marketing Research* (New York: McGraw-Hill, 1974), 102.

37. Fletcher, K., 'Jump on the omnibus', *Marketing* (15 June 1995), 25–28.

38. Bednall, D., 'CATI: what researchers, interviewers and clients can do to improve response rates', *Research News* (December 2004), 10.

39. Heeg, R., 'Rigid data-protection and closed doors', *Research World* (April 2004), 6–7.

40. Groves, R.M., 'Nonresponse rates and nonresponse bias in household surveys', *Public Opinion Quarterly* 70 (5) (2006), 646–675; Roy, A. and Berger, P., 'E-mail and mixed mode database surveys revisited: exploratory analyses of factors affecting response rates', *Journal of Database Marketing & Customer Strategy Management* 12 (21) (January 2005), 153–171; Smith, J., 'How to boost DM response rates quickly', *Marketing News* 35 (9) (23 April 2001), 5; Columbo, R., 'A model for diagnosing and reducing non-response bias', *Journal of Advertising Research* (January/April 2000), 85–93.

41. ESOMAR, 'Global Market Research', ESOMAR Industry Report (2010), 48.

42. Fowler, F.J. Jr., *Survey Research Methods*, 3rd edn (Thousand Oaks, CA: Sage, 2001); Guengel, P.C., Berchman, T.R. and Cannell, C.E., *General Interviewing*

Techniques: A Self Instructional Workbook for Telephone and Personal Interviewer Training (Ann Arbor, MI: Survey Research Center, University of Michigan, 1983).

43. Graeff, T.R., 'Uninformed response bias in telephone surveys', *Journal of Business Research* 55 (3) (March 2002), 251; Singer, E., 'Experiments with incentives in telephone surveys', *Public Opinion Quarterly* 64 (2) (Summer 2000), 171–188; Cannell, C.E., Miller, P.U., Oksenberg, L. and Leinhardt, S. (eds), 'Research on interviewing techniques', *Sociological Methodology* (San Francisco, CA: Jossey-Bass, 1981); Miller, P.U. and Cannell, C.E., 'A study of experimental techniques for telephone interviewing', *Public Opinion Quarterly* 46 (Summer 1982), 250–269.

44. Fink, A., *How to conduct surveys: A step by step guide*, 3rd edn (Thousand Oaks, CA: Sage, 2005); McMaster, M., 'E-Marketing poll vault', *Sales and Marketing Management* 153 (8) (August 2001), 25; Fink, A., *A Survey Handbook* (Thousand Oaks, CA: Sage, 1995).

45. Lee, Z. and Sargeant, A., 'Dealing with social desirability bias: an application to charitable giving', *European Journal of Marketing* 45 (5) (2011), 703–719.

46. Anon., 'Random sampling: homework – yeah right', *Marketing News* 36 (6) (18 March 2002), 4; Vinten, G., 'The threat in the question', *Credit Control* 18 (1) (1997), 25–31; Raghubir, P. and Menon, G., 'Asking sensitive questions: the effects of type of referent and frequency wording in counterbiasing method', *Psychology & Marketing* 13 (7) (October 1996), 633–652.

47. 'Audi – born of powerful ideas', European Association of Communications Agencies Bronze winner (2008).

48. Vicente, P., Reis, E. and Santos, M., 'Using mobile phones for survey research; a comparison with fixed phones', *International Journal of Market Research* 51 (5) (2009), 613–634; Eva, G. and Jowell, R., 'Conference notes – prospects for mixed-mode data collection in cross-national surveys', *International Journal of Market Research* 51 (2) (2009), 267–269.

49. Blyth, B., 'Mixed mode: the only "fitness" regime?', *International Journal of Market Research* 50 (2) (2008), 241–266.

50. Macer, T., 'Different strokes', *Research in Business* (March 2004), 20.

51. Pettit, R., 'Digital anthropology: how ethnography can improve online research', *Journal of Advertising Research*, 50 (3) (2010), 240–242; Milat, A.J., 'Measuring physical activity in public open space – an electronic device versus direct observation', *Australian & New Zealand Journal of Public Health* 26 (1) (February 2002), 1; Wilcox, S.B., 'Trust, but verify', *Appliance Manufacturer* 46 (1) (January 1998), 8, 87.

52. Healy, M.J., Beverland, M.B., Oppewal, H. and Sands, S., 'Understanding retail experiences – the case for ethnography', *International Journal of Market Research* 49 (6) (2007), 751–778; Travers, M., *Qualitative Research through Case Studies* (London: Sage, 2001), 4.

53. Smith, A., Brown, L. and Garner, S., 'Charities and the not-for-profit sector', *Admap* 495 (June 2008), 38–40.

54. McNeil, R., 'The mystery squad's tougher challenge', *ResearchPlus* (April 1994), 13.

55. Smit, E.G. and Neijens, P.C., 'The march to reliable metrics: a half century of coming closer to the truth', *Journal of Advertising Research* 51 (1)50th Anniversary Supplement (2011), 124–135.

56. Poynter, R., 'A taxonomy of NewMR', Market Research Society, Annual Conference (2010).

57. Baverstock, A., Bywater, H., Halliwell, P. and Boyle, B., 'Stripping the wallpaper – using technology to reach the "out of reach" answers', ESOMAR, Qualitative, Marrakech (November 2009); Kurcina, B., 'Use videos to obtain crucial POP info', *Marketing News* 34 (24) (20 November 2000), 16; Seaton, A.V., 'Unobtrusive observational measures as a qualitative extension of visitor surveys at festivals and events: mass observation revisited', *Journal of Travel Research* 35 (4) (Spring 1997), 25–30.

58. Kasari, H.J., 'People-meter systems in the changing TV climate', *Admap* 476 (October 2006) 55–56; Ephron, E., 'Nielsen's secret passive meter', *Mediaweek* 10 (36) (18 September 2000).

59. Zigmond, D., Dorai-Raj, S., Interian, Y. and Naverniouk, I., 'Measuring advertising quality on television: deriving meaningful metrics from audience retention data', *Journal of Advertising Research* 49 (4) (December 2009), 419–428.

60. Blackadder, J., 'Through the shopper's eyes', *Research News* (November 2006), 26.

61. Addie, I. and Lewis-Hodgson, D., 'Bioshopping: revolutionising shopper insight', Market Research Society Annual Conference (2010).

62. Moellmann, A., Carter, S. and Binet, L., 'Philips – girl power: how a female robot grew sales for the Philips MSS shaver', Institute of Practitioners in Advertising, Entrant, IPA Effectiveness Awards (2010).

63. For examples of an application of GSR, see Ohme, R.K., Reykowska, D., Wiener, D. and Choromanska, A., 'Analysis of neurophysiological reactions to advertising stimuli by means of EEG and Galvanic Skin Responses measures', *Journal of Neuroscience, Psychology, and Economics* 2 (1) (2009), 21–31; Anthes, G.H., 'Smile, you're on Candid Computer', *Computerworld* 35 (49) (3 December 2001), 50.

64. Pullen, J.P., 'Truth down to a science', *ANA Magazine* (October 2006), 78–82; Croal, N'G., 'Moviefone learns to listen,' *Newsweek* 135 (19) (8 May 2000), 84.

65. Romaniuk, J. and Wight, S., 'The influences of brand usage on response to advertising awareness measures', *International Journal of Market Research* 51 (2) (2009), 203–218; Haaijer, R., 'Response latencies in the analysis of conjoint choice experiments', *Journal of Marketing Research* (August 2000), 376–382; Vasilopoulos, N. 'The influence of job familiarity and impression management on self-report measure scale scores and response latencies', *Journal of Applied Psychology* 85 (1) (February 2000), 50.

66. Verton, D., 'SafeWeb users vulnerable', *Computerworld* 36 (8) (18 February 2002), 6; Bayan, R., 'Privacy means knowing your cookies,' *Link-Up* 18 (1) (January/February 2001), 22–23.

67. McPhee, N., 'Is there a future for "real" qualitative market research interviewing in the digital age?', ESOMAR, Congress Odyssey, Athens (September 2010).

68. ESOMAR, 'Global Market Research', ESOMAR Industry Report (2010), 102.

69. ESOMAR, 'Global Market Research', ESOMAR Industry Report (2010), 97.

70. Phillips, A., 'IJMR Research Methods Forum: "Start listening, stop asking" – research snoopers and spies – the legal and ethical challenges facing observational research', *International Journal of Market Research* 52 (2) (2010), 275–281.

71. ESOMAR, 'Global Market Research', ESOMAR Industry Report (2010), 46.

72. Case, S., 'How social media is democratizing research', ESOMAR, Congress Odyssey, Athens (September 2010).

73. EFS Survey, 'Warner Music customer panel community drives key business decisions', *GlobalPark Case Study* (2011), **www.globalpark.co.uk**, accessed 23 March 2011.

74. Lavine, S., 'Mobile interviewing – the next frontier of data collection', ESOMAR, Online Research, Chicago (October 2009).

11 Causal research design: experimentation

Causality can never be proved; in other words, it can never be demonstrated decisively. Inferences of cause-and-effect relationships are the best that can be achieved.

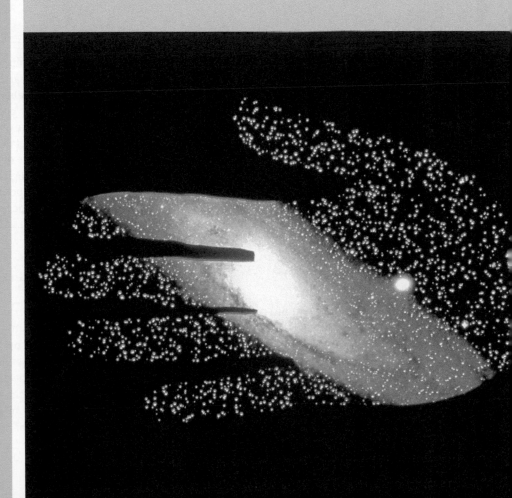

Objectives

After reading this chapter, you should be able to:

1 explain the concept of causality as defined in marketing research and distinguish between the ordinary meaning and the scientific meaning of causality;

2 define and differentiate two types of validity: internal validity and external validity;

3 discuss the various extraneous variables that can affect the validity of results obtained through experimentation and explain how the researcher can control extraneous variables;

4 describe and evaluate experimental designs and the differences among pre-experimental, true experimental, quasi-experimental and statistical designs;

5 compare and contrast the use of laboratory versus field experimentation and experimental versus non-experimental designs in marketing research;

6 describe test marketing and its various forms: standard test market, controlled test market, simulated test market, electronic and other forms of test marketing;

7 understand the problems of internal and external validity of field experiments when conducted in international markets;

8 describe the ethical issues involved in conducting causal research and the role of debriefing in addressing some of these issues;

9 appreciate how digital developments are shaping the manner in which experiments are managed and applied.

Overview

We introduced causal designs in Chapter 3, where we discussed their relationship to exploratory and descriptive designs and defined experimentation as the primary method employed in causal designs. This chapter explores the concept of causality further. We identify the necessary conditions for causality, examine the role of validity in experimentation, and consider the extraneous variables and procedures for controlling them. We present a classification of experimental designs and consider specific designs, along with the relative merits of laboratory and field experiments. An application in the area of test marketing is discussed in detail. The considerations involved in conducting experimental research when researching international markets are discussed. Several ethical issues, which arise in experimentation, are identified. The chapter also discusses how digital developments in marketing research are enabling researchers to conduct improved and/or new forms of experimentation. We begin with an example that encapsulates the opportunities inherent in the application and process of experimentation.

Real research   How the tone and wording of advertisements interact[1]

There are many examples of positive and negative advertisements. For instance, in a positive advert, Sony Ericsson showed a young woman sitting in a café chatting on the phone. It would seem she was enjoying her leisure time by using her mobile phone. In contrast, the Red Cross showed an advert with one of its volunteers holding a young boy while the characters look at a war-torn landscape. The caption read, 'Whatever the future holds, we'll be there.' By focusing on negative aspects, and how the Red Cross can overcome such a situation, the advert was taking a sad affective tone. Affective tone is defined here as the overall feeling of the advertisement. In a study to draw together the two constructs of message affect and framing, an experiment was conducted to discover whether and how they interact. The experiment was undertaken in the context of television advertisements for mobile phones. The researchers set two hypotheses for this study: **H1**: For advertisements with a happy or sad affective tone, positive message frames are more persuasive than negative message frames. **H2**: Advertisements with the incongruous positive (negative) frame and sad (happy) tone are more persuasive than the congruous negative (positive) frame and sad (happy) tone. The method designed to test these competing hypotheses was a 2 (affective tone: happy, sad) × 2 (message framing: positive, negative) between-subjects factorial design. A total of 187 participants were randomly assigned to treatment conditions. Mobile telephones were chosen as the context for the advert as they were known to be important but not crucial items to the participant sample. Message framing was manipulated by inserting three attributes of information on a black screen background (i.e. convenience, business productivity and personal security). For the positive framing conditions this meant the following words being displayed on screen (negative framing in parentheses).

A MOBILE OFFERS YOU:	**(NO MOBILE MEANS):**
Convenience	*(Inconvenience)*
Greater productivity	*(Being unproductive)*
Personal security in emergencies	*(Isolation in emergencies)*

Participants were told that the purpose of the study was to find out how people evaluate TV programmes and adverts. An episode of *The Simpsons* was then played, followed by the advert, after which participants completed a questionnaire. The choice of TV programme was based on showing the participants a programme that would keep the attention levels high, distract participants away from the purpose of the experiment and minimise the biases associated with lab experimentation. The entire procedure took less than 37 minutes to complete. The results showed that for adverts with a positive affective tone, it was negative frames rather than positive frames that produced the most favourable attitudes. This result was in accordance with hypothesis 2. By contrast, for adverts with a negative affective tone, using positive framing appeared to be the most persuasive, which supported the negative state avoidance rationale for hypothesis 1 and the incongruity rationale for hypothesis 2. The experiment revealed two alternative yet complementary perspectives of the relationship between message affect and framing.

Concept of causality

Causality
Causality applies when the occurrence of X increases the probability of the occurrence of Y.

Experimentation is commonly used to infer causal relationships. The concept of causality requires some explanation. The scientific concept of causality is complex. 'Causality' means something very different to the average person on the street than to a scientist.[2] A statement such as 'X causes Y' will have the following meaning to an ordinary person and to a scientist:

Ordinary meaning	Scientific meaning
X is the only cause of Y	X is only one of a number of possible causes of Y
X must always lead to Y	The occurrence of X makes the occurrence of Y more probable (X is a probabilistic cause of Y)
It is possible to prove that X is a cause of Y	We can never prove that X is a cause of Y. At best, we can infer that X is a cause of Y

The scientific meaning of causality is more appropriate to marketing research than is the everyday meaning. Marketing effects are caused by multiple variables and the relationship between cause and effect tends to be probabilistic. Moreover, we can never prove causality (i.e. demonstrate it conclusively); we can only infer a cause-and-effect relationship. In other words, it is possible that the true causal relation, if one exists, will not have been identified. We further clarify the concept of causality by discussing the conditions for causality.

Conditions for causality

Before making causal inferences, or assuming causality, three conditions must be satisfied: (1) concomitant variation, (2) time order of occurrence of variables, and (3) elimination of other possible causal factors. These conditions are necessary but not sufficient to demonstrate causality. No one of these three conditions, or all three conditions combined, can demonstrate decisively that a causal relationship exists.[3] These conditions are explained in more detail in the following sections.

Concomitant variation

Concomitant variation
A condition for inferring causality that requires that the extent to which a cause, X, and an effect, Y, occur together or vary together is predicted by the hypothesis under consideration.

Concomitant variation is the extent to which a cause, X, and an effect, Y, occur together or vary together in the way predicted by the hypothesis under consideration. Evidence pertaining to concomitant variation can be obtained in a qualitative or quantitative manner.

For example, in the qualitative case, the management of a travel company may believe that the retention of customers is highly dependent on the quality of its service. This hypothesis could be examined by assessing concomitant variation. Here, the causal factor X is service level and the effect factor Y is retention level. A concomitant variation supporting the hypothesis would imply that travel companies with satisfactory levels of service would also have a satisfactory retention of customers. Likewise, travel companies with unsatisfactory service would exhibit unsatisfactory retention of customers. If, on the other hand, the opposite pattern was found, we would conclude that the hypothesis was untenable.

For a quantitative example, consider a random survey of 1,000 participants questioned on the purchase of a skiing holiday. This survey yields the data in Table 11.1. The participants have been classified into high- and low-education groups based on a median or even split. This table suggests that the purchase of a skiing holiday is influenced by education level. Participants with high education are more likely to purchase a skiing holiday: 73% of the participants with high education have a high purchase level, whereas only 64% of those with low education have a high purchase level. Furthermore, this is based on a relatively large sample of 1,000 participants.

Based on this evidence, can we conclude that high education causes a high purchasing level of skiing holidays? Certainly not! All that can be said is that association makes the hypothesis more tenable; it does not prove it. What about the effect of other possible causal factors

Table 11.1	Evidence of concomitant variation between purchase of a skiing holiday and education		
		Purchase of a skiing holiday from a travel company, Y	
		High	*Low*	*Total*
Education, X	*High*	363 (73%)	137 (27%)	500 (100%)
	Low	322 (64%)	178 (36%)	500 (100%)

such as income? Skiing holidays can be expensive, so people with higher incomes may be more able to afford them. Table 11.2 shows the relationship between the purchase of a skiing holiday and education for different income segments. This is equivalent to holding the effect of income constant. Here again, the sample has been split at the median to produce high- and low-income groups of equal size. Table 11.2 shows that the difference in purchasing levels of a skiing holiday between high- and low-education participants has been reduced considerably. This suggests that the association indicated by Table 11.1 may be spurious.

We could give similar examples to show why the absence of initial evidence of concomitant variation does not imply that there is no causation. It is possible that considering a third variable will crystallise an association that was originally obscure. The time order of the occurrence of variables provides additional insights into causality.

Time order of occurrence of variables

The time order of occurrence condition states that the causing event must occur either before or simultaneously with the effect; it cannot occur afterwards. By definition, an effect cannot be produced by an event that occurs after the effect has taken place. It is possible, however, for each event in a relationship to be both a cause and an effect of the other event. In other words, a variable can be both a cause and an effect in the same causal relationship. To illustrate, customers who shop frequently in a particular supermarket are more likely to have a loyalty card for that supermarket. In addition, customers who have a loyalty card for a supermarket are likely to shop there frequently.

Consider travel companies and the challenge of retaining their customers. If the quality of their service offering is the cause of retention, then improvements in service must be

Table 11.2		Purchase of skiing holiday by income and education			
		Low-income			
		Purchase			
		High	Low	Total	
Education	High	122 (61%)	78 (39%)	200 (100%)	
	Low	171 (57%)	129 (43%)	300 (100%)	
		High-income			
		Purchase			
		High	Low	Total	
Education	High	241 (80%)	59 (20%)	300 (100%)	
	Low	151 (76%)	49 (24%)	200 (100%)	

made before, or at least simultaneously with, an increase in retention. These improvements might consist of training or hiring more staff in their branches. Then, in subsequent months, the retention of customers should increase. Alternatively, retention may increase simultaneously with the training or hiring of additional branch staff. On the other hand, suppose that a travel company experienced an appreciable increase in the level of retaining customers and then decided to use some of that money generated to retrain its branch staff, leading to an improvement in service. In this case, the improved service quality cannot be a cause of increased retention; rather, just the opposite hypothesis might be plausible.

Absence of other possible causal factors

The absence of other possible causal factors means that the factor or variable being investigated should be the only possible causal explanation. Travel company service quality may be a cause of retention if we can be sure that changes in all other factors affecting retention – pricing, advertising, promotional offers, product characteristics, competition and so forth – were held constant or were otherwise controlled.

In an after-the-fact examination of a situation, we can never confidently rule out all other causal factors. In contrast, with experimental designs it is possible to control some of the other causal factors. It is also possible to balance the effects of some of the uncontrolled variables so that only random variations resulting from these uncontrolled variables will be measured. These aspects are discussed in more detail later in this chapter.

The difficulty of establishing a causal relationship is illustrated by the following example. If you were to design this experiment, imagine trying to pinpoint what 'creativity' means in the context of designing an advertisement.

Real research   **Advertising creativity matters[4]**

A common view is that creativity is a mission of the entire advertising industry, its *raison d'être*. In a frequently cited study,[5] wasteful advertising creativity in advertising agencies in the form of an abundance of creative ideas yielded more effective advertisements in the long term. An experiment was undertaken to test the notion of wasteful advertising. The aim was to see whether an abundance of creativity in a single advertisement yielded positive effects. To test their hypotheses, the researchers wished to compare responses between consumers who had been exposed to a more creative versus a less creative advertisement for the same brand with the same message. To do this they chose a 2 (more creative/less creative advertisement) × 2 (perceived creativity before/after) experimental design where participants were randomly assigned to one of the four cells. To avoid stimulus-specific effects, four different brands and accompanying messages were used for a total of 16 experiment cells. All four brands were established and well known in their respective product categories (pain relief, coffee, vodka and condoms). Four pairs of print advertisements were developed, one pair for each brand. Print advertisements usually have three main elements: the brand, text and visuals. In creating test material, the brand and the visuals were kept constant, while the text was varied to communicate the same message in a more (employing rhetorical figures) or less (without rhetorical figures) creative way. The number of words was kept constant. The participants were recruited from an access panel to represent the adult working population. In total, 1,284 consumers participated in the study, making a cell size of approximately 80 participants. Participants were randomly exposed to one of the stimulus print advertisements online and then directly completed a questionnaire. The results showed that waste in advertising creativity mattered. Rather than improving the functionality of an advertisement and pushing the message into consumers' minds (which conventional wisdom held to be the major benefit of creativity), an extra degree of creativity may send signals about the advertiser that rub off on consumer perceptions of the brand. More versus less creative advertising signalled greater effort on the advertiser's behalf and was taken as proof of the brand's smartness, and ability to solve problems and develop valuable products. As a result, consumers became more interested in the brand and perceived it to be of higher quality.

The visual characteristics of 'creativity' were not tested in this example, which could have had a major impact upon how participants view the creativity of an advert. This does not mean that the experiment has no value, far from it, but it does illustrate the challenges inherent in establishing cause-and-effect relationships. If, as this example indicates, it is difficult to establish cause-and-effect relationships, what is the role of evidence obtained in experimentation?

Evidence of concomitant variation, time order of occurrence of variables and elimination of other possible causal factors, even if combined, still do not demonstrate conclusively that a causal relationship exists. If all the evidence is strong and consistent, however, it may be reasonable to conclude that there is a causal relationship. Accumulated evidence from several investigations increases our confidence that a causal relationship exists. Confidence is further enhanced if the evidence is interpreted in light of intimate conceptual knowledge of the problem situation. Controlled experiments can provide strong evidence on all three conditions.

Definitions and concepts

In this section, we define some basic concepts and illustrate them using the *Real Research* 'Advertising creativity' experiment detailed above:

Independent variables
Variables that are manipulated by the researcher and whose effects are measured and compared.

- **Independent variables.** Independent variables are variables or alternatives that are manipulated (i.e. the levels of these variables are changed by the researcher) and whose effects are measured and compared. These variables, also known as treatments, may include price levels, package designs and advertising themes. In the advertising creativity example, the independent variable was the text used to communicate a message (i.e. 'more' or 'less' creative).

Test units
Individuals, organisations or other entities whose responses to independent variables or treatments are being studied.

- **Test units.** Test units are individuals, organisations or other entities whose response to the independent variables or treatments is being examined. Test units may include consumers, stores or geographical areas. In the advertising creativity example, the test units were consumers.

Dependent variables
Variables that measure the effect of the independent variables on the test units.

- **Dependent variables.** Dependent variables are the variables that measure the effect of the independent variables on the test units. These variables may include sales, profits and market shares. In the advertising creativity example, the dependent variable was a measure of favourable attitudes towards the brand being advertised.

Extraneous variables
Variables, other than dependent and independent variables, which may influence the results of the experiment.

- **Extraneous variables.** Extraneous variables are all variables other than the independent variables that affect the response of the test units. These variables can confound the dependent variable measures in a way that weakens or invalidates the results of the experiment. In the advertising creativity example, product categories, brands, visuals and number of words were extraneous variables that had to be controlled.

Experiment
The process of manipulating one or more independent variables and measuring their effect on one or more dependent variables, while controlling for the extraneous variables.

- **Experiment.** An experiment is formed when the researcher manipulates one or more independent variables and measures their effect on one or more dependent variables, while controlling for the effect of extraneous variables.[6] The advertising creativity research project qualifies as an experiment based on this definition.

Experimental design
The set of experimental procedures specifying (1) the test units and sampling procedures, (2) the independent variables, (3) the dependent variables, and (4) how to control the extraneous variables.

- **Experimental design.** An experimental design is a set of procedures specifying: (1) the test units and how these units are to be divided into homogeneous subsamples; (2) what independent variables or treatments are to be manipulated; (3) what dependent variables are to be measured; and (4) how the extraneous variables are to be controlled.[7]

As a further illustration of these definitions, consider the following example.

Real research	Engaging consumers through 'advergames'[8]

Advertisers are engaging consumers in a game of 'hide-and-seek' by embedding brand messages. This strategy, known as branded entertainment, involves integrating elements of brand communication into content that consumers seek out for entertainment. One form of branded entertainment is the advergame, a videogame designed around a brand. Researchers felt that a high degree of thematic connection between an advergame and a brand should strengthen the bond between the game and the brand. This could result in a stronger connection between conditioned brand attitudes and attitude towards the game. This pattern of attitude conditioning should become manifest in a **stronger observed relationship between attitude towards the game and attitude towards the brand** (*dependent variable*) as a result of playing advergames with a high degree of thematic connection to the brand, compared with playing advergames with low thematic connection to the brand. The primary hypothesis of an experiment to test this connection was:

H1: *There is a stronger positive relationship between attitude towards the game and attitude towards the brand for advergames with a high thematic connection between the game and the brand than for advergames with low thematic connection.*

To test this hypothesis, an experiment was created by the travel company Orbitz (**www. orbitz.com**) in which **adult participants** (*test units*) played two advergames. The manipulation of the thematic connection involved **randomly assigning participants to one of two groups, such that they play either games with a travel-related theme or games that have little to do with travel** (*experimental design*). Attitude towards Orbitz was measured both before the experiment and after participants finished playing the games, at which point they also indicated how much they enjoyed the gaming experience. Participants played two randomly assigned advergames, both with either **high or low thematic connection** (*independent variables*). Participants in the high thematic connection advergame condition played 'Find Your Hotel' and 'Gondoliero', both of which had a travel-related theme that reinforced the association between Orbitz and travel. The object of 'Find Your Hotel' was to negotiate a series of obstacles and find a hotel; the object of 'Gondoliero' was to win a series of gondola races set in the canals of Venice. Participants in the low thematic connection advergame condition played 'Paper Football' and 'Sink The Putt'. 'Paper Football' was based on a table game in which one person tries to flick a folded paper triangle between a set of goalposts that another person has made with their fingers. 'Sink The Putt' was a computerised version of miniature golf, in which participants tried to putt a ball into a hole in the fewest possible shots. After entering the laboratory, participants sat at **computers** (*extraneous variable*) and provided their informed consent. The study instructions told participants that the researchers were interested in their attitudes towards different online travel companies and indicated how to complete a brand attitude pretest. When participants had finished playing and evaluating both games, they filled out a post-test measure of brand attitude. The entire experiment lasted approximately one hour. The results suggested that the most effective advergame executions involved the design of product-relevant games. This could be done by building games that engaged players in activities related to a behaviour they would do if they purchased the sponsoring brand's product. Such efforts may be easier in some product categories than in others. Travel, the category used in this experiment, should be a fairly easy context around which to build product-relevant games.

In the preceding experiment, the independent variable that was manipulated was the level of thematic connection between the brand and game. The dependent variable was the strength of the observed relationship between attitude towards the game and attitude towards the brand. An extraneous variable that was controlled was the device that the advergame was played on – the computer. Games players may engage in different manners dependent upon the gaming device they use. The test units were adult participants. The experimental design required the random assignment of participants to treatment groups (travel related or little to do with travel).

Definition of symbols

To facilitate our discussion of extraneous variables and specific experimental designs, we define a set of symbols now commonly used in marketing research:

X = the exposure of a group to an independent variable, treatment or event, the effects of which are to be determined

O = the process of observation or measurement of the dependent variable on the test units or group of units

R = the random assignment of participants or groups to separate treatments

In addition, the following conventions are adopted:

- Movement from left to right indicates movement through time.
- Horizontal alignment of symbols implies that all those symbols refer to a specific treatment group.
- Vertical alignment of symbols implies that those symbols refer to activities or events that occur simultaneously.

For example, the symbolic arrangement

$$X\,O_1\,O_2$$

means that a given group of participants was exposed to the treatment variable (X) and the response was measured at two different points in time O_1 and O_2.

Likewise, the symbolic arrangement

$$R\,X_1\,O_1$$
$$R\,X_2\,O_2$$

means that two groups of participants were randomly assigned to two different treatment groups at the same time, and the dependent variable was measured in the two groups simultaneously.

Validity in experimentation

When conducting an experiment, a researcher has two goals: (1) to draw valid conclusions about the effects of independent variables on the study group; and (2) to make valid generalisations to a larger population of interest. The first goal concerns internal validity, the second external validity.[9]

Internal validity

Internal validity
A measure of accuracy of an experiment. It measures whether the manipulation of the independent variables, or treatments, actually caused the effects on the dependent variable(s).

External validity
A determination of whether the cause-and-effect relationships found in the experiment can be generalised.

Internal validity refers to whether the manipulation of the independent variables or treatments actually caused the observed effects on the dependent variables. Thus, internal validity refers to whether the observed effects on the test units could have been caused by variables other than the treatment. If the observed effects are influenced or confounded by extraneous variables, it is difficult to draw valid inferences about the causal relationship between the independent and dependent variables. Internal validity is the basic minimum that must be present in an experiment before any conclusion about treatment effects can be made. Without internal validity, the experimental results are confounded. Control of extraneous variables is a necessary condition for establishing internal validity.

External validity

External validity refers to whether the cause-and-effect relationships found in the experiment can be generalised. In other words, can the results be generalised beyond the experimental situation and, if so, to what populations, settings, times, independent variables and dependent variables can the results be projected?[10] Threats to external validity arise when the specific set of experimental conditions does not realistically take into account the interactions of other relevant variables in the real world.

It is desirable to have an experimental design that has both internal and external validity, but in applied marketing research we often have to trade one type of validity for another.[11] To control for extraneous variables, a researcher may conduct an experiment in an artificial environment. This enhances internal validity, but it may limit the generalisability of the results, thereby reducing external validity. For example, pizza restaurants test customers' preferences for new formulations of menu items in test kitchens. Can the effects measured in this environment be generalised to pizza restaurants that may operate in a variety of other environments? (Further discussion on the influence of artificiality on external validity may be found in the section of this chapter on laboratory versus field experimentation.) Regardless of the deterrents to external validity, if an experiment lacks internal validity, it may not be meaningful to generalise the results. Factors that threaten internal validity may also threaten external validity, the most serious of these being extraneous variables.

Extraneous variables

In this section, we classify extraneous variables in the following categories: history, maturation, testing effects, instrumentation, statistical regression, selection bias and mortality.

History

History
Specific events that are external to the experiment but that occur at the same time as the experiment.

Contrary to what the name implies, history (H) does not refer to the occurrence of events before the experiment. Rather, history refers to specific events that are external to the experiment but that occur at the same time as the experiment. These events may affect the dependent variable. Consider the following experiment:

$$O_1 \, X_1 \, O_2$$

where O_1 and O_2 are measures of ticket sales to a weekend break built around visiting the Christmas market in Nuremberg, Germany, and X_1 represents a new promotional campaign. The difference $(O_2–O_1)$ is the treatment effect. Suppose that the experiment revealed that there was no difference between O_2 and O_1. Can we then conclude that the promotional campaign was ineffective? Certainly not! The promotional campaign X_1 is not the only possible explanation of the difference between O_2 and O_1. The campaign might well have been effective. What if general economic conditions declined during the experiment and the local area was particularly hard hit by redundancies through several employers closing down their operations (history)? Conversely, even if there was some difference between O_2 and O_1, it may be incorrect to conclude that the campaign was effective if history was not controlled, because the experimental effects might have been confounded by history. The longer the time interval between observations, the greater the possibility that history will confound an experiment of this type.[12]

Maturation

Maturation

An extraneous variable attributable to changes in the test units themselves that occur with the passage of time.

Testing effects

Effects caused by the process of experimentation.

Main testing effect

An effect of testing occurring when a prior observation affects a later observation.

Interactive testing effect

An effect in which a prior measurement affects the test unit response to the independent variable.

Maturation (MA) is similar to history except that it refers to changes in participants themselves. These changes are not caused by the impact of independent variables or treatments but occur with the passage of time. In an experiment involving people, maturation takes place as people become older, more experienced, tired, bored or uninterested. Tracking and market studies that span several months are vulnerable to maturation, since it is difficult to know how participants are changing over time.

Maturation effects also extend to test units other than people. For example, consider the case in which the participants or test units are travel companies. Travel companies change over time in terms of personnel, physical layout, decoration, and the range of holidays and services they have to offer.

Testing effects

Testing effects are caused by the process of experimentation. Typically, these are the effects on the experiment of taking a measure on the dependent variable before and after the presentation of the treatment. There are two kinds of testing effects: (1) main testing effect (MT), and (2) interactive testing effect (IT).

The **main testing effect** (MT) occurs when a prior observation affects a later observation. Consider an experiment to measure the effect of advertising on attitudes towards taking a holiday in Egypt. Imagine that participants are given a pre-treatment questionnaire measuring background information and attitude towards holidaying in Egypt. They are then exposed to the test advertisement embedded in a TV programme. After viewing the advertisement, the participants again answer a questionnaire measuring, among other things, attitude towards holidaying in Egypt.

Suppose that there was no difference between the pre- and post-treatment attitudes. Can we conclude that the advertisement was ineffective? An alternative explanation might be that the participants tried to maintain consistency between their pre- and post-treatment attitudes. As a result of the main testing effect, post-treatment attitudes were influenced more by pre-treatment attitudes than by the treatment itself. The main testing effect may also be reactive, causing the participants to change their attitudes simply because these attitudes have been measured. The main testing effect compromises the internal validity of the experiment.

In the **interactive testing effect** (IT), a prior measurement affects the participants response to the independent variable. Continuing with our advertising experiment, when people are asked to indicate their attitudes towards taking a holiday in Egypt, they become more aware of Egyptian holidays: they are sensitised to Egyptian holidays and become more likely to pay attention to the test advertisement than are people who were not included in the experiment. The measured effects are then not generalisable to the population; therefore, the interactive testing effects influence the experiment's external validity.[13]

Instrumentation

Instrumentation (I) refers to changes in the measuring instrument, in the observers or in the scores themselves. Sometimes measuring instruments are modified during the course of an experiment. In the Egyptian holiday experiment, using a newly designed questionnaire to measure the post-treatment attitudes could lead to variations in the responses obtained. Consider an experiment in which sales at a shoe shop are measured before and after exposure to a promotional offer of a discounted music festival ticket (treatment). If there is a non-experimental price change between O_1 and O_2, this could result in a change in instrumentation, because European sales may be measured using different unit prices. In this case, the treatment effect $(O_2 - O_1)$ could be attributed to a change in instrumentation.

Instrumentation effects are likely when interviewers make pre- and post-treatment measurements. The effectiveness of interviewers can be different at different times.

Statistical regression

Statistical regression (SR) effects occur when participants with extreme scores move closer to the average score during the course of the experiment. In the Egyptian holiday advertising experiment, suppose that in a pretest measurement some participants had either very favourable or very unfavourable attitudes towards the country of Egypt. On post-treatment measurement, their attitudes might have moved towards the average. Consumer attitudes change continuously for a wide variety of reasons. Consumers with extreme attitudes have more room for change, so variation may be more likely. This has a confounding effect on the experimental results, because the observed effect (change in attitude) may be attributable to statistical regression rather than to the treatment (test advertisement).

Selection bias

Selection bias (SB) refers to the improper assignment of participants to treatment conditions. This bias occurs when selection or assignment of participants results in treatment groups that differ on the dependent variable before the exposure to the treatment condition. If participants self-select their own groups or are assigned to groups on the basis of the researchers' judgement, selection bias is possible. For example, consider an experiment in which two different merchandising displays (old *static display* and new *audio-visual display*) are assigned to different branches of a travel company. The branches in the two groups may not be equivalent to begin with. They may vary with respect to a key characteristic, such as branch size. Branch size is likely to affect the sales of holidays, regardless of which merchandising display was assigned to a branch.

Mortality

Mortality (MO) refers to the loss of participants while the experiment is in progress. This happens for many reasons, such as participants refusing to continue in the experiment. Mortality confounds results because it is difficult to determine whether the lost participants would respond in the same manner to the treatments as those that remain. Consider again the merchandising display experiment. Suppose that during the course of the experiment, three branches in the new *audio-visual display* drop out because they feel the noise is not conducive to negotiations with certain types of client (e.g. the type of customer that would spend €10,000 on a luxury cruise). The researcher could not determine whether the average sales of holidays for the new display would have been higher or lower if these three branches had continued in the experiment.

The various categories of extraneous variables are not mutually exclusive; they can occur jointly and also interact with each other. To illustrate, testing–maturation–mortality refers to a situation in which, because of pre-treatment measurement, the participants' beliefs and attitudes change over time and there is a differential loss of participants from the various treatment groups.

Controlling extraneous variables

Extraneous variables represent alternative explanations of experimental results. They pose a serious threat to the internal and external validity of an experiment. Unless they are controlled, they affect the dependent variable and thus confound the results. For this reason, they are also called confounding variables. There are four ways of controlling extraneous variables: randomisation, matching, statistical control and design control.

Randomisation

Randomisation refers to the random assignment of participants to experimental groups by using random numbers. Treatment conditions are also randomly assigned to experimental groups. In the three *Real Research* examples presented above, participants were randomly assigned. To illustrate further in an experiment of a test advertisement, participants may be randomly assigned to one of three experimental groups. One of the three versions of the test advertisement, selected at random, is administered to each group. As a result of random assignment, extraneous factors can be represented equally in each treatment condition. Randomisation is the preferred procedure for ensuring the prior equality of experimental groups,[14] but it may not be effective when the sample size is small because it merely produces groups that are equal on average. It is possible, though, to check whether randomisation has been effective by measuring the possible extraneous variables and comparing them across the experimental groups.

Matching

Matching involves comparing participants on a set of key background variables before assigning them to the treatment conditions. In the merchandising display (old *static display* and new *audio-visual display*) experiment, travel company branches could be matched on the basis of turnover, size, proportion of retail to corporate clients, or location. Then one branch from each matched pair would be assigned to each experimental group.

Matching has two drawbacks. First, participants can be matched on only a few characteristics, so the participants may be similar on the variables selected but unequal on others. Second, if the matched characteristics are irrelevant to the dependent variable, then the matching effort has been futile.[15]

Statistical control

Statistical control involves measuring the extraneous variables and adjusting for their effects through statistical analysis. This was illustrated in Table 11.2, which examined the relationship (association) between purchase of skiing holidays and education, controlling for the effect of income. More advanced statistical procedures, such as analysis of covariance (ANCOVA), are also available. In ANCOVA, the effects of the extraneous variable on the dependent variable are removed by an adjustment of the dependent variable's mean value within each treatment condition. ANCOVA is discussed in more detail in Chapter 19.

Design control

Design control involves the use of experiments designed to control specific extraneous variables. The types of controls made possible by suitably designing the experiment are illustrated with the following example.

| Real research | **Experimenting with new products[16]** |

Controlled-distribution electronic test markets are used increasingly to conduct experimental research on new products. This method makes it possible to create a design that controls for several extraneous factors. The control can allow for the manipulation of variables that can affect the success of new products. In manipulating variables, it is possible to ensure that a new product:

- obtains the right level of supermarket acceptance and all commodity volume distribution;
- is positioned in the correct aisle in each supermarket;
- receives the right number of facings on the shelf;
- has the correct everyday price;
- never has out-of-stock problems;
- obtains the planned level of trade promotion, display and price features on the desired time schedule.

By being able to control these variables, a high degree of internal validity can be obtained.

This example shows that controlled-distribution electronic test markets can be effective in controlling for specific extraneous variables. Extraneous variables can also be controlled by adopting specific experimental designs, as described in the next section.

A classification of experimental designs

Pre-experimental designs
Designs that do not control for extraneous factors by randomisation.

Experimental designs may be classified as pre-experimental, true experimental, quasi-experimental and statistical designs; see Figure 11.1.

Figure 11.1	

A classification of experimental designs

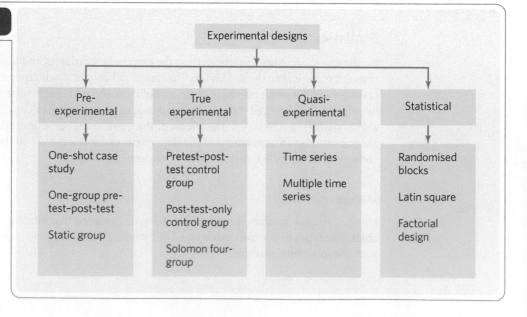

True experimental designs
Experimental designs distinguished by the fact that the researcher can randomly assign participants to experimental groups and also randomly assign treatments to experimental groups.

Quasi-experimental designs
Designs that apply part of the procedures of true experimentation but lack full experimental control.

Statistical designs
Designs that allow for the statistical control and analysis of external variables.

Pre-experimental designs do not employ randomisation procedures to control for extraneous factors. Examples of these designs include the one-shot case study, the one-group pretest–post-test design and the static group. In true experimental designs, the researcher can randomly assign participants to experimental groups and treatments to experimental groups. Included in this category are the pretest–post-test control group design, the post-test-only control group design and the Solomon four-group design. Quasi-experimental designs result when the researcher is unable to achieve full manipulation of scheduling or allocation of treatments to participants but can still apply part of the apparatus of the experimentation. Two such designs are time series and multiple time series designs. A statistical design is a series of basic experiments that allows for statistical control and analysis of external variables. Statistical designs are classified based on their characteristics and use. The important statistical designs include randomised block, Latin square and factorial.[17] These designs are illustrated in the context of a possible extension of the IFM Sports Marketing Surveys Racetrack study.* It measures the effectiveness of a test advertisement 'Sunday Driver' with Michael Schumacher and Mika Häkkinen for the Mercedes E-Class Estate car. The test advertisement could be evaluated in preparation to run in conjunction with TV coverage of Formula One races.

We begin our discussion with the first type of experimental design: pre-experimental.

---

* The Racetrack Project did not use experimental techniques. The example illustrates how they could have been applied.

Pre-experimental designs

These designs are characterised by an absence of randomisation. Three specific designs are described: the one-shot case study, the one-group pretest–post-test design and the static group design.

One-shot case study

One-shot case study
A pre-experimental design in which a single group of participants is exposed to a treatment **X**, and then a single measurement of the dependent variable is taken.

Also known as the after-only design, the one-shot case study may be symbolically represented as

$$X_1 \ O_1$$

A single group of participants is exposed to a treatment **X**, and then a single measurement on the dependent variable is taken (O_1). There is no random assignment of participants. Note that the symbol **R** is not used, because the participants are self-selected or selected arbitrarily by the researcher.

The danger of drawing valid conclusions from experiments of this type can be easily seen. They do not provide a basis of comparing the level of O_1 with what would happen if **X** were absent. In addition, the level of O_1 might be affected by many extraneous variables, including history, maturation, selection and mortality. Lack of control for these extraneous variables undermines the internal validity. For these reasons, the one-shot case study is more appropriate for exploratory than for conclusive research.

Focus on   **IFM Sports Marketing Surveys**

One-shot case study
A one-shot case study to measure the effectiveness of test advertisements for a Mercedes E-Class car would be implemented as follows. Online interviews are conducted with a national sample of participants from an access panel who have reported watching

a particular TV programme the previous night, e.g. The Shanghai Grand Prix. The programme selected is one that contains the selected test advertisement, e.g. a Mercedes E-Class advertisement (X). The dependent variables (O_s) are unaided and aided recall. First, unaided recall is measured by asking the participants whether they recall seeing a car advertisement, e.g. 'do you recall seeing a car advertisement last night?' If they recall the test advertisement, details about the advertisement content and execution are solicited. Participants who do not recall the test advertisement are asked about it specifically, e.g. 'do you recall seeing a Mercedes E-Class advertisement last night?' (aided recall). The results of aided and unaided recall are compared with norm scores to develop an index for interpreting the scores.

One-group pretest–post-test design

One-group pretest–post-test design

A pre-experimental design in which a group of participants is measured twice.

The one-group pretest–post-test design may be symbolised as

$$O_1 \; X \; O_2$$

In this design, a group of participants is measured twice. There is no control group. First a pre-treatment measure is taken (O_1), then the group is exposed to the treatment (X). Finally, a post-treatment measure is taken (O_2). The treatment effect is computed as ($O_2 - O_1$) but the validity of this conclusion is questionable since extraneous variables are largely uncontrolled. History, maturation, testing (both main and interactive testing effects), instrumentation, selection, mortality and regression could possibly be present. The following example shows how this design is used.

Focus on | **IFM Sports Marketing Surveys**

One-group pretest–post-test design

A one-group pretest–post-test design to measure the effectiveness of a test advertisement for a Mercedes would be implemented as follows. Participants are recruited to central cinema locations in different test cities. At the central location, participants are first administered a personal interview to measure, among other things, attitudes towards the Mercedes E-Class (O_1). Then they watch a TV programme containing the test advertisement (X). After viewing the TV programme, the participants are again administered a personal interview to measure attitudes towards the Mercedes E-Class (O_2). The effectiveness of the test advertisement is measured as ($O_2 - O_1$).

Static group design

Static group

A pre-experimental design in which there are two groups: the experimental group (EG), which is exposed to the treatment, and the control group (CG). Measurements on both groups are made only after the treatment, and participants are not assigned at random.

The static group is a two-group experimental design. One group, called the experimental group (EG), is exposed to the treatment, and the other, called the control group (CG), is not. Measurements on both groups are made only after the treatment, and participants are not assigned at random. This design may be symbolically described as

$$EG: X \; O_1$$
$$CG: O_2$$

The treatment effect would be measured as ($O_1 - O_2$). Notice that this difference could also be attributed to at least two extraneous variables (selection and mortality). Because participants are not randomly assigned, the two groups (EG and CG) may differ before the treatment, and selection bias may be present. There may also be mortality effects, as more participants may withdraw from the experimental group than from the control group. This would be particularly likely to happen if the treatment were unpleasant.

In practice, a control group is sometimes defined as the group that receives the current level of marketing activity, rather than a group that receives no treatment at all. The control group is defined in this way because it is difficult to reduce current marketing activities such as advertising and personal selling to zero.

Focus on   **IFM Sports Marketing Surveys**

Static group

A static group comparison to measure the effectiveness of a test advertisement for the Mercedes E-Class would be conducted as follows. Two groups of participants would be recruited on the basis of convenience. Only the experimental group would be exposed to the TV programme containing the advertisement. Then, attitudes towards the Mercedes E-Class of both the experimental and control group participants would be measured. The effectiveness of the test advertisement would be measured as (O_1-O_2).

True experimental designs

The distinguishing feature of true experimental designs, compared with pre-experimental designs, is randomisation. In true experimental designs, the researcher randomly assigns participants to experimental groups and treatments to experimental groups. True experimental designs include the pretest–post-test control group design, the posttest-only control group design and the Solomon four-group design.

Pretest–post-test control group design

Pretest–post-test control group design
An experimental design in which the experimental group is exposed to the treatment but the control group is not. Pretest and post-test measures are taken on both groups.

In the pretest–post-test control group design, participants are randomly assigned to either the experimental or the control group and a pre-treatment measure is taken on each group. Then the treatment is applied to the experimental group, and a post-treatment measure is taken from both groups. This design is symbolised as

$$\text{EG:} \quad R \quad O_1 \quad X \quad O_2$$
$$\text{CG:} \quad R \quad O_3 \qquad \ O_4$$

The treatment effect (TE) is measured as

$$(O_2\text{–}O_1) - (O_4\text{–}O_3)$$

This design controls for most extraneous variables. Selection bias is eliminated by randomisation. The other extraneous effects are controlled as follows:

$$O_2\text{–}O_1 = TE + H + MA + MT + IT + I + SR + MO$$
$$O_4\text{–}O_3 = H + MA + MT + I + SR + MO$$
$$= EV \text{ (extraneous variables)}$$

where the symbols for the extraneous variables are as defined previously. The experimental result is obtained by

$$(O_2\text{–}O_1) - (O_4\text{–}O_3) = TE + IT$$

The interactive testing effect is not controlled, because of the effect of the pretest measurement on the reaction of participants in the experimental group to the treatment.

Focus on

IFM Sports Marketing Surveys

Pretest–post-test control group

In the context of measuring the effectiveness of a test advertisement for the Mercedes E-Class, a pretest–post-test control group design would be implemented as follows. A sample of participants would be selected at random. Half of these would be randomly assigned to the experimental group, and the other half would form the control group. Participants in both groups would be administered a questionnaire to obtain a pretest measurement on attitudes towards the Mercedes E-Class. Only the participants in the experimental group would be exposed to the TV programme featuring the test advertisement. Then, a questionnaire would be administered to participants in both groups to obtain post-test measures on attitudes towards the Mercedes E-Class.

As this example shows, the pretest–post-test control group design involves two groups and two measurements on each group. A simpler design is the post-test-only control group design.

Post-test-only control group design

Post-test-only control group design
Experimental design in which the experimental group is exposed to the treatment but the control group is not and no pretest measure is taken.

The post-test-only control group design does not involve any pre-measurement. It may be symbolised as

$$\text{EG: R X } O_1$$
$$\text{CG: R   } O_2$$

The treatment effect is obtained by

$$TE = O_1 - O_2$$

This design is fairly simple to implement. Because there is no pre-measurement, the testing effects are eliminated, but this design is sensitive to selection bias and mortality. It is assumed that the two groups are similar in terms of pre-treatment measures on the dependent variable because of the random assignment of participants to groups. Because there is no pre-treatment measurement, this assumption cannot be checked. This design is also sensitive to mortality. It is difficult to determine whether those in the experimental group who discontinue the experiment are similar to their counterparts in the control group. Yet another limitation is that this design does not allow the researcher to examine changes in individual participants.

It is possible to control for selection bias and mortality through carefully designed experimental procedures. Examination of individual cases is often not of interest. On the other hand, this design possesses significant advantages in terms of time, cost and sample size requirements. It involves only two groups and only one measurement per group. Because of its simplicity, the post-test-only control group design is probably the most popular design in marketing research. Note that, except for pre-measurement, the implementation of this design is very similar to that of the pretest–post-test control group design.

Focus on

IFM Sports Marketing Surveys

Post-test-only control group

In the context of measuring the effectiveness of a test advertisement for the Mercedes E-Class, a post-test-only control group design would be implemented as follows. A sample of participants would be selected at random. The sample would be randomly split, with half the subjects forming the experimental group and the other half constituting the control group. Only the participants in the experimental group would be exposed to the TV programme containing the test Mercedes E-Class advertisement. Then, a questionnaire would be administered to both groups to obtain post-test measures on attitudes towards the Mercedes E-Class. The differences in the attitudes of the experimental group and the control group would be used as a measure of the effectiveness of the test advertisement.

Solomon four-group design
An experimental design that explicitly controls for interactive testing effects, in addition to controlling for all the other extraneous variables.

In this example, the researcher is not concerned with examining the changes in the attitudes of individual participants. When this information is desired, the Solomon four-group design should be considered. The Solomon four-group design overcomes the limitations of the pretest–post-test control group and post-test-only control group designs in that it explicitly controls for the interactive testing effect, in addition to controlling for all the other extraneous variables. However, this design has practical limitations: it is expensive and time consuming to implement. Hence, it is not considered further.[18]

In all true experimental designs, the researcher exercises a high degree of control. In particular, the researcher can control when the measurements are taken, on whom they are taken and the scheduling of the treatments. Moreover, the researcher can randomly select the test units and randomly expose test units to the treatments. In some instances, the researcher cannot exercise this kind of control; then quasi-experimental designs should be considered.

Quasi-experimental designs

A quasi-experimental design results under the following conditions. First, the researcher can control when measurements are taken and on whom they are taken. Second, the researcher lacks control over the scheduling of the treatments and also is unable to expose participants to the treatments randomly.[19] Quasi-experimental designs are useful because they can be used in cases when true experimentation cannot be used, and because they are quicker and less expensive. An application of a quasi-experiment is illustrated in the following example.

Real research   ## Measuring the effectiveness of food advertisements[20]

A quasi-experiment was performed to explore the relationships between dominant types claims made in advertising and two advertising effectiveness measures: attitude towards the brand and purchase intention. To start the study, claims in food advertisements from selected women's magazines were content analysed. Three magazines, *Better Homes & Gardens, Good Housekeeping* and the *Ladies' Home Journal,* were selected as representative of the larger population of women's magazines. The researchers focused on women's magazines because they felt that women aged 25 to 64 were most often found to be the primary decision-makers in food consumption. In addition, magazine advertisements were analysed because they typically provided detailed product information and because print media were frequently ranked among the sources from which consumers sought nutrition and health information. The criteria for selection included a wide circulation with monthly publication, an abundance of food advertisements and the availability of full-page, slick, colour advertisements. The study became a quasi-experiment because the chosen stimulus advertisements were not manipulated, but carefully selected from the sample of advertisements used in the content analysis. The overall design of the quasi-experiment mirrored a 2 × 2 factorial design, with two independent variables –

product category (i.e. hedonic vs. functional foods) and advertising claims (i.e. taste claims vs. specific nutrition claims). Overall, a total of 20 different stimulus advertisements – five stimulus advertisements for each of the four experiment conditions – were rated. Of the 20 advertisements, 10 were promoting hedonic foods and the other 10 were promoting functional foods. Of the 10 advertisements promoting hedonic and functional foods, respectively, 5 advertisements incorporated taste claims (e.g. 'deliciously rich, silky smooth taste'), whereas the other 5 advertisements incorporated specific nutrition claims (e.g. '44% less fat'). Taste claims and specific nutrition claims were selected for the quasi-experiment, as they turned out to be the most dominant types of advertising claim, employed in 69% and 65% of the total advertisements examined, respectively. The findings from the quasi-experiment called into question food advertising practices revealed in the content analysis. It was found that specific nutrition claims were more effective when promoting hedonic (vs. functional) foods and taste claims were more effective when promoting functional (vs. hedonic) foods.

Because full experimental control is lacking, the researcher must consider the specific variables that are not controlled. Popular forms of quasi-experimental designs are time series and multiple time series designs.

Time series design

Time series design
A quasi-experimental design that involves periodic measurements of the dependent variable for a group of participants. Then the treatment is administered by the researcher or occurs naturally. After the treatment, periodic measurements are continued to determine the treatment effect.

Multiple time series design
A time series design that includes another group of participants to serve as a control group.

The **time series design** involves a series of periodic measurements on the dependent variable for a group of participants. The treatment is then administered by the researcher or occurs naturally. After the treatment, periodic measurements are continued to determine the treatment effect. A time series experiment may be symbolised as

$$O_1 \, O_2 \, O_3 \, O_4 \, O_5 \, O_6 \, O_7 \, O_8 \, O_9 \, O_{10}$$

This is a quasi-experiment, because there is no randomisation of participants to treatments, and the timing of treatment presentation, as well as which participants are exposed to the treatment, may not be within the researcher's control (hence no specific X symbolised above).

Taking a series of measurements before and after the treatment provides at least partial control for several extraneous variables. Maturation is at least partially controlled, because it would not affect O_5 and O_6 alone but would also influence other observations. By similar reasoning, the main testing effect and statistical regression are controlled as well. If the participants are selected randomly or by matching, selection bias can be reduced. Mortality may pose a problem, but it can be largely controlled by paying a premium or offering other incentives to participants.

The major weakness of the time series design is the failure to control history. Another limitation is that the experiment may be affected by the interactive testing effect because multiple measurements are being made on the participants. Nevertheless, time series designs are useful, as illustrated by this case. The effectiveness of a test advertisement (**X**) may be examined by broadcasting the advertisement a predetermined number of times and examining the data from a pre-existing test panel. Although the marketer can control the scheduling of the test advertisement, it is uncertain when or whether the panel members are exposed to it. The panel members' purchases before, during and after the campaign are examined to determine whether the test advertisement has a short-term effect, a long-term effect or no effect.

Multiple time series design

The **multiple time series design** is similar to the time series design except that another group of participants is added to serve as a control group. Symbolically, this design may be described as

$$\text{EG:} \quad O_1 \ O_2 \ O_3 \ O_4 \ O_5 \quad X \quad O_6 \ O_7 \ O_8 \ O_9 \ O_{10}$$
$$\text{CG:} \quad O_{11} \ O_{12} \ O_{13} \ O_{14} \ O_{15} \qquad O_{16} \ O_{17} \ O_{18} \ O_{19} \ O_{20}$$

If the control group is carefully selected, this design can be an improvement over the simple time series experiment. The improvement lies in the ability to test the treatment effect twice: against the pre-treatment measurements in the experimental group and against the control group. To use the multiple time series design to assess the effectiveness of an advertisement, the test panel example would be modified as follows. The test advertisement would be shown in only a few of the test cities. Panel members in these cities would make up the experimental group. Panel members in cities where the advertisement was not shown would constitute the control group.

In concluding our discussion of pre-experimental, true experimental and quasi-experimental designs, we summarise in Table 11.3 the potential sources of invalidity that may affect each of these designs. In this table, a minus sign indicates a definite weakness, a plus sign indicates that the factor is controlled, a question mark denotes a possible source of concern, and

Table 11.3	Potential sources of invalidity of experimental designs

	Source of invalidity							
			Internal variables					External variables
Design	History	Maturation	Testing	Instrumentation	Regression	Selection	Mortality	Interaction of testing and X
Pre-experimental designs								
One-shot case study X O	-	-				-	-	
One-group pretest–post-test design O X O	-	-	-	-	?			-
Static group comparison X O 　O	+	?	+	+	+	-	-	
True experimental designs								
Pretest–post-test control group R O X O R O　O	+	+	+	+	+	+	+	-
Post-test-only control group design R X O R　O	+	+	+	+	+	+	+	+
Quasi-experimental designs								
Time series O O O X O O O	-	+	+	?	+	+	+	-
Multiple time series O O O X O O O O O O　O O O	+	+	+	+	+	+	+	

Note: A minus sign indicates a definite weakness, a plus sign indicates that the factor is controlled, a question mark denotes a possible source of concern, and a blank means that the factor is not relevant.

a blank means that the factor is not relevant. It should be remembered that potential sources of invalidity are not the same as actual errors.

Statistical designs

Statistical designs consist of a series of basic experiments that allow for statistical control and analysis of external variables. In other words, several basic experiments are conducted simultaneously. Thus, statistical designs are influenced by the same sources of invalidity that affect the basic designs being used. Statistical designs offer the following advantages:

1   The effects of more than one independent variable can be measured.

2   Specific extraneous variables can be statistically controlled.

3   Economical designs can be formulated when each participant is measured more than once.

The most common statistical designs are the randomised block design, the Latin square design and the factorial design.

Randomised block design

Randomised block design
A statistical design in which the participants are blocked on the basis of an external variable to ensure that the various experimental and control groups are matched closely on that variable.

A randomised block design is useful when there is only one major external variable – such as sales, store size or income of the participant – that might influence the dependent variable. The participants are blocked or grouped on the basis of the external variable. The researcher must be able to identify and measure the blocking variable. By blocking, the researcher ensures that the various experimental and control groups are matched closely on the external variable.

As the following example illustrates, in most marketing research situations, external variables such as sales, store size, store type, location, income, occupation and social class of the participant can influence the dependent variable. Therefore, generally speaking, randomised block designs are more useful than completely random designs. Their main limitation is that the researcher can control for only one external variable. When more than one variable must be controlled, the researcher must use Latin square or factorial designs.

Focus on   **IFM Sports Marketing Surveys**

Randomised block design

In the context of measuring the effectiveness of a Mercedes E-Class 'Sunday Driver' test advertisement starring Michael Schumacher and Mika Häkkinen, we extend the example to measure the impact of humour on the effectiveness of advertising.[21] Three test advertisements, A, B and C, have respectively no humour, some humour and high levels of humour. Which of these would be the most effective? Management feel that the participants' evaluation of the advertisements will be influenced by the extent to which they have driven Mercedes cars in the past (work vehicle, owning, hire/rental). So, Mercedes driving experience is identified as the blocking variable, and the randomly selected participants are classified into four blocks (heavy, medium, light or never driven a Mercedes car). Participants from each block are randomly assigned to the treatment groups (test advertisements A, B and C). The results reveal that the 'some humour' advertisement B was the most effective (Table 11.4).

| Table 11.4 | An example of a randomised block design |

		Treatment groups		
Block number	Mercedes usage	*Advertisement A*	*Advertisement B*	*Advertisement C*
1	*High*	A	B	C
2	*Medium*	A	B	C
3	*Light*	A	B	C
4	*None*	A	B	C

Latin square design

Latin square design
A statistical design that allows for the statistical control of two non-interacting external variables in addition to the manipulation of the independent variable.

A **Latin square design** allows the researcher to control statistically two non-interacting external variables as well as to manipulate the independent variable. Each external or blocking variable is divided into an equal number of blocks or levels. The independent variable is also divided into the same number of levels. A Latin square is conceptualised as a table (see Table 11.5), with the rows and columns representing the blocks in the two external variables. The levels of the independent variable are then assigned to the cells in the table. The assignment rule is that each level of the independent variable should appear only once in each row and each column, as shown in Table 11.5.

| Table 11.5 | An example of a Latin square design |

	Interest in watching Formula One races		
Mercedes usage	*High*	*Medium*	*Low*
High	B	A	C
Medium	C	B	A
Light and none	A	C	B

Note: A, B and C denote the three test advertisements, which have respectively no humour, some humour and high humour.

| **Focus on** | **IFM Sports Marketing Surveys** |

Latin square design

To illustrate the Latin square design, suppose that in the previous example, in addition to controlling for Mercedes usage, the researcher also wanted to control for interest in watching Formula One races (defined as high, medium or low). To implement a Latin square design, Mercedes usage would also have to be blocked at three rather than four levels (e.g. by combining the low and non-users into a single block). Assignments of the three test advertisements could then be made as shown in Table 11.5. Note that each advertisement – A, B or C – appears once, and only once, in each row and each column.

Although Latin square designs are popular in marketing research, they are not without limitations. They require an equal number of rows, columns and treatment levels, which is sometimes problematic. Note that, in the above example, the low users and non-patrons had to be combined to satisfy this requirement. In addition, only two external variables can be controlled simultaneously. Latin squares do not allow the researcher to examine interactions of the external variables with each other or with the independent variable. To examine interactions, factorial designs should be used.

Factorial design

Factorial design
A statistical experimental design used to measure the effects of two or more independent variables at various levels and to allow for interactions between variables.

A factorial design is used to measure the effects of two or more independent variables at various levels. Unlike the randomised block design and the Latin square, factorial designs allow for interactions between variables.[22] An interaction is said to take place when the simultaneous effect of two or more variables is different from the sum of their separate effects. For example, an individual's favourite drink might be coffee and favourite temperature level might be cold, but this individual might not prefer cold coffee, leading to an interaction. The following example presents a situation where variables interacted and a factorial design was used.

Real research	**Choosing a tour route in South America**[23]

A study was conducted by Spanish researchers on students in their last year of university who wished to make an end-of-year trip for 15 days during their Easter holiday. An experiment was conducted to determine how a holiday package should be designed. More specifically the researchers wished to to determine the tour route and services in South America that would best satisfy the needs of their target market. Four relevant and very specific attributes were chosen for the study: the meal plan (four to eight days on half-board and the rest on bed and breakfast), accommodation at an Amazon lodge, an excursion to Colca Canyon and a sightseeing flight over the Nazca Lines. If all four relevant attributes were chosen, the cost of delivering this would exceed what could be afforded by this target market. Thus, the researchers had to find the exact combination of attributes that gave the best deal as seen by their target market. To ascertain exactly which of these four attributes determined the process of choosing a route, and what effect their interaction generated, they proposed an experiment using a two-level factorial design. The advantages of such a design were that it required very few elemental experiments for each factor, providing them with trends for determining the direction for future experiments, allowing the sequential investigation required by causal analysis.

A factorial design may also be conceptualised as a table. In a two-factor design, each level of one variable represents a row and each level of another variable represents a column. Multi-dimensional tables can be used for three or more factors. Factorial designs involve a cell for every possible combination of treatment variables. Suppose that in the Mercedes example, in addition to examining the effect of humour, the researcher was also interested in simultaneously examining the effect of the amount of information about the performance of the Mercedes E-Class that came over in the advertisement. Further, the amount of information was also varied at three levels (high, medium and low). As shown in Table 11.6, this would require $3 \times 3 = 9$ cells. The participants would be randomly selected and randomly assigned to the nine cells. Participants in each cell would receive a specific treatment combination. For example, participants in the upper left corner cell would view an advertisement that had no-humour and low information about the performance of the Mercedes E-Class. The results revealed a significant interaction between the two factors or variables. Participants with a low amount of Mercedes information preferred the high-humour advertisement (C). Those with a high amount of Mercedes information, however, preferred the no humour film clip (G). Notice that, although Table 11.6 may appear somewhat similar to Table 11.4, the random assignment of participants and data analysis are very different for the randomised block design and the factorial design.[24]

Table 11.6	An example of a factorial design		
Amount of Mercedes E-Class information	**Amount of humour**		
	No humour	*Some humour*	*High humour*
Low	A	B	C
Medium	D	E	F
High	G	H	I

The main disadvantage of a factorial design is that the number of treatment combinations increases multiplicatively with an increase in the number of variables or levels. In our example of Table 11.6, if the amount of humour and Mercedes information had five levels each instead of three, the number of cells would jump from 9 to 25. All the treatment combinations are required if all the main effects and interactions are to be measured. If the researcher is interested in only a few of the interactions or main effects, fractional factorial designs may be used. As their name implies, these designs consist of only a fraction or portion of the corresponding full factorial design.

Laboratory versus field experiments

Laboratory environment
An artificial setting for experimentation in which the researcher constructs the desired conditions.

Field environment
An experimental location set in actual market conditions.

Demand artefacts
Responses given because participants attempt to guess the purpose of the experiment and respond accordingly.

Experiments may be conducted in a laboratory or field environment. A laboratory environment is an artificial one that the researcher constructs with the desired conditions specific to the experiment. A field environment is synonymous with actual market conditions. The earlier example of the advergame experiment of designing a videogame around a brand was conducted in a laboratory environment where participants sat at computers in a given room to play the tested games. The same experiment could also be conducted in a field environment by allowing the participants to play the games on devices wherever they felt comfortable. The differences between the two environments are summarised in Table 11.7.

Laboratory experiments have the following advantages over field experiments:

- The laboratory environment offers a high degree of control because it isolates the experiment in a carefully monitored environment. Therefore, the effects of history can be minimised.

- A laboratory experiment also tends to produce the same results if repeated with similar participants, leading to high internal validity.

- Laboratory experiments tend to use a small number of participants, last for a shorter time, be more restricted geographically, and are easier to conduct than field experiments. Hence, they are generally less expensive as well.

Compared with field experiments, laboratory experiments suffer from some main disadvantages:

- The artificiality of the environment may cause reactive error in that participants react to the situation itself rather than to the independent variable.[25]

- The environment may cause demand artefacts, a phenomenon in which participants attempt to guess the purpose of the experiment and respond accordingly. For example, while viewing a film clip, participants may recall pre-treatment questions about the brand and guess that the advertisement is trying to change their attitudes towards the brand.[26]

Table 11.7	Laboratory versus field experiments	
Factor	Laboratory	Field
Environment	Artificial	Realistic
Control	High	Low
Reactive error	High	Low
Demand artefacts	High	Low
Internal validity	High	Low
External validity	Low	High
Time	Short	Long
Number of participants	Small	Large
Ease of implementation	High	Low
Cost	Low	High

- Finally, laboratory experiments are likely to have lower external validity than field experiments. Because a laboratory experiment is conducted in an artificial environment, the ability to generalise the results to the real world may be diminished.

It has been argued that artificiality or lack of realism in a laboratory experiment need not lead to lower external validity. One must be aware of the aspects of the laboratory experiment that differ from the situation to which generalisations are to be made. External validity will be reduced only if these aspects interface with the independent variables explicitly manipulated in the experiment, as is often the case in applied marketing research. Another consideration, however, is that laboratory experiments allow for more complex designs than field experiments. Hence, the researcher can control for more factors or variables in the laboratory setting, which increases external validity.[27]

The researcher must consider all these factors when deciding whether to conduct laboratory or field experiments. Field experiments are less common in marketing research than laboratory experiments, although laboratory and field experiments play complementary roles.[28]

Experimental versus non-experimental designs

In Chapter 3, we discussed three types of research designs: exploratory, descriptive and causal. Of these, it may be argued that causal designs are the most appropriate for inferring and measuring cause-and-effect relationships (though not the only way, as may be argued by the adherents to grounded research approaches, introduced in Chapter 6). Although descriptive survey data are often used to provide evidence of 'causal' relationships, these studies do not meet all the conditions required for causality. For example, it is difficult in descriptive studies to establish the prior equivalence of the participant groups with respect to both the independent and dependent variables. On the other hand, an experiment can establish this equivalence by random assignment of participants to groups. In descriptive research, it is also difficult to establish the time order of occurrence of variables. In an experiment, however, the researcher controls the timing of the measurements and the introduction of the treatment. Finally, descriptive research offers little control over other possible causal factors.

We do not wish to undermine the importance of descriptive research designs in marketing research. As mentioned in Chapter 3, descriptive research constitutes the most popular research design in marketing research, and we do not want to imply that it should never be used to examine causal relationships. Indeed, some authors have suggested procedures for drawing causal inferences from descriptive (non-experimental) data.[29] Rather, our intent is to alert the reader to the limitations of descriptive research for examining causal relationships. Likewise, we also want to make the reader aware of the limitations of experimentation.[30]

Experimentation is an important research design that gives the ability to infer causal relationships. In marketing research terms, it has been used primarily in the field of communications and advertising.[31] However, it has limitations of time, cost and administration of an experiment, with these limitations meaning that experimental techniques have a relatively low penetration into marketing research practice.[32]

Time

Experiments can be time consuming, particularly if the researcher is interested in measuring the long-term effects of the treatment, such as the effectiveness of an advertising campaign. Experiments should last long enough so that the post-treatment measurements include most or all of the effects of the independent variables.

Cost

Test marketing
An application of a controlled experiment done in limited, but carefully selected, test markets. It involves a replication of the planned national marketing programme for a product in test markets.

Experiments are often expensive. The requirements of experimental group, control group and multiple measurements significantly add to the cost of research.

Administration

Test market
A carefully selected part of the marketplace particularly suitable for test marketing.

Experiments can be difficult to administer. It may be impossible in measuring human activity to control for the effects of the extraneous variables, particularly in a field environment. Field experiments often interfere with a company's ongoing operations, and obtaining cooperation from the retailers, wholesalers and others involved may be difficult. Finally, competitors may deliberately contaminate the results of a field experiment. These limitations have given rise to the use of grounded theory approaches, especially in developing an understanding of consumer behaviour that may be impossible to encapsulate through experiments.

Application: test marketing

Test marketing, also called market testing, is an application of a controlled experiment conducted in limited but carefully selected parts of the marketplace called test markets. The following example illustrates what decisions may be supported through a test market and some of the challenges faced.

Real research | **Developing the Boots brand for a European launch[33]**

Boots (**www.boots.com**) was a virtually unknown consumer brand in mainland Europe. Where it existed, any brand awareness associated it with a 'drugstore' health and beauty retailing, a far cry from the traditional, specialist, advice-led European pharmacy. A key challenge faced by Boots was how to leverage its expertise in product development, manufacturing, sourcing and distribution to build brand equity for the Boots brand across Europe. Boots planned a major international brand creation involving four key markets (France, Spain, Italy and Portugal) with a key business objective of launching a master brand and supporting product portfolio. This would involve concept and positioning development, naming approaches and an identity that could be communicated through product, range, packaging and collateral design. Initial research among some 1,500 European pharmacy and consumer targets indicated that pharmacy consumers had a very specific set of needs and look for particular attributes in their choice of brands. While virtually unknown as a consumer brand in Europe, Boots Healthcare had developed equity and heritage for Boots as a 'laboratory' with pharmacists in key markets. Based upon this awareness, the master brand positioning was developed under the name of 'Boots Laboratories', building on the brand's heritage and awareness among health care professionals. The Boots Laboratories visual identity was created to reflect the 'scientific' heritage and health care credentials. France was selected as the lead and test market for the brand. France had a strong and established range of skincare brands and was notoriously difficult to 'crack'. All agreed that it would provide a challenging test market for the new brand. The research and launch programme covered the following stages: (1) quantitative strategic research (August 2007), (2) qualitative concept research, (3) quantitative concept/design test (February 2008), (4) trade launch (April and May 2008) and (5) consumer launch in France and Portugal (September 2008). The test reactions to the brand were very positive with a strong appeal and very good levels of unpriced purchase intent. The Boots range was seen as a good fit with the pharmacy environment, with 94% describing it as being appropriate to be sold in French pharmacies.

Test marketing involves a replication of a planned national or, as in the Boots example, an international marketing programme in selected test markets. Often, the marketing mix variables (independent variables) are varied in test marketing and the sales (dependent variable) are monitored so that an appropriate national marketing strategy can be identified. The two major objectives of test marketing are (1) to determine market acceptance of the product and (2) to test alternative levels of marketing mix variables. Test-marketing procedures may be classified as standard test markets, controlled and mini-market tests, and simulated test marketing.

Standard test market

Standard test market
A test market in which the product is sold through regular distribution channels. For example, no special considerations are given to products simply because they are being test marketed.

In a standard test market, test markets are selected and the product is sold through regular distribution channels which could include online outlets. Typically, the company's own sales force is responsible for distributing the product. Sales personnel manage the stocking, restocking and monitoring inventory at regular intervals. One or more combinations of marketing mix variables (product, price, distribution and promotional levels) are employed.

Designing a standard test market involves deciding what criteria are to be used for selecting test markets, how many test markets to use and the duration of the test. Care must be taken in establishing the rationale for the choice of a test market. In general, the more test markets that can be used, the better. If resources are limited, at least two test markets should be used for each programme variation to be tested. Where external validity is important, however, at least four test markets should be used. The criteria for the ideal selection of test markets may be summarised as:[34]

1 Large enough to produce meaningful projections. They should contain at least 2% of the potential target population.

2 Representative demographically.

3 Representative with respect to product consumption behaviour.

4 Representative with respect to media usage.

5 Representative with respect to competition.

6 Relatively isolated in terms of media and physical distribution.

7 Having normal historical development in the product class.

8 Having marketing research and auditing services available.

9 Not overtested.

The duration of the test depends on the repurchase cycle for the product, the probability of competitive response, cost considerations, the initial consumer response and company philosophy. The test should last long enough for repurchase activity to be observed. This indicates the long-term impact of the product. If competitive reaction to the test is anticipated, the duration should be short. The cost of the test is also an important factor. The longer a test is, the more it costs, and at some point the value of additional information is outweighed by its costs. Recent evidence suggests that tests of new brands whose product lifecycle is projected in 'years' should run for at least 10 months. An empirical analysis found that the final test-market share was reached in 10 months 85% of the time and in 12 months 95% of the time.[35] Test marketing is not without risks, but it can be very beneficial to a product's successful introduction.

A standard test market constitutes a one-shot case study. In addition to the problems associated with this design, test marketing faces two unique problems. First, competitors often take actions such as increasing their promotional efforts to contaminate the test-marketing programme. When Procter & Gamble test marketed a hand-and-body lotion, Wondra, the market leader, Cheeseborough Ponds, started a competitive buy-one-get-one-free promotion for its flagship brand, Vaseline Intensive Care lotion. This encouraged consumers to stock up on Vaseline Intensive Care lotion and, as a result, Wondra did poorly in the test market. In spite of this, Procter & Gamble still launched the line nationally. Ponds again countered with the same promotional strategy. Vaseline Intensive Care settled with a market share of 22% while Procter & Gamble achieved just 4%.[36] Another problem is that, while a firm's test marketing is in progress, competitors have an opportunity to beat it to the national market. Sometimes it is not feasible to implement a standard test market using the company's personnel. Instead, the company must seek help from an outside supplier, in which case the controlled test market may be an attractive option.

Controlled test market

Controlled test market
A test-marketing programme conducted by an outside research company in field experimentation. The research company guarantees distribution of the product in retail outlets that represent a predetermined percentage of the market.

In a **controlled test market**, the entire test-marketing programme is conducted by an outside research company. The research company guarantees distribution of the product in retail outlets that represent a predetermined percentage of the market. It handles warehousing and field sales operations, such as stocking shelves, selling and stock control. The controlled test market includes both mini-market (or forced distribution) tests and the smaller controlled store panels. An excellent example of this is provided by the German research firm, GfK (**www.gfk.com**).

Simulated test market

Simulated test market
A quasi-test market in which participants are preselected; they are then interviewed and observed on their purchases and attitudes towards the product.

Also called a laboratory test or test-market simulation, a **simulated test market** yields mathematical estimates of market share based on the initial reaction of consumers to a new product. The procedure works as follows. Typically, participants are intercepted in busy locations, such as shopping centres, and pre-screened for product usage. The selected individuals are exposed to the proposed new product concept and given an opportunity to buy the new product in a real-life or laboratory environment. Those who purchase the new product are interviewed about their evaluation of the product and repeat purchase intentions. The trial and repeat purchase estimates so generated are combined with data on proposed promotion and distribution levels to project a share of the market. Simulated test markets can be conducted in 16 weeks or less. The information they generate is confidential and the competition cannot obtain it. They are also relatively inexpensive. Simulated test markets became widely adopted by major manufacturers around the world as an alternative to test marketing, which was slower, more expensive and less secure.[37]

However, the role of simulated test markets has changed. In the past the focus was helping to decide on the go/no decision and providing diagnostics to improve the product performance (communication, package, price and product) before launch. More recently the go/no decisions are typically made in advance of a simulated test market and it serves primarily as a disaster check. Also, improvements in product performance need to be made earlier in the process and are based on other research (concept, copy, product, price, or package studies). By the time a simulated test market is performed, it may be too late and it changes its role to become more focused on marketing plan optimisation.[38]

International marketing research

If field experiments are difficult to conduct in developed Western economies, the challenge they pose is greatly increased in international markets. In many countries, the marketing, economic, structural, information and technological environment is not developed to the extent that it is in Europe and the USA. In some countries in Asia, Africa and South America, a majority of the population live in small towns and villages. Yet basic infrastructure such as roads, transportation and warehouse facilities are lacking, making it difficult to achieve desired levels of distribution. Even when experiments are designed in such countries, it is difficult to control for the time order of occurrence of variables and the absence of other possible causal factors, two of the necessary conditions for causality. Because the researcher has little control over the environment, control of extra-neous variables is particularly problematic. Furthermore, it may not be possible to address this problem by adopting the most appropriate experimental design, as environmental constraints may make that design infeasible.

Thus, the internal and external validity of field experiments conducted in international markets is generally lower than in Europe and the USA. Although pointing to the difficulties of conducting field experiments in other countries, we do not wish to imply that such causal research cannot or should not be conducted. On the contrary, there are many international locations that may have more advanced infrastructure than many parts of Europe and the USA. The use of Singapore as a test market in the Asia-Pacific region is illustrated in the following example.

Real research   Local cultural and media tastes[39]

The fact that Asian consumers quickly adopt emerging technology into their daily lives has led to many improvements by governments around the region. Singapore is a shining example, not just for Asia but globally, in the provision of online government services; Accenture has consistently ranked it as one of the world's top three countries in this field. The more than 1,600 government services available online have become a necessity for Singaporeans, while the city state's small, densely populated nature makes it an ideal e-government test market. More recently, Singapore has started putting up free wireless broadband kiosks in shopping malls and public buildings.

Ethics in marketing research

As was explained in Chapter 10, it is often believed that, if participants are aware of the purpose of a research project, they may give biased responses. In these situations, a deliberate attempt is made by the researcher to disguise the purpose of the research. This is often necessary with experimentation, where disguise is needed to produce valid results. Take, for instance, the *Real Research* example at the start of this chapter. The study aimed to measure the interaction of tone and wording in advertisements but participants were told that the purpose of the study was to find out how people evaluate TV programmes and advertisements. In the advergames *Real Research* example, the study sought to measure the link between the theme of a videogame and the nature of a brand linked to that game. The advergames study instructions told participants that the researchers were interested in their attitudes towards different online travel companies. If participants knew the true purpose of these two studies their responses might be biased. Disguising the purpose of the research, however, should not lead to deception.

Although this seems like a paradox, one solution is to disclose the possible existence of deception before the start of the experiment and allow the participants the right to redress at the conclusion of the experiment. The following four items should be conveyed: (1) inform participants that in an experiment of this nature a disguise of the purpose is often required for valid results; (2) inform them of the general nature of the experiment and what they will be asked to do; (3) make sure they know that they can leave the experiment at any time; and (4) inform them that the study will be fully explained after the data have been gathered and at that time they may request that their information be withdrawn.

The procedure outlined in item (4) is called debriefing. It could be argued that disclosure in this way would also bias results. There is evidence, however, indicating that data collected from subjects informed of the possibility of deception and those not informed are similar.[40] Debriefing can alleviate the stress caused by the experiment and make the experiment a learning experience for the participants. However, if not handled carefully, debriefing itself can be unsettling to subjects. In the advergames example above, participants may find it disheartening that they spent their time helping to build brands that were embedded into the videogames they enjoy. The researcher should anticipate and address this issue in the debriefing session.

Debriefing
After a disguised experiment, informing participants what the experiment was about and how the experimental manipulations were performed.

Digital applications in marketing research

The Internet can be a useful vehicle for conducting causal research. Different experimental treatments can be displayed on different websites. Participants can then be recruited to visit these sites and respond to a questionnaire that obtains information on the dependent and extraneous variables. Thus, the Internet can provide a mechanism for controlled experimentation, which may be in a laboratory environment but, especially with the use of mobile devices, could also be a field experiment.

An example of testing the effectiveness of advertisements can be used to illustrate the use of the Internet in causal research. Different advertisements can be posted on different websites. Matched or randomly selected participants can be recruited to visit these sites, with one group visiting only one site. If any pre-treatment measures have to be obtained, participants can answer a questionnaire posted on the site. Then they are exposed to a particular advertisement on that site. After viewing the advertisement, participants answer additional questions providing post-treatment measures. Control groups can also be implemented in a similar way. Thus, all types of experimental designs that we have considered can be implemented in this manner.

Digital developments are also enabling the development of experiments through virtual test markets and virtual shopping experiences. Experiments in virtual environments can be conducted using mobile devices. They can be designed to be an engaging and enjoyable research experience. With the use of access panels or online research communities, experimental treatments can be applied to specific types of participant on a global basis. Virtual experiments can be conducted much more quickly and cheaply than conventional marketing research experiments.

The following example illustrates why and how Kraft Foods used simulated shopping behaviour to conduct experiments. Of particular note is also the digital developments that enabled Kraft to share its knowledge with decision-makers across the globe.

Simulated shopping behaviour at Kraft Foods[41]

The Shopper Insight Teams of Kraft Foods were directly affected by the demands of international expansion as they were expected to bring relevant shopper and market knowledge quickly and cost-effectively. The task of the Shopper Insight Teams was to gain, accumulate, and synthesise relevant shopper insights that helped innovations, in-store environments, improved differentiation and raised loyalty. They recognised that not all available shopper insights were equally reliable, valid and trustworthy. They classified evidence at three levels. Level 1 represented the most valid insights addressing sales-oriented outcomes. Examples included rigorous controlled store tests, test-market comparisons, or randomised in-store experiments which clearly and unambiguously identified the key drivers of sales effects in an otherwise tightly controlled test environment, with sufficiently large sample sizes to support robust and generalisable conclusions. Level 2 represented weaker and more indirect methods of scientific investigation, not quite meeting the quality criteria to achieve level 1 evidence. Examples include focus groups, interviews based on retrospective reports of in-store behaviour or smaller-scaled studies without adequate reference standards. Level 3 represented reports that were not based on scientific analysis of shoppers' in-store behaviour. Examples included case studies, anecdotal observations, subjective impressions, expert opinions, and conclusions extrapolated indirectly from other (often undocumented) sources. Gaining level 1 evidence was challenging as conventional sales-oriented shopper research conducted in physical stores tended to be expensive, time consuming and complex to manage. As a result they turned to virtual shopper simulations as an alternative to traditional tools in shopper research. Simulations provided photo-realistic 3D simulations of product categories and store departments with high-resolution graphics, and usually let participants manoeuvre freely through the environment. Shopping behaviour of participants was tracked on a second-to-second basis, yielding detailed information about product contacts and purchases, which when aggregated to summary metrics, gave estimates of the sales volume and value performance of specific in-store interventions. One of the primary benefits of this approach, beyond considerable savings both in time and increased flexibility and maximum confidentiality, was experimental control: virtual simulations let researchers completely manipulate both the environment and participants' interaction with it. This approach promised the much sought-after high-quality level 1 conclusive evidence base to shopper marketing, with unequivocal causal links between directly controllable in-store variables and their sales impact on shoppers. After some internal validation work, Kraft Foods relied extensively on virtual shopper simulations which have helped it with the missing evidence base for recommendations to shopper marketing, e.g. for optimal shelf placement of brands, or the positioning of point-of-sale communication inside stores. A by-product of creating virtual store scenarios was the ability to reuse the test material for subsequent presentation and visualisation purposes. Kraft's teams realised that to achieve maximum impact of sharing and disseminating their shopper insights in a multi-country context, a communication platform for effective knowledge transfer was needed. Given their presence in more than 160 countries, the solution had to be Web-based and embeddable in their existing intranet. They also wished to share this knowledge on as many media types as possible: online, but also offline, for easy distribution via memory sticks, CDs, etc., in individual viewer sessions, face-to-face interactions, small-group tutorials, or larger seminars. Another display option was to be on mobile phones.

Summary

The scientific notion of causality implies that we can never prove that X causes Y. At best, we can only infer that X is one of the causes of Y in that it makes the occurrence of Y probable. Three conditions must be satisfied before causal inferences can be made: (1) concomitant variation, which implies that X and Y must vary together in a hypothesised way; (2) the time order of occurrence of variables, which implies that X must precede Y; and (3) elimination of other possible causal factors, which implies that competing explanations must be ruled out. Experiments provide the most convincing evidence of all three conditions. An experiment is formed when one or more independent variables are manipulated or controlled by the researcher and their effect on one or more dependent variables is measured.

In designing an experiment, it is important to consider internal and external validity. Internal validity refers to whether the manipulation of the independent variables actually caused the effects on the dependent variables. External validity refers to the generalisability of experimental results. For the experiment to be valid, the researcher must control the threats imposed by extraneous variables, such as history, maturation, testing (main and interactive testing effects), instrumentation, statistical regression, selection bias and mortality. There are four ways of controlling extraneous variables: randomisation, matching, statistical control and design control.

Experimental designs may be classified as pre-experimental, true experimental, quasi-experimental and statistical designs. An experiment may be conducted in a laboratory environment or under actual market conditions in a real-life setting. Only causal designs encompassing experimentation are appropriate for inferring cause-and-effect relationships.

Although experiments have limitations in terms of time, cost and administration, they continue to be popular in marketing, especially in the testing of communications and advertising. Test marketing is an important example of research monies spent on the application of experimental design.

The internal and external validity of field experiments conducted in developing nations is generally lower than in the developed Western economies. The level of development in many countries can be lower where the researcher lacks control over many of the marketing variables. Care has to be taken with this generalisation as the application of experimentation and test markets grows in online and virtual environments. Many nations beyond developed Western economies have the infrastructure and consumer engagement in online environments that can enable well-crafted experiments. The ethical issues involved in conducting causal research include disguising the purpose of the experiment. Debriefing can be used to address some of these issues.

Questions

1 What are the requirements for inferring a causal relationship between two variables?

2 Differentiate between internal and external validity.

3 List any five extraneous variables and give an example to show how each can reduce internal validity.

4 Describe the various methods for controlling extraneous sources of variation.

5 What is the key characteristic that distinguishes true experimental designs from pre-experimental designs?

6 List the steps involved in implementing the post-test-only control group design. Describe the design symbolically.

7 What is a time series experiment? When is it used?

8 How is a multiple time series design different from a basic time series design?

9 What advantages do statistical designs have over basic designs?

10 What are the limitations of the Latin square design?

11 Compare the characteristics of laboratory and field experimentation.

12 Should descriptive research be used for investigating causal relationships? Why or why not?

13 What is test marketing? What are the major types of test marketing?

14 What is the main difference between a standard test market and a controlled test market?

15 Describe how simulated test marketing works.

Exercises

1   You are the marketing research manager for Louis Vuitton (**www.vuitton. com**). The company would like to determine whether it should increase, decrease or maintain the current spend level of advertising. Design a field experiment to address this issue.

2   What potential difficulties do you see in conducting the experiment above? To what extent could the Louis Vuitton management help you overcome these difficulties?

3   Select two different perfume advertisements for any brand of perfume. Design and conduct an experiment to determine which advertisement is the most effective. Use a student sample with 10 students being exposed to each advertisement (treatment condition). Develop your own measures of advertising effectiveness in this context.

4   Red Bull (**www.redbull.com**) has developed three alternative package designs to replace its current can design. Design an online-based experiment to determine which, if any, of these new package designs is superior to the current one.

5   In a small group discuss the following issues: 'Is it possible to prove causality in any aspects of consumer behaviour?' and 'The potential to observe consumer buying behaviour electronically using the Internet has created great growth potential for the application of experimental techniques.'

Video case exercise: Electrolux

Electrolux uses macro-trend forecasting and ethnographic techniques to help it develop consumer insight. These approaches help Electrolux to create design solutions for problems that its consumers 'do not overtly know they have'. The chief innovation officer wishes to take this insight further through the use of causal research designs. These could be applied in developing an understanding of Electrolux's: brand personality (perhaps related to its Swedish heritage), use of social media as part of the communications mix, new product development. Choose any one of these applications and make the case for a particular causal design that you think would help Electrolux gain greater consumer insight.

Notes

1. Veer, E. and Pervan, S., 'How the tone and wording of advertisements interact', *International Journal of Advertising* 27 (2) (2008), 191–207.

2. Moreno, R. and Martinez, R., 'Causality as validity: some implications for the social sciences', *Quality & Quantity* 42 (5) (October 2008), 597–604: Viswanathan, M., *Measurement Error and Research Design* (Thousand Oaks, CA: Sage, 2005); Sobel, M., 'Causal inference in the social sciences', *Journal of the American Statistical Association* 95 (450) (June 2000), 647–651.

3. Heckman, J.J., 'The scientific model of causality', *Sociological Methodology* 35 (1) (2007), 1–98; Boruch, R.F., *Randomized Experiments for Planning and Evaluation* (Thousand Oaks, CA: Sage, 1994).

4. Dahlen, M., Törn, F. and Rosengren, S., 'Advertising creativity matters', *Journal of Advertising Research* 48 (3) (September 2008), 392–403.

5. Gross, I., 'The creative aspects of advertising', *Sloan Management Review* 14 (1) (1972), 83–109.

6. Viswanathan, M., *Measurement Error and Research Design* (Thousand Oaks, CA: Sage, 2005); Leichty, J., Ramaswamy, V. and Cohen, S.H., 'Choice menus for mass customization: an experimental approach for analyzing customer demand with an application to a web-based information service', *Journal of Marketing Research* 38 (2) (May 2001), 183–196; Wyner, G.A., 'Experimental design', *Marketing Research: A Magazine of Management and Applications* 9 (3) (Fall 1997), 39–41; Brown, S.R. and Melamed, L.E., *Experimental Design and Analysis* (Newbury Park, CA: Sage, 1990).

7. Farris, P.W., 'Overcontrol in advertising experiments', *Journal of Advertising Research* (November/December 2000), 73–78.

8. Wise, K., Bolls, P.D., Kim, H., Venkataraman, A. and Meyer, R., 'Enjoyment of advergames and brand attitudes: the impact of thematic relevance', *Journal of Interactive Advertising* 9 (1) (Fall 2008), 27–36.

9. In addition to internal and external validity, there also exist construct and statistical conclusion validity. Construct validity addresses the question of what construct, or characteristic, is in fact being measured and is discussed in Chapter 12 on measurement and scaling. Statistical conclusion validity addresses the extent and statistical significance of the covariation that exists in the data and is discussed in the chapters on data analysis. See Treadwell, K.R.H., 'Demonstrating experimenter "Ineptitude" as a means of teaching internal and external validity', *Teaching of Psychology* 35 (3) (August 2008), 184–188; Klink, R.R. and Smith, D.C., 'Threats to the external validity of brand extension research', *Journal of Marketing Research* 38 (3) (August 2001), 326–335; Campbell, D.T. and Stanley, J.C., *Experimental and Quasi Experimental Designs for Research* (Chicago: Rand McNally, 1966).

10. Blanton, H. and Jaccard, J., 'Representing versus generalizing: two approaches to external validity and their implications for the study of prejudice', *Psychological Inquiry* 19 (2) (2008), 99–105; Laurent, G., 'Improving the external validity of marketing models: a plea for more qualitative input', *International Journal of Research*

in Marketing 17 (2) (September 2000), 177; Bordia, P., 'Face-to-face computer-mediated communication: a synthesis of the experimental literature', *Journal of Business Communication* 34 (1) (January 1997), 99–120; Bowen, D.M., 'Work group research: past strategies and future opportunities', *IEEE Transactions on Engineering Management* 42 (1) (February 1995), 30–38; Lynch, J.G. Jr, 'On the external validity of experiments in consumer research', *Journal of Consumer Research* 9 (December 1982), 225–244.

11. Winer, R., 'Experimentation in the 21st century: the importance of external validity', *Academy of Marketing Science* 27 (3) (Summer 1999), 349–358; Argyris, C., 'Actionable knowledge: design causality in the service of consequential theory', *Journal of Applied Behavioural Science* 32 (4) (December 1966), 390–406; Lynch, J.G. Jr, 'The role of external validity in theoretical research', Calder, B.J., Phillips, L.W. and Tybout, A., 'Beyond external validity', and McGrath, J.E and Brinberg, D., 'External validity and the research process', *Journal of Consumer Research* 10 (1) (June 1983), 109–111, 112–114 and 115–124 respectively.

12. Berger, P. and Maurer, R., *Experimental Design with Applications in Management, Engineering and the Sciences* (Boston, MA: Boston University Press, 2002).

13. Berger, P. and Maurer, R., *Experimental design with applications in management, engineering and the sciences* (Boston, MA: Boston University Press, 2002); Dholakia, U.M. and Morwitz, V.G., 'The scope and persistence of mere-measurement effects: evidence from a field study of consumer satisfaction measurement', *Journal of Consumer Research* 29 (2) (2002), 159–167.

14. Small, D.S., Have, T.R.T., and Rosenbaum, P.R., 'Randomization inference in a group-randomized trial of treatments for depression: covariate adjustment, noncompliance and quantile effects', *Journal of the American Statistical Association* 103 (481) (March 2008), 271–279; Rosenbaum, P.R., 'Attributing effects to treatment in matched observational studies', *Journal of the American Statistical Association* 97 (457) (March 2002), 183–192; Durier, C., Monod, H. and Bruetschy, A., 'Design and analysis of factorial sensory experiments with carry-over effects', *Food Quality and Preference* 8 (2) (March 1997), 141–149; Nelson, L.S., 'Notes on the use of randomization in experimentation', *Journal of Quality Technology* 28 (1) (January 1996), 123–126.

15. Glick, R., Guo, X. and Hutchison, M., 'Currency crises, capital-account liberalization and selection bias', *Review of Economics and Statistics* 88 (4) (November 2006), 698–714; Rosenbaum, P.R., 'Attributing effects to treatment in matched observational studies', *Journal of the American Statistical Association* 97 (457) (March 2002), 183–192; Selart, M., 'Structure compatibility and restructuring in judgement and choice', *Organisation Behaviour and Human Decision Processes* 65 (2) (February 1996), 106–116; Barker Bausell, R., *Conducting Meaningful Experiments* (Thousand Oaks, CA: Sage, 1994).

16. Kim, B., 'Virtual field experiments for a digital economy: a new research methodology for exploring an information economy', *Decision Support Systems* 32 (3) (January 2002), 215; Chamis, E., 'Auto dealers test online

sales in 90 day experiment', *Washington Business Journal* 19 (11 May 2001), 15; Spethmann, B., 'Choosing a test market', *Brandweek* 36 (19) (8 May 1995), 42–43; Tarshis, A.M., 'Natural sell-in avoids pitfalls of controlled tests', *Marketing News* (24 October 1986), 14.

17. Other experimental designs are also available. See Borror, C.M., 'Evaluation of statistical designs for experiments involving noise variables', *Journal of Quality Technology* 34 (1) (January 2002), 54–70; Campbell, D.T. and Russo, M.J., *Social Experimentation* (Thousand Oaks, CA: Sage, 1999); Gunter, B., 'Fundamental issues in experimental design', *Quality Progress* 29 (6) (June 1996), 105–113.

18. For an application of the Solomon four-group design, see Ayres, J., 'Are reductions in CA an experimental artifact? A Solomon four group answer', *Communications Quarterly* 48 (1) (Winter 2000), 19–26.

19. Simester, D., 'Implementing quality improvement programs designed to enhance customer satisfaction: quasi experiments in the United States and Spain', *Journal of Marketing Research* 37 (1) (February 2000), 102–112; Moorman, C., 'A quasi-experiment to assess the consumer and informational determinants of nutrition information-processing activities – the case of the Nutrition Labeling and Education Act', *Journal of Public Policy and Marketing* 15 (1) (Spring 1996), 28–44.

20. Kim, K., Cheong, Y. and Zheng, L., 'The current practices in food advertising – the usage and affectiveness of different advertising claims', *International Journal of Advertising* 28 (3) (2009), 527–553.

21. See, for example, Vanden Bergh, B.G., Lee, M., Quilliam, E.T. and Hove, T., 'The multidimensional nature and brand impact of user-generated ad parodies in social media', *International Journal of Advertising* 30 (1) (2011), 103–131; Vagnoni, A., 'Fear of funny abating', *Advertising Age* 73 (10) (11 March 2002), 8–9; Weinberger, M.G., Spotts, H., Campbell, L. and Parsons, A.L., 'The use and effect of humor in different advertising media', *Journal of Advertising Research* 35 (3) (May/June 1995), 44–56.

22. For applications of factorial designs, see Chung-Chau, C. and Yu-Jen, C., 'Goal orientation and comparative valence in persuasion', *Journal of Advertising* 37 (1) (Spring 2008), 73–87; Sengupta, J. and Gorn, G.J., 'Absence makes the mind grow sharper: effects of element omission on subsequent recall', *Journal of Marketing Research* 39 (2) (May 2002), 186–201.

23. Huertas-Garcia, R. and Consolación-Segura, C., 'Using statistical design experiment methodologies to identify customers' needs', *International Journal of Market Research* 51 (1) (2009), 115–136.

24. Roehm, M.L., Pullins, E.B. and Roehm, H.A. Jr, 'Designing loyalty building programs for packaged goods brands', *Journal of Marketing Research* 39 (2) (May 2002), 202–213; Jones, G.E. and Kavanagh, M.J., 'An experimental examination of the effects of individual and situational factors on unethical behavioural intentions in the workplace', *Journal of Business Ethics* 15 (5) (May 1996), 511–523.

25. Krishna, A. and Unver, M.U., 'Improving the efficiency of course bidding at business schools: field and laboratory studies', *Marketing Science* 27 (2) (March/April 2008), 262–282: Dawar, N., 'Impact of product harm crises on brand equity: the moderating role of consumer

expectations', *Journal of Marketing Research* 37 (2) (May 2000), 215–226.

26. Allen, C.T., 'A theory based approach for improving demand artifact assessment in advertising experiments', *Journal of Advertising* 33 (2) (Summer 2004), 63–73; Lane, V.R., 'The impact of ad repetition and ad content on consumer perceptions of incongruent extensions', *Journal of Marketing* (April 2000), 80–91; Perrien, J., 'Repositioning demand artifacts in consumer research', *Advances in Consumer Research* 24 (1997), 267–271.

27. Ofir, C. and Simonson, I., 'In search of negative customer feedback: the effect of expecting to evaluate on satisfaction evaluations', *Journal of Marketing Research* 38 (2) (May 2001), 170–182; Laurent, G., 'Improving the external validity of marketing models: a plea for more qualitative input', *International Journal of Research in Marketing* 17 (2–3) (September 2000), 177–182.

28. Blumenschein, K., 'Hypothetical versus real willingness to pay in the health care sector: results from a field experiment', *Journal of Health Economics* 20 (3) (May 2001), 441; Alston, R.M. and Nowell, C., 'Implementing the voluntary contribution game: a field experiment', *Journal of Economic Behaviour and Organisation* 31 (3) (December 1996), 357–368.

29. Spanos, A., 'On theory testing in econometrics: modeling with nonexperimental data', *Journal of Econometrics* 67 (1) (May 1995), 189–226; Blalock, H.M. Jr, *Causal Inferences in Non-experimental Research* (Chapel Hill, NC: University of North Carolina Press, 1964).

30. In some situations, surveys and experiments can complement each other and may both be used. For example, the results obtained in laboratory experiments may be further examined in a field survey. See Johnston, W.J. and Kim, K., 'Performance, attribution, and expectancy linkages in personal selling', *Journal of Marketing* 58 (October 1994), 68–81.

31. Farris, P.W. and Reibstein, D.J., 'Overcontrol in advertising experiments', *Journal of Advertising Research* 40 (6) (November/December 2000), 73–78.

32. Ryals, L. and Wilson, H., 'Experimental methods in market research: from information to insight', *International Journal of Market Research* 47 (4) (2005), 347–366.

33. Boots Laboratories Serum 7 – Alliance Boots, Design Business Association, Gold, Design Effectiveness Awards (2009).

34. Vinarsky, C., 'Test market for smokeless tobacco', *Knight Ridder Tribune Business News* (11 March 2002), 1; Romeo, P., 'Testing, testing', *Restaurant Business* 97 (2) (15 January 1998), 12.

35. Hitsch, G.J., 'An empirical model of optimal dynamic product launch and exit under demand uncertainty', *Marketing Science* 25 (1) (January/February 2006), 25–50; Lawrence, K., 'Owensboro, Kentucky could be next test market for new McDonald's eatery concept', *Knight Ridder Tribune Business News* (7 February 2002), 1.

36. Anon., 'Vaseline to back Dermacare with Llm Ads activity', *Marketing* (10 January 2002), 4; Mehegan, S., 'Vaseline ups ante via anti-bacterial', *Brandweek* 38 (21) (26 May 1997), 1, 6.

37. Willke, J.J., 'The future of simulated test markets', ESOMAR, Consumer Insight Congress, Barcelona, (September 2002); Hayes, D.J., Shogren, J.F., Fox, J.A. and Kliebenstein, B., 'Test marketing new food products using a multitrial nonhypothetical experimental auction', *Psychology and Marketing* 13 (4) (July 1996), 365–379.

38. Markowitz, L., 'The future of forecasting is here: did simulated test markets evolve as anticipated...and what are the new expectations?', ESOMAR, Congress Odyssey, Athens (Sepember 2010).

39. Eschenbacher, D., 'Local cultural and media tastes need differing creative approaches', *Admap, South East Asia Supplement* (February 2009), 25–26.

40. Hansen, D.E., 'Knowledge transfer in online learning environments', *Journal of Marketing Education*, 30 (2) (August 2008), 93–105; Anon., 'The disclosure dilemma', *Workspan* 45 (1) (January 2002), 72.

41. Grootenhuis, S. and Treiber, B., 'Incite to action: encouraging effective utilization of shopper insights in a global context', ESOMAR, Insights, Brussels (February 2011).

12

Measurement and scaling: fundamentals, comparative and non-comparative scaling

Stage 1

Problem definition

Stage 2

Research approach developed

Stage 3

Research design developed

Stage 4

Fieldwork or data collection

Stage 5

Data integrity and analysis

Stage 6

Report preparation and presentation

When you can measure what you are speaking about and express it in numbers, you know something about it.

Lord Kelvin

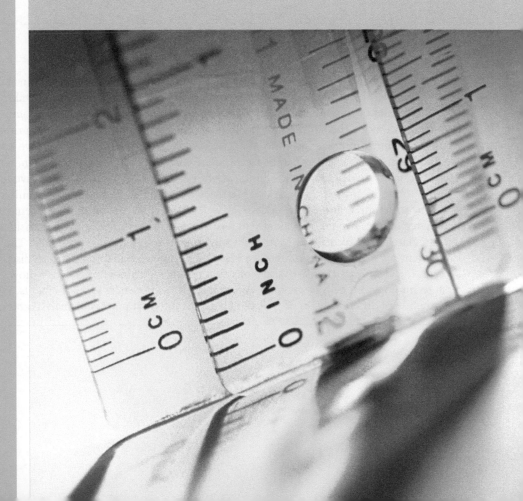

Objectives

After reading this chapter, you should be able to:

1 introduce the concepts of measurement and scaling and show how scaling may be considered an extension of measurement;

2 explain the characteristics of description, order, distance, and origin and how they define the level of measurement in a scale;

3 discuss the primary scales of measurement and differentiate nominal, ordinal, interval and ratio scales;

4 classify and discuss scaling techniques as comparative and non-comparative and describe the comparative techniques of paired comparison, rank order, constant sum and Q-sort scaling;

5 describe the non-comparative scaling techniques, distinguish between continuous and itemised rating scales, and explain Likert, semantic differential and Stapel scales;

6 discuss the decisions involved in constructing itemised rating scales;

7 discuss the criteria used for scale evaluation and explain how to assess reliability, validity and generalisability;

8 discuss the considerations involved in implementing the primary scales of measurement in an international setting;

9 understand the ethical issues involved in selecting scales of measurement;

10 appreciate how digital developments are shaping the manner in which scales may be designed, delivered and experienced.

Overview

Once researchers have a clear understanding of what they wish to encapsulate in their target participants, they should consider the concepts of scaling and measurement. These concepts are vital in developing questionnaires or 'instruments of measurement' that will fulfil their research objectives in the most accurate manner. In this chapter we describe the concepts of scaling and measurement and discuss four primary scales of measurement: nominal, ordinal, interval and ratio. We describe and illustrate both comparative and non-comparative scaling techniques in detail. The comparative techniques, consisting of paired comparison, rank order, constant sum and Q-sort scaling, are discussed and illustrated with examples. The non-comparative techniques are composed of continuous and itemised rating scales. We discuss and illustrate the popular itemised rating scales – the Likert, semantic differential and Stapel scales – as well as the construction of multi-item rating scales. We show how scaling techniques should be evaluated in terms of reliability and validity and consider how the researcher selects a particular scaling technique. Mathematically derived scales are also presented. The considerations involved in implementing scaling techniques when researching international markets are discussed. The chapter presents several ethical issues that arise in scale construction and concludes by examining how visual forms of scaling using flash technology can help create more engaging survey experiences for participants. We begin with an example of how the use of different types of scale can give quite different powers of analysis and interpretation.

Real research	## Numbers, rankings and ratings: Spain is on top

According to the international football federation (FIFA) (**www.fifa.com**) post-2010 World Cup rankings, the world champions Spain reigned supreme at the top of the rankings with 1,880 points and the runners-up, the Netherlands, took second spot with 1,730 points. The top 10 countries were as follows:

Number	Country	March 2011 ranking	Points
1	Argentina	4	1,412
2	Brazil	5	1,411
3	Croatia	8	1,071
4	England	6	1,212
5	Germany	3	1,486
6	Greece	10	1,038
7	Netherlands	2	1,730
8	Portugal	9	1,060
9	Spain	1	1,880
10	Uruguay	7	1,172

Note that the countries have been placed in alphabetical order and that at first glance this gives the impression that South American countries have performed better than European countries. An alphabetical order is used to illustrate the first column 'Number'. The 'number' assigned to denote countries is not in any way related to their football-playing capabilities but simply serves the purpose of identification, e.g. drawing numbered balls to decide which teams may play each other in a competition. This identification number constitutes a nominal scale, which says nothing about the respective performances of the countries. So while England is numbered 4 and Germany is numbered 5, this does not reflect the superior performance of Germany.

A much clearer way to present the list would be to place the countries in the order of their ranking, with Spain at the top and Greece at the bottom of the table. The ranking would represent an ordinal scale, where it would be clear to see that the lower the number, the better the performance. But what is still missing from the ranking is the magnitude of differences between the countries.

The only way really to understand how much one country is better than another is to examine the points awarded to each country. The points awarded represent an interval scale. Based on the points awarded, note that only 1 point separates the closely ranked Argentina (1,412) and Brazil (1,411), or 11 points between Croatia (1,071) and Portugal (1,060), but that the difference between the Netherlands (1,730) ranked at number 2 and Germany (1,486) ranked at number 3 is 244 points.

Measurement and scaling

Measurement
The assignment of numbers or other symbols to characteristics of objects according to certain pre-specified rules.

Measurement means assigning numbers or other symbols to characteristics of objects according to certain pre-specified rules.[1] Note that what we measure is not the object but some characteristic of it. Thus, we do not measure consumers, only their perceptions, attitudes, preferences or other relevant characteristics. In marketing research, numbers are usually assigned for one of two reasons. First, numbers permit statistical analysis of the resulting data. Second, numbers facilitate a universal and transparent communication of measurement rules and results.

The most important aspect of measurement is the specification of rules for assigning numbers to the characteristics. The assignment process must be isomorphic, i.e. there must be one-to-one correspondence between the numbers and the characteristics being measured. For example, the same euro (€) figures can be assigned to households with identical annual incomes. Only then can the numbers be associated with specific characteristics of the measured object, and vice versa. In addition, the rules for assigning numbers should be standardised and applied uniformly. They must not change over objects or time.

Scaling
The generation of a continuum upon which measured objects are located.

Scaling may be considered an extension of measurement. Scaling involves creating a continuum upon which measured objects are located. To illustrate, consider a scale for locating consumers according to the characteristic 'attitude towards visiting a cinema'. Each participant is assigned a number indicating an unfavourable attitude (measured as 1), a neutral attitude (measured as 2) or a favourable attitude (measured as 3). Measurement is the actual assignment of 1, 2 or 3 to each participant. Scaling is the process of placing the participants on a continuum with respect to their attitude towards visiting a cinema. In our example, scaling is the process by which participants would be classified as having an unfavourable, neutral or positive attitude.

Scale characteristics and levels of measurement

All the scales used in marketing research can be described in terms of four basic characteristics. These characteristics are description, order, distance and origin, and together they define the level of measurement of a scale. The level of measurement denotes what properties of an object the scale is measuring or not measuring. An understanding of the scale characteristics is fundamental to understanding the primary type of scales.

Description

Description
The unique labels or descriptors that are used to designate each value of the scale. All scales possess description.

By **description**, we mean the unique labels or descriptors that are used to designate each value of the scale. Some examples of descriptors are as follows: 1. Female, 2. Male; 1 = Strongly disagree, 2 = Disagree, 3 = Neither agree nor disagree, 4 = Agree and 5 = Strongly agree; and the numbers of euros earned annually by a household. Female and Male are unique descriptors used to describe values 1 and 2 of the gender scale. All scales possess this characteristic of description, i.e. all scales have unique labels or descriptors that are used to define the scale values or response options.

Order

Order
The relative sizes or positions of the descriptors. Order is denoted by descriptors such as greater than, less than and equal to.

By **order**, we mean the relative sizes or positions of the descriptors. There are no absolute values associated with order, only relative values. Order is denoted by descriptors such as 'greater than', 'less than' and 'equal to'. For example, a participant's preference for art forms that they visit can be expressed by the following order, with the most preferred art form being listed first and the least preferred last:

Cinema

Theatre

Pop concert

For this participant, the preference for the cinema is greater than the preference for the theatre. Likewise, the preference for a pop concert is less than the preference for the theatre. Participants who fall into the same age category, say 35 to 49, are considered to be equal to each other in terms of age, and greater than participants in the 20 to 34 age group. All scales do not possess the order characteristic. In the gender scale (1. Female, 2. Male) considered above, we have no way of determining whether a female is greater or less than a male. Thus the gender scale does not possess order.

Distance

Distance
The characteristic of distance means that absolute differences between the scale descriptors are known and may be expressed in units.

The characteristic of distance means that absolute differences between the scale descriptors are known and may be expressed in units. A five-person household has one person more than a four-person household, which in turn has one person more than a three-person household. Thus the following scale possesses the distance characteristic:

Number of persons living in your household _____

Notice that a scale that has distance also has order. We know that a five-person household is greater than the four-person household in terms of the number of persons living in the household. Likewise, a three-person household is less than a four-person household. Thus, distance implies order but the reverse may not be true.

Origin

Origin
The origin characteristic means that the scale has a unique or fixed beginning or true zero point.

The origin characteristic means that the scale has a unique or fixed beginning or true zero point. Thus, an exact measurement of income by a scale such as

What is the annual income of your household before taxes? €_____

has a fixed origin or a true zero point. An answer of zero would mean that the household has no income at all. A scale that has origin also has distance (and order and description). Many scales used in marketing research do not have a fixed notice or true zero point, as in the disagree–agree scale considered earlier under description. Notice that such a scale was defined as 1 = Strongly disagree, 2 = Disagree, 3 = Neither agree nor disagree, 4 = Agree and 5 = Strongly agree. However, 1 is an arbitrary origin or starting point. This scale could just as easily been defined as 0 = Strongly disagree, 1 = Disagree, 2 = Neither agree nor disagree, 3 = Agree and 4 = Strongly agree, with 0 as the origin. Alternatively, shifting the origin to –2 will result in an equivalent scale: –2 = Strongly disagree, –1 = Disagree, 0 = Neither agree nor disagree, 1 = Agree and 2 = Strongly agree. All these three forms of the agree–disagree scale, with the origin at 1, 0, or –2, are equivalent. Thus this scale does not have a fixed origin or a true zero point and consequently does not possess the characteristic of origin.

You may have observed that description, order, distance and origin represent successively higher level characteristics, with origin being the highest scale characteristic. Description is the most basic characteristic that is present in all scales. If a scale has order, it also has description. If a scale has distance, it also has order and description. Finally, a scale that that has origin also has distance, order and description. Thus, if a scale has a higher level characteristic, it also has all the lower level characteristics. However, the reverse may not be true, i.e. if a scale has a lower level characteristic, it may or may not have a higher level characteristic. With an understanding of scale characteristics, we are ready to discuss the primary types of scale.

Primary scales of measurement

There are four primary scales of measurement: nominal, ordinal, interval and ratio.[2] These scales are illustrated in Figure 12.1, and their properties are summarised in Table 12.1 and discussed in the following sections.

Nominal scale

Nominal scale

A scale whose numbers serve only as labels or tags for identifying and classifying objects with a strict one-to-one correspondence between the numbers and the objects.

A **nominal scale** is a figurative labelling scheme in which the numbers serve only as labels or tags for identifying and classifying objects. For example, the numbers assigned to the participants in a study constitute a nominal scale; thus a female participant may be assigned a number 1 and a male participant 2. When a nominal scale is used for the purpose of identification, there is a strict one-to-one correspondence between the numbers and the objects. Each number is assigned to only one object, and each object has only one number assigned to it.

Common examples include student registration numbers at a college or university and numbers assigned to football players or jockeys in a horse race. In marketing research, nominal scales are used for identifying participants, brands, attributes, websites and other objects.

When used for classification purposes, the nominally scaled numbers serve as labels for classes or categories. For example, you might classify the control group as group 1 and the experimental group as group 2. The classes are mutually exclusive and collectively exhaustive. The objects in each class are viewed as equivalent with respect to the characteristic represented by the nominal number. All objects in the same class have the same number, and no two classes have the same number. However, a nominal scale need not involve the assignment of numbers; alphabets or symbols could be assigned as well.

The numbers in a nominal scale do not reflect the amount of the characteristic possessed by the objects. For example, a high number on a football player's shirt does not imply that the footballer is a better player than one with a low number, or vice versa. The same applies to numbers assigned to classes. The only permissible operation on the numbers in a nominal scale is counting. Only a limited number of statistics, all of which are based on frequency

Figure 12.1

An illustration of primary scales of measurement

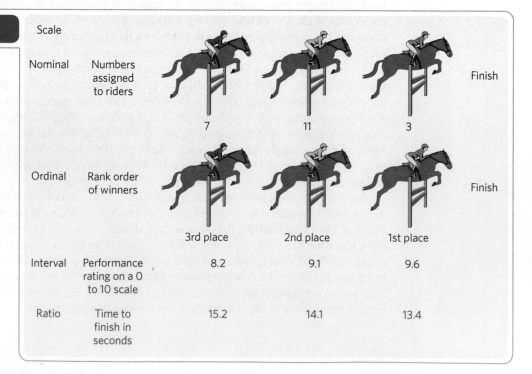

Scale					
Nominal	Numbers assigned to riders				Finish
		7	11	3	
Ordinal	Rank order of winners				Finish
		3rd place	2nd place	1st place	
Interval	Performance rating on a 0 to 10 scale	8.2	9.1	9.6	
Ratio	Time to finish in seconds	15.2	14.1	13.4	

Table 12.1	Primary scales of measurement				

Scale	Basic characteristics	Common examples	Marketing example	Permissible statistics	
				Descriptive	Inferential
Nominal	Numbers identify and classify objects	Student registration numbers, numbers on football players' shirts	Gender classification of retail outlet types	Percentages, mode	Chi-square, binomial test
Ordinal	Numbers indicate the relative positions of the objects but not the magnitude of differences between them	Rankings of the top four teams in the football World Cup	Ranking of service quality delivered by a number of shops. Rank order of favourite TV programmes	Percentile, median	Rank order correlation, Friedman, ANOVA
Interval	Differences between objects can be compared; zero point is arbitrary	Temperature (Fahrenheit, Celsius)	Attitudes, opinions, index numbers	Range, mean, standard deviation	Product moment correlations, t tests, ANOVA, regression, factor analysis
Ratio	Zero point is fixed; ratios of scale values can be computed	Length, weight	Age, income, costs, sales, market shares	Geometric mean, harmonic mean	Coefficient of variation

counts, are permissible. These include percentages, mode, chi-square and binomial tests (see Chapter 18). It is not meaningful to compute an average student registration number, the average gender of participants in a survey, or the number assigned to an average film genre, as in the example below.

Focus on | **IFM Sports Marketing Surveys**

S:Comm Leisure Time Survey

Nominal scale

In a study of how UK adults spend their leisure time, questions were related to the arts, sport, visitor attractions and leisure breaks. One key area was devoted to the cinema and the popularity of types of films. The numbers 1 to 10 were assigned to different film genres (see extracts from the list in Table 12.2). Thus, genre 2 referred to Animated. It did not imply that Animated was in any way superior or inferior to Comedy, which was assigned the number 3. Any reassignment of the numbers, such as transposing the numbers assigned to Animated and Comedy, would have no effect on the numbering system, because the numerals did not

reflect any characteristics of the genres. It is meaningful to make statements such as '95% of young, affluent and family free' named Comedy as their favourite genre. Although the average of the assigned numbers is 5.5, it is not meaningful to state that the number of the average cinema genre is 5.5.

Table 12.2 **Illustration of primary scales of measurement**

Nominal scale		Ordinal scale		Interval scale		Ratio scale
No.	Film genre	Preference rankings		Preference ratings		Amount (€) spent on cinema visits in the past three months
				1–7	11–17	
1	Action	1	10	7	17	200
2	Animated	5	53	5	15	35
3	Comedy	2	25	7	17	200
4	Drama	3	30	6	16	100
5	Factual	4	45	6	16	0
6	Fantasy	6	61	5	15	100
7	Light drama	7	79	5	15	0
8	Romance	8	82	4	14	0
9	Sci-fi	9	95	4	14	0
10	Suspense	10	115	2	12	10

Ordinal scale

Ordinal scale
A ranking scale in which numbers are assigned to objects to indicate the relative extent to which some characteristic is possessed. Thus, it is possible to determine whether an object has more or less of a characteristic than some other object.

An **ordinal scale** is a ranking scale in which numbers are assigned to objects to indicate the relative extent to which the objects possess some characteristic. An ordinal scale allows you to determine whether an object has more or less of a characteristic than some other object, but not how much more or less. Thus, an ordinal scale indicates relative position, not the magnitude of the differences between the objects. The object ranked first has more of the characteristic as compared with the object ranked second, but whether the object ranked second is a close second or a poor second is not known. Common examples of ordinal scales include quality rankings, rankings of teams in a tournament and occupational status. In marketing research, ordinal scales are used to measure relative attitudes, opinions, perceptions and preferences. Measurements of this type include 'greater than' or 'less than' judgements from participants.

In an ordinal scale, as in a nominal scale, equivalent objects receive the same rank. Any series of numbers can be assigned that preserves the ordered relationships between the objects. Ordinal scales can be transformed in any way as long as the basic ordering of the objects is maintained.[3] In other words, any monotonic positive (order-preserving) transformation of the scale is permissible, since the differences in numbers are void of any meaning other than order (see the example below). For these reasons, in addition to the counting operation allowable for nominal scale data, ordinal scales permit the use of statistics based on centiles. It is meaningful to calculate percentile, quartile, median (Chapter 18), rank order correlation (Chapter 20) or other summary statistics from ordinal data.

Focus on

IFM Sports Marketing Surveys

S:Comm Leisure Time Survey

Ordinal scale

Table 12.2 gives a particular participant's preference rankings. Participants ranked the film genres in order of who they preferred, by assigning a rank 1 to the first, rank 2 to the second, and so on. Note that Action (ranked 1) is preferred to Comedy (ranked 2), but how much it is preferred we do not know. Also, it is not necessary that we assign numbers from 1 to 10 to obtain a preference ranking. The second ordinal scale, which assigns a number 10 to Action, 25 to Comedy and 30 to Drama, is an equivalent scale, as it was obtained by a monotonic positive transformation of the first scale. The two scales result in the same ordering of the genres according to preference.

Interval scale

Interval scale
A scale in which the numbers are used to rank objects such that numerically equal distances on the scale represent equal distances in the characteristic being measured.

Ratio scale
The highest scale. This scale allows the researcher to identify or classify objects, rank-order the objects, and compare intervals or differences. It is also meaningful to compute ratios of scale values.

In an interval scale, numerically equal distances on the scale represent equal values in the characteristic being measured. An interval scale contains all the information of an ordinal scale, but it also allows you to compare the differences between objects. The difference between any two scale values is identical to the difference between any other two adjacent values of an interval scale. There is a constant or equal interval between scale values. The difference between 1 and 2 is the same as the difference between 2 and 3, which is the same as the difference between 5 and 6. A common example in everyday life is a temperature scale. In marketing research, attitudinal data obtained from rating scales are often treated as interval data.[4]

In an interval scale, the location of the zero point is not fixed. Both the zero point and the units of measurement are arbitrary. Hence, any positive linear transformation of the form $y = a + bx$ will preserve the properties of the scale. Here, x is the original scale value, y is the transformed scale value, b is a positive constant and a is any constant. Therefore, two interval scales that rate objects A, B, C and D as 1, 2, 3 and 4 or as 22, 24, 26 and 28 are equivalent. Note that the latter scale can be derived from the former by using $a = 20$ and $b = 2$ in the transforming equation.

Because the zero point is not fixed, it is not meaningful to take ratios of scale values. As can be seen, the ratio of D to B values changes from 2:1 to 7:6 when the scale is transformed. Yet, ratios of differences between scale values are permissible. In this process, the constants a and b in the transforming equation drop out in the computations. The ratio of the difference between D and B values to the difference between C and B values is 2:1 in both the scales.

Statistical techniques that may be used on interval scale data include all those that can be applied to nominal and ordinal data in addition to the arithmetic mean, standard deviation (Chapter 18), product moment correlations (Chapter 20), and other statistics commonly used in marketing research. Certain specialised statistics such as geometric mean, harmonic mean and coefficient of variation, however, are not meaningful on interval scale data. The IFM Sports Marketing Surveys example gives a further illustration of an interval scale.

Ratio scale

A ratio scale possesses all the properties of the nominal, ordinal and interval scales, and, in addition, an absolute zero point. Thus, ratio scales possess the characteristic of origin (and distance, order and description). With ratio scales we can identify or classify objects, rank the objects, and compare intervals or differences. It is also meaningful to compute ratios of scale values. Not only is the difference between 2 and 5 the same as the difference between 14 and 17, but also 14 is seven times as large as 2 in an absolute sense. Common examples of ratio

Focus on　**IFM Sports Marketing Surveys**

S:Comm Leisure Time Survey

Interval scale

In Table 12.2, a participant's preferences for the 10 film genres are expressed on a seven-point rating scale (where a higher number represents a greater preference for a genre). We can see that although Drama received a preference rating of 6 and Suspense a rating of 2, this does not mean that Drama is preferred three times as much as Suspense. When the ratings are transformed to an equivalent 11 to 17 scale (next column), the ratings for those genres become 16 and 12, and the ratio is no longer 3:1. In contrast, the ratios of preference differences are identical on the two scales. The ratio of preference difference between Comedy and Suspense to the preference difference between Fantasy and Suspense is 5:3 on both the scales.

scales include height, weight, age and money. In marketing research, sales, costs, market share and number of customers are variables measured on a ratio scale.

Ratio scales allow only proportionate transformations of the form $y = bx$, where b is a positive constant. One cannot add an arbitrary constant, as in the case of an interval scale. An example of this transformation is provided by the conversion of metres to yards ($b = 1.094$). The comparisons between the objects are identical whether made in metres or yards.

All statistical techniques can be applied to ratio data. These include specialised statistics such as geometric mean, harmonic mean and coefficient of variation. The ratio scale is further illustrated in the context of an IFM Sports Marketing Surveys example.

Focus on　**IFM Sports Marketing Surveys**

S:Comm Leisure Time Survey

Ratio scale

In the ratio scale illustrated in Table 12.2, a participant is asked to indicate how much had been spent on cinema visits (i.e. the whole visit experience, not just the cinema ticket) in the last three months. Note that this participant spent €200 on Action films and only €10 on Suspense. The participant spent 20 times more euros on Action compared with Suspense. Also, the zero point is fixed because 0 means that the participant did not spend any money on films such as Factual and Romance. Multiplying these numbers by 100 to convert euros to cents results in an equivalent scale.

The four primary scales discussed above do not exhaust the measurement-level categories. It is possible to construct a nominal scale that provides partial information on order (the partially ordered scale). Likewise, an ordinal scale can convey partial information on distance, as in the case of an ordered metric scale. A discussion of these scales is beyond the scope of this text.[5]

Metric scale
A scale that is either interval or ratio in nature.

A comparison of scaling techniques

The scaling techniques commonly employed in marketing research can be classified into comparative and non-comparative scales (see Figure 12.2).

Comparative scales involve the direct comparison of stimulus objects. For example, participants may be asked whether they prefer to visit a cinema or a theatre. Comparative scale data must be interpreted in relative terms and have only ordinal or rank order properties. For this reason, comparative scales are also referred to as non-metric scales. As shown in Figure 12.2, comparative scales include paired comparisons, rank order, constant sum scales, Q-sort and other procedures.

The major benefit of comparative scaling is that small differences between stimulus objects can be detected. As they compare the stimulus objects, participants are forced to choose between them. In addition, participants approach the rating task from the same known reference points. Consequently, comparative scales are easily understood and can be applied easily. Other advantages of these scales are that they involve fewer theoretical assumptions, and they also tend to reduce halo or carryover effects from one judgement to another.[6] The major disadvantages of comparative scales include the ordinal nature of the data and the inability to generalise beyond the stimulus objects scaled. For instance, to compare a visit to a pop concert to a cinema or theatre visit, the researcher would have to do a new study. These disadvantages are substantially overcome by the non-comparative scaling techniques.

In non-comparative scales, also referred to as monadic or metric scales, each object is scaled independently of the others in the stimulus set. The resulting data are generally assumed to be interval or ratio scaled.[7] For example, participants may be asked to evaluate a cinema visit on a 1 to 6 preference scale (1 = Not at all preferred, 6 = Greatly preferred). Similar evaluations would be obtained for a theatre visit and a pop concert visit. As can be seen in Figure 12.2, non-comparative scales can be continuous rating or itemised rating scales. The itemised rating scales can be further classified as Likert, semantic differential or Stapel scales. Non-comparative scaling is the most widely used scaling technique in marketing research.

Comparative scales
One of two types of scaling techniques in which there is direct comparison of stimulus objects with one another.

Non-metric scale
A scale that is either nominal or ordinal in nature.

Carryover effects
Where the evaluation of a particular scaled item significantly affects the participant's judgement of subsequent scaled items.

Non-comparative scale
One of two types of scaling technique in which each stimulus object is scaled independently of the other objects in the stimulus set. Also called monadic scale.

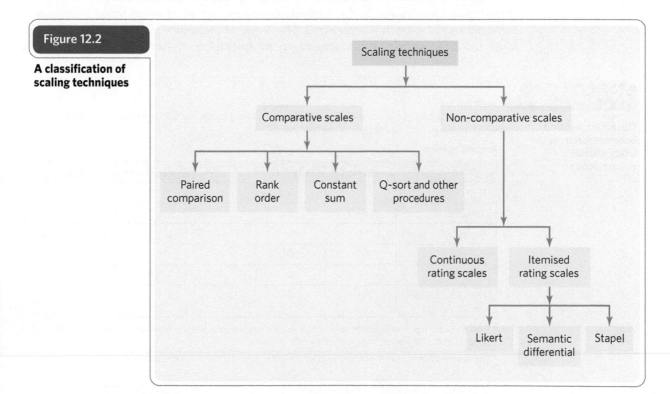

Figure 12.2

A classification of scaling techniques

Comparative scaling techniques

Paired comparison scaling

Paired comparison scaling
A comparative scaling technique in which a participant is presented with two objects at a time and asked to select one object in the pair according to some criterion. The data obtained are ordinal in nature.

Transitivity of preference
An assumption made to convert paired comparison data to rank order data. It implies that if Brand A is preferred to Brand B, and Brand B is preferred to Brand C, then Brand A is preferred to Brand C.

As its name implies, in paired comparison scaling a participant is presented with two objects and asked to select one according to some criterion.[8] The data obtained are ordinal in nature. A participant may state that they prefer Belgian chocolate to Swiss, likes Kellogg's cereals better than supermarket home brands, or likes Adidas more than Nike. Paired comparison scales are frequently used when the stimulus objects are physical products. Coca-Cola is reported to have conducted more than 190,000 paired comparisons before introducing New Coke.[9]

Figure 12.3 shows paired comparison data obtained to assess a participant's bottled beer preferences. As can be seen, this participant made 10 comparisons to evaluate five brands. In general, with n brands, $[n(n-1)/2]$ paired comparisons include all possible pairings of objects.[10]

Paired comparison data can be analysed in several ways.[11] The researcher can calculate the percentage of participants who prefer one stimulus over another by summing the matrices of Figure 12.3 for all the participants, dividing the sum by the number of participants, and multiplying by 100. Simultaneous evaluation of all the stimulus objects is also possible. Under the assumption of transitivity, it is possible to convert paired comparison data to a rank order.

Transitivity of preference implies that if Brand A is preferred to B, and Brand B is preferred to C, then Brand A is preferred to C. To arrive at a rank order, the researcher determines the number of times each brand is preferred by summing the column entries in Figure 12.3. Therefore, this participant's order of preference, from most to least preferred, is Carlsberg, Holsten, Stella Artois, Budvar and Grolsch. It is also possible to derive an interval scale from paired comparison data using the Thurstone case V procedure. Refer to the appropriate literature for a discussion of this procedure.[12]

Several modifications of the paired comparison technique have been suggested. One involves the inclusion of a neutral/no difference/no opinion response. Another extension is graded pairs comparisons. In this method, participants are asked which brand in the pair is preferred and how much it is preferred. The degree of preference may be expressed by how much more the participant is willing to pay for the preferred brand. The resulting scale is

Figure 12.3

Obtaining bottled beer preferences using paired comparisons

Instructions
We are going to present you with 10 pairs of bottled beer brands. For each pair, please indicate which of the two brands of beer in the pair you prefer.

Recording form

	Holsten	Stella Artois	Grolsch	Carlsberg	Budvar
Holsten		0	0	1	0
Stella Artois	1[a]		0	1	0
Grolsch	1	1		1	1
Carlsberg	0	0	0		0
Budvar	1	1	0	1	
Number of times preferred[b]	3	2	0	4	1

[a] 1 in a particular box means that the brand in that column was preferred over the brand in the corresponding row. 0 means that the row brand was preferred over the column brand.

[b] The number of times a brand was preferred is obtained by summing the 1s in each column

a euro metric scale. Another modification of paired comparison scaling is widely used in obtaining similarity judgements in multidimensional scaling (see Chapter 24).

Paired comparison scaling is useful when the number of brands is limited, since it requires direct comparison and overt choice. With a large number of brands, however, the number of comparisons becomes unwieldy. Other disadvantages are that violations of the assumption of transitivity may occur, and the order in which the objects are presented may bias the results. Paired comparisons bear little resemblance to the marketplace situation, which involves selection from multiple alternatives. Also participants may prefer one object over certain others, but they may not like it in an absolute sense.[13]

Rank order scaling

Rank order scaling
A comparative scaling technique in which participants are presented with several objects simultaneously and asked to order or rank them according to some criterion.

In rank order scaling, participants are presented with several objects simultaneously and asked to order or rank them according to some criterion. For example, participants may be asked to rank according to overall preference. As shown in Figure 12.4, these rankings are typically obtained by asking the participants to assign a rank of 1 to the most preferred film genre, 2 to the second most preferred, and so on, until a rank of n is assigned to the least preferred genre. Like paired comparison, this approach is also comparative in nature, and it is possible that the participants may dislike the genre ranked 1 in an absolute sense. Furthermore, rank order scaling also results in ordinal data. See Table 12.2, which uses rank order scaling to derive an ordinal scale.

Rank order scaling is commonly used to measure attributes of products and services as well as preferences for brands. Rank order data are frequently obtained from participants in conjoint analysis (see Chapter 24), since rank order scaling forces the participants to discriminate among the stimulus objects. Moreover, compared with paired comparisons, this type of scaling

Figure 12.4	**Instructions**
	Rank the listed film genres in order of preference. Begin by picking out the genre that you like the most and assign it a number 1. Then find the second most preferred genre and assign it a number 2. Continue this procedure until you have ranked all the genres in order of preference. The least preferred genre should be assigned a rank of 10.
Preference for film genres using rank order sampling	

No two genres should receive the same rank number

The criterion of preference is entirely up to you. There is no right or wrong answer. Just try to be consistent

Genre	Rank order
Action	
Animated	
Comedy	
Drama	
Factual	
Fantasy	
Light drama	
Romance	
Sci-fi	
Suspense	

process more closely resembles the shopping environment. It also takes less time and eliminates intransitive responses. If there are n stimulus objects, only $(n-1)$ scaling decisions need be made in rank order scaling. However, in paired comparison scaling, $[n(n-1)/2]$ decisions would be required. Another advantage is that most participants easily understand the instructions for ranking. The major disadvantage is that this technique produces only ordinal data.

Finally, under the assumption of transitivity, rank order data can be converted to equivalent paired comparison data, and vice versa. This point was illustrated by examining the 'Number of times preferred' in Figure 12.3. Hence, it is possible to derive an interval scale from rankings using the Thurstone case V procedure. Other approaches for deriving interval scales from rankings have also been suggested.[14]

Constant sum scaling

Constant sum scaling
A comparative scaling technique in which participants are required to allocate a constant sum of units such as points, euros, chits, stickers or chips among a set of stimulus objects with respect to some criterion.

In constant sum scaling, participants allocate a constant sum of units, such as points or euros, among a set of stimulus objects with respect to some criterion. As shown in Figure 12.5, participants may be asked to allocate 100 points to attributes of bottled beers in a way that reflects the importance they attach to each attribute. If an attribute is unimportant, the participant assigns it zero points. If an attribute is twice as important as some other attribute, it receives twice as many points. The sum of all the points is 100, hence the name of the scale.

The attributes are scaled by counting the points assigned to each one by all the participants and dividing by the number of participants. These results are presented for three groups, or segments, of participants in Figure 12.5. Segment I attaches overwhelming importance to price. Segment II considers a high alcohol level to be of prime importance. Segment III values bitterness, hop flavours, fragrance and the aftertaste. Such information cannot be obtained

---

Figure 12.5

Importance of bottled beer attributes using a constant sum scale

Instructions
Below are eight attributes of bottled beers. Please allocate 100 points among the attributes so that your allocation reflects the relative importance you attach to each attribute. The more points an attribute receives, the more important an attribute is. If an attribute is not at all important, assign it no points. If an attribute is twice as important as some other attribute, it should receive twice as many points.

Note: the figures below represent the mean points allocated to bottled beers by three segments of a target market.

Form

	Attribute	MEAN POINTS ALLOCATED		
		Segment I	**Segment II**	**Segment III**
1	Bitterness	8	2	17
2	Hop flavours	2	4	20
3	Fragrance	3	9	19
4	Country where brewed	9	17	4
5	Price	53	5	7
6	High alcohol level	7	60	9
7	Aftertaste	5	0	15
8	Package design	13	3	9
	Sum	**100**	**100**	**100**

from rank order data unless they are transformed into interval data. Note that the constant sum also has an absolute zero; 10 points are twice as many as 5 points, and the difference between 5 and 2 points is the same as the difference between 57 and 54 points. For this reason, constant sum scale data are sometimes treated as metric. Although this may be appropriate in the limited context of the stimuli scaled, these results are not generalisable to other stimuli not included in the study. Hence, strictly speaking, the constant sum should be considered an ordinal scale because of its comparative nature and the resulting lack of generalisability. It can be seen that the allocation of points in Figure 12.5 is influenced by the specific attributes included in the evaluation task.

The main advantage of the constant sum scale is that it allows for fine discrimination among stimulus objects without requiring too much time. It has two primary disadvantages, however. Participants may allocate more or fewer units than those specified. For example, a participant may allocate 108 or 94 points. The researcher must modify such data in some way or eliminate this participant from the analysis. Another potential problem is rounding error if too few units are used. On the other hand, the use of a large number of units may be too taxing on the participant and cause confusion and fatigue.[15]

Q-sort and other procedures

Q-sort scaling
A comparative scaling technique that uses a rank order procedure to sort objects based on similarity with respect to some criterion.

Verbal protocol
A technique used to understand participants' cognitive responses or thought processes by having them think aloud while completing a task or making a decision.

Q-sort scaling was developed to discriminate among a relatively large number of objects quickly. This technique uses a rank order procedure in which objects are sorted into piles based on similarity with respect to some criterion. For example, participants are given 100 attitude statements on individual cards and asked to place them into 11 piles, ranging from 'most highly agreed with' to 'least highly agreed with'. The number of objects to be sorted should not be less than 60 nor more than 140; a reasonable range is 60 to 90 objects. The number of objects to be placed in each pile is pre-specified, often to result in a roughly normal distribution of objects over the whole set.

Another comparative scaling technique is magnitude estimation.[15] In this technique, numbers are assigned to objects such that ratios between the assigned numbers reflect ratios on the specified criterion. For example, participants may be asked to indicate whether they agree or disagree with each of a series of statements measuring attitude towards different film genres. Then they assign a number between 0 and 100 to each statement to indicate the intensity of their agreement or disagreement. Providing this type of number imposes a cognitive burden on the participants.

Another particularly useful procedure (that could be viewed as a very structured combination of observation and in-depth interviewing) for measuring cognitive responses or thought processes consists of verbal protocols. Participants are asked to 'think out loud' and verbalise anything going through their heads while making a decision or performing a task. The researcher says, 'If you think anything, say it aloud, no matter how trivial the thought may be.' Even with such an explicit instruction, the participants may be silent. At these times, the researcher will say, 'Remember to say aloud everything you are thinking.' Everything that the participants say is recorded. This record of the participants' verbalised thought processes is referred to as a protocol.[16]

Protocols have been used to measure consumers' cognitive responses in actual shopping trips as well as in simulated shopping environments. An interviewer accompanies the participant and holds a recording device into which the participant talks. Protocols, thus collected, have been used to determine the attributes and cues used in making purchase decisions, product usage behaviour and the impact of the shopping environment on consumer decisions. Protocol analysis has also been employed to measure consumer response to advertising. Immediately after seeing an advertisement, the participant is asked to list all the thoughts that came to mind while watching it. The participant is given a limited amount of time to list the thoughts so as to minimise the probability of collecting thoughts generated after, rather than during, the message. After the protocol has been collected, the individual's thoughts or cognitive responses can be coded into three categories as illustrated in Table 12.3.[18]

Table 12.3	Coded verbal protocols	
Category	**Definition**	**Example**
Support argument	Support the claim made by the message	'Diet Coke tastes great'
Counter-argument	Refute the claim made by the message	'Diet Coke has an aftertaste'
Source derogation	Negative opinion about the source of the message	'Coca-Cola is not an honest company'

Protocols are, typically, incomplete. The participant has many thoughts that they cannot or will not verbalise. The researcher must take the incomplete record and infer from it a measure of the underlying cognitive response.

Non-comparative scaling techniques

Continuous rating scale
A measurement scale that has participants rate the objects by placing a mark at the appropriate position on a line that runs from one extreme of the criterion variable to the other. The form may vary considerably. Also called graphic rating scale.

Participants using a non-comparative scale employ whatever rating standard seems appropriate to them. They do not compare the object being rated either with another object or with some specified standard, such as 'your ideal brand'. They evaluate only one object at a time; thus, non-comparative scales are often referred to as monadic scales. Non-comparative techniques consist of continuous and itemised rating scales, which are described in Table 12.4 and discussed in the following sections.

Continuous rating scale

In a continuous rating scale, also referred to as a graphic rating scale, participants rate the objects by placing a mark at the appropriate position on a line that runs from one extreme of

Table 12.4	Basic non-comparative scales			
Scale	**Basic characteristics**	**Examples**	**Advantages**	**Disadvantages**
Continuous rating scale	Place a mark on a continuous line	Reaction to TV advertisements	Easy to construct	Scoring can be cumbersome unless computerised
Itemised rating scales				
Likert scale	Degree of agreement on a 1 (strongly disagree) to 5 (strongly agree) scale	Measurement of attitudes	Easy to construct, administer and understand	More time consuming
Semantic differential scale	Seven-point scale with bipolar labels	Brand, product and company images	Versatile	Controversy as to whether the data are interval
Stapel scale	Unipolar 10-point scale, –5 to +5, without a neutral point (zero)	Measurement of attitudes and images	Easy to construct, administered over the phone	Confusing and difficult to apply

the criterion variable to the other. Thus, the participants are not restricted to selecting from marks previously set by the researcher. The form of the continuous scale may vary considerably. For example, the line may be vertical or horizontal: scale points, in the form of numbers or brief descriptions, may be provided; and if provided, the scale points may be few or many. Three versions of a continuous rating scale are illustrated in Figure 12.6.

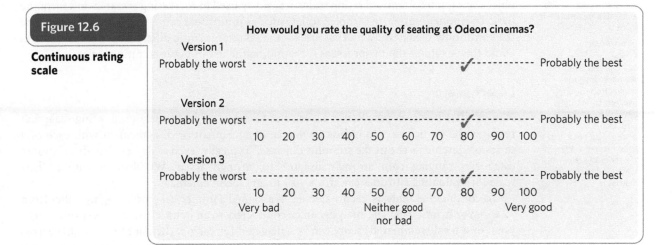

Figure 12.6

Continuous rating scale

How would you rate the quality of seating at Odeon cinemas?

Version 1
Probably the worst --✓----------- Probably the best

Version 2
Probably the worst -------------------------------------✓----------- Probably the best
                    10   20   30   40   50   60   70   80   90   100

Version 3
Probably the worst -------------------------------------✓----------- Probably the best
                    10   20   30   40   50   60   70   80   90   100
                    Very bad   Neither good   Very good
                                       nor bad

Once the participant has provided the ratings, the researcher divides the line into as many categories as desired and assigns scores based on the categories into which the ratings fall. In Figure 12.6, the participant exhibits a favourable attitude towards the seating at the Odeon cinema. These scores are typically treated as interval data. The advantage of continuous scales is that they are easy to construct; however, scoring is cumbersome and unreliable. Moreover, continuous scales provide little new information. Recently however, with the increase of computer-assisted personal interview (CAPI), kiosk, online and mobile device surveys their use is becoming more frequent. Continuous rating scales can be easily implemented in such surveys. The cursor or point of screen is touched in a continuous fashion to select the exact position on the scale that best describes the participant's evaluation. Moreover, the scale values can be automatically scored, thus increasing the speed and accuracy of processing the data.

The following example illustrates how a technological development has enabled the use of continuous rating scales in a marketing research context.

Real research

Continuous measurement and analysis of perceptions: The Perception Analyzer

The Perception Analyzer (**www.perceptionanalyzer.com**) by Dialsmith is a computer-supported, interactive feedback system composed of wireless or wired handheld dials for each participant, a console and software that edits questions, collects data and analyses participant responses. Used in the context of a focus group for example, participants can record their emotional responses to test advertisements, instantly and continuously. Each participant is given a dial and instructed to record continuously their reaction to the material being tested. As participants turn the dial, the information is fed to a computer. Thus, the researcher can determine the second-by-second response of participants as a test advertisement is run. Furthermore, this response can be superimposed on the advertisement to see the participants' reactions to various frames and parts of the advert.

Itemised rating scales

Itemised rating scale
A measurement scale having numbers or brief descriptions associated with each category. The categories are ordered in terms of scale position.

Likert scale
A measurement scale with typically five response categories ranging from 'strongly disagree' to 'strongly agree' that requires participants to indicate a degree of agreement or disagreement with each of a series of statements related to the stimulus objects.

In an itemised rating scale, participants are provided with a scale that has a number or brief description associated with each category. The categories are ordered in terms of scale position, and the participants are required to select the specified category that best describes the object being rated. Itemised rating scales are widely used in marketing research and form the basic components of more complex scales, such as multi-item rating scales. We first describe the commonly used itemised rating scales – the Likert, semantic differential and Stapel scales – and then examine the major issues surrounding the use of itemised rating scales.

Likert scale

Named after its developer, Rensis Likert, the Likert scale is a widely used rating scale that requires the participants to indicate a degree of agreement or disagreement with each of a series of statements about the stimulus objects.[19] Typically, each scale item has five response categories, ranging from 'strongly disagree' to 'strongly agree'. We illustrate with a Likert scale for evaluating attitudes towards a visit to an Odeon cinema.

To conduct the analysis, each statement is assigned a numerical score, ranging either from –2 to +2 or from 1 to 5. The analysis can be conducted on an item-by-item basis (profile analysis), or a total (summated) score can be calculated for each participant by summing across items. Suppose that the Likert scale in Figure 12.7 was used to measure attitudes towards Odeon as well as a local arts-based cinema. Profile analysis would involve comparing the two cinema experiences in terms of the average participant ratings for each item. The summated approach is most frequently used, and, as a result, the Likert scale is also referred to as a summated scale.[20] When using this approach to determine the total score for each participant on each cinema, it is important to use a consistent scoring procedure so that a high (or low) score consistently reflects a favourable response. This requires that the categories assigned to the negative statements by the participants be scored by reversing the scale. Note that for a negative statement, an agreement reflects an unfavourable response, whereas for a posi-

---

Figure 12.7

The Likert scale

Instructions
Listed below are different beliefs about the Odeon cinema. Please indicate how strongly you agree or disagree with each by using the following scale:

1 = Strongly disagree, 2 = Disagree, 3 = Neither agree nor disagree, 4 = Agree, 5 = Strongly agree

	1	2	3	4	5
1 I like to visit Odeon cinemas		✓			
2 The Odeon sells poor-quality food		✓			
3 The Odeon presents a wide variety of film genres			✓		
4 I do not like Odeon advertisements				✓	
5 The Odeon charges fair prices				✓	
6 Booking a seat at the Odeon is difficult	✓				
7 The acoustics at Odeon cinemas are excellent				✓	
8 Odeon staff serve their customers very well				✓	
9 The Odeon is a great place for families to enjoy films		✓			

tive statement, agreement represents a favourable response. Accordingly, a 'strongly agree' response to a favourable statement and a 'strongly disagree' response to an unfavourable statement would both receive scores of 5.[21] In the example in Figure 12.7, if a higher score is to denote a more favourable attitude, the scoring of items 2, 4 and 6 will be reversed. The participant to this set of statements has an attitude score of 26. Each participant's total score for each cinema is calculated. A participant will have the most favourable attitude towards a cinema with the highest score. The procedure for developing summated Likert scales is described later in the section on the development and evaluation of scales.

The Likert scale has several advantages. It is easy to construct and administer, and participants readily understand how to use the scale, making it suitable for online surveys, kiosk, mobile, mail, telephone or personal interviews. The major disadvantage of the Likert scale is that it takes longer to complete than other itemised rating scales because participants have to read and fully reflect upon each statement. Sometimes, it may be difficult to interpret the response to a Likert item, especially if it was an unfavourable statement. In our example, the participant disagrees with statement number 2 that the Odeon sells poor quality food. In reversing the score of this item prior to summing, it is assumed that this participant would agree with a statement that the Odeon sells high-quality food. This, however, may not be true; the disagreement merely indicates that the participant would not make statement 2.

Semantic differential scale

Semantic differential
A seven-point rating scale with end points associated with bipolar labels.

The semantic differential is typically a seven-point rating scale with end points associated with bipolar labels that have semantic meaning. In a typical application, participants rate objects on a number of itemised, seven-point rating scales bounded at each end by one of two bipolar adjectives, such as 'boring' and 'exciting'.[22] We illustrate this scale in Figure 12.8 by presenting a participant's evaluation of a visit to the Odeon cinema on six attributes.

The participants mark the blank that best indicates how they would describe the object being rated.[23] Thus, in our example, an Odeon visit is evaluated as exciting, special, indulgent, cosy and youthful though noisy. The negative adjective or phrase sometimes appears at the left side of the scale and sometimes at the right. In this example they are mixed and the adjectives of 'youthful' and 'mature' may not readily be classified as positive or negative. By mixing the position of positive and negative adjectives, the tendency of some participants, particularly those with very positive or very negative attitudes, to mark the right- or left-hand sides without reading the labels is controlled.

Figure 12.8

Semantic differential scale

Instructions
What does visiting an Odeon cinema mean to you? The following descriptive scales, bounded at each end by bipolar adjectives, summarise characteristics of a visit. Please mark X the blank that best indicates what a visit to an Odeon cinema means to you.

Boring	|__|__|__|__|__| X |__| Exciting
Special	|__| X |__|__|__|__|__| Routine
Thrifty	|__|__| X |__|__|__|__| Indulgent
Cosy	|__| X |__|__|__|__|__| Uncomfortable
Peaceful	|__|__|__|__|__| X |__| Noisy
Youthful	|__| X |__|__|__|__|__| Mature

Individual items on a semantic differential scale may be scored either on a −3 to +3 or on a 1 to 7 scale. The resulting data are commonly analysed through profile analysis. In profile analysis, means or median values on each rating scale are calculated and compared by plotting or statistical analysis. This helps determine the overall differences and similarities among the objects. To assess differences across segments of participants, the researcher can compare mean responses of different segments. Although the mean is most often used as a summary statistic, there is some controversy as to whether the data obtained should be treated as an interval scale.[24] On the other hand, in cases when the researcher requires an overall comparison of objects, such as to determine cinema preference, the individual item scores are summed to arrive at a total score. As in the case of the Likert scale, the scores for the negative items are reversed before summing.

Its versatility makes the semantic differential a popular rating scale in marketing research. It has been widely used in comparing brand, product and company images. It has also been used to develop advertising and promotion strategies and in new product development studies.[25]

Stapel scale

Stapel scale
A scale for measuring attitudes that consists of a single adjective in the middle of an even-numbered range of values.

The Stapel scale, named after its developer, Jan Stapel, is a unipolar rating scale with 10 categories numbered from −5 to +5, without a neutral point (zero).[26] This scale is usually presented vertically. Participants are asked to indicate, by selecting an appropriate numerical response category, how accurately or inaccurately each term describes the object. The higher the number, the more accurately the term describes the object, as shown in Figure 12.9. In this example, a visit to an Odeon cinema is perceived as being full of energy but not a special event.

The data obtained by using a Stapel scale can be analysed in the same way as semantic differential data. The Stapel scale produces results similar to the semantic differential. The Stapel scale's advantages are that it does not require a pretest of the adjectives or phrases to ensure true bipolarity and that it can be administered over the telephone. Some researchers, however, believe the Stapel scale is confusing and difficult to apply. Of the three itemised rating scales considered, the Stapel scale is used least. Nonetheless, this scale merits more attention than it has received.

Figure 12.9

The Stapel scale

Instructions
Please evaluate how accurately each phrase describes a visit to an Odeon cinema. Select a positive number for the phrases you think describe a visit accurately. The more accurately you think the phrase describes a visit, the larger the positive number you should choose. You should select a minus number if you do not think the phrase accurately describes a visit. The less accurately you think it describes a visit, the larger the negative number you should choose. You can select any number from +5 for phrases you think are very accurate, to −5 for phrases you think are very inaccurate.

A visit to an Odeon cinema

+5	+5
+4	+4
+3	+3
+2	+2 ✗
+1	+1
A special event	**Full of energy**
−1	−1
−2 ✗	−2
−3	−3
−4	−4
−5	−5

Itemised rating scale decisions

As is evident from the discussion so far, non-comparative itemised rating scales can take many different forms. The researcher must make six major decisions when constructing any of these scales:

1 The number of scale categories to use.

2 Balanced versus unbalanced scale.

3 Odd or even number of categories.

4 Forced versus non-forced choice.

5 The nature and degree of the verbal description.

6 The physical form of the scale.

Number of scale categories

Two conflicting considerations are involved in deciding the number of scale categories or response options. The greater the number of scale categories, the finer the discrimination among stimulus objects that is possible. On the other hand, most participants cannot handle more than a few categories. Traditional guidelines suggest that the appropriate number of categories should be between five and nine.[27] Yet there is no single optimal number of categories. Several factors should be taken into account in deciding on the number of categories.

If the participants are interested in the scaling task and are knowledgeable about the objects, many categories may be employed. On the other hand, if the participants are not very knowledgeable or engaged with the task, fewer categories should be used. Likewise, the nature of the objects is also relevant. Some objects do not lend themselves to fine discrimination, so a small number of categories are sufficient. Another important factor is the mode of data collection. If telephone interviews are involved, many categories may confuse the participants. Likewise, space limitations may restrict the number of categories in mail questionnaires. If online surveys are used, there is scope for more visual treatment of scale items and categories; this will be presented in more detail later in this chapter.

How the data are to be analysed and used should also influence the number of categories. In situations where several scale items are added together to produce a single score for each participant, five categories are sufficient. The same is true if the researcher wishes to make broad generalisations or group comparisons. If, however, individual responses are of interest or if the data will be analysed by sophisticated statistical techniques, seven or more categories may be required. The size of the correlation coefficient, a common measure of relationship between variables (Chapter 20), is influenced by the number of scale categories. The correlation coefficient decreases with a reduction in the number of categories. This, in turn, has an impact on all statistical analysis based on the correlation coefficient.[28]

Balanced versus unbalanced scale

Balanced scale
A scale with an equal number of favourable and unfavourable categories.

In a balanced scale, the number of favourable and unfavourable categories is equal; in an unbalanced scale, the categories are unequal.[29] Examples of balanced and unbalanced scales are given in Figure 12.10.

In general, in order to obtain the most objective data, the scale should be balanced. If the distribution of responses is likely to be skewed, however, either positively or negatively, an unbalanced scale with more categories in the direction of skewness may be appropriate. If an unbalanced scale is used, the nature and degree of imbalance in the scale should be taken into account in data analysis.

Figure 12.10

Balanced and unbalanced scales

Balanced scale	
Clinique moisturiser for men is:	
Extremely good	
Very good	✓
Good	
Bad	
Very bad	
Extremely bad	

Unbalanced scale	
Clinique moisturiser for men is:	
Extremely good	
Very good	✓
Good	
Somewhat good	
Bad	
Very bad	

Odd or even number of categories

With an odd number of categories, the middle scale position is generally designated as neutral or impartial. The presence, position and labelling of a neutral category can have a significant influence on the response. The Likert scale is a balanced rating scale with an odd number of categories and a neutral point.[30]

The decision to use an odd or even number of categories depends on whether some of the participants may be neutral on the response being measured. If a neutral or indifferent response is possible from at least some of the participants, an odd number of categories should be used. If, on the other hand, the researcher wants to force a response or believes that no neutral or indifferent response exists, a rating scale with an even number of categories should be used. A related issue is whether the choice should be forced or non-forced.

Forced versus non-forced choice

Forced rating scale
A rating scale that forces participants to express an opinion because a 'no opinion' or 'no knowledge' option is not provided.

On forced rating scales the participants are forced to express an opinion because a 'no opinion' option is not provided. In such a case, participants without an opinion may mark the middle scale position. If a sufficient proportion of the participants do not have opinions on the topic, marking the middle position will distort measures of central tendency and variance. In situations where the participants are expected to have no opinion, as opposed to simply being reluctant to disclose it, the accuracy of data may be improved by a non-forced scale that includes a 'no opinion' category.[31]

Nature and degree of verbal description

The nature and degree of verbal description associated with scale categories varies considerably and can have an effect on the responses. Scale categories may have verbal, numerical or pictorial descriptions. Furthermore, the researcher must decide whether to label every scale category, label only some scale categories, or label only extreme scale categories. If they are to use pictorial descriptions (which in online surveys may be moving pictures), researchers have to decide whether they are to use labels at all. Providing a verbal description for each scale category may not improve the accuracy or reliability of the data. Yet, an argument can be made for labelling all or many scale categories to reduce scale ambiguity. The category descriptions should be located as close to the response categories as possible.

The strength of the adjectives used to anchor the scale may influence the distribution of the responses. With strong anchors (1 = Completely disagree, 7 = Completely agree), participants are less likely to use the extreme scale categories. This results in less variable and more peaked response distributions. Weak anchors (1 = Generally disagree, 7 = Generally agree), in contrast, produce uniform or flat distributions. Procedures have been developed to assign values to category descriptors to result in balanced or equal interval scales.[32]

Physical form of the scale

A number of options are available with respect to scale form or configuration. Scales can be presented vertically or horizontally. Categories can be expressed by boxes, discrete lines or units on a continuum and may or may not have numbers assigned to them. If numerical values are used, they may be positive, negative or both. Several possible configurations are presented in Figure 12.11.

Two unique rating scale configurations used in marketing research are the thermometer scale and the smiling face scale. For the thermometer scale, the higher the temperature, the

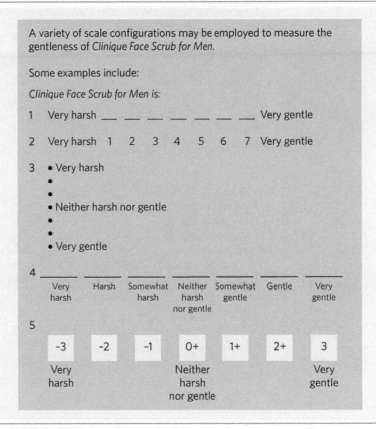

Figure 12.11

Rating scale configurations

A variety of scale configurations may be employed to measure the gentleness of *Clinique Face Scrub for Men*.

Some examples include:

Clinique Face Scrub for Men is:

1 Very harsh ___ ___ ___ ___ ___ ___ ___ Very gentle

2 Very harsh 1 2 3 4 5 6 7 Very gentle

3 • Very harsh
   •
   •
   • Neither harsh nor gentle
   •
   •
   • Very gentle

4 _____
   Very   Harsh   Somewhat   Neither   Somewhat   Gentle   Very
   harsh   harsh   harsh   gentle   gentle
                                 nor gentle

5
   | -3 | -2 | -1 | 0+ | 1+ | 2+ | 3 |
   Very   Neither   Very
   harsh   harsh   gentle
                            nor gentle

Table 12.5	**Summary of itemised rating scale decisions**
1 **Number of categories**	Although there is no single, optimal number, traditional guidelines suggest that there should be between five and nine categories
2 **Balanced versus unbalanced**	In general, the scale should be balanced to obtain the most objective data
3 **Odd or even number of categories**	If a neutral or indifferent scale response is possible from at least some of the participants, an odd number of categories should be used
4 **Forced versus unforced**	In situations where the participants are expected to have no opinion, the accuracy of the data may be improved by a non-forced scale
5 **Verbal description**	An argument can be made for labelling all or many scale categories. The category descriptions should be located as close to the response categories as possible
6 **Physical form**	A number of options should be tried and the best one selected

more favourable the evaluation. Likewise, happier faces indicate evaluations that are more favourable. These scales are especially useful for children.[33] Examples of these scales are shown in Figure 12.12. Table 12.5 summarises the six decisions in designing rating scales. Table 12.6 presents some commonly used scales. Although we show these as having five categories, the number of categories can be varied depending upon the judgement of the researcher.

Figure 12.12

Some unique rating scale configurations

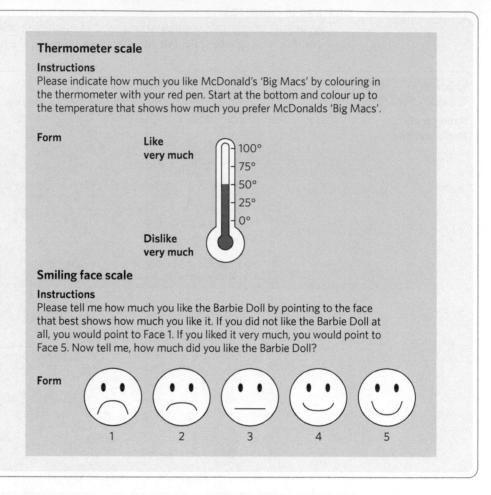

Thermometer scale

Instructions

Please indicate how much you like McDonald's 'Big Macs' by colouring in the thermometer with your red pen. Start at the bottom and colour up to the temperature that shows how much you prefer McDonalds 'Big Macs'.

Form

Like very much — 100°, 75°, 50°, 25°, 0° — Dislike very much

Smiling face scale

Instructions

Please tell me how much you like the Barbie Doll by pointing to the face that best shows how much you like it. If you did not like the Barbie Doll at all, you would point to Face 1. If you liked it very much, you would point to Face 5. Now tell me, how much did you like the Barbie Doll?

Form 1 2 3 4 5

Table 12.6   Some commonly used scales in marketing

Construct	Scale descriptors				
Attitude	Very bad	Bad	Neither bad nor good	Good	Very good
Importance	Not at all important	Not important	Neutral	Important	Very important
Satisfaction	Very dissatisfied	Dissatisfied	Neither dissatisfied nor satisfied	Satisfied	Very satisfied
Purchase Intent	Definitely will not buy	Probably will not buy	Might or might not buy	Probably will buy	Definitely will buy
Purchase Frequency	Never	Rarely	Sometimes	Often	Very often

Multi-item scales

Multi-item scale
A multi-item scale consists of multiple items, where an item is a single question or statement to be evaluated.

Construct
A specific type of concept that exists at a higher level of abstraction than do everyday concepts.

A multi-item scale consists of multiple items, where an item is a single question or statement to be evaluated. The Likert, semantic differential and Stapel scales presented earlier to measure attitudes towards a visit to an Odeon cinema were examples of multi-item scales. Note that each of these scales has multiple items. The development of multi-item rating scales requires considerable technical expertise.[34] Figure 12.13 presents a sequence of operations needed to construct multi-item scales. The researcher begins by developing the construct of interest. A construct is a specific type of concept that exists at a higher level of abstraction than everyday concepts. Examples of such constructs in marketing include 'brand loyalty', 'product involvement' and 'satisfaction'. Next, the researcher must develop a theoretical definition of the construct that establishes the meaning of the central idea or concept of interest. For this we need an underlying theory of the construct being measured. A theory is necessary not only for constructing the scale, but also for interpreting the resulting scores. For example, brand loyalty may be theoretically defined as the *consistent repurchase of a brand prompted by a favourable attitude towards the brand*. The construct of brand loyalty must be operationalised in a way that is consistent with this theoretical definition. The operational definition specifies which observable characteristics will be measured and the process of assigning value to the construct. For example, in a context of buying fashion items, consumers could be characterised as brand loyal if they exhibit a highly favourable attitude (top quartile) and have purchased the same fashion brand on at least four of the last five purchase occasions.

The next step is to generate an initial pool of scale items. Typically, this is based on theory, analysis of secondary data and qualitative research. From this pool, a reduced set of potential

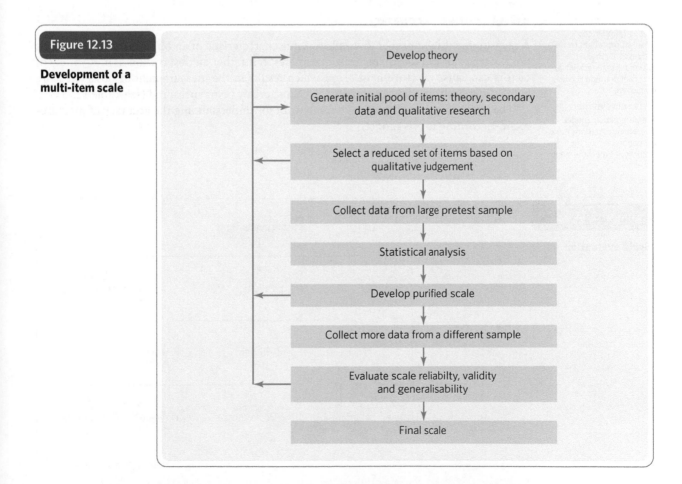

Figure 12.13

Development of a multi-item scale

scale items is generated by the judgement of the researcher and other knowledgeable individuals. Some qualitative criterion is adopted to aid their judgement. The reduced set of items may still be too large to constitute a scale. Thus, further reduction is achieved in a quantitative manner.

Data are collected on the reduced set of potential scale items from a large pretest sample of participants. The data are analysed using techniques such as correlations, factor analysis, cluster analysis, discriminant analysis and statistical tests discussed later in this book. As a result of these statistical analyses, several more items are eliminated, resulting in a purified scale. The purified scale is evaluated for reliability and validity by collecting more data from a different sample. On the basis of these assessments, a final set of scale items is selected. As can be seen from Figure 12.13, the scale development process is an iterative one with several feedback loops.[35]

Scale evaluation

A multi-item scale should be evaluated for accuracy and applicability.[36] As shown in Figure 12.14, this involves an assessment of reliability, validity and generalisability of the scale. Approaches to assessing reliability include test–retest reliability, alternative-forms reliability and internal consistency reliability. Validity can be assessed by examining content validity, criterion validity and construct validity.

Before we can examine reliability and validity we need an understanding of measurement accuracy; it is fundamental to scale evaluation.

Measurement accuracy

Measurement error
The variation in the information sought by the researcher and the information generated by the measurement process employed.

True score model
A mathematical model that provides a framework for understanding the accuracy of measurement.

A measurement is a number that reflects some characteristic of an object. A measurement is not the true value of the characteristic of interest but rather an observation of it. A variety of factors can cause measurement error, which results in the measurement or observed score being different from the true score of the characteristic being measured (see Table 12.7).

The true score model provides a framework for understanding the accuracy of measurement. According to this model,

$$X_O = X_T + X_S + X_R$$

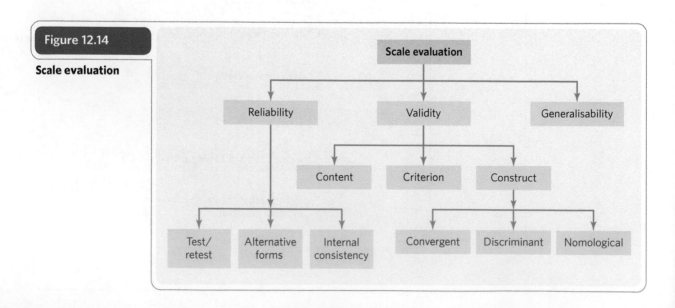

Figure 12.14

Scale evaluation

where X_O = the observed score or measurement
  X_T = the true score of the characteristic
  X_S = systematic error
  X_R = random error

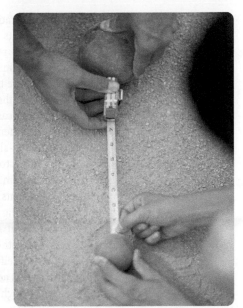

Note that the total measurement error includes the systematic error, X_S, and the random error, X_R. **Systematic error** affects the measurement in a constant way. It represents stable factors that affect the observed score in the same way each time the measurement is made, such as mechanical factors (see Table 12.7). **Random error**, on the other hand, is not constant. It represents transient factors that affect the observed score in different ways each time the measurement is made, such as short-term transient personal factors or situational factors (see Table 12.7). The distinction between systematic and random error is crucial to our understanding of reliability and validity.

Systematic error
An error that affects the measurement in a constant way and represents stable factors that affect the observed score in the same way each time the measurement is made.

Random error
An error that arises from random changes or differences in participants or measurement situations.

Table 12.7	Potential sources of error in measurement

1 Other relatively stable characteristics of the individual that influence the test score such as intelligence social desirability and education

2 Short-term or transient personal factors such as health, emotions and fatigue

3 Situational factors such as the presence of other people, noise and distractions

4 Sampling of items included in the scale: addition, deletion or changes in the scale items

5 Lack of clarity of the scale including the instructions or the items themselves

6 Mechanical factors such as poor printing, overcrowding items in the questionnaire and poor design

7 Administration of the scale such as differences among interviewers

8 Analysis factors such as differences in scoring and statistical analysis

Reliability

Reliability
The extent to which a scale produces consistent results if repeated measurements are made on the characteristic.

Test–retest reliability
An approach for assessing reliability, in which participants are administered identical sets of scale items at two different times, under as nearly equivalent conditions as possible.

Reliability refers to the extent to which a scale produces consistent results if repeated measurements are made.[37] Systematic sources of error do not have an adverse impact on reliability, because they affect the measurement in a constant way and do not lead to inconsistency. In contrast, random error produces inconsistency, leading to lower reliability. Reliability can be defined as the extent to which measures are free from random error, X_R. If $X_R = 0$, the measure is perfectly reliable.

Reliability is assessed by determining the proportion of systematic variation in a scale. This is done by determining the association between scores obtained from different administrations of the scale. If the association is high, the scale yields consistent results and is therefore reliable. Approaches for assessing reliability include the test–retest, alternative-forms and internal consistency methods.

In **test–retest reliability**, participants are administered identical sets of scale items at two different times, under as nearly equivalent conditions as possible. The time interval between tests or administrations is typically two to four weeks. The degree of similarity between the two measurements is determined by computing a correlation coefficient (see Chapter 20). The higher the correlation coefficient, the greater the reliability.

Several problems are associated with the test–retest approach to determining reliability. First, it is sensitive to the time interval between testing. Other things being equal, the longer the time interval, the lower the reliability. Second, the initial measurement may alter the characteristic being measured. For example, measuring participants' attitude towards low-alcohol beer may cause them to become more health conscious and to develop a more positive attitude towards low-alcohol beer. Third, it may be impossible to make repeated measurements (e.g. the research topic may be the participant's initial reaction to a new product). Fourth, the first measurement may have a carryover effect to the second or subsequent measurements. Participants may attempt to remember answers they gave the first time. Fifth, the characteristic being measured may change between measurements. For example, favourable information about an object between measurements may make a participant's attitude more positive. Finally, the test–retest reliability coefficient can be inflated by the correlation of each item with itself. These correlations tend to be higher than correlations between different scale items across administrations. Hence, it is possible to have high test–retest correlations because of the high correlations between the same scale items measured at different times even though the correlations between different scale items are quite low. Because of these problems, a test–retest approach is best applied in conjunction with other approaches, such as alternative-forms reliability.[38]

Alternative-forms reliability

An approach for assessing reliability that requires two equivalent forms of the scale to be constructed and then the same participants to be measured at two different times.

In **alternative-forms reliability**, two equivalent forms of the scale are constructed. The same participants are measured at two different times, usually two to four weeks apart with a different scale form being administered each time. The scores from the administrations of the alternative scale forms are correlated to assess reliability.[39]

The two forms should be equivalent with respect to content, i.e. each scale item should attempt to measure the same items. There are two major problems with this approach. First, it is time consuming and expensive to construct an equivalent form of the scale. Second, it is difficult to construct two equivalent forms of a scale. The two forms should be equivalent with respect to content. In a strict sense, it is required that the alternative sets of scale items should have the same means, variances and intercorrelations. Even if these conditions are satisfied, the two forms may not be equivalent in content. Thus, a low correlation may reflect either an unreliable scale or non-equivalent forms.

Internal consistency reliability

An approach for assessing the internal consistency of a set of items, where several items are summated in order to form a total score for the scale.

Internal consistency reliability is used to assess the reliability of a summated scale where several items are summed to form a total score. In a scale of this type, each item measures some aspect of the construct measured by the entire scale, and the items should be consistent in what they indicate about the construct.[40] This measure of reliability focuses on the internal consistency of the set of items forming the scale.

Split-half reliability

A form of internal consistency reliability in which the items constituting the scale are divided into two halves and the resulting half scores are correlated.

The simplest measure of internal consistency is **split-half reliability**. The items on the scale are divided into two halves and the resulting half scores are correlated. High correlations between the halves indicate high internal consistency.[41] The scale items can be split into halves based on odd- and even-numbered items or randomly. The problem is that the results will depend on how the scale items are split. A popular approach to overcoming this problem is to use the coefficient alpha.

Coefficient alpha

A measure of internal consistency reliability that is the average of all possible split-half coefficients resulting from different splittings of the scale items.

The **coefficient alpha**, or Cronbach's alpha, is the average of all possible split-half coefficients resulting from different ways of splitting the scale items.[42] This coefficient varies from 0 to 1, and a value of 0.6 or less generally indicates unsatisfactory internal consistency reliability. An important property of coefficient alpha is that its value tends to increase with an increase in the number of scale items. Therefore, coefficient alpha may be artificially, and inappropriately, inflated by including several redundant scale items.[43] Another coefficient that can be employed in conjunction with coefficient alpha is coefficient beta. Coefficient beta assists in determining whether the averaging process used in calculating coefficient alpha is masking any inconsistent items.

Some multi-item scales include several sets of items designed to measure different aspects of a multidimensional construct. For example, fashion boutique image is a multidimensional construct that includes brand image(s) of stocked merchandise, quality of merchandise, assortment of merchandise, layout and merchandising, service of boutique personnel, prices, physical location, and characteristics of other shoppers in the boutique. Hence, a scale designed to measure fashion boutique image could contain items measuring each of these dimensions. Because these dimensions are somewhat independent, a measure of internal consistency computed across dimensions would be inappropriate. If several items are used to measure each dimension, however, internal consistency reliability can be computed for each dimension.

The following example illustrates how researchers developed scale items to encapsulate newspaper reading behaviour. It shows how they performed reliability tests and the subject of our next section, validity tests.

Real research	**Reading digital newspapers: establishing reliability and validity[44]**

The advantages of digital media have brought about a revolution in journalism. Digital media have impacted upon the speed with which news items reach readers, the low cost of distributing information, and the opportunities to establish more direct contact and interaction with readers. These advantages have boosted the supply of digital newspapers in both quantitative and qualitative terms, resulting in a proliferation of increasingly specialised electronic journals. In a study of digital journalism, the main objective was to analyse the possible influence of reader motivations in reading newspapers on the degree of substitutability between digital and traditional media. In order to develop scales to measure their chosen variables, researchers undertook an exhaustive review of the literature including a search for existing scales that could be suitably adapted. They also conducted a series of in-depth interviews with readers. They then designed a series of questions that would measure the multiple dimensions involved.

Before testing any hypotheses, the scales initially proposed were subjected to a sifting process in order to obtain measurement instruments that would allow the researchers to quantify the concepts they wanted to encapsulate. **Exploratory analysis of reliability**: The first step in assessing reliability was to calculate the Cronbach's alpha value and the item-total correlation of each of the variables analysed. The initial scales were refined and the results of the Cronbach's alpha test showed an acceptable degree of internal consistency in the four scales they considered, being in all the cases over the 0.7 recommended by Cronbach. As a second stage the researchers carried out a study of unidimensionality by means of an exploratory factor analysis. **Confirmatory analysis of reliability**: In order to guarantee the proposed scales' reliability and validity, the researchers carried out a series of confirmatory analyses. This enabled them to sift scales by the development of successive confirmatory factor analyses. The goodness of fit of the complete confirmatory model was checked and was acceptable. Lastly, the scales that had varied in structure since the exploratory analysis were subjected to a fresh reliability assessment using Cronbach's alpha criteria and item-total correlation. The reliability levels for each indicator, expressed in terms of R^2, were at acceptable levels. In order to confirm the definitive reliability of the scales, the researchers carried out tests of the composite reliability coefficient and the average variance extracted.

In order to verify whether the designed scales were measuring the concepts correctly, analyses of validity were carried out. In this study, researchers considered validity to be guaranteed not only in view of the rigour used in the design of the initial scales on the basis of the literature, but also because they took into account the findings of their in-depth interviews, which were endorsed by various experts in the subject. **Construct**

> **validity**: This type of validity analysis was formed by two fundamental categories of validity: convergent and discriminatory. **Convergent validity**: The standardised coefficients in each scale were over 0.5 and significant. To assess the discriminatory validity the researchers used several tests, such as checking that value '1' was not in the confidence interval of the correlations between different constructs. Likewise, they checked that correlations between different scales were not over 0.8.

Validity

Validity
The extent to which a measurement represents characteristics that exist in the phenomenon under investigation.

The validity of a scale may be considered as the extent to which differences in observed scale scores reflect true differences among objects on the characteristic being measured, rather than systematic or random error. Perfect validity requires that there be no measurement error ($X_O = X_T$, $X_R = 0$, $X_S = 0$). Researchers may assess content validity, criterion validity or construct validity.[45]

Content validity
A type of validity, sometimes called face validity, that consists of a subjective but systematic evaluation of the representativeness of the content of a scale for the measuring task at hand.

Content validity, sometimes called face validity, is a subjective but systematic evaluation of how well the content of a scale represents the measurement task at hand. The researcher or someone else examines whether the scale items adequately cover the entire domain of the construct being measured. Thus, a scale designed to measure fashion boutique image would be considered inadequate if it omitted any of the major dimensions (brand image(s) of stocked merchandise, quality of merchandise, assortment of merchandise, layout and merchandising, service of boutique personnel, prices, etc.). Given its subjective nature, content validity alone is not a sufficient measure of the validity of a scale, yet it aids in a common-sense interpretation of the scale scores.[46] A more formal evaluation can be obtained by examining criterion validity.

Criterion validity
A type of validity that examines whether the measurement scale performs as expected in relation to other selected variables as meaningful criteria.

Criterion validity reflects whether a scale performs as expected in relation to other selected variables (criterion variables) as meaningful criteria. If, for example, a scale is designed to measure loyalty in customers, criterion validity might be determined by comparing the results generated by this scale with results generated by observing the extent of repeat purchasing. Based on the time period involved, criterion validity can take two forms, concurrent validity and predictive validity.

Concurrent validity
A type of validity that is assessed when the data on the scale being evaluated and on the criterion variables are collected at the same time.

Concurrent validity is assessed when the data on the scale being evaluated (e.g. loyalty scale) and the criterion variables (e.g. repeat purchasing) are collected at the same time. The scale being developed and the alternative means of encapsulating the criterion variables would be administered simultaneously and the results compared.[47]

Predictive validity
A type of validity that is concerned with how well a scale can forecast a future criterion.

Predictive validity is concerned with how well a scale can forecast a future criterion. To assess predictive validity, the researcher collects data on the scale at one point in time and data on the criterion variables at a future time. For example, attitudes towards how loyal customers feel to a particular brand could be used to predict future repeat purchases of that brand. The predicted and actual purchases (which could be tracked on CRM databases or scanned purchases) are compared to assess the predictive validity of the attitudinal scale.[48]

Construct validity
A type of validity that addresses the question of what construct or characteristic the scale is measuring. An attempt is made to answer theoretical questions of why a scale works and what deductions can be made concerning the theory underlying the scale.

Construct validity addresses the question of what construct or characteristic the scale is, in fact, measuring. When assessing construct validity, the researcher attempts to answer theoretical questions about why the scale works and what deductions can be made concerning the underlying theory. Thus, construct validity requires a sound theory of the nature of the construct being measured and how it relates to other constructs.[49] Construct validity is the most sophisticated and difficult type of validity to establish. As Figure 12.14 shows, construct validity includes convergent, discriminant and nomological validity.

Convergent validity
A measure of construct validity that measures the extent to which the scale correlates positively with other measures of the same construct.

Convergent validity is the extent to which the scale correlates positively with other measurements of the same construct. It is not necessary that all these measurements be obtained by

Discriminant validity
A type of construct validity that assesses the extent to which a measure does not correlate with other constructs from which it is supposed to differ.

Nomological validity
A type of validity that assesses the relationship between theoretical constructs. It seeks to confirm significant correlations between the constructs as predicted by a theory.

Generalisability
The degree to which a study based on a sample applies to the population as a whole.

using conventional scaling techniques.[50] Discriminant validity is the extent to which a measure does not correlate with other constructs from which it is supposed to differ. It involves demonstrating a lack of correlation among differing constructs.[51] Nomological validity is the extent to which the scale correlates in theoretically predicted ways with measures of different but related constructs. A theoretical model is formulated that leads to further deductions, tests and inferences.[52] Gradually a nomological net is built in which several constructs are systematically interrelated.

An instance of construct validity can be evaluated in the following example. A researcher seeks to provide evidence of construct validity in a multi-item scale, designed to measure the concept of 'self-image'. These findings would be sought:[53]

- High correlations with other scales designed to measure self-concepts and with reported classifications by friends (convergent validity).

- Low correlations with unrelated constructs of brand loyalty and variety seeking (discriminant validity).

- Brands that are congruent with the individual's self-concept are preferred, as postulated by the theory (nomological validity).

- A high level of reliability.

Note that a high level of reliability was included as evidence of construct validity in this example. This illustrates the relationship between reliability and validity.

Relationship between reliability and validity

The relationship between reliability and validity can be understood in terms of the true score model. If a measure is perfectly valid, it is also perfectly reliable. In this case, $X_O = X_T$, $X_R = 0$ and $X_S = 0$. Thus, perfect validity implies perfect reliability. If a measure is unreliable, it cannot be perfectly valid, since at a minimum $X_O = X_T + X_R$. Furthermore, systematic error may also be present, i.e. $X_S \neq 0$. Thus, unreliability implies invalidity. If a measure is perfectly reliable, it may or may not be perfectly valid, because systematic error may still be present ($X_O = X_T + X_S$). In other words, a reliable scale can be constructed to measure 'customer loyalty' but it may not necessarily be a valid measurement of 'customer loyalty'. Conversely, a valid measurement of 'customer loyalty' has to be reliable. Reliability is a necessary, but not sufficient, condition for validity.

Generalisability

Generalisability refers to the extent to which one can generalise from the observations at hand to a universe of generalisations. The set of all conditions of measurement over which the investigator wishes to generalise is the universe of generalisation. These conditions may include items, interviewers and situations of observation. A researcher may wish to generalise a scale developed for use in personal interviews to other modes of data collection, such as kiosk and online interviews. Likewise, one may wish to generalise from a sample of items to the universe of items, from a sample of times of measurement to the universe of times of measurement, from a sample of observers to a universe of observers, and so on.[54]

In generalisability studies, measurement procedures are designed to investigate each universe of interest by sampling conditions of measurement from each of them. For each universe of interest, an aspect of measurement called a facet is included in the study. Traditional reliability methods can be viewed as single-facet generalisability studies. A test–retest correlation is concerned with whether scores obtained from a measurement scale are generalisable to the universe scores across all times of possible measurement. Even if the test–retest correlation is high, nothing can be said about the generalisability of the scale to other universes. To generalise to other universes, generalisability theory procedures must be employed.

Choosing a scaling technique

In addition to theoretical considerations and evaluation of reliability and validity, certain practical factors should be considered in selecting scaling techniques for a particular marketing research problem.[55] These include the level of information (nominal, ordinal, interval or ratio) desired, the capabilities and willingness of participants, the characteristics of the stimulus objects, method of administration, the context and cost. Selecting an appropriate rating scale is a necessary first step in developing a good measurement instrument; establishing statistical reliability and validity through a multi-step testing and retesting process should be accorded the highest priority in selecting a scale. A good rating scale should have the following characteristics:[56] minimal response bias, participant interpretation and understanding, discriminating power, ease of administration, ease of use by participants, credibility and usefulness of results.

As a general rule, using the scaling technique that will yield the highest level of information feasible in a given situation will permit using the greatest variety of statistical analyses. Also, regardless of the type of scale used, whenever feasible, several scale items should measure the characteristic of interest. This provides more accurate measurement than a single-item scale. In many situations, it is desirable to use more than one scaling technique or to obtain additional measures using mathematically derived scales.

Mathematically derived scales

All the scaling techniques discussed in this chapter require the participants to evaluate directly the constructs that the researcher believes to comprise the object of study, e.g. the cognitive state of brand loyalty. In contrast, mathematical scaling techniques allow researchers to infer participants' evaluations of the constructs of the object of study. These evaluations are inferred from the participants' overall judgements. Two popular mathematically derived scaling techniques are multidimensional scaling and conjoint analysis, which are discussed in detail in Chapter 24.

International marketing research

In designing the scale or response format for international research projects, participants' cultural backgrounds should be taken into account.[57] Researchers should aim to develop scales that are free of cultural biases. Of the scaling techniques we have considered, the semantic differential scale may be the simplest to use in a consistent manner over many cultures. It has been tested in a number of countries and has consistently produced similar results. Even so, when developing a scale, cultural values that may affect how a scale is perceived should be tested, as illustrated in the following example.

Although the semantic differential worked well in this Chinese context, an alternative approach

Exploring cosmetics advertising in southern China[58]

Chinese people's perceptions of advertisements are changing rapidly, and are made ever more complex by the socio-economic disparities that exist among communities from the many different geographical regions within China. Despite modernisation, traditional Chinese values have persisted, posing dilemmas for advertising executives to develop creative campaigns that can work within a Chinese cultural context. A study was designed to assist international cosmetics companies by providing a framework to design effective advertising strategies in targeting women in Hong Kong and Shenzhen. The study aimed to explore the notions of advertising appeals, the use of endorsers, and the reliance on product information and media selection. Study questions were categorised into four areas: media selection, standardisation and adaptation, reference groups and endorsers, and product information. In order to measure consumer preferences in these areas, five-point semantic differential scales were developed. Due to Confucian values, five or seven point scales may bias the Chinese towards midpoint responses; a pilot test with 10 Chinese women did not reveal any tendencies to respond centrally. Neither was this recognised as being a problem when the instrument was pretested with a further 30 participants. Therefore it was decided to retain the five-item measures, as the midpoint was considered to represent a valid measure. Overall the pilot and pretest proved worthwhile, and several modifications relating to an improved structure, layout and wording content of the instrument were implemented. A mall-intercept survey was undertaken in eight major shopping malls throughout Hong Kong and Shenzhen. This study has highlighted that the cosmetics markets for these cities were prima facie similar in terms of how products should be advertised, yet further cross-comparison revealed that subtle differences did exist despite the close proximity of the two cities. The findings indicated that there was an overwhelming influence from the West in terms of how cosmetics may appeal to Chinese consumers. Women from both cities, by and large, aspired to Western-branded cosmetics, advertisements that featured Western music, and formats with Western image appeals – as they afforded more status and modernity. However, this study has also revealed that the continued allure of Chinese-looking models and celebrities needed to be considered, particularly for the Shenzhen market.

is to develop scales that use a self-defined cultural norm as a base referent. For example, participants may be required to indicate their own anchor point and position relative to a culture-specific stimulus set. This approach is useful for measuring attitudes that are defined relative to cultural norms (e.g. attitude towards marital roles). In developing response formats, verbal rating scales appear to be the most suitable. Special attention should be devoted to determining equivalent verbal descriptors in different languages and cultures. The end points of the scale are particularly prone to different interpretations. In some cultures, 1 may be interpreted as best, whereas in others it may be interpreted as worst, regardless of how it is scaled. It is important that the scale end points and the verbal descriptors be employed in a manner consistent with the culture. In international marketing research, it is critical to establish the equivalence of scales and measures used to obtain data from different countries. This topic is complex and is discussed in some detail in Chapter 26.

Ethics in marketing research

Researchers have an ethical responsibility to use scales that have reasonable reliability, validity and generalisability. Research findings generated by scales that are unreliable, invalid or not generalisable to stated target populations are questionable and at best raise serious ethical issues. Moreover, researchers should not bias scales so as to slant the findings in any particular direction. This is easy to do by biasing the wording of statements (Likert-type scales), the scale descriptors or other aspects of the scales. Consider, for example, the use of scale descriptors. The descriptors used to frame a scale can be chosen to bias results in a desired direction, e.g. to generate a positive view of the client's brand or a negative view of a competitor's brand. A researcher who wants to project the client's brand favourably can ask participants to indicate their opinion of the brand on several attributes using seven-point scales framed by the descriptors 'extremely poor' to 'good'. In such a case, participants may be reluctant to rate the product extremely poorly. Using a strongly negative descriptor with only a mildly positive one has an interesting effect. As long as the product is not the worst, participants will be reluctant to rate the product extremely poorly. In fact, participants who believe the product to be only mediocre will end up responding favourably. Try this yourself. How would you rate BMW cars on the following attributes?

Reliability	Horrible	1	2	3	4	5	6	7 Good
Performance	Very poor	1	2	3	4	5	6	7 Good
Quality	One of the worst	1	2	3	4	5	6	7 Good
Prestige	Very low	1	2	3	4	5	6	7 Good

Did you find yourself rating BMW cars positively? Using this same technique, a researcher can negatively bias evaluations of competitors' products by providing a mildly negative descriptor (somewhat poor) against a strong positive descriptor (extremely good).

Thus we see how important it is to use balanced scales with comparable positive and negative descriptors. When this guide is not practised, responses can be biased and should be interpreted accordingly. This concern also underscores the need to establish adequately the reliability, validity and generalisability of scales before using them in a research project. Scales that are invalid, unreliable or not generalisable to the target population provide the client with flawed results and misleading findings, thus raising serious ethical issues. The researcher has a responsibility to both the client and participants to ensure the applicability and usefulness of the scale.

Digital applications in marketing research

Poor scale and survey design can cause low levels of participant engagement resulting in incomplete surveys and low response rates. Participants are generally developing more technological know-how, and can interpret ideas and concepts in different manners, especially in visual formats. They also are becoming more accustomed to faster speeds in engaging with technology and multitasking. Researchers need to appreciate how participants relate to technology and find ways to retain their attention and interest, especially in the design of online surveys. Evidence is growing that the use of new questionnaire design tools, like Flash and Java, can create a much more enjoyable and engaging research experience.[59] Survey designs can be created that are on par with the most engaging appli- cations such as games. Designing a survey encapsulating the gaming type user interface, by the help of an animated questionnaire, can help enormously with participant engagement. Adding more flash elements into the survey and animating the characters can allow surveys to mimic a game or a puzzle. One way to do this has been through the use of fusion surveys (online surveys incorporating rich media techniques).[60] The following example illustrates how award-winning technology developments can be used to create fusion surveys. This technology can help to improve existing formats of scales but also to create new forms of scale that are totally visually based, opening up many possibilities for cross-cultural studies where language and literacy have created a barrier.

Real research

SurveyFlashToolsSM

Annik (**www.anniksystems.com**) was the winner of the 2010 Market Research Society (**www.mrs.org.uk**) and Association for Survey Computing (**www.asc. org.uk**) MRS/ASC Technology Effectiveness Award. This prestigious technology award was given to Annik's division SurveyFlashToolsSM (**www.surveyflash-tools.com**). SurveyFlashToolsSM makes interactive, animation-based tools for online surveys. This is normally a cumbersome and time-consuming process. SurveyFlashTools makes visually stimulating scale and question types readily available to embed into online surveys requiring no knowledge of Flash programming. Survey designers can browse, customise and then embed Flash Tools into surveys, in just a few clicks. This technology does much to raise participant enjoyment, thus increasing engagement and ultimately survey response rates. Survey designers can select Flash Tools to embed in their surveys that include:

Sliders (for continuous rating scales) – this vertical or horizontal slider can be used for rating multiple products. A text rating tool can be used for rating multiple attributes of a product.

Rating and ranking tools, including visual rating and ranking – this tool can be used for rating custom images where participants can rate each image. An image ranking tool can be used for custom product where participants can rank images.

Video rating – this tool can be used for assessment of a given videoclip.

Visit **www.surveyflashtools.com** to see examples of these tools and Confirmit (**www.confirmit.com**) to see a survey design company that uses this technology as part of their online surveys.

Summary

Measurement is the assignment of numbers or other symbols to characteristics of objects according to set rules. Scaling involves the generation of a continuum upon which measured objects are located. The fundamental scale characteristics are description, order, distance and origin. The four primary scales of measurement are nominal, ordinal, interval and ratio. Of these, the nominal scale is the most basic in that the numbers are used only for identifying or classifying objects and the only characteristic possessed is description. In the ordinal scale, the numbers indicate the relative position of the objects but not the magnitude of difference between them. Thus, only the order and description characteristics are present. The interval scale permits a comparison of the differences between the objects. Because it has an arbitrary zero point, however, it is not meaningful to calculate ratios of scale values on an interval scale. The highest level of measurement is represented by the ratio scale in which the zero point is fixed. The researcher can compute ratios of scale values using this scale. The ratio scale incorporates all the properties of the lower level scales and also has the origin characteristic.

Scaling techniques can be classified as comparative or non-comparative. Comparative scaling involves a direct comparison of stimulus objects. Comparative scales include paired comparisons, rank order, constant sum and the Q-sort. The data obtained by these procedures have only ordinal properties. Verbal protocols, where the participant is instructed to think out loud, can be used for measuring cognitive responses. In non-comparative scaling, each object is scaled independently of the other objects in the stimulus set. The resulting data are generally assumed to be interval or ratio scaled. Non-comparative rating scales can be either continuous or itemised. The itemised rating scales are further classified as Likert, semantic differential or Stapel scales. The data from all these three types of scale are typically treated as interval. Thus, these scales possess the characteristics of description, order and distance. When using non-comparative itemised rating scales, the researcher must decide on the number of scale categories, balanced versus unbalanced scales, an odd or even number of categories, forced versus non-forced choices, the nature and degree of verbal description, and the physical form or configuration.

Multi-item scales consist of a number of rating scale items. These scales should be evaluated in terms of reliability and validity. Reliability refers to the extent to which a scale produces consistent results if repeated measurements are made. Approaches to assessing reliability include test–retest, alternative forms and internal consistency. The validity of a measurement may be assessed by evaluating content validity, criterion validity and construct validity.

The choice of a particular scaling technique in a given situation should be based on theoretical and practical considerations. Generally, the scaling technique used should be the one that will yield the highest level of information feasible. Also, multiple measures should be obtained.

In international marketing research, special attention should be devoted to determining equivalent verbal descriptors in different languages and cultures. The misuse of scale descriptors also raises serious ethical concerns. The researcher has a responsibility to both the client and participants to ensure the applicability and usefulness of scales. There is a growing use of visually based scales used in online surveys. These offer great potential in being both engaging for participants and able to capture views that may be difficult to express in words alone.

Questions

1   What is measurement?

2   Highlight any marketing phenomena that you feel may be problematic in terms of assigning numbers to characteristics of those phenomena.

3   Describe and illustrate, with examples, the differences between a nominal and an ordinal scale.

4   What are the advantages of a ratio scale over an interval scale? Are these advantages significant?

5   What is a comparative rating scale?

6   What is a paired comparison? What are the advantages and disadvantages of paired comparison scaling?

7   Describe the constant sum scale. How is it different from the other comparative rating scales?

8 Identify the type of scale (nominal, ordinal, interval or ratio) used in each of the following. Give reasons for your choice.

a I like to listen to the radio when I am revising for exams

Disagree   Agree

1   2   3   4   5

b How old are you? _____

c Rank the following activities in terms of your preference by assigning a rank from 1 to 5 (1 = Most preferred, 2 = Second most preferred, etc.):

(i) Reading magazines.

(ii) Watching television.

(iii) Going to the cinema.

(iv) Shopping for clothes.

(v) Eating out.

d What is your university/college registration number? _____

e In an average weekday, how much time do you spend doing class assignments?

(i) Less than 15 minutes

(ii) 15 to 30 minutes

(iii) 31 to 60 minutes

(iv) 61 to 120 minutes

(v) More than 120 minutes.

f How much money did you spend last week in the Student Union shop? _____

9 Describe the semantic differential scale and the Likert scale. For what purposes are these scales used?

10 What are the major decisions involved in constructing an itemised rating scale? How many scale categories should be used in an itemised rating scale? Why?

11 Should an odd or even number of categories be used in an itemised rating scale?

12 How does the nature and degree of verbal description affect the response to itemised rating scales?

13 What is reliability? What are the differences between test–retest and alternative-forms reliability?

14 What is validity? What is criterion validity? How is it assessed?

15 How would you select a particular scaling technique?

Exercises

1   You work in the marketing research department of a luxury watch brand. Your firm would like to measure the attitudes of retailers towards your brand and your main competitors. The attitudes would be measured using an online survey. You have been asked to develop an appropriate scale for this purpose. You have also been asked to explain and justify your reasoning in constructing this scale.

2   Develop three comparative (paired comparison, rank order and constant sum) scales to measure attitude towards five popular brands of beer (e.g. Heineken, Guinness, Carlsberg, Stella and Holsten). Administer each scale to five students. No student should be administered more than one scale. Note the time it takes each student to respond. Which scale was the easiest to administer? Which scale took the shortest time?

3   Develop a constant sum scale to determine preferences for restaurants. Administer this scale to a pilot sample of 20 students to determine their preferences for some of the popular restaurants in your town or city. Based on your pilot, evaluate the efficacy of the scale items you chose, and design new scale items that could be used for a full survey.

4   Design Likert scales to measure the usefulness of the Louis Vuitton Möet Hennessy website. Visit the site at **www.lvmh.com** and rate it on the scales that you have developed. After your site visit, were there any aspects of usefulness that you had not considered in devising your scales, what were they and why were they not apparent before you made your site visit?

5   In a small group discuss the following issues: 'A brand could receive the highest median rank on a rank order scale of all the brands considered and still have poor sales' and 'It really does not matter which scaling technique you use. As long as your measure is reliable, you will get the right results.'

Video case exercise: St Paul's Cathedral

St Paul's is planning a survey to measure the characteristics of visitors, their experience of the cathedral and their image of the brand. Make a case for what scales would work for this challenge and why you think they would be successful.

Notes

1. Bartholomew, D.J., *Measurement* (Thousand Oaks, CA: Sage, 2006); Wyner, G.A., 'The right side of metrics', *Marketing Management* 13 (1) (2004), 8–9; Newell, S.J., 'The development of a scale to measure perceived corporate credibility', *Journal of Business Research* (June 2001), 235; Gofton, K., 'If it moves measure it', *Marketing* (Marketing Technique Supplement) (4 September 1997), 17; Nunnally, J.C., *Psychometric Theory*, 2nd edn (New York: McGraw-Hill, 1978), 3.

2. Schuster, C. and Smith, D.A., 'Estimating with a latent class model the reliability of nominal judgments upon which two raters agree', *Educational and Psychological Measurement* 66 (5) (October 2006), 739; Stevens, S., 'Mathematics, measurement and psychophysics', in Stevens, S. (ed.), *Handbook of Experimental Psychology* (New York: Wiley, 1951).

3. Giovagnoli, A., Marzialetti, J. and Wynn, H.P., 'A new approach to inter-rater agreement through stochastic orderings: the discrete case', *Metrika* 67 (3) (April 2008), 349–370; Kurpius, S.E., *Testing and measurement* (Thousand Oaks, CA: Sage, 2002); Moshkovich, H.M., 'Ordinal judgments in multiattribute decision analysis', *European Journal of Operational Research* 137 (3) (16 March 2002), 625; Cook, W.D., Kress, M. and Seiford,

L.M., 'On the use of ordinal data in data envelopment analysis', *Journal of the Operational Research Society* 44 (2) (February 1993), 133–140; Barnard, N.R. and Ehrenberg, A.S.C., 'Robust measures of consumer brand beliefs', *Journal of Marketing Research* 27 (November 1990), 477–484; Perreault, W.D. Jr and Young, F.W., 'Alternating least squares optimal scaling: analysis of nonmetric data in marketing research', *Journal of Marketing Research* 17 (February 1980), 1–13.

4. Halme, M., 'Dealing with interval scale data in data envelopment analysis', *European Journal of Operational Research* 137 (1) (16 February 2002), 22; Lynn, M. and Harriss, J., 'The desire for unique consumer products: a new individual difference scale', *Psychology and Marketing* 14 (6) (September 1997), 601–616.

5. For a discussion of these scales, refer to Miller, D.C. and Salkind, N.J., *Handbook of Research Design and Social Measurement*, 6th edn (Thousand Oaks, CA: Sage, 2002); Taiwo, A., 'Overall evaluation rating scales: an assessment', *International Journal of Market Research* (Summer 2000), 301–311; Coombs, C.H., 'Theory and methods of social measurement', in Festinger, L. and Katz, D. (eds), *Research Methods in the Behavioral Sciences* (New York: Holt, Rinehart & Winston, 1953).

6. Tellis, G.J., 'Generalizations about advertising effectiveness in markets', *Journal of Advertising Research* 49 (2) (June 2009), 240–245.

7. There is, however, some controversy regarding this issue. See Louviere, J.J. and Islam, T., 'A comparison of importance weights and willingness-to-pay measures derived from choice based conjoint, constant sum scales and best-worst scaling', *Journal of Business Research* 61 (9) (September 2008), 903–911; Campbell, D.T. and Russo, M.J., *Social Measurement* (Thousand Oaks, CA: Sage, 2001); Amoo, T., 'Do the numeric values influence subjects' responses to rating scales?', *Journal of International Marketing and Marketing Research* (February 2001), 41.

8. Tavares, S., Cardoso, M. and Dias, J.G., 'The heterogeneous best-worst choice method in market research', *International Journal of Market Research* 52 (4) (2010), 533–546.

9. Anon., 'Competition between Coca-Cola and Pepsi to start,' *Asiainfo Daily China News* (19 March 2002), 1; Rickard, L., 'Remembering New Coke', *Advertising Age* 66 (16) (17 April 1995), 6; 'Coke's flip-flop underscores risks of consumer taste tests', *Wall Street Journal* (18 July 1985), 25.

10. It is not necessary to evaluate all possible pairs of objects, however. Procedures such as cyclic designs can significantly reduce the number of pairs evaluated. A treatment of such procedures may be found in Bemmaor, A.C. and Wagner, U., 'A multiple-item model of paired comparisons: separating chance from latent performance', *Journal of Marketing Research* 37 (4) (November 2000), 514–524; Malhotra, N.K., Jain, A.K. and Pinson, C., 'The robustness of MDS configurations in the case of incomplete data', *Journal of Marketing Research* 25 (February 1988), 95–102.

11. For an advanced application involving paired comparison data, see Bemmaor, A.C. and Wagner, U., 'A multiple-item model of paired comparisons: separating chance from latent performance', *Journal of Marketing Research* 37 (4) (November 2000), 514–524.

12. For the assumption of transitivity, see Voorhoeve, A. and Binmore, K., 'Transitivity, the Sorites paradox, and similarity based decision making', *Erkenntnis* 64 (1) (January 2006), 101–114; Miljkovic, D., 'Rational choice and irrational individuals or simply an irrational theory: a critical review of the hypothesis or perfect rationality', *Journal of Socio-Economics* 34 (5) (October 2005), 621–634. For Thurstone scaling, see Viswanathan, M., *Measurement error and research design* (Thousand Oaks, CA: Sage, 2005): Campbell, D.T. and Russo, M.J., *Social Measurement* (Thousand Oaks, CA: Sage, 2001); Likert, R., Roslow, S. and Murphy, G., 'A simple and reliable method of scoring the Thurstone Attitude Scales', *Personnel Psychology* 46 (3) (Autumn 1993), 689–690; Thurstone, L.L., *The Measurement of Values* (Chicago: University of Chicago Press, 1959). For an application of the case V procedure, see Malhotra, N.K., 'Marketing linen services to hospitals: a conceptual framework and an empirical investigation using Thurstone's case V analysis', *Journal of Health Care Marketing* 6 (March 1986), 43–50.

13. Yvert-Blanchet, N. and Fournier, A., 'Likeability, liking is not enough', ESOMAR, Fragrance Conference, Paris (November 2007).

14. Bottomley, P.A., 'Testing the reliability of weight elicitation methods: direct rating versus point allocation', *Journal of Marketing Research* 37 (4) (November 2000), 508–513; Herman, M.W. and Koczkodaj, W.W., 'A Monte Carlo study of pairwise comparison', *Information Processing Letters* 57 (1) (15 January 1996), 25–29.

15. Chrzan, K. and Golovashkina, N., 'An empirical test of six stated importance measures', *International Journal of Market Research* 48 (6) (2006), 717–740.

16. Siciliano, T., 'Magnitude estimation', *Quirk's Marketing Research Review* (November 1999); Noel, N.M. and Nessim, H., 'Benchmarking consumer perceptions of product quality with price: an exploration', *Psychology & Marketing* 13 (6) (September 1996), 591–604; Steenkamp, J.-B. and Wittink, D.R., 'The metric quality of full-profile judgments and the number of attribute levels effect in conjoint analysis', *International Journal of Research in Marketing* 11 (3) (June 1994), 275–286.

17. For an application of verbal protocols, see Shao, W., Lye, A. and Rundle-Thiele, S., 'Decisions, decisions, decisions: multiple pathways to choice', *International Journal of Market Research* 50 (6) (2008), 797–816.

18. Mick, D.G., 'Levels of subjective comprehension in advertising processing and their relations to ad perceptions, attitudes, and memory', *Journal of Consumer Research* 18 (March 1992), 411–424; Wright, P.L., 'Cognitive processes mediating acceptance of advertising', *Journal of Marketing Research* 10 (February 1973), 53–62; Wright, P.L., 'Cognitive responses to mass media advocacy and cognitive choice processes', in Petty, R., Ostrum, T. and Brock, T. (eds), *Cognitive Responses to Persuasion* (New York: McGraw-Hill, 1978).

19. Swain, S.D., Weathers, D. and Niedrich, R.W., 'Assessing three sources of misresponse to reversed Likert items', *Journal of Marketing Research* 45 (1) (February 2008), 116–131; Bartholomew, D.J., *Measurement* (Thousand Oaks, CA: Sage, 2006); Amoo, T. and Friedman, H.H., 'Overall evaluation rating scales: an assessment,' *International Journal of market Research* 42 (3) (Summer 2000),

301–310; Albaum, G., 'The Likert scale revisited – an alternative version', *Journal of the Market Research Society* 39 (2) (April 1997), 331–348; Brody, C.J. and Dietz, J., 'On the dimensionality of 2-question format Likert attitude scales', *Social Science Research* 26 (2) (June 1997), 197–204; Likert, R., 'A technique for the measurement of attitudes', *Archives of Psychology* 140 (1932).

20. However, when the scale is multidimensional, each dimension should be summed separately. See Braunsberger, K., Buckler, R.B. and Ortinau, D.J., 'Categorizing cognitive responses: an empirical investigation of the cognitive intent congruency between independent raters and original subject raters', *Journal of the Academy of Marketing Science* 33 (4) (September 2005), 620–632; Stanton, J.M., 'Issues and strategies for reducing the length of self-report scales', *Personnel Psychology* 55 (1) (Spring 2002), 167–194; Aaker, J.L., 'Dimensions of brand personality', *Journal of Marketing Research* 34 (August 1997), 347–356.

21. Herche, J. and Engelland, B., 'Reversed-polarity items and scale unidimensionality', *Journal of the Academy of Marketing Science* 24 (4) (Fall 1996), 366–374.

22. Sethi, R., Smith, D.C. and Whan Park, C., 'Cross-functional product development teams, creativity and the innovativeness of new consumer products', *Journal of Marketing Research* 38 (1) (February 2001), 73–85; Chandler, T.A. and Spies, C.J., 'Semantic differential comparisons of attributions and dimensions among participants from 7 nations', *Psychological Reports* 79 (3 pt 1) (December 1996), 747–758.

23. Kurpius, S.E., *Testing and measurement* (Thousand Oaks, CA: Sage, 2002); Miller, D.C. and Salkind, N.J., *Handbook of research design and social measurement*, 6th edn (Thousand Oaks, CA: Sage, 2002); Bearden, W.O. and Netemeyer, R.G., *Handbook of Marketing Scales: Multi-item measures for marketing and consumer behaviour research* (Thousand Oaks, CA: Sage, 1999), 456–464.

24. There is little difference in the results based on whether the data are ordinal or interval; however, see Nishisato, S., *Measurement and multivariate analysis* (New York: Springer-Verlag, 2002); Gaiton, J., 'Measurement scales and statistics: resurgence of an old misconception', *Psychological Bulletin* 87 (1980), 567.

25. Swenson, M., Yu, J.H. and Albaum, G., 'Is a central tendency error inherent in the use of semantic differential scales in different cultures?', *International Journal of Market Research* 45 (2) (2003), 213–228; Ofir, C., 'In search of negative customer feedback: the effect of expecting to evaluate on satisfaction evaluations', *Journal of Marketing Research* (May 2001), 170–182; Reisenwitz, T.H. and Wimbush, G.J. Jr, 'Over-the-counter pharmaceuticals: exploratory research of consumer preferences toward solid oral dosage forms', *Health Marketing Quarterly* 13 (4) (1996), 47–61; Malhotra, S., Van Auken, S. and Lonial, S.C., 'Adjective profiles in television copy testing', *Journal of Advertising Research* (August 1981), 21–25.

26. Brady, M.K., 'Performance only measurement of service quality: a replication and extension', *Journal of Business Research* 55 (1) (January 2002), 17; Stapel, J., 'About 35 years of market research in the Netherlands', *Markonderzock Kwartaalschrift* 2 (1969), 3–7.

27. Dawes, J., 'Do data characteristics change according to the number of scale points used?', *International Journal of Market Research* 50 (1) (2008), 61–77; Anderson, E.W., 'Foundations of the American customer satisfaction index', *Total Quality Management* 11 (7) (September 2000), 5869–5882; Coleman, A.M., Norris, C.E. and Peterson, C.C., 'Comparing rating scales of different lengths – equivalence of scores from 5-point and 7-point scales', *Psychological Reports* 80 (2) (April 1997), 355–362; Viswanathan, M., Bergen, M. and Childers, T., 'Does a single response category in a scale completely capture a response?', *Psychology and Marketing* 13 (5) (August 1996), 457–479; Cox, E.P., III, 'The optimal number of response alternatives for a scale: a review', *Journal of Marketing Research* 17 (November 1980), 407–422.

28. Dawes, J., 'Do data characteristics change according to the number of scale points used? An experiment using 5-point, 7-point and 1-point scales', *International Journal of Market Research* 50 (1) (2008), 61–104; Coelho, P.S. and Esteves, S.P., 'The choice between a five-point and a ten-point scale in the framework of customer satisfaction measurement', *International Journal of Market Research* 49 (3) (2007), 313–339; Dodge, Y., 'On asymmetric properties of the correlation coefficient in the regression setting', *American Statistician* 55 (1) (February 2001), 51–54; Alwin, D.F., 'Feeling thermometers versus 7-point scales – which are better?', *Sociological Methods and Research* 25 (3) (February 1997), 318–340.

29. Joshi, A., Tamang, S. and Vashisthaz, H., 'You can't judge a book by its cover! A way to tackle the severe acquiescence bias among Arab respondents', ESOMAR, Annual Congress, Montreal (September 2008); Jones, B.S., 'Modeling direction and intensity in semantically balanced ordinal scales: an assessment of Congressional incumbent approval', *American Journal of Political Science* 44 (1) (January 2000), 174.

30. Morrel-Samuels, P., 'Getting the truth into workplace surveys', *Harvard Business Review* 80 (2) (February 2002), 111; and Spagna, G.J., 'Questionnaires: which approach do you use?', *Journal of Advertising Research* (February–March 1984), 67–70.

31. Kulas, J., Stachowski, A. and Haynes, B. 'Middle response functioning in Likert responses to personality items', *Journal of Business and Psychology* 22 (3) (March 2008), 251–259; McColl-Kennedy, J., 'Measuring customer satisfaction: why, what and how', *Total Quality Management* 11 (7) (September 2000), 5883–5896.

32. Kruger, J. and Vargas, P., 'Consumer confusion of percent differences', *Journal of Consumer Psychology* 18 (1) (January 2008) 49–61; Amoo, T., 'Do numeric values influence subjects' responses to rating scales?', *Journal of International Marketing and Market Research* (February 2001), 41; Gannon, K.M. and Ostrom, T.M., 'How meaning is given to rating scales – the effects of response language on category activation', *Journal of Experimental Social Psychology* 32 (4) (July 1996), 337–360.

33. Alwin, D.F., 'Feeling thermometers versus 7-point scales – which are better?', *Sociological Methods and Research* 25 (3) (February 1997), 318–340.

34. For an example of a multi-item scale, see Bruner II, G.C. and Kumar, A., 'Attitude toward location based advertising', *Journal of Interactive Advertising* 7 (2) (Spring 2007), 3–15; Rossiter, J.R., 'The C-OAR-SE procedure for

scale development in marketing', *International Journal of Research in Marketing* 19 (4) (2002), 305–335; Brown, T., 'The customer orientation of service workers: personality trait effects on self and supervisor-performance ratings', *Journal of Marketing Research* 39 (1) (February 2002), 110–119.

35. For example, see Kidwell, B., Hardesty, D.M. and Childers, T.L., 'Consumer emotional intelligence: conceptualisation, measurement and the prediction of consumer decision making', *Journal of Consumer Research* 35 (1) (June 2008), 154–166; Delgado-Ballester, E., Munuera-Alemán, J.L. and Yagüe-Guillén, M.J., 'Development and validation of brand trust scale', *International Journal of Market Research* 45 (1) (2003) 35–53; Flynn, L.R. and Pearcy, D., 'Four subtle sins in scale development: some suggestions for strengthening the current paradigm', *International Journal of Market Research* 43 (4) (Fourth Quarter 2001), 409–423; King, M.F., 'Social desirability bias: a neglected aspect of validity testing', *Psychology and Marketing* 17 (2) (February 2000), 79.

36. Bassi, F., 'Latent class analysis for marketing scale development', *International Journal of Market Research* 53 (2) (2011) 211–232 ; Malhotra, N.K., Kim, S. and Agarwal, J. 'Internet users' information privacy concerns (IUIPC): The construct, the scale and the causal model', *Information Systems Research* 15 (4) (December 2004), 336–355; Borman, W.C., 'An examination of the comparative reliability, validity and accuracy and performance ratings made using computerised adaptive rating scales', *Journal of Applied Psychology* 86 (5) (October 2001), 965.

37. Clancy, K.J. and Rabino, S., 'The effects of visual enhancement on attribute/benefit desirability and brand perception measures: implications for reliability and validity', *Journal of Advertising Research* 47 (1) (March 2007), 95–102; Thompson, B., *Score Reliability: Contemporary thinking on reliability issues* (Thousand Oaks, CA: Sage, 2002); Sinha, P., 'Determination of reliability of estimations obtained with survey research: a method of simulation', *International Journal of Market Research* 42 (3) (Summer 2000), 311–317.

38. Sturman, M.C., Cheramie, R.A. and Cashen, L.H., 'The impact of job complexity and performance measurement on the temporal consistency, stability, and test-retest reliability of employee job performance rating', *Journal of Applied Psychology* 90 (2) (2005), 269–283; Viswanathan, M., *Measurement error and research design* (Thousand Oaks, CA: Sage, 2005), 269–283; Campbell, D.T. and Russo, M.J., *Social Measurement* (Thousand Oaks, CA: Sage, 2001).

39. Hunt, D., *Measurement and scaling in statistics* (London: Edward Arnold, 2001); Armstrong, D., Gosling, A., Weinman, J. and Marteau, T., 'The place of inter-rater reliability in qualitative research: an empirical study', *Sociology: The Journal of the British Sociological Association* 31 (3) (August 1997), 597–606; Segal, M.N., 'Alternate form conjoint reliability', *Journal of Advertising Research* 4 (1984), 31–38.

40. Kim, K., Cheong, Y. and Zheng, L., 'The current practices in food advertising – the usage and effectiveness of different advertising claims', *International Journal of Advertising* 28 (3) (2009), 527–553.

41. Singh, N., Baack, D.W., Pereira, A. and Baack, D., 'Culturally customizing websites for US Hispanic online consumers', *Journal of Advertising Research* 48 (2) (June 2008), 224–234.

42. Cronbach, L.J., 'Coefficient alpha and the internal structure of tests', *Psychometrika* 16 (1951), 297–334.

43. Waller, N.G., 'Commingled samples: a neglected source of bias in reliability analysis', *Applied Psychological Measurement* 32 (3) (May 2008), 211–223; Duhachek, A., Coughlan, A.T. and Iacobucci, D., 'Results on the standard error of the coefficient alpha index of reliability', *Marketing Science* 24 (2) (Spring 2005), 294–301; Peterson, R.A., 'A meta-analysis of Cronbach's coefficient alpha', *Journal of Consumer Research* 21 (September 1994), 381–391.

44. Flavián, C. and Gurrea, R., 'Digital versus traditional newspapers: influences on perceived substitutability', *International Journal of Market Research* 51 (5) (2009), 635–657.

45. Chandon, P., Morwitz, V.G. and Reinartz, W.J., 'Do intentions really predict behaviour? Self-generated validity effects in survey research', *Journal of Marketing* 69 (2) (April 2005), 1–14; Chen, G., 'Validation of a new general self-efficacy scale', *Organizational Research Methods* 4 (1) (January 2001), 62–83; McTavish, D.G., 'Scale validity – a computer content analysis approach', *Social Science Computer Review* 15 (4) (Winter 1997), 379–393; Peter, J.P., 'Construct validity: a review of basic issues and marketing practices', *Journal of Marketing Research* 18 (May 1981), 133–145.

46. Voorveld, H., Neijens, P. and Smit, E., 'The interactive authority of brand websites: a new tool provides new insights', *Journal of Advertising Research* 50 (3) (2010), 292–304.

47. Li, F., Zhou, N., Kashyap, R. and Yang, Z., 'Brand trust as a second order factor: an alternative measurement model', *International Journal of Market Research* 50 (6) (2008), 817–839.

48. Bergkvist, L. and Rossiter, J., 'Tailor made single-item measures of doubly concrete constructs', *International Journal of Advertising* 28 (4) (2009), 607–621.

49. Terblanche, N.S. and Boshoff, C., 'Improved scale development in marketing: an empirical illustration', *International Journal of Market Research* 50 (1) (2008), 105–119.

50. Shi, G., Shi, Y.-Z., Chan, A.K.K. and Wang, Y., 'Relationship strength in service industries: a measurement model', *International Journal of Market Research* 51 (5) (2009), 659–686.

51. Yan, J. and She, Q., 'Developing a trichotomy model to measure socially responsible behaviour in China', *International Journal of Market Research* 53 (2) (2011), 255–276.

52. Brandt, C., Pahud de Mortanges, C., Bluemelhuber, C. and van Riel, A.C.R., 'Associative networks: a new approach to market segmentation', *International Journal of Market Research* 53 (2) (2011), 189–210.

53. For further details on validity, see Kidwell, B., Hardesty, D.M. and Childers, T.L., 'Consumer emotional intelligence: conceptualisation, measurement and the prediction of consumer decision making', *Journal of*

Consumer Research 35 (1) (June 2008), 154–166; Alford, B.L. and Engelland, B.T., 'Measurement validation in marketing research: a review and commentary', *Journal of Business Research* 57 (2) (2004), 95–97; Keillor, B., 'A cross-cultural/cross national study of influencing factors and socially desirable response biases', *International Journal of Market Research* (1st Quarter 2001), 63–84; Sirgy, M.J., Grewal, D., Mangleburg, T.F., Park, J., Chon, K.-S., Claiborne, C.B., Johar, J.S. and Berkman, H., 'Assessing the predictive ability of two methods of measuring self-image congruence', *Journal of the Academy of Marketing Science* 25(3) (Summer 1997), 229–241.

54. For a discussion of the generalisability theory and its applications in marketing research, see Peng, L. and Finn, A., 'How far can you rely on a concept test? The generalisability of testing over occasions', *International Journal of Market Research* 52 (3) (2010), 353–372; Middleton, K.L., 'Socially desirable response sets: the impact of country culture', *Psychology and Marketing* (February 2000), 149; Abe, S., Bagozzi, R.P. and Sadarangani, P., 'An investigation of construct validity and generalizability in the self concept: self consciousness in Japan and the United States', *Journal of International Consumer Marketing* 8 (3, 4) (1996), 97–123.

55. Myers, M., 'Academic insights: an application of multiple-group causal models in assessing cross-cultural measurement equivalence', *Journal of International Marketing* 8 (4) (2000), 108–121; Hinkin, T.R., 'A review of scale development practices in the study of organisations', *Journal of Management* 21 (5) (1995), 967–988.

56. Devlin, S.J., Dong, H.K. and Brown, M., 'Selecting a scale for measuring quality', *Marketing Research* (Fall 2003), 13–16.

57. Van Auken, S., Barry, T.E. and Bagozzi, R.P., 'A cross-country construct validation of cognitive age', *Journal of the Academy of Marketing Science* 34 (3) (Summer 2006), 439–455; Page Fisk, A., 'Using individualism and collectivism to compare cultures – a critique of the validity and measurement of the constructs: Comment on Oyserman', *Psychological Bulletin* 128 (1) (January 2002), 78.

58. Barnes, B.R., Siu, N.Y.M., Yu, Q. and Chan, S.S.Y., 'Exploring cosmetics advertising in southern China – an investigation of Hong Kong and Shenzhen', *International Journal of Advertising* 28 (2) (2009), 369–393.

59. Swahar, G. and Swahar, J., 'Designing innovation: maximizing online respondent engagement through a game-way research design', ESOMAR, Innovate, Barcelona (November 2010); Cooke, M., Johnson, A., Rolfe, G. and Parker, K., 'Association for Survey Computing (ASC): "Pizzazz in research: renewing the rules of engagement"', *International Journal of Market Research* 53 (1) (2011) 115–125.

60. Reid, J., Morden, M. and Reid, A., 'Maximizing respondent engagement: the use of rich media', ESOMAR, Annual Congress, Berlin (September 2007).

13

Questionnaire design

Stage 1
Problem definition

Stage 2
Research approach developed

Stage 3
Research design developed

Stage 4
Fieldwork or data collection

Stage 5
Data integrity and analysis

Stage 6
Report preparation and presentation

The questionnaire must motivate the participant to cooperate, become involved, and provide complete, honest and accurate answers.

Objectives

After reading this chapter, you should be able to:

1 explain the purpose of a questionnaire and its objectives of asking questions that participants can and will answer, engaging participants and minimising response error;

2 understand the array of trade-offs that have to be made in the total process of questionnaire design;

3 describe the process of designing a questionnaire, the steps involved and guidelines that must be followed at each step;

4 discuss the considerations involved in designing questionnaires for international marketing research;

5 understand the ethical issues involved in questionnaire design;

6 appreciate how digital developments are shaping the manner in which questionnaires may be designed, delivered and experienced.

Overview

This chapter discusses the importance of questionnaire design and how researchers must put themselves 'in the shoes' of target participants in order to create an effective questionnaire. There are no scientific principles that can guarantee an optimal questionnaire; it is more of a craft that is honed through experience. Through experience, questionnaire designers will see that, given the information needs of the decision-makers they support and characteristics of target participants, they must make a series of trade-offs. These trade-offs are described and illustrated. Next, we describe the objectives of a questionnaire and the steps involved in designing questionnaires. We provide several guidelines for developing sound questionnaires. The considerations involved in designing questionnaires when conducting international marketing research are discussed. Several ethical issues that arise in questionnaire design are evaluated. The chapter concludes by examining how digital developments can help in the design of more engaging questionnaires for participants.

We begin with an example that articulates some of the main challenges of good questionnaire design and the impact of poor design. The second example illustrates an academic study where characteristics of the questionnaire design could provide an engaging experience for participants.

Real research | ## Digital versus traditional newspapers: establishing reliability and validity[1]

Survey Sampling International is a global provider of sampling solutions – online and telephone, both fixed/landline and wireless/mobile, multimode and postal mail (**www. surveysampling.com**). A key part of its operations is the management of access panels. There has been much criticism of sampling quality issues addressed at the use of access panels. Online panel companies have done much to tackle quality issues and conduct research necessary to understand online panellists, their motivation, behaviour, needs and wants. Researchers from Survey Sampling International presented the following views of some of the questionnaires that they have to work with, as designed by professional researchers:

As panel providers we are well aware of some of the quality issues surrounding questionnaire design; we see the questionnaires for ourselves and receive feedback on them from our panellists (some of whom 'vote with their feet' and drop out of the survey or worse, leave the panel). At the same time as we strive to develop algorithms to identify poor quality data we must endeavour not to penalise otherwise good panellists who treat poor questionnaires with the disdain they deserve. We recognise that by the time we get to see the questionnaire there are very real 'political' and practical issues impacting the ability to make changes to questionnaire design. In addition, full service (programming and hosting) offerings from panel companies have allowed end-clients to directly access fieldwork and tabulation services without the need to engage a research company. At this level the breadth of quality in questionnaire design becomes even more apparent.

Real research

Brands in songs[2]

The insertion of brands in songs is one of the most ignored forms of product placement, an idea that has aroused the interest of many advertisers. Researchers analysed the memorisation of 17 brands cited in two French songs. The study evaluated perceptions of placement, examining whether the approval of a song and the artist generated a more favourable attitude towards the use of brands. In order to test the researchers' hypotheses, an online survey was undertaken. The general principle was to invite participants to listen to two songs, then to question about the brands mentioned. The choice of songs, 'Tes Parents' by Vincent Delerm and 'Wonderbra' by MC Solaar, met several objectives. The idea was to choose songs in French that mentioned several brands and had comparable broadcast rates. Ten brands were counted in the song by Delerm and seven in the song by MC Solaar. The songs chosen were from different musical genres (French chanson and rap) in order to improve the external validity of the study, and to examine differences according to musical preferences. In designing the survey, the aim was to limit the length of the questionnaire without compromising the quality of the measurement of the variables. The average time required to complete the questionnaire was around 15 minutes. The clarity and the context of the use of the brand involved some subjectivity, and were measured on three-point scales developed by a brand specialist and a linguist. Familiarity with the song, approval or appreciation of the singer, of the song and of the music genre, were variables that the participants had no difficulty in understanding, and were therefore measured in a direct manner. The questionnaire was placed on a personal website and designed in the form of three successive web pages. The first screen contained general questions and questions that referred to the participants' interest in music, and it allowed them to listen to the songs. The second screen concerned the knowledge and appreciation of the songs and their singers, and the spontaneous memorisation of the brands. The final screen dealt with the assisted memorisation of brands, the perception of brand placement and with spontaneous memorisation (with the indication of the title and extracts from the texts) of the brands in several other songs. Compared with a continuous form layout, this presentation on three screens had the advantage of not revealing immediately the length of the questionnaire. It also prevented participants from modifying the responses they had already given, and made it possible to keep the object of the study secret until they had listened to the two songs.

Questionnaire definition

As discussed in Chapter 10, survey and observation are the two sets of techniques for obtaining quantitative primary data in descriptive research. Both methods require some procedure for standardising the data collection process so that the data obtained are internally consistent and can be analysed in a uniform and coherent manner. If 40 different interviewers conduct face-to-face interviews or make observations in different parts of the country, the data they collect will not be comparable unless they follow specific guidelines and ask questions and record answers in a standard way. A standardised questionnaire or form will ensure comparability of the data, increase the speed and accuracy of recording, and facilitate data processing.

Questionnaire
A structured technique for data collection consisting of a series of questions, written or verbal, that a participant answers.

A questionnaire, whether it is called a schedule, interview form or measuring instrument, is a formalised set of questions for obtaining information from participants. Typically, a questionnaire is only one element of a data collection package that might also include: (1) fieldwork procedures, such as instructions for selecting, approaching and questioning participants (see Chapter 16); (2) some reward, gift or payment offered to participants; and (3) communication aids, such as maps, pictures, music, advertisements and products (as in many online and face-to-face interviews) and return envelopes (in postal surveys).

Any questionnaire has three specific objectives. First, it must translate the information needed into a set of specific questions that participants can and will answer. Developing questions that participants can and will answer and that will yield the desired information is difficult. Two apparently similar ways of posing a question may yield different information. Hence, this objective is most challenging.

Second, a questionnaire must uplift, motivate and encourage the participant to become involved, to cooperate and to complete the task. Figure 13.1 uses a basic marketing model of exchange of values between two parties to illustrate this point. Before designing any questionnaire or indeed any research technique, the researcher must evaluate 'what is the participant going to get out of this?' In other words, the researcher must have an empathy with target participants and appreciate what they think when approached and questioned. Such an apprecia-

---

Figure 13.1

Exchange of values between researchers and participants

What the participant may want from the researcher:

- Tangible reward
- Confidentiality
- Interesting subject and experience
- Personal benefits from seeing the research completed
- Social benefits from seeing the research completed
- Being 'chosen' as a participant with expertise on a subject
- Research organisation known for excellence in research
- Rapport and trust

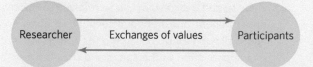

Researcher   Exchanges of values   Participants

What the researcher may want from the participant:

- Honesty
- Takes in reasons for the study
- Follows the instructions in completing the study
- Thinks through the issues before forming an answer
- Social benefits from seeing the research completed
- Says good things about the rationale for marketing research
- Says good things about the research process

tion of what participants go through affects the design of how they are approached, the stated purpose of the research, the rewards for taking part, and the whole process of questioning and question design.[3]

Not all participants are the same in what they seek from a questionnaire or interview process. In Figure 13.1, some participants may want to see some personal benefit, perhaps a tangible reward, while others may be happy to see the social benefits. Taking care in appreciating what participants expect from the questioning process can nurture responses that have been well thought through, are stated in honesty and are accurate.

Third, a questionnaire should minimise response error. The potential sources of error in research designs were discussed in Chapter 3, where response error was defined as the error that arises when participants give inaccurate answers or when their answers are mis-recorded or mis-analysed. A questionnaire can be a major source of response error. Minimising this error is an important objective of questionnaire design.

Questionnaire design process

The great weakness of questionnaire design is a lack of theory. Because there are no scientific principles that guarantee an optimal or ideal questionnaire, questionnaire design is a skill acquired through experience. Similarly, the correct grammatical use of language does not guarantee the optimal questionnaire. There may be certain participants who do not communicate in a 'correct' grammatical manner; such questionnaires may be confusing and meaningless. Therefore, this section presents guidelines and rules to help develop the craft of questionnaire design. Although these guidelines and rules can help you avoid major mistakes, the 'fine tuning' of a questionnaire comes from the creativity of a skilled researcher.[4] Developing the craft of questionnaire design requires the creative 'trade-off' of many factors. Figure 13.2 helps to illustrate some of the trade-offs that the questionnaire designer faces and that collectively make the design process problematic.

The design process is founded upon generating information that will effectively support marketing decision-makers. Establishing the nature of marketing problems and corresponding marketing research problems, i.e. defining the nature of effective support, was discussed in Chapter 2. Different techniques and sources of information were outlined to help in the diagnosis process, which feed directly into the stages set out below:

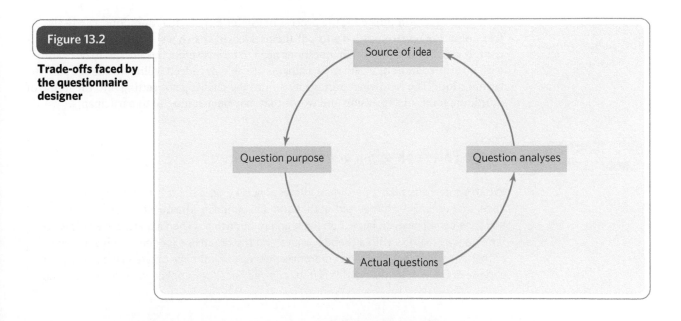

Figure 13.2

Trade-offs faced by the questionnaire designer

1 The 'source of idea' represents the culmination of the marketing decision-maker's and researchers' diagnoses and the information they have available at the time of commissioning a marketing research project.

2 From the diagnoses, and the statement of marketing and research problems, emerge specific research questions. Based upon the diagnoses, the purpose of each potential question should be established, i.e. 'question purpose'. Some research questions may be addressed through actual measurements in questionnaires. Other research questions may not be addressed by the use of questionnaires. The following example illustrates how a large global team of stakeholders established priorities for the questionnaire design of an online survey.

Real research   **Establishing question priorities[5]**

In an online survey to support the commercial vision for the Durex brand, research needed to address a number of discrete research objectives. These ranged from understanding sexual well-being and how it fits into people's lives, through exploring the sexual activities they take part in, to future trends. The stakeholder audiences in this study included internal business teams and divisions, sexual well-being and health experts, clinicians, politicians, opinion-formers and teachers. A first stage of awareness and communication on the project was undertaken by Durex to ensure that all parties were informed, convinced of the value of the study and kept up to date with key developments. To ensure that all business units brought their support to this initiative, managers across the globe were involved in the design phase, providing feedback on the questionnaire as well as by checking that the questionnaire translation was satisfactory for their country. Face-to-face meetings were instrumental in bringing the team together and ensuring they worked effectively. Regular day-long workshops and summits were used throughout the project. These sessions ensured that the coverage and output of the research were tailored to the needs of individual stakeholders. However, dealing with the needs of each stakeholder presented a challenge for the research, i.e. how to cover all needs within a finite questionnaire length and budget? In the end, they worked around this issue through prioritisation of needs and compromise. On discussing the consequences with the team, a solution was agreed which addressed each stakeholder's priority needs and which worked well in full fielding.

---

3 With clear question purposes, the process of establishing 'actual questions' can begin. At this point, the researchers have to put themselves 'in the shoes' of the potential participant. It is fine to say that certain questions need to be answered, but this has to be balanced with an appreciation of whether participants are able or indeed willing to answer particular questions. The following example illustrates the challenge of getting into the frame of mind, the forms of expression and words that may be meaningful to participants.

Real research   **Tango Facebook application questionnaire[6]**

When someone is taking part in an intercept survey on a brand's site or Facebook Fan Page, the research becomes part of that brand experience. The questionnaire's look, feel and tone can all have an impact on the brand relationship. When a questionnaire is written in a way that fits with a brand's values and the creative experience, the experience of the research is less likely to compromise feelings of intimacy between the participant and the brand. An example of this is from a Tango Facebook application that was created by collaboration between research experts from the brand and communications agency Hall and Partners (**www.hall-and-partners.com**), digital agency Nudge (**www.nudge digital.co.uk**) and advertising agency BBH (**www.bartleboglehegarty.com**). The introduction or invitation to participate reads:

> *Bongiorno! So, we both know you've used the Tango Head Masher 3000 facebook app to mash more heads than a Zombie DJ at a funeral themed rave. The voices in your head gave permission for us to talk to you so we're going to - Listen, we're even doing it now. You can hear us in your head can't you. Stop picking your nose, because we wanna ask you some questions about Tango, the facebook application and why your dad spends so long on the toilet. If you manage to complete all of the questionnaire without fainting or farting, then you'll be entered into a PRIZE DRAW for a Tango iPod. Yup, it's an orange iPod. Not one that you drink. Now, let the questions begin? Oh, that wasn't supposed to be the first one.*

Examples of Tango Facebook application question phrasing included: *It made me feel that I could marry a can of Tango* and *It made me feel Tango was pretty bloody good.*

4 Deciding how the data collected are to be analysed does not happen when questionnaires have been returned from participants. 'Question analyses' must be thought through from an early stage. The connections between questions and the appropriate statistical tests that fulfil the question purposes should be established as the questionnaire is designed. Again, trade-offs have to be considered. In Chapter 12, different scale types were linked to different statistical tests. As one progresses from nominal through ordinal to interval and then ratio scales, more sophisticated statistical analyses can be performed. However, as one progresses through these scale types, the task for participants becomes more onerous. This trade-off can be illustrated again in the following example.

Real research | **Trading off the participant task with statistical power**

In the study of banking practices in Europe, participants were asked who they thought were the top four banks in their country (ordinal scale). They were then asked why they thought the top two banks were perceived to be best and second best. This could be completed in a number of ways. A list of characteristics could be given and participants asked to tick those that they thought matched the bank. This would be easy for participants to undertake and produce nominal data. The same set of characteristics could be listed with participants asked to rank-order them. This task requires more thought and effort, though now produces the more powerful ordinal data. The same list could have been presented and participants asked to allocate 100 points using a constant sum scale. This would have been an even more onerous task but would have produced the more powerful interval scale. The questionnaire designer has to consider how onerous the task is for participants, especially when set in the context of all the other questions the participant is being asked, and trade this off against the meaning and interpretations that decision-makers would get from the findings.

5 The understanding that is taken from the data comes back to the 'source of idea'. By now the researcher or questionnaire designers may have collected other data, interpreted existing data differently, or been exposed to new forces in the marketplace. They may even now see what questions they should have been asking!

There can be no theory to encapsulate the trade-offs illustrated in Figure 13.2. Each research project will have different demands and emphases. With the experience of designing a number of questionnaires, the 'craft' of questionnaire design is developed and the balance understood to meet different demands and emphases.

In order to develop a further understanding of questionnaire design, the process will be presented as a series of steps, as shown in Figure 13.3, and we present guidelines for each step. The process outlined in Figure 13.2 shows that in practice the steps are interrelated and the development of a questionnaire involves much iteration and interconnection between stages.[7]

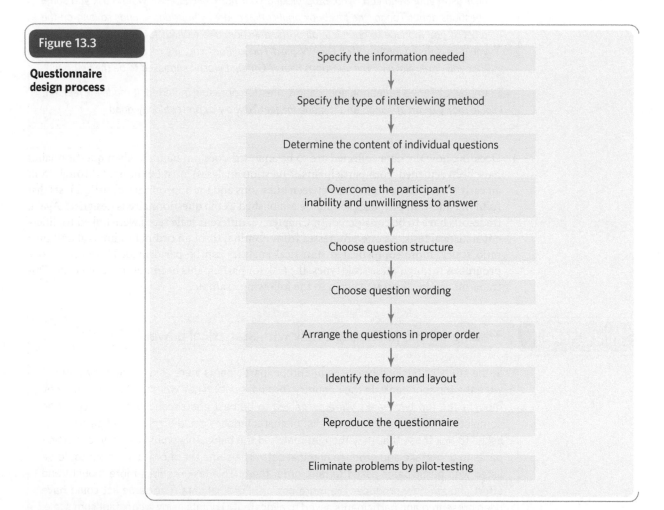

Figure 13.3

Questionnaire design process

Specify the information needed

↓

Specify the type of interviewing method

↓

Determine the content of individual questions

↓

Overcome the participant's inability and unwillingness to answer

↓

Choose question structure

↓

Choose question wording

↓

Arrange the questions in proper order

↓

Identify the form and layout

↓

Reproduce the questionnaire

↓

Eliminate problems by pilot-testing

Specify the information needed

The first step in questionnaire design is to specify the information needed. This is also the first step in the research design process. Note that, as the research project progresses, the information needed can become more clearly defined. It is helpful to review the components of the problem and the approach, particularly the research questions, hypotheses and characteristics that influence the research design. To ensure further that the information obtained fully addresses all the components of the problem, the researcher should prepare a set of dummy tables. A dummy table is a blank table used to present findings. It portrays how the analysis will be structured once the data have been collected.

It is also vital to have a clear idea of the target participants. The characteristics of the participant group have a great influence on questionnaire design. The wording and style of questions that may be appropriate for finance directors being surveyed about their IT needs may not be appropriate for retired persons being surveyed about their holiday needs or school-children being surveyed about games they play on mobile devices. The more diversified the participant group, the more difficult it is to design a single questionnaire appropriate for the entire group.

Specify the type of interviewing method

An appreciation of how the type of interviewing method influences questionnaire design can be obtained by considering how the questionnaire is administered under each method (see Chapter 10). Online and postal surveys are self-administered, so the questions must be simple, and detailed instructions must be provided. In online surveys and computer-assisted interviewing (CAPI and CATI), complex skip patterns and randomisation of questions to eliminate order bias can be easily accommodated. In face-to-face interviews, participants see the questionnaire and interact with the interviewer. Thus, lengthy, complex and varied questions can be asked. In telephone interviews the participants interact with the interviewer, but they do not see the questionnaire. This limits the type of questions that can be asked to short and simple ones. Questionnaires designed for face-to-face and telephone interviews should be written in a conversational style.[8]

Focus on | **IFM Sports Marketing Surveys**

Effect of interviewing method on

Online and postal questionnaire design

Please rank order the following film genres in order of your preference. Begin by picking out the genre that you like the most and assign it a number 1. Then find the second most preferred genre and assign it a number 2. Continue until you have ranked all genres in order of preference. Your least preferred genre should be assigned a rank of 10. No two genres should receive the same rank number. The criteria you use to establish your preference are entirely up to you. There are no right or wrong answers. Just try to be consistent.

	Film genre	Rank order
1	Action	_____
2	Animated	_____
3	Comedy	_____
4	Drama	_____
5	Factual	_____
6	Fantasy	_____
7	Light drama	_____
8	Romance	_____
9	Sci-fi	_____
10	Suspense	_____

Telephone questionnaire design

I will read you the names of film genres. Please rate them in terms of your preference on a scale of 1 to 10: 10 represents 'greatly preferred' and 1 represents 'not so preferred'. The higher the number, the greater the degree of preference for that genre. Now, please tell me your preference for these genres ... (READ ONE GENRE AT A TIME.)

	Film genre	Not so preferred									Greatly preferred
1	Action	1	2	3	4	5	6	7	8	9	10
2	Animated	1	2	3	4	5	6	7	8	9	10
3	Comedy	1	2	3	4	5	6	7	8	9	10
4	Drama	1	2	3	4	5	6	7	8	9	10
5	Factual	1	2	3	4	5	6	7	8	9	10
6	Fantasy	1	2	3	4	5	6	7	8	9	10
7	Light drama	1	2	3	4	5	6	7	8	9	10
8	Romance	1	2	3	4	5	6	7	8	9	10
9	Sci-fi	1	2	3	4	5	6	7	8	9	10
10	Suspense	1	2	3	4	5	6	7	8	9	10

Face-to-face questionnaire design

(HAND GENRE NAME CARDS TO THE PARTICIPANT.) Here is a set of film genres, each written on a separate card. Please examine these cards carefully. (GIVE PARTICIPANT TIME.) Now, give me the card with the film genre that you prefer the most. (RECORD THE GENRE AND TAKE THE CARD FROM THE PARTICIPANT.) Would you carry on through the cards and hand over, in order, your second, third, fourth, etc.? (REPEAT THIS PROCESS SEQUENTIALLY UNTIL THE PARTICIPANT HAS ONLY ONE CARD LEFT.)

	Genre rank	Genre name
1	1	_____
2	2	_____
3	3	_____
4	4	_____
5	5	_____
6	6	_____
7	7	_____
8	8	_____
9	9	_____
10	10	_____

In the S:Comm Leisure Time study where we focused upon cinema visits, ranking 10 film genres could be easily administered in an online survey, postal survey and on some mobile devices. Such a ranking may be too complex a task to be administered over the telephone or as an email survey. Instead, the simpler ranking task, where the genres are rated one at a time, could be selected to measure preferences. Note the use of cards to facilitate the ranking task in the face-to-face interview. Interviewer instructions (typed in capital letters) are much more extensive in the face-to-face interview. Another difference is that whereas the participant records the ranks in online and postal surveys, the interviewer records the film genres in the face-to-face interview. The type of interviewing method also influences the content of individual questions.

Determine the content of individual questions

Once the information needed is specified and the type of interviewing method decided, the next step is to determine individual question content: what to include in individual questions?

Is the question necessary?

Every question in a questionnaire should contribute to the information needed or serve some specific purpose that will help to elicit the desired information from participants. If there is no explicit and satisfactory use for the data resulting from a question, that question should be eliminated. In certain situations, however, questions may be asked that are not directly related to the needed information. It is useful to ask some neutral questions at the beginning of the questionnaire to establish involvement and rapport, particularly when the topic of the questionnaire is sensitive or controversial. Sometimes filter questions are asked to disguise the purpose or sponsorship of the project. For example, a survey on mobile devices sponsored by Nokia may also include filler questions related to Apple and BlackBerry. Questions unrelated to the immediate problem may sometimes be included to generate client support for the project. At times, certain questions may be duplicated for the purpose of assessing reliability or validity.[9]

Are several questions needed instead of one?

Double-barrelled question
A single question that attempts to cover two issues. Such questions can be confusing to respondents and result in ambiguous responses.

Once we have ascertained that a question is necessary, we must make sure that it is sufficient to get the desired information. Sometimes several questions are needed to obtain the required information in an unambiguous manner. Consider the question 'Do you think Coca-Cola is a tasty and refreshing soft drink?' A yes answer will presumably be clear, but what if the answer is no? Does this mean that the participant thinks that Coca-Cola is not tasty, that it is not refreshing, or that it is neither tasty nor refreshing? Such a question is called a double-barrelled question, because two or more questions are combined into one. To obtain the required information, two distinct questions should be asked: 'Do you think Coca-Cola is a tasty soft drink?' and 'Do you think Coca-Cola is a refreshing soft drink?'

Another example of multiple questions embedded in a single question is the 'why' question. The 'why' question seems very simple to write in a questionnaire and may be very simple to pose in an interview. It may not be a simple task in responding to such a question as it may tap into many constructs that for the participant may be difficult to conceive and/or articulate. In the context of the leisure time study focusing on cinemas, consider the question 'Why do you like the Odeon cinema?' The possible answers may include: 'I was taken there by my mother and have such happy memories of that visit', 'the Odeon is conveniently located for me to just drop in when I feel like it' and 'it has the best assortment of snacks and sweets'. Each answer relates to a different question embedded in the 'why' question. The first tells how the participant first learnt about the Odeon, the second reveals what the participant likes about the Odeon compared with other cinemas, and the third reveals what features of the cinema the participant favours. The three answers are not comparable and any one answer may not be sufficient. Complete information may be obtained by asking two or even more separate questions: 'What do you like about the Odeon compared with other cinemas?' and 'How did you first happen to visit an Odeon cinema?' Most 'why' questions about the use of a product or choice alternative involve two aspects: (1) attributes of the product and (2) influences leading to knowledge of it.[10]

Overcoming the participant's inability and unwillingness to answer

Researchers should not assume that participants can provide accurate or well-reasoned answers to all questions posed to them (assuming that they are willing to!). The researcher should attempt to overcome the participants' inability to answer. Certain factors limit the participants' ability to provide the desired information. The participants may not be informed, may not remember, or may be unable to articulate certain types of responses.

Is the participant informed?

Participants are often asked about topics on which they are not informed. Marketers and brand designers may have a deep and well-informed knowledge of the characteristics that shape their industries and environments. Their target consumers, however, may have little inclination to spend their time understanding such intricacies. Even if they do wish to understand issues like, for example, the environmental impact of the use of pesticides on the growth of cotton used in a shirt they are considering buying, there may be many complexities that make them uninformed. The following example illustrates how in issues such as social responsibility and environmental sustainability, there can be many different stories and 'facts' that lead to uninformed participants.

Real research	Understanding corporate social responsibility[11]

In a Global Change Network (**www.the-globalchangenetwork.com**) survey among communications professionals, more than two-thirds of participants believed that consumers would be increasingly interested in social and environmental efforts, not, however, at the expense of economic concerns, but in concert with them. Those products that demonstrated a clear value and were good for society and the environment were likely to prosper. Proper communications can help to clear up the confusion while boosting a company's revenues. How companies tell social and environmental stories is critical. Consumers are often uninformed or confused by much of the news and information they get. They do not necessarily understand green terminology, or how a company or product is really 'giving back'.

Filter question

An initial question in a questionnaire that screens potential participants to ensure they meet the requirements of the sample.

In situations where not all participants are likely to be informed about the topic of interest, filter questions that measure familiarity, product use and past experience should be asked before questions about the topics themselves.[12] Filter questions enable the researcher to filter out participants who are not adequately informed. The use of online, CATI and CAPI surveys allows extensive filtering to produce a variety of questionnaire formats that can be tailored to the familiarity, product use and past experiences of participants.

In the S:Comm Leisure Time study that covered the arts, sport and visitor attractions, the questionnaire could include questions related to the sponsors of art and sport. In different age groups there may be no awareness of who sponsored a team, individual or an event. This could be vital information for a brand designer and a sponsor and so questions on 'familiarity' or 'awareness' could be obtained for each sponsor. This would allow for separate analysis of data on sponsors about which the participants were not informed. A 'don't know' option appears to reduce uninformed responses without reducing the overall response rate or the response rate for questions about which the participants have information. Hence this option should be provided when the researcher expects that participants may not be adequately informed about the subject of the question.[13]

Can the participant remember?

Many things that we might expect everyone to know are remembered by only a few. Test this on yourself. Can you remember the brand name of the socks you are wearing (assuming you are wearing socks), what you had for lunch a week ago, or what you were doing a month ago at noon? Further, do you know how many litres of soft drinks you consumed during the last four weeks? Evidence indicates that consumers are particularly poor at remembering quantities of products consumed. In situations where factual data were available for comparison, it was found that consumer reports of product usage exceeded actual usage by 100% or more.[14] Thus, soft drink consumption may be better obtained by asking:

How often do you consume soft drinks in a typical week?

○ *Less than once a week*

○ *1 to 3 times a week*

○ *4 to 6 times a week*

○ *7 or more times per week*

Telescoping

A psychological phenomenon that takes place when an individual telescopes or compresses time by remembering an event as occurring more recently than it actually occurred.

The inability to remember leads to errors of omission, telescoping and creation. Omission is the inability to recall an event that actually took place. Telescoping takes place when an individual telescopes or compresses time by remembering an event as occurring more recently than it actually occurred.[15] For example, a participant reports three trips to the supermarket in the last two weeks when, in fact, one of these trips was made 18 days ago. Creation error takes place when a participant 'remembers' an event that did not actually occur.

The ability to remember an event is influenced by (1) the event itself, (2) the time elapsed since the event, and (3) the presence or absence of things that would aid memory. We tend to remember events that are important or unusual or that occur frequently. People remember their wedding anniversary and birthday. Likewise, more recent events are remembered better. A fashion shopper is more likely to remember what he or she purchased on the last shopping trip than what was bought three shopping trips ago.

Research indicates that questions that do not provide the participant with cues to the event, and that rely on unaided recall, can underestimate the actual occurrence of an event. For example, testing whether participants were exposed to a beer advertisement at the cinema could be measured in an unaided manner by questions like 'What brands of beer do you remember being advertised last night at the cinema?' (having established that the participant was at a cinema last night). Naming a brand shows that the participant saw the advert, took in the brand name and could recall it – three different stages. An aided recall approach attempts to stimulate the participant's memory by providing cues related to the event of interest. Thus, the important features to measure may be that the participant saw the advert and took in the brand name – the fact that the participant cannot say the brand name may not affect his or her purchasing intentions. The aided recall approach would list a number of beer brands and then ask 'Which of these brands were advertised last night at the cinema?' In presenting cues, the researcher must guard against biasing the responses by testing out several successive levels of stimulation. The influence of stimulation on responses can then be analysed to select an appropriate level of stimulation.[16]

Is the participant able to articulate?

Participants may be unable to articulate certain types of responses. For example, if asked to describe the 'atmosphere' of a cinema they would prefer to frequent, most participants may be unable to phrase their answers. On the other hand, if the participants are provided with alternative descriptions of cinema atmosphere, they will be able to indicate the one they like the best. If the participants are unable to articulate their responses to a question, they are likely to ignore that question and refuse to respond to the rest of the questionnaire. Thus, participants should be given aids such as pictures, maps and descriptions to help them articulate their responses.

Even if participants are able to answer a particular question, they may be unwilling to do so, because too much effort is required, the situation or context may not seem appropriate for disclosure, no legitimate purpose or need for the information requested is apparent, or the information requested is sensitive.

Effort required of the participants

Most participants are unwilling to devote much effort to providing information. Hence, the researcher should minimise the effort required of the participants.[17] Suppose that the researcher is interested in determining from which shops a participant bought goods on the most recent shopping trip. This information can be obtained in at least two ways. The researcher could ask the participant to list all the items purchased on the most recent shopping trip, or the researcher could provide a list of shops and ask the participant to indicate the applicable ones. The second option is preferable, because it requires less effort from participants.

Context

Some questions may seem appropriate in certain contexts but not in others. For example, questions about personal hygiene habits may be appropriate when asked in a survey sponsored by a health organisation but not in one sponsored by a breakfast cereal manufacturer. Participants are unwilling to respond to questions they consider being inappropriate for the given context. Sometimes, the researcher can manipulate the context in which the questions are asked so that the questions seem appropriate. For example, before asking for information on personal hygiene in a survey for a fast-food restaurant, the context could be manipulated by making the following statement: 'As a fast-food restaurant, we are very concerned about providing a clean and hygienic environment for our customers. Therefore, we would like to ask you some questions related to personal hygiene.'

Legitimate purpose

Participants are also unwilling to divulge information that they do not see as serving a legitimate purpose. Why should a firm marketing breakfast cereals want to know their age, income and occupation? Explaining why the data are needed can make the request for the information seem legitimate and may increase the participants' willingness to answer. A statement such as 'To determine how the preferences for cereal brands vary among people of different ages, we need information on …' can make the request for information seem more legitimate.

Sensitive information

Participants may be unwilling to disclose, at least accurately, sensitive information because this may cause embarrassment or threaten the participants' prestige or self-image, or be seen as too personal and an invasion of privacy. If pressed for the answer, participants may give biased responses, especially during personal interviews[18] (see Table 10.2). Sensitive topics include money, personal hygiene, family life, political and religious beliefs, and involvement in accidents or crimes. In industrial surveys, sensitive questions may encompass much of what a company does, especially if it reveals strategic activities and plans. The techniques described in the following subsection can be adopted to increase the likelihood of obtaining information that participants are unwilling to give.

Increasing the willingness of participants

Participants may be encouraged to provide information which they are unwilling to give by the following techniques:[19]

1   Place sensitive topics at the end of the questionnaire. By then, initial mistrust has been overcome, rapport has been created, legitimacy of the project has been established, and participants are more willing to give information. In this context, consider how sensitive classification questions such as gender, age and income may be perceived.

2   Preface the question with a statement that the behaviour of interest is common. For example, before requesting information on credit card debt, say 'Recent studies show that most European consumers are in debt.' This technique describes the use of counter-biasing statements.

3   Ask the question using the third-person technique (see Chapter 7): phrase the question as if it referred to other people.

4   Hide the question in a group of other questions that participants are willing to answer. The entire list of questions can then be asked quickly.

5   Provide response categories rather than asking for specific figures.[20] Do not ask 'What is your household's annual income?' Instead, ask the participant to indicate an appropriate income category. In face-to-face interviews, give the participants cards that list the numbered choices. The participants then indicate their responses by number.

6   Use randomised techniques. In these techniques, participants are presented with two questions, one sensitive and the other a neutral question with a known probability of yes responses (e.g. 'Is your birthday in March?'). The participants are asked to select one question randomly by flipping a coin, for example. They then answer the selected question yes or no, without telling the researcher which question is being answered. Given the overall probability of a yes response, the probability of selecting the sensitive question, and the probability of a yes response to the neutral question, the researcher can determine the probability of a yes response to the sensitive question using the law of probability. The researcher cannot, however, determine which participants have answered yes to the sensitive question.[21]

Choose question structure

A question may be unstructured or structured. We define unstructured questions and discuss their relative advantages and disadvantages and then consider the major types of structured questions: multiple choice, dichotomous and scales.[22]

Unstructured questions

Unstructured questions
Open-ended questions that participants answer in their own words.

Unstructured questions are open-ended questions that participants answer in their own words. They are also referred to as free-response or free-answer questions. The following are some examples:

- What is your occupation?
- What do you think of people who patronise secondhand clothes shops?
- Who is your favourite film personality?

Open-ended questions can be good first questions on a topic. They enable the participants to express general attitudes and opinions that can help the researcher interpret the responses to structured questions. They can also be useful as a final question in a questionnaire. After participants have thought through and given all their answers in a questionnaire, there may be other issues that are important to them and that may not have been covered. Having an open-ended question at the end allows participants to express these issues. As well as providing material to help the researcher interpret other responses, the participants have the chance to express what they feel to be important. Unstructured questions have a much less biasing influence on response than structured questions. Participants are free to express any views. Their comments and explanations can provide the researcher with rich insights.

A principal disadvantage in the case of face-to-face interviews is that the potential for bias is high. Whether the interviewers record the answers verbatim or write down only the main points, the data depend on the skills of the interviewers. Recorders should be used if verbatim reporting is important.

Another major disadvantage of unstructured questions is that the coding of responses is costly and time consuming. This was discussed in the context of analysing qualitative data in Chapter 9. We discussed how there is more use of software to cope with coding open-ended responses. This can be time and cost efficient if the research design employed uses a multiple cross-sectional or longitudinal design, but for the ad hoc survey, such approaches can still be very labour intensive.[23] The coding procedures required to summarise responses in a format useful for data analysis and interpretation can be extensive. Implicitly, unstructured or open-ended questions give extra weight to participants who are more articulate. Also, unstructured questions are not very suitable for self-administered questionnaires (online, CAPI, email and postal), because participants tend to be briefer in writing than in speaking.

Pre-coding can overcome some of the disadvantages of unstructured questions. Expected responses are recorded in multiple-choice format, although the question is presented to the participants as an open-ended question. In the case of a face-to-face interview, based on the participant's reply, the interviewer selects the appropriate response category. Because the response alternatives are limited, this approach may be satisfactory when the participant can easily formulate the response and when it is easy to develop pre-coded categories. In general, open-ended questions are useful in exploratory research and as opening or closing questions. They should be chosen with great care as their disadvantages can outweigh their advantages in a large ad hoc survey.[24] Open-ended questions do not necessarily have to contain large amounts of qualitative data and may involve simple but effective forms of analysis, as illustrated in the following example.

Real research   ## Comparing mobile with fixed phones for surveys[25]

A study targeted at Portuguese adults (aged 15 years and over) aimed to compare mobile survey with fixed telephone survey methods. The study focused on Internet usage, attitudes towards the Internet, cultural practices and demographics. Two surveys were conducted by the same survey company in order to overcome problems that might confuse the assessment of survey results if multiple sources of data collection were used. The survey introduction identified Marktest (**www.marktest.com**) as the sponsor, one of the best-known survey companies operating in Portugal. For both surveys, interviews were conducted at the company's CATI centre over the same time period and with the same set of interviewers working simultaneously on both surveys. Both for the fixed sample and the mobile sample, 1,000 interviews were conducted. In the fixed sample, interviews were conducted with the person who celebrated their birthday most recently or, in the absence of this adult, with any other adult available at the time of contact. In the mobile sample, interviews were conducted with the person who answered the phone, though only persons aged 15 years or older were eligible. A common measurement instrument was used for both surveys. The questionnaire included eight questions based upon nominal scales, three batteries of ordinal scales (25 items overall), one open-ended quantitative question on time spent on the Internet per week (participants were to report the hours they spend on the Internet as a number, integer or not) and a section on demographics. The open-ended quantitative question on the number of hours a week spent on the Internet revealed that, in the mobile phone sample, 50% of participants spent less than 5 hours a week online, while for the fixed phone sample the same proportion of participants spent less than 6 hours. In both samples, 25% of the participants spent more than 14 hours. The significance test for the mean revealed no significant differences at $p < 0.05$, which meant that mobile and fixed phone participants had similar Internet usage intensity: on average nearly 10 hours a week.

Structured questions

Structured questions
Questions that pre-specify the set of response alternatives and the response format. A structured question could be multiple choice, dichotomous or a scale.

Order bias (position bias)
A participant's tendency to choose an alternative merely because it occupies a certain position or is listed in a certain order.

Structured questions specify the set of response alternatives and the response format. A structured question may be multiple choice, dichotomous or a scale.

Multiple-choice questions. In multiple-choice questions, the researcher provides a choice of answers and participants are asked to select one or more of the alternatives given. Consider the following question:

Do you intend to buy a new watch within the next six months?

○ *Definitely will not buy*

○ *Probably will not buy*

○ *Undecided*

○ *Probably will buy*

○ *Definitely will buy*

Other (please specify)

Of concern in designing multiple-choice questions are the number of alternatives that should be included and the order of potential responses, known as position bias. The response alternatives should include the set of all possible choices. The general guideline is to list all alternatives that may be of importance and to include an alternative labelled 'other (please specify)', as shown above. The response alternatives should be mutually exclusive. Participants should also be able to identify one, and only one, alternative, unless the researcher specifically allows two or more choices (e.g. 'Please indicate all the brands of soft drinks that you have consumed in the past week'). If the response alternatives are numerous, consider using more than one question to reduce the information processing demands on the participants.

Order bias or position bias is the participants' tendency to tick an alternative merely because it occupies a certain position or is listed in a certain order. Participants may tend to tick the first or the last statement in a list, particularly the first. For a list of numbers (quantities or prices), there is a bias towards the central value on the list. To control for order bias, with many online or electronic forms of survey, alternative responses or scale items can be positioned randomly for each participant.[26] For manually prepared forms of the questionnaire, different versions can be prepared in which the alternatives vary from form to form. Each alternative should appear once in each of the extreme positions, once in the middle and once somewhere in between.[27]

Multiple-choice questions overcome many of the disadvantages of open-ended questions because these questions are administered quickly and, where used, interviewer bias is reduced. In self-administered questionnaires, participant cooperation is improved if the majority of the questions are structured. Also, coding and processing of data are much less costly and time consuming. The following example illustrates how a questionnaire built upon a large bank of multiple-choice questions proved to be an engaging and successful survey experience.

Real research   **IKEA – love where you live**[28]

In planning the launch of a new IKEA store in Perth, research showed that the main barriers for new customers visiting the old store were: (1) store too far away/journey took too long; (2) parking problem/no ease of shopping; (3) IKEA did not have the products that suited particular tastes. A new bigger store (26,600 m² vs. 6,640 m² at the old store) and its location (improved access to the freeway/train) was the starting point to addressing these barriers, but their key challenge was the third barrier indicating that a proportion of Perth's population did not see IKEA as a brand for them. This instigated the thinking that a communications campaign needed to be so much more than simply the launch of a new store; it was

about changing people's perceptions of IKEA. To underpin this, IKEA conducted an online survey, carried out two weeks prior to the launch campaign, hosted on a purpose-built microsite, set in a virtual suburban house. The survey aimed to measure views from Perth residents about their homes, habits, likes and IKEA. To promote the survey they chose online banners, radio advertising, in-store, electronic direct mail and a promotional tie-in with local radio station NOVA. The survey comprised 28 multiple-choice questions. By the time the survey phase had finished, there had been over 30,600 microsite visits spending an average of over 8 minutes on the site, 13,850 survey attempts and 9,474 completed surveys – against an initial target of 1,000.

Multiple-choice questions are not without disadvantages. Considerable effort is required to design effective multiple-choice questions. Qualitative techniques may be required to determine the appropriate wording and/or images for response alternatives. It may difficult to obtain information on alternatives not listed. Even if an 'other (please specify)' category is included, participants tend to choose among the listed alternatives. In addition, showing participants the list of possible answers produces biased responses.[29] There is also the potential for order bias.

Dichotomous question
A structured question with only two response alternatives, such as yes and no.

Dichotomous questions. A dichotomous question has only two response alternatives, such as yes or no, or agree or disagree. Often, the two alternatives of interest are supplemented by a neutral alternative, such as 'no opinion', 'don't know', 'both' or 'none', as in this example.[30]

The question asked before about intentions to buy a new watch as a multiple-choice question can also be asked as a dichotomous question.

Do you intend to buy a new watch within the next six months?

○ *Yes*

○ *No*

○ *Don't know*

Note that this question could also be framed as a multiple-choice question using response alternatives 'Definitely will buy', 'Probably will buy', 'Probably will not buy', and so forth. The decision to use a dichotomous question should be guided by whether the participants approach the issue as a yes-or-no issue. Although decisions are often characterised as series of binary or dichotomous choices, the underlying decision-making process may reflect uncertainty that can best be captured by multiple-choice responses. For example, two individuals may be equally likely to buy a new car within the next six months if the economic conditions remain favourable. One individual, who is being optimistic about the economy, will answer 'yes', while the other, feeling pessimistic, will answer 'no'.

Another issue in the design of dichotomous questions is whether to include a neutral response alternative. If it is not included, participants are forced to choose between yes and no even if they feel indifferent. On the other hand, if a neutral alternative is included, participants can avoid taking a position on the issue, thereby biasing the results. We offer the following guidelines. If a substantial proportion of the participants can be expected to be neutral, include a neutral alternative. If the proportion of neutral participants is expected to be small, avoid the neutral alternative.[31]

The general advantages and disadvantages of dichotomous questions are very similar to those of multiple-choice questions. Dichotomous questions are the easiest types of questions to code and analyse, but they have one acute problem. The response can be influenced by the wording of the question. To illustrate, 59.6% of participants in a survey agreed with the statement 'Individuals are more to blame than social conditions for crime and lawlessness in this country'. On a matched sample using an opposing statement, 'Social conditions are more to blame than individuals for crime and lawlessness in this country', 43.2% agreed.[32] To overcome this problem, the question should be framed in one way on one-half of the questionnaires and in the opposite way on the other half. This is referred to as the split-ballot technique.

Scales. Scales were discussed in detail in Chapter 12. To illustrate the difference between scales and other kinds of structural questions, consider the question about intentions to buy a new watch. One way of framing this using a scale is as follows:

Do you intend to buy a new watch within the next six months?

Definitely will not buy	*Probably will not buy*	*Undecided*	*Probably will buy*	*Definitely will buy*
○	○	○	○	○

This is only one of several scales that could be used to ask this question (see Chapter 12 for more examples).

Choose question wording

Question wording is the translation of the desired question content and structure into words that participants can clearly and easily understand. Deciding on question wording is perhaps the most critical and difficult task in developing a questionnaire. If a question is worded poorly, participants may refuse to answer it or answer it incorrectly. The first condition, known as item non-response, can increase the complexity of data analysis.[33] The second condition leads to response error, discussed earlier. Unless the participants and the researcher assign exactly the same meaning to the question, the results will be seriously biased.[34]

To avoid these problems, we offer the following guidelines:

1   Define the issue.

2   Use ordinary words.

3   Use unambiguous words.

4   Avoid leading or biasing questions.

5   Avoid implicit alternatives.

6   Avoid implicit assumptions.

7   Avoid generalisations and estimates.

8   Use positive and negative statements.

Define the issue

A question should clearly define the issue being addressed. Trainee journalists are cautioned to define issues in terms of who, what, when, where, why and way (the six Ws).[35] Consider the following question:

Which brand of shampoo do you use?

On the surface, this may seem to be a well-defined question, but we may reach a different conclusion when we examine it in terms of 'who', 'what', 'when' and 'where'. 'Who' in this question refers to the participant. It is not clear, though, whether the researcher is referring to the brand the participant uses personally or the brand used by the household. 'What' is the brand of shampoo. But what if more than one brand of shampoo is being used? Should the participant mention the most preferred brand, the brand used most often, the brand used most recently, or the brand that comes to mind first? 'When' is not clear; does the researcher mean last time, last week, last month, last year, or ever? As for 'where', it is implied that the shampoo is used at home, but this is not stated clearly. A better wording for this question would be:

Which brand or brands of shampoo have you personally used at home during the last month? In the case of more than one brand, please list all the brands that apply.

Use ordinary words

Ordinary words should be used in a questionnaire. They should match the vocabulary level of the target participants and/or be supplemented with graphic/visual support to convey issues simply.[36] In other words, even though we may speak the same language as our potential participants, there may be particular colloquialisms and ways of using words and terms they use which we should acquaint ourselves with. When choosing words, bear in mind the intellectual level of the target group of participants, and how comfortable they are with technical terms related to any products or services we are measuring. Most participants do not understand technical marketing words. For example, instead of asking 'Do you think the distribution of soft drinks is adequate?' ask 'Do you think soft drinks are easily available when you want to buy them?' Never forget that you are imposing your language upon participants in the form of a questionnaire. Your language communicates and puts participants in a particular frame of mind as they answer the questions you pose. Unless that language is meaningful to participants, they will be put in a frame of mind that you may not intend, and be answering different questions from those you set. The following example illustrates something of the magnitude of the challenge of using 'ordinary' words in questionnaire design.

Real research	**The forgotten 12 million**[37]

There are 12 million adults in the UK whose first language is English, but who have a reading and writing age between 9 and 14. This represents almost a third of the adult population. It is a large and diverse audience yet all have literacy issues which in some way limit their lives. Importantly, these people can read and write, they are not illiterate or necessarily interested in improving their skill levels. They may be pretty comfortable as they are, and not publicly acknowledge that they have a problem, and may not even be aware of any need to change existing behaviour patterns. Many are likely to feel isolated and defined by their skills deficit and will have almost certainly developed strategies to cover up the fact that they are limited in reading and writing. The implications for research and questionnaire design are considerable. First, individuals will not take part in research that requires reading and writing skills. They are not going simply to volunteer the information that they have literacy issues. They are not going to tell you why they do not come to groups or take part in research. They are just not going to participate. Similarly, they are rarely going to say '*I'm sorry, but the reason I don't want to do that questionnaire is because it's got too many words.*' If they think they are going to look at something complicated, they are just not going to participate. Second, you will not get the most out of them if they do take part. Questionnaires and forms may be completed by the partner or friend of a participant rather than the participant him- or herself. In short, these adults and their views will be forgotten. One third of the adult population – forgotten. Researchers need to consider how the views of these participants may be represented. How can the researchers create a research environment that is more appropriate to their needs and conducive to participation? How can they develop stimulus materials that are effective yet more suited to their needs?

Use unambiguous words

The words used in a questionnaire should have a single meaning that is known to the participants. A number of words that appear to be unambiguous have different meanings for different people.[38] These include 'usually', 'normally', 'frequently', 'often', 'regularly', 'occasionally' and 'sometimes'. Consider the following question:

In a typical month, how often do you visit a boutique?

○ *Never*
○ *Occasionally*
○ *Sometimes*
○ *Often*
○ *Regularly*

The answers to this question are fraught with response bias, because the words used to describe category labels have different meanings for different participants. Three participants who visit a boutique once a month may tick three different categories: occasionally, sometimes and often. A much better wording for this question would be the following:

In a typical month, how often do you visit a boutique?

○ *Less than once*
○ *1 or 2 times*
○ *3 or 4 times*
○ *More than 4 times*

Note that this question provides a consistent frame of reference for all participants. Response categories have been objectively defined, and participants are no longer free to interpret them in their own way. Additionally, all-inclusive or all-exclusive words may be understood differently by various people. Some examples of such words are 'all', 'always', 'any', 'anybody', 'ever' and 'every'. Such words should be avoided. To illustrate, 'any' could mean 'every', 'some', or 'one only' to different participants, depending on how they look at it.

In deciding on the choice of words, researchers should consult a dictionary and thesaurus and ask the following questions:

1 Does the word mean what we intend?

2 Does the word mean the same to our target participants?

3 Does the word have any other meanings?

4 If so, does the context make the intended meaning clear?

5 Does the word have more than one pronunciation?

6 Is there any word or similar pronunciations that might be confused with this word?

7 Is a simpler word or phrase suggested that may be more meaningful to our target participants?

Avoid leading or biasing questions

Leading question
A question that gives the participant a clue as to what answer is desired or leads the participant to answer in a certain way.

Acquiescence bias (yea-saying)
This bias is the result of some participants' tendency to agree with the direction of a leading question (yea-saying).

A leading question is one that clues the participant to what answer is desired or leads the participant to answer in a certain way. Some participants have a tendency to agree with whatever way the question is leading them to answer. This tendency is known as yea-saying and results in a bias called acquiescence bias. Consider the following question:

Do you think that patriotic French people should buy imported cars when that would put French workers out of employment?

○ *Yes*

○ *No*

○ *Don't know*

This question would tend to lead participants to a 'No' answer. After all, how could patriotic French people put French people out of work? Therefore, this question would not help determine the preferences of French people for imported versus domestic cars. A better question (though to determine preferences Likert scales could work better that a binary choice) would be:

Do you think that French people should buy imported cars?

○ *Yes*

○ *No*

○ *Don't know*

Bias may also arise when participants are given clues about the sponsor of the project. Participants may tend to respond favourably towards the sponsor. The question 'Is Colgate your favourite toothpaste?' could bias the responses in favour of Colgate. A more unbiased way of obtaining this information would be to ask 'What is your favourite toothpaste brand?' Likewise, the mention of a prestigious or non-prestigious name can bias the response, as in 'Do you agree with the British Dental Association that Colgate is effective in preventing cavities?' An unbiased question would be to ask 'Is Colgate effective in preventing cavities?'[39]

Avoid implicit alternatives

Implicit alternative
An alternative that is not explicitly expressed.

Implicit assumptions
An assumption that is not explicitly stated in a question.

An alternative that is not explicitly expressed in the options is an implicit alternative. Making an implied alternative explicit may increase the percentage of people selecting that alternative, as in the following two questions:

1 *Do you like to fly when travelling short distances?*

2 *Do you like to fly when travelling short distances, or would you rather drive?*

In the first question, the alternative of driving is only implicit, but in the second question it is explicit. The first question is likely to yield a greater preference for flying than the second question.

Questions with implicit alternatives should be avoided unless there are specific reasons for including them. When the alternatives are close in preference or large in number, the alternatives at the end of the list have a greater chance of being selected. To overcome this bias, the split-ballot technique should be used to rotate the order in which the alternatives appear.[40]

Avoid implicit assumptions

Questions should not be worded so that the answer is dependent on implicit assumptions about what will happen as a consequence. Implicit assumptions are assumptions that are not explicitly stated in the question, as in the following example:[41]

1 *Are you in favour of a balanced national budget?*

2 *Are you in favour of a balanced national budget if it would result in an increase in personal income tax?*

Implicit in question 1 are the consequences that will arise as a result of a balanced national budget. There might be a cut in defence expenditure, an increase in personal income tax, a cut in health spending, and so on. Question 2 is a better way to word this question. Question 1's failure to make its assumptions explicit would result in overestimating the participants' support for a balanced national budget.

Avoid generalisations and estimates

Questions should be specific, not general. Moreover, questions should be worded so that the participant does not have to make generalisations or compute estimates. Suppose that we were interested in households' annual per capita expenditure on clothing. If we asked participants the question:

> *What is the annual per capita expenditure on clothing in your household?*

they would first have to determine the annual expenditure on clothing by multiplying the monthly expenditure on clothing by 12 or even the weekly expenditure by 52. Then they would have to divide the annual amount by the number of persons in the household. Most participants would be unwilling or unable to perform these calculations. A better way of obtaining the required information would be to ask the participants two simple questions:

> *What is the monthly (or weekly) expenditure on clothing in your household?*

and

> *How many members are there in your household?*

The researcher can then perform the necessary calculations.

Use positive and negative statements

Many questions, particularly those measuring attitudes and lifestyles, are presented as statements with which participants indicate their degree of agreement or disagreement. Evidence indicates that the response obtained is influenced by the directionality of the statements: whether they are stated positively or negatively. In these cases, it is better to use dual statements, some of which are positive and others negative. Two different questionnaires could be prepared. One questionnaire would contain half-negative and half-positive statements in an interspersed way. The direction of these statements would be reversed in the other questionnaire. An example of dual statements was provided in the summated Likert scale in Chapter 12 designed to measure attitudes towards the Odeon cinema.

Arrange the questions in proper order

The order of questions is of equal importance to the wording used in the questions. As noted in the previous section, questions communicate and set participants in a particular frame of mind. This frame of mind is set at the start of the questioning process and can change as each question is posed and responded to. It affects how participants perceive individual questions and respond to those questions. As well as understanding the characteristics of language in target participants, questionnaire designers must be aware of the logical connections between questions, as perceived by target participants. The following issues help to determine the order of questions.

Opening questions

The opening questions can be crucial in gaining the confidence and cooperation of participants. These questions should be interesting, simple and non-threatening. Questions that ask participants for their opinions can be good opening questions, because most people like to express their opinions. Sometimes such questions are asked although they are unrelated to the research problem and their responses are not analysed.[42] Though classification questions seem simple to start a questionnaire, issues like age, gender and income can be seen as very sensitive issues. Opening a questionnaire with these questions tends to make participants concerned about the purpose of these questions and indeed the whole survey. They can also give the questionnaire a feel of an 'official form' to be completed (like a national census or a tax form), rather than a positive engagement and experience with a particular topic. However, in some instances it is necessary to qualify participants to determine whether they are eligible to participate in the interview. In this case the qualifying questions serve as the opening questions, and they may have to be classification questions such as the age of the participant.

Type of information

Classification information
Socio-economic and demographic characteristics used to classify participants.

Identification information
A type of information obtained in a questionnaire that includes name, address and phone number.

The type of information obtained in a questionnaire may be classified as (1) basic information, (2) classification information and (3) identification information. Basic information relates directly to the research problem. Classification information, consisting of socio-economic and demographic characteristics, is used to classify the participants, understand the results and validate the sample (see Chapter 14). Identification information includes name, postal address, email address and telephone number. Identification information may be obtained for a variety of purposes, including verifying that the participants listed were actually interviewed and to send promised incentives or prizes. As a general guideline, basic information should be obtained first, followed by classification and finally identification information. The basic information is of greatest importance to the research project and should be obtained first, before risking alienation of the participants by asking a series of personal questions.

Difficult questions

Difficult questions or questions that are sensitive, embarrassing, complex or dull should be placed late in the sequence. After rapport has been established and the participants become involved, they are less likely to object to these questions. Thus, in the S:Comm Leisure Time study where we focused upon cinema visits, information about the nature of film merchandise that has been purchased should be asked at the end of the section on basic information. Had participants perceived (incorrectly) that the survey was being used as a means to sell them merchandise, their trust in the survey and the nature of their subsequent responses could have been impaired. Likewise, income should be the last question in the classification section (if it is to be used at all).

Effect on subsequent questions

Questions asked early in a sequence can influence the responses to subsequent questions. As a rule of thumb, general questions should precede specific questions. This prevents specific questions from biasing responses to the general questions. Consider the following sequence of questions:

Q1: *What considerations are important to you in selecting a boutique?*
Q2: *In selecting a boutique, how important is convenience of its location?*

Note that the first question is general whereas the second is specific. If these questions were asked in the reverse order, participants would be clued about convenience of location and would be more likely to give this response to the general question.

Going from general to specific is called the funnel approach. The funnel approach is particularly useful when information has to be obtained about participants' general choice behaviour and their evaluations of specific products.[43] Sometimes the inverted funnel approach may be useful. In this approach, questioning starts with specific questions and concludes with the general questions. The participants are compelled to provide specific information before making general evaluations. This approach is useful when participants have no strong feelings or have not formulated a point of view.

Logical order

Questions should be asked in a logical order. This may seem a simple rule, but as the researcher takes time to understand participants and how they use language, the researcher should also take time to understand their logic, i.e. what 'logical order' means to target participants. All questions that deal with a particular topic should be asked before beginning a new topic. When switching topics, brief transitional phrases should be used to help participants switch their train of thought.

Branching questions should be designed with attention to logic, making the questionnaire experience more relevant to individual participants.[44] Branching questions direct participants to different places in the questionnaire based on how they respond to the question at hand. These questions ensure that all possible contingencies are covered. They also help reduce interviewer and participant error and encourage complete responses. Skip patterns based on the branching questions can become quite complex. A simple way to account for all contingencies is to prepare a flow chart of the logical possibilities and then develop branching questions and instructions based on it. A flow chart used to assess the use of electronic payments in online clothes purchases is shown in Figure 13.4.

Placement of branching questions is important and the following guidelines should be followed: (1) the question being branched (the one to which the participants are being directed) should be placed as close as possible to the question causing the branching; and (2) the branching questions should be ordered so that the participants cannot anticipate what additional information will be required. Otherwise, the participants may discover that they

---

Funnel approach
A strategy for ordering questions in a questionnaire in which the sequence starts with the general questions, which are followed by progressively specific questions, to prevent specific questions from biasing general questions.

Branching question
A question used to guide an interviewer (or participant) through a survey by directing the interviewer (or participant) to different spots on the questionnaire depending on the answers given.

Figure 13.4

Flow chart for questionnaire design

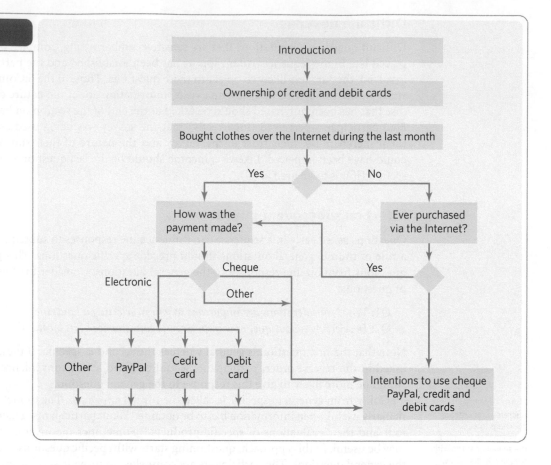

can avoid detailed questions by giving certain answers to branching questions. For example, the participants should first be asked if they have seen any of the listed advertisements before they are asked to evaluate advertisements. Otherwise, the participants will quickly discover that stating that they have seen an advertisement leads to detailed questions about that advertisement and that they can avoid detailed questions by stating that they have not seen the advertisement.

Identify the form and layout

The format, spacing and positioning of questions can have a significant effect on the results, particularly in self-administered questionnaires.[45] It is good practice to divide a questionnaire into several parts. Several parts may be needed for questions pertaining to the basic information. The questions in each part should be numbered, particularly when branching questions are used. Numbering of questions also makes the coding of responses easier. In addition, if the survey is conducted by post, the questionnaires should preferably be pre-coded. In pre-coding, the codes to enter in the computer can be printed on the questionnaire. Note that when conducting online, CATI and CAPI surveys, pre-coding of the questionnaire is built into the questionnaire design software. Coding of questionnaires is explained in more detail in Chapter 17 on data preparation.

Pre-coding
In questionnaire design, assigning a code to every conceivable response before data collection.

In surveys where there are hard copies of questionnaires, they should be numbered serially. This facilitates the control of questionnaires in the field as well as the coding and analysis. Numbering makes it easy to account for the questionnaires and to determine whether any have been lost. A possible exception to this rule is postal questionnaires. If these are numbered, participants assume that a given number identifies a particular participant. Some participants may refuse to participate or may answer differently under these conditions.

With the majority of questionnaires being administered online, researchers should not think of form and structure of a questionnaire in terms of designing a paper or postal survey experience. Such thinking can lead to a dull and monotonous survey experience for online participants. With many people experiencing rich, varied and exciting websites, to move then into a flat, text-based questionnaire experience can be most off-putting. An analogy may be in terms of games technology. Imagine a participant being used to a highly interactive, perhaps 3D games experience, and then being expected to engage with a 'Pong' (one of the earliest arcade videogames, a tennis sports game featuring simple two-dimensional graphics). There may be a moment of nostalgia for such an experience but it would be quickly dismissed as being boring and irrelevant. The following example illustrates how questionnaire software designers have to follow the use of devices with an eye to developing a positive participant experience.

Real research | **Surveys beyond SMS**[46]

A mobile technology that has been around for nearly as long as SMS (Short Message Service) is WAP (Wireless Application Protocol). WAP 1.0 is a decidedly monochrome affair (although colour is possible) and uses a very rudimentary markup language allowing for little sophistication. WAP 2.0 is a more sophisticated offering altogether which uses a subset of XHTML. This means that WAP 2 embraces colour and is capable of providing the benefits of rich media experience along with images, movies and the like, handset capabilities permitting. For the researcher, WAP offers a number of possibilities. It can provide a richer experience for the end user with all the niceties of interface elements such as dropdown lists and checkboxes, rich media such as graphics and better layout control. These all make slightly longer surveys more feasible, although thought has to be given to the nature of the mobile device. Merely translating a lengthy web survey onto a mobile handset does not fit with usage patterns or interface practicalities. There are other benefits compared with SMS, such as reduced service complexity and cost. For example, SMS connections can be time consuming and expensive to set up and run for a single overseas project. Apple's iPhone set a new standard for mobile browsing and catapulted the industry forward, as has Google's Android technology.

Reproduce the questionnaire

The above example and the arguments about the form and layout of an online, SMS and CAPI survey relate to reproducing the questionnaire. In the design of an online questionnaire, variations of language, branching, graphics and visuals and the survey experience can be almost tailored to individual participants. Time and money that in the past may have been devoted to the printing of paper-based questionnaires can now be avoided and invested in designing the form, layout and look to give participants the most engaging experience. In surveys where there are hard copies of questionnaires (or even in multimode surveys where participant have a choice of survey type), how a questionnaire is reproduced for administration can influence the results. For example, if the questionnaire is reproduced on poor-quality paper or is otherwise shabby in appearance, participants will think that the project is unimportant and the quality of response will be adversely affected. Therefore, the questionnaire should be reproduced on good-quality paper and have a professional appearance.

In face-to-face interviews and postal surveys, when a printed questionnaire runs to several pages, it should take the form of a booklet rather than a number of sheets of paper clipped or stapled together. Booklets are easier for the interviewer and the participants to handle and do not easily come apart with use. They allow the use of a double-page format for questions and look more professional. Each question should be reproduced on a single page (or double-page spread). Researchers should avoid splitting a question, including its response categories. Split questions can mislead the interviewer or the participant into thinking that the question has ended at the end of a page. This will result in answers based on incomplete questions.

Vertical response columns should be used for individual questions. It is easier for interviewers and participants to read down a single column rather than reading sideways across several columns. Sideways formatting and splitting, done frequently to conserve space, should be avoided. The tendency to crowd questions together to make the questionnaire look shorter should be avoided. Overcrowded questions with little blank space between them can lead to errors in data collection and yield shorter and less informative replies. Moreover, it gives the impression that the questionnaire is complex and can result in lower cooperation and completion rates. Although shorter questionnaires are more desirable than longer ones, the reduction in size should not be obtained at the expense of crowding.

Directions or instructions for individual questions should be placed as close to the questions as possible. Instructions relating to how the question should be administered or answered by the participant should be placed just before the question. Instructions concerning how the answer should be recorded or how the probing should be done should be placed after the question (for more information on probing and other interviewing procedures, see Chapter 16). It is common practice to distinguish instructions from questions by using different typefaces (such as capital, italic or boldfaced letters).

Pilot-testing

Testing the questionnaire on a small sample of participants for the purpose of improving the questionnaire by identifying and eliminating potential problems.

Although colour does not generally influence response rates to questionnaires, it can be employed advantageously in many respects. Colour coding is useful for branching questions. The next question to which the participant is directed is printed in a colour that matches the space in which the answer to the branching question was recorded. The questionnaire should be reproduced in such a way that it is easy to read and answer. The type should be large and clear. Reading the questionnaire should not impose a strain.

Eliminate problems by pilot-testing

Pilot-testing refers to testing the questionnaire on a small sample of participants to identify and eliminate potential problems as illustrated in the following example.[47]

Real research   ## Re inventing long-haul travel[48]

Air New Zealand worked with Synovate (**www.synovate.com**) to conduct a survey on all areas of designing the flying experience: seats, in-flight entertainment, food and beverage specification, service flow, kitchen design. The researchers also helped realise other ideas that had not been considered before, such as on-board events. The actual questionnaire had to be relatively straightforward in structure, but it was critical that the attitudinal statements at the core of the questionnaire were sufficiently discriminatory to separate out what might be quite soft attitudes and feelings. The researchers set up a series of statements for the questionnaire which were a combination of both the findings from a study conducted by the design consultancy IDEO (**www.ideo.com**) and their learning from previous Air New Zealand research. Lengthy discussions between Air New Zealand and IDEO, as well as the inclusion of the Qualitative Research Director, Grant Storry (**www.grantstorry.com**), led to the final draft. An online pilot questionnaire was tested on 40 long-haul travellers, who were clearly informed that they were testing the questionnaire. The test questionnaire contained only the attitudinal statements. Pilot participants were asked to pause after each block of attitudinal questions and reflect on whether these statements were clear, easy to understand, and whether they captured the concept of the wider need that Air New Zealand was interested in. Their open-ended responses were reviewed by the researchers and used to refine the statements. In addition, the pilot participants' actual ratings were analysed to determine whether each statement was sufficiently discriminative across the sample to be useful for segmentation purposes. The final questionnaire included a total of 50 attitudinal statements across the whole long-haul experience.

Even the best questionnaire can be improved by pilot-testing. As a general rule, a questionnaire should not be used in the field survey without adequate pilot-testing. A pilot-test should be extensive. All aspects of the questionnaire should be tested, including question content, wording, sequence, form and layout, question difficulty, and instructions. The participants in the pilot-test should be similar to those who will be included in the actual survey in terms of background characteristics, familiarity with the topic, and attitudes and behaviours of interest.[49] In other words, participants for the pilot-test and for the actual survey should be drawn from the same population.

Pilot-tests are best done by face-to-face interviews, even if the actual survey is to be conducted by online, postal or telephone methods, because interviewers can observe participants' reactions and attitudes. After the necessary changes have been made, another pilot-test could be conducted by online, postal or telephone methods if those methods are to be used in the actual survey. The latter pilot-tests should reveal problems peculiar to the interviewing method. To the extent possible, a pilot-test should involve administering the questionnaire in the environment and context similar to that of the actual survey.

A variety of interviewers should be used for pilot-tests. The project director, the researcher who developed the questionnaire and other key members of the research team should conduct some pilot-test interviews. This will give them a good feel for potential problems and the nature of the expected data. If the survey involves face-to-face interviews, pilot-tests should be conducted by regular interviewers. It is good practice to employ both experienced and novice interviewers. Experienced interviewers can easily perceive uneasiness, confusion and resistance in the participants, and novice interviewers can help the researcher identify interviewer-related problems. The sample size of the pilot-test is typically small, varying from 15 to 30 participants for the initial testing, depending on the heterogeneity (e.g. a wide array of education levels) of the target population. The sample size can increase substantially if the pilot-testing involves several stages or waves.

Protocol analysis and debriefing are two commonly used procedures in pilot-testing. In protocol analysis, the participant is asked to 'think aloud' while answering the questionnaire, as explained in Chapter 12. Typically, the participant's remarks are recorded and analysed to determine the reactions invoked by different parts of the questionnaire. Debriefing occurs after the questionnaire has been completed. Participants are told that the questionnaire they just completed was a pilot-test and the objectives of pilot-testing are described to them. They are then asked to describe the meaning of each question, to explain their answers, and to state any problems they encountered while answering the questionnaire.

Editing involves correcting the questionnaire for the problems identified during pilot-testing. After each significant revision of the questionnaire, another pilot-test should be conducted, using a different sample of participants. Sound pilot-testing involves several stages. One pilot-test is a bare minimum. Ideally, pilot-testing should be continued until no further changes are needed.

Finally, the responses obtained from the pilot-test should be analysed. The analysis of pilot-test responses can serve as a check on the adequacy of the problem definition and the data and analysis required to obtain the necessary information. The dummy tables prepared before developing the questionnaire will point to the need for the various sets of data. If the response to a question cannot be related to one of the preplanned dummy tables, either those data are superfluous or some relevant analysis has not been foreseen. If part of a dummy table remains empty, a necessary question may have been omitted. Analysis of pilot-test data helps to ensure that all data collected will be utilised and that the questionnaire will obtain all the necessary data.[50]

Summarising the questionnaire design process

Table 13.1 summarises the questionnaire design process in the form of a checklist.

Table 13.1	Questionnaire design checklist

Step 1: Specify the Information Needed

1   Ensure that the information obtained fully addresses all the components of the problem. Review components of the problem and the approach, particularly the research questions, hypotheses and characteristics that influence the research design.
2   Prepare a set of dummy tables.
3   Have a clear idea of the characteristics and motivations of the target participants.

Step 2: Specify the Type of Interviewing Method

1   Review the type of interviewing method determined based on considerations discussed in Chapter 10.

Step 3: Determine the Content of Individual Questions

1   Is the question necessary?
2   Are several questions needed instead of one to obtain the required information in an unambiguous manner?
3   Do not use double-barrelled questions.

Step 4: Overcome the Participant's Inability and Unwillingness to Answer

1   Is the participant informed?
2   If the participant is not likely to be informed, filter questions that measure familiarity, product use and past experience should be asked before questions about the topics themselves.
3   Can the participant remember?
4   Avoid errors of omission, telescoping and creation.
5   Questions that do not provide the participant with cues can underestimate the actual occurrence of an event.

Table 13.1	**Continued**

6   Can the participant articulate?

7   Minimise the effort required of the participant.

8   Is the context in which the questions are asked appropriate?

9   Make the request for information seem legitimate.

10 If the information is sensitive:

   (a) Place sensitive topics at the end of the questionnaire.

   (b) Preface the question with a statement that the behaviour of interest is common.

   (c) Ask the question using the third-person technique.

   (d) Hide the question in a group of other questions that participants are willing to answer.

   (e) Provide response categories rather than asking for specific figures.

   (f) Use randomised techniques, if appropriate.

Step 5: Choose Question Structure

1   Open-ended questions are useful in exploratory research and as closing questions.

2   Use structured questions whenever possible.

3   In multiple-choice questions, the response alternatives should include the set of all possible choices and should be mutually exclusive.

4   In a dichotomous question, if a substantial proportion of the participants can be expected to be neutral, include a neutral alternative.

5   Consider the use of the split-ballot technique to reduce order bias in dichotomous and multiple-choice questions.

6   If the response alternatives are numerous, consider using more than one question to reduce the information processing demands on the participants.

Step 6: Choose Question Wording

1   Define the issue in terms of 'who', 'what', 'when' and 'where'.

2   Use ordinary words. Words should match the vocabulary level of the participants.

3   Avoid ambiguous words such as 'usually', 'normally', 'frequently', 'often', 'regularly', 'occasionally', 'sometimes', etc.

4   Avoid leading or biasing questions that cue the participant to what the answer should be.

5   Avoid implicit alternatives that are not explicitly expressed in the options.

6   Avoid implicit assumptions.

7   Participants should not have to make generalisations or compute estimates.

8   Use positive and negative statements.

Step 7: Arrange the Questions in Proper Order

1   The opening questions should be interesting, simple and non-threatening.

2   Qualifying questions should serve as the opening questions.

3   Basic information should be obtained first, followed by classification and finally identification information.

4   Difficult, sensitive or complex questions should be placed late in the sequence.

5   General questions should precede specific questions.

6   Questions should be asked in a logical order.

7   Branching questions should be designed carefully to cover all possible contingencies.

8   The question being branched should be placed as close as possible to the question causing the branching, and the branching questions should be ordered so that the participants cannot anticipate what additional information will be required.

Table 13.1	Continued

Step 8: Design the Form and Layout

1 Divide a questionnaire into several parts.
2 Questions in each part should be numbered.
3 If hard copies of the questionnaires are used, coding should be printed on the forms to facilitate manual data entry.

Step 9: Publish the Questionnaire

1 The questionnaire should be designed to be visually engaging.
2 Vertical response columns should be used.
3 Grids are useful when there are a number of related questions that use the same set of response categories.
4 The tendency to crowd questions to make the questionnaire look shorter should be avoided.
5 Directions or instructions for individual questions should be placed as close to the questions as possible.
6 If hard copies of the questionnaires are used, a booklet format should be used for long questionnaires; each question should be reproduced on a single page (or double-page spread).

Step 10: Eliminate Problems by Pilot-testing

1 Pilot-testing should always be done.
2 All aspects of the questionnaire should be tested, including question content, wording, sequence, form and layout, question difficulty, instructions and rewards for taking part in the survey.
3 The participants in the pilot-test should be similar to those who will be included in the actual survey.
4 Begin the pilot-test by using face-to-face interviews.
5 The pilot-test should also be conducted by online, postal or telephone methods if those methods are to be used in the actual survey.
6 A variety of interviewers should be used for pilot-tests.
7 The pilot-test sample size should be small, varying from 15 to 30 participants for the initial testing.
8 Use protocol analysis and debriefing to identify problems.
9 After each significant revision of the questionnaire, another pilot-test should be conducted, using a different sample of participants.
10 The responses obtained from the pilot-test should be analysed to check the setup of tables and charts.
11 The responses obtained from the pilot-test should not be aggregated with responses from the final survey.

International marketing research

Questionnaire design should be adapted to specific cultural environments and all efforts made to avoid bias in terms of any one culture. This requires careful attention to each step of the questionnaire design process. The information needed should be clearly specified and form the focus of the questionnaire design. This should be balanced by taking into account any participant differences in terms of underlying consumer behaviour, decision-making processes, psychographics, lifestyles and demographic variables. In the context of demographic characteristics, information on marital status, education, household size, occupation, income and dwelling unit may have to be specified differently for different countries, as these variables may not be directly comparable across countries. For example, household definition and size vary greatly, given the extended family structure in some countries and the practice of two or even three families living under the same roof.

Although online surveys may dominate as a survey method in many Western countries, different survey methods may be favoured or more prevalent in different countries for a variety of reasons. Hence, the questionnaire may have to be suitable for administration by more than one mode. Using different survey modes can be readily facilitated by the use of online research communities. The following example illustrates a study on the use of online research communities in different countries and how online research is used in different countries.

Real research

Online research communities: a cross-cultural review of participants' perceptions[51]

Online research communities have been described as the fastest growing sector of marketing research. Among the benefits credited to online research communities are phrases such as *'authentic voice of the consumer'* and *'increased engagement'*. These benefits were unsupported by data, raising questions about whether participants really felt better about online research communities. A study examined this issue and compared views of different survey modes across five countries: Australia, Canada, China, Indonesia and the USA. The study represented a collaboration of four companies: Australia (Colmar Brunton, **www.cbr.com.au**), Canada (Social Data Research), China (SSI, **www.surveysampling.com**), Indonesia (Nielsen, **www.nielsen.com**), USA (SSI). An online survey looked at the perceptions of interviews conducted face to face, by telephone, online access panels, focus groups and online research communities. In Indonesia and China, research could be conducted online but infrastructure issues and access problems for some socio-economic groups continued to make the challenges for online research formidable. There were considerable similarities between the countries. This suggested that once a citizen of any of the five countries became a member of an online access panel, the citizen started to be like members of panels in other countries, at least in terms of views about the different ways to conduct research. It was possible to draw a distinction between the three more developed research markets (Australia, Canada, USA) and the two less developed research markets (Indonesia and China), with China being part-way between Indonesia and the three more developed markets. The two less developed research markets showed higher degrees of participants being members of online access panels and also being participants for other survey modes, suggesting that they represented a highly researched minority. This change probably reflected the fact that in Australia, Canada and the USA, research started by using random sampling approaches based on face-to-face, migrating to telephone, and more recently to online access panels. In China, and even more so in Indonesia, marketing research had jumped the earlier phases and has arrived online much earlier (and with the complexity of telephone research being identified with mobile phones from the outset). Chinese participants were the least positive about face-to-face research, and Indonesia was the most positive about telephone research. Across all countries, participants reported lower levels of satisfaction with telephone surveys than with any of the other survey modes. While research online communities were seen as having several strengths, they needed to be more engaging or they may turn participants off. One key area for improvement for online research communities was the need to ensure that participants felt the return they received was worth their effort. This may require both improvements to incentives and processes that increased other types of rewards, including recognition, feedback and the provision of information. One major caveat that should be borne in mind was that this study focused on online participants and their views of all modes. In Australia, Canada, and the USA, online was the single largest mode. However, in China, and even more so in Indonesia, online was a relatively smaller mode, but one that was growing rapidly.

Even if there is a global trend that questionnaires have to be designed to be administered in online surveys, there still remains a need for cultural adaptation of questionnaires. Examples of such adaptation can include the challenges of comprehension and translation. It is desirable to have two or more simple questions rather than a single complex question. In overcoming the inability to answer, the variability in the extent to which participants in different cultures are informed about the subject matter of the survey should be taken into account. Participants in some parts of the world may not be as well informed on many issues as people in Europe (and vice versa of course!). The use of unstructured or open-ended questions may be desirable if the researcher lacks knowledge about the determinants of response in other countries. Because they do not impose any response alternatives, unstructured questions also reduce cultural bias, but they are more affected by differences in educational levels than structured questions. They should be used with caution in countries with low literacy and indeed low readership levels.

The questionnaire may have to be translated for administration in different cultures. The researcher must ensure that the questionnaires in different languages are equivalent. The special procedures designed for this purpose are discussed in Chapter 26. Pilot-testing the questionnaire is complicated in international research because linguistic equivalence must be pilot-tested. Two sets of pilot-tests are recommended. The translated questionnaire should be pilot-tested on monolingual subjects in their native language, and the original and translated versions should also be administered to bilingual subjects. The pilot-test data from administering the questionnaire in different countries or cultures should be analysed and the pattern of responses compared to detect any cultural biases.

Ethics in marketing research

Several ethical issues related to the researcher–participant relationship and the researcher–client relationship may have to be addressed in questionnaire design. Of particular concern are the use of overly long questionnaires, asking sensitive questions, combining questions of more than one client in the same questionnaire or survey (piggy-backing) and deliberately biasing the questionnaire. Participants are volunteering their time and should not be overburdened by soliciting too much information. The researcher should avoid overly long questionnaires. An overly long questionnaire may vary in length or completion time depending upon variables such as the topic of the survey, the effort required, the number of open-ended questions, the frequency of use of complex scales and the method of administration. According to the guidelines of the Professional Marketing Research Society of Canada (**www.pmrs-aprm.com**), with the exception of home face-to-face interviews, questionnaires that take more than 30 minutes to complete are generally considered 'overly long'. Face-to-face home interviews can take up to 60 minutes without overloading the participants. Overly long questionnaires are burdensome on the participants and adversely affect the quality of responses. Similarly, questions that are confusing, exceed the participants' ability, are difficult, or are otherwise improperly worded should be avoided.

Sensitive questions deserve special attention. A real ethical dilemma exists for researchers investigating social problems such as poverty, drug use and sexually transmitted diseases such as AIDS, or conducting studies of highly personal products like feminine hygiene products or financial products.[52] Candid and truthful responses are needed to generate meaningful results. But how do researchers obtain such data without asking sensitive questions that invade participants' privacy? When asking sensitive questions, researchers should attempt to minimise the discomfort of the participants. It should be made clear at the beginning of the questionnaire that participants are not obligated to answer any question that makes them uncomfortable.[53]

An important researcher–client issue is piggy-backing, which occurs when a questionnaire contains questions pertaining to more than one client. This is often done in omnibus surveys (see Chapter 4) that different clients can use to field their questions. One sponsor's questions may take up a part of the questionnaire, while a second sponsor's study takes up the rest. Although there is some risk that one study will contaminate the other or that the questionnaire may not be very coherent, piggybacking can substantially reduce the cost. Thus, it can be a good way for clients with limited research budgets to collect primary data they would not be able to afford otherwise. In these cases all clients must be aware of and consent to the arrangement. Unfortunately, piggybacking is sometimes used without disclosure to the clients for the sole purpose of increasing the researcher's income. This is unethical.

Finally, the researcher has the ethical responsibility of designing the questionnaire so as to obtain the required information in an unbiased manner. Deliberately biasing the questionnaire in a desired direction, e.g. by asking leading questions, cannot be condoned. In deciding the question structure, the most appropriate rather than the most convenient option should be adopted, as illustrated in the next example. Also, the questionnaire should be thoroughly pilot-tested before fieldwork begins, or an ethical breach has occurred.

| Real research | **Questioning international marketing ethics**[54] |

In designing a questionnaire, open-ended questions may be most appropriate if the response categories are not known. In a study designed to identify ethical problems in international marketing, a series of open-ended questions was used. The objective of the survey was to elicit the three most frequently encountered ethical problems, in order of priority, to Australian firms that engage in international marketing activities. After reviewing the results, the researcher tabulated and categorised them into 10 categories that occurred most often: traditional small-scale bribery; large-scale bribery; gifts, favours, entertainment; pricing; inappropriate products or technology; tax evasion practices; illegal or immoral practices; questionable commissions to channel members; cultural differences; and involvement in political affairs. The sheer number of categories indicated that international marketing ethics should have probably been questioned more closely. The use of structured questions in this case, although more convenient, would have been inappropriate, raising ethical concerns.

Digital applications in marketing research

Software is widely used to design, create and administer questionnaires, for all survey modes. Although we describe the use of software for the most predominant mode, online surveys, the functions are essentially the same for questionnaires designed for other modes. Questionnaire design software systems help automatically to perform a variety of tasks such as:

Personalisation. The participant's name and personal responses are automatically inserted into key questions.

Complex branching. Responses to specific questions can trigger routes to other specific questions and sets of responses.

Randomise response choices. The order of presentation of response options in multiple-choice questions can be randomised for each participant to control for order bias.

Consistency checks. Inconsistent responses can be identified while the interview is in progress so that corrective action can be taken if needed.

Add new response categories as the interviewing progresses. If many participants give a particular response to a 'Other, please specify' category, that response will be automatically converted into a check-off category and added to the set of pre-specified response options.

In addition, questionnaire software has a variety of features that facilitate questionnaire design:

Question list. The user can select a variety of formats from a menu of question types such as open ended, multiple choice, scales, dichotomous questions, numerical. Moreover, one can use buttons, drop-down boxes (closed position or open position), checkboxes, or open-ended scrolling text boxes.

Question libraries. The user can select predefined questions or save questions used often in the question library. For example, the question library may contain predefined questions for measuring satisfaction, purchase intention and other commonly used constructs in marketing.

Questionnaire appearance. The user can select the background colours, graphics and flash applications used in a questionnaire from a range of available templates or create a customised template using the template manager.

Preview. The questionnaire can be previewed as it is developed to examine the content, interactivity, type of questions, branching and background design, and make any changes that may be needed.

Publish. The designer can create an HTML questionnaire, post it to a unique web page, create a database to collect the data on the hosting server, and obtain a unique URL to which participants can be directed.

Notification. The designer can create, personalise, send and track email and social-media-based invitations to participate in the survey.

As each participant completes the survey, the data are transferred online to the data file on the host server. The data can be analysed at any time, even when the survey is running, thus results can be examined in real time.

These features have given questionnaire designers the facility to craft surveys that, given their potential complexities and international reach, are far more cost and time efficient in comparison with approaches that depend upon hard copies of questionnaires. They have also enabled designers to create more personalised and appealing surveys for participants. These features, however, are not enough to create questionnaires that are engaging to participants. By examining other online experiences and what may engage users, questionnaire designers can use techniques and experiences to enhance their designs. The following example illustrates how ideas from online game designs can and are being developed for online questionnaires. Such approaches need much pilot-testing and it is not suggested that a questionnaire should be designed to be packed with quizzes, games and flash technology. The intent of this example is to reflect on the experience that participants' gain from completing a questionnaire. From an understanding of that experience the questionnaire designer should try to enhance that experience to keep participants in an honest, reflective and happy state.

Maximising online participant engagement through a game-way research design[55]

Online survey research faces a great deal of competition for participant attention and expression, ranging from online games to online social networks and alternative opinion sites. Social network sites, in spite of their high engagement levels, use games to further engagement among their participants. Extrapolating the idea to marketing research, ideas from gaming can improve engagement among online survey participants. Creating a fun element to an online survey could mean creating a relaxed atmosphere and motivating participants to put effort into completing a survey without resentment. For example, instead of asking about demographics in a question format, the participants could be allowed to create their own avatar; they could create the person who they are in terms of age, gender, hair colour, skin tone, dress. This could generate the information sought and at the same time be fun for the participants. Household details could be ascertained by allowing the participant to drag their household members using a cursor, and as they drag each household member onto the screen the participants could be questioned for the details of the member and the appearance of each household member could be customised accordingly. For example, a son aged 10 years could be made to look taller than a son aged 5 years. By this, the details of an entire household, its size, number of children and family type, could be generated in one go. Using advanced animation technologies, the participants could upload pictures or capture pictures using a webcam and cartoonise their pictures to use in the profile of their avatar for the questionnaire. Extending the fun element to give it a sense of 'play' could also be developed. When the participants create their profile, when they choose a particular option to change the avatar, e.g. change its dress, they could be allowed to shoot the option from among a set of swinging or bouncing (like a ball) options across the screen. The play element could be extended to other parts of the questionnaire: for example, in indicating levels of satisfaction for Brand X, participants could garland Brand X, shower X with roses or applaud, and the negatives could be indicated by punching or throwing tomatoes. The play element could be developed by introducing small puzzles and games in between sections of the questionnaire in the right combination to keep the participants in a playful state of mind. Participants could also earn reward points for small play exercises. Problem solving can be seen as a game and, in the case of a questionnaire, the participants could be allowed to face real-life problems, such as if their most often used brand was not available in the shop, then trade-off shopping scenarios could be set with limited access to money. These scenarios would enable participants to earn, spend and save reward points accumulated. The scenarios could be challenged by having a number of distracters to saving. This could be useful when measuring usage behaviour: the participants could be asked to make coffee; do their laundry; go shopping without asking questions. This could give spontaneity to their responses.

Summary

A questionnaire has three objectives. It must translate the information needed into a set of specific questions that the participants can and will answer. It must motivate participants to complete the interview. It must also minimise response error.

Designing a questionnaire is more of a craft than a science. This is primarily due to the interrelationship of stages and the trade-offs that questionnaire designers make in balancing the source of ideas, question purposes, actual questions and question analyses. The steps involved in the questionnaire design process involve:

1 Specifying the information needed. Understanding what information decision-makers need and the priorities they face.

2 Specifying the type of interviewing method. Understanding which means of eliciting the information will work best, given the research design constraints that the researcher has to work with.

3 Determining the content of individual questions. Understanding the purpose of each question and working out how a posed question may fulfil that purpose.

4 Overcoming the participants' inability and unwillingness to answer questions. Understanding the process of approaching and questioning participants – from their perspective. Knowing what benefits they get from taking part in the survey process. Knowing what they find engaging and/or boring as a questionnaire experience.

5 Choosing the question structure. Understanding how individual questions help to elicit information from participants and help them to express their feelings.

6 Choosing the question wording. Understanding the meaning of words from the perspective of the participant.

7 Arranging the questions in a proper order. Understanding what 'proper' means from the perspective of the participant. Recognising that, as each question is posed to a participant and the participant thinks about the response, he or she changes. Information is not only drawn out of participants, it is communicated to them and they change as each question is tackled.

8 Identifying the form and layout of the questionnaire. Understanding how in a self-completion scenario the form and layout motivate and help the participant to answer the questions in an honest and reflective manner. Understanding when needed how the form and layout help the interviewer to conduct and record the interview.

9 Publishing the questionnaire. Understanding how the professional appearance of a questionnaire affects the perceived credibility and professional ability of researchers.

10 Eliminating problems by pilot-testing. Understanding that no matter how much experience the researcher has in designing questionnaires – the issues, participant characteristics and context of questioning make each survey unique – pilot-testing is vital.

Questions

1 What is the purpose of a questionnaire?

2 What expectations does the researcher have of potential questionnaire participants – in terms of how they will react to the experience of completing a questionnaire?

3 What does the researcher have to offer potential questionnaire participants? Why should this question be considered?

4 How would you determine whether a specific question should be included in a questionnaire?

5 What are the reasons why participants may be (a) unable to answer and (b) unwilling to answer the question asked?

6 Explain the errors of omission, telescoping and creation. What can be done to reduce such errors?

7 Explain the concepts of aided and unaided recall.

8 What can a researcher do to make the request for information seem legitimate?

9 What are the advantages and disadvantages of unstructured questions?

10 What are the issues involved in designing multiple-choice questions?

11 What are the guidelines available for deciding on question wording?

12 What is a leading question? Give an example.

13 What is the proper order for questions intended to obtain basic, classification and identification information?

14 What guidelines are available for deciding on the form and layout of a questionnaire?

15 Describe the issues involved in pilot-testing a questionnaire.

Exercises

1 Visit the website of one of the online marketing research firms, e.g. **www. hostedsurvey.com**. Choose one of the sample surveys and critically analyse the questionnaire using the principles discussed in this chapter.

2 Heineken beer would like to conduct a survey of 18–25-year-old Europeans to determine the characteristics of its corporate image. Design a full questionnaire using survey software such as SNAP. Administer this questionnaire in a mode of your choice to 25 fellow students. Write a short report based upon your experience of using the software, the findings you have generated and any limitations you see in the whole process (i.e. how would you do this differently if you were to repeat it?).

3 Develop a questionnaire for determining household preferences for popular brands of cold breakfast cereals. Administer the questionnaire to five adult females, five adult males and five children. How would you modify the questionnaire if it was to be administered by telephone? What changes would be necessary if it was to be administered online? Are there distinctive characteristics of your different participant types that could affect your questionnaire design?

4 You have been hired as a management trainee by a firm that manufactures major household appliances. Your boss has asked you to develop a questionnaire to determine how households plan, purchase and use major appliances. This questionnaire is to be used in five European countries. However, you feel that you do not have the expertise or the experience to construct such a complex questionnaire. Present your case to your boss.

5 In a small group discuss the following issues: 'Because questionnaire design is a craft, it is useless to follow a rigid set of guidelines. Rather the process should be left entirely to the creativity and ingenuity of the researcher.' And 'Asking classification questions at the start of a questionnaire only upsets the sensibilities of older participants; young participants are not concerned about where these questions are asked.'

Video case exercise: St Paul's Cathedral

The head of marketing and PR wishes to design a number of kiosks to administer a visitor survey but is concerned about response rates and the quality of responses from participants. What advice would you give to the head to ensure that participants find value and are fully engaged in the survey experience?

Notes

1. Flavián, C. and Gurrea, R., 'Digital versus traditional newspapers: influences on perceived substitutability', *International Journal of Market Research* 51 (5) (2009), 635–657.

2. Delattre, E. and Colovic, A., 'Memory and perception of brand mentions and placement of brands in songs', *International Journal of Advertising* 28 (5) (2009), 807–842.

3. Livin, J., 'Improving response rates in web surveys with default setting: the effects of default on web survey participation and permission', *International Journal of Market Research* 53 (1) (2011), 75–94; Balabanis, G., Mitchell, V.-W. and Heinonen-Mavrovouniotis, S., 'SMS-based surveys: strategies to improve participation', *International Journal of Advertising* 26 (3) (2007), 369–385.

4. The founding reference to this subject is Payne, S.L., *The Art of Asking Questions* (Princeton, NJ: Princeton University Press, 1951). See also Lietz, P., 'Research into questionnaire design: a summary of the literature', *International Journal of Market Research* 52 (2) (2010), 249–272; Schrage, M., 'Survey says', *Adweek Magazines' Technology Marketing* 22 (1) (January 2002), 11; Gillham, B., *Developing a questionnaire* (New York: Continuum International, 2000).

5. Murray, D. and Manuel, L., 'Coming together . . .', Market Research Society, Annual Conference (2008).

6. Woodnutt, T. and Owen, R., 'The research industry needs to embrace radical change in order to thrive and survive in the digital era', Market Research Society: Annual Conference (2010).

7. These guidelines are drawn from several books on questionnaire design: Dillman, D.A., Smyth, J.D. and Melani, L., *Internet, Mail, and Mixed-Mode Surveys: The Tailored Design Method*, 3rd edn (Hoboken, NJ: Wiley, 2008); Bradburn, N.M., Sudman, S. and Wansink, B., *Asking Questions: The Definitive Guide to Questionnaire Design – For Market Research, Political Polls, and Social and Health Questionnaires* (San Francisco: Jossey-Bass, 2004); Gillham, B., *Developing a questionnaire* (New York: Continuum International, 2000); Peterson, R.A., *Constructing Effective Questionnaires* (Thousand Oaks, CA: Sage, 2000); Schuman, H. and Presser, S., *Questions and Answers in Attitude Surveys* (Thousand Oaks, CA: Sage, 1996); Fink, A., *How to Ask Survey Questions* (Thousand Oaks, CA: Sage, 1995); Sudman, S. and Bradburn, N.M., *Asking Questions* (San Francisco: Jossey-Bass, 1983).

8. Cierpicki, S., Davis, C., Eddy, C., Lorch, J., Phillips, K., Poynter, R., York, S. and Zuo, B., 'From clipboards to online research communities: a cross cultural review of respondents' perceptions', ESOMAR, Congress Odyssey, Athens (September 2010).

9. Biering, P., Becker, H., Calvin, A. and Grobe, S.J., 'Casting light on the concept of patient satisfaction by studying the construct validity and the sensitivity of a questionnaire', *International Journal of Health Care Quality Assurance* 19 (3) (2006), 246–258; Clark, B.H., 'Bad examples', *Marketing Management* 12 (2) (2003), 34–38; Bordeaux, D.B., 'Interviewing – part II: Getting the most out of interview questions', *Motor Age* 121 (2) (February 2002), 38–40.

10. Bressette, K., 'Deeply understanding the mind to unmask the inner human', ESOMAR, Qualitative, Marrakech (November 2009); Reynolds, T.J., 'Methodological

and strategy development implications of decision segmentation', *Journal of Advertising Research* 46 (4) (December 2006) 445–461; Healey, B., Macpherson, T. and Kuijten, B., 'An empirical evaluation of three web survey design principles', *Marketing Bulletin*, 16 (May 2005), 1–9; Hess, J., 'The effects of person-level versus household-level questionnaire design on survey estimates and data quality', *Public Opinion Quarterly* 65 (4) (Winter 2001), 574–584.

11. Fairfield, A., 'Doing the right thing is a brand communicator's imperative', *Admap* 504 (April 2009), 32–35.

12. Alioto, M.F. and Parrett, M., 'The use of "respondent-based intelligent" surveys in cross-national research', ESOMAR, Latin American Conference, São Paulo (May 2002), 157–220; Knauper, B., 'Filter questions and question interpretation: presuppositions at work', *Public Opinion Quarterly* 62 (1) (Spring 1998), 70–78; Stapel, J., 'Observations: a brief observation about likeability and interestingness of advertising', *Journal of Advertising Research* 34 (2) (March/April 1994), 79–80.

13. Graeff, T.R., 'Reducing uninformed responses: the effects of product class familiarity and measuring brand knowledge on surveys', *Psychology and Marketing* 24 (8) (August 2007), 681–702; Graeff, T.R., 'Uninformed response bias in telephone surveys', *Journal of Business Research* 55 (3) (March 2002), 251.

14. Braunsberger, K., Gates, R. and Ortinau, D.J., 'Prospective respondent integrity behaviour in replying to direct mail questionnaires: a contributor in overestimating nonresponse rates', *Journal of Business Research* 58 (3) (March 2005), 260–267; Lee, E., Hu, M.Y. and Toh, R.S., 'Are consumer survey results distorted? Systematic impact of behavioural frequency and duration on survey response errors', *Journal of Marketing Research* 37 (1) (February 2000), 125–133.

15. Wilson, E.J. and Woodside, A.G., 'Respondent inaccuracy', *Journal of Advertising Research* 42 (5) (September/October 2002), 7–18; Gaskell, G.D., 'Telescoping of landmark events: implications for survey research', *Public Opinion Quarterly* 64 (1) (Spring 2000), 77–89; Menon, G., Raghubir, P. and Schwarz, N., 'Behavioural frequency judgments: an accessibility-diagnosticity framework', *Journal of Consumer Research* 22 (2) (September 1995), 212–228; Cook, W.A., 'Telescoping and memory's other tricks', *Journal of Advertising Research* (February–March 1987), 5–8.

16. Goodrich, K., 'What's up? Exploring upper and lower visual field advertising effects', *Journal of Advertising Research* 50 (1) (2010), 91–106.

17. Bednall, D.H.B., Adam, S. and Plocinski, K., 'Ethics in practice: using compliance techniques to boost telephone response rates', *International Journal of Market Research* 52 (2) (2010), 155–168.

18. Nancarrow, C. and Brace, I., 'Let's get ethical: dealing with socially desirable responding online', Market Research Society, Annual Conference (2008); Tourangeau, R. and Yan, T., 'Sensitive questions in surveys', *Psychological Bulletin* 133 (5) (September 2007), 859–883; France, M., 'Why privacy notices are a sham', *Business Week* (18 June 2001), 82.

19. Manfreda, K.L., Bosnjak, M., Berzelak, J., Haas, I. and Vehovar, V., 'Web surveys versus other survey modes: a meta analysis comparing response rates', *International Journal of*

Market Research 50 (1) (2008), 79–104; Hanrahan, P., 'Mine your own business', *Target Marketing* (February 2000), 32; Tourangeau, R. and Smith, T.W., 'Asking sensitive questions: the impact of data collection mode, question format, and question context', *Public Opinion Quarterly* 60 (20) (Summer 1996), 275–304.

20. Maehle, N., and Supphellen, M., 'In search of the sources of brand personality', *International Journal of Market Research* 53 (1) (2011), 95–114; Peterson, R.A., 'Asking the age question: a research note', *Public Opinion Quarterly* (Spring 1984), 379–383.

21. Nancarrow, C. and Brace, I., 'Let's get ethical: dealing with socially desirable responding online', Market Research Society, Annual Conference (2008); Larkins, E.R., Hume, E.C. and Garcha, B.S., 'The validity of the randomized response method in tax ethics research', *Journal of Applied Business Research* 13 (3) (Summer 1997), 25–32; Mukhopadhyay, P., 'A note on UMVU-estimation under randomized-response model', *Communications in Statistics – Theory and Methods* 26 (10) (1997), 2415–2420.

22. Millican, P. and Kolb, C., 'Connecting with Elizabeth: using artificial intelligence as a data collection aid', Market Research Society, Annual Conference (2006); Patten, M.L., *Questionnaire Research: A practical guide* (Los Angeles: Pyrczak, 2001); Newman, L.M., 'That's a good question', *American Demographics* (Marketing Tools) (June 1995), 10–13.

23. Esuli, A. and Sebastiani, F., 'Machines that learn how to code open-ended survey data', *International Journal of Market Research* 52 (6) (2010), 775–800; Popping, R., *Computer-assisted text analysis* (Thousand Oaks, CA: Sage, 2000); Luyens, S., 'Coding verbatims by computers', *Marketing Research: A Magazine of Management and Applications* 7 (2) (Spring 1995), 20–25.

24. Verhaeghe, A., De Ruyck, T. and Schillewaert, N., 'Join the research – participant-led open-ended questions', *International Journal of Market Research* 50 (5) (2008), 655–678; Pothas, A.-M., 'Customer satisfaction: keeping tabs on the issues that matter', *Total Quality Management* 12 (1) (January 2001), 83.

25. Vicente, P., Reis, E. and Santos, M., 'Using mobile phones for survey research: a comparison with fixed phones', *International Journal of Market Research* 51 (5) (2009), 613–634.

26. Bellman, S., Schweda, A. and Varan, D., 'The importance of social motives for watching and interacting with digital television', *International Journal of Market Research* 52 (1) (2010), 67–87.

27. Russell, M., Fischer, M.J., Fischer, C.M. and Premo, K., 'Exam question sequencing effects on marketing and management sciences student performance', *Journal for Advancement of Marketing Education* 3 (Summer 2003), 1–10; Javeline, D., 'Response effects in polite cultures', *Public Opinion Quarterly* 63 (1) (Spring 1999), 1–27; Krosnick, J.A. and Alwin, D.F., 'An evaluation of a cognitive theory of response order effects in survey measurement', *Public Opinion Quarterly* (Summer 1987), 201–219; Blunch, N.J., 'Position bias in multiple-choice questions', *Journal of Marketing Research* 21 (May 1984), 216–220, has argued that position bias in multiple-choice questions cannot be eliminated by rotating the order of the alternatives. This viewpoint is contrary to common practice.

28. 'IKEA – love where you live', The Communications Council, Bronze, Australian Effie Awards (2009).

29. DeMoranville, C.W. and Bienstock, C.C., 'Question order effects in measuring service quality', *International Journal of Research in Marketing* 20 (3) (2003), 457–466; Singer, E., 'Experiments with incentives in telephone surveys', *Public Opinion Quarterly* 64 (2) (Summer 2000), 171–188; Schuman, H. and Presser, S., *Questions and Answers in Attitude Surveys* (Thousand Oaks, CA: Sage, 1996).

30. Dolnicar, S., Grün, B. and Leisch, F., 'Quick, simple and reliable: forced binary survey questions', *International Journal of Market Research* 53 (2) (2011), 233–254; Blumenschein, K., 'Hypothetical versus real willingness to pay in the health care sector: results from a field experiment', *Journal of Health Economics* 20 (3) (May 2001), 441; Herriges, J.A. and Shogren, J.F., 'Starting point bias in dichotomous choice valuation with follow-up questioning', *Journal of Environmental Economics and Management* 30 (1) (January 1996), 112–131.

31. Kalton, G. and Schuman, H., 'The effect of the question on survey responses: a review', *Journal of the Royal Statistical Society Series A* 145, Part 1 (1982), 44–45.

32. Albaum, G., Roster, C., Yu, J.H. and Rogers, R.D., 'Simple rating scale formats: exploring extreme response', *International Journal of Market Research* 49 (5) (2007), 1–17; Vriends, M., Wedel, M. and Sandor, Z., 'Split-questionnaire design', *Marketing Research* 13 (2) (2001), 14–19; Conrad, F.G., 'Clarifying question meaning in a household telephone survey', *Public Opinion Quarterly* 64 (1) (Spring 2000), 1–27; McBurnett, M., 'Wording of questions affects responses to gun control issue', *Marketing News* 31 (1) (6 January 1997), 12.

33. Cape, P., Lorch, J. and Piekarski, L., 'A tale of two questionnaires', ESOMAR, Panel Research, Orlando, (October 2007); Colombo, R., 'A model for diagnosing and reducing nonresponse bias', *Journal of Advertising Research* 40 (1/2) (January/April 2000), 85–93; Etter, J.F. and Perneger, T.V., 'Analysis of nonresponse bias in a mailed health survey', *Journal of Clinical Epidemiology* 50 (10) (25 October 1997), 1123–1128; Omura, G.S., 'Correlates of item non-response', *Journal of the Market Research Society* (October 1983), 321–330.

34. Manfreda, K.L., Bosnjak, M., Berzelak, J., Haas, I. and Vehovar, V., 'Web surveys versus other survey modes: a meta-analysis comparing response rates', *International Journal of Market Research* 50 (1) (2008), 79–104; Bollinger, C.R., 'Estimation with response error and nonresponse: food-stamp participation in the SIPP', *Journal of Business and Economic Statistics* 19 (2) (April 2001), 129–141.

35. Gillham, B., *Developing a questionnaire* (New York: Continuum International, 2000); Saltz, L.C., 'How to get your news release published', *Journal of Accountancy* 182 (5) (November 1996), 89–91.

36. Reid, J., Morden, M. and Reid, A., 'Maximising respondent engagement: the use of rich media', ESOMAR, Annual Congress, Berlin (September 2007); Couper, M.P., 'Web surveys: a review of issues and approaches', *Public Opinion Quarterly* 64 (4) (Winter 2000), 464–494; Edmondson, B., 'How to spot a bogus poll', *American Demographics* 8 (10) (October 1996), 10–15; O'Brien, J., 'How do market researchers ask questions?', *Journal of the Market Research Society* 26 (April 1984), 93–107.

37. Cohen, J., 'Reading and writing: the forgotten 12 million', Market Research Society, Annual Conference (2006).

38. Snowden, D., and Stienstra, J., 'Stop asking questions: understanding how consumers make sense of it all', ESOMAR, Annual Congress, Berlin (September 2007); Chisnall, P.M., 'Marketing research: state of the art perspectives', *International Journal of Marketing Research* 44 (1) (First Quarter 2002), 122–125; Abramson, P.R. and Ostrom, C.W., 'Question wording and partisanship', *Public Opinion Quarterly* 58 (1) (Spring 1994), 21–48.

39. Charney, C., 'Top ten ways to get misleading poll results', *Campaigns and Elections* 28 (7) (July 2007), 66–67; Dubelaar, C. and Woodside, A.G., 'Increasing quality in measuring advertising effectiveness: a meta analysis of question framing in conversion studies', *Journal of Advertising Research* 43 (1) (March 2003), 78–85; Becker, B., 'Take direct route when data gathering', *Marketing News* 33 (20) (27 September 1999), 29–30.

40. Brinkmann, S., 'Could interviews be epistemic? An alternative to qualitative opinion polling', *Qualitative Inquiry* 13 (8) (December 2007), 1116–1138; Gillham, B., *Developing a questionnaire* (New York: Continuum International, 2000); Adamek, R.J., 'Public opinion and Roe v. Wade: measurement difficulties', *Public Opinion Quarterly* 58 (3) (Fall 1994), 409–418.

41. Chen, S., Poland, B. and Skinner, H.A., 'Youth voices: evaluation of participatory action research', *Canadian Journal of Program Evaluation* 22 (1) (March 2007), 125; Ouyang, M., 'Estimating marketing persistence on sales of consumer durables in China', *Journal of Business Research* 55 (4) (April 2002), 337; Jacoby, J. and Szybillo, G.J., 'Consumer research in FTC versus Kraft (1991): a case of heads we win, tails you lose?', *Journal of Public Policy and Marketing* 14 (1) (Spring 1995), 1–14.

42. Phillips, S. and Hamburger S., 'A quest for answers: the campaign against Why', ESOMAR, Annual Congress, Berlin (September 2007); Glassman, N.A. and Glassman, M., 'Screening questions', *Marketing Research* 10 (3) (1998), 25–31; Schuman, H. and Presser, S., *Questions and Answers in Attitude Surveys* (Thousand Oaks, CA: Sage, 1996).

43. Rating a brand on specific attributes early in a survey may affect responses to a later overall brand evaluation. For example, see Gendall, P. and Hoek, J., 'David takes on Goliath: an overview of survey evidence in a trademark dispute', *International Journal of Market Research* 45 (1) (2003), 99–122; Bartels, L.M., 'Question order and declining faith in elections', *Public Opinion Quarterly* 66 (1) (Spring 2002), 67–79. See also McAllister, I. and Wattenberg, M.P., 'Measuring levels of party identification: does question order matter?', *Public Opinion Quarterly* 59 (2) (Summer 1995), 259–268.

44. Watson, P.D., 'Adolescents' perceptions of a health survey using multimedia computer-assisted self administered interview', *Australian & New Zealand Journal of Public Health* 25 (6) (December 2001), 520; Bethlehem, J., 'The routing structure of questionnaires', *International Journal of Market Research* 42 (1) 2000, 95–110; Willits, F.K. and Ke, B., 'Part-whole question order effects: views of rurality', *Public Opinion Quarterly* 59 (3) (Fall 1995), 392–403.

45. Puleston, J. and Sleep, D., 'Measuring the value of respondent engagement – innovative techniques to improve panel quality', ESOMAR, Panel Research, Dublin (October 2008).

46. Denitto, M., Walsh, L. and Martin, P. (ed. by Macer, T.), 'Technology futures: perspectives on how technology will transform the market research of tomorrow', Market Research Society, Annual Conference (2009).

47. Schlegelmilch, B.B., Diamantopoulos, A. and Reynolds, N., 'Pre-testing in questionnaire design: a review of the literature and suggestions for further research', *International Journal of Market Research* 35 (2) (1993), 171–182.

48. Feldhaeuser, H. and Smales, H., 'Flying with the Simpsons: an award winning research paper that helped Air New Zealand reinvent the long haul air travel', ESOMAR, Asia Pacific, Melbourne (2011).

49. Blair, J. and Srinath, K.P., 'A note on sample size for behaviour coding pretests', *Field Methods* 85 (11) (February 2008), 20; Conrad, F.G., 'Clarifying question meaning in a household telephone survey', *Public Opinion Quarterly* 64 (1) (Spring 2000), 1–27; Diamantopoulos, A., Schlegelmilch, B.B. and Reynolds, N., 'Pre-testing in questionnaire design: the impact of participant characteristics on error detection', *Journal of the Market Research Society* 36 (October 1994), 295–314.

50. Meir, D., 'The seven stages of effective survey research', *American Marketing Association* (2002); Gillham, B., *Developing a questionnaire* (New York: Continuum International, 2000).

51. Cierpicki, S., Davis, C., Eddy, C., Lorch, J., Phillips, K., Poynter, R., York, S. and Zuo, B., 'From clipboards to online research communities: a cross-cultural review of participants' perceptions', ESOMAR, Congress Odyssey, Athens (September 2010).

52. Manceau, D. and Tissier-Desbordes, E., 'Are sex and death taboos in advertising? An analysis of taboos in advertising and a survey of French consumer perceptions', *International Journal of Advertising* 25 (1) (2006), 9–33; Laczniak, G.R. and Murphy, P.E., *Ethical Marketing Decisions: The Higher Road* (Needham Heights, MA: Allyn and Bacon, 1993).

53. Birenbaum-Carmeli, D., Carmeli, Y., and Gornostayev, S., 'Researching sensitive fields: some lessons from a study of sperm donors in Israel', *International Journal of Sociology and Social Policy* 28 (11/12) (2008), 425–439; Morris, M.H., Marks, A.S., Allen, J.A. and Peery, N.S., 'Modeling ethical attitudes and behaviours under conditions of environmental turbulence – case of South Africa', *Journal of Business Ethics* 15 (10) (October 1996), 1119–1130.

54. Tsalikis, J. and Seaton, B., 'Business Etics Index: Measuring consumer sentiments toward ethical business practices', *Journal of Business Ethics* 64 (4) (April 2006), 317–326; David, M.A., 'Measuring ethical ideology in business ethics: a critical analysis of the ethics position questionnaire', *Journal of Business Ethics* 32 (1) (July 2001), 35–53; Armstrong, R.W., 'An empirical investigation of international marketing ethics: problems encountered by Australian firms', *Journal of Business Ethics* 11 (1992), 161–171.

55. Swahar, G. and Swahar, J., 'Designing innovation: maximizing online respondent engagement through a game-way research design', ESOMAR, Innovate, Barcelona (November 2010).

14 Sampling: design and procedures

Stage 1

Problem definition

Stage 2

Research approach developed

Stage 3

Research design developed

Stage 4

Fieldwork or data collection

Stage 5

Data integrity and analysis

Stage 6

Report preparation and presentation

> *There is no hope of making scientific statements about a population based on the knowledge obtained from a sample, unless we are circumspect in choosing a sampling method.*

Objectives

After reading this chapter, you should be able to:

1 differentiate a sample from a census and identify the conditions that favour the use of a sample versus a census;

2 discuss the sampling design process: definition of the target population, determination of the sampling frame, selection of sampling technique(s), determination of sample size, execution of the sampling process and validating the sample;

3 classify sampling techniques as non-probability and probability sampling techniques;

4 describe the non-probability sampling techniques of convenience, judgemental, quota and snowball sampling;

5 describe the probability sampling techniques of simple random, systematic, stratified and cluster sampling;

6 identify the conditions that favour the use of non-probability sampling versus probability sampling;

7 understand the sampling design process and the use of sampling techniques in international marketing research;

8 identify the ethical issues related to the sampling design process and the use of appropriate sampling techniques;

9 appreciate how digital developments are shaping the manner in which sampling may be designed and executed.

Overview

Sampling is a key component of any research design. Sampling design involves several basic questions:

1 Should a sample be taken?

2 If so, what process should be followed?

3 What kind of sample should be taken?

4 How large should it be?

5 What can be done to control and adjust for non-response errors?

This chapter introduces the fundamental concepts of sampling and the qualitative considerations necessary to answer these questions. We address the question of whether or not to sample and describe the steps involved in sampling. Included in questions of the steps involved in sampling are the use, benefits and limitations of the access panel in sample design. We present the nature of non-probability and probability sampling and related sampling techniques. We discuss the use of sampling techniques in international marketing research and identify the relevant ethical issues. We conclude by examining digital developments that are enabling researchers to design and execute well-focused samples, especially in the context of conducting online surveys. Statistical determination of sample size, and the causes for control of and adjustments for non-response error, are discussed in Chapter 15.

We begin with two examples. The first illustrates the choice of a sampling method in a complex international study, with hard-to-access participants. The second illustrates a key debate that challenges many researchers. Given the demand for researchers to sample 'willing' participants to match specific profiles, the use of the access panel has grown enormously in the research industry. As you progress through questions of the nature, purpose and techniques of sampling, the key debates in this example should be addressed.

Real research **Measuring the impact of empowerment[1]**

Research by the United Nations has demonstrated that in most economies of the world, women are the lyinchpin to the advancement of many indicators of prosperity. In the West, it is often believed that greater financial prosperity always equates to greater happiness. In those countries where women appear to be doing well financially, are these women really happier? In societies where women's pursuit of prosperity and happiness is not supported, research has a role to play both in providing them with a voice to let their hopes and dreams be heard and in public policy designed to support them. To address some of these issues, D3 Systems (**www.d3systems.com**) launched the Women In Muslim Countries study (WIMC). WIMC consisted of annually repeated, nationally representative quantitative research in 22 Muslim-majority countries of the globe. The questions used for the WIMC were designed to measure women's empowerment in actual daily practice, providing a deep look into the gap between current public policy and empowerment initiatives and actual practice on the personal and local level. In some cases, WIMC got at the issues indirectly, as in many Muslim countries asking with direct wording would not yield honest answers. Individual country surveys were conducted either face to face or via CATI as appropriate. Each country's sampling frame was designed to provide the best possible representation of the attitudes and experience of that country's women. In all cases, the sample was two-stage, stratified random. In the case of Egypt, the sampling frame was limited to urban areas only. At its launch WIMC focused upon 10 countries that included the following:

Country	Mode	Women only, n
Afghanistan	Face-to-face nationwide	1175
Bangladesh	Face-to-face nationwide	753
Egypt	Face-to-face nationwide, seven main cities and suburbs	500
Iran	CATI nationwide	1003
Iraq	Face-to-face nationwide	1093
Jordan	Face-to-face nationwide	500
Kosovo	Face-to-face nationwide	538
Pakistan	Face-to-face nationwide	960
Saudi Arabia	CATI nationwide	514
Turkey	CATI nationwide	490

Real research **Down with random sampling**

Peter Kellner, President of YouGov (**www.yougov.co.uk**), the online political polling company, presented the contentious views on the challenges of conducting random sampling:[2]

*We know that perfection does not exist. Pure random samples are too expensive. Besides 100% response rates belong to the world of fantasy. So we are told to do the best we can. There are two separate phenomena to address: the quality of the **designed** sample and the quality of the **achieved** sample. When we deliver results to our clients, what matters is the second, not the first. If the achieved sample is badly skewed, it is no defence to say that we used impeccably random samples to obtain it. Our aim should be to present our clients with **representative achieved samples**. This means developing a much more purposive* *approach to sampling and weighting. At YouGov we have been forced into this approach by the very nature of our business. Our samples are drawn from a panel of more than 150,000 people throughout Great Britain. By definition, we don't approach the remaining 45 million adults who have not joined our panel. Random sample purists look at our methods with scorn. Yet our record demonstrates an overall accuracy that our rivals envy.*

We draw on existing knowledge of a population in question to construct samples that are representative of that population. We also apply weights that are relevant to each group, not simply all purpose demographic weights. Of course, the non-response problem can never be completely eliminated. We can never be sure of the views of people who never respond to pollsters of any kind.

In response Harmut Schffler of TNS Infratest www.tns-infratest.com commented:[3]

Whilst we need to develop our expertise, and refusal rates are a growing problem, to say random sampling is obsolete and then present modulated access panels as the solution is astounding. Yes, Peter Kellner will want to defend his business model. He at least hints that access panels can produce enormous distortion with respect to who does and does not participate. Instead of declaring the death of random sampling, we should improve its quality through better promoting our industry to the public and finding more intelligent ways to address potential participants so we can increase response rates. We need random methods. And so does Peter Kellner's model or he will find no solution to his own recruitment distortion problem.

Andrew Zelin and Patten Smith of Ipsos MORI (**www.ipsos-mori.com**) added:

We agree that a high quality of designed sample does not guarantee a high quality of achieved sample, that poor response rates coupled with differences between responders and non-responders lead to non-response bias and that demographic weighting may be a poor tool for removing this bias. However, his arguments depend upon the implication that random probability samples produce unacceptable levels of non-response bias. For some samples and some variables this will be true, but often it will not. Unless we are certain that the alternatives to random probability sampling are superior, we should investigate non-response bias on a variable-by-variable survey-by-survey basis.

This example infers that the 'best' form of sampling is the probability random sample. It may be an ideal that researchers would prefer to administer. However, researchers have long recognised the balance between what may be seen as the scientific ideal of sampling and the administrative constraints in achieving that ideal. This balance will be addressed throughout this chapter. Before we discuss these issues in detail, we address the question of whether the researcher should sample or take a census.

Sample or census

Population
The aggregate of all the elements, sharing some common set of characteristics, that comprise the universe for the purpose of the marketing research problem.

The objective of most marketing research projects is to obtain information about the characteristics or parameters of a population. A population is the aggregate of all the elements that share some common set of characteristics and that comprise the universe for the purpose of the marketing research problem. The population parameters are typically numbers, such as the proportion of consumers who are loyal to a particular fashion brand. Information about

Census

A complete enumeration of the elements of a population or study objects.

Sample

A subgroup of the elements of the population selected for participation in the study.

population parameters may be obtained by taking a census or a sample. A census involves a complete enumeration of the elements of a population. The population parameters can be calculated directly in a straightforward way after the census is enumerated. A sample, on the other hand, is a subgroup of the population selected for participation in the study. Sample characteristics, called statistics, are then used to make inferences about the population parameters. The inferences that link sample characteristics and population parameters are estimation procedures and tests of hypotheses. These inference procedures are considered in Chapters 18 to 24.

Table 14.1 summarises the conditions favouring the use of a sample versus a census. Budget and time limits are obvious constraints favouring the use of a sample. A census is both costly and time consuming to conduct. A census is unrealistic if the population is large, as it is for most consumer products. In the case of many industrial products, however, the population is small, making a census feasible as well as desirable. For example, in investigating the use of certain machine tools by Italian car manufacturers, a census would be preferred to a sample. Another reason for preferring a census in this case is that variance in the characteristic of interest is large. For example, machine tool usage of Fiat may vary greatly from the usage of Ferrari. Small population sizes as well as high variance in the characteristic to be measured favour a census.

If the cost of sampling errors is high (e.g. if the sample omitted a major manufacturer like

Table 14.1	Sample versus census		
Factors		*Conditions favouring the use of*	
		Sample	*Census*
1 Budget		Small	Large
2 Time available		Short	Long
3 Population size		Large	Small
4 Variance in the characteristic		Small	Large
5 Cost of sampling errors		Low	High
6 Cost of non-sampling errors		High	Low
7 Nature of measurement		Destructive	Non-destructive
8 Attention to individual cases		Yes	No

Ford, the results could be misleading), a census, which eliminates such errors, is desirable. If the cost of non-sampling errors is high (e.g. interviewers incorrectly questioning target participants) a sample, where fewer resources would have been spent, would be favoured.

A census can greatly increase non-sampling error to the point that these errors exceed the sampling errors of a sample. Non-sampling errors are found to be the major contributor to total error, whereas random sampling errors have been relatively small in magnitude.[4] Hence, in most cases, accuracy considerations would favour a sample over a census.

A sample may be preferred if the measurement process results in the destruction or contamination of the elements sampled. For example, product usage tests result in the consumption of the product. Therefore, taking a census in a study that requires households to use a new brand of toothpaste would not be feasible. Sampling may also be necessary to focus attention on individual cases, as in the case of in-depth interviews. Finally, other pragmatic considerations, such as the need to keep the study secret, may favour a sample over a census.

The sampling design process

The sampling design process includes six steps, which are shown sequentially in Figure 14.1. These steps are closely interrelated and relevant to all aspects of the marketing research project, from problem definition to the presentation of the results. Therefore, sample design decisions should be integrated with all other decisions in a research project.[5]

Figure 14.1

The sampling design process

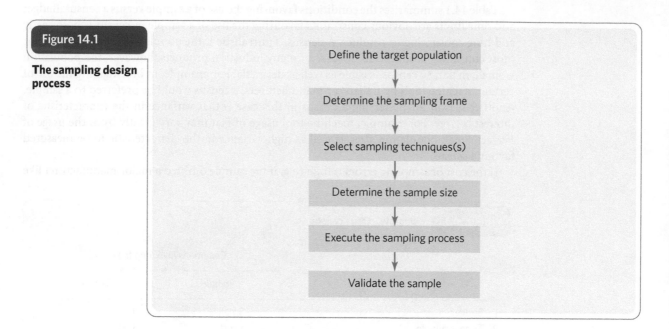

Define the target population

↓

Determine the sampling frame

↓

Select sampling techniques(s)

↓

Determine the sample size

↓

Execute the sampling process

↓

Validate the sample

Define the target population

Target population

The collection of elements or objects that possess the information sought by the researcher and about which inferences are to be made.

Element

An object that possesses the information sought by the researcher and about which inferences are to be made.

Sampling unit

An element, or a unit containing the element, that is available for selection at some stage of the sampling process.

Sampling design begins by specifying the target population. This is the collection of elements or objects that possess the information sought by the researcher and about which inferences are to be made. The target population must be defined precisely. Imprecise definition of the target population will result in research that is ineffective at best and misleading at worst. Defining the target population involves translating the problem definition into a precise statement of who should and should not be included in the sample.

The target population should be defined in terms of elements, sampling units, extent and time. An element is the object about which or from which the information is desired. In survey research, the element is usually the participant. A sampling unit is an element, or a unit containing the element, that is available for selection at some stage of the sampling process. Suppose that Clinique wanted to assess consumer response to a new line of lipsticks and wanted to sample females over 25 years of age. It may be possible to sample females over 25 directly, in which case a sampling unit would be the same as an element. Alternatively, the sampling unit might be households. In the latter case, households would be sampled and all females over 25 in each selected household would be interviewed. Here, the sampling unit and the population element are different. Extent refers to the geographical boundaries of the research, and the time refers to the period under consideration. We use the Formula One Racetrack Project to illustrate.

IFM Sports Marketing Surveys

Target population

In a Brand Tracker study for the International Basketball Federation FIBA, the target population for its online survey was defined as follows:

Elements:	male or female aged 16–45
Sampling units:	individual participants
Extent:	Brazil, China, Italy, Spain, Turkey, UK, USA
Time:	2009

Defining the target population may not be as easy as it was in this example. Consider a marketing research project assessing consumer response to a new brand of men's moisturiser. Who should be included in the target population? All men? Men who have used a moisturiser during the last month? Men of 17 years of age or older? Should females be included, because some women buy moisturiser for men whom they know? These and similar questions must be resolved before the target population can be appropriately defined.[6] This challenge is further illustrated in the following example.

Kiasma: the insightful museum[7]

Kiasma Museum of Contemporary Art (**www.kiasma.fi**) in Finland is dedicated to contemporary art. Throughout its existence Kiasma has been the most visited museum in Finland. Kiasma's marketing and management team wanted to explore the museum's marketing strategy, contextual development and changes in the external working environment. Research was planned between Kiasma and the media agency Dagmar (**www.dagmar.fi**) with whom it had been working for over 10 years. One of the first challenges was to establish what the population for the research would be. Would it be the total population for Finland? Kiasma had a public duty to serve the whole population, but it was unfeasible in the context of the research to segment the whole Finnish population, since the museum was located in Helsinki and just pure distance was a hindrance for visiting and/or visiting regularly. The approach the researchers chose was to first gauge the interest in contemporary art in an online panel. The question they posed was a simple 'are you interested in contemporary art – yes/no?' The result was that a discouraging 33% had an interest in contemporary art. A follow-up question was open-ended, about why the participant was interested or not interested. The results helped the researchers to define a population for their planned survey as 'people living a maximum of 60 km from Helsinki, 15–74 years of age and interested in any form of cultural activities, or, failing that, are interested in new experiences'. The reasoning behind this was that a person who was interested in at least some form of culture would more easily be persuaded to come to Kiasma.

Determine the sampling frame

Sampling frame
A representation of the elements of the target population that consists of a list or set of directions for identifying the target population.

A sampling frame is a representation of the elements of the target population. It consists of a list or set of directions for identifying the target population. Examples of a sampling frame include the telephone book, an association directory listing the firms in an industry, a customer database, a mailing list on a database purchased from a commercial organisation, a city directory, a map or, most frequently in marketing research, an access panel.[8] If a list cannot be compiled, then at least some directions for identifying the target population should be specified, such as random-digit dialling procedures in telephone surveys.

With growing numbers of individuals, households and businesses, it may be possible to compile or obtain a list of population elements, but the list may omit some elements of the population or may include other elements that do not belong. Therefore, the use of a list will lead to sampling frame error, which was discussed in Chapter 3.[9]

In some instances, the discrepancy between the population and the sampling frame is small enough to ignore. In most cases, however, the researcher should recognise and attempt to treat the sampling frame error. One approach is to redefine the population in terms of the sampling frame. For example, if a specialist business directory is used as a sampling frame, the population of businesses could be redefined as those with a correct listing in a given location. Although this approach is simplistic, it does prevent the researcher from being misled about the actual population being investigated.[10] Ultimately, the major drawback of redefining the population based upon available sampling frames is that the nature of the research problem may be compromised. Who is being measured and ultimately to whom the research findings may be generalised may not match the target group of individuals identified in a research problem definition. Evaluating the accuracy of sampling frames matches the issues of evaluating the quality of secondary data (see Chapter 4).

Another way is to account for sampling frame error by screening the participants in the data collection phase. The participants could be screened with respect to demographic characteristics, familiarity, product usage and other characteristics to ensure that they satisfy the criteria for the target population. Screening can eliminate inappropriate elements contained in the sampling frame, but it cannot account for elements that have been omitted. Yet another approach is to adjust the data collected by a weighted scheme to counterbalance the sampling frame error. These issues were presented in the opening example 'Down with random sampling' and will be further discussed in Chapters 15 and 17. Regardless of which approach is used, it is important to recognise any sampling frame error that exists, so that inappropriate inferences can be avoided.

Select a sampling technique

Selecting a sampling technique involves several decisions of a broader nature. The researcher must decide whether to use a Bayesian or traditional sampling approach, to sample with or without replacement, and to use non-probability or probability sampling.

Bayesian approach

A selection method where the elements are selected sequentially. The Bayesian approach explicitly incorporates prior information about population parameters as well as the costs and probabilities associated with making wrong decisions.

Sampling with replacement

A sampling technique in which an element *can* be included in the sample more than once.

Sampling without replacement

A sampling technique in which an element *cannot* be included in the sample more than once.

In the Bayesian approach, the elements are selected sequentially. After each element is added to the sample, the data are collected, sample statistics computed and sampling costs determined. The Bayesian approach explicitly incorporates prior information about population parameters as well as the costs and probabilities associated with making wrong decisions.[11] This approach is theoretically appealing. Yet it is not used widely in marketing research because much of the required information on costs and probabilities is not available. In the traditional sampling approach, the entire sample is selected before data collection begins. Because the traditional approach is the most common approach used, it is assumed in the following sections.

In sampling with replacement, an element is selected from the sampling frame and appropriate data are obtained. Then the element is placed back in the sampling frame. As a result, it is possible for an element to be included in the sample more than once. In sampling without replacement, once an element is selected for inclusion in the sample, it is removed from the sampling frame and therefore cannot be selected again. The calculation of statistics is done somewhat differently for the two approaches, but statistical inference is not very different if the sampling frame is large relative to the ultimate sample size. Thus, the distinction is important only when the sampling frame is small compared with the sample size.

The most important decision about the choice of sampling technique is whether to use non-probability or probability sampling. Non-probability sampling relies on the judgement of the researcher, while probability sampling relies on chance. Given its importance, the issues involved in this decision are discussed in detail below, in the next section.

If the sampling unit is different from the element, it is necessary to specify precisely how the elements within the sampling unit should be selected. With home face-to-face interviews and telephone interviews, merely specifying the address or the telephone number may not be sufficient. For example, should the person answering the doorbell or the telephone be interviewed, or someone else in the household? Often, more than one person in a household may qualify. For example, both the male and female head of household, and even their children, may be eligible to participate in a study examining family leisure-time activities. When a probability sampling technique is being employed, a random selection must be made from all the eligible persons in each household. A simple procedure for random selection is the 'next birthday' method. The interviewer asks which of the eligible persons in the household has the next birthday and includes that person in the sample.

Determine the sample size

Sample size
The number of elements to be included in a study.

Sample size refers to the number of elements to be included in the study. Determining the sample size involves several qualitative and quantitative considerations. The qualitative factors are discussed in this subsection, and the quantitative factors are considered in Chapter 15. Important qualitative factors to be considered in determining the sample size include (1) the importance of the decision, (2) the nature of the research, (3) the number of variables, (4) the nature of the analysis, (5) sample sizes used in similar studies, (6) incidence rates, (7) completion rates and (8) resource constraints.

In general, for more important decisions, more information is necessary, and that information should be obtained very precisely. This calls for larger samples, but as the sample size increases, each unit of information is obtained at greater cost. The degree of precision may be measured in terms of the standard deviation of the mean, which is inversely proportional to the square root of the sample size. The larger the sample, the smaller the gain in precision by increasing the sample size by one unit.

The nature of the research also has an impact on the sample size. For exploratory research designs, such as those using qualitative research, the sample size is typically small. For conclusive research, such as descriptive surveys, larger samples are required. Likewise, if data are being collected on a large number of variables, i.e. many questions are asked in a survey, larger samples are required. The cumulative effects of sampling error across variables are reduced in a large sample.

If sophisticated analysis of the data using multivariate techniques is required, the sample size should be large. The same applies if the data are to be analysed in great detail. Thus, a larger sample would be required if the data are being analysed at the subgroup or segment level than if the analysis is limited to the aggregate or total sample.

Sample size is influenced by the average size of samples in similar studies. Table 14.2 gives an idea of sample sizes used in different marketing research studies. These sample sizes have been determined based on experience and can serve as rough guidelines, particularly when non-probability sampling techniques are used.

Finally, the sample size decision should be guided by a consideration of the resource constraints. In any marketing research project, money and time are limited. The sample size required should be adjusted for the incidence of eligible participants and the completion rate. The quantitative decisions involved in determining the sample size are covered in detail in the next chapter.

Execute the sampling process

Execution of the sampling process requires a detailed specification of how the sampling design decisions with respect to the population, sampling unit, sampling frame, sampling technique and sample size are to be implemented. While individual researchers may know how they are going to execute their sampling process, once more than one individual is involved, a specification for execution is needed to ensure that the process is conducted in a consistent manner.

For example, if households are the sampling unit, an operational definition of a household is needed. Procedures should be specified for empty housing units and for call-backs in case no one is at home.

Table 14.2	Usual sample sizes used in marketing research studies	
Type of study	Minimum size	Typical range
Problem identification	500	1,000–2,500 research (e.g. market potential)
Problem-solving research	200	300–500 (e.g. pricing)
Product tests	200	300–500
Test marketing studies	200	300–500
TV, radio, print or online advertising	150	200–300 (per advertisement tested)
Test-market audits	10 stores	10–20 stores
Focus groups	6 groups	6–12 groups

Validate the sample

Sample validation aims to account for sampling frame error by screening the participants in the data collection phase. Participants can be screened with respect to demographic characteristics, familiarity, product usage and other characteristics to ensure that they satisfy the criteria for the target population. Screening can eliminate inappropriate elements contained in the sampling frame, but it cannot account for elements that have been omitted. The success of the validation process depends upon the accuracy of base statistics that describe the structure of a target population.

Once data are collected from a sample, comparisons between the structure of the sample and the target population should be made, as practised in the following example. Once data have been collected and it is found that the structure of a sample does not match the target population, a weighting scheme can be used (this is discussed in Chapter 17).

Real research	**How consumers are affected by online banking layouts[12]**

A study was conducted to examine banking store layout effects on consumer behaviour. The target population for this study was adult heavy Internet users that used either offline or online banking services in Greece. Three versions of a web banking store were developed and tested. Two of the layout types were transformed from conventional banking and one type was designed by incorporating users' preferences and suggestions. The study was conducted in three phases. Phase 1 involved a series of semi-structured in-depth interviews with design experts from four major multinational banks in Greece. Phase 2 involved a series of focus groups with banking users and heavy online shoppers to evaluate requirements as far as the most preferred layout type was concerned. Phase 3 consisted of a within-group laboratory experiment to test three alternative versions of a virtual e-banking store. Sample validation was conducted, enabling the researchers to demonstrate that the sample used satisfied the population criteria. Validation was further strengthened as participants were further questioned upon completion of their questionnaires in a semi-structured face-to-face interview conducted by the experiment's administrator.

A classification of sampling techniques

Non-probability sampling
Sampling techniques that do not use chance selection procedures but rather rely on the personal judgement of the researcher.

Probability sampling
A sampling procedure in which each element of the population has a fixed probabilistic chance of being selected for the sample.

Confidence intervals
The range into which the true population parameter will fall, assuming a given level of confidence.

Sampling techniques may be broadly classified as non-probability and probability (see Figure 14.2). Non-probability sampling relies on the personal judgement of the researcher rather than on chance to select sample elements. The researcher can arbitrarily or consciously decide which elements to include in the sample. Non-probability samples may yield good estimates of the population characteristics, but they do not allow for objective evaluation of the precision of the sample results. Because there is no way of determining the probability of selecting any particular element for inclusion in the sample, the estimates obtained are not statistically projectable to the population. Commonly used non-probability sampling techniques include convenience sampling, judgemental sampling, quota sampling and snowball sampling.

In probability sampling, sampling units are selected by chance. It is possible to pre-specify every potential sample of a given size that could be drawn from the population, as well as the probability of selecting each sample. Every potential sample need not have the same probability of selection, but it is possible to specify the probability of selecting any particular sample of a given size. This requires not only a precise definition of the target population, but also a general specification of the sampling frame. Because sample elements are selected by chance, it is possible to determine the precision of the sample estimates of the characteristics of interest. Confidence intervals, which contain the true population value with a given level of certainty, can be calculated. This permits the researcher to make inferences or projections about the target population from which the sample was drawn. Classification of probability sampling techniques is based on:

- element versus cluster sampling
- equal unit probability versus unequal probabilities
- unstratified versus stratified selection
- random versus systematic selection
- one-stage versus multistage techniques.

All possible combinations of these five aspects result in 32 different probability sampling techniques. Of these techniques, we consider simple random sampling, systematic sampling,

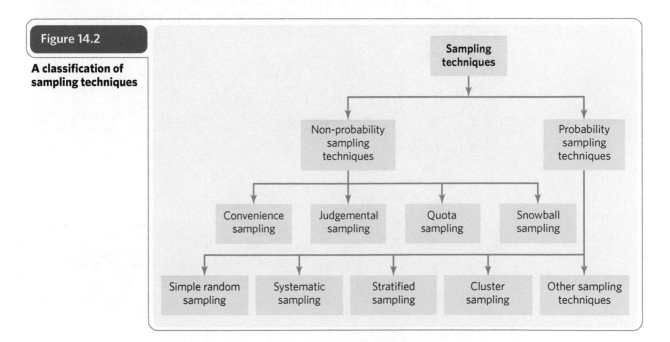

Figure 14.2

A classification of sampling techniques

stratified sampling and cluster sampling in depth and briefly touch on some others. First, however, we discuss non-probability sampling techniques.

Non-probability sampling techniques

Figure 14.3 presents a graphical illustration of the various non-probability sampling techniques. The population consists of 25 elements and we have to select a sample of size 5: A, B, C, D and E represent groups and can also be viewed as strata or clusters.

Convenience sampling
A non-probability sampling technique that attempts to obtain a sample of convenient elements. The selection of sampling units is left primarily to the interviewer.

Convenience sampling

Convenience sampling attempts to obtain a sample of convenient elements. The selection of sampling units is left primarily to the interviewer. Often, participants are selected because they happen to be in the right place at the right time. Examples of convenience sampling include: (1) use of students, religious groups and members of social organisations; (2) street

---

Figure 14.3

A graphical illustration of non-probability sampling techniques

A graphical illustration of non-probability techniques

1 Convenience sampling

A	B	C	D	E	
1	6	11	16	21	Group D happens to assemble at a convenient time and place. So all the elements in this group are selected. The resulting sample consists of elements 16, 17, 18, 19 and 20. Note that no elements are selected from groups A, B, C, E
2	7	12	17	22	
3	8	13	18	23	
4	9	14	19	24	
5	10	15	20	25	

2 Judgemental sampling

A	B	C	D	E	
1	6	11	16	21	The researcher considers groups B, C and E to be typical and convenient. Within each of these groups one or two elements are selected based on typicality and convenience. The resulting sample consists of elements 8, 10, 11, 13 and 24. Note that no elements are selected from groups A and D
2	7	12	17	22	
3	8	13	18	23	
4	9	14	19	24	
5	10	15	20	25	

3 Quota sampling

A	B	C	D	E	
1	6	11	16	21	A quota of one element from each group, A to E, is imposed. Within each group, one element is selected based on judgement or convenience. The resulting sample consists of elements 3, 6, 13, 20 and 22. Note that one element is selected from each column or group
2	7	12	17	22	
3	8	13	18	23	
4	9	14	19	24	
5	10	15	20	25	

4 Snowball sampling

	Random				
Selection			Referrals		
A	B	C	D	E	
1	6	11	16	21	Elements 2 and 9 are selected randomly from groups A and B. Element 2 refers elements 12 and 13. Element 9 refers element 18. The resulting sample consists of elements 2, 9 12, 13 and 18. Note that no element is selected from group E
2	7	12	17	22	
3	8	13	18	23	
4	9	14	19	24	
5	10	15	20	25	

interviews without qualifying the participants; (3) some forms of online and email surveys; (4) tear-out questionnaires included in a newspaper or magazine; and (5) journalists interviewing 'people on the street', or on radio or TV shows.[13]

Convenience sampling is the least expensive and least time consuming of all sampling techniques. The sampling units are accessible, easy to measure and cooperative. Despite these advantages, this form of sampling has serious limitations. Many potential sources of selection bias are present, including participant self-selection. Convenience samples are not representative of any definable population.[14] Hence, it is not theoretically meaningful to generalise any population from a convenience sample, and convenience samples are not appropriate for marketing research projects involving population inferences. Convenience samples are not recommended for descriptive or causal research, but they can be used in exploratory research for generating ideas, insights or hypotheses. Convenience samples can be used for pretesting questionnaires, or pilot studies. Even in these cases, caution should be exercised in interpreting the results. Nevertheless, this technique is sometimes used even in large surveys. For example, in the following case, samples ranging in size from 200 to 1,500 were selected to represent visitors to different Olympic Games. With no means to validate these samples, how confident would you be in using these findings to represent all of the visitors?

| Real research | **Olympic convenience**[15] |

The International Olympic Committee (IOC) (**www.olympic.org**) used surveys at the 2000 Olympic Games in Sydney to find out what visitors thought about the level of commercialism in Sydney. One survey was given to a convenience sample of 200 visitors to the games and they were asked about the level of commercialism they find appropriate, whether they thought the event was too commercial, and whether company sponsorship of the games was perceived to be positive. The survey, conducted by Performance Research (**www.performanceresearch.com**), revealed that 77% of the visitors found the presence of large corporations such as Coca-Cola and McDonald's to be appropriate. Furthermore, 88% of the visitors thought the sponsors contributed to the Olympics positively. About 33% said that they thought a company's involvement in Sydney made them feel more positive about that company in general. Performance Research continued its study of Olympic sponsorship by conducting 300 on-site, 900 telephone and 1,500 online surveys using convenience samples in conjunction with the 2002 Winter Olympics in Salt Lake City, Utah. The results with respect to companies' sponsorship and involvement in the Olympics were again positive. A survey was also conducted at the 2004 Olympics in Athens to assess spectators' satisfaction with the Games. A convenience sample of 1,024 persons (46% Greeks, 13% Americans and the rest different nationalities) was used and the results indicated an overwhelming seal of approval for the Olympic Games in Athens. Surveys based on convenience samples were conducted for the 2008 Olympics in Beijing. According to a survey by Survey Sampling International (**www.surveysampling.com**), more than 80% of Chinese citizens agreed that having the 2008 Olympic Games held in their country strengthened people's participation in sports activities.

Judgemental sampling

Judgemental sampling
A form of convenience sampling in which the population elements are purposely selected based on the judgement of the researcher.

Judgemental sampling is a form of convenience sampling in which the population elements are selected based on the judgement of the researcher. The researcher, exercising judgement or expertise, chooses the elements to be included in the sample because it is believed that they are representative of the population of interest or are otherwise appropriate as illustrated in the following example.

Establishing marketing relationships in the advertising agency business[16]

For long-term success, relationships must be nurtured and developed between a client and an advertising agency. There are numerous advantages that such relationships can bring to both sides including transaction cost savings, strengthening competitive or collaborative advantages, and achieving growth in exchange volume. A Slovenian study explored how partnerships between clients and advertising agencies develop into long-term relationships. A questionnaire was tested on a small sample of agency experts, marketing academics, and on a small sample of agency clients. The starting point for the sample was a list of 300 leading Slovenian enterprises according to revenues and/or profits, out of which a judgemental sample of 200 main advertisers was drawn. Participants were marketing managers and other managers, selected by title, responsible for decision making with regard to their cooperation with advertising agencies. Revenues of companies in the sample ranged from €60 to €485 million. The sample included the vast majority of advertisers from the area plus subsidiaries of international companies, and was seen as representative of advertisers among leading Slovenian enterprises.

Common examples of judgemental sampling include: (1) test markets selected to determine the potential of a new product; (2) purchasing professionals selected in business-to-business marketing research because they are considered to be representative of particular companies; (3) product testing with individuals who may be particularly fussy or who hold extremely high expectations; (4) expert witnesses used in court; and (5) boutiques or fashion flagship stores selected to test a new merchandising display system.

Judgemental sampling is inexpensive, convenient and quick, yet it does not allow direct generalisations to a specific population, usually because the population is not defined explicitly. Judgemental sampling is subjective and its value depends entirely on the researcher's judgement, expertise and creativity. It can be useful if broad population inferences are not required. Judgemental samples are frequently used in business-to-business marketing research projects, given that in many projects the target population is relatively small (see Chapter 27).

Quota sampling

Quota sampling
A non-probability sampling technique that is a two-stage restricted judgemental sampling. The first stage consists of developing control categories or quotas of population elements. In the second stage, sample elements are selected based on convenience or judgement.

Quota sampling may be viewed as two-stage restricted judgemental sampling that has traditionally been associated with street interviewing. It is now used extensively and with much debate in drawing samples from access panels.[17] The first stage consists of developing control characteristics, or quotas, of population elements such as age or gender. To develop these quotas, the researcher lists relevant control characteristics and determines the distribution of these characteristics in the target population, such as Males 48%, Females 52% (resulting in 480 men and 520 women being selected in a sample of 1,000 participants). Often, the quotas are assigned so that the proportion of the sample elements possessing the control characteristics is the same as the proportion of population elements with these characteristics. In other words, the quotas ensure that the composition of the sample is the same as the composition of the population with respect to the characteristics of interest.

In the second stage, sample elements are selected based on convenience or judgement. Once the quotas have been assigned, there is considerable freedom in selecting the elements to be included in the sample. The only requirement is that the elements selected fit the control characteristics.[18] This technique is illustrated with the following example.

| Real research | **How is epilepsy perceived?** |

A study was undertaken by the Scottish Epilepsy Association to determine the perceptions of the condition of epilepsy by the adult population in the Scottish city of Glasgow. A quota sample of 500 adults was selected. The control characteristics were gender, age and propensity to donate to a charity. Based on the composition of the adult population of the city, the quotas assigned were as follows:

Propensity to donate		Male 48%		Female 52%		Totals
		Have a flag	No flag	Have a flag	No flag	
Age		50%	50%	50%	50%	
18 to 30	25%	30	30	33	32	**125**
31 to 45	40%	48	48	52	52	**200**
46 to 60	15%	18	18	19	20	**75**
Over 60	20%	24	24	26	26	**100**
Totals		**120**	**120**	**130**	**130**	
Totals		**240**		**260**		**500**

Note that the percentages of gender and age within the target population were taken from local census statistics. The percentages of 'propensity to donate' could not be gleaned from secondary data sources and so were split on a 50/50 basis. The interviews were conducted on a Saturday when it was customary to see charity 'flag sellers' operating. One of the hypotheses to be tested in the study was the extent to which those who donated to charities on flag days were more aware of the condition of epilepsy and how to treat epileptic sufferers. Thus the instruction to interviewers was to split interviews between those who wore the 'flag' that they had bought from a street collector and those who had not bought a flag. It was recognised that this was a crude measure of propensity to donate to a charity but was the only tangible clue that could be consistently observed.

In this example, quotas were assigned such that the composition of the sample mirrored the population. In certain situations, however, it is desirable either to under- or over-sample elements with certain characteristics. To illustrate, it may be desirable to over-sample heavy users of a product so that their behaviour can be examined in detail. Although this type of sample is not representative, nevertheless it may be very relevant to allow a particular group of individuals to be broken down into subcategories and analysed in depth.

Even if the sample composition mirrors that of the population with respect to the control characteristics, there is no assurance that the sample is representative. If a characteristic that is relevant to the problem is overlooked, the quota sample will not be representative. Relevant control characteristics are often omitted because there are practical difficulties associated with including certain control characteristics. For example, suppose a sample was sought that was representative of the different strata of socio-economic classes in a population. Imagine street interviewers approaching potential participants who they believe would fit into the quota they have been set. Could interviewers 'guess' (from their clothes, accessories, posture?) which potential participants fit into different socio-economic classes, in the same way that they may guess the gender and age of participants? The initial questions of a street interview could establish the characteristics of potential participants to see whether they fit a set quota. But given the levels of non-response and ineligibility found by such an approach, this is not an ideal solution.

Because the elements within each quota are selected based on convenience or judgement, many sources of selection bias are potentially present. The interviewers may go to selected areas where eligible participants are more likely to be found. Likewise, they may avoid people who look unfriendly or are not well dressed or those who live in undesirable locations. Quota sampling does not permit assessment of sampling error.[19] Quota sampling attempts to obtain representative samples at a relatively low cost. Its advantages are the lower costs and greater convenience to the interviewers in selecting elements for each quota. Under certain conditions, quota sampling obtains results close to those for conventional probability sampling.[20]

Snowball sampling

Snowball sampling
A non-probability sampling technique in which an initial group of participants is selected randomly. Subsequent participants are selected based on the referrals or information provided by the initial participants. By obtaining referrals from referrals, this process may be carried out in waves.

In snowball sampling, an initial group of participants is selected, sometimes on a random basis, but more typically targeted at a few individuals who are known to possess the desired characteristics of the target population. After being interviewed, these participants are asked to identify others who also belong to the target population of interest. Subsequent participants are selected based on the referrals. By obtaining referrals from referrals, this process may be carried out in waves, thus leading to a snowballing effect. Even though probability sampling can be used to select the initial participants, the final sample is a non-probability sample. The referrals will have demographic and psychographic characteristics more similar to the persons referring them than would occur by chance.[21]

The main objective of snowball sampling is to estimate characteristics that are rare in the wider population. Examples include users of particular government or social services, such as parents who use nurseries or child minders, whose names cannot be revealed; special census groups, such as widowed males under 35; and members of a scattered minority ethnic group. Another example is research in industrial buyer–seller relationships, using initial contacts to identify buyer–seller pairs and then subsequent 'snowballed' pairs. The major advantage of snowball sampling is that it substantially increases the likelihood of locating the desired characteristic in the population. It also results in relatively low sampling variance and costs.[22] Snowball sampling is illustrated by the following example.

Real research | **Sampling horse owners**

Dalgety Animal Feeds wished to question horse owners about the care and feeding of their horses. The firm could not locate any sampling frame that listed all horse owners, with the exception of registers of major racing stables. However, the firm wished to contact owners who had one or two horses as it believed this group was not well understood and held great marketing potential. The initial approach involved locating interviewers at horse feed outlets. The interviewers ascertained basic characteristics of horse owners but more importantly they invited them along to focus groups. When the focus groups were conducted, issues of horse care and feeding were developed in greater detail to allow the construction of a meaningful postal questionnaire. As a rapport and trust was built up with those who attended the focus groups, names as referrals were given that allowed a sampling frame for the first wave of participants to the subsequent postal survey. The process of referrals continued, allowing a total of four waves and a response of 800 questionnaires.

In this example, note the non-random selection of the initial group of participants through focus group invitations. This procedure was more efficient than random selection, which given the absence of an appropriate sampling frame would be very cumbersome. In other cases where an appropriate sampling frame exists (appropriate in terms of identifying the desired characteristics in a number of participants, not in terms of being exhaustive – if it were exhaustive, a snowball sample would not be needed), random selection of participants through probability sampling techniques may be more appropriate.

Probability sampling techniques

Probability sampling techniques vary in terms of sampling efficiency. Sampling efficiency is a concept that reflects a trade-off between sampling cost and precision. Precision refers to the level of uncertainty about the characteristic being measured. Precision is inversely related to sampling errors but positively related to cost. The greater the precision, the greater the cost, and most studies require a trade-off. The researcher should strive for the most efficient sampling design, subject to the budget allocated. The efficiency of a probability sampling

Figure 14.4

A graphical illustration of probability sampling techniques

A graphical illustration of probability sampling techniques

1 Simple random sampling

A	B	C	D	E	
1	6	11	16	21	Select five random numbers from 1 to 25. The
2	7	12	17	22	resulting sample consists of population elements
3	8	13	18	23	3, 7, 9, 16 and 24. Note that there is no element
4	9	14	19	24	from group C
5	10	15	20	25	

2 Systematic sampling

A	B	C	D	E	
1	6	11	16	21	Select a random number between 1 and 5, say 2.
2	7	12	17	22	The resulting sample consists of a population 2,
3	8	13	18	23	$(2 + 5) = 7$, $(2 + 5 \times 2) = 12$, $(2 + 5 \times 3) = 17$ and
4	9	14	19	24	$(2 + 5 \times 4) = 22$. Note that all the elements are
5	10	15	20	25	selected from a single row

3 Stratified sampling

A	B	C	D	E	
1	6	11	16	21	Randomly select a number from 1 to 5 from each
2	7	12	17	22	stratum, A to E. The resulting sample consists of
3	8	13	18	23	population elements 4, 7, 13, 19 and 21. Note that
4	9	14	19	24	one element is selected from each column
5	10	15	20	25	

4 Cluster sampling (two stage)

A	B	C	D	E	
1	6	11	16	21	Randomly select three clusters, B, D and E. Within
2	7	12	17	22	each cluster, randomly select one or two elements.
3	8	13	18	23	The resulting sample consists of population elements
4	9	14	19	24	7, 18, 20, 21 and 23. Note that no elements are
5	10	15	20	25	selected from clusters A and C

technique may be assessed by comparing it with that of simple random sampling. Figure 14.4 presents a graphical illustration of the various probability sampling techniques. As in the case of non-probability sampling, the population consists of 25 elements and we have to select a sample of size 5; A, B, C, D and E represent groups and can also be viewed as strata or clusters.

Simple random sampling

Simple random sampling (SRS)
A probability sampling technique in which each element has a known and equal probability of selection. Every element is selected independently of every other element, and the sample is drawn by a random procedure from a sampling frame.

In **simple random sampling** (SRS), each element in the population has a known and equal probability of selection. Furthermore, each possible sample of a given size (n) has a known and equal probability of being the sample actually selected. This implies that every element is selected independently of every other element. The sample is drawn by a random procedure from a sampling frame. This method is equivalent to a lottery system in which names are placed in a container, the container is shaken and the names of the winners are then drawn out in an unbiased manner.

To draw a simple random sample, the researcher first compiles a sampling frame in which each element is assigned a unique identification number. Then random numbers are generated to determine which elements to include in the sample. The random numbers may be generated with a computer routine or a table (see Table 1 in the Appendix of statistical tables). Suppose that a sample of size 10 is to be selected from a sampling frame containing 800 elements. This could be done by starting with row 1 and column 1 of Table 1, considering the three rightmost digits, and going down the column until 10 numbers between 1 and 800 have been selected. Numbers outside this range are ignored. The elements corresponding to the random numbers generated constitute the sample. Thus, in our example, elements 480, 368, 130, 167, 570, 562, 301, 579, 475 and 553 would be selected. Note that the last three digits of row 6 (921) and row 11 (918) were ignored, because they were out of range. Using these tables is fine for small samples, but can be very tedious. A more pragmatic solution is to turn to random-number generators in most data analysis packages. For example, in Excel, the Random Number Generation Analysis Tool allows you to set a number of characteristics of your target population, including the nature of distribution of the data, and to create a table of random numbers on a separate worksheet.

SRS has many desirable features. It is easily understood and the sample results may be projected to the target population. Most approaches to statistical inference assume that the data have been collected by SRS. However, SRS suffers from at least four significant limitations. First, it is often difficult to construct a sampling frame that will permit a simple random sample to be drawn. Second, SRS can result in samples that are very large or spread over large geographical areas, thus increasing the time and cost of data collection. Third, SRS often results in lower precision with larger standard errors than other probability sampling techniques. Fourth, SRS may or may not result in a representative sample. Although samples drawn will represent the population well on average, a given simple random sample may grossly misrepresent the target population. This is more likely if the size of the sample is small. For these reasons, SRS is not widely used in marketing research[23] though there exceptions as illustrated in the following example.

Real research

An attitudinal segmentation of parents and young people[24]

In the UK, the Department of Education (**www.education.gov.uk**) was looking for more effective ways to understand its key audiences of parents & carers and children & young people. Its Customer Insight Unit (CIU) identified a need for a robust quantitative segmentation study that gave it a better understanding of underlying attitudes and values of its audiences. It felt that such a study could be used for policy and communications development across a range of issues. Specifically, the aims of the segmentation were to enable staff and stakeholders to: think about parents and young people in a new way (as an alternative to demographics), uncovering new 'target groups' and issues that required action; identify new insights affecting families; provide insights to guide communications with different groups; and identify knowledge gaps and new areas for further research. Researchers developed the National Survey of Parents and Children, using qualitative findings to inform their questionnaire design fully. They wished to collect a robust, nationally representative dataset of the various types of parenting conduct and parenting values. To capture both sides of the parent–child relationship, the survey needed a linked sample of parents and children belonging to the same household. In order to achieve this the researchers selected a random addresses in England, drawn from the Postcode Address File. Parents of children aged 19 or under were randomly chosen from those households for an adult interview, and asked about their relationship with one of their children. Then a selected child (as long as they were resident in the household and over the age of 10) was invited for the child interview. The 'link' connecting the adult to the child added a vital extra dimension to the analysis and segmentations, while the random probability sampling approach ensured that all sections of society were represented: fathers as well as mothers from all social backgrounds, with various levels of parenting experience, as well as dependent children of all ages.

Systematic sampling

Systematic sampling
A probability sampling technique in which the sample is chosen by selecting a random starting point and then picking every *i*th element in succession from the sampling frame.

In systematic sampling, the sample is chosen by selecting a random starting point and then picking every ith element in succession from the sampling frame.[25] The sampling interval, i, is determined by dividing the population size N by the sample size n and rounding to the nearest whole number. For example, there are 100,000 elements in the population and a sample of 1,000 is desired. In this case, the sampling interval, i, is 100. A random number between 1 and 100 is selected. If, for example, this number is 23, the sample consists of elements 23, 123, 223, 323, 423, 523, and so on.[26]

Systematic sampling is similar to SRS in that each population element has a known and equal probability of selection. It is different from SRS, however, in that only the permissible samples of size n that can be drawn have a known and equal probability of selection. The remaining samples of size n have a zero probability of being selected. For systematic sampling, the researcher assumes that the population elements are ordered in some respect. In some cases, the ordering (e.g. alphabetical listing in a telephone book) is unrelated to the characteristic of interest. In other instances, the ordering is directly related to the characteristic under investigation. For example, credit card customers may be listed in order of outstanding balance, or firms in a given industry may be ordered according to annual sales. If the population elements are arranged in a manner unrelated to the characteristic of interest, systematic sampling will yield results quite similar to SRS.

On the other hand, when the ordering of the elements is related to the characteristic of interest, systematic sampling increases the representativeness of the sample. If firms in an industry are arranged in increasing order of annual sales, a systematic sample will include some small and some large firms. A simple random sample may be unrepresentative because it may contain, for example, only small firms or a disproportionate number of small firms. If the ordering of the elements produces a cyclical pattern, systematic sampling may decrease the representativeness of the sample. To illustrate, consider the use of systematic sampling to generate a sample of monthly sales from the Harrods store in London. In such a case, the sampling frame could contain monthly sales for the last 60 years or more. If a sampling interval of 12 were chosen, the resulting sample would not reflect the month-to-month and seasonal variations in sales.[27]

Systematic sampling is less costly and easier than SRS because random selection is done only once to establish a starting point. Moreover, random numbers do not have to be matched with individual elements as in SRS. Because some lists contain millions of elements, considerable time can be saved, which reduces the costs of sampling. If information related to the characteristic of interest is available for the population, systematic sampling can be used to obtain a more representative and reliable (lower sampling error) sample than SRS. Another relative advantage is that systematic sampling can even be used without knowledge of the elements of the sampling frame. For example, every ith person accessing a website, leaving a shop or passing a point in the street can be intercepted (provided very strict control of the flow of potential participants is exercised). For these reasons, systematic sampling is often employed in online surveys, postal, telephone and street interviews, as illustrated by the following example.

Real research	**Service quality expectations of Hong Kong Chinese shoppers[28]**

Global retailers in the last century have focused on the presumed similarities of consumers across borders, and used the management of product novelty or newness to attract foreign customers. When novelty and newness fades, however, success moves to a dependence on understanding differences among consumers in different cultures. A study examined how cultural differences affected retail customers' service quality perception in a cultural context distinctly different from Western culture, the Hong Kong Chinese retail supermarket. The key research objective was to examine underlying service quality dimensions of experienced shoppers in two supermarkets. The population was defined as all Chinese shoppers who had previously shopped in the selected Park'N Shop and Wellcome stores. The sample was a systematic sample using a random start with the selection of Chinese shoppers occurring as they approached the stores. Each potential participant was qualified by being asked if they had previously shopped at the store, with an alternative line of questionning if they did not qualify. A total of 100 interviews were completed at each of four stores for a total of 400 completed interviews.

Stratified sampling

Stratified sampling
A probability sampling technique that uses a two-step process to partition the population into subsequent subpopulations, or strata. Elements are selected from each stratum by a random procedure.

Stratified sampling is a two-step process in which the population is partitioned into subpopulations, or strata. The strata should be mutually exclusive and collectively exhaustive in that every population element should be assigned to one and only one stratum and no population elements should be omitted. Next, elements are selected from each stratum by a random procedure, usually SRS. Technically, only SRS should be employed in selecting the elements from each stratum. In practice, sometimes systematic sampling and other probability sampling procedures are employed. Stratified sampling differs from quota sampling in that the sample elements are selected probabilistically rather than based on convenience or judgement. A major objective of stratified sampling is to increase precision without increasing cost.[29]

The variables used to partition the population into strata are referred to as stratification variables. The criteria for the selection of these variables consist of homogeneity, heterogeneity, relatedness and cost. The elements within a stratum should be as homogeneous as possible, but the elements in different strata should be as heterogeneous as possible. The stratification variables should also be closely related to the characteristic of interest. The more closely these criteria are met, the greater the effectiveness in controlling extraneous sampling variation. Finally, the variables should decrease the cost of the stratification process by being easy to measure and apply. Variables commonly used for stratification include demographic characteristics (as illustrated in the example for quota sampling), type of customer (e.g. credit card versus non-credit card), size of firm, or type of industry. It is possible to use more than one variable for stratification, although more than two are seldom used because of pragmatic and cost considerations. Although the number of strata to use is a matter of judgement, experience suggests the use of no more than six. Beyond six strata, any gain in precision is more than offset by the increased cost of stratification and sampling.

Another important decision involves the use of proportionate or disproportionate sampling. In proportionate stratified sampling, the size of the sample drawn from each stratum is proportionate to the relative size of that stratum in the total population. In disproportionate stratified sampling, the size of the sample from each stratum is proportionate to the relative size of that stratum and to the standard deviation of the distribution of the characteristic of interest among all the elements in that stratum. The logic behind disproportionate sampling is simple. First, strata with larger relative sizes are more influential in determining the population mean, and these strata should also exert a greater influence in deriving the sample estimates. Consequently, more elements should be drawn from strata of larger relative size. Second, to increase precision, more elements should be drawn from strata with larger standard deviations and fewer elements should be drawn from strata with smaller standard deviations. (If all the elements in a stratum are identical, a sample size of one will result in perfect information.) Note that the two methods are identical if the characteristic of interest has the same standard deviation within each stratum.

Disproportionate sampling requires that some estimate of the relative variation, or standard deviation of the distribution of the characteristic of interest, within strata be known. As this information is not always available, the researcher may have to rely on intuition and logic to determine sample sizes for each stratum. For example, large fashion stores might be expected to have greater variation in the sales of some products as compared with small boutiques. Hence, the number of large stores in a sample may be disproportionately large. When the researcher is primarily interested in examining differences between strata, a common sampling strategy is to select the same sample size from each stratum.

Stratified sampling can ensure that all the important subpopulations are represented in the sample. This is particularly important if the distribution of the characteristic of interest in the population is skewed. For example, very few households have annual incomes that allow them to own a second home overseas. If a simple random sample is taken, households that have a second home overseas may not be adequately represented. Stratified sampling would guarantee that the sample contains a certain number of these households. Stratified sampling combines the simplicity of SRS with potential gains in precision. Therefore, it is a popular sampling technique and is illustrated in the following example.

Real research	**Consumer attitudes towards advertising in Romania**[30]

Significant changes in social values, mindsets and behavioural patterns have taken place in central and eastern European countries in the transition from a centrally planned system to a free market economy. These changes impacted upon ideologies that underpinned not only product involvement and brand experimentation, but also consumer attitudes to advertising. In this context, a study investigated consumer attitudes towards advertising in Romania, which became a new member state of the EU as of January 2007. A questionnaire was developed to be administered by face-to-face interviews with adult participants. The sampling method consisted of two stages. In the first stage, three cities from distinctive socio-cultural areas were selected. This sampling plan capitalised on the significant differences in the economic development and lifestyles that had been reported between Bucharest, Lasi and Cluj. In the second stage, participants in each city were selected. The data collection method used was stratified random sampling. Education, gender and age strata were identified to reflect the specific socio-demographic characteristics of each city.

Cluster sampling

Cluster sampling
A two-step probability
sampling technique where
the target population is
first divided into mutually
exclusive and collectively
exhaustive subpopulations
called clusters, and then
a random sample of
clusters is selected based
on a probability sampling
technique such as SRS.
For each selected cluster,
either all the elements are
included in the sample, or
a sample of elements is
drawn probabilistically.

Area sampling
A common form of
cluster sampling in which
the clusters consist of
geographical areas such
as counties, housing
tracts, blocks or other area
descriptions.

In cluster sampling, the target population is first divided into mutually exclusive and collectively exhaustive subpopulations, or clusters. These subpopulations or clusters are assumed to contain the diversity of participants held in the target population. A random sample of clusters is selected, based on a probability sampling technique such as SRS. For each selected cluster, either all the elements are included in the sample or a sample of elements is drawn probabilistically. If all the elements in each selected cluster are included in the sample, the procedure is called one-stage cluster sampling. If a sample of elements is drawn probabilistically from each selected cluster, the procedure is two-stage cluster sampling. As shown in Figure 14.5, two-stage cluster sampling can be either simple two-stage cluster sampling involving SRS or probability proportionate to size sampling. Furthermore, a cluster sample can have multiple (more than two) stages, as in multistage cluster sampling.

The key distinction between cluster sampling and stratified sampling is that in cluster sampling only a sample of subpopulations (clusters) is chosen, whereas in stratified sampling all the subpopulations (strata) are selected for further sampling. The objectives of the two methods are also different. The objective of cluster sampling is to increase sampling efficiency by decreasing costs, but the objective of stratified sampling is to increase precision. With respect to homogeneity and heterogeneity, the criteria for forming clusters are just the opposite of those for strata. Elements within a cluster should be as heterogeneous as possible, but clusters themselves should be as homogeneous as possible. Ideally, each cluster should be a small-scale representation of the population. In cluster sampling, a sampling frame is needed only for those clusters selected for the sample. The differences between stratified sampling and cluster sampling are summarised in Table 14.3.

A common form of cluster sampling is area sampling, in which the clusters consist of geographical areas, such as counties, housing districts or residential blocks. If only one level of sampling takes place in selecting the basic elements (e.g. if the researcher samples blocks and then all the households within the selected blocks are included in the sample), the design is called one-stage area sampling. If two or more levels of sampling take place before the basic elements are selected (if the researcher samples blocks and then samples households within the sampled blocks), the design is called two-stage (or multistage) area sampling. The distinguishing feature of one-stage area sampling is that all the households in the selected blocks (or geographical areas) are included in the sample.

There are two types of two-stage cluster sampling designs, as shown in Figure 14.5. Simple two-stage cluster sampling involves SRS at the first stage (e.g. sampling blocks) as well as the second stage (e.g. sampling households within blocks). This design is called *simple two-stage cluster sampling*. In this design the fraction of elements (e.g. households) selected at the second stage is the same for each sample cluster (e.g. selected blocks). This process was

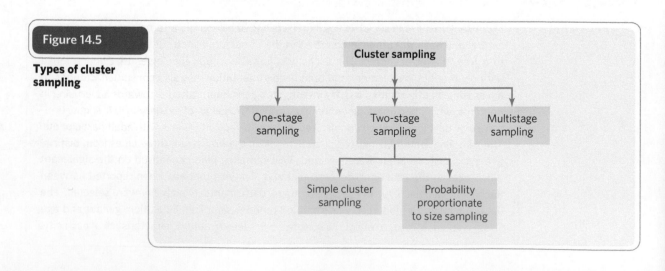

Figure 14.5

Types of cluster sampling

Table 14.3	Differences between stratified and cluster sampling	
Factor	**Stratified sampling**	**Cluster sampling (one stage)**
Objective	Increase precision	Decrease cost
Subpopulations	All strata are included	A sample of clusters is chosen
Within subpopulations	Each stratum should be homogeneous	Each cluster should be heterogeneous
Across subpopulations	Strata should be heterogeneous	Clusters should be homogeneous
Sampling frame	Needed for the entire population	Needed only for the selected clusters
Selection of elements	Elements selected from each stratum randomly	All elements from each selected cluster are included

administered in a project that investigated the behaviour of high net worth consumers. A simple random sample of 800 block groups was selected from a listing of neighbourhoods with average incomes exceeding €35,000 in locations ranked in the top half by income according to census data. Commercial database companies supplied head of household names for approximately 95% of the census-tabulated homes in the 800 block groups. From the 213,000 enumerated households, 9000 were selected by SRS.[31]

This design is appropriate when the clusters are equal in size; that is, when the clusters contain approximately the same number of sampling units. If they differ greatly in size, however, simple two-stage cluster sampling can lead to biased estimates. Sometimes the clusters can be made of equal size by combining clusters. When this option is not feasible, probability proportionate to size (PPS) sampling can be used.

Probability proportionate to size (PPS)
A selection method where the probability of selecting a sampling unit in a selected cluster varies inversely with the size of the cluster. Therefore, the size of all the resulting clusters is approximately equal.

In probability proportionate to size (PPS) sampling, the clusters are sampled with probability proportional to size. The size of a cluster is defined in terms of the number of sampling units within that cluster. Thus, in the first stage, large clusters are more likely to be included than small clusters. In the second stage, the probability of selecting a sampling unit in a selected cluster varies inversely with the size of the cluster. Thus, the probability that any particular sampling unit will be included in the sample is equal for all units, because the unequal first-stage probabilities are balanced by the unequal second-stage probabilities. The numbers of sampling units included from the selected clusters are approximately equal. This type of multistage sampling is presented in the following example.

Real research | **Teleuse on a shoestring[32]**

In the telecommunications industries, companies are beginning to understand the needs of low-income consumers, adapting their products and business models to better serve their needs. Many commentators predict that the low-income, developing markets will be where new telecom growth will come from. A study addressing the needs of these consumers was conducted in five emerging Asian countries, namely Pakistan, India, Sri Lanka, Philippines and Thailand. Given the necessity for cross-country comparisons among the less privileged strata of society, the target groups had to be defined as close as possible in a universal manner. Target participants of the study were telecom users, defined as those who had used a phone (own or someone else's; paid for or free of charge) during the preceding three months. Participants were males and females between the ages of

18 and 60 years, from rural and urban locations. A multistage stratified cluster sampling by probability proportionate to size (PPS) was used to select the target number of urban and rural centres. After determining the number of centres to be selected from each cell (strata in respective provinces), urban and rural areas were selected again using PPS on a constant population interval on geographically ordered centres within each cell. In each selected centre, a common place such as a road, park, hospital was designated the starting point for contacting households. Only one participant was selected from each household. In households with more than one valid participant, a random-number chart was used to select the participant. Within each country, data were weighted by gender, province group/zone and socio-economic group to correct over- or under-sampling in certain areas and socio-economic groups.

Cluster sampling has two major advantages: feasibility and low cost. In many situations the only sampling frames readily available for the target population are clusters, not population elements. It is often impossible to compile a list of all consumers in a population, given the resources and constraints. Lists of geographical areas, telephone exchanges and other clusters of consumers, however, can be constructed relatively easily. Cluster sampling is the most cost-effective probability sampling technique. This advantage must be weighed against several limitations.[33] Cluster sampling results in relatively imprecise samples, and it is difficult to form clusters in which the elements are heterogeneous, because, for example, households in a block tend to be similar rather than dissimilar.[34] It can be difficult to compute and interpret statistics based on clusters.

Other probability sampling techniques

In addition to the four basic probability sampling techniques, there is a variety of other sampling techniques. Most of these may be viewed as extensions of the basic techniques and were developed to address complex sampling problems. Two techniques with some relevance to marketing research are sequential sampling and double sampling.

Sequential sampling
A probability sampling technique in which the population elements are sampled sequentially, data collection and analysis are done at each stage, and a decision is made as to whether additional population elements should be sampled.

Double sampling
A sampling technique in which certain population elements are sampled twice.

In sequential sampling, the population elements are sampled sequentially, data collection and analysis are done at each stage, and a decision is made as to whether additional population elements should be sampled. The sample size is not known in advance, but a decision rule is stated before sampling begins. At each stage, this rule indicates whether sampling should be continued or whether enough information has been obtained. Sequential sampling has been used to determine preferences for two competing alternatives. In one study, participants were asked which of two alternatives they preferred, and sampling was terminated when sufficient evidence was accumulated to validate a preference. It has also been used to establish the price differential between a standard model and a de luxe model of a consumer durable.[35]

In double sampling, also called two-phase sampling, certain population elements are sampled twice. In the first phase, a sample is selected and some information is collected from all the elements in the sample. In the second phase, a subsample is drawn from the original sample and additional information is obtained from the elements in the sub sample. The process may be extended to three or more phases, and the different phases may take place simultaneously or at different times. Double sampling can be useful when no sampling frame is readily available for selecting final sampling units but when the elements of the frame are known to be contained within a broader sampling frame. For example, a researcher wants to select households in a given city that consume apple juice. The households of interest are contained within the set of all households, but the researcher does not know which ones they are. In applying double sampling, the researcher would obtain a sampling frame of all households in the first phase. This would be constructed from a directory of city addresses. Then a sample of households would be drawn, using systematic random sampling to determine the amount of apple juice consumed. In the second phase, households that consume apple juice would be selected and stratified according to the amount of apple juice consumed. Then a stratified random sample would be drawn and detailed questions regarding apple juice consumption asked.[36]

Choosing non-probability versus probability sampling

The choice between non-probability and probability samples should be based on considerations such as the nature of the research, relative magnitude of non-sampling versus sampling errors, and variability in the population, as well as statistical and operational considerations (see Table 14.4). For example, in exploratory research, the judgement of the researcher in selecting participants with particular qualities may be far more effective than any form of probability sampling. On the other hand, in conclusive research where the researcher wishes to use the results to estimate overall market shares or the size of the total market, probability sampling is favoured. Probability samples allow statistical projection of the results to a target population.

For some research problems, highly accurate estimates of population characteristics are required. In these situations, the elimination of selection bias and the ability to calculate sampling error make probability sampling desirable. However, probability sampling will not always result in more accurate results. If non-sampling errors are likely to be an important factor, then non-probability sampling may be preferable because the use of judgement may allow greater control over the sampling process.

Another consideration is the homogeneity of the population with respect to the variables of interest. A heterogeneous population would favour probability sampling because it would be more important to secure a representative sample. Probability sampling is preferable from a statistical viewpoint, as it is the basis of most common statistical techniques.

Probability sampling generally requires statistically trained researchers, generally costs more and takes longer than non-probability sampling, especially in the establishment of accurate sampling frames. In many marketing research projects, it is difficult to justify the additional time and expense. Therefore, in practice, the objectives of the study dictate which sampling method will be used.

Non-probability sampling is used in concept tests, package tests, name tests and copy tests where projections to the populations are usually not needed. In such studies, interest centres on the proportion of the sample that gives various responses or expresses various attitudes.

Table 14.4	Choosing non-probability vs. probability sampling	
	Conditions favouring the use of:	
Factors	*Non-probability sampling*	*Probability sampling*
Nature of research	Exploratory	Conclusive
Relative magnitude of sampling and non-sampling errors	Non-sampling errors are larger	Sampling errors are larger
Variability in the population	Homogeneous (low)	Heterogeneous (high)
Statistical considerations	Unfavourable	Favourable
Operational considerations	Favourable	Unfavourable

Samples for these studies can be drawn using access panels and employing methods such as online surveys, street interviewing and quota sampling. On the other hand, probability sampling is used when there is a need for highly accurate estimates of market share or sales volume for the entire market. National market tracking studies, which provide information on product category and brand usage rates as well as psychographic and demographic profiles of users, use probability sampling.

Summary of sampling techniques

The strengths and weaknesses of basic sampling techniques are summarised in Table 14.5. Table 14.6 describes the procedures for drawing probability samples.

Table 14.5	Strengths and weaknesses of sampling techniques	
Technique	*Strengths*	*Weaknesses*
Non-probability sampling		
Convenience sampling	Least expensive, least time consuming, most convenient	Selection bias, sample not representative, not recommended for descriptive or causal research
Judgemental sampling	Low cost, convenient, not time consuming. Ideal for exploratory research designs	Does not allow generalisation, subjective
Quota sampling	Sample can be controlled for certain characteristics	Selection bias, no assurance of representativeness
Snowball sampling	Can estimate rare characteristics	Time consuming
Probability sampling		
Simple random sampling (SRS)	Easily understood, results projectable	Difficult to construct sampling frame, expensive, lower precision, no assurance of representativeness
Systematic sampling	Can increase representativeness, easier to implement than SRS, sampling frame not always necessary	Can decrease representativeness depending upon 'order' in the sampling frame
Stratified sampling	Includes all important subpopulations, precision	Difficult to select relevant stratification variables, not feasible to stratify on many variables, expensive
Cluster sampling	Easy to implement, cost effective	Imprecise, difficult to compute and interpret results

| Table 14.6 | **Procedures for drawing probability samples** |

Simple random sampling

1 Select a suitable sampling frame.
2 Each element is assigned a number from 1 to N (population size).
3 Generate n (sample size) different random numbers between 1 and N using a software package or a table of simple random numbers (Table 1 in the Appendix of statistical tables). To use Table 1, select the appropriate number of digits (e.g. if $N = 900$, select three digits). Arbitrarily select a beginning number. Then proceed up or down until n different numbers between 1 and N have been selected. Discard 0, duplicate numbers and numbers greater than N.
4 The numbers generated denote the elements that should be included in the sample.

Systematic sampling

1 Select a suitable sampling frame.
2 Each element is assigned a number from 1 to N (population size).
3 Determine the sampling interval i, where $i = N/n$. If i is a fraction, round to the nearest whole number.
4 Select a random number, r, between 1 and i, as explained in simple random sampling.
5 The elements with the following numbers will comprise the systematic random sample:
$r, r + i, r + 2i, r + 3i, r + 4i, ..., r + (n-1)i$

Stratified sampling

1 Select a suitable sampling frame.
2 Select the stratification variable(s) and the number of strata, H.
3 Divide the entire population into H strata. Based on the classification variable, each element of the population is assigned to one of the H strata.
4 In each stratum, number the elements from 1 to N_h (the population size of stratum h).
5 Determine the sample size of each stratum, n_h, based on proportionate or disproportionate stratified sampling, where

$$\sum_{h=1}^{H} n_h = n$$

6 In each stratum, select a simple random sample of size n_h.

Cluster sampling

We describe the procedure for selecting a simple two-stage sample, because this represents the most commonly used general case:

1 Assign a number from 1 to N to each element in the population.
2 Divide the population into C clusters of which c will be included in the sample.
3 Calculate the sampling interval i, where $i = N/c$. If i is a fraction, round to the nearest whole number.
4 Select a random number, r, between 1 and i, as explained in simple random sampling.
5 Identify elements with the following numbers: $r, r + i, r + 2i, r + 3i, ..., r + (c - 1)i$.
6 Select the clusters that contain the identified elements.
7 Select sampling units within each selected cluster based on SRS or systematic sampling. The number of sampling units selected from each sample cluster is approximately the same and equal to n/c.
8 If the population of the cluster exceeds the sampling interval i, that cluster is selected with certainty. That cluster is removed from further consideration. Calculate the new proportion size, N^*, the number of clusters to be selected, $c^* (= c - 1)$, and the new sampling interval i^*. Repeat this process until each of the remaining clusters has a population less than the relevant sampling interval. If b clusters have been selected with certainty, select the remaining $c - b$ clusters according to steps 1 to 7. The fraction of units to be sampled from each cluster selected with certainty is the overall sampling fraction n/N. Thus, for clusters selected with certainty, we would select $n_s(n/N)(N_1 + N_2 + ... + N_b)$ units. The units selected from clusters selected under two-stage sampling will therefore be $n^* = n - n_s$.

International marketing research

Many of the examples used in this chapter have illustrated the use of sampling in international markets. Implementing the sampling design process in international marketing research can be most challenging and rewarding as illustrated in the following example.[37]

Real research   ## Measuring the business elite of India[38]

The objectives of Business Elite surveys (**www.ipsos-mori.com**) were threefold: (1) to estimate the size and scope of a business elite audience in India; (2) to measure their media consumption and business decision-making influence; and (3) to support campaign planning targeted at the most senior business executives. The research design consisted of three broad steps; (1) identify eligible companies using a variety of local business directories and other sources; (2) sample these companies by telephone to identify and confirm contact details for the most senior executives and to identify the existence or not of certain job functions within the organisation; and (3) send a short self-completion questionnaire by post or email to identified participants. Ipsos MORI was approached by a leading Indian business newspaper to investigate the possibility of extending the coverage of the Business Elite survey to India. The agency identified a list of 17,456 qualifying companies across eight major cities (Mumbai, New Delhi, Kolkata, Chennai, Bangalore, Hyderabad, Ahmedabad and Pune). A systematic random sample was drawn from a cleaned-up database of companies which Ipos MORI researchers endeavoured to

contact by telephone. Controls were set by industry sector at the weighting stage to correct any bias in the sources. In the initial telephoning screening exercise, the researchers targeted 1,714 companies and made successful contact with 859 of them (50.1%). From the interviews they estimated that the universe of eligible business executives in qualifying companies across the eight Indian cities totalled 106,307. This was based on the incidence at each of the companies sampled, of a randomly generated list of job functions. They also pinpointed 1,499 executives to contact, of whom 600 (40%) agreed to be interviewed face to face. This was a response rate in line with that found in recent Business Elite studies in Asia (37%) and Europe (31%).

This example illustrated many of the challenges faced in defining a target population. The relevant element (participant) may differ from country to country. Accessibility also varies across countries. Sampling through face-to-face contact can be complex in developing countries that have limited census data or no postcode system. This can demand more training with senior interviewers versed in sampling design needed to ensure that the sample reflects the desired population. This is especially important in markets with strong population growth and changing classification of urban areas. In Vietnam for example, people are flooding into urban areas as a result of new wealth-generating opportunities and birth rates remaining high. It should not be assumed that developing countries are simply behind the pace of change in marketing research simply because they have not progressed from 'door-to-door, pen-and-paper' interviewing to CATI or online research. While face-to-face interviewing remains important in these markets, it will not be the only method of data collection. Cambodia, for example, has very limited fixed-line coverage for telecoms, but it has bypassed the development of fixed-line communications and moved straight to a mobile infrastructure. The situation is the same across Africa and many other developing countries and signifies a different evolution in the development of technology that can be used for data capture in research, to that for developed countries.[39]

Developing an appropriate sampling frame is a difficult task. In many countries, particularly developing countries, reliable information about the target population may not be available from secondary sources. Government data may be unavailable or highly biased. Population lists may not be available commercially. The time and money required to compile these lists may be prohibitive. The census data available (even for demographics at household level) in some countries have one or more of the following problems: limited availability of variables, outdated data, unreliable data, outdated or unavailable maps. Reliable and updated information from the National Economic Census is not necessarily available for business-to-business, agricultural or industrial studies. It is possible to find countries where the information at household level is quite reliable, updated and available online or on CD-ROM. Mexico for example was the first country in the Latin American region to provide this.[40]

Given the lack of suitable sampling frames, the inaccessibility of certain participants, such as women in some cultures, and the dominance of face-to-face interviewing, probability sampling techniques are uncommon in international marketing research. New modes of data collection, namely email, online, SMS, mobile devices, have necessitated new sampling methods primarily through the use of access panels. With such approaches the validation of survey findings or provision of relevant weighting is not generally feasible, especially in international studies where there may be a lack of valid population data. In international research, the growth of online surveys has caused concern when used with online panels where sampling is usually based upon non-probability methods. What constitutes an adequate sampling frame includes adequate coverage, known probabilities of selection, and being up to date. Access panels with adequate sampling frames, adequate selection/recruitment procedures and adequate controls can provide verifiable research findings. However, the American Association for Public Opinion Research[41] reported:

The majority of studies comparing results from surveys using non-probability online panels with those using probability-based methods (most often RDD [Random-Digit Dialling] telephone) often report significantly different results on a wide array of behaviour and attitudes.

One common element in almost all panels being evaluated is that the recruitment of the panel members is self-selecting, from either direct contact by potential panel members to a particular panel provider, or after seeing an invitation on certain web pages. Good-quality access panels can be specified and created but there are major challenges in achieving such standards across international markets. This can only be achieved by adequate investment in design, process, IT systems, skills and management control.[42]

Ethics in marketing research

The researcher has several ethical responsibilities to both the client and the participants pertaining to sampling.[43] With regard to the client, the researcher must develop a sampling design that best fits the project in an effort to minimise the sampling and non-sampling errors (see Chapter 3). When probability sampling can be used, it should be. When non-probability design such as convenience sampling is used, the limitations of the design should be explicit in any findings that are presented. It is unethical and misleading to treat non-probability samples as probability samples and to project the results to a target population. Appropriate definitions of the population and the sampling frame, and application of the correct sampling techniques, are essential if the research is to be conducted and the findings used ethically.

Researchers must be extremely sensitive to preserving the anonymity of the participants when conducting business-to-business research with small populations, particularly when reporting the findings to the client. When the population size is small, it is easier to discern the identities of the participants than when the samples are drawn from a large population. Special care must be taken when sample details are too revealing and when using verbatim quotations in reports to the client. This problem is acute in areas such as employee research. Here a breach of a participant's anonymity can cost the participant a pay rise, a promotion, or even their employment. In such situations, special effort should be made to protect the identities of the participants. In such situations, the researcher has the ethical obligation to protect the identities of participants, even if it means limiting the level of sampling detail that is reported to the client and other parties.

Digital applications in marketing research

A major sampling issue for online research is representativeness because of a lack of ownership or access to online devices. Heavy users of the Internet may have a disproportionately higher probability of being included in studies. Unrestricted online samples in which any visitor can participate are convenience samples and suffer from self-selection bias in that participants can initiate their own selection. To avoid sampling errors, the researcher must be able to control the pool from which the participants are selected. Also, it must be ensured that the participants do not respond more than once. These requirements are met by many online, SMS and mobile device surveys, in which the researcher selects specific participants. This can be accomplished with online surveys by sending invitations to selected participants and asking them to visit the website on which a survey is posted. In this case, the survey is posted in a hidden location on the Web, which is protected by a password. Hence, non-invited web surfers are unable to access it.

The sampling techniques commonly used online may be classified as online intercept (non-random and random), online recruited and other techniques as shown in Figure 14.6. Online recruited techniques can be further classified as panel (recruited or opt-in) or non-panel (list rentals). In online intercept sampling, visitors to a website are intercepted and given an opportunity to participate in a survey. The interception can be made at one or more websites, including high-traffic sites such as Yahoo!. In non-random sampling, every visitor is intercepted. This may be meaningful if the website traffic is low, the survey has to be completed in a short time, and little incentive is being offered. However, this results in a convenience sample. Quotas can be imposed to increase representativeness. In random intercept sampling, the software selects visitors at random and a 'pop-up' window asks whether the person wants to participate in the survey. The selection can be made based on simple random or systematic random sampling. If the population is defined as visitors to a particular website, then this procedure results in a probability sample. However, if the population is other than visitors to a particular site, the resulting sample is more similar to a non-probability sample. Nevertheless, randomisation improves representativeness and discourages multiple responses from the same participant.

| Figure 14.6 | A classification of online sampling |

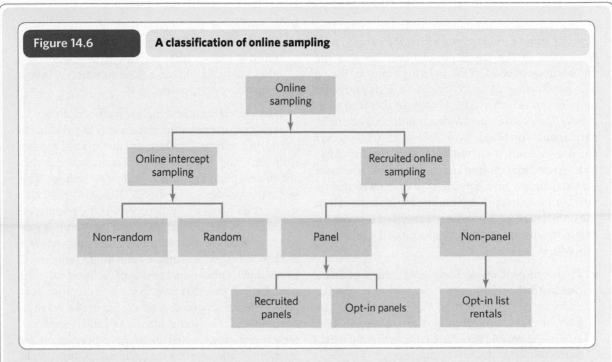

Online panels function in ways similar to non-online panels and share many of the same advantages and disadvantages. In recruited panels, typically termed as access panels, members can be recruited online or even by traditional means (postal, telephone). Based on the researcher's judgement, certain qualifying criteria can be introduced to pre-screen participants. Participants can be offered incentives such as sweepstake prizes, redeemable points and other types of online currencies. Members typically provide detailed psychographic, demographic, online usage and product consumption information at the time of joining. Opt-in panels operate similarly except that members choose to opt in as opposed to being recruited. To select a sample, the online company sends an email to those panellists who qualify based upon sample specifications given by the researcher. In the following example, online panels across the globe can be accessed through one source, enabling detailed sample specifications in cross-cultural studies.

| Real research | **Accessing panels across the globe**[44] |

Cint (**www.cint.com**) is a Swedish software company that produces and sells online marketing research products. Cint developed Direct Sample as an open marketplace platform. This enables online research to be conducted by bringing together panel owners and sample buyers. Together they can can buy and sell access to over 5 million members of research panels in more than 40 countries. The company has an extensive list of clients and partners spanning most of the large market research groups, media and Web-based companies, branding and advertising agencies, plus medium and small research agencies and other organisations involved in marketing research. The panels accessed through Cint were built by several major brands such as Habbo, Bounty, MSN and Metro, plus leading research agencies. These brands have strong relationships with their customers so the affinity levels and participant engagement were high. Cint performs quality checks for surveys (language, logic, adherence to the industry standards) for online questionnaires coming to the Cint Panel Exchange (Cint's global marketplace for buyers and sellers of samples) from market research professionals, before allowing these surveys to be dispatched to the panels.

The success of probability sampling techniques depends upon the extent to which the panel is representative of the target population. This was the argument developed in the opening example 'Down with random sampling'. With panels, highly targeted samples can be achieved, e.g. teenage girls who shop at boutiques more than twice a month. For example, participants for Harris Poll Online (HPOL) surveys are drawn from their multi-million-member database **www.harrispollonline.com**. Email addresses for participants in the database are obtained from a number of sources including the HPOL registration site and HPOL banner advertisements. To maintain reliability and integrity in the sample, the following procedures are used:

- *Password protection.* Each invitation contains a password that is uniquely assigned to that email address. A participant is required to enter the password at the beginning of the survey to gain access. Password protection ensures that a participant completes the survey only once.
- *Reminder invitations.* To increase the number of participants in the survey and to improve overall response rates, up to two additional reminder invitations are typically emailed at two- to four-day intervals to those participants who have not responded.

- *Summary of the survey findings.* To increase the number of participants in the survey and to improve overall response rates, participants are often provided with an online summary of some of the survey responses.

Non-panel recruited sampling methods can also be used that require potential participants to go online to complete a survey. To illustrate, the Spanish fashion store Zara may hand its customers an invite as they complete a purchase (either in-store or online). This invite directs them to a specific password-protected site to respond to a questionnaire. If the population is defined as the company's customers, as in a customer satisfaction survey, and a random procedure is used to select participants, a probability sample will be obtained. Other non-panel approaches involve the use of email lists that have been bought from suppliers. Presumably (and great care must be taken in establishing the ethical credentials of such suppliers), these participants opted in or gave permission for their email addresses to be circulated. Offline techniques such as short telephone screening interviews are also used for recruiting online samples. Many companies routinely collect email addresses in their CRM databases through telephone interactions, product registration cards, on-site registrations, special promotions and competitions.

Summary

Information about the characteristics of a population may be obtained by carrying out either a sample or a census. Budget and time limits, large population size and small variance in the characteristic of interest favour the use of a sample. Sampling is also preferred when the cost of sampling error is low, the cost of non-sampling error is high, the nature of measurement is destructive, and attention must be focused on individual cases. The opposite set of conditions favours the use of a census.

Sampling design begins by defining the target population in terms of elements, sampling units, extent and time. Then the sampling frame should be determined. A sampling frame is a representation of the elements of the target population. It consists of a list of directions for identifying the target population. At this stage, it is important to recognise any sampling frame errors that may exist. The next step involves selecting a sampling technique and determining the sample size. In addition to quantitative analysis, several qualitative considerations should be taken into account in determining the sample size. Execution of the sampling process requires detailed specifications for each step in the sampling process. Finally, the selected sample should be validated by comparing characteristics of the sample with known characteristics of the target population.

Sampling techniques may be classified as non-probability and probability techniques. Non-probability sampling techniques rely on the researcher's judgement. Consequently, they do not permit an objective evaluation of the precision of the sample results, and the estimates obtained are not statistically projectable to the population. The commonly used non-probability sampling techniques include convenience sampling, judgemental sampling, quota sampling and snowball sampling.

In probability sampling techniques, sampling units are selected by chance. Each sampling unit has a non-zero chance of being selected, and the researcher can pre-specify every potential sample of a given size that could be drawn from the population as well as the probability of selecting each sample. It is also possible to determine the precision of the sample estimates and inferences and make projections to the target population. Probability sampling techniques include simple random sampling, systematic sampling, stratified sampling, cluster sampling, sequential sampling and double sampling. The choice between probability and non-probability sampling should be based on the nature of the research, degree of error tolerance, relative magnitude of sampling and non-sampling errors, variability in the population, and statistical and operational considerations.

When conducting international marketing research, it is desirable to achieve comparability in sample composition and representativeness even though this may require the use of different sampling techniques in different countries. It is unethical and misleading to treat non-probability samples as probability samples and to project the results to a target population. The growth of online research has seen a corresponding growth in the use of online panels. Such panels have offered many advantages to researchers wishing to access samples of sufficient size and structure, from across the globe, quickly and relatively cheaply. Such panels create much debate about representativeness, the challenges of working primarily with non-probability samples and the actions required to create probability samples.

Questions

1 Under what conditions would a sample be preferable to a census? A census preferable to a sample?

2 Describe the sampling design process.

3 How should the target population be defined? How does this definition link with the definition of a marketing research problem?

4 What is a sampling unit? How is it different from the population element?

5 To what extent may the availability of sampling frames determine the definition of a population?

6 What qualitative factors should be considered in determining the sample size?

7 How do probability sampling techniques differ from non-probability sampling techniques? What factors should be considered in choosing between probability and non-probability sampling?

8 What is the least expensive and least time consuming of all sampling techniques? What are the major limitations of this technique?

9 What is the major difference between judgemental and convenience sampling? Give examples of where each of these techniques may be successfully applied.

10 Describe snowball sampling. How may the technique be supported by qualitative research techniques?

11 What are the distinguishing features of simple random sampling?

12 Describe the procedure for selecting a systematic random sample.

13 Describe stratified sampling. What are the criteria for the selection of stratification variables?

14 What are the differences between proportionate and disproportionate stratified sampling?

15 Describe the cluster sampling procedure. What is the key distinction between cluster sampling and stratified sampling?

Exercises

1 Examine online databases and secondary data sources to determine all of the airlines operating in the EU. If a survey of airlines were conducted to determine their future plans to purchase/lease aircraft, would you take a sample or census? Explain why.

2 Visit **www.ralphlauren.com** and collect further secondary data and intelligence to obtain information on the segmentation strategy of Ralph Lauren. As the Vice President of Marketing for Ralph Lauren, what information would you like to support decisions around an idea to launch a new line of unisex shirts in Europe? Imagine that the company had launched these shirts and wanted to determine initial consumer reactions. If non-probability sampling were used, which sampling technique would you recommend, and why?

3 The Alumni Office of your university would like to conduct a survey of on-campus students who are in their final year of study. The office wishes to determine attitudes to joining alumni associations as students progress through further study and their careers. As a consultant you must develop a quota sample. What quota variables would you use? Design a quota matrix. Base this matrix upon your chosen variables and the proportions of these variables within your university.

4 You work as the Marketing Research Manager for ABN AMRO in Amsterdam. Managers would like to know if the attitudes towards saving differ between ethnic groups. They wonder whether, given the varied population of the Netherlands, it is meaningful to segment the market according to ethnic background. A survey is planned. You have been asked to design a sampling plan for this task. Present your plan to a group of students representing the board of ABN AMRO.

5 In a small group discuss the following issues: 'Given that many governments use sampling to check the accuracy of various censuses and that non-response rates to censuses are growing, national decennial censuses should be abolished in favour of the use of existing databases and sample surveys' and 'Because non-sampling errors are greater in magnitude than sampling errors, it really does not matter which sampling method is used.'

Video case exercise: Wild Planet

What sampling challenges does Wild Planet face in conducting surveys with children and parents? Evaluate the use of online access panels in resolving these challenges.

Notes

1. Feld, K., 'Women in the world's Muslim economies: measuring the effectiveness of empowerment', ESOMAR, Annual Congress, Berlin (September 2007).

2. Kellner, P., 'Down with random samples', *ResearchWorld* (May 2009), 31.

3. Anon., 'Down with random sampling?', *ResearchWorld* (November 2007), 44–45.

4. Kent, R., 'Rethinking data analysis – part one: the limitations of frequentist approaches', *International Journal of Market Research* 51 (1) (2009), 51–69; Semon, T.T., 'Nonresponse bias affects all survey research', *Marketing News* 38 (12) (July 2004), 7; Anon., 'Random sampling', *Marketing News* (16 July 2001), 10; Wilcox, S., 'Sampling and controlling a TV audience measurement panel', *International Journal of Market Research* 42 (4) (Winter 2000), 413–430; Verma, V. and Le, T., 'An analysis of sampling errors for the demographic and health surveys', *International Statistical Review* 64 (3) (December 1966), 265–294; Assael, H. and Keon, J., 'Non-sampling vs. sampling errors in sampling research', *Journal of Marketing* (Spring 1982), 114–123.

5. Wywial, J.L., 'Sampling design proportional to order statistic of auxiliary variable', *Statistical Papers* 49 (2) (April 2008), 277–289; Huizing, L., van Ossenbruggen, R., Muller, M., van der Wal, C., Gerty, J.L.M. Lensvelt-Mulders and Hubregtse, M., 'Improving panel sampling: embedding propensity scores and response behaviour in sampling frames', ESOMAR, Panel Research, Orlando (October 2007); Anon., 'Random sampling: bruised, battered, bowed,' *Marketing News* 36 (5) (4 March 2002), 12; Fink, A., *How to Sample in Surveys* (Thousand Oaks, CA: Sage, 1995); Frankel, M.R., 'Sampling theory', in Rossi, P.H., Wright, J.D. and Anderson, A.B. (eds), *Handbook of Survey Research* (Orlando, FL: Academic Press, 1983), 21–67.

6. Coleman, L., 'Preferences towards sex education and information from a religiously diverse sample of young people', *Health Education* 108 (1) (2007), 72–91; Reiter, J.P., 'Topics in survey sampling/finite population sampling and inference: a prediction approach', *Journal of the American Statistical Association* 97 (457) (March 2002), 357–358; Henry, G.T., *Practical Sampling* (Thousand Oaks, CA: Sage, 1995); Sudman, S., 'Applied sampling', in Rossi, P.H., Wright, J.D. and Anderson, A.B. (eds), *Handbook of Survey Research* (Orlando, FL: Academic Press, 1983), 145–194.

7. Jäntti, S.-M. and Järn, C., 'The insightful museum – how to create a customer centred marketing strategy', ESOMAR, Consumer Insights, Dubai (February 2009).

8. Körner, T. and Nimmergut, A., 'Using an access panel as a sampling frame for voluntary household surveys', *Statistical Journal of the United Nations* 21 (2004), 33–52;. Cage, R., 'New methodology for selecting CPI outlet samples', *Monthly Labor Review* 119 (12) (December 1996), 49–83.

9. Wyner, G.A., 'Survey errors', *Marketing Research* 19 (1) (April 2007), 6–8; Couper, M.P., 'Web surveys: a review of issues and approaches,' *Public Opinion Quarterly* 64 (4) (Winter 2000), 464–494; Smith, W., Mitchell, P., Attebo, K. and Leeder, S., 'Selection bias from sampling frames:

telephone directory and electoral roll compared with door-to-door population census: results from the Blue Mountain eye study', *Australian & New Zealand Journal of Public Health* 21 (2) (April 1997), 127–133.

10. For the effect of sample frame error on research results, see Murphy, G.B., 'The effects of organizational sampling frame selection', *Journal of Business Venturing* 17 (3) (May 2002), 237; Fish, K.E., Barnes, J.H. and Banahan, B.F., III, 'Convenience or calamity', *Journal of Health Care Marketing* 14 (Spring 1994), 45–49.

11. Kent, R., 'Rethinking data analysis – part two: some alternatives to frequentist approaches', *International Journal of Market Research* 51 (2) (2009), 181–202; Bakken, D.G., 'The Bayesian revolution in marketing research', Innovate! Conference, Paris (February 2005).

12. Vrechopoulos, A. and Atherinos, E., 'Web banking layout effects on consumer behavioural intentions', *International Journal of Bank Marketing* 27 (7) (2009), 524–546.

13. For an application of convenience sampling, see Schwaiger, M., Sarstedt, M. and Taylor, C.R., 'Art for the sake of the corporation: Audi, BMW Group, Daimler Chrysler, Montblanc, Siemens and Volkswagen help explore the effect of sponsorship on corporate reputations', *Journal of Advertising Research* 50 (1) (2010), 77–91; Ritchie, L., 'Empowerment and Australian community health nurses' work with aboriginal clients: the sociopolitical context', *Qualitative Health Research* 11 (2) (March 2001), 190–205; Ho, F., Ong, B.S. and Seonsu, A., 'A multicultural comparison of shopping patterns among Asian consumers', *Journal of Marketing Theory and Practice* 5 (1) (Winter 1997), 42–51.

14. Kerr, G. and Schultz, D., 'Maintenance person or architect? The role of academic advertising research in building better understanding', *International Journal of Advertising* 29 (4) (2010), 547–568.

15. Maddox, K., 'XIX Winter Olympics: marketing hot spot', *B to B* 87 (2) (11 February 2002), 1–2.

16. Jancic, Z. and Zabkar, V., 'Establishing marketing relationships in the advertising agency business: a transitional economy case', *Journal of Advertising Research* 38 (6) (November/December 1998).

17. Huizing, L., van Ossenbruggen, R., Muller, M., van der Wal, C., Lensvelt-Mulders, G.J.L.M. and Hubregtse, M., 'Improving panel sampling: embedding propensity scores and response behavior in sampling frames', ESOMAR, Panel Research, Orlando (October 2007).

18. Thompson, S.K., *Sampling* (New York: Wiley, 2002); Sudman, S., 'Sampling in the twenty-first century', *Academy of Marketing Science Journal* 27 (2) (Spring 1999), 269–277; Kish, L., *Survey Sampling* (New York: Wiley, 1965), 552.

19. Curtice, J. and Sparrow, N., 'How accurate are traditional quota opinion polls?', *Journal of the Market Research Society* 39 (3) (July 1997), 433–448.

20. de Gaudemar, O., 'Benefits and challenges of multi-sourcing – understanding differences between sample sources', ESOMAR, Panel Research, Barcelona (November 2006); Getz, P.M., 'Implementing the new sample design for the current employment statistics survey', *Business*

Economics 35 (4) (October 2000), 47–50; Anon., 'Public opinion: polls apart', *The Economist* 336 (7927) (12 August 1995), 48; Kalton, G., *Introduction to Survey Sampling* (Beverly Hills, CA: Sage, 1982); Sudman, S., 'Improving the quality of shopping center sampling', *Journal of Marketing Research* 17 (November 1980), 423–431.

21. For applications of snowball sampling, see Zeng, F., Huang, L. and Dou, W., 'Social factors in user perceptions and responses to advertising in online social networking', *Journal of Interactive Advertising* 10 (1) (Fall 2009); Winkler, T. and Buckner, K., 'Receptiveness of gamers to embedded brand messages in advergames: attitudes towards product placement', *Journal of Interactive Advertising* 7 (1) (Fall 2006); Maher, L., 'Risk behaviours of young Indo-Chinese injecting drug users in Sydney and Melbourne', *Australian & New Zealand Journal of Public Health* (February 2001), 50–54; Frankwick, G.L., Ward, J.C., Hutt, M.D. and Reingen, P.H., 'Evolving patterns of organisational beliefs in the formation of strategy', *Journal of Marketing* 58 (April 1994), 96–110.

22. If certain procedures for listing members of the rare population are followed strictly, the snowball sample can be treated as a probability sample. See Sampath, S., *Sampling Theory and Methods* (Boca Raton, FL: CRC Press, 2000); Henry, G.T., *Practical Sampling* (Thousand Oaks, CA: Sage, 1995); Kalton, G. and Anderson, D.W., 'Sampling rare populations', *Journal of the Royal Statistical Association* 149 (1986), 65–82; Biemacki, P. and Waldorf, D., 'Snowball sampling: problems and techniques of chain referred sampling', *Sociological Methods and Research* 10 (November 1981), 141–163.

23. Campbell, C., Parent, M. and Plangger, K., 'Instant innovation; from zero to full speed in fifteen years – how online offerings have reshaped marketing research', *Journal of Advertising Research* 51 (1) 50th Anniversary Supplement (2011), 72–86.

24. Clark, J., Jones, S., Romanou, E. and Harrison, M., 'Segments, hugs and rock'n'roll: An attitudinal segmentation of parents and young people', *Market Research Society, Annual Conference* (2009).

25. Lavrakas, P.J., Mane, S. and Laszlo, J., 'Does anyone really know if online ad campaigns are working? An evaluation of methods used to assess the effectiveness of advertising on the internet', *Journal of Advertising Research* 50 (4) (2010), 354–373.

26. When the sampling interval, *i*, is not a whole number, the easiest solution is to use as the interval the nearest whole number below or above *i*. If rounding has too great an effect on the sample size, add or delete the extra cases.

27. For an application of systematic random sampling, see Man, Y.S. and Prendergast, G., 'Perceptions of handbills as a promotional medium: an exploratory study', *Journal of Advertising Research* 45 (1) (March 2005), 124–131; MacFarlane, P., 'Structuring and measuring the size of business markets', *International Journal of Market Research* 44 (1) (First Quarter 2002), 7–30; Qu, H. and Li, I., 'The characteristics and satisfaction of mainland Chinese visitors to Hong Kong', *Journal of Travel Research* 35 (4) (Spring 1997), 37–41; Chakraborty, G., Ettenson, R. and Gaeth, G., 'How consumers choose health insurance', *Journal of Health Care Marketing* 14 (Spring 1994), 21–33.

28. Meng, J., Summey, J.H., Herndon, N.C. and Kwong, K.K., 'On the retail service quality expectations of Chinese shoppers', *International Journal of Market Research* 51 (6) (2009), 773–796.

29. For applications of stratified random sampling, see Truong, Y., 'Personal aspirations and the consumption of luxury goods', *International Journal of Market Research* 52 (5) (2010), 655–673; Okazaki, S., 'Social influence model and electronic word of mouth: PC versus mobile internet', *International Journal of Advertising* 28 (3) (2009), 439–472; Kjell, G., 'The level-based stratified sampling plan', *Journal of the American Statistical Association* 95 (452) (December 2000), 1185–1191.

30. Petrovici, D. and Paliwoda, S., 'An empirical examination of public attitudes towards advertising in a transitional economy', *International Journal of Advertising* 26 (2) (2007), 247–276.

31. Opdyke, J.D. and Mollenkamp, C., 'Yes, you are "High Net Worth"', *Wall Street Journal* (May 21, 2002), D1, D3.

32. de Silva, H., Zainudeen, A. and Cader, S., 'Teleuse on a shoestring', ESOMAR, Telecoms Conference, Barcelona (November 2006).

33. Zelin, A. and Stubbs, R., 'Cluster sampling: a false economy?', *International Journal of Market Research* 47 (5) (2005), 501–522.

34. Geographic clustering of rare populations, however, can be an advantage. See Laaksonen, S., 'Retrospective two-stage cluster sampling for mortality in Iraq', *International Journal of Market Research* 50 (3) (2008), 403–417; Rao, P.S., *Sampling methodologies with applications* (Boca Raton, FL: CRC Press, 2001); Carlin, J.B., 'Design of cross-sectional surveys using cluster sampling: an overview with Australian case studies', *Australian & New Zealand Journal of Public Health* 23 (5) (October 1999), 546–551; Raymondo, J.C., 'Confessions of a Nielsen Housechild', *American Demographics* 19 (3) (March 1997), 24–27; Sudman, S., 'Efficient screening methods for the sampling of geographically clustered special populations', *Journal of Marketing Research* 22 (February 1985), 20–29.

35. Sergeant, J. and Bock, T., 'Small sample market research', *International Journal of Market Research* 44 (2) (2002), 235–244; Walker, J., 'A sequential discovery sampling procedure', *Journal of the Operational Research Society* 53 (1) (January 2002), 119; Park, J.S., Peters, M. and Tang, K., 'Optimal inspection policy in sequential screening', *Management Science* 37 (8) (August 1991), 1058–1061; Anderson, E.J., Gorton, K. and Tudor, R., 'The application of sequential analysis in market research', *Journal of Marketing Research* 17 (February 1980), 97–105.

36. For more discussion of double sampling, see Brewer, K., *Design and Estimation in Survey Sampling* (London: Edward Arnold, 2001); Shade, J., 'Sampling inspection tables: single and double sampling', *Journal of Applied Statistics* 26 (8) (December 1999), 1020; Baillie, D.H., 'Double sampling plans for inspection by variables when the process standard deviation is unknown', *International Journal of Quality & Reliability Management* 9 (5) (1992), 59–70; Frankel, M.R. and Frankel, L.R., 'Probability sampling', in Ferber, R. (ed.), *Handbook of Marketing Research* (New York: McGraw-Hill, 1974), 2–230–2–246.

37. For the use and challenges faced by using different non-probability sampling techniques in cross-cultural

research, see Wichers, B. and Zengerink, E., 'It's the culture, stupid! A cross cultural comparison of data collection methods', ESOMAR, Panel Research, Barcelona (November 2006); Malhotra, N.K. and Peterson, M., 'Marketing research in the new millennium: emerging issues and trends', *Market Intelligence and Planning* 19 (4) (2001), 216–235; Malhotra, N.K., Agarwal, J. and Peterson, M., 'Cross-cultural marketing research: methodological issues and guidelines', *International Marketing Review* 13 (5) (1996), 7–43; Saeed, S. and Jeong, I., 'Cross-cultural research in advertising: an assessment of methodologies', *Journal of the Academy of Marketing Science* 22 (Summer 1994), 205–215.

38. Green, A., Heak, J. and Staplehurst, S., 'Measuring the business elites of India and China: powerhouse methodology meets powerhouse economies', ESOMAR, Asia Pacific Conference, Singapore (April 2008).

39. Worthington, P., 'Research in developing markets: upwardly mobile', *Admap* (July/August 2010), 28–29.

40. García-González, J., 'How to avoid the pitfalls of multi-country research', ESOMAR, Latin America Conference, Buenos Aires (September 2005).

41. 'Report on online panels', AAPOR (March 2010).

42. Passingham, J. and Blyth, B., 'A small rock holds back a great wave: unleashing our potential', ESOMAR, Congress Odyssey, Athens (September 2010).

43. Bednall, D.H.B., Adam, S. and Plocinski, K., 'Ethics in practice: using compliance techniques to boost telephone response rates', *International Journal of Market Research* 52 (2) (2010), 155–168.

44. Davison, L. and Thornton, R., 'DIY – new life or the death of research? It's like giving the keys to a Ferrari to a child who has just learned to drive', ESOMAR, Congress Odyssey, *Athens* (September 2010).

15

Sampling: final and initial sample size determination

Stage 1
Problem definition

Stage 2
Research approach developed

Stage 3
Research design developed

Stage 4
Fieldwork or data collection

Stage 5
Data integrity and analysis

Stage 6
Report preparation and presentation

Making a sample too big wastes resources, making it too small diminishes the value of findings – a dilemma resolved only with the judicious use of sampling theory.

Objectives

After reading this chapter, you should be able to:

1   define key concepts and symbols pertinent to sampling;

2   understand the concepts of the sampling distribution, statistical inference and standard error;

3   discuss the statistical approach to determining sample size based on simple random sampling and the construction of confidence intervals;

4   derive the formulae to determine statistically the sample size for estimating means and proportions;

5   discuss the non-response issues in sampling and the procedures for improving response rates and adjusting for non-response;

6   understand the difficulty of statistically determining the sample size in international marketing research;

7   identify the ethical issues related to sample size determination, particularly the estimation of population variance;

8   appreciate how digital developments are shaping the manner in which response rates may be improved.

Overview

This chapter focuses on the determination of sample size in simple random sampling. We define various concepts and symbols and discuss the properties of the sampling distribution. Additionally, we describe statistical approaches to sample size determination based on confidence intervals. We present the formulae for calculating the sample size with these approaches and illustrate their use. We briefly discuss the extension to determining sample size in other probability sampling designs. The sample size determined statistically is the final or net sample size; that is, it represents the completed number of interviews or observations. To obtain this final sample size, however, a much larger number of potential participants have to be initially contacted. We describe the adjustments that need to be made to the statistically determined sample size to account for incidence and completion rates and calculate the initial sample size. We also cover the non-response issues in sampling, with a focus on improving response rates and adjusting for non-response. We discuss the difficulty of statistically determining the sample size in international marketing research, identify relevant ethical issues and discuss how digital developments in marketing research are enabling a better participant research experience, maintaining or improving response rates and quality.

Statistical determination of sample size requires knowledge of the normal distribution and the use of normal probability tables. The normal distribution is bell shaped and symmetrical. Its mean, median and mode are identical (see Chapter 18). Information on the normal distribution and the use of normal probability tables is presented in the Appendix to this chapter. The first example illustrates the statistical aspects of sampling. The second example illustrates how an online survey was administered in terms of the sample selected, response rate and validation. The example says that the survey method was 'random'. Given the sampling frame was an online panel, would you consider this to be a probability sample?

Has there been a shift in opinion?

The sample size used in opinion polls commissioned and published by most national newspapers is influenced by statistical considerations. The allowance for sampling error may be limited to around 3 percentage points.

The table that follows can be used to determine the allowances that should be made for sampling error. These intervals indicate the range (plus or minus the figure shown) within which the results of repeated samplings in the same time period could be expected to vary, 95% of the time, assuming that the sample procedure, survey execution and questionnaire used were the same.

Recommended allowance for sampling error of a percentage

In percentage points (at 95% confidence level for a sample size of 355)

Percentage near 10	3
Percentage near 20	4
Percentage near 30	4
Percentage near 40	5
Percentage near 50	5
Percentage near 60	5
Percentage near 70	4
Percentage near 80	4
Percentage near 90	3

The table should be used as follows. If a reported percentage is 43 (e.g. 43% of French chief executives believe their company will have to lay off workers in the next 12 months), look at the row labelled 'percentages near 40'. The number in this row is 5, so the 43% obtained in the sample is subject to a sampling error of 5 percentage points. Another way of saying this is that very probably (95 times out of 100) the average of repeated samplings would be somewhere between 38% and 48%. The reader can be 95% confident that in the total population of French chief executives, between 38% and 48% believe their company will have to lay off workers in the next 12 months, with the most likely figure being 43%.

The fortunes of political parties measured through opinion polls are regularly reported in newspapers throughout Europe. The next time that you read a report of a political opinion poll, examine the sample size used, the confidence level assumed and the stated margin of error. When comparing the results of a poll with a previous poll, consider whether a particular political party or politician has *really* grown or slumped in popularity. If there is a news item that the popularity of Party X has grown or the approval of President Y has diminished, is there really anything to report? Can the reported change be accounted for within the set margin of error as summarised in this example?

| Real research | **Are product placements ethical?**[1] |

In a US study, a sample of 3,340 consumers was surveyed to measure attitudes towards ethical standards of product placement in films, support for regulation of this practice, and the level of acceptability for various types of products to be placed. The study was based upon an online survey administered via an access panel. Potential participants were randomly selected from the panel, with a total of 18,640 active panel members receiving a survey invitation via email. Among them, 2,859 panel members completed the survey. Two weeks later, a reminder email was sent to the remaining 15,781 members and a total of 3,722 completed the survey. The final sample size (n = 3,340) reflected a reduction in the initial number of participants eliminated due to incomplete surveys, and represented a response rate of almost 20%. This was in line with reviews of online panel response rates (typically in the 16–25% range).[2] Among the 3,340 participants, 64.6% were female and 34.3% were male. Approximately 28% of the participants were aged 26–35, followed by those aged 36–45 (27.0%) and 46–55 (23.1%). In order to check the validity and representativeness of the sample, researchers compared their profile with the US national population, US cinema-going audiences, TV-viewing audiences and videotape/DVD film renters.

Definitions and symbols

Confidence intervals and other statistical concepts that play a central role in sample size determination are defined in the following list:

- *Parameter.* A parameter is a summary description of a fixed characteristic or measure of the target population. A parameter denotes the true value that would be obtained if a census rather than a sample were undertaken.

- *Statistic.* A statistic is a summary description of a characteristic or measure of the sample. The sample statistic is used as an estimate of the population parameter.

- *Finite population correction.* The finite population correction (fpc) is a correction for overestimation of the variance of a population parameter – for example, a mean or proportion – when the sample size is 10% or more of the population size.

- *Precision level.* When estimating a population parameter by using a sample statistic, the precision level is the desired size of the estimating interval. This is the maximum permissible difference between the sample statistic and the population parameter.

- *Confidence interval.* The confidence interval is the range into which the true population parameter will fall, assuming a given level of confidence.

- *Confidence level.* The confidence level is the probability that a confidence interval will include the population parameter.

Table 15.1	Symbols for population and sample variables		
Variable		Population	Sample
Mean		μ	$\bar{x}$
Proportion		π	p
Variance		σ^2	s^2
Standard deviation		σ	s
Size		N	n
Standard error of the mean		$\sigma_{\bar{x}}$	$s_{\bar{x}}$
Standard error of the proportion		σ_p	s_p
Standardised variate (z)		$\dfrac{X-\mu}{\sigma}$	$\dfrac{X-\bar{X}}{s}$
Coefficient of variation (C)		$\dfrac{\sigma}{\mu}$	$\dfrac{s}{x}$

The symbols used in statistical notation for describing population and sample characteristics are summarised in Table 15.1.

The sampling distribution

Sampling distribution
The distribution of the values of a sample statistic computed for each possible sample that could be drawn from the target population under a specified sampling plan.

Statistical inference
The process of generalising the sample results to a target population.

Normal distribution
A basis for classical statistical inference that is bell shaped and symmetrical in appearance. Its measures of central tendency are all identical.

The **sampling distribution** is the distribution of the values of a sample statistic computed for each possible sample that could be drawn from the target population under a specified sampling plan.[3] Suppose that a simple random sample of 5 sponsors is to be drawn from a population of 20 sponsors of the Paris Fashion Week. There are $(20 \times 19 \times 18 \times 17 \times 16)/(1 \times 2 \times 3 \times 4 \times 5)$, or 15,504, different samples of size 5 that can be drawn. The relative frequency distribution of the values of the mean of these 15,504 different samples would specify the sampling distribution of the mean.

An important task in marketing research is to calculate statistics, such as the sample mean and sample proportion, and use them to estimate the corresponding true population values. This process of generalising the sample results to a target population is referred to as **statistical inference**. In practice, a single sample of predetermined size is selected, and the sample statistics (such as mean and proportion) are computed. Theoretically, to estimate the population parameter from the sample statistic, every possible sample that could have been drawn should be examined. If all possible samples were actually to be drawn, the distribution of the statistic would be the sampling distribution. Although in practice only one sample is actually drawn, the concept of a sampling distribution is still relevant. It enables us to use probability theory to make inferences about the population values.

The important properties of the sampling distribution of the mean, and the corresponding properties for the proportion, for large samples (30 or more) are as follows:

1 The sampling distribution of the mean is a **normal distribution** (see the Appendix at the end of the chapter). Strictly speaking, the sampling distribution of a proportion is a binomial. For large samples ($n = 30$ or more), however, it can be approximated by the normal distribution.

2   The mean of the sampling distribution of the mean

$$\overline{X} = \left(\sum_{i=1}^{n} X_i / n \right)$$

or the proportion $p = X/n$ (X = the count of the characteristic of interest) equals the corresponding population parameter value, μ or π, respectively.

Standard error
The standard deviation of the sampling distribution of the mean or proportion.

z value
The number of standard errors a point is away from the mean.

3   The standard deviation is called the standard error of the mean or the proportion to indicate that it refers to a sampling distribution of the mean or the proportion and not to a sample or a population. The formulae are

Mean   Proportion

$$\sigma_{\overline{x}} = \frac{\sigma}{\sqrt{n}} \qquad \sigma_p = \sqrt{\frac{\pi(1-\pi)}{n}}$$

4   Often the population standard deviation, σ, is not known. In these cases, it can be estimated from the sample by using the following formula:

$$s = \sqrt{\frac{\sum_{i=1}^{n}(X_i - \overline{X})^2}{n-1}}$$

or

$$s = \sqrt{\frac{\sum_{i=1}^{n} X_i^2 - (\sum_{i=1}^{n} X_i)^2 / n}{n-1}}$$

In cases where σ is estimated by s, the standard error of the mean becomes

$$\text{est. } s_x = \frac{s}{\sqrt{n}}$$

Assuming no measurement error, the reliability of an estimate of a population parameter can be assessed in terms of its standard error.

5   Likewise, the standard error of the proportion can be estimated by using the sample proportion p as an estimator of the population proportion, π, as

$$\text{est. } s_p = \sqrt{\frac{p(1-p)}{n}}$$

6   The area under the sampling distribution between any two points can be calculated in terms of z values. The z value for a point is the number of standard errors a point is away from the mean. The z values may be computed as follows:

$$z = \frac{\overline{X} - \pi}{\sigma_{\overline{x}}} \quad \text{and} \quad z = \frac{p - \pi}{\sigma_n}$$

For example, the areas under one side of the curve between the mean and points that have z values of 1.0, 2.0 and 3.0 are, respectively, 0.3413, 0.4772 and 0.4986. (See Table 2 in the Appendix of statistical tables.)

7   When the sample size is 10% or more of the population size, the standard error formulae will overestimate the standard deviation of the population mean or proportion. Hence, these should be adjusted by a finite population correction factor defined by

$$\sqrt{\frac{N-n}{N-1}}$$

In this case,

$$\sigma_{\bar{x}} = \frac{\sigma}{\sqrt{n}}\sqrt{\frac{N-n}{N-1}} \quad \text{and} \quad \sigma_p = \sqrt{\frac{\pi(1-\pi)}{n}}\sqrt{\frac{N-n}{N-1}}$$

Statistical approaches to determining sample size

Several qualitative factors should also be taken into consideration when determining the sample size (see Chapter 14). These include the importance of the decision, the nature of the research, the number of variables, the nature of the analysis, sample sizes used in similar studies, incidence rates (the occurrence of behaviour or characteristics in a population), completion rates and resource constraints. The statistically determined sample size is the net or final sample size: the sample remaining after eliminating potential participants who do not qualify or who do not complete the interview. Depending on incidence and completion rates, the size of the initial sample may have to be much larger. In commercial marketing research, limits on time, money and expert resources can exert an overriding influence on sample size determination.

The statistical approach to determining sample size that we consider is based on traditional statistical inference.[4] In this approach the precision level is specified in advance. This approach is based on the construction of confidence levels around sample means or proportions.

The confidence interval approach

The confidence interval approach to sample size determination is based on the construction of confidence intervals around the sample means or proportions using the standard error formula. As an example, suppose that a researcher has taken a simple random sample of 300 households to estimate the monthly amount invested in savings schemes and found that the mean household monthly investment for the sample is €182. Past studies indicate that the population standard deviation σ can be assumed to be €55.

We want to find an interval within which a fixed proportion of the sample means would fall. Suppose that we want to determine an interval around the population mean that will include 95% of the sample means, based on samples of 300 households. The 95% could be divided into two equal parts, half below and half above the mean, as shown in Figure 15.1.

Calculation of the confidence interval involves determining a distance below ($\bar{X}_L$) and above ($\bar{X}_L$) the population mean (μ), which contains a specified area of the normal curve.

Figure 15.1

The 95% confidence interval

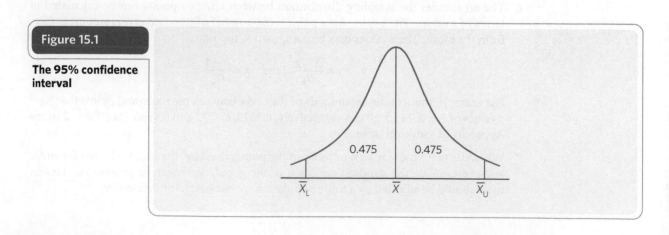

The z values corresponding to $\overline{X}_L$ and $\overline{X}_U$ may be calculated as:

$$z_L = \frac{\overline{X}_L - \mu}{\sigma_{\overline{x}}}$$

$$Z_U = \frac{\overline{X}_U - \mu}{\sigma_{\overline{x}}}$$

where $z_L = -z$ and $z_U = +z$. Therefore, the lower value of is $\overline{X}$ is

$$\overline{X}_L = \mu - z\sigma_{\overline{x}}$$

and the upper value of $\overline{X}$ is

$$\overline{X}_U = \mu + z\sigma_{\overline{x}}$$

Note that μ is estimated by $\overline{X}$. The confidence interval is given by

$$\overline{X} \pm z\sigma_{\overline{x}}$$

We can now set a 95% confidence interval around the sample mean of €182. As a first step, we compute the standard error of the mean:

$$\sigma_{\overline{x}} = \frac{\sigma}{\sqrt{n}} = \frac{55}{\sqrt{300}} = 3.18$$

From Table 2 in the Appendix of statistical tables, it can be seen that the central 95% of the normal distribution lies within ±1.96 z values. The 95% confidence interval is given by

$$\overline{X} \pm 1.96\sigma_{\overline{x}} = 182.00 \pm 1.96(3.18)$$

$$= 182.00 \pm 6.23$$

Thus, the 95% confidence interval ranges from €175.77 to €188.23. The probability of finding the true population mean to be within €175.77 and €188.23 is 95%.

Sample size determination: means

The approach used here to construct a confidence interval can be adapted to determine the sample size that will result in a desired confidence interval.[5] Suppose that the researcher wants to estimate the monthly household savings investment more precisely so that the estimate will be within ±€5.00 of the true population value. What should be the size of the sample? The following steps, summarised in Table 15.2, will lead to an answer.

1   Specify the level of precision. This is the maximum permissible difference (D) between the sample mean and the population mean. In our example, $D = \pm€5.00$.

2   Specify the level of confidence. Suppose that a 95% confidence level is desired.

3   Determine the z value associated with the confidence level using Table 2 in the Appendix of statistical tables. For a 95% confidence level, the probability that the population mean will fall outside one end of the interval is 0.025 (0.05/2). The associated z value is 1.96.

4   Determine the standard deviation of the population. This may be known from secondary sources. If not, it might be estimated by conducting a pilot study. Alternatively, it might be estimated on the basis of the researcher's judgement. For example, the range of a normally distributed variable is approximately equal to ±3 standard deviations, and one can thus estimate the standard deviation by dividing the range by 6. The researcher can often estimate the range based on knowledge of the phenomenon.

Table 15.2	Summary of sample size determination for means and proportions	
Steps	Means	Proportions
Specify the level of precision.	$D = \pm €5.00$	$D = p - \pi = \pm 0.05$
Specify the confidence level (CL)	CL = 95%	CL = 95%
Determine the z value associated with the CL	z value is 1.96	z value is 1.96
Determine the standard deviation of the population	Estimate σ: $\sigma = 55$	Estimate π: $\pi = 0.64$
Determine the sample size using the formula for the standard error	$n = \dfrac{\sigma^2 z^2}{D^2}$ $= \dfrac{55^2 (1.96)^2}{5^2}$ $= 465$	$n = \dfrac{\pi(1-\pi)z^2}{D^2}$ $= \dfrac{0.64(1-0.64)(1.96)^2}{(0.05)^2}$ $= 355$
If the sample size represents ≥10% of the population, apply the finite factor popular correction (fpc) If necessary, re-estimate the confidence interval by employing s to estimate σ	$n_c = \dfrac{nN}{N+n-1}$ $= \overline{X} \pm z s_{\overline{x}}$	$n_c = \dfrac{nN}{N+n-1}$ $= p \pm z s_p$
If precision is specified in relative rather than absolute terms, determine the sample size by substituting for D	$D = R\mu$ $n = \dfrac{C^2 z^2}{R^2}$	$D = R\pi$ $n = \dfrac{z^2(1-\pi)}{R^2 \pi}$

5 Determine the sample size using the formula for the standard error of the mean:

$$z = \frac{\overline{X} - \mu}{\sigma_{\overline{x}}}$$

$$= \frac{D}{\sigma_{\overline{x}}}$$

or

$$\sigma_{\overline{x}} = \frac{D}{z}$$

$$\frac{\sigma}{\sqrt{n}} = \frac{D}{z}$$

or

$$n = \frac{\sigma^2 z^2}{D^2}$$

In our example,

$$n = \frac{55^2 (1.96)^2}{5^2}$$

$$= 464.83$$
$$= 465 \text{ (rounded to the next highest integer)}$$

It can be seen from the formula for sample size that sample size increases with an increase in the population variability, the degree of confidence and the precision level required of the estimate. Because the sample size is directly proportional to σ^2, the larger the population variability, the larger the sample size. Likewise, a higher degree of confidence implies a larger value of z, and thus a larger sample size. Both σ^2 and z appear in the numerator. Greater precision means a smaller value of D, and thus a larger sample size because D appears in the denominator.

6　If the resulting sample size represents 10% or more of the population, the finite population correction (fpc) should be applied.[6] The required sample size should then be calculated from the formula

$$n_c = \frac{nN}{(N+n-1)}$$

where　n = sample size without fpc
　　　　n_c = sample size with fpc

7　If the population standard deviation, σ^2, is unknown and an estimate is used, it should be re-estimated once the sample has been drawn. The sample standard deviation, s, is used as an estimate of σ. A revised confidence interval should then be calculated to determine the precision level actually obtained.

Suppose that the value of 55.00 used for σ was an estimate because the true value was unknown. A sample of $n = 465$ is drawn, and these observations generate a mean $\bar{X}$ of 180.00 and a sample standard deviation s of 50.00. The revised confidence interval is then

$$\bar{X} \pm ZS_{\bar{X}} = 180 \pm 1.96(50.0 / \sqrt{465})$$

$$= 180 \pm 4.55$$

or

$$175.45 \leq \mu \leq 184.55$$

Note that the confidence interval obtained is narrower than planned, because the population standard deviation was overestimated, as judged by the sample standard deviation.

8　In some cases, precision is specified in relative rather than absolute terms. In other words, it may be specified that the estimate be within plus or minus R percentage points of the mean. Symbolically,

$$D = R\mu$$

In these cases, the sample size may be determined by

$$n = \frac{\sigma^2 z^2}{D^2}$$

$$= \frac{C^2 z^2}{R^2}$$

where the coefficient of variation $C = \sigma/\mu$ would have to be estimated.

The population size, N, does not directly affect the size of the sample, except when the fpc factor has to be applied. Although this may be counter-intuitive, upon reflection it makes sense. For example, if all the population elements are identical on the characteristics of interest, then a sample size of one will be sufficient to estimate the mean perfectly. This is true whether there are 50, 500, 5,000 or 50,000 elements in the population. What directly affects the sample size is the variability of the characteristic in the population. This variability enters into the sample size calculation by way of population variance σ^2 or sample variance s^2. Also, note that the larger the sample size, the more accurate the parameter estimation (sample mean), i.e. the smaller the precision level (error) for a given level of confidence. This can be seen from the formula in step 5. A larger sample will also result in a narrower confidence level. This can be seen from the formula for the confidence interval in step 7.

Sample size determination: proportions

If the statistic of interest is a proportion rather than a mean, the approach to sample size determination is similar. Suppose that the researcher is interested in estimating the proportion of households in a particular region that have bought fashion apparel online. The following steps, also summarised in Table 15.2, should be followed:[7]

1 Specify the level of precision. Suppose that the desired precision is such that the allowable interval is set as $D = p - \pi = \pm 0.05$.

2 Specify the level of confidence. Suppose that a 95% confidence level is desired.

3 Determine the z value associated with the confidence level. As explained in the case of estimating the mean, this will be $z = 1.96$.

4 Estimate the population proportion π. As explained earlier, the population proportion may be estimated from secondary sources, or from a pilot study, or may be based on the judgement of the researcher. Suppose that, based on secondary data, the researcher estimates that 64% of the households in the target population have bought fashion apparel online. Hence, $\pi = 0.64$.

5 Determine the sample size using the formula for the standard error of the proportion:

$$\sigma_p = \frac{p - \pi}{z}$$

$$= \frac{D}{z}$$

$$= \sqrt{\frac{\pi(1-\pi)}{n}}$$

or

$$n = \frac{\pi(1-\pi)z^2}{D^2}$$

In our example,

$$n = \frac{0.64(1-0.64)(1.96)^2}{(0.05)^2}$$

$$= 354.04$$
$$= 355 \text{ (rounded to the next highest integer)}$$

6 If the resulting sample size represents 10% or more of the population, the fpc should be applied. The required sample size should then be calculated from the formula

$$n_c = \frac{nN}{(N+n-1)}$$

where n = sample size without fpc
n_c = sample size with fpc

7 If the estimate of π turns out to be poor, the confidence interval will be more or less precise than desired. Suppose that after the sample has been taken, the proportion p is calculated to have a value of 0.55. The confidence interval is then re-estimated by employing s_p to estimate the unknown σ_p as

$$p \pm zs_p$$

where

$$s_p = \sqrt{\frac{p(1-p)}{n}}$$

In our example

$$s_p = \sqrt{\frac{0.55(1-0.55)}{355}}$$

$$= 0.0264$$

The confidence interval, then, is

$$0.55 \pm 1.96(0.0264) = 0.55 \pm 0.052$$

which is wider than that specified. This could be attributed to the fact that the sample standard deviation based on $p = 0.55$ was larger than the estimate of the population standard deviation based on $\pi = 0.64$.

If a wider interval than specified is unacceptable, the sample size can be determined to reflect the maximum possible variation in the population. This occurs when the product $\pi(1 - \pi)$ is the greatest, which happens when π is set at 0.5. This result can also be seen intuitively. Since half of the population has one value of the characteristic and the other half the other value, more evidence would be required to obtain a valid inference than if the situation was more clear cut and the majority had one particular value. In our example, this leads to a sample size of

$$n = \frac{0.5(0.5)(1.96)^2}{(0.05)^2}$$

$$= 384.16$$

$$= 385 \text{ (rounded to the next higher integer)}$$

8 Sometimes, precision is specified in relative rather than absolute terms. In other words, it may be specified that the estimate be within plus or minus R percentage points of the population proportion. Symbolically,

$$D = R\pi$$

In such a case, the sample size may be determined by

$$n = \frac{z^2(1-\pi)}{R^2\pi}$$

| Real research | **The impact of organic labelling[8]** |

Huober Brezeln (**www.huoberbrezel.de**) is a traditional Swabian business with a long history, including the introduction of the 'Dauerbrezel' (a long-lasting dry pretzel). In a study Huober wished to test the assumption that an organic seal of approval was needed to associate 'sustainability' into a brand image; 175 participants were interviewed in a face-to-face survey. In the sample 33.1% were male, 66.9% were female. These quotas were agreed upon with Huober, since the majority of snack buyers were women. Of all participants, 66.3% came from the areas of Bavaria, Baden-Württemberg and Hesse. The northern area was represented by 23.4%, the eastern area by 10.3%. This roughly equated with the German sales area of Huober, which was mainly focused on southern Germany. In evaluating the survey findings, Huober wished to determine what the maximum margin of error was in this study using a 95% confidence interval. Understanding at this confidence level would enable Huober to determine that if all German consumers were to participate in a similar survey, the responses would change by no more than ±X%. To confirm a maximum margin of error with a sample size of 175, calculations for sample size determination by proportions were made as follows. The calculation uses the maximum population variation (π = 0.5). To estimate the unknown ±X% or σ_p, the calculation makes the estimate employing s_p:

$$s_p = \sqrt{\frac{p(1-p)}{n}}$$

$$= 0.074$$

Therefore, the confidence interval is 0.5 ± 0.074, i.e. a rather large margin of ±7.4%. If Huober were concerned by this maximum error of margin, it could form estimates for individual questions, such as those that addressed the effects of an organic seal of approval on a brand.

There are a number of websites and apps that offer free use of sample size and confidence interval calculators, for example Survey System (**www.surveysystem.com**) or MaCorr Research Solutions (**www.macorr.com**). You can use these calculators to determine how many participants you need to interview in order to get results that reflect the target population as precisely as needed. By incorporating the cost of each sampling unit, the sample size can be adjusted based upon budget considerations.

Multiple characteristics and parameters

In the preceding examples, we focused on the estimation of a single parameter. In most marketing research projects, several characteristics are of interest. The researcher is required to estimate several parameters and not just one. The calculation of sample size in these cases should be based on a consideration of all the parameters to be estimated.

For example, suppose that in addition to the mean household spend at a supermarket, it was decided to estimate the mean household spend on clothes and on gifts. The sample sizes needed to estimate each of the three mean monthly expenses are given in Table 15.3

Table15.3	Sample size for estimating multiple parameters		
	Variable monthly household spend on:		
	Supermarket	Clothes	Gifts
Confidence level	95%	95%	95%
z value	1.96	1.96	1.96
Precision level (*D*)	€5	€5	€4
Standard deviation of the population (*σ*)	€55	€40	€30
Required sample size (*n*)	465	246	217

and are 465 for supermarket shopping, 246 for clothes and 217 for gifts. If all three variables were equally important, the most conservative approach would be to select the largest value of $n = 465$ to determine the sample size. This will lead to each variable being estimated at least as precisely as specified. If the researcher was most concerned with the mean household monthly expense on clothes, however, a sample size of $n = 246$ could be selected.

Other probability sampling techniques

So far, the discussion of sample size determination has been based on the methods of traditional statistical inference and has assumed simple random sampling. Next, we discuss the determination of sample size when other sampling techniques are used. The determination of sample size for other probability sampling techniques is based on the same underlying principles. The researcher must specify the level of precision and the degree of confidence and estimate the sampling distribution of the test statistic.

In simple random sampling, cost does not enter directly into the calculation of sample size. In the case of stratified or cluster sampling however, cost has an important influence. The cost per observation varies by strata or cluster, and the researcher needs some initial estimates of these costs.[9] In addition, the researcher must take into account within-strata variability or within- and between-cluster variability. Once the overall sample size is determined, the sample is apportioned among strata or clusters. This increases the complexity of the sample size formulae. The interested reader is referred to standard works on sampling theory for more information.[10] In general, to provide the same reliability as simple random sampling, sample sizes are the same for systematic sampling, smaller for stratified sampling and larger for cluster sampling.

Adjusting the statistically determined sample size

Sample size determined statistically represents the final sample size that must be achieved to ensure that the parameters are estimated with the desired degree of precision and set level of confidence. In surveys, this represents the number of completed interviews or questionnaires. To achieve this final sample size, a much greater number of potential participants have to be contacted. In other words, the initial sample size has to be much larger because typically the incidence rates and completion rates are less than 100%.[11]

Incidence rate

Incidence rate refers to the rate of occurrence or the percentage of persons eligible to participate in a study.

Completion rate

The percentage of qualified participants who complete the interview. It enables researchers to take into account anticipated refusals by people who qualify.

Incidence rate refers to the rate of occurrence or the percentage of persons eligible to participate in the study. Incidence rate determines how many contacts need to be screened for a given sample size requirement.[12] For example, suppose that a study of pet ownership targets a sample of households. Of the households that might be approached to see if they qualify, approximately 75% own a pet. This means that, on average, 1.33 households would be approached to obtain one qualified participant. Additional criteria for qualifying participants (e.g. product usage behaviour) will further increase the number of contacts. Suppose that an added eligibility requirement is that the household should have bought a toy for their pet during the last two months. It is estimated that 60% of the households contacted would meet this criterion. Then the incidence rate is $0.75 \times 0.6 = 0.45$. Thus the final sample size will have to be increased by a factor of (1/0.45) or 2.22.

Similarly, the determination of sample size must take into account anticipated refusals by people who qualify. The completion rate denotes the percentage of qualified participants who complete the interview.[13] If, for example, the researcher expects an interview completion rate of 80% of eligible participants, the number of contacts should be increased by a factor of 1.25. The incidence rate and the completion rate together imply that the number of potential participants contacted, i.e. the initial sample size, should be 2.22×1.25 or 2.78 times the sample size required. In general, if there are c qualifying factors with an incidence of $Q_1 \times Q_2 \times Q_3 \dots \times Q_c$, each expressed as a proportion, the following are true:

$$\text{Incidence rate} = Q_1 \times Q_2 \times Q_3 \times \dots \times Q_c$$

$$\text{Initial sample size} = \frac{\text{final sample size}}{\text{incidence rate} \times \text{completion rate}}$$

The number of units that will have to be sampled will be determined by the initial sample size. These calculations assume that an attempt to contact a participant will result in a determination as to whether the participant is eligible. However, this may not be the case. An attempt to contact the participant may be inconclusive as the participant may refuse to answer, not be at home, be busy, or for many other reasons. Such instances will further increase the initial sample size. These instances are considered later when we calculate the response rate. Often a number of variables are used for qualifying potential participants, thereby decreasing the incidence rate. Completion rates are affected by non-response issues. These issues deserve particular attention and are detailed in the next section. Some of the challenges of qualifying potential participants through incidence and completion are illustrated in the following example.

Real research   **Sampling cosmetic surgery consumers[14]**

The German Federal Ministry of Food, Agriculture and Consumer Protection funded a study of suppliers and customers of cosmetic surgery, examining market supply, the quality of surgery results and any needs for consumer-oriented political action. The low prevalence of cosmetic surgery made it clear that a multiple-mode approach was needed to engage sufficient qualified participants. As the intention of the study was to analyse not only demand but supply as well, the size of the market was estimated by a survey of all physicians and institutions offering cosmetic surgery. For that purpose, a sampling frame of all suppliers was built. Following that, a questionnaire was sent to 1,712 physicians and institutions covering the number, type, costs and risks of operations as well as age and gender of their patients. Due to mistrust of the physicians, who expected negative consequences by the tax authorities, the response rate was lower than usual (8.8%). In examining demand issues, customer data were collected by a survey of 620 patients from all over Germany who had undergone cosmetic surgery between 2004 and 2006. The mix of data collection modes included face-to-face as well as telephone, online and postal surveys. The majority were completed using the online mode which used a screening process with a covering question to define the target population. Postal questionnaires were used for patients of cosmetics who declared their willingness to participate in the study. Consumers of cosmetic surgery for the face-to-face interviews were identified randomly and participants were recruited for telephone interviews through approaches to chat rooms of patients.

Calculation of response rates

Response rate can be defined as:[15]

$$\text{Response rate} = \frac{\text{number of completed interviews}}{\text{number of eligible units in sample}}$$

To illustrate how the formula is used, consider the following simple example involving a single-stage online survey with individuals where no screening is involved. The sample consists of 2,000 email addresses, generated from an access panel. Three attempts are made to reach each participant. The results are summarised as follows:

Call #	Attempts	Participants who complete survey	Cumulative	Response rate
1	2,000	1,200	1,200	60%
2	800	400	1,600	80%
3	400	100	1,700	85%

In this example, the number of eligible units is 2,000 and the response rate after three emails is 85%. Now consider the case of a single-stage sample where screening is required to determine the eligibility of participants, i.e., to ascertain whether the participant is qualified for the survey. The attempt to screen each participant will result in one of three outcomes: (1) eligible, (2) ineligible, (3) not ascertained (NA). The NA category will include refusals or participants not able to access their email accounts. In this case we determine the number of eligible participants in the NAs by distributing NAs in the ratio of (1) to (1 + 2). Suppose that we sent out 2,000 emails that resulted in the following outcomes:

Number of completed surveys = 800
Number of eligible participants = 900
Number of ineligible participants = 600
Not ascertained (NA) = 500

The first step is to determine the number of eligible units in the NAs. This can be calculated as

$$500 \times [900/(900 + 600)] = 300$$

Thus the total number of eligible units in the sample is 900 + 300 = 1200.
Thus the response rate is 800/1200 = 66.7%.

Although we illustrate the calculation of response rates for online surveys, the calculations for other survey methods are similar. Response rates are affected by non-response, which is a major issue for marketing researchers.[16]

Non-response issues in sampling

The two major non-response issues in sampling are improving response rates and adjusting for non-response. Non-response error arises when some of the potential participants included in the sample do not respond (see Chapter 3). This is one of the most significant problems in survey research. Non-participants may differ from participants in terms of demographic, psychographic, personality, attitudinal, motivational and behavioural variables.[17] Evaluating these differences was detailed in Chapter 14 in the process of sample validation. For a given study, if the non-participants differ from the participants on the characteristics of interest, the sample estimates can be seriously biased. Higher response rates, in general, imply lower rates of non-response bias, yet response rate may not be an adequate indicator of non-response bias. Response rates themselves do not indicate whether the participants are representative of the original sample.[18] Increasing the response rate may not reduce non-response bias if the additional participants are no different from those who have already responded but do differ from those who still do not respond. As low response rates increase the probability of non-response bias, an attempt should be made to improve the response rate.[19] This is not an issue that should be considered after a survey approach has been decided and a questionnaire designed. Factors that improve response rates are integral to survey and questionnaire design. As detailed in Chapter 13, the researchers should build up an awareness of what motivates their target participants to participate in a research study. The researchers should ask themselves what their target participants get in return for spending time and effort, answering set questions in a full and honest manner. The following subsection details the techniques involved in improving response rates and adjusting for non-response. There is no definitive formula or theory that explains why the non-response occurs or what to do about it. There have been many practitioner and academic studies about non-response in individual survey modes, in cross-comparisons between modes and in specific contexts, e.g. particular countries, participant types and the nature of topic. We continue with ideas to improve non-response, based upon this body of studies. The following two examples illustrate academic and practitioner views of non-response in specific contexts.

Real research

Comparing mobile with fixed phones for surveys[20]

A study targeted at Portuguese adults (aged 15 years and over) aimed to compare mobile survey with fixed telephone survey methods. The study focused on Internet usage, attitudes towards the Internet, cultural practices and demographics. Two surveys were conducted by the same survey company in order to overcome problems that might confuse the assessment of survey results if multiple sources of data collection were used. There were no conclusive results regarding the performance of mobile phone surveys as opposed to fixed phone surveys in terms of response rates. However, there were several features of mobile phones that could induce lower overall response rates. First, a mobile phone was seen as a personal device and many users may consider receiving a call from strangers on their mobile phone an invasion of their privacy. The reaction may be a refusal or even a hang-up-without-answering as soon as they see an unfamiliar number on the phone screen. Second, the participant may be more or less willing to cooperate depending on the tariff that has been contracted for the mobile phone. Charging for receiving calls may discourage the acceptance of some calls, namely those from unknown sources. Mobile phones have the advantage of making the person accessible at any time of the day because it is a personal device carried at all times. Those participants who were previously difficult to reach are now reachable thanks to the mobile phone. The time period for contacts can be extended and is not restricted mainly to evenings and weekends; even the holiday period, typically connected with high non-response, may become a good or even a better period to conduct surveys. However, this advantage may become less salient because subscribers, especially lower income customers, are more likely to turn off their phone and set it to voicemail so as to control the costs incurred by receiving calls.

Real research

'No time' main reason for refusal[21]

Research conducted by Paul Lavrakas, Vice President of Nielsen Media Research (**www.nielsenmedia.com**), showed that there were four basic 'causes' for non-cooperation. These were 'no time or interest', 'privacy and confidentiality concerns', 'not enjoying the survey experience' and 'not believing one's opinions are important'. Paul says it is known that mentioning the survey's topic could significantly affect response rates:

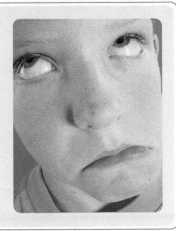

Response rates for surveys on topics that are of higher interest to participants can be up to 40% higher. Health issue surveys for instance, usually get high response rates. But is it acceptable to mention the topic in the introduction to a survey? One professor at the Ohio State University Survey Center insisted that we not mention the survey topic because of the risk of non-response due to only people being interested in the survey being willing to be interviewed. Balancing effective measures to improve response rates and concerns about non-response errors will always be a very difficult trade-off.

Improving the response rates

The primary causes of low response rates are refusals and not-at-homes, as shown in Figure 15.2.

Refusals. Refusals, which result from the unwillingness or inability of people included in the sample to participate, result in lower response rates and increased potential for non-response bias. Given the potential differences between participants and non-participants, researchers should attempt to lower refusal rates. This can be done by prior notification, incentives, good questionnaire design and administration, follow-up and other facilitators:

- *Prior notification.* In prior notification, potential participants are sent an email, a letter or are telephoned notifying them of the imminent online, postal, telephone or face-to-face survey. Prior notification increases response rates, as the participant's attention is drawn to the purpose of a study and the potential benefits, without the apparent 'chore' of the questionnaire. With the potential participant's attention focused upon the purpose and benefits, the chances increase for a greater reception when approached actually to complete a survey.[22] A key element of notifying potential participants lies in how surveys are introduced as illustrated in the following example.

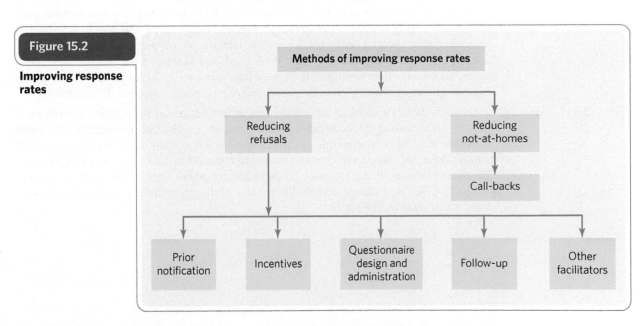

Figure 15.2

Improving response rates

Real research	**Only incentives increase response rates?**[23]

In a study organised by a New Zealand marketing research agency that conducted omnibus surveys using CATI, a measure of the effectiveness of 'introductions' upon response rates was made. Four introduction elements were tested: an incentive (prize draw for a weekend holiday); an assurance that the survey was not a sales pitch; an assurance of confidentiality; and a short versus longer description of the survey topic. Overall, only the incentive significantly increased the response rate. In combination, the best result and the only one to achieve a significantly higher response rate was the use of the incentive coupled with a 'no-sales' assurance. The use of the incentive did not appear to encourage people to lie about their eligibility as participants.

- *Incentives.* Response rates can be increased by offering monetary as well as non-monetary incentives to potential participants. Monetary incentives can be prepaid or promised. The prepaid incentive is included with the survey or questionnaire. The promised incentive is sent to only those participants who complete the survey. The most commonly used non-monetary incentives are premiums and rewards, such as pens, pencils, books and offers of survey results.[24] Prepaid incentives have been shown to increase response rates to a greater extent than promised incentives. The amount of incentive can vary from trivial amounts to tens of euros. The amount of incentive has a positive relationship with response rate, but the cost of large monetary incentives may outweigh the value and quality of additional information obtained.

- *Questionnaire design and administration.* A well-designed questionnaire can decrease the overall refusal rate as well as refusals to specific questions (see Chapter 13). If the questionnaire and experience of answering the questions are interesting for the participants, using words, logic and visual appeal that are meaningful to them, the response rate can improve. Likewise, the skill used to administer the questionnaire in telephone and face-to-face interviews can increase the response rate. Trained interviewers are skilled in refusal conversion or persuasion. They do not accept a no response without an additional plea. The additional plea might emphasise the brevity of the questionnaire or importance of the participant's opinion. Interviewing procedures are discussed in more detail in Chapter 16.

- *Follow-up.* Follow-up, or contacting the non-participants periodically after the initial contact, is particularly effective in decreasing refusals in online, SMS and postal surveys. The researcher might send a reminder to non-participants to complete and return the questionnaire. Two or three mailings may be needed in addition to the original one. With proper follow-up, the response rate in postal surveys can be increased to 80% or more. Follow-ups can be done by postcard, letter, telephone, email or face-to-face contacts.[25]

- *Other facilitators.* Personalisation, or sending letters addressed to specific individuals, is effective in increasing response rates, especially when practised in conjunction with prior notification.[26] The only downside of such an approach is actually obtaining the names and contact details of those to whom a questionnaire should be sent. The following example illustrates elements of the approach to increasing response rates at the German research company GfK. The example is set in the context of the company changing from a postal-based panel to an online panel.

Real research

GfK's online panel[27]

The Web Portal is the 'web presence' of an online panel. This is where the panel members go to interact with a research agency and thus is a hugely important aspect of online research. The portal is used to build a relationship with the panel members and achieve the high panel retention that is necessary for the quality of continuous research. When communicating with the panel members it is important to retain the personal 'feel'. The GfK website is compared by their panel members with every site they visit, not just those of other research companies. Therefore, the Web Portal had to offer a comparable experience to that offered by, for example, banks and retailers, in terms of functionality and user experience. The system must also be extremely reliable as any problems will have a direct effect on response rates and panel retention. Response levels have been raised to well above the industry average for online access panels, although still below their postal panel peak of 85%. GfK has seen response rates rise directly in line with its increase in the understanding of the differences between the online and offline postal panel. The online panel has a 'core' of panellists from which GFK experiences an 80% response rate. Outside this group there is a continuous influx of panellists who participate for about a year and then drop off. When analysing this against its experience with the postal panels GFK offered the following lessons:

- Receiving a questionnaire through the post is a much more tangible experience. The questionnaire sits on a 'to-do' pile and this is a constant reminder to complete it. The participant is also able to see the entirety of the questionnaire and can easily make an estimation of the time required to complete it.

- People are much more likely to change their email address than they are to move. It is therefore much easier to lose contact with participants. 'Spam' mailing is a major reason for switching email address and is therefore a major issue for companies running continuous panels.

- The Internet is a rapidly changing environment and it is very easy for panellists to become tired of a website. There are many more distractions for people when they are online. Community sites such as MySpace and Facebook take up increasing amounts of online time. There has also been an increase in entertainment available online, such as gaming and online TV services such as the BBC iPlayer.

Taking these factors into account means that the panellist communication strategy and incentive schemes are constantly under review. It is always necessary to value the importance of building and maintaining the relationship with the panellists and ensuring they feel valued for the help they provide in conducting the research.

Not-at-homes. The second major cause of low response rates is not-at-homes. This factor has contributed to the growth of online and mobile surveys. Where telephone and home face-to-face interviews are planned, low response rates can result if the potential participants are not at home when contact is attempted. A study analysing 182 commercial telephone surveys involving a total sample of over 1 million consumers revealed that a large percentage of potential participants were never contacted. The median non-contact rate was 40%. In nearly 40% of the surveys, only a single attempt was made to contact potential participants. The results of 259,088 first-call attempts using a sophisticated random-digit dialling system show that less than 10% of the calls resulted in completed interviews, and 14.3% of those contacted refused to participate.[28]

The likelihood that potential participants will not be at home varies with several factors. People with small children are more likely to be at home. Consumers are more likely to be at home at weekends than on weekdays and in the evening as opposed to during the afternoon. Pre-notification and appointments increase the likelihood that the participant will be at home when contact is attempted.

The percentage of not-at-homes can be substantially reduced by employing a series of call-backs, or periodic follow-up attempts, to contact non-participants. The decision about the number of call-backs should weigh the benefits of reducing non-response bias against the additional costs. As call-backs are completed, the call-back participants should be compared with those who have already responded to determine the usefulness of making further call-backs. In most consumer surveys, three or four call-backs may be desirable. Although the first call yields the most responses, the second and third calls have a higher response per call. It is important that call-backs be made and controlled according to a prescribed plan.[29]

Adjusting for non-response

Low response rates increase the probability that non-response bias will be substantial. Response rates should always be reported, and, whenever possible, the effects of non-response should be estimated. This can be done by linking the non-response rate to estimated differences between participants and non-participants. Information on differences between the two groups may be obtained from the sample itself. For example, differences found through call-backs could be extrapolated, or a concentrated follow-up could be conducted on a subsample of the non-participants. Alternatively, it may be possible to estimate these differences from other sources.[30] To illustrate, in a survey of owners of vacuum cleaners, demographic and other information may be obtained for participants and non-participants from their guarantee cards. For a postal panel, a wide variety of information is available for both groups from syndicate organisations. If the sample is supposed to be representative of the general population, then comparisons can be made with census figures. Even if it is not feasible to estimate the effects of non-response, some adjustments can still be made during data analysis and interpretation.[31] The strategies available to adjust for non-response error include subsampling of non-participants, replacement, substitution, subjective estimates, trend analysis, simple weighting and imputation.

Subsampling of non-participants. Subsampling of non-participants, particularly in the case of postal surveys, can be effective in adjusting for non-response bias. In this technique, the researcher contacts a subsample of the non-participants, usually by means of telephone, face-to-face interviews or by email. This often results in a high response rate within that subsample. The values obtained for the subsample are then projected to all the non-participants, and the survey results are adjusted to account for non-response. This method can estimate the effect of non-response on the characteristic of interest.

Replacement. In replacement, the non-participants in the current survey are replaced with non-participants from an earlier, similar survey. The researcher attempts to contact these non-participants from the earlier survey and administer the current survey questionnaire to them, possibly by offering a suitable incentive. It is important that the nature of non-response in the current survey be similar to that of the earlier survey. The two surveys should use similar kinds of participants, and the time interval between them should be short. As an example, as the S:Comm, IFM Sports Marketing Surveys Leisure Time study is repeated each year, the non-participants in the present survey may be replaced by the non-participants in the original survey.

Substitution
A procedure that substitutes for non-participants other elements from the sampling frame who are expected to respond.

Substitution. In substitution, the researcher substitutes for non-participants other elements from the sampling frame who are expected to respond. The sampling frame is divided into subgroups that are internally homogeneous in terms of participant characteristics but heterogeneous in terms of response rates. These subgroups are then used to identify substitutes who are similar to particular non-participants but dissimilar to participants already in the sample. Note that this approach would not reduce non-response bias if the substitutes are similar to participants already in the sample.

Subjective estimates. When it is no longer feasible to increase the response rate by subsampling, replacement or substitution, it may be possible to arrive at subjective estimates of the nature and effect of non-response bias. This involves evaluating the likely effects of non-response based on experience and available information. For example, married adults with young children are more likely to be at home than single or divorced adults or than married adults with no children. This information provides a basis for evaluating the effects of non-response due to not-at-homes in face-to-face or telephone surveys.

Trend analysis. Trend analysis is an attempt to discern a trend between early and late participants. This trend is projected to non-participants to estimate where they stand on the characteristic of interest. For example, Table 15.4 presents the results of several waves of a postal survey. The characteristic of interest is money spent on shopping in supermarkets during the last two months. The known value of the characteristic for the total sample is given at the bottom of the table. The value for each successive wave of participants becomes closer to the value for non-participants. For example, those responding to the second mailing spent 79% of the amount spent by those who responded to the first mailing. Those responding to the third mailing spent 85% of the amount spent by those who responded to the second mailing. Continuing this trend, one might estimate that those who did not respond spent 91% [85 + (85 − 79)] of the amount spent by those who responded to the third mailing. This results in an estimate of €252 (277 × 0.91) spent by non-participants and an estimate of €288 [(0.12 × 412) + (0.18 × 325) + (0.13 × 277) + (0.57 × 252)] for the average amount spent in shopping at supermarkets during the last two months for the overall sample. Suppose we knew from consumer panel records that the actual amount spent by non-participants was €230 rather than €252, and that the actual sample average was €275 rather than the €288 estimated by trend analysis. Although the trend estimates are wrong, the error is smaller than the error that would have resulted from ignoring the non-participants. Had the non-participants been ignored, the average amount spent would have been estimated at €335 [(0.12 × 412) + (0.18 × 325) + (0.13 × 277)]/(0.12 + 0.18 + 0.13) for the sample.

Weighting. Weighting attempts to account for non-response by assigning differential weights to the data depending on the response rates.[32] For example, in a survey on personal computers, the sample was stratified according to income. The response rates were 85%, 70% and 40%, respectively, for the high-, medium- and low-income groups. In analysing the data, these subgroups are assigned weights inversely proportional to their response rates. That is,

Trend analysis
A method of adjusting for non-response in which the researcher tries to discern a trend between early and late participants. This trend is projected to non-participants to estimate their characteristic of interest.

Weighting
A statistical procedure that attempts to account for non-response by assigning differential weights to the data depending on the response rates.

Table 15.4	Use of trend analysis in adjusting for non-response		
	Percentage response	*Average euro expenditure*	*Percentage of previous wave's response*
First mailing	12	412	–
Second mailing	18	325	79
Third mailing	13	277	85
Non-response	(57)	(230)	91
Total	100	275	

the weights assigned would be 100/85, 100/70 and 100/40, respectively, for the high, medium- and low-income groups. Although weighting can correct for the differential effects of non-response, it destroys the self-weighting nature of the sampling design and can introduce complications.[33] Weighting is further discussed in Chapter 17 on data integrity.

Imputation

A method to adjust for non-response by assigning the characteristic of interest to the non-participants based on the similarity of the variables available for both non-participants and participants.

Imputation. Imputation involves imputing, or assigning, the characteristic of interest to the non-participants based on the similarity of the variables available for both non-participants and participants.[34] For example, a participant who does not report brand usage may be imputed based on the usage of a participant with similar demographic characteristics. Often there is a high correlation between the characteristic of interest and some other variables. In such cases, this correlation can be used to predict the value of the characteristic for the non-participants (see Chapter 14).

International marketing research

When conducting marketing research in international environments, statistical estimation of sample size may be difficult because estimates of the population variance in particular countries may be unavailable. Hence, the sample size is often determined by qualitative considerations, as discussed in Chapter 14: (1) the importance of the decision, (2) the nature of the research, (3) the number of variables, (4) the nature of the analysis, (5) sample sizes used in similar studies, (6) incidence rates, (7) completion rates, and (8) resource constraints. If statistical estimation of sample size is attempted at all, it should be realised that the estimates of the population variance may vary from country to country. For example, in measuring consumer preferences, a greater degree of heterogeneity may be encountered in countries where consumer preferences are not well developed. Thus, it may be a mistake to assume that the population variance is the same or to use the same sample size in different countries.

It is important to realise that survey response rates can vary widely across countries. The following example illustrates how researchers are faced with response rate challenges in China. It is worth noting how attitudes to participation may change in a developing nation, forcing researchers to consider the motivations of and rewards demanded by participants. There are also indications of environmental factors that can shape levels of response to individual survey modes.

Real research   Chinese marketing research in a global context[35]

As in the rest of the world, survey completion rates have dropped year by year in China. In the early days, Chinese consumers were just curious about research activities. They participated in surveys full of interest and were eager to share their opinions. Currently an interviewer would have to knock on 80 doors in a residential part of Beijing to find one potential participant, or approach 200 pedestrians on a downtown Shanghai street to find one person interested in participating in a survey, let alone screen whether they are qualified. Smaller cities seem in general to have better response rates, but travelling to those areas and putting together teams of experienced interviewers to conduct the surveys does not save as much money or energy as could be hoped. Those who answer a door knock and accepted an interview during a typical workday were very often retired, and at the front gate of an upscale residential complex, interviewers were often stopped outside by security guards even though more affluent participants were definitely listed and targeted on a quota sheet. Telephone became a natural alternative and many research firms established their own telephone interviewing facilities, and

CATI became a popular approach in projects conducted in the larger (tier 1) and medium size (tier 2) cities where the high telephone penetration has enabled a robust enough pool for sampling. At the same time, telephone interviews brought greater flexibility and faster speed in recruiting participants even though the refusal rate and drop out rate was not low at all. However, telephone interviews were generally still not recommended for surveys among low-penetration populations or for unsolicited longer interviews. For some surveys, CATI was found to serve well as a supplement to face-to-face approaches. For example, in a typical car clinic project, participants were often pre-recruited by telephone and then invited to join a face-to-face interview conducted at a central location. These car clinic tests often required a specific composition of participant profiles, i.e. by the model of car owned, and the fieldwork often required a quick turnaround to produce results. Pre-recruitment thus helped achieve these needed samples to agree to interviews at the available times, and research buyers understood they would have to pay extra to accomplish this. Researchers rarely gain good response rates through postal surveys. People did not seem to have as much enthusiasm in responding to a postal survey and taking the trouble to mail it back, especially when the survey was commercial in nature. Results were relatively better for those surveys organised by government entities or large state-owned companies with government sponsorship. Another issue that limited the application of postal surveys was with the address database. Residential addresses had never been maintained to a good level of detail and accuracy. Further, due to the residential registration control in China, a person's residence was officially registered to an address where they were born or where the household residence officially belonged to – the *hukou* (officially registered residence) and did not necessarily connect to where they were currently living. A young professional who had lived and worked in Beijing for more than 10 years could still be registered with an address in a small town in Anhui Province where their parents resided. The *hukou* addressee maintenance system placed a serious hurdle in the way of postal survey development in China and remains so.

Ethics in marketing research

Although the statistical determination of sample size is mainly objective, it is nonetheless susceptible to ethical concerns. As can be seen from the formula, the sample size is heavily dependent on the standard deviation of the variable and there is no way of knowing the standard deviation until the data have been collected. An estimate of the standard deviation is used to calculate the sample size. This estimate is derived based on secondary data, judgement or a small pilot study. By inflating the standard deviation, it is possible to increase the sample size and thus the project revenue. Using the sample size formula, it can be seen that increasing the standard deviation by 20%, for example, will increase the sample size by 44%. It is clearly unethical to inflate the standard deviation, and thereby increase the sample size, simply to enhance the revenue of a research company. Ethical dilemmas can arise even when the standard deviation is estimated honestly. It is possible, indeed common, that the standard deviation in the actual study is different from that estimated initially. When the standard deviation is larger than initially estimated, the confidence interval will also be larger than desired. In such a situation, the researcher has the responsibility to discuss this with the client and jointly decide on a course of action.

Researchers also have the ethical responsibility to investigate the possibility of non-response bias, and make a reasonable effort to adjust for non-response. The research design adopted and the extent of non-response bias found should be clearly communicated. There are ethical ramifications of poor communications that affect non-response and confidence intervals of survey estimates based on statistical samples. These are illustrated in the following example that looks at some of the specific challenges faced in political polling. Though parts of the example may seem dated, the lessons are still relevant in the manner that researchers cope with non-response bias.

Real research | Surveys serve up elections[36]

The dissemination of some survey results has been strongly criticised as manipulative and unethical. In particular, the ethics of releasing political poll results before and during an election have been questioned. Opponents of such surveys claim that voters are misled by these results. First, before the election, voters are influenced by whom the polls predict will win. If they see that the candidate they favour is trailing, they may decide not to vote; they assume that there is no way their candidate can win. The attempt to predict the election results while the election is in progress has come under even harsher criticism. Opponents of this practice feel that this predisposes voters to vote for the projected winner or that it may even discourage voters from voting, even though the polls have not closed, because the media project that there is already a winner. Furthermore, not only are the effects of these projections questionable, but frequently the accuracy of the projections is questionable as well. Although voters may be told a candidate has a certain percentage of the votes within 1 per cent, the confidence interval may be much larger, depending on the sample size.

In 1994, and with opinion polls consistently failing to predict the outcome of the UK General Election, the Market Research Society and the Royal Statistical Society launched an enquiry into why this had happened. David Butler (Emeritus Fellow of Nuffield College, Oxford), who chaired the committee, wrote in the introduction to the report that:

The standards of accuracy which are demanded of pre-election polls and which pollsters seem forced implicitly to accept are far more stringent than those applied to any other form of survey research and may well be unrealistic . . . and this must be understood by those who use the polls. They made the following recommendations.[37]

- *Pollsters should use reliable, regularly updated sources for sample quotas and target weights, and should explore variables more closely related to voting behaviour than those, primarily demographic, variables that were being used at that time.*
- *Efforts should be made to get a clearer understanding of the profile and attitudes of those who refuse to participate in surveys, since the quota sampling method universally used was likely to conceal significant non-response biases.*
- *Participants who refuse to answer the voting question should be encouraged to express a party preference, and the use of claimed past voting behaviour should be explored as a way to get a more accurate measure of voting intention from this group of people. In any case, 'don't know' levels should always be reported since there were major differences in the levels of 'don't know' between different providers.*

Digital applications in marketing research

Digital developments in marketing have meant a huge growth of databases in terms of directories and lists of existing and potential customers. Many of these have been compiled for direct marketing applications that may be questionable to researchers. With the ethical considerations and critical sense in evaluating secondary data sources adopted by bone fide researchers, there is much of value in these databases. From the researcher's perspective, these databases can be seen and evaluated as sampling frames. Researchers can track down many potential sampling frames that could be used to define and classify a population. With different sampling frames collected and 'cleaned' in a database package, an ultimate population can be defined, classified and its ultimate size can be determined. If there is a finite size to a population, such searches can play a vital role in tracking down all elements of that population. Using database packages to build rich details of survey participants, the researcher can also keep track of non-participants. The database can help to determine whether there are particular geographical locations or types of non-participant that are problematic and have to be dealt with in a particular manner. The rapid identification of non-participants enables researchers to develop tactics to encourage a response.

Online surveys have grown in number and clearly lead other modes of conducting surveys. With the opportunities this growth has afforded to researchers has come added complexity in designing surveys. Much of this complexity is due to the variety of the devices used by participants, how participants engage with these devices, and what these devices are capable of doing. With new technological developments and participants abilities to engage with new technology come opportunities and threats. ESOMAR sees the opportunities as a means to improve methods and engage participants, fuelled by the strong growth in Internet and mobile penetration and advances in the sophistication of mobile devices and online platforms. ESOMAR sees threats as there may be an overreliance on new techniques that rely on impersonal communications with participants growing tired of lengthy, arduous surveys.[38] ESOMAR has noted a general decline in completion and response rates. For researchers, this means that to maintain and improve response rates, they have to use new technologies in ways that engage with increasingly demanding participants. In Chapter 1 we detailed the broader context of these challenges and potential responses of the research industry. In the context of improving response rates, the following example illustrates how Diageo and its researchers improved their methods and engaged participants. Though many of the rewards and motivations they used were not new, it was the totality of the participant experience they managed, using digital technologies.

Real research

Understanding, embracing and evolving marketing research online communities[39]

Diageo's Altitude Lounge was an online community run by Virtual Surveys (**www.virtualsurveys.com**). Diageo manages a premium drinks business with a collection of international brands across spirits, wine and beer. It traded in approximately 180 markets and employed over 20,000 people around the world. Diageo Global Travel and Middle East (GTME) was Diageo's business unit responsible for the Global Travel Retail channel as well as the Middle East region. This channel was made up largely of airports, but also included cruise lines, airlines and border stores. Online communities were new to Diageo and the GTME team was keen to lead the way in this field. The online community covered five markets: China, Germany, South Korea, the UK and the USA. Members were recruited from existing online panels in each of the countries. Before developing the community the team wanted to ensure that it was able to understand the cultural context of the countries in question. To make this work, it spoke to professionals and experts with a good knowledge of Chinese, South Korean and German culture. This helped the team improve how it communicated with participants in these countries and learn more about what might motivate them to take part. As the project unfolded, it took a number of steps to engage with its members:

- *Online guide.* The team created a visual help guide and translated this into all the different languages so it was easier for people to understand how the community worked.

- *Native language.* The team sent out emails about topics in native languages (although topics largely stayed in English) and styled the text so it was a more appropriate way to speak to members in each country (e.g. the UK focused more on feedback around how it would be helping the brand by taking part; the USA was more focused on the prize draw and the chances of winning).

- *Private comments.* The team made it easier for people to make comments privately by enabling them to reply to its email address with further comments rather than leaving these publicly in the discussion.

- *Shared results.* The team offered specific feedback on the concepts it had tested, explaining the impact the research had on Diageo's strategies.

- *Incentives.* The team offered premium alcohol as additional incentives to participation, matching brands to the types of participant taking part. There were high levels of affinity to these brands and this was a reason many were returning to the site.

- *Prizes.* The team conducted country-specific prize draws which guaranteed a prize per country.

- *User feedback.* After the community had been running for four months, the team undertook a review of the community with members, asking what they liked about taking part and how they could improve the community. Members liked the following: feedback and having an impact on Diageo; the incentives (this was the biggest motivation to joining); being able to express views; finding out about new products and ideas.

Diageo saw response rates improve substantially as participants became more interested in taking part in research. A number of experts it spoke to said that the whole idea of a marketing research community was problematic for people in South Korea and China because it was alien to what they were accustomed to. However, while the recruitment has proved slower and more challenging, the interest that has been shown from these countries was testament to the success that international marketing research communities could have.

Summary

The statistical approaches to determining sample size are based on confidence intervals. These approaches may involve the estimation of the mean or proportion. When estimating the mean, determination of sample size using the confidence interval approach requires the specification of precision level, confidence level and population standard deviation. In the case of proportion, the precision level, confidence level and an estimate of the population proportion must be specified. The sample size determined statistically represents the final or net sample size that must be achieved. To achieve this final sample size, a much greater number of potential participants have to be contacted to account for a reduction in response due to incidence rates and completion rates.

Non-response error arises when some of the potential participants included in the sample do not respond. The primary causes of low response rates are refusals and not-at-homes. Refusal rates may be reduced by prior notification, incentives, excellent questionnaire design and administration, and follow-up. The percentage of not-at-homes can be substantially reduced by call-backs. Adjustments for non-response can be made by subsampling non-participants, replacement, substitution, subjective estimates, trend analysis, simple weighting and imputation.

The statistical estimation of sample size is even more complicated in international marketing research because the population variance may differ from one country to the next. The preliminary estimation of population variance for the purpose of determining the sample size also has ethical ramifications. Digital developments in marketing research can assist in determining the sample size and adjusting it to account for expected incidence and completion rates. Digital developments can also afford opportunities to design questionnaires, surveys and research experiences that engage with more sophisticated and demanding participants.

Questions

1 Define:
   a   the sampling distribution
   b   finite population correction
   c   confidence intervals.

2 What is the standard error of the mean?

3 What is the procedure for constructing a confidence interval around a mean?

4 Describe the difference between absolute precision and relative precision when estimating a population mean.

5 How do the degree of confidence and the degree of precision differ?

6 Describe the procedure for determining the sample size necessary to estimate a population mean, given the degree of precision and confidence and a known population variance. After the sample is selected, how is the confidence interval generated?

7 Describe the procedure for determining the sample size necessary to estimate a population mean, given the degree of precision and confidence but where the population variance is unknown. After the sample is selected, how is the confidence interval generated?

8 How is the sample size affected when the absolute precision with which a population mean is estimated is doubled?

9   How is the sample size affected when the degree of confidence with which a population mean is estimated increases from 95% to 99%?

10 Define what is meant by absolute precision and relative precision when estimating a population proportion.

11 Describe the procedure for determining the sample size necessary to estimate a population proportion given the degree of precision and confidence. After the sample is selected, how is the confidence interval generated?

12 How can the researcher ensure that the generated confidence interval will be no larger than the desired interval when estimating a population proportion?

13 When several parameters are being estimated, what is the procedure for determining the sample size?

14 Define incidence rate and completion rate. How do these rates affect the determination of the final sample size?

15 What strategies are available for adjusting for non-response?

Exercises

1   Using a spreadsheet (e.g. Excel), program the formulae for determining the sample size under the various approaches described in this chapter.

2   Using the website of a major newspaper in your country, search for reports of three recent major surveys. Write a report on the sample sizes used and the extent to which details of precision, confidence levels and any other factors affecting the sample were reported. Note any reporting that sensationalises statistical changes over time that are within the margin of error tolerances.

3   Examine online databases and secondary data sources to determine the average monthly household spend on broadband services in your country. Assuming a confidence level of €10, and a standard deviation of €100, what should be the sample size to determine the average monthly household expenditure on broadband services?

4   You work as the marketing research manager for a chain of themed restaurants. A new menu has been developed based upon organic and fair-trade produce. Before the new menu is introduced, management are concerned about how existing and potential customers will react. How would you approach the sample size calculations for this task? Present your plan to a group of students representing the board of the chain.

5   In a small group discuss the following issues: 'Statistical considerations are more important than administrative considerations in determining sample size' and 'The real determinant of sample size is what managers feel confident with; it has little to do with statistical confidence.'

Video case exercise: Subaru

Evaluate the reasons for the high response rates to Subaru's surveys. What lessons of Subaru's success can be generalised to other survey designs?

Appendix: The normal distribution

In this appendix, we provide a brief overview of the normal distribution and the use of the normal distribution table. The normal distribution is used in calculating the sample size, and it serves as the basis for classical statistical inference. Many continuous phenomena follow the normal distribution or can be approximated by it. The normal distribution can, likewise, be used to approximate many discrete probability distributions.[40]

The normal distribution has some important theoretical properties. It is bell shaped and symmetrical in appearance. Its measures of central tendency (mean, median and mode) are all identical. Its associated random variable has an infinite range ($-\infty < x < +\infty$).

The normal distribution is defined by the population mean μ and population standard deviation σ. Since an infinite number of combinations of μ and σ exist, an infinite number of normal distributions exist and an infinite number of tables would be required. By standardising the data, however, we need only one table, such as Table 2 in the Appendix of statistical tables. Any normal random variable X can be converted to a standardised normal random variable z by the formula

$$z = \frac{X - \pi}{\sigma}$$

Note that the random variable z is always normally distributed with a mean of 0 and a standard deviation of 1. The normal probability tables are generally used for two purposes: (1) finding probabilities corresponding to known values of X or z, and (2) finding values of X or z corresponding to known probabilities. Each of these uses is discussed.

Finding probabilities corresponding to known values

Suppose that Figure 15A.1 represents the distribution of the number of engineering contracts received per year by an engineering firm. Because the data span the entire history of the firm, Figure 15A.1 represents the population. Therefore, the probabilities or proportion of area under the curve must add up to 1.0. The marketing director wishes to determine the probability that the number of contracts received next year will be between 50 and 55. The answer can be determined by using Table 2 of the Appendix of statistical tables.

Table 2 gives the probability or area under the standardised normal curve from the mean (zero) to the standardised value of interest, z. Only positive entries of z are listed in the table. For a symmetrical distribution with zero mean, the area from the mean to +z (i.e. z standard

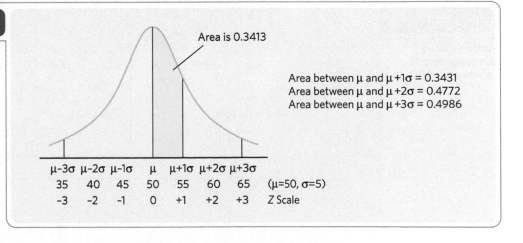

Figure 15.A1

Finding probability corresponding to a known value

Area is 0.3413

Area between μ and $\mu+1\sigma$ = 0.3431
Area between μ and $\mu+2\sigma$ = 0.4772
Area between μ and $\mu+3\sigma$ = 0.4986

	$\mu-3\sigma$	$\mu-2\sigma$	$\mu-1\sigma$	μ	$\mu+1\sigma$	$\mu+2\sigma$	$\mu+3\sigma$	
	35	40	45	50	55	60	65	(μ=50, σ=5)
	-3	-2	-1	0	+1	+2	+3	Z Scale

deviations above the mean) is identical to the area from the mean to $-z$ (z standard deviations below the mean).

Note that the difference between 50 and 55 corresponds to a z value of 1.00. Note that, to use Table 2, all z values must be recorded to two decimal places. To read the probability or area under the curve from the mean to $z = +1.00$, scan down the z column of Table 2 until the z value of interest (in tenths) is located. In this case, stop in the row $z = 1.00$. Then read across this row until you intersect the column containing the hundredths place of the z value. Thus, in Table 2, the tabulated probability for $z = 1.00$ corresponds to the intersection of the row $z = 1.0$ with the column $z = 0.00$. This probability is 0.3413. As shown in Figure 15A.1, the probability is 0.3413 that the number of contracts received by the firm next year will be between 50 and 55. It can also be concluded that the probability is 0.6826 (2 × 0.3413) that the number of contracts received next year will be between 45 and 55.

This result could be generalised to show that for any normal distribution the probability is 0.6826 that a randomly selected item will fall within ±1 standard deviations above or below the mean. Also, it can be verified from Table 2 that there is a 0.9544 probability that any randomly selected, normally distributed observation will fall within ±2 standard deviations above or below the mean, and a 0.9973 probability that the observation will fall within ±3 standard deviations above or below the mean.

Finding values corresponding to known properties values

Suppose that the marketing director wishes to determine how many contracts must come in so that this number represents 5% of the contracts expected for the year. If 5% of the contracts have come in, 95% of the contracts have yet to come. As shown in Figure 15A.2, this 95% can be broken down into two parts: contracts above the mean (i.e. 50%) and contracts between the mean and the desired z value (i.e. 45%). The desired z value can be determined from Table 2, since the area under the normal curve from the standardised mean, 0, to this z must be 0.4500. From Table 2, we search for the area or probability 0.4500. The closest value is 0.4495 or 0.4505. For 0.4495, we see that the z value corresponding to the particular z row (1.6) and z column (0.04) is 1.64. The z value, however, must be recorded as negative (i.e. $z = -1.64$), since it is below the standardised mean of 0. Similarly, the z value corresponding to the area of 0.4505 is -1.65. Since 0.4500 is midway between 0.4495 and 0.4505, the appropriate z value could be midway between the two z values and estimated as -1.645. The corresponding X value can then be calculated from the standardisation formula, as follows:

$$X = \mu + z\sigma$$
$$= 50 + (-1.645)5$$
$$= 41.775$$

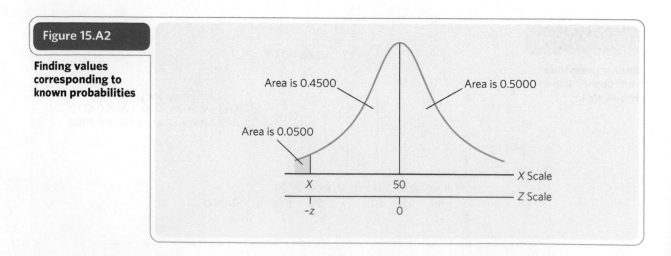

Figure 15.A2

Finding values corresponding to known probabilities

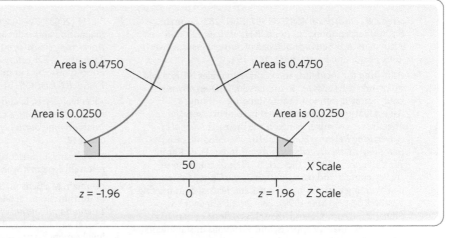

Figure 15.A3

Finding values corresponding to known probabilities: confidence interval

Suppose that the marketing director wanted to determine the interval in which 95% of the contracts for the next year are expected to lie. As can be seen from Figure 15A.3, the corresponding z values are ± 1.96. This corresponds to X values of $50 \pm (1.96)5$, or 40.2 and 59.8. This range represents the 95% confidence interval.

Notes

1. Sung, Y., de Gregorio, F. and Jung, J.-H., 'Non-student consumer attitudes towards product placement – implications for public policy and advertisers', *International Journal of Advertising* 28 (2) (2009), 257–285.

2. Joinson, A.H. and Reips, U., 'Personalized salutation, power of sender and response rates to web-based surveys', *Computers in Human Behavior* 23 (3) (2007), 1372–1383; Couper, M.P., 'Web surveys: a review of issues and approaches', *Public Opinion Quarterly* 64 (4) (2000), 464–494.

3. A discussion of the sampling distribution may be found in any basic statistics textbook. For example, see Berenson, M.L., Levine, D.M. and Krehbiel, T., *Basic Business Statistics: Concepts and Applications*, 9th edn (Englewood Cliffs, NJ: Prentice Hall, 2009).

4. Other statistical approaches are also available. A discussion of these is beyond the scope of this book, however. The interested reader is referred to Rohm, A.J., Milne, G.R. and McDonald, M.A., 'A mixed-method approach to developing market segmentation typologies in the sports industry', *Sport Marketing Quarterly* 15 (1) (2006), 29–39; Reynolds, M.R. Jr. ,'EWMA control charts with variable sample sizes and variable sampling intervals', *IIE Transactions* 33 (6) (June 2001), 511–530; Sampath, S., *Sampling theory and methods* (Boca Raton, FL: CRC Press, 2000); Yeh, L. and Van, L.C., 'Bayesian double-sampling plans with normal distributions', *Statistician* 46 (2) (1997), 193–207; Blyth, W.G. and Marchant, L.J., 'A self -weighting random sampling technique', *Journal of the Market Research Society* 38 (4) (October 1996), 473–479; Nowell, C. and Stanley, L.R., 'Length-biased sampling in mall intercept surveys', *Journal of Marketing Research* 28 (November 1991), 475–479; Gillett, R., 'Confidence interval construction by Stein's method: a practical and economical approach to sample size determination', *Journal of Marketing Research* 26 (May 1989), 237.

5. Sharot, T., 'The design and precision of data-fusion studies', *International Journal of Market Research* 49 (4) (2007), 449–470; Kelley, K., 'Sample size planning for the coefficient of variation from the accuracy in parameter estimation approach', *Behavior Research Methods* 39 (4) (November 2007), 755–766; Thompson, S.K., *Sampling* (New York: Wiley, 2002); Wall, M.M., 'An effective confidence interval for the mean with samples of size one and two', *American Statistician* (May 2001), 102–105; Chow, S.L., *Statistical Significance* (Thousand Oaks, CA: Sage, 1996).

6. Valliant, R.L., Dorfinan, A.H. and Royall, R.M., *Finite Population Sampling and Inference: A Prediction Approach* (New York: Wiley, 2000).

7. Joseph, L. and Wolfson, D.B., 'Interval based versus decision-theoretic criteria for the choice of a sample size', *Statistician* 46 (2) (1997), 145–149; Frankel, M., 'Sampling theory', in Rossi, P.H., Wright, J.D. and Anderson, A.B. (eds), *Handbook of Survey Research* (New York: Academic Press, 1983), 21–67.

8. Götze, S., 'Sustainability as a monetary brand value – a social-psychological and economical framework', ESOMAR, Congress, Montreux (September 2009).

9. For a discussion of estimating sample costs, see Davies, R.J. and McIntosh, A., 'The sampling on non-domestic populations', *International Journal of Market Research* 38 (4) (1996); Sudman, S., *Applied Sampling* (New York: Academic Press, 1976); Kish, L., *Survey Sampling* (New York: Wiley, 1965).

10. See, for example, Sampath, S., *Sampling theory and methods*, 2nd edn (Oxford: Alpha Science International, 2005); Bradley, N., 'Sampling for internet surveys: an examination of participant selection for internet research', *Journal of the Market Research Society* 41 (4) (October 1999), 387–395; Adcock, C.J., 'Sample size determination:

a review', *Statistician* 46 (2) (1997), 261–283; Sudman, S., 'Applied sampling', in Rossi, P.H., Wright, J.D. and Anderson, A.B. (eds), *Handbook of Survey Research* (New York: Academic Press, 1983), 145–194.

11. Adjusting for incidence and completion rates is discussed in Lavrakas, P.J., Mane, S. and Laszlo, J., 'Does anyone really know if online ad campaigns are working? An evaluation of methods used to used to assess the effectiveness of advertising on the internet', *Journal of Advertising Research* 50 (4) (2010) 354–373; Rao, P.S., *Sampling Methodologies with Applications* (Boca Raton, FL: CRC Press, 2001); Bickart, B., 'The distribution of survey contact and participation in the United States: constructing a survey based estimate', *Journal of Marketing Research* 36 (2) (May 1999), 286–294; Dillman, D.A., Singer, E., Clark, J.R. and Treat, J.B., 'Effects of benefits appeals, mandatory appeals, and variations in statements of confidentiality on completion rates for census questionnaires', *Public Opinion Quarterly* 60 (3) (Fall 1996), 376–389.

12. Stevens, C., Jethwani, T. and Renaud, D., 'Online = research nirvana?', ESOMAR, Conference on Panel Research, Budapest (April 2005); Lee, K.G., 'Incidence is a key element', *Marketing News* (13 September 1985), 50.

13. Till, A., Souza, F. and Mele, S., 'Right here… right now… – location specific mobile research', ESOMAR, Annual Congress, London (September 2006).

14. Korczak, D., 'Do I want to be beautiful? Consumer decision making for cosmetic surgery', ESOMAR, Healthcare Conference, Rome (February 2008).

15. Council of American Survey Research Organisations, **www.casro.org**.

16. ESOMAR, 'Global Market Research', ESOMAR Industry Report (2010), 48.

17. Cooke, M., Johnson, A., Rolfe, G. and Parker, K., 'Association for Survey Computing (ASC): Pizzazz in research: renewing the rules of engagement', *International Journal of Market Research* 53 (1) (2011), 115–125; Van Kenhove, P., 'The influence of topic involvement on mail-survey response behaviour', *Psychology & Marketing* 19 (3) (March 2002), 293; Fisher, M.R., 'Estimating the effect of nonresponse bias on angler surveys', *Transactions of the American Fisheries Society* 125 (1) (January 1996), 118–126; Martin, C., 'The impact of topic interest on mail survey response behaviour', *Journal of the Market Research Society* 36 (October 1994), 327–338.

18. Heerwegh, D., 'Effects of personal salutations in email invitations to participate in a web survey', *Public Opinion Quarterly* 69 (4) (Winter 2005), 588–598; Cummings, S.M., 'Reported response rates to mailed physician questionnaires', *Health Services Research* 35 (6) (February 2001), 1347–1355; Hill, A., Roberts, J., Ewings, P. and Gunnell, D., 'Nonresponse bias in a lifestyle survey', *Journal of Public Health Medicine* 19 (2) (June 1997), 203–207; McDaniel, S.W., Madden, C.S. and Verille, P., 'Do topic differences affect survey non-response?', *Journal of the Market Research Society* (January 1987), 55–66.

19. For minimising the incidence of non-response and adjusting for its effects, see Lozar Manfreda, K., Bosnjak, M., Berzelak, J., Haas, I. and Vehovar, V., 'Web surveys versus other survey modes: a meta-analysis comparing response rates', *International Journal of Market Research*

50 (1) (2008), 79–104; Columbo, R., 'A model for diagnosing and reducing non-response bias', *Journal of Advertising Research* 40 (1/2) (January/April 2000), 85–93; Chen, H.C., 'Direction, magnitude, and implications of nonresponse bias in mail surveys', *Journal of the Market Research Society* 38 (3) (July 1996), 267–276.

20. Vicente, P., Reis, E. and Santos, M., 'Using mobile phones for survey research: a comparison with fixed phones', *International Journal of Market Research* 51 (5) (2009), 613–634.

21. Havermans, J., 'Strict rules for telemarketers may help research', *Research World* (June 2004), 14.

22. Brennan, M., Benson, S. and Kearns, Z., 'The effect of introductions on telephone survey response rates', *International Journal of Market Research* 47 (1) (2005), 65–74; Van Kenhove, P., 'The influence of topic involvement on mail-survey response behaviour', *Psychology & Marketing* 19 (3) (March 2002), 293; Groves, R.M., 'Leverage-saliency theory of survey participation: description and an illustration', *Public Opinion Quarterly* 64 (3) (Fall 2000), 299–308; Everett, S.A., Price, J.H., Bedell, A.W. and Telljohann, S.K., 'The effect of a monetary incentive in increasing the return rate of a survey of family physicians', *Evaluation and the Health Professions* 20 (2) (June 1997), 207–214; Armstrong, J.S. and Lusk, E.J., 'Return postage in mail surveys: a meta-analysis', *Public Opinion Quarterly* (Summer 1987), 233–248; Yu, J. and Cooper, H., 'A quantitative review of research design effects on response rates to questionnaires', *Journal of Marketing Research* 20 (February 1983), 36–44.

23. Brennan, M., Benson, S. and Kearns, Z., 'The effect of introductions on telephone survey participation rates', *International Journal of Market Research* 47 (1) (January 2005), 65–74.

24. Gendall, P. and Healey, B., 'Effect of a promised donation to charity on survey response', *International Journal of Market Research* 52 (5) (2010), 565–577; Rose, D.S., Sidle, S.D. and Griffith, K.H., 'A penny for your thoughts: monetary incentives improve response rates for company-sponsored employee surveys', *Organizational Research Methods* 10 (2) (April 2007), 225–240; Hansen, K.M., 'The effects of incentives, interview length and interviewer characteristics on response rates in a CATI study', *International Journal of Public Opinion Research* 19 (1) (April 2007), 112–121; Saunders, J., Jobber, D. and Mitchell, V., 'The optimum prepaid monetary incentives for mail surveys', *Journal of the Operational Research Society* 57 (10) (October 2006), 1224–1230; Shaw, M.J., 'The use of monetary incentives in a community survey: impact on response rates, data, quality and cost', *Health Services Research* 35 (6) (February 2001), 1339–1346.

25. McCarty, C., House, M., Harman, J. and Richards, S., 'Effort in phone survey response rates: the effects of vendor and client controlled factors', *Field Methods* 18 (2) (May 2006), 172; Zafer Erdogan, B., 'Increasing mail survey response rates from an industrial population: a cost effectiveness analysis of four follow-up techniques', *Industrial Marketing Management* 31 (1) (January 2002), 65.

26. Ladik, D.M., Carrillat, F.A. and Solomon, P.J., 'The effectiveness of university sponsorship in increasing survey response rate', *Journal of Marketing Theory & Practice* 15 (3) (July 2007), 263–271; Byrom, J., 'The effect

of personalization on mailed questionnaire response rates', *International Journal of Market Research* (Summer 2000), 357–359; Dillman, D.A., Singer, E., Clark, J.R. and Treat, J.L.B., 'Effects of benefits appeals, mandatory appeals, and variations in statements of confidentiality on completion rates for census questionnaires', *Public Opinion Quarterly* 60 (3) (Fall 1996), 376–389; Gendall, P., Hoek, J. and Esslemont, D., 'The effect of appeal, complexity and tone in a mail survey covering letter', *Journal of the Market Research Society* 37 (3) (July 1995), 251–268; Greer, T.V. and Lohtia, R., 'Effects of source and paper color on response rates in mail surveys', *Industrial Marketing Management* 23 (February 1994), 47–54.

27. Van Walwyk, M. and Garland, C., 'Turning the super tanker – the migration from a postal to online methodology', ESOMAR, Panel Research, Dublin (October 2008).

28. Keeter, S., 'Consequences of reducing non-response in a national telephone survey', *Public Opinion Quarterly* 64 (2) (Summer 2000), 125–148; Bowen, G.L., 'Estimating the reduction in nonresponse bias from using a mail survey as a backup for nonparticipants to a telephone interview survey', *Research on Social Work Practice* 4 (1) (January 1994), 115–128; Kerin, R.A. and Peterson, R.A., 'Scheduling telephone interviews', *Journal of Advertising Research* (May 1983), 44.

29. van Goor, H. and van Goor, A., 'The usefulness of the basic question – procedure for determining nonresponse bias in substantive variables: a test of four telephone questionnaires', *International Journal of Market Research* 49 (2) (2007), 221–236.

30. Phillips, A., Curtice, J., Sparrow, N., Whiteley, P., Clarke, H., Sanders, D., Stewart, M. and Moon, N., 'Lessons from the polls: retrospective views on the performance of the opinion polls conducted in the run-up to the 2010 UK General Election', *International Journal of Market Research* 52 (5) (2010), 675–696; Groves, R.M., 'Nonresponse rates and nonresponse bias in household surveys', *Public Opinion Quarterly* 70 (5) (2006), 646–675; Columbo, R., 'A model for diagnosing and reducing nonresponse bias', *Journal of Advertising Research* (January/April 2000), 85–93.

31. Abraham, K.G., Maitland, A. and Bianchi, S.M., 'Nonresponse in the American Time Use Survey', *Public Opinion Quarterly* 70 (5) (2006), 676–703; Larsen, M.D., 'The psychology of survey response', *Journal of the American Statistical Association* 97 (457) (March 2002), 358–359; Dey, E.L., 'Working with low survey response rates the efficacy of weighting adjustments', *Research in Higher Education* 38 (2) (April 1997), 215–227.

32. de Jong, M.G., Steenkamp, J.-B.E.M., Fox, J.-P. and Baumgartner, H., 'Using item response theory to measure extreme response style in marketing research: a global investigation', *Journal of Marketing Research* 45 (1) (February 2008), 104–115; Sobh, R. and Perry, C.,

'Research design and data analysis in realism research', *European Journal of Marketing* 40 (11) (January 2006), 1194; Qin, J., 'Estimation with survey data under non-ignorable non-response or informative sampling', *Journal of the American Statistical Association* 97 (457) (March 2002), 193–200; Kessler, R.C., Little, R.J. and Grover, R.M., 'Advances in strategies for minimising and adjusting for survey nonresponse', *Epidemiologic Reviews* 17 (1) (1995), 192–204.

33. Sparrow, N., 'Developing reliable online polls', *International Journal of Market Research* 48 (6) (2006), 659–680.

34. Groves, R.M. and Peytcheva, E., 'The impact of nonresponse rates on nonresponse bias: a meta-analysis', *Public Opinion Quarterly* 72 (2) (Summer 2008), 167–189; Brewer, K., *Design and estimation in survey sampling* (London: Edward Arnold, 2001); Sao, J., 'Variance estimation for survey data with composite imputation and non-negligible sampling fractions', *Journal of American Statistical Association* (March, 1999), 254–265; Drane, J.W., Richter, D. and Stoskopf, C., 'Improved imputation of nonresponse to mailback questionnaires', *Statistics in Medicine* 12 (34) (February 1993), 283–288.

35. Fine, B., Ellis, R.S. and Xu, D., 'Research methodologies in China – past, present and future', ESOMAR, Asia Pacific, Beijing (April 2009).

36. Christensen, W.F. and Florence, L.W., 'Predicting presidential and other multistage election outcomes using state-level pre-election polls', *American Statistician* 62 (1) (February 2008), 1; Taylor, H., 'Using internet polling to forecast the 2000 elections', *Marketing Research* 13 (1) (Spring 2001), 26–30; Morwitz, V.G., and Pluzinski, C., 'Do polls reflect opinions or do opinions reflect polls? The impact of political polling on voters' expectations, preferences and behaviour', *Journal of Consumer Research* 23 (1) (June 1996), 53–67.

37. Phillips, A., Curtice, J., Sparrow, N., Whiteley, P., Clarke, H., Sanders, D., Stewart, M. and Moon, N., 'Lessons from the polls: retrospective views on the performance of the opinion polls conducted in the run-up to the 2010 UK General Election', *International Journal of Market Research* 52 (5) (2010), 675–696.

38. ESOMAR, 'Global Market Research', ESOMAR Industry Report (2010), 48.

39 Child, P., Fleming, K., Shaw, R. and Skilbeck, T., 'Vive la difference: understanding, embracing and evolving MROCs globally', ESOMAR, Congress Odyssey, Athens (September 2010).

40 This material is drawn from Berenson, M.L., Levine, D.M. and Krehbiel, T., *Basic Business Statistics: Concepts and Applications*, 11th edn (Upper Saddle River, NJ: Prentice Hall, 2000).

16 Survey fieldwork

Stage 1

Problem definition

Stage 2

Research approach developed

Stage 3

Research design developed

Stage 4

Fieldwork or data collection

Stage 5

Data integrity and analysis

Stage 6

Report preparation and presentation

No matter how well the research process is designed, the individuals working in the field hold the key to quality data.

Objectives

After reading this chapter, you should be able to:

1 describe the survey fieldwork process and explain the selecting, training and supervising of fieldworkers, validating fieldwork and evaluating fieldworkers;

2 discuss the training of fieldworkers in making the initial contact, asking the questions, probing, recording the answers and concluding the interview;

3 discuss supervising fieldworkers in terms of quality control and editing, sampling control, control of cheating and central office control;

4 describe evaluating fieldworkers in areas of cost and time, response rates, quality of interviewing and the quality of data;

5 explain the issues related to fieldwork when conducting international marketing research;

6 discuss ethical aspects of survey fieldwork;

7 appreciate how digital developments are shaping the manner and quality of fieldwork.

Overview

Survey fieldwork is a vital process, helping to generate sound marketing research data. During this phase, fieldworkers make contact with potential participants, administer questionnaires or observation forms, record data, and turn in completed forms for processing. A worker managing online research engagements, a face-to-face interviewer administering questionnaires door to door, an interviewer intercepting shoppers in the street, a telephone interviewer calling from a central location, a worker mailing questionnaires from an office, an observer counting customers in a particular section of a store, a mystery shopper experiencing the service of a retail outlet, and others involved in data collection and supervision of the process are all fieldworkers.

The researcher faces two major problems when managing fieldwork operations. First of all, fieldwork should be carried out in a consistent manner so that regardless of who administers a questionnaire, the same process is adhered to. This is vital to allow comparisons between all completed questionnaires. Second, fieldworkers to some extent have to approach and motivate potential participants in a manner that sets the correct purpose for a study and motivates the participant to spend time answering the questions properly. This cannot be done in a 'robotic' manner; it requires good communication skills and an amount of empathy with participants, but could be interpreted as a means to bias responses. These two problems may be seen as conflicting, but, for the researcher, fieldwork management means resolving these conflicts for each individual data gathering process. This makes survey fieldwork an essential task in the generation of sound research data.

This chapter describes the nature of survey fieldwork and the general survey fieldwork/data collection process. This process involves selecting, training and supervising fieldworkers, validating fieldwork and evaluating fieldworkers. We briefly discuss survey fieldwork in the context of international marketing research and identify the relevant ethical issues. We conclude by discussing how digital developments in marketing research are enabling more efficient and effective fieldwork. To begin, we present two examples. The first example illustrates the role of fieldwork in the administration of an online panel. The second illustrates the challenges faced by fieldwork managers. There is much pressure on fieldwork managers to achieve high response rates and this example illustrates a study designed to understand how they feel about methods to gain compliance from participants.

The Clubhouse: a panel of out-of-home sports TV viewers[1]

The broadcaster BSkyB appointed the research company Ipsos MORI (**www.ipsos-mori. com**) to measure out-of-home viewing of Sky Sports. The research objectives were to: (1) provide analysis of out-of-home viewing on a game-by-game basis; (2) provide out-of-home viewing figures for all major sporting events; (3) establish the demographic profile, reach and audience share for Sky Sports in an out-of-home environment; (4) determine the environment in which out-of-home viewing was taking place (e.g. local pub, other pub, clubs, at work, etc.); (5) provide a research design that did not rely so heavily on participant recall as the then current two-weekly telephone survey; and (6) determine which were the most popular pub channels for out-of-home viewing. The research approach to fulfil these objectives included:

Universe. Out-of-home sports viewers aged 18 years or over (15.5 million).
Method. Online panel of viewers to sporting events on TV in out-of-home locations.

Sample size. 7,000.

Recruitment. Primarily online.

Panel interface. Panellists logged on to their own home page with access to the message boards, latest survey, report summaries and the latest incentives.

Incentives. Mixture of points, prize draws, charity donations and vouchers.

Fieldwork. The panel was subdivided into four matched panels and each was surveyed weekly. The questionnaire content was agreed by Tuesday each week; fieldwork ran from Thursday to Wednesday and was reported on a Thursday.

Questionnaire. Each week 8-10 fixtures were measured along with ad hoc questions which included advertisement testing, pub visiting habits, brand awareness and usage. Questionnaires were agreed weekly.

Reporting. Weekly reporting included viewing of football fixtures only. Monthly reporting includes viewing of all other sports, ad hoc questions and incorporate qualitative insights from the message boards. Quarterly reports summarise key trends and viewing patterns and were enhanced with qualitative insight from the message boards.

In order to engage with participants throughout the key fieldwork period (English football season August–May) a competition was held to predict the score of one match each week. In taking part in this competition participants were taken back to their home page and could complete their survey if eligible to do so, contribute to the message boards and were reminded of their link to The Clubhouse.

Using compliance techniques to boost response rates[2]

Survey researchers use a variety of compliance appeals to boost response rates. Where they involve deliberate deception or misinformation they clearly violate marketing research ethics and codes of practice. Where researchers use what might be called sharp practice, in making exaggerated claims or in making participants uncomfortable if they do not comply, it is contrary to the broader aspirations of codes of practice. Such practices may be considered detrimental to building long-term cooperation with participants. In light of these issues, an Australian study sought answers to the following questions: (1) To what extent are these compliance techniques considered contrary to the commercial researchers' Code of Professional Behaviour? (2) To what extent do marketing research companies actually use them in seeking to improve cooperation? In asking participants about their own ethical behaviour, it was recognised that a social desirability bias was possible. The method adopted aimed to identify not only reported behaviours, but also the reasons for them. The study focused on the field managers of telephone surveys in marketing research firms. They had the responsibility for managing interviewers and implementing survey designs. The study was conducted in two stages. The first involved eight in-depth interviews with participants from companies with extensive experience in telephone survey facilities in Australia. This stage was used to generate the items included in a survey. This survey formed the second stage of the study, targeted at Australian marketing research companies. The field managers disliked the use of most of the compliance principles. They were concerned about the ethics of misleading participants about the true duration of an interview. Concerns were also raised about the use of a social validation compliance principle, which involved interviewers mentioning to participants that the survey had met with 'great enthusiasm and cooperation from others'. Managers saw the industry as trying to distance itself from telemarketing because the public's confusion of the two activities worked against marketing research. A principle of 'liking' was commonly engaged in telephone research as interviewers were instructed to sound friendly, pleasant and courteous, but not to sound too familiar as a telemarketer may do. They believed that in the current climate of participants being concerned about privacy, appealing to 'scarcity' by making participants feel that they have been specially chosen might make them feel even more nervous and suspicious about how a research company acquired their details. The managers indicated that when appropriate they would be likely to emphasise a survey's sponsorship by an authority such as a government department or a university to increase cooperation. It could also help to assure participants about confidentiality.

The nature of survey fieldwork

Marketing research data are rarely collected by the persons who design the research. Researchers have two major options for collecting their data: they can manage this within their own organisations or they can contract with a fieldwork agency. In either case, data collection involves the use of some kind of field force. The field force may operate either from an office (online, telephone and postal surveys) or in the field (face-to-face interviews at home or a workplace, street interview, CAPI and observation). The fieldworkers who collect data typically may have little formal marketing research or marketing training. Their training primarily focuses upon the essential tasks of selecting the correct participants, motivating them to take part in the research, eliciting the correct answers from them, accurately recording the answers and conveying those answers for analysis. An appreciation of why these tasks fit into the overall context of conducting marketing research is important, but it is not necessary for the survey fieldworker to be trained in the whole array of research skills.

The growth in online research has changed the nature and emphasis of fieldwork. Traditionally, marketing research used a 'personal attention' approach in which every interviewer paid attention to nurturing and addressing each specific participant. Online research has shifted the service design from a personalised to a more 'self-service' approach. Analogous to transactions like self-service petrol stations, company websites, or e-tickets for airlines, the participant becomes a 'partial interviewer' participating in the production of the service. Conducting online research eliminates the bias and the pressure that are usually introduced by the presence of the interviewer in the participant's environment. The intentional or unintentional behaviour and appearance of the interviewer does not influence the participants and how they respond. As a corollary, the participants may provide more truthful answers than would be the case in the presence of another party. Many participants like online research because it puts them in control. For many other participants the 'self-service' form of engaging with researchers is treated with much scepticism. Many participants need to develop a sense of trust, and the benefits of participation need to be clearly promoted by human contact.[3] For these participants, telephone or face-to-face interviews will be required, using traditional forms of fieldwork.

Survey fieldwork and the data collection process

All survey fieldwork involves selecting, training and supervising persons who collect and manage data.[4] The validation of fieldwork and the evaluation of fieldworkers are also parts of the process. Figure 16.1 represents a general framework for the survey fieldwork and data collection process. Even though we describe a general process, it should be recognised that the nature of survey fieldwork can vary widely with the mode of data collection and that the relative emphasis on the different steps will be different for online, telephone, face-to-face and postal surveys.

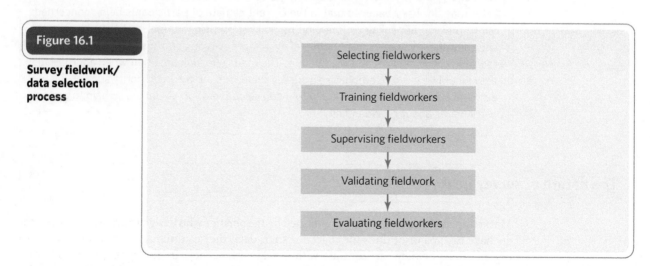

Figure 16.1

Survey fieldwork/ data selection process

Selecting survey fieldworkers

The first step in the survey fieldwork process is the selection of fieldworkers. The researcher should: (1) develop job specifications for the project, taking into account the mode of data collection; (2) decide what characteristics the fieldworkers should have; and (3) recruit appropriate individuals. Interviewers' background characteristics, opinions, perceptions, expectations and attitudes can affect the responses they elicit.[5]

For example, the social acceptability of a fieldworker to the participant may affect the quality of data obtained, especially in face-to-face interviewing. Researchers generally agree that the appearance and demeanour of the interviewer have a direct impact upon participants' willingness to take part in an interview. This factor is illustrated in the following example.

| Real research | **Barclays Brand Health Monitor[6]** |

Barclays Bank decided to establish a consistent framework across business divisions which integrated strategic measures of brand health and advertising tracking. This was conducted in the context of a concern that the role of interviewers in the research process was being neglected, resulting in a detrimental effect on the quality of information collected. Barclays felt there was an opportunity to draw these elements together and so developed a survey that addressed both interviewer and participant issues while providing a sound basis of understanding from which the business could make strategic decisions. The result was the Barclays Brand Health Monitor (BHM). The BHM interviewed 600 individuals with either a current account or a savings account each month, of which two-thirds were representative of the sample universe and the remainder were recruited to boost a survey of Barclays customers, the impact of which was weighted at analysis. Interviews were conducted at home. The extent to which the interview truly engaged participants was established, to some extent, by the degree to which they felt the interview covered their views on the subject. The majority (in excess of 80%) responded positively on this measure and there was a direct relationship between this and enjoyment. There was a fair understanding of marketing research and its role and this supported participants' initial interest in taking part. In addition, the appearance and demeanour of the interviewer were also key influences on initial participation; interviewers must be friendly and approachable as well as appearing trustworthy, professional and polite in order to be allowed into participants' homes.

Training survey fieldworkers

Training survey fieldworkers is critical to the quality of data collected. Training may be conducted in person at a central location or, if the interviewers are geographically dispersed, online, by video-conferencing or even by mail. Training ensures that all interviewers administer the questionnaire in the same manner so that the data can be collected uniformly. Training should cover making the initial contact, asking the questions, probing, recording the answers and concluding the interview.[7]

Making the initial contact

The initial contact can result in cooperation or the loss of potential participants.[8] It also sets the potential participant in a 'frame of mind' to answer subsequent questions. Thus interviewers should be trained to make opening remarks that will convince potential participants that their participation is important. Interviewers should also motivate potential participants to reflect properly upon the questions posed to them and to answer honestly.

Asking the questions

Even a slight change in the wording, sequence or manner in which a question is asked can distort its meaning and bias the response. Training in asking questions can yield high dividends in eliminating potential sources of bias. Changing the phrasing or order of questions during the interview can make significant differences in the response obtained:

> While we could be faulted for not writing as perfect a questionnaire as we possibly could, still it must be asked in the exact way it is written. It's a challenge for us to try to get the interviewers to be more conversational, but despite this, the field force absolutely must ask questions as they are written![9]

It was argued in Chapter 13 that questionnaire design is a craft. The researchers have to understand and step into the shoes of the participants they hope to elicit information from. Researchers impose their language and logic onto participants as they lead them through a questionnaire. If the interviewer is to behave as stated in the above quotation, researchers must appreciate what interviewers go through as they pose questions, probe and motivate participants. This is because asking questions is also a craft. The subtle smiles, body language, tone of voice all get the most out of the vast array of personalities, intellects and contexts in which the interviewer must work. The craft of interviewing develops with experience, allowing questions to be posed in a consistent manner.[10]

The following are guidelines for interviewers in becoming consistent in asking questions:[11]

1 Be thoroughly familiar with the purpose of the questionnaire.

2 Be thoroughly familiar with the structure of the questionnaire.

3 Ask the questions in the order in which they appear in the questionnaire.

4 Use the exact wording given in the questionnaire.

5 Read each question slowly.

6 Repeat questions that are not understood.

7 Ask every applicable question.

8 Follow instructions, working through any filter questions, and probe carefully.

Probing

Probing
A motivational technique used when asking questions to induce the participants to enlarge on, clarify or explain their answers.

Probing is intended to motivate participants to enlarge on, clarify or explain their answers. Probing also helps participants focus on the specific content of the interview and provide only relevant information. Probing should not introduce any bias. An example of the effect of interviewer bias comes from a survey in which one of the authors helped in data analysis (but not in the design of the questionnaire or in the management of the whole research process!). The survey related to bread and cake buying habits with one particular question focusing upon 'large cakes' that participants had bought over the previous 12 months. In analysing the data a percentage of participants had replied '*Christmas cake*'. When analysed further, all the participants who said '*Christmas cake*' had been interviewed by the same interviewer. The conclusion from this analysis was that the interviewer in question had used their own probe in a manner that would have answered the question, and, in the interviewer's view, to make the interview process work. None of the other interviewers had used this probe, which meant there was an inconsistent approach in eliciting answers from participants. The paradox faced by the survey designers in this example was that the 'rogue' interviewer *may* have used a probe that elicited a true representation of large cake purchasing, the other interviewers consistently failing to draw out a 'true' response.

To help in the process of probing, the following list details some commonly used techniques:[12]

1 *Repeating the question.* Repeating the question in the same words can be effective in eliciting a response.

2 *Repeating the participant's reply.* Participants can be stimulated to provide further comments by repeating their replies verbatim. This can be done as the interviewer records the replies.

3 *Using a pause or silent probe.* A silent probe, or an expectant pause or look, can cue the participant to provide a more complete response. The silence should not become embarrassing, however.

4 *Boosting or reassuring the participant.* If the participant hesitates, the interviewer should reassure the participant with comments such as 'There are no right or wrong answers. We are just trying to get your opinions.' If the participant needs an explanation of a word or phrase, the interviewer should not offer an interpretation, unless written instructions to do so have been provided. Rather, the responsibility for the interpretation should be returned to the participant. This can be done with a comment such as 'Just whatever it means to you.'

5 *Eliciting clarification.* The participant's motivation to cooperate with the interviewer and provide complete answers can be aroused with a question: 'I don't quite understand what you mean by that. Could you please tell me a little more?'

6 *Using objective or neutral questions or comments.* Table 16.1 provides several examples of the common questions or comments used as probes.[13] Corresponding abbreviations are also provided. The interviewer should record the abbreviations in parentheses next to the question asked.

The above list may seem to be simple, but there are hidden dangers. For example, probing '*why*' participants behave in a particular manner or feel about a particular issue takes the interview into the realms of the qualitative interview. Compare the context of the street interview with a short structured questionnaire with the context of the qualitative interview with a questioning approach structured to the participant and where a greater amount of rapport may be developed. The latter scenario is much more conducive to eliciting '*why*' participants behave or feel as they do. The question '*why*' is an example of a seemingly simple question that can create many problems of consistency in fieldwork. In the greater majority of circumstances, '*why*' should be treated as a qualitative issue. The following example illustrates the challenges of probing. Trying to uncover how participants really feel about an issue may be beyond simple probing?

Table 16.1	Commonly used probes and abbreviations
Standard interviewer's probe	*Abbreviation*
Any other reason?	(AO?)
Any others?	(Other?)
Anything else?	(AE or Else?)
Could you tell me more about your thinking on that?	(Tell more)
How do you mean?	(How mean?)
Repeat question	(RQ)
What do you mean?	(What mean?)
Which would be closer to the way you feel?	(Which closer?)
Why do you feel this way?	(Why?)
Would you tell me what you have in mind?	(What in mind?)

The emerging digital frontier: does probing help?[14]

TNS Global (**www.tnsglobal.com**) managed an ongoing conversation or community with young people in China for over six months. To set up and run an online community meant adapting and adopting conversational research techniques, moving away from some of the question formats TNS used in focus groups. Typically in a focus group, the conversation topics and flow are pre set with the moderator very much in charge. It was more challenging to manage the discussion in the same way online where probing by the researcher may actually interrupt the atmosphere and create 'distance' between researcher and participants. TNS found it more insight-ful to give young people the space and time to talk about topics that they found engaging. Although they may have talked about completely irrelevant things from the desired topic, sometimes insightful informa-tion emerged unexpectedly. 'Stories' and 'pictures' were found to be more helpful than 'what do you think . . .' or 'in your opinion . . .' kind of questions. The participants would only engage  when they liked the community, and they were willing to understand more about other participants in the community and to introduce more about themselves. There was no hurry to 'probe', as researchers always had the opportunity to re-ask a question from a different angle or in a different way. TNS found with this community that young people were much more spontaneous online than in offline conversation. They were also very likely to answer a question very abruptly if they were not in the mood to elaborate; from time to time it was found difficult to gain responses with 'depth', but highly possible on another day when the participants initiated a relevant topic and some very interesting discussion took place voluntarily.

Recording the answers

Although recording participant answers seems simple, several mistakes are common.[15] All interviewers should use the same format and conventions to record the interviews and edit completed interviews. Although the rules for recording answers to structured questions vary with each specific questionnaire, the general rule is to check the box that reflects the partici-pant's answer. The general rule for recording answers to unstructured questions is to record the responses verbatim. The following guidelines help to record answers to unstructured questions.

1   Record responses during the interview.

2   Use the participant's own words.

3   Do not summarise or paraphrase the participant's answers.

4   Include everything that pertains to the question objectives.

5   Include all probes and comments.

6   Repeat the response as it is written down.

Concluding the interview

The interview should not be closed before all the information is obtained. Any spontaneous comments the participant offers after all the formal questions have been asked should be recorded. The interviewer should answer the participant's questions about the project. The participant should be left with a positive feeling about the interview. It is important to thank the participant and express appreciation.

Saying 'thank you' can take many forms. As well as genuinely thanking participants for their cooperation, it serves the purpose of educating participants about the nature and purpose of marketing research, distinguishing marketing research from 'sugging' and 'frugging' as explained in the ethics section of Chapter 10. The following example illustrates a format of saying 'thank you' that works online but could be readily modified for use in all survey modes.

Real research | **RONIN's way of saying thank you**

The research company RONIN (**www.ronin.com**) says 'thank you' to its research participants in the following manner:

> As adherents to The ICC/ESOMAR International Code of Marketing and Social Research Practice, RONIN Corporation takes the privacy of all contributors of research information very seriously. RONIN Corporation would like to thank you for taking part in this genuine market research survey and for visiting our web site. We are not trying to sell or promote anything in our surveys. We promise that, in obtaining your cooperation, we will not mislead you about the nature of the research or the use, which will be made of the findings. The answers you give us will be treated as confidential unless you have given your consent to the contrary. In the relatively few instances where we ask you for permission to pass data on in a form which allows you to be personally identified, we will ensure that the information will be used only for the purposes stated. We will not send you unsolicited mail or pass on your email addresses to others for this purpose. Taking part in our surveys will cost you nothing apart from your normal internet connection. As with all forms of marketing and opinion research, your cooperation is voluntary at all times. We will not seek any personal information from or about you, without your prior knowledge and agreement. You are entitled at any stage of the interview, or subsequently, to ask that part or all of the record of your interview be destroyed or deleted. Wherever reasonable and practical we will carry out such a request. We try our best not to interview children without first getting the permission of their parents, though we cannot always assure this to be the case. We use cookies and other similar devices sparingly and only for quality control, validation and to prevent bothersome repeat surveying. You can configure your browser to notify you when cookies are being placed on your computer. You can also delete cookies by adjusting your browser settings. We automatically capture information about your browser type in order to deliver an interview best suited to your software. We do no other invisible processing of data from your computer.

Summary of training issues

To encapsulate the process of interviewer training, the following list summarises the nature and scope of areas in which a marketing research interviewer should be trained:

1 The marketing research process: how a study is developed, implemented and reported.

2 The importance of the interviewer to this process; the need for honesty, objectivity, organisational skills and professionalism.

3 Confidentiality of the participant and the client.

4 Familiarity with marketing research terminology.

5 The importance of following the exact wording and recording responses verbatim.

6 The purpose and use of probing and clarifying techniques.

7 The reason for and use of classification and participant information questions.

8 A review of samples of instructions and questionnaires.

9 The importance of the participant's positive feelings about survey research.

Conversely, researchers should be trained in the 'experience' of gathering data in the field with a practical knowledge of what works in terms of:

- Motivating potential participants to take part in a survey.
- Questions that will elicit the required data.
- Probes that can be consistently applied.
- An interview process that does not confuse or cause boredom in the participant.

The researcher needs to appreciate what the participant and the interviewer go through in the interview process. Without such an understanding, the questionnaires and interview procedures, which seem fine on paper, can lead to very poor-quality data. The following example illustrates the experiences of a 'typical' participant and researcher. While the feelings expressed cannot be generalised to all interview situations, the lesson from this is that the researcher should aim to understand how the target participants and interviewers feel about the process. These feelings must form an integral part of any research design that generates sound and accurate data.

Real research	**How was it for you?**[16]

A participant and an interviewer describe what their interview experiences were like for them.

The participant

I felt sorry for the interviewer, she was going around all these houses and nobody was in, so I agreed to take part in the survey. The interview did not take that long, only about 10 to 15 minutes, slightly less time than the interviewer said it would. The interviewer was smartly dressed, professional and helpful. She prompted me but did not actually push me. The experience was enjoyable, it was fun, and not a bad way to spend 10 to 15 minutes, although I think that was long enough. I like taking part in a survey if the subject matter is relevant to your life and you feel that your views are being taken into account. I think a lot of women prefer other females (or gay men) to interview them as there is an empathy there, and they might not feel they can be as honest or chatty with men. The age of the interviewer should relate to the subject matter. For example, if you are asking about children, then you should have an interviewer in a mother's age group. I think it is important to actually be in the same position as someone being surveyed. In an interview, you should be honest, do not tell them what you think they want to hear, relax, be friendly and go with the flow. A lot depends on the participant as well as the interviewer. There has to be a bit of banter between the two of you.

The interviewer

I do not have a typical day. If I am doing quota sampling I will do around 10 interviews a day. If it is preselected, then I will do 3 to 4 in-depth interviews. But if it's exit interviewing, I can do as many as 20 in a shift. There are pressures to the job sometimes. Getting your quota is like looking for a needle in a haystack. People are much more suspicious, and fewer will open the doors these days. I have interviewed through wrought iron gates, letter boxes, front room windows, and with the chain on the door. For your own safety, you must be aware of where you are and what's around you. Technology has not made my job easier, I feel that interviewing using pen and paper flows better.

My job could be made easier by keeping questionnaires short, and using proper screening questions. The essence is to keep it interesting. The worst thing in the world is when you have got a survey that repeats itself and is boring; huge lists are our worst enemy. All I ask of a participant is that they are honest, they do not have to be articulate or have strong opinions. There are two keys to successful interviewing, smile and be polite at all times, so that it is very hard for people to be rude to you, and be firm and in control of the interview.

Supervising survey fieldworkers

Supervising survey fieldworkers means making sure that they are following the procedures and techniques in which they were trained. Supervision involves quality control and editing, sampling control, control of cheating and central office control.

Quality control and editing

Quality control of fieldworkers requires checking to see whether the field procedures are being properly implemented.[17] If any problems are detected, the supervisor should discuss them with the fieldworkers and if necessary provide additional training. To understand the interviewers' problems related to a specific study, the supervisors should also do some interviewing. Supervisors should ensure that there are no technical problems in recording and transferring data through electronic means. If a survey is being conducted with hard copies of questionnaires, the supervisors should collect and check them daily. They should examine the questionnaires to make sure all appropriate questions have been completed, that unsatisfactory or incomplete answers have not been accepted. Supervisors should also keep a record of hours worked and expenses. This will allow a determination of the cost per completed interview, whether the job is moving on schedule and whether any interviewers are having problems.

Sampling control

Sampling control
An aspect of supervising that ensures that the interviewers strictly follow the sampling plan rather than select sampling units based on convenience or accessibility.

An important aspect of supervision is sampling control, which attempts to ensure that the interviewers are strictly following the sampling plan rather than selecting sampling units based on convenience or accessibility.[18] Interviewers tend to avoid homes, workplaces and people (sampling units) that they perceive as difficult or undesirable. If the sampling unit is not at home, for example, interviewers may be tempted to substitute the next available unit rather than call back. Interviewers sometimes stretch the requirements of quota samples. For example, a 58-year-old person may be placed in the 46–55 category and interviewed to fulfil quota requirements. To control these problems, supervisors should keep daily records of the number of calls made, the number of not-at-homes, the number of refusals, the number of completed interviews for each interviewer and the total for all interviewers under their control.

Central office control

Supervisors provide quality and cost-control information to the central office so that a total progress report can be maintained. In addition to the controls initiated in the field, other controls may be added at the central office to identify potential problems. Central office control includes tabulation of quota variables, important demographic characteristics and answers to key variables.

Validating survey fieldwork

An interviewer may falsify part of an answer to make it acceptable or may fake answers. The most blatant form of cheating occurs when the interviewer falsifies the entire questionnaire, merely filling in fake answers, either on their own or through the use of friends or family members. Cheating can be minimised through proper training, supervision and by rewarding interviewers properly. Most importantly their work should be validated, which includes recording the names and contact details of participants.[19] Supervisors usually call 10–25% of the participants to enquire whether the fieldworkers actually conducted the interviews. The supervisors ask about the length and quality of the interview, reaction to the interviewer and basic demographic data. The demographic information is cross-checked against the information reported by the interviewers on the questionnaires. The major drawback of this approach is that participants may not trust interviewers with a name and telephone number, perhaps believing that it is to be used to generate a sale, i.e. it can be confused with a 'sugging' or 'frugging' approach.

Evaluating survey fieldworkers

It is important to evaluate survey fieldworkers to provide them with feedback on their performance as well as to identify the better fieldworkers and build a better, high-quality field force. The evaluation criteria should be clearly communicated to the fieldworkers during their training. The evaluation of fieldworkers should be based on the criteria of cost and time, response rates, quality of interviewing and quality of data.[20]

Cost and time

Interviewers can be compared in terms of the total cost (salary and expenses) per completed interview. If the costs differ by city size, comparisons should be made only among fieldworkers working in comparable cities. Fieldworkers should also be evaluated on how they spend their time. Time should be broken down into categories such as actual interviewing, travel and administration.

Response rates

It is important to monitor response rates on a timely basis so that corrective action can be taken if these rates are too low.[21] Supervisors can help interviewers with an inordinate number of refusals by listening to the introductions they use and providing immediate feedback. When all the interviews are over, different fieldworkers' percentage of refusals can be compared to identify the more able interviewers and to help understand what has impacted upon non-response for particular types of participant. Interviewers can be a rich source of understanding why a particular survey works well or not.

Quality of interviewing

To evaluate interviewers on the quality of interviewing, the supervisor must directly observe the interviewing process. The supervisor can do this in person or the fieldworker can record the interview. The quality of interviewing should be evaluated in terms of: (1) the appropriateness of the introduction; (2) the precision with which the fieldworker asks questions; (3) the ability to probe in an unbiased manner; (4) the ability to ask sensitive questions; (5) interpersonal skills displayed during the interview, and (6) the manner in which the interview is terminated.

Quality of data

The completed questionnaires of each interviewer should be evaluated for the quality of data. Some indicators of quality data are that: (1) the recorded data are legible; (2) all instructions, including skip patterns, are followed; (3) the answers to unstructured questions are recorded verbatim; (4) the answers to unstructured questions are meaningful and complete enough to be coded; and (5) item non-response occurs infrequently.

International marketing research

The selection, training, supervision and evaluation of survey fieldworkers are critical in international marketing research. The quality of local fieldwork agencies can vary a great deal across many countries and so it may be necessary to recruit and train local fieldworkers. The use of local fieldworkers is desirable, because they are familiar with the subtleties of language and culture. They can create an appropriate climate for the interview and sensitivity to the concerns of the participants. Even with these advantages, extensive training may be required and close supervision in order to ensure that the questions are presented as intended. As observed in many countries, local interviewers may help the participant with answers or select households or sampling units based on personal considerations rather than the sampling plan. This means that the validation of fieldwork is critical. Proper application of fieldwork procedures can greatly reduce these difficulties and result in consistent and useful findings. International marketing research studies add more complexity regardless of how simple a survey may seem. Collecting data that is comparable between countries may be difficult, but it can be done using some conventional research techniques, with adaptations when needed and/or using mixed-mode approaches. Equivalent research procedures enable researchers to detect, analyse and better understand the world's socio-cultural differences. Such differences were explored in the following example.

Real research

International fieldwork challenges in an Olympic Interest Survey[22]

ResearchNow (**www.researchnow.com**) conducted a study that had fieldwork challenges to test its online access panels across the world. Specific countries were selected to ensure an interesting and likely diverse representation across five continents, including both established and emerging consumer markets. The countries examined were Australia, Brazil, China, the UK, and the USA. The sample size was based upon 4,542 participants. The length of the interview was five minutes, covering interests and attitudes towards the Olympic Games. One of the prime considerations when designing the Olympic Interest Survey was whether consumers in the countries selected could be reached via online access panels. Panel members were sourced from a mix of email marketing, search engine optimisation, website banners, co-registration, affiliate and viral marketing. Panels were also sourced by offline methods such as converting telephone call lists and in-person interviews. However, as the majority of panels tended to be sourced online and future response rates depended on participating in an online modality, the extent of a country's online penetration was considered. In designing the questionnaire and interview format, it could have been argued that an informal language style would be more appropriate for the 'informal' environment of the Internet and social networking sites. How-

ever, Research Now recognised that in surveys designed to engage a wide range of consumers in a population, 'informal' may not always be suitable. For the Olympic Interest Survey therefore, a formal style was used as the target was a broad swathe of age groups and an informal style would have potentially appeared to be disrespectful to older participants. Interviews were conducted in the mainstream language of the country in which they were living. In Brazil, all were interviewed in Brazilian Portuguese; in China the interviews were in Mandarin. In Australia, the UK and the USA, all were interviewed in localised English.

Ethics in marketing research

Researchers and survey fieldworkers should make participants feel comfortable when participating in research activities. This is vital in order to elicit the correct responses for a specific project but also more broadly for the health of the marketing research industry. A participant who feels that their trust has been abused, who found an interview to be cumbersome and boring, or who fails to see the purpose of a particular study, is less likely to participate in further marketing research efforts. Collectively, the marketing research industry has the responsibility to look after its most precious assets – willing and honest participants. Understanding how participants feel about a survey and why this so important is illustrated in the example opposite.

Many researchers that craft research designs do not meet participants face to face, or if they have, it may have occurred many years ago. Not being in the field, researchers can lose an awareness of what it is like actually to collect data in the field. Without this awareness, research designs that on paper seem feasible are difficult to administer in the field in a consist-

ent manner. If there are problems in collecting data in the field, these may not always be attributable to the training and quality of fieldworkers; the blame may lie with the research designer. The researcher, therefore, has an ethical responsibility to the fieldworker and the participant. The researcher's responsibility lies in an awareness of the process that the fieldworker and participant go through in the field for each individual piece of research they design. Poor design can leave fieldworkers facing very disgruntled participants and can cause great damage.

Good researchers have an awareness of their responsibilities to fieldworkers and participants. The researcher may take great care in understanding the difficulties of collecting data in the field and go to great pains to ensure that the data gathering process works well for the fieldworker and participant alike. The fieldworker may have been told about the purpose of the study, the purpose of particular questions, the means to select and approach participants, and the means to elicit responses correctly from participants. However, fieldworkers may behave in an unethical

Real research	**The challenges of researching body image**[23]

The research company Family Kids and Youth (**www.kidsandyouth.com**) carried out a study with adolescents about body image. Aware that this would be a highly sensitive subject, the company wanted to explore how the participants felt about the research. As well as the Market Research Society and ESOMAR guidelines, the nature of its studies meant that it also abided by the codes of conduct of the British Association for Counselling and Psychotherapy and the British Educational Research Association. The study explored many areas that affected young people such as friendship, relationship with family and how they felt about the way they looked. The first stage of the study was qualitative, and

included friendship triads with 11 to 15 year olds. The second stage of the research was an online survey. The first part of this survey was carried out with mothers who were told what the research was about and that with their permission the interviewers would also like to talk to their daughter/son. Having completed approximately five minutes of questioning, they were asked once again whether their child aged 11 to 15 was prepared to take part in the study. The child then read an explanation of the research and a reassurance that there were no right or wrong answers, and was asked if they would like to take part in the survey. A total of 705 children took part in the survey. The questionnaire was designed by Dr Barbie Clarke, a trained child psychotherapist, with a link to the young people's helpline Get Connected (**www.getconnected.org.uk**) at the end of the survey. As the study dealt with a such a sensitive topic, Family Kids and Youth was concerned to find out whether the questions might have left participants with a sense of disquiet. In all, 95% of participants agreed that the survey wanted to find out about their lives, and nearly all the children were pleased to be asked their opinion. The interviewers also asked children whether some of the questions might be too personal, and while 74% did not agree, 26% did feel this to be the case, which may have implied that some of the questions were too intrusive.

manner. They may cut corners in terms of selecting the correct participants, posing questions and probes, and recording responses. In such circumstances the fieldworker can cause much damage to an individual study and to the long-term relationship with potential participants. Thus it becomes a vital part of fieldworker training to demonstrate the ethical responsibilities that fieldworkers have in collecting data.

Researchers and fieldworkers have an ethical responsibility to respect participants' privacy, feelings and dignity.[24] Moreover, participants should be left with a positive and pleasant experience. This will enhance goodwill and future cooperation from participants. Researchers and fieldwork agencies are also responsible to their clients for following the accepted procedures for the selection, training, supervision, validation and evaluation of fieldworkers. They must ensure the integrity and fit with research codes of practice, e.g. ESOMAR, of the data collection process. The fieldwork procedures should be documented and made available to clients. Appropriate actions by researchers and fieldwork agencies can go a long way in addressing ethical concerns associated with fieldwork.

Digital applications in marketing research

The majority of survey research is now conducted online and the fieldwork related to such approaches occurs in a virtual world. The skills and demands of fieldworkers where there may be no face-to-face, audio or visual contact are different from the more traditional telephone and face-to-face survey techniques. The underlying principles of fieldwork in terms of building a relationship with participants, eliciting data, managing and validating data, remain the same whatever mode of collection is adopted. What differs is the nature of fieldwork tasks. The following example illustrates the administration of a digital diary that contained survey elements. In evaluating this case, consider what fieldwork means and how quality fieldwork standards could be relevant for the target participants.

Real research   Careers, relationships and bullying[25]

The digital marketing agency Brass (**www.brassagency.com**) helped to develop a strategy for how the UK government should communicate online with young people aged 14 to 19. The research project required panellists to keep a weekly diary of their lives in order to understand the challenges young people faced over a six-month period. Paper diary methods were not deemed suitable; cumbersome hard-copy documents were not easy to use or sufficiently private. The solution was to design a bespoke project website to facilitate the diary process. The site was an extranet, effectively a 'walled garden' accessed via a username and password. The panellists could log on and write their entries which would then be visible only to the project team. This ensured privacy, an important consideration as the project team was keen to make them feel comfortable and to get them to open up and share the details of their lives with the team. Each entry was recorded so the large number of entries could be categorised and analysed with relative ease. The website also allowed the project team to communicate with the panellists should they have any queries. To support participants, a 16-page booklet was created containing all the relevant project information such as the website's URL, the contact details of their moderator, the dates they could expect their incentives once they had completed their blog entries, as well as the relevant Market Research Society information for reference. The aim was that the booklet would act as an aide-memoire for the six-month fieldwork period. As the project progressed, the team needed to get feedback from participants on the hypotheses that the creative team had developed. The team felt it important to ensure that the hypotheses were clearly explained, concisely and in a replicable manner, ensuring each participant was given the same description in order to be consistent. Brass created an interactive media player (similar to Windows Media Player) for participants to interact with. This took the form of a chaptered case study video. It was filmed from a central character's perspective showing a young person's decision-making process about what career to choose, set over a six-week summer holiday. Different hypotheses were included in the narrative as the person progressed, e.g. taking part in an online careers fair. As each hypothesis was shown, an 'information point' icon appeared on the player; participants could click this to find out more about any third-party site being described (e.g. Habbo Hotel) if they were not familiar with it. Presenting ideas in this way was more user-centric, allowing participants a degree of active involvement in the process. They could pause the narrative to ask questions, repeat sections to recap on the ideas or look at an 'information point' where they were unsure about a third-party website being described.

Note in this case how much work would be needed to build and maintain a good relationship with participants, and in this context what materials were designed and 'fed' to participants. This relationship was vital to draw out what participants felt about particular issues; managing this in a consistent manner was a key fieldwork task.

In fieldwork activities where face-to-face or telephone contact is made, online systems can play a valuable role in all the phases of survey fieldwork: selection, training, supervision, validation and evaluation of fieldworkers. As far as selection is concerned, interviewers can be located, interviewed and hired online. This process can be initiated, for example, by posting job vacancy notices for interviewers on company websites, social networking sites, bulletin boards and at other suitable locations. While this would confine the search to only online-savvy interviewers, this may well be a qualification to look for in the current marketing research environment.

Similarly, multimedia capabilities offered by online engagements can be a good supplementary tool for training fieldworkers in all aspects of interviewing. Training in this manner can complement personal training programmes and add value to the process. Supervision is enhanced by facilitating communication between the supervisors and the interviewers via email and secured chat rooms. Central office control can be strengthened by posting progress reports and quality and cost-control information at a secured location on a website, so that they are easily available to all the relevant parties.

Validation of fieldwork, especially for face-to-face and telephone interviews, can be easily accomplished for those participants who have an email address or online access. These participants can be sent a short verification survey by email or asked to visit a website where the survey is posted. Finally, the evaluation criteria can be communicated online to fieldworkers during their training stage, and performance feedback can also be provided to them by using this medium.

Summary

Researchers have two major options in the generation of sound research data: developing their own organisations or contracting with fieldwork agencies. In either case, data collection involves the use of a field force. The growth in online research has changed the nature and emphasis of fieldwork. Traditionally, marketing research used a 'personal attention' approach in which every interviewer paid attention to nurturing and addressing each specific participant. Online research has shifted the service design from a personalised to a more 'self-service' approach. Though fieldwork tasks differ between survey modes, especially comparing face-to-face with online approaches, the underlying principles of good fieldwork remain the same. Fieldworkers should be trained in important aspects of fieldwork, including making the initial contact, asking the questions, probing, recording the answers and concluding the interview. Supervising fieldworkers involves quality control and editing, sampling control, control of cheating and central office control. Validating fieldwork can be accomplished by calling 10–25% of those who have been identified as interviewees and enquiring whether the interviews took place. Fieldworkers should be evaluated on the basis of cost and time, response rates, quality of interviewing and quality of data collection.

Fieldwork should be carried out in a consistent manner so that, regardless of who administers a questionnaire, the same process is adhered to. This is vital to allow comparisons between collected data. Fieldworkers to some extent have to approach and motivate potential participants in a manner that sets the correct purpose for a study and motivates the participant to spend time answering the questions properly. This cannot be done in a 'robotic' manner; it requires good communication skills and an amount of empathy with participants. This makes the issue of managing fieldwork an essential task in the generation of sound research data.

Selecting, training, supervising and evaluating fieldworkers is even more critical in international marketing research because the quality of local fieldwork agencies can be highly variable between countries. Ethical issues include making the participants feel comfortable in the data collection process so that their experience is positive. The growth of online survey techniques has meant that the nature of participant engagement has changed. The skills and demands of fieldworkers where there may be no face-to-face, audio or visual contact are changing but the underlying principles of quality fieldwork remain the same.

Questions

1   Why do researchers need to use survey fieldworkers?

2   Describe the survey fieldwork/data collection process.

3   What qualifications should survey fieldworkers possess?

4   What are the guidelines for asking questions?

5   Describe and illustrate the differences between probing in a survey and in an in-depth interview.

6   Evaluate what may be done to help interviewers probe correctly and consistently.

7   Outline the advantages and disadvantages of the interviewer developing a rapport with participants.

8   How should the answers to unstructured questions be recorded?

9   How should the survey fieldworker conclude an interview?

10   What aspects are involved in the supervision of survey fieldworkers?

11   How can participant selection problems be controlled?

12   What is validation of survey fieldwork? How is this done?

13   Describe the criteria that should be used for evaluating survey fieldworkers.

14   Describe the major sources of error related to survey fieldwork.

15   Comment on the following field situations, making recommendations for corrective action:

   a   One of the interviewers has an excessive rate of refusals in face-to-face home interviews.

   b   In a CATI situation, many phone numbers are giving a busy signal during the first dialling attempt.

   c   An interviewer reports that at the end of the interviews many participants asked if they had answered the questions correctly.

   d   During validation of the fieldwork, a participant reports that they cannot remember being interviewed over the telephone, but the interviewer insists that the interview was conducted.

Exercises

1   Visit the websites of three major marketing research agencies. Evaluate how they present their quality management of fieldwork. Write a report that details what you feel to be the best elements of their respective practices. Note also what additional practices they should be highlighting to reassure potential marketing research buyers and users.

2   You are a field supervisor. Ask a fellow student to assume the role of an interviewer and another student the role of a participant. Train the interviewer to conduct a home interview by giving a live demonstration.

3   In teams of four, design a questionnaire to be used in a street interview. One of the team then takes on the role of the interviewer, the other three act as participants. Conduct three interviews and video the process. Replay the video and write a report that focuses upon:

   a   The questionnaire design
   b   Stopping and motivating participants
   c   Interviewer instructions
   d   The consistency of the process
   e   Ethical issues involved in the process.

4   Visit **www.clinique.com** and examine online databases, secondary data and intelligence sources to obtain information on men's usage of moisturisers, soaps and shampoos. As a brand manager for Clinique, what information would you like to have to formulate brand extension strategies, targeted at men? How would you select and train fieldworkers to conduct a face-to-face survey (home, office or street) to determine mens' usage of 'grooming products'?

5   In a small group discuss the following issues: 'What makes street interviewing a craft?' and 'Why do interviewers cheat?'

Video case exercise: HSBC

HSBC wishes to understand the changing expectations and lifestyles of its target customers and the social events they attend. It plans to target the rising wealthy strata of India to conduct a face-to-face home survey. HSBC has chosen three cities to conduct the fieldwork: Chennai, Delhi and Mumbai. What challenges would HSBC face in conducting fieldwork for this survey? What advice would you offer to help overcome these fieldwork challenges?

Notes

1. Malagoni, L. and Barnsdale, A., 'A pint of lager and panel membership: measurement of out-of-home TV viewing', ESOMAR, Panel Research, Orlando (October 2007).

2. Bednall, D.H.B., Adam, S. and Plocinski, K., 'Ethics in practice: using compliance techniques to boost response rates', *International Journal of Market Research* 52 (2) (2010), 155–168.

3. Akaoui, J., 'Brand experience on the pitch: how the sponsors fared in the World Cup', *Journal of Advertising Research* 47 (2) (June 2007), 147–157.

4. Guest, G., Bunce, A. and Johnson, L., 'How many interviews are enough? An experiment with data saturation and variability', *Field Methods* 18 (1) (February 2006), 59–83; Gubrium, J.F. and Holstein, J.A., *Handbook of Survey Research: Context and Method* (Thousand Oaks, CA: Sage, 2000); Frey, J.H. and Oishi, S.M., *How to Conduct Interviews by Telephone and In Person* (Thousand Oaks, CA: Sage, 1995).

5. Dommeyer, C.J., 'The effects of the researcher's physical attractiveness and gender on mail survey response', *Psychology and Marketing* 25 (1) (January 2008), 47–70; Sacco, J.M., Scheu, C.R., Ryan, A.M. and Schmitt, N., 'An investigation of race and sex similarity effects in interviews: a multilevel approach to relational demography', *Journal of Applied Psychology* 88 (5) (2003), 852–865; McCombie, S.C., 'The influences of sex of interviewer on the results of an AIDS survey in Ghana', *Human Organization* 61 (1) (Spring 2002), 51–55; Catania, J.A., Binson, D., Canchola, J., Pollack, L.M., Hauck, W. and Coates, T.J., 'Effects of interviewer gender, interviewer choice, and item wording on responses to questions concerning sexual behaviour', *Public Opinion Quarterly* 60 (3) (Fall 1996), 345–375; Coulter, P.B., 'Race of interviewer effects on telephone interviews', *Public Opinion Quarterly* 46 (Summer 1982), 278–284; Singer, E., Frankel, M.R. and Glassman, M.B., 'The effect of interviewer characteristics and expectations on response', *Public Opinion Quarterly* 41 (Spring 1983), 68–83.

6. Miles, K., 'Improving the research interview experience', Market Research Society, Annual Conference (2000).

7. Lai, J. and Shuttles, C., 'Improving cooperation of Asian households through cultural sensitivity training for field interviewers', *Conference Papers – American Association for Public Opinion Research* (2004); Anon., 'Renewing your interviewing skills', *Healthcare Executive* 17 (1) (January/February 2002), 29; Kiecker, P. and Nelson, J.E., 'Do interviewers follow telephone survey instructions?', *Journal of the Market Research Society* 38 (2) (April 1996), 161–176; Guenzel, P.I., Berkmans, T.R. and Cannell, C.F., *General Interviewing Techniques* (Ann Arbor, MI: Institute for Social Research, 1983).

8. Rogelberg, S.G. and Stanton, J.M., 'Introduction, understanding and dealing with organizational survey nonresponse', *Organizational Research Methods* 10 (2) (April 2007), 195–209; Robertson, B., 'The effect of an introductory letter on participation rates using telephone recruitment', *Australian & New Zealand Journal of Public Health* 24 (5) (October 2000), 552; Feld, K., 'Good introductions save time, money', *Marketing News* 34 (5) (28 February 2000), 19–20; Couper, M.P., 'Survey introductions and data quality', *Public Opinion Quarterly* (Summer 1997), 317–338.

9. Bordeaux, D.B., 'Interviewing Part II: Getting the most out of interview questions', *Motor Age* 121 (2) (February 2002), 38–40; Anon., 'Market research industry sets up interviewing quality standards', *Management Auckland* 44 (2) (March 1997), 12.

10. Sethuraman, R., Kerin, R.A. and Cron, W.L., 'A field study comparing online and offline data collection methods for identifying product attribute preferences using conjoint analysis', *Journal of Business Research* 58 (5) (May 2005), 602–610.

11. This list follows closely the material in *Interviewer's Manual*, rev. edn (Ann Arbor, MI: Survey Research Center, Institute for Social Research, University of Michigan, 1976); Guenzel, P.J., Berkmans, T.R. and Cannell, C.E., *General Interviewing Techniques* (Ann Arbor, MI: Institute for Social Research, 1983).

12. For an extensive treatment of probing, see Henderson, N.R., 'The power of probing', *Marketing Research* 19 (4) (January 2007), 38–39; Gubrium, J.F. and Holstein, J.A., *Handbook of Interview Research: Context and method* (Thousand Oaks, CA: Sage, 2001), 15–19.

13. Ting, D.H., 'Further probing of higher order in satisfaction construct', *International Journal of Bank Marketing* 24 (2/3) (2006) 98–113; Institute for Social Research, University of Michigan, *Interviewer's Manual*, rev. edn (Ann Arbor, MI: Survey Research Center, 1976), 16.

14. Ryan, L. and Klaassen, B., 'Mapping the emerging digital frontier', ESOMAR, Annual Congress, Montreal (September 2008).

15. Trembly, A.C., 'Poor data quality: a $600 billion issue', *National Underwriter* 106 (11) (18 March 2002), 48; Anon., 'Market research industry sets up interviewing quality standards', *Management Auckland* 44 (2) (March 1997), 12; Morton-Williams, J. and Sykes, W., 'The use of interaction coding and follow-up interviews to investigate comprehension of survey questions', *Journal of the Market Research Society* 26 (April 1984), 109–127.

16. Park, C., 'How was it for you?', *Research*, Fieldwork Supplement (July 2000), 8–9.

17. Sparrow, N., 'Quality issues in online research', *Journal of Advertising Research* 47 (2) (June 2007), 179–182; Cri, D. and Micheaux, A., 'From customer data to value: what is lacking in the information chain?', *Journal of Database Marketing and Customer Strategy Management* 13 (4) (July 2006), 282–299; Pallister, J., 'Navigating the righteous course: a quality issue', *Journal of the Market Research Society* 41 (3) (July 1999), 327–343; Hurley, R.F. and Laitamaki, J.M., 'Total quality research: integrating markets and the organization', *California Management Review* 38 (1) (Fall 1995), 59–78.

18. Sparrow, N., 'What is an opinion anyway? Finding out what people really think', *International Journal of Market Research* 53 (1) (2011), 25–39; Czaja, R., Blair, J. and Sebestik, J.P., 'Participant selection in telephone survey: a comparison of three techniques', *Journal of Marketing Research* (August 1982), 381–385.

19. de Jong, K., 'CSI Berlin: the strange case of the death of panels', ESOMAR, Online Research, Berlin (October 2010); Frost-Norton, T., 'The future of mall research: current trends affecting the future of marketing research in malls', *Journal of Consumer Behaviour* 4 (4) (June 2005), 293–301; Fielding, N.G., *Interviewing: Four volume set* (Thousand Oaks, CA: Sage, 2003); Greengard, S., '50% of your employees are lying, cheating & stealing', *Workforce* 76 (10) (October 1997), 44–53; Tull, D.S. and Richards, L.E., 'What can be done about interviewer bias?', in Sheth, J. (ed.), *Research in Marketing* (Greenwich, CT: SAT Press, 1980), 143–162.

20. Chapman, D.S. and Rowe, P.M., 'The impact of videoconference technology, interview structure and interviewer gender on interviewer evaluations in the employment interview: a field experiment', *Journal of Occupational and Organizational Psychology* 74 (3) (September 2001), 279–298; Johnson, C., 'Making sure employees measure up', *HRMagazine* 46 (3) (March 2001), 36–41; Pulakos, E.D., Schmitt, N., Whitney, D. and Smith, M., 'Individual differences in interviewer ratings: the impact of standardization, consensus discussion and sampling error on the validity of a structured interview', *Personnel Psychology* 49 (1) (Spring 1996), 85–102.

21. Manfreda, K.L., Bosnjak, M., Berzelak, J., Haas, I. and Vehovar, V., 'Web surveys versus other survey modes: a meta analysis comparing response rates', *International Journal of Market Research* 50 (1) (2008), 79–104; Smith, J., 'How to boost DM response rates quickly', *Marketing News* 35 (9) (23 April 2001), 5; Turley, S.K., 'A case of response rate success', *Journal of the Market Research Society* 41 (3) (July 1999), 301–309; Edmonston, S., 'Why response rates are declining', *Advertising Age's Business Marketing* 82 (8) (September 1997), 12.

22. Pearson, C., Smith, E., Ridlen, R., Zhang, H. and Cooper, A., 'Using global online panels: a comparative study on the Beijing 2008 Olympics', ESOMAR, Asia Pacific Conference, Singapore (April 2008).

23. Clarke, B. and Nairn, A., 'Researching children: are we getting it right? A discussion of ethics', Market Research Society, Annual Conference (2011).

24. Davenport, T.H., Harris, J.G., Jones, G.L. and Lemon, K.N., 'HBR Case Study: The dark side of customer analytics', *Harvard Business Review* 85 (5) (May 2007), 37; Al-Khatib, J.A., D'Auria Stanton, A. and Rawwas, M.Y.A., 'Ethical segmentation of consumers in developing countries: a comparative analysis', *International Marketing Review* 22 (2) (2005), 225–246.

25. Shaw, S., 'Communicating creatively: from digital media to stains on the bedroom floor', Market Research Society, Annual Conference (2010).

17 Data integrity

Stage 1

Problem definition

Stage 2

Research approach developed

Stage 3

Research design developed

Stage 4

Fieldwork or data collection

Stage 5

Data integrity and analysis

Stage 6

Report integrity and presentation

Perhaps the most neglected series of activities in the marketing research process. Handled with care, data integrity can substantially enhance the quality of statistical results.

Objectives

After reading this chapter, you should be able to:

1 discuss the nature and scope of data integrity and the data integrity process;

2 explain questionnaire checking and editing and the treatment of unsatisfactory responses by returning to the field, assigning missing values and discarding unsatisfactory responses;

3 describe the guidelines for coding questionnaires, including the coding of structured and unstructured questions;

4 discuss the data cleaning process and the methods used to treat missing responses: substitution of a neutral value, imputed response, casewise deletion and pairwise deletion;

5 state the reasons for and methods of statistically adjusting data: weighting, variable respecification and scale transformation;

6 describe the procedure for selecting a data analysis strategy and the factors influencing the process;

7 classify statistical techniques and give a detailed classification of univariate techniques as well as a classification of multivariate techniques;

8 understand the intra-cultural, pan-cultural and cross-cultural approaches to data analysis in international marketing research;

9 identify the ethical issues related to data processing, particularly the discarding of unsatisfactory responses, violation of the assumptions underlying the data analysis techniques, and evaluation and interpretation of results and paired samples;

10 appreciate how the use of SPSS and SAS software can shape the manner and quality of data integrity.

Overview

Decisions related to data integrity and analysis should not take place after data have been collected. Before the raw data contained in questionnaires can be subjected to statistical analysis, they must be converted into a form suitable for analysis. The suitable form and the means of analysis should be considered as a research design is developed. This ensures that the output of the analyses will satisfy the research objectives set for a particular project. The care exercised in the data integrity phase has a direct effect upon the quality of statistical results and ultimately the support offered to marketing decision-makers. Paying inadequate attention to data integrity can seriously compromise statistical results, leading to biased findings and incorrect interpretation. Most of the data integrity process and the quality checks inherent in this process are now completed automatically. Online modes which form the majority of surveys have in-built parameters to ensure the quality of data prepared for statistical analysis. Survey software helps researchers to perform quality checks at all stages of data integrity, whatever the mode of collection. With software developments, many researchers will not have to intervene manually in the data integrity process. However, it is important to understand what this process entails and what survey software does to monitor data quality.

This chapter describes the data collection process, which begins with checking the questionnaires for completeness. Then we discuss the editing of data and provide guidelines for handling illegible, incomplete, inconsistent, ambiguous or otherwise unsatisfactory responses. We also describe coding, transcribing and data cleaning, emphasising the treatment of missing responses and statistical adjustment of data. We discuss the selection of a data analysis strategy and classify statistical techniques. The intra-cultural, pan-cultural and cross-cultural approaches to data analysis in international marketing research are explained. The ethical issues related to data processing are identified with emphasis on discarding unsatisfactory responses, violation of the assumptions underlying the data analysis techniques, and evaluation and interpretation of results.

We begin with an illustration of the data integrity process set in the context of a Formula One Racetrack study conducted by IFM Sports Marketing Surveys.

| Focus on | IFM Sports Marketing Surveys |

Data integrity

In a Formula One Racetrack Project, the data were obtained by face-to-face and telephone interviews. As the questionnaire was developed and finalised, a preliminary plan was drawn up of how the findings could be analysed. The questionnaires were edited by a supervisor as they were being returned from Australia, Brazil, France, Germany, Italy, Japan, Spain and the UK. The questionnaires were checked for incomplete, inconsistent and ambiguous responses. Questionnaires with problematic responses were queried with supervisors in each of the eight countries. In some circumstances, the supervisors were asked to recontact the participants to clarify certain issues. Thirty-five questionnaires were discarded because the proportion of incomplete or unsatisfactory responses rendered them too poor to use. This resulted in a final sample size of 2,050.

A codebook was developed for coding the questionnaires; this was done automatically as the questionnaire was designed using the SNAP software (fully integrated survey software with on-screen questionnaire design, data collection and analysis for all types of surveys, **www.snapsurveys.com**). Data were transcribed by being directly keyed in as the telephone interview mode was conducted. In the face-to-face mode, data were transcribed using personal digital assistants (PDAs) as the interviews were conducted. The software has a built-in error check that identified out-of-range responses; 10% of the data were verified for other data entry errors. The data were cleaned by identifying logically inconsistent responses. Most of the rating information was obtained using five-point scales, so responses of 0, 6 and 7 were considered out of range and a code of 9 was assigned to missing responses. If an out-of-range response was keyed in, the SNAP software issued an audible warning and prohibited any continuation of data entry. New variables were created that were composites of original variables. Finally, a data analysis strategy was developed.

The Formula One Racetrack example describes the various phases of the data integrity process. Note that the process was initiated while the fieldwork was still in progress. A systematic description of the data integrity process follows.

The data integrity process

Editing
A review of the questionnaires with the objective of increasing accuracy and precision.

Coding
Assigning a code to represent a specific response to a specific question along with the data record and column position that the code will occupy.

The data integrity process is shown in Figure 17.1. The entire process is guided by the preliminary plan of data analysis that was formulated in the research design phase. The first step is to check for acceptable questionnaires. This is followed by editing, coding and transcribing the data. The data are cleaned and a treatment for missing responses is prescribed. Often, after the stage of sample validation, statistical adjustment of the data may be necessary to make them representative of the population of interest. The researcher should then select an appropriate data analysis strategy. The final data analysis strategy differs from the preliminary plan of data analysis due to the information and insights gained since the preliminary plan was formulated. Data integrity should begin as soon as the first batch of questionnaires is received from the field, while the fieldwork is still going on. Thus, if any problems are detected, the fieldwork can be modified to incorporate corrective action.

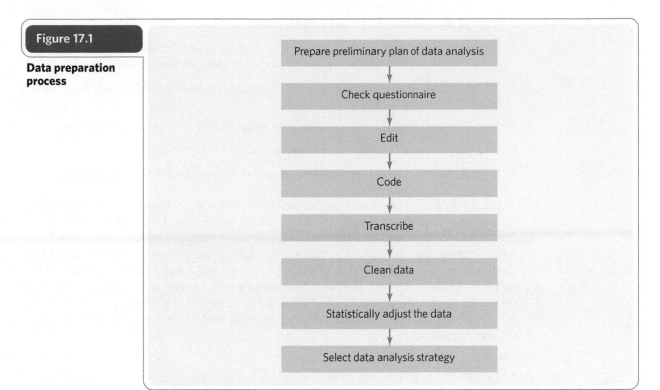

Checking the questionnaire

The initial step in questionnaire checking involves reviewing all questionnaires to assess how well they have been completed, as illustrated in the following example.

Custom cleaning[1]

According to Johan Harristhal of Gfk Custom Research (**www.gfk.com/gfkcr**), completed questionnaires from the field often have many small errors because of the inconsistent quality of interviewing. For example, qualifying responses are not circled, or skip patterns are not followed accurately. These small errors can be costly. When responses from such questionnaires are put onto a computer, Custom Research runs a cleaning program that checks for completedness and logic. Discrepancies are identified on a computer printout, which is checked by the tabulation supervisors. Once the errors are identified, appropriate corrective action is taken before data analysis is carried out. Custom research has found that this procedure substantially increases the quality of statistical results.

Researchers do not just depend upon error checks at the data entry stage; checks should be made while fieldwork is still under way. If the fieldwork was contracted to a data collection agency, the researcher should make an independent check after it is over. A questionnaire returned from the field may be unacceptable for several reasons:

1   Parts of the questionnaire may be incomplete.

2   The pattern of responses may indicate that the participant did not understand or follow the instructions. For example, filter questions may not have been followed.

3   The responses show little variance. For example, a participant has ticked only 4s on a series of seven-point rating scales.

4   The returned questionnaire is physically incomplete: one or more pages is missing.

5   The questionnaire is received after a pre-established cut-off date.

6   The questionnaire is answered by someone who does not qualify for participation.

If quotas or cell group sizes have been imposed, the acceptable questionnaires should be classified and counted accordingly. Any problems in meeting the sampling requirements should be identified, and corrective action, such as conducting additional interviews in the under-represented cells, should be taken where this is possible, before the data are edited. Note that in online surveys, each of the above factors will usually be automatically monitored. Participants may not be allowed to continue with a survey, e.g. leaving gaps in their responses, or an error report will be automatically generated, e.g. when participants have a pattern of responses that demonstrates they have not read the instructions or engaged with the survey process.

Editing

Editing is the review of the questionnaires with the objective of increasing accuracy and precision. It consists of screening questionnaires to identify illegible, incomplete, inconsistent or ambiguous responses. Responses may be illegible if they have been poorly recorded. This is particularly common in questionnaires with a large number of unstructured questions. The replies must be legible if they are to be properly coded. Likewise, questionnaires may be incomplete to varying degrees. A few or many questions may be unanswered.

At this stage, the researcher makes a preliminary check for consistency. Certain obvious inconsistencies can be easily detected. For example, participants in a financial survey may have answered a whole series of questions relating to their perceptions of a particular bank, yet in other questions may have indicated that they have not used that particular bank or even heard of it.

Responses to unstructured questions may be ambiguous and difficult to interpret clearly. The answer may be abbreviated, or some ambiguous words may have been used. For structured questions, more than one response may be marked for a question designed to elicit a single response. Suppose that a participant circles 2 and 3 on a five-point rating scale. Does this mean that 2.5 was intended? To complicate matters further, the coding procedure may allow for only a single-digit response.

Treatment of unsatisfactory responses

Unsatisfactory responses are commonly handled by returning to the field to get better data, assigning missing values and discarding unsatisfactory participants.

Returning to the field. Questionnaires with unsatisfactory responses may be returned to the field, where the interviewers recontact the participants. This approach is particularly attractive for business and industrial marketing surveys, where the sample sizes are small and the participants are easily identifiable. The data obtained the second time, however, may be different from those obtained during the original survey. These differences may be attributed to changes over time or differences in the mode of questionnaire administration (e.g. online versus a face-to-face interview).

Assigning missing values. If returning the questionnaires to the field is not feasible, the editor may assign missing values to unsatisfactory responses. This approach may be desirable if: (1) the number of participants with unsatisfactory responses is small; (2) the proportion of unsatisfactory responses for each of these participants is small; or (3) the variables with unsatisfactory responses are not the key variables.

Discarding unsatisfactory participants. In another approach, the participants with unsatisfactory responses are simply discarded. This approach may have merit when: (1) the proportion of unsatisfactory participants is small (less than 10%); (2) the sample size is large; (3) the unsatisfactory participants do not differ from satisfactory participants in obvious ways (e.g. demographics, product usage characteristics); (4) the proportion of unsatisfactory responses for each of these participants is large; or (5) responses on key variables are missing. Unsatisfactory participants may differ from satisfactory participants in systematic ways, however, and the decision to designate a participant as unsatisfactory may be subjective. Both these factors bias the results. If the researcher decides to discard unsatisfactory participants, the procedure adopted to identify these participants and their number should be reported, as in the following example.

Real research	**Declaring 'discards'[2]**

In a cross-cultural survey of marketing managers from English-speaking African countries, questionnaires were mailed to 565 firms. A total of 192 completed questionnaires were returned, of which four were discarded because participants suggested that they were not in charge of overall marketing decisions. The decision to discard the four questionnaires was based on the consideration that the sam-

ple size was sufficiently large and the proportion of unsatisfactory participants was small.

Coding

Many questionnaire design and data entry software packages code data automatically. Learning how to use such packages or even using spreadsheet packages means that the process of coding is now a much simpler task for the researcher. Many of the principles of coding are based on the days of data processing using 'punched cards' or even, much more recently, DOS files. While there may be many data analysts who could present coherent cases for the use of original forms of data entry, the greater majority of researchers enjoy the benefits of a simpler, speedier and less error-prone form of data entry, using proprietary software packages. The nature and importance of coding for qualitative data were introduced in Chapters 6 and 9. For quantitative data, which can include coping with open-ended responses or responses to 'Other – Please State…', it is still important to understand the principles of coding, as reference to the process is made by so many in the marketing research industry.

Coding means assigning a code, usually a number, to each possible answer to each question. For example, a question on the gender of participants may be assigned a code of 1 for females and 2 for males. For every individual question in a questionnaire, the researcher decides which codes should be assigned to all its possible answers.

If the question posed has only two possible answers, the codes assigned of 1 or 2 take up one digit space. If the question posed had 25 possible answers such as '*Apart from Formula One, what other sports do you follow on TV or through any other media?*', the possible answers and assigned codes of 1 to 25 would take up two digit spaces. The reason for focusing upon the digit spaces required for any particular question relates to an old convention in marketing research to record the answers from individual questionnaire participants in 'flat ASCII files'. Such files were typically 80 columns wide. The columns would be set out into 'fields', i.e. assigned columns that relate to specific questions. Thus the task for the researcher after assigning codes to individual question responses was to set out a consecutive series of fields or columns. These fields would represent where the answers to particular questions would be positioned in the ASCII file. In each row of a computer file would be the coded responses from individual questionnaire participants. Each row is termed a 'record', i.e. all the fields that make up the response from one participant. All the attitudinal, behavioural, demographic and other classification characteristics of a participant may be contained in a single record.

Table 17.1 shows an extract from the Formula One Racetrack questionnaire and Table 17.2 illustrates the answers to these questions from a selection of participants as set out in codes, fields and records. The classification questions set out on Table 17.1 were placed at the start of the questionnaire, forming the 'Screening' part of the questionnaire. It is followed by the first question in the section on 'Attitudes and Opinions towards F1'.

Question 2 has two possible answers, coded 1 to 2, that take up one digit space (there could be a space for 'Refused' to cope with the very rare occasions where the participants refuse to state their gender and the interviewer cannot discern their gender). Non-responses to gender and age questions are usually more prevalent in postal questionnaires.[3] Question 3 has eight possible answers, coded 1 to 8, that take up one digit space. Question 4 has seven possible answers, coded 1 to 7, that take up one digit space. Note that if the actual number of Grands Prix viewed were entered (rather than a category), two digit spaces would be needed. Question 5 has 12 possible answers which are coded 01 to 12, taking up two digit spaces. Note that to the right of each question is a number in parentheses. These numbers represent the first field positions of each question as illustrated in Table 17.2.

Table 17.1	**Classification questions from the Formula One Racetrack survey**

Question 1 – *Have you watched at least one hour of a Formula One race on television in the 2010 season?*

(5)

1 ☐   Yes

2 ☐   No (terminate interview)

Question 2 – *Please enter gender*

(6)

1 ☐   Male

2 ☐   Female

3 ☐   Refused

Table 17.1	Continued

Question 3 – Please could you tell me how old you are? (7)

1 ☐ 18–24
2 ☐ 25–29
3 ☐ 30–34
4 ☐ 35–39
5 ☐ 40–44
6 ☐ 45–49
7 ☐ 50–55
8 ☐ Refused

Question 4 – Out of 16 Formula One Grands Prix held in the 2010 season, how many have you watched on television? (8)

1 ☐ 1–2
2 ☐ 3–4
3 ☐ 5–6
4 ☐ 7–9
5 ☐ 10–12
6 ☐ 13–15
7 ☐ 16

Question 5 – Which one Formula One team do you support?
(DO NOT READ OUT AND TICK ONLY ONE.) (9–10)

01 ☐ Don't have a favourite team
02 ☐ Don't know
03 ☐ Ferrari
04 ☐ Force India-Mercedes
05 ☐ Lotus-Renault
06 ☐ McLaren-Mercedes
07 ☐ Renault
08 ☐ RBR Renault
09 ☐ Sauber
10 ☐ STR Ferrari
11 ☐ Williams Cosworth
12 ☐ Virgin Cosworth

Table 17.2	Illustrative computer file held on a flat ASCII file					
	Fields					
Records	*1–4*	*5*	*6*	*7*	*8*	*9–10*
Record #1	0001	1	1	2	2	01
Record #11	0011	1	1	3	1	03
Record #21	0021	1	2	7	6	04
Record #2050	2050	1	1	5	4	11

In Table 17.2, the columns represent the fields and the rows represent the records of each participant. The field space 1–4 is used to record an assigned number to each participant. Table 17.3 illustrates how the same data may be entered using a spreadsheet. Each row represents an individual participant and each column represents the fields required to hold the response to an individual question. Note that there is a column that identifies a specific number attached to each record. Many survey analysis packages record a unique ID for each record so that, as the answers to an individual questionnaire are entered, the ID is automatically updated. However, if a unique ID is attached to each questionnaire before it is sent out (e.g. in a postal survey), the ID may be entered as a distinct field (see column A).

Table 17.3	Example of computer file held on a spreadsheet program					
Records in rows	*Individual fields in columns*					
	A	*B*	*C*	*D*	*E*	*F*
	ID	Question 1	Question 2	Question 3	Question 4	Question 5
2	1	1	1	2	2	01
12	11	1	1	3	1	03
22	21	1	2	7	6	04
2051	2050	1	1	5	4	11

Coding is still required to identify the individual responses to individual questions. Spreadsheets are normally wide enough to allow an individual record to be recorded on one line, and they can be set up so that whoever is entering the data can clearly keep track of which questions relate to which columns. Spreadsheets can be used as a format to analyse data in a number of data analysis packages and so are very versatile. They do, however, have shortcomings. The next paragraph will go on to illustrate these.

In many surveys, multiple-response questions are widely used. An example of a multiple-response question is shown in Table 17.4, a question from the Formula One Racetrack survey which examines participants' perceptions of Formula One.

In essence, each of the options presented in question 8 is an individual 'yes' or 'no' question. In the example shown, the participant has replied 'yes' to the second, fifth, sixth and ninth variables. Using a spreadsheet, this question would be coded as shown in Table 17.5

Table 17.4	Multiple-response question from the Formula One Racetrack survey

Question 8 – Please tell me which of the following words you think best describe Formula One.
(READ OUT AND TICK ALL THAT APPLY.)

01		Boring
02	✓	Competitive
03		Dangerous
04		Dynamic
05	✓	Elitist
06	✓	Exciting
07		Expensive
08		Extravagant
09	✓	Innovative
10		Inspirational
11		Prestigious
12		Safe
13		Sexy
14		Too technical

where the response in Table 17.4 is represented as 'Record 1'. The 'ticks' have been coded as a '1' to represent 'yes' and '0' as 'no'.

Entering data for multiple-response questions is a fairly simple task on a spreadsheet, provided that there are not so many of these question types in a survey. In the Formula One

Table 17.5	Formula One Racetrack, Question 8 spreadsheet presentation

Records	Individual fields in columns								
	Question 8								
	AJ	AK	AL	AM	AN	AO	AP	AQ	AU
	Q8(1)	Q8(2)	Q8(3)	Q8(4)	Q8(5)	Q8(6)	Q8(7)	Q8(8)	Q8(9)
1	1	0	0	0	1	1	0	0	1
2	1	1	0	0	0	1	1	0	0
3	0	0	1	1	1	0	0	0	0
4	1	1	0	0	1	0	1	1	1
... n	0	1	1	0	0	1	1	0	0

Racetrack questionnaire there was one question related to which cars 'belonged' (owned, leased or a company car) to particular households. Had the open-ended question been closed into a multiple-response question of 38 different car manufacturers, this would have meant a spreadsheet of 38 columns. Had the question gone beyond the manufacturer, e.g. Renault, to the type of Renault, e.g. Clio, the number of columns could have run to thousands. If participants had indicated that they had a Renault, this would mean finding the precise column to enter a '1' and then 37 '0s'. This is a lengthy and potentially error-prone task. This is where proprietary questionnaire design and survey packages really hold many advantages, i.e. they make the data entry task very simple for multiple-response questions of any length and check for errors. Again, the use of proprietary packages will be outlined at the end of this chapter.

Codebook

Whether the researcher uses DOS-based systems or a spreadsheet, a summary of the whole questionnaire, showing the position of the fields and the key to all the codes, should be produced. With proprietary software packages, this summary is created automatically as the questionnaire is designed. Such a summary is called a codebook. Table 17.6 shows an extract from the Formula One Racetrack codebook. The codebook shown is based upon using a spreadsheet to enter the data. Depending upon which type of data entry is used, the codebook style will change, but in essence the type of information recorded is the same.

Table 17.6	Extract from the Formula One Racetrack survey codebook		
Column identifier	Question name	Question number	Coding instructions
A	Participant ID		Enter handwritten number from top right-hand corner of the questionnaire
B	Watched Formula One	1	Yes = '1' No = '2'
C	Gender	2	Male = '1' Female = '2' Refused = '3'
D	Age band	3	Enter number as seen alongside ticked box: 18–24 = '1' 25–29 = '2' 30–34 = '3' 35–39 = '4' 40–44 = '5' 45–49 = '6' 50–55 = '7' Refused = '8'
E	Viewing frequency	4	Enter number as seen alongside ticked box: 1–2 = '1' 3–4 = '2' 5–6 = '3' 7–9 = '4' 10–12 = '5' 13–15 = '6' 16 = '7'

Codebook
A book containing coding instructions and the necessary information about the questions and potential answers in a survey.

A **codebook** contains instructions and the necessary information about the questions and potential answers in a survey. A codebook guides the 'coders' in their work and helps the researcher identify and locate the questions properly. Even if the questionnaire has been pre-coded, it is helpful to prepare a formal codebook. As illustrated in Table 17.6, a codebook generally contains the following information: (1) column identifier, (2) question name, (3) question number, and (4) coding instructions.

Coding open-ended questions

The coding of structured questions, be they single or multiple choice, is relatively simple because the options are predetermined. The researcher assigns a code for each response to each question and specifies the appropriate field or column in which it will appear; this is termed 'pre-coding'.[4] The coding of unstructured or open-ended questions is more complex; this is termed 'post-coding'. Participants' verbatim responses are recorded on the questionnaire. One option the researcher has is to go through all the completed questionnaires, list the verbatim responses, and then develop and assign codes to these responses. Another option that is allowed on some data entry packages is to enter the verbatim responses directly onto the computer, allowing a print-off of the collective responses and codes to be assigned before all of the questionnaires have been entered. The coding process here is similar to the process of assigning codes in the analysis of qualitative data as described in Chapter 9.[5] The verbatim responses to 1,000 questionnaires may generate 1,000 different answers. The words may be different but the essence of the response may mean that 20 issues have been addressed. The researcher decides what those 20 issues are, names the issues and assigns codes from 1 to 20, and then goes through all the 1,000 questionnaires to enter the code alongside the verbatim response.

The following guidelines are suggested for coding unstructured questions and questionnaires in general.[6] Category codes should be mutually exclusive and collectively exhaustive. Categories are mutually exclusive if each response fits into one and only one category code. Categories should not overlap. Categories are collectively exhaustive if every response fits into one of the assigned category codes. This can be achieved by adding an additional category code of 'other' or 'none of the above'. An absolute maximum of 10% of responses should fall into the 'other' category; the researcher should strive to assign all responses into meaningful categories.

Category codes should be assigned for critical issues even if no one has mentioned them. It may be important to know that no one has mentioned a particular response. For example, a car manufacturer may be concerned about its new website design. In a question 'How did you learn about the new Renault Clio?', key responses such as 'Google' or 'Facebook' should be included as a distinct category, even if no participants gave these answers.

Transcribing

Transcribing data involves keying the coded data from the collected questionnaires into computers. If the data have been collected online or via CATI or CAPI, this step is unnecessary because the data are entered directly into the computer as they are collected. Besides the direct keying of data, they can be transferred by using optical recognition, digital technologies, bar codes or other technologies (see Figure 17.2).

Optical character recognition programs transcribe handwritten text onto computer files. Optical scanning is a data transcribing process by which answers recorded on computer-readable forms are scanned to form a data record. This requires responses to be recorded in a pre-designated area and for a device then to read that response. A more flexible process is optical mark recognition, where a spreadsheet type of interface is used to read and process forms created by users. These mark-sensed forms are then processed by optical scanners and the data are stored in a computer file. Digital technology has resulted in computerised sensory analysis systems, which automate the data collection process. The questions appear on a

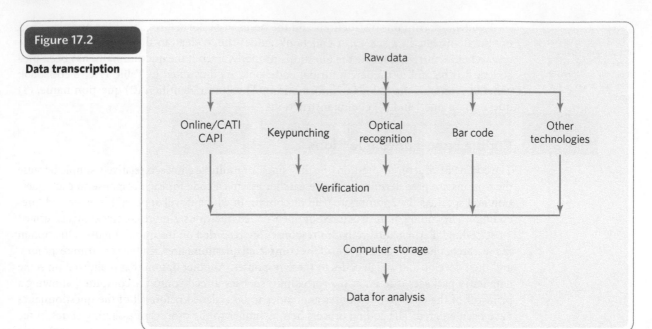

Figure 17.2

Data transcription

computerised grid pad, and responses are recorded directly into the computer using a sensing device. Field interviewers use iPads, notebook computers, PDAs and other handheld devices to record responses, which are then sent via a built-in communication modem, wireless LAN or cellular link directly to another computer in the field or a remote location. Bar codes involve direct machine reading of the codes and simultaneous transcription. Many national censuses use bar codes to identify participants.

Several other technologies may also be used to transcribe the data. Voice recognition and voice response systems can translate recorded voice responses into data files. For example, Microsoft Windows software now includes advanced speech recognition functions and can be used to transcribe data by speaking into a microphone. When online, CATI or CAPI modes are employed, data are verified as they are collected. In the case of inadmissible responses, the computer will prompt the interviewer or participant. In the case of admissible responses, the interviewer or the participant can see the recorded response on the screen and verify it before proceeding.

The selection of a data transcription method is guided by the type of interviewing method used and the availability of technology. If online, CATI or CAPI modes are used, the replies are entered directly into the computer. Keypunching via a computer terminal is most frequently used for ordinary telephone, home and street interviewing and postal surveys. However, the use of digital technology in face-to-face interviews is growing with the increasing use of handheld devices. Optical scanning can be used in structured and repetitive surveys, and mark-sensed forms are used in special cases.[7] The following example illustrates the use of scanned data and the advantage it can have over keypunching.

Real research   ## Scanning the seas[8]

As of 2009, Princess Cruises (**www.princess.com**) annually carried more than a million passengers. Princess wished to know what passengers thought of the cruise experience, but wanted to determine this information in a cost-effective way. A scannable questionnaire was developed that allowed the cruise line to transcribe the data quickly from thousands of responses, thus expediting data integrity and analysis. The questionnaire was designed and distributed to measure customer satisfaction on all voyages. In addition to saving time as compared with keypunching, scanning also increased the accuracy of survey results. The Senior Researcher for Princess Cruises, Jamie Goldfarb, commented:

> When we compared the data files from the two methods, we found that although the scanned system occasionally missed marks because they had not been filled in properly, the scanned data was still more accurate than the keypunched file.

A monthly report with analyses based upon cruise destination and ship was produced. This report identified any specific problems that had been noticed, and steps were taken to make sure these problems were addressed.

Cleaning the data

Data cleaning
Thorough and extensive checks for consistency and treatment of missing responses.

Data cleaning includes consistency checks and treatment of missing responses. Even though preliminary consistency checks have been made during editing, the checks at this stage are more thorough and extensive, because they are made by computer.

Consistency checks

Consistency checks
A part of the data cleaning process that identifies data that are out of range, logically inconsistent or have extreme values. Data with values not defined by the coding scheme are inadmissible.

Consistency checks identify data that are out of range or logically inconsistent or have extreme values. Out-of-range data values are inadmissible and must be corrected. For example, participants may be asked to express their degree of agreement with a series of lifestyle statements on a 1–5 scale. Assuming that 9 has been designated for missing values, data values of 0, 6, 7 and 8 would be out of range. Computer packages can be programmed to identify out-of-range values for each variable and will not progress to another variable within a record until a value in the set range is entered. Other packages can be programmed to print out the participant code, variable code, variable name, record number, column number and out-of-range value. This makes it easy to check each variable systematically for out-of-range values. The correct responses can be determined by going back to the edited and coded questionnaire.

Responses can be logically inconsistent in various ways. For example, participants may indicate that they charge long-distance calls to a calling card from a credit card company, although they do not have such a credit card. Alternatively participants might report both unfamiliarity with and frequent usage of the very same product. The necessary information (participant code, variable code, variable name, record number, column number and inconsistent values) can be printed to locate these responses and to take corrective action.

Finally, extreme values should be closely examined. Not all extreme values result from errors, but they may point to problems with the data. For example, in the Formula One Racetrack survey, participants were asked to name the manufacturer of the cars that 'belonged' to their households. Certain participants recorded 10 or more cars. In these circumstances the extreme values can be identified and the actual figure validated in many cases by recontacting the participant.[9]

Treatment of missing responses

Missing responses represent values of a variable that are unknown either because participants provided ambiguous answers or because their answers were not properly recorded. Treatment of missing responses poses problems, particularly if the proportion of missing responses is more than 10%. The following options are available for the treatment of missing responses.[10]

Substitute a neutral value. A neutral value, typically the mean response to the variable, is substituted for the missing responses. Thus, the mean of the variable remains unchanged, and other statistics such as correlations are not affected much. Although this approach has some merit, the logic of substituting a mean value (say 4) for participants who, if they had answered, might have used either high ratings (6 or 7) or low ratings (1 or 2) is questionable.[11]

Substitute an imputed response. The participants' pattern of responses to other questions is used to impute or calculate a suitable response to the missing questions. The researcher attempts to infer from the available data the responses that the individuals would have given if they had answered the questions. This can be done statistically by determining the relationship of the variable in question to other variables based on the available data. For example, product usage could be related to household size for participants who have provided data on both variables. Given that participant's household size, the missing product usage response for a participant could then be calculated. This approach, however, requires considerable effort and can introduce serious bias. Sophisticated statistical procedures have been developed to calculate imputed values for missing responses.[12]

Real research   ## Imputation increases integrity[13]

A project was undertaken to assess the willingness of households to implement the recommendations of an energy audit (dependent variable) having been given the financial implications (independent variables). Five financial factors were used as independent variables and they were manipulated at known levels. The values of these factors were always known by virtue of the design adopted. However, several values of the dependent variable were missing. These missing values were replaced with imputed values. The imputed values were statistically calculated, given the corresponding values of the independent variables. The treatment of missing responses in this manner greatly increased the simplicity and validity of subsequent analysis.

Casewise deletion. In casewise deletion, cases or participants with any missing responses are discarded from the analysis. Because many participants may have some missing responses, this approach could result in a small sample. Throwing away large amounts of data is undesirable because it is costly and time consuming to collect data. Furthermore, participants with missing responses could differ from participants with complete responses in systematic ways. If so, casewise deletion could seriously bias the results.

Pairwise deletion. In pairwise deletion, instead of discarding all cases with any missing responses, the researcher uses only the cases or participants with complete responses for each calculation. As a result, different calculations in an analysis may be based on different sample sizes. This procedure may be appropriate when (1) the sample size is large, (2) there are few missing responses, and (3) the variables are not highly related. However, this procedure can produce unappealing or even infeasible results.

The different procedures for the treatment of missing responses may yield different results, particularly when the responses are not missing at random and the variables are related.

Hence, missing responses should be kept to a minimum. The researcher should carefully consider the implications of the various procedures before selecting a particular method for the treatment of non-response.

Statistically adjusting the data

Procedures for statistically adjusting the data consist of weighting, variable respecification and scale transformation. These adjustments are not always necessary but can enhance the quality of data analysis.

Weighting

Weighting
A statistical procedure that attempts to account for non-response by assigning differential weights to the data depending on the response rates.

In **weighting**, each case or participant in the database is assigned a weight to reflect its importance relative to other cases or participants.[14] The value 1.0 represents the unweighted case. The effect of weighting is to increase or decrease the number of cases in the sample that possess certain characteristics. (See Chapter 15, which discussed the use of weighting to adjust for non-response bias.)

Weighting is most widely used to make the sample data more representative of a target population on specific characteristics. For example, it may be used to give greater importance to cases or participants with higher quality data. Yet another use of weighting is to adjust the sample so that greater importance is attached to participants with certain characteristics. If a study is conducted to determine what modifications should be made to an existing product, the researcher might want to attach greater weight to the opinions of heavy users of the product. This could be accomplished by assigning weights of 3.0 to heavy users, 2.0 to medium users and 1.0 to light users and non-users. Because it destroys the self-weighting nature of the sample design, weighting should be applied with caution. If used, the weighting procedure should be documented and made a part of the project report.[15]

Real research

Determining the weight of community centre users

A postal survey was conducted in the Scottish city of Edinburgh to determine the patronage of a community centre. The resulting sample composition differed in age structure from the area population distribution as compiled from recent census data. Therefore, the sample was weighted to make it representative in terms of age structure. The weights applied were determined by dividing the population percentage by the corresponding sample percentage. The distribution of age structure for the sample and population, as well as the weights applied, are given in the following table.

Age group percentage	Sample percentage	Population	Weight
13–18	4.32	6.13	1.42
19–24	5.89	7.45	1.26
25–34	12.23	13.98	1.14
35–44	17.54	17.68	1.01
45–54	14.66	15.59	1.06
55–64	13.88	13.65	0.98
65–74	15.67	13.65	0.87
75 plus	15.81	11.87	0.75
Totals	100.00	100.00	

Age groups under-represented in the sample received higher weights, whereas over-represented age groups received lower weights. Thus, the data for a participant aged 13–18 would be overweighted by multiplying by 1.42, whereas the data for a participant aged 75 plus would be underweighted by multiplying by 0.75.

Variable respecification

Variable respecification

The transformation of data to create new variables or the modification of existing variables so that they are more consistent with the objectives of the study.

Dummy variables

A respecification procedure using variables that take on only two values, usually 0 or 1.

Variable respecification involves the transformation of data to create new variables or to modify existing variables. The purpose of respecification is to create variables that are consistent with the objectives of the study. For example, suppose that the original variable was product usage, with 10 response categories. These might be collapsed into four categories: heavy, medium, light and non-user. Or the researcher may create new variables that are composites of several other variables. For example, the researcher may create an Index of Information Search (ISS), which is the sum of information new car customers seek from dealers, promotional sources, online and other independent sources. Likewise, one may take the ratio of variables. If the number of purchases at a clothes shop (X_1) and the number of purchases where a credit card was used (X_2) have been measured, the proportion of purchases charged to a credit card can be a new variable, created by taking the ratio of the two (X_2/X_1). Other respecifications of variables include square root and log transformations, which are often applied to improve the fit of the model being estimated.

An important respecification procedure involves the use of **dummy variables** for respecifying categorical variables.[16] Dummy variables are also called binary, dichotomous, instrumental or qualitative variables. They are variables that may take on only two values, such as 0 or 1. The general rule is that to respecify a categorical variable with K categories, $K-1$ dummy variables are needed. The reason for having $K-1$, rather than K, dummy variables is that only $K-1$ categories are independent. Given the sample data, information about the Kth category can be derived from information about the other $K-1$ categories. Consider gender, a variable having two categories. Only one dummy variable is needed. Information on the number or percentage of males in the sample can be readily derived from the number or percentage of females. The following example further illustrates the concept of dummy variables.

| Real research | **'Frozen' consumers treated as dummies** |

In a survey of consumer preferences for frozen foods, the participants were classified as heavy users, medium users, light users and non-users, and they were originally assigned codes of 4, 3, 2 and 1, respectively. This coding was not meaningful for several statistical analyses. To conduct these analyses, product usage was represented by three dummy variables, X_1, X_2 and X_3, as shown in the table.

Product usage	Original variable code	Dummy variable code category		
		X_1	X_2	X_3
Non-users	1	1	0	0
Light users	2	0	1	0
Medium users	3	0	0	1
Heavy users	4	0	0	0

Note that $X_1 = 1$ for non-users and 0 for all others. Likewise, $X_2 = 1$ for light users and 0 for all others, and $X_3 = 1$ for medium users and 0 for all others. In analysing the data, X_1, X_2 and X_3 are used to represent all user/non-user groups.

Scale transformation

Scale transformation
A manipulation of scale values to ensure compatibility with other scales or otherwise to make the data suitable for analysis.

Scale transformation involves a manipulation of scale values to ensure comparability with other scales or otherwise to make the data suitable for analysis.[17] Frequently, different scales are employed for measuring different variables. For example, image variables may be measured on a seven-point semantic differential scale, attitude variables on a continuous rating scale, and lifestyle variables on a five-point Likert scale. Therefore, it would not be meaningful to make comparisons across the measurement scales for any participant. To compare attitudinal scores with lifestyle or image scores, it would be necessary to transform the various scales. Even if the same scale is employed for all the variables, different participants may use the scale differently. For example, some participants consistently use the upper end of a rating scale whereas others consistently use the lower end. These differences can be corrected by appropriately transforming the data as illustrated in the following example.

Real research | **Health care services: transforming consumers[18]**

In a study examining preference segmentation of health care services, participants were asked to rate the importance of 18 factors affecting preferences for hospitals on a three-point scale (very, somewhat, or not important). Before analysing the data, each individual's ratings were transformed. For each individual, preference responses were averaged across all 18 items. Then this mean was $\overline{X}$ subtracted from each item rating X_i, and a constant C was added to the difference. Thus, the transformed data, X_t, were obtained by

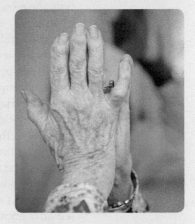

$$X_t = X_i - \overline{X} + C$$

Subtraction of the mean value corrected for any uneven use of the importance scale. The constant C was added to make all the transformed values positive, since negative importance ratings are not meaningful conceptually. This transformation was desirable because some participants, especially those with low incomes, had rated almost all the preference items as very important. Others, high-income participants in particular, had assigned the very important rating to only a few preference items. Thus, subtraction of the mean value provided a more accurate idea of the relative importance of the factors.

Standardisation
The process of correcting data to reduce them to the same scale by subtracting the sample mean and dividing by the standard deviation.

In this example, the scale transformation is corrected only for the mean response. A more common transformation procedure is standardisation. To standardise a scale X_i, we first subtract the mean, $\overline{X}$, from each score and then divide by the standard deviation, s_x. Thus, the standardised scale will have a mean of 0 and a standard deviation of 1. This is essentially the same as the calculation of z scores (see Chapter 15). Standardisation allows the researcher to compare variables that have been measured using different types of scales.[19] Mathematically, standardised scores, z_i, may be obtained as

$$z_i = \frac{(X_i - \overline{X})}{S}$$

Selecting a data analysis strategy

The process of selecting a data analysis strategy is described in Figure 17.3. The selection of a data analysis strategy should be based on the earlier steps of the marketing research process, known characteristics of the data, properties of statistical techniques, and the background and philosophy of the researcher.

Data analysis is not an end in itself. Its purpose is to produce information that will help address the problem at hand and support effective decision making. The selection of a data analysis strategy must begin with a consideration of the earlier steps in the research process: problem definition (step 1), development of an approach (step 2) and research design (step 3). The preliminary plan of data analysis prepared as part of the research design should be used to facilitate a richer engagement and understanding of meaning that may lie within collected data. Changes in analysis techniques may be necessary in the light of additional information generated in subsequent stages of the research process.

The next step is to consider the known characteristics of the data. The measurement scales used exert a strong influence on the choice of statistical techniques (see Chapter 12). In addition, the research design may favour certain techniques. For example, analysis of variance (see Chapter 19) is suited for analysing experimental data from causal designs. The insights into the data obtained during data integrity can be valuable for selecting a strategy for analysis.

It is also important to take into account the properties of the statistical techniques, particularly their purpose and underlying assumptions. Some statistical techniques are appropriate for examining differences in variables, others for assessing the magnitudes of the relationships between variables, and still others for making predictions. The techniques also involve different assumptions, and some techniques can withstand violations of the underlying assumptions better than others. A classification of statistical techniques is presented below.

Finally, the researcher's background and philosophy affect the choice of a data analysis strategy. The experienced, statistically trained researcher will employ a range of techniques, including advanced statistical methods. Researchers differ in their willingness to make assumptions about the variables and their underlying populations. Researchers who are conservative about making assumptions will limit their choice of techniques to distribution-free methods. In general, several techniques may be appropriate for analysing the data from a given project. We use the Formula One Racetrack Project to illustrate how a data analysis strategy can be developed.

Figure 17.3

Selecting a data analysis strategy

Earlier stages of marketing research process:
- problem definition
- development of a research approach
- research design

↓

Known characteristics of the data

↓

Properties of statistical techniques

↓

Background and philosophy of the researcher

↓

Data analysis strategy

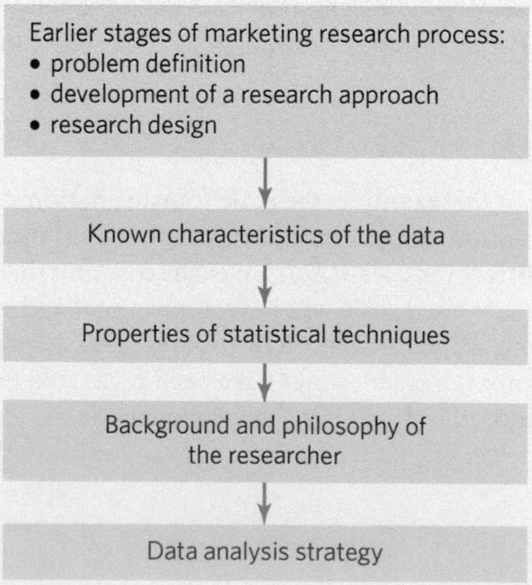

Focus on	**IFM Sports Marketing Surveys**

Data analysis strategy[20]

As part of the analysis conducted in the Formula One Racetrack Project, Formula One Image was modelled in terms of the most important issues that shaped perceptions of the sport. The sample was split into halves. The participants in each half were clustered on the basis of their perceptions. Statistical tests for clusters were conducted, and eight segments were identified. Formula One Image was modelled in terms of the evaluations of the race teams. The model was estimated separately for each segment. Differences between segment preference functions were statistically tested. Finally, model verification and cross-validation were conducted for each segment. The data analysis strategy adopted is depicted in this figure:

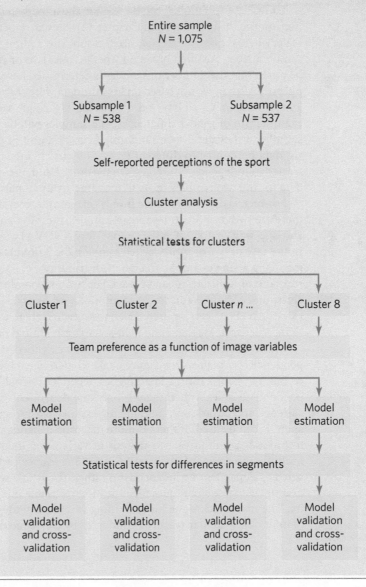

A classification of statistical techniques

Statistical techniques can be classified as univariate or multivariate. Univariate techniques are appropriate when there is a single measurement of each element in the sample or when there are several measurements of each element but each variable is analysed in isolation. Multivariate techniques, on the other hand, are suitable for analysing data when there are two or more measurements of each element and the variables are analysed simultaneously. Multivariate techniques are concerned with the simultaneous relationships among two or more phenomena. Multivariate techniques differ from univariate techniques in that they shift the focus away from the levels (averages) and distributions (variances) of the phenomena, concentrating instead on the degree of relationships (correlations or covariances) among these phenomena.[21] The univariate and multivariate techniques are described in detail in Chapters 18 to 24, but here we show how the various techniques relate to each other in an overall scheme of classification.

Univariate techniques can be further classified based on whether the data are metric or non-metric (as introduced in Chapter 12). Metric data are measured on an interval or ratio scale, whereas non-metric data are measured on a nominal or ordinal scale. These techniques can be further classified based on whether one, two or more samples are involved. It should be noted that the number of samples is determined based on how the data are treated for the purpose of analysis, not based on how the data were collected. For example, the data for males and females may well have been collected as a single sample, but if the analysis involves an examination of gender differences, two samples will be used. The samples are independent samples if they are drawn randomly from different populations. For the purpose of analysis, data pertaining to different groups of participants, e.g. males and females, are generally treated as independent samples. On the other hand, the samples are paired samples when the data for the two samples relate to the same group of participants.

For metric data, when there is only one sample, the z test and the t test can be used. When there are two or more independent samples, the z test and t test can be used for two samples, and one-way analysis of variance (one-way ANOVA) can be used for more than two samples. In the case of two or more related samples, the paired t test can be used. For non-metric data involving a single sample, frequency distribution, chi-square, Kolmogorov–Smirnov (K–S), runs and binomial tests can be used. For two independent samples with non-metric data, the chi-square, Mann–Whitney, median, K–S and Kruskal–Wallis one-way analysis of variance (K–W ANOVA) can be used. In contrast, when there are two or more related samples, the sign, Wilcoxon, McNemar and chi-square tests should be used (see Figure 17.4).

Multivariate statistical techniques can be classified as dependence techniques or interdependence techniques (see Figure 17.5). Dependence techniques are appropriate when one or more variables can be identified as dependent variables and the remaining ones as independent variables. When there is only one dependent variable, cross-tabulation, analysis of variance and covariance, multiple regression, two-group discriminant analysis and conjoint analysis can be used. If there is more than one dependent variable, however, the appropriate techniques are multivariate analysis of variance and covariance, canonical correlation and multiple discriminant analysis. In interdependence techniques, the variables are not classified as dependent or independent; rather, the whole set of interdependent relationships is examined. These techniques focus on either variable interdependence or inter object similarity. The major technique for examining variable interdependence is factor analysis. Analysis of inter object similarity can be conducted by cluster analysis and multidimensional scaling.[22]

Figure 17.4

A classification of univariate techniques

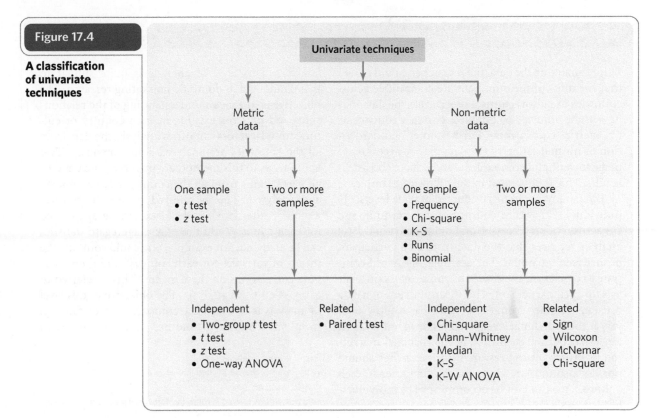

Figure 17.5

A classification of multivariate techniques

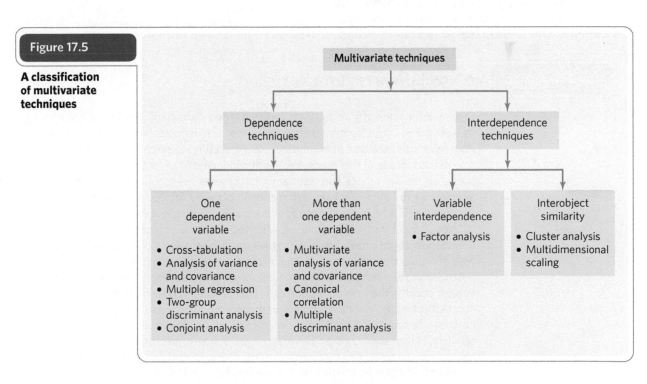

International marketing research

Before analysing the data, the researcher should ensure that the units of measurement are comparable across countries or cultural units. For example, the data may have to be adjusted to establish currency equivalents or metric equivalents. Furthermore, standardisation or normalisation of the data may be necessary to make meaningful comparisons and achieve consistent results. This is illustrated in the following example.

Data analysis can be conducted at three levels: (1) individual, (2) within country or cultural unit, and (3) across countries or cultural units. Individual-level analysis requires that the data from each participant be analysed separately. For example, one might compute a correlation coefficient or run a regression analysis for each participant. This means that enough data must be obtained from each individual to allow analysis at the individual level, which is often not feasible. Yet it has been argued that, in international marketing or cross-cultural research, the researcher should possess a sound knowledge of the consumer in each culture. This can best be accomplished by individual-level analysis.[23]

In within-country or cultural unit analysis, the data are analysed separately for each country or cultural unit. This is also referred to as intra-cultural analysis. This level of analysis is quite similar to that conducted in domestic marketing research. The objective is to gain an understanding of the relationships and patterns existing in each country or cultural unit. In across-countries analysis, the data from all the countries are analysed simultaneously. Two approaches to this method are possible. The data for all participants from all the countries can be pooled and analysed. This is referred to as pan-cultural analysis. Alternatively, the data can be aggregated for each country, and then these aggregate statistics can be analysed. For example, one could compute the means of variables for each country, and then compute correlations on these means. This is referred to as cross-cultural analysis. The objective of this level of analysis is to assess the comparability of findings from one country to another. The similarities as

Intra-cultural analysis
Within-country analysis of international data.

Pan-cultural analysis
Across-countries analysis in which the data for all participants from all the countries are pooled and analysed.

Cross-cultural analysis
A type of across-countries analysis in which the data could be aggregated for each country and these aggregate statistics analysed.

Real research   A worldwide scream for ice cream[24]

Over half the sales of Häagen-Dazs (**www.haagen-dazs.com**), the US ice cream manufacturer, come from markets outside the USA. Its sales across Europe and Asia have increased at a phenomenal rate. Marketing research has played a key role in the success of this brand. Research conducted in several European countries (e.g. the UK, France and Germany) and several Asian countries (e.g. Japan, Singapore and Taiwan) revealed that consumers were hungry for a high-quality ice cream with a high-quality image and were willing to pay a premium price for it. These consistent findings emerged after the price of ice cream in each country was standardised to have a mean of zero and a standard deviation of unity. Standardisation was desirable because the prices were specified in different local currencies and a common basis was needed for comparison across countries. Also, in each country, the premium price had to be defined in relation to the prices of competing brands. Standardisation accomplished both of these objectives. Based on these findings, Häagen-Dazs first introduced the brand at a few high-end retailers; it then built company-owned stores in high-traffic areas; and finally it rolled into convenience stores and supermarkets. It maintained the premium-quality brand name by starting first with a few high-end retailers. It also supplied free freezers to retailers. Hungry for quality products, consumers in the new markets paid double or triple the price of home brands. Häagen-Dazs remains popular, although faced with intense competition and health-conscious consumers.

well as the differences between countries should be investigated. When examining differences, not only differences in means but also differences in variance and distribution should be assessed. All the statisti-cal techniques that have been discussed in this book can be applied to within-country or across-countries analysis and, subject to the amount of data available, to individual-level analysis as well.[25]

Ethics in marketing research

Ethical issues that arise during the data integrity and analysis step of the marketing research process per-tain mainly to the researcher. While checking, editing, coding, transcribing and cleaning, researchers should try to get some idea about the quality of the data. An attempt should be made to identify participants who have provided data of questionable quality. Consider, for example, a participant who ticks the '7' response to all the 20 items measuring attitude to spectator sports on a 1–7 Likert scale. Apparently, this participant did not realise that some of the statements were nega-tive whereas others were positive. Thus, this partici-pant has indicated an extremely favourable attitude towards spectator sports on all the positive statements and an extremely negative attitude on the statements that were reversed. Decisions on whether such par-ticipants should be discarded, i.e. not included in the analysis, can raise ethical concerns. A good rule of thumb is to make such decisions during the data integrity phase before conducting any analysis.

In contrast, suppose that the researcher conducted the analysis without first attempting to identify unsat-isfactory responses. The analysis, however, does not reveal the expected relationship; the analysis does not show that attitude towards spectator sports influences attendance at spectator sports. The researcher then decides to examine the quality of data obtained. In checking the questionnaires, a few participants with unsatisfactory data are identified. In addition to the type of unsatisfactory responses mentioned earlier, there were responses as '4', the 'neither agree nor disa-gree' response, to all the 20 items measuring attitude towards spectator sports. When these participants are eliminated and the reduced dataset is analysed, the expected results are obtained showing a positive influ-ence of attitude on attendance of spectator sports. Discarding participants after analysing the data raises ethical concerns, particularly if the report does not state that the initial analysis was inconclusive. Moreover, the procedure used to identify unsatisfactory participants and the number of participants discarded should be clearly disclosed, as in the following example.

While analysing the data, the researcher may also have to deal with ethical issues. The assump-

Real research   The ethics of downsizing[26]

A study was conducted on perceptual differences between chief executives and employees as to whether the downsizing of companies was seen as ethical or not. A total of 410 questionnaires were mailed to employees of US companies, 231 com-pleted questionnaires were returned but 53 were determined to be unusable. The unusable questionnaires either contained incomplete responses to questions or were completed by unqualified participants. This resulted in an employee sample size of 178. The questionnaire was also mailed to 179 chief executives of companies that had been identified as going through at least one downsizing during the last five years. Out of the 179, only 36 questionnaires were returned, of which five par-ticipants indicated they had never actually been with a company during downsizing. Only 31 chief executives had responded in a manner that was deemed 'usable'. This was an example of ethical editing of the data. The criterion for unusable or unsatis-factory responses was clearly stated, the unsatisfactory participants were identified before the analysis, and the number of participants eliminated was disclosed.

tions underlying the statistical techniques used to analyse the data must be satisfied to obtain meaningful results. Any departure from these assumptions should be critically examined to determine the appropriateness of the technique for analysing the data at hand. The researcher has the responsibility of justifying the statistical techniques used for analysis. When this is not done, ethical questions can be raised. Moreover, there should be no intentional or deliberate misrepresentation of research methods or results. Similarly, ethical issues can arise in interpreting the results, drawing conclusions,

making recommendations, and in implementation. For example, the error terms in bivariate regression must be normally distributed about zero, with a constant variance, and be uncorrelated (Chapter 20). The researcher has the responsibility to test these assumptions and take appropriate corrective actions if necessary. Although interpretations, conclusions, recommendations and implementations necessarily involve subjective judgement, this judgement must be exercised honestly, free from personal biases or agendas of the researcher or the client.

SPSS and SAS Learning Editions

We have developed demonstration movies that give step-by-step instructions to run all the SPSS and SAS Learning Edition programs that are discussed in this book. These demonstrations can be downloaded from the website for this book. The instructions for running these demonstrations are given in Exhibit 17.2 below. The step-by-step instructions for running the various SPSS and SAS Learning Edition programs are also illustrated in screen captures with appropriate notes. These screen captures can be downloaded from the website for this book.

SPSS Windows

Using the Base module of SPSS, out-of-range values can be selected using the SELECT IF command. These cases, with the identifying information (subject ID, record number, variable name and variable value) can then be printed using the LIST or PRINT commands. The PRINT command will save active cases to an external file. If a formatted list is required, the SUMMARIZE command can be used.

SPSS Data Entry can facilitate data integrity. You can verify that participants have answered completely by setting rules. These rules can be used on existing datasets to validate and check the data, whether or not the questionnaire used to collect the data was constructed in Data Entry. Data Entry allows you to control and check the entry of data through three types of rules: validation, checking, and skip and fill rules. Although the missing values can be treated within the context of the Base module, SPSS Missing Values Analysis can assist in diagnosing missing

values with estimates. TextSmart by SPSS can help in the coding and analysis of open-ended responses.

Creating a variable called *Overall Evaluation*

We illustrate the use of the Base module in creating new variables and recoding existing ones using the data of Exhibit 17.1. We want to create a variable called *Overall Evaluation* (*Overall*) that is the sum of the ratings on quality, quantity, value and service. Thus,

Overall = Quality + Quantity + Value + Service

These steps are as follows:

1 Select TRANSFORM.
2 Click COMPUTE VARIABLE.
3 Type 'overall' in the TARGET VARIABLE box.
4 Click 'quality' and move it to the NUMERIC EXPRESSIONS box.
5 Click the '+' sign.
6 Click 'quantity' and move it to the NUMERIC EXPRESSIONS box.
7 Click the '+' sign.
8 Click 'value' and move it to the NUMERIC EXPRESSIONS box.
9 Click the '+' sign.
10 Click 'service' and move it to the NUMERIC EXPRESSIONS box.
11 Click TYPE & LABEL under the TARGET VARIABLE box and type 'Overall Evaluation'. Click CONTINUE.
12 Click OK.

Exhibit 17.1	Restaurant preference

ID	Preference	Quality	Quantity	Value	Service	Income
1	2	2	3	1	3	6
2	6	5	6	5	7	2
3	4	4	3	4	5	3
4	1	2	1	1	2	5
5	7	6	6	5	4	1
6	5	4	4	5	4	3
7	2	2	3	2	3	5
8	3	3	4	2	3	4
9	7	6	7	6	5	2
10	2	3	2	2	2	5
11	2	3	2	1	3	6
12	6	6	6	6	7	2
13	4	4	3	3	4	3
14	1	1	3	1	2	4
15	7	7	5	5	4	2
16	5	5	4	5	5	3
17	2	3	1	2	3	4
18	4	4	3	3	3	3
19	7	5	5	7	5	5
20	3	2	2	3	3	3

Exhibit 17.2	Instructions for running computerised demonstrations

To initiate an SPSS demonstration, pick the folder with the appropriate name. For example, to create the Overall Evaluation variable using the data of Exhibit 17.1, use the '14-Transform_demo' folder. Each folder will have several files. All the files in a folder are required to run the demonstration. For example, '14-Transform_demo' has four files. However, some folders have more files. All the files in each folder should be downloaded and saved in the same separate folder. The file that you should select to run the demonstration movie is the one that has the same name as the the folder, but with the '.htm' extension appended to its name. For example, if you want to run a demonstration of creating the Overall Evaluation variable using the data of Exhibit 17.1 using SPSS, then double-click the file '14-Transform_demo.htm' in the '14-Transform_demo' folder. Once you double click, Internet Explorer (or your default web browser) will be loaded, and your demonstration movie will start automatically. Note that the other three files that also need to be in the same folder are '14-Transform_demo_skin.swf' '14-Transform_demo.swf,' and 'standard.js'.

If you want to stop the demonstration movie at any specific point in the demonstration, simply click the ⏸ button. The demonstration stops at that point. The button now changes form and looks like ▶. To continue viewing the demonstration from that point on, simply click the ▶ button. To fast-forward the demonstration, you can click the ⏩ button. Click it multiple times if you need to fast-forward through longer intervals. To rewind the demonstration, simply click the ⏪ button. Click it multiple times if you need to rewind through longer intervals. At any time, if you want to replay the demonstration, right from the beginning, then simply click the ↺ button. Finally, you can also move the slide ▭ left or right to navigate through the demonstration. The slider achieves the same purpose as that of the fast-forward and rewind buttons.

Recoding to create new variable called *Recoded Income*

We also want to illustrate the recoding of variables to create new variables. Income category 1 occurs only once and income category 6 occurs only twice. So we want to combine income categories 1 and 2, and categories 5 and 6, and create a new income variable 'rincome' labelled 'Recoded Income'. Note that rincome has only four categories that are coded as 1 to 4. This can be done in SPSS Windows as follows:

1 Select TRANSFORM.
2 Click RECODE and select INTO DIFFERENT VARIABLES.
3 Click income and move it to NUMERIC VARIABLE → OUTPUT VARIABLE box.
4 Type 'rincome' in OUTPUT VARIABLE NAME box.
5 Type 'Recode Income' in OUTCOME VARIABLE LABEL box.
6 Click OLD AND NEW VALUES box.
7 Under OLD VALUES on the left, click RANGE. Type '1' and '2' in the range boxes. Under NEW VALUES on the right, click VALUE and type '1' in the value box. Click ADD.
8 Under OLD VALUES on the left, click VALUE. Type '3' in the value box. Under NEW VALUES on the right, click VALUE and type '2' in the value box. Click ADD.
9 Under OLD VALUES on the left, click VALUE. Type '4' in the value box. Under NEW VALUES on the right, click VALUE and type '3' in the value box. Click ADD.
10 Under OLD VALUES on the left, click RANGE. Type '5' and '6' in the range boxes. Under NEW VALUES on the right, click VALUE and type '4' in the value box. Click ADD.
11 Click CONTINUE.
12 Click CHANGE.
13 Click OK.

SAS Learning Edition

The instructions given here and in all the data analysis chapters (17 to 25) will work with the SAS Learning Edition as well as with the SAS Enterprise Guide. Within BASE SAS the IF, IF–THEN and IF–THEN ELSE statements can be used to select cases with missing or out-of-range values. The LIST statement is useful for printing suspicious input lines.[27] SAS Learning Edition allows the user to identify missing out-of-range values with the Filter Data tab within

the Query and Filter Data task. The procedures MI and MIANALYZE in SAS/STAT also offer the capability of imputing missing values when a more sophisticated approach is required. We illustrate the use of the Base module in creating new variables and recoding existing ones using the data of Exhibit 17.1.

Creating a variable called *Overall Evaluation*

(*TIP: Before completing the following tasks, go to TOOLS Q OPTIONS Q QUERY and be sure 'Automatically add columns from input tables to result set of query' is checked.*)

1 Select DATA.
2 Click FILTER AND QUERY.
3 Move all variables to SELECT DATA tab.
4 Select the COMPUTED COLUMNS button.
5 Click NEW.
6 Select BUILD EXPRESSION.
7 Select 'QUALITY' and click on ADD TO EXPRESSION.
8 Click the '+' sign.
9 Select 'QUANTITY' and click ADD TO EXPRESSION.
10 Click the '+' sign.
11 Select 'VALUE' and click ADD TO EXPRESSION.
12 Click the '+' sign.
13 Select 'SERVICE' and click ADD TO EXPRESSION.
14 Click OK.
15 Select 'CALCULATION1' and click RENAME.
16 Type OVERALL.
17 Click CLOSE.
18 Select RUN.

Recoding to create new variable called *Recorded Income*

1 Select DATA.
2 Click FILTER AND QUERY.
3 Move all variables to SELECT DATA tab.
4 Right-click INCOME.
5 Select RECODE.
6 In NEW COLUMN NAME box, type 'RINCOME'.
7 Click ADD.
8 Under REPLACE VALUES enter 2.
9 Under WITH THIS VALUE enter 1.
10 Click OK.
11 Click ADD.
12 Under REPLACE VALUES enter 3.

13 Under WITH THIS VALUE enter 2.	20 Under REPLACE A RANGE tab.
14 Click OK.	21 Check SET A LOWER LIMIT and enter 5.
15 Click ADD.	22 Check SET A UPPER LIMIT and enter 6.
16 Under REPLACE VALUES enter 4.	23 Under WITH THIS VALUE enter 4.
17 Under WITH THIS VALUE enter 3.	24 Click OK.
18 Click OK.	25 Click OK.
19 Click ADD.	26 Click RUN.

Summary

Data integrity begins with a preliminary check of all questionnaires for completeness and interviewing quality. Then more thorough editing takes place. Editing consists of screening questionnaires to identify illegible, incomplete, inconsistent or ambiguous responses. Such responses may be handled by returning questionnaires to the field, assigning missing values or discarding unsatisfactory participants.

The next step is coding. A numeric or alphanumeric code is assigned to represent a specific response to a specific question along with the column position or field that code will occupy. It is often helpful to print off a codebook containing the coding instructions and the necessary information about the variables in the dataset. The coded data are transcribed onto computer memory, disks, other storage devices or entered directly into a data analysis package. For this purpose, keypunching, optical recognition, digital technologies, bar codes or other technologies may be used. Survey design software packages completely automate the coding process.

Cleaning the data requires consistency checks and treatment of missing responses. Options available for treating missing responses include substitution of a neutral value such as a mean, substitution of an imputed response, casewise deletion and pairwise deletion. Statistical adjustments such as weighting, variable respecification and scale transformations often enhance the quality of data analysis. The selection of a data analysis strategy should be based on the earlier steps of the marketing research process, known characteristics of the data, properties of statistical techniques, and the background and philosophy of the researcher. Statistical techniques may be classified as univariate or multivariate.

Before analysing the data in international marketing research, the researcher should ensure that the units of measurement are comparable across countries or cultural units. The data analysis could be conducted at three levels: (1) individual, (2) within-country or cultural unit (intra-cultural analysis), and (3) across countries or cultural units (pan-cultural or cross-cultural analysis). Several ethical issues are related to data processing, particularly the discarding of unsatisfactory responses, violation of the assumptions underlying the data analysis techniques, and evaluation and interpretation of results.

Questions

1 Describe the data integrity process. Why is this process needed?

2 What activities are involved in the preliminary checking of questionnaires that have been returned from the field?

3 What is meant by editing a questionnaire?

4 How are unsatisfactory responses that are discovered in editing treated?

5 What is the difference between pre-coding and post-coding?

6 Describe the guidelines for the coding of unstructured questions.

7 What does transcribing the data involve?

8 What kinds of consistency checks are made in cleaning the data?

9 What options are available for the treatment of missing data?

10 What kinds of statistical adjustments are sometimes made to the data?

11 Describe the weighting process. What are the reasons for weighting?

12 What are dummy variables? Why are such variables created?

13 Explain why scale transformations are made.

14 Which scale transformation procedure is most commonly used? Briefly describe this procedure.

15 What considerations are involved in selecting a data analysis strategy?

Exercises

1 Visit **www.ettinger.co.uk** and examine online databases, secondary data and intelligence sources to obtain information on the criteria buyers use in selecting luxury leather accessories. Demographic and psychographic data were obtained in a survey designed to explain the choice of luxury leather accessories. What kind of consistency checks, treatment of missing responses, and variable respecification should be conducted?

2 To a sample of five male and five female fellow students, pose the question 'Which of the following sports have you participated in over the last 12 months?' Create a list of what you think may be the top 10 sports that fellow students may have participated in, with space for 'Others – please specify'. After conducting the 10 interviews, how would you cope with the coding of the 'Others'? How would you rewrite this question and potential list of sports if you were to repeat the exercise?

3 You are the Marketing Research Manager for AGA (**www.agaliving.com**). AGA has developed a luxury refrigerator and matching freezer at €4,000 each. A European survey was conducted to determine consumer response to the proposed models. The data were obtained by conducting a face-to-face survey at shopping malls in 10 European capital cites. Although the resulting sample of 2,500 is fairly representative on all other demographic variables, it under-represents the upper income households. The marketing research analyst who reports to you feels that weighting is not necessary. Discuss this question with the analyst (a student in your class).

4   You are the project manager for a data analysis firm. You are supervising the data integrity process for a large survey on personal hygiene issues. The data were collected via a postal survey and 1,823 questionnaires have been returned. The response rate was excellent, partially due to an excellent prize draw that accompanied the survey. However, you are suspicious about the quality of many responses and 290 questionnaires have missing responses. The data analyst preparing the data has not seen such a level of missing data and does not know how to cope with this survey. Explain to the data analyst how the missing responses and checks on the quality of data to be analysed should be performed.

5   In a small group discuss the following issues: 'Data processing is tedious, time consuming and costly; it should be circumvented whenever possible' and 'Conducting robust sampling is tedious, time consuming and costly; any structural problems in a sample can be simply resolved through weighting.'

Video case exercise: HSBC

HSBC plans to target the rising wealthy strata of India through a face-to-face home survey. It has chosen three cities to conduct the fieldwork, Chennai, Delhi and Mumbai. Do you feel that by targeting these three cities HSBC could have a representative view of the rising wealthy strata of India? Would you advise HSBC to weight its data in any way? How could it weight its data?

Notes

1. Trembly, A.C., 'Poor data quality: a $600 billion issue', *National Underwriter* 106 (11) (18 March 2002), 48; Higgins, K.T., 'Never ending journey', *Marketing Management* 6 (1) (Spring 1997), 4–7; Harristhal, J., 'Interviewer tips', *Applied Marketing Research* 28 (Fall 1988), 42–45.

2. Keillor, B., Owens, D. and Pettijohn, C., 'A cross-cultural/cross-national study of influencing factors and socially desirable response biases', *International Journal of Market Research* 43 (1) (First Quarter 2001), 63–84; Dadzie, K.Q., 'Demarketing strategy in shortage marketing environment', *Journal of the Academy of Marketing Science* (Spring 1989), 157–165. See also Nishisato, S., *Measurement and multivariate analysis* (New York: Springer-Verlag, 2002).

3. Healey, B. and Gendall, P., 'Forum – Asking the age question in mail and online surveys', *International Journal of Market Research* 50 (3) (2008), 309–317.

4. Schmidt, M., 'Quantification of transcripts from depth interviews, open ended responses and focus groups: challenges, accomplishments, new applications and perspectives for market research', *International Journal of Market Research* 52 (4) (2010), 483–509; Jenkins, S., 'Automating questionnaire design and construction', *Journal of the Market Research Society* 42 (1) (Winter 1999–2000), 79–85; Fink, A., *How to analyze survey data* (Thousand Oaks, CA: Sage, 1995).

5. Esuli, A. and Sebastiani, F., 'Machines that learn how to code open-ended survey data', *International Journal of Market Research* 52 (6) (2010), 775–800.

6. Kearney, I., 'Measuring consumer brand confusion to comply with legal guidelines', *International Journal of Market Research* 43 (1) (First Quarter 2001), 85–91; Luyens, S., 'Coding verbatims by computer', *Marketing Research: A Magazine of Management and Applications* 7(2) (Spring 1995), 20–25.

7. Hammett, Y.C., 'Voters in Hillsborough County, Florida try out touch-screen voting machines', *Knight Ridder Tribune Business News* (3 April 2007), 1; Studt, T., 'Exclusive survey reveals move to high-tech solutions', *Research & Development* 43 (3) (March 2001), 37–38; Frendberg, N., 'Scanning questionnaires efficiently', *Marketing Research: A Magazine of Management and Applications* 5 (2) (Spring 1993), 38–42.

8. Rydholm, J., 'Scanning the seas', *Marketing Research Review* (May 1993), **www.princess.com**, accessed 23 May 2002.

9. Albaum, G., Roster, C., Yu, J.H. and Rogers, R.D., 'Simple rating scale formats: exploring extreme response', *International Journal of Market Research* 49 (5) (2007), 633–650.

10. Vicente, P., Reis, E. and Santos, M., 'Using mobile phones for survey research: a comparison with fixed phones', *International Journal of Market Research* 51 (5) (2009), 613–634; Allison, P.D., *Missing data* (Thousand Oaks, CA: Sage, 2001); Lee, B.-J., 'Sample selection bias correction for missing response observations', *Oxford Bulletin of Economics and Statistics* 62 (2) (May 2000), 305; Freedman, V.A. and Wolf, D.A., 'A case study on the use of multiple imputation', *Demography* 32 (3) (August 1995), 459–470; Malhotra, N.K., 'Analysing marketing research data with incomplete information on the dependent variable', *Journal of Marketing Research* 24 (February 1987), 74–84.

11. A meaningful and practical value should be imputed. The value imputed should be a legitimate response code. For example, a mean of 3.86 may not be practical if only single-digit response codes have been developed. In such cases, the mean should be rounded to the nearest integer. See Allen, N.J., Williams, H., Stanley, D.J. and Ross, S.J., 'Assessing dissimilarity relations under missing data conditions: evidence from computer simulations', *Journal of Applied Psychology* 92 (5) (September 2007), 1414–1426.

12. Kent, R.A., 'Cases as configurations: using combinatorial and fuzzy logic to analyse marketing data', *International Journal of Market Research* (47) 2 (2005), 205–228; Murphy, K.M., 'Estimation and inference in two-step econometric models', *Journal of Business & Economic Statistics* 20 (1) (January 2002), 88–97; Kara, A., Nielsen, C., Sahay, S. and Sivasubramaniam, N., 'Latent information in the pattern of missing observations in global mail surveys', *Journal of Global Marketing* 7 (4) (1994), 103–126.

13. Zeithammer, R. and Lenk, P., 'Bayesian estimation of multivariate-normal models when dimensions are absent', *Quantitative Marketing and Economics* 4 (3) (September 2006), 241–264.

14. Sparrow, N., 'Quality issues on online research', *Journal of Advertising Research* 47 (2) (June 2007), 179–182.

15. Some weighting procedures require adjustments in subsequent data analysis techniques. See Curtice, J. and Sparrow, N., 'The past matters: eliminating the pro-Labour bias in British opinion polls', *International Journal of Market Research* 52 (2) (2010), 169–189; Dawes, J., 'Do data characteristics change according to the number of scale points used?', *International Journal of Market Research* 50 (1) (2008), 61–77; Tucker, C., Brick, M. and Meekins, B., 'Household telephone service and usage patterns in the United States in 2004: implications for telephone samples', *Public Opinion Quarterly* 71 (1) (April 2007), 3–22; Bartholomew, D.J., Steele, F., Moustaki, I and Galbraith, J.I., *The analysis and interpretation of multivariate data for social scientists*, 2nd edn (Boca Raton, FL: CRC Press, 2008).

16. Labeaga-Azcona, J.M., Lado-Cousté, N. and Martos-Partal, M., 'The double jeopardy loyalty effect using discrete choice models', *International Journal of Market Research* 52 (5) (2010), 635–654.

17. Dolnicar, S., Grün, B. and Leisch, F., 'Quick, simple and reliable: forced binary survey questions', *International Journal of Market Research* 53 (2) (2011), 233–254.

18. Akinci, F. and Healey, B.J., 'The role of social marketing in understanding access to primary health care services: perceptions and experiences', *Health Marketing Quarterly* 21 (4) (January 2004), 3–30; Bradford, M., 'Health care access services for expats gain in popularity', *Business Insurance* 36 (1) (7 January 2002), 19–20; Woodside, A.G., Nielsen, R.L., Walters, F. and Muller, G.D., 'Preference segmentation of health care services: the old-fashioneds, value conscious, affluents, and professional want-it-alls', *Journal of Health Care Marketing* (June 1988), 14–24. See also Jayanti, R., 'Affective responses toward service providers: implications for service encounters', *Health Marketing Quarterly* 14 (1) (1996), 49–65.

19. See, for specific transformations frequently used in marketing research, Gomez, M. and Okazaki, S., 'Estimating store brand shelf space: a new framework using neural networks and partial least squares', *International Journal of Market Research* 51 (2) (2009), 243–266; Johnson, R.A. and Wichern, D.W., *Applied Multivariate Statistical Analysis* (Paramus, NJ: Prentice Hall, 2001); Swift, B., 'Preparing numerical data', in Sapsford, R. and Jupp, V. (eds), *Data Collection and Analysis* (Thousand Oaks, CA: Sage, 1996); Frank, R.E., 'Use of transformations', *Journal of Marketing Research* 3 (August 1966), 247–253.

20. Vesset, D., 'Trends in the market for analytic applications', *KM World* 11 (4) (April 2002), 14. For a similar data analysis strategy, see Malhotra, N.K., 'Modelling store choice based on censored preference data', *Journal of Retailing* (Summer 1986), 128–144; Birks, D.F. and Birts, A.N., 'Service quality in domestic banks', in Birks, D.F. (ed.), *Global Cash Management in Europe* (Basingstoke: Macmillan, 1998), 175–205.

21. Bivariate techniques have been included here with multivariate techniques. Although bivariate techniques are concerned with pairwise relationships, multivariate techniques examine more complex simultaneous relationships among phenomena. See DeSarbo, W.S., Hausman, R.E. and Kukitz, J.M., 'Restricted principal components analysis for marketing research', *Journal of Modeling in Management* 2 (3) (2007), 305; Spicer, J., *Making Sense of Multivariate Data Analysis: An intuitive approach* (Thousand Oaks, CA: Sage, 2004); Tacq, J., *Multivariate Analysis Techniques in Social Science Research Analysis* (Thousand Oaks, CA: Sage, 1996).

22. Drossos, D., Giaglis, G.M., Lekakos, G., Kokkinaki, F. and Stavraki, M.G., 'Determinants of effective SMS advertising: an experimental study', *Journal of Interactive Advertising* 7 (2) (Spring 2007), 16–27; DeSarbo, W.S., 'The joint spatial representation of multiple variable batteries collected in marketing research', *Journal of Marketing Research* 38 (2) (May 2001), 244–253; Carroll, J.D. and Green, P.E., 'Psychometric methods in marketing research: Part II, multidimensional scaling', *Journal of Marketing Research* 34 (2) (May 1997), 193–204.

23. Ford, J.B., Mueller, B., Taylor, C.R. and Hollis, N., 'The tension between strategy and execution: challenges for international advertising research – globalization is much more than universal branding', *Journal of Advertising Research* 51 (1), 50th Anniversary Supplement (2011), 27–41; Dolnicar, S. and Grun, B., 'Cross-cultural differences in survey response patterns', *International Marketing Review* 24 (2) (2007), 127; McDonald, G., 'Cross-cultural methodological issues in ethical research', *Journal of Business Ethics* 27 (1/2) (September 2000), 89–104;

Alasuutari, P., *Researching Culture* (Thousand Oaks, CA: Sage, 1995).

24. Slavens, R., 'Haagen-Dazs tastes success with crème de la crème campaign', *B to B* 92 (1) (January 2007), 23; Anon., 'For a scoop of their own', *Businessline* (17 January 2002), 1; Kilburn, D., 'Häagen-Dazs is flavor of month', *Marketing Week* 20 (23) (4 September 1997), 30.

25. See, for example, McCarty, J.A., Horn, M.I., Szenasy, M.K. and Feintuch, J., 'An exploratory study of consumer style: country differences and international segments', *Journal of Consumer Behaviour* 6 (1) (February 2007), 48; Tian, R.G., 'Cross-cultural issues in Internet marketing', *Journal of American Academy of Business* 1 (2) (March 2002), 217–224; Spiller, L.D. and Campbell, A.J., 'The use of international direct marketing by small businesses in Canada, Mexico, and the United States: a comparative analysis', *Journal of Direct Marketing* 8 (Winter 1994), 7–16; Nyaw, M.K. and Ng, I., 'A comparative analysis of ethical beliefs: a four country study', *Journal of Business Ethics* 13 (July 1994), 543–556.

26. Barnes, R., 'Downsizing, increased competition has employees working longer, feeling anger', *Knight Ridder Tribune Business News* (May 8, 2004), 1; Hopkins, W.E. and Hopkins, S.A., 'The ethics of downsizing: perception of rights and responsibilities', *Journal of Business Ethics* 18 (2) (January 1999), 145–154.

27. The help of Pamela Prentice of SAS in writing these and the SAS instructions in all the chapters (17 to 25) is gratefully acknowledged.

18 Frequency distribution, cross-tabulation and hypothesis testing

Frequency distribution, cross-tabulation and hypothesis testing are the fundamental building blocks of quantitative data analysis. They provide insights into the data, guide subsequent analyses and aid the interpretation of results.

Objectives

After reading this chapter, you should be able to:

1 describe the significance of preliminary data analysis and the insights that can be obtained from such analyses;

2 discuss data analysis associated with frequencies, including measures of location, measures of variability and measures of shape;

3 explain data analysis associated with cross-tabulations and the associated statistics: chi-square, phi coefficient, contingency coefficient, Cramer's *V* and lambda coefficient;

4 describe data analysis associated with parametric hypothesis testing for one sample, two independent samples and paired samples;

5 understand data analysis associated with non-parametric hypothesis testing for one sample, two independent samples and paired samples;

6 appreciate how the SPSS and SAS software is used in analyses of frequency distribution, cross-tabulations and hypothesis testing.

Overview

Once the data have been prepared for analysis (Chapter 17), the researcher should conduct basic analyses. This chapter describes basic data analyses, including frequency distribution, cross-tabulation and hypothesis testing. First, we describe the frequency distribution and explain how it provides both an indication of the number of out-of-range, missing or extreme values as well as insights into the central tendency, variability and shape of the underlying distribution. Next, we introduce hypothesis testing by describing the general procedure. Hypothesis testing procedures are classified as tests of associations or tests of differences. We consider the use of cross-tabulation for understanding the associations between variables taken two or three at a time. Although the nature of the association can be observed from tables, statistics are available for examining the significance and strength of the association. We present tests for examining hypotheses related to differences based on one or two samples. Finally, help is provided to run the SPSS and SAS Learning Editions in the data analysis challenges presented in this chapter.

Many marketing research projects do not go beyond basic data analysis. These findings are often displayed using tables and graphs, as discussed further in Chapter 25. Although the findings of basic analysis are valuable in their own right, they also provide guidance for conducting multivariate analysis. The insights gained from the basic analysis are also invaluable in interpreting the results obtained from more sophisticated statistical techniques. The following examples provide a 'flavour' of basic data analysis techniques. We illustrate the use of cross-tabulation, chi-square analysis and hypothesis testing.

Focus on	**IFM Sports Marketing Surveys**

FIBA Brand Tracker

In 2009, the International Basketball Federation FIBA commissioned IFM Sports Marketing Surveys to conduct a Brand Health Tracker study. FIBA wished to monitor perceptions of the FIBA brand and FIBA events. It wanted to know what affected the development of its brand. FIBA was particularly interested in how perceptions of basketball differed in the countries under study and whether any differences were statistically significant. IFM Sports Marketing Surveys classified its sample of sports fans based upon the number of games they had watched in the previous year. The following table focuses upon the levels of interest in basketball of Chinese, Italian, Spanish and UK participants.

Cross-tabulation and chi-square analysis provided the following:

Sports fans level of interest in basketball	Country (absolute numbers of participants – and column %)			
	China	Italy	Spain	UK
Avid	187 (31%)	146 (24%)	83 (15%)	85 (14%)
Occasional	115 (19%)	158 (26%)	226 (41%)	219 (36%)
Low	242 (40%)	238 (39%)	187 (34%)	194 (32%)
None	60 (10%)	67 (11%)	55 (10%)	115 (19%)
Totals	604 (100%)	645 (100%)	609 (100%)	607 (100%)
	$\chi^2 = 145.56$		$p \leq 0.0001$	

These results indicate that there was little difference across the four countries in terms of 'Low' or 'No' levels of interest in basketball. However, there was a much higher proportion of Chinese and Italians that had an 'Avid' interest. UK sports fans had the lowest levels of 'Avids' and the highest levels of fans with no interest in basketball. The chi-square test indicated that there were statistically significant differences in levels of interest in basketball across the countries studied.

Real research

Catalogues are risky business[1]

Twelve product categories were examined to compare shopping by catalogue with store shopping. The hypothesis that there is no significant difference in the overall amount of risk perceived when buying products by catalogue compared with buying the same products in a retail store was rejected. The hypothesis was tested by computing 12 (one for each product) paired observation t tests. Mean scores for overall perceived risk for some of the products in both buying situations are presented in the following table, with higher scores indicating greater risk.

Product	Overall perceived risk	
	Catalogue	Store
Shoes	58.60	50.80*
Pocket calculator	49.62	42.00*
Hi-fi	48.89	41.98*
Portable TV	48.53	40.91*
Digital camera	48.13	39.52*
Athletic socks	35.22	30.22*
Perfume	34.85	29.79*
CDs	32.65	28.74*

* Significant at 0.01 level.

As can be seen, a significantly ($p < 0.01$) higher overall amount of perceived risk was attached to products purchased by catalogue as compared with those purchased from a retail store. Although this study reveals risk associated with buying from a catalogue, terrorist threats, time shortage and increased convenience have increased the amount of products that are purchased from catalogues as well as online.

These two examples show how basic data analysis can be useful in its own right. The cross-tabulation and chi-square analysis in the FIBA example and the paired *t* tests in the catalogue shopping example enabled us to draw specific conclusions from the data. These and other concepts discussed in this chapter are illustrated in the context of explaining Internet usage for personal (non-professional) reasons. Table 18.1 contains data for 30 participants giving the gender (1 = male, 2 = female), familiarity with the Internet (1 = very unfamiliar, 7 = very familiar), Internet usage in hours per week, attitude towards the Internet and towards technology, both measured on a seven-point scale (1 = very unfavourable, 7 = very favourable), and whether the participants have done online shopping or banking (1 = yes, 2 = no). For illustrative purposes, we consider only a small number of observations. In actual practice, frequencies, cross-tabulations and hypothesis tests are performed on much larger samples. For example, the FIBA study sample size was 4,288.

Table 18.1	Internet usage data						
Participant no.	Gender	Familiarity	Internet usage	Attitude towards Internet	Attitude towards technology	Usage of Internet shopping	Usage of Internet banking
1	1	7	14	7	6	1	1
2	2	2	2	3	3	2	2
3	2	3	3	4	3	1	2
4	2	3	3	7	5	1	2
5	1	7	13	7	7	1	1
6	2	4	6	5	4	1	2
7	2	2	2	4	5	2	2
8	2	3	6	5	4	2	2
9	2	3	6	6	4	1	2
10	1	9	15	7	6	1	2
11	2	4	3	4	3	2	2
12	2	5	4	6	4	2	2
13	1	6	9	6	5	2	1
14	1	6	8	3	2	2	2
15	1	6	5	5	4	1	2
16	2	4	3	4	3	2	2
17	1	6	9	5	3	1	1
18	1	4	4	5	4	1	2
19	1	7	14	6	6	1	1
20	2	6	6	6	4	2	2
21	1	6	9	4	2	2	2
22	1	5	5	5	4	2	1
23	2	3	2	4	2	2	2
24	1	7	15	6	6	1	1
25	2	6	6	5	3	1	2
26	1	6	13	6	6	1	1
27	2	5	4	5	5	1	1
28	2	4	2	3	2	2	2
29	1	4	4	5	3	1	2
30	1	3	3	7	5	1	2

Frequency distribution

Marketing researchers often need to answer questions about a single variable. For example:

- How many users of the brand may be characterised as brand loyal?
- What percentage of the market consists of heavy users, medium users, light users and non-users?
- How many customers are very familiar with a new product offering? How many are familiar, somewhat familiar, or unfamiliar with the brand? What is the mean familiarity rating? Is there much variance in the extent to which customers are familiar with the new product?
- What is the income distribution of brand users? Is this distribution skewed towards low-income brackets?

Frequency distribution
A mathematical distribution whose objective is to obtain a count of the number of responses associated with different values of one variable and to express these counts in percentage terms.

The answers to these kinds of questions can be determined by examining frequency distributions. In a frequency distribution, one variable is considered at a time.

The objective is to obtain a count of the number of responses associated with different values of the variable. The relative occurrence, or frequency, of different values of the variable is expressed in percentages. A frequency distribution for a variable produces a table of frequency counts, percentages and cumulative percentages for all the values associated with that variable.

Table 18.2 gives the frequency distribution of familiarity with the Internet. In the table, the first column contains the labels assigned to the different categories of the variable and the second column indicates the codes assigned to each value. Note that a code of 9 has been assigned to missing values. The third column gives the number of participants ticking each value. For example, three participants ticked value 5, indicating that they were somewhat familiar with the Internet. The fourth column displays the percentage of participants ticking each value. The fifth column shows percentages calculated by excluding the cases with missing values. If there are no missing values, the fourth and fifth columns are identical. The last column represents cumulative percentages after adjusting for missing values. As can be seen, of the 30 participants who participated in the survey, 10% entered a figure of '5'. If the one participant with a missing value is excluded, this changes to 10.3%. The cumulative percentage corresponding to the value of 5 is 58.6. In other words, 58.6% of the participants with valid responses indicated a familiarity value of 5 or less.

A frequency distribution helps determine the extent of item non-response (1 participant out of 30 in Table 18.1). It also indicates the extent of illegitimate responses. Values of 0 and

Table 18.2	Frequency distribution of 'Familiarity with the Internet'				
Value label	Value	Frequency (N)	Percentage	Valid percentage	Cumulative percentage
Very unfamiliar	1	0	0.0	0.0	0.0
	2	2	6.7	6.9	6.9
	3	6	20.0	20.7	27.6
	4	6	20.0	20.7	48.3
	5	3	10.0	10.3	58.6
	6	8	26.7	27.6	86.2
Very familiar	7	4	13.3	13.8	100.0
Missing	9	1	3.3		
Total		30	100.0	100.0	

8 would be illegitimate responses, or errors. The cases with these values could be identified and corrective action could be taken. The presence of outliers or cases with extreme values can also be detected. For example, in the case of a frequency distribution of household size, a few isolated families with household sizes of nine or more might be considered outliers. A frequency distribution also indicates the shape of the empirical distribution of the variable. The frequency data may be used to construct a histogram, or a vertical bar chart in which the values of the variable are portrayed along the X axis and the absolute or relative frequencies of the values are placed along the Y axis.

Figure 18.1 is a histogram of the frequency data in Table 18.1. From the histogram, one could examine whether the observed distribution is consistent with an expected or assumed distribution.

Figure 18.1

Frequency histogram

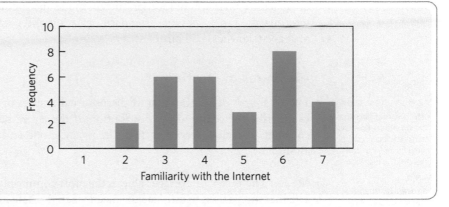

Focus on

IFM Sports Marketing Surveys

FIBA Brand Tracker

In the FIBA branding study, avid fans of basketball were asked how they followed basketball. Of the sample of 4,288, there were 900 classified as avid fans of the sport.

The results showed that the top three forms of media favoured by avid basketball fans were: 'watch dedicated TV', 'read newspaper articles' and 'visit websites'. Of particular interest was the use of new media in terms of 'visit websites', 'read blogs' and 'receive results via mobile'. FIBA took particular note of these new media forms and the differences between countries in how forms of media were favoured. In subsequent brand health studies, FIBA would take particular note of changes in media usage, especially in the use of new media.

All countries – avid fans regularly follow basketball through...

Media used	Frequency	Percentage
Watch dedicated TV	495	55
Read newspaper articles	423	47
Visit websites	315	35
Participate	270	30
Read specialist magazines	234	26
Read blogs	234	26
Listen to radio broadcasts	225	25
Attend events	180	20
Receive results via mobile	126	14
Did not respond	10	0.01
Total	900*	100.0

* This refers to participants' responses to a multiple-choice question.

Note that the numbers and percentages in the preceding example indicate the extent of media usage to follow basketball by avid fans of the sport. Because numbers are involved, a frequency distribution can be used to calculate descriptive or cumulative statistics.

Statistics associated with frequency distribution

As illustrated in the previous section, a frequency distribution is a convenient way of looking at different values of a variable. A frequency table is easy to read and provides basic information, but sometimes this information may be too detailed and the researcher must summarise it by the use of descriptive statistics. The most commonly used statistics associated with frequencies are measures of location (mean, mode and median), measures of variability (range, interquartile range, variance, standard deviation and coefficient of variation) and measures of shape (skewness and kurtosis).[2]

Measures of location

Measure of location

A statistic that describes a location within a dataset. Measures of central tendency describe the centre of the distribution.

The **measures of location** that we discuss are measures of central tendency because they tend to describe the centre of the distribution. If the entire sample is changed by adding a fixed constant to each observation, then the mean, mode and median change by the same fixed amount.

Mean

The average; that value obtained by summing all elements in a set and dividing by the number of elements.

Mean. The **mean**, or average value, is the most commonly used measure of central tendency. The measure is used to estimate the mean when the data have been collected using an interval or ratio scale. The data should display some central tendency, with most of the responses distributed around the mean.

The mean, $\overline{X}$, is given by

Mode

A measure of central tendency given as the value that occurs with the most frequency in a sample distribution.

$$\overline{X} = \frac{\sum_{i=1}^{n} X_i}{n}$$

Median

A measure of central tendency given as the value above which half of the values fall and below which half of the values fall.

where X_i = observed values of the variable X
n = number of observations (sample size)

Generally, the mean is a robust measure and does not change markedly as data values are added or deleted. For the frequencies given in Table 18.1, the mean value is calculated as follows:

$$\overline{X} = (2 \times 2) + (6 \times 3) + (6 \times 4) + (3 \times 5) + (8 \times 6) + (4 \times 7)/29$$
$$= (4 + 18 + 24 + 15 + 48 + 28)/29$$
$$= 137/29$$
$$= 4.724$$

Mode. The **mode** is the value that occurs most frequently. It represents the highest peak of the distribution. The mode is a good measure of location when the variable is inherently categorical or has otherwise been grouped into categories. The mode in Table 18.2 is 6.

Median. The **median** of a sample is the middle value when the data are arranged in ascending or descending order. If the number of data points is even, the median is usually estimated as the midpoint between the two middle values by adding the two middle values and dividing their sum by 2. The median is the 50th percentile. The median is an appropriate measure of central tendency for ordinal data. In Table 18.2, the middle value is 5, so the median is 5.

As can be seen from Table 18.1, the three measures of central tendency for this distribution are different (mean = 4.724, mode = 6, median = 5). This is not surprising, since each measure defines central tendency in a different way. So which measure should be used? If the variable is measured on a nominal scale, the mode should be used. If the variable is measured on an ordinal scale, the median is appropriate. If the variable is measured on an interval or ratio scale, the mode is a poor measure of central tendency. This can be seen from Table 18.2. Although the modal value of 6 has the highest frequency, it represents only 27.6% of the sample. In general, for interval or ratio data, the median is a better measure of central tendency, although it too ignores available information about the variable. The actual values of the variable above and below the median are ignored. The mean is the most appropriate measure of central tendency for interval or ratio data. The mean makes use of all the information available since all of the values are used in computing it. However, it is sensitive to extremely small or extremely large values (outliers). When there are outliers in the data, the mean is not a good measure of central tendency, and it is useful to consider both the mean and the median. In Table 18.2, since there are no extreme values and the data are treated as interval, the mean value of 4.724 is a good measure of location or central tendency. Although this value is greater than 4, it is still not high (i.e. it is less than 5).

Measures of variability

Measure of variability
A statistic that indicates the distribution's dispersion.

Range
The difference between the smallest and largest values of a distribution.

Interquartile range
The range of a distribution encompassing the middle 50% of the observations.

Variance
The mean squared deviation of all the values of the mean.

Standard deviation
The square root of the variance.

The measures of variability, which are calculated on interval or ratio data, include the range, interquartile range, variance or standard deviation and coefficient of variation.

Range. The range measures the spread of the data. It is simply the difference between the largest and smallest values in the sample:

$$\text{Range} = X_{\text{largest}} - X_{\text{smallest}}$$

As such, the range is directly affected by outliers. If all the values in the data are multiplied by a constant, the range is multiplied by the same constant. The range in Table 18.2 is $7 - 2 = 5$.

Interquartile range. The interquartile range is the difference between the 75th and 25th percentiles. For a set of data points arranged in order of magnitude, the pth percentile is the value that has p% of the data points below it and $(100 - p)$% above it. If all the data points are multiplied by a constant, the interquartile range is multiplied by the same constant. The interquartile range in Table 18.2 is $6 - 3 = 3$.

Variance. The difference between the mean and an observed value is called the deviation from the mean. The variance is the mean squared deviation from the mean. The variance can never be negative. When the data points are clustered around the mean, the variance is small. When the data points are scattered, the variance is large. If all the data values are multiplied by a constant, the variance is multiplied by the square of the constant.

Standard deviation. The standard deviation is the square root of the variance. Thus, the standard deviation is expressed in the same units as the data, rather than in squared units. The standard deviation of a sample, S_x, is calculated as

$$S_x = \sqrt{\frac{\sum_{i-1}^{n}(X_i - \bar{X})^2}{n-1}}$$

We divide by $n - 1$ instead of n because the sample is drawn from a population and we are trying to determine how much the responses vary from the mean of the entire population. The population mean is unknown, however; therefore, the sample mean is used instead. The use of the sample mean makes the sample seem less variable than it really is. By dividing by

$n-1$ instead of by n, we compensate for the smaller variability observed in the sample. For the data given in Table 18.1, the variance is calculated as follows:

$$
\begin{aligned}
s_x^2 &= [2 \times (2-4.724)^2 + 6 \times (3-4.724)^2 + 6 \times (4-4.724)^2 + 3 \times (5-4.724)^2 \\
&\quad + 8 \times (6-4.724)^2 + 4 \times (7-4.724)^2]/28 \\
&= [14.840 + 17.833 + 3.145 + 0.229 + 13.025 + 20.721]/28 \\
&= 69.793/28 \\
&= 2.493
\end{aligned}
$$

The standard deviation, therefore, is calculated as

$$
\begin{aligned}
s_x &= \sqrt{2.493} \\
&= 1.579
\end{aligned}
$$

Coefficient of variation

A useful expression in sampling theory for the standard deviation as a percentage of the mean.

Coefficient of variation. The coefficient of variation is the ratio of the standard deviation to the mean expressed as a percentage, and it is a unitless measure of relative variability. The coefficient of variation, CV, is expressed as

$$
CV = \frac{s_x}{\overline{X}}
$$

The coefficient of variation is meaningful only if the variable is measured on a ratio scale. It remains unchanged if all the data values are multiplied by a constant. Because familiarity with the Internet is not measured on a ratio scale, it is not meaningful to calculate the coefficient of variation for the data in Table 18.2. From a managerial viewpoint, measures of variability are important because if a characteristic shows good variability, then perhaps the market could be segmented based on that characteristic.

Measures of shape

In addition to measures of variability, measures of shape are also useful in understanding the nature of the distribution. The shape of a distribution is assessed by examining skewness and kurtosis.

Skewness

A characteristic of a distribution that assesses its symmetry about the mean.

Kurtosis

A measure of the relative peakedness of the curve defined by the frequency distribution.

Skewness. Distributions can be either symmetric or skewed. In a symmetric distribution, the values on either side of the centre of the distribution are the same, and the mean, mode and median are equal. The positive and corresponding negative deviations from the mean are also equal. In a skewed distribution, the positive and negative deviations from the mean are unequal. Skewness is the tendency of the deviations from the mean to be larger in one direction than in the other. It can be thought of as the tendency for one tail of the distribution to be heavier than the other (see Figure 18.2). The skewness value for the data of Table 18.2 is −0.094, indicating a slight negative skew.

Kurtosis. Kurtosis is a measure of the relative peakedness or flatness of the curve defined by the frequency distribution. The kurtosis of a normal distribution is zero. If the kurtosis is positive, then the distribution is more peaked than a normal distribution. A negative value means that the distribution is flatter than a normal distribution. The value of this statistic for Table 18.2 is −1.261, indicating that the distribution is flatter than a normal distribution. Measures of shape are important because if a distribution is highly skewed or markedly peaked or flat, then statistical procedures that assume normality should be used with caution.

A general procedure for hypothesis testing

Basic analysis invariably involves some hypothesis testing. Examples of hypotheses generated in marketing research abound:

- A cinema is being patronised by more than 10% of the households in a city.
- The heavy and light users of a brand differ in terms of psychographic characteristics.
- One hotel has a more 'luxurious' image than its close competitor.
- Familiarity with a restaurant results in greater preference for that restaurant.

Chapter 15 covered the concepts of the sampling distribution, standard error of the mean or the proportion, and the confidence interval.[3] All these concepts are relevant to hypothesis testing and should be reviewed. We now describe a general procedure for hypothesis testing that can be applied to test hypotheses about a wide range of parameters.

The following steps are involved in hypothesis testing (Figure 18.3).

1 Formulate the null hypothesis H_0 and the alternative hypothesis H_1.

2 Select an appropriate statistical technique and the corresponding test statistic.

3 Choose the level of significance, α.

4 Determine the sample size and collect the data. Calculate the value of the test statistic.

5 Determine the probability associated with the test statistic under the null hypothesis, using the sampling distribution of the test statistic. Alternatively, determine the critical values associated with the test statistic that divide the rejection and non-rejection regions.

6 Compare the probability associated with the test statistic with the level of significance specified. Alternatively, determine whether the test statistic has fallen into the rejection or the non-rejection region.

7 Make the statistical decision to reject or not reject the null hypothesis.

8 Express the statistical decision in terms of the marketing research problem.

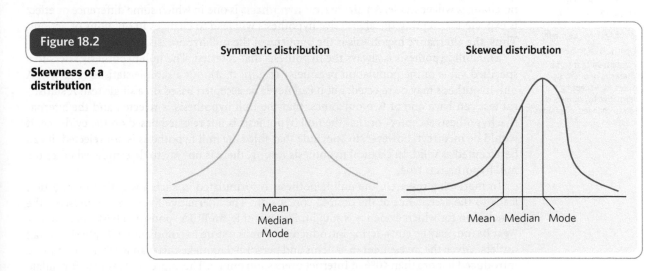

Figure 18.2

Skewness of a distribution

Symmetric distribution

Mean
Median
Mode

Skewed distribution

Mean Median Mode

Figure 18.3

A general procedure for hypothesis testing

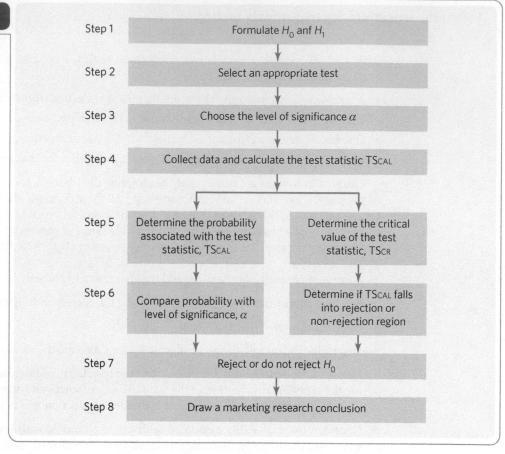

Step 1: Formulate the hypothesis

Null hypothesis
A statement in which no difference or effect is expected. If the null hypothesis is not rejected, no changes will be made.

Alternative hypothesis
A statement that some difference or effect is expected. Accepting the alternative hypothesis will lead to changes in opinions or actions.

The first step is to formulate the null and alternative hypotheses. A null hypothesis is a statement of the status quo, one of no difference or no effect. If the null hypothesis is not rejected, no changes will be made. An alternative hypothesis is one in which some difference or effect is expected. Accepting the alternative hypothesis will lead to changes in opinions or actions. Thus, the alternative hypothesis is the opposite of the null hypothesis.

The null hypothesis is always the hypothesis that is tested. The null hypothesis refers to a specified value of the population parameter (e.g. μ, σ, π), not a sample statistic (e.g. $\overline{X}$,). A null hypothesis may be rejected, but it can never be accepted based on a single test. A statistical test can have one of two outcomes: that the null hypothesis is rejected and the alternative hypothesis accepted, or that the null hypothesis is not rejected based on the evidence. It would be incorrect, however, to conclude that since the null hypothesis is not rejected, it can be accepted as valid. In classical hypothesis testing, there is no way to determine whether the null hypothesis is true.

In marketing research, the null hypothesis is formulated in such a way that its rejection leads to the acceptance of the desired conclusion. The alternative hypothesis represents the conclusion for which evidence is sought. For example, an FIBA sponsor, a basketball sportswear brand, may be considering introducing an online store to complement its physical retail outlets. Given the investment in systems and personnel to make this plan work, it will only be introduced if more than 40% of Internet users shop online. The appropriate way to formulate the hypotheses is

$$H_0: \pi \leq 0.40$$
$$H_1: \pi > 0.40$$

If the null hypothesis H_0 is rejected, then the alternative hypothesis H_1 will be accepted and the new online shopping service introduced. On the other hand, if H_0 is not rejected, then a planned online shopping service should not be introduced until additional supporting evidence is obtained. The test of the null hypothesis is a one-tailed test because the alternative hypothesis is expressed directionally: the proportion of customers who express a preference is greater than 0.40.

On the other hand, suppose that the researcher wanted to determine whether the proportion of Internet users who shop via the Internet is different than 40%. Then a two-tailed test would be required, and the hypotheses would be expressed as

$$H_0: \pi = 0.40$$
$$H_1: \pi \neq 0.40$$

In commercial marketing research, the one-tailed test is used more often than a two-tailed test. Typically, there is some preferred direction for the conclusion for which evidence is sought. For example, the higher the profits, sales and product quality, the better. The one-tailed test is more powerful than the two-tailed test. The power of a statistical test is discussed further in step 3.

Step 2: Select an appropriate statistical technique

To test the null hypothesis, it is necessary to select an appropriate statistical technique. The researcher should take into consideration how the test statistic is computed and the sampling distribution that the sample statistic (e.g. the mean) follows. The test statistic measures how close the sample has come to the null hypothesis. The test statistic often follows a well-known distribution, such as the normal, t, or chi-square distribution. Guidelines for selecting an appropriate test or statistical technique are discussed later in this chapter. In our example, the z statistic, which follows the standard normal distribution, would be appropriate. This statistic would be computed as follows:

$$z = \frac{p - \pi}{\sigma_p} \quad \text{where } \sigma_p = \sqrt{\frac{\pi(1 - \pi)}{n}}$$

Step 3: Choose the level of significance, α

Whenever we draw inferences about a population, there is a risk that an incorrect conclusion will be reached. Two types of error can occur.

Type I error occurs when the sample results lead to the rejection of the null hypothesis when it is in fact true. In our example, a Type I error would occur if we concluded, based on sample data, that the proportion of customers preferring an online store was greater than 0.40, when in fact it was less than or equal to 0.40. The probability of Type I error (α) is also called the level of significance. The Type I error is controlled by establishing the tolerable level of risk of rejecting a true null hypothesis. The selection of a particular risk level should depend on the cost of making a Type I error.

Type II error occurs when, based on the sample results, the null hypothesis is not rejected when it is in fact false. In our example, the Type II error would occur if we concluded, based on sample data, that the proportion of customers preferring an online store was less than or equal to 0.40 when in fact it was greater than 0.40. The probability of Type II error is denoted by β. Unlike α, which is specified by the researcher, the magnitude of β depends on the actual value of the population parameter (proportion). The probability of Type I error (α) and the probability of Type II error (β) are shown in Figure 18.4.

The complement $(1 - \beta)$ of the probability of a Type II error is called the power of a statistical test. The power of a test is the probability $(1 - \beta)$ of rejecting the null hypothesis when it is false and should be rejected. Although β is unknown, it is related to α. An extremely low value of α (e.g. 0.001) will result in intolerably high β errors. So it is necessary to balance the

Marginal glossary

One-tailed test
A test of the null hypothesis where the alternative hypothesis is expressed directionally.

Two-tailed test
A test of the null hypothesis where the alternative hypothesis is not expressed directionally.

Test statistic
A measure of how close the sample has come to the null hypothesis. It often follows a well-known distribution, such as the normal, t, or chi-square distribution.

Type I error
An error that occurs when the sample results lead to the rejection of a null hypothesis that is in fact true. Also called alpha error (α).

Level of significance
The probability of making a Type I error.

Type II error
An error that occurs when the sample results lead to acceptance of a null hypothesis that is in fact false. Also called beta error (β).

Power of a statistical test
The probability of rejecting the null hypothesis when it is in fact false and should be rejected.

Figure 18.4

**Type I error (α) and
Type II error (β)**

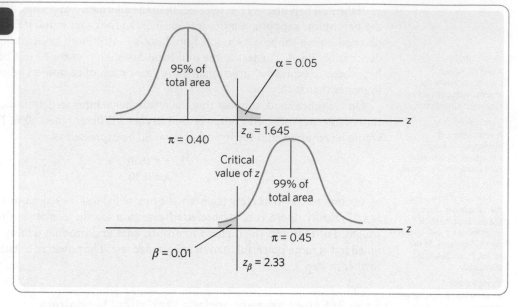

two types of errors. As a compromise, α is often set at 0.05; sometimes it is 0.01; other values of α are rare. The level of α along with the sample size will determine the level of β for a particular research design. The risk of both α and β can be controlled by increasing the sample size. For a given level of α, increasing the sample size will decrease β, thereby increasing the power of the test.

Step 4: Collect the data and calculate the test statistic

Sample size is determined after taking into account the desired α and β errors and other qualitative considerations, such as budget constraints. Then the required data are collected and the value of the test statistic is computed. In our example, 30 users were surveyed and 17 indicated that they shopped online. Thus the value of the sample proportion is $p = 17/30 = 0.567$. The value of σ_p can be determined as follows:

$$\sigma_p = \sqrt{\pi(1-\pi)/n}$$
$$= \sqrt{0.4 \times 0.6/30}$$
$$= 0.089$$

The test statistic z can be calculated as follows:

$$z = p - \pi/\sigma_p$$
$$= 0.567 - 0.40/0.089$$
$$= 1.88$$

Step 5: Determine the probability or the critical value

p value

This is the probability of observing a value of the test statistic as extreme as, or more extreme than, the value actually observed, assuming that the null hypothesis is true.

Using standard normal tables (Table 2 of the Appendix of statistical tables), the probability of obtaining a z value of 1.88 can be calculated (see Figure 18.5). The shaded area between $-\infty$ and 1.88 is 0.9699. Therefore, the area to the right of $z = 1.88$ is $1.0000 - 0.9699 = 0.0301$. This is also called the *p value* and is the probability of observing a value of the test statistic as extreme as, or more extreme than, the value actually observed, assuming the null hypothesis is true.

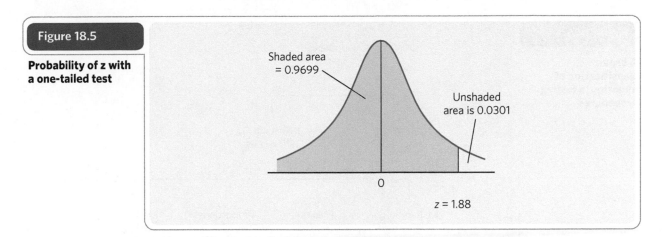

Figure 18.5

Probability of z with a one-tailed test

Shaded area = 0.9699

Unshaded area is 0.0301

0

$z = 1.88$

Alternatively, the critical value of z, which will give an area to the right side of the critical value of 0.05, is between 1.64 and 1.65 and equals 1.645. Note that, in determining the critical value of the test statistic, the area to the right of the critical value is either α or $\alpha/2$. It is α for a one-tailed test and $\alpha/2$ for a two-tailed test.

Steps 6 and 7: Compare the probability or critical values and make the decision

The probability associated with the calculated or observed value of the test statistic is 0.0301. This is the probability of getting a p value of 0.567 when $\pi = 0.40$. This is less than the level of significance of 0.05. Hence, the null hypothesis is rejected. Alternatively, the calculated value of the test statistic $z = 1.88$ lies in the rejection region, beyond the value of 1.645. Again, the same conclusion to reject the null hypothesis is reached. Note that the two ways of testing the null hypothesis are equivalent but mathematically opposite in the direction of comparison. If the probability associated with the calculated or observed value of the test statistic (TS_{CAL}) is less than the level of significance (α), the null hypothesis is rejected. If the calculated value of the test statistic is greater than the critical value of the test statistic (TS_{CR}), however, the null hypothesis is rejected. The reason for this sign shift is that the larger the value of TS_{CAL}, the smaller the probability of obtaining a more extreme value of the test statistic under the null hypothesis. This sign shift can be easily seen:

if probability of TS_{CAL} < significance level (α), then reject H_0

but

if $|TS_{CAL}| > |TS_{CR}|$, then reject H_0

Step 8: Draw the marketing research conclusion

The conclusion reached by hypothesis testing must be expressed in terms of the marketing research problem. In our example, we conclude that there is evidence that the proportion of Internet users who shop online is significantly greater than 0.40. Hence, the recommendation would be to launch the new online store.

As can be seen from Figure 18.6, hypothesis testing can be related to either an examination of associations or an examination of differences. In tests of associations the null hypothesis is that there is no association between the variables (H_0: ... is *not* related to ...). In tests of differences the null hypothesis is that there is no difference (H_0: ... is *not* different than ...). Tests of differences could relate to distributions, means, proportions, or medians or rankings. First, we discuss hypotheses related to associations in the context of cross-tabulations.

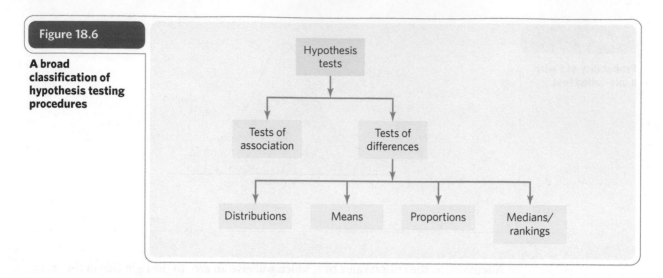

Figure 18.6

A broad classification of hypothesis testing procedures

Cross-tabulations

Although answers to questions related to a single variable are interesting, they often raise additional questions about how to link that variable to other variables. To introduce the frequency distribution, we posed several representative marketing research questions. For each of these, a researcher might pose additional questions to relate these variables to other variables. For example:

- How many brand-loyal users are males?
- Is product use (measured in terms of heavy users, medium users, light users and non-users) related to interest in outdoor leisure activities (high, medium and low)?
- Is familiarity with a new product related to age and income levels?
- Is product ownership related to income (high, medium and low)?

Cross-tabulation
A statistical technique that describes two or more variables simultaneously and results in tables that reflect the joint distribution of two or more variables that have a limited number of categories or distinct values.

Contingency table
A cross-tabulation table. It contains a cell for every combination of categories of the two variables.

The answers to such questions can be determined by examining cross-tabulations. A frequency distribution describes one variable at a time, but a cross-tabulation describes two or more variables simultaneously. A cross-tabulation is the merging of the frequency distribution of two or more variables in a single table. It helps us to understand how one variable such as brand loyalty relates to another variable such as gender. Cross-tabulation results in tables that reflect the joint distribution of two or more variables with a limited number of categories or distinct values. The categories of one variable are cross-classified with the categories of one or more other variables. Thus, the frequency distribution of one variable is subdivided according to the values or categories of the other variables.

Suppose we are interested in determining whether Internet usage is related to gender. For the purpose of cross-tabulation, participants are classified as 'light' or 'heavy' users. Those reporting five hours or less usage were classified as 'light' users, and the remaining were 'heavy' users. The cross-tabulation is shown in Table 18.3. A cross-tabulation includes a cell for every combination of the categories of the two variables. The number in each cell shows how many participants gave that combination of responses. In Table 18.3, 10 participants were females who reported light Internet usage. The marginal totals in this table indicate that of the 30 participants with valid responses on both variables, 15 reported light usage and 15 were heavy users. In terms of gender, 15 participants were females and 15 were males. Note that this information could have been obtained from a separate frequency distribution for each variable. In general, the margins of a cross-tabulation show the same information as the frequency tables for each of the variables. Cross-tabulation tables are also called contingency tables. The data are considered to be qualitative or categorical data, because each variable is assumed to have only a nominal scale.[4]

Cross-tabulation is widely used in commercial marketing research because: (1) cross-tabulation analysis and results can be easily interpreted and understood by managers who are not statistically oriented; (2) the clarity of interpretation provides a stronger link between research results and managerial action; (3) a series of cross-tabulations may provide greater insights into a complex phenomenon than a single multivariate analysis; (4) cross-tabulation may alleviate the problem of sparse cells, which could be serious in discrete multivariate analysis; and (5) cross-tabulation analysis is simple to conduct and appealing to both qualitative and quantitative researchers.[5] We discuss cross-tabulation for two and three variables.

Two variables

Cross-tabulation with two variables is also known as bivariate cross-tabulation. Consider again the cross-classification of Internet usage with gender given in Table 18.3. Is usage related to gender? It appears to be from Table 18.3. We see that disproportionately more of the participants who are male are heavy Internet users as compared with females. Computation of percentages can provide more insight.

Because two variables have been cross-classified, percentages could be computed either column-wise, based on column totals (Table 18.4), or row-wise, based on row totals (Table 18.5). Which table is more useful?

Table 18.3	Gender and Internet usage		
	Gender		Row total
Internet usage	Male	Female	
Light (1)	5	10	15
Heavy (2)	10	5	15
Column totals	15	15	

Table 18.4	Gender and Internet usage – column totals	
	Gender	
Internet usage	Male	Female
Light (1)	33.3%	66.7%
Heavy (2)	66.7%	33.3%
Column totals	100%	100%

Table 18.5	Gender and Internet usage – row totals		
	Gender total		Row total
Internet usage	Male	Female	
Light (1)	33.3%	66.7%	100%
Heavy (2)	66.7%	33.3%	100%

The answer depends on which variable will be considered as the independent variable and which as the dependent variable.[6] The general rule is to compute the percentages in the direction of the independent variable, across the dependent variable. In our analysis, gender may be considered as the independent variable and Internet usage as the dependent variable, and the correct way of calculating percentages is shown in Table 18.4. Note that whereas 66.7% of the males are heavy users, only 33.3% of females fall into this category. This seems to indicate that males are more likely to be heavy users of the Internet as compared with females.

Note that computing percentages in the direction of the dependent variable across the independent variable, as shown in Table 18.5, is not meaningful in this case. Table 18.5 implies that heavy Internet usage causes people to be males. This latter finding is implausible. It is possible, however, that the association between Internet usage and gender is mediated by a third variable, such as age or income. This kind of possibility points to the need to examine the effect of a third variable.

Three variables

Often the introduction of a third variable clarifies the initial association (or lack of it) observed between two variables. As shown in Figure 18.7, the introduction of a third variable can result in four possibilities:

1 It can refine the association observed between the two original variables.

2 It can indicate no association between the two variables, although an association was initially observed. In other words, the third variable indicates that the initial association between the two variables was spurious.

3 It can reveal some association between the two original variables, although no association was initially observed. In this case, the third variable reveals a suppressed association between the first two variables: a suppressor effect.

4 It can indicate no change in the initial association.[7]

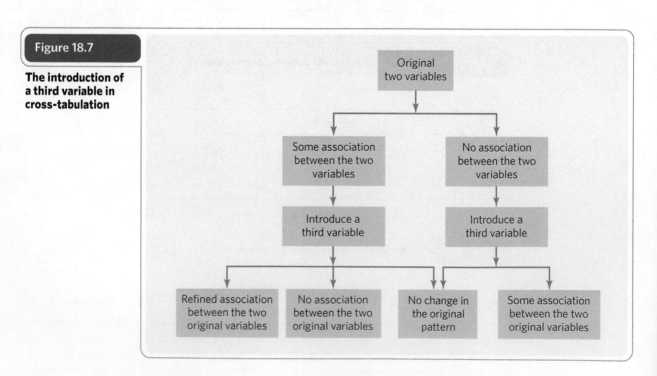

Figure 18.7

The introduction of a third variable in cross-tabulation

These cases are explained with examples based on a sample of 1,000 participants. Although these examples are contrived to illustrate specific cases, such sample sizes are not uncommon in commercial marketing research.

Refine an initial relationship. An examination of the relationship between the purchase of luxury branded clothing and marital status resulted in the data reported in Table 18.6. The participants were classified into either high or low categories based on their purchase of luxury branded clothing. Marital status was also measured in terms of two categories: currently married or unmarried. As can be seen from Table 18.6, 52% of unmarried participants fell in the high-purchase category as opposed to 31% of the married participants. Before concluding that unmarried participants purchase more luxury branded clothing than those who are married, a third variable, the buyer's gender, was introduced into the analysis.

The buyer's gender was selected as the third variable based on past research. The relationship between purchase of luxury branded clothing and marital status was re-examined in light of the third variable, as shown in Table 18.7. In the case of females, 60% of the unmarried participants fall in the high-purchase category compared with 25% of those who are married. On the other hand, the percentages are much closer for males, with 40% of the unmarried participants and 35% of the married participants falling in the high-purchase category. Hence, the

Table 18.6	Purchase of luxury branded clothing by marital status	
Purchase of luxury branded clothing	Marital status	
	Married	Unmarried
High	31%	52%
Low	69%	48%
Column	100%	100%
Number of participants	700	300

Table 18.7	Purchase of luxury branded clothing by marital status and gender			
Purchase of luxury branded clothing	Gender			
	Male marital status		Female marital status	
	Married	Unmarried	Married	Unmarried
High	35%	40%	25%	60%
Low	65%	60%	75%	40%
Column	100%	100%	100%	100%
Number of participants	400	120	300	180

introduction of gender (third variable) has refined the relationship between marital status and purchase of luxury branded clothing (original variables). Unmarried participants are more likely to fall into the high-purchase category than married ones, and this effect is much more pronounced for females than for males.

Initial relationship was spurious. A researcher working for an advertising agency promoting a car brand costing more than €80,000 was attempting to explain the ownership of expensive cars (see Table 18.8). The table shows that 32% of those with university degrees own an expensive (more than €80,000) car compared with 21% of those without university degrees. The researcher was tempted to conclude that education influenced ownership of expensive cars. Realising that income may also be a factor, the researcher decided to re-examine the relationship between education and ownership of expensive cars in the light of income level. This resulted in Table 18.9. Note that the percentages of those with and without university degrees who own expensive cars are the same for each income group. When the data for the high-income and low-income groups are examined separately, the association between education and ownership of expensive cars disappears, indicating that the initial relationship observed between these two variables was spurious.

Reveal suppressed association. A researcher suspected that desire to travel abroad may be influenced by age. A cross-tabulation of the two variables produced the results in Table 18.10, indicating no association. When gender was introduced as the third variable, Table 18.11 was obtained. Among men, 60% of those under 45 indicated a desire to travel abroad compared with 40% of those 45 or older. The pattern was reversed for women, where 35% of those under 45 indicated a desire to travel abroad as opposed to 65% of those 45 or older.

Table 18.8	Ownership of expensive cars by education level	
Own expensive car	Education	
	Degree	No degree
Yes	32%	21%
No	68%	79%
Column	100%	100%
Number of participants	250	750

Table 18.9	Ownership of expensive cars by education and income levels			
	Income			
Own expensive car	Low-income education		High-income education	
	Degree	No degree	Degree	No degree
Yes	20%	20%	40%	40%
No	80%	80%	60%	60%
Column totals	100%	100%	100%	100%
Number of participants	100	700	150	50

Since the association between desire to travel abroad and age runs in the opposite direction for males and females, the relationship between these two variables is masked when the data are aggregated across gender as in Table 18.10. But when the effect of gender is controlled, as in Table 18.11, the suppressed association between preference and age is revealed for the separate categories of males and females.

No change in initial relationship. In some cases, the introduction of the third variable does not change the initial relationship observed, regardless of whether the original variables were associated. This suggests that the third variable does not influence the relationship between the first two. Consider the cross-tabulation of family size and the tendency to eat in

Table 18.10	Desire to travel abroad by age	

Desire to travel abroad	Age	
	Under 45	45 or older
Yes	50%	50%
No	50%	50%
Column totals	100%	100%
Number of participants	500	500

Table 18.11	Desire to travel abroad by age and gender			

Desire to travel abroad	Gender			
	Male age		Female age	
	Under 45	45 or older	Under 45	45 or older
Yes	60%	40%	35%	65%
No	40%	60%	65%	35%
Column totals	100%	100%	100%	100%
Number of participants	300	300	200	200

Table 18.12	Eating frequently in fast-food restaurants by family size	

Eat frequently in fast-food restaurants	Family size	
	Small	Large
Yes	65%	65%
No	35%	35%
Column totals	100%	100%
Number of participants	500	500

fast-food restaurants frequently, as shown in Table 18.12. The participants' families were classified into small- and large-size categories based on a median split of the distribution, with 500 participants in each category. No association is observed. The participants were further classified into high- or low-income groups based on a median split. When income was introduced as a third variable in the analysis, Table 18.13 was obtained. Again, no association was observed.

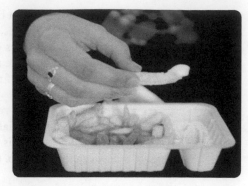

Table 18.13	Eating frequently in fast-food restaurants by family size and income			
	Income			
Eat frequently in fast-food restaurants	*Low-income family size*		*High-income family size*	
	Small	*Large*	*Small*	*Large*
Yes	65%	65%	65%	65%
No	35%	35%	35%	35%
Column total	100%	100%	100%	100%
Number of participants	250	250	250	250

General comments on cross-tabulation

More than three variables can be cross-tabulated; the interpretation is quite complex. Also, because the number of cells increases multiplicatively, maintaining an adequate number of participants or cases in each cell can be problematic. As a general rule, there should be at least five expected observations in each cell for the computed statistics to be reliable. Thus, cross-tabulation is an inefficient way of examining relationships when there are more than a few variables. Note that cross-tabulation examines association between variables, not causation. To examine causation, the causal research design framework should be adopted (see Chapter 11).

Statistics associated with cross-tabulation

We now discuss the statistics commonly used for assessing the statistical significance and strength of association of cross-tabulated variables. The statistical significance of the observed association is commonly measured by the chi-square statistic. The strength of association, or degree of association, is important from a practical or substantive perspective. Generally, the strength of association is of interest only if the association is statistically significant. The strength of the association can be measured by the phi correlation coefficient, the contingency coefficient, Cramer's V and the lambda coefficient. These statistics are described in detail.

Chi-square statistic
The statistic used to test the statistical significance of the observed association in a cross-tabulation. It assists us in determining whether a systematic association exists between the two variables.

Chi-square

The chi-square statistic (χ^2) is used to test the statistical significance of the observed association in a cross-tabulation. It assists us in determining whether a systematic association exists between the two variables. The null hypothesis, H_0, is that there is no association between the variables. The test is conducted by computing the cell frequencies that would be expected if no association were present between the variables, given the existing row and column totals. These expected cell frequencies, denoted f_e, are then compared with the actual observed frequencies, f_o, found in the cross-tabulation to calculate the chi-square statistic. The greater the discrepancies between the expected and observed frequencies, the larger the value of the statistic. Assume that a cross-tabulation has r rows and c columns and a random sample of n observations. Then the expected frequency for each cell can be calculated by using a simple formula:

$$f_e = \frac{n_r n_c}{n}$$

where n_r = total number in the row
n_c = total number in the column
n = total sample size

For the data in Table 18.3, the expected frequencies for the cells, going from left to right and from top to bottom, are

$$15 \times 15/30 = 7.50, \ 15 \ 15/30 = 7.50, \ 15 \times 15/30 = 7.50, \ 15 \times 15/30 = 7.50$$

Then the value of χ^2 is calculated as follows:

$$\chi^2 = \sum_{all\ cells} \frac{\left(f_o - f_e\right)^2}{f_e}$$

For the data in Table 18.2, the value of χ^2 is calculated as

$$\chi^2 = (5 - 7.5)^2/7.5 + (10 - 7.5)^2/7.5 + (10 - 7.5)^2/7.5 + (5 - 7.5)^2/7.5$$
$$= 0.833 + 0.833 + 0.833 + 0.833$$
$$= 3.333$$

To determine whether a systematic association exists, the probability of obtaining a value of chi-square as large as or larger than the one calculated from the cross-tabulation is estimated. An important characteristic of the chi-square statistic is the number of degrees of freedom (df) associated with it. In general, the number of degrees of freedom is equal to the number of observations less the number of constraints needed to calculate a statistical term. In the case of a chi-square statistic associated with a cross-tabulation, the number of degrees of freedom is equal to the product of number of rows (r) less one and the number of columns (c) less one. That is, $df = (r - 1) \times (c - 1)$.[8] The null hypothesis (H_0) of no association between the two variables will be rejected only when the calculated value of the test statistic is greater than the critical value of the chi-square distribution with the appropriate degrees of freedom, as shown in Figure 18.8.

The **chi-square distribution** is a skewed distribution whose shape depends solely on the number of degrees of freedom.[9] As the number of degrees of freedom increases, the chi-square distribution becomes more symmetrical. Table 3 in the Appendix of statistical tables contains

Chi-square distribution
A skewed distribution whose shape depends solely on the number of degrees of freedom. As the number of degrees of freedom increases, the chi-square distribution becomes more symmetrical.

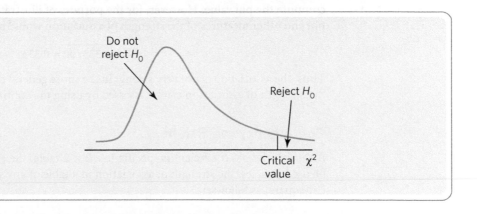

Figure 18.8

Chi-square test of association

Do not reject H_0

Reject H_0

Critical value χ^2

upper tail areas of the chi-square distribution for different degrees of freedom. In this table, the value at the top of each column indicates the area in the upper portion (the right side, as shown in Figure 18.8) of the chi-square distribution. To illustrate, for 1 degree of freedom, the value for an upper tail area of 0.05 is 3.841. This indicates that for 1 degree of freedom the probability of exceeding a chi-square value of 3.841 is 0.05. In other words, at the 0.05 level of significance with 1 degree of freedom, the critical value of the chi-square statistic is 3.841.

For the cross-tabulation given in Table 18.3, there are $(2 - 1) \times (2 - 1) = 1$ degree of freedom. The calculated chi-square statistic had a value of 3.333. Because this is less than the critical value of 3.841, the null hypothesis of no association cannot be rejected, indicating that the association is not statistically significant at the 0.05 level. Note that this lack of significance is mainly due to the small sample size (30). If, instead, the sample size were 300 and each data entry of Table 18.3 were multiplied by 10, it can be seen that the value of the chi-square statistic would be multiplied by 10 and would be 33.33, which is significant at the 0.05 level.

The chi-square statistic can also be used in goodness-of-fit tests to determine whether certain models fit the observed data. These tests are conducted by calculating the significance of sample deviations from assumed theoretical (expected) distributions and can be performed on cross-tabulations as well as on frequencies (one-way tabulations). The calculation of the chi-square statistic and the determination of its significance are the same as illustrated above.

The chi-square statistic should be estimated only on counts of data. When the data are in percentage form, they should first be converted to absolute counts or numbers. In addition, an underlying assumption of the chi-square test is that the observations are drawn independently. As a general rule, chi-square analysis should not be conducted when the expected or theoretical frequency in any of the cells is less than five. If the number of observations in any cell is less than 10, or if the table has two rows and two columns (a 2×2 table), a correction factor should be applied.[10] With the correction factor, the value is 2.133, which is not significant at the 0.05 level. In the case of a 2×2 table, the chi-square is related to the phi coefficient.

Phi coefficient

Phi coefficient (ϕ)
A measure of the strength of association in the special case of a table with two rows and two columns (a 2×2 table).

Contingency coefficient
A measure of the strength of association in a table of any size.

The **phi coefficient** (ϕ) is used as a measure of the strength of association in the special case of a table with two rows and two columns (a 2×2 table). The phi coefficient is proportional to the square root of the chi-square statistic. For a sample of size n, this statistic is calculated as

$$\phi = \sqrt{\frac{\chi^2}{n}}$$

It takes the value of 0 when there is no association, which would be indicated by a chi-square value of 0 as well. When the variables are perfectly associated, phi assumes the value of 1 and all the observations fall just on the main or minor diagonal. (In some computer programs, phi assumes a value of –1 rather than +1 when there is perfect negative association.) In our case, because the association was not significant at the 0.05 level, we would not normally compute the phi value. However, for the purpose of illustration, we show how the values of phi and other measures of the strength of association would be computed. The value of phi is

$$\phi = \sqrt{3.333 / 30} = 0.333$$

Thus, the association is not very strong. In the more general case involving a table of any size, the strength of association can be assessed by using the contingency coefficient.

Contingency coefficient

Although the phi coefficient is specific to a 2×2 table, the **contingency coefficient** (C) can be used to assess the strength of association in a table of any size. This index is also related to chi-square, as follows:

$$C = \sqrt{\frac{\chi^2}{\chi^2 + n}}$$

The contingency coefficient varies between 0 and 1. The value of 0 occurs in the case of no association (i.e. the variables are statistically independent), but the maximum value of 1 is never achieved. Rather, the maximum value of the contingency coefficient depends on the size of the table (number of rows and number of columns). For this reason, it should be used only to compare tables of the same size. The value of the contingency coefficient for Table 18.3 is

$$C = \sqrt{3.333/(3.333 + 30)} = 0.316$$

This value of C indicates that the association is not very strong. Another statistic that can be calculated for any table is Cramer's V.

Cramer's V

Cramer's V
A measure of the strength of association used in tables larger than 2 × 2.

Asymmetric lambda
A measure of the percentage improvement in predicting the value of the dependent variable given the value of the independent variable in contingency table analysis. Lambda also varies between 0 and 1.

Symmetric lambda
The symmetric lambda does not make an assumption about which variable is dependent. It measures the overall improvement when prediction is done in both directions.

Cramer's V is a modified version of the phi correlation coefficient, ϕ, and is used in tables larger than 2 × 2. When phi is calculated for a table larger than 2 × 2, it has no upper limit. Cramer's V is obtained by adjusting phi for either the number of rows or the number of columns in the table based on which of the two is smaller. The adjustment is such that V will range from 0 to 1. A large value of V merely indicates a high degree of association. It does not indicate how the variables are associated. For a table with r rows and c columns, the relationship between Cramer's V and the phi correlation coefficient is expressed as

$$V = \sqrt{\frac{\phi^2}{\min(r-1),\ (c-1)}}$$

or

$$V = \sqrt{\frac{\chi^2/n}{\min(r-1),\ (c-1)}}$$

The value of Cramer's V for Table 18.3 is

$$V = \sqrt{(3.333/30)/1} = 0.333$$

Thus, the association is not very strong. As can be seen, in this case $V = \phi$. This is always the case for a 2 × 2 table. Another statistic commonly estimated is the lambda coefficient.

Lambda coefficient

The lambda coefficient assumes that the variables are measured on a nominal scale. Asymmetric lambda measures the percentage improvement in predicting the value of the dependent variable, given the value of the independent variable. The lambda coefficient also varies between 0 and 1. A value of 0 means no improvement in prediction. A value of 1 indicates that the prediction can be made without error. This happens when each independent variable category is associated with a single category of the dependent variable.

Asymmetric lambda is computed for each of the variables (treating it as the dependent variable). In general, the two asymmetric lambdas are likely to be different, since the marginal distributions are not usually the same. A symmetric lambda is also computed, which is a kind of average of the two asymmetric values. The symmetric lambda does not make an assumption about which variable is dependent. It measures the overall improvement when prediction is done in both directions.[11] The value of asymmetric lambda in Table 18.3, with usage as the dependent variable, is 0.333. This indicates that knowledge of gender increases our predictive ability by the proportion of 0.333, i.e. a 33% improvement. The symmetric lambda is also 0.333.

Other statistics

tau *b*

A test statistic that measures the association between two ordinal-level variables. It makes an adjustment for ties and is the most appropriate when the table of variables is square.

tau *c*

A test statistic that measures the association between two ordinal-level variables. It makes an adjustment for ties and is most appropriate when the table of variables is not square but a rectangle.

Gamma

A test statistic that measures the association between two ordinal-level variables. It does not make an adjustment for ties.

Note that in the calculation of the chi-square statistic the variables are treated as being measured only on a nominal scale. Other statistics such as **tau** *b*, **tau** *c* and **gamma** are available to measure association between two ordinal-level variables. All these statistics use information about the ordering of categories of variables by considering every possible pair of cases in the table. Each pair is examined to determine whether its relative ordering on the first variable is the same as its relative ordering on the second variable (concordant), the ordering is reversed (discordant), or the pair is tied. The manner in which the ties are treated is the basic difference between these statistics. Both tau *b* and tau *c* adjust for ties. Tau *b* is the most appropriate with square tables in which the number of rows and the number of columns are equal. Its value varies between +1 and –1. Thus the direction (positive or negative) as well as the strength (how close the value is to 1) of the relationship can be determined. For a rectangular table in which the number of rows is different from the number of columns, tau *c* should be used. Gamma does not make an adjustment for either ties or table size. Gamma also varies between +1 and –1 and generally has a higher numerical value than tau *b* or tau *c*. For the data in Table 18.3, as gender is a nominal variable, it is not appropriate to calculate ordinal statistics. All these statistics can be estimated by using the appropriate analysis software that incorporates cross-tabulation. Other statistics for measuring the strength of association, namely product moment correlation and non-metric correlation, are discussed in Chapter 20.

Cross-tabulation in practice

While conducting cross-tabulation analysis in practice, it is useful to proceed through the following steps:

1 Test the null hypothesis that there is no association between the variables using the chi-square statistic. If you fail to reject the null hypothesis, then there is no relationship.

2 If H_0 is rejected, then determine the strength of the association using an appropriate statistic (phi coefficient, contingency coefficient, Cramer's *V*, lambda coefficient, or other statistics).

3 If H_0 is rejected, interpret the pattern of the relationship by computing the percentages in the direction of the independent variable, across the dependent variable.

4 If the variables are treated as ordinal rather than nominal, use tau *b*, tau *c* or gamma as the test statistic. If H_0 is rejected, then determine the strength of the association using the magnitude, and the direction of the relationship using the sign of the test statistic.

5 Translate the results of hypothesis testing, strength of association and pattern of association into managerial implications and recommendations.

Hypothesis testing related to differences

The previous section considered hypothesis testing related to associations. We now focus on hypothesis testing related to differences. A classification of hypothesis testing procedures for examining differences is presented in Figure 18.9. Note that this figure is consistent with the classification of univariate techniques presented in Figure 17.4. The major difference is that Figure 17.4 also accommodates more than two samples and thus deals with techniques such as one-way ANOVA and K–W ANOVA (Chapter 17), whereas Figure 18.9 is limited to no more than two samples. Also, one-sample techniques such as frequencies, which do not involve statistical testing, are not covered in Figure 18.9.

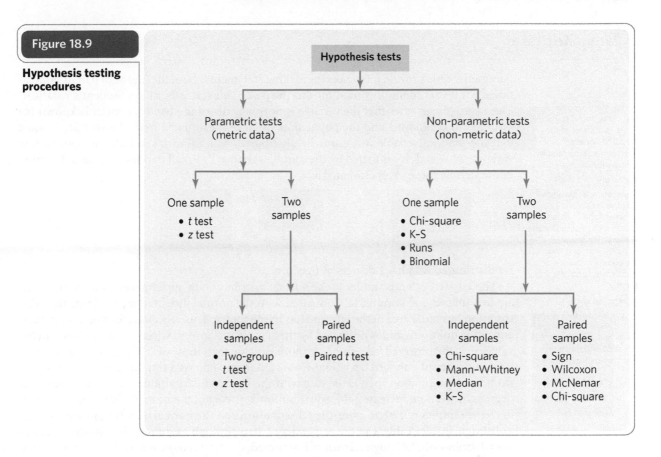

Figure 18.9

Hypothesis testing procedures

Hypothesis testing procedures can be broadly classified as parametric or non-parametric, based on the measurement scale of the variables involved. Parametric tests assume that the variables of interest are measured on at least an interval scale. Non-parametric tests assume that the variables are measured on a nominal or ordinal scale. These tests can be further classified based on whether one or two or more samples are involved. As explained in Chapter 17, the number of samples is determined based on how the data are treated for the purpose of analysis, not based on how the data were collected. The samples are independent if they are drawn randomly from different populations. For the purpose of analysis, data pertaining to different groups of participants, e.g. males and females, are generally treated as independent samples. On the other hand, the samples are paired when the data for the two samples relate to the same group of participants.

The most popular parametric test is the *t* test conducted for examining hypotheses about means. The *t* test could be conducted on the mean of one sample or two samples of observations. In the case of two samples, the samples could be independent or paired. Non-parametric tests based on observations drawn from one sample include the chi-square test, the Kolmogorov–Smirnov test, the runs test and the binomial test. In the case of two independent samples, the chi-square test, the Mann–Whitney *U* test, the median test and the Kolmogorov–Smirnov two-sample test are used for examining hypotheses about location. These tests are non-parametric counterparts of the two-group *t* test. For paired samples, non-parametric tests include the Wilcoxon matched-pairs signed-ranks test and the sign test. These tests are the counterparts of the paired *t* test. In addition, the McNemar and chi-square tests can also be used. Parametric as well as non-parametric tests are also available for evaluating hypotheses relating to more than two samples. These tests are considered in later chapters.

Parametric tests
Hypothesis testing procedures that assume that the variables of interest are measured on at least an interval scale.

Non-parametric tests
Hypothesis testing procedures that assume that the variables are measured on a nominal or ordinal scale.

Parametric tests

Parametric tests provide inferences for making statements about the means of parent populations. A *t* test is commonly used for this purpose. This test is based on Student's *t* statistic. The *t* statistic assumes that the variable is normally distributed and the mean is known (or assumed to be known) and the population variance is estimated from the sample. Assume that the random variable X is normally distributed, with mean μ and unknown population variance σ^2, which is estimated by the sample variance s^2. Recall that the standard deviation of the sample mean, $\overline{X}$, is estimated as

$$s_{\overline{X}} = s/\sqrt{n}$$

Then

$$t = (\overline{X} - \mu)/s_{\overline{X}}$$

is t distributed with $n-1$ degrees of freedom.

The *t distribution* is similar to the normal distribution in appearance. Both distributions are bell shaped and symmetric. Compared with the normal distribution, however, the *t* distribution has more area in the tails and less in the centre. This is because the population variance σ^2 is unknown and is estimated by the sample variance s^2. Given the uncertainty in the value of s^2, the observed values of *t* are more variable than those of *z*. Thus, we must go out a larger number of standard deviations from zero to encompass a certain percentage of values from the *t* distribution than is the case with the normal distribution. Yet, as the number of degrees of freedom increases, the *t* distribution approaches the normal distribution. In fact, for large samples of 120 or more, the *t* distribution and the normal distribution are virtually indistinguishable. Table 4 in the Appendix of statistical tables shows selected percentiles of the *t* distribution. Although normality is assumed, the *t* test is quite robust to departures from normality.

The procedure for hypothesis testing, for the special case when the *t* statistic is used, is as follows:

1 Formulate the null (H_0) and the alternative (H_1) hypotheses.

2 Select the appropriate formula for the *t* statistic.

3 Select a significance level, α, for testing H_0. Typically, the 0.05 level is selected.[12]

4 Take one or two samples and compute the mean and standard deviation for each sample.

5 Calculate the *t* statistic assuming that H_0 is true.

6 Calculate the degrees of freedom and estimate the probability of getting a more extreme value of the statistic from Table 4 in the Appendix. (Alternatively, calculate the critical value of the *t* statistic.)

7 If the probability computed in step 6 is smaller than the significance level selected in step 3, reject H_0. If the probability is larger, do not reject H_0. (Alternatively, if the absolute value of the calculated *t* statistic in step 5 is larger than the absolute critical value determined in step 6, reject H_0. If the absolute calculated value is smaller than the absolute critical value, do not reject H_0.) Failure to reject H_0 does not necessarily imply that H_0 is true. It only means that the true state is not significantly different from that assumed by H_0.[13]

8 Express the conclusion reached by the *t* test in terms of the marketing research problem.

We illustrate the general procedure for conducting *t* tests in the following sections, beginning with the one-sample case.

One sample

In marketing research, the researcher is often interested in making statements about a single variable against a known or given standard. Examples of such statements are that the market share for a new product will exceed 15%, at least 65% of customers will like a new package design, and 80% of retailers will prefer a new pricing policy. These statements can be translated to null hypotheses that can be tested using a one-sample test, such as the *t* test or the *z* test. In the case of a *t* test for a single mean, the researcher is interested in testing whether the population mean conforms to a given hypothesis (H_0). For the data in Table 18.2, suppose we wanted to test the hypothesis that the mean familiarity rating exceeds 4.0, the neutral value on a seven-point scale. A significance level of $\alpha = 0.05$ is selected. The hypothesis may be formulated as

$$H_0: \mu \leq 4.0$$
$$H_1: \mu > 4.0$$
$$t = (\overline{X} - \mu)/s_{\overline{X}}$$
$$s_{\overline{X}} = s/\sqrt{n}$$
$$s_{\overline{X}} = 1.579/\sqrt{29} = 1.579/5.385 = 0.293$$
$$t = (4.724 - 4.0)/0.293 = 0.724/0.293 = 2.471$$

The degrees of freedom for the t statistic to test the hypothesis about one mean are $n - 1$. In this case, $n - 1 = 29 - 1$, or 28. From Table 4 in the Appendix, the probability of getting a more extreme value than 2.471 is less than 0.05. (Alternatively, the critical *t* value for 28 degrees of freedom and a significance level of 0.05 is 1.7011, which is less than the calculated value.) Hence, the null hypothesis is rejected. The familiarity level does not exceed 4.0.

Note that if the population standard deviation was assumed to be known as 1.5, rather than estimated from the sample, a *z* test would be appropriate. In this case, the value of the *z* statistic would be

z test
A univariate hypothesis test using the standard normal distribution.

$$z = \frac{\overline{X} - \mu}{\sigma_{\overline{X}}}$$

where

$$\sigma_{\overline{X}} = 1.5/\sqrt{29} = 1.5/5.385 = 0.279$$

and

$$z = (4.724 - 4.0)/0.279 = 0.724/0.279 = 2.595$$

From Table 2 in the Appendix of statistical tables, the probability of getting a more extreme value of *z* than 2.595 is less than 0.05. (Alternatively, the critical *z* value for a one-tailed test and a significance level of 0.05 is 1.645, which is less than the calculated value.) Therefore, the null hypothesis is rejected, reaching the same conclusion arrived at earlier by the *t* test.

The procedure for testing a null hypothesis with respect to a proportion was illustrated earlier in this chapter when we introduced hypothesis testing.

Two independent samples

Several hypotheses in marketing relate to parameters from two different populations: for example, the users and non-users of a brand differ in terms of their perceptions of the brand, high-income consumers spend more on leisure activities than low-income consumers, or the proportion of brand-loyal users in segment I is more than the proportion in segment II. Samples drawn randomly from different populations are termed **independent samples**. As in the case for one sample, the hypotheses could relate to means or proportions.

Independent samples
The samples are independent if they are drawn randomly from different populations.

Means. In the case of means for two independent samples, the hypotheses take the following form:

$$H_0: \mu_1 = \mu_2$$
$$H_1: \mu_1 \neq \mu_2$$

The two populations are sampled and the means and variances are computed based on samples of sizes n_1 and n_2. If both populations are found to have the same variance, a pooled variance estimate is computed from the two sample variances as follows:

$$s^2 = \frac{\sum_{i=1}^{n_1}\left(X_{i_1} - \overline{X}_1\right)^2 + \sum_{i=1}^{n_2}\left(X_{i_2} - \overline{X}_2\right)^2}{n_1 + n_2 - 2} \qquad s^2 = \frac{\left(n_1 - 1\right)s_1^2 + \left(n^2 - 1\right)s_2^2}{n_1 + n_2 - 2}$$

The standard deviation of the test statistic can be estimated as

$$s_{\overline{X}_1 - \overline{X}_2} = \sqrt{s^2\left(\frac{1}{n_1} + \frac{1}{n_2}\right)}$$

The appropriate value of t can be calculated as

$$t = \frac{\left(\overline{X}_1 - \overline{X}_2\right) - \left(\mu_1 - \mu_2\right)}{s_{\overline{X}_1 - \overline{X}_2}}$$

The degrees of freedom in this case are $(n_1 + n_2 - 2)$.

If the two populations have unequal variances, an exact t cannot be computed for the difference in sample means. Instead, an approximation to t is computed. The number of degrees of freedom in this case is usually not an integer, but a reasonably accurate probability can be obtained by rounding to the nearest integer.[14]

An *F* test of sample variance may be performed if it is not known whether the two populations have equal variance. In this case the hypotheses are

$$H_0: \sigma_1^2 = \sigma_2^2$$
$$H_1: \sigma_1^2 \neq \sigma_2^2$$

The *F* statistic is computed from the sample variances as follows:

$$F\left(n_1 - 1\right),\left(n_2 - 1\right) = \frac{s_1^2}{s_2^2}$$

where
  n_1 = size of sample 1
  n_2 = size of sample 2
  $n_1 - 1$ = degrees of freedom for sample 1
  $n_2 - 1$ = degrees of freedom for sample 2
  s_1^2 = sample variance for sample 1
  s_2^2 = sample variance for sample 2

As can be seen, the critical value of the *F distribution* depends on two sets of degrees of freedom: those in the numerator and those in the denominator. The critical values of F for various degrees of freedom for the numerator and denominator are given in Table 5 of the Appendix of statistical tables. If the probability of F is greater than the significance level α, H_0 is not rejected and t based on the pooled variance estimate can be used. On the other hand, if the probability of F is less than or equal to α, H_0 is rejected and t based on a separate variance estimate is used.

F test
A statistical test of the equality of the variances of two populations.

F statistic
The ratio of two sample variances.

F distribution
A frequency distribution that depends upon two sets of degrees of freedom: the degrees of freedom in the numerator and the degrees of freedom in the denominator.

Using the data in Table 18.1, suppose we wanted to determine whether Internet usage was different for males as compared with females. A two-independent-samples t test can be conducted. The results of this test are presented in Table 18.14. Note that the F test of sample variances has a probability that is less than 0.05. Accordingly H_0 is rejected and the t test based on the 'equal variances not assumed' should be used. The t value is -4.492 and, with 18.014 degrees of freedom, this gives a probability of 0.000, which is less than the significance level of 0.05. Therefore, the null hypothesis of equal means is rejected. Because the mean usage for males (gender = 1) is 9.333 and that for females (gender = 2) is 3.867, males use the Internet to a significantly greater extent than females. We also show the t test assuming equal variances because most software packages automatically conduct the t test both ways.

Table 18.14	Two independent-samples t test

Summary statistics

	Number of cases	Mean	Standard error mean
Male	15	9.333	1.137
Female	15	3.867	0.435

F test for equality of variances

F value	Two-tail probability
15.507	0.000

t test

Equal variances assumed			Equal variances not assumed		
t value	Degrees of freedom	Two-tail probability	t value	Degrees of freedom	Two-tail probability
−4.492	28	0.000	−4.492	18.014	0.000

For another application of the t test, consider the following example.

Real research	**Shops seek to suit elderly to a 't'[15]**

A study based on a sample of 789 participants who were 65 or older attempted to determine the effect of a lack of mobility on shop patronage. A major research question related to the differences in the physical requirements of dependent and self-reliant elderly persons. That is, did the two groups require different things to get to the shop or after they arrived at the shop? A more detailed analysis of the physical requirements conducted by the t tests of two independent samples (shown in the table) indicated that dependent elderly persons were more likely to look for shops that offer home delivery and phone orders and for shops to which they have accessible transportation. They were also more likely to look for a variety of shops located close together.

Differences in physical requirements between dependent and self-reliant elderly

| | Mean* | | |
Physical requirement items	Self-reliant	Dependent	t test probability
Delivery to home	1.787	2.000	0.023
Phone in order	2.030	2.335	0.003
Transportation to store	2.188	3.098	0.000
Convenient parking	4.001	4.095	0.305
Location close to home	3.177	3.325	0.137
Variety of shops close together	3.456	3.681	0.023

*Measured on a five-point scale from not important (1) to very important (5).

In this example, we tested the difference between means. A similar test is available for testing the difference between proportions for two independent samples.

Proportions. A case involving proportions for two independent samples is also illustrated using the data from Table 18.1, which gives the number of males and females who shop online. Is the proportion of participants who shop online the same for males and females? The null and alternative hypotheses are

$$H_0: \pi_1 = \pi_2$$
$$H_1: \pi_1 \neq \pi_2$$

A z test is used as in testing the proportion for one sample. In this case, however, the test statistic is given by

$$z = \frac{P_1 - P_2}{s_{\bar{P}_1 - \bar{P}_2}}$$

In the test statistic, the numerator is the difference between the proportions in the two samples, P_1 and P_2. The denominator is the standard error of the difference in the two proportions and is given by

$$s_{\bar{P}_1 - \bar{P}_2} = \sqrt{p(1-p)\left(\frac{1}{n_1} + \frac{1}{n_2}\right)}$$

where

$$p = \frac{n_1 P_1 + n_2 P_2}{n_1 + n_2}$$

A significance level of $\alpha = 0.05$ is selected. Given the data in Table 18.1, the test statistic can be calculated as

$$P_1 - P_2 = (11/15) - (6/15)$$
$$= 0.733 - 0.400 = 0.333$$
$$p = (15 \times 0.733 + 15 \times 0.4)/(15+15) = 0.567$$
$$S_{P_1 - P_2} = \sqrt{0.567 \times 0.433(1/15 + 1/15)} = 0.181$$
$$z = 0.333/0.181 = 1.84$$

Given a two-tail test, the area to the right of the critical value is $\alpha/2$, or 0.025. Hence, the critical value of the test statistic is 1.96. Because the calculated value is less than the critical value, the null hypothesis cannot be rejected. Thus, the proportion of users (0.733) for males and (0.400) for females is not significantly different for the two samples. Note that although the difference is substantial, it is not statistically significant due to the small sample sizes (15 in each group).

Paired samples

In many marketing research applications, the observations for the two groups are not selected from independent samples. Rather, the observations relate to **paired samples** in that the two sets of observations relate to the same participants. A sample of participants may rate competing brands, may indicate the relative importance of two attributes of a product, or may evaluate a brand at two different times. The differences in these cases are examined by a **paired samples *t* test**. To compute *t* for paired samples, the paired difference variable, denoted by *D*, is formed and its mean and variance calculated. Then the *t* statistic is computed. The degrees of freedom are $n - 1$, where n is the number of pairs. The relevant formulae are

$$H_0: \mu_D = 0$$
$$H_1: \mu_D \neq 0$$

$$t_{n-1} = \frac{\bar{D} - \mu_D}{\frac{s_{\bar{D}}}{\sqrt{n}}}$$

where

$$\bar{D} = \frac{\sum_{i=1}^{n} D_i}{n}$$

$$s_{\bar{D}} = \sqrt{\sum_{i=1}^{n} (D_i - \bar{D})^2}$$

$$s_{\bar{D}} = s_D / \sqrt{n}$$

In the Internet usage example (Table 18.1), a paired *t* test could be used to determine whether the participants differed in their attitude towards the Internet and attitude towards technology. The resulting output is shown in Table 18.15. The mean attitude towards the Internet is 5.167 and that towards technology is 4.10. The mean difference between the variables is 1.067, with a standard deviation of 0.828 and a standard error of 0.1511. This results in a *t* value of $(1.067/0.1511) = 7.06$, with $30 - 1 = 29$ degrees of freedom and a probability of less than 0.001. Therefore the participants have a more favourable attitude towards the Internet as compared with technology in general. An implication, if this were a large and representative

Table 18.15	Paired samples *t* test

Variable	Number of cases	Mean	Standard deviation	Standard error
Internet attitude	30	5.167	1.234	0.225
Technology attitude	30	4.100	1.398	0.255

Difference = Internet – Technology

Difference mean	Standard deviation	Standard error	Correlation	Two-tail probability	t value	Degrees of freedom	Two-tail probability
1.067	0.828	0.1511	0.809	0.000	7.059	29	0.000

sample, would be that Internet service providers should not hesitate to market their services to consumers who do not have a very positive attitude towards technology and do not consider themselves to be technologically savvy. Another application is provided in the context of determining the relative effectiveness of 15-second versus 30-second TV commercials.

Real research

Seconds count[16]

A survey of 83 media directors of the largest Canadian advertising agencies was conducted to determine the relative effectiveness of 15-second versus 30-second commercial advertisements. By use of a five-point rating scale (1 being excellent and 5 being poor), 15- and 30-second commercials were rated by each participant for brand awareness, main idea recall, persuasion, and ability to tell an emotional story. The table indicates that 30-second commercials were rated more favourably on all the dimensions. Paired *t* tests indicated that these differences were significant, and the 15-second commercials were evaluated as less effective.

Mean rating 15- and 30-second commercials on four communication variables

Brand awareness		Main idea recall		Persuasion		Ability to tell an emotional story	
15	30	15	30	15	30	15	30
2.5	1.9	2.7	2.0	3.7	2.1	4.3	1.9

The difference in proportions for paired samples can be tested by using the McNemar test or the chi-square test, as explained in the following section on non-parametric tests.

Non-parametric tests

Non-parametric tests are used when the variables are non-metric. Like parametric tests, non-parametric tests are available for testing variables from one sample, two independent samples or two related samples.

One sample

Kolmogorov–Smirnov (K–S) one-sample test
A one-sample non-parametric goodness-of-fit test that compares the cumulative distribution function for a variable with a specified distribution.

Sometimes the researcher wants to test whether the observations for a particular variable could reasonably have come from a particular distribution, such as the normal, uniform or Poisson distribution. Knowledge of the distribution is necessary for finding probabilities corresponding to known values of the variable, or variable values corresponding to known probabilities (see the Appendix at the end of Chapter 15). The Kolmogorov–Smirnov (K–S) one-sample test is one such goodness-of-fit test. The K–S test compares the cumulative distribution function for a variable with a specified distribution. A_i denotes the cumulative relative frequency for each category of the theoretical (assumed) distribution, and O_i denotes the comparable value of the sample frequency. The K–S test is based on the maximum value of the absolute difference between A_i and O_i. The test statistic is

$$K = \max|A_i - O_i|$$

The decision to reject the null hypothesis is based on the value of K. The larger K is, the more confidence we have that H_0 is false. Note that this is a one-tailed test, since the value of K is always positive, and we reject H_0 for large values of K. For $\alpha = 0.05$, the critical value of

K for large samples (over 35) is given by $1.36/\sqrt{n}$.[17] Alternatively, K can be transformed into a normally distributed z statistic and its associated probability determined.

In the context of the Internet usage example, suppose we wanted to test whether the distribution of Internet usage was normal. A K–S one-sample test is conducted, yielding the data shown in Table 18.16. The largest absolute difference between the observed and normal distribution was $K = 0.222$. Although our sample size is only 30 (less than 35), we can use the approximate formula and the critical value of K is $1.36/\sqrt{30} = 0.248$. Because the calculated value of K is smaller than the critical value, the null hypothesis cannot be rejected. Alternatively, Table 18.16 indicates that the probability of observing a K value of 0.222, as determined by the normalised z statistics, is 0.103. Because this is more than the significance level of 0.05, the null hypothesis cannot be rejected, leading to the same conclusion. Hence the distribution of Internet usage does not deviate significantly from the normal distribution. The implication is that we are safe in using statistical tests (e.g., the z test) and procedures that assume the normality of this variable.

As mentioned earlier, the chi-square test can also be performed on a single variable from one sample. In this context, the chi-square serves as a goodness-of-fit test. It tests whether a significant difference exists between the observed number of cases in each category and the expected number. Other one-sample non-parametric tests include the **runs test** and the **binomial test**. The runs test is a test of randomness for dichotomous variables. This test is conducted by determining whether the order or sequence in which observations are obtained is random. The binomial test is also a goodness-of-fit test for dichotomous variables. It tests the goodness of fit of the observed number of observations in each category to the number expected under a specified binomial distribution. For more information on these tests, refer to the standard statistical literature.[18]

Two independent samples

When the difference in the location of two populations is to be compared based on observations from two independent samples and the variable is measured on an ordinal scale, the

Runs test

A test of randomness for a dichotomous variable.

Binominal test

A goodness-of-fit statistical test for dichotomous variables. It tests the goodness of fit of the observed number of observations in each category to the number expected under a specified binominal distribution.

Table 18.16	K-S one-sample test for normality for Internet usage				
Test distribution, normal					
Mean					6.600
Standard deviation					4.296
Cases					30
Most extreme differences					
Absolute	Positive	Negative		K-S z	Two-tailed p
0.222	0.222	–0.142		1.217	0.103

Mann–Whitney *U* test
A statistical test for a variable measured on an ordinal scale, comparing the differences in the location of two populations based on observations from two independent samples.

Mann–Whitney *U* test can be used.[19] This test corresponds to the two-independent-samples *t* test, for interval-scale variables, when the variances of the two populations are assumed equal.

In the Mann–Whitney *U* test, the two samples are combined and the cases are ranked in order of increasing size. The test statistic, *U*, is computed as the number of times a score from sample or group 1 precedes a score from group 2. If the samples are from the same population, the distribution of scores from the two groups in the rank list should be random. An extreme value of *U* would indicate a non-random pattern pointing to the inequality of the two groups. For samples of less than 30, the exact significance level for *U* is computed. For larger samples, *U* is transformed into a normally distributed *z* statistic. This *z* can be corrected for ties within ranks.

We examine again the difference in the Internet usage of males and females. This time, though, the Mann–Whitney test is used. The results are given in Table 18.17. Again, a significant difference is found between the two groups, corroborating the results of the two-independent-samples *t* test reported earlier. Because the ranks are assigned from the smallest observation to the largest, the higher mean rank of males (20.93) indicates that they use the Internet to a greater extent than females (mean rank = 10.07).

Table 18.17	Mann–Whitney *U* and Wilcoxon rank sum *W* tests: Internet usage by gender

Gender	Mean rank	Cases
Male	20.93	15
Female	10.07	15
Total		30

U	*W*	*z*	Corrected for ties, two-tailed *p*
31.000	151.000	-3.406	0.001

Note: *U* = Mann–Whitney test statistics, *W* = Wilcoxon *W* statistic, *z* = *U* transformed into normally distributed *z* statistics.

Two-sample median test
Non-parametric test statistic that determines whether two groups are drawn from populations with the same median. This is not as powerful as the Mann–Whitney *U* test.

Kolmogorov–Smirnov (K–S) two-sample test
Non-parametric test statistic that determines whether two distributions are the same. It takes into account any differences in the two distributions, including median, dispersion and skewness.

Researchers often wish to test for a significant difference in proportions obtained from two independent samples. In this case, as an alternative to the parametric *z* test considered earlier, one could also use the cross-tabulation procedure to conduct a chi-square test.[20] In this case, we will have a 2 × 2 table. One variable will be used to denote the sample and will assume a value of 1 for sample 1 and a value of 2 for sample 2. The other variable will be the binary variable of interest.

Two other independent-samples non-parametric tests are the median test and the Kolmogorov–Smirnoff test. The two-sample median test determines whether the two groups are drawn from populations with the same median. It is not as powerful as the Mann–Whitney *U* test because it merely uses the location of each observation relative to the median, and not the rank, of each observation. The Kolmogorov–Smirnoff two-sample test examines whether the two distributions are the same. It takes into account any differences between the two distributions, including the median, dispersion and skewness, as illustrated by the following example.

In this example, the marketing research directors and users comprised two independent samples. The samples, however, are not always independent. In the case of paired samples, a different set of tests should be used.

| Real research | **Directors change direction**[21] |

How do marketing research directors and users in Fortune 500 manufacturing firms perceive the role of marketing research in initiating changes in marketing strategy formulation? A study found that marketing research directors were more strongly in favour of initiating changes in strategy and less in favour of holding back than were users of marketing research. The percentage responses to one of the items, 'Initiate change in the marketing strategy of the firm whenever possible', are given in the following table. Using the K–S test, these differences of role definition were statistically significant at the 0.05 level, as shown below.

The role of marketing research in strategy formulation

		Responses (%)				
Sample	*n*	*Absolutely must*	*Preferably should*	*May or may not*	*Preferably should not*	*Absolutely must not*
D	77	7	26	43	19	5
U	68	2	15	32	35	16

K–S significance = 0.05. D = directors, U = users.

Paired samples

Wilcoxon matched-pairs signed-ranks test
A non-parametric test that analyses the differences between the paired observations, taking into account the magnitude of the differences.

Sign test
A non-parametric test for examining differences in the location of two populations, based on paired populations, that compares only the signs of the differences between pairs of variables without taking into account the magnitude of the differences.

An important non-parametric test for examining differences in the location of two populations based on paired observations is the Wilcoxon matched-pairs signed-ranks test. This test analyses the differences between the paired observations, taking into account the magnitude of the differences. So it requires that the data are measured at the interval level of measurement. However, it does not require assumptions about the form of the distribution of the measurements. It should therefore be used whenever the distributional assumptions that underlie the *t* test cannot be satisfied. The test computes the differences between the pairs of variables and ranks the absolute differences. The next step is to sum the positive and negative ranks. The test statistic, *z*, is computed from the positive and negative rank sums. Under the null hypothesis of no difference, *z* is a standard normal variate with mean 0 and variance 1 for large samples. This test corresponds to the paired *t* test considered earlier.[22]

The example considered for the paired *t* test, whether the participants differed in terms of attitude towards the Internet and attitude towards technology, is considered again. Suppose we assume that both these variables are measured on ordinal rather than interval scales. Accordingly, we use the Wilcoxon test. The results are shown in Table 18.18. Again, a significant difference is found in the variables, and the results are in accordance with the conclusion reached by the paired *t* test. There are 23 negative differences (attitude towards technology is less favourable than attitude towards the Internet). The mean rank of these negative differences is 12.72. On the other hand, there is only one positive difference (attitude towards technology is more favourable than attitude towards the Internet). The mean rank of the difference is 7.50. The are six ties, or observations with the same value for both variables. These numbers indicate that the attitude towards the Internet is more favourable than that towards technology. Furthermore, the probability associated with the *z* statistic is less than 0.05, indicating that the difference is indeed significant.

Another paired sample non-parametric test is the sign test.[23] This test is not as powerful as the Wilcoxon matched-pairs signed-ranks test because it compares only the signs of the differences between pairs of variables without taking into account the ranks. In the special case of a binary variable where the researcher wishes to test differences in proportions, the McNemar test can be used. Alternatively, the chi-square test can also be used for binary variables.

Table 18.18	Wilcoxon matched-pairs signed-ranks test		
	Internet with technology		
(Technology–Internet)		*Cases*	*Mean rank*
– Ranks		23	12.72
+ Ranks		1	7.50
Ties		6	
Total		30	
$z = -4.207$			Two-tailed $p = 0.000$

The various parametric and non-parametric tests are summarised in Table 18.19. The tests in Table 18.19 can be easily related to those in Figure 18.9. Table 18.19 classifies the tests in more detail, as parametric tests (based on metric data) are classified separately for means and proportions. Likewise, non-parametric tests (based on non-metric data) are classified separately for distributions and rankings/medians. The final example illustrates the use of hypothesis testing in international branding strategy.

Table 18.19	A summary of hypothesis testing		
Sample	*Application*	*Level of scaling*	*Test/comments*
One sample			
One sample	Distributions	Non-metric	K–S and chi-square for goodness of fit
			Runs test for randomness
			Binomial test for goodness of fit for dichotomous variables
One sample	Means	Metric	t test, if variance is unknown
			z test, if variance is known
One sample	Proportions	Metric	z test
Two independent samples			
Two independent samples	Distributions	Non-metric	K–S two-sample test for examining equivalence of two distributions
Two independent samples	Means	Metric	Two-group t test
			F test for equality of variances
Two independent samples	Proportions	Metric	z test
		Non-metric	Chi-square test
Two independent samples	Rankings/medians	Non-metric	Mann–Whitney U test more powerful than median test

Table 18.19	Continued		
Paired samples			
Paired samples	Means	Metric	Paired *t* test
Paired samples	Proportions	Non-metric	McNemar test for binary variables
			Chi-square test
Paired samples	Rankings/medians	Non-metric	Wilcoxon matched-pairs ranked-signs test more powerful than sign test

---

Real research	**International brand equity – the name of the game[24]**

In an era of global marketing, how can marketers develop theirs brands in diverse social, cultural and historical envirnoments? A study showed that, in general, a firm's international brand structure includes firm-based characteristics, product market characteristics, and market dynamics. More specifically, according to Bob Kroll, the former President of Del Monte International, uniform packaging may be an asset to marketing internationally, but catering to the culinary taste preferences of individual countries is more important. One survey on international product marketing made this clear. Participants included 100 brand and product managers and marketing executives from some of the world's largest food, pharmaceutical and personal product companies. For international markets, 39% said it was not a good idea to use uniform packaging and 38% said it was a good idea. Those who said it was not a good idea mentioned, however, the desirability of maintaining as much brand equity and package consistency from market to market. But they also believed it was necessary to tailor the package to fit the linguistic and regulatory needs of different markets.

Based on this finding, a suitable research question could be: 'Do consumers in different countries prefer to buy global name brands with different packaging customised to suit their local needs?' Based on this research question, one could frame a hypothesis that, other things being constant, standardised branding with customised packaging for a well-established brand name will result in a greater market share. The hypotheses may be formulated as follows:

H_0: Standardised branding with customised packaging for a well-established brand name will not lead to greater market share in an international market.
H_1: Other factors remaining equal, standardised branding with customised packaging for a well-established brand name will lead to greater market share in the international market.

To test the null hypothesis, a well-established brand such as Colgate toothpaste, which has followed a mixed strategy, could be selected. The market share in countries with standardised branding and standardised packaging can be compared with market share in countries with standardised branding and customised packaging, after controlling for the effect of other factors. A two-independent-samples t test could be used.

SPSS and SAS Learning Editions

SPSS Windows

The main program in SPSS is FREQUENCIES. It produces a table of frequency counts, percentages and cumulative percentages for the values of each variable. It gives all of the associated statistics except for the coefficient of variation. If the data are interval scaled and only the summary statistics are desired, the DESCRIPTIVES procedure can be used. All of the statistics computed by DESCRIPTIVES are available in FREQUENCIES. However, DESCRIPTIVES is more efficient because it does not sort values into a frequency table. Moreover, the DESCRIPTIVES procedure displays summary statistics for several variables in a single table and can also calculate standardised values (z scores). The EXPLORE procedure produces summary statistics and graphical displays, either for all the cases or separately for groups of cases. Mean, median, variance, standard deviation, minimum, maximum and range are some of the statistics that can be calculated.

To select these procedures, click

Analyze>Descriptive Statistics>Frequencies
Analyze>Descriptive Statistics>Descriptives
Analyze>Descriptive Statistics>Explore

We give detailed steps for running frequencies on familiarity with the Internet (Table 18.1) and plotting the histogram (Figure 18.1):

1 Select ANALYZE on the SPSS menu bar.
2 Click DESCRIPTIVE STATISTICS and select FREQUENCIES.
3 Move the variable 'Familiarity [familiar]' to the VARIABLE(S) box.
4 Click STATISTICS.
5 Select MEAN, MEDIAN, MODE, STD. DEVIATION, VARIANCE and RANGE.
6 Click CONTINUE.
7 Click CHARTS.
8 Click HISTOGRAMS, then click CONTINUE.
9 Click OK.

The major cross-tabulation program is CROSS-TABS. This program will display cross-classification tables and provides cell counts, row and column percentages, the chi-square test for significance, and all the measures of the strength of the association that have been discussed.

To select these procedures, click

Analyze>Descriptive Statistics>Crosstabs

We give detailed steps for running the cross-tabulation of gender and usage of the Internet given in Table 18.3 and calculating the chi-square, contingency coefficient, and Cramer's V:

1 Select ANALYZE on the SPAA menu bar.
2 Click on DESCRIPTIVE STATISTICS and select CROSSTABS.
3 Move the variable 'Internet Usage Group [iusagegr]' to the ROW(S) box.
4 Move the variable 'Sex [sex]' to the COLUMN(S) box.
5 Click CELLS.
6 Select OBSERVED under COUNTS and COLUMN under PERCENTAGES.
7 Click CONTINUE.
8 Click STATISTICS.
9 Click CHI-SQUARE, PHI and CRAMER'S V.
10 Click CONTINUE.
11 Click OK.

The major program for conducting parametric tests in SPSS is COMPARE MEANS. This program can be used to conduct t tests on one sample or independent or paired samples. To select these procedures using SPSS for Windows, click

Analyze>Compare Means>Means . . .
Analyze>Compare Means>One-Sample T Test . . .
Analyze>Compare Means>Independent-Samples T Test . . .
Analyze>Compare Means>Paired-Samples T Test . . .

We give detailed steps for running a one-sample test on the data of Table 18.1. We wanted to test the hypothesis that the mean familiarity rating exceeds 4.0. The null hypothesis is that the mean familiarity rating is less than or equal to 4.0.

1 Select ANALYZE from the SPSS menu bar.
2 Click COMPARE MEANS and then ONE SAMPLE T TEST.
3 Move 'Familiarity [familiar]' into the TEST VARIABLE(S) box.
4 Type '4' in the TEST VALUE box.
5 Click OK.

We give the detailed steps for running a two-independent-samples t test on the data of Table 18.1. The null hypothesis is that the Internet usage for males and females is the same.

1   Select ANALYZE from the SPSS menu bar.
2   Click COMPARE MEANS and then INDE-PENDENT SAMPLES T TEST.
3   Move 'Internet Usage Hrs/Week [iusage]' into the TEST VARIABLE(S) box.
4   Move 'Sex [sex]' to the GROUPING VARIABLE box.
5   Click DEFINE GROUPS.
6   Type '1' in box GROUP 1 and '2' in box GROUP 2.
7   Click CONTINUE.
8   Click OK.

We give the detailed steps for running a paired samples *t* test on the data of Table 18.1. The null hypothesis is that there is no difference in the attitude towards the Internet and attitude towards technology.

1   Select ANALYZE from the SPSS menu bar.
2   Click COMPARE MEANS and then PAIRED SAMPLES T TEST.
3   Move 'Attitude toward Internet [iattitude]' and then select 'Attitude toward technology [tattitude]'. Move these variables into the PAIRED VARIABLE(S) box.
4   Click OK.

The non-parametric tests discussed in this chapter can be conducted using NONPARAMETRIC TESTS. To select these procedures using SPSS for Windows, click

Analyze>Nonparametric Tests>Chi-Square . . .
Analyze>Nonparametric Tests>Binomial . . .
Analyze>Nonparametric Tests>Runs . . .
Analyze>Nonparametric Tests>1-Sample K-S . . .
Analyze>Nonparametric Tests>2 Independent Samples . . .
Analyze>Nonparametric Tests>2 Related Samples . . .

The detailed steps for the non-parametric tests are similar to those for parametric tests.

SAS Learning Edition

The instructions given here and in all the data analysis chapters (17 to 25) work with the SAS Learning Edition as well as the SAS Enterprise Guide. The Summary Statistics task provides summary statistics including basic summary statistics, percentile summary statistics and more advanced summary statistics including confidence intervals, *t* statistics, coefficient of variation and sums of squares. It also provides graphical displays including histograms and box-and-whisker plots. The One-Way Frequencies task can be used to generate frequency tables as well as binomial and chi-square tests.

To select these tasks, click

Describe>Summary Statistics
Describe>One-Way Frequencies

We give detailed steps for running frequencies on familiarity with the Internet and plotting the histogram.

1   Select DESCRIBE on the SAS Learning Edition menu bar.
2   Click SUMMARY STATISTICS.
3   Move the variable 'FAMILIARITY' to the Analysis variables role.
4   Click BASIC.
5   Select MEAN, STANDARD DEVIATION, VARIANCE and RANGE.
6   Click PLOTS.
7   Click HISTOGRAM.
8   Click RUN.

The major cross-tabulation task is called TABLE ANALYSIS. This task will display the cross-classification table and provide cell counts, row and column percentages, the chi-square test for significance, and all the measures of strength of the association that have been discussed.

To select this task, click

Describe>Table Analysis

We give detailed steps for running the cross-tabulation of sex and usage of the Internet given in Table 18.3 and calculating the chi-square, contingency coefficient and Cramer's *V*:

1   Select DESCRIBE on the SAS Learning Edition menu bar.
2   Click TABLE ANALYSIS.
3   Move the variables 'IUSAGEGOUP' and 'SEX' to the Tables variables role.
4   Click TABLES.
5   Move 'SEX' and then 'IUSAGEGROUP'.
6   Click CELL STATISTICS.
7   Select COLUMN PERCENTAGES and CELL FREQUENCIES.
8   Click ASSOCIATION under TABLE STATISTICS.
9   Click CHI_SQUARE TESTS under TESTS OF ASSOCIATION.
10 Click RUN.

The major task for conducting parametric tests is called T TEST. This task can be used to conduct *t* tests on one sample or independent or paired samples. To select this task, click

Analyze>ANOVA>*t* Test

We give detailed steps for running a one-sample test on the data of Table 18.1. We wanted to test the hypothesis that the mean familiarity ratings exceed 4.0. The null hypothesis is that the mean familiarity rating is less than or equal to 4.0.

1 Select ANALYZE from the SAS Learning Edition menu bar.
2 Click ANOVA and then T TEST.
3 Click ONE SAMPLE.
4 Click TASK ROLES.
5 Move FAMILIARITY to the Analysis variables role.
6 Click ANALYSIS.
7 Enter '4' into the Null Hypothesis field.
8 Click RUN.

We give detailed steps for running a two-sample *t* test on the data of Table 18.1. The null hypothesis is that the Internet usage for males and females is the same.

1 Select ANALYZE from the SAS Learning Edition menu bar.
2 Click ANOVA and then T TEST.
3 Click TWO SAMPLE.
4 Click TASK ROLES.
5 Move 'IUSAGE' to the Analysis variables role.
6 Move 'SEX' to the Group by role.
7 Click RUN.

We give detailed steps for running paired samples *t* test on the data of Table 18.1. The null hypothesis is that there is no difference in the attitude towards the Internet and attitude towards technology.

1 Select ANALYZE from the SAS Learning Edition menu bar.
2 Click ANOVA and then T TEST.
3 Click PAIRED.
4 Click TASK ROLES.
5 Move 'IATTITUDE' and 'TATTITUDE' to the Paired variables role.
6 Click RUN.

The non-parametric tests discussed in this chapter can be conducted as follows.

Non-parametric one-sample test (Kolmogorov–Smirnov one-sample test):

1 Select DESCRIBE from the SAS Learning Edition menu bar.
2 Click DISTRIBUTION ANALYSIS.
3 Click TASK ROLES.
4 Move 'IUSAGE' to the Analysis variables role.
5 Click TABLES.
6 Check on TESTS FOR NORMALITY.
7 Click RUN.

Note that you check TEST FOR NORMALITY if you want a one-way test of distribution. If you want a non-parametric test for location, perform the same steps above except select TEST FOR LOCATION in step 6. In addition to the (parametric) *t* test, you will get the sign test and the Wilcoxon signed ranks test (also known as the Mann–Whitney test).

Non-parametric two-independent-samples test (Wilcoxon test, which is also known as the Mann–Whitney test):

1 Select ANALYZE from the SAS Learning Edition menu bar.
2 Click ANOVA and then NONPARAMETRIC ONE-WAY ANOVA.
3 Click TASK ROLES.
4 Move 'IUSAGE' to the Dependent variable role.
5 Move 'SEX' to the Independent variable role.
6 Click ANALYSIS.
7 Click WILCOXON.
8 Click RUN.

Non-parametric two paired samples test (Wilcoxon matched-pairs signed-ranks test): create a 'difference score' that is calculated as DIFF=IATTITUDE-TATTITUDE and then use one-sample method to describe DIFF:

1 Select DESCRIBE from the SAS Learning Edition menu bar.
2 Click DISTRIBUTION ANALYSIS.
3 Click TASK ROLES.
4 Move 'DIFF' to the Analysis variable role.
5 Click TABLES.
6 Check on TESTS FOR NORMALITY.
7 Click RUN.

Summary

Basic data analysis provides valuable insights and guides the rest of the data analysis as well as the interpretation of the results. A frequency distribution should be obtained for each variable in the data. This analysis produces a table of frequency counts, percentages and cumulative percentages for all the values associated with that variable. It indicates the extent of out-of-range, missing or extreme values. The mean, mode and median of a frequency distribution are measures of central tendency. The variability of the distribution is described by the range, the variance or standard deviation, coefficient of variation and interquartile range. Skewness and kurtosis provide an idea of the shape of the distribution.

The general procedure for hypothesis testing involves eight steps. Formulate the null and alternative hypotheses, select an appropriate test statistic, choose the level of significance (α), calculate the value of the test statistic, and determine the probability associated with the test statistic calculated from the sample data under the null hypothesis. Alternatively, determine the critical value associated with the test statistic. Compare the probability associated with the test statistic with the level of significance specified or, alternatively, determine whether the calculated value of the test statistic falls into the rejection or the non-rejection region. Accordingly, make the decision to reject or not reject the null hypothesis, and arrive at a conclusion.

Cross-tabulations are tables that reflect the joint distribution of two or more variables. In cross-tabulation, the percentages can be computed either by column, based on column totals, or by row, based on row totals. The general rule is to compute the percentages in the direction of the independent variable, across the dependent variable. Often the introduction of a third variable can provide additional insights. The chi-square statistic provides a test of the statistical significance of the observed association in a cross-tabulation. The phi coefficient, contingency coefficient, Cramer's V and lambda coefficient provide measures of the strength of association between the variables.

Parametric and non-parametric tests are available for testing hypotheses related to differences. In the parametric case, the t test is used to examine hypotheses related to the population mean. Different forms of the t test are suitable for testing hypotheses based on one sample, two independent samples or paired samples. In the non-parametric case, popular one-sample tests include the Kolmogorov–Smirnov, chi-square, runs test and the binomial test. For two independent non-parametric samples, the Mann–Whitney U test, median test, Kolmogorov–Smirnov and the chi-square tests can be used. For paired samples, the sign, Wilcoxon matched-pairs signed-ranks, McNemar and chi-square tests are useful for examining hypotheses related to measures of location.

Questions

1 Describe the procedure for computing frequencies.
2 What measures of location are commonly computed?
3 What measures of variability are commonly computed?
4 How is the relative flatness or peakedness of a distribution measured?
5 What is a skewed distribution? What does it mean?
6 What is the major difference between cross-tabulation and frequency distribution?
7 What is the general rule for computing percentages in cross-tabulations?
8 Define a spurious correlation.
9 What is meant by a suppressed association? How is it revealed?
10 Discuss the reasons for the frequent use of cross-tabulations. What are some of the limitations?
11 Present a classification of hypothesis testing procedures.
12 Describe the general procedure for conducting a t test.
13 What is the major difference between parametric and non-parametric tests?
14 Which non-parametric tests are the counterparts of the two-independent-samples t test for parametric data?
15 Which non-parametric tests are the counterparts of the paired samples t test for parametric data?

Exercises

1 In each of the following situations, indicate the statistical analysis you would conduct and the appropriate test or test statistic that should be used:

   a Consumer preferences for The Body Shop shampoo were obtained on an 11-point Likert scale. The same consumers were then shown a commercial about The Body Shop. After the commercial, preferences for The Body Shop were again measured. Has the commercial been successful in inducing a change in preferences?

   b Does the preference for The Body Shop shampoo follow a normal distribution?

   c Participants in a survey of 1,000 households were classified as heavy, medium, light and non-users of ice cream. They were also classified as being in high-, medium- or low-income categories. Is the consumption of ice cream related to income level?

   d In a survey of 2,000 households, participants were asked to rank 10 supermarkets, including Lidl, in order of preference. The sample was divided into small and large households based on a median split of the household size. Does preference for shopping in Lidl vary by household size?

2 The current advertising campaign for Red Bull would be changed if less than 30% of consumers like it.

   a Formulate the null and alternative hypotheses.

   b Discuss the Type I and Type II errors that could occur in hypothesis testing.

c Which statistical test would you use? Why?

d A random sample of 300 consumers was surveyed and 84 participants indicated that they liked the campaign. Should the campaign be changed? Why?

3 An electrical goods chain is having a New Year sale of refrigerators. The number of refrigerators sold during this sale at a sample of 10 stores was

   80   110   0   40   70   80   100   50   80   30

a Is there evidence that an average of more than 50 refrigerators per store was sold during this sale? Use $\alpha = 0.05$.

b What assumption is necessary to perform this test?

4 In a survey pretest, data were obtained from 45 participants on Benetton clothes. These data are given in the table overleaf, which gives the usage, gender, awareness, attitude, preference, intention and loyalty towards Benetton of a sample of Benetton users. Usage was coded as 1, 2 or 3, representing light, medium or heavy users. Gender was coded as 1 for females and 2 for males. Awareness, attitude, preference, intention and loyalty were measured on a seven point Likert type scale (1 = very unfavourable, 7 = very favourable). Note that five participants have missing values that are denoted by 9.

Analyse the Benetton data to answer the following questions. In each case, formulate the null and alternative hypotheses and conduct the appropriate statistical test(s).

a Obtain a frequency distribution for each of the following variables and calculate the relevant statistics: awareness, attitude, preference, intention and loyalty towards Benetton.

b Conduct a cross-tabulation of the usage with gender. Interpret the results.

c Does the awareness for Benetton exceed 3.0?

d Do males and females differ in their awareness of Benetton? Their attitude towards Benetton? Their loyalty to Benetton?

e Do the participants in the pretest have a higher level of awareness than loyalty?

f Does awareness of Benetton follow a normal distribution?

g Is the distribution of preference for Benetton normal?

h Assume that awareness towards Benetton was measured on an ordinal scale rather than an interval scale. Do males and females differ in their loyalty towards Benetton?

i Assume that loyalty towards Benetton was measured on an ordinal scale rather than an interval scale. Do males and females differ in their loyalty towards Benetton?

j Assume that attitude and loyalty towards Benetton were measured on an ordinal scale rather than an interval scale. Do the participants have a greater awareness of Benetton than loyalty to Benetton?

Number	Usage	Gender	Awareness	Attitude	Preference	Intention	Loyalty
1	3	2	7	6	5	5	6
2	1	1	2	2	4	6	5
3	1	1	3	3	6	7	6
4	3	2	6	5	5	3	2
5	3	2	5	4	7	4	3
6	2	2	4	3	5	2	3
7	2	1	5	4	4	3	2
8	1	1	2	1	3	4	5
9	2	2	4	4	3	6	5
10	1	1	3	1	2	4	5
11	3	2	6	7	6	4	5
12	3	2	6	5	6	4	4
13	1	1	4	3	3	1	1
14	3	2	6	4	5	3	2
15	1	2	4	3	4	5	6
16	1	2	3	4	2	4	2
17	3	1	7	6	4	5	3
18	2	1	6	5	4	3	2
19	1	1	1	1	3	4	5
20	3	1	5	7	4	1	2
21	3	2	6	6	7	7	5
22	2	2	2	3	1	4	2
23	1	1	1	1	3	2	2
24	3	1	6	7	6	7	6
25	1	2	3	2	2	1	1
26	2	2	5	3	4	4	5
27	3	2	7	6	6	5	7
28	2	1	6	4	2	5	6
29	1	1	9	2	3	1	3
30	2	2	5	9	4	6	5
31	1	2	1	2	9	3	2
32	1	2	4	6	5	9	3
33	2	1	3	4	3	2	9
34	2	1	4	6	5	7	6
35	3	1	5	7	7	3	3
36	3	1	6	5	7	3	4
37	3	2	6	7	5	3	4
38	3	2	5	6	4	3	2
39	3	2	7	7	6	3	4
40	1	1	4	3	4	6	5
41	1	1	2	3	4	5	6
42	1	1	1	3	2	3	4
43	1	1	2	4	3	6	7
44	1	1	3	3	4	6	5
45	1	1	1	1	4	5	3

5   In a small group discuss the following issues: 'Why waste time doing basic forms of data analysis? Why not just go straight to performing multivariate analyses – whose outputs from most software packages will include basic analyses?' and 'Why do managers find cross-tabulations so appealing? What would it take to make managers more appreciative of statistical analyses that go beyond the cross-tabulation?'.

Notes

1. Keen, C., Wetzels, M., de Ruyter, K. and Feinberg, R., 'E-tailers versus retailers: which factors determine consumer preferences', *Journal of Business Research* 57 (7) (July 2004), 685; Mathwick, C., Malhotra, N.K. and Rigdon, E., 'The effect of dynamic retail experience on experiential perceptions of value: an Internet and catalog comparison', *Journal of Retailing* 78 (2002), 51–60.

2. See any introductory statistics book for a more detailed description of these statistics; for example, see Berenson, M.L., Levine, D.M. and Krehbiel, T.C., *Basic Business Statistics: Concepts and Applications*, 11th edn (Upper Saddle River, NJ: Prentice Hall, 2009).

3. For our purposes, no distinction will be made between formal hypothesis testing and statistical inference by means of confidence intervals. See, for example, Larocque, D. and Randles, R.H., 'Confidence intervals for a discrete population median', *American Statistician* 62 (1) (February 2008), 32–39.

4. Excellent discussions of ways to analyse cross-tabulations can be found in Wagner, W.W., *Using SPSS for Social Statistics and Research Methods* (Thousand Oakes, CA: Pine Forge Press, 2007); Denman, B.E., 'Advanced categorical statistics: issues and applications in communication research', *Journal of Communication* 52 (1) (March 2002), 162; Hellevik, O., *Introduction to Casual Analysis: Exploring Survey Data by Crosstabulation* (Beverley Hills, CA: Sage, 1984).

5. McKechnie, D.S., Grant, J., Korepina, V. and Sadykova, N., 'Women: segmenting the home fitness equipment market', *Journal of Consumer Marketing* 24 (1) (2007), 18–26; Kivetz, R. and Simonson, I., 'Earning the right to indulge: effort as a determinant of customer preferences toward frequency program rewards', *Journal of Marketing Research* 39 (2) (May 2002), 155–170; Feick, L.F., 'Analyzing marketing research data with association models', *Journal of marketing Research* 21 (November 1984), 376–386.

6. Lenell, W. and Boissoneau, R., 'Using causal-comparative and correlational designs in conducting market research', *Journal of Professional Services Marketing* 13 (2) (1996), 59–69. See also the classic book by Zeisel, H., *Say It with Figures*, 5th edn (New York: Harper & Row, 1968).

7. Sirkin, R.M., *Statistics for the Social Sciences*, 3rd edn (Thousand Oaks, CA: Sage, 2005); Wright, D.B., *First steps in statistics* (Thousand Oaks, CA: Sage, 2002); Sirkin, R.M., *Statistics for the Social Sciences* (Thousand Oaks, CA: Sage, 1994).

8. Higgins, J.J., *Introduction to modern nonparametric statistics* (Pacific Grove, CA: Duxbury, 2002); Pet, M.A., *Nonparametric Statistics for Health Care Research* (Thousand Oaks, CA: Sage, 1997). For a more extensive treatment see Lancaster, H.O., *The Chi Squared Distribution* (New York: Wiley, 1969). For a recent application, see Bakir, A., 'Some assembly required: comparing disclaimers in children's TV advertising in Turkey and the United States', *Journal of Advertising Research* 49 (1) (March 2009), 93–103.

9. Berenson, M.L., Levine, D.M. and Krehbiel, T.C., *Basic Business Statistics: Concepts and Applications*, 11th edn (Upper Saddle River, NJ: Prentice Hall, 2009).

10. Some statisticians, however, disagree. They feel that a correction should not be applied. See, for example, Overall, J.E., 'Power of chi-square tests for 2 × 2 contingency tables with small expected frequencies', *Psychological Bulletin* (January 1980), 132–135. See also Betancourt, R.R., Cortinas, M., Elorz, M. and Mugica, J.M., 'The demand for and the supply of distribution services: a basis for the analysis of customer satisfaction in retailing', *Quantitative Marketing and Economics* 5 (3) (September 2007), 293–312.

11. Significance tests and confidence intervals are also available for either asymmetric lambda or symmetric lambda. See Goodman, L.A. and Kruskal, W.H., 'Measures of association for cross classification: appropriate sampling theory', *Journal of the American Statistical Association* 88 (June 1963), 310–364.

12. Fields, A., *Discovering statistics using SPSS*, 2nd edn (Thousand Oaks, CA: Sage, 2005); Hoenig, J.M., 'The abuse of power: the pervasive fallacy of power calculation for data analysis', *American Statistician* 55 (1) (February 2001), 19–24; Cowles, M. and Davis, C., 'On the origins of the .05 level of statistical significance', *American Psychologist* 37 (5) (May 1982), 553–558. See also Kotabe, M., Duhan, D.E., Smith, D.K. Jr and Wilson, R.I.D., 'The perceived veracity of PIMS strategy principles in Japan: an empirical inquiry', *Journal of Marketing* 55 (January 1991), 26–41.

13. Technically, a null hypothesis cannot be accepted. It can be either rejected or not rejected. This distinction, however, is inconsequential in marketing research.

14. The condition when the variances cannot be assumed to be equal is known as the Behrens–Fisher problem. There is some controversy over the best procedure in this case. For an example, see Hulten, B., 'Customer segmentation: the concepts of trust commitment and relationships', *Journal of Targeting, Measurement and Analysis for Marketing* 15 (4) (September 2007), 256–269; Heilman, C.M., Nakamoto, K. and Rao, A.G., 'Pleasant surprises: consumer response to unexpected in-store coupons', *Journal of Marketing Research* 39 (2) (May 2002), 242–252.

15. Iyer, R. and Eastman, J.K., 'The elderly and their attitudes toward the internet: the impact on internet use, purchase and comparison shopping', *Journal of Marketing Theory and Practice* 14 (1) (January 2006), 57–66; Chandler, S., 'Some retailers begin to cater to growing group of aging shoppers', *Knight Ridder Tribune Business News* (17 March 2001), 1; Lumpkin, J.R. and Hunt, J.B., 'Mobility as an influence on retail patronage behavior of the elderly: testing conventional wisdom', *Journal of the Academy of Marketing Science* (Winter 1989), 1–12.

16. Schleis, P., 'Startup bets on Super Bowl: local entrepreneurs hope pricey 15-second ad draws viewers to new website', *McClatchy-Tribune Business News* (January 2008); Ives, N., 'In a TV world filled with clutter, some commercials are running longer, hoping to be noticed', *New York Times* (28 July 2004), C.11; Dunst, L., 'Is it possible to get creative in 15 seconds?', *Advertising Age* 64 (50) (29 November 1993), 18; Rosenblatt, J.A. and Mainprize, J., 'The history and future of 15-second commercials: an empirical investigation of the perception of ad agency media directors', in Lazer, W., Shaw, E. and

Wee, C.H. (eds), *World Marketing Congress*, International Conference Series, Vol. 4 (Boca Raton, FL: Academy of Marketing Science, 1989), 169–177.

17. Grover, R. and Vriens, M., *The Handbook of Marketing Research: Uses, misuses and future advances* (Thousand Oaks, CA: Sage, 2006); Kanji, G.K., *100 Statistical Tests* (Thousand Oaks, CA: Sage, 1999); Harnett, D.L., *Statistical Methods*, 3rd edn (Reading, MA: Addison-Wesley, 1982).

18. Higgins, J.J., *Introduction to modern nonparametric statistics* (Pacific Grove, CA: Duxbury, 2002); Pen, M.A., *Nonparametric Statistics for Health Care Research* (Thousand Oaks, CA: Sage, 1997).

19. There is some controversy over whether non-parametric statistical techniques should be used to make inferences about population parameters.

20. The *t* test in this case is equivalent to a chi-square test for independence in a 2 × 2 contingency table. The relationship is

$$\chi^2.95(1) = t^2.0005(n_1 + n_2 - 2)$$

For large samples, the *t* distribution approaches the normal distribution and so the *t* test and the *z* test are equivalent.

21. Swaddling, D., 'Good data still worth the investment', *Marketing News* 35 (2) (15 January 2001), 20–21; Krum, J.R., Rau, P.A. and Keiser, S.K., 'The marketing research process: role perceptions of researchers and users', *Journal of Advertising Research* (December–January 1988), 9–21. See also Miller, C., 'Gallup Brothers analyze the research industry', *Marketing News* 31 (1) (6 January 1997), 2.

22. Bergmann, R., 'Different outcomes of the Wilcoxon–Mann–Whitney test from different statistics packages', *American Statistician* 54 (1) (February 2000), 72–77; for an example of Wilcoxon matched-pairs signed-ranks test, see Kalwani, M.U. and Narayandas, N., 'Long-term manufacturer-supplier relationships: do they pay off for supplier firms?', *Journal of Marketing* 59 (January 1995), 1–16.

23. Bailey, W., 'Data use: nonparametric tests: Sturdy alternatives', **www.quirks.com/articles/a2002/20020509.aspx?searchID=3435634**, accessed 23 March 2008; Pett, M.A., *Nonparametric Statistics for Health Care Research* (Thousand Oaks, CA: Sage, 1997); Field, J.G., 'The world's simplest test of significance', *Journal of the Market Research Society* (July 1971), 170–172.

24. Strange, R., 'Branding and externalization of production', *International Marketing Review* 23 (6) (2006), 578; Miles, L., 'Finding a balance in global research', Marketing (29 November 2001), 33; de Chernatony, L., Halliburton, C. and Bernath, R., 'International branding: demand or supply driven?', *International Marketing Review* 12 (2) (1995), 9–21.

19 Analysis of variance and covariance

Analysis of variance is a straightforward way to examine the differences between groups of responses that are measured on interval or ratio scales.

Objectives

After reading this chapter, you should be able to:

1   discuss the scope of the analysis of variance (ANOVA) technique and its relationship to the *t* test, and regression;

2   describe one-way analysis of variance, including decomposition of the total variation, measurement of effects significance testing and interpretation of results;

3   describe *n*-way analysis of variance and the testing of the significance of the overall effect, the interaction effect and the main effect of each factor;

4   describe analysis of covariance and show how it accounts for the influence of uncontrolled independent variables;

5   explain key factors pertaining to the interpretation of results with emphasis on interactions, relative importance of factors and multiple comparisons;

6   discuss specialised ANOVA techniques applicable to marketing, such as repeated measures ANOVA, non-metric ANOVA and multivariate analysis of variance (MANOVA);

7   appreciate how SPSS and SAS software are used in analyses of variance and covariance.

Overview

In Chapter 18, we examined tests of differences between two means or two medians. In this chapter, we discuss procedures for examining differences between more than two means or medians. These procedures are called analysis of variance and analysis of covariance. These procedures have traditionally been used for analysing experimental data, but they are also used for analysing survey or observational data.

We describe analysis of variance and covariance procedures and discuss their relationship to other techniques. Then we describe one-way analysis of variance, the simplest of these procedures, followed by *n*-way analysis of variance and analysis of covariance. Special attention is given to issues in interpretation of results as they relate to interactions, relative importance of factors and multiple comparisons. Some specialised topics such as repeated measures analysis of variance, non-metric analysis of variance and multivariate analysis of variance are briefly discussed. Finally, help is provided to run the SPSS and SAS Learning Editions in the data analysis challenges presented in this chapter. We begin with two examples that illustrate applications of analysis of variance.

Real research   ### Analysis of tourism destinations[1]

A survey conducted by EgeBank in Istanbul, Turkey, focused upon the importance of tour operators' and travel agents' perceptions of selected Mediterranean tourist destinations (Egypt, Greece, Italy and Turkey). Operators/travel agents were mailed questionnaires based on the location of tours, broken down as follows: Egypt (53), Greece (130), Italy (150) and Turkey (65). The survey consisted of questions on affective and cognitive evaluations of the four destinations. The four  affective questions were asked on a seven-point semantic differential scale, whereas the 14 cognitive evaluations were measured on a five-point Likert scale (1 = offers very little,

2 = offers somewhat little, 3 = offers neither little nor much, 4 = offers somewhat much, and 5 = offers very much). The differences in the evaluations of the four locations were examined using one-way analysis of variance (ANOVA) as seen in the following table.

The ANOVA table shows that 'unpleasant–pleasant' and 'distressing–relaxing' affective factors had significant differences among the four destinations. For instance, Greece and Italy were perceived as being significantly more relaxing than Egypt. As for the perceptual factors, 8 of the 14 factors were significant. Turkey was perceived as significantly better value for money than Greece and Italy. Turkey's main strength appeared to be 'good value', and the country's tourist agencies should promote this in their marketing strategies. On the other hand, Turkey needed to improve the perception of its infrastructure, cleanliness and entertainment to attract more tour operators and travel agencies.

Image variations of destinations promoted to tour operators and travel agencies

Image items	Turkey (n=36)	Egypt (n=29)	Greece (n=37)	Italy (n=34)	Sig.
Affective (scale 1–7)					
Unpleasant–pleasant	6.14	5.62	6.43	6.50	0.047*
Sleepy–arousing	6.24	5.61	6.14	6.56	0.053
Distressing–relaxing	5.60	4.86	6.05	6.09	0.003*
Gloomy–exciting	6.20	5.83	6.32	6.71	0.061
Perceptual (scale 1–5)					
Good value for money	4.62	4.32	3.89	3.27	0.000*
Beautiful scenery and natural attractions	4.50	4.04	4.53	4.70	0.011*
Good climate	4.29	4.00	4.41	4.35	0.133
Interesting cultural attractions	4.76	4.79	4.67	4.79	0.781
Suitable accommodations	4.17	4.28	4.35	4.62	0.125
Appealing local food (cuisine)	4.44	3.57	4.19	4.85	0.000*
Great beaches and water sports	3.91	3.18	4.27	3.65	0.001*
Quality of infrastructure	3.49	2.97	3.68	4.09	0.000*
Personal safety	3.83	3.28	4.19	4.15	0.000*
Interesting historical attractions	4.71	4.86	4.81	4.82	0.650
Unpolluted and unspoiled environment	3.54	3.34	3.43	3.59	0.784
Good nightlife and entertainment	3.44	3.15	4.06	4.27	0.000*
Standard hygiene and cleanliness	3.29	2.79	3.76	4.29	0.000*
Interesting and friendly people	4.34	4.24	4.35	4.32	0.956

*Significant at 0.05 level.

Real research

Online shopping risks[2]

Analysis of variance was used to test differences in preferences for online shopping for products with different economic and social risks. In a 2 × 2 design, economic risk and social risk were varied at two levels each (high, low). Preference for online shopping served as the dependent variable. The results indicated a significant interaction of social risk with economic risk. Online shopping was not perceived favourably for high-social-risk products, regardless of the level of economic product risk, but it was preferred for low-economic-risk over high-economic-risk products, when the level of social risk was low.

The tourist destination example presented a situation with four categories. The *t* test was not appropriate for examining the overall difference in category means, so analysis of variance was used instead. The online shopping study involved a comparison of means when there were two factors (independent variables), each of which was varied at two levels. In this example *t* tests were not appropriate, because the effect of each factor was not independent of the effect of the other factor (in other words, interactions were significant). Analysis of variance provided meaningful conclusions in these studies. The relationship of analysis of variance to the *t* test and other techniques are considered in the next section.

Relationship among techniques

Analysis of variance (ANOVA)

A statistical technique for examining the differences among means for two or more populations.

Factors

Categorical independent variables in ANOVA. The independent variables must all be categorical (non-metric) to use ANOVA.

Treatment

In ANOVA, a particular combination of factor levels or categories.

One-way analysis of variance

An ANOVA technique in which there is only one factor.

n-way analysis of variance

An ANOVA model where two or more factors are involved.

Analysis of covariance (ANCOVA)

An advanced ANOVA procedure in which the effects of one or more metric-scaled extraneous variables are removed from the dependent variable before conducting the ANOVA.

Covariate

A metric-independent variable used in ANCOVA.

Analysis of variance and analysis of covariance are used for examining the differences in the mean values of the dependent variable associated with the effect of the controlled independent variables, after taking into account the influence of the uncontrolled independent variables. Essentially, analysis of variance (ANOVA) is used as a test of means for two or more populations. The null hypothesis, typically, is that all means are equal. For example, suppose that the researcher was interested in examining whether heavy users, medium users, light users and non-users of yogurt differed in their preference for Müller yogurt, measured on a nine-point Likert scale. The null hypothesis that the four groups were not different in preference for Müller could be tested using ANOVA.

In its simplest form, ANOVA must have a dependent variable (preference for Müller yogurt) that is metric (measured using an interval or ratio scale). There must also be one or more independent variables (product use: heavy, medium, light and non-users). The independent variables must all be categorical (non-metric). Categorical independent variables are also called factors. A particular combination of factors, or categories, is called a treatment. One-way analysis of variance involves only one categorical variable, or a single factor. The differences in preference of heavy users, medium users, light users and non-users would be examined by one-way ANOVA. In this, a treatment is the same as a factor level (medium users constitute a treatment). If two or more factors are involved, the analysis is termed *n*-way analysis of variance. If, in addition to product use, the researcher also wanted to examine the preference for Müller yogurt of customers who are loyal and those who are not, an *n*-way ANOVA would be conducted.

If the set of independent variables consists of both categorical and metric variables, the technique is called analysis of covariance (ANCOVA). For example, analysis of covariance would be required if the researcher wanted to examine the preference of product use groups and loyalty groups, taking into account the participants' attitudes towards nutrition and the importance they attached to dairy products. The latter two variables would be measured on nine-point Likert scales. In this case, the categorical independent variables (product use and brand loyalty) are still referred to as factors, whereas the metric-independent variables (attitude towards nutrition and importance attached to dairy products) are referred to as covariates.

The relationship of ANOVA to *t* tests and other techniques, such as regression (see Chapter 20), is shown in Figure 19.1. These techniques all involve a metric-dependent variable. ANOVA and ANCOVA can include more than one independent variable (product use, brand loyalty, attitude, importance, etc.). Furthermore, at least one of the independent variables must be categorical, and the categorical variables may have more than two categories (in our example, product use has four categories). A *t* test, on the other hand, involves a single, binary independent variable. For example, the difference in the preferences of loyal and non-loyal participants could be tested by conducting a *t* test. Regression analysis, like ANOVA and ANCOVA, can also involve more than one independent variable. All the independent variables, however, are generally interval scaled, although binary or categorical variables can be accommodated using dummy variables. For example, the relationship between preference for

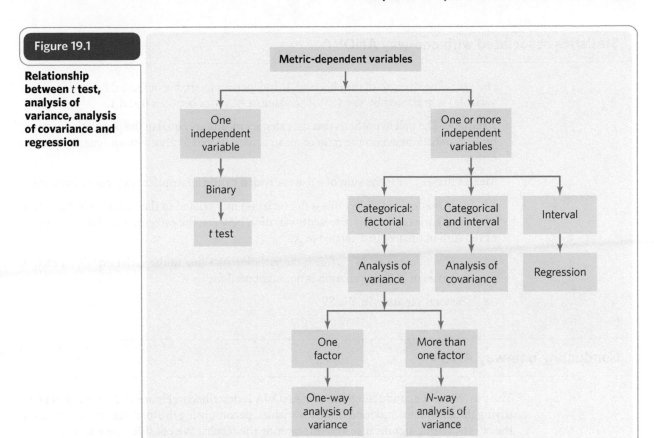

Figure 19.1

Relationship between *t* test, analysis of variance, analysis of covariance and regression

Müller yogurt, attitude towards nutrition, and importance attached to dairy products could be examined via regression analysis, with preference for Müller serving as the dependent variable and attitude and importance as independent variables.

One-way ANOVA

Researchers are often interested in examining the differences in the mean values of the dependent variable for several categories of a single independent variable or factor. For example:

- Do various market segments differ in terms of their volume of product consumption?
- Do brand evaluations of groups exposed to different advertisements vary?
- Do retailers, wholesalers and agents differ in their attitudes towards the firm's distribution policies?
- How do consumers' intentions to buy the brand vary with different price levels?
- What is the effect of consumers' familiarity with a car manufacturer (measured as high, medium and low) on preference for the car?

The answer to these and similar questions can be determined by conducting one-way ANOVA. Before describing the procedure, we define the important statistics associated with one-way ANOVA.[3]

Statistics associated with one-way ANOVA

eta² (η^2). The strength of the effects of X (independent variable or factor) on Y (dependent variable) is measured by eta² (η^2). The value of η^2 varies between 0 and 1.

F **statistic.** The null hypothesis that the category means are equal in the population is tested by an *F statistic* based on the ratio of mean square related to X and mean square related to error.

Mean square. This is the sum of squares divided by the appropriate degrees of freedom.

$SS_{between}$. Also denoted as SS_x, this is the variation in Y related to the variation in the means of the categories of X. This represents variation between the categories of X or the portion of the sum of squares in Y related to X.

SS_{within}. Also denoted as SS_{error}, this is the variation in Y due to the variation within each of the categories of X. This variation is not accounted for by X.

SS_y. The total variation in Y is SS_y.

Conducting one-way ANOVA

The procedure for conducting one-way ANOVA is described in Figure 19.2. It involves identifying the dependent and independent variables, decomposing the total variation, measuring the effects, testing significance and interpreting the results. We consider these steps in detail and illustrate them with some applications.

Identifying the dependent and independent variables

The dependent variable is denoted by Y and the independent variable by X, and X is a categorical variable having c categories. There are n observations on Y for each category of X, as shown in Table 19.1. As can be seen, the sample size in each category of X is n, and the total sample size $N = n \times c$. Although the sample sizes in the categories of X (the group sizes) are assumed to be equal for the sake of simplicity, this is not a requirement.

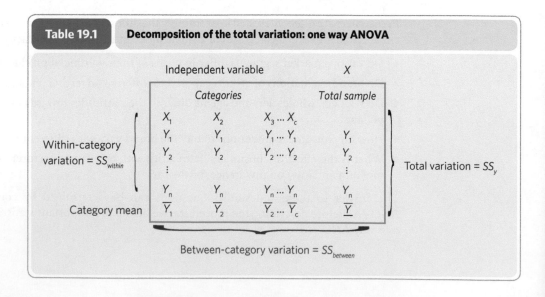

| Table 19.1 | Decomposition of the total variation: one way ANOVA |

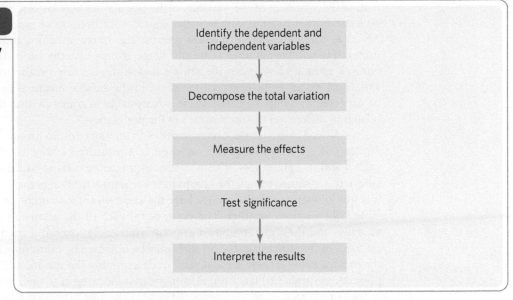

Figure 19.2

Conducting one-way ANOVA

Decompose the total variation

In examining the differences among means, one-way ANOVA involves the decomposition of the total variation observed in the dependent variable. This variation is measured by the sums of squares corrected for the mean (SS). ANOVA is so named because it examines the variability or variation in the sample (dependent variable) and, based on the variability, determines whether there is reason to believe that the population means differ.

Decomposition of the total variation

In one-way ANOVA, separation of the variation observed in the dependent variable into the variation due to the independent variables plus the variation due to error.

The total variation in Y, denoted by SS_y, can be decomposed into two components:

$$SS_y = SS_{between} + SS_{within}$$

where the subscripts *between* and *within* refer to the categories of X. $SS_{between}$ is the variation in Y related to the variation in the means of the categories of X. It represents variation between the categories of X. In other words, $SS_{between}$ is the portion of the sum of squares in Y related to the independent variable or factor X. For this reason, $SS_{between}$ is also denoted as SS_x. SS_{within} is the variation in Y related to the variation within each category of X. SS_{within} is not accounted for by X. Therefore, it is referred to as SS_{error}. The total variation in Y may be decomposed as

$$SS_y = SS_x + SS_{error}$$

where

$$SS_y = \sum_{i=1}^{N} (Y_i - \bar{Y})^2$$

$$SS_x = \sum_{j=1}^{c} n(Y_j - \bar{Y}_j)^2$$

$$SS_{error} = \sum_{j=1}^{c} (Y_{ij} - \bar{Y}_j)^2$$

and Y_i = individual observation
$\bar{Y}_j$ = mean for category j
$\bar{Y}$ = mean over the whole sample or grand mean
Y_{ij} = ith observation in the jth category

The logic of decomposing the total variation in Y, SS_y, into $SS_{between}$ and SS_{within} in order to examine differences in group means can be intuitively understood. Recall from Chapter 18 that, if the variation of the variable in the population was known or estimated, one could estimate how much the sample mean should vary because of random variation alone. In ANOVA, there are several different groups (e.g. heavy, medium and light users and non-users). If the null hypothesis is true and all the groups have the same mean in the population, one can estimate how much the sample means should vary because of sampling (random) variations alone. If the observed variation in the sample means is more than what would be expected by sampling variation, it is reasonable to conclude that this extra variability is related to differences in group means in the population.

In ANOVA, we estimate two measures of variation: within groups (SS_{within}) and between groups ($SS_{between}$). Within-group variation is a measure of how much the observations, Y values, within a group vary. This is used to estimate the variance within a group in the population. It is assumed that all the groups have the same variation in the population. But because it is not known that all the groups have the same mean, we cannot calculate the variance of all the observations together. The variance for each of the groups must be calculated individually, and these are combined into an 'average' or 'overall' variance. Likewise, another estimate of the variance of the Y values may be obtained by examining the variation between the means. (This process is the reverse of determining the variation in the means, given the population variances.) If the population mean is the same in all the groups, then the variation in the sample means and the sizes of the sample groups can be used to estimate the variance of Y. The reasonableness of this estimate of the Y variance depends on whether the null hypothesis is true. If the null hypothesis is true and the population means are equal, the variance estimate based on between-group variation is correct. On the other hand, if the groups have different means in the population, the variance estimate based on between-group variation will be too large. Thus, by comparing the Y variance estimates based on between-group and within-group variation, we can test the null hypothesis. Decomposition of the total variation in this manner also enables us to measure the effects of X on Y.

Measuring the effects

The effects of X on Y are measured by SS_x. Because SS_x is related to the variation in the means of the categories of X, the relative magnitude of SS_x increases as the differences among the means of Y in the categories of X increase. The relative magnitude of SS_x also increases as the variations in Y within the categories of X decrease. The strength of the effects of X on Y is measured as follows:

$$\eta^2 = \frac{SS_x}{SS_y} = \frac{SS_y - SS_{error}}{SS_y}$$

The value of η^2 varies between 0 and 1. It assumes a value of 0 when all the category means are equal, indicating that X has no effect on Y. The value of η^2 will be 1 when there is no variability within each category of X but there is some variability between categories. Thus, η^2 is a measure of the variation in Y that is explained by the independent variable X. Not only can we measure the effects of X on Y, but we can also test for their significance.

Testing the significance

In one-way ANOVA, the interest lies in testing the null hypothesis that the category means are equal in the population.[4] In other words,

$$H_0: \mu_1 = \mu_2 = \mu_3 = \ldots = \mu_c$$

Under the null hypothesis, SS_x and SS_{error} come from the same source of variation. In such a case, the estimate of the population variance of Y can be based on either between-category variation or within-category variation. In other words, the estimate of the population variance of Y,

$$s_y^2 = \frac{SS_x}{c-1}$$
$$= \text{mean square due to } X$$
$$= MS_x$$

or

$$s_y^2 = \frac{SS_{error}}{N-c}$$
$$= \text{mean square due to error}$$
$$= MS_{error}$$

The null hypothesis may be tested by the F statistic based on the ratio between these two estimates:

$$F = \frac{SS_x/(c-1)}{SS_{error}/(N-c)} = \frac{MS_x}{MS_{error}}$$

This statistic follows the F distribution, with $(c-1)$ and $(N-c)$ degrees of freedom (df). A table of the F distribution is given as Table 5 in the Appendix of statistical tables at the end of the book. As mentioned in Chapter 18, the F distribution is a probability distribution of the ratios of sample variances. It is characterised by degrees of freedom for the numerator and degrees of freedom for the denominator.[5]

Interpreting results

If the null hypothesis of equal category means is not rejected, then the independent variable does not have a significant effect on the dependent variable. On the other hand, if the null hypothesis is rejected, then the effect of the independent variable is significant. In other words, the mean value of the dependent variable will be different for different categories of the independent variable. A comparison of the category mean values will indicate the nature of the effect of the independent variable. Other salient issues in the interpretation of results, such as examination of differences among specific means, are discussed later.

Illustrative data

We illustrate the concepts discussed in this section using the data presented in Table 19.2. For illustrative purposes, we consider only a small number of observations. In actual practice, ANOVA is performed on a much larger sample. These data were generated by an experiment in which Mercedes wanted to examine the effect of direct mail offers and dealership promotions upon the level of sales of new cars. Dealership promotion was varied at three levels: high (1), medium (2) and low (3). Direct mail efforts were manipulated at two levels. Either an exclusive set of leather-bound books that detailed the history of Mercedes was offered to customers who bought a new car (denoted by 1) or it was not (denoted by 2 in Table 19.2). Dealership promotion and direct mail offer were crossed, resulting in a 3 × 2 design with six cells. Thirty Mercedes dealerships were randomly selected, and five dealerships were randomly assigned to each treatment condition. The experiment ran for two months. The sales levels of new cars were measured, normalised to account for extraneous factors (e.g. dealership size, competitive dealerships in town) and converted to a 1 to 10 scale (10 representing the highest level of sales). In addition, a qualitative assessment was made of the relative affluence of the clientele of each dealership, again using a 1 to 10 scale. In these scales, higher numbers denote higher sales or more affluent clientele.

Table 19.2	Direct mail offer, dealership promotion, sales of new cars and clientele rating			
Dealership number	Direct mail offer	Dealership promotion	Sales	Clientele rating
1	1	1	10	9
2	1	1	9	10
3	1	1	10	8
4	1	1	8	4
5	1	1	9	6
6	1	2	8	8
7	1	2	8	4
8	1	2	7	10
9	1	2	9	6
10	1	2	6	9
11	1	3	5	8
12	1	3	7	9
13	1	3	6	6
14	1	3	4	10
15	1	3	5	4
16	2	1	8	10
17	2	1	9	6
18	2	1	7	8
19	2	1	7	4
20	2	1	6	9
21	2	2	4	6
22	2	2	5	8
23	2	2	5	10
24	2	2	6	4
25	2	2	4	9
26	2	3	2	4
27	2	3	3	6
28	2	3	2	10
29	2	3	1	9
30	2	3	2	8

Illustrative applications of one-way ANOVA

We illustrate one-way ANOVA, first with an example showing calculations done by hand, and then by computer. Suppose that only one factor, namely dealership promotion, was manipulated; that is, let us ignore the direct mail efforts for the purpose of this illustration. Mercedes is attempting to determine the effect of dealership promotion (X) on the sales of new cars (Y). For the purpose of illustrating hand calculations, the data of Table 19.2 are transformed in Table 19.3 to show the dealership (Y_{ij}) for each level of promotion.

The null hypothesis is that the category means are equal:

$$H_0: \mu_1 = \mu_2 = \mu_3$$

Table 19.3	Effect of dealership promotion on sales of new cars		

	Level of dealership promotion		
Dealership number	High	Medium	Low
	Normalised sales		
1	10	8	5
2	9	8	7
3	10	7	6
4	8	9	4
5	9	6	5
6	8	4	2
7	9	5	3
8	7	5	2
9	7	6	1
10	6	4	2
Column totals	83	62	37
Category means: $\overline{Y}_j$	$\frac{83}{10}=8.3$	$\frac{62}{10}=6.2$	$\frac{37}{10}=3.7$

Grand means: $\overline{Y}=\dfrac{83+62+37}{30}=6.067$

To test the null hypothesis, the various sums of squares are computed as follows:

$$SS_y = (10-6.067)^2 +(9-6.067)^2 +(10-6.067)^2 +(8-6.067)^2 +(9-6.067)^2 +(8-6.067)^2$$
$$+(8-6.067)^2 +(7-6.067)^2 +(9-6.067)^2 +(6-6.067)^2 +(5-6.067)^2 +(7-6.067)^2$$
$$+(6-6.067)^2 +(4-6.067)^2 +(5-6.067)^2 +(8-6.067)^2 +(9-6.067)^2 +(7-6.067)^2$$
$$+(7-6.067)^2 +(6-6.067)^2 +(4-6.067)^2 +(5-6.067)^2 +(5-6.067)^2 +(6-6.067)^2$$
$$+(4-6.067)^2 +(2-6.067)^2 +(3-6.067)^2 +(2-6.067)^2 +(1-6.067)^2 +(2-6.067)^2$$
$$=185.867$$

$$SS_x = 10(8.3-6.067)^2 + 10(6.2-6.067)^2 + 10(3.7-6.067)^2$$
$$= 106.067$$

$$SS_{error} = (10-8.3)^2 + (9-8.3)^2 + (10-8.3)^2 + (8-8.3)^2 + (9-8.3)^2 + (8-8.3)^2$$
$$+ (9-8.3)^2 + (7-8.3)^2 + (7-8.3)^2 + (6-8.3)^2 + (8-8.3)^2 + (8-8.3)^2$$
$$+ (7-8.3)^2 + (9-8.3)^2 + (6-8.3)^2 + (4-8.3)^2 + (5-8.3)^2 + (5-8.3)^2$$
$$+ (6-8.3)^2 + (4-8.3)^2 + (5-8.3)^2 + (7-8.3)^2 + (6-8.3)^2 + (4-8.3)^2$$
$$+ (5-8.3)^2 + (2-8.3)^2 + (3-8.3)^2 + (2-8.3)^2 + (1-8.3)^2 + (2-8.3)^2$$
$$= 79.80$$

It can be verified that

$$SS_y = SS_x + SS_{error}$$

as follows:

$$185.867 = 106.067 + 79.80$$

The strength of the effects of X on Y are measured as follows:

$$\eta^2 = \frac{SS_x}{SS_y}$$

$$= \frac{106.067}{185.897}$$

$$= 0.571$$

In other words, 57.1% of the variation in sales (Y) is accounted for by dealership promotion (X), indicating a modest effect. The null hypothesis may now be tested:

$$F = \frac{SS_x/(c-1)}{SS_{error}/(N-c)} = \frac{MS_x}{MS_{error}}$$

$$= \frac{106.067/(3-1)}{79.8/(30-3)}$$

$$= 17.944$$

From Table 5 in the Appendix of statistical tables we see that, for 2 and 27 degrees of freedom, the critical value of F is 3.35 for $\alpha = 0.05$. Because the calculated value of F is greater than the critical value, we reject the null hypothesis. We conclude that the population means for the three levels of dealership promotion are indeed different. The relative magnitudes of the means for the three categories indicate that a high level of dealership promotion leads to significantly higher sales of new car sales.

We now illustrate the ANOVA procedure using a computer program. The results of conducting the same analysis by computer are presented in Table 19.4.

Table 19.4	One-way ANOVA: effect of dealership promotion on the sale of new cars				
Source of variation	Sum of squares	df	Mean square	F ratio	F probability
Between groups (dealership promotion)	106.067	2	53.033	17.944	0.000
Within groups (error)	79.800	27	2.956		
Total	185.867	29	6.409		

Cell means

Level of dealership promotion	Count	Mean
High (1)	10	8.300
Medium (2)	10	6.200
Low (3)	10	3.700
Total	30	6.067

The value of SS_x denoted by main effects is 106.067 with 2 df; that of SS_{error} (within-group sums of squares) is 79.80 with 27 df. Therefore, $MSx = 106.067/2 = 53.033$ and $MS_{error} = 79.80/27 = 2.956$. The value of $F = 53.033/2.956 = 17.944$ with 2 and 27 df, resulting in a probability of 0.000. Since the associated probability is less than the significance level of 0.05, the null hypothesis of equal population means is rejected. Alternatively, it can be seen from Table 5 in the Appendix that the critical value of F for 2 and 27 df is 3.35. Since the calculated value of F (17.944) is larger than the critical value, the null hypothesis is rejected. As can be seen from Table 19.4, the sample means with values of 8.3, 6.2 and 3.7 are quite different. Dealerships with a high level of promotions have the highest average sales (8.3) and dealerships with a low level of promotions have the lowest average sales (3.7). Dealerships with a medium level of promotions have an intermediate level of sales (6.2). These findings seem plausible.

Assumptions in ANOVA

The procedure for conducting one-way ANOVA and the illustrative applications help us understand the assumptions involved. The salient assumptions in ANOVA can be summarised as follows:

1   Ordinarily, the categories of the independent variable are assumed to be fixed. Inferences are made only to the specific categories considered. This is referred to as the *fixed-effects model*. Other models are also available. In the *random-effects model*, the categories or treatments are considered to be random samples from a universe of treatments. Inferences are made to other categories not examined in the analysis. A *mixed-effects model* results if some treatments are considered fixed and others random.[6]

2   The error term is normally distributed, with a zero mean and a constant variance. The error is not related to any of the categories of X. Modest departures from these assumptions do not seriously affect the validity of the analysis. Furthermore, the data can be transformed to satisfy the assumption of normality or equal variances.

3   The error terms are uncorrelated. If the error terms are correlated (i.e. the observations are not independent), the F ratio can be seriously distorted.

In many data analysis situations, these assumptions are reasonably met. ANOVA is therefore a common procedure as illustrated in the following example.

Real research   ## Viewing ethical perceptions from different lenses[7]

A survey was conducted to examine differences in perceptions of ethical issues. The data were obtained from 31 managers, 21 faculty, 97 undergraduate business students and 48 MBA students. As part of the survey, participants were required to rate five ethical items on a scale of 1 = Strongly Agree to 5 = Strongly Disagree with 3 representing a neutral response. The means for each group are shown. One-way analysis of variance was conducted to examine the significance of differences between groups for each survey item, and the F and p values obtained are shown.

Item no.	Survey item	Managers	Faculty	MBA students	Undergrad students	F value	p value
1	Students caught cheating should receive an F	3.7	3.8	3.8	4.0	0.94	0.42
2	Plagiarism should be reported	4.1	3.4	3.8	3.5	2.2	0.09
3	Student grades should be raised to get employer pay for course	1.6	1.7	2.7	2.8	18.3	0.00
4	Use of school printers for personal printing should be stopped	4.5	3.4	3.5	3.2	11.0	0.00
5	Coursework should be simplified to accommodate weaker students	1.7	1.8	2.4	2.8	13.4	0.00

The findings indicating significant differences on three of the five ethics items point to the need for more communication among the four groups so as to better align perceptions of ethical issues in management education.

N-way ANOVA

In marketing research, one is often concerned with the effect of more than one factor simultaneously.[8] For example:

- How do consumers' intentions to buy a brand vary with different levels of price and different levels of distribution?
- How do advertising levels (high, medium and low) interact with price levels (high, medium and low) to influence a brand's sale?
- Do income levels (high, medium and low) and age (younger than 35, 35–55, older than 55) affect consumption of a brand?
- What is the effect of consumers' familiarity with a bank (high, medium and low) and bank image (positive, neutral and negative) on preference for taking a loan out with that bank?

Interaction
When assessing the relationship between two variables, an interaction occurs if the effect of X_1 depends on the level of X_2, and vice versa.

In determining such effects, n-way ANOVA can be used. A major advantage of n-way ANOVA is that it enables the researcher to examine **interactions** between the factors. Interactions occur when the effects of one factor on the dependent variable depend on the level (category) of the other factors. The procedure for conducting n-way ANOVA is similar to that for one-way ANOVA. The statistics associated with n-way ANOVA are also defined similarly. Consider the simple case of two factors X_1 and X_2 having categories c_1 and c_2. The total variation in this case is partitioned as follows:

$$SS_{total} = SS \text{ due to } X_1 + SS \text{ due to } X_2 + SS \text{ due to interaction of } X_1 \text{ and } X_2 + SS_{within}$$

or

$$SS_y = SS_{x_1} + SS_{x_2} + SS_{x_1x_2} + SS_{error}$$

A larger effect of X_1 will be reflected in a greater mean difference in the levels of X_1 and a larger SSx_1. The same is true for the effect of X_2. The larger the interaction between X_1 and X_2, the larger SS_{x1x2} will be. On the other hand, if X_1 and X_2 are independent, the value of SS_{x1x2} will be close to zero.[9]

Multiple η^2

The strength of the joint effect of two (or more) factors, or the overall effect.

Significance of the overall effect

A test that some differences exist between some of the treatment groups.

Significance of the interaction effect

A test of the significance of the interaction between two or more independent variables.

Significance of the main effect of each factor

A test of the significance of the main effect for each individual factor.

The strength of the joint effect of two factors, called the overall effect, or **multiple η^2**, is

$$\text{Multiple } \eta^2 = (SS_{x_1} + SS_{x_2} + SS_{x_1 x_2})/SS_y$$

The **significance of the overall effect** may be tested by an F test, as follows:

$$F = \frac{(SS_{x_1} + SS_{x_2} + SS_{x_1 x_2})/df_n}{SS_{error}/df_d}$$

$$= \frac{SS_{x_1,x_2,x_1x_2}/df_n}{SS_{error}/df_d}$$

$$= \frac{MS_{x_1,x_2,x_1x_2}}{MS_{error}}$$

where df_n = degrees of freedom for the numerator
$$= (c_1 - 1) + (c_2 - 1) + (c_1 - 1)(c_2 - 1)$$
$$= c_1 c_2 - 1$$
df_d = degrees of freedom for the denominator
$$= N - c_1 c_2$$
MS = mean square

If the overall effect is significant, the next step is to examine the **significance of the interaction effect**. Under the null hypothesis of no interaction, the appropriate F test is

$$F = \frac{SS_{x_1x_2}/df_n}{SS_{error}/df_d}$$

$$= \frac{MS_{x_1x_2}}{MS_{error}}$$

where $df_n = (c_1 - 1)(c_2 - 1)$
$df_d = N - c_1 c_2$

If the interaction effect is found to be significant, then the effect of X_1 depends on the level of X_2, and vice versa. Since the effect of one factor is not uniform but varies with the level of the other factor, it is not generally meaningful to test the **significance of the main effect of each factor**. It is meaningful to test the significance of each main effect of each factor, if the interaction effect is not significant.[10]

The significance of the main effect of each factor may be tested as follows for X_1:

$$F = \frac{SS_{x_1}/df_n}{SS_{error}/df_d}$$

$$= \frac{MS_{x_1}}{MS_{error}}$$

where $df_n = c_1 - 1$
$df_d = N - c_1 c_2$

The foregoing analysis assumes that the design was orthogonal, or balanced (the number of cases in each cell was the same). If the cell size varies, the analysis becomes more complex.

Illustrative example of *N*-way ANOVA

Returning to the data in Table 19.2, let us now examine the effect of the level of dealership promotion and direct mail efforts on the sales of new cars. The results of running a 3×2 ANOVA on the computer are presented in Table 19.5.

For the main effect of level of promotion, the sum of squares SS_{xp}, degrees of freedom and mean square MS_{xp} are the same as determined earlier in Table 19.4. The sum of squares for direct mail is $SS_{xd} = 53.333$ with 1 *df*, resulting in an identical value for the mean square MS_{xd}. The combined main effect is determined by adding the sum of squares due to the two main effects ($SS_{xp} + SS_{xd} = 106.067 + 53.333 = 159.400$) as well as adding the degrees of freedom (2 + 1 = 3). For the promotions and direct mail interaction effect, the sum of squares is $SS_{xpxd} = 3.267$ with $(3 - 1) \times (2 - 1) = 2$ *df*, resulting in $MS_{xpxd} = 3.267/2 = 1.633$. For the overall (model) effect, the sum of squares is the sum of squares for promotions main effect, direct

Table 19.5	**Two-way ANOVA**

Source of variation	Sum of squares	df	Mean squares	F	Sig. of F	ω^2
			Main effects			
Dealer promotions	106.067	2	53.033	54.843	0.000	0.557
Direct mail	53.333	1	53.333	55.153	0.000	0.280
Combined	159.400	3	53.133	54.966	0.000	
Two-way interaction	3.267	2	1.633	1.690	0.206	
Model	162.667	5	32.533	33.643	0.000	
Residual (error)	23.200	24	0.967			
Total	185.867	29	6.409			

Cell means

Dealership promotions	Direct mail	Count	Mean
High	Yes	5	9.200
High	No	5	7.400
Medium	Yes	5	7.600
Medium	No	5	4.800
Low	Yes	5	5.400
Low	No	5	2.000

Factor-level means

Dealership promotions	Direct mail	Count	Mean
High		10	8.300
Medium		10	6.200
Low		10	3.700
	Yes	15	7.400
	No	15	4.733
Grand mean		30	6.067

mail main effect and interaction effect = 106.067 + 53.333 + 3.267 = 162.667 with 2 + 1 + 2 = 5 *df*, resulting in a mean square of 162.667/5 = 32.533. Note, however, that the error statistics are now different from those in Table 19.4. This is due to the fact that we now have two factors instead of one, SS_{error} = 23.2 with [30 − (3 × 2)] or 24 *df* resulting in MS_{error} = 23.2/24 = 0.967. The test statistic for the significance of the overall effect is

$$F = \frac{32.533}{0.967}$$
$$= 33.643$$

with 5 and 24 degrees of freedom, which is significant at the 0.05 level.

The test statistic for the significance of the interaction effect is

$$F = \frac{1.633}{0.967}$$
$$= 1.69$$

with 2 and 24 degrees of freedom, which is not significant at the 0.05 level.

As the interaction effect is not significant, the significance of the main effects can be evaluated. The test statistic for the significance of the main effect of promotion is

$$F = \frac{53.033}{0.967}$$
$$= 54.843$$

with 2 and 24 degrees of freedom, which is significant at the 0.05 level.

The test statistic for the significance of the main effect of direct mail is

$$F = \frac{53.333}{0.967}$$
$$= 55.153$$

with 1 and 24 degrees of freedom, which is significant at the 0.05 level. Thus, higher levels of promotions result in higher sales. The use of a direct mail campaign results in higher sales. The effect of each is independent of the other.

The following example illustrates the use of *n*-way analysis.

Real research   **Country affects TV reception**[11]

A study examined the impact of country affiliation on the credibility of product-attribute claims for TVs. The dependent variables were the following product-attribute claims: good sound, reliability, crisp-clear picture and stylish design. The independent variables which were manipulated consisted of price, country affiliation and store distribution. A 2 × 2 × 2 between-subjects design was used. Two levels of price, 'low' and 'high', two levels of country affiliation, South Korea and Germany, and two levels of store distribution, Kaufhof and without Kaufhof, were specified.

Data were collected from two shopping centres in a large German city. Thirty participants were randomly assigned to each of the eight treatment cells for a total of 240 subjects. Table 1 presents the results for manipulations that had significant effects on each of the dependent variables.

The directions of country-by-distribution interaction effects for the three dependent variables are shown in Table 2. Although the credibility ratings for the crisp-clear picture, reliability and stylish design claims are improved by distributing the Korean-made TV set through Kaufhof rather than some other distributor, the same is not true of a German-made set. Similarly, the directions of country-by-price interaction effects for the two dependent variables are shown in Table 3. At the 'high' price level, the credibility ratings for the 'good sound' and 'reliability' claims are higher for the German-made TV set than for its Korean counterpart, but there is little difference related to country affiliation when the product is at the 'low' price.

Table 1 Analyses for significant manipulations

		Univariate		
Effect	Dependent variable	F	df	p
Country × price	Good sound	7.57	1.232	0.006
Country × price	Reliability	6.57	1.232	0.011
Country × distribution	Crisp-clear picture	6.17	1.232	0.014
Country × distribution	Reliability	6.57	1.232	0.011
Country × distribution	Stylish design	10.31	1.232	0.002

Table 2 Country-by-distribution interaction means

Country × distribution	Crisp-clear picture	Reliability	Stylish design
South Korea			
Kaufhof	3.67	3.42	3.82
Without Kaufhof	3.18	2.88	3.15
Germany			
Kaufhof	3.60	3.47	3.53
Without Kaufhof	3.77	3.65	3.75

Table 3 Country-by-price interaction means

Country × price	Good sound	Reliability
Low price		
Kaufhof	3.75	3.40
Without Kaufhof	3.53	3.45
High price		
Kaufhof	3.15	2.90
Without Kaufhof	3.73	3.67

This study demonstrates that credibility of attribute claims, for products tradition-ally exported to Germany by a company in a relatively newly industrialised country, can be significantly improved if the same company distributes the product through a pres-tigious German retailer and considers making manufacturing investments in Europe. Specifically, three product-attribute claims (crisp-clear picture, reliability and stylish design) are perceived as more credible when the TVs are made in South Korea if they are also distributed through a prestigious German retailer. Also, the 'good sound' and 'reliability' claims for TVs are perceived to be more credible for a German-made set sold at a higher price, possibly offsetting the potential disadvantage of higher manufacturing costs in Europe.

Analysis of covariance (ANCOVA)

When examining the differences in the mean values of the dependent variable related to the effect of the controlled independent variables, it is often necessary to take into account the influence of uncontrolled independent variables. For example:

- In determining how consumers' intentions to buy a brand vary with different levels of price, attitude towards the brand may have to be taken into consideration.
- In determining how different groups exposed to different advertisements evaluate a brand, it may be necessary to control for prior knowledge.
- In determining how different price levels will affect a household's breakfast cereal consumption, it may be essential to take household size into account.

In such cases, ANCOVA should be used. ANCOVA includes at least one categorical independent variable and at least one interval or metric-independent variable. The categorical independent variable is called a *factor*, whereas the metric-independent variable is called a *covariate*. The most common use of the covariate is to remove extraneous variation from the dependent variable, because the effects of the factors are of major concern. The variation in the dependent variable due to the covariates is removed by an adjustment of the dependent variable's mean value within each treatment condition. An ANOVA is then performed on the adjusted scores.[12] The significance of the combined effect of the covariates, as well as the effect of each covariate, is tested by using the appropriate *F* tests. The coefficients for the covariates provide insights into the effect that the covariates exert on the dependent variable. ANCOVA is most useful when the covariate is linearly related to the dependent variable and is not related to the factors.[13]

Illustrative application of covariance

We again use the data of Table 19.2 to illustrate ANCOVA. Suppose that we wanted to determine the effect of dealership promotion and direct mail on sales while controlling for the affluence of clientele. It is felt that the affluence of the clientele may also have an effect on the sales of new cars. The dependent variable consists of new car sales. As before, promotion has three levels and direct mail has two. Clientele affluence is measured on an interval scale and serves as the covariate. The results are shown in Table 19.6.

Table 19.6	ANCOVA				
Source of variation	Sum of squares	df	Mean square	F	Sig. of F
Covariates					
Clientele	0.838	1	0.838	0.862	0.363
Main effects					
Promotions	106.067	2	53.033	54.546	0.000
Direct mail	53.333	1	53.333	54.855	0.000
Combined	159.400	3	53.133	54.649	0.000
Two-way interaction					
Promotions × Direct mail	3.267	2	1.633	1.680	0.208
Model	163.505	6	27.251	28.028	0.000
Residual (error)	22.362	23	0.972		
Total	185.867	29	6.409		
Covariate	Raw coefficient				
Clientele	−0.078				

As can be seen, the sum of squares attributable to the covariate is very small (0.838) with 1 *df* resulting in an identical value for the mean square. The associated *F* value is 0.838/0.972 = 0.862, with 1 and 23 *df*, which is not significant at the 0.05 level. Thus, the conclusion is that the affluence of the clientele does not have an effect on the sales of new Mercedes cars (which may be a tough conclusion to draw, demanding further investigation). If the effect of the covariate is significant, the sign of the raw coefficient can be used to interpret the direction of the effect on the dependent variable.

Issues in interpretation

Important issues involved in the interpretation of ANOVA results include interactions, relative importance of factors, and multiple comparisons.

Interactions

The different interactions that can arise when conducting ANOVA on two or more factors are shown in Figure 19.3. One outcome is that ANOVA may indicate that there are no interactions (the interaction effects are not found to be significant). The other possibility is that the interaction is significant. An interaction effect occurs when the effect of an independent variable on a dependent variable is different for different categories or levels of another independent variable. The interaction may be ordinal or disordinal. In ordinal interaction, the rank order of the effects related to one factor does not change across the levels of the second factor. Disordinal interaction, on the other hand, involves a change in the rank order of the effects of one factor across the levels of another. If the interaction is disordinal, it could be of a non-crossover or crossover type.[14] These interaction cases are displayed in Figure 19.4, which assumes that there are two factors, X_1 with three levels (X_{11}, X_{12} and X_{13}) and X_2 with two levels (X_{21} and X_{22}). Case 1 depicts no interaction.

The effects of X_1 on Y are parallel over the two levels of X_2. Although there is some departure from parallelism, this is not beyond what might be expected from chance. Parallelism implies that the net effect of X_{22} over X_{21} is the same across the three levels of X_1. In the absence of interaction, the joint effect of X_1 and X_2 is simply the sum of their individual main effects.

Case 2 depicts an ordinal interaction. The line segments depicting the effects of X_1 and X_2 are not parallel. The difference between X_{22} and X_{21} increases as we move from X_{11} to X_{12} and

Ordinal interaction
An interaction where the rank order of the effects attributable to one factor does not change across the levels of the second factor.

Disordinal interaction
The change in the rank order of the effects of one factor across the levels of another.

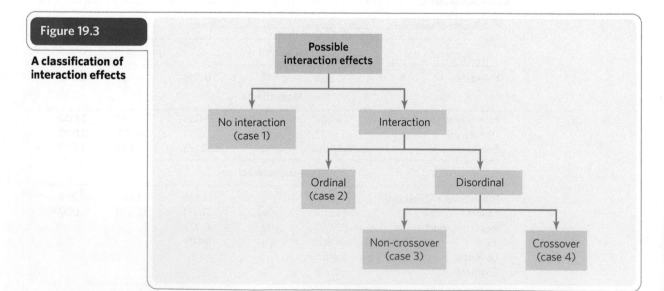

Figure 19.3

A classification of interaction effects

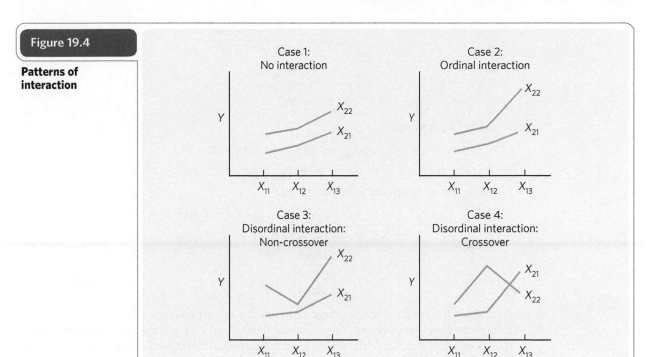

Figure 19.4

Patterns of interaction

from X_{12} to X_{13}, but the rank order of the effects of X_1 is the same over the two levels of X_2. This rank order, in ascending order, is X_{11}, X_{12}, X_{13}, and it remains the same for X_{21} and X_{22}.

Disordinal interaction of a non-crossover type is displayed by case 3. The lowest effect of X_1 at level X_{21} occurs at X_{11}, and the rank order of effects is X_{11}, X_{12}, X_{13}. At level X_{22}, however, the lowest effect of X_1 occurs at X_{12}, and the rank order is changed to X_{12}, X_{11}, X_{13}. Because it involves a change in rank order, disordinal interaction is stronger than ordinal interaction.

In disordinal interactions of a crossover type, the line segments cross each other, as shown by case 4 in Figure 19.4. In this case, the relative effect of the levels of one factor changes with the levels of the other. Note that X_{22} has a greater effect than X_{21} when the levels of X_1 are X_{11} and X_{12}. When the level of X_1 is X_{13}, the situation is reversed, and X_{21} has a greater effect than X_{22}. (Note that in cases 1, 2 and 3, X_{22} had a greater impact than X_{21} across all three levels of X_1.) Hence, disordinal interactions of a crossover type represent the strongest interactions.[15]

Relative importance of factors

Experimental designs are usually balanced in that each cell contains the same number of participants. This results in an orthogonal design in which the factors are uncorrelated. Hence, it is possible to determine unambiguously the relative importance of each factor in explaining the variation in the dependent variable. The most commonly used measure in ANOVA is omega squared (ω^2). This measure indicates what proportion of the variation in the dependent variable is related to a particular independent variable or factor. The relative contribution of a factor X is calculated as follows:[16]

Omega squared (ω^2)
A measure indicating the proportion of the variation in the dependent variable that is related to a particular independent variable or factor.

$$\omega_x^2 = \frac{SS_x - (df_x \times MS_{error})}{SS_{total} + MS_{error}}$$

Note that the estimated value of ω^2 can be negative, in which case the estimated value of ω^2 is set equal to zero. Normally, ω^2 is interpreted only for statistically significant effects.[17] In Table 19.4, ω^2 associated with level of dealership promotions is calculated as follows:

$$\omega_p^2 = \frac{106.067 - (2 \times 0.967)}{185.867 + 0.967}$$

$$= \frac{104.133}{186.834}$$

$$= 0.557$$

In Table 19.5 note that

$$SS_{total} = 106.067 + 53.333 + 3.267 + 23.2$$

$$= 185.867$$

Likewise, the ω^2 associated with direct mail is

$$\omega^2 = \frac{53.333 - (1 \times 0.967)}{185.867 + 0.967}$$

$$= \frac{52.366}{186.834}$$

$$= 0.280$$

As a guide to interpreting ω^2, a large experimental effect produces an ω^2 of 0.15 or greater, a medium effect produces an index of around 0.06, and a small effect produces an index of 0.01.[18] In Table 19.5, while the effects of promotions and direct mail are both large, the effect of promotions is much larger. Therefore, dealership promotions will be more effective in increasing sales than direct mail.

Multiple comparisons

Contrasts

In ANOVA, a method of examining differences among two or more means of the treatment groups.

A priori contrasts

Contrasts determined before conducting the analysis, based on the researcher's theoretical framework.

A posteriori contrasts

Contrasts made after conducting the analysis. These are generally multiple comparison tests.

Multiple comparison tests

A posteriori contrasts that enable the researcher to construct generalised confidence intervals that can be used to make pairwise comparisons of all treatment means.

The ANOVA F test examines only the overall difference in means. If the null hypothesis of equal means is rejected, we can only conclude that not all the group means are equal. Only some of the means may be statistically different, however, and we may wish to examine differences among specific means. This can be done by specifying appropriate contrasts, or comparisons used to determine which of the means are statistically different. Contrasts may be a priori or a posteriori. A priori contrasts are determined before conducting the analysis, based on the researcher's theoretical framework. Generally, a priori contrasts are used in lieu of the ANOVA F test. The contrasts selected are orthogonal (they are independent in a statistical sense).

A posteriori contrasts are made after the analysis. These are generally multiple comparison tests. They enable the researcher to construct generalised confidence intervals that can be used to make pairwise comparisons of all treatment means. These tests, listed in order of decreasing power, include least significant difference, Duncan's multiple range test, Student–Newman–Keuls, Tukey's alternate procedure, honestly significant difference, modified least significant difference and Scheffé's tests. Of these tests, least significant difference is the most powerful and Scheffé's the most conservative. For further discussion on a priori and a posteriori contrasts, refer to the literature.[19]

Our discussion so far has assumed that each subject is exposed to only one treatment or experimental condition. Sometimes subjects are exposed to more than one experimental condition, in which case repeated measures ANOVA should be used.

Repeated measures ANOVA

In marketing research, there are often large differences in the background and individual characteristics of participants. If this source of variability can be separated from treatment effects (effects of the independent variable) and experimental error, then the sensitivity of the experiment can be enhanced. One way of controlling the differences between subjects is by observing each subject under each experimental condition (see Table 19.7). In this sense, each subject serves as its own control. For example, in a survey attempting to determine differences in evaluations of various airlines, each participant evaluates all the major competing airlines. Because repeated measurements are obtained from each participant, this design is referred to as within-subjects design or **repeated measures ANOVA**. This differs from the assumption we made in our earlier discussion that each participant is exposed to only one treatment condition, also referred to as between-subjects design.[20] Repeated measures ANOVA may be thought of as an extension of the paired samples t test to the case of more than two related samples.

Repeated measures ANOVA

An ANOVA technique used when participants are exposed to more than one treatment condition and repeated measurements are obtained.

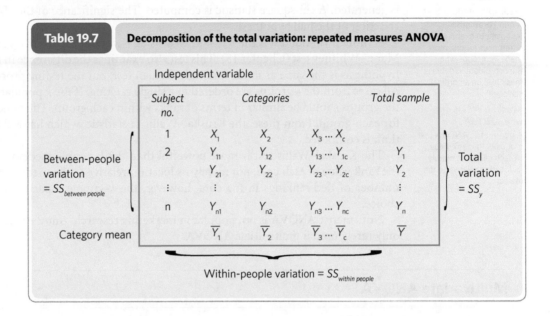

Table 19.7	Decomposition of the total variation: repeated measures ANOVA

In the case of a single factor with repeated measures, the total variation, with $n(c - 1)$ degrees of freedom, may be split into between-people variation and within-people variation:

$$SS_{total} = SS_{between\ people} + SS_{within\ people}$$

The between-people variation, which is related to the differences between the means of people, has $n - 1$ degrees of freedom. The within-people variation has $n(c - 1)$ degrees of freedom. The within-people variation may, in turn, be divided into two different sources of variation. One source is related to the differences between treatment means, and the second consists of residual or error variation. The degrees of freedom corresponding to the treatment variation are $c - 1$ and those corresponding to residual variation are $(c - 1)(n - 1)$. Thus,

$$SS_{within\ people} = SS_x + SS_{error}$$

A test of the null hypothesis of equal means may now be constructed in the usual way:

$$F = \frac{SS_x / (c-1)}{SS_{error} / (n-1)(c-1)}$$
$$= \frac{MS_x}{MS_{error}}$$

So far we have assumed that the dependent variable is measured on an interval or ratio scale. If the dependent variable is non-metric, however, a different procedure should be used.

Non-metric ANOVA

Non-metric ANOVA
An ANOVA technique for examining the difference in the central tendencies of more than two groups when the dependent variable is measured on an ordinal scale.

k-sample median test
A non-parametric test used to examine differences among more than two groups when the dependent variable is measured on an ordinal scale.

Kruskal–Wallis one-way ANOVA
A non-metric ANOVA test that uses the rank value of each case, not merely its location relative to the median.

Non-metric ANOVA examines the difference in the central tendencies of more than two groups when the dependent variable is measured on an ordinal scale. One such procedure is the k-sample median test. As its name implies, this is an extension of the median test for two groups, which was considered in Chapter 18. The null hypothesis is that the medians of the k populations are equal. The test involves the computation of a common median over the k samples. Then, a $2 \times k$ table of cell counts based on cases above or below the common median is generated. A chi-square statistic is computed. The significance of the chi-square implies a rejection of the null hypothesis.

A more powerful test is the Kruskal–Wallis one-way ANOVA. This is an extension of the Mann–Whitney test (Chapter 18). This test also examines the difference in medians. The null hypothesis is the same as in the k-sample median test, but the testing procedure is different. All cases from the k groups are ordered in a single ranking. If the k populations are the same, the groups should be similar in terms of ranks within each group. The rank sum is calculated for each group. From these, the Kruskal–Wallis H statistic, which has a chi-square distribution, is computed.

The Kruskal–Wallis test is more powerful than the k-sample median test because it uses the rank value of each case, not merely its location relative to the median. If there are a large number of tied rankings in the data, however, the k-sample median test may be a better choice.

Non-metric ANOVA is not popular in marketing research. Another procedure that is also only rarely used is multivariate ANOVA.

Multivariate ANOVA

Multivariate analysis of variance (MANOVA)
An ANOVA technique using two or more metric dependent variables.

Multivariate analysis of variance (MANOVA) is similar to ANOVA except that instead of one metric-dependent variable we have two or more. The objective is the same, since MANOVA is also concerned with examining differences between groups. Although ANOVA examines group differences on a single dependent variable, MANOVA examines group differences across multiple dependent variables simultaneously. In ANOVA, the null hypothesis is that the means of the dependent variables are equal across the groups. In MANOVA, the null hypothesis is that the vector of the means of multiple dependent variables is equal across groups. MANOVA is appropriate when there are two or more dependent variables that are correlated. If there are multiple dependent variables that are uncorrelated or orthogonal, ANOVA on each of the dependent variables is more appropriate than MANOVA.[21]

As an example, suppose that four groups, each consisting of 100 randomly selected individuals, were exposed to four different advertisements about the 'B Class' Mercedes. After seeing the advertisement, each individual provided ratings on preference for the 'B Class', preference for Mercedes and preference for the advertisement itself. Because these three preference variables are correlated, MANOVA should be conducted to determine which advertisement is the most effective (produced the highest preference across the three preference variables). The following example illustrates the application of ANOVA and MANOVA in international marketing research.

Real research

The commonality of unethical research practices worldwide[22]

A study examined marketing professionals' perceptions of how common unethical practices in marketing research were across different countries, i.e. 'the commonality of unethical marketing research practices'. A sample of marketing professionals was drawn from Australia, the UK, Canada and the USA. Participants' evaluations were analysed using MANOVA and ANOVA techniques. The predictor variable was the 'country of participant' and 15 evaluations of 'commonality' served as the criterion variables. The F values from the ANOVA analyses indicated that only 2 of the 15 commonality evaluations achieved significance ($p < 0.05$ or better). Further, the MANOVA F value was not statistically significant, implying the lack of overall differences in commonality evaluations across participants of the four countries. It was concluded that marketing professionals in the four countries demonstrate similar perceptions of the commonality of unethical research practices. This finding was not surprising, given other research evidence that organisations in the four countries reflect similar corporate cultures.

Real research

'MAN'OVA demonstrates that man is different from woman[23]

In order to investigate differences between research ethics judgements In men and women, the statistical techniques of MANOVA and ANOVA were used. Participants were asked to indicate their degree of approval with regard to a series of scenarios involving decisions of an ethical nature. These evaluations served as the dependent variable in the analysis, and participant gender as the independent variable. MANOVA was used  for multivariate analysis and its resultant F value was significant at the $p < 0.001$ level, indicating that there was an 'overall' difference between males and females in research ethics judgements. Univariate analysis was conducted via ANOVA, and F values indicated that three items were the greatest contributors to the overall gender difference in ethical evaluations: the use of ultraviolet ink to precode a mail questionnaire, the use of an advertisement that encourages consumer misuse of a product, and unwillingness of a researcher to offer data help to an inner city advisory group. Another recent study examined how ethical beliefs were related to age and gender of business professionals. The results of this particular study indicated that, overall, younger business professionals exhibited a lower standard of ethical beliefs. In the younger age group, females demonstrated a higher level of ethical beliefs to males. However, in the older age group, results showed that males had a slightly higher level of ethical beliefs. Thus companies should emphasise ethical values and training to the younger professionals, especially men.

SPSS and SAS Learning Editions

SPSS Windows

One-way ANOVA can be efficiently performed using the program COMPARE MEANS and then ONE-WAY ANOVA. To select this procedure click

Analyze>Compare Means>One-Way ANOVA . . .

The following are the detailed steps for running a one-way ANOVA on the data of Table 19.2. The null hypothesis is that there is no difference in mean normalised sales for the three levels of dealership promotion.

1 Select ANALYZE from the SPSS menu bar.
2 Click COMPARE MEANS and then ONE-WAY ANOVA.
3 Move 'Sales [sales]' into the DEPENDENT LIST box.
4 Move 'Dealership Promotion [promotion]' to the FACTOR box.
5 Click OPTIONS.
6 Click Descriptive.
7 Click CONTINUE.
8 Click OK.

   N-way ANOVA, analysis of covariance, MANOVA and repeated measures ANOVA can be preformed using GENERAL LINEAR MODEL. To select this procedure, click

Analyze>General Linear Model>Univariate. . .
Analyze>General Linear Model>Multivariate. . .
Analyze>General Linear Model>Repeated Measures. . .

We show the detailed steps for performing the analysis of covariance given in Table 19.6:

1 Select ANALYZE from the SPSS menu bar.
2 Click GENERAL LINEAR MODEL and then UNIVARIATE.
3 Move 'Sales [sales]' into the DEPENDENT LIST box.
4 Move 'Dealership Promotion [promotion]' to the FIXED FACTOR(S) box. Then move 'Direct Mail [coupon]' to the FIXED FACTOR(S) box.
5 Move 'Clientele [clientel]' to the COVARIATE(S) box.
6 Click OK.

For non-metric ANOVA, including k-sample median test and Kruskal–Wallis one-way ANOVA, the program Nonparametric Tests should be used.

Analyze>Nonparametric Tests>K Independent Samples . . .
Analyze>Nonparametric Tests>K Related Samples . . .

The detailed steps for the other procedures are similar to those shown.

SAS Learning Edition

The ANOVA task offers one-way ANOVA, non-parametric one-way ANOVA, and mixed and linear models. One-way ANOVA can be efficiently performed using One-Way ANOVA within the ANOVA task. To select this task click:

Analyze>ANOVA>One-Way ANOVA

The following are the detailed steps for running a one-way ANOVA on the data of Table 19.2. The null hypothesis is that there is no difference in mean normalised sales for the three levels of dealership promotion.

1 Select ANALYZE from the SAS Learning Edition menu bar.
2 Click ANOVA and then One-way ANOVA.
3 Move SALES to the dependent variable task role.
4 Move PROMOTION to the independent variable task role.
5 Click RUN.

   N-way ANOVA, analysis of covariance, MANOVA, and repeated measures ANOVA can be performed using the Linear Models task:

Analyze>ANOVA>Linear Models.

We show the detailed steps for performing the analysis of covariance given in Table 19.6:

1 Select ANALYZE from the SAS Learning Edition menu bar.
2 Click ANOVA and then Linear Models.
3 Move SALES to the dependent variable task role.
4 Move PROMOTION and COUPON to the quantitative variables task role.

5 Move CLIENTEL to the classification variable task role.
6 Click Model.
7 Select PROMOTION and COUPON and then click Main.
8 Select PROMOTION and COUPON and then click Cross.
9 Click RUN.

For non-metric ANOVA, including the k-sample median task and Kruskal–Wallis one-way ANOVA, the Nonparametric One-Way ANOVA task should be used:

Analyze>ANOVA>Nonparametric One-Way ANOVA

Summary

In ANOVA and ANCOVA, the dependent variable is metric and the independent variables are all categorical and metric variables. One-way ANOVA involves a single independent categorical variable. Interest lies in testing the null hypothesis that the category means are equal in the population. The total variation in the dependent variable may be decomposed into two components: variation related to the independent variable and variation related to error. The variation is measured in terms of the sum of squares corrected for the mean (SS). The mean square is obtained by dividing the SS by the corresponding degrees of freedom (df). The null hypothesis of equal means is tested by an F statistic, which is the ratio of the mean square related to the independent variable to the mean square related to error.

N-way analysis of variance involves the simultaneous examination of two or more categorical independent variables. A major advantage is that the interactions between the independent variables can be examined. The significance of the overall effect, interaction terms and the main effects of individual factors are examined by appropriate F tests. It is meaningful to the significance of main effects only if the corresponding interaction terms are not significant.

ANCOVA includes at least one categorical independent variable and at least one interval or metric-independent variable. The metric-independent variable, or covariate, is commonly used to remove extraneous variation from the dependent variable.

When ANOVA is conducted on two or more factors, interactions can arise. An interaction occurs when the effect of an independent variable on a dependent variable is different for different categories or levels of another independent variable. If the interaction is significant, it may be ordinal or disordinal. Disordinal interaction may be of a non-crossover or crossover type. In balanced designs, the relative importance of factors in explaining the variation in the dependent variable is measured by omega squared (ω^2). Multiple comparisons in the form of a priori or a posteriori contrasts can be used for examining differences among specific means.

In repeated measures analysis of variance, observations on each subject are obtained under each treatment condition. This design is useful for controlling for the differences in subjects that exist prior to the experiment. Non-metric analysis of variance involves examining the differences in the central tendencies of two or more groups when the dependent variable is measured on an ordinal scale. Multivariate analysis of variance (MANOVA) involves two or more metric-dependent variables.

Questions

1 Discuss the similarities and differences between analysis of variance and analysis of covariance.

2 What is the relationship between analysis of variance and the *t* test?

3 What is total variation? How is it decomposed in a one-way analysis of variance?

4 What is the null hypothesis in one-way ANOVA? What basic statistic is used to test the null hypothesis in one-way ANOVA? How is this statistic computed?

5 How does *n*-way analysis of variance differ from the one-way procedure?

6 How is the total variation decomposed in *n*-way analysis of variance?

7 What is the most common use of the covariate in ANCOVA?

8 What is the difference between ordinal and disordinal interaction?

9 How is the relative importance of factors measured in a balanced design?

10 What is an a priori contrast?

11 What is the most powerful test for making a posteriori contrasts? Which test is the most conservative?

12 What is meant by repeated measures ANOVA? Describe the decomposition of variation in repeated measures ANOVA.

13 What are the differences between metric and non-metric analyses of variance?

14 Describe two tests used for examining differences in central tendencies in non-metric ANOVA.

15 What is multivariate analysis of variance? When is it appropriate?

Exercises

1 A researcher wants to test the hypothesis that there is no difference in the importance attached to shopping by consumers living in Belgium, France, Germany and the Netherlands. A study is conducted and analysis of variance is used to analyse the data. The results obtained are presented in the following table:

Source	df	Sum of squares	Mean squares	F ratio	F probability
Between groups	3	70.212	23.404	1.12	0.3
Within groups	996	20,812.416	20.896		

a Is there sufficient evidence to reject the null hypothesis?

b What conclusion can be drawn from the table?

c If the average importance was computed for each group, would you expect the sample means to be similar or different?

d What was the total sample size in this study?

2 In a pilot study examining the effectiveness of three advertisements (A, B and C), 10 consumers were assigned to view each advertisement and rate it on a nine-point Likert scale. The data obtained from the 30 participants are shown in the following table:

Advertisement A	Advertisement B	Advertisement C
4	7	8
5	4	7
3	6	7
4	5	6
3	4	8
4	6	7
4	5	8
3	5	8
5	4	5
5	4	6

a Calculate the category means and the grand mean.
b Calculate SS_y into SS_x and SS_{error}.
c Calculate η^2.
d Calculate the value of F.
e Are the three advertisements equally effective?

3 An experiment tested the effects of package design and shelf display on the likelihood of buying a breakfast cereal. Package design and shelf display were varied at two levels each, resulting in a 2 × 2 design. Purchase likelihood was measured on a seven-point scale. The results are partially described in the following table:

Source of variation	Sum of squares	df	Mean square	F	Sig. of F	ω^2
Package design	68.76	1				
Shelf display	320.19	1				
Two-way interaction	55.05	1				
Residual error	176.00	40				

a Complete the table by calculating the mean square, F, significance of F, and ω^2 values.
b How should the main effects be interpreted?

4 In an experiment designed to measure the effect of gender and frequency of travel on preference for long-haul holidays, a 2 (gender) × 3 (frequency of travel) between-subjects design was adopted. Five participants were assigned to each cell for a total sample size of 30. Preference for long-haul holidays was measured on a nine-point scale (1 = no preference, 9 = strong preference). Gender was coded as male = 1 and female = 2. Frequency of travel was coded as light = 1, medium = 2 and heavy = 3. The data obtained are shown in the table:

Number	Gender	Travel group	Preference
1	1	1	2
2	1	1	3
3	1	1	4
4	1	1	4
5	1	1	2
6	1	2	4
7	1	2	5
8	1	2	5
9	1	2	3
10	1	2	3
11	1	3	8
12	1	3	9
13	1	3	8
14	1	3	7
15	1	3	7
16	2	1	6
17	2	1	7
18	2	1	6
19	2	1	5
20	2	1	7
21	2	2	3
22	2	2	4
23	2	2	5
24	2	2	4
25	2	2	5
26	2	3	6
27	2	3	6
28	2	3	6
29	2	3	7
30	2	3	8

Using software of your choice, perform the following analysis:

a Do males and females differ in their preference for long-haul travel?

b Do the light, medium and heavy travellers differ in their preference for long-haul travel?

c Conduct a 2 × 3 analysis of variance with preference for long-haul travel as the dependent variable and gender and travel frequency as the independent variables or factors. Interpret the results.

5 In a small group discuss the following issues: 'Which procedure is more useful in marketing research – analysis of variance or analysis of covariance?' and 'There are few marketing research applications where *t* tests are used; the complexity of marketing phenomena means that analysis of variance or analysis of covariance are much more commonplace.'

Notes

1. Wang, Y., 'Web based destination marketing systems: assessing the critical factors for management and implementation', *International Journal of Tourism Research* 10 (1) (February 2008), 55; Mangaloglu, S.B.M., 'Tourism destination images of Turkey, Egypt, Greece and Italy as perceived by US based tour operators and travel agents', *Tourism Management* 22 (1) (February 2001), 1–9.

2. Weltevreden, J.W.J. and Boschma, R.A., 'Internet strategies and performance of Dutch retailers', *Journal of Retailing and Consumer Services* 15 (3) (May 2008), 163–178.

3. For applications of ANOVA, see Ahmed, S.A. and d'Astous, A., 'Antecedents, moderators and dimensions of country of origins evaluations', *International Marketing Review* 25 (1) (2008), 75; Swait, J. and Erdem, T., 'Brand effects on choice and choice set formation under uncertainty', *Marketing Science* 26 (5) (October 2007), 679–700; Sengupta, J. and Gorn, G.J., 'Absence makes the mind grow sharper: effects of element omission on subsequent recall', *Journal of Marketing Research* 39 (2) (May 2002), 186–201.

4. Sirkin, R.M., *Statistics for the Social Sciences*, 3rd edn (Thousand Oaks, CA: Sage 2005); Janky, D.G., 'Sometimes pooling for analysis of variance hypothesis tests: a review and study of a split level model', *American Statistician* 54 (4) (November 2000), 269–279; Driscoll, W.C., 'Robustness of the ANOVA and Tukey-Kramer statistical tests', *Computers and Industrial Engineering* 31 (1, 2) (October 1996), 265–268.

5. The *F* test is a generalised form of the *t* test. If a random variable is *t* distributed with *N* degrees of freedom, then t^2 is *F* distributed with 1 and *N* degrees of freedom. Where there are two factor levels or treatments, ANOVA is equivalent to the two-sided *t* test.

6. Although computations for the fixed-effects and random-effects models are similar, interpretations of results differ. A comparison of these approaches is found in Turner, J.R. and Thayer, J., *Introduction to Analysis of Variance: Design, Analysis and Interpretation* (Thousand Oaks, CA: Sage, 2001); Erez, A., Bloom, M.C. and Wells, M.T., 'Using random rather than fixed effects models in meta-analysis: implications for situational specificity and validity generalization', *Personnel Psychology* 49 (2) (Summer 1996), 275–306; Neter, J.W., *Applied Linear Statistical Models*, 4th edn (Burr Ridge, IL: Irwin, 1996).

7. Hall, A. and Berardino, L., 'Teaching professional behaviours: differences in the perceptions of faculty, students and employers', *Journal of Business Ethics* 63 (2006), 407–415.

8. We consider only the full factorial designs, which incorporate all possible combinations of factor levels. For example, see Menon, G., 'Are the parts better than the whole? The effects of decompositional questions on judgments of frequent behaviors', *Journal of Marketing Research* 34 (August 1997), 335–346.

9. Pecotich, A. and Ward, S., 'Global branding, country of origin and expertise: an experimental evaluation', *International Marketing Review* 24 (3) (2007), 271; Kamins, M.A., Dreze, X. and Folkes, V.S., 'Effects of seller-supplied prices on buyers' product evaluations: reference prices in an internet auction context', *Journal of Consumer*

Research 30 (March 2004), 622–628; Jaccard, J., *Interaction Effects in Factorial Analysis of Variance* (Thousand Oaks, CA: Sage, 1997); Mayers, J.L., *Fundamentals of Experimental Design*, 3rd edn (Boston, MA: Allyn & Bacon, 1979).

10. Field, A., *Discovering Statistics Using SPSS*, 2nd edn (Thousand Oaks, CA: Sage, 2005); Nishisato, S., *Measurement and Multivariate Analysis* (New York: Springer-Verlag, 2002).

11. Maheswaran, D. and Chen, C.Y., 'Nation equity: incidental emotions in country of origin effects', *Journal of Consumer Research* 33 (3) (December 2006), 370–376; Desai, K.K., 'The effects of ingredient branding strategies on host brand extendibility', *Journal of Marketing* 66 (1) (January 2002), 73–93; Peterson, R.A. and Jolibert, A.J.P., 'A meta-analysis of country-of-origin effects', *Journal of International Business Studies* 26 (4) (Fourth Quarter 1995), 883–900; Chao, P., 'The impact of country affiliation on the credibility of product attribute claims', *Journal of Advertising Research* (April–May 1989), 35–41.

12. Although this is the most common way in which analysis of covariance is performed, other situations are also possible. For example, covariate and factor effects may be of equal interest, or the set of covariates may be of major concern. For applications, see Sharot, T., 'The design and precision of data-fusion studies', *International Journal of Market Research* 49 (4) (2007), 449–470; Bolton, L.E. and Reed, A., 'Sticky priors: the perseverance of identity effects on judgment', *Journal of Marketing Research* 41 (November 2004), 397–410.

13. For more detailed discussions, see Turner, J.R. and Thayer, J., *Introduction to Analysis of Variance: Design, Analysis and Interpretation* (Thousand Oaks, CA: Sage, 2001); Glantz, S.A. and Slinker, B.K., *Primer of Applied Regression and Analysis of Variance* (Blacklick, OH: McGraw-Hill, 2000); Neter, J.W., *Applied Linear Statistical Models*, 4th edn (Burr Ridge, IL: Irwin, 1996); Wildt, A.R. and Ahtola, O.T., *Analysis of Covariance* (Beverly Hills, CA: Sage, 1978).

14. See Zhang, S. and Schmitt, B.H., 'Creating local brands in multilingual international markets', *Journal of Marketing Research* 38 (3) (August 2001), 313–325; Umesh, U.N., Peterson, R.A., McCann-Nelson, M. and Vaidyanathan, R., 'Type IV error in marketing research: the investigation of ANOVA interactions', *Journal of the Academy of Marketing Science* 24 (1) (Winter 1966), 17–26; Ross, W.T. Jr and Creyer, E.H., 'Interpreting interactions: raw means or residual means', *Journal of Consumer Research* 20 (2) (September 1993), 330–338; Leigh, J.H. and Kinnear, T.C., 'On interaction classification', *Educational and Psychological Measurement* 40 (Winter 1980), 841–843.

15. For an examination of interactions using an ANOVA framework, see Jaccard, J., *Interaction Effects in Factorial Analysis of Variance* (Thousand Oaks, CA: Sage, 1997); Wansink, B., 'Advertising's impact on category substitution', *Journal of Marketing Research* 31 (November 1994), 505–515.

16. This formula does not hold if repeat measurements are made on the dependent variable. See Fern, E.F. and Monroe, K.B., 'Effect size estimates: issues and problems in interpretation', *Journal of Consumer Research* 23 (2)

(September 1996), 89–105; Dodd, D.H. and Schultz, R.F. Jr, 'Computational procedures for estimating magnitude of effect for some analysis of variance designs', *Psychological Bulletin* (June 1973), 391–395.

17. The ω^2 formula is attributed to Hays. See Hays, W.L., *Statistics for Psychologists* (New York: Holt, Rinehart & Winston, 1963).

18. Johnson, R.A. and Wichern, D.W., *Applied Multivariate Statistical Analysis* (Paramus, NJ: Prentice Hall, 2001); Fern, E.F. and Monroe, K.B., 'Effect-size estimates: issues and problems in interpretation', *Journal of Consumer Research* 23 (2) (September 1996), 89–105; Cohen, J., *Statistical Power Analysis for the Behavioral Sciences* (Mahwah, NJ: Lawrence Erlbaum Associates, 1988).

19. Ximnez, C. and Revuelta, J., 'Extending the CLAST sequential rule to one-way ANOVA under group sampling', *Behaviour Research Methods* 39 (1) (February 2007), 86–100; Turner, J.R. and Thayer, J., *Introduction to Analysis of Variance: Design, Analysis and Interpretation* (Thousand Oaks, CA: Sage, 2001); Neter, J.W., *Applied Linear Statistical Models*, 4th edn (Burr Ridge, IL: Irwin, 1996); Winer, B.J., Brown, D.R. and Michels, K.M., *Statistical Principles in Experimental Design*, 3rd edn (New York: McGraw-Hill, 1991).

20. It is possible to combine between-subjects and within-subjects factors in a single design. See, for example, Vickner, F. and Hofmann, J., 'The price-perceived quality relationship: a meta analytic review and assessment of its determinants', *Marketing Letters* 18 (3) (July 2007), 181–196; Ahluwalia, R., Unnava, H.R. and Burnkrant, R.E., 'The moderating role of commitment on the spillover effect of marketing communications', *Journal of Marketing Research* 38 (4) (November 2001), 458–470.

21. See Schott, J.R., 'Some high-dimensional tests for a one-way MANOVA', *Journal of Multivariate Analysis* 98 (9) (October 2007), 1825–1839; Kim, S. and Olejnik, S., 'Bias and precision of measures of association for a fixed-effect multivariate analysis of variance model', *Multivariate Behavioural Research* 40 (4) (October 2005), 401–425; Roehm, M.L., Pullins, E.B. and Roehm, H.A. Jr, 'Designing loyalty-building programs for packaged goods brands', *Journal of Marketing* 39 (2) (May 2002), 202–213; Bray, J.H. and Maxwell, S.E., *Multivariate Analysis of Variance* (Beverly Hills, CA: Sage, 1985). For an application of MANOVA, see Piercy, N.F., 'Sales manager behaviour control strategy and its consequences: the impact of gender differences', *Journal of Personal Selling & Sales Management* 21(1) (Winter 2001), 39–49.

22. Kimmel, A.J. and Smith, N.C., 'Deception in marketing research: ethical, methodological and disciplinary implications', *Psychology and Marketing* 18 (7) (July 2001), 663–689; Abramson, N.R., Keating, R.J. and Lane, H.W., 'Cross-national cognitive process differences: a comparison of Canadian, American and Japanese managers', *Management International Review* 36 (2) (Second Quarter 1996), 123–147; Akaah, I.P., 'A cross-national analysis of the perceived commonality of unethical practices in marketing research', in Lazer, L., Shaw, E. and Wee, C.-H. (eds), *World Marketing Congress*, International Conference Series, Vol. 4 (Boca Raton, FL: Academy of Marketing Science, 1989), 2–9.

23. Peterson, D., Rhoads, A. and Vaught, B.C., 'Ethical beliefs of business professionals: a study of gender, age and external factors', *Journal of Business Ethics* 31 (3) (June 2001), 1; Akaah, I.P., 'Differences in research ethics judgments between male and female marketing professionals', *Journal of Business Ethics* 8 (1989), 375–381.

20 Correlation and regression

Correlation is the simplest way to understand the association between two metric variables. When extended to multiple regression, the relationship between one variable and several others becomes more clear.

Objectives

After reading this chapter, you should be able to:

1 discuss the concepts of product moment correlation, partial correlation and part correlation, and show how they provide a foundation for regression analysis;

2 explain the nature and methods of bivariate regression analysis and describe the general model, estimation of parameters, standardised regression coefficient, significance testing, prediction accuracy, residual analysis and model cross-validation;

3 explain the nature and methods of multiple regression analysis and the meaning of partial regression coefficients;

4 describe specialised techniques used in multiple regression analysis, particularly stepwise regression, regression with dummy variables, and analysis of variance and covariance with regression;

5 discuss non-metric correlation and measures such as Spearman's rho and Kendall's tau;

6 appreciate how SPSS and SAS software are used in analyses of correlation and regression.

Overview

Chapter 19 examined the relationship among the *t* test, analysis of variance and covariance, and regression. This chapter describes regression analysis, which is widely used for explaining variation in market share, sales, brand preference and other marketing results. This is done in terms of marketing management variables such as advertising, price, distribution and product quality. Before discussing regression, however, we describe the concepts of product moment correlation and partial correlation coefficient, which lay the conceptual foundation for regression analysis.

In introducing regression analysis, we discuss the simple bivariate case first. We describe estimation, standardisation of the regression coefficients, and testing and examination of the strength and significance of association between variables, prediction accuracy and the assumptions underlying the regression model. Next, we discuss the multiple regression model, emphasising the interpretation of parameters, strength of association, significance tests and examination of residuals.

We then cover topics of special interest in regression analysis, such as stepwise regression, multicollinearity, relative importance of predictor variables and cross-validation. We describe regression with dummy variables and the use of this procedure to conduct analysis of variance and covariance. Finally, help is provided to run the SPSS and SAS Learning Editions in the data analysis challenges presented in this chapter. We begin with two examples that illustrate applications of regression analysis.

Real research   Regression hits the right bell for Avon[1]

Avon Products (**www.avon.com**) was having significant problems with its sales staff. The company's business, dependent upon sales representatives, was facing a shortage of sales staff without much hope of getting new ones. Regression models were developed to reveal the possible variables that were fuelling this situation. The models revealed that the most significant variable was the level of appointment fee that representatives pay for materials, and second was the employee benefits. With data to back up its actions, the company lowered the fee. Avon also recruited a senior manager to improve the way it communicated to new recruits its employee benefits package. The 'Guide to your personal benefits' was an informative and easy-to-navigate information source. These changes resulted in an improvement in the recruitment and retention of sales representatives.

Retailing revolution[2]

Many experts argue that online shopping has revolutionised retailing. Whereas many traditional retailers experienced sluggish, single-digit sales growth in the 2000s, online sales records were off the charts. Although online shopping continues to make up a small portion of overall retail sales, the prospects look very promising for the future. A research project investigating this trend looked for correlates of consumers' preferences for online shopping. The sample was made up of participants who were familiar with online shopping. The explanation of consumers' preferences was sought in psychographic, demographic and communications variables suggested in the literature. Multiple regression was used to analyse the data. The overall multiple regression model was significant at a 0.05 level. Univariate t tests indicated that the following variables in the model were significant at a 0.05 level or better: price orientation, gender, age, occupation, ethnicity and education. None of the three communication variables (mass media, word of mouth and publicity) was significantly related to consumer preference, the dependent variable. The results suggested that electronic shopping was preferred by white females who were older, better educated, working in supervisory or higher level occupations, and price oriented.

These example illustrate some of the uses of regression analysis in determining which independent variables explain a significant variation in the dependent variable of interest, the structure and form of the relationship, the strength of the relationship, and predicted values of the dependent variable. Fundamental to regression analysis is an understanding of product moment correlation.

Product moment correlation

In marketing research, we are often interested in summarising the strength of association between two metric variables, as in the following situations:

- How strongly are sales related to advertising expenditures?
- Is there an association between market share and size of the sales force?
- Are consumers' perceptions of quality related to their perceptions of prices?

Product moment correlation (r)
A statistic summarising the strength of association between two metric variables.

In situations like these, the **product moment correlation** (r) is the most widely used statistic, summarising the strength of association between two metric (interval- or ratio-scaled) variables, say X and Y. It is an index used to determine whether a linear or straight line relationship exists between X and Y. It indicates the degree to which the variation in one variable, X, is related to the variation in another variable, Y. Because it was originally proposed by Karl Pearson, it is also known as the *Pearson correlation coefficient* and also referred to as *simple correlation, bivariate correlation* or merely the *correlation coefficient*. From a sample of n observations, X and Y, the product moment correlation, r, can be calculated as

$$r = \frac{\sum_{i=1}^{n}(X_i - \overline{X})(Y_i - \overline{Y})}{\sqrt{\sum_{i=1}^{n}(X_i - \overline{X})^2 \sum_{i=1}^{n}(Y_i - \overline{Y})^2}}$$

Division of the numerator and denominator by $n-1$ gives

$$r = \frac{\displaystyle\sum_{i=1}^{n}\frac{(X_i-\overline{X})(Y_i-\overline{Y})}{n-1}}{\sqrt{\displaystyle\sum_{i=1}^{n}\frac{(X_i-\overline{X})^2}{n-1}\sum_{i=1}^{n}\frac{(Y_i-\overline{Y})^2}{n-1}}}$$

$$= \frac{COV_{xy}}{s_x s_y}$$

Covariance

A systematic relationship between two variables in which a change in one implies a corresponding change in the other (COV_{xy}).

In these equations $\overline{X}$ and $\overline{Y}$ denote the sample means, and s_x and s_y the standard deviations. COV_{xy}, the **covariance** between X and Y, measures the extent to which X and Y are related. The covariance may be either positive or negative. Division by $s_x s_y$ achieves standardisation so that r varies between -1.0 and $+1.0$. Note that the correlation coefficient is an absolute number and is not expressed in any unit of measurement. The correlation coefficient between two variables will be the same regardless of their underlying units of measurement.

As an example, suppose that a researcher wants to explain attitudes towards a participant's city of residence in terms of duration of residence in the city. The attitude is measured on an 11-point scale (1 = do not like the city, 11 = very much like the city), and the duration of residence is measured in terms of the number of years the participant has lived in the city. In a pretest of 12 participants, the data shown in Table 20.1 are obtained. For illustrative purposes, we consider only a small number of observations so that we can show the calculations by hand. In practice, correlation and regression analyses are performed on much larger samples.

Table 20.1	Explaining attitude towards the city of residence		
Participant number	Attitude towards the city	Duration of residence	Importance attached to weather
1	6	10	3
2	9	12	11
3	8	12	4
4	3	4	1
5	10	12	11
6	4	6	1
7	5	8	7
8	2	2	4
9	11	18	8
10	9	9	10
11	10	17	8
12	2	2	5

The correlation coefficient may be calculated as follows:

$$\overline{X} = (10+12+12+4+12+6+8+2+18+9+17+2)/12$$
$$= 9.333$$
$$\overline{Y} = (6+9+8+3+10+4+5+2+11+9+10+2)/12$$
$$= 6.583$$

$$\sum_{i=1}^{n}(X_i-\overline{X})\,(Y_i-\overline{Y})=(10-9.33)(6-6.58)$$
$$+(12-9.33)(9-6.58)$$
$$+(12-9.33)(8-6.58)+(4-9.33)(3-6.58)$$
$$+(12-9.33)(10-6.58)+(6-9.33)(4-6.58)$$
$$+(8-9.33)(5-6.58)+(2-9.33)(2-6.58)$$
$$+(18-9.33)(11-6.58)+(9-9.33)(9-6.58)$$
$$+(17-9.33)(10-6.58)+(2-9.33)(2-6.58)$$
$$=-0.3886+6.4614+3.7914+19.0814+9.1314+8.5914$$
$$+\ 2.1014+33.5714+38.3214-0.7986+26.2314+33.5714$$
$$=179.6668$$

$$\sum_{i=1}^{n}(X_i-X)^2=(10-9.33)^2+(12-9.33)^2+(12-9.33)^2+(4-9.33)^2$$
$$+(12-9.33)^2+(6-9.33)^2+(8-9.33)^2+(2-9.33)^2+(18-9.33)^2$$
$$+(9-9.33)^2+(17-9.33)^2+(2-9.33)^2$$
$$=0.4489+7.1289+7.1289+28.4089+7.1289+11.0889+1.7689$$
$$+\ 53.7289+75.1689+0.1089+58.8289+53.7289$$
$$=304.6668$$

$$\sum_{i=1}^{n}(Y_i-\overline{Y})^2=(6-6.58)^2+(9-6.58)^2+(8-6.58)^2+(3-6.58)^2+(3-6.58)^2$$
$$+(10-6.58)^2+(4-6.58)^2+(5-6.58)^2+(2-6.58)^2+(11-6.58)^2$$
$$+(9-6.58)^2+(10-6.58)^2+(2-6.58)^2$$
$$=0.3364+5.8564+2.0164+12.8164+11.6964+6.6564+2.4964$$
$$+\ 20.9764+19.5364+5.8564+11.6964+20.9764$$
$$=120.9168$$

Thus,

$$r=\frac{179.6668}{\sqrt{(304.6668)(120.9168)}}$$
$$=0.9361$$

In this example, $r = 0.9361$, a value close to 1.0. This means that participants' duration of residence in the city is strongly associated with their attitude towards the city. Furthermore, the positive sign of r implies a positive relationship; the longer the duration of residence, the more favourable the attitude and vice versa.

Since r indicates the degree to which variation in one variable is related to variation in another, it can also be expressed in terms of the decomposition of the total variation (see Chapter 19). In other words,

$$r^2=\frac{\text{explained variation}}{\text{total variation}}$$
$$=\frac{SS_x}{SS_y}$$
$$=\frac{\text{total variation}-\text{error variation}}{\text{total variation}}$$
$$=\frac{SS_y-SS_{error}}{SS_y}$$

Hence, r^2 measures the proportion of variation in one variable that is explained by the other. Both r and r^2 are symmetric measures of association. In other words, the correlation of X with Y is the same as the correlation of Y with X. It does not matter which variable is considered to be the dependent variable and which the independent. The product moment coefficient measures the strength of the linear relationship and is not designed to measure non-linear relationships. Thus $r = 0$ merely indicates that there is no linear relationship between X and Y. It does not mean that X and Y are unrelated. There could well be a non-linear relationship between them, which would not be captured by r (see Figure 20.1).

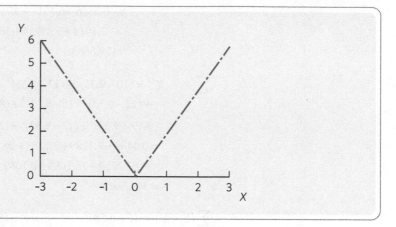

Figure 20.1

A non-linear relationship for which $r = 0$

When computed for a population rather than a sample, the product moment correlation is denoted by the Greek letter rho, ρ. The coefficient r is an estimator of ρ. Note that the calculation of r assumes that X and Y are metric variables whose distributions have the same shape. If these assumptions are not met, r is deflated and underestimates ρ. In marketing research, data obtained by using rating scales with a small number of categories may not be strictly interval. This tends to deflate r, resulting in an underestimation of ρ.[3]

The statistical significance of the relationship between two variables measured by using r can be conveniently tested. The hypotheses are

$$H_0: \rho = 0$$
$$H_1: \rho \neq 0$$

The test statistic is

$$t = r\left(\frac{n-2}{1-r^2}\right)^{\frac{1}{2}}$$

which has a t distribution with $n - 2$ degrees of freedom.[4] For the correlation coefficient calculated based on the data given in Table 20.1,

$$t = 0.9361\left(\frac{12-2}{1-(0.9361^2)}\right)^{\frac{1}{2}}$$

$$= 8.414$$

and the degrees of freedom $df = 12 - 2 = 10$. From the t distribution table (Table 4 in the Appendix of statistical tables), the critical value of t for a two-tailed test and $\alpha = 0.05$ is 2.228. Hence, the null hypothesis of no relationship between X and Y is rejected. This, along with the positive sign of r, indicates that attitude towards the city is positively related to the duration of residence in the city. Moreover, the high value of r indicates that this relationship is strong. If this were a large and representative sample, the implication would be that managers, city officials and politicians wishing to reach people with a favourable attitude to the city should target long-term residents of that city.

In conducting multivariate data analysis, it is often useful to examine the simple correlation between each pair of variables. These results are presented in the form of a correlation matrix, which indicates the coefficient of correlation between each pair of variables. Usually, only the lower triangular portion of the matrix is considered. The diagonal elements all equal 1.00, since a variable correlates perfectly with itself. The upper triangular portion of the matrix is a mirror image of the lower triangular portion, since r is a symmetric measure of association. The form of a correlation matrix for five variables, V_1 to V_5, is as follows:

	V_1	V_2	V_3	V_4	V_5
V_1					
V_2	0.5				
V_3	0.3	0.4			
V_4	0.1	0.3	0.6		
V_5	0.2	0.5	0.3	0.7	

Although a matrix of simple correlations provides insights into pairwise associations, sometimes researchers want to examine the association between two variables after controlling for one or more other variables. In the latter case, partial correlation should be estimated.

Partial correlation

Partial correlation coefficient

A measure of the association between two variables after controlling or adjusting for the effects of one or more additional variables.

Whereas the product moment or simple correlation is a measure of association describing the linear association between two variables, a partial correlation coefficient measures the association between two variables after controlling for or adjusting for the effects of one or more additional variables. This statistic is used to answer the following questions:

- How strongly are sales related to advertising expenditures when the effect of price is controlled?
- Is there an association between market share and size of the sales force after adjusting for the effect of sales promotion?
- Are consumers' perceptions of quality related to their perceptions of prices when the effect of brand image is controlled?

As in these situations, suppose that a researcher wanted to calculate the association between X and Y after controlling for a third variable, Z. Conceptually, one would first remove the effect of Z from X. To do this, one would predict the values of X based on knowledge of Z by using the product moment correlation between X and Z, r_{xz}. The predicted value of X is then subtracted from the actual value of X to construct an adjusted value of X. In a similar manner, the values of Y are adjusted to remove the effects of Z. The product moment correlation between the adjusted values of X and the adjusted values of Y is the partial correlation coefficient between X and Y, after controlling for the effect of Z, and is denoted by $r_{xy \cdot z}$. Statistically, since the simple correlation between two variables completely describes the linear relationship between them, the partial correlation coefficient can be calculated from knowledge of the simple correlations alone, without using individual observations:

$$r_{xy \cdot z} = \frac{r_{xy} - (r_{xz})(r_{yz})}{\sqrt{1 - r_{xz}^2} \sqrt{1 - r_{yz}^2}}$$

To continue our example, suppose that the researcher wanted to calculate the association between attitude towards the city, Y, and duration of residence, X_1, after controlling for a third variable, importance attached to weather, X_2. These data are presented in Table 20.1.

The simple correlations between the variables are

$$r_{yx_1} = 0.9361 \quad r_{yx_2} = 0.7334 \quad r_{x_1x_2} = 0.5495$$

The required partial correlation may be calculated as follows:

$$r_{xy_1 \cdot x_2} = \frac{0.9361 - (0.5495)(0.7334)}{\sqrt{1-(0.5495)^2}\sqrt{1-(0.7334)^2}}$$

$$= 0.9386$$

As can be seen, controlling for the effect of importance attached to weather has little effect on the association between attitude towards the city and duration of residence. Thus, regardless of the importance they attach to weather, those who have stayed in a city longer have more favourable attitudes towards the city and vice versa.

Partial correlations have an *order* associated with them. The order indicates how many variables are being adjusted or controlled. The simple correlation coefficient, *r*, has a zero order, because it does not control for any additional variables while measuring the association between two variables. The coefficient $r_{xy \cdot z}$ is a first-order partial correlation coefficient, because it controls for the effect of one additional variable, *Z*. A second-order partial correlation coefficient controls for the effects of two variables, a third-order for the effects of three variables, and so on. The higher order partial correlations are calculated similarly. The (*n* + 1)-th-order partial coefficient may be calculated by replacing the simple correlation coefficients on the right side of the preceding equation with the *n*th-order partial coefficients.

Partial correlations can be helpful for detecting spurious relationships (see Chapter 18). The relationship between *X* and *Y* is spurious if it is solely because *X* is associated with *Z*, which is indeed the true predictor of *Y*. In this case, the correlation between *X* and *Y* disappears when the effect of *Z* is controlled. Consider a case in which consumption of a breakfast cereal brand (*C*) is positively associated with income (*I*), with r_{ci} = 0.28. Because this brand was popularly priced, income was not expected to be a significant factor. Therefore, the researcher suspected that this relationship was spurious. The sample results also indicated that income is positively associated with household size (*H*), r_{hi} = 0.48, and that household size is associated with breakfast cereal consumption, r_{ch} = 0.56. These figures seem to indicate that the real predictor of breakfast cereal consumption is not income but household size. To test this assertion, the first-order partial correlation between cereal consumption and income is calculated, controlling for the effect of household size. The reader can verify that this partial correlation, $r_{ci \cdot h}$, is 0.02, and the initial correlation between cereal consumption and income vanishes when the household size is controlled. Therefore, the correlation between income and cereal consumption is spurious. The special case when a partial correlation is larger than its respective zero-order correlation involves a suppressor effect (see Chapter 18).[5]

Part correlation coefficient

A measure of the correlation between Y and X when the linear effects of the other independent variables have been removed from X (but not from Y).

Another correlation coefficient of interest is the **part correlation coefficient**. This coefficient represents the correlation between *Y* and *X* when the linear effects of the other independent variables have been removed from *X* but not from *Y*. The part correlation coefficient, $r_{y(x \cdot z)}$, is calculated as follows:

$$r_{y(x \cdot y)} = \frac{r_{xy} - r_{xz}r_{yz}}{\sqrt{1-r_{xz}^2}}$$

The part correlation between attitude towards the city and the duration of residence, when the linear effects of the importance attached to weather have been removed from the duration of residence, can be calculated as

$$r_{y(x1 \cdot x2)} = \frac{0.9361 - (0.5495)(0.7334)}{\sqrt{1-(0.5495)^2}}$$

$$= 0.63806$$

The partial correlation coefficient is generally viewed as more important than the part correlation coefficient. The product moment correlation, partial correlation and part correlation coefficients all assume that the data are interval or ratio scaled. If the data do not meet these requirements, the researcher should consider the use of non-metric correlation.

Real research	# Selling ads to home shoppers[6]

Advertisements play a very important role in forming attitudes and preferences for brands. Often advertisers use celebrity endorsement to present hopefully a credible source to influence consumers' attitudes and purchase intentions. Another type of source credibility is corporate credibility, which can also influence consumer reactions to advertisements and shape brand attitudes. In general, it has been found that for low-involvement products, attitude towards the advertisement mediates brand cognition (beliefs about the brand) and attitude towards the brand. What would happen to the effect of this mediating variable when products are purchased through a home shopping network? Home

Shopping Budapest in Hungary conducted research to assess the impact of advertisements towards purchase. A survey was conducted in which several measures were taken, such as attitude towards the product, attitude towards the brand, attitude towards the ad characteristics and brand cognitions. It was hypothesised that in a home shopping network, advertisements largely determined attitude towards the brand. To find the degree of association of attitude towards the ad with both attitude towards the brand and brand cognition, a partial correlation coefficient was computed. The partial correlation was calculated between attitude towards the brand and brand cognitions after controlling for the effects of attitude towards the ad on the two variables. If attitude towards the ad was significantly high, then the partial correlation coefficient should have been significantly less than the product moment correlation between brand cognition and attitude towards the brand. Research was conducted which supported this hypothesis. Then Saatchi & Saatchi (**www.saatchi.com**) designed the advertisements aired on Home Shopping Budapest to generate a positive attitude towards the advertising. This turned out to be a major competitive weapon for the network.

Non-metric correlation

At times the researcher may have to compute the correlation coefficient between two variables that are non-metric. It may be recalled that non-metric variables do not have interval or ratio scale properties and do not assume a normal distribution. If the non-metric variables are ordinal and numeric, Spearman's rho, ρ_s, and Kendall's tau, τ, are two measures of non-metric correlation which can be used to examine the correlation between them. Both these measures use rankings rather than the absolute values of the variables, and the basic concepts underlying them are quite similar. Both vary from –1.0 to +1.0. (See Chapter 18.)

Non-metric correlation
A correlation measure for two non-metric variables that relies on rankings to compute the correlation.

In the absence of ties, Spearman's ρ_s yields a closer approximation to the Pearson product moment correlation coefficient, ρ, than does Kendall's τ. In these cases, the absolute magnitude of τ tends to be smaller than Pearson's ρ. On the other hand, when the data contain a large number of tied ranks, Kendall's τ seems more appropriate. As a rule of thumb, Kendall's τ is to be preferred when a large number of cases fall into a relatively small number of categories (thereby leading to a large number of ties). Conversely, the use of Spearman's ρ_s is preferable when we have a relatively larger number of categories (thereby having fewer ties).[7]

The product moment as well as the partial and part correlation coefficients provide a conceptual foundation for bivariate as well as multiple regression analysis.

Regression analysis

Regression analysis
A statistical procedure for analysing associative relationships between a metric-dependent variable and one or more independent variables.

Regression analysis is a powerful and flexible procedure for analysing associative relationships between a metric-dependent variable and one or more independent variables. It can be used in the following ways:

1   To determine whether the independent variables explain a significant variation in the dependent variable: whether a relationship exists.

2   To determine how much of the variation in the dependent variable can be explained by the independent variables: strength of the relationship.

3   To determine the structure or form of the relationship: the mathematical equation relating the independent and dependent variables.

4   To predict the values of the dependent variable.

5   To control for other independent variables when evaluating the contributions of a specific variable or set of variables.

Although the independent variables may explain the variation in the dependent variable, this does not necessarily imply causation. The use of the terms *dependent* or *criterion variables* and *independent* or *predictor variables* in regression analysis arises from the mathematical relationship between the variables. These terms do not imply that the criterion variable is dependent on the independent variables in a causal sense. Regression analysis is concerned with the nature and degree of association between variables and does not imply or assume any causality. Bivariate regression is discussed first, followed by multiple regression.

Bivariate regression

Bivariate regression
A procedure for deriving a mathematical relationship, in the form of an equation, between a single metric-dependent variable and a single metric-independent variable.

Bivariate regression is a procedure for deriving a mathematical relationship, in the form of an equation, between a single metric-dependent or criterion variable and a single metric-independent or predictor variable. The analysis is similar in many ways to determining the simple correlation between two variables. Since an equation has to be derived, however, one variable must be identified as the dependent variable and the other as the independent variable. The examples given earlier in the context of simple correlation can be translated into the regression context:

● Can variation in sales be explained in terms of variation in advertising expenditures? What is the structure and form of this relationship, and can it be modelled mathematically by an equation describing a straight line?

● Can the variation in market share be accounted for by the size of the sales force?

● Are consumers' perceptions of quality determined by their perceptions of price?

Before discussing the procedure for conducting bivariate regression, we define some important statistics associated with bivariate regression analysis.

Statistics associated with bivariate regression analysis

The following statistics and statistical terms are associated with bivariate regression analysis:

Bivariate regression model. The basic regression equation is $Y_i = \beta_0 + \beta_1 X_i + e_i$, where Y = dependent or criterion variable, X = independent or predictor variable, β_0 = intercept of the line, β_1 = slope of the line, and e_i is the error term associated with the ith observation.

Coefficient of determination. The strength of association is measured by the coefficient of determination, r^2. It varies between 0 and 1 and signifies the proportion of the total variation in Y that is accounted for by the variation in X.

Estimated or predicted value. The estimated or predicted value of Y_i is $\hat{Y} \beta_i = a + bx$, where $\hat{Y}_i$ is the predicted value of Y_i, and a and b are estimators of β_0 and β_1, respectively.

Regression coefficient. The estimated parameter b is usually referred to as the non-standardised regression coefficient.

Scattergram. A scatter diagram, or scattergram, is a plot of the values of two variables for all the cases or observations.

Standard error of estimate. This statistic, the SEE, is the standard deviation of the actual Y values from the predicted $\hat{Y}$ values.

Standard error. The standard deviation of b, SE_b, is called the standard error.

Standardised regression coefficient. Also termed the beta coefficient or beta weight, this is the slope obtained by the regression of Y on X when the data are standardised.

Sum of squared errors. The distances of all the points from the regression line are squared and added together to arrive at the sum of squared errors, which is a measure of total error, $\sum e_j^2$

t statistic. A t statistic with $n - 2$ degrees of freedom can be used to test the null hypothesis that no linear relationship exists between X and Y, or

$$H_0 : \beta_1 = 0, \text{ where } t = \frac{b}{SE_b}$$

Conducting bivariate regression analysis

The steps involved in conducting bivariate regression analysis are described in Figure 20.2. Suppose that the researcher wants to explain attitudes towards the city of residence in terms of the duration of residence (see Table 20.2). In deriving such relationships, it is often useful first to examine a scatter diagram.

Plot the scatter diagram

A scatter diagram, or scattergram, is a plot of the values of two variables for all the cases or observations. It is customary to plot the dependent variable on the vertical axis and the independent variable on the horizontal axis. A scatter diagram is useful for determining the form of the relationship between the variables. A plot can alert the researcher to patterns in the data or to possible problems. Any unusual combinations of the two variables can be easily identified. A plot of Y (attitude towards the city) against X (duration of residence) is given in

Figure 20.3. The points seem to be arranged in a band running from the bottom left to the top right. One can see the pattern: as one variable increases, so does the other. It appears from this scattergram that the relationship between X and Y is linear and could be well described by a straight line. However, as seen in Figure 20.4, several straight lines can be drawn through the data. How should the straight line be fitted to best describe the data?

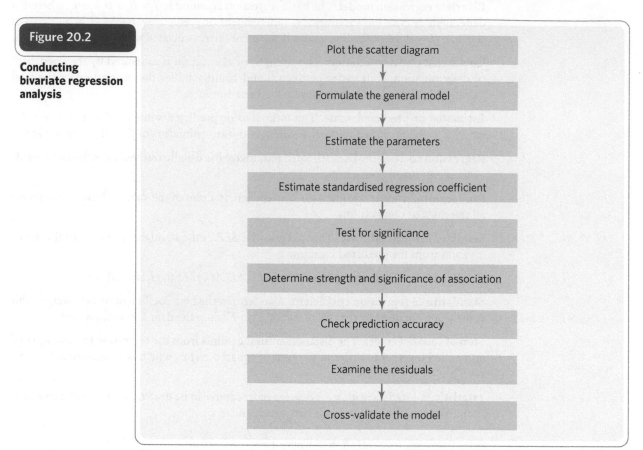

Figure 20.2

Conducting bivariate regression analysis

Plot the scatter diagram

Formulate the general model

Estimate the parameters

Estimate standardised regression coefficient

Test for significance

Determine strength and significance of association

Check prediction accuracy

Examine the residuals

Cross-validate the model

Table 20.2   **Bivariate regression**

Multiple R	0.93608
R^2	0.87624
Adjusted R^2	0.86387
Standard error	1.22329

Analysis of variance

	df	Sum of squares	Mean square
Regression	1	105.95222	105.95222
Residual	10	14.96444	1.49644

$F = 70.80266$ Significance of $F = 0.0000$

Variables in the equation

Variable	b	SE_B	Beta (β)	t	Sig. of t
Duration	0.58972	0.07008	0.93608	8.414	0.0000
(Constant)	1.07932	0.74335		1.452	0.1772

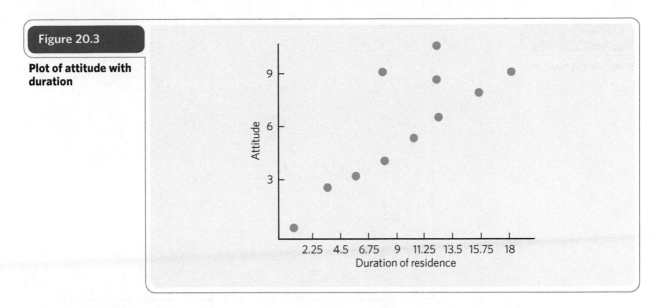

Figure 20.3

Plot of attitude with duration

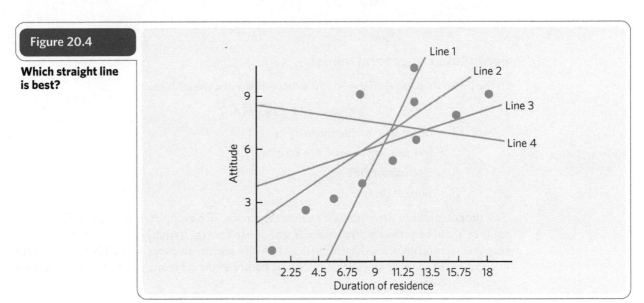

Figure 20.4

Which straight line is best?

Least squares procedure

A technique for fitting a straight line to a scattergram by minimising the vertical distances of all the points from the line.

The most commonly used technique for fitting a straight line to a scattergram is the **least squares procedure**. This technique determines the best-fitting line by minimising the square of the vertical distances of all the points from the line; the procedure is called ordinary least squares (OLS) regression. The best-fitting line is called the regression line. Any point that does not fall on the regression line is not fully accounted for. The vertical distance from the point to the line is the error, e_j (see Figure 20.5). The distances of all the points from the line are squared and added together to arrive at the sum of squared errors, which is a measure of total error, $\sum e_j^2$. In fitting the line, the least squares procedure minimises the sum of squared errors. If Y is plotted on the vertical axis and X on the horizontal axis, as in Figure 20.4, the best-fitting line is called the regression of Y on X, since the vertical distances are minimised. The scatter diagram indicates whether the relationship between Y and X can be modelled as a straight line and, consequently, whether the bivariate regression model is appropriate.

Figure 20.5

Bivariate regression

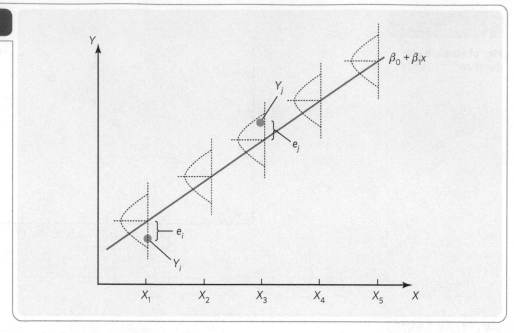

Formulate the general model

In the bivariate regression model, the general form of a straight line is

$$Y = \beta_0 + \beta_1 X$$

where Y = dependent or criterion variable

X = independent or predictor variable

β_0 = intercept of the line

β_1 = slope of the line

This model implies a deterministic relationship in that Y is completely determined by X. The value of Y can be perfectly predicted if β_0 and β_1 are known. In marketing research, however, very few relationships are deterministic. Thus, the regression procedure adds an error term to account for the probabilistic or stochastic nature of the relationship. The basic regression equation becomes

$$Y_i = \beta_0 + \beta_1 X_i + e_i$$

where e_i is the error term associated with the ith observation.[8] Estimation of the regression parameters, β_0 and β_1, is relatively simple.

Estimate the parameters

In most cases, β_0 and β_1 are unknown and are estimated from the sample observations using the equation

$$\hat{Y}_i = a + bx_i$$

Estimated or predicted value

The value $Y_i = a + b_x$, where a and b are, respectively, estimators of β_0 and β_1, the corresponding population parameters.

where $\hat{Y}_i$ is the estimated or predicted value of Y_i, and a and b are estimators of β_0 and β_1 respectively. The constant b is usually referred to as the non-standardised regression coefficient. It is the slope of the regression line, and it indicates the expected change in Y when X is changed by one unit. The formulae for calculating a and b are simple.[9] The slope, b, may be computed in terms of the covariance between X and Y (COV_{xy}) and the variance of X as:

$$b = \frac{COV_{xy}}{s_x^2}$$

$$= \frac{\sum_{i=1}^{n}(X_i - \bar{X})(Y_i - \bar{Y})}{\sum_{i=1}^{n}(X_i - \bar{X})^2}$$

$$= \frac{\sum_{i=1}^{n}X_iY_i - n\bar{X}\bar{Y}}{\sum_{i=1}^{n}X_i^2 - n\bar{X}^2}$$

The intercept, *a*, may then be calculated using

$$a = \bar{Y} - b\bar{X}$$

For the data in Table 20.2, the estimation of parameters may be illustrated as follows:

$$\sum_{i=1}^{12}X_iY_i = (10)(6)+(12)(9)+(12)(8)+(4)(3)+(12)(10)+(6)(4)+(8)(5)+(2)(2)$$

$$+(18)(11)+(9)(9)+(17)(10)+(2)(2)$$

$$= 917$$

$$\sum_{i=1}^{12}X_i^2 = 10^2+12^2+12^2+4^2+12^2+6^2+8^2+2^2+18^2+9^2+17^2+2^2$$

$$= 1350$$

It may be recalled from earlier calculations of the simple correlation that

$$\bar{X} = 9.333$$

$$\bar{Y} = 6.583$$

Given *n* = 12, *b* can be calculated as

$$b = \frac{917 - (12)(9.333)(6.583)}{1350 - (12)(9.333)^2}$$

$$= 0.5897$$

$$a = \bar{Y} - b\bar{X}$$

$$= 6.583 - (0.5897)(9.333)$$

$$= 1.0793$$

Note that these coefficients have been estimated on the raw (untransformed) data. Should standardisation of the data be considered desirable, the calculation of the standardised coefficients is also straightforward.

Estimate the standardised regression coefficient

Standardisation is the process by which the raw data are transformed into new variables that have a mean of 0 and a variance of 1 (Chapter 17). When the data are standardised, the intercept assumes a value of 0. The term *beta coefficient* or *beta weight* is used to denote the standardised regression coefficient. In this case, the slope obtained by the regression of *Y* on *X*, B_{yx}, is the same as the slope obtained by the regression of *X* on *Y*, B_{xy}. Moreover, each of these regression coefficients is equal to the simple correlation between *X* and *Y*:

$$B_{yx} = B_{xy} = r_{xy}$$

There is a simple relationship between the standardised and non-standardised regression coefficients:

$$B_{yx} = b_{yx} \left(\frac{s_x}{s_y} \right)$$

For the regression results given in Table 20.2, the value of the beta coefficient is estimated as 0.9361. Note that this is also the value of r calculated earlier in this chapter.

Once the parameters have been estimated, they can be tested for significance.

Test for significance

The statistical significance of the linear relationship between X and Y may be tested by examining the hypotheses

$$H_0: \beta_1 = 0$$
$$H_1: \beta_1 \neq 0$$

The null hypothesis implies that there is no linear relationship between X and Y. The alternative hypothesis is that there is a relationship, positive or negative, between X and Y. Typically, a two-tailed test is done. A t statistic with $n - 2$ degrees of freedom can be used, where

$$t = \frac{b}{SE_b}$$

and SE_b denotes the standard deviation of b, called the *standard error*.[10] The t distribution was discussed in Chapter 18.

Using quantitative data analysis software, the regression of attitude on duration of residence, using the data shown in Table 20.1, yielded the results shown in Table 20.2. The intercept, a, equals 1.0793, and the slope, b, equals 0.5897. Therefore, the estimated equation is

$$\text{attitude}(\hat{Y}) = 1.0793 + 0.5897(\text{duration of residence})$$

The standard error or standard deviation of b is estimated as 0.07008, and the value of the t statistic, $t = 0.5897/0.0701 = 8.414$, with $n - 2 = 10$ df. From Table 4 in the Appendix of statistical tables, we see that the critical value of t with 10 df and $\rho = 0.05$ is 2.228 for a two-tailed test. Since the calculated value of t is larger than the critical value, the null hypothesis is rejected. Hence, there is a significant linear relationship between attitude towards the city and duration of residence in the city. The positive sign of the slope coefficient indicates that this relationship is positive. In other words, those who have lived in the city for a longer time have more positive attitudes towards it.

Determine strength and significance of association

A related inference involves determining the strength and significance of the association between Y and X. The strength of association is measured by the coefficient of determination, r^2. In bivariate regression, r^2 is the square of the simple correlation coefficient obtained by correlating the two variables. The coefficient r^2 varies between 0 and 1. It signifies the proportion of the total variation in Y that is accounted for by the variation in X. The decomposition of the total variation in Y is similar to that for analysis of variance (Chapter 19). As shown in Figure 20.6, the total variation SS_y may be decomposed into the variation accounted for by the regression line, SS_{reg}, and the error or residual variation, SS_{error} or SS_{res}, as follows:

$$SS_y = SS_{reg} + SS_{res}$$

where

$$SS_y = \sum_{i=1}^{n}(Y_i - \overline{Y})^2$$

$$SS_{reg} = \sum_{i=1}^{n}(\hat{Y}_i - \overline{Y})^2$$

$$SS_{res} = \sum_{i=1}^{n}(Y_i - \hat{Y}_i)^2$$

The strength of the association may then be calculated as follows:

$$r^2 = \frac{SS_{reg}}{SS_y}$$

$$= \frac{SS_y - SS_{res}}{SS_y}$$

To illustrate the calculations of r^2, let us consider again the effect of attitude towards the city on the duration of residence. It may be recalled from earlier calculations of the simple correlation coefficient that

$$SS_y = \sum_{i=1}^{n}(Y_i - \overline{Y})^2 = 120.9168$$

The predicted values ($\hat{Y}$) can be calculated using the regression equation

$$\text{attitude}(\hat{Y}) = 1.0793 + 0.5897(\text{duration of residence})$$

For the first observation in Table 20.1, this value is

$$(\hat{Y}) = 1.0793 + (0.5897 \times 10) = 6.9763$$

For each successive observation, the predicted values are, in order, 8.1557, 8.1557, 3.4381, 8.1557, 4.6175, 5.7969, 2.2587, 11.6939, 6.3866, 11.1042, 2.2587. Therefore,

$$
\begin{aligned}
SS_{reg} &= \sum_{i=1}^{n}(\hat{Y}_i - \overline{Y})^2 \\
&= (6.9763 - 6.5833)^2 + (8.1557 - 6.5833)^2 + (8.1557 - 6.5833)^2 \\
&\quad + (3.4381 - 6.5833)^2 + (8.1557 - 6.5833)^2 + (4.6175 - 6.5833)^2 \\
&\quad + (5.7969 - 6.5833)^2 + (2.2587 - 6.5833)^2 + (11.6939 - 6.5833)^2 \\
&\quad + (6.3866 - 6.5833)^2 + (11.1042 - 6.5833)^2 + (2.2587 - 6.5833)^2 \\
&= 0.1544 + 2.4724 + 2.4724 + 9.8922 + 2.4724 + 3.8643 + 0.6184 \\
&\quad + 18.7021 + 26.1182 + 0.0387 + 20.4385 + 18.7021 \\
&= 105.9466
\end{aligned}
$$

$$
\begin{aligned}
SS_{res} &= \sum_{i=1}^{n}(Y_i - \hat{Y}_i)^2 \\
&= (6 - 6.9763)^2 + (9 - 8.1557)^2 + (8 - 8.1557)^2 + (3 - 3.4381)^2 \\
&\quad + (10 - 8.1557)^2 + (4 - 4.6175)^2 + (5 - 5.7969)^2 + (2 - 2.2587)^2 \\
&\quad + (11 - 11.6939)^2 + (9 - 6.3866)^2 + (10 - 11.1042)^2 + (2 - 2.2587)^2 \\
&= 14.9644
\end{aligned}
$$

It can be seen that $SS_y = SS_{reg} + SS_{res}$. Furthermore,

$$r^2 = \frac{SS_{reg}}{SS_y}$$

$$= \frac{105.9466}{120.9168}$$

$$= 0.8762$$

Figure 20.6

Decomposition of the total variation in bivariate regression

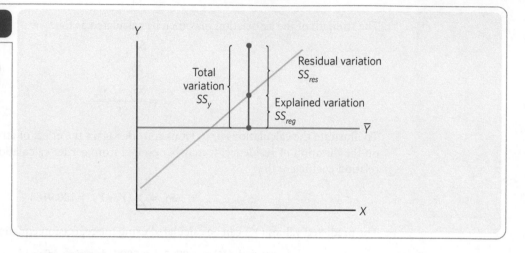

Another equivalent test for examining the significance of the linear relationship between X and Y (significance of b) is the test for the significance of the coefficient of determination. The hypotheses in this case are

$$H_0: R^2_{pop} = 0$$

$$H_1: R^2_{pop} > 0$$

The appropriate test statistic is the F statistic

$$F = \frac{SS_{reg}}{SS_{res}/(n-2)}$$

which has an F distribution with 1 and $(n-2)$ df. The F test is a generalised form of the t test (see Chapter 18). If a random variable is t distributed with n degrees of freedom, then t^2 is F distributed with 1 and n df. Hence, the F test for testing the significance of the coefficient of determination is equivalent to testing the following hypotheses:

$$H_0: \beta_1 = 0$$

$$H_1: \beta_1 \neq 0$$

or

$$H_0: \rho = 0$$

$$H_1: \rho \neq 0$$

From Table 20.2, it can be seen that

$$r^2 = \frac{105.9522}{105.9522 + 14.9644}$$

$$= 0.8762$$

which is the same as the value calculated earlier. The value of the F statistic is

$$F = \frac{105.9522}{14.9644/10}$$
$$= 70.8028$$

with 1 and 10 df. The calculated F statistic exceeds the critical value of 4.96 determined from Table 5 in the Appendix. Therefore, the relationship is significant at $\alpha = 0.05$, corroborating the results of the t test. If the relationship between X and Y is significant, it is meaningful to predict the values of Y based on the values of X and to estimate prediction accuracy.

Check prediction accuracy

To estimate the accuracy of predicted values, $\hat{Y}$, it is useful to calculate the standard error of estimate, SEE. This statistic is the standard deviation of the actual Y values from the predicted $\hat{Y}$ values:

$$SEE = \sqrt{\frac{\sum_{i=1}^{n}(Y_i - \hat{Y})^2}{n-2}}$$

$$SEE = \sqrt{\frac{SS_{res}}{n-2}}$$

or, more generally, if there are k independent variables

$$SEE = \sqrt{\frac{SS_{res}}{n-k-1}}$$

SEE may be interpreted as a kind of average residual or average error in predicting Y from the regression equation.[11]

Two cases of prediction may arise. The researcher may want to predict the mean value of Y for all the cases with a given value of X, say X_0, or predict the value of Y for a single case. In both situations, the predicted value is the same and is given by $\hat{Y}$, where

$$\hat{Y} = a + bX_0$$

But the standard error is different in the two situations, although in both situations it is a function of SEE. For large samples, the standard error for predicting the mean value of Y is $SEE/\sqrt{n}$ and for predicting individual Y values it is SEE. Hence, the construction of confidence intervals (see Chapter 15) for the predicted value varies, depending upon whether the mean value or the value for a single observation is being predicted. For the data given in Table 20.2, SEE is estimated as follows:

$$SEE = \sqrt{\frac{14.9644}{12-2}}$$
$$= 1.22329$$

The final two steps in conducting bivariate regression, namely examination of residuals and model cross-validation, are considered later, and we now turn to the assumptions underlying the regression model.

Assumptions

The regression model makes a number of assumptions in estimating the parameters and in significance testing, as shown in Figure 20.5:

1 The error term is normally distributed. For each fixed value of X, the distribution of Y is normal.[12]

2 The means of all these normal distributions of Y, given X, lie on a straight line with slope b.

3   The mean of the error term is 0.

4   The variance of the error term is constant. This variance does not depend on the values assumed by X.

5   The error terms are uncorrelated. In other words, the observations have been drawn independently.

Insights into the extent to which these assumptions have been met can be gained by an examination of residuals, which is covered in the next section on multiple regression.[13]

Multiple regression

Multiple regression
A statistical technique that simultaneously develops a mathematical relationship between two or more independent variables and an interval-scaled dependent variable.

Multiple regression involves a single dependent variable and two or more independent variables. The questions raised in the context of bivariate regression can also be answered via multiple regression by considering additional independent variables:

- Can variation in sales be explained in terms of variation in advertising expenditures, prices and level of distribution?
- Can variation in market shares be accounted for by the size of the sales force, advertising expenditures and sales promotion budgets?
- Are consumers' perceptions of quality determined by their perceptions of prices, brand image and brand attributes?

Additional questions can also be answered by multiple regression:

- How much of the variation in sales can be explained by advertising expenditures, prices and level of distribution?
- What is the contribution of advertising expenditures in explaining the variation in sales when the levels of prices and distribution are controlled?
- What levels of sales may be expected given the levels of advertising expenditures, prices and level of distribution?

Real research   ## Global brands, local ads[14]

European consumers welcome brands from across the globe, but when it comes to advertising, they seem to prefer brands from their own country. A survey conducted by Yankelovich and Partners (**www.yankelovich.com**) and its affiliates found that most European consumers' favourite advertisements were for local brands even though they were more than likely to buy brands from other countries. Participants in the UK, France and Germany named Coca-Cola as the most often purchased soft drink. The French, however, selected the famous award-winning spot for France's Perrier bottled water as their favourite advertisement. Similarly, in Germany, the favourite advertising was for a German brand of non-alcoholic beer, Clausthaler. In the UK, though, Coca-Cola was the favourite soft drink and also the favourite advertising. In the light of such findings, the important question was: does advertising help? Does it help increase the purchase probability of the brand or does it merely maintain the brand recognition rate high? One way of finding out was by running a regression where the dependent variable was the likelihood of brand purchase and the independent variables were brand attribute evaluations and advertising evaluations. Separate models with and without advertising could be run to assess any significant difference in the contribution. Individual t tests could also be examined to find out the significant contribution of both the brand attributes and advertising. The results could indicate the degree to which advertising plays an important part in brand purchase decisions.

In conjunction with these results, a study revealed that attempting to build brand loyalty purchases by means of a sales promotion is not a desirable way to achieve such an objective. According to the study, sales promotions only encourage momentary brand switching and merely enhance short-term performance for companies. Furthermore, over the long run a sales promotion may imply a low quality or unstable brand image to consumers or it may confuse them, which could also lead to a decline in brand loyalty. The results of this study show that sacrificing advertising and relying on sales promotions reduces brand associations, which ultimately leads to a decrease in brand loyalty purchases.

Multiple regression model

An equation used to explain the results of multiple regression analysis.

The general form of the **multiple regression model** is as follows:

$$Y = \beta_0 + \beta_1 X_1 + \beta_2 X_2 + \beta_3 X_3 + \ldots + \beta_k X_k + e$$

which is estimated by the following equation:

$$\hat{Y} = a + b_1 X_1 + b_2 X_2 + b_3 X_3 + \ldots + b_k X_k$$

As before, the coefficient a represents the intercept, but the bs are now the partial regression coefficients. The least squares criterion estimates the parameters in such a way as to minimise the total error, SS_{res}. This process also maximises the correlation between the actual values of Y and the predicted values of $\hat{Y}$. All the assumptions made in bivariate regression also apply in multiple regression. We define some associated statistics and then describe the procedure for multiple regression analysis.[15]

Statistics associated with multiple regression

Most of the statistics and statistical terms described under bivariate regression also apply to multiple regression. In addition, the following statistics are used:

Adjusted R^2. R^2, the coefficient of multiple determination, is adjusted for the number of independent variables and the sample size to account for the diminishing returns. After the first few variables, the additional independent variables do not make much contribution.

Coefficient of multiple determination. The strength of association in multiple regression is measured by the square of the multiple correlation coefficient, R^2, which is also called the *coefficient of multiple determination.*

F test. The F test is used to test the null hypothesis that the coefficient of multiple determination in the population, R^2_{pop}, is zero. This is equivalent to testing the null hypothesis H_0: $\beta_1 = \beta_2 = \beta_3 = \ldots = \beta_k = 0$. The test statistic has an F distribution with k and $(n - k - 1)$ *df*.

Partial F test. The significance of a partial regression coefficient, β_i, of X_i may be tested using an incremental F statistic. The incremental F statistic is based on the increment in the explained sum of squares resulting from the addition of the independent variable X_i to the regression equation after all the other independent variables have been included.

Partial regression coefficient. The partial regression coefficient, b_1, denotes the change in the predicted value, $\hat{Y}$, per unit change in X_1 when the other independent variables, X_2 to X_k, are held constant.

Conducting multiple regression analysis

The steps involved in conducting multiple regression analysis are similar to those for bivariate regression analysis. The discussion focuses on partial regression coefficients, strength of association, significance testing and examination of residuals.

Estimating the partial regression coefficients

To understand the meaning of a partial regression coefficient, let us consider a case in which there are two independent variables, so that

$$\hat{Y} = a + b_1 X_1 + b_2 X_2$$

First, note that the relative magnitude of the partial regression coefficient of an independent variable is, in general, different from that of its bivariate regression coefficient. In other words, the partial regression coefficient, b_1, will be different from the regression coefficient, b, obtained by regressing Y on only X_1. This happens because X_1 and X_2 are usually correlated. In bivariate regression, X_2 was not considered, and any variation in Y that was shared by X_1 and X_2 was attributed to X_1. In the case of multiple independent variables, however, this is no longer true.

The interpretation of the partial regression coefficient, b_1, is that it represents the expected change in Y when X_1 is changed by one unit but X_2 is held constant or otherwise controlled. Likewise, b_2 represents the expected change in Y for a unit change in X_2 when X_1 is held constant. Thus, calling b_1 and b_2 partial regression coefficients is appropriate. It can also be seen that the combined effects of X_1 and X_2 on Y are additive. In other words, if X_1 and X_2 are each changed by one unit, the expected change in Y would be $(b_1 + b_2)$.

Conceptually, the relationship between the bivariate regression coefficient and the partial regression coefficient can be illustrated as follows. Suppose that one were to remove the effect of X_2 from X_1. This could be done by running a regression of X_1 on X_2. In other words, one would estimate the equation $\hat{X}_1 = a + bX_2$ and calculate the residual $X_r = (X_1 - \hat{X}_1)$. The partial regression coefficient, b_1, is then equal to the bivariate regression coefficient, b_r, obtained from the equation $\hat{Y} = a + b_r X_r$. In other words, the partial regression coefficient, b_1, is equal to the regression coefficient, b_r, between Y and the residuals of X_1 from which the effect of X_2 has been removed. The partial coefficient, b_2, can also be interpreted along similar lines.

Extension to the case of k variables is straightforward. The partial regression coefficient, b_1, represents the expected change in Y when X_1 is changed by one unit and X_2 to X_k are held constant. It can also be interpreted as the bivariate regression coefficient, b, for the regression of Y on the residuals of X_1, when the effect of X_2 to X_k has been removed from X_1.

The beta coefficients are the partial regression coefficients obtained when all the variables $(Y, X_1, X_2, \ldots, X_k)$ have been standardised to a mean of 0 and a variance of 1 before estimating the regression equation. The relationship of the standardised to the non-standardised coefficients remains the same as before:

$$B_1 = b_1 \left(\frac{s_{x1}}{s_y} \right)$$

$$\vdots$$

$$B_k = b_k \left(\frac{s_{xk}}{s_y} \right)$$

The intercept and the partial regression coefficients are estimated by solving a system of simultaneous equations derived by differentiating and equating the partial derivatives to zero. Since these coefficients are automatically estimated by various computer programs, we will not present the details. Yet it is worth noting that the equations cannot be solved if (1) the sample size, n, is smaller than or equal to the number of independent variables, k, or (2) one independent variable is perfectly correlated with another.

Suppose that in explaining the attitude towards the city we now introduce a second variable, importance attached to the weather. The data for the 12 pretest participants on attitude towards the city, duration of residence and importance attached to the weather are given in Table 20.1. The results of multiple regression analysis are depicted in Table 20.3. The partial regression coefficient for duration (X_1) is now 0.4811, different from what it was in the bivariate case. The corresponding beta coefficient is 0.7636.

Table 20.3	Multiple regression

Multiple R	0.97210
R^2	0.94498
Adjusted R^2	0.93276
Standard error	0.85974

Analysis of variance

	df	Sum of squares	Mean square
Regression	2	114.26425	57.13213
Residual	9	6.65241	0.73916
$F = 77.29364$		Significance of $F = 0.0000$	

Variables in the equation

Variable	b	SE_B	Beta (β)	t	Sig. of t
Importance	0.28865	0.08608	0.31382	3.353	0.0085
Duration	0.48108	0.05895	0.76363	8.160	0.0000
(Constant)	0.33732	0.56736		0.595	0.5668

The partial regression coefficient for importance attached to weather (X_2) is 0.2887, with a beta coefficient of 0.3138. The estimated regression equation is

$$(\hat{Y}) = 0.33732 + 0.48108X_1 + 0.28865X_2$$

or

$$\text{attitude} = 0.33732 + 0.48108(\text{duration}) + 0.28865(\text{importance})$$

This equation can be used for a variety of purposes, including predicting attitudes towards the city, given a knowledge of the participants' duration of residence in the city and the importance they attach to weather. Note that duration and importance are significant and useful in the prediction.

Strength of association

The strength of the relationship stipulated by the regression equation can be determined by using appropriate measures of association. The total variation is decomposed as in the bivariate case:

$$SS_y = SS_{reg} + SS_{res}$$

where

$$SS_y = \sum_{i=1}^{n}(Y_i - \overline{Y})^2$$

$$SS_{reg} = \sum_{i=1}^{n}(\hat{Y}_i - \overline{Y})^2$$

$$SS_{res} = \sum_{i=1}^{n}(Y_i - \hat{Y})^2$$

The strength of association is measured by the square of the multiple correlation coefficient, R^2, which is also called the coefficient of multiple determination:

$$R^2 = \frac{SS_{reg}}{SS_y}$$

The multiple correlation coefficient, R, can also be viewed as the simple correlation coefficient, r, between Y and $\hat{Y}$. Several points about the characteristics of R^2 are worth noting. The coefficient of multiple determination, R^2, cannot be less than the highest bivariate, r^2, of any individual independent variable with the dependent variable. R^2 will be larger when the correlations between the independent variables are low. If the independent variables are statistically independent (uncorrelated), then R^2 will be the sum of bivariate r^2 of each independent variable with the dependent variable. R^2 cannot decrease as more independent variables are added to the regression equation. Yet diminishing returns set in, so that after the first few variables, the additional independent variables do not make much of a contribution.[16] For this reason, R^2 is adjusted for the number of independent variables and the sample size by using the following formula:

$$\text{adjusted } R^2 = R^2 - \frac{k(1-R^2)}{n-k-1}$$

For the regression results given in Table 20.3, the value of R^2 is

$$R^2 = \frac{114.2643}{114.2643 + 6.6524}$$
$$= 0.9450$$

This is higher than the r^2 value of 0.8762 obtained in the bivariate case. The r^2 in the bivariate case is the square of the simple (product moment) correlation between attitude towards the city and duration of residence. The R^2 obtained in multiple regression is also higher than the square of the simple correlation between attitude and importance attached to weather (which can be estimated as 0.5379). The adjusted R^2 is estimated as

$$\text{adjusted } R^2 = 0.9450 - \frac{2(1.0-0.9450)}{12-2-1}$$
$$= 0.9328$$

Note that the value of adjusted R^2 is close to R^2 and both are higher than r^2 for the bivariate case. This suggests that the addition of the second independent variable, importance attached to weather, makes a contribution in explaining the variation in attitude towards the city.

Test for significance

Significance testing involves testing the significance of the overall regression equation as well as specific partial regression coefficients. The null hypothesis for the overall test is that the coefficient of multiple determination in the population, R^2_{pop}, is zero:

$$H_0: R^2_{pop} = 0$$

This is equivalent to the following null hypothesis:

$$H_0: \beta_1 = \beta_2 = \beta_3 = \ldots = \beta_k = 0$$

The overall test can be conducted by using an F statistic

$$F = \frac{SS_{reg}/k}{SS_{reg}/(n-k-1)}$$

$$= \frac{R^2/k}{(1-R^2)/(n-k-1)}$$

which has an F distribution with k and $(n - k - 1)$ df.[17] For the multiple regression results given in Table 20.3,

$$F = \frac{114.2642/2}{6.6524/9} = 77.2937$$

which is significant at $\alpha = 0.05$.

If the overall null hypothesis is rejected, one or more population partial regression coefficients have a value different from 0. To determine which specific coefficients (the β_is) are non-zero, additional tests are necessary. Testing for the significance of the β_is can be done in a manner similar to that in the bivariate case by using t tests. The significance of the partial coefficient for importance attached to weather may be tested by the following equation:

$$t = \frac{b}{SE_b}$$

$$= \frac{0.2887}{0.08608} = 3.354$$

which has a t distribution with $(n - k - 1)$ df. This coefficient is significant at $\alpha = 0.05$. The significance of the coefficient for duration of residence is tested in a similar way and found to be significant. Therefore, both the duration of residence and importance attached to weather are important in explaining attitude towards the city.

Some data analysis programs provide an equivalent F test, often called the partial F test, which involves a decomposition of the total regression sum of squares, SS_{reg}, into components related to each independent variable. In the standard approach, this is done by assuming that each independent variable has been added to the regression equation after all the other independent variables have been included. The increment in the explained sum of squares, resulting from the addition of an independent variable, X_i, is the component of the variation attributed to that variable and is denoted by SS_{Xi}.[18] The significance of the partial regression coefficient for this variable, b_i, is tested using an incremental F statistic

$$F = \frac{SS_{Xi}/1}{SS_{res}/(n-k-1)}$$

which has an F distribution with 1 and $(n - k - 1)$ df.

Although high R^2 and significant partial regression coefficients are comforting, the efficacy of the regression model should be evaluated further by an examination of the residuals.

Examine the residuals

Residual

The difference between the observed value of Y_i and the value predicted by the regression equation $\hat{Y}_i$.

A **residual** is the difference between the observed value of Y_i and the value predicted by the regression equation $\hat{Y}_i$. Residuals are used in the calculation of several statistics associated with regression. In addition, scattergrams of the residuals – in which the residuals are plotted against the predicted values, $\hat{Y}_i$, time, or predictor variables – provide useful insights in examining the appropriateness of the underlying assumptions and regression model fitted.[19]

The assumption of a normally distributed error term can be examined by constructing a histogram of the standardised residuals. A visual check reveals whether the distribution is normal. It is also useful to examine the normal probability plot of standardised residuals compared with the expected standardised residuals from a normal distribution. If the observed residuals are normally distributed, they will fall on a 45° line. Also, look at the table of residual statistics and identify any standardised predicted values or standardised residuals that are more than plus or minus one or two standard deviations. These percentages can be compared with what would be expected under the normal distribution (68% and 95%, respectively). More formal assessment can be made by running the K–S one-sample test.

The assumption of constant variance of the error term can be examined by plotting the residuals against the predicted values of the dependent variable, $\hat{Y_i}$. If the pattern is not random, the variance of the error term is not constant. Figure 20.7 shows a pattern whose variance is dependent on the $\hat{Y_i}$ values.

Figure 20.7

Residual plot indicating that variance is not constant

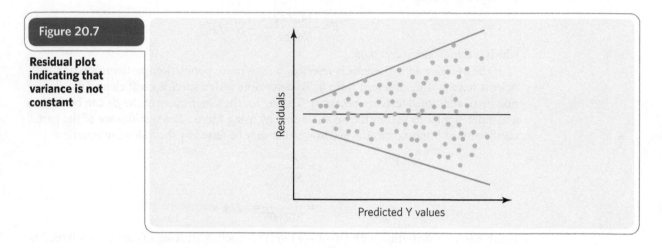

A plot of residuals against time, or the sequence of observations, will throw some light on the assumption that the error terms are uncorrelated. A random pattern should be seen if this assumption is true. A plot like the one in Figure 20.8 indicates a linear relationship between residuals and time. A more formal procedure for examining the correlations between the error terms is the Durbin–Watson test.[20]

Figure 20.8

Plot indicating a linear relationship between residuals and time

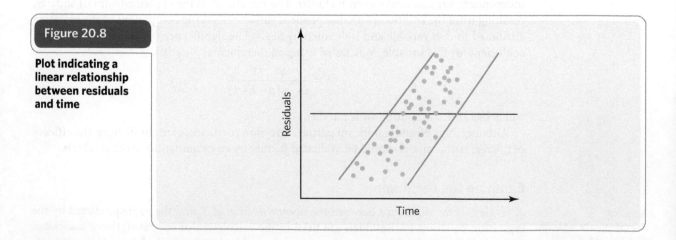

Plotting the residuals against the independent variables provides evidence of the appropriateness or inappropriateness of using a linear model. Again, the plot should result in a random pattern. The residuals should fall randomly, with relatively equal distribution dispersion about zero. They should not display any tendency to be either positive or negative.

To examine whether any additional variables should be included in the regression equation, one could run a regression of the residuals on the proposed variables. If any variable explains a significant proportion of the residual variation, it should be considered for inclusion. Inclusion of variables in the regression equation should be strongly guided by the researcher's theory. Thus, an examination of the residuals provides valuable insights into the appropriateness of the underlying assumptions and the model that is fitted. Figure 20.9 shows a plot that indicates that the underlying assumptions are met and that the linear model is appropriate. If an examination of the residuals indicates that the assumptions underlying linear regression are not met, the researcher can transform the variables in an attempt to satisfy the assumptions. Transformations, such as taking logs, square roots or reciprocals, can stabilise the variance, make the distribution normal or make the relationship linear.

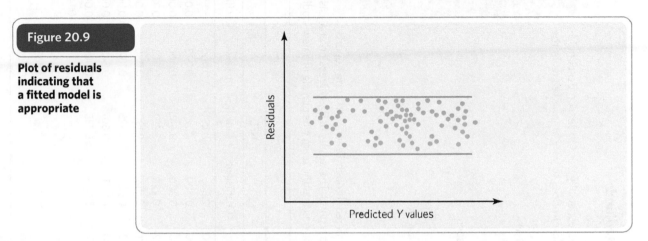

Figure 20.9

Plot of residuals indicating that a fitted model is appropriate

The plots and residual table can be requested when the regression is run, e.g. when using SPSS. It is worth conducting these analyses for multiple regression on the data of Table 20.1. From the histogram, it can be seen that five residuals are positive, whereas seven residuals are negative. By comparing the frequency distribution with the normal distribution that is plotted in the same output, it can be seen that the assumption of normality might not be severe. It is possible to conduct a more formal test for normality if that is warranted. All the standardised residuals are within plus or minus two standard deviations. Furthermore, many of the residuals are relatively small, which means that most of the model predictions are quite good.

The normal probability plot shows that the residuals are quite close to the 45° line shown in the graph. When the plot of the standardised residuals is compared with the standardised predicted values, no systematic pattern can be discerned in the spread of the residuals. Finally, the table of residual statistics indicates that all the standardised predicted values and all the standardised residuals are within plus or minus two standard deviations. Hence, it can be concluded that multiple regression on the data of Table 20.1 does not appear to result in gross violations of the assumptions. This suggests that the relationship we are trying to predict is linear and that the error terms are more or less normally distributed.

As in this example, some independent variables considered in a study often turn out not to be significant. When there are a large number of independent variables and the researcher suspects that not all of them are significant, stepwise regression should be used.

Stepwise regression

Stepwise regression
A regression procedure in which the predictor variables enter or leave the regression equation one at a time.

The purpose of stepwise regression is to select, from a large number of predictor variables, a small subset of variables that account for most of the variation in the dependent or criterion variable. In this procedure, the predictor variables enter or are removed from the regression equation one at a time.[21] There are several approaches to stepwise regression:

| Real research | What influences sports ticket prices? A new stadium![22] |

A major source of revenue from any professional sports team is through ticket sales, especially sales to season ticket holders. A study performed a regression analysis to determine what factors caused ticket prices to vary among teams in the same league within a given year. The regression equation was

$$LTIX = a_0 + a_1 HWIN + a_2 INCOME + a_3 PAY + a_4 POPL + a_5 TREND + a_6 CAP + a_7 STAD$$

where LTIX = natural log of average ticket price

TIX = average ticket price

HWIN = average number of wins by the team in the previous three seasons

INCOME = average income level of city population

PAY = team payroll

POPL = population size of city

TREND = trends in the industry

CAP = attendance as a percentage of capacity

STAD = if the team is playing in a new stadium

The research gathered data over a period of seven years. The financial data were gathered through Team Marketing Reports and the rest of the data were collected using publicly available sources such as sports reports. The results of the regression analysis can be seen in the table below. The results suggest that several factors influenced ticket prices, and the largest factor was that the team was playing in a new stadium.

Regression results

Variable	MLB			NBA			NFL			NHL		
	Coefficient	t statistic	p value	Coefficient	t statistic	p value	Coefficient	t statistic	p value	Coefficient	t statistic	p value
Constant	1.521	12.012	0.000	2.965	20.749	0.000	2.886	18.890	0.000	3.172	16.410	0.000
POPL	0.000	5.404	0.000	0.000	5.036	0.000	0.000	-2.287	0.023	0.000	2.246	0.026
INCOME	0.000	3.991	0.000	0.000	0.208	0.836	0.000	3.645	0.000	0.000	0.669	0.504
STAD	0.337	5.356	0.000	0.108	3.180	0.002	0.226	3.357	0.001	0.321	4.087	0.000
HWIN	0.000	0.091	0.927	0.004	3.459	0.001	0.013	2.190	0.030	0.001	0.369	0.713
CAP	0.006	8.210	0.000	0.000	2.968	0.003	0.002	1.325	0.187	0.005	3.951	0.000
PAY	0.004	4.192	0.000	0.008	5.341	0.000	0.001	0.607	0.545	0.002	1.099	0.273
TREND	0.047	6.803	0.000	0.016	1.616	0.100	0.058	6.735	0.000	0.009	0.718	0.474
CAN (Canada)										-0.146	-3.167	0.002
Adjusted R^2	0.778			0.488			0.443			0.292		
F statistic	98.366			28.227			24.763			9.545		
F significance	0.000			0.000			0.000			0.000		

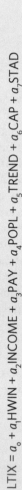

1 *Forward inclusion.* Initially, there are no predictor variables in the regression equation. Predictor variables are entered one at a time, only if they meet certain criteria specified in terms of F ratio. The order in which the variables are included is based on the contribution to the explained variance.

2 *Backward elimination.* Initially, all the predictor variables are included in the regression equation. Predictors are then removed one at a time based on the F ratio.

3 *Stepwise solution.* Forward inclusion is combined with the removal of predictors that no longer meet the specified criterion at each step.

Stepwise procedures do not result in regression equations which are optimal, in the sense of producing the largest R^2, for a given number of predictors. Because of the correlations between predictors, an important variable may never be included or less important variables may enter the equation. To identify an optimal regression equation, one would have to compute combinatorial solutions in which all possible combinations are examined. Nevertheless, stepwise regression can be useful when the sample size is large in relation to the number of predictors, as shown in the following example.

Real research | **Browsers step out**[23]

Many commentators consider store-based retailers to have an advantage over online retailers when it comes to browsing, because store-based retailers are larger in size and product offerings. Online retailing has great attractions to many shoppers but the shopping centre can remain a dominant force having so many entertainment factors being built into the shopping experience. A profile of browsers in regional shopping centres was constructed using three sets of independent variables: demographics, shopping behaviour, and psychological and attitudinal variables. The dependent variable consisted of a browsing index. In a stepwise regression including all three sets of variables, demographics were found to be the most powerful predictors of browsing behaviour. The final regression equation, which contained 20 of the possible 36 variables, included all the demographics. The table presents the regression coefficients, standard errors of the coefficients, and their significance levels.

In interpreting the coefficients, it should be recalled that the smaller the browsing index (the dependent variable), the greater the tendency to exhibit behaviours associated with browsing. The two predictors with the largest coefficients were gender and employment status. Browsers were more likely to be employed females. They also tend to be somewhat 'downscale', compared with other shopping centre patrons, exhibiting lower levels of education and income, after accounting for the effects of gender and employment status. Although browsers tend to be somewhat younger than non-browsers, they are not necessarily single; those who reported larger family sizes tended to be associated with smaller values of the browsing index.

The 'downscale' profile of browsers relative to other patrons indicates that speciality stores in shopping centres should emphasise moderately priced products. This may explain the historically low rate of failure in shopping centres among such stores and the tendency of high-priced speciality shops to be located in only the prestigious shopping centres or 'upscale' non-enclosed shopping centres.

Regression of browsing index on descriptive and attitudinal variables by order of entry into stepwise regression

Variable description	Coefficient	SE	Significance
Gender (0 = male, 1 = female)	−0.485	0.164	0.001
Employment status (0 = employed)	0.391	0.182	0.003
Self-confidence	−0.152	0.128	0.234
Education	0.079	0.072	0.271
Brand intention	−0.063	0.028	0.024
Watch daytime TV? (0 = yes)	0.232	0.144	0.107
Tension	−0.182	0.069	0.008
Income	0.089	0.061	0.144
Frequency of shopping centre visits	−0.130	0.059	0.028
Fewer friends than most	0.162	0.084	0.054
Good shopper	−0.122	0.090	0.174
Others' opinions important	−0.147	0.065	0.024
Control over life	−0.069	0.069	0.317
Family size	−0.086	0.062	0.165
Enthusiastic person	−0.143	0.099	0.150
Age	0.036	0.069	0.603
Number of purchases made	−0.068	0.043	0.150
Purchases per store	0.209	0.152	0.167
Shop on tight budget	−0.055	0.067	0.412
Excellent judge of quality	−0.070	0.089	0.435
Constant	3.250		
Overall R^2 = 0.477			

Multicollinearity

Multicollinearity
A state of high intercorrelations among independent variables.

Stepwise regression and multiple regression are complicated by the presence of multicollinearity. Virtually all multiple regression analyses done in marketing research involve predictors or independent variables that are related. Multicollinearity, however, arises when intercorrelations among the predictors are very high. Multicollinearity can result in several problems, including the following:

1   The partial regression coefficients may not be estimated precisely. The standard errors are likely to be high.

2   The magnitudes as well as the signs of the partial regression coefficients may change from sample to sample.

3   It becomes difficult to assess the relative importance of the independent variables in explaining the variation in the dependent variable.

4   Predictor variables may be incorrectly included or removed in stepwise regression.

What constitutes serious multicollinearity is not always clear, although several rules of thumb and procedures have been suggested in the literature. Procedures of varying complexity have also been suggested to cope with multicollinearity.[24] A simple procedure consists of using only one of the variables in a highly correlated set of variables. Alternatively, the set of independent variables can be transformed into a new set of predictors that are mutually independent by using techniques such as principal components analysis (see Chapter 22). More specialised techniques, such as ridge regression and latent root regression, can also be used.[25]

Relative importance of predictors

When multicollinearity is present, special care is required in assessing the relative importance of independent variables. In marketing research, it is valuable to determine the *relative importance of the predictors*. In other words, how important are the independent variables in accounting for the variation in the criterion or dependent variable?[26] Unfortunately, because the predictors are correlated, there is no unambiguous measure of relative importance of the predictors in regression analysis.[27] Several approaches however, are commonly used to assess the relative importance of predictor variables:

1 *Statistical significance.* If the partial regression coefficient of a variable is not significant, as determined by an incremental F test, that variable is judged to be unimportant. An exception to this rule is made if there are strong theoretical reasons for believing that the variable is important.

2 *Square of the simple correlation coefficient.* This measure, r^2, represents the proportion of the variation in the dependent variable explained by the independent variable in a bivariate relationship.

3 *Square of the partial correlation coefficient.* This measure, $R^2_{yxi.xj.xk}$, is the coefficient of determination between the dependent variable and the independent variable, controlling for the effects of the other independent variables.

4 *Square of the part correlation coefficient.* This coefficient represents an increase in R^2 when a variable is entered into a regression equation that already contains the other independent variables.

5 *Measures based on standardised coefficients or beta weights.* The most commonly used measures are the absolute values of the beta weights, $|\beta_i|$, or the squared values, β_i^2. Because they are partial coefficients, beta weights take into account the effect of the other independent variables. These measures become increasingly unreliable as the correlations among the predictor variables increase (multicollinearity increases).

6 *Stepwise regression.* The order in which the predictors enter or are removed from the regression equation is used to infer their relative importance.

Given that the predictors are correlated, at least to some extent, in virtually all regression situations, none of these measures is satisfactory. It is also possible that the different measures may indicate a different order of importance of the predictors.[28] Yet if all the measures are examined collectively, useful insights may be obtained into the relative importance of the predictors.

Cross-validation

Cross-validation
A test of validity that examines whether a model holds on comparable data not used in the original estimation.

Before assessing the relative importance of the predictors or drawing any other inferences, it is necessary to cross-validate the regression model. Regression and other multivariate procedures tend to capitalise on chance variations in the data. This could result in a regression model or equation that is unduly sensitive to the specific data used to estimate the model. One approach for evaluating the model for this and other problems associated with regression is cross-validation. Cross-validation examines whether the regression model continues to hold on comparable data not used in the estimation. The typical cross-validation procedure used in marketing research is as follows:

1 The regression model is estimated using the entire dataset.

2 The available data are split into two parts, the *estimation sample* and the *validation sample*. The estimation sample generally contains 50–90% of the total sample.

3 The regression model is estimated using the data from the estimation sample only. This model is compared with the model estimated on the entire sample to determine the agreement in terms of the signs and magnitudes of the partial regression coefficients.

4 The estimated model is applied to the data in the validation sample to predict the values of the dependent variable, $\hat{Y}_i$, for the observations in the validation sample.

5 The observed values, Y_i, and the predicted values, $\hat{Y}_i$, in the validation sample are correlated to determine the simple r^2. This measure, r^2, is compared with R^2 for the total sample and with R^2 for the estimation sample to assess the degree of shrinkage.

A special form of validation is called **double cross-validation**. In double cross-validation the sample is split into halves. One half serves as the estimation sample, and the other is used as a validation sample in conducting cross-validation. The roles of the estimation and validation halves are then reversed, and the cross-validation is repeated.

Double cross-validation

A special form of validation in which the sample is split into halves. One half serves as the estimation sample and the other as a validation sample. The roles of the estimation and validation halves are then reversed and the cross-validation process is repeated.

Regression with dummy variables

Cross-validation is a general procedure that can be applied even in some special applications of regression, such as regression with dummy variables. Nominal or categorical variables may be used as predictors or independent variables by coding them as dummy variables. The concept of dummy variables was introduced in Chapter 17. In that chapter, we explained how a categorical variable with four categories (heavy users, medium users, light users and non-users) can be coded in terms of three dummy variables, D_1, D_2 and D_3, as shown.

Suppose that the researcher was interested in running a regression analysis of the effect of attitude towards the brand on product use. The dummy variables D_1, D_2 and D_3 would be used as predictors. Regression with dummy variables would be modelled as follows:

$$\hat{Y}_i = a + b_1 D_1 + b_2 D_2 + b_3 D_3$$

Product usage category	Original variable code	Dummy variable code		
		D1	D2	D3
Non-users	1	1	0	0
Light users	2	0	1	0
Medium users	3	0	0	1
Heavy users	4	0	0	0

In this case, 'heavy users' have been selected as a reference category and have not been directly included in the regression equation. Note that for heavy users, D_1, D_2 and D_3 assume a value of 0, and the regression equation becomes

$$\hat{Y}_i = a$$

For non-users, $D_1 = 1$ and $D_2 = D_3 = 0$, and the regression equation becomes

$$\hat{Y}_i = a + b_1$$

Thus, the coefficient b_1 is the difference in predicted $\hat{Y}_i$ for non-users, as compared with heavy users. The coefficients b_2 and b_3 have similar interpretations. Although 'heavy users' was selected as a reference category, any of the other three categories could have been selected for this purpose.[29]

Analysis of variance and covariance with regression

Regression with dummy variables provides a framework for understanding the analysis of variance and covariance. Although multiple regression with dummy variables provides a general procedure for the analysis of variance and covariance, we show only the equivalence of regression with dummy variables to one-way analysis of variance. In regression with dummy variables, the predicted $\hat{Y}$ for each category is the mean of Y for each category. To illustrate using the dummy variable coding of product use we just considered, the predicted $\hat{Y}$ and mean values for each category are as follows:

Product usage category	Predicted value $\hat{Y}$	Mean value $\hat{Y}$
Non-users	$a + b_1$	$a + b_1$
Light users	$a + b_2$	$a + b_2$
Medium users	$a + b_3$	$a + b_3$
Heavy users	a	a

Given this equivalence, it is easy to see further relationships between dummy variable regression and one-way ANOVA.[30]

Thus, we see that regression in which the single independent variable with c categories has been recoded into $c - 1$ dummy variables is equivalent to one-way ANOVA. Using similar correspondences, one can also illustrate how n-way ANOVA and analysis of covariance can be performed using regression with dummy variables:

Dummy variable regression	One-way ANOVA
$SS_{res} = \sum_{i=1}^{n}(Y_i - \hat{Y}_i)^2$	$= SS_{within} = SS_{error}$
$SS_{reg} = \sum_{i=1}^{n}(\hat{Y}_i - \bar{Y})^2$	$= SS_{between} = SS_x$
R^2	$= \eta^2$
Overall F test	$= F$ test

Regression analysis in its various forms is a widely used technique as further illustrated in the following two examples. The first example illustrates an application in the context of international marketing research. The second example shows how regression can be used in investigating ethics in marketing research.

Frequent fliers – fly from the clouds to the clear[31]

As with all airline companies across the globe, airlines in Asia had been facing uncertainty and tough competition. They had been hit by high fuel costs, global recession and pre-emptive competitive deals. A group of airlines realised that they could combine efforts to increase air patronage. Secondary data revealed that among the important factors leading to airline selection by consumers were price, on-time schedules, destinations,

deals available, kitchen and food service, and on-flight service. Qualitative research in the form of focus groups revealed that the frequent flier programme was a critical factor for a broad segment of passengers and the business passenger in particular. A survey of international passengers was conducted and a series of multiple regression analyses were used to analyse the data. The likelihood of flying and other choice measures served as the dependent variable and the set of service factors, including the frequent flier programme, were the independent variables. The results indicated that the frequent flier programme indeed had a significant effect on the choice of airline. Based upon these findings, Cathay Pacific, Singapore International Airlines, Thai Airways International and Malaysian Airlines introduced a cooperative frequent flier programme called Asia Plus, available to all travellers. A multimillion-euro marketing and advertising campaign was started to promote Asia Plus. Frequent fliers thus flew from the clouds to the clear and the airlines involved experienced increased passenger traffic.

Reasons for researchers regressing to unethical behaviour[32]

More marketing research studies are being conducted online. It has been recognised for some time that the research community needs a coherent ethical code of practice to guide research activities conducted online. Many online researchers are distressed at the manner in which some researchers abuse the Internet as a means of collecting data. In particular, marketing research has been charged with engaging in deception, conflict of interest, violation of anonymity, invasion of privacy, data falsifications, dissemination of faulty research findings and the use of research as a guise to sell merchandise. It has been posited that when a researcher chooses to participate in unethical activities, that decision may be influenced by organisational factors. Therefore, a study using multiple regression analysis was designed to examine organisational factors as determinants of the incidence of unethical research practices. Six organisational variables were used as the independent variables, namely: extent of ethical problems within the organisation, top management actions on ethics, code of ethics, organisational rank, industry category and organisational role. The participant's evaluation of the incidence of unethical marketing research practices served as the dependent variable. Regression analysis of the data suggested that four of the six organisational variables influenced the extent of unethical research practice: extent of ethical problems within the organisation, top management actions on ethics, industry category and organisational role. Thus to reduce the incidence of unethical research practice, top management should take stern actions, clarificational roles and responsibilities for ethical violations, and address the extent of general ethical problems within the organisation.

SPSS and SAS Learning Editions

SPSS Windows

The CORRELATE program computes Pearson product moment correlations with significance levels. Univariate statistics, covariance and cross-product deviations may also be requested. Significance levels are included in this output. To select this procedure click

> Analyze>Correlate>Bivariate . . .
> Analyze>Correlate>Partial . . .

Scatterplots can be obtained by clicking:

> Graphs>Scatter> . . . >Simple>Define

The following are the detailed steps for running a correlation between attitude towards the city and duration of residence given in Table 20.1. A positive correlation is to be expected.

1 Select ANALYZE from the SPSS menu bar.
2 Click CORRELATE and then BIVARIATE.
3 Move 'Attitude[attitude]' into the VARIABLES box. Then move 'Duration[duration]' into the VARIABLES box.
4 Click PEARSON under CORRELATION COEFFICIENTS.
5 Check ONE_TAILED under TEST OF SIGNIFICANCE.
6 Check FLAG SIGNIFICANT CORRELATIONS.
7 Click OK.

REGRESSION calculates bivariate and multiple regression equations, associated statistics and plots. It allows easy examination of residuals. To select this procedure click

> Analyze>Regression>Linear . . .

The following are the detailed steps for running a bivariate regression with attitude towards the city as the dependent variable and duration of residence as the independent variable using the data of Table 20.1:

1 Select ANALYZE from the SPSS menu bar.
2 Click REGRESSION and then LINEAR.
3 Move 'Attitude[attitude]' into the DEPENDENT box.
4 Move 'Duration[duration]' into the INDEPENDENT(S) box.
5 Select ENTER in the METHOD box.
6 Click STATISTICS and check ESTIMATES under REGRESSION COEFFICIENTS.
7 Check MODEL FIT.

8 Click CONTINUE.
9 Click PLOTS.
10 In the LINEAR REGRESSION:PLOTS box, move *ZRESID into the Y: box and *ZPRED into the X: box.
11 Check HISTOGRAM and NORMAL PROBABILITY PLOT in the STANDARDIZED RESIDUAL PLOTS.
12 Click CONTINUE.
13 Click OK.

The steps for running multiple regression are similar except for step 4. In step 4, move 'Duration[duration]' and 'Importance[importance]' into the INDEPENDENT(S) box.

SAS Learning Edition

The instructions given here and in all the quantitative data analysis chapters will work with the SAS Learning Edition as well as with the SAS Enterprise Guide. For a point-and-click approach for performing metric and non-metric correlations, use the Analyze task within the SAS Learning Edition. The Multivariate>Correlations task offers these correlation types: Pearson product moment correlations, Kendall tau-b and Spearman rank order correlations. The task also offers Pearson, Spearman and Kendall partial correlations. To select this task click

> Analyze>Multivariate>Correlations

(*You can do correlations, partial correlations and scatterplots within this task.*)

The following are the detailed steps for running a correlation between attitude towards the city and duration of residence given in Table 20.1. A positive correlation is to be expected.

1 Select ANALYZE from the SAS Learning Edition menu bar.
2 Click MULTIVARIATE and then CORRELATIONS.
3 Move CITY and DURATION to the analysis variable task role.
4 Click OPTIONS.
5 Click PEARSON under correlation types.
6 Click RUN.

For a point-and-click approach for performing regression analysis, use the Analyze task within the SAS Learning Edition. The Regression task calculates bivariate and multiple regression equations, associated statistics, and plots. It allows an easy examination of residuals. The Regression task offers not only Linear, but also Nonlinear and Logistic Regression as well as Generalised Linear Models. To select this task click

Analyze>Regression>Linear

The following are the detailed steps for running a bivariate regression with attitude towards the city as the dependent variable and duration of residence as the independent variable using the data given in Table 20.1:

1 Select ANALYZE from the SAS Learning Edition menu bar.

2 Click REGRESSION and then LINEAR.
3 Move CITY to the dependent variable task role.
4 Move DURATION to the explanatory variables task role.
5 Click MODEL.
6 Select Full model fitted (no selection) under Model selection method.
7 Click RUN. (*The model fit stats and the estimates are part of the automatic output.*)

The steps for running multiple regression are similar except for step 4. In step 4, move DURATION and WEATHER to the explanatory variables task role.

Summary

The product moment correlation coefficient, r, measures the linear association between two metric (interval- or ratio-scaled) variables. Its square, r^2, measures the proportion of variation in one variable explained by the other. The partial correlation coefficient measures the association between two variables after controlling, or adjusting for, the effects of one or more additional variables. The order of a partial correlation indicates how many variables are being adjusted or controlled. Partial correlations can be very helpful for detecting spurious relationships.

Bivariate regression derives a mathematical equation between a single metric criterion variable and a single metric predictor variable. The equation is derived in the form of a straight line by using the least squares procedure. When the regression is run on standardised data, the intercept assumes a value of 0, and the regression coefficients are called *beta weights*. The strength of association is measured by the coefficient of determination, r^2, which is obtained by computing a ratio of SS_{reg} to SS_y. The standard error of estimate is used to assess the accuracy of prediction and may be interpreted as a kind of average error made in predicting Y from the regression equation.

Multiple regression involves a single dependent variable and two or more independent variables. The partial regression coefficient, b_1, represents the expected change in Y when X_1 is changed by one unit and X_2 to X_k are held constant. The strength of association is measured by the coefficient of multiple determination, R^2. The significance of the overall regression equation may be tested by the overall F test. Individual partial regression coefficients may be tested for significance using the incremental F test. Scattergrams of the residuals, in which the residuals are plotted against the predicted values, $\hat{Y}_i$ time, or predictor variables, are useful for examining the appropriateness of the underlying assumptions and the regression model fitted. It is also useful to examine the histogram of standardised residuals, normal probability plot of standardised residuals and the table of residual statistics.

In stepwise regression, the predictor variables are entered or removed from the regression equation one at a time for the purpose of selecting a smaller subset of predictors that account for most of the variation in the criterion variable. Multicollinearity, or very high intercorrelations among the predictor variables, can result in several problems. Because the predictors are correlated, regression analysis provides no unambiguous measure of relative importance of the predictors. Cross-validation examines whether the regression model continues to hold true for comparable data not used in estimation. It is a useful procedure for evaluating the regression model. Nominal or categorical variables may be used as predictors by coding them as dummy variables. Multiple regression with dummy variables provides a general procedure for the analysis of variance and covariance.

Questions

1   What is the product moment correlation coefficient? Does a product moment correlation of zero between two variables imply that the variables are not related to each other?

2   What are the main uses of regression analysis?

3   What is the least squares procedure?

4   Explain the meaning of standardised regression coefficients.

5   How is the strength of association measured in bivariate regression? In multiple regression?

6   What is meant by prediction accuracy? What is the standard error of the estimate?

7   What is multiple regression? How is it different from bivariate regression?

8   Explain the meaning of a partial regression coefficient. Why is it called that?

9   State the null hypothesis in testing the significance of the overall multiple regression equation. How is this null hypothesis tested?

10 What is gained by an examination of residuals?

11 Explain the stepwise regression approach. What is its purpose?

12 What is multicollinearity? What problems can arise because of multicollinearity?

13 Describe the cross-validation procedure. Describe double cross-validation.

14 What are some of the measures used to assess the relative importance of predictors in multiple regression?

15 Demonstrate the equivalence of regression with dummy variables to one-way ANOVA.

Exercises

1   A supermarket chain wants to determine the effect of promotion on relative competitiveness. Data were obtained from 15 cities on the promotional expenses relative to a major competitor (competitor expenses = 100) and on sales relative to this competitor (competitor sales = 100).

City number	Relative promotional expense	Relative sales
1	95	98
2	92	94
3	103	110
4	115	125
5	77	82
6	79	84
7	105	112
8	94	99
9	85	93
10	101	107
11	106	114
12	120	132
13	118	129
14	75	79
15	99	105

You are assigned the task of telling the manager whether there is any relationship between relative promotional expense and relative sales.

a Plot the relative sales (Y axis) against the relative promotional expense (X axis), and interpret the diagram.

b Which measure would you use to determine whether there is a relationship between the two variables? Why?

c Run a bivariate regression analysis of relative sales on relative promotional expense.

d Interpret the regression coefficients.

e Is the regression relationship significant?

f If the company matched the competitor in terms of promotional expense (if the relative expense was 100), what would the company's relative sales be?

g Interpret the resulting r^2.

2 To understand the role of quality and price in influencing the patronage of shoe shops, 14 major shoe shops in a large city were rated in terms of preference to shop, quality of shoes sold and price fairness. All the ratings were obtained on an 11-point scale, with higher numbers indicating more positive ratings.

Shoe shop number	Preference	Quality	Price
1	6	5	3
2	9	6	11
3	8	6	4
4	3	2	1
5	10	6	11
6	4	3	1
7	5	4	7
8	2	1	4
9	11	9	8
10	9	5	10
11	10	8	8
12	2	1	5
13	9	8	5
14	5	3	2

a Run a multiple regression analysis explaining shoe shop preference in terms of shoe quality and price fairness.

b Interpret the partial regression coefficients.

c Determine the significance of the overall regression.

d Determine the significance of the partial regression coefficients.

e Do you think that multicollinearity is a problem in this case? Why or why not?

3 You come across a magazine article reporting the following relationship between annual expenditure on prepared dinners (PD) and annual income (INC):

$$PD = 23.4 + 0.003INC$$

The coefficient of the *INC* variable is reported as significant.

a Does this relationship seem plausible? Is it possible to have a coefficient that is small in magnitude and yet significant?

b From the information given, can you tell how good the estimated model is?

c What are the expected expenditures on prepared dinners of a family earning €30,000?

d If a family earning €40,000 spent €130 annually on prepared dinners, what is the residual?

e What is the meaning of the negative residual?

4 In a survey pretest, data were obtained from 20 participants on preference for boots on a seven-point scale (1 = not preferred, 7 = greatly preferred) (V_1). The participants also provided their evaluations of the boots on comfort (V_2), style (V_3) and durability (V_4), also on seven-point scales (1 = poor, 7 = excellent). The resulting data are given in the following table:

Number	V_1	V_2	V_3	V_4
1	6	6	3	5
2	2	3	2	4
3	7	5	6	7
4	4	6	4	5
5	1	3	2	2
6	6	5	6	7
7	5	6	7	5
8	7	3	5	4
9	2	4	6	3
10	3	5	3	6
11	1	3	2	3
12	5	4	5	4
13	2	2	1	5
14	4	5	4	6
15	6	5	4	7
16	3	3	4	2
17	4	4	3	2
18	3	4	3	2
19	4	4	3	2
20	2	3	2	4

a Calculate the simple correlations between V_1 and V_4 and interpret the results.

b Run a bivariate regression with preference for boots (V_1) as the dependent variable and evaluation on comfort (V_2) as the independent variable. Interpret the results.

c Run a bivariate regression with preference for boots (V_1) as the dependent variable and evaluation on style (V_3) as the independent variable. Interpret the results.

d Run a bivariate regression with preference for boots (V_1) as the dependent variable and evaluation on durability (V_4) as the independent variable. Interpret the results.

e Run a multiple regression with preference for boots (V_1) as the dependent variable and V_2 to V_4 as the independent variables. Interpret the results. Compare the coefficients for V_2, V_3 and V_4 obtained in the bivariate and the multiple regressions.

5 In a small group discuss the following issues: 'Regression is such a basic technique that it should always be used in analysing data' and 'What is the relationship between bivariate correlation, bivariate regression, multiple regression and analysis of variance?'

Notes

1. Harrington, A. and Bartsiewicz, P., 'Who's up? Who's down?', *Fortune* 150 (8) (18 October, 2004), 181–186; Wojcik, J., 'Avon's benefits booklet presents easily understood information to all levels of the corporation', *Business Insurance* 35 (47) (19 November, 2001), 14; Miller, C., 'Computer modeling rings the right bell for Avon', *Marketing News* (9 May, 1988), 14.

2. Maddox, K., 'Online ad sales expected to keep growing in '05', *B to B* 89 (11) (11 October, 2004), 12; Korgaonkar, P.K. and Smith, A.E., 'Shopping orientation, demographic and media preference correlates of electronic shopping', in Balm, K.D. (ed.), *Developments in Marketing Science* Vol. 11 (Blacksburg, VA: Academy of Marketing Science, 1988), 52–55.

3. Chen, P.Y. and Popovich, P.M., *Correlation: Parametric and Nonparametric Measures* (Thousand Oaks, CA: Sage, 2002); Bobko, P., Roth, P.L. and Bobko, C., 'Correcting the effect size of *d* for range restriction and unreliability', *Organizational Research Methods* 4 (1) (January 2001), 46–61; Draper, N.R. and Smith, H., *Applied Regression Analysis*, 3rd edn (New York: Wiley, 1998); Doherty, M.E. and Sullivan, J.A., 'rho = p', *Organizational Behaviour and Human Decision Processes* 43 (1) (February 1989), 136–144; Martin, W.S., 'Effects of scaling on the correlation coefficient: additional considerations', *Journal of Marketing Research* 15 (May 1978), 304–308; Bollen, K.A. and Barb, R.H., 'Pearson's *R* and coarsely categorized measures', *American Sociological Review* 46 (1981), 232–239.

4. Cox, T. and Branco, J., *Introduction to multivariate analysis* (New York: Oxford University Press, 2002); Tacq, J., *Multivariate Analysis Techniques in Social Science Research* (Thousand Oaks, CA: Sage, 1997).

5. Although the topic is not discussed here, partial correlations can also be helpful in locating intervening variables and making certain types of causal inferences.

6. 'Global gallery', *Advertising Age* 78 (9) (February 2007), S-10; Goldsmith, R.E., 'The impact of corporate credibility and celebrity credibility on consumer reaction to advertisements and brands', *Journal of Advertising* 29 (3) (Fall 2000), 43–54; 'Bates Saatchi & Saatchi, Budapest: accounting for change', *Accountancy* 116 (224) (August 1995), 31; Kasriel, K., 'Hungary's million-dollar slap', *Advertising Age* (8 June 1992).

7. Another advantage to τ is that it can be generalised to a partial correlation coefficient. Higgins, J.J., *Introduction to modern nonparametric statistics* (Pacific Grove, CA: Duxbury, 2002); Pett, M.A., *Nonparametric Statistics for Health Care Research* (Thousand Oaks, CA: Sage, 1997); Siegel, S. and Castellan, N.J., *Nonparametric Statistics*, 2nd edn (New York: McGraw-Hill, 1988).

8. In a strict sense, the regression model requires that errors of measurement be associated only with the criterion variable and that the predictor variables be measured without error. For serially correlated errors, see Berk, R.A., *Regression* (Thousand Oaks, CA: Sage, 2003); Canjels, E. and Watson, M.W., 'Estimating deterministic trends in the presence of serially correlated errors', *Review of Economics and Statistics* 79 (2) (May 1997), 184–200. See also Bobko, P., *Correlation and Regression: Applications for Industrial/Organizational Psychology and Management*, 2nd edn (Thousand Oaks, CA: Sage, 2001). See also Fox, J., *Applied Regression Analysis and Generalized Linear Models*, 2nd edn (Thousand Oaks, CA: Sage, 2008).

9. See any text on regression, such as Kahane, L.H., *Regression Basics*, 2nd edn (Thousand Oaks, CA: Sage, 2007).

10. Technically, the numerator is $b - \beta$. Since it has been hypothesised that $\beta = 0.0$, however, it can be omitted from the formula.

11. The larger the *SEE*, the poorer the fit of the regression.

12. The assumption of fixed levels of predictors applies to the 'classical' regression model. It is possible, if certain conditions are met, for the predictors to be random variables. Their distribution is not allowed to depend on the parameters of the regression equation. See Allison, P.D., *Fixed effects regression models* (Thousand Oaks, CA: Sage, 2009); Miles, J. and Shevlin, M., *Applying Regression and Correlation: A guide for students and researchers* (Thousand Oaks, CA: Sage, 2001); Draper, N.R. and Smith, H., *Applied Regression Analysis*, 3rd edn (New York: Wiley, 1998).

13. For an approach to handling the violations of these assumptions, see Fong, D.K.H. and DeSarbo, W.S., 'A Bayesian methodology for simultaneously detecting and estimating regime change points and variable selection in multiple regression models for marketing research', *Quantitative Marketing and Economics* 5 (4) (December

2007), 427–453; Zellner, A., 'Further results on Bayesian method of moments analysis of the multiple regression model', *International Economic Review* 42 (1) (February 2001), 121–140; Dispensa, G.S., 'Use logistic regression with customer satisfaction data', *Marketing News* 31 (1) (6 January 1997), 13; Reddy, S.K., Holak, S.L. and Bhat, S., 'To extend or not to extend: success determinants of line extensions', *Journal of Marketing Research* 31 (May 1994), 243–262.

14. da Silva Lopes, T. and Casson, M., 'Entrepreneurship and the development of global brands', *Business History Review* 81 (4) (January 2007), 651–680; Fan, Y., 'The national image of global brands', *Journal of Brand Management* 9 (3) (January 2002), 180–192; Donthu, N., Lee, S. and Yoo, B., 'An examination of selected marketing mix elements and brand equity', *Academy of Marketing Science* 28 (2) (Spring 2000), 195–211; Giges, N., 'Europeans buy outside goods, but like local ads', *Advertising Age International* (27 April 1992).

15. For other applications of multiple regression see Binninger, A.-S., 'Exploring the relationships between retail brands and consumer store loyalty', *International Journal of Retail & Distribution Management* 36 (2) (2008), 94; Kirca, A.H., Jayachandran, S. and Bearden, W.O., 'Market orientation: a meta-analytic review and assessment of its antecedents and impact upon performance', *Journal of Marketing* 69 (April 2005), 24–41; Wertenbroch, K. and Skiera, B., 'Measuring consumers' willingness to pay at the point of purchase', *Journal of Marketing Research* 39 (2) (May 2002), 228–241.

16. Yet another reason for adjusting R^2 is that, as a result of the optimising properties of the least squares approach, it is a maximum. Thus, to some extent, R^2 always overestimates the magnitude of a relationship.

17. If R^2_{pop} is zero, then the sample R^2 reflects only sampling error, and the F ratio will tend to be equal to unity.

18. Another approach is the hierarchical method, in which the variables are added to the regression equation in an order specified by the researcher.

19. Sirkin, R.M., *Statistics for the Social Sciences*, 3rd edn (Thousand Oaks, CA: Sage, 2005); Irwin, J.R. and McClelland, G.H., 'Misleading heuristics and moderated multiple regression models', *Journal of Marketing Research* 38 (1) (February 2001), 100–109; Atkinson, A.C., Koopman, S.J. and Shephard, N., 'Detecting shocks: outliers and breaks in time series', *Journal of Econometrics* 80 (2) (October 1997), 387–422; Wang, G.C.S. and Akabay, C.K., 'Autocorrelation: problems and solutions in regression modeling', *Journal of Business Forecasting Methods and Systems* 13 (4) (Winter 1994/95), 18–26; Belsley, D., Kub, E. and Walsh, R.E., *Regression Diagnostics* (New York: Wiley, 1980).

20. The Durbin–Watson test is discussed in virtually all regression textbooks. See also Allison, P.D., *Fixed Effects Regression Models* (Thousand Oaks, CA: Sage, 2009); Halkos, G.E. and Kevork, I.S., 'A comparison of alternative root tests', *Journal of Applied Statistics* 32 (1) (January 2005), 45–60.

21. Meiri, R. and Zahavi, J., 'Using simulated annealing to optimize the feature selection problem in marketing applications', *European Journal of Operational Research* 171 (3) (June 2006), 842–858; Fox, E.J. and Hoch, S.J.,

'Cherry-picking', *Journal of Marketing* 69 (January 2005), 46–62; Schmitt, N., 'Estimates for cross-validity for stepwise regression and with predictor selection', *Journal of Applied Psychology* 84 (1) (February 1999), 50; Fox, J., *Applied Regression Analysis, Linear Models and Related Methods* (Thousand Oaks, CA: Sage, 1997); McIntyre, S.H., Montgomery, D.B., Srinivasan, V. and Weitz, B.A., 'Evaluating the statistical significance of models developed by stepwise regression', *Journal of Marketing Research* 20 (February 1983), 1–11.

22. Mondello, M. and Rishe, P., 'Ticket price determination in professional sports: an empirical analysis of the NBA, NFL, NHL and Major League Baseball', *Sports Marketing Quarterly* 13 (2004), 104–112.

23. Forseter, M. and Mahler, D.Q., 'The Roper Starch Report', *Drug Store News* (2000), 46–63; Jarboe, G.R. and McDaniel, C.D., 'A profile of browsers in regional shopping malls', *Journal of the Academy of Marketing Science* (Spring 1987), 46–53.

24. Possible procedures are given in Echambadi, R. and Hess, J.D., 'Mean-centering does not alleviate collinearity problems in moderated multiple regression models', *Marketing Science* 26 (3) (June 2007), 438–445; Sethi, R., Smith, D.C. and Whan Park, C., 'Cross-functional product development teams, creativity and the innovations of new consumer products', *Journal of Marketing Research* 38 (1) (February 2001), 73–85; Grapentine, T., 'Path analysis vs. structural equation modeling', *Journal of Business Forecasting Methods and Systems* 15 (1) (Spring 1996), 23–27; Wang, G.C.S., 'How to handle multicollinearity in regression modelling', *Journal of Business Forecasting Methods and Systems* 15 (1) (Spring 1996), 23–27; Mason, C.H. and Perreault, W.D. Jr, 'Collinearity, power, and interpretation of multiple regression analysis', *Journal of Marketing Research* 28 (August 1991), 268–280; Hocking, R.R., 'Developments in linear regression methodology: 1959–1982', *Technometrics* 25 (August 1983), 219–230; Snee, R.D., 'Discussion', *Technometrics* 25 (August 1983), 230–237.

25. Billor, N., 'An application of the local influence approach to ridge regression', *Journal of Applied Statistics* 26 (2) (February 1999), 177–183; Holzworth, J.R., 'Policy capturing with ridge regression', *Organizational Behavior and Human Decision Processes* 68 (2) (November 1996), 171–179; Wildt, A.R., 'Equity estimation and assessing market response', *Journal of Marketing Research* 31 (February 1994), 437–451; Shanna, S. and James, W.L., 'Latent root regression: an alternative procedure for estimating parameters in the presence of multicollinearity', *Journal of Marketing Research* 18 (May 1981), 154–161.

26. Only relative importance can be determined, since the importance of an independent variable depends upon all the independent variables in the regression model.

27. Field, A., *Discovering Statistics using SPSS*, 2nd edn (Thousand Oaks, CA: Sage, 2005); McClendon, M.J., *Multiple Regression and Causal Analysis* (Prospect Heights, IL: Waveland Press, 2002); Rugimbana, R., 'Predicting automated teller machine usage: the relative importance of perceptual and demographic factors', *International Journal of Bank Marketing* 13 (4) (1995), 26–32; Green, P.E., Carroll, S.D. and DeSarbo, W.S., 'A new measure of predictor variable importance in multiple regression', *Journal of Marketing Research* 15 (August 1978), 356–360;

Jackson, B.B., 'Comment on "A new measure of predictor variable importance in multiple regression"', *Journal of Marketing Research* 17 (February 1980), 116–118.

28. In the rare situation in which all the predictors are uncorrelated, simple correlations = partial correlations = part correlations = betas. Hence, the squares of these measures will yield the same rank order of the relative importance of the variables.

29. For further discussion and applications of dummy variable regression, see Mauro, J., Hernandez, C. and Mazzon, J.A., 'Adoption of internet banking: proposition and implementation of an integrated methodology approach', *International Journal of Bank Marketing* 25 (3) (2007), 72–82; Glantz, S.A. and Slinker, B.K., *Primer of applied regression and analysis of variance* (Blacklick, OH: McGraw-Hill, 2000); Yavas, U., 'Demand forecasting in a service setting', *Journal of International Marketing and Marketing Research* 21 (1) (February 1996), 3–11. For further discussion on dummy variable coding, see Cohen, J. and Cohen, P., *Applied Multiple Regression Correlation Analysis for the Behavioural Sciences*, 2nd edn (Hillsdale, NJ: Lawrence Erlbaum Associates, 1983), 191–222.

30. Goode, M.M.H. and Harris, L.C., 'Online behavioural intentions: an empirical investigation of antecedents and moderators', *European Journal of Marketing* 41 (5/6) (2007), 512; Aguinis, H., Beaty, J.C., Boik, R.J. and Pierce, C.A., 'Effect size and power in assessing moderating effects of categorical variables using multiple regression: a 30 year review', *Journal of Applied Psychology* 90 (1) (2005), 94–107; Glantz, S.A. and Slinker, B.K., *Primer of applied regression and analysis of variance* (Blacklick, OH: McGraw-Hill, 2000); Fox, J., *Applied Regression Analysis, Linear Models and Related Methods* (Thousand Oaks, CA: Sage, 1997). For an application of regression analysis to conduct analysis of covariance, see Barone, M.J., Manning, K.C. and Miniard, P.W., 'Consumer response to retailers' use of partially comparative pricing', *Journal of Marketing* 68 (July 2004), 37–47.

32. Anon., 'World airline performance: Asia Pacific-transpacific recovery continues', *Interavia* 58 (671) (May/June 2003), 35; Flottau, J., 'Asian carriers advised to seek new formulas', *Aviation Week & Space* 155 (23) (3 December, 2001), 45.

33. Barnett, T. and Valentine, S., 'Issue contingencies and marketers' recognition of ethical issues, ethical judgments and behavioural intentions', *Journal of Business Research* 57 (4) (April 2004), 338; Delorme, D.E., Zinkhan, G.M. and French, W., 'Ethics and the internet: issues associated with qualitative research', *Journal of Business Ethics* 33 (4) (October 2001), 2.

21

Discriminant and logit analysis

Stage 1

Problem definition

Stage 2

Research approach developed

Stage 3

Research design developed

Stage 4

Fieldwork or data collection

Stage 5

Data integrity and analysis

Stage 6

Report preparation and presentation

Discriminant analysis is used to estimate the relationship between a categorical dependent variable and a set of interval-scaled independent variables.

Objectives

After reading this chapter, you should be able to:

1 describe the concept of discriminant analysis, its objectives and its applications in marketing research;

2 outline the procedures for conducting discriminant analysis, including the formulation of the problem, estimation of the discriminant function coefficients, determination of significance, interpretation and validation;

3 discuss multiple discriminant analysis and the distinction between two-group and multiple discriminant analysis;

4 explain stepwise discriminant analysis and describe the Mahalanobis procedure;

5 describe the binary logit model and its advantages over discriminant and regression analysis;

6 appreciate how SPSS and SAS software are used in discriminant and logit analysis.

Overview

This chapter discusses the technique of discriminant analysis. We begin by examining the relationship of this procedure to regression analysis (Chapter 20) and analysis of variance (Chapter 19). We present a model and describe the general procedure for conducting discriminant analysis, with an emphasis on formulation, estimation, determination of significance, interpretation, and validation of the results. The procedure is illustrated with an example of two-group discriminant analysis, followed by an example of multiple (three-group) discriminant analysis. The stepwise discriminant analysis procedure is also covered. When the dependent variable is binary, the logit model can also be used instead of two-group discriminant analysis. We explain the logit model and discuss its relative merits versus discriminant and regression analyses. Finally, help is provided to run the SPSS and SAS Learning Editions in the data analysis challenges presented in this chapter. We begin with an example that illustrates an application of multiple discriminant analysis.

Real research | ## An eye for a bargain[1]

A study of 294 consumers was undertaken to determine the correlates of 'rebate proneness': in other words, the characteristics of consumers who respond favourably to direct mail promotions that offer a discount on the normal purchase price. The predictor variables were four factors related to household shopping attitudes and behaviour and selected demographic characteristics (gender, age and income). The dependent variable was the extent to which participants were predisposed to take up the offer of a rebate, of which three levels were identified. Participants who reported no purchases triggered by a rebate during the past 12 months were classified as *non-users*, those who reported one or two such purchases as *light users*, and those with more than two purchases as *frequent users* of discounts. Multiple discriminant analysis was used to analyse the data. Two primary findings emerged. First, consumers' perception of the effort/value relationship was the most effective variable in discriminating among frequent users, light users and non-users of rebate offers. Clearly, 'rebate-prone' consumers associate less effort with fulfilling the requirements of the rebated purchase, and are willing to accept a relatively smaller refund than other customers. Second, consumers who were aware of the regular prices of products, so that they recognise bargains, are more likely than others to respond to rebate offers. These findings were used by Dell (**www.dell.com**) when it offered up to $150 cash rebates on its notebook computers during April 2009. The company felt that this would encourage rebate-sensitive customers to choose Dell notebooks.

In this example, significant intergroup differences were found using multiple predictor variables. An examination of differences across groups lies at the heart of the basic concept of discriminant analysis.

Basic concept of discriminant analysis

Discriminant analysis
A technique for analysing marketing research data when the criterion or dependent variable is categorical and the predictor or independent variables are interval in nature.

Discriminant function
The linear combination of independent variables developed by discriminant analysis that will best discriminate between the categories of the dependent variable.

Two-group discriminant analysis
Discriminant analysis technique where the criterion variable has two categories.

Multiple discriminant analysis
Discriminant analysis technique where the criterion variable involves three or more categories.

Discriminant analysis is a technique for analysing data when the criterion or dependent variable is categorical and the predictor or independent variables are interval in nature.[2] For example, the dependent variable may be the choice of the make of a new car (A, B or C) and the independent variables may be ratings of attributes of mobile phones on a seven-point Likert scale. The objectives of discriminant analysis are as follows:

1 Development of discriminant functions, or linear combinations of the predictor or independent variables, that best discriminate between the categories of the criterion or dependent variable (groups).

2 Examination of whether significant differences exist among the groups, in terms of the predictor variables.

3 Determination of which predictor variables contribute to most of the intergroup differences.

4 Classification of cases to one of the groups based on the values of the predictor variables.

5 Evaluation of the accuracy of classification.

Discriminant analysis techniques are described by the number of categories possessed by the criterion variable. When the criterion variable has two categories, the technique is known as two-group discriminant analysis. When three or more categories are involved, the technique is referred to as multiple discriminant analysis. The main distinction is that in the two-group case it is possible to derive only one discriminant function, but in multiple discriminant analysis more than one function may be computed.[3]

Examples of discriminant analysis abound in marketing research. This technique can be used to answer questions such as:

• In terms of demographic characteristics, how do customers who exhibit loyalty to a particular fashion brand differ from those who do not?

• Do heavy users, medium users and light users of soft drinks differ in terms of their consumption of frozen foods?

• What psychographic characteristics help differentiate between price-sensitive and non-price-sensitive buyers of groceries?

• Do market segments differ in their media consumption habits?

• What are the distinguishing characteristics of consumers who respond to direct mail offers?

Relationship of discriminant and logit analysis to ANOVA and regression

The relationships among discriminant analysis, analysis of variance (ANOVA) and regression analysis are shown in Table 21.1. We explain these relationships with an example in which the researcher is attempting to explain the amount of life insurance purchased in terms of age and income. All three procedures involve a single criterion or dependent variable and multiple predictor or independent variables. The nature of these variables differs, however. In ANOVA and regression analysis, the dependent variable is metric or interval scaled (amount of life insurance purchased in euros), whereas in discriminant analysis, it is categorical (amount of life insurance purchased classified as high, medium or low). The independent variables are categorical in the case of ANOVA (age and income are each classified as high, medium or low) but metric in the case of regression and discriminant analysis (age in years and income in euros, i.e. both measured on a ratio scale).

Table 21.1	Similarities and differences among ANOVA, regression and discriminant analysis		
	ANOVA	*Regression*	*Discriminant/Logit analysis*
Similarities			
Number of dependent variables	One	One	One
Number of independent variables	Multiple	Multiple	Multiple
Differences			
Nature of the dependent variable	Metric	Metric	Categorical/binary
Nature of the independent variable	Categorical	Metric	Metric

Two-group discriminant analysis, in which the dependent variable has only two categories, is closely related to multiple regression analysis. In this case, multiple regression, in which the dependent variable is coded as a 0 or 1 dummy variable, results in partial regression coefficients that are proportional to discriminant function coefficients (see the following section on the discriminant analysis model). The nature of dependent and independent variables in the binary logit model is similar to that in the two-group discriminant analysis.

Discriminant analysis model

Discriminant analysis model

The statistical model on which discriminant analysis is based.

The **discriminant analysis model** involves linear combinations of the following form:

$$D = b_0 + b_1 X_1 + b_2 X_2 + b_3 X_3 + \ldots + b_k X_k$$

where D = discriminant score
         bs = discriminant coefficients or weight
         Xs = predictor or independent variable

The coefficients or weights (b) are estimated so that the groups differ as much as possible on the values of the discriminant function. This occurs when the ratio of between-group sum of squares to within-group sum of squares for the discriminant scores is at a maximum. Any other linear combination of the predictors will result in a smaller ratio.

We give a brief geometrical exposition of two-group discriminant analysis. Suppose we had two groups, G1 and G2, and each member of these groups was measured on two variables

X_1 and X_2. A scatter diagram of the two groups is shown in Figure 21.1, where X_1 and X_2 are the two axes. Members of G1 are denoted by 1 and members of G2 by 2. The resultant ellipses encompass some specified percentage of the points (members), say 93% in each group. A straight line is drawn through the two points where the ellipses intercept and then projected to a new axis, D. The overlap between the univariate distributions G1' and G2', represented by the shaded area in Figure 21.1, is smaller than would be obtained by any other line drawn through the ellipses representing the scatterplots. Thus the groups differ as much as possible on the D axis. Several statistics are associated with discriminant analysis.

Figure 21.1

A geometric interpretation of two-group discriminant analysis

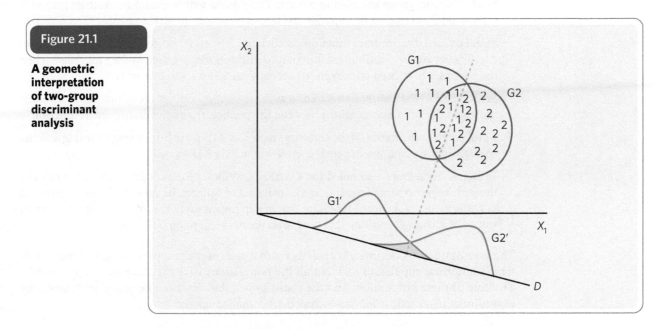

Statistics associated with discriminant analysis

The important statistics associated with discriminant analysis include the following:

Canonical correlation. Canonical correlation measures the extent of association between the discriminant scores and the groups. It is a measure of association between the single discriminant function and the set of dummy variables that define the group membership.

Centroid. The centroid is the mean values for the discriminant scores for a particular group. There are as many centroids as there are groups, as there is one for each group. The means for a group on all the functions are the *group centroids*.

Classification matrix. Sometimes also called the confusion or prediction matrix, the classification matrix contains the number of correctly classified and misclassified cases. The correctly classified cases appear on the diagonal, because the predicted and actual groups are the same. The off-diagonal elements represent cases that have been incorrectly classified. The sum of the diagonal elements divided by the total number of cases represents the *hit ratio*.

Discriminant function coefficients. The discriminant function coefficients (unstandardised) are the multipliers of variables, when the variables are in the original units of measurement.

Discriminant scores. The unstandardised coefficients are multiplied by the values of the variables. These products are summed and added to the constant term to obtain the discriminant scores.

Eigenvalue. For each discriminant function, the eigenvalue is the ratio of between-group to within-group sums of squares. Large eigenvalues imply superior functions.

F values and their significance. F values are calculated from a one-way ANOVA, with the grouping variable serving as the categorical independent variable. Each predictor, in turn, serves as the metric-dependent variable in the ANOVA.

Group means and group standard deviations. Group means and group standard deviations are computed for each predictor for each group.

Pooled within-group correlation matrix. The pooled within-group correlation matrix is computed by averaging the separate covariance matrices for all the groups.

Standardised discriminant function coefficients. The standardised discriminant function coefficients are the discriminant function coefficients that are used as the multipliers when the variables have been standardised to a mean of 0 and a variance of 1.

Structure correlations. Also referred to as *discriminant loadings*, the structure correlations represent the simple correlations between the predictors and the discriminant function.

Total correlation matrix. If the cases are treated as if they are from a single sample and the correlations are computed, a total correlation matrix is obtained.

Wilks' λ. Sometimes also called the U statistic, Wilks' λ for each predictor is the ratio of the within-group sum of squares to the total sum of squares. Its value varies between 0 and 1. Large values of λ (near 1) indicate that group means do not seem to be different. Small values of λ (near 0) indicate that the group means seem to be different.

The assumptions in discriminant analysis are that each of the groups is a sample from a multivariate normal population and that all the populations have the same covariance matrix. The role of these assumptions and the statistics just described can be better understood by examining the procedure for conducting discriminant analysis.

Conducting discriminant analysis

The steps involved in conducting discriminant analysis consist of formulation, estimation, determination of significance, interpretation and validation (see Figure 21.2). These steps are discussed and illustrated within the context of two-group discriminant analysis. Discriminant analysis with more than two groups is discussed later in this chapter.

Formulate the problem

The first step in discriminant analysis is to formulate the problem by identifying the objectives, the criterion variable and the independent variables. The criterion variable must consist of two or more mutually exclusive and collectively exhaustive categories. When the dependent variable is interval or ratio scaled, it must first be converted into categories. For example, attitude towards the brand, measured on a seven-point scale, could be categorised as unfavourable (1, 2, 3), neutral (4) or favourable (5, 6, 7). Alternatively, one could plot the distribution of the dependent variable and form groups of equal size by determining the appropriate cut-off points for each category. The predictor variables should be selected based on a theoretical model or previous research, or, in the case of exploratory research, the experience of the researcher should guide their selection.

The next step is to divide the sample into two parts. One part of the sample, called the *estimation* or analysis sample, is used for estimation of the discriminant function. The other part, called the *holdout* or validation sample, is reserved for validating the discriminant function. When the sample is large enough, it can be split in half. One half serves as the analysis

Analysis sample
Part of the total sample used to check the results of the discriminant function.

Validation sample
That part of the total sample used to check the results of the estimation sample.

Figure 21.2
Conducting discriminant analysis

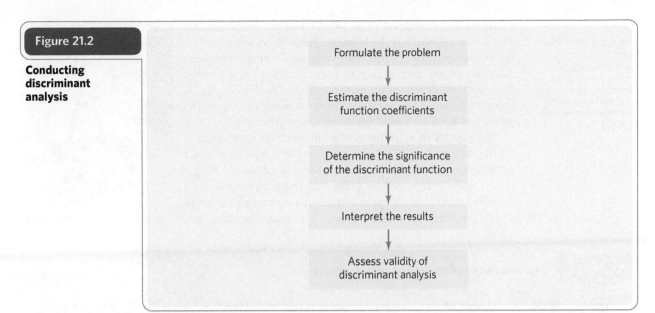

sample and the other is used for validation. The roles of the halves are then interchanged and the analysis is repeated. This is called double cross-validation and is similar to the procedure discussed in regression analysis (Chapter 20).

Often, the distribution of the number of cases in the analysis and validation samples follows the distribution in the total sample. For instance, if the total sample contained 50% loyal and 50% non-loyal consumers, then the analysis and validation samples would each contain 50% loyal and 50% non-loyal consumers. On the other hand, if the sample contained 25% loyal and 75% non-loyal consumers, the analysis and validation samples would be selected to reflect the same distribution (25% vs. 75%).

Finally, it has been suggested that the validation of the discriminant function should be conducted repeatedly. Each time, the sample should be split into different analysis and validation parts. The discriminant function should be estimated and the validation analysis carried out. Thus, the validation assessment is based on a number of trials. More rigorous methods have also been suggested.[4]

To better illustrate two-group discriminant analysis, let us look at an example. Suppose we want to determine the salient characteristics of families that have visited a skiing resort during the last two years. Data were obtained from a pretest sample of 42 households. Of these, 30 households, shown in Table 21.2, were included in the analysis sample and the remaining 12, shown in Table 21.3, were part of the validation sample. The households that visited a resort during the last two years were coded as 1; those that did not, as 2 (VISIT). Both the analysis and validation samples were balanced in terms of VISIT. As can be seen, the analysis sample contains 15 households in each category, whereas the validation sample had 6 in each category. Data were also obtained on annual family income (INCOME), attitude towards travel (TRAVEL, measured on a nine-point scale), importance attached to a family skiing holiday (HOLIDAY, measured on a nine-point scale), household size (HSIZE) and age of the head of the household (AGE).

Estimate the discriminant function coefficients

Direct method
An approach to discriminant analysis that involves estimating the discriminant function so that all the predictors are included simultaneously.

Once the analysis sample has been identified, as in Table 21.2, we can estimate the discriminant function coefficients. Two broad approaches are available. The **direct method** involves estimating the discriminant function so that all the predictors are included simultaneously. In this case, each independent variable is included, regardless of its discriminating power. This method is appropriate when, based on previous research or a theoretical model, the researcher

Stepwise discriminant analysis

Discriminant analysis in which the predictors are entered sequentially based on their ability to discriminate between the groups.

wants the discrimination to be based on all the predictors. An alternative approach is the stepwise method. In stepwise discriminant analysis, the predictor variables are entered sequentially, based on their ability to discriminate among groups. This method, described in more detail later in this chapter, is appropriate when the researcher wants to select a subset of the predictors for inclusion in the discriminant function.

The results of running two-group discriminant analysis on the data of Table 21.2 using a popular statistical analysis package are presented in Table 21.4. Some intuitive feel for the results may be obtained by examining the group means and standard deviations. It appears that the two groups are more widely separated in terms of income than other variables, and

Table 21.2	Information on skiing holiday: analysis sample					
Number	Resort visit	Annual family income (€000)	Attitude towards travel	Importance attached to family skiing holiday	Household size	Age of head of household	Amount spent on family skiing holiday
1	1	50.2	5	8	3	43	M (2)
2	1	70.3	6	7	4	61	H (3)
3	1	62.9	7	5	6	52	H (3)
4	1	48.5	7	5	5	36	L (1)
5	1	52.7	6	6	4	55	H (3)
6	1	75.0	8	7	5	68	H (3)
7	1	46.2	5	3	3	62	M (2)
8	1	57.0	2	4	6	51	M (2)
9	1	64.1	7	5	4	57	H (3)
10	1	68.1	7	6	5	45	H (3)
11	1	73.4	6	7	5	44	H (3)
12	1	71.9	5	8	4	64	H (3)
13	1	56.2	1	8	6	54	M (2)
14	1	49.3	4	2	3	56	H (3)
15	1	62.0	5	6	2	58	H (3)
16	2	32.1	5	4	3	58	L (1)
17	2	36.2	4	3	2	55	L (1)
18	2	43.2	2	5	2	57	M (2)
19	2	50.4	5	2	4	37	M (2)
20	2	44.1	6	6	3	42	M (2)
21	2	38.3	6	6	2	45	L (1)
22	2	55.0	1	2	2	57	M (2)
23	2	46.1	3	5	3	51	L (1)
24	2	35.0	6	4	5	64	L (1)
25	2	37.3	2	7	4	54	L (1)
26	2	41.8	5	1	3	56	M (2)
27	2	57.0	8	3	2	36	M (2)
28	2	33.4	6	8	2	50	L (1)
29	2	37.5	3	2	3	48	L (1)
30	2	41.3	3	3	2	42	L (1)

Table 21.3	Information on skiing holiday: validation sample						
Number	Resort visit	Annual family income (€000)	Attitude towards travel	Importance attached to family skiing holiday	Household size	Age of head of household	Amount spent on family skiing holiday
1	1	50.8	4	7	3	45	M (2)
2	1	63.6	7	4	7	55	H (3)
3	1	54.0	6	7	4	58	M (2)
4	1	45.0	5	4	3	60	M (2)
5	1	68.0	6	6	6	46	H (3)
6	1	62.1	5	6	3	56	H (3)
7	2	35.0	4	3	4	54	L (1)
8	2	49.6	5	3	5	39	L (1)
9	2	39.4	6	5	3	44	H (3)
10	2	37.0	2	6	5	51	L (1)
11	2	54.5	7	3	3	37	M (2)
12	2	38.2	2	2	3	49	L (1)

Table 21.4	Results of two-group discriminant analysis

Group means

Visit	INCOME	TRAVEL	HOLIDAY	HSIZE	AGE
1	60.52000	5.40000	5.80000	4.33333	53.73333
2	41.91333	4.33333	4.06667	2.80000	50.13333
Total	51.21667	4.86667	4.93333	3.56667	51.93333

Group standard deviations

	INCOME	TRAVEL	HOLIDAY	HSIZE	AGE
1	9.83065	1.91982	1.82052	1.23443	8.77062
2	7.55115	1.95180	2.05171	0.94112	8.27101
Total	12.79523	1.97804	2.09981	1.33089	8.57395

Pooled within-groups correlation matrix

	INCOME	TRAVEL	HOLIDAY	HSIZE	AGE
INCOME	1.00000				
TRAVEL	0.19745	1.00000			
HOLIDAY	0.09148	0.08434	1.00000		
HSIZE	0.08887	-0.01681	0.07046	1.00000	
AGE	-0.01431	-0.19709	0.01742	-0.04301	1.00000

Table 21.4	**Continued**

Wilks' λ (*U* statistic) and univariate *F* ratio with 1 and 28 degrees of freedom

Variable	Wilks' λ	F	Significance
INCOME	0.45310	33.800	0.0000
TRAVEL	0.92479	2.277	0.1425
HOLIDAY	0.82377	5.990	0.0209
HSIZE	0.65672	14.640	0.0007
AGE	0.95441	1.338	0.2572

Canonical discriminant functions

Function	Eigenvalue	Per cent of variance	Cumulative percentage	Canonical correlation	After function	Wilks' λ	Chi-square	df	Sig.
1*	1.7862	100.00	100.00	0.8007	0	0.3589	26.13	5	0.0001

*Marks the one canonical discriminant function remaining in the analysis.

Standard canonical discriminant function coefficients

	Func 1
INCOME	0.74301
TRAVEL	0.09611
HOLIDAY	0.23329
HSIZE	0.46911
AGE	0.20922

Structure matrix: pooled within-groups correlations between discriminating variables and canonical discriminant functions (variables ordered by size of correlation within function)

	Func 1
INCOME	0.82202
HSIZE	0.54096
HOLIDAY	0.34607
TRAVEL	0.21337
AGE	0.16354

Unstandardised canonical discriminant function coefficients

	Func 1
INCOME	0.8476710E-01
TRAVEL	0.4964455E-01
HOLIDAY	0.1202813
HSIZE	0.4273893
AGE	0.2454380E-01
(Constant)	−7.975476

Table 21.4	**Continued**

Canonical discriminant functions evaluated at group means (group centroids)

Group	Func 1
1	1.29118
2	–1.29118

Classification results

		Visit	Predicted group membership 1	2	Total
Original	Count	1	12	3	15
		2	0	15	15
	%	1	80.0	20.0	100.0
		2	0.0	100.0	100.0
Cross-validated	Count	1	11	4	15
		2	2	13	15
	%	1	73.3	26.7	100.0
		2	13.3	86.7	100.0

[a] Cross-validation is done only for those cases in the analysis. In cross-validation, each case is classified by the functions derived from all cases other than that case.

[b] 90.0% of original grouped cases correctly classified.

[c] 80.0% of cross-validated grouped cases correctly classified.

Classification results for cases not selected for use in analysis (holdout sample)

Actual group		No. of cases	Predicted group membership 1	2
Group	1	6	4	2
			66.7%	33.3%
Group	2	6	0	6
			0.0%	100%

Percentage of grouped cases correctly classified: 83.33%

there appears to be more of a separation on the importance attached to the family skiing holiday than on attitude towards travel. The difference between the two groups on age of the head of the household is small, and the standard deviation of this variable is large.

The pooled within-groups correlation matrix indicates low correlations between the predictors. Multicollinearity is unlikely to be a problem. The significance of the univariate F ratios indicates that, when the predictors are considered individually, only income, importance of holiday and household size significantly differentiate between those who visited a resort and those who did not.

Because there are two groups, only one discriminant function is estimated. The eigenvalue associated with this function is 1.7862, and it accounts for 100% of the explained variance. The canonical correlation associated with this function is 0.8007. The square of this correlation, $(0.8007)^2 = 0.64$, indicates that 64% of the variance in the dependent variable (VISIT) is explained or accounted for by this model. The next step is determination of significance.

Determine the significance of the discriminant function

It would not be meaningful to interpret the analysis if the discriminant functions estimated were not statistically significant. The null hypothesis that, in the population, the means of all discriminant functions in all groups are equal can be statistically tested. In SPSS, this test is based on Wilks' λ. If several functions are tested simultaneously (as in the case of multiple discriminant analysis), the Wilks' λ statistic is the product of the univariate λ for each function. The significance level is estimated based on a chi-square transformation of the statistic. In testing for significance in the holiday resort example (see Table 21.4), it may be noted that the Wilks' λ associated with the function is 0.3589, which transforms to a chi-square of 26.13 with 5 degrees of freedom. This is significant beyond the 0.05 level. In SAS, an approximate F statistic, based on an approximation to the distribution of the likelihood ratio, is calculated. If the null hypothesis is rejected, indicating significant discrimination, one can proceed to interpret the results.[5]

Interpret the results

The interpretation of the discriminant weights, or coefficients, is similar to that in multiple regression analysis. The value of the coefficient for a particular predictor depends on the other predictors included in the discriminant function. The signs of the coefficients are arbitrary, but they indicate which variable values result in large and small function values and associate them with particular groups.

Given the multicollinearity in the predictor variables, there is no unambiguous measure of the relative importance of the predictors in discriminating between the groups.[6] With this caveat in mind, we can obtain some idea of the relative importance of the variables by examining the absolute magnitude of the standardised discriminant function coefficients. Generally, predictors with relatively large standardised coefficients contribute more to the discriminating power of the function, as compared with predictors with smaller coefficients, and are therefore more important.

Some idea of the relative importance of the predictors can also be obtained by examining the structure correlations, also called *canonical loadings* or *discriminant loadings*. These simple correlations between each predictor and the discriminant function represent the variance that the predictor shares with the function. Like the standardised coefficients, these correlations must also be interpreted with caution.

An examination of the standardised discriminant function coefficients for the holiday resort example is instructive. Given the low intercorrelations between the predictors, one might cautiously use the magnitudes of the standardised coefficients to suggest that income is the most important predictor in discriminating between the groups, followed by household size and importance attached to the family skiing holiday. The same observation is obtained from examination of the structure correlations. These simple correlations between the predictors and the discriminant function are listed in order of magnitude.

The unstandardised discriminant function coefficients are also given. These can be applied to the raw values of the variables in the holdout set for classification purposes. The group centroids, giving the value of the discriminant function evaluated at the group means, are also shown. Group 1, those who have visited a resort, has a positive value, whereas group 2 has an equal negative value. The signs of the coefficients associated with all the predictors are positive, which suggests that higher family income, household size, importance attached to family skiing holiday, attitude towards travel and age are more likely to result in the family visiting the resort. It would be reasonable to develop a profile of the two groups in terms of the three predictors that seem to be the most important: income, household size and importance of holiday. The values of these three variables for the two groups are given at the beginning of Table 21.4.

The determination of relative importance of the predictors is further illustrated by the following example.

| Real research | **Satisfied salespeople stay[7]** |

A survey asked business people about the climate of hiring and maintaining employees in harsh economic conditions. It was reported that 85% of participants were concerned about recruiting employees and 81% said they were concerned about retaining employees. When the economy is down, turnover is rapid. Generally speaking, if an organisation wants to retain its employees, it must learn why people leave their jobs and why others stay and are satisfied with their jobs. Discriminant analysis was used to determine what factors explained the differences between salespeople who left a large computer

manufacturing company and those who stayed. The independent variables were company rating, job security, seven job satisfaction dimensions, four role-conflict dimensions, four role-ambiguity dimensions and nine measures of sales performance. The dependent variable was the dichotomy between those who stayed and those who left. The canonical correlation, an index of discrimination ($R = 0.4572$), was significant (Wilks' $\lambda = 0.7909$, $F_{26,173} = 1.7588$, $p = 0.0180$). This result indicated that the variables discriminated between those who left and those who stayed.

Discriminant analysis results

	Variable	Coefficients	Standardised coefficients	Structure correlations
1	Work[a]	0.0903	0.3910	0.5446
2	Promotion[a]	0.0288	0.1515	0.5044
3	Job security	0.1567	0.1384	0.4958
4	Customer relations[b]	0.0086	0.1751	0.4906
5	Company rating	0.4059	0.3240	0.4824
6	Working with others[b]	0.0018	0.0365	0.4651
7	Overall performance[b]	-0.0148	-0.3252	0.4518
8	Time-territory management[b]	0.0126	0.2899	0.4496
9	Sales produced[b]	0.0059	0.1404	0.4484
10	Presentation skill[b]	0.0118	0.2526	0.4387
11	Technical information[b]	0.0003	0.0065	0.4173
12	Pay benefits[a]	0.0600	0.1843	0.3788
13	Quota achieved[b]	0.0035	0.2915	0.3780
14	Management[a]	0.0014	0.0138	0.3571

Variable		Coefficients	Standardised coefficients	Structure correlations
15	Information collection[b]	-0.0146	-0.3327	0.3326
16	Family[c]	-0.0684	-0.3408	-0.3221
17	Sales manager[a]	-0.0121	-0.1102	0.2909
18	Coworker[a]	0.0225	0.0893	0.2671
19	Customer[c]	-0.0625	-0.2797	-0.2602
20	Family[d]	0.0473	0.1970	0.2180
21	Job[d]	0.1378	0.5312	0.2119
22	Job[c]	0.0410	0.5475	-0.1029
23	Customer[d]	-0.0060	-0.0255	0.1004
24	Sales manager[c]	-0.0365	-0.2406	-0.0499
25	Sales manager[d]	-0.0606	-0.3333	0.0467
26	Customer[a]	-0.0338	-0.1488	0.0192

Note: Rank order of importance is based on the magnitude of the canonical loadings:

[a] Satisfaction

[b] Performance

[c] Ambiguity

[d] Conflict.

The results from simultaneously entering all variables in discriminant analysis are presented in the table above. The rank order of importance, as determined by the relative magnitude of the canonical loadings, is presented in the first column. Satisfaction with the job and promotional opportunities were the two most important discriminators, followed by job security. Those who stayed in the company found the job to be more exciting, satisfying, challenging and interesting than those who left.

In this example, promotion was identified as the second most important variable based on the canonical loadings. However, it is not the second most important variable based on the absolute magnitude of the standardised discriminant function coefficients. This anomaly results from multicollinearity.

Characteristic profile
An aid to interpreting discriminant analysis results by describing each group in terms of the group means for the predictor variables.

Another aid to interpreting discriminant analysis results is to develop a characteristic profile for each group by describing each group in terms of the group means for the predictor variables. If the important predictors have been identified, then a comparison of the group means on these variables can assist in understanding the intergroup differences. Before any findings can be interpreted with confidence, however, it is necessary to validate the results.

Assess the validity of discriminant analysis

Many programs such as SPSS offer a leave-one-out cross-validation option. In this option, the discriminant model is re-estimated as many times as there are participants in the sample. Each re-estimated model leaves out one participant and the model is used to predict for that participant. When a large holdout sample is not possible, this gives a sense of the robustness of the estimate using each participant in turn, as a holdout.

As explained earlier, the data should be randomly divided into two subsamples: analysis and validation. The analysis sample is used for estimating the discriminant function; the validation sample is used for developing the classification matrix. The discriminant weights, estimated by using the analysis sample, are multiplied by the values of the predictor variables in the holdout sample to generate discriminant scores for the cases in the holdout sample.

Hit ratio

The percentage of cases correctly classified by discriminant analysis.

The cases are then assigned to groups based on their discriminant scores and an appropriate decision rule. For example, in two-group discriminant analysis, a case will be assigned to the group whose centroid is the closest. The **hit ratio**, or the percentage of cases correctly classified, can then be determined by summing the diagonal elements and dividing by the total number of cases.[8]

It is helpful to compare the percentage of cases correctly classified by discriminant analysis with the percentage that would be obtained by chance. When the groups are equal in size, the percentage of chance classification is one divided by the number of groups. How much improvement should be expected over chance? No general guidelines are available, although some authors have suggested that classification accuracy achieved by discriminant analysis should be at least 25% greater than that obtained by chance.[9]

Most discriminant analysis programs also estimate a classification matrix based on the analysis sample. Because they capitalise on chance variation in the data, such results are invariably better than the classification obtained on the holdout sample.

Table 21.4, for the holiday resort example, also shows the classification results based on the analysis sample. The hit ratio, or the percentage of cases correctly classified, is $(12 + 15)/30 = 0.90$, or 90%. One might suspect that this hit ratio is artificially inflated, as the data used for estimation were also used for validation. Leave-one-out cross-validation correctly classifies only $(11 + 13)/30 = 0.80$ or 80% of the cases. Conducting classification analysis on an independent holdout set of data results in the classification matrix with a slightly lower hit ratio of $(4 + 6)/12 = 0.833$, or 83.3% (see Table 21.4). Given two groups of equal size, by chance one would expect a hit ratio of $1/2 = 0.50$, or 50%. Hence, the improvement over chance is more than 25%, and the validity of the discriminant analysis is judged as satisfactory.

Another application of two-group discriminant analysis is provided by the following example.

Real research

Home bodies and couch potatoes[10]

Two-group discriminant analysis was used to assess the strength of each of five dimensions used in classifying individuals as TV users or non-users. The discriminant analysis procedure was appropriate for this use because of the nature of the predefined categorical groups (users and non-users) and the interval scales used to generate individual factor scores.

Two equal groups of 185 elderly consumers, users and non-users (total $n = 370$) were created. The discriminant equation for the analysis was estimated by using a subsample of 142 participants from the sample of 370. Of the remaining participants, 198 were used as a validation subsample in a cross-validation of the equation. Thirty participants were excluded from the analysis because of missing discriminant values.

The canonical correlation for the discriminant function was 0.4291, significant at the $p < 0.0001$ level. The eigenvalue was 0.2257. The table below summarises the standardised canonical discriminant coefficients. A substantial portion of the variance is explained by the discriminant function. In addition, as the table shows, the home-orientation dimension made a fairly strong contribution to classifying individuals as users or non-users of TV. Morale, security and health, and respect also contributed significantly. The social factor appeared to make little contribution.

The cross-validation procedure using the discriminant function from the analysis sample gave support to the contention that the dimensions aided researchers in discriminating between users and non-users of TV. As the table shows, the discriminant function was successful in classifying 75.76% of the cases. This suggests that consideration of the identified dimensions will help marketers understand elderly consumers.

Summary of discriminant analysis

Standard canonical discriminant function coefficients

Morale	0.27798
Security and health	0.39850
Home orientation	0.77496
Respect	0.32069
Social	−0.01996

Classification results for cases selected for use in the analysis

		Predicted group membership	
Actual group	No. of cases	Non-users	Users
TV non-users	77	56	21
		72.7%	27.3%
TV users	65	24	41
		36.9%	63.1%

Per cent of grouped cases correctly classified: 68.31%

Classification results for cases selected for cross-validation

		Predicted group membership	
Actual group	No. of cases	Non-users	Users
TV non-users	108	85	23
		78.7%	21.3%
TV users	90	25	65
		27.8%	72.2%

Per cent of grouped cases correctly classified: 75.76%

The extension from two-group discriminant analysis to multiple discriminant analysis involves similar steps and is illustrated with an application.

Conducting multiple discriminant analysis

Formulate the problem

The data presented in Tables 21.2 and 21.3 can also be used to illustrate three-group discriminant analysis. In the last column of these tables, the households are classified into three categories, based on the amount spent on their family skiing holiday (high, medium or low).

Ten households fall in each category. The question of interest is whether the households that spend high, medium or low amounts on their holidays (AMOUNT) can be differentiated in terms of annual family income (INCOME), attitude towards travel (TRAVEL), importance attached to family skiing holiday (HOLIDAY), household size (HSIZE) and age of the head of household (AGE).[11]

Estimate the discriminant function coefficients

Table 21.5 presents the results of estimating three-group discriminant analysis. An examination of group means indicates that income appears to separate the groups more widely than any other variable. There is some separation on travel and holiday. Groups 1 and 2 are very close in terms of household size and age. Age has a large standard deviation relative to the separation between the groups. The pooled within-groups correlation matrix indicates some correlation of holiday and household size with income. Age has some negative correlation with travel. Yet these correlations are on the lower side, indicating that, although multicollinearity may be of some concern, it is not likely to be a serious problem. The significance attached to the univariate F ratios indicates that, when the predictors are considered individually, only income and travel are significant in differentiating between the two groups.

In multiple discriminant analysis, if there are G groups, $G - 1$ discriminant functions can be estimated if the number of predictors is larger than this quantity. In general, with G groups and k predictors, it is possible to estimate up to the smaller of $G - 1$, or k, discriminant functions. The first function has the highest ratio of between-groups to within-groups sum of squares. The second function, uncorrelated with the first, has the second highest ratio, and so on. Not all the functions may be statistically significant, however.

Because there are three groups, a maximum of two functions can be extracted. The eigenvalue associated with the first function is 3.8190, and this function accounts for 93.93% of variance in the data. The eigenvalue is large, so the first function is likely to be superior. The second function has a small eigenvalue of 0.2469 and accounts for only 6.07% of the variance.

Table 21.5	Results of three-group discriminant analysis

Group means

Amount	INCOME	TRAVEL	HOLIDAY	HSIZE	AGE
1	38.57000	4.50000	4.70000	3.10000	50.30000
2	50.11000	4.00000	4.20000	3.40000	49.50000
3	64.97000	6.10000	5.90000	4.20000	56.00000
Total	51.21667	4.86667	4.93333	3.56667	51.93333

Group standard deviations

	INCOME	TRAVEL	HOLIDAY	HSIZE	AGE
1	5.29718	1.71594	1.88856	1.19722	8.09732
2	6.00231	2.35702	2.48551	1.50555	9.25263
3	8.61434	1.19722	1.66333	1.13529	7.60117
Total	12.79523	1.97804	2.09981	1.33089	8.57395

Table 21.5 **Continued**

Pooled within-groups correlation matrix

	INCOME	TRAVEL	HOLIDAY	HSIZE	AGE
INCOME	1.00000				
TRAVEL	0.05120	1.00000			
HOLIDAY	0.30681	0.03588	1.00000		
HSIZE	0.38050	0.00474	0.22080	1.00000	
AGE	-0.20939	-0.34022	-0.01326	-0.02512	1.00000

Wilks' λ (U statistic) and univariate F ratio with 2 and 27 degrees of freedom

Variable	Wilks' λ	F	Significance
INCOME	0.26215	38.000	0.0000
TRAVEL	0.78790	3.634	0.0400
HOLIDAY	0.88060	1.830	0.1797
HSIZE	0.87411	1.944	0.1626
AGE	0.88214	1.804	0.1840

Canonical discriminant functions

Function	Eigenvalue	Per cent of variance	Cumulative percentage	Canonical correlation	After function	Wilks' λ	Chi-square	df	Sig.
					0	0.1664	44.831	10	0.00
1*	3.8190	93.93	93.93	0.8902	1	0.8020	5.517	4	0.24
2*	0.2469	6.07	100.00	0.4450					

* Marks the two canonical discriminant functions remaining in the analysis.

Standardised canonical discriminant function coefficients

	Func 1	Func 2
INCOME	1.04740	-0.42076
TRAVEL	0.33991	0.76851
HOLIDAY	-0.14198	0.53354
HSIZE	-0.16317	0.12932
AGE	0.49474	0.52447

Structure matrix: pooled within-groups correlations between discriminating variables and canonical discriminant functions (variables ordered by size of correlation within function)

	Func 1	Func 2
INCOME	0.85556*	-0.27833
HSIZE	0.19319*	0.07749
HOLIDAY	0.21935	0.58829*
TRAVEL	0.14899	0.45362*
AGE	0.16576	0.34079*

Table 21.5	Continued

Unstandardised canonical discriminant function coefficients

	Func 1	Func 2
INCOME	0.1542658	-0.6197148E-01
TRAVEL	0.1867977	0.4223430
HOLIDAY	-0.6952264E-01	0.2612652
HSIZE	-0.1265334	0.1002796
AGE	0.5928055E-01	0.6284206E-01
(Constant)	-11.09442	-3.791600

Canonical discriminant functions evaluated at group means (group centroids)

Group	Func 1	Func 2
1	-2.04100	0.41847
2	-0.40479	-0.65867
3	2.44578	0.24020

Classification results

		Amount	Predicted group membership 1	2	3	Total
Original	Count	1	9	1	0	10
		2	1	9	0	10
		3	0	2	8	10
	%	1	90.0	10.0	0.0	100.0
		2	10.0	90.0	0.0	100.0
		3	0.0	20.0	80.0	100.0
Cross-validated	Count	1	7	3	0	10
		2	4	5	1	10
		3	0	2	8	10
	%	1	70.0	30.0	0.0	100.0
		2	40.0	50.0	10.0	100.0
		3	0.0	20.0	80.0	100.0

[a] Cross-validation is done only for those cases in the analysis. In cross-validation, each case is classified by the functions derived from all cases other than that case.

[b] 86.7% of original grouped cases correctly classified.

[c] 66.7% of cross-validated grouped cases correctly classified.

Determine the significance of the discriminant function

To test the null hypothesis of equal group centroids, both the functions must be considered simultaneously. It is possible to test the means of the functions successively by first testing all means simultaneously. Then one function is excluded at a time, and the means of the remaining functions are tested at each step. In Table 21.5, the 0 below the 'After function'

Table 21.5	**Continued**

Classification results for cases not selected for use in analysis

			Predicted group membership		
	Actual group	No. of cases	1	2	3
Group	1	4	3	1	0
			75.0%	25.0%	0.0%
Group	2	4	0	3	1
			0.0%	75.0%	25.0%
Group	3	4	1	0	3
			25.0%	0.0%	75.0%

Percentage of grouped cases correctly classified: 75.00%

heading indicates that no functions have been removed. The value of Wilks' λ is 0.1644. This transforms to a chi-square of 44.831, with 10 degrees of freedom, which is significant beyond the 0.05 level. Thus, the two functions together significantly discriminate among the three groups. When the first function is removed, however, the Wilks' λ associated with the second function is 0.8020, which is not significant at the 0.05 level. Therefore, the second function does not contribute significantly to group differences.

Interpret the results

The interpretation of the results is aided by an examination of the standardised discriminant function coefficients, the structure correlations and certain plots. The standardised coefficients indicate a large coefficient for income on function 1, whereas function 2 has relatively larger coefficients for travel, holiday and age. A similar conclusion is reached by an examination of the structure matrix (see Table 21.5). To help interpret the functions, variables with large coefficients for a particular function are grouped together. These groupings are shown with asterisks. Thus income and household size have asterisks for function 1 because these variables have coefficients which are larger for function 1 than for function 2. These variables are associated primarily with function 1. On the other hand, travel, holiday and age are predominantly associated with function 2, as indicated by the asterisks.

Figure 21.3 is a scattergram plot of all the groups on function 1 and function 2. It can be seen that group 3 has the highest value on function 1, and group 1 the lowest. Because function 1 is primarily associated with income and household size, one would expect the three groups to be ordered on these two variables. Those with higher incomes and higher household size are likely to spend large amounts of money on holidays. Conversely, those with low incomes and smaller household size are likely to spend small amounts on holidays. This interpretation is further strengthened by an examination of group means on income and household size.

Figure 21.3 further indicates that function 2 tends to separate group 1 (highest value) and group 2 (lowest value). This function is primarily associated with travel, holiday and age. Given the positive correlations of these variables with function 2 in the structure matrix, we expect to find group 1 to be higher than group 2 in terms of travel, holiday and age. This is indeed true for travel and holiday, as indicated by the group means of these variables. If fami-

Figure 21.3

All-groups scattergram

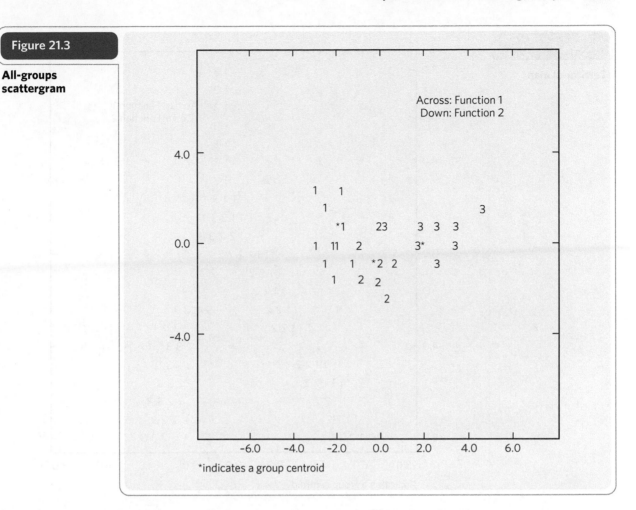

Across: Function 1
Down: Function 2

*indicates a group centroid

lies in group 1 have more favourable attitudes towards travel and attach more importance to a family skiing holiday than group 2, why do they spend less? Perhaps they would like to spend more on holidays but cannot afford it because they have low incomes.

A similar interpretation is obtained by examining a **territorial map**, as shown in Figure 21.4. In a territorial map, each group centroid is indicated by an asterisk. The group boundaries are shown by numbers corresponding to the groups. Thus, group 1 centroid is bounded by ls, group 2 centroid by 2s and group 3 centroid by 3s.

Territorial map
A tool for assessing discriminant analysis results by plotting the group membership of each case on a graph.

Assess the validity of discriminant analysis

The classification results based on the analysis sample indicate that $(9 + 9 + 8)/30 = 86.67\%$ of the cases are correctly classified. Leave-one-out cross-validation correctly classifies only $(7 + 5 + 8)/30 = 0.667$ or 66.7% of the cases. When the classification analysis is conducted on the independent holdout sample of Table 21.3, a hit ratio of $(3 + 3 + 3)/12 = 75\%$ is obtained. Given three groups of equal size, by chance alone one would expect a hit ratio of $1/3 = 0.333$ or 33.3%. The improvement over chance is more than 25%, indicating at least satisfactory validity.

Further illustration of multiple group discriminant analysis is provided by the following example.

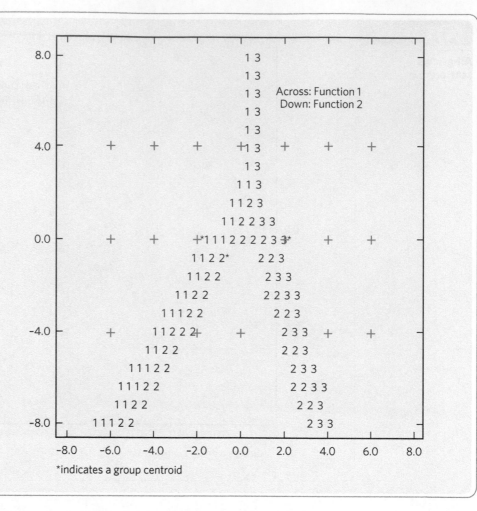

Figure 21.4

Territorial map

*indicates a group centroid

The home is where the patient's heart is[12]

In the majority of developed nations, the largest sector in the economy is the health care industry. Over the next decade, it is expected that spending on health care services will grow significantly faster than national economies. Contributing to this growth are demographic forces, with shrinking birth rates, ageing populations, longer life expectancies and with rapidly growing numbers of elderly patients seeking health support of some kind. Consumers were surveyed to determine their attitudes towards four systems of health care delivery (home health care, hospitals, nursing homes and outpatient clinics) along 10

attributes. A total of 102 responses were obtained, and the results were analysed using multiple discriminant analysis (Table 1). Three discriminant functions were identified. Chi-square tests performed on the results indicated that all three discriminant functions were significant at the 0.01 level. The first function accounted for 63% of the total discriminative power, and the remaining two functions contributed 29.4% and 7.6%, respectively.

Table 1 gives the standardised discriminant function coefficients of the 10 variables in the discriminant equations. Coefficients ranged in value from –1 to +1. In determining the ability of each attribute to classify the delivery system, absolute values were used. In the first discriminant function, the two variables with the largest coefficients were comfort (0.53) and privacy (0.40). Because both related to personal attention and care, the first dimension was labelled 'personalised care'. In the second function, the two variables with the largest coefficients were quality of medical care (0.67) and likelihood of faster recovery (0.32). Hence, this dimension was labelled 'quality of medical care'. In the third discriminant function, the most significant attributes were sanitation (–0.70) and expense (0.52). Because these two attributes represent value and price, the third discriminant function was labelled 'value'.

The four group centroids are shown in Table 2. This table shows that home health care was evaluated most favourably along the dimension of personalised care, and hospitals were evaluated least favourably. Along the dimension of quality of medical care, there was a substantial separation between nursing homes and the other three systems. Also, home health care received higher evaluations on the quality of medical care than did outpatient clinics. Outpatient clinics, on the other hand, were judged to offer the best value.

Classification analysis of the 102 responses, reported in Table 3, showed correct classifications ranging from 86% for hospitals to 68% for outpatient clinics. The misclassifications for hospitals were 6% each to nursing homes and outpatient clinics and 2% to home health care. Nursing homes showed misclassifications of 9% to hospitals, 10% to outpatient clinics and 3% to home health care. For outpatient clinics, 9% misclassifications were made to hospitals, 13% to nursing homes and 10% to home health care. For home health care, the misclassifications were 5% to hospitals, 4% to nursing homes and 13% to outpatient clinics. The results demonstrated that the discriminant functions were fairly accurate in predicting group membership.

Table 1 Standardised discriminant function coefficients

Variable system	Discriminant function		
	1	2	3
Safe	–0.20	–0.04	0.15
Convenient	0.08	0.08	0.07
Chance of medical complications[a]	–0.27	0.10	0.16
Expensive[a]	0.30	–0.28	0.52
Comfortable	0.53	0.27	–0.19
Sanitary	–0.27	–0.14	–0.70
Best medical care	–0.25	0.67	–0.10
Privacy	0.40	0.08	0.49
Faster recovery	0.30	0.32	–0.15
Staffed with best medical personnel	–0.17	–0.03	0.18
Percentage of variance explained	63.0	29.4	7.6
Chi-square	663.3[b]	289.2[b]	70.1[b]

[a] These two items were worded negatively on the questionnaire. They were reverse coded for purposes of data analysis.
[b] $p < 0.01$.

Table 2 Centroids of health care systems in discriminant space

System	Discriminant function		
	1	2	3
Hospital	-1.66	0.97	-0.08
Nursing home	-0.60	-1.36	-0.27
Outpatient clinic	0.54	-0.13	0.77
Home health care	1.77	0.50	-0.39

Table 3 Classification table

System	Classification (%)			
	Hospital	Nursing home	Outpatient clinic	Home health care
Hospital	86	6	6	2
Nursing home	9	78	10	3
Outpatient clinic	9	13	68	10
Home health care	5	4	13	78

Stepwise discriminant analysis

Stepwise discriminant analysis is analogous to stepwise multiple regression (see Chapter 20) in that the predictors are entered sequentially based on their ability to discriminate between the groups. An F ratio is calculated for each predictor by conducting a univariate ANOVA in which the groups are treated as the categorical variable and the predictor as the criterion variable. The predictor with the highest F ratio is the first to be selected for inclusion in the discriminant function, if it meets certain significance and tolerance criteria. A second predictor is added based on the highest adjusted or partial F ratio, taking into account the predictor already selected.

Each predictor selected is tested for retention based on its association with other predictors selected. The process of selection and retention is continued until all predictors meeting the significance criteria for inclusion and retention have been entered in the discriminant function. Several statistics are computed at each stage. In addition, at the conclusion, a summary of the predictors entered or removed is provided. The standard output associated with the direct method is also available from the stepwise procedure.

Mahalanobis procedure

A stepwise procedure used in discriminant analysis to maximise a generalised measure of the distance between the two closest group.

The selection of the stepwise procedure is based on the optimising criterion adopted. The Mahalanobis procedure is based on maximising a generalised measure of the distance between the two closest groups. This procedure allows researchers to make maximum use of the available information.[13]

The Mahalanobis method was used to conduct a two-group stepwise discriminant analysis on the data pertaining to the visit variable in Tables 21.2 and 21.3. The first predictor variable to be selected was income, followed by household size and then holiday. The order in which the variables were selected also indicates their importance in discriminating between the groups. This was further corroborated by an examination of the standardised discriminant function coefficients and the structure correlation coefficients. Note that the findings of the stepwise analysis agree with the conclusions reported earlier by the direct method.

The logit model

When the dependent variable is binary and there are several independent variables that are metric, in addition to two-group discriminant analysis one can also use ordinary least squares (OLS) regression, and the logit and the probit models for estimation. The data preparation for running OLS regression and the logit and probit models is similar in that the dependent variable is coded as 0 or 1. OLS regression was discussed in Chapter 20. The probit model is less commonly used and will not be discussed, but we give an explanation of the binary logit model.

Conducting binary logit analysis

The steps involved in conducting binary logit analysis are given in Figure 21.5.[14]

Formulate the problem

Binary logit model
The binary logit model commonly deals with the issue of how likely an observation is to belong to each group. It estimates the probability of an observation belonging to a particular group.

As discussed earlier under the basic concept of discriminant analysis, there are several instances in marketing where we want to explain a binary dependent variable in terms of metric independent variables. (Note that logit analysis can also handle categorical independent variables when these are recoded using dummy variables, as discussed in Chapters 17 and 20.) Discriminant analysis deals with the issue of which group an observation is likely to belong to. On the other hand, the binary logit model commonly deals with the issue of how likely an observation is to belong to each group. Thus, the logit model falls somewhere between regression and discriminant analysis in application. We can estimate the probability of a binary event taking place using the binary logit model, also called *logistic regression*. Consider an event that has two outcomes: success and failure. The probability of success may be modelled using the logit model as

$$\log_e \left(\frac{p}{1-p} \right) = a_0 + a_1 X_1 + a_2 X_2 + \ldots + a_k X_k$$

or

$$\log_e \left(\frac{p}{1-p} \right) = \sum_{i=0}^{k} a_i X_i$$

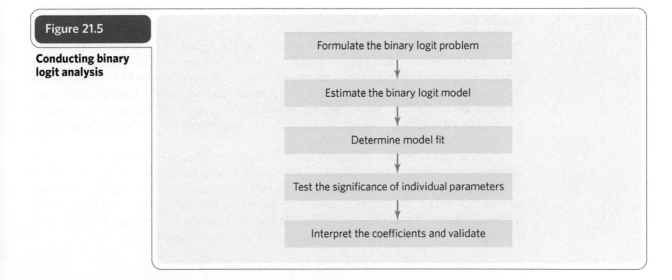

Figure 21.5

Conducting binary logit analysis

Formulate the binary logit problem

↓

Estimate the binary logit model

↓

Determine model fit

↓

Test the significance of individual parameters

↓

Interpret the coefficients and validate

or

$$p = \frac{\exp\left(\displaystyle\sum_{i=0}^{k} a_i X_i\right)}{1 + \exp\left(\displaystyle\sum_{i=0}^{k} a_i X_i\right)}$$

where p = probability of success
X_i = independent variable i
a_i = parameter to be estimated

It can be seen from the third equation that although X_i may vary from $-\infty$ to $+\infty$, p is constrained to lie between 0 and 1. When X_i approaches $-\infty$, p approaches 0, and when X_i approaches $+\infty$, p approaches 1. This is desirable because p is a probability and must lie between 0 and 1. On the other hand, when OLS regression is used the estimation model is

$$p = \sum_{i=0}^{n} a_i X_i$$

Thus, when OLS regression is used, p is not constrained to lie between 0 and 1; it is possible to obtain estimated vales of p that are less than 0 or greater than 1. These values, are of course, conceptually and intuitively unappealing. We demonstrate this phenomenon in our illustrative application. As in the case of discriminant analysis, the researcher should specify the objectives and clearly identify the binary criterion variables and the independent variables that will be considered in the analysis. Moreover, the sample may have to be divided into analysis and validation subsamples.

Estimating the binary logit model

As discussed in Chapter 20, the linear regression model is fit by the OLS procedure. In OLS regression, the parameters are estimated so as to minimise the sum of squared errors of prediction. The error terms in regression can take on any values and are assumed to follow a normal distribution when conducting statistical tests. In contrast, in the binary logit model, each error can assume only two values. If $Y = 0$, the error is p, and if $Y = 1$, the error is $1-p$. Therefore, we would like to estimate the parameters in such a way that the estimated values of p would be close to 0 when $Y = 0$ and close to 1 when $Y = 1$. The procedure that is used to achieve this and estimate the parameters of the binary logit model is called the *maximum likelihood method*. This method is so called because it estimates the parameters so as to maximise the likelihood or probability of observing the actual data.

Model fit

In multiple regression the model fit is measured by the square of the multiple correlation coefficient, R^2, which is also called the *coefficient of multiple determination* (see Chapter 20). In logistic regression (binary logit), commonly used measures of model fit are based on the likelihood function and are the Cox and Snell R square and Nagelkerke R square. Both these measures are similar to R^2 in multiple regression. The Cox and Snell R square is constrained in such a way that it cannot equal 1.0, even if the model perfectly fits the data. This limitation is overcome by the Nagelkerke R square.

As discussed earlier in the chapter, in discriminant analysis, the model fit is assessed by determining the proportion of correct prediction. A similar procedure can also be used for the binary logit model. If the estimated probability is greater than 0.5, then the predicted value of Y is set to 1. On the other hand, if the estimated probability is less than 0.5, then the predicted value of Y is set to 0. The predicted values of Y can then be compared with the corresponding actual values to determine the percentage of correct predictions.

Significance testing

The testing of individual estimated parameters or coefficients for significance is similar to that in multiple regression. In this case, the significance of the estimated coefficients is based on Wald's statistic. This statistic is a test of significance of the logistic regression coefficient based on the asymptotic normality property of maximum likelihood estimates and is estimated as

$$\text{Wald} = (a_i/SE_{ai})^2$$

where a_i = logistical coefficient for that predictor variable
SE_{ai} = standard error of the logistical coefficient

The Wald statistic is chi-square distributed with 1 degree of freedom if the variable is metric and the number of categories minus 1 if the variable is non-metric.

The associated significance has the usual interpretation. For practical purposes, the significance of the null hypothesis that a_i can also be tested using a t test where the degrees of freedom equal the number of observations minus the number of estimated parameters. The ratio of the coefficient to its standard error is compared with the critical t value. For a large number of observations, the z test can be used.

Interpretation of the coefficients and validation

The interpretation of the coefficients or estimated parameters is similar to that in multiple regression, taking into account of course that the nature of the dependent variable is different. In logistic regression, the log odds, that is $\log_e(p/1-p)$, is a linear function of the estimated parameters. Thus, if X_i is increased by one unit, the log odds will increase by a_i units, when the effect of other independent variables is held constant. Thus a_i is the size of the increase in the log odds of the dependent variable event when the corresponding independent variable X_i is increased by one unit and the effect of the other independent variables is held constant. The sign of a_i will determine whether the probability increases (if the sign is positive) or decreases (if the sign is negative). The validation process is very similar to that discussed for discriminant analysis. The analysis sample is used for estimating the model coefficients; the validation sample is used for developing the classification matrix. As before, the hit ratio is the percentage of cases correctly classified.

An illustrative application of logistic regression

We illustrate the logit model by analysing the data of Table 21.6. This table gives the data for 30 participants, 15 of whom are brand loyal (indicated by 1) and 15 of whom are not (indicated by 0). We also measure attitude towards the brand (Brand), attitude towards the product category (Product) and attitude towards shopping (Shopping), all on a 1 (unfavourable) to 7 (favourable) scale. The objective is to estimate the probability of a consumer being brand loyal as a function of attitude towards the brand, the product category and shopping.

First we run an OLS regression on the data of Table 21.6 to illustrate the limitations of this procedure for analysing binary data. The estimated equation is given by

$$p = -0.684 + 0.183 \text{ (Brand)} + 0.020 \text{ (Product)} + 0.074 \text{ (Shopping)}$$

where

$$p = \text{probability of a consumer being brand loyal}$$

Only the constant term and Brand are significant at the 0.05 level. It can be seen from the estimated regression equation that the estimated values of p are negative for the low values of the independent variables (e.g. when Brand = 1, Product = 1 and Shopping = 1, and for many other values of Brand = 1, 2 or 3). Likewise, the estimated values of p are greater than 1 for high values of the independent variables (e.g. when Brand = 7, Product = 7 and Shopping = 7). This

Table 21.6	Explaining brand loyalty			
No.	Loyalty	Brand	Product	Shopping
1	1	4	3	5
2	1	6	4	4
3	1	5	2	4
4	1	7	5	5
5	1	6	3	4
6	1	3	4	5
7	1	5	5	5
8	1	5	4	2
9	1	7	5	4
10	1	7	6	4
11	1	6	7	2
12	1	5	6	4
13	1	7	3	3
14	1	5	1	4
15	1	7	5	5
16	0	3	1	3
17	0	4	6	2
18	0	2	5	2
19	0	5	2	4
20	0	4	1	3
21	0	3	3	4
22	0	3	4	5
23	0	3	6	3
24	0	4	4	2
25	0	6	3	6
26	0	3	6	3
27	0	4	3	2
28	0	3	5	2
29	0	5	5	3
30	0	1	3	2

is intuitively and conceptually unappealing because p is a probability and must lie between 0 and 1.

This limitation of OLS regression is overcome by logistic regression. The output for logistic regression when analysing the data for Table 21.6 is shown in Table 21.7. The Cox and Snell R square and Nagelkerke R square measures indicate a reasonable fit of the model to the data. This is further verified by the classification table that reveals that 24 of the 30, cases i.e. 80%, are correctly classified. The significance of the estimated coefficients is based on Wald's statistic. We note that only attitude towards the brand is significant in explaining brand loyalty. Unlike discriminant analysis, logistic regression results in standard error estimates for the estimated coefficients and hence their significance can be assessed. The positive sign for the coefficient indicates that positive attitude towards the brand results in higher loyalty towards the brand. Attitude towards the product category and attitude towards shopping do not influence brand loyalty. Thus, a manager seeking to increase brand loyalty should focus

Table 21.7	Results of binary logit model or logistic regression

Dependent variable encoding

Original value	Internal value
Not loyal	0
Loyal	1

Model summary

Step	−2 log likelihood	Cox and Snell R square	Nagelkerke R square
1	23.471[a]	0.453	0.604

[a] Estimation terminated at iteration number 6 because parameter estimates changed by less than 0.001.

Classification table[a]

		Predicted		
		Loyalty to the brand		
		Not loyal	Loyal	Percentage correct
Step 1	Loyalty to the brand　Not loyal	12	3	80.0
	Loyal	3	12	80.0
	Overall percentage			80.0

[a] The cut value is 0.500.

Variables in the equation

		B	SE	Wald	df	Sig.	Exp(B)
Step 1[a]	Brand	1.274	0.479	7.075	1	0.008	3.575
	Product	0.186	0.322	0.335	1	0.563	1.205
	Shopping	0.590	0.491	1.442	1	0.230	1.804
	Constant	−8.642	3.346	6.672	1	0.010	0.000

[a] Variable(s) entered on step 1: Brand, Product, Shopping.

on fostering a more positive attitude towards the brand and not worry about attitude towards the product category or attitude towards shopping. The logit model can also be used when the dependent variable has more than two categories. In this case, the model is termed the *multinomial logit*.[15]

Discriminant analysis in its various forms is a widely used technique as further illustrated in the following two examples. The first example illustrates an application in the context of international marketing research. The second example shows how discriminant analysis can be used in investigating ethical behaviour.

Real research

Satisfactory results of satisfaction programmes[16]

In their marketing strategies, computer companies are emphasising the quality of their customer service programmes rather than focusing upon computer features and capabilities. Hewlett-Packard learned this lesson in Europe. Research conducted across Europe revealed that there was a difference in emphasis on service requirements across age segments. Focus groups revealed that customers above 40 years of age had a hard time with the technical aspects of the computer and greatly required the customer service programmes. On the other hand, younger customers appreciated the technical aspects of the product that added to their satisfaction. To uncover the factors leading to differences in the two segments, further research in the form of a large single cross-sectional survey was undertaken. A two-group discriminant analysis was conducted with satisfied and dissatisfied customers as the two groups, with several independent variables such as technical information, ease of operation, variety and scope of customer service programmes. Results confirmed the fact that the variety and scope of customer satisfaction programmes was indeed a strong differentiating factor. This was a crucial finding because Hewlett-Packard could better handle dissatisfied customers by focusing more on customer services than on technical details. Consequently, Hewlett-Packard successfully started three programmes on customer satisfaction: customer feedback, customer satisfaction surveys and total quality control. This effort resulted in increased customer satisfaction.

Real research

Discriminant analysis discriminates ethical and unethical behaviour[17]

In order to identify the important variables that predict ethical and unethical behaviour, discriminant analysis was used. Prior research suggested that the variables that affect ethical decisions were attitudes, leadership, the presence or absence of ethical codes of conduct and the organisation's size. To determine which of these variables were the best predictors of ethical behaviour, 149 firms were surveyed and asked to indicate how their firm operated in 18 different ethical situations. Of these 18 situations, 9 related to marketing activities. These activities included using misleading sales presentations, accepting gifts for preferential treatment, pricing below out-of-pocket expenses. Based on these nine issues, the participating firms were classified into two groups: 'never practice' and 'practice'. An examination of the variables that influenced classification via two-group discriminant analysis indicated that attitudes and a company's size were the best predictors of ethical behaviour. Evidently, smaller firms tended to demonstrate more ethical behaviour on marketing issues.

SPSS and SAS Learning Editions

SPSS Windows

The DISCRIMINANT program performs both two-group and multiple discriminant analysis. To select this procedure, click

Analyze>Classify>Discriminant . . .

The following are the detailed steps for running a two-group discriminant analysis with Resort Visit (visit) as the dependent variable and annual family income (income), attitude towards travel (attitude), importance attached to family vacation (vacation), household size (hsize), and age of the household (age) as the independent variables, using the data in Table 21.2:

1 Select ANALYZE from the SPSS menu bar.
2 Click CLASSIFY and then DISCRIMINANT.
3 Move 'visit' into the GROUPING VARIABLE box.
4 Click DEFINE RANGE. Enter 1 for MINIMUM and 2 for MAXIMUM. Click CONTINUE.
5 Move 'income,' 'travel,' 'vacation,' 'hsize' and 'age' into the INDEPENDENTS box.
6 Select ENTER INDEPENDENTS TOGETHER (default option).
7 Click on STATISTICS. In the pop-up window, in the DESCRIPTIVES box check MEANS and UNIVARIATE ANOVAS. In the MATRICES box check WITHIN-GROUP CORRELATIONS. Click CONTINUE.
8 Click CLASSIFY . . . In the pop-up window in the PRIOR PROBABILITIES box check ALL GROUPS EQUAL (default). In the DISPLAY box check SUMMARY TABLE and LEAVE-ONE-OUT CLASSIFICATION. In the USE COVARIANCE MATRIX box check WITHIN-GROUPS. Click CONTINUE.
9 Click OK.

The steps for running three-group discriminant analysis are similar. Select the appropriate dependent and independent variables. In step 4, click DEFINE RANGE. Enter 1 for MINIMUM and 3 for MAXIMUM. Click CONTINUE. For running stepwise discriminant analysis, in step 6 select USE STEPWISE METHOD.

To run logit analysis or logistic regression, click

Analyze>Regression>Binary Logistic . . .

The following are the detailed steps for running logit analysis with brand loyalty as the dependent variable and attitude towards the brand (brand), attitude towards the product category (product) and attitude toward shopping (shopping) as the independent variables using the data of Table 21.6:

1 Select ANALYZE from the SPSS menu bar.
2 Click REGRESSION and then BINARY LOGISTIC.
3 Move 'Loyalty to the Brand [Loyalty]' into the DEPENDENT VARIABLE box.
4 Move 'Attitude towards the Brand [Brand]', 'Attitude towards the Product category [Product]' and 'Attitude towards Shopping [Shopping]' into the COVARIATES (S box).

5 Select ENTER for METHOD (default option).
6 Click OK

SAS Learning Edition

The instructions given here and in all the quantitative data analysis chapters will work with the SAS Learning Edition as well as with the SAS Enterprise Guide. For a point-and-click approach for performing discriminant analysis, use the Analyze task within the SAS Learning Edition. The Multivariate>Discriminant Analysis task offers both two-group and multiple discriminant analysis. Both two-group and multiple discriminant analysis can be performed using the Discriminant Analysis task within the SAS Learning Edition. To select this task click

Analyze>Multivariate>Discriminant Analysis . . .

The following are the detailed steps for running a two-group discriminant analysis with Resort Visit (VISIT) as the dependent variable and annual family income (INCOME), attitude towards travel (TRAVEL), importance attached to family vacation (VACATION), household size (HSIZE) and age of the household (AGE) as the independent variables, using the data in Table 21.2:

1 Select ANALYZE from the SAS Learning Edition menu bar.
2 Click MULTIVARIATE and then DISCRIMINANT ANALYSIS.
3 Move VISIT to the Classification variable task role.
4 Move INCOME, TRAVEL, VACATION, HSIZE and AGE to the analysis variables task role.
5 Click OPTIONS.
6 Select UNIVARIATE test for equality of class means and SUMMARY results of cross-validation classification. (If means are desired, then use the Summary Statistics task.)
7 Click the PREVIEW CODE button.
8 Click the Insert Code . . . button.
9 Double-click to insert code before the CROSS-VALIDATE option.
10 Add the CAN and PCORE options in the pop-up box and then click OK.
11 Click OK and then close the PREVIEW CODE window.
12 Click RUN.

The steps for running three-group discriminant analysis are similar to these steps. To run logit analysis or logistic regression, click

Analyze>Regression>Logistic . . .

The following are the detailed steps for running logit analysis with brand loyalty as the dependent variable and attitude towards the brand, attitude towards the product category and attitude towards shopping as the independent variables using the data of Table 18.6:

1 Select ANALYZE from the SAS Learning Edition menu bar.
2 Click REGRESSION and then LOGISTIC.
3 Move LOYALTY to the Dependent variable task role.
4 Move BRAND, PRODUCT and SHOPPING to the QUANTITATIVE variables task role.
5 Select MODEL EFFECTS.
6 Choose BRAND, PRODUCT and SHOPPING as Main Effects.
7 Select MODEL OPTIONS.
8 Check SHOW CLASSIFICATION TABLE and enter 0.5 as the critical probability value.
9 Click RUN.

Summary

Discriminant analysis is useful for analysing data when the criterion or dependent variable is categorical and the predictor or independent variables are interval scaled. When the criterion variable has two categories, the technique is known as two-group discriminant analysis. Multiple discriminant analysis refers to the case when three or more categories are involved.

Conducting discriminant analysis is a five-step procedure. First, formulating the discriminant problem requires identification of the objectives and the criterion and predictor variables. The sample is divided into two parts. One part, the analysis sample, is used to estimate the discriminant function. The other part, the holdout sample, is reserved for validation. Estimation, the second step, involves developing a linear combination of the predictors, called discriminant functions, so that the groups differ as much as possible on the predictor values.

Determination of statistical significance is the third step. It involves testing the null hypothesis that, in the population, the means of all discriminant functions in all groups are equal. If the null hypothesis is rejected, it is meaningful to interpret the results.

The fourth step, the interpretation of discriminant weights or coefficients, is similar to that in multiple regression analysis. Given the multicollinearity in the predictor variables, there is no unambiguous measure of the relative importance of the predictors in discriminating between the groups. Some idea of the relative importance of the variables, however, may be obtained by examining the absolute magnitude of the standardised discriminant function coefficients and by examining the structure correlations or discriminant loadings. These simple correlations between each predictor and the discriminant function represent the variance that the predictor shares with the function. Another aid to interpreting discriminant analysis results is to develop a characteristic profile for each group, based on the group means for the predictor variables.

Validation, the fifth step, involves developing the classification matrix. The discriminant weights estimated by using the analysis sample are multiplied by the values of the predictor variables in the holdout sample to generate discriminant scores for the cases in the holdout sample. The cases are then assigned to groups based on their discriminant scores and an appropriate decision rule. The percentage of cases correctly classified is determined and compared with the rate that would be expected by chance classification.

Two broad approaches are available for estimating the coefficients. The direct method involves estimating the discriminant function so that all the predictors are included simultaneously. An alternative is the stepwise method in which the predictor variables are entered sequentially, based on their ability to discriminate among groups.

In multiple discriminant analysis, if there are G groups and k predictors, it is possible to estimate up to the smaller of $G - 1$, or k, discriminant functions. The first function has the highest ratio of between-group to within-group sums of squares; the second function, uncorrelated with the first, has the second highest ratio; and so on.

Logit analysis, also called *logistic regression*, is an alternative to two-group discriminant analysis when the dependent variable is binary. The logit model estimates the probability of a binary event. Unlike OLS regression, the logit model constrains the probability to lie between 0 and 1. Unlike discriminant analysis, logistic regression results in standard error estimates for the estimated coefficients and hence their significance can be assessed.

Questions

1 What are the objectives of discriminant analysis?
2 Describe four examples of the application of discriminant analysis.
3 What is the main distinction between two-group and multiple discriminant analysis?
4 Describe the relationship of discriminant analysis to regression and ANOVA.
5 What are the steps involved in conducting discriminant analysis?
6 How should the total sample be split for estimation and validation purposes?
7 What is Wilks' λ? For what purpose is it used?
8 Define discriminant scores.
9 Explain what is meant by an eigenvalue.
10 What is a classification matrix?
11 Explain the concept of structure correlations.
12 How is the statistical significance of discriminant analysis determined?
13 Describe a common procedure for determining the validity of discriminant analysis.
14 When the groups are of equal size, how is the accuracy of chance classification determined?
15 How does the stepwise discriminant procedure differ from the direct method?

Exercises

1 In investigating the differences between heavy and light or non-users of frozen foods, it was found that the two largest standardised discriminant function coefficients were 0.97 for convenience orientation and 0.61 for income. Is it correct to conclude that convenience orientation is more important than income when each variable is considered by itself?

2 Given the following information, calculate the discriminant score for each participant. The value of the constant is 2.04.

Unstandardised discriminant function coefficients	
Age	0.38
Income	0.44
Risk taking	-0.39
Optimistic	1.26

Participant ID	Age	Income	Risk taking	Optimistic
0246	36	43.7	21	65
1337	44	62.5	28	56
2375	57	33.5	25	40
2454	63	38.7	16	36

3 Analyse the Benetton data (taken from Exercise 4, Chapter 18). Do the three usage groups differ in terms of awareness, attitude, preference, intention and loyalty towards Benetton when these variables are considered simultaneously?

4 Conduct a two-group discriminant analysis on the data given in Tables 21.2 and 21.3 using different statistical analysis packages, e.g. SPSS, SAS and Minitab. Compare the output from all the packages. Discuss the similarities and differences.

5 In a small group discuss the following issue: 'Is it meaningful to determine the relative importance of predictors in discriminating between the groups? Why or why not?'

Notes

1. Qiang, L. and Moorthy, S., 'Coupons versus rebates', *Marketing Science* 26 (1)(February 2007), 67–82; Michealree, J., 'Incentive programs mean more than money to retailers', *Agri Marketing* 42 (5) (June 2004), 32; Lichtenstein, D.R., Burton, S. and Netemeyer, R.G., 'An examination of deal proneness across sales promotion types: a consumer segmentation perspective', *Journal of Retailing* 73 (2) (Summer 1997), 283–297; Jolson, M.A., Wiener, J.L. and Rosecky, R.B., 'Corrleates of rebate proness', *Journal of Advertising Research* (February–March 1987), 33–43.

2. A detailed discussion of discriminant analysis may be found in McLachlan, G.J., *Discriminant Analysis and Statistical Pattern Recognition* (Hoboken, NJ: Wiley, 2004); Kemsley, E.K., *Discriminant Analysis and Class Modeling*

of Spectroscopic Data (New York: Wiley, 1998); Tacq, J., *Multivariate Analysis Techniques in Social Science Research* (Thousand Oaks, CA: Sage, 1996); Lachenbruch, P.A., *Discriminant Analysis* (New York: Hafner Press, 1975). For an application, see Ofir, C., 'Reexamining latitude of price acceptability and price thresholds: predicting basic consumer reaction to price', *Journal of Consumer Research* 30 (March 2004), 612–621.

3. See Johnson, R.A. and Wichern, D.W., *Applied Multivariate Statistical Analysis*, 5th edn (Paramus, NJ: Prentice Hall, 2001); Klecka, W.A., *Discriminant Analysis* (Beverly Hills, CA: Sage, 1980). See also Sinclair, S.A. and Stalling, E.C., 'How to identify differences between market segments with attribute analysis', *Industrial Marketing Management* 19 (February 1990), 31–40.

4. Ping, R., 'Second-order latent variables: interactions, specification, estimation and an example', *American Marketing Association, Conference Proceedings, Chicago*, 18 (January 2007), 286; Yoon, S.-J. and Kang, J.W., 'Validation of marketing performance model for service industries in Korea', *Services Marketing Quarterly* 26 (4) (2005), 57; Franses, P.H., 'A test for the hit rate in binary response models', *International Journal of Market Research* 42 (2) (Spring 2000), 239–245; Mitchell, V.-W., 'How to identify psychographic segments: Part 2', *Marketing Intelligence and Planning* 12 (7) (1994), 11–16; Crask, M.R. and Perrault, W.D. Jr, 'Validation of discriminant analysis in marketing research', *Journal of Marketing Research* 14 (February 1977), 60–68.

5. Strictly speaking, before testing for the equality of group means, the equality of group covariance matrices should be tested. Box's M test can be used for this purpose. If the equality of group covariance means is rejected, the results of discriminant analysis should be interpreted with caution. In this case, the power of the test for the equality of group means decreases.

6. See Hanna, N., 'Brain dominance and the interpretation of advertising messages', *International Journal of Commerce & Management* 9 (3/4) (1999), 19–32; Fok, L., Angelidis, J.P., Ibrahim, N.A. and Fok, W.M., 'The utilization and interpretation of multivariate statistical techniques in strategic management', *International Journal of Management* 12 (4) (December 1995), 468–481; Morrison, D.G., 'On the interpretation of discriminant analysis', *Journal of Marketing Research* 6 (May 1969), 156–163.

7. Miodonski, B., 'Retaining good employees starts at the top', *Contractor* 51 (10) (October 2004), 7–8; Fern, E.E., Avila, R.A. and Grewal, D., 'Salesforce turnover: those who left and those who stayed', *Industrial Marketing Management* (1989), 1–9.

8. For the validation of discriminant analysis, see Yoon, S.-J. and Kang, J.-W., 'Validation of marketing performance model for service industries in Korea', *Service Marketing Quarterly* 26 (4) (2005), 57; Reinartz, W.J. and Kumar, V., 'On the profitability of long life customers in a non-contractual setting: an empirical investigation and implications for marketing', *Journal of Marketing* 64 (4) (October 2000), 17–35.

9. Hair, J.E. Jr, Black, W.C., Babin, B.J. and Anderson, R.E., *Multivariate Data Analysis with Readings*, 7th edn (Upper Saddle River, NJ: Prentice Hall, 2010). See also Glen, J.J., 'Classification accuracy in discriminant analysis: a mixed integer programming approach', *Journal of the Operational Research Society* 52 (3) (March 2001), 328.

10. Anon., 'Interactive TV growth to erupt over the next five years', *Satellite News* 24 (2) (8 January, 2001), 1; Rahtz, D.R., Sirgy, M.J. and Kosenko, R., 'Using demographics and psychographic dimensions to discriminate between mature heavy and light television users: an exploratory analysis', in Bahn, K.D. (ed.), *Developments in Marketing Science*, Vol. 11 (Blacksburg, VA: Academy of Marketing Science, 1988), 2–7.

11. For advanced discussion of multiple discriminant analysis, see Johnson, R.A. and Wichern, D.W., *Applied Multivariate Statistical Analysis*, 5th edn (Upper Saddle River, NJ: Prentice Hall, 2002). For an application, see Duffy, R.S., 'Towards a better understanding of partnership attributes: an exploratory analysis of relationship type classification', *Industrial Marketing Management* 37 (2) (April 2008), 228–244; Shoham, A. and Ruvio, A., 'Opinion leaders and followers: a replication and extension', *Psychology & Marketing* 25 (3) (March 2008), 280–297.

12. Tudor, J., 'Valuation of the health services industry', *Weekly Corporate Growth Report* (1133) (26 March, 2001), 11237–11238; Dansky, K.H. and Brannon, D., 'Discriminant analysis: a technique for adding value to patient satisfaction surveys', *Hospital and Health Services Administration* 41 (4) (Winter 1996), 503–513; Lim, J.S. and Zallocco, R., 'Determinant attributes in formulation of attitudes toward four health care systems', *Journal of Health Care Marketing* 8 (June 1988), 25–30.

13. Hair, J.E. Jr, Black, W.C., Babin, B.J. and Anderson, R.E., *Multivariate Data Analysis with Readings*, 7th edn (Upper Saddle River, NJ: Prentice Hall, 2010); Johnson, R.A. and Wichern, D.A., *Applied Multivariate Statistical Analysis*, 5th edn (Upper Saddle River, NJ: Prentice Hall, 2002).

14. For a discussion of the logit model, see Malhotra, N.K., 'The use of linear logit models in marketing research', *Journal of Marketing Research* 21 (February 1984), 20–31. For a comparison of OLS regression, discriminant, logit and probit models, see Malhotra, N.K., 'A comparison of the predictive validity of procedures for analyzing binary data', *Journal of Business and Economic Statistics* 1 (October 1983), 326–336.

15. Richards, T.J., 'A nested logit model of strategic promotion', *Quantitative Marketing and Economics* 5 (1) (March 2007), 63–91; Sriram, S., Chintagunta, P.K. and Neelamegham, R., 'Effects of brand preference, product attributes and marketing mix variables in technology product markets', *Marketing Science* 25 (5) (June 2006), 440; Malhotra, N.K., 'The use of linear logit models in marketing research', *Journal of Marketing Research* 21 (February 1984), 20–31.

16. Sterlicchi, J., 'Customer satisfaction just catching on in Europe', *Marketing News* (May 28, 1990).

17. Segal, M.N. and Giacobbe, R.W., 'Ethical issues in Australian marketing research services: an empirical investigation', *Services Marketing Quarterly* 28 (3) (2007), 33; Schwepker, C.H. and Hartline, M.D., 'Managing the ethical climate of customer-contact service employees', *Journal of Service Research* 7 (4) (May 2005), 377–396; Murphy, P.R., Smith, J.E. and Daley, J.M., 'Executive attitudes, organisational size and ethical issues: perspectives on a service industry', *Journal of Business Ethics* 11 (1982), 11–19.

22

Factor analysis

Factor analysis allows an examination of the potential interrelationships among a number of variables and the evaluation of the underlying reasons for these relationships.

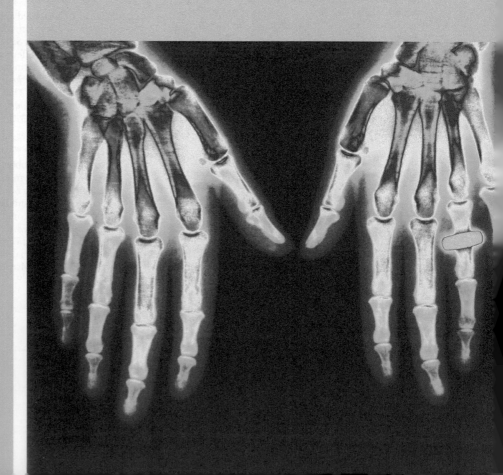

Objectives

After reading this chapter, you should be able to:

1 describe the concept of factor analysis and explain how it is different from analysis of variance, multiple regression and discriminant analysis;

2 discuss the procedure for conducting factor analysis, including problem formulation, construction of the correlation matrix, selection of an appropriate method, determination of the number of factors, rotation and interpretation of factors;

3 understand the distinction between principal component factor analysis and common factor analysis methods;

4 explain the selection of surrogate variables and their application with emphasis on their use in subsequent analysis;

5 describe the procedure for determining the fit of a factor analysis model using the observed and the reproduced correlations;

6 appreciate how SPSS and SAS software are used in factor analysis.

Overview

In analysis of variance (Chapter 19), regression (Chapter 20) and discriminant analysis (Chapter 21), one of the variables is clearly identified as the dependent variable. We now turn to a procedure, factor analysis, in which variables are not classified as independent or dependent. Instead, the whole set of interdependent relationships among variables is examined. This chapter discusses the basic concept of factor analysis and gives an exposition of the factor model. We describe the steps in factor analysis and illustrate them in the context of principal components analysis. Next, we present an application of common factor analysis. Finally, help is provided to run the SPSS and SAS Learning Editions in the data analysis challenges presented in this chapter. We begin with an example that illustrates an application of factor analysis.

| Real research | **Personal alarms**[1] |

In a study of personal alarms, women were asked to rate eight personal alarms using the following 15 statements:

1   Feels comfortable in the hand.
2   Could be easily kept in the pocket.
3   Would fit easily into a handbag.
4   Could be easily worn on the person.
5   Could be carried to be very handy when needed.
6   Could be set off almost as a reflex action.
7   Would be difficult for an attacker to take it off me.
8   Could keep a very firm grip on it if attacked.
9   An attacker might be frightened that I might attack him with it
10 Would be difficult for an attacker to switch off.
11 Solidly built.
12 Would be difficult to break.

13   Looks as if it would give off a very loud noise.

14   An attacker might have second thoughts about attacking me if he saw me with it.

15   I would be embarrassed to carry it around with me.

The question was 'Could these 15 variables be reduced to a smaller number of derived variables, known as factors, in such a way that too much information was not lost?' Factor analysis enabled these 15 variables to be reduced to four underlying dimensions or factors that women used to evaluate the alarms. Factor 1 seemed to measure a dimension of *size*, on a continuum of small to large. Factor 2 tapped into aspects of the *appearance* of a personal alarm. Factor 3 revealed *robustness* characteristics, with factor 4 related to *hand feel*.

Basic concept

Factor analysis
A class of procedures primarily used for data reduction and summarisation.

Factor
An underlying dimension that explains the correlations among a set of variables.

Interdependence technique
A multivariate statistical technique in which the whole set of interdependent relationships is examined.

Factor analysis is a general name denoting a class of procedures primarily used for data reduction and summarisation. In marketing research, there may be a large number of variables, most of which are correlated and which must be reduced to a manageable level. Relationships among sets of many interrelated variables are examined and represented in terms of a few underlying factors. For example, the image of a fashion brand may be measured by asking participants to evaluate competing fashion brands on a series of items on a semantic differential scale or a Likert scale. These item evaluations may then be analysed to determine the **factors** underlying the image of a fashion brand.

In analysis of variance, multiple regression and discriminant analysis, one variable is considered the dependent or criterion variable, and the others are considered independent or predictor variables. But no such distinction is made in factor analysis. Rather, factor analysis is an interdependence technique in that an entire set of **interdependent relationships** is examined.[2]

Factor analysis is used in the following circumstances:

1   To identify underlying dimensions, or factors, that explain the correlations among a set of variables. For example, a set of lifestyle statements may be used to measure the psychographic profiles of consumers. These statements may then be factor analysed to identify the underlying psychographic factors as illustrated in the opening example. This is also illustrated in Figure 22.1 based upon empirical analysis, where seven psychographic variables can be represented by two factors. In this figure, factor 1 can be interpreted as homebody vs. socialite, and factor 2 can be interpreted as sports vs. cinema/theatre.

Figure 22.1

Factors underlying selected psychographics and lifestyles

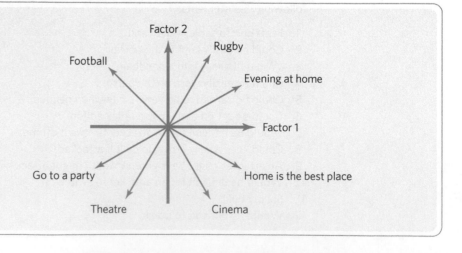

2 To identify a new, smaller, set of uncorrelated variables to replace the original set of correlated variables in subsequent multivariate analysis (regression or discriminant analysis). For example, the psychographic factors identified may be used as independent variables in explaining the differences between loyal and non-loyal consumers. Thus, instead of the seven correlated psychographic variables of Figure 22.1, we can use the two uncorrelated factors, i.e. homebody versus socialite, and sports versus cinema/theatre, in subsequent analysis.

3 To identify a smaller set of salient variables from a larger set for use in subsequent multivariate analysis. For example, a few of the original lifestyle statements that correlate highly with the identified factors may be used as independent variables to explain the differences between the loyal and non-loyal users. Specifically, based upon theory and empirical results (Figure 22.1), we can select home is the best place and football as independent variables, and drop the other five variables to avoid problems due to multicollinearity (see Chapter 20)

All these uses are exploratory in nature and therefore factor analysis is also called exploratory factor analysis (EFA). Factor analysis has numerous applications in marketing research. For example:

- It can be used in market segmentation for identifying the underlying variables on which to group the customers. New car buyers might be grouped based on the relative emphasis they place on economy, convenience, performance, comfort and luxury. This might result in five segments: economy seekers, convenience seekers, performance seekers, comfort seekers and luxury seekers.

- In product research, factor analysis can be employed to determine the brand attributes that influence consumer choice. Toothpaste brands might be evaluated in terms of protection against cavities, whiteness of teeth, taste, fresh breath and price.

- In advertising studies, factor analysis can be used to understand the media consumption habits of the target market. The users of frozen foods may be heavy viewers of horror films, play a lot of electronic games, and listen to rock music.

- In pricing studies, factor analysis can be used to identify the characteristics of price-sensitive consumers. For example, these consumers might be methodical, economy minded and home centred.

Factor analysis model

Mathematically, factor analysis is somewhat similar to multiple regression analysis in that each variable is expressed as a linear combination of underlying factors. The amount of variance a variable shares with all other variables included in the analysis is referred to as *communality*. The covariation among the variables is described in terms of a small number of common factors plus a unique factor for each variable. These factors are not overtly observed. If the variables are standardised, the factor model may be represented as

$$X_i = A_{i1}F_1 + A_{i2}F_2 + A_{i3}F_3 + \ldots + A_{im}F_m + V_iU_i$$

where
X_i = ith standardised variable
A_{ij} = standardised multiple regression coefficient of variable i on common factor j
F = common factor
V_i = standardised regression coefficient of variable i on unique factor i
U_i = the unique factor for variable i
m = number of common factors

The unique factors are correlated with each other and with the common factors.[3] The common factors themselves can be expressed as linear combinations of the observed variables

$$F_i = W_{i1}X_1 + W_{i2}X_2 + W_{i3}X_3 + \dots + W_{ik}X_k$$

where F_i = estimate of ith factor
W_i = weight or factor score coefficient
k = number of variables

It is possible to select weights or factor score coefficients so that the first factor explains the largest portion of the total variance. Then a second set of weights can be selected so that the second factor accounts for most of the residual variance, subject to being uncorrelated with the first factor. This same principle could be applied to selecting additional weights for the additional factors. Thus, the factors can be estimated so that their factor scores, unlike the values of the original variables, are not correlated. Furthermore, the first factor accounts for the highest variance in the data, the second factor for the second highest, and so on. A simplified graphical illustration of factor analysis in the case of two variables is presented in Figure 22.2. Several statistics are associated with factor analysis.

Figure 22.2

Graphical illustration of factor analysis

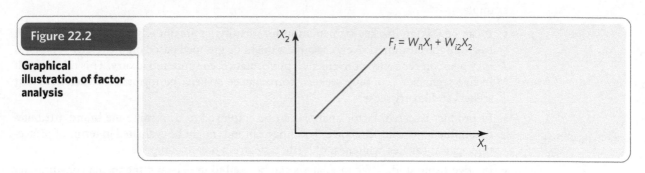

Statistics associated with factor analysis

The key statistics associated with factor analysis are as follows:

Bartlett's test of sphericity. This is a test statistic used to examine the hypothesis that the variables are uncorrelated in the population. In other words, the population correlation matrix is an identity matrix; each variable correlates perfectly with itself ($r = 1$) but has no correlation with the other variables ($r = 0$).

Communality. This is the amount of variance a variable shares with all the other variables being considered. It is also the proportion of variance explained by the common factors.

Correlation matrix. A correlation matrix is a lower triangular matrix showing the simple correlations, r, between all possible pairs of variables included in the analysis. The diagonal elements, which are all one, are usually omitted.

Eigenvalue. The eigenvalue represents the total variance explained by each factor.

Factor loadings. These are simple correlations between the variables and the factors.

Factor loading plot. A factor loading plot is a plot of the original variables using the factor loadings as coordinates.

Factor matrix. A factor matrix contains the factor loadings of all the variables on all the factors extracted.

Factor scores. These are composite scores estimated for each participant on the derived factors.

Factor scores coefficient matrix. This matrix contains the weights, or factor score coefficients, used to combine the standardised variables to obtain factor scores.

Kaiser–Meyer–Olkin (KMO) measure of sampling adequacy. The KMO measure of sampling adequacy is an index used to examine the appropriateness of factor analysis. High values (between 0.5 and 1.0) indicate that factor analysis is appropriate. Values below 0.5 imply that factor analysis may not be appropriate.

Percentage of variance. This is the percentage of the total variance attributed to each factor.

Residuals. These are the differences between the observed correlations, as given in the input correlation matrix, and the reproduced correlations, as estimated from the factor matrix.

Scree plot. A scree plot is a plot of the eigenvalues against the number of factors in order of extraction.

We describe the uses of these statistics in the next section, in the context of the procedure for conducting factor analysis.

Conducting factor analysis

The steps involved in conducting factor analysis are illustrated in Figure 22.3. The first step is to define the factor analysis problem and identify the variables to be factor analysed. Then a correlation matrix of these variables is constructed and a method of factor analysis is selected. The researcher decides on the number of factors to be extracted and the method of rotation. Next, the rotated factors should be interpreted. Depending on the objectives, the factor scores

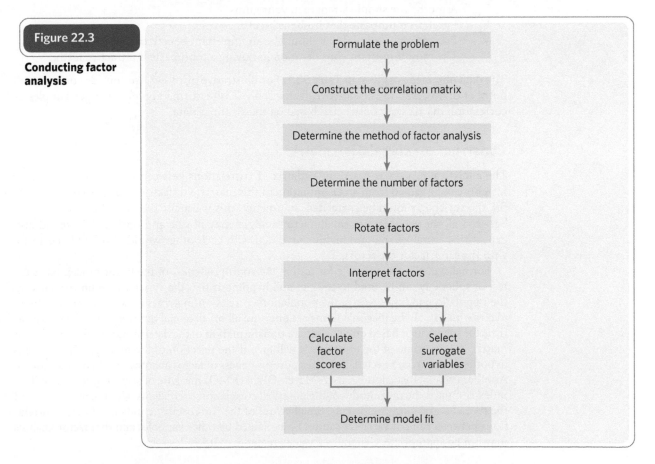

Figure 22.3

Conducting factor analysis

may be calculated, or surrogate variables selected, to represent the factors in subsequent multivariate analysis. Finally, the fit of the factor analysis model is determined. We discuss these steps in more detail in the following subsections.[4]

Formulate the problem

Formulating the problem includes several tasks. First, the objectives of factor analysis should be identified. The variables to be included in the factor analysis should be specified based on past research (quantitative or qualitative), theory and judgement of the researcher. It is important that the variables be appropriately measured on an interval or ratio scale. An appropriate sample size should be used. As a rough guide, there should be at least four or five times as many observations (sample size) as there are variables.[5] In many marketing research situations, the sample size is small, and this ratio is considerably lower. In these cases, the results should be interpreted cautiously.

To illustrate factor analysis, suppose that the researcher wants to determine the underlying benefits that consumers seek from the purchase of a toothpaste. A sample of 30 participants was interviewed using street interviewing. The participants were asked to indicate their degree of agreement with the following statements using a seven-point scale (1 = strongly disagree, 7 = strongly agree):

V_1 It is important to buy a toothpaste that prevents cavities.
V_2 I like a toothpaste that gives shiny teeth.
V_3 A toothpaste should strengthen your gums.
V_4 I prefer a toothpaste that freshens breath.
V_5 Prevention of tooth decay should be an important benefit offered by a toothpaste.
V_6 The most important consideration in buying a toothpaste is attractive teeth.

The data obtained are given in Table 22.1. For illustrative purposes, we consider only a small number of observations. In practice, factor analysis is performed on much larger samples. A correlation matrix was constructed based on these ratings data.

Construct the correlation matrix

The analytical process is based on a matrix of correlations between the variables. Valuable insights can be gained from an examination of this matrix. For factor analysis to be meaningful, the variables should be correlated. In practice, this is usually the case. If the correlations between all the variables are small, factor analysis may not be appropriate. We would also expect that variables that are highly correlated with each other would also highly correlate with the same factor or factors.

Formal statistics are available for testing the appropriateness of the factor model. Bartlett's test of sphericity can be used to test the null hypothesis that the variables are uncorrelated in the population; in other words, the population correlation matrix is an identity matrix. In an identity matrix, all the diagonal terms are one, and all off-diagonal terms are zero. The test statistic for sphericity is based on a chi-square transformation of the determinant of the correlation matrix. A large value of the test statistic will favour the rejection of the null hypothesis. If this hypothesis cannot be rejected, then the appropriateness of factor analysis should be questioned. Another useful statistic is the Kaiser–Meyer–Olkin (KMO) measure of sampling adequacy. This index compares the magnitudes of the observed correlation coefficients with the magnitudes of the partial correlation coefficients. Small values of the KMO statistic indicate that the correlations between pairs of variables cannot be explained by other variables and that factor analysis may not be appropriate. Generally, a value greater than 0.5 is desirable.

Table 22.1	Toothpaste attribute ratings					
Participant number	V_1	V_2	V_3	V_4	V_5	V_6
1	7	3	6	4	2	4
2	1	3	2	4	5	4
3	6	2	7	4	1	3
4	4	5	4	6	2	5
5	1	2	2	3	6	2
6	6	3	6	4	2	4
7	5	3	6	3	4	3
8	6	4	7	4	1	4
9	3	4	2	3	6	3
10	2	6	2	6	7	6
11	6	4	7	3	2	3
12	2	3	1	4	5	4
13	7	2	6	4	1	3
14	4	6	4	5	3	6
15	1	3	2	2	6	4
16	6	4	6	3	3	4
17	5	3	6	3	3	4
18	7	3	7	4	1	4
19	2	4	3	3	6	3
20	3	5	3	6	4	6
21	1	3	2	3	5	3
22	5	4	5	4	2	4
23	2	2	1	5	4	4
24	4	6	4	6	4	7
25	6	5	4	2	1	4
26	3	5	4	6	4	7
27	4	4	7	2	2	5
28	3	7	2	6	4	3
29	4	6	3	7	2	7
30	2	3	2	4	7	2

The correlation matrix, constructed from the data obtained to understand toothpaste benefits, is shown in Table 22.2. There are relatively high correlations among V_1 (prevention of cavities), V_3 (strong gums) and V_5 (prevention of tooth decay). We would expect these variables to correlate with the same set of factors. Likewise, there are relatively high correlations among V_2 (shiny teeth), V_4 (fresh breath) and V_6 (attractive teeth). These variables may also be expected to correlate with the same factors.[6]

The results of factor analysis are given in Table 22.3. The null hypothesis, that the population correlation matrix is an identity matrix, is rejected by Bartlett's test of sphericity. The approximate chi-square statistic is 111.314 with 15 degrees of freedom, which is significant at the 0.05 level. The value of the KMO statistic (0.660) is also large (>0.5). Thus factor analysis may be considered an appropriate technique for analysing the correlation matrix of Table 22.2.

Table 22.2	**Correlation matrix**

Participant	V_1	V_2	V_3	V_4	V_5	V_6
V_1	1.00					
V_2	-0.053	1.00				
V_3	0.873	-0.155	1.00			
V_4	-0.086	0.572	-0.248	1.00		
V_5	-0.858	0.020	-0.778	-0.007	1.00	
V_6	0.004	0.640	-0.018	0.640	-0.136	1.00

Table 22.3	**Results of principal components analysis**

Bartlett test of sphericity
Approximate chi-square = 111.314, df = 15, significance = 0.00000
Kaiser–Meyer–Olkin measure of sampling adequacy = 0.660

Communalities

Variable	Initial	Extraction
V_1	1.000	0.926
V_2	1.000	0.723
V_3	1.000	0.894
V_4	1.000	0.739
V_5	1.000	0.878
V_6	1.000	0.790

Initial eigenvalues

Factor	Eigenvalue	Percentage of variance	Cumulative percentage
1	2.731	45.520	45.520
2	2.218	36.969	82.488
3	0.442	7.360	89.848
4	0.341	5.688	95.536
5	0.183	3.044	98.580
6	0.085	1.420	100.000

Extraction sums of squared loadings

Factor	Eigenvalue	Percentage of variance	Cumulative percentage
1	2.731	45.520	45.520
2	2.218	36.969	82.488

Table 22.3	Continued

Factor matrix

	Factor 1	Factor 2
V_1	0.928	0.253
V_2	-0.301	0.795
V_3	0.936	0.131
V_4	-0.342	0.789
V_5	-0.869	-0.351
V_6	-0.177	0.871

Rotation sums of squared loadings

Factor	Eigenvalue	Percentage of variance	Cumulative percentage
1	2.688	44.802	44.802
2	2.261	37.687	82.488

Rotated factor matrix

	Factor 1	Factor 2
V_1	0.962	-0.027
V_2	-0.057	0.848
V_3	0.934	-0.146
V_4	-0.098	0.854
V_5	-0.933	-0.084
V_6	0.083	0.885

Factor score coefficient matrix

	Factor 1	Factor 2
V_1	0.358	0.011
V_2	-0.001	0.375
V_3	0.345	-0.043
V_4	-0.017	0.377
V_5	-0.350	-0.059
V_6	0.052	0.395

Reproduced correlation matrix

Variables	V_1	V_2	V_3	V_4	V_5	V_6
V_1	0.926*	0.024	-0.029	0.031	0.038	-0.053
V_2	-0.078	0.723*	0.022	-0.158	0.038	-0.105
V_3	0.902	-0.177	0.894*	-0.031	0.081	0.033
V_4	-0.117	0.730	-0.217	0.739*	-0.027	-0.107
V_5	-0.895	-0.018	0.859	0.020	0.878*	0.016
V_6	0.057	-0.746	-0.051	0.748	-0.152	0.790

*The lower left triangle contains the reproduced correlation matrix; the diagonal, the communalities; and the upper right triangle, the residuals between the observed correlations and the reproduced correlations.

Determine the method of factor analysis

Principal components analysis
An approach to factor analysis that considers the total variance in the data.

Common factor analysis
An approach to factor analysis that estimates the factors based only on the common variance. Also called principal axis factoring.

Once it has been determined that factor analysis is an appropriate technique for analysing the data, an appropriate method must be selected. The approach used to derive the weights or factor score coefficients differentiates the various methods of factor analysis. The two basic approaches are principal components analysis and common factor analysis. In principal components analysis, the total variance in the data is considered. The diagonal of the correlation matrix consists of unities, and full variance is brought into the factor matrix. Principal components analysis is recommended when the primary concern is to determine the minimum number of factors that will account for maximum variance in the data for use in subsequent multivariate analysis. The factors are called *principal components*.

In common factor analysis, the factors are estimated based only on the common variance. Communalities are inserted in the diagonal of the correlation matrix. This method is appropriate when the primary concern is to identify the underlying dimensions and the common variance is of interest. This method is also known as *principal axis factoring*.

Other approaches for estimating the common factors are also available. These include the methods of unweighted least squares, generalised least squares, maximum likelihood, alpha method and image factoring. These methods are complex and are not recommended for inexperienced users.[7]

Table 22.3 shows the application of principal components analysis to the toothpaste example.

Under 'Communalities', 'Initial' column, it can be seen that the communality for each variable, V_1 to V_6, is 1.0 as unities were inserted in the diagonal of the correlation matrix. The table labelled 'Initial eigenvalues' gives the eigenvalues. The eigenvalues for the factors are, as expected, in decreasing order of magnitude as we go from factor 1 to factor 6. The eigenvalue for a factor indicates the total variance attributed to that factor. The total variance accounted for by all the six factors is 6.00, which is equal to the number of variables. Factor 1 accounts for a variance of 2.731, which is (2.731/6) or 45.52% of the total variance. Likewise, the second factor accounts for (2.218/6) or 36.97% of the total variance, and the first two factors combined account for 82.49% of the total variance. Several considerations are involved in determining the number of factors that should be used in the analysis.

Determine the number of factors

It is possible to compute as many principal components as there are variables, but, in doing so, no parsimony is gained, i.e. we would not have summarised the information nor revealed any underlying structure. To summarise the information contained in the original variables, a smaller number of factors should be extracted. The question is: how many? Several procedures have been suggested for determining the number of factors. These included a priori determination and approaches based on eigenvalues, scree plot, percentage of variance accounted for, split-half reliability and significance tests:

A priori determination. Sometimes, because of prior knowledge, the researcher knows how many factors to expect and thus can specify the number of factors to be extracted beforehand. The extraction of factors ceases when the desired number of factors has been extracted. Most computer programs allow the user to specify the number of factors, allowing for an easy implementation of this approach.

Determination based on eigenvalues. In this approach, only factors with eigenvalues greater than 1.0 are retained; the other factors are not included in the model. An eigenvalue represents the amount of variance associated with the factor. Hence, only factors with a variance greater than 1.0 are included. Factors with a variance less than 1.0 are no better than a single variable because, due to standardisation, each variable has a variance of 1.0. If the number of variables is less than 20, this approach will result in a conservative number of factors.

Determination based on scree plot. A scree plot is a plot of the eigenvalues against the number of factors in order of extraction. The shape of the plot is used to determine the number of factors. Typically, the plot has a distinct break between the steep slope of factors, with large eigenvalues and a gradual trailing off associated with the rest of the factors. This gradual trailing off is referred to as the scree. Experimental evidence indicates that the point at which the scree begins denotes the true number of factors. Generally, the number of factors determined by a scree plot will be one or a few more than that determined by the eigenvalue criterion.

Determination based on percentage of variance. In this approach, the number of factors extracted is determined so that the cumulative percentage of variance extracted by the factors reaches a satisfactory level. What level of variance is satisfactory depends upon the problem. It is recommended that the factors extracted should account for at least 60% of the variance.

Determination based on split-half reliability. The sample is split in half, and factor analysis is performed on each half. Only factors with high correspondence of factor loadings across the two subsamples are retained.

Determination based on significance tests. It is possible to determine the statistical significance of the separate eigenvalues and retain only those factors that are statistically significant. A drawback is that with large samples (size greater than 200) many factors are likely to be statistically significant, although from a practical viewpoint many of these account for only a small proportion of the total variance.

In Table 22.3, we see that the eigenvalue greater than 1.0 (default option) results in two factors being extracted. Our a priori knowledge tells us that toothpaste is bought for two major reasons. The scree plot associated with this analysis is given in Figure 22.4. From the scree plot, a distinct break occurs at three factors. Finally, from the cumulative percentage of variance accounted for, we see that the first two factors account for 82.49% of the variance and that the gain achieved in going to three factors is marginal. Furthermore, split-half reliability also indicates that two factors are appropriate. Thus, two factors appear to be reasonable in this situation.

The second column under the 'Communalities' heading in Table 22.3 gives relevant information after the desired number of factors has been extracted. The communalities for the variances under 'Extraction' are different from those under 'Initial' because all of the variances associated with the variables are not explained unless all the factors are retained. The 'Extraction sums of squared loadings' table gives the variances associated with the factors that are retained.

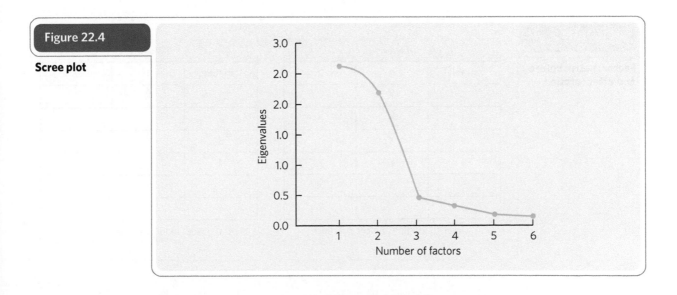

Figure 22.4

Scree plot

Note that these are the same as those under 'Initial eigenvalues'. This is always the case in principal components analysis. The percentage variance accounted for by a factor is determined by dividing the associated eigenvalue by the total number of factors (or variables) and multiplying by 100. Thus, the first factor accounts for $(2.731/6) \times 100$ or 45.52% of the variance of the six variables. Likewise, the second factor accounts for $(2.218/6) \times 100$ or 36.967% of the variance. Interpretation of the solution is often enhanced by a rotation of the factors.

Rotate factors

An important output from factor analysis is the factor matrix, also called the *factor pattern matrix*. The factor matrix contains the coefficients used to express the standardised variables in terms of the factors. These coefficients, the factor loadings, represent the correlations between the factors and the variables. A coefficient with a large absolute value indicates that the factor and the variable are closely related. The coefficients of the factor matrix can be used to interpret the factors.

Although the initial or unrotated factor matrix indicates the relationship between the factors and individual variables, it seldom results in factors that can be interpreted, because the factors are correlated with many variables. For example, in Table 22.3, factor 1 is at least somewhat correlated with five of the six variables (absolute value of factor loading greater than 0.3). Likewise, factor 2 is at least somewhat correlated with four of the six variables. Moreover, variables 2 and 5 load at least somewhat on both the factors. This is illustrated in Figure 22.5(a). How should this factor be interpreted? In such a complex matrix, it is difficult to interpret the factors. Therefore, through rotation, the factor matrix is transformed into a simpler one that is easier to interpret.

In rotating the factors, we would like each factor to have non-zero, or significant, loadings or coefficients for only some of the variables. Likewise, we would like each variable to have non-zero or significant loadings with only a few factors, and if possible with only one. If several factors have high loadings with the same variable, it is difficult to interpret them. Rotation does not affect the communalities and the percentage of total variance explained. The percentage of variance accounted for by each factor does change, however. This is seen in Table 22.3 by comparing 'Extraction sums of squared loadings' with ' Rotation sums of squared loadings'. The variance explained by the individual factors is redistributed by rotation. Hence, different methods of rotation may result in the identification of different factors.

The rotation is called **orthogonal rotation** if the axes are maintained at right angles. The most commonly used method for rotation is the **varimax procedure**. This is an orthogonal

Orthogonal rotation
Rotation of factors in which the axes are maintained at right angles.

Varimax procedure
An orthogonal method of factor rotation that minimises the number of variables with high loadings on a factor, thereby enhancing the interpretability of the factors.

Figure 22.5
Factor matrix before and after rotation

	Factors				Factors	
Variables	1	2		Variables	1	2
1	X			1	X	
2	X	X		2		X
3	X			3	X	
4	X	X		4		X
5	X	X		5	X	
6		X		6		X

(a) High loadings before rotation   (b) High loadings after rotation method of rotation that minimises the number of variables with high loadings on a factor, thereby enhancing the interpretability of the factors.[8] Orthogonal rotation results in factors that are uncorrelated. The rotation is called oblique rotation when the axes are not maintained at right angles, and the factors are correlated. Sometimes, allowing for correlations among factors can simplify the factor pattern matrix. Oblique rotation should be used when factors in the population are likely to be strongly correlated.

Oblique rotation
Rotation of factors when the axes are not maintained at right angles.

In Table 22.3, by comparing the varimax rotated factor matrix with the unrotated matrix (entitled 'Factor matrix'), we can see how rotation achieves simplicity and enhances interpretability. Whereas five variables correlated with factor 1 in the unrotated matrix, only variables V_1, V_3 and V_5 correlate highly with factor 1 after rotation. The remaining variables, V_2, V_4 and V_6, correlate highly with factor 2. Furthermore, no variable correlates highly with both the factors. The rotated factor matrix forms the basis for interpretation of the factors.

Interpret factors

Interpretation is facilitated by identifying the variables that have large loadings on the same factor. That factor can then be interpreted in terms of the variables that load high on it. Another useful aid in interpretation is to plot the variables, using the factor loadings as coordinates. Variables at the end of an axis are those that have high loadings on only that factor and hence describe the factor. Variables near the origin have small loadings on both the factors. Variables that are not near any of the axes are related to both the factors. If a factor cannot be clearly defined in terms of the original variables, it should be labelled as an undefined or a general factor.

In the rotated factor matrix of Table 22.3, factor 1 has high coefficients for variables V_1 (prevention of cavities) and V_3 (strong gums), and a negative coefficient for V_5 (prevention of tooth decay is not important). Therefore, this factor may be labelled a health benefit factor. Note that a negative coefficient for a negative variable (V_5) leads to a positive interpretation that prevention of tooth decay is important. Factor 2 is highly related with variables V_2 (shiny teeth), V_4 (fresh breath) and V_6 (attractive teeth). Thus factor 2 may be labelled a social benefit factor. A plot of the factor loadings, given in Figure 22.6, confirms this interpretation. Variables V_1, V_3 and V_5 (denoted 1, 3 and 5, respectively) are at the end of the horizontal axis (factor 1), with V_5 at the end opposite to V_1 and V_3, whereas variables V_2, V_4 and V_6 (denoted 2, 4 and 6) are at the end of the vertical axis (factor 2). One could summarise the data by stating that consumers appear to seek two major kinds of benefits from toothpaste: health benefits and social benefits.

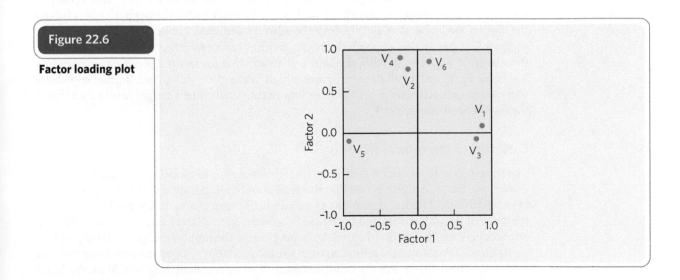

Figure 22.6

Factor loading plot

Calculate factor scores

Factor scores
Composite scores estimated for each participant on the derived factors.

Following interpretation, factor scores can be calculated, if necessary. Factor analysis has its own stand-alone value. If the goal of factor analysis is to reduce the original set of variables to a smaller set of composite variables (factors) for use in subsequent multivariate analysis, however, it is useful to compute factor scores for each participant. A factor is simply a linear combination of the original variables. The factor scores for the ith factor may be estimated as follows:

$$F_i = W_{i1}X_1 + W_{i2}X_2 + W_{i3}X_3 + \ldots + W_{ik}X_k$$

These symbols were defined earlier in the chapter.

The weights or factor score coefficients used to combine the standardised variables are obtained from the factor score coefficient matrix. Most computer programs allow you to request factor scores. Only in the case of principal components analysis is it possible to compute exact factor scores. Moreover, in principal components analysis, these scores are uncorrelated. In common factor analysis, estimates of these scores are obtained, and there is no guarantee that the factors will be uncorrelated with each other. Factor scores can be used instead of the original variables in subsequent multivariate analysis. For example, using the 'Factor score coefficient matrix' in Table 22.3, one could compute two factor scores for each participant. The standardised variable values would be multiplied by the corresponding factor score coefficients to obtain the factor scores.

Select surrogate variables

Surrogate variables
A subset of original variables selected for use in subsequent analysis.

Sometimes, instead of computing factor scores, the researcher wishes to select surrogate variables. Selection of substitute or surrogate variables involves singling out some of the original variables for use in subsequent analysis. This allows the researcher to conduct subsequent analysis and to interpret the results in terms of original variables rather than factor scores. By examining the factor matrix, one could select for each factor the variable with the highest loading on that factor. That variable could then be used as a surrogate variable for the associated factor. This process works well if one factor loading for a variable is clearly higher than all other factor loadings. The choice is not as easy, however, if two or more variables have similarly high loadings. In such a case, the choice between these variables should be based on theoretical and measurement considerations. For example, theory may suggest that a variable with a slightly lower loading is more important than one with a slightly higher loading. Likewise, if a variable has a slightly lower loading but has been measured more precisely, it should be selected as the surrogate variable. In Table 22.3, the variables V_1, V_3 and V_5 all have high loadings on factor 1, and all are fairly close in magnitude, although V_1 has relatively the highest loading and would therefore be a likely candidate. However, if prior knowledge suggests that prevention of tooth decay is a very important benefit, V_5 would be selected as the surrogate for factor 1. Also, the choice of a surrogate for factor 2 is not straightforward. Variables V_2, V_4 and V_6 all have comparable high loadings on this factor. If prior knowledge suggests that attractive teeth are the most important social benefit sought from a toothpaste, the researcher would select V_6.

Determine the model fit

The final step in factor analysis involves the determination of model fit. A basic assumption underlying factor analysis is that the observed correlation between variables can be attributed to common factors. Hence, the correlations between the variables can be deduced or reproduced from the estimated correlations between the variables and the factors. The differences between the observed correlations (as given in the input correlation matrix) and the reproduced correlations (as estimated from the factor matrix) can be examined to determine model fit. These differences are called *residuals*. If there are many large residuals, the factor model does not provide a good fit to the data and the model should be reconsidered. In the upper right triangle of the 'Reproduced correlation matrix' of Table 22.3, we see that only five residuals are larger than 0.05, indicating an acceptable model fit.

The following example further illustrates principal components factoring in the context of trade promotion.

Real research | **Manufacturing promotion components[9]**

The objective of this study was to develop a comprehensive inventory of manufacturer-controlled trade promotion variables and to demonstrate that an association exists between these variables and the retailers' promotion support decision. Retailer support was defined operationally as the trade buyers' attitude towards the promotion.

Factor analysis was performed on the explanatory variables with the primary goal of data reduction. The principal components method, using varimax rotation, reduced the 30 explanatory variables to eight factors having eigenvalues greater than 1.0. For the purpose of interpretation, each factor was composed of variables that loaded 0.40 or higher on that factor. In two instances, where variables loaded 0.40 or above on two factors, each variable was assigned to the factor where it had the highest loading. Only one variable, 'ease of handling/stocking at retail', did not load at least 0.40 on any factor. In all, the eight factors explained 62% of the total variance. Interpretation of the factor loading matrix was straightforward. Table 1 lists the factors in the order in which they were extracted.

Stepwise discriminant analysis was conducted to determine which, if any, of the eight factors predicted trade support to a statistically significant degree. The factor scores for the eight factors were the explanatory variables. The dependent variable consisted of the retail buyer's overall rating of the deal (rating), which was collapsed into a three-group (low, medium and high) measure of trade support. The results of the discriminant analyses are shown in Table 2. All eight entered the discriminant functions. Goodness-of-fit measures indicated that, as a group, the eight factors discriminated between high, medium and low levels of trade support. Multivariate F ratios, indicating the degree of discrimination between each pair of groups, were significant at $p < 0.001$. Correct classification into high, medium and low categories was achieved for 65% of the cases. The order of entry into discriminant analysis was used to determine the relative importance of factors as trade support influencers, as shown in Table 3.

Table 1 Factors influencing trade promotional support

Factor	Factor interpretation (% variance explained)	Loading	Variables included in the factor
F1	Item importance (16.3%)	0.77	Item is significant enough to warrant promotion
		0.75	Category responds well to promotion
		0.66	Closest trade competitor is likely to promote item
		0.64	Importance of promoted product category
		0.59	Item regular (non-deal) sales volume
		0.57	Deal meshes with trade promotional requirements
			Buyer's estimate of sales increase on the basis of:
F2	Promotion elasticity (9.3%)	0.86	Price reduction and display
		0.82	Display only
		0.80	Price reduction only
		0.70	Price reduction, display and advertising

Factor	Factor interpretation (% variance explained)	Loading	Variables included in the factor
			Manufacturer's brand support in the form of:
F3	Manufacturer brand support (8.2%)	0.85	Coupons
		0.81	Radio and television advertising
		0.80	Newspaper advertising
		0.75	Point of purchase promotion (e.g. display)
F4	Manufacturer reputation (7.3%)	0.72	Manufacturer's overall reputation
		0.72	Manufacturer's cooperation in meeting trade's promotional needs
		0.64	Manufacturer's cooperation on emergency orders
		0.55	Quality of sales presentation
		0.51	Manufacturer's overall product quality
F5	Promotion wearout (6.4%)	0.93	Product category is overpromoted
		0.93	Item is overpromoted
F6	Sales velocity (5.4%)	−0.81	Brand market share rank*
		0.69	Item regular sales volume*
		0.46	Item regular sales volume
F7	Item profitability (4.5%)	0.79	Item regular gross margin
		0.72	Item regular gross margin*
		0.49	Reasonableness of deal performance requirements
F8	Incentive amount (4.2%)	0.83	Absolute amount of deal allowances
		0.81	Deal allowances as per cent of regular trade cost*
		0.49	Absolute amount of deal allowances*

* Denotes objectives (archival) measure.

Table 2 Discriminant analysis results: analysis of rating (n = 564)

		Standardised discrimination coefficients Analysis of rating	
Factor		Function 1	Function 2
F1	Item importance	0.861	−0.253
F2	Promotion elasticity	0.081	0.398
F3	Manufacturer brand support	0.127	−0.036
F4	Manufacturer reputation	0.394	0.014
F5	Promotion wearout	−0.207	0.380
F6	Sales velocity	0.033	−0.665
F7	Item profitability	0.614	0.357
F8	Incentive amount	0.461	0.254
Wilks' λ (for each factor)		All significant at $p < 0.001$	
Multivariate F ratios		All significant at $p < 0.001$	
Percentage of cases correctly classified		65% correct	

Table 3 Relative importance of trade support influencers (as indicated by order of entry into the discriminant analysis)

Analysis of rating	
Order of entry	Factor name
1	Item importance
2	Item profitability
3	Incentive amount
4	Manufacturer reputation
5	Promotion wearout
6	Sales velocity
7	Promotion elasticity
8	Manufacturer brand support

Applications of common factor analysis

The data of Table 22.1 were analysed using the common factor analysis model. Instead of using unities in the diagonal, the communalities were inserted. The output, shown in Table 22.4, is similar to the output from principal components analysis presented in Table 22.3. Beneath the 'Communalities' heading, below the 'Initial' column, the communalities for the variables are no longer 1.0. Based on the eigenvalue criterion, again two factors are extracted. The variances, after extracting the factors, are different from the initial eigenvalues. The first factor accounts for 42.84% of the variance, whereas the second accounts for 31.13%, in each case a little less than what was observed in principal components analysis.

The values in the unrotated factor pattern matrix of Table 22.4 are a little different from those in Table 22.3, although the pattern of the coefficients is similar. Sometimes, however, the pattern of loadings for common factor analysis is different from that for principal

Table 22.4	**Results of common factor analysis**

Bartlett test of sphericity
Approximate chi-square = 111.314, df = 15, significance = 0.00000
Kaiser–Meyer–Olkin measure of sampling adequacy = 0.660

Communalities

Variable	Initial	Extraction
V_1	0.859	0.928
V_2	0.480	0.562
V_3	0.814	0.836
V_4	0.543	0.600
V_5	0.763	0.789
V_6	0.587	0.723

Table 22.4	Continued

Initial eigenvalues

Factor	Eigenvalue	Percentage of variance	Cumulative percentage
1	2.731	45.520	45.520
2	2.218	36.969	82.488
3	0.442	7.360	89.848
4	0.341	5.688	95.536
5	0.183	3.044	98.580
6	0.085	1.420	100.000

Extraction sums of squared loadings

Factor	Eigenvalue	Percentage of variance	Cumulative percentage
1	2.570	42.837	42.837
2	1.868	31.126	73.964

Factor matrix

	Factor 1	Factor 2
V_1	0.949	0.168
V_2	-0.206	0.720
V_3	0.914	0.038
V_4	-0.246	0.734
V_5	-0.850	-0.259
V_6	-0.101	0.844

Rotation sums of squared loadings

Factor	Eigenvalue	Percentage of variance	Cumulative percentage
1	2.541	42.343	42.343
2	1.897	31.621	73.964

Rotated factor matrix

	Factor 1	Factor 2
V_1	0.963	-0.030
V_2	-0.054	0.747
V_3	0.902	-0.150
V_4	-0.090	0.769
V_5	-0.885	-0.079
V_6	0.075	0.847

Table 22.4	Continued

Factor score coefficient matrix

	Factor 1	Factor 2
V_1	0.628	0.101
V_2	-0.024	0.253
V_3	0.217	-0.169
V_4	-0.023	0.271
V_5	-0.166	-0.059
V_6	0.083	0.500

Reproduced correlation matrix

	V_1	V_2	V_3	V_4	V_5	V_6
V_1	0.928*	0.022	-0.000	0.024	-0.008	-0.042
V_2	-0.075	0.562*	0.006	-0.008	0.031	0.012
V_3	0.873	-0.161	0.836*	-0.051	0.008	0.042
V_4	-0.110	0.580	-0.197	0.600*	-0.025	-0.004
V_5	-0.850	-0.012	0.786	0.019	0.789*	-0.003
V_6	0.046	0.629	-0.060	0.645	-0.133	0.723*

* The lower left triangle contains the reproduced correlation matrix; the diagonal, the communalities; and the upper right triangle, the residuals between the observed correlations and the reproduced correlations.

components analysis, with some variables loading on different factors. The rotated factor matrix has the same pattern as that in Table 22.3, leading to a similar interpretation of the factors. We end with another application of common factor analysis, in the context of consumer perception of rebates.

Real research	**'Common' rebate perceptions[10]**

Rebates are effective in obtaining new users, brand switching and repeat purchases among current users. AT&T deployed a rebate programme as a means to draw new users to its Internet services. AT&T's intent behind this rebate plan was to acquire new users from rivals such as Verizon. The question faced by decision-makers at AT&T was: 'What makes rebates effective?'

A study was undertaken to determine the factors underlying consumer perception of rebates. A set of 24 items measuring consumer perceptions of rebates was constructed. Participants were asked to express their degree of agreement with these items on five-point Likert scales. The data were collected by telephone survey, with a total of 303 usable questionnaires.

The 24 items measuring perceptions of rebates were analysed using common factor analysis. The initial factor solution did not reveal a simple structure of underlying rebate perceptions. Therefore, items that had low loadings were deleted from the scale, and the factor analysis was performed on the remaining items. This second solution yielded three interpretable factors. The factor loadings are presented in the accompanying table, where large loadings have been underscored. The three factors contained four, four and three items, respectively. Factor 1 was defined as a representation of consumers' faith in the rebate system (**Faith**). Factor 2 seemed to capture the consumers' perceptions of the efforts and difficulties associated with rebate redemption (**Efforts**). Factor 3 represented consumers' perceptions of the manufac-

turers' motives for offering rebates (**Motives**). The loadings of items on their respective factors ranged from 0.527 to 0.744. Significant loadings are underscored.

Therefore, companies such as AT&T that employ rebates should ensure that the effort and difficulties of consumers in taking advantage of the rebates are minimised. Companies should also try to build consumers' faith in the rebate system and portray honest motives for offering rebates.

Factor analysis of perceptions of rebates

Scale items[a]	Factor loading		
	Factor 1	Factor 2	Factor 3
Manufacturers make the rebate process too complicated	0.194	0.671	-0.127
Postal rebates are not worth the trouble involved	-0.031	0.612	0.352
It takes too long to receive the rebate from the manufacturer	0.013	0.718	0.051
Manufacturers could do more to make rebates easier to use	0.205	0.616	0.173
Manufacturers offer rebates because consumers want them	0.660	0.172	0.101[b]
Today's manufacturers take real interest in consumer welfare[b]	0.569	0.203	0.334
Consumer benefit is usually the primary consideration in rebate offers[b]	0.660	0.002	0.318
In general, manufacturers are sincere in their rebate offers to consumers[b]	0.716	0.047	-0.033
Manufacturers offer rebates to get consumers to buy something they do not really need	0.099	0.156	0.744
Manufacturers use rebate offers to induce consumers to buy slow-moving items	0.090	0.027	0.702
Rebate offers require you to buy more of a product than you need	0.230	0.066	0.527
Eigenvalues	2.030	1.344	1.062
Percentage of explained variance	27.500	12.200	9.700

[a] The response categories for all items were strongly agree (I), agree (2), neither agree nor disagree (3), disagree (4), strongly disagree (5) and don't know (6). 'Don't know' responses were excluded from data analysis.
[b] The scores of these items were reversed.

In this example, when the initial factor solution was not interpretable, items which had low loadings were deleted and the factor analysis was performed on the remaining items. If the number of variables is large (greater than 15), principal components analysis and common factor analysis result in similar solutions. Principal components analysis is less prone to misinterpretation, however, and is recommended for the non-expert user. Factor analysis in its various forms is a widely used technique as further illustrated in the following two examples. The first example illustrates an application in the context of international marketing research. The second example shows how factor analysis can be used in investigating ethical behaviour.

Real research   ## Driving nuts for Beetles[11]

Consumer preferences for cars need to be continually tracked to identify changing demands and specifications. However, there is one car that is quite an exception – the Volkswagen Beetle. More than 22 million have been built since it was introduced in 1938. Surveys have been conducted in different countries to determine the reasons why people purchase Beetles. Principal components analysis of the variables measuring the reasons for owning Beetles have consistently revealed one factor – fanatical loyalty. The company had long wished for the car's natural death but without any effect. The noisy and cramped 'bug' has inspired devotion in drivers across the generations. Now old bugs are being sought across the globe. VW reintroduced the brand in 1998 as the New Beetle. The New Beetle has proven itself as much more than a sequel to its legendary namesake, winning several distinguished automotive awards.

Real research   ## Factors predicting unethical marketing research practices[12]

Unethical employee behaviour was identified as a root cause for the global banking and financial mess of 2008–2009. If companies want ethical employees, then they themselves must conform to high ethical standards. This also applies to the marketing research industry. In order to identify organisational variables that are determinants of the incidence of unethical marketing research practices, a sample of 420 marketing professionals was surveyed. These marketing professionals were asked to provide responses on several scales, and to provide evaluations of incidence of 15 research practices that have been found to pose research ethics problems. One of these scales included 11 items pertaining to the extent that ethical problems plagued the organisation, and what top management's actions were towards ethical situations. A principal components analysis with varimax rotation indicated that the data could be represented by two factors. These two factors were then used in a multiple regression along with four other predictor variables. They were found to be the two best predictors of unethical marketing research practices.

Factor analysis of ethical problems and top management action scales

	Extent of ethical problems within the organisation (Factor 1)	Top management actions on ethics (Factor 2)
1 Successful executives in my company make rivals look bad in the eyes of important people in my company	0.66	
2 Peer executives in my company often engage in behaviours that I considered to be unethical	0.68	
3 There are many opportunities for peer executives in my company to engage in unethical behaviours	0.43	
4 Successful executives in my company take credit for the ideas and accomplishment of others	0.81	
5 In order to succeed in my company, it is often necessary to compromise one's ethics	0.66	
6 Successful executives in my company are generally more unethical than unsuccessful executives	0.64	
7 Successful executives in my company look for a 'scapegoat' when they feel they may be associated with failure	0.78	
8 Successful executives in my company withold information that is detrimental to their self-interest	0.68	
9 Top management in my company have let it be known in no uncertain terms that unethical behaviours will not be tolerated		0.73
10 If an executive in my company is discovered to have engaged in unethical behaviour that results primarily in personal gain (rather than corporate gain), he or she will be promptly reprimanded		0.80
11 If an executive in my company is discovered to have engaged in unethical behaviour that results primarily in corporate gain (rather than personal gain), he or she will be promptly reprimanded		0.78
Eigenvalues	5.06	1.17
Percentage of explained variance	46%	11%
Coefficient alpha	0.87	0.75

To simplify the table, only varimax rotated loadings of 0.40 or greater are reported. Each was rated on a five-point scale with 1 = 'strongly agree' and 5 = 'strongly disagree'.

SPSS and SAS Learning Editions

SPSS Windows

To select this procedure, click

Analyze>Data Reduction>Factor . . .

The following are the detailed steps for running principal components analysis on the toothpaste attribute ratings (V_1 to V_6) using the data of Table 22.1:

1 Select ANALYZE from the SPSS menu bar.
2 Click DIMENSION REDUCTION and then FACTOR.
3 Move 'Prevents Cavities [v1]' 'Shiny Teeth [v2]', 'Strengthen Gums [v3]', 'Freshens Breath [v4]', 'Tooth Decay Unimportant [v5]' and 'Attractive Teeth [v6]' into the VARIABLES box.
4 Click DESCRIPTIVES. In the pop-up window, in the STATISTICS box check INITIAL SOLUTION. In the CORRELATION MATRIX box check KMO AND BARTLETT'S TEST OF SPHERICITY and also check REPRODUCED. Click CONTINUE.
5 Click EXTRACTION. In the pop-up window, for METHOD select PRINCIPAL COMPONENTS (default). In the ANALYZE box, check CORRELATION MATRIX. In the EXTRACT box, select BASED ON EIGENVALUE and enter 1 in EIGENVALUES GREATER THAN box. In the DISPLAY box check UNROTATED FACTOR SOLUTION. Click CONTINUE.
6 Click ROTATION. In the METHOD box check VARIMAX. In the display box check ROTATED SOLUTION. Click CONTINUE.
7 Click SCORES. In the pop-up window, check DISPLAY FACTOR SCORE COEFFICIENT MATRIX. Click CONTINUE.
8 Click OK.

The procedure for running common factor analysis is similar, except that, in step 5, for METHOD select PRINCIPAL AXIS FACTORING.

SAS Learning Edition

The instructions given here and in all the quantitative data analysis chapters will work with the SAS Learning Edition as well as with the SAS Enterprise Guide. For a point-and-click approach for performing principal components analysis and factor analysis, use the Analyze task within the SAS Learning Edition. The Multivariate>Factor Analysis task performs both principal components analysis and factor analysis. The Multivariate>Principal Components task also performs principal components analysis. To select this task click

Analyze>Multivariate>Factor Analysis . . .

The following are the detailed steps for running principal components analysis on the toothpaste attribute ratings (V_1 to V_6) using the data in Table 21.2:

1 Select ANALYZE from the SAS Learning Edition menu bar.
2 Click MULTIVARIATE and then FACTOR ANALYSIS.
3 Move V_1–V_6 to the ANALYSIS variables task role.
4 Click FACTORING METHOD and change the SMALLEST EIGENVALUE to 1.
5 Click ROTATION AND PLOTS and select ORTHOGONAL VARIMAX as the Rotation method and the SCREE PLOT under the PLOTS TO SHOW.
6 Click RESULTS and EIGENVECTORS, FACTOR SCORING COEFFICIENTS under FACTOR RESULTS, and MEANS AND STANDARD DEVIATIONS of input columns, CORRELATION MATRIX of input columns and KAISER'S MEASURE OF SAMPLING ADEQUACY under RELATED STATISTICS.
7 Click RUN.

The procedure for running common factor analysis is similar, except that, in step 5, select PRINCIPAL AXIS FACTORING as the ROTATION METHOD.

Summary

Factor analysis, also called exploratory factor analysis (EFA), is a class of procedures used for reducing and summarising data. Each variable is expressed as a linear combination of the underlying factors. Likewise, the factors themselves can be expressed as linear combinations of the observed variables. The factors are extracted in such a way that the first factor accounts for the highest variance in the data, the second for the next highest, and so on. Additionally, it is possible to extract the factors so that the factors are uncorrelated, as in principal components analysis.

In formulating the factor analysis problem, the variables to be included in the analysis should be specified based on past research, theory and the judgement of the researcher. These variables should be measured on an interval or ratio scale. Factor analysis is based on a matrix of correlation between the variables. The appropriateness of the correlation matrix for factor analysis can be statistically tested.

The two basic approaches to factor analysis are principal components analysis and common factor analysis. In principal components analysis, the total variance in the data is considered. Principal components analysis is recommended when the researcher's primary concern is to determine the minimum number of factors that will account for maximum variance in the data for use in subsequent multivariate analysis. In common factor analysis, the factors are estimated based only on the common variance. This method is appropriate when the primary concern is to identify the underlying dimensions and when the common variance is of interest. This method is also known as principal axis factoring.

The number of factors that should be extracted can be determined a priori or based on eigenvalues, scree plots, percentage of variance, split-half reliability or significance tests. Although the initial or unrotated factor matrix indicates the relationships between the factors and individual variables, it seldom results in factors that can be interpreted, because the factors are correlated with many variables. Therefore, rotation is used to transform the factor matrix into a simpler one that is easier to interpret. The most commonly used method of rotation is the varimax procedure, which results in orthogonal factors. If the factors are highly correlated in the population, oblique rotation can be used. The rotated factor matrix forms the basis for interpreting the factors.

Factor scores can be computed for each participant. Alternatively, surrogate variables may be selected by examining the factor matrix and selecting for each factor a variable with the highest or near highest loading. The differences between the observed correlations and the reproduced correlations, as estimated from the factor matrix, can be examined to determine model fit.

Questions

1   How is factor analysis different from multiple regression and discriminant analysis?

2   What are the major uses of factor analysis?

3   Describe the factor analysis model.

4   What hypothesis is examined by Bartlett's test of sphericity? For what purpose is this test used?

5   What is meant by the term 'communality of a variable'?

6   Briefly define the following: eigenvalue, factor loadings, factor matrix and factor scores.

7 For what purpose is the Kaiser–Meyer–Olkin measure of sampling adequacy used?

8 What is the major difference between principal components analysis and common factor analysis?

9 Explain how eigenvalues are used to determine the number of factors.

10 What is a scree plot? For what purpose is it used?

11 Why is it useful to rotate the factors? Which is the most common method of rotation?

12 What guidelines are available for interpreting the factors?

13 When is it useful to calculate factor scores?

14 What are surrogate variables? How are they determined?

15 How is the fit of the factor analysis model examined?

Exercises

1 Complete the following portion of an output from principal components analysis:

Variable	Communality	Factor	Eigenvalue	% of variance
V_1	1.0	1	3.25	
V_2	1.0	2	1.78	
V_3	1.0	3	1.23	
V_4	1.0	4	0.78	
V_5	1.0	5	0.35	
V_6	1.0	6	0.30	
V_7	1.0	7	0.19	
V_8	1.0	8	0.12	

a Draw a scree plot based on these data.

b How many factors should be extracted? Explain your reasoning.

2 In a study of the relationship between household behaviour and shopping behaviour, data on the following lifestyle statements were obtained on a seven-point scale (1 = disagree, 7 = agree):

V_1 I would rather spend a quiet evening at home than go out to a party.
V_2 I always check prices, even on small items.
V_3 Magazines are more interesting than movies.
V_4 I would not buy products advertised on billboards.
V_5 I am a homebody.
V_6 I save and cash coupons.
V_7 Companies waste a lot of money advertising.

The data obtained from a pretest sample of 25 participants are given below:

No.	V_1	V_2	V_3	V_4	V_5	V_6	V_7
1	6	2	7	6	5	3	5
2	5	7	5	6	6	6	4
3	5	3	4	5	6	6	7
4	3	2	2	5	1	3	2
5	4	2	3	2	2	1	3
6	2	6	2	4	3	7	5
7	1	3	3	6	2	5	7
8	3	5	1	4	2	5	6
9	7	3	6	3	5	2	4
10	6	3	3	4	4	6	5
11	6	6	2	6	4	4	7
12	3	2	2	7	6	1	6
13	5	7	6	2	2	6	1
14	6	3	5	5	7	2	3
15	3	2	4	3	2	6	5
16	2	7	5	1	4	5	2
17	3	2	2	7	2	4	6
18	6	4	5	4	7	3	3
19	7	2	6	2	5	2	1
20	5	6	6	3	4	5	3
21	2	3	3	2	1	2	6
22	3	4	2	1	4	3	6
23	2	6	3	2	1	5	3
24	6	5	7	4	5	7	2
25	7	6	5	4	6	5	3

a Analyse these data using principal components analysis, using the varimax rotation procedure.

b Interpret the factors extracted.

c Calculate factor scores for each participant.

d If surrogate variables were to be selected, which ones would you select?

e Examine the model fit.

f Analyse the data using common factor analysis, and answer parts b to e.

3 Analyse the Benetton data (taken from Exercise 4, Chapter 18). Consider only the following variables: awareness, attitude, preference, intention and loyalty towards Benetton.

a Analyse these data using principal components analysis, using the varimax rotation procedure.

b Interpret the factors extracted.

c Calculate factor scores for each participant.

d If surrogate variables were to be selected, which ones would you select?

e Examine the model fit.

f Analyse the data using common factor analysis, and answer parts b to e.

4   You are a marketing research analyst for a manufacturer of fashion clothing targeted at teenage boys. You have been asked to develop a set of 10 statements for measuring psychographic characteristics and lifestyles that you feel would relate to their fashion personas. The participants would be asked to indicate their degree of agreement with the statements using a seven-point scale (1 = completely disagree, 7 = completely agree). Question 40 students on campus using these scale items. Factor analyse the data to identify the underlying psychographic factors.

5   In a small group identify the uses of factor analysis in each of the following major decision areas in marketing:

   a Market segmentation

   b Product decisions

   c Promotions decisions

   d Pricing decisions

   e Distribution decisions

   f Service delivery decisions.

Notes

1. Magnusson, P.R., 'Benefits of involving users in service innovation', *European Journal of Innovation Management* 6 (4) (2003), 228–238; Alt, M., *Exploring Hyperspace* (New York: McGraw-Hill, 1990), 74.

2. For a detailed discussion of factor analysis, see Loehlin, J.C., *Latent Variable Models: An introduction to factor, path, and structural equation analysis* (Mahwah, NJ: Lawrence Erlbaum Associates, 2004); Tacq, J., *Multivariate Analysis Techniques in Social Science Research* (Thousand Oaks, CA: Sage, 1996); Dunteman, G.H., *Principal Components Analysis* (Newbury Park, CA: Sage, 1989). For applications, see Aaker, J.L., 'Dimensions of brand personality', *Journal of Marketing Research* 34 (August 1997), 347–356; Birks, D.F. and Birts, A.N., 'Service quality in domestic cash management banks', in Birks, D.F. (ed.), *Global Cash Management in Europe* (Basingstoke: Macmillan, 1998), 175–205. See also Cudeck, R. and MacCallum, R.C., *Factor Analysis at 100: Historical developments and future directions* (Mahwah, NJ: Lawrence Erlbaum Associates, 2007).

3. See Cudeck, R. and MacCallum, R.C., *Factor Analysis at 100: Historical developments and future directions* (Mahwah, NJ: Lawrence Erlbaum Associates, 2007); Pett, M.A., Lackey, N. and Sullivan, J., *Making Sense of Factor Analysis: The use of factor analysis for instrument development in health care research* (Thousand Oaks, CA: Sage, 2006); Ding, A.A., 'Prediction intervals, factor analysis models and high-dimensional empirical linear prediction', *Journal of the American Statistical Association* 94 (446) (June 1999), 446–455; Gaur, S., 'Adelman and Morris factor analysis of developing countries', *Journal of Policy Modeling* 19 (4) (August 1997), 407–415; Lastovicka, J.L. and Thamodaran, K., 'Common factor score estimates in multiple regression problems', *Journal*

of Marketing Research 28 (February 1991), 105–112; Dillon, W.R. and Goldstein, M., *Multivariate Analysis: Methods and Applications* (New York: Wiley, 1984), 23–99.

4. For applications of factor analysis, see Logan, K., 'Hulu. com or NBC? Streaming videos versus traditional TV: a study of an industry in its infancy', *Journal of Advertising Research* 51 (1) (2011), 276–287; Vanden Bergh, B.G., Lee, M., Quilliam, E.T. and Hove, T., 'The multidimensional nature and brand impact of user-generated ad parodies in social media', *International Journal of Advertising* 30 (1) (2011), 103–131; Bellman, S., Schweda, A. and Varan, D., 'The importance of social motives for watching and interacting with digital television', *International Journal of Market Research* 52 (1) (2010), 67–87.

5. Child, D., *The essentials of factor analysis*, 3rd edn (New York: Continuum, 2006); Bartholomew, D.J. and Knott, M., *Latent variable models and factor analysis* (London: Edward Arnold, 1999); Hair, J.E. Jr, Anderson, R.E., Tatham, R.L. and Black, W.C., *Multivariate Data Analysis with Readings*, 5th edn (Englewood Cliffs, NJ: Prentice Hall, 1999), 364–419; Basilevsky, A., *Statistical Factor Analysis and Related Methods: Theory and Applications* (New York: Wiley, 1994).

6. Factor analysis is influenced by the relative size of the correlations rather than the absolute size.

7. See Wu, J., DeSarbo, W., Chen, P.-J. and Fu, Y.-Y., 'A latent structure factor analytic approach for customer satisfaction measurement', *Marketing Letters* 17 (3) (July 2006), 221–237; Henderson, P.W., Giese, J.L. and Cote, J., 'Impression management using typeface design', *Journal of Marketing* 68 (October 2004), 60–72; Kamakura, W.A. and Wedel, M., 'Factor analysis and missing data', *Journal of Marketing Research* 37 (4) (November 2000), 490–498; Roberts, J.A.

and Beacon, D.R., 'Exploring the subtle relationships between environmental concern and ecologically conscious behavior', *Journal of Business Research* 40 (1) (September 1997), 79–89; Chatterjee, S., Jamieson, L. and Wiseman, F., 'Identifying most influential observations in factor analysis', *Marketing Science* (Spring 1991), 145–160; Acito, F. and Anderson, R.D., 'A Monte Carlo comparison of factor analytic methods', *Journal of Marketing Research* 17 (May 1980), 228–236.

8. Other methods of orthogonal rotation are also available. The quartimax method minimises the number of factors needed to explain a variable. The equimax method is a combination of varimax and quartimax.

9. Park, H., 'US retailers' cooperation with manufacturer promotional support', *Journal of Fashion Management* 8 (4) (2004), 412–424; Silva-Risso, J.M., Bucklin, R.E. and Morrison, D.G., 'A decision support system for planning manufacturers' sales promotion calendars', *Marketing Science* 18 (3) (1999), 274; Curhan, R.C. and Kopp, R.J., 'Obtaining retailer support for trade deals: key success

factors', *Journal of Advertising Research* (December 1987–January 1988), 51–60.

10. Chtourou, M.S., Chandon, J.L. and Zollinger, M., 'Effect of price information and promotion on click-through rate for internet banners', *Journal of Euromarketing* 11 (2) (2002), 23–40; Tat, P., Cunningham, W.A. III and Babakus, E., 'Consumer perceptions of rebates', *Journal of Advertising Research* (August–September 1988), 45–50.

11. Guyer, L., 'Fitting in at VW: try "Raumwunder"', *Advertising Age* 77 (16) (April 2006), S-8 (2); Hammonds, D., 'Volkswagen's new Beetle acquits itself well in sporting world', *Knight Ridder Tribune Business News* (July 23, 2004), 1.

12. Rittenburg, T., Valentine, S. and Faircloth, J., 'An ethical decision-making framework for competitor intelligence gathering', *Journal of Business Ethics* 70 (3) (February 2007), 235–245; Akaah, I.P and Riordan, E.A., 'The incidence of unethical practices in marketing research: an empirical investigation', *Journal of the Academy of Marketing Science* 18 (1990), 143–152.

23 Cluster analysis

Stage 1
Problem definition

Stage 2
Research approach developed

Stage 3
Research design developed

Stage 4
Fieldwork or data collection

Stage 5
Data integrity and analysis

Stage 6
Report preparation and presentation

Cluster analysis aims to identify and classify similar entities, based upon the characteristics they possess. It helps the researcher to understand patterns of similarity and difference that reveal naturally occurring groups.

Objectives

After reading this chapter, you should be able to:

1 describe the basic concept and scope of cluster analysis and its importance in marketing research;

2 discuss the statistics associated with cluster analysis;

3 explain the procedure for conducting cluster analysis, including formulating the problem, selecting a distance measure, selecting a clustering procedure, deciding on the number of clusters, interpreting clusters and profiling clusters;

4 describe the purpose and methods for evaluating the quality of clustering results and assessing reliability and validity;

5 discuss the applications of non-hierarchical clustering and clustering of variables;

6 appreciate how SPSS and SAS software are used in factor analysis.

Overview

Like factor analysis (Chapter 22), cluster analysis examines an entire set of interdependent relationships. Cluster analysis makes no distinction between dependent and independent variables. Rather, interdependent relationships between the whole set of variables are examined. The primary objective of cluster analysis is to classify objects into relatively homogeneous groups based on the set of variables considered. Objects in a group are relatively similar in terms of these variables and different from objects in other groups. When used in this manner, cluster analysis is the obverse of factor analysis in that it reduces the number of objects, not the number of variables, by grouping them into a much smaller number of clusters.

This chapter describes the basic concept of cluster analysis. The steps involved in conducting cluster analysis are discussed and illustrated in the context of hierarchical clustering. Then an application of non-hierarchical clustering is presented, followed by a discussion of clustering of variables. Finally, help is provided to run the SPSS and SAS Learning Editions in the data analysis challenges presented in this chapter. We begin with an example that illustrates the use of clustering to aid the process of defining target markets.

Real research　　**Ice cream 'hot spots'[1]**

Häagen-Dazs Shoppe Co. (**www.haagen-dazs.com**) with more than 850 retail ice cream shops in over 50 countries was interested in expanding its customer base. The objective was to identify potential consumer segments that could generate additional sales. It used geodemographic techniques (as discussed in Chapter 5), which are based upon clustering consumers, using geographic, demographic and lifestyle data. Additional primary data were collected to develop an understanding of the demographic, lifestyle and behavioural characteristics of Häagen-Dazs Shoppe users, which included frequency of purchase, time of day to visit café, day of the week and a range of other

product variables. The postcodes or zip codes of participants were also obtained. The participants were then assigned to 40 geodemographic clusters based upon a clustering procedure developed by Nielsen Claritas (**www.claritas.com**). Häagen-Dazs compared its profile of customers with the profile of geodemographic classifications to develop a clearer picture of the types of consumer it was attracting. From this it decided which profiles of consumer or target markets it believed to hold the most potential for additional sales. New products were developed and advertising was established and profiled to target specific consumer types.

Basic concept

Cluster analysis is a class of techniques used to classify objects or cases into relatively homogeneous groups called *clusters*. Objects in each cluster tend to be similar to each other and dissimilar to objects in the other clusters. Cluster analysis is also called *classification analysis* or numerical taxonomy.[2] We are concerned with clustering procedures that assign each object to one and only one cluster.[3] Figure 23.1 shows an ideal clustering situation in which the clusters are distinctly separated on two variables: quality consciousness (variable 1) and price sensitivity (variable 2). Note that each consumer falls into one cluster and there are no overlapping areas. Figure 23.2, on the other hand, presents a clustering situation more likely to be encountered in practice. In Figure 23.2, the boundaries for some of the clusters are not clear cut, and the classification of some consumers is not obvious, because many of them could be grouped into one cluster or another.

Figure 23.1

An ideal clustering solution

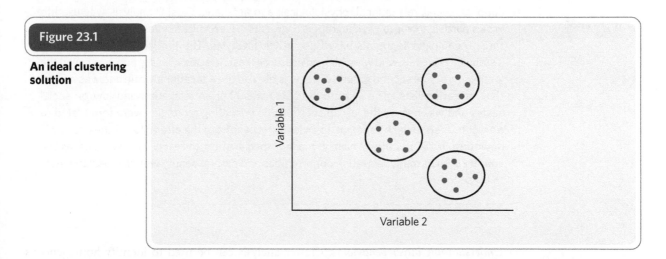

Both cluster analysis and discriminant analysis are concerned with classification. Discriminant analysis, however, requires prior knowledge of the cluster or group membership for each object or case included, to develop the classification rule. In contrast, in cluster analysis there is no a priori information about the group or cluster membership for any of the objects. Groups or clusters are suggested by the data, not defined a priori.[4] Cluster analysis has been used in marketing for a variety of purposes, including the following:[5]

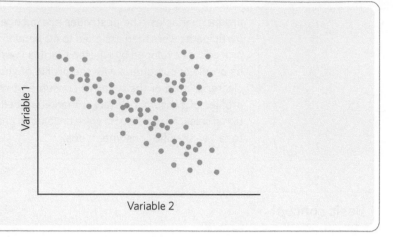

Figure 23.2

A practical clustering solution

- *Segmenting the market.* For example, consumers may be clustered on the basis of benefits sought from the purchase of a product. Each cluster would consist of consumers who are relatively homogeneous in terms of the benefits they seek.[6] This approach is called *benefit segmentation* as illustrated in the following example.

Real research   **Thailand escapists[7]**

In a study examining decision-making patterns among international tourists, 260 participants provided information on six psychographic orientations: psychological, educational, social, relaxational, physiological, and aesthetic. Cluster analysis was used to group participants into psychographic segments. The results suggested that there were three meaningful segments based upon their lifestyles. The first segment (53%) consisted of individuals who were high on nearly all lifestyle scales. This group was called the 'demanders'. The second group (20%) was high on the educational scale and was named the 'educationalists'. The last group (26%) was high on relaxation and low on social scales and was named the 'escapists'. Specific marketing strategies were formulated to attract tourists in each segment. In order to recover from the aftermath of the economic downturn in 2008–2009, Thailand made a special effort to reach the 'escapists' as the country with its many relaxation opportunities and natural beauty would appeal the most to these tourists.

- *Understanding buyer behaviours.* Cluster analysis can be used to identify homogeneous groups of buyers. Then the buying behaviour of each group may be examined separately, as can happen for example with different types of car buyers. Cluster analysis has been used to identify the kinds of strategies car buyers use to obtain information to support their buying decisions.
- *Identifying new product opportunities.* By clustering brands and products, competitive sets within the market can be determined. Brands in the same cluster compete more fiercely with each other than with brands in other clusters. A firm can examine its current offerings compared with those of its competitors to identify potential new product opportunities.
- *Selecting test markets.* By grouping cities into homogeneous clusters, it is possible to select comparable cities to test various marketing strategies.

● *Reducing data.* Cluster analysis can be used as a general data reduction tool to develop clusters or subgroups of data that are more manageable than individual observations. Subsequent multivariate analysis is conducted on the clusters rather than on the individual observations. For example, to describe differences in consumers' product usage behaviour, the consumers may first be clustered into groups. The differences among the groups may then be examined using multiple discriminant analysis.

Statistics associated with cluster analysis

Before discussing the statistics associated with cluster analysis, it should be mentioned that most clustering methods are relatively simple procedures that are not supported by an extensive body of statistical reasoning. Rather, most clustering methods are heuristics, which are based on algorithms. Thus, cluster analysis contrasts sharply with analysis of variance, regression, discriminant analysis and factor analysis, which are based upon an extensive body of statistical reasoning. Although many clustering methods have important statistical properties, the fundamental simplicity of these methods needs to be recognised.[8] The following statistics and concepts are associated with cluster analysis:

Agglomeration schedule. An agglomeration schedule gives information on the objects or cases being combined at each stage of a hierarchical clustering process.

Cluster centroid. The cluster centroid is the mean values of the variables for all the cases or objects in a particular cluster.

Cluster centres. The cluster centres are the initial starting points in non-hierarchical clustering. Clusters are built around these centres or seeds.

Cluster membership. This indicates the cluster to which each object or case belongs.

Dendrogram. A dendrogram, or tree graph, is a graphical device for displaying clustering results. Vertical lines represent clusters that are joined together. The position of the line on the scale indicates the distances at which clusters were joined. The dendrogram is read from left to right. Figure 23.8 later in this chapter is a dendrogram.

Distances between cluster centres. These distances indicate how separated the individual pairs of clusters are. Clusters that are widely separated are distinct and therefore desirable.

Icicle diagram. An icicle diagram is a graphical display of clustering results, so called because it resembles a row of icicles hanging from the eaves of a house. The columns correspond to the objects being clustered, and the rows correspond to the number of clusters. An icicle diagram is read from bottom to top. Figure 23.7 later in this chapter is an icicle diagram.

Similarity/distance coefficient matrix. A similarity/distance coefficient matrix is a lower triangular matrix containing pairwise distances between objects or cases.

Conducting cluster analysis

The steps involved in conducting cluster analysis are listed in Figure 23.3. The first step is to formulate the clustering problem by defining the variables on which the clustering will be based. Then, an appropriate distance measure must be selected. The distance measure determines how similar or dissimilar the objects being clustered are. Several clustering procedures have been developed, and the researcher should select one that is appropriate for the problem

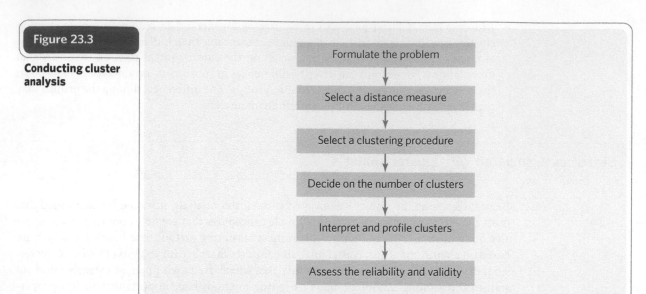

Figure 23.3

Conducting cluster analysis

at hand. Deciding on the number of clusters requires judgement on the part of the researcher. The derived clusters should be interpreted in terms of the variables used to cluster them and profiled in terms of additional salient variables. Finally, the researcher must assess the validity of the clustering process.

Formulate the problem

Perhaps the most important part of formulating the clustering problem is selecting the variables on which the clustering is based. Inclusion of even one or two irrelevant variables may distort an otherwise useful clustering solution. Basically, the set of variables selected should describe the similarity between objects in terms that are relevant to the marketing research problem. The variables should be selected based on past research, theory or a consideration of the hypotheses being developed or tested. If cluster analysis is used as an exploratory approach, the researcher naturally exercises their judgement and intuition.

To illustrate, we consider a clustering of consumers based on attitudes towards shopping. Based on past research, six attitudinal variables were identified as being the most relevant to the marketing research problem. Consumers were asked to express their degree of agreement with the following statements on a seven-point scale (1 = disagree, 7 = agree):

V_1 Shopping is fun.

V_2 Shopping is bad for your budget.

V_3 I combine shopping with eating out.

V_4 I try to get the best buys while shopping.

V_5 I don't care about shopping.

V_6 You can save a lot of money by comparing prices.

Data obtained from a pretest sample of 20 participants are shown in Table 23.1. Note that, in practice, clustering is done on much larger samples of 100 or more. A small sample size has been used to illustrate the clustering process.

Table 23.1	Attitudinal data for clustering					
Case number	V_1	V_2	V_3	V_4	V_5	V_6
1	6	4	7	3	2	3
2	2	3	1	4	5	4
3	7	2	6	4	1	3
4	4	6	4	5	3	6
5	1	3	2	2	6	4
6	6	4	6	3	3	4
7	5	3	6	3	3	4
8	7	3	7	4	1	4
9	2	4	3	3	6	3
10	3	5	3	6	4	6
11	1	3	2	3	5	3
12	5	4	5	4	2	4
13	2	2	1	5	4	4
14	4	6	4	6	4	7
15	6	5	4	2	1	4
16	3	5	4	6	4	7
17	4	4	7	2	2	5
18	3	7	2	6	4	3
19	4	6	3	7	2	7
20	2	3	2	4	7	2

Select a distance measure

Because the objective of clustering is to group similar objects together, some measure is needed to assess how similar or different the objects are. The most common approach is to measure similarity in terms of distance between pairs of objects. Objects with smaller distances between them are more similar to each other than are those at larger distances. There are several ways to compute the distance between two objects.[9]

Euclidean distance
The square root of the sum of the squared differences in values for each variable.

The most commonly used measure of similarity is the Euclidean distance or its square. The Euclidean distance is the square root of the sum of the squared differences in values for each variable. Other distance measures are also available. The city-block or Manhattan distance between two objects is the sum of the absolute differences in values for each variable. The *Chebychev distance* between two objects is the maximum absolute difference in values for any variable. For our example, we use the squared Euclidean distance.

If the variables are measured in vastly different units, the clustering solution will be influenced by the units of measurement. In a supermarket shopping study, attitudinal variables may be measured on a nine-point Likert-type scale; patronage, in terms of frequency of visits per month and the amount spent; and brand loyalty, in terms of percentage of grocery shopping expenditure allocated to the favourite supermarket. In these cases, before clustering participants, we must standardise the data by rescaling each variable to have a mean of 0 and a standard deviation of 1. Although standardisation can remove the influence of the unit of measurement, it can also reduce the differences between groups on variables that may best discriminate groups or clusters. It is also desirable to eliminate outliers (cases with atypical values).[10]

Use of different distance measures may lead to different clustering results. Hence, it is advisable to use different measures and to compare the results. Having selected a distance or similarity measure, we can next select a clustering procedure.

Hierarchical clustering
A clustering procedure characterised by the development of a hierarchy or treelike structure.

Agglomerative clustering
A hierarchical clustering procedure where each object starts out in a separate cluster. Clusters are formed by grouping objects into bigger and bigger clusters.

Divisive clustering
A hierarchical clustering procedure where all objects start out in one giant cluster. Clusters are formed by dividing this cluster into smaller and smaller clusters.

Linkage methods
Agglomerative methods of hierarchical clustering that cluster objects based on a computation of the distance between them.

Single linkage
A linkage method based on minimum distance or the nearest neighbour rule.

Complete linkage
A linkage method that is based on maximum distance or the farthest neighbour approach.

Select a clustering procedure

Figure 23.4 is a classification of clustering procedures. Clustering procedures can be hierarchical or non-hierarchical, or other procedures. Hierarchical clustering is characterised by the development of a hierarchy or treelike structure. Hierarchical methods can be agglomerative or divisive. Agglomerative clustering starts with each object in a separate cluster. Clusters are formed by grouping objects into bigger and bigger clusters. This process is continued until all objects are members of a single cluster. Divisive clustering starts with all the objects grouped in a single cluster. Clusters are divided or split until each object is in a separate cluster.

Agglomerative methods are commonly used in marketing research. They consist of linkage methods, error sums of squares or variance methods, and centroid methods. Linkage methods include single linkage, complete linkage and average linkage. The single linkage method is based on minimum distance or the nearest neighbour rule. The first two objects clustered are those that have the smallest distance between them. The next shortest distance is identified, and either the third object is clustered with the first two or a new two-object cluster is formed. At every stage, the distance between two clusters is the distance between their two closest points (see Figure 23.5). Two clusters are merged at any stage by the single shortest link between them. This process is continued until all objects are in one cluster. The single linkage method does not work well when the clusters are poorly defined. The complete linkage method is similar to single linkage, except that it is based on the maximum distance or the farthest neighbour approach. In complete linkage, the distance between two clusters is calculated as the distance between their two farthest points (see Figure 23.5). The average linkage method works similarly. In this method, however, the distance between two clusters is defined as the average of the distances between all pairs of objects, where one member of the pair is from each of the clusters (Figure 23.5). As can be seen, the average linkage method uses information on all pairs of distances, not merely the minimum or maximum distances. For this reason, it is usually preferred to the single and complete linkage methods.

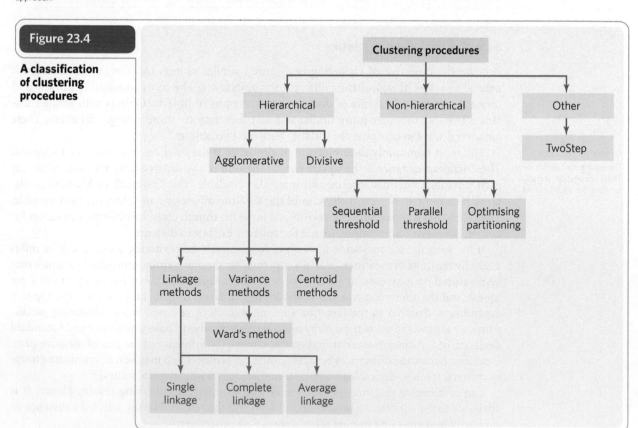

Figure 23.4

A classification of clustering procedures

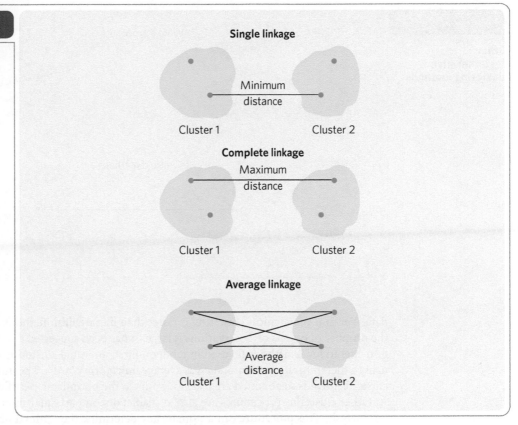

Figure 23.5

Linkage methods of clustering

Average linkage

A linkage method based on the average distance between all pairs of objects, where one member of the pair is from each of the clusters.

Variance method

An agglomerative method of hierarchical clustering in which clusters are generated to minimise the within-cluster variance.

Ward's procedure

A variance method in which the squared Euclidean distance to the cluster means is minimised.

Centroid methods

A method of hierarchical clustering in which clusters are generated so as to maximise the distances between the centres or centroids of clusters.

Non-hierarchical clustering

A procedure that first assigns or determines a cluster centre and then groups all objects within a pre-specified threshold value from the centre(s).

Sequential threshold method

A non-hierarchical clustering method in which a cluster centre is selected and all objects within a pre-specified threshold value from the centre are grouped together.

Parallel threshold method

A non-hierarchical clustering method that specifies several cluster centres at once. All objects that are within a pre-specified threshold value from the centre are grouped together.

Optimising partitioning method

A non-hierarchical clustering method that allows for later reassignment of objects to clusters to optimise an overall criterion.

The variance methods attempt to generate clusters to minimise the within-cluster variance. A commonly used variance method is Ward's procedure. For each cluster, the means for all the variables are computed. Then, for each object, the squared Euclidean distance to the cluster means is calculated (Figure 23.6), and these distances are summed for all the objects. At each stage, the two clusters with the smallest increase in the overall sum of squares within cluster distances are combined. In the centroid method, the distance between two clusters is the distance between their centroids (means for all the variables), as shown in Figure 23.6. Every time objects are grouped, a new centroid is computed. Of the hierarchical methods, the average linkage method and Ward's procedure have been shown to perform better than the other procedures.[11]

The second type of clustering procedures, the non-hierarchical clustering methods, are frequently referred to as k-means clustering. These methods include sequential threshold, parallel threshold and optimising partitioning. In the sequential threshold method, a cluster centre is selected and all objects within a pre-specified threshold value from the centre are grouped together. A new cluster centre or seed is then selected, and the process is repeated for the unclustered points. Once an object is clustered with a seed, it is no longer considered for clustering with subsequent seeds. The parallel threshold method operates similarly except that several cluster centres are selected simultaneously and objects within the threshold level are grouped with the nearest centre. The optimising partitioning method differs from the two threshold procedures in that objects can later be reassigned to clusters to optimise an overall criterion, such as average within-cluster distance for a given number of clusters.

Two major disadvantages of the non-hierarchical procedures are that the number of clusters must be pre-specified and that the selection of cluster centres is arbitrary. Furthermore, the clustering results may depend on how the centres are selected. Many non-hierarchical programs select the first k cases (k = number of clusters) without missing values as initial cluster centres. Thus, the clustering results may depend on the order of observations in the

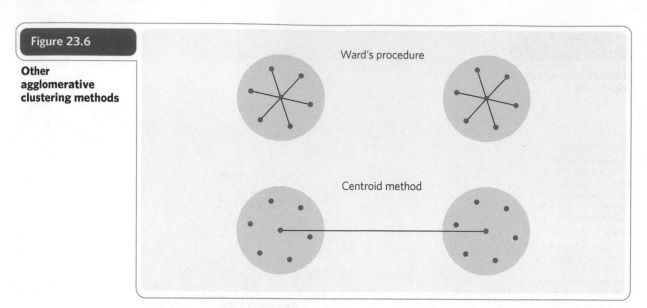

Figure 23.6

Other agglomerative clustering methods

Ward's procedure

Centroid method

data. Yet non-hierarchical clustering is faster than hierarchical methods and has merit when the number of objects or observations is large. It has been suggested that the hierarchical and non-hierarchical methods be used in tandem. First, an initial clustering solution is obtained using a hierarchical procedure, such as average linkage or Ward's. The number of clusters and cluster centroids so obtained are used as inputs to the optimising partitioning method.[12]

Other clustering procedures are also available; one of particular interest is TwoStep cluster analysis. This procedure can automatically determine the optimal number of clusters by comparing the values of model-choice criteria across different clustering solutions. It also has the ability to create cluster models based on categorical and continuous variables. In addition to Euclidean distance, the TwoStep procedure also uses the log-likelihood measure. The log-likelihood measure places a probability distribution on the variables. It also accommodates two clustering criteria: Schwarz's Bayesian Information Criterion (BIC) or the Akaike Information Criterion (AIC).[13]

The choice of a clustering method and the choice of a distance measure are interrelated. For example, squared Euclidean distances should be used with Ward's and the centroid methods. Several non-hierarchical procedures also use squared Euclidean distances. In the TwoStep procedure, the Euclidean measure can be used only when all of the variables are continuous.

We will use Ward's procedure to illustrate hierarchical clustering. The output obtained by clustering the data of Table 23.1 is given in Table 23.2. Useful information is contained in the agglomeration schedule, which shows the number of cases or clusters being combined at each stage. The first line represents stage 1, with 19 clusters. Participants 14 and 16 are combined at this stage, as shown in the columns labelled 'Clusters combined'. The squared Euclidean distance between these two participants is given under the column labelled 'Coefficients'. The columns entitled 'Stage cluster first appears' indicate the stage at which a cluster is first formed. To illustrate, an entry of 1 at stage 6 indicates that participant 14 was first grouped at stage 1. The last column, 'Next stage', indicates the stage at which another case (participant) or cluster is combined with this one. Because the number in the first line of the last column is 6, we see that, at stage 6, participant 10 is combined with 14 and 16 to form a single cluster. Similarly, the second line represents stage 2 with 18 clusters. In stage 2, participants 6 and 7 are grouped together.

Another important part of the output is contained in the icicle plot given in Figure 23.7. The columns correspond to the objects being clustered; in this case, they are the participants labelled 1 to 20. The rows correspond to the number of clusters. This figure is read from bottom

Table 23.2	Results of hierarchical clustering

Case processing summary[a,b]

Valid		Missing		Total	
N	*%*	*N*	*%*	*N*	*%*
20	100.0	0	0.0	20	100.0

[a] Squared Euclidean distance used.
[b] Ward linkage.

Ward linkage: agglomeration schedule

	Clusters combined			Stage cluster first appears		
Stage	Cluster 1	Cluster 2	Coefficients	Cluster 1	Cluster 2	Next stage
1	14	16	1.000	0	0	6
2	6	7	2.000	0	0	7
3	2	13	3.500	0	0	15
4	5	11	5.000	0	0	11
5	3	8	6.500	0	0	16
6	10	14	8.167	0	1	9
7	6	12	10.500	2	0	10
8	9	20	13.000	0	0	11
9	4	10	15.583	0	6	12
10	1	6	18.500	0	7	13
11	5	9	23.000	4	8	15
12	4	19	27.750	9	0	17
13	1	17	33.100	10	0	14
14	1	15	41.333	13	0	16
15	2	5	51.833	3	11	18
16	1	3	64.500	14	5	19
17	4	18	79.667	12	0	18
18	2	4	172.667	15	17	19
19	1	2	328.600	16	18	0

Cluster membership

	Number of clusters		
Case	Four clusters	Three clusters	Two clusters
1	1	1	1
2	2	2	2
3	1	1	1
4	3	3	2
5	2	2	2
6	1	1	1
7	1	1	1
8	1	1	1
9	2	2	2
10	3	3	2
11	2	2	2
12	1	1	1
13	2	2	2
14	3	3	2
15	1	1	1
16	3	3	2
17	1	1	1
18	4	3	2
19	3	3	2
20	2	2	2

Figure 23.7 | **Vertical icicle plot using Ward's procedure**

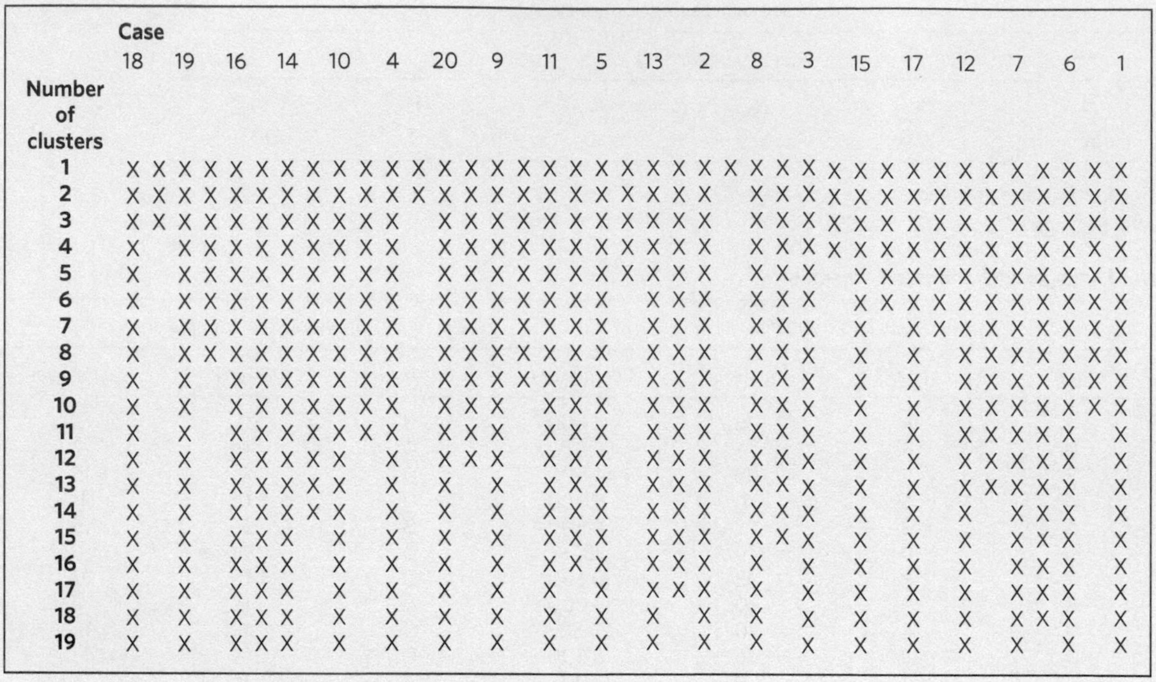

```
          Case
          18  19  16  14  10  4  20  9  11  5  13  2  8  3  15  17  12  7  6  1
Number
  of
clusters
   1   X X X X X X X X X X X X X X X X X X X X X X X X X X X X X X X X X X X X X X X
   2   X X X X X X X X X X X X X X X X X X X X X X X X X X X   X X X X X X X X X X X X X X X X
   3   X X X X X X X X X X X       X X X X X X X X X X X X X   X X X X X X X X X X X X X X X
   4   X   X X X X X X X X X       X X X X X X X X X X X X X   X X X X X X X X X X X X X X X
   5   X   X X X X X X X X X       X X X X X X X X X X X X X   X X X   X X X X X X X X X X X
   6   X   X X X X X X X X X       X X X X X X X   X X X       X X X   X X X X X X X X X
   7   X   X X X X X X X X X       X X X X X X X   X X X       X X X   X     X X X X X X X X
   8   X   X X X X X X X X X       X X X X X X X   X X X       X X X   X     X     X X X X X X X
   9   X   X     X X X X X X X     X X X X X X X   X X X       X X X   X     X     X X X X X X X
  10   X   X     X X X X X X X     X X X         X X X       X X X   X     X     X X X X X X X
  11   X   X     X X X X X X X     X X X         X X X       X X X   X     X     X X X X X   X
  12   X   X     X X X X X X X     X X X         X X X       X X X   X     X     X X X X X   X
  13   X   X     X X X X X X       X     X     X     X X X       X X X   X X   X     X     X X X       X
  14   X   X     X X X X X X       X     X     X     X X X       X X X   X     X     X     X X X       X
  15   X   X     X X X X         X     X     X     X X X       X X X   X     X     X     X X X       X
  16   X   X     X X X X         X     X     X     X X X       X X X   X     X     X     X X X       X
  17   X   X     X X X X         X     X     X     X     X     X X X       X     X     X     X     X X X       X
  18   X   X     X X X X         X     X     X     X     X     X     X       X     X     X     X     X X X       X
  19   X   X     X X X X         X     X     X     X     X     X     X       X     X     X     X     X     X       X
```

to top. At first, all cases are considered as individual clusters. Since there are 20 participants, there are 20 initial clusters. At the first step, the two closest objects are combined, resulting in 19 clusters. The last line of Figure 23.7 shows these 19 clusters. The two cases, participants 14 and 16, that have been combined at this stage have no blank space separating them. Row number 18 corresponds to the next stage, with 18 clusters. At this stage, participants 6 and 7 are grouped together. Thus, at this stage there are 18 clusters; 16 of them consist of individual participants, and 2 contain two participants each. Each subsequent step leads to the formation of a new cluster in one of three ways: (1) two individual cases are grouped together, (2) a case is joined to an already existing cluster, or (3) two clusters are grouped together.

Another graphic device that is useful in displaying clustering results is the dendrogram (see Figure 23.8). The dendrogram is read from left to right. Vertical lines represent clusters that are joined together. The position of the line on the scale indicates the distances at which clusters were joined. Because many distances in the early stages are of similar magnitude, it is difficult to tell the sequence in which some of the early clusters are formed. It is clear, however, that in the last two stages, the distances at which the clusters are being combined are large. This information is useful in deciding on the number of clusters.

It is also possible to obtain information on cluster membership of cases if the number of clusters is specified. Although this information can be discerned from the icicle plot, a tabular display is helpful. Table 23.2 contains the cluster membership for the cases, depending on whether the final solution contains two, three or four clusters. Information of this type can be obtained for any number of clusters and is useful for deciding on the number of clusters.

Decide on the number of clusters

A major issue in cluster analysis is deciding on the number of clusters. Although there are no hard and fast rules, some guidelines are available:

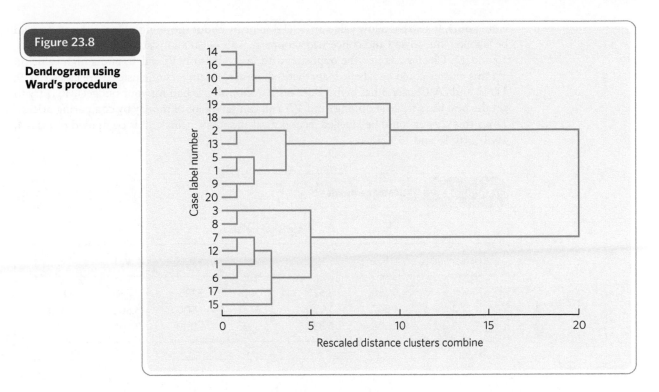

Figure 23.8

Dendrogram using Ward's procedure

1   Theoretical, conceptual or practical considerations may suggest a certain number of clusters. For example, if the purpose of clustering is to identify market segments, management may want a particular number of clusters.

2   In hierarchical clustering, the distances at which clusters are combined can be used as criteria. This information can be obtained from the agglomeration schedule or from the dendrogram. In our case, we see from the agglomeration schedule in Table 23.2 that the value in the 'Coefficients' column suddenly more than doubles between stages 17 (three clusters) and 18 (two clusters). Likewise, at the last two stages of the dendrogram in Figure 23.8, the clusters are being combined at large distances. Therefore, it appears that a three-cluster solution is appropriate.

3   In non-hierarchical clustering, the ratio of total within-group variance to between-group variance can be plotted against the number of clusters. The point at which an elbow or a sharp bend occurs indicates an appropriate number of clusters. Increasing the number of clusters beyond this point is usually not worthwhile.

4   The relative sizes of the clusters should be meaningful. In Table 23.2, by making a simple frequency count of cluster membership, we see that a three-cluster solution results in clusters with eight, six and six elements. If we go to a four-cluster solution, however, the sizes of the clusters are eight, six, five and one. It is not meaningful to have a cluster with only one case, so a three-cluster solution is preferable in this situation.

Interpret and profile clusters

Interpreting and profiling clusters involves examining the cluster centroids. The centroids represent the mean values of the objects contained in the cluster on each of the variables. The centroids enable us to describe each cluster by assigning it a name or label. If the clustering program does not print this information, it may be obtained through discriminant analysis. Table 23.3 gives the centroids or mean values for each cluster in our example. Cluster 1 has relatively high values on variables V_1 (Shopping is fun) and V_3 (I combine shopping with eating out). It also has a low value on V_5 (I don't care about shopping). Hence cluster 1 could be labelled 'fun-loving and concerned shoppers'. This cluster consists of cases 1, 3, 6, 7, 8, 12, 15 and 17. Cluster 2 is just the opposite, with low values on V_1 and V_3 and a high value on V_5; this cluster could be labelled 'apathetic shoppers'. Members of cluster 2 are cases 2, 5, 9, 11, 13 and 20. Cluster 3 has high values on V_2 (Shopping is bad for your budget), V_4 (I try to get the best buys while shopping) and V_6 (You can save a lot of money by comparing prices). Thus, this cluster could be labelled 'economical shoppers'. Cluster 3 is composed of cases 4, 10, 14, 16, 18 and 19.

Table 23.3	Cluster centroids					
	Means of variables					
Cluster number	V_1	V_2	V_3	V_4	V_5	V_6
1	5.750	3.625	6.000	3.125	1.750	3.875
2	1.667	3.000	1.833	3.500	5.500	3.333
3	3.500	5.833	3.333	6.000	3.500	6.000

It is often helpful to profile the clusters in terms of variables that were not used for clustering, such as demographic, psychographic, product usage, media usage or other variables. For example, the clusters may have been derived based on benefits sought. Further profiling may be done in terms of demographic and psychographic variables to target marketing efforts for each cluster. The variables that significantly differentiate between clusters can be identified via discriminant analysis and one-way analysis of variance.

Assess the reliability and validity

Given the several judgements entailed in cluster analysis, no clustering solution should be accepted without some assessment of its reliability and validity. Formal procedures for assessing the reliability and validity of clustering solutions are complex and not fully defensible.[14] Hence, we omit them here. The following procedures, however, provide adequate checks on the quality of clustering results. These are vital if managers are to appreciate what constitutes robust clustering solutions.[15]

1 Perform cluster analysis on the same data using different distance measures. Compare the results across measures to determine the stability of the solutions.

2 Use different methods of clustering and compare the results.

3 Split the data randomly into halves. Perform clustering separately on each half. Compare cluster centroids across the two subsamples.

4 Delete variables randomly. Perform clustering based on the reduced set of variables. Compare the results with those obtained by clustering based on the entire set of variables.

5 In non-hierarchical clustering, the solution may depend on the order of cases in the dataset. Make multiple runs using different order of cases until the solution stabilises.

We further illustrate hierarchical clustering with a study of differences in marketing strategy among British, Japanese and American companies.

It is a small world[16]

Data for a study of Bristish, Japanese and American competitors were obtained from detailed face-to-face interviews with chief executives and top marketing decision-makers for defined product groups in 90 companies. To control for market differences, the methodology was based upon matching 30 British companies with their major Japanese and American competitors in the British market. The study involved 30 triads of companies, each composed of a British, Japanese and American business that competed directly with one another. Most of the data on the characteristics of the companies' performance, strat-

egy and organisation were collected on five-point semantic differential scales. The first stage of the analysis involved factor analysis of variables describing the firms' strategies and marketing activities. The factor scores were used to identify groups of similar companies using Ward's hierarchical clustering routine. A six-cluster solution was developed.

Cluster	I	II	III	IV	V	VI
Name	Innovators	Quality marketers	Price promoters	Product marketers	Mature marketers	Aggressive pushers
Size	22	11	14	13	13	17
Successful (%)	55	100	36	38	77	41
Nationality (%)						
British	23	18	64	38	31	29
Japanese	59	46	22	31	15	18
American	18	36	14	31	54	53

Membership in the six clusters was then interpreted against the original performance, strategy and organisational variables. All the clusters contained some successful companies, although some contained significantly more than others. The clusters lent support to the hypothesis that successful companies were similar irrespective of nationality, since British, Japanese and American companies were found in all the clusters. There was, however, a preponderance of Japanese companies in the more successful clusters and a predominance of British companies in the two least successful clusters. Apparently, Japanese companies did not deploy strategies that were unique to them; rather, more of them pursued strategies that worked effectively in the British market. The findings indicated that there were generic strategies that described successful companies irrespective of their industry. Three successful strategies could be identified. The first is the quality marketing strategy. These companies had strengths in marketing and research and development. They concentrated their technical developments on achieving high quality rather than pure innovation. These companies were characterised by entrepreneurial organisations, long-range planning and a well-communicated sense of mission. The second generic strategy was that of the innovators who are weaker on advanced research and development but were entrepreneurial and driven by a quest for innovation. The last successful group were the mature marketers, who were highly profit oriented and had in-depth marketing skills. All three appeared to consist of highly marketing-oriented businesses.

Applications of non-hierarchical clustering

We illustrate the non-hierarchical procedure using the data in Table 23.1 and an optimising partitioning method. Based on the results of hierarchical clustering, a three-cluster solution was pre-specified. The results are presented in Table 23.4.

Table 23.4	Results of non-hierarchical clustering

Initial cluster centres

	Cluster		
	1	**2**	**3**
V_1	4	2	7
V_2	6	3	2
V_3	3	2	6
V_4	7	4	4
V_5	2	7	1
V_6	7	2	3

Iteration history*
Change in cluster centres

Iteration	**1**	**2**	**3**
1	2.154	2.102	2.550
2	0.000	0.000	0.000

*Convergence achieved due to no or small distance change. The maximum distance by which any centre has changed is 0.000. The current iteration is 2. The minimum distance between initial centres is 7.746.

Cluster membership

Case number	Cluster	Distance
1	3	1.414
2	2	1.323
3	3	2.550
4	1	1.404
5	2	1.848
6	3	1.225
7	3	1.500
8	3	2.121
9	2	1.756
10	1	1.143
11	2	1.041
12	3	1.581
13	2	2.598
4	1	1.404
15	3	2.828
16	1	1.624
17	3	2.598
18	1	3.555
19	1	2.154
20	2	2.102

Table 23.4	Continued

Final cluster centres

	Cluster		
	1	2	3
V_1	4	2	6
V_2	6	3	4
V_3	3	2	6
V_4	6	4	3
V_5	4	6	2
V_6	6	3	4

Distances between final cluster centres

Cluster	1	2	3
1	0.000		
2	5.568	0.000	
3	5.698	6.928	0.000

Analysis of variance

Variable	Cluster Mean Square	df	Error Mean Square	df	F	Sig.
V_1	29.108	2	0.608	17	47.888	0.000
V_2	13.546	2	0.630	17	21.505	0.000
V_3	31.392	2	0.833	17	37.670	0.000
V_4	15.713	2	0.728	17	21.585	0.000
V_5	22.537	2	0.816	17	27.614	0.000
V_6	12.171	2	1.071	17	11.363	0.001

The F tests should be used only for descriptive purposes because the clusters have been chosen to maximise the differences among cases in different clusters. The observed significance levels are not corrected for this and thus cannot be interpreted as tests of the hypothesis that the cluster means are equal.

Number of cases in each cluster

Cluster	
1	6
2	6
3	8
Missing	0
Total	20

The 'Initial cluster centres' are the values of three randomly selected cases. In some programs, the first three cases are selected. The classification cluster centres are interim centres used for the assignment of cases. Each case is assigned to the nearest classification cluster centre. The classification centres are updated until the stopping criteria are reached. The 'Final cluster centres' represent the variable means for the cases in the final clusters. In SPSS Windows, these are rounded to the nearest integer.

Table 23.4 also displays 'Cluster membership' and the distance between each case and its classification centre. Note that the cluster memberships given in Table 23.2 (hierarchical clustering) and Table 23.4 (non-hierarchical clustering) are identical. (Cluster 1 of Table 23.2 is labelled cluster 3 in Table 23.4, and cluster 3 of Table 23.2 is labelled cluster 1 in Table 23.4.) The 'Distances between the final cluster centres' indicate that the pairs of clusters are well separated. The univariate F test for each clustering variable is presented. These F tests are only descriptive. Because the cases or objects are systematically assigned to clusters to maximise differences on the clustering variables, the resulting probabilities should not be interpreted as testing the null hypothesis of no differences among clusters.

The following example of hospital choice further illustrates non-hierarchical clustering.

Real research	**Segmentation with surgical precision**[17]

Cluster analysis was used to classify and segment participants, based upon their preferences for hospitals that provide inpatient care. The clustering was based on the reasons participants gave for preferring a particular hospital. The demographic profiles of the grouped participants were compared to learn whether the segments could be identified more efficiently. The k-means clustering method (SPSS) was used for grouping the participants based on their answers to the hospital preference items. The squared Euclidean distances between all clustering variables were minimised. Because different individuals perceive scales of importance differently, each individual's ratings were normalised before clustering. The results indicated that the participants could be best classified into four clusters. The cross-validation procedure for cluster analysis was run twice, on halves of the total sample. As expected, the four groups differed substantially by their distributions and average responses to the reasons for their hospital preferences. The names assigned to the four groups reflected the demographic characteristics and reasons for hospital preferences: 'old-fashioned', 'affluent', 'value conscious' and 'professional want-it-alls'.

Applications of TwoStep clustering

The data of Table 23.1 were also analysed using the TwoStep procedure in SPSS. Since all of the variables were continuous, we used the Euclidean distance measure. The clustering criterion was the Akaike Information Criterion (AIC). The number of clusters was determined automatically. The results are shown in Table 23.5. As can be seen, the three-cluster solution was obtained, similar to that in hierarchical and non-hierarchical clustering. Note that the AIC is at a minimum (97.594) for a three-cluster solution. A comparison of cluster centroids in Table 23.5 with those in Table 23.3 shows that cluster 1 of Table 23.5 corresponds to cluster 2 in Table 23.3 (hierarchical clustering), cluster 2 of Table 23.5 corresponds to cluster 3 of Table 23.3 and cluster 3 of TwoStep corresponds to cluster 1. The interpretation and implications are similar to those discussed earlier. In this case all three methods (hierarchical, non-hierarchical and TwoStep) give similar results. In other cases, different methods may yield different results. It is a good idea to analyse a given dataset using different methods to examine the stability of clustering solutions.

Table 23.5	Results of TwoStep clustering

Auto-clustering

Number of clusters	Akaike's information criterion (AIC)	AIC change[a]	Ratio of AIC changes[b]	Ratio of distance measures[c]
1	104.140			
2	101.171	−2.969	1.000	0.847
3	97.594	−3.577	1.205	1.583
4	116.896	19.302	−6.502	2.115
5	138.230	21.335	−7.187	1.222
6	158.586	20.355	−6.857	1.021
7	179.340	20.755	−6.991	1.224
8	201.628	22.288	−7.508	1.006
9	224.055	22.426	−7.555	1.111
10	246.522	22.467	−7.568	1.588
11	269.570	23.048	−7.764	1.001
12	292.718	23.148	−7.798	1.055
13	316.120	23.402	−7.883	1.002
14	339.223	23.103	−7.782	1.044
15	362.650	23.427	−7.892	1.004

[a] The changes are from the previous number of clusters in the table.
[b] The ratios of changes are relative to the change for the two-cluster solution.
[c] The rations of distance measures are based on the current number of clusters against the previous number of clusters.

Cluster distribution

Cluster	N	% of combined	% of total
1	6	30	30
2	6	30	30
3	8	40	40
Combined	20	100	100
Total	20		100

Centroids

Cluster	Fun		Bad for budget	
	Mean	Std deviation	Mean	Std deviation
1	1.67	0.516	3.00	0.632
2	3.50	0.548	5.83	0.753
3	5.75	1.035	3.63	0.916
Combined	3.85	1.899	4.10	1.410

| Table 23.5 | Continued |

Centroids

| | Eating out | | Best buys | |
Cluster	Mean	Std deviation	Mean	Std deviation
1	1.83	0.753	3.50	1.049
2	3.33	0.816	6.00	0.632
3	6.00	1.089	3.13	0.835
Combined	3.95	2.012	4.10	1.518

Centroids

| | Don't care | | Compare prices | |
Cluster	Mean	Std deviation	Mean	Std deviation
1	5.50	1.049	3.33	0.816
2	3.50	0.837	6.00	1.549
3	1.80	0.835	3.88	0.641
Combined	3.45	1.761	4.35	1.496

Clustering variables

Sometimes cluster analysis is also used for clustering variables to identify homogeneous groups. In this instance, the units used for analysis are the variables, and the distance measures are computed for all pairs of variables. For example, the correlation coefficient, either the absolute value or with the sign, can be used as a measure of similarity (the opposite of distance) between variables.

Hierarchical clustering of variables can aid in the identification of unique variables, or variables that make a unique contribution to the data. Clustering can also be used to reduce the number of variables. Associated with each cluster is a linear combination of the variables in the cluster, called the *cluster component*. A large set of variables can often be replaced by the set of cluster components with little loss of information. A given number of cluster components does not generally explain as much variance as the same number of principal components, however. Why, then, should the clustering of variables be used? Cluster components are usually easier to interpret than the principal components, even if the latter are rotated.[18] We illustrate the clustering of variables with an example from advertising research.

Real research	**Feelings – nothing more than feelings[19]**

As it faced stiff competition in digital cameras, Nikon (**www.nikon.com**) was marketing its Coolpix line with the tag lines 'passion made powerful', 'brilliance made beautiful' and 'memories made easy'. The advertising campaign was designed to evoke emotional feelings in consumers. Nikon based this campaign on a study conducted to identify feelings that were intuitively evoked. A total of 655 feelings were reduced to a set of 180 that were judged by participants to be most
likely to be stimulated by advertising. This group was clustered on the basis of judgements of similarity between feelings resulting in 31 'feelings' clusters. These were divided into 16 positive and 15 negative clusters, as shown in the table.

Positive feelings		Negative feelings	
1	Playful/childish	1	Fear
2	Friendly	2	Bad/sick
3	Humorous	3	Confused
4	Delighted	4	Indifferent
5	Interested	5	Bored
6	Strong/confident	6	Sad
7	Warm/tender	7	Anxious
8	Relaxed	8	Helpless/timid
9	Energetic/impulsive	9	Ugly/stupid
10	Eager/excited	10	Pity/deceived
11	Contemplative	11	Mad
12	Pride	12	Disagreeable
13	Persuaded/expectant	13	Disgusted
14	Vigorous/challenged	14	Irritated
15	Amazed	15	Moody/frustrated
16	Set/informed		

Thus, 655 feelings responses to advertising were reduced to a core set of 31 feelings. In this way, advertisers now have a manageable set of feelings for understanding and measuring responses to advertising. When measured, these feelings can provide information on a commercial's ability to persuade target consumers, as in the case of Nikon cameras.

Cluster analysis in its various forms is a widely used technique as further illustrated in the following two examples. The first example illustrates an application in the context of international marketing research. The second example shows how cluster analysis can be used in researching ethical evaluations.

Real research

Perceived product parity – once rarity, now reality[20]

How do consumers in different countries perceive brands in different product categories? Surprisingly, the answer is that the product perception parity rate is quite high. Perceived product parity means that consumers perceive all/most of the brands in a product category as similar to each other, or at par. A study by BBDO Worldwide (**www.bbdo.com**) showed that two-thirds of consumers surveyed in 28 countries considered brands in 13 product categories to be at parity. The product categories ranged from airlines to credit cards to coffee. Perceived parirty averaged 63% for all categories in all countries. The Japanese had the highest perception of parity across all product categories at 99%, and the Colombians the lowest at 28%. Viewed by product category, credit cards had the highest parity perception at 76% and cigarettes the lowest at 52%.

BBDO clustered the countries based on product parity perceptions to arrive at clusters that exhibited similar levels and patterns of parity perceptions. The highest perception parity figure came from the Asia–Pacific region (83%) that included Australia, Japan, Malaysia and South Korea, and also France. It was no surprise that France was in this list because, for most products, it used highly emotional, visual advertising that was 'feelings oriented'. The next cluster was US-influenced markets (65%) which included Argentina, Canada, Hong Kong, Kuwait, Mexico, Singapore and the USA. The third cluster, primarily European countries (60%) included Austria, Belgium, Denmark, Italy, the Netherlands, South Africa, Spain, the UK and Germany. What all this means is that in order to differentiate a brand, advertising cannot just focus on product performance, but also must relate the product to the consumer's life in an important way. Also, much greater marketing effort would be required in the Asia–Pacific region and France in order to differentiate the brand from the competition and establish a unique image.

Real research

Clustering marketing professionals based on ethical evaluations[21]

Cluster analysis can be used to explain differences in ethical perceptions by using a large multi-item, multidimensional scale developed to measure how ethical different situations are. One such scale was developed by Reidenbach and Robin.[22] This scale has 29 items that compose five dimensions that measure how a participant judges a certain action. To illustrate, a given participant will read about a researcher who has provided proprietary information on one of their clients to another client. The participant is then asked to complete the 29-item ethics scale. For example, the participant marks the following semantic differential scale to indicate if this action is:

Just   ___ : ___ : ___ : ___ : ___ : ___ Unjust
Traditionally acceptable ___ : ___ : ___ : ___ : ___ : ___ Unacceptable
Violates   ___ : ___ : ___ : ___ : ___ : ___ Does not violate an
                                                                                    unwritten contract

The scale could be administered to a sample of marketing professionals. By clustering participants based on these 29 items, two important questions could be investigated. First, how do the clusters differ with respect to five ethical dimensions that have been recognised, i.e. 'Justice', 'Relativist', 'Egoism', 'Utilitarianism' and 'Deontology'? Second, what types of firms compose each cluster? The participants in the clusters could be described in terms of their industrial category, size and profitability. Answers to these questions should provide insight into the differences between types of firms in their use of criteria to evaluate ethical situations.

SPSS and SAS Learning Editions

SPSS Windows

In SPSS, the main program for hierarchical clustering of objects or cases is HIERARCHICAL CLUSTER. Different distance measures can be computed, and all the hierarchical clustering procedures discussed here are available. For non-hierarchical clustering, the K-MEANS CLUSTER program can be used. This program is particularly helpful for clustering a large number of cases. The TWOSTEP CLUSTER procedure is also available. To select these procedure, click

Analyze>Classify>Hierarchical Cluster . . .
Analyze>Classify>K-Means Cluster . . .
Analyze>Classify>TwoStep Cluster . . .

The following are the detailed steps for running hierarchical cluster analysis on the attitudinal data (V_1 to V_6) of Table 23.1:

1 Select ANALYZE from the SPSS menu bar.
2 Click CLASSIFY and then HIERARCHICAL CLUSTER.
3 Move 'Fun [v1]', 'Bad for Budget [v2]', 'Eating Out [v3]', 'Best Buys [v4]', 'Don't Care [v5]' and 'Compare Prices [v6]' into the VARIABLES box.
4 In the CLUSTER box check CASES (default option). In the DISPLAY box check STATISTICS and PLOTS (default options).
5 Click STATISTICS. In the pop-up window, check AGGLOMERATION SCHEDULE. In the CLUSTER MEMBERSHIP box check RANGE OF SOLUTIONS. Then for MINIMUM NUMBER OF CLUSTERS enter '2', and for MAXIMUM NUMBER OF CLUSTERS enter '4'. Click CONTINUE.
6 Click PLOTS. In the pop-up window, check DENDROGRAM. In the ICICLE box check ALL CLUSTERS (default). In the ORIENTATION box, check VERTICAL. Click CONTINUE.
7 Click METHOD. For CLUSTER METHOD select WARD'S METHOD. In the MEASURE box check INTERVAL and select SQUARED EUCLIDEAN DISTANCE. Click CONTINUE.
8 Click OK.

The procedure for clustering of variables is the same as that for hierarchical clustering except that, in step 4, in the CLUSTER box check VARIABLES.

The following are the detailed steps for running non-hierarchical (k-means) cluster analysis on the attitudinal data (V_1 to V_6) of Table 23.1:

1 Select ANALYZE from the SPSS menu bar.
2 Click CLASSIFY and then K-MEANS CLUSTER.
3 Move 'Fun [v1]', 'Bad for Budget [v2]', 'Eating Out [v3]', 'Best Buys [v4]', 'Don't Care [v5]' and 'Compare Prices [v6]' into the VARIABLES box.
4 For NUMBER OF CLUSTERS select 3.
5 Click OPTIONS. In the pop-up window, in the STATISTICS box check INITIAL CLUSTER CENTERS and CLUSTER INFORMATION FOR EACH CASE. Click CONTINUE.
6 Click OK.

The following are the detailed steps for running TwoStep cluster analysis on the attitudinal data (V_1 to V_6) of Table 23.1:

1 Select ANALYZE from the SPSS menu bar.
2 Click CLASSIFY and then TWOSTEP CLUSTER.
3 Move 'Fun [v1]', 'Bad for Budget [v2]', 'Eating Out [v3]', 'Best Buys [v4]', 'Don't Care [v5]' and 'Compare Prices [v6]' into the CONTINUOUS VARIABLES box.
4 For DISTANCE MEASURE select EUCLIDEAN.
5 For NUMBER OF CLUSTERS select DETERMINE AUTOMATICALLY.
6 For CLUSTERING CRITERION select AKAIKE'S INFORMATION CRITERION (AIC).
7 Click OK.

SAS Learning Edition

The instructions given here and in all the quantitative data analysis chapters will work with the SAS Learning Edition as well as with the SAS Enterprise Guide. For a point-and-click approach for performing principal components analysis and factor analysis, use the Analyze task within the SAS Learning Edition. The Multivariate>Cluster Analysis task creates hierarchical clusters from data that contains either coordinate or distance data. If the dataset contains coordinate data, the task computes Euclidean distances before applying the clustering methods. Alternatively, the task can create non-hierarchical clusters of coordinate data by using the *k*-means methods. The task also produces dendrograms. To select this procedure click

Analyze>Multivariate>Cluster Analysis...

The following are the detailed steps for running hierarchical cluster analysis on the attitudinal data (V_1 to V_6) of Table 23.1:

1. Select ANALYZE from the SAS Learning Edition menu bar.
2. Select MULTIVARIATE>CLUSTER ANALYSIS.
3. Move V1–V6 to the ANALYSIS VARIABLES task role.
4. Click CLUSTER and select WARD'S MINIMUM VARIANCE METHOD under CLUSTER METHOD.
5. Click RESULTS and select SIMPLE SUMMARY STATISTICS.
6. Click RUN.

The following are the detailed steps for running non-hierarchical (*k*-means) cluster analysis on the attitudinal data (V_1 to V_6) of Table 23.1:

1. Select ANALYZE from the SAS Learning Edition menu bar.
2. Select MULTIVARIATE>CLUSTER ANALYSIS.
3. Move V1–V6 to the ANALYSIS VARIABLES task role.
4. Click CLUSTER and select K-MEANS ALGORITHM as the CLUSTER METHOD and 3 for the MAXIMUM NUMBER OF CLUSTERS.
5. Click RUN.

SAS does not provide TwoStep cluster analysis.

Summary

Cluster analysis is used for classifying objects or cases, and sometimes variables, into relatively homogeneous groups. The groups or clusters are suggested by the data and are not defined a priori.

The variables on which the clustering is based should be selected based on past research, theory, the hypotheses being tested, or the judgement of the researcher. An appropriate measure of distance or similarity should be selected. The most commonly used measure is the Euclidean distance or its square.

Clustering procedures may be hierarchical or non-hierarchical. Hierarchical clustering is characterised by the development of a hierarchy or treelike structure. Hierarchical methods can be agglomerative or divisive. Agglomerative methods consist of linkage methods, variance methods and centroid methods. Linkage methods are composed of single linkage, complete linkage and average linkage. A commonly used variance method is Ward's procedure. The non-hierarchical methods are frequently referred to as k-means clustering. These methods can be classified as sequential threshold, parallel threshold and optimising partitioning. Hierarchical and non-hierarchical methods can be used in tandem. The TwoStep procedure can automatically determine the optimal number of clusters by comparing the values of model-choice criteria across different clustering solutions. The choice of a clustering procedure and the choice of a distance measure are interrelated.

The number of clusters may be based on theoretical, conceptual or practical considerations. In hierarchical clustering, the distance at which the clusters are being combined is an important criterion. The relative sizes of the clusters should be meaningful. The clusters should be interpreted in terms of cluster centroids. It is often helpful to profile the clusters in terms of variables that were not used for clustering. The reliability and validity of the clustering solutions may be assessed in different ways.

Questions

1 Discuss the similarity and difference between cluster analysis and discriminant analysis.

2 What is a 'cluster'?

3 What are some of the uses of cluster analysis in marketing?

4 Briefly define the following terms: dendrogram, icicle plot, agglomeration schedule and cluster membership.

5 What is the most commonly used measure of similarity in cluster analysis?

6 Present a classification of clustering procedures.

7 Upon what basis may a researcher decide which variables should be selected to formulate a clustering problem?

8 Why is the average linkage method usually preferred to single linkage and complete linkage?

9 What are the two major disadvantages of non-hierarchical clustering procedures?

10 What guidelines are available for deciding the number of clusters?

11 What is involved in the interpretation of clusters?

12 What role may qualitative methods play in the interpretation of clusters?

13 What are some of the additional variables used for profiling the clusters?

14 Describe some procedures available for assessing the quality of clustering solutions.

15 How is cluster analysis used to group variables?

Exercises

1 Analyse the data in Table 23.1 using the following hierarchical methods:
   a Single linkage (nearest neighbour).
   b Complete linkage (furthest neighbour).
   c Method of centroid.
   Use SPSS, SAS or Minitab. Compare your results with those given in Table 20.2.

2 Conduct the following analysis on the boots data (taken from Exercise 4, Chapter 20). Consider only the following variables: evaluations of the boots on comfort (V_2), style (V_3) and durability (V_4).
   a Cluster the participants based on the identified variables using hierarchical clustering. Use Ward's method and squared Euclidean distances. How many clusters do you recommend and why?
   b Cluster the participants based on the identified variables using k-means clustering and the number of clusters identified in part a. Compare the results to those obtained in part a.

3   Analyse the Benetton data (taken from Exercise 4, Chapter 18). Consider only the following variables: awareness, attitude, preference, intention and loyalty towards Benetton.

    a   Cluster the participants based on the identified variables using hierarchical clustering. Use Ward's method and squared Euclidean distances. How many clusters do you recommend and why?

    b   Cluster the participants based on the identified variables using *k*-means clustering and the number of clusters identified in part **a**. Compare the results to those obtained in part **a**.

4   You are a marketing research analyst for a major airline. You have been set the task of determining consumers' attitudes towards budget airlines. Construct a 15-item scale for this purpose. In a group of five students, obtain data on this scale and standard demographic characteristics from 25 males and 25 females in your community. These data should then be used to cluster participants and to cluster the 15 variables measuring consumer attitudes towards budget airlines.

5   In a small group discuss the following issues: 'The consequences of inappropriate validation of cluster analysis solutions can be disastrous' and 'User-friendly statistical packages can create cluster solutions in situations where naturally occurring clusters do not exist'.

Notes

1. Slavens, R., 'Häagen-Dazs tastes success with Crème de la Crème campaign', *B to B* 92 (1) (January 2007), 23; Reynolds, E., 'Is Häagen-Dazs shrewd to drop its sexy image?', *Marketing* (6 September, 2001), 17; Stuart, L., 'Häagen-Dazs aims to scoop a larger share', *Marketing Week* 19 (46/2) (21 February 1997), 26.

2. For applications of cluster analysis, see Bassi, F., 'Latent class factor models for market segmentation: an application to pharmaceuticals', *Statistical Methods and Applications* 16 (2) (January 2007), 279–287; Mathwick, C. and Rigdon, E., 'Play, flow, and the online search experience', *Journal of Consumer Research* 31 (September 2004), 324–332; Moe, W.W. and Fader, P.S., 'Modeling hedonic portfolio products: a joint segmentation analysis of music compact disc sales', *Journal of Marketing Research* 38 (3) (August 2001), 376–388; Arimond, G., 'A clustering method for categorical data in tourism market segmentation research', *Journal of Travel Research* 39 (4) (May 2001), 391–397; Birks, D.F. and Birts, A.N., 'Cash management market segmentation', in Birks, D.F. (ed.), *Global Cash Management in Europe* (Basingstoke: Macmillan, 1998), 83–109.

3. Overlapping clustering methods that permit an object to be grouped into more than one cluster are also available. See Curry, B., Davies, F., Evans, M., Moutinho, L. and Phillips, P., 'The Kohonen self-organising map as an alternative to cluster analysis: An application to direct marketing', *International Journal of Market Research* 45 (2)

(February 2003), 191–211; Chaturvedi, A., Carroll, J.D., Green, P.E. and Rotondo, J.A., 'A feature based approach to market segmentation via overlapping k-centroids clustering', *Journal of Marketing Research* 34 (August 1997), 370–377.

4. Excellent discussions on the various aspects of cluster analysis may be found in Abonyi, J. and Feil, B., *Cluster Analysis for Data Mining and System Identification* (Basle: Birkhäuser, 2007); Kaufman, L. and Rousseeuw, P.J., *Finding Groups in Data: An introduction to cluster analysis* (Hoboken, NJ: Wiley, 2005); Romsburg, H.C., *Cluster Analysis for Researchers* (Melbourne: Krieger, 2004); Everitt, B.S., Landau, S. and Leese, M., *Cluster Analysis*, 4th edn (Oxford: Oxford University Press, 2001).

5. Ali, J. and Rao, C.P., 'Micro-market segmentation using a neural network model approach', *Journal of International Consumer Marketing* 13 (2001), 7–27; Douglas, V., 'Questionnaires too long? Try variable clustering', *Marketing News* 29 (5) (27 February 1995), 38; Punj, G. and Stewart, D., 'Cluster analysis in marketing research: review and suggestions for application', *Journal of Marketing Research* 20 (May 1983), 134–148.

6. For use of cluster analysis for segmentation, see Tuma, M.N., Decker, R. and Scholz, S.W., 'A survey of the challenges and pitfalls of cluster analysis application in market segmentation', *International Journal of Market Research* 53 (3) (2011), 391–414; Clark, J., Jones, S., Romanou, E. and Harrison, M., 'Segments, hugs and rock 'n' roll: An

attitudinal segmentation of parents and young people', Market Research Society, Annual Conference (2009).

7. Hyde, K.F., 'Contemporary information search strategies of destination-naïve international vacationers', *Journal of Travel and Tourism Marketing* 21 (2/3) (2006), 63–76; Brown, T.J., Qu, H. and Rittichainuwat, B.N., 'Thailand's international travel image: mostly favourable', *Cornell Hotel and Restaurant Administration Quarterly* 42 (2) (April 2001), 85–95.

8. Caragea, P.C. and Smith, R.L., 'Asymptotic properties of computationally efficient alternative estimators for a class of multivariate normal models', *Journal of Multivariate Analysis* 98 (104) (August 2007), 1417–1440; Sambandam, R., 'Cluster analysis gets complicated', *Marketing Research* (Spring 2003), 16–21; Everitt, B.S., Landau, S. and Leese, M., *Cluster Analysis*, 4th edn (Oxford: Oxford University Press, 2001).

9. For a detailed discussion on the different measures of similarity, and formulae for computing them, see Brandt, C., de Mortanges, C.P., Bluemelhuber, C. and van Riel, A.C.R., 'Associative networks: a new approach to market segmentation', *International Journal of Market Research* 53 (2) (2011), 189–210; Bradlow, E.T. and Fitzsimmons, G.J., 'Subscale distance and item clustering effects in self-administered surveys: a new metric', *Journal of Marketing Research* 38 (May 2001), 254–261; Chepoi, V. and Dragan, F., 'Computing a median point of a simple rectilinear polygon', *Information Processing Letters* 49 (6) (22 March 1994), 281–285; Romsburg, H.C., *Cluster Analysis for Researchers* (Belmont, CA: Lifetime Learning, 1984).

10. For further discussion of the issues involved in standardisation, see Hair, J.E. Jr, Anderson, R.E., Tatham, R.L. and Black, W.C., *Multivariate Data Analysis with Readings*, 5th edn (Englewood Cliffs, NJ: Prentice Hall, 1999), 364–419; Romsburg, H.C., *Cluster Analysis for Researchers* (Melbourne: Krieger, 1990).

11. Everitt, B.S., Landau, S. and Leese, M., *Cluster Analysis*, 4th edn (Oxford: Oxford University Press, 2001); Johnson, R.A. and Wichern, D.W., *Applied Multivariate Statistical Analysis*, 5th edn (Paramus, NJ: Prentice Hall, 2001); Milligan, G., 'An examination of the effect of six types of error perturbation on fifteen clustering algorithms', *Psychometrika* 45 (September 1980), 325–342.

12. MacLachlan, D.L. and Mulhern, M.G., 'Segment optimization: an empirical comparison', ESOMAR, Marketing Conference, Warsaw (October 2004); Everitt, B.S., Landau, S. and Leese, M., *Cluster Analysis*, 4th edn (Oxford: Oxford University Press, 2001); Punj, G. and Stewart, D., 'Cluster analysis in marketing research: reviews and suggestions for application', *Journal of Marketing Research* 20 (May 1983), 134–148.

13. Tuma, M.N., Decker, R. and Scholz, S.W., 'A survey of the challenges and pitfalls of cluster analysis application in market segmentation', *International Journal of Market Research* 53 (3) (2011), 391–414.

14. For a formal discussion of reliability, validity and significance testing in cluster analysis, see Barnes, S., Bauer, H.H., Neumann, M.M. and Huber, F., 'Segmenting cyberspace: a customer typology for the internet', *European Journal of Marketing* 41 (1/2) (2007), 71–93; Brusco, M.J., Cradit, J.D. and Stahl, S., 'A simulated annealing heuristic for a bicriterion partitioning problem in market segmentation', *Journal of Marketing Research* 39 (1) (February 2002), 99–109; Chen, H.-M., 'Using clustering techniques to detect usage patterns in a web-based information system', *Journal of the American Society for Information Science and Technology* 52 (11) (September 2001), 888; Dibbs, S. and Stern, P., 'Questioning the reliability of market segmentation techniques', *Omega* 23 (6) (December 1995), 625–636; Funkhouser, G.R., 'A note on the reliability of certain clustering algorithms', *Journal of Marketing Research* 30 (February 1983), 99–102; Klastorin, T.D., 'Assessing cluster analysis results', *Journal of Marketing Research* 20 (February 1983), 92–98; Arnold, S.J., 'A test for clusters', *Journal of Marketing Research* 16 (November 1979), 545–551.

15. Bottomley, P. and Nairn, A., 'Blinded by science: the managerial consequences of inadequately validated cluster analysis solutions,' *International Journal of Market Research* 46 (2) (2004), 171–187.

16. Saunders, J. and Forrester, R.H., 'Capturing learning and applying knowledge: an investigation of the use of innovation teams in Japanese and American automotive firms', *Journal of Business Research* 47 (1) (January 2000), 35; Saunders, J., Wong, V. and Doyle, P., 'The congruence of successful international competitors: a study of the marketing strategies and organizations of Japanese and US competitors in the UK', *Journal of Global Marketing* 7 (3) (1994), 41–59; Doyle, P., Saunders, J. and Wong, V., 'International marketing strategies and organizations: a study of U.S., Japanese, and British competitors', in Bloom, P., Winer, R., Kassarjian, H.H., Scammon, D.L., Weitz, B., Spekman, R.E., Mahajan, V. and Levy, M. (eds), *Enhancing Knowledge Development in Marketing*, Series No. 55 (Chicago: American Marketing Association, 1989), 100–104.

17. Moschis, G.P., Bellenger, D.N. and Folkman Curasi, C., 'What influences the mature consumer?', *Marketing Health Services* 23 (4) (January 2003), 16; Lin, A., Lenert, L.A., Haltky, M.A. and McDonald, K.M., 'Clustering and the design of preference-assessment surveys in healthcare', *Health Services Research* 34 (5) (December 1999), 1033–1045; Holohean, E.J. Jr, Banks, S.M. and Maddy, B.A., 'System impact and methodological issues in the development of an empirical typology of psychiatric hospital residents', *Journal of Mental Health Administration* 22 (2) (Spring 1995), 177–188.

18. Liu, H.H., 'Variable selection in clustering for marketing segmentation using genetic algorithms', *Expert Systems with Applications: An International Journal Archive* 34 (1) (January 2008), 502–510; Barnes, S., Bauer, H.H., Neumann, M.M. and Huber, F., 'Segmenting cyberspace: a customer typology for the internet', *European Journal of Marketing* 41 (1/2) (2007), 71–93; Everitt, B.S., Landau, S. and Leese, M., *Cluster Analysis*, 4th edn (Oxford: Oxford University Press, 2001); Douglas, V., 'Questionnaire too long? Try variable clustering', *Marketing News* 29 (5) (27 February 1995), 38.

19. Mooradian, T.A., Matzler, K. and Szykman, L., 'Empathetic responses to advertising: testing a network of antecedents and consequences', *Marketing Letters* 19 (2) (June 2008), 79–92; Baar, A., 'Polaroid ads play up emotion', *Adweek* 42 (15) (9 April 2001); Helgesen, T., 'The power of advertising – myths and realities', *Marketing and Research Today* 24 (2) (May 1996), 63–71; Aaker,

D.A., Stayman, D.M. and Vezina, R., 'Identifying feelings elicited by advertising', *Psychology and Marketing* (Spring 1988), 1–16.

20. Pickett, G.M., 'The impact of product type and parity on the informational content of advertising', *Journal of Marketing Theory and Practice* 9 (3) (Summer 2001), 32–43; Zandpour, F. and Harich, K.R., 'Think and feel country clusters: a new approach to international advertising standardisation', *International Journal of Advertising* 15 (4) (1996), 325–344.

21. Fraedrich, J.P., Herndon, N.C. Jr and Yeh, Q.-J., 'An investigation of moral values and the ethical content of the corporate culture', *Journal of Business Ethics* 30 (1) (March 2001), 73–85; Akaah, I.P., 'Organizational culture and ethical research behavior', *Journal of the Academy of Marketing Science* 21 (1) (Winter 1993), 59–63.

22. Reidenbach, R.E. and Robin, D.P., 'Some initial steps toward improving the measurement of ethical evaluations of marketing activities', *Journal of Business Ethics* 7 (1988), 871–879.

24

Multidimensional scaling and conjoint analysis

Stage 1

Problem definition

Stage 2

Research approach developed

Stage 3

Research design developed

Stage 4

Fieldwork or data collection

Stage 5

Data integrity and analysis

Stage 6

Report preparation and presentation

Multidimensional scaling allows the perceptions and preferences of consumers to be clearly represented in a spatial map. Conjoint analysis helps to determine the relative importance of attributes that consumers use in choosing products.

Objectives

After reading this chapter, you should be able to:

1 discuss the basic concept and scope of multidimensional scaling (MDS) in marketing research and describe its various applications;

2 describe the steps involved in MDS of perception data, including formulating the problem, obtaining input data, selecting an MDS procedure, deciding on the number of dimensions, labelling the dimensions and interpreting the configuration, and assessing reliability and validity;

3 explain the MDS scaling of preference data and distinguish between internal and external analysis of preferences;

4 explain correspondence analysis and discuss its advantages and disadvantages;

5 understand the relationship between MDS discriminant analysis and factor analysis;

6 discuss the basic concepts of conjoint analysis, contrast it with MDS and discuss its various applications;

7 describe the procedure for conducting conjoint analysis, including formulating the problem, constructing the stimuli, deciding the form of input data, selecting a conjoint analysis procedure, interpreting the results, and assessing reliability and validity;

8 define the concept of hybrid conjoint analysis and explain how it simplifies the data collection task;

9 appreciate how SPSS and SAS software are used in multidimensional scaling and conjoint analysis.

Overview

This chapter presents two related techniques for analysing consumer perceptions and preferences: multidimensional scaling (MDS) and conjoint analysis. We outline and illustrate the steps involved in conducting MDS and discuss the relationships among MDS, factor analysis and discriminant analysis. Then we describe conjoint analysis and present a step-by-step procedure for conducting it. We also provide brief coverage of hybrid conjoint models. Finally, help is provided to run the SPSS and SAS Learning Editions in the data analysis challenges presented in this chapter. We begin with examples illustrating MDS and conjoint analysis.

Real research   ## Colas collide[1]

In a survey, participants were asked to rank-order all the possible pairs of nine brands of soft drinks in terms of their similarity. These data were analysed via multidimensional scaling and resulted in the following spatial representation of soft drinks.

From other information obtained in the questionnaire, the horizontal axis was labelled 'cola flavour'. Diet Coke was perceived to be the most cola flavoured and 7-Up the least cola flavoured. The vertical axis was labelled 'dietness', with Diet Coke being perceived to be the most dietetic and Dr Pepper the least dietetic. Note that Coke and Pepsi were perceived to be very similar as indicated by their closeness in the perceptual map. Close similarity was also perceived between 7-Up and Tango, Diet 7-Up and Diet Tango, and Diet Coke and Diet Pepsi. Notice that Dr Pepper is perceived to be relatively dissimilar to the other brands. Such MDS maps are very useful in understanding the competitive structure of the soft drink market.

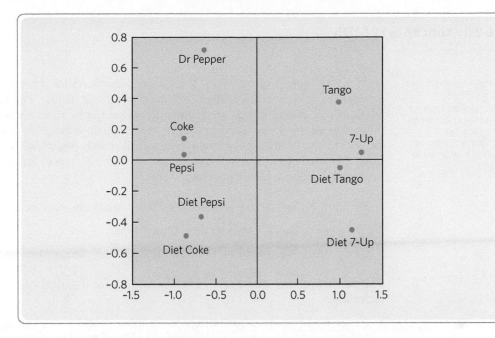

Real research

The conjoint path over the cultural divide[2]

Boots the Chemist was considering whether to open new stores in the Netherlands, Japan and Thailand. Research was conducted to help decide whether to enter these markets and also to decide which element of Boots' product and service offerings to prioritise.

The key research objectives were to:

- Understand the key drivers of store choice.
- Assess the performance of main competitors already in the market.
- Estimate the proportion of shoppers likely to visit new Boots stores.

Conjoint analysis was used to understand the key drivers of store choice, the impact of features such as range, price, quality, service and convenience, and the trade-offs made in prioritising these features. To understand the strengths and weaknesses of existing retailers, participants stated for each of the attributes under review what the named competitors offered. To enable take-up of the new stores to be forecast, participants were first shown a video of the Boots concept store. The concept store was then assessed on the same series of attributes used for the existing competitors. Over 1,000 interviews were conducted in each country. The research results found:

- The characteristics of the target market in terms of age, sex, income and lifestage, frequency of and attitudes to shopping.
- The key success factors in each product area, which influenced store design, merchandising, staff training and marketing decisions.
- Which existing players posed the greatest threat, in terms of being differentiated from current competitors and having possible areas of leverage against Boots.

The first example illustrates the derivation and use of perceptual maps, which lie at the heart of MDS. The Boots example involves the trade-offs that participants make while evaluating alternatives in choosing stores and desirable features within those stores. The conjoint analysis procedure is based on these trade-offs.

Basic concepts in MDS

Multidimensional scaling (MDS)
A class of procedures for representing perceptions and preferences of participants spatially by means of a visual display.

Multidimensional scaling (MDS) is a class of procedures for representing perceptions and preferences of participants spatially by means of a visual display. Perceived or psychological relationships among stimuli are represented as geometric relationships among points in a multidimensional space. These geometric representations are often called spatial maps. The axes of the spatial map are assumed to denote the psychological bases or underlying dimensions that participants use to form perceptions and preferences for stimuli.[3] MDS has been used in marketing to identify the following:

1 The number and nature of dimensions that consumers use to perceive different brands.

2 The positioning of brands on these dimensions.

3 The positioning of consumers' ideal brand on these dimensions.

Information provided by MDS has been used for a variety of marketing applications, including:

- *Image measurement.* Comparing the customers' and non-customers' perceptions of a company with the company's perceptions of itself and thus identifying perceptual gaps.
- *Market segmentation.* Positioning brands and consumers in the same space and then identifying groups of consumers with relatively homogeneous perceptions.
- *New product development.* Looking for gaps in a spatial map, which indicate potential opportunities for positioning new products. Also to evaluate new product concepts and existing brands on a test basis to determine how consumers perceive the new concepts. The proportion of preferences for each new product is one indicator of its success.
- *Assessing advertising effectiveness.* Spatial maps can be used to determine whether advertising has been successful in achieving the desired brand positioning.
- *Pricing analysis.* Spatial maps developed with and without pricing information can be compared to determine the impact of pricing.
- *Channel decisions.* Judgements on compatibility of brands with different retail outlets could lead to spatial maps useful for making channel decisions.
- *Attitude-scale construction.* MDS techniques can be used to develop the appropriate dimensionality and configuration of the attitude space.

Statistics and terms associated with MDS

The important statistics and terms associated with MDS include the following:

Similarity judgements. These are ratings on all possible pairs of brands or other stimuli in terms of their similarity using a Likert-type scale.

Preference rankings. These are rank orderings of the brands or other stimuli from the most preferred to the least preferred. They are normally obtained from participants.

Stress. This is a lack-of-fit measure; higher values of stress indicate poorer fits.

R-square. This is a squared correlation index that indicates the proportion of variance of the optimally scaled data that can be accounted for by the MDS procedure. *R*-square is a goodness-of-fit measure.

Spatial map. Perceived relationships among brands or other stimuli are represented as geometric relationships among points in a multidimensional space.

Coordinates. These indicate the positioning of a brand or a stimulus in a spatial map.

Unfolding. The representation of both brands and participants as points in the same space.

Conducting MDS

Figure 24.1 shows the steps in MDS. The researcher must formulate the MDS problem carefully because a variety of data may be used as input into MDS. The researcher must also determine an appropriate form in which data should be obtained and select an MDS procedure for analysing the data. An important aspect of the solution involves determining the number of dimensions for the spatial map. Also, the axes of the map should be labelled and the derived configuration interpreted. Finally, the researcher must assess the quality of the results obtained.[4] We describe each of these steps, beginning with problem formulation.

Figure 24.1

Conducting MDS

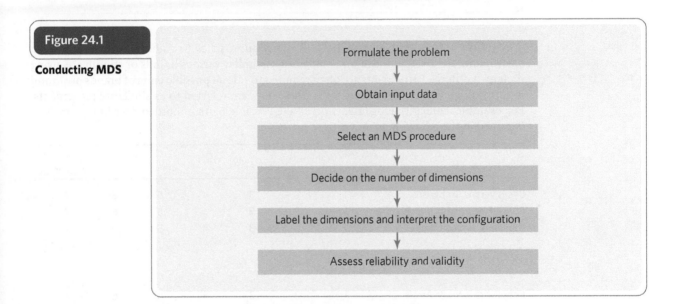

Formulate the problem
↓
Obtain input data
↓
Select an MDS procedure
↓
Decide on the number of dimensions
↓
Label the dimensions and interpret the configuration
↓
Assess reliability and validity

Formulate the problem

Formulating the problem requires that the researcher specify the purpose for which the MDS results would be used and select the brands or other stimuli to be included in the analysis. The number of brands or stimuli selected and the specific brands included determine the nature of the resulting dimensions and configurations. At a minimum, eight brands or stimuli should be included to obtain a well-defined spatial map. Including more than 25 brands is likely to be cumbersome and may result in participant fatigue.[5]

The decision regarding which specific brands or stimuli to include should be made carefully. Suppose that a researcher is interested in obtaining consumer perceptions of fashion brands. If luxury fashion brands were not included in the stimulus set, this dimension may not emerge in the results. The choice of the number and specific brands or stimuli to be included should be based on the statement of the marketing research problem, theory and the judgement of the researcher.

MDS will be illustrated in the context of obtaining a spatial map for 10 brands of beer. These brands are Becks, Budvar, Budweiser, Carlsberg, Corona, Grolsch, Harp, Holsten, San Miguel and Stella Artois. Given the list of brands, the next question is: how should we obtain data on these 10 brands?

Obtain input data

As shown in Figure 24.2, input data obtained from the participants may be related to perceptions or preferences. Perception data, which may be direct or derived, are discussed first.

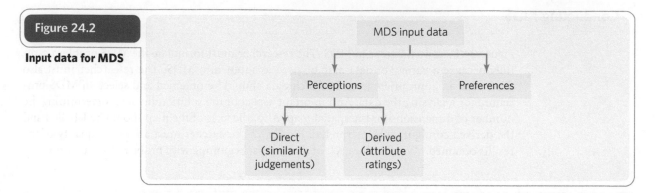

Figure 24.2

Input data for MDS

Perception data: direct approaches. In direct approaches to gathering perception data, participants are asked to judge how similar or dissimilar various brands or stimuli are, using their own criteria. Participants are often required to rate all possible pairs of brands or stimuli in terms of similarity on a Likert scale. These data are referred to as similarity judgements. For example, similarity judgements on all the possible pairs of bottled beer brands may be obtained in the following manner:

	Very dissimilar						Very similar
Becks versus Budweiser	1	2	3	4	5	6	7
Budweiser versus Carlsberg	1	2	3	4	5	6	7
Carlsberg versus Corona	1	2	3	4	5	6	7
.	.	.	.	.	.	.	.
.	.	.	.	.	.	.	.
.	.	.	.	.	.	.	.
Becks versus Stella Artois	1	2	3	4	5	6	7

The number of pairs to be evaluated is $n(n-1)/2$, where n is the number of stimuli. Other procedures are also available. Participants could be asked to rank-order all the possible pairs from the most similar to the least similar. In another method, the participant rank orders the brands in terms of their similarity to an anchor brand. Each brand, in turn, serves as the anchor. In our example, the direct approach was adopted. Subjects were asked to provide similarity judgements for all 45 ($10 \times 9/2$) pairs of bottled beer brands, using a seven-point scale. The data obtained from one participant are given in Table 24.1.[6]

Derived approaches

In MDS, attribute-based approaches to collecting perception data requiring participants to rate the stimuli on the identified attributes using semantic differential or Likert scales.

Perception data: derived approaches. Derived approaches to collecting perception data are attribute-based approaches requiring the participants to rate the brands or stimuli on the identified attributes using semantic differential or Likert scales. For example, the different brands of bottled beer may be rated on attributes like these:

Best drunk with food   ___:___:___:___:___:___:___ Best drunk on its own
Bottle feels good to hold   ___:___:___:___:___:___:___ Bottle does not feel good to hold
.
.
.
Has a strong smell of hops ___:___:___:___:___:___:___ No smell of hops

Sometimes an ideal brand is also included in the stimulus set. The participants are asked to evaluate their hypothetical ideal brand on the same set of attributes. If attribute ratings are obtained, a similarity measure (such as Euclidean distance) is derived for each pair of brands.

Direct vs. derived approaches. Direct approaches have the advantage that the researcher does not have to identify a set of salient attributes. Participants make similarity judgements using their own criteria, as they would under normal circumstances. The disadvantages are that the criteria are influenced by the brands or stimuli being evaluated. If various fashion brands being evaluated are in the same price range, then price will not emerge as an important factor. It may be difficult to determine before analysis if and how the individual participant's judgements should be combined. Furthermore, it may be difficult to label the dimensions of the spatial map.

Table 24.1	Similarity ratings of bottled beer brands

	Becks	Budvar	Budweiser	Carlsberg	Corona	Grolsch	Harp	Holsten	San Miguel	Stella Artois
Becks										
Budvar	5									
Budweiser	6	7								
Carlsberg	4	6	6							
Corona	2	3	4	5						
Grolsch	3	3	4	4	5					
Harp	2	2	2	3	5	5				
Holsten	2	2	2	2	6	5	6			
San Miguel	2	2	2	2	6	6	7	6		
Stella Artois	1	2	4	2	4	3	3	4	3	

The advantage of the attribute-based approach is that it is easy to identify participants with homogeneous perceptions. The participants can be clustered based on the attribute ratings. It is also easier to label the dimensions. A disadvantage is that the researcher must identify all the salient attributes, a difficult task. The spatial map obtained depends on the attributes identified.

The direct approaches are more frequently used than the attribute-based approaches. It may, however, be best to use both these

approaches in a complementary way. Direct similarity judgements may be used for obtaining the spatial map, and attribute ratings may be used as an aid to interpreting the dimensions of the perceptual map. Similar procedures are used for preference data.

Preference data. Preference data order the brands or stimuli in terms of participants' preference for some property. A common way in which such data are obtained is preference rankings. Participants are required to rank the brands from the most preferred to the least preferred. Alternatively, participants may be required to make paired comparisons and indicate which brand in a pair they prefer. Another method is to obtain preference ratings for the various brands. (The rank order, paired comparison and rating scales were discussed in Chapter 12 on scaling techniques.) When spatial maps are based on preference data, distance implies differences in preference. The configuration derived from preference data may differ greatly from that obtained from similarity data. Two brands may be perceived as different in a similarity map yet similar in a preference map, and vice versa. For example, Becks and Harp may be perceived by a group of participants as very different brands and thus appear far apart on a perception map. But these two brands may be about equally preferred and may appear close together on a preference map. We continue using the perception data obtained in the bottled beer example to illustrate the MDS procedure and then consider the scaling of preference data.

Select an MDS procedure

Selecting a specific MDS procedure depends on whether perception or preference data are being scaled or whether the analysis requires both kinds of data. The nature of the input data is also a determining factor. Non-metric MDS procedures assume that the input data are ordinal, but they result in metric output. The distances in the resulting spatial map may be assumed to be interval scaled. These procedures find, in a given dimensionality, a spatial map whose rank orders of estimated distances between brands or stimuli best preserve or reproduce the input rank orders. In contrast, metric MDS methods assume that input data are metric. Since the output is also metric, a stronger relationship between the output and input data is maintained, and the metric (interval or ratio) qualities of the input data are preserved. The metric and non-metric methods produce similar results.[7]

Another factor influencing the selection of a procedure is whether the MDS analysis will be conducted at the individual participant level or at an aggregate level. In individual-level analysis, the data are analysed separately for each participant, resulting in a spatial map for each participant. Although individual-level analysis is useful from a research perspective, it is not appealing from a managerial standpoint. With some exceptions, especially in luxury goods and business-to-business relationships, marketing strategies are typically formulated at the segment or aggregate level, rather than at the individual level. If aggregate-level analysis is conducted, some assumptions must be made in aggregating individual data. Typically, it is assumed that all participants use the same dimensions to evaluate the brands or stimuli, but that different participants weight these common dimensions differentially.

The data of Table 24.1 were treated as rank ordered and scaled using a non-metric procedure. Because these data were provided by one participant, an individual-level analysis was conducted. Spatial maps were obtained in one to four dimensions, and then a decision on an appropriate number of dimensions was made. This decision is central to all MDS analyses; therefore, it is explored in greater detail in the following subsection.

Decide on the number of dimensions

The objective in MDS is to obtain a spatial map that best fits the input data in the smallest number of dimensions. However, spatial maps are computed in such a way that the fit improves as the number of dimensions increases, which means that a compromise has to be made. The fit of an MDS solution is commonly assessed by the stress measure. Stress is a lack-of-fit measure; higher values of stress indicate poorer fits. The following guidelines are suggested for determining the number of dimensions:

1 *A priori knowledge.* Theory or past research may suggest a particular number of dimensions.

2 *Interpretability of the spatial map.* Generally, it is difficult to interpret configurations or maps derived in more than three dimensions.

Non-metric MDS
A type of MDS which assumes that the input data are ordinal.

Metric MDS
An MDS method that assumes that input data are metric.

Elbow criterion

A plot of stress versus dimensionality used in MDS. The point at which an elbow or a sharp bend occurs indicates an appropriate dimensionality.

3 *Elbow criterion.* A plot of stress versus dimensionality should be examined. The points in this plot usually form a convex pattern, as shown in Figure 24.3. The point at which an elbow or a sharp bend occurs indicates an appropriate number of dimensions. Increasing the number of dimensions beyond this point is usually not worth the improvement in fit. This criterion for determining the number of dimensions is called the elbow criterion.

4 *Ease of use.* It is generally easier to work with two-dimensional maps or configurations than with those involving more dimensions.

5 *Statistical approaches.* For the sophisticated user, statistical approaches are also available for determining the dimensionality.[8]

Based on the plot of stress versus dimensionality (Figure 24.3), interpretability of the spatial map and ease-of-use criteria, it was decided to retain a two-dimensional solution. This is shown in Figure 24.4.

Figure 24.3

Plot of stress versus dimensionality

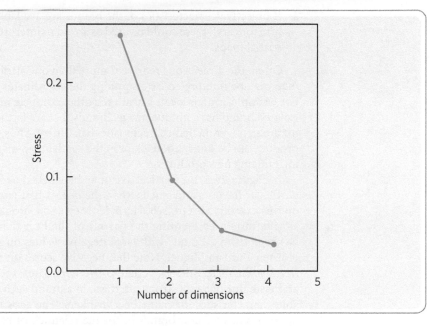

Figure 24.4

A spatial map of beer brands

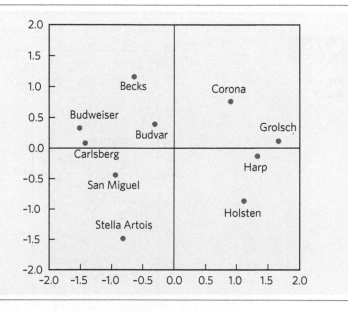

Label the dimensions and interpret the configuration

Once a spatial map is developed, the dimensions must be labelled and the configuration interpreted. Labelling the dimensions requires subjective judgement on the part of the researcher. The following guidelines can assist in this task:

1   Even if *direct* similarity judgements are obtained, ratings of the brands on researcher-supplied attributes may still be collected. Using statistical methods such as regression these attribute vectors may be fitted in the spatial map (see Figure 24.5). The axes may then be labelled for the attributes with which they are most closely aligned.

2   After providing direct similarity or preference data, the participants may be asked to indicate the criteria they used in making their evaluations. These criteria may then be subjectively related to the spatial map to label the dimensions.

3   If possible, the participants can be shown their spatial maps and asked to label the dimensions by inspecting the configurations.

4   If objective characteristics of the brands are available (e.g. horsepower or kilometres per litre for cars), these could be used as an aid in interpreting the subjective dimensions of the spatial maps.

Often, the dimensions represent more than one attribute. The configuration or the spatial map may be interpreted by examining the coordinates and relative positions of the brands. For example, brands located near each other compete more fiercely than brands far apart. An isolated brand has a unique image. Brands that are farther along in the direction of a descriptor are stronger on that characteristic than others. Thus, the strengths and weaknesses of each product can be understood. Gaps in the spatial map may indicate potential opportunities for introducing new products.

In Figure 24.5, the vertical axis may be labelled as 'strength', representing the power of particular flavours and smells when the beer is first tasted. Brands with high positive values on this axis include Grolsch, Harp, Holsten and Corona. The horizontal axis may be labelled as 'aftertaste', representing the flavour of the beer that lingers on the palate after the beer has been drunk. Brands with large negative values on this dimension include Stella Artois, Holsten and San Miguel. Note that negative scores on the map do not necessarily represent negative characteristics for certain consumers. Thus, the strength of flavour from initial smell and taste through to a strong aftertaste in a brand such as Stella Artois may be seen as desirable characteristics for many beer drinkers. The gaps in the spatial map indicate potential opportunities for new brands or for the relaunch or repositioning of an existing brand: for example, a brand that has a strong initial taste but does not have a strong lingering aftertaste.

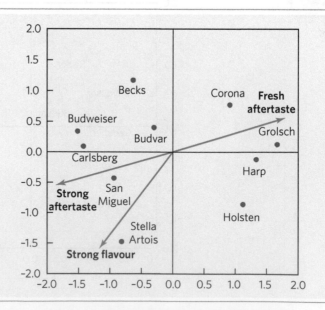

Figure 24.5

Using attribute vectors to label dimensions

Assess reliability and validity

The input data, and consequently the MDS solutions, are invariably subject to substantial random variability. Hence, it is necessary that some assessment be made of the reliability and validity of MDS solutions. The following guidelines are suggested:

1   The index of fit, or R-square, should be examined. This is a squared correlation index that indicates the proportion of variance of the optimally scaled data that can be accounted for by the MDS procedure. Thus, it indicates how well the MDS model fits the input data. Although higher values of R-square are desirable, values of 0.60 or better are considered acceptable.

2   Stress values are also indicative of the quality of MDS solutions. Whereas R-square is a measure of goodness of fit, stress measures badness of fit, or the proportion of variance of the optimally scaled data that is not accounted for by the MDS model. Stress values vary with the type of MDS procedure and the data being analysed. For Kruskal's stress formula 1, the recommendations for evaluating stress values are as follows:[9]

Stress (%)	Goodness of fit
20	Poor
10	Fair
5	Good
2.5	Excellent
0	Perfect

3   If an aggregate-level analysis has been done, the original data should be split into two or more parts. MDS analysis should be conducted separately on each part and the results compared.

4   Stimuli can be selectively eliminated from the input data and the solutions determined for the remaining stimuli.

5   A random error term could be added to the input data. The resulting data are subjected to MDS analysis and the solutions compared.

6   The input data could be collected at two different points in time and the test–retest reliability determined.

Figure 24.6

Assessment of stability by deleting one brand

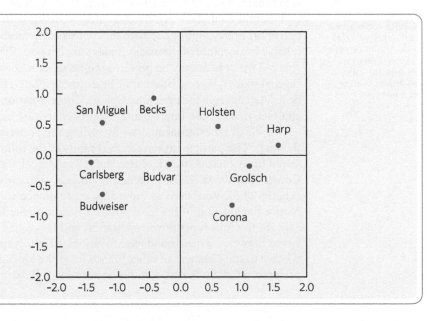

Formal procedures are available for assessing the validity of MDS. In the case of our illustrative example, the stress value of 0.095 indicates a fair fit. One brand, namely Stella Artois, is different from the others. Would the elimination of Stella Artois from the stimulus set appreciably alter the relative configuration of the other brands? The spatial map obtained by deleting Stella Artois is shown in Figure 24.6. There is some change in the relative positions of the brands, particularly Corona and Holsten, yet the changes are modest, indicating fair stability.[10]

Assumptions and limitations of MDS

It is worthwhile to point out some assumptions and limitations of MDS. It is assumed that the similarity of stimulus A to B is the same as the similarity of stimulus B to A. There are some instances where this assumption may be violated. For example, New Zealand is perceived as more similar to Australia than Australia is to New Zealand. MDS assumes that the distance (similarity) between two stimuli is some function of their partial similarities on each of several perceptual dimensions. Not much research has been done to test this assumption. When a spatial map is obtained, it is assumed that inter-point distances are ratio scaled and that the axes of the map are multidimensional interval scaled. A limitation of MDS is that dimension interpretation relating physical changes in brands or stimuli to changes in the perceptual map is difficult at best. These limitations also apply to the scaling of preference data.

Scaling preference data

Internal analysis of preferences
A method of configuring a spatial map such that the spatial map represents both brands or stimuli and participant points or vectors and is derived solely from the preference data.

External analysis of preferences
A method of configuring a spatial map such that the ideal points or vectors based on preference data are fitted in a spatial map derived from the perception data.

Analysis of preference data can be internal or external. In internal analysis of preferences, a spatial map representing both brands or stimuli and participant points or vectors is derived solely from the preference data. Thus, by collecting preference data, both brands and participants can be represented in the same spatial map. In external analysis of preferences, the ideal points or vectors based on preference data are fitted in a spatial map derived from perception (e.g. similarities) data. To perform external analysis, both preference and perception data must be obtained. The representation of both brands and participants as points in the same space, by using internal or external analysis, is referred to as *unfolding*.

External analysis is preferred in most situations. In internal analysis, the differences in perceptions are confounded with differences in preferences. It is possible that the nature and relative importance of dimensions may vary between the perceptual space and the preference space. Two brands may be perceived to be similar (located closely to each other in the perceptual space), yet one brand may be distinctly preferred over the other (i.e. the brands may be located apart in the preference space). These situations cannot be accounted for in internal analysis. In addition, internal analysis procedures are beset with computational difficulties.[11]

We illustrate external analysis by scaling the preferences of our participant into the spatial map. The participant ranked the brands in the following order of preference (most preferred first): Stella Artois, Holsten, Harp, San Miguel, Carlsberg, Grolsch, Budvar, Budweiser, Corona and Becks. These preference rankings, along with the coordinates of the spatial map (Figure 24.5), were used as input into a preference scaling program to derive Figure 24.7. Notice the location of the ideal point. It is close to Stella Artois, Holsten, Carlsberg and San Miguel, the four most preferred brands, and far from Corona and Becks, the two least preferred brands. If a new brand were to be located in this space, its distance from the ideal point, relative to the distances of other brands from the ideal point, would determine the degree of preference for this brand. Another application is illustrated in the following example.

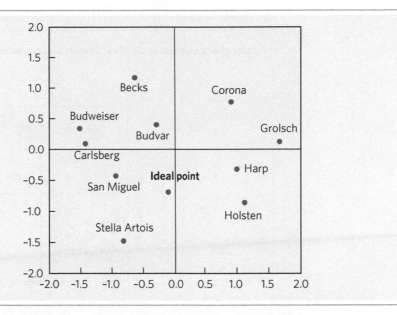

Figure 24.7

External analysis of preference data

Real research | **Participants park in different spaces[12]**

A study examined consumer perceptions of car brands using multidimensional scaling. Participants rated several attributes of cars and the effect those attributes had on their final choice in buying a car. Ratings were conducted using a five-point scale, and each participant's responses were summed across each dimension. The five highest scoring attributes overall were: price, fuel economy, net horsepower, braking and acceleration. The use of MDS can help car brands better understand what attributes are most important to consumers and then make segmentation, targeting and postioning decisions.

An illustrative MDS map of selected car brands derived from similarity data is shown. In this spatial representation, each brand is identified by its distance from the other brands. The closer two brands are (e.g. VW and Chrysler), the more similar they are perceived to be. The farther apart two brands are (e.g. VW and Mercedes), the less similar they are perceived to be. Small distance (i.e. similarity) may also indicate competition. To illustrate, Honda competes closely with Toyota but not with Porsche. The dimensions can be interpreted as economy/prestige and sportiness/non-sportiness. The position of each car on these dimensions can be easily determined.

The preference data consisted of a simple rank order of the brands according to consumers' preferences. Participants' ideal points are also located in the same spatial representation. Each ideal point represents the preferred position of a particular participant. Thus, participant 1 (denoted by P1) prefers the sporty cars: Porsche, Jaguar and Audi. Participant 2 (denoted by P2), on the other hand, prefers luxury cars: Mercedes, Lexus and Cadillac. Such analysis can be done at the individual participant level, enabling the researcher to segment the market according to similarities in participants' ideal positions. Alternatively, participants can be clustered based upon their similarity with respect to the original preference ranking and ideal points established for each segment.

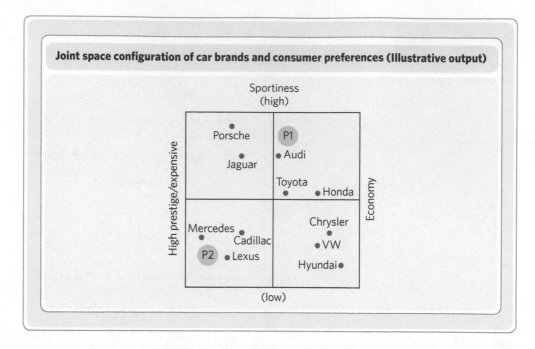

Joint space configuration of car brands and consumer preferences (Illustrative output)

Although we have considered only quantitative data so far, qualitative data can also be mapped using procedures such as correspondence analysis.

Correspondence analysis

Correspondence analysis
An MDS technique for scaling qualitative data that scales the rows and columns of the input contingency table in corresponding units so that each can be displayed in the same low-dimensional space.

Correspondence analysis is an MDS technique for scaling qualitative data in marketing research. The input data are in the form of a contingency table indicating a qualitative association between the rows and columns. Correspondence analysis scales the rows and columns in corresponding units so that each can be displayed graphically in the same low-dimensional space. These spatial maps provide insights into:

1 Similarities and differences within the rows with respect to a given column category.

2 Similarities and differences within the column categories with respect to a given row category.

3 Relationships among the rows and columns.[13]

The interpretation of results in correspondence analysis is similar to that in principal components analysis (Chapter 22), given the similarity of the algorithms. Correspondence analysis results in the grouping of categories (activities, brands or other stimuli) found within the contingency table, just as principal components analysis involves the grouping of the independent variables. The results are interpreted in terms of proximities among the rows and columns of the contingency table. Categories that are closer together than others are more similar in underlying structure.

Compared with other MDS techniques, the advantage of correspondence analysis is that it reduces the data collection demands imposed on the participants, since only binary or categorical data are obtained. Participants are merely asked to tick which attributes apply to each of several brands. The input data are the number of 'yes' responses for each brand on each attribute. The brands and the attributes are then displayed in the same multidimensional space. The disadvantage is that between-set (i.e. between column and row) distances cannot be meaningfully interpreted. Other users have criticised the technique as causing confusion when interpreting attribute–brand relationships and complications in the tracking of perceptual changes.[14] Ultimately, it must be remembered that correspondence analysis is an exploratory data analysis technique (with the many advantages that exploration holds) and so it is not suitable for hypothesis testing.[15]

MDS, including correspondence analysis, is not the only procedure available for obtaining perceptual maps. Two other techniques that we have discussed before, discriminant analysis (Chapter 21) and factor analysis (Chapter 22), can also be used for this purpose.

Relationship among MDS, factor analysis and discriminant analysis

If the attribute-based approaches are used to obtain input data, spatial maps can also be obtained by using factor or discriminant analysis. In this approach, each participant rates n brands on m attributes. By factor analysing the data, one could derive for each participant n factor scores for each factor, one for each brand (see Chapter 22). By plotting brand scores on the factors, a spatial map could be obtained for each participant. If an aggregate map is desired, the factor score for each brand for each factor can be averaged across participants. The dimensions would be labelled by examining the factor loadings, which are estimates of the correlations between attribute ratings and underlying factors.

The goal of discriminant analysis is to select the linear combinations of attributes that best discriminate between the brands or stimuli (Chapter 21). To develop spatial maps by means of discriminant analysis, the dependent variable is the brand rated and the independent or predictor variables are the attribute ratings. A spatial map can be obtained by plotting the discriminant scores for the brands. The discriminant scores are the ratings on the perceptual dimensions, based on the attributes which best distinguish the brands. The dimensions can be labelled by examining the discriminant weights, or the weightings of attributes that make up a discriminant function or dimension.[16]

Basic concepts in conjoint analysis

Conjoint analysis
A technique that attempts to determine the relative importance that consumers attach to salient attributes and the utilities they attach to the levels of attributes.

Conjoint analysis attempts to determine the relative importance that consumers attach to salient attributes and the utilities they attach to the levels of attributes. This information is derived from consumers' evaluations of brands or from brand profiles composed of these attributes and their levels. The participants are presented with stimuli that consist of combinations of attribute levels. They are asked to evaluate these stimuli in terms of their desirability. Conjoint procedures attempt to assign values to the levels of each attribute so that the resulting values or utilities attached to the stimuli match, as closely as possible, the input evaluations provided by the participants. The underlying assumption is that any set of stimuli – such as products, brands or companies – is evaluated as a bundle of attributes.[17]

Like MDS, conjoint analysis relies on participants' subjective evaluations. In MDS, however, the stimuli are products or brands. In conjoint analysis, the stimuli are combinations of attribute levels determined by the researcher. The goal in MDS is to develop a spatial map depicting the stimuli in a multidimensional perceptual or preference space. Conjoint analysis, on the other hand, seeks to develop the part-worth or utility functions describing the utility that consumers attach to the levels of each attribute. The two techniques are complementary.

Conjoint analysis has been used in marketing for a variety of purposes, including the following:

- *Determining the relative importance of attributes in the consumer choice process.* A standard output from conjoint analysis consists of derived relative importance weights for all the attributes used to construct the stimuli presented in an evaluation task. The relative importance weights indicate which attributes are important in influencing consumer choice.

- *Estimating market share of brands that differ in attribute levels.* The utilities derived from conjoint analysis can be used as input into a choice simulator to determine the share of choices, and hence the market share, of different brands.

- *Determining the composition of the most preferred brand.* Brand features can be varied in terms of attribute levels and the corresponding utilities determined. The brand features that yield the highest utility indicate the composition of the most preferred brand.

- *Segmenting the market based on similarity of preferences for attribute levels.* The part-worth functions derived for the attributes may be used as a basis for clustering participants to arrive at homogeneous preference segments.[18]

Applications of conjoint analysis have been made in consumer goods, industrial goods and financial and other services. Moreover, these applications have spanned all areas of marketing. A survey of conjoint analysis reported applications in the areas of new product and concept identification, competitive analysis, pricing, market segmentation, advertising and distribution.[19]

Statistics and terms associated with conjoint analysis

The important statistics and terms associated with conjoint analysis include the following:

Part-worth functions. The part-worth or *utility functions* describe the utility that consumers attach to the levels of each attribute.

Relative importance weights. The relative importance weights are estimated and indicate which attributes are important in influencing consumer choice.

Attribute levels. These levels denote the values assumed by the attributes.

Full profiles. Full or complete profiles of brands are constructed in terms of all the attributes by using the attribute levels specified by the design.

Pairwise tables. Participants evaluate two attributes at a time until all the required pairs of attributes have been evaluated.

Cyclical designs. These designs are employed to reduce the number of paired comparisons.

Fractional factorial designs. These designs are employed to reduce the number of stimulus profiles to be evaluated in the full-profile approach.

Orthogonal arrays. These are a special class of fractional designs that enable the efficient estimation of all main effects.

Internal validity. This involves correlations of the predicted evaluations for the holdout or validation stimuli with those obtained from the participants.

Conducting conjoint analysis

Figure 24.8 lists the steps in conjoint analysis. Formulating the problem involves identifying the salient attributes and their levels. These attributes and levels are used for constructing the stimuli to be used in a conjoint evaluation task. The participants rate or rank the stimuli using a suitable scale, and the data obtained are analysed. The results are interpreted and their reliability and validity assessed. We now describe each of the steps of conjoint analysis in detail.

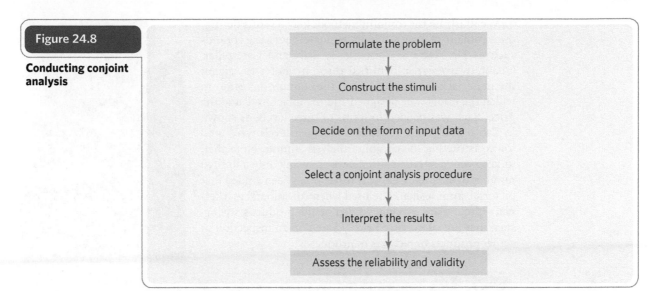

Figure 24.8

Conducting conjoint analysis

Formulate the problem

In formulating the conjoint analysis problem, the researcher must identify the attributes and attribute levels to be used in constructing the stimuli. Attribute levels denote the values assumed by the attributes. From a theoretical standpoint, the attributes selected should be salient in influencing consumer preference and choice. For example, in the choice of a car, price, fuel efficiency, interior space and so forth should be included. From a managerial perspective, the attributes and their levels should be characteristics that management can change and take action upon. To tell a manager that consumers prefer a sporty car to one that is conservative looking is not helpful, unless sportiness and conservativeness are defined in terms of attributes over which a manager has control. The attributes can be identified through discussions with management and industry experts, analysis of secondary data, qualitative research and pilot surveys. A typical conjoint analysis study may involve six or seven attributes.

Once the salient attributes have been identified, their appropriate levels should be selected. The number of attribute levels determines the number of parameters that will be estimated and also influences the number of stimuli that will be evaluated by the participants. To minimise the participant evaluation task and yet estimate the parameters with reasonable accuracy, it is desirable to restrict the number of attribute levels. The utility or part-worth function for the levels of an attribute may be non-linear. For example, a consumer may prefer a medium-sized car to either a small or a large one. Likewise, the utility for price may be non-linear. The loss of utility in going from a low price to a medium price may be much smaller than the loss in utility in going from a medium price to a high price. In these cases, at least three levels should be used. Some attributes, though, may naturally occur in binary form (two levels): a car does or does not have a sunroof.

The attribute levels selected will affect the consumer evaluations. If the price of a car brand is varied at €14,000, €16,000 and €18,000, price will be relatively unimportant. On the other hand, if the price is varied at €20,000, €30,000 and €40,000, it will be an important factor. Hence, the researcher should take into account the attribute levels prevalent in the marketplace and the objectives of the study. Using attribute levels that are beyond the range reflected in the marketplace will decrease the believability of the evaluation task, but it will increase the accuracy with which the parameters are estimated. The general guideline is to select attribute levels so that the ranges are somewhat greater than those prevalent in the marketplace but not so large as to impact adversely upon the believability of the evaluation task.

We illustrate the conjoint methodology by considering the problem of how students evaluate boots, e.g. brands such as Dr Martens, Timberland, Bally and Caterpillar. Qualitative research identified three attributes as salient: the material used for the upper, the country or region in which the boots were designed and manufactured, and the price. Each was defined in terms of three levels, as shown in Table 24.2. These attributes and their levels were used for constructing the conjoint analysis stimuli. Note that, to keep the illustration simple, we are using only a limited number of attributes, i.e. only three. It has been argued that pictorial stimuli should be used when consumers' market-place choices are strongly guided by the product's styling, such that the choices are heavily based on an inspection of actual products or pictures of products.[20]

Table 24.2	**Boot attributes and levels**		

| | | Level | |
Attribute		Number	Description
Uppers		3	Leather
		2	Suede
		1	Imitation leather
Country		3	Italy
		2	USA
		1	Far East
Price		3	€50
		2	€125
		1	€200

Construct the stimuli

Two broad approaches are available for constructing conjoint analysis stimuli: the pairwise approach and the full-profile procedure. In the pairwise approach, also called *two-factor evaluations*, participants evaluate two attributes at a time until all the possible pairs of attributes have been evaluated. This approach is illustrated in the context of the boots example in Figure 24.9. For each pair, participants evaluate all the combinations of levels of both the attributes, which are presented in a matrix.

In the full-profile approach, also called *multiple-factor evaluations*, full or complete profiles of brands are constructed for all the attributes. Typically, each profile is described on a separate index card. This approach is illustrated in the context of the boots example in Table 24.3.

Table 24.3	**Full-profile approach to collecting conjoint data**

Example of boot product profile	
Upper	Made of leather
Country	Designed and made in Italy
Price	Costing €200

Figure 24.9

Pairwise approach to collecting conjoint data

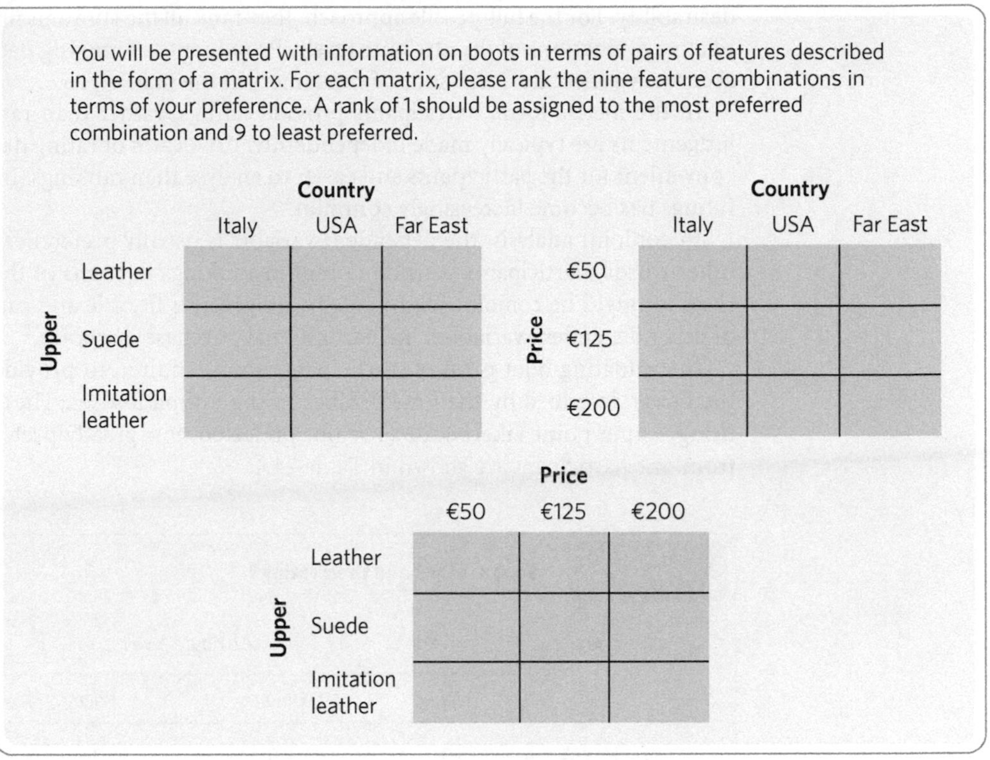

You will be presented with information on boots in terms of pairs of features described in the form of a matrix. For each matrix, please rank the nine feature combinations in terms of your preference. A rank of 1 should be assigned to the most preferred combination and 9 to least preferred.

It is not necessary to evaluate all the possible combinations, nor is it feasible in all cases.[21] In the pairwise approach, it is possible to reduce the number of paired comparisons by using cyclical designs. Likewise, in the full-profile approach, the number of stimulus profiles can be greatly reduced by means of fractional factorial designs. A special class of fractional designs, *orthogonal arrays*, allows for the efficient estimation of all main effects. Orthogonal arrays permit the measurement of all main effects of interest on an uncorrelated basis. These designs assume that all interactions are negligible.[22] Generally, two sets of data are obtained. One, the *estimation set*, is used to calculate the part-worth functions for the attribute levels. The other, the *holdout set*, is used to assess reliability and validity.

The advantage of the pairwise approach is that it is easier for the participants to provide these judgements. Its relative disadvantage, however, is that it requires more evaluations than the full-profile approach. Also, the evaluation task may be unrealistic when only two attributes are being evaluated simultaneously. Studies comparing the two approaches indicate that both methods yield comparable utilities, yet the full-profile approach is more commonly used.

The boots example follows the full-profile approach. Given three attributes, defined at three levels each, a total of $3 \times 3 \times 3 = 27$ profiles can be constructed. To reduce the participant evaluation task, a fractional factorial design was employed and a set of nine profiles was constructed to constitute the estimation stimuli set (see Table 24.4). Another set of nine stimuli was constructed for validation purposes. Input data were obtained for both the estimation and validation stimuli. Before the data could be obtained, however, it was necessary to decide on the form of the input data.

Decide on the form of input data

As in the case of MDS, conjoint analysis input data can be either non-metric or metric. For non-metric data, participants are typically required to provide rank order evaluations. For the pairwise approach, participants rank all the cells of each matrix in terms of their desirability. For the full-profile approach, they rank all the stimulus profiles. Rankings involve relative evaluations of the attribute levels. Proponents of ranking data believe that such data accurately reflect the behaviour of consumers in the marketplace.

In the metric form, participants provide ratings, rather than rankings. In this case, the judgements are typically made independently. Advocates of rating data believe they are more convenient for the participants and easier to analyse than rankings. In recent years, the use of ratings has become increasingly common.

In conjoint analysis, the dependent variable is usually preference or intention to buy. In other words, participants provide ratings or rankings in terms of their preference or intentions to buy. The conjoint methodology, however, is flexible and can accommodate a range of other dependent variables, including actual purchase or choice.

In evaluating boot profiles, participants were required to provide preference ratings for the boots described by the nine profiles in the estimation set. These ratings were obtained using a nine-point Likert scale (1 = not preferred, 9 = greatly preferred). Ratings obtained from one participant are shown in Table 24.4.

Table 24.4	Boot profiles and their ratings			
Profile number	Attribute levels[a]			
	Upper	Country	Price	Preference rating
1	1	1	1	9
2	1	2	2	7
3	1	3	3	5
4	2	1	2	6
5	2	2	3	5
6	2	3	1	6
7	3	1	3	5
8	3	2	1	7
9	3	3	2	6

[a] The attribute levels correspond to those in Table 24.2.

Select a conjoint analysis procedure

Conjoint analysis model

The mathematical model expressing the fundamental relationship between attributes and utility in conjoint analysis.

The basic conjoint analysis model may be represented by the following formula:[23]

$$U(X) = \sum_{i=1}^{m} \sum_{j=1}^{k_i} \alpha_{ij} x_{ij}$$

where $U(X)$ = overall utility of an alternative

α_{ij} = the part-worth contribution or utility associated with the jth level ($j = 1, 2, \ldots, k_j$) of the ith attribute ($i = 1, 2, \ldots, m$)

k_i = number of levels of attribute i

m = number of attributes

x_{ij} = 1 if the jth level of the ith attribute is present

= 0 otherwise

The importance of an attribute, I_p is defined in terms of the range of the part-worths, α_{ij}, across the levels of that attribute:

$$I_j = \{\max(\alpha_{ij}) - \min(\alpha_{ij})\} \text{ for each } i$$

The attribute's importance is normalised to ascertain its importance relative to other attributes, W_i:

$$W_i = \frac{I_i}{\sum\limits_{i=1}^{m} I_i}$$

so that

$$\sum\limits_{i=1}^{m} W_i = 1$$

Several different procedures are available for estimating the basic model. The simplest, and one which is gaining in popularity, is dummy variable regression (see Chapter 20). In this case, the predictor variables consist of dummy variables for the attribute levels. If an attribute has k_i levels, it is coded in terms of $k_i - 1$ dummy variables (see Chapter 17). If metric data are obtained, the ratings, assumed to be interval scaled, form the dependent variable. If the data are non-metric, the rankings may be converted to 0 or 1 by making paired comparisons between brands. In this case, the predictor variables represent the differences in the attribute levels of the brands being compared. Other procedures that are appropriate for non-metric data include LINMAP, MONANOVA and the LOGIT model (see Chapter 21).[24]

The researcher must also decide whether the data will be analysed at the individual participant or the aggregate level. At the individual level, the data of each participant are analysed separately. If an aggregate-level analysis is to be conducted, some procedure for grouping the participants must be devised. One common approach is to estimate individual-level part-worth or utility functions first. Participants are then clustered on the basis of the similarity of their part-worth functions. Aggregate analysis is then conducted for each cluster. An appropriate model for estimating the parameters should be specified.[25]

The data reported in Table 24.4 were analysed using ordinary least squares (OLS) regression with dummy variables. The dependent variable was the preference ratings. The independent variables or predictors were six dummy variables, two for each variable. The transformed data are shown in Table 24.5. Since the data pertain to a single participant, an individual-level analysis was conducted. The part-worth or utility functions estimated for each attribute, as well as the relative importance of the attributes, are given in Table 24.6.[26]

| Table 24.5 | **Boot data coded for dummy variable regression** |

Preference ratings	Attributes					
	Upper		Country		Price	
Y	X_1	X_2	X_3	X_4	X_5	X_6
9	1	0	1	0	1	0
7	1	0	0	1	0	1
5	1	0	0	0	0	0
6	0	1	1	0	0	1
5	0	1	0	1	0	0
6	0	1	0	0	1	0
5	0	0	1	0	0	0
7	0	0	0	1	1	0
6	0	0	0	0	0	1

Table 24.6	**Results of conjoint analysis**

Attribute	Level			Importance
	Number	Description	Utility	
Uppers	3	Leather	0.778	
	2	Suede	-0.556	
	1	Imitation leather	-0.222	0.268
Country	3	Italy	0.445	
	2	USA	0.111	
	1	Far East	-0.556	0.214
Price	3	€50	1.111	
	2	€125	0.111	
	1	€200	-1.222	0.500

The model estimated may be represented as

$$U = b_0 + b_1 X_1 + b_2 X_2 + b_3 X_3 + b_4 X_4 + b_5 X_5 + b_6 X_6$$

where X_1, X_2 = dummy variables representing uppers
X_3, X_4 = dummy variables representing country
X_5, X_6 = dummy variables representing price

For uppers, the attribute levels were coded as follows:

	X_1	X_2
Level 1	1	0
Level 2	0	1
Level 3	0	0

The levels of the other attributes were coded similarly. The parameters were estimated as follows:

$$b_0 = 4.222$$
$$b_1 = 1.000$$
$$b_2 = -0.333$$
$$b_3 = 1.000$$
$$b_4 = 0.667$$
$$b_5 = 2.333$$
$$b_6 = 1.333$$

Given the dummy variable coding, in which level 3 is the base level, the coefficients may be related to the part-worths. As explained in Chapter 20, each dummy variable coefficient represents the difference in the part-worth for that level minus the part-worth for the base level. For uppers, we have the following:

$$\alpha_{11} - \alpha_{13} = b_1$$
$$\alpha_{12} - \alpha_{13} = b_2$$

To solve for the part-worths, an additional constraint is necessary. The part-worths are estimated on an interval scale, so the origin is arbitrary. Therefore, the additional constraint imposed is of the form

$$\alpha_{11} + \alpha_{12} + \alpha_{13} = 0$$

These equations for the first attribute, uppers, are

$$\alpha_{11} - \alpha_{13} = 1.000$$
$$\alpha_{12} - \alpha_{13} = -0.333$$
$$\alpha_{11} + \alpha_{12} + \alpha_{13} = 0$$

Solving these equations, we get

$$\alpha_{11} = 0.778$$
$$\alpha_{12} = -0.556$$
$$\alpha_{13} = -0.222$$

The part-worths for other attributes reported in Table 24.6 can be estimated similarly. For country, we have

$$\alpha_{21} - \alpha_{23} = b_3$$
$$\alpha_{22} - \alpha_{23} = b_4$$
$$\alpha_{21} + \alpha_{22} + \alpha_{23} = 0$$

For the third attribute, price, we have

$$\alpha_{31} - \alpha_{33} = b_5$$
$$\alpha_{32} - \alpha_{33} = b_6$$
$$\alpha_{31} + \alpha_{32} + \alpha_{33} = 0$$

The relative importance weights were calculated based on ranges of part-worths, as follows:

$$\text{Sum of ranges of part-worths} = [0.778\,(-0.556)] + [0.445 - (-0.556)]$$
$$+ [1.111 - (-1.222)]$$
$$= 4.668$$

$$\text{Relative importance of uppers} = \frac{[0.778 - (-0.556)]}{4.668} = \frac{1.334}{4.668} = 0.286$$

$$\text{Relative importance of country} = \frac{[0.445 - (-0.556)]}{4.668} = \frac{1.001}{4.668} = 0.214$$

$$\text{Relative importance of price} = \frac{[1.111 - (-1.222)]}{4.668} = \frac{2.333}{4.668} = 0.500$$

The estimation of the part-worths and the relative importance weights provides the basis for interpreting the results.

Interpret the results

For interpreting the results, it is helpful to plot the part-worth functions. The part-worth function values for each attribute given in Table 24.6 are graphed in Figure 24.10. As can be seen from Table 24.6 and Figure 24.10, this participant has the greatest preference for leather uppers when evaluating boots. Second preference is for imitation leather uppers, and suede uppers are least preferred. An Italian boot is most preferred, followed by American boots and boots from the Far East. As may be expected, a price of €50.00 has the highest utility and a price of €200.00 the lowest. The utility values reported in Table 24.6 have only interval scale properties, and their origin is arbitrary. In terms of relative importance of the attributes, we see that price is number one. Second most important is uppers, followed closely by country. Because price is by far the most important attribute for this participant, this person could be labelled as price sensitive.

Figure 24.10

**Part-worth
functions**

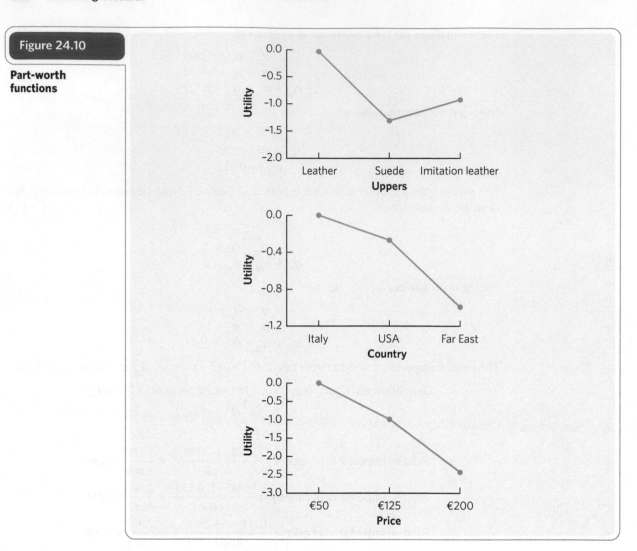

Assess the reliability and validity

Several procedures are available for assessing the reliability and validity of conjoint analysis results:[27]

1 The goodness of fit of the estimated model should be evaluated. For example, if dummy variable regression is used, the value of R^2 will indicate the extent to which the model fits the data. Models with poor fit are suspect.

2 Test–retest reliability can be assessed by obtaining a few replicated judgements later in data collection. In other words, at a later stage in the interview, the participants are asked to evaluate certain selected stimuli again. The two values of these stimuli are then correlated to assess test–retest reliability.

3 The evaluations for the holdout or validation stimuli can be predicted by the estimated part-worth functions. The predicted evaluations can then be correlated with those obtained from the participants to determine internal validity.

4 If an aggregate-level analysis has been conducted, the estimation sample can be split in several ways and conjoint analysis conducted on each subsample. The results can be compared across subsamples to assess the stability of conjoint analysis solutions.

In running a regression analysis on the data of Table 24.5, an R^2 of 0.934 was obtained, indicating a good fit. The preference ratings for the nine validation profiles were predicted from the utilities reported in Table 24.6. These were correlated with the input ratings for these profiles obtained from the participant. The correlation coefficient was 0.95, indicating a good predictive ability. This correlation coefficient is significant at $\alpha = 0.05$.

Assumptions and limitations of conjoint analysis

Although conjoint analysis is a popular technique, like MDS it carries a number of assumptions and limitations. Conjoint analysis assumes that the important attributes of a product can be identified. Furthermore, it assumes that consumers evaluate the choice alternatives in terms of these attributes and make trade-offs. In situations where image or brand name is important, however, consumers may not evaluate the brands or alternatives in terms of attributes. Even if consumers consider product attributes, the trade-off model may not be a good representation of the choice process. Another limitation is that data collection may be complex, particularly if a large number of attributes are involved and the model must be estimated at the individual level. This problem has been mitigated to some extent by procedures such as interactive or adaptive conjoint analysis and hybrid conjoint analysis. It should also be noted that the part-worth functions are not unique.

Hybrid conjoint analysis

Hybrid conjoint analysis
A form of conjoint analysis that can simplify the data collection task and estimate selected interactions as well as all main effects.

Hybrid conjoint analysis is an attempt to simplify the burdensome data collection task required in traditional conjoint analysis. Each participant evaluates a large number of profiles, yet usually only simple part-worth functions, without any interaction effects, are estimated. In the simple part-worths or main-effects model, the value of a combination is simply the sum of the separate main effects (simple part-worths). In actual practice, two attributes may interact in the sense that the participant may value the combination more than the average contribution of the separate parts. Hybrid models have been developed to serve two main purposes: (1) to simplify the data collection task by imposing less of a burden on each participant; and (2) to permit the estimation of selected interactions (at the subgroup level) as well as all main (or simple) effects at the individual level.

In the hybrid approach, the participants evaluate a limited number, generally no more than nine, of conjoint stimuli, such as full profiles. These profiles are drawn from a large master design and different participants evaluate different sets of profiles so that, over a group of participants, all the profiles of interest are evaluated. In addition, participants directly evaluate the relative importance of each attribute and desirability of the levels of each attribute. By combining the direct evaluations with those derived from the evaluations of the conjoint stimuli, it is possible to estimate a model at the aggregate level and still retain some individual differences.[28]

MDS and conjoint analysis are complementary techniques and may be used in combination, as in the following example.

Weeding out the competition[29]

ICI Agricultural Products did not know whether it should lower the price of Fusilade, its herbicide. It knew that it had developed a potent herbicide, but it was not sure that its weedkiller would survive in a price-conscious market. So a survey was designed to assess the relative importance of different attributes in selecting herbicides and to measure and map perceptions of major herbicides on the same attributes. Face-to-face interviews were conducted with

601 soybean and cotton farmers who had at least 200 hectares dedicated to growing these crops and who had used herbicides during the past growing season. First, conjoint analysis was used to determine the relative importance of the attributes farmers use when selecting herbicides. Then MDS was used to map farmers' perceptions of herbicides. The study showed that price greatly influenced herbicide selections, and participants were particularly sensitive when costs were more than €10 per hectare. But price was not the only determinant. Farmers also considered how much weed control the herbicide provided. They were willing to pay higher prices to keep weeds off their land. The study showed that herbicides that failed to control even one of the four most common weeds would have to be very inexpensive to attain a reasonable market share. Fusilade promised good weed control. Furthermore, MDS indicated that one of Fusilade's competitors was considered to be expensive. Hence, ICI kept its original pricing plan and did not lower the price of Fusilade.

Both MDS and conjoint analysis are widely used techniques as further illustrated in the following two examples. The first example illustrates an application of conjoint analysis in the context of international marketing research. The second example shows how MDS can be used in researching ethical perceptions.

Fab's fabulous foamy fight[30]

Competition in the detergent market was intensifying in Thailand. Market potential research in Thailand indicated that superconcentrates would continue to grow at a healthy rate, although the detergent market had slowed. In addition, this category had already dominated other Asian markets such as Taiwan, Hong Kong and Singapore. Consequently, Colgate entered this new line of competition with Fab Power Plus with the objective of capturing 4% market share. Based on secondary data and qualitative research, Colgate assessed the critical factors for the success of superconcentrates. Some of these factors were: environmental appeal; hand washing and machine washing convenience; superior cleaning abilities; optimum level of suds for hand washing; and brand name. Research also revealed that no brand had both hand and machine wash capabilities and a formula that had both these qualities was desirable. A conjoint study was designed and these factors varied at either two or three levels. Preference ratings were gathered from participants and part-worths for the factors estimated at both the individual and group level. Results showed that the factor of hand–machine capability had a substantial contribution, supporting earlier claims. Based on these findings, Fab Power Plus was successfully introduced as a brand with both hand and machine wash capabilities.

Real research	**Ethical perceptions of marketing research firms[31]**

In a refined scale to measure the degree to which a certain situation is ethical or unethical, three factors have been found to have acceptable validity and parsimony. Two of these dimensions are particularly interesting. These were a broad-based moral equity dimension (factor 1) and a relativistic dimension (factor 2). Using multidimensional scaling, one can plot the perceived ethics of marketing research firms using these dimensions. For example, an MDS plot might look like the diagram here.

An MDS plot might look like this . . .

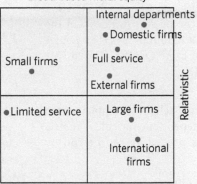

In this example, internal marketing research departments were perceived to be the most ethical on both dimensions. Large marketing research firms were perceived to be more ethical on the relativistic dimension, whereas small firms were more ethical on the moral equity factor. International research firms were more ethical on relativistic terms (*coping in an environment where there are no absolute truths*), whereas domestic firms were higher on the moral equity dimension. Full-service research firms were perceived to be more ethical on both the dimensions as compared with limited-service firms.

SPSS and SAS Learning Editions

SPSS Windows

The multidimensional scaling program allows individual differences as well as aggregate analysis using ALSCAL. The level of measurement can be ordinal, interval or ratio. Both the direct and derived approaches can be accommodated. To select multidimensional scaling procedures, click

Analyze>Scale>Multidimensional Scaling . . .

Following are the detailed steps for running multidimensional scaling on the similarity rating using the data from Table 24.1. First, convert similarity ratings to distances by subtracting each value of Table

24.1 from 8. The form of the data matrix has to be square symmetric (diagonal elements zero and distances above and below the diagonal; see SPSS file Table 24.1 Input). Note that SPSS gives solutions that are different from those presented in this chapter using different software. Note also that the example in Table 24.1 is based upon beer preferences. In the following, the example is based upon toothpaste preferences. The dataset is identical.

1 Select ANALYZE from the SPSS menu bar.
2 Click SCALE and then MULTIDIMENSIONAL SCALING (ALSCAL).

3 Move 'Aqua-Fresh [var00001]', 'Crest [var00002]', 'Colgate [var00003]', 'Aim [var00004]', 'Gleem [var00005]', 'Plus White [var00006]', 'Ultra-Brite [var00007]', 'Close-Up [var00008]', 'Pepsodent [var00009]' and 'Sensodyne [var00010]' into the VARIABLES box.

4 In the DISTANCES box check DATA ARE DISTANCES. SHAPE should be SQUARE SYMMETRIC (default).

5 Click MODEL. In the pop-up window, in the LEVEL OF MEASUREMENT box, check INTERVAL. In the SCALING MODEL box, check EUCLIDEAN DISTANCE. In the CONDITIONALITY box, check MATRIX. Click CONTINUE.

6 Click OPTIONS. In the pop-up window, in the DISPLAY box, check GROUP PLOTS, DATA MATRIX and MODEL AND OPTIONS SUMMARY. Click CONTINUE.

7 Click OK.

The conjoint analysis approach can be implemented using regression if the dependent variable is metric (interval or ratio). This procedure can be run by clicking

    Analyze>Regression>Linear . . .

Detailed steps for running a regression are given in Chapter 20. SPSS Conjoint is a specialised program that is available as a separate module.

SAS Learning Edition

The instructions given here and in all the quantitative data analysis chapters will work with the SAS Learning Edition as well as with the SAS Enterprise Guide. In SAS, the MDS procedure is available and shares many of the features of the ALSCAL (a program that incorporates several different MDS models and can be used for conducting individual or aggregate-level analysis). Within SAS, the MDS procedure generally produces results similar to those from the ALSCAL procedure if you use the following options in PROC MDS:

    FIT=SQUARED
    FORMULA = 1 except for unfolding data, which require FORMULA = 2
    PFINAL to get output similar to that from ALSCAL

The MDS and ALSCAL procedures may sometimes produce different results for the following reasons:

- With the LEVEL = INTERVAL option, PROC MDS fits a regression model while PROC ALSCAL fits a measurement model. These models are not equivalent if there is more than one partition, although the differences in the parameter estimates are usually minor.

- PROC MDS and PROC ALSCAL use different algorithms for internalisation and optimisation. Hence different local optima may be found by PROC MDS and PROC ALSCAL for some datasets with poor fit. Using the INAV = SSCP option causes the initial estimates from PROC MDS to be more like those from PROC ALSCAL.

- The default convergence criteria in PROC MDS are stricter than those in PROC ALSCAL. The convergence measure in PROC ALSCAL may cause PROC ALSCAL to stop iterating because a local optimum has been reached. Even if you run PROC ALSCAL with a very small convergence criterion and a very large iteration limit, PROC ALSCAL may never achieve the same degree of precision as PROC MDS. For most applications, this problem is of no practical consequence since two- or three-digit precision is sufficient. If the model does not fit well, obtaining higher precision may require hundreds of iterations.

Also, PROC MDS produces no plots so you must use output datasets to produce the plots.

Following are the detailed steps for running MDS on the similarity ratings with the data in Table 24.1. Again note that the example in Table 24.1 is based upon beer preferences. In the following, the example is based upon toothpaste preferences. The dataset is identical.

1 Select File>New>Code. (Note that MDS is not available as an SAS Learning Edition task and that SAS code needs to be submitted to run this analysis.)

2 Type the following SAS statements into the Code window and enter the physical location of Table 24.1 in the libname statement:

```
libname mdsdata 'Location of MDS Data';
proc mds data=mdsdata.table_21_1
  fit=squared
  formula=1
  pfinal
    out=out
;
run;
%plotit(data=out(where=
(_type_='CONFIG')), datatype=mds,
            labelvar=_name_,vtoh=1.75);
```

3 Select Code>Run Code on Local.

The conjoint analysis approach can be implemented using regression if the dependent variable is metric (interval or ratio). This procedure can be run within SAS Learning Edition by clicking

Analyze>Regression>Linear . . .

Note that the Learning Edition of SAS does not have a specific function for MDS or conjoint, so SAS code has to be inserted. The screen captures, which can be downloaded from the Website for this book, show how to do that.

Summary

Multidimensional scaling (MDS) is used for obtaining spatial representations of participants' perceptions and preferences. Perceived or psychological relationships among stimuli are represented as geometric relationships among points in a multidimensional space. Formulating the MDS problem requires a specification of the brands or stimuli to be included. The number and nature of brands selected influence the resulting solution. Input data obtained from participants can be related to perceptions or preferences. Perception data can be direct or derived. The direct approaches are more common in marketing research.

The selection of an MDS procedure depends on the nature (metric or non-metric) of the input data and whether perceptions or preferences are being scaled. Another determining factor is whether the analysis will be conducted at the individual or aggregate level. The decision about the number of dimensions in which to obtain a solution should be based on theory, interpretability, elbow criterion and ease-of-use considerations. Labelling of the dimensions is a difficult task that requires subjective judgement. Several guidelines are available for assessing the reliability and validity of MDS solutions. Preference data can be subjected to either internal or external analysis. If the input data are of a qualitative nature, they can be analysed via correspondence analysis. If the attribute-based approaches are used to obtain input data, spatial maps can also be obtained by means of factor or discriminant analysis.

Conjoint analysis is based on the notion that the relative importance that consumers attach to salient attributes, and the utilities they attach to the levels of attributes, can be determined when consumers evaluate brand profiles that are constructed using these attributes and their levels. Formulating the problem requires an identification of the salient attributes and their levels. The pairwise and the full-profile approaches are commonly employed for constructing the stimuli. Statistical designs are available for reducing the number of stimuli in the evaluation task. The input data can be either non-metric (rankings) or metric (ratings). Typically, the dependent variable is preference or intention to buy.

Although other procedures are available for analysing conjoint analysis data, regression using dummy variables is becoming increasingly important. Interpreting the results requires an examination of the part-worth functions and relative importance weights. Several procedures are available for assessing the reliability and validity of conjoint analysis results.

Questions

1   For what purposes are MDS procedures used?
2   Identify two marketing research problems where MDS could be applied. Explain how you would apply MDS in these situations.
3   What is meant by a spatial map?
4   Describe the steps involved in conducting MDS.
5   Describe the direct and derived approaches to obtaining MDS input data.
6   What factors influence the choice of an MDS procedure?
7   What guidelines are used for deciding on the number of dimensions in which to obtain an MDS solution?
8   Describe the ways in which the reliability and validity of MDS solutions can be assessed.
9   What is the difference between internal and external analysis of preference data?
10 What is involved in formulating a conjoint analysis problem?
11 Describe the full-profile approach to constructing stimuli in conjoint analysis.
12 Describe the pairwise approach to constructing stimuli in conjoint analysis.
13 How can regression analysis be used for analysing conjoint data?
14 Graphically illustrate what is meant by part-worth functions.
15 What procedures are available for assessing the reliability and validity of conjoint analysis results?

Exercises

1   Identify two marketing research problems where MDS could be applied and two where conjoint analysis could be applied. Explain how you would use these techniques in these situations.

2   A participant's ratings of nine luxury car brands on four dimensions are shown. Each brand was evaluated on each dimension (prestige, performance, luxury and value) on a seven-point scale with '1 = poor' and '7 = excellent'. Develop an MDS plot in two dimensions. Explain the plot.

Brand	Prestige	Performance	Luxury	Value
Ferrari	5	7	5	7
Jaguar	5	6	5	7
BMW	5	7	6	5
Mercedes	6	6	6	6
Audi	5	5	6	5
Lexus	6	6	5	5
Porsche	5	6	5	4
Bentley	7	4	7	3
Rolls	7	4	7	1

3 Consider 12 brands of bath soap (you can use the following – or other brands that you are more familiar with): Dove, Zest, Dial, Imperial Leather, Body Shop, Camay, Ivory, Palmolive, Irish Spring, Lux, Safeguard, Fairy. Form all the possible 66 pairs of these brands. Rate these pairs of brands in terms of similarity using a seven-point scale. Write a report on what you would see as the participant experience in completing the task of comparing these brands.

4 Construct the nine boot profiles given in Table 24.4. Rate these nine profiles in terms of your preference, using a nine-point rating scale.

5 In a small group discuss the similarities and differences between MDS, factor analysis and discriminant analysis, and 'simplifying MDS solutions to two-dimensional graphics works well in conveying a solution, but they can only rarely convey the complexity of how consumers differentiate between brands'.

Notes

1. Foote, A, 'Another wake up call', *Beverage World* 124 (3) (March 2005), 4; Foust, D., 'Things go better with… Juice: Coke's new CEO will have to move quickly to catch up in noncarbonated drink', *Business Week* 3883 (17 May, 2004), 81; Green, P.E., Carmone, F.J. Jr and Smith, S.M., *Multidimensional Scaling: Concepts and Applications* (Boston, MA: Allyn & Bacon, 1989), 16–17.

2. Anon., 'Boots Laboratories Serum 7 – Alliance Boots', Design Business Association, Gold, Design Effectiveness Awards (2009); Kara, A., Kaynak, E. and Kucukemiroglu, O., 'Credit card development strategies for the youth market: the use of conjoint analysis', *International Journal of Bank Marketing* 12 (6) (1994), 30–36; Barrett, P., Burr, P. and Dolman, N., 'The conjoint path over the cultural divide', *Marketing Week* (14 October 1997).

3. For a review of MDS studies in marketing, see Howaldt, K. and Mitchell, A., 'Can segmentation ever deliver the goods?', *Market Leader* 36 (Spring 2007), 54–58; DeSarbo, W. and Wu, J., 'The joint spatial representation of multiple variable batteries collected in marketing research', *Journal of Marketing Research* 38 (2) (May 2001), 244; Andrews, R.L. and Manrai, A.K., 'MDS maps for product attributes and market response: an application to scanner panel data', *Marketing Science* 18 (4) (1999), 584–604; Bijmolt, T.H.A. and Wedel, M., 'A comparison of multidimensional scaling methods for perceptual mapping', *Journal of Marketing Research* 36 (2) (May 1999), 277–285; Carroll, J.D. and Green, P.E., 'Psychometric methods in marketing research: Part II. Multidimensional scaling', *Journal of Marketing Research* 34 (February 1997), 193–204; Cooper, L.G., 'A review of multidimensional scaling in marketing research', *Applied Psychological Measurement* 7 (Fall 1983), 427–450.

4. An excellent discussion of the various aspects of MDS may be found in Borg, I. and Groenen, P.J.F., *Modern Multidimensional Scaling: Theory and Applications*, 2nd edn (New York: Springer-Verlag, 2005); Kruskal, J.B. and Wish, M., *Multidimensional Scaling* (Newbury Park, CA:

Sage, 2005); Green, P.E. and Wind, Y., *Marketing Research and Modeling: Progress and Prospects: A tribute to Paul E. Green* (New York: Springer-Verlag, 2005); Bijmolt, T.H.A. and Wedel, M., 'A comparison of multidimensional scaling methods for perceptual mapping', *Journal of Marketing Research* 36 (2) (May 1999), 277–285.

5. Lines, R. and Denstadli, J.M., 'Information overload in conjoint experiments', *International Journal of Market Research* 46 (3) (2004), 297–310.

6. The data are commonly treated as symmetric. For an asymmetric approach, see Desarbo, W.S. and Grewal, R., 'An alternative efficient representation of demand based competitive asymmetry', *Strategic Management Journal* 28 (7) (July 2007), 755–766; Desarbo, W.S. and Manrai, A.K., 'A new multidimensional scaling methodology for the analysis of asymmetric proximity data in marketing research', *Marketing Science* 11 (1) (Winter 1992), 1–20. For other approaches to MDS data, see Juvoung, K., 'Incorporating context effects in the multidimensional scaling of "Pick Any/N" choice data', *International Journal of Research in Marketing* 16 (1) (February 1999), 35–55; Bijmolt, T.H.A. and Wedel, M., 'The effects of alternative methods of collecting similarity data for multidimensional scaling', *International Journal of Research in Marketing* 12 (4) (November 1995), 363–371.

7. See Borg, I. and Groenen, P.J.F., *Modern Multidimensional Scaling: Theory and Applications*, 2nd edn (New York: Springer-Verlag, 2005); Cox, T.F. and Cox, M.A., *Multidimensional scaling*, 2nd edn (New York: Chapman & Hall, 2000); Steenkamp, J.-B.E.M. and Van Trijp, H.C.M., 'Task experience and validity in perceptual mapping: a comparison of two consumer-adaptive techniques', *International Journal of Research in Marketing* 13 (3) (July 1996), 265–276; Malhotra, N.K., Jain, A.K. and Pinson, C., 'The robustness of MDS configurations in the case of incomplete data', *Journal of Marketing Research* 25 (February 1988), 95–102.

8. See Cox, T.F. and Cox, M.A., *Multidimensional scaling*, 2nd edn (New York: Chapman & Hall, 2000). For an application see Dreyfuss, L., Danilo, S. and Garrel, C., 'Fragrance innovation – understanding consumer perceptions of fragrance', ESOMAR, Fragrance Research, Cannes (June 2009); d'Astous, A. and Boujbel, L., 'Positioning countries on personality dimensions: scale development and implications for country marketing', *Journal of Business Research* 60 (3) (March 2007), 231–239.

9. Kruskal's stress is probably the most commonly used measure for lack of fit. See Kruskal, J.B. and Wish, M., *Multidimensional Scaling* (Newbury Park, CA: Sage, 2005). For the original article, see Kruskal, J.B., 'Multidimensional scaling by optimising goodness of fit to a nonmetric hypothesis', *Psychometrika* 29 (March 1964), 1–27.

10. For an examination of the reliability and validity of MDS solutions, see DeSarbo, W.S., 'The joint spatial representation of multiple variable batteries collected in marketing research', *Journal of Marketing Research* 38 (2) (May 2001), 244–253; Carroll, J.D. and Green, P.E., 'Psychometric methods in marketing research: Part II. Multidimensional scaling', *Journal of Marketing Research* 34 (February 1997), 193–204; Malhotra, N.K., 'Validity and structural reliability of multidimensional scaling', *Journal of Marketing Research* 24 (May 1987), 164–173.

11. See, for example, Desarbo, W.S. and Grewal, R., 'An alternative efficient representation of demand based competitive asymmetry', *Strategic Management Journal* 28 (7) (July 2007), 755–766; Lee, J.K.H., Sudhir, K. and Steckel, J.H., 'A multiple ideal point model: capturing multiple preference effects from within an ideal point framework', *Journal of Marketing Research* 39 (1) (February 2002), 73–86; DeSarbo, W.S., Hoffman, D. and Rangaswamy, A., 'A parametric multidimensional unfolding procedure for incomplete nonmetric preference/choice set data marketing research', *Journal of Marketing Research* 34 (4) (November 1997), 499–516; Mackay, D.B., Easley, R.F. and Zinnes, J.L., 'A single ideal point model for market structure analysis', *Journal of Marketing Research* 32 (4) (November 1995), 433–443.

12. Ferris, P., 'All the right designs', *Marketing* 109 (15) (26 April, 2004), 3; Odekerken-Schroder, G., Ouwersloot, H., Lemmink, J. and Semeijn, J., 'Consumers' trade-off between relationship, service and package and price: an empirical study in the car industry', *European Journal of Marketing* 37 (1/2) (2003), 219–244.

13. For an application of correspondence analysis, see Gomez, M. and Benito, N.R., 'Manufacturer's characteristics that determine the choice of producing store brands', *European Journal of Marketing* 42 (1/2) (2008), 154–177; Inman, J., Shankar, V. and Ferraro, R., 'The roles of channel-category associations and geodemographics in channel patronage', *Journal of Marketing* 68 (April 2004), 51–71; Malhotra, N.K. and Charles, B., 'Overcoming the attribute prespecification bias in international marketing research by using nonattribute based correspondence analysis', *International Marketing Review* 19 (1) (2002), 65–79; Reed, K., 'The use of correspondence analysis to develop a scale to measure workplace morale from multi-level data', *Social Indicators Research* 57 (3) (March 2002), 339.

14. Whitlark, D.B. and Smith, S.M., 'Using correspondence analysis to map relationships', *Marketing Research: A Magazine of Management and Applications* 13 (4) (Fall 2001), 22–27.

15. See Bartholomew, D.J., *Analysis of Multivariate Social Science Data*, 2nd edn (Boca Raton, FL: CRC Press, 2008); Blasius, J. and Greenacre, M.J., *Visualization of Categorical Data* (New York: Academic Press, 1998); Greenacre, M.J., *Correspondence Analysis in Practice* (New York: Academic Press, 1993); Greenacre, M.J., 'The Carroll–Green–Schaffer scaling in correspondence analysis: a theoretical and empirical appraisal', *Journal of Marketing Research* 26 (August 1989), 358–365; Greenacre, M.J., *Theory and Applications of Correspondence Analyses* (New York: Academic Press, 1984); Hoffman, D.L. and Franke, G.R., 'Correspondence analysis: graphical representation of categorical data in marketing research', *Journal of Marketing Research* 23 (August 1986), 213–227.

16. Borg, I. and Groenen, P.J.F., *Modern Multidimensional Scaling: Theory and Application*, 2nd edn (New York: Springer-Verlag, 2005); Bijmolt, T.H.A. and Wedel, M., 'A comparison of multidimensional scaling methods for perceptual mapping', *Journal of Marketing Research* 36 (2) (May 1999), 277–285; Hauser, J.R. and Koppelman, F.S., 'Alternative perceptual mapping techniques: relative accuracy and usefulness', *Journal of Marketing Research* 16 (November 1979), 495–506. Hauser and Koppelman conclude that factor analysis is superior to discriminant analysis.

17. For applications and issues in conjoint analysis, see Meißner, M. and Decker, R., 'Eye-tracking information processing in choice-based conjoint analysis', *International Journal of Market Research* 52 (5) (2010), 593–612; Mønness, E. and Coleman, S., 'Comparing a survey and a conjoint study: the future vision of water intermediaries', *Journal of Applied Statistics* 35 (1) (January 2008), 19–30; Orth, U.R. and Malkewitz, K., 'Holistic package design and consumer brand impressions', *Journal of Marketing* 72 (3) (July 2008), 64–81; Backhaus, K., Hillig, T. and Wilken, R., 'Predicting purchase decisions with different conjoint analysis methods: a Monte Carlo simulation', *International Journal of Market Research* 49 (3) (2007), 341–364; Poynter, R., 'The power of conjoint analysis and choice modeling in online surveys', Market Research Society, Annual Conference (2006).

18. Wilsom-Jeanselme, M. and Reynolds, J., 'The advantages of preference based segmentation: an investigation of online grocery retailing', *Journal of Targeting, Measurement & Analysis for Marketing* 14 (4) (July 2006), 297–308; Dickson, M.A., Lennon, S.J., Montalto, C.P., Shen, D. and Zhang, L., 'Chinese consumer market segments for foreign apparel products', *Journal of Consumer Marketing* 21 (4/5) (2004), 301; Vriens, M., 'Linking attributes, benefits, and consumer values', *Marketing Research* 12 (3) (Fall 2000), 4–10; Thomas-Miller, J., Ogden, J.R. and Latshaw, C.A., 'Using trade-off analysis to determine value–price sensitivity of custom calling features', *American Business Review* 16 (1) (January 1998), 8–13. For an overview of conjoint analysis in marketing, see Carroll, J.D. and Green, P.E., 'Psychometric methods in marketing research: Part I. Conjoint analysis', *Journal of Marketing Research* 32 (November 1995), 385–391; Green, P.E. and Srinivasan, V., 'Conjoint analysis in marketing: new developments with implications for research and practice', *Journal of Marketing* 54 (October 1990), 3–19.

19. Hatzinger, R. and Mazanec, J.A., 'Measuring the part worth of the mode of transport in a trip package: an extended Bradley Terry model for paired comparison conjoint data', *Journal of Business Research* 60 (12) (December 2007), 1290–1302; Liechty, J.C., Fong, D.K.H. and DeSarbo, W.S., 'Dynamic models incorporating individual heterogeneity: utility evolution in conjoint analysis', *Marketing Science* 24 (2) (March 2005), 285–293; Bloch, P.H., Brunel, F.F. and Arnold, T.J., 'Individual differences in the centrality of visual product aesthetics: concept and measurement', *Journal of Consumer Research* 29 (March 2003), 551–565; Sandor, Z. and Wedel, M., 'Designing conjoint choice experiments using managers' prior beliefs', *Journal of Marketing Research* 38 (4) (November 2001), 430–444; Srinivasan, V., 'Predictive validation of multiattribute choice models', *Marketing Research* 11 (4) (Winter 1999/Spring 2000), 29–34; Wittink, D.R., Vriens, M. and Burhenne, W., 'Commercial uses of conjoint analysis in Europe: results and critical reflections', *International Journal of Research in Marketing* 11 (1) (January 1994), 41–52.

20. Jansson, C., Bointon, B. and Marlow, N., 'An exploratory conjoint analysis study of consumers' aesthetic responses of point of purchase materials', *International Review of Retail, Distribution and Consumer Research* 13 (1) (January 2003), 59–76; Wetzels, M., 'Measuring service quality trade-offs in Asian distribution channels: a multilayer perspective', *Total Quality Management* 11 (3) (May 2000), 307–318; Loosschilder, G.H., Rosbergen, E., Vriens, M. and Wittink, D.R., 'Pictorial stimuli in conjoint analysis – to support product styling decisions', *Journal of the Market Research Society* 37 (January 1995), 17–34.

21. McCullough, D., 'A users guide to conjoint analysis', *Marketing Research* (Summer 2002), 19–23.

22. See Grunert, K.G., Esbjerg, L., Bech-Larsen, T., Bruns, K. and Juhl, H., 'Consumer preferences for retail brand architectures: results from a conjoint study', *International Journal of Retail and Distribution Management* 34 (8) (2006), 597–608; Toubia, O., Hauser, J.R. and Simester, D.I., 'Polyhedral methods for adaptive choice based conjoint analysis', *Journal of Marketing Research* 41 (1) (February 2004), 116–131; Green, P.A., Krieger, A.M. and Wind, Y., 'Thirty years of conjoint analysis: reflections and prospects', *Interfaces* 31 (3) (May/June 2001), S56; Carroll, J.D. and Green, P.E., 'Psychometric methods in marketing research: Part I. Conjoint analysis', *Journal of Marketing Research* 32 (November 1995), 385–391; Kuhfeld, W.F., Tobias, R.D. and Garratt, M., 'Efficient experimental designs with marketing applications', *Journal of Marketing Research* 31 (November 1994), 545–557; Addleman, S., 'Orthogonal main-effect plans for asymmetrical factorial experiments', *Technometrics* 4 (February 1962), 21–36; Green, P.E., 'On the design of choice experiments involving multifactor alternatives', *Journal of Consumer Research* 1 (September 1974), 61–68.

23. Iyengar, R.I., Jedidi, K. and Kohli, R., 'A conjoint approach to multipart pricing', *Journal of Marketing Research* 45 (2) (May 2008), 195–210; Haaijer, R., Kamakura, W. and Wedel, M., 'Response latencies in the analysis of conjoint choice experiments', *Journal of Marketing Research* 37 (3) (August 2000), 376–382; Carroll, J.D. and Green, P.E., 'Psychometric methods in marketing research: Part I. Conjoint analysis', *Journal of Marketing Research* 32 (November 1995), 385–391.

24. Helm, R., Scholl, A. and Manthey, L., 'A comparative empirical study on common methods for measuring preferences', *International Journal of Management and Decision Making* 9 (3) (2008), 242–265; Ding, M., 'An incentive aligned mechanism for conjoint analysis', *Journal of Marketing Research* 44 (2) (May 2007), 214; Sandor, Z. and Wedel, M., 'Designing conjoint choice experiments using managers' prior beliefs', *Journal of Marketing Research* 38 (4) (November 2001), 430–444; Oppewal, H., Timmermans, H.J. and Louviere, J.J., 'Modeling the effect of shopping center size and store variety in consumer choice behaviour', *Environment and Planning* 29 (6) (June 1997), 1073–1090.

25. Evgeniou, T., Boussios, C. and Zacharia, G., 'Generalised robust conjoint estimation', *Marketing Science* 24 (3) (June 2005), 415–429; Arora, N. and Allenby, G.M., 'Measuring the influence of individual preference structures in group decision making', *Journal of Marketing Research* 36 (4) (November 1999), 476–487; Brice, R., 'Conjoint analysis: a review of conjoint paradigms and discussion of the outstanding design issues', *Marketing and Research Today* 25 (4) (November 1997), 260–266; Carroll, J.D. and Green, P.E., 'Psychometric methods in marketing research: Part I. Conjoint analysis', *Journal of Marketing Research* 32 (November 1995), 385–391; Carmone, E.J. and Green, P.E., 'Model mis-specification in multiattribute parameter estimation', *Journal of Marketing Research* 18 (February 1981), 87–93.

26. Chhajed, D. and Kim, K., 'The role of inclination and part worth differences across segments is designing a price-discriminating product line', *International Journal of Research in Marketing* 21 (3) (September 2004), 313. For an application of conjoint analysis using OLS regression, see Haaijer, R., Kamakura, W. and Wedel, M., 'The "No-Choice" alternative to conjoint choice experiments', *International Journal of Market Research* 43 (1) (First Quarter 2001), 93–106; Ostrom, A. and Iacobucci, D., 'Consumer trade-offs and the evaluation of services', *Journal of Marketing* 59 (January 1995), 17–28; Danaher, P.J., 'Using conjoint analysis to determine the relative importance of service attributes measured in customer satisfaction surveys', *Journal of Retailing* 73 (2) (Summer 1997), 235–260.

27. Ding, M., Grewal, R. and Liechty, J., 'Incentive aligned conjoint analysis', *Journal of Marketing Research* 42 (1) (February 2005), 67; Moore, W.L., 'A cross-validity comparison of rating-based and choice-based conjoint analysis models', *International Journal of Research in Marketing* 21 (3) (2004), 299–312; Andrews, R.L., 'Hierarchical Bayes versus finite mixture conjoint analysis: a comparison of fit, prediction and partworth recovery', *Journal of Marketing Research* 39 (1) (February 2002), 87–98; Carroll, J.D. and Green, P.E., 'Psychometric methods in marketing research: Part I. Conjoint analysis', *Journal of Marketing Research* 32 (November 1995), 385–391; Malhotra, N.K., 'Structural reliability and stability of nonmetric conjoint analysis', *Journal of Marketing Research* 19 (May 1982), 199–207; Leigh, T.W., MacKay, D.B. and Summers, J.O., 'Reliability and validity of conjoint analysis and self-explicated weights: a comparison', *Journal of Marketing Research* 21 (November 1984), 456–462; Segal, M.N., 'Reliability of conjoint analysis: contrasting data collection procedures', *Journal of Marketing Research* 19 (February 1982), 139–143.

28. Hofstede, F.T., Kim, Y. and Wedel, M., 'Bayesian prediction in hybrid conjoint analysis', *Journal of Marketing Research* 39 (2) (May 2002), 253–261; Vavra, T.G., Green, P.E. and Krieger, A.M., 'Evaluating EZPass', *Marketing Research* 11 (2) (Summer 1999), 4–14; Hu, C. and Hiemstra, S.J., 'Hybrid conjoint analysis as a research technique to measure meeting planners' preferences in hotel selection', *Journal of Travel Research* 35 (2) (Fall 1996), 62–69; Green, P.E. and Krieger, A.M., 'Individualized hybrid models for conjoint analysis', *Management Science* 42 (6) (June 1996), 850–867; Green, P.E., 'Hybrid models for conjoint analysis: an expository review', *Journal of Marketing Research* 21 (May 1984), 155–169.

29. Lusk, J.L., Fields, D. and Prevatt, W., 'An incentive compatible conjoint ranking mechanism', *American Journal of Agricultural Economics* 90 (2) (May 2008), 487–498; Boyle, K.J., 'A comparison of conjoint analysis response formats', *American Journal of Agricultural Economics* 83 (2) (May 2001), 441–454; McDonald, D., 'Industry giants', *Farm Industry News* 34 (3) (February 2001), 6; Schneidman, D., 'Research method designed to determine price for new products, line extensions', *Marketing News* (23 October 1987), 11.

30. Anon., 'Lever Faberge plans major softener launch', *Marketing Week* (September 9, 2004), 5; Jitpleecheep, S., 'Thailand's detergent market growth rate slows', *Knight Ridder Tribune Business News* (24 May, 2002), 1; Grant, L., 'Outmarketing P & G', *Fortune* 137 (1) (12 January, 1998), 150–152; Butler, D., 'Thai superconcentrates foam', *Advertising Age* (18 January, 1993).

31. Srnka, K.J., 'Culture's role in marketers' ethical decision making: an integrated theoretical framework', *Academy of Marketing Science Review* (2004) No. 1; Peterson, D., Rhoads, A. and Vaught, B.C., 'Ethical beliefs of business professionals: a study of gender, age and external factors', *Journal of Business Ethics* 31 (3) (June 2001), 1; Vitell, S.J. and Ho, F.N., 'Ethical decision making in marketing: a synthesis and evaluation of scales measuring the various components of decision making in ethical situations', *Journal of Business Ethics* 16 (7) (May 1997), 699–717.

Structural equation modelling and path analysis

Structural equation modelling can test the descriptive ability of different models, thus allowing them to be compared.

Objectives

After reading this chapter, you should be able to:

1 define the nature and unique characteristics of structural equation modelling (SEM);

2 explain the basic concepts in SEM such as theory, model, path diagram, exogenous versus endogenous constructs, dependence and correlational relationships, model fit and model identification;

3 discuss the basic statistics associated with SEM;

4 describe the process of conducting SEM and explain the various steps involved;

5 know how to specify a measurement model and assess its validity;

6 explain the concept of model fit and the differences between absolute, incremental and parsimony fit indices;

7 describe how to specify a structural model and assess its validity;

8 discuss the relationship of SEM to other multivariate techniques;

9 explain path analysis and discuss its relationship to SEM;

10 appreciate how SPSS and SAS software are used in structural equation modelling.

Overview

This chapter provides an overview of structural equation modelling (SEM), a procedure for estimating a series of dependence relationships among a set of concepts or constructs represented by multiple measured variables and incorporated into an integrated model. The principles of regression (Chapter 20) and factor analysis (Chapter 22) provide a foundation for understanding SEM. We start by discussing the basic concepts of SEM, followed by an explanation of the key statistics and terms associated with the procedure. Then we describe the procedure for conducting SEM. We also cover second-order confirmatory factor analysis (CFA) and present illustrative applications of SEM. Then, we describe the related technique of path analysis. Finally, help is provided to run the SPSS and SAS Learning Editions in the data analysis challenges presented in this chapter. We begin with an example of the use of SEM and confirmatory factor analysis.[1]

Real research | **Personal aspirations and the consumption of luxury goods[2]**

The market for luxury goods and services has been enlarging, steadily and strongly, since the early 1990s. The economic factors driving this trend include increasing disposable income, lower unemployment, reducing production costs and increasing female employment, as well as a growing wealthy class in developing nations. Studies have found significant and meaningful relationships between luxury consumption and a conspicuous consumption motive, but few have investigated other social motivations. A

study proposed to develop and validate an empirical model that included both extrinsic and intrinsic antecedents to buying luxury goods. Extrinsic goals included financial success (money and luxury), social recognition (fame) and appealing appearance (image); intrinsic goals were self-acceptance (growth), affiliation (relatedness), community feeling (helpfulness) and physical fitness (health). Research hypotheses were set to assess the effects of antecedents on consumer preference for luxury goods. A theoretical model was built, depicting the relationships between intrinsic and extrinsic aspirations, quality search, conspicuous consumption behaviour and self-directed pleasure. It was validated and tested by means of confirmatory factor analysis and structural equation modelling. Validation of the structural and measurement models was by means of discriminant and convergent validity tests.

Structural equation modelling (SEM)

Structural equation modelling (SEM) is a procedure for estimating a series of dependence relationships among a set of concepts or constructs represented by multiple measured variables and incorporated into an integrated model.

Basic concepts in SEM

In many instances, researchers must answer a set of interrelated questions. For example, a hotel company may be interested in the following questions: What variables determine service quality? How does service quality influence service attitude and service satisfaction? How does satisfaction with the service result in patronage intention? How does attitude towards the service combine with other variables to affect intention to patronise the service? Such interrelated questions cannot be examined in a unified analysis by any single statistical technique we have discussed so far. To answer such questions in a unified and integrated manner, the researcher must make use of structural equation modelling (SEM). SEM can help us assess the measurement properties and test the proposed theoretical relationships by using a single technique.[3] For example, based upon theory and previous research, we could contend that service quality has five dimensions or factors such tangibility, reliability, responsiveness, assurance and empathy. Service quality could be depicted as a latent construct that is not directly observed or measured. Rather, service quality is represented by the five dimensions that are observed or measured. SEM can determine the contribution of each dimension in representing service quality and evaluate how well a set of observed variables measuring these dimensions represents quality, i.e. how reliable the construct is. We can then incorporate this information into the estimation of the relationships between service quality and other constructs. Service quality has a direct and positive influence on both attitude and satisfaction towards the service. Service attitude and satisfaction, in turn, determine attitude to patronise the service. Thus service attitude and service satisfaction are both dependent and independent variables in our theory. A hypothesised dependent variable (service attitude/satisfaction) can become an independent variable in a subsequent dependence relationship (explaining patronage intention). Later in this chapter we give an empirical application of service quality in the context of personal banking.

SEM examines the structure of these interrelationships, which are expressed in a series of structural equations. This concept is similar to estimating a series of multiple regression equations (see Chapter 20). These equations model all the relationships among constructs, dependent as well as independent. In SEM, the constructs are unobservable or latent factors that are represented by multiple variables. This is similar to the concept of variables representing a factor in factor analysis (see Chapter 22), but SEM explicitly takes into account the measurement error. Measurement error is the degree to which the observed variables do not describe the latent constructs of interest in SEM.

SEM is distinguished from the other multivariate techniques we have discussed by the following characteristics:[4]

Construct

In SEM, a construct is a latent or unobservable concept that can be defined conceptually but cannot be measured directly or without error. Also called a *factor*, a construct is measured by multiple indicators or observed variables.

Measurement error

The degree to which the observed variables do not describe the latent constructs of interest in SEM.

1 Representation of constructs as unobservable or latent factors in dependence relationships.

2 Estimation of multiple and interrelated dependence relationships incorporated in an integrated model.

3 Incorporation of measurement error in an explicit manner. SEM can explicitly account for less than perfect reliability of the observed variables, providing analyses of attenuation and estimation bias due to measurement error.

4 Explanation of the covariance among the observed variables. SEM seeks to represent hypotheses about the means, variances and covariances of observed data in terms of a smaller number of structural parameters defined by a hypothesised underlying model.

SEM is also known by other names such as *covariance structure analysis, latent variable analysis* and *causal modelling*. However, it should be noted that SEM by itself cannot establish causality, although it can assist in that process. To make causal inferences, all of the three conditions of causality discussed in Chapter 11 must be satisfied. This is seldom the case in SEM as such models are generally estimated on single cross-sectional data (Chapter 3) collected by surveys at a single point in time. However, SEM can provide evidence of systematic covariation.[5] SEM is mainly used as a confirmatory, rather than exploratory, technique. Generally we use SEM to determine whether a certain model is valid, rather than using SEM to 'find' a suitable model. However, SEM analyses often involve an exploratory aspect.

Statistics and terms associated with SEM

The following statistics and statistical terms are associated with SEM:

Absolute fit indices. These indices measure the overall goodness of fit or badness of fit for both the measurement and structural models. Larger values of goodness of fit and smaller values of badness of fit represent better fits.

Average variance extracted (*AVE*). A measure used to assess convergent and discriminant validity, which is defined as the variance in the indicators or observed variables that is explained by the latent construct.

Chi-square difference statistic ($\Delta\chi^2$). A statistic used to compare two competing, nested SEM models. It is calculated as the difference between the models' chi-square values. Its degrees of freedom equal the difference in the models' degrees of freedom.

Composite reliability (*CR*). This is defined as the total amount of true score variation in relation to the total score variance. Thus composite reliability corresponds to the conventional notion of reliability in classical test theory.

Confirmatory factor analysis (*CFA*). A technique used to estimate the measurement model. It seeks to confirm whether the number of factors (or constructs) and the loadings of observed (indicator) variables on them conform to what is expected on the basis of theory. Indicator variables are selected on the basis of theory, and *CFA* is used to see if they load as predicted on the expected number of factors.

Endogenous construct. This is a latent, multi-item equivalent of a dependent variable. It is determined by constructs or variables within the model and thus it is dependent on other constructs.

Estimated covariance matrix. Denoted by Σ_k, this matrix consists of the predicted covariances between all observed variables based on equations estimated in SEM.

Exogenous construct. This is the latent, multi-item equivalent of an independent variable in traditional multivariate analysis. An exogenous construct is determined by factors outside of the model and it cannot be explained by any other construct or variable in the model.

First-order factor model. Covariances between observed variables are explained with a single latent factor or construct layer.

Incremental fit indices. These measures assess how well a model specified by the researcher fits relative to some alternative baseline model. Typically, the baseline model is a null model in which all observed variables are unrelated to each other.

Measurement model. The first two models estimated in SEM. This represents the theory that specifies the observed variables for each construct and permits the assessment of construct validity.

Modification index. An index calculated for each possible relationship that is not freely estimated but is fixed. The index shows the improvement in the overall model χ^2 if that path was freely estimated.

Nested model. A model is nested within another model if it has the same number of constructs and variables and can be derived from the other model by altering relationships, as by adding or deleting relationships.

Non-recursive model. A structural model that contains feedback loops or dual dependences.

Parsimony fit indices. Designed to assess fit in relation to model complexity and useful in evaluating competing models, these indices are goodness-of-fit measures and can be improved by a better fit or by a simpler, less complex model that estimates fewer parameters.

Parsimony ratio. This is calculated as the ratio of degrees of freedom used by the model to the total degrees of freedom available.

Path analysis (*PA*). A special case of SEM with only single indicators for each of the variables in the causal model. In other words, path analysis is SEM with a structural model, but no measurement model.

Path diagram. A graphical representation of a model showing the complete set of relationships among the constructs. Dependence relationships are portrayed by straight arrows and correlational relationships by curved arrows.

Recursive model. A structural model that does not contain any feedback loops or dual dependencies.

Sample covariance matrix. Denoted by S, this matrix consists of the variances and covariances for the observed variables.

Second-order factor model. There are two levels or layers. A second-order latent construct causes multiple first-order latent constructs, which in turn cause the observed variables. Thus, the first-order constructs now act as indicators or observed variables for the second-order factor.

Squared multiple correlations. Similar to communality, these values denote the extent to which an observed variable's variance is explained by a latent construct or factor.

Structural error. This is similar to an error term in regression analysis. In the case of completely standardised estimates, squared multiple correlation is equal to 1 − the structural error.

Structural model. The second of two models estimated in SEM. It represents the theory that specifies how the constructs are related to each other, often with multiple dependence relationships.

Structural relationship. Dependence relationship between an endogenous construct and another exogenous or endogenous construct.

Unidimensionality. A notion that a set of observed variables represent only one underlying construct. All cross-loadings are zero.

Foundations of SEM

Foundational to the understanding of SEM are the concepts of theory, model, path diagram, exogenous versus endogenous constructs, dependence and correlational relationships, model fit and model identification. These fundamental concepts are discussed next.

Theory, model, and path diagram

The role of theory and models in developing an approach to the problem was discussed in Chapter 2. There we defined a theory as a conceptual scheme based on foundational statements or axioms that are assumed to be true. A theory serves as a conceptual foundation for developing a model. It is very important that an SEM model be based on theory because all relationships must be specified before the SEM model can be estimated. In SEM, models are often constructed to test certain hypotheses derived from the theory. An SEM model consists of two models: the measurement model and the structural model.[6] The measurement model depicts how the observed (measured) variables represent constructs. It represents the theory that specifies the observed variables for each construct and permits the assessment of construct validity (Chapter 12). The observed variables are measured by the researcher and are also referred to as *measured variables*, *manifest variables*, *indicators* or *items* of the construct. Typically, observed variables are assumed to be dependent upon constructs.[7] Thus, straight arrows are drawn from a construct to the observed variables that are indicators of the construct (Figure 25.1). No single indicator can completely represent a construct but is used as an indication of that construct. The measurement model uses the technique of CFA in which the researcher specifies which variables define each construct (or factor). It seeks to confirm whether the number of factors (or constructs) and the loadings of observed (indicator) variables on them conform to what is expected on the basis of theory. Thus, CFA is used to verify the factor structure of a set of observed variables. CFA allows the researcher to test the hypothesis that a relationship between observed variables and their underlying latent constructs exists. The researcher uses knowledge of the theory, empirical research, or both; postulates the relationship pattern a priori; and then tests the hypothesis statistically. Indicator variables are selected on the basis of theory, and CFA is used to see if they load as predicted on the expected number of factors. The terms *construct* and *factor* are used interchangeably.

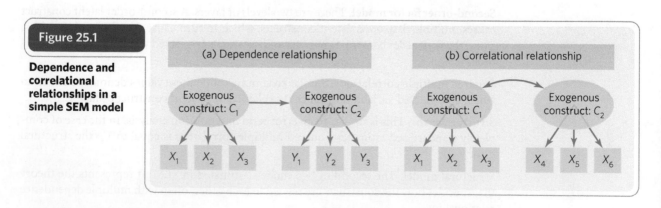

Figure 25.1

Dependence and correlational relationships in a simple SEM model

In other words, in testing for the measurement model, the researcher has complete control over which indicators describe each construct. On the other hand, a structural model shows how the constructs are related to each other, often with multiple dependence relationships. It specifies whether a relationship exists or does not exist. If a relationship is hypothesised by the theory, then an arrow is drawn. If a relationship is not hypothesised, then no arrow is drawn.

A model is portrayed in a graphical form (see Chapter 2) known as a path diagram. The following norms are followed in constructing a path diagram for a measurement model. Constructs are represented by ovals or circles while measured variables are represented by squares. Straight arrows are drawn from the constructs to the measured variables, as in Figure 25.1(a). Dependence relationships are portrayed by straight arrows (Figure 25.1(a)) and correlational relationships by curved arrows (Figure 25.1(b)).

Exogenous versus endogenous constructs

As stated earlier, in SEM a construct is an unobservable or latent variable that can be defined in conceptual terms but cannot be measured directly, e.g. by asking questions in a questionnaire. Also, a construct cannot be measured without error. Rather, a construct is measured approximately and indirectly by examining the consistency among multiple observed or measured variables.

An exogenous construct is the latent, multi-item equivalent of an independent variable in traditional multivariate analysis. Multiple observed variables or items are used to represent an exogenous construct that acts as an independent variable in the model. An exogenous construct is determined by factors outside of the model, and it cannot be explained by any other construct or variable in the model. Graphically, an exogenous construct does not have any paths (single-headed arrows) coming into it from any other construct or variable in the model: it will only have paths (single-headed arrows) going out of it. In a measurement model, the indicators or measured variables for an exogenous construct are referred to as X variables. Thus, the construct C_1 in Figure 25.1(a) is an exogenous variable.

In contrast, an endogenous construct is the latent, multi-item equivalent of a dependent variable. It is determined by constructs or variables within the model and thus it is dependent on other constructs. Graphically, an endogenous construct has one or more paths (single-headed arrows) coming into it from one or more exogenous constructs or from other endogenous constructs. In a measurement model, the indicators or measured variables for an endogenous construct are referred to as Y variables, as in the case of construct C_2 in Figure 25.1(a).

Dependence and correlational relationships

A dependence relationship is shown by straight arrows. The arrows flow from the antecedent (independent) to the subsequent effect (dependent) measured variable or latent construct. In a measurement model, the straight arrows are drawn from the construct to its measured variables. In a structural model, the dependence occurs between constructs and so straight arrows are drawn between constructs, as shown in Figure 25.1(a). The specification of dependence relationships is also related to whether a construct is considered exogenous or endogenous, as explained earlier. Thus construct C_2 is endogenous in this case. It should be noted that an endogenous construct can be an antecedent of other endogenous constructs.

A correlational relationship, also called *covariance relationship*, specifies a simple correlation between exogenous constructs. The theory posits that these constructs are correlated but it is not assumed that one construct is dependent upon another. A correlation relationship is depicted by a two-headed curved arrow, as shown in Figure 25.1(b). Note that both constructs, C_1 and C_2, are exogenous in this case. A path diagram typically involves a combination of dependence and correlational relationships among endogenous and exogenous constructs, as stipulated by theory.

Model fit

SEM tests a set of multiple relationships that are represented by multiple equations. Therefore, the fit or predictive accuracy has to be determined for the model as a whole, not for any single relationship. Other multivariate techniques decompose variance, as explained in Chapter 19 for analysis of variance and covariance, and in Chapter 20 for multiple regression. In contrast, SEM analyses correlation or covariance. SEM determines how well the proposed theory explains the observed correlation or covariance matrix among measured variables. The data analysis is primarily based on a correlation or covariance matrix at the item level. Thus, one of the preparatory steps for SEM is to produce correlations or covariances among the items (measured or observed variables). Most contemporary SEM programs automatically generate correlations or covariances for subsequent analysis and thus this step may not be apparent to most users of such software. Yet it is important to note that SEM analysis is based on a correlation or covariance matrix, rather than raw data. As compared with correlations, we advocate the estimation of SEM based on covariances. A correlation matrix is a special case of the covariance matrix when the data are standardised (see Chapter 20). As compared with correlations, covariances contain greater information and provide more flexibility. Based on the proposed measurement and structural models, it is possible to estimate the covariance matrix between the observed variables Σ_k. Model fit is then determined by comparing how closely the estimated covariance matrix Σ_k matches the observed (sample) covariance matrix S, i.e. the fit statistics are based on $|S - \Sigma_k|$. A residual in SEM is the difference between the observed value and the estimated value of a covariance. Specific fit indices used in SEM are discussed later in the chapter.[8]

Model identification

Model identification concerns whether there is enough information in the covariance matrix to enable us to estimate a set of structural equations. We can estimate one model parameter for each unique variance or covariance among the observed variables. If there are p observed variables, then up to a maximum of $(p(p+1))/2$ parameters can be estimated. Note that this number is the sum of all the unique covariances ($p(p+1)/2$ and all the variances, p. Thus,

$$(p(p+1))/2 = p(p-1))/2 + p$$

If the actual number of estimated parameters, k, is less than $(p(p+1))/2$, the model is over identified. In that case, we have positive degrees of freedom. Conversely, if k is greater than $(p(p+1))/2$, the model is underidentified and a unique solution cannot be found. As a general guideline, having at least three observed variables for each latent construct helps in model identification, i.e. results in an overidentified model. This practice is therefore recommended.

Model fit
Model fit is determined by comparing how closely the estimated covariance matrix Σ_k matches the observed (sample) covariance matrix S, i.e. the fit statistics are based on $|S - \Sigma_k|$.

Residuals
In SEM, the residuals are the differences between the observed and estimated covariance matrices.

Model identification
Model identification concerns whether there is enough information in the covariance matrix to enable us to estimate a set of structural equations.

Conducting SEM

The process of conducting SEM is described in Figure 25.2. The steps involved in conducting SEM are: (1) define the individual constructs; (2) specify the measurement model; (3) assess measurement model reliability and validity; (4) specify the structural model if the measurement model is valid; (5) assess structural model validity; and (6) draw conclusions and make recommendations if the structural model is valid. We will describe each of these steps and discuss the relevant issues involved.

Define the individual constructs

As already mentioned, it is very important that SEM analysis be grounded in theory. The specific constructs, how each construct will be defined and measured, and the interrelationships

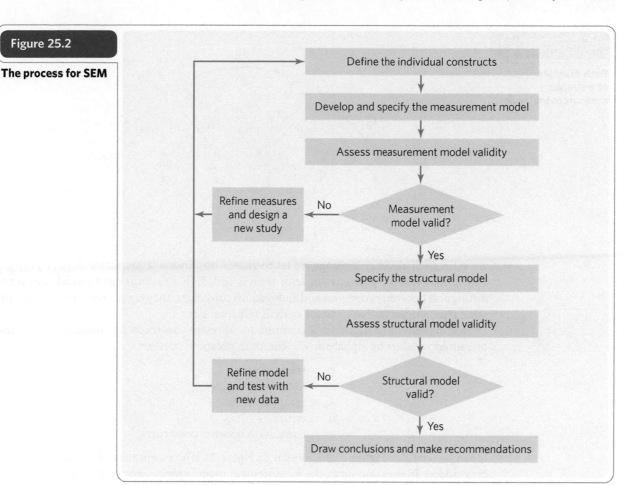

Figure 25.2

The process for SEM

among constructs must all be specified based on theory. Generally, the interest in SEM is to test both the measurement theory and the structural theory. Measurement theory specifies how the constructs are represented; structural theory posits how the constructs are interrelated. Structural relationships posited by theory are converted to hypotheses (see Chapter 2) that are then tested using SEM. The test of these hypotheses will be valid only if the underlying measurement model specifying how these constructs are represented is valid. Hence, great care should be taken in operationalising, measuring and scaling the relevant variables as identified and defined by theory. The measurement and scaling considerations involved, including the development of multi-item scales, were discussed in Chapter 12. This process results in scales used to measure the observed variables or indicators.

Specify the measurement model

Once the constructs have been defined and their observed or indicator variables measured, we are in a position to specify the measurement model. This involves the assignment of the relevant measured variables to each latent construct. The measurement model is usually represented by a diagram, as indicated in Figure 25.3. Figure 25.3 represents a simple measurement model having two correlated constructs with each construct being represented by three indicator or measured variables. The assignment of measured variables to each latent construct is graphically equivalent to drawing arrows from each construct to the measured variables that represent that construct. The degree to which each measured variable is related to its construct is represented by that variable's loading, also shown in Figure 25.3. Only the loadings linking each measured variable to its latent construct as specified by the arrows

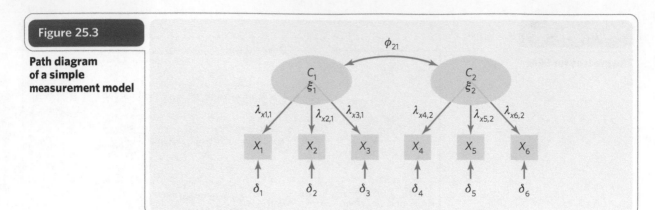

Figure 25.3

Path diagram of a simple measurement model

are estimated; all other loadings are set to zero. Also, since a latent factor does not explain a measured variable perfectly, an error term is added. In a measurement model, we do not distinguish between exogenous and endogenous constructs; they are all treated as being of the same type, similar to that in factor analysis (Chapter 22).

In a measurement model, it is common to represent constructs by Greek characters and measured variables by alphabets. The common notations used are

$$\xi = \text{latent factors}$$
$$X = \text{measured variables}$$
$$\lambda_x = \text{factor loadings}$$
$$\delta = \text{errors}$$
$$\phi = \text{correlation between constructs}$$

It can be seen that Figure 25.3 is similar to Figure 25.1(b) except that all the notations have been added. In equation form, the measurement model may be represented as

$$X_1 = \lambda_{x1,1}\xi_1 + \delta_1$$

In the model of Figure 25.3, a total of 13 parameters need to be estimated. The parameters consist of six loading estimates, six error estimates and one between-construct correlation. All the other paths have not been specified, i.e. no arrows have been shown. These paths will be set to zero, i.e. they will not be estimated. For each possible parameter in the model, the researcher should specify whether it is estimated or not. A free parameter is one that is estimated in the analysis. A fixed parameter is one which is not estimated by SEM but whose value is set by the researcher. Often, the value of a fixed parameter is set at zero, indicating that the specific relationship is not estimated. Specifying the observed variables or indicators for each latent construct requires 'setting the scale' of the latent construct. Because a latent construct is not observed, it has no metric scale, i.e. no range of values. Therefore this must be provided and either one of the following two options may be used:

1   One of the factor loadings can be fixed, generally to a value of 1.

2   The construct variance can be fixed, generally to a value of 1. In this case, the relationships between constructs are represented by a correlation matrix.

Sample size requirements

The sample size required for SEM depends upon several considerations, including the complexity of the model, estimation technique, amount of missing data, amount of average error variance among the indicators or measured variables, and multivariate distribution of the data. In terms of complexity, models with more constructs or more measured variables require larger samples. Larger samples are also needed if there are less than three measured variables for each construct. Regarding estimation technique, if maximum likelihood estimation (MLE – see Chapter 21) is used, the sample size should be generally in the range of 200 to 400, subject to other considerations.[9] If the extent of missing data is higher than 10%, then problems may be encountered and larger samples are required. The impact of the average error variance of indicators can be understood in terms of communality. Similar to the notion in factor analysis (see Chapter 22), communality is the variance of a measured variable that is explained by the construct on which it loads. Research shows that as communalities become smaller, larger samples are required. In particular, when the communalities are less than 0.5, larger samples will be required. The problem is magnified when the constructs have been measured with fewer than three indicators. Finally, as the data deviate more and more from the assumption of multivariate normality, larger samples are needed. To minimise problems with deviations from normality, it has been suggested that there should be at least 15 participants for each parameter estimated in the model.[10]

We offer the following simplified guidelines. SEM models with five or fewer constructs, each with more than three measured variables, and communalities of at least 0.5 should be estimated with sample sizes of at least 200. For five or fewer constructs, when even some of the constructs are measured with fewer than three indicators, or the communalities are less than 0.5, the sample size should be at least 300. When there are more than five constructs, with several constructs being measured with fewer than three indicators, and there are multiple low (less than 0.5) communalities, the sample size should be at least 400. In general, larger samples produce more stable solutions and the researcher should ensure that the SEM model is being estimated on an adequate sample size.[11]

Communality
Communality is the variance of a measured variance that is explained by the construct on which it loads.

Assess measurement model reliability and validity

The validity of the measurement model depends on the goodness-of-fit results, reliability and evidence of construct validity, especially convergent and discriminant validity.

Assess measurement model fit. As stated earlier, goodness of fit means how well the specified model reproduces the covariance matrix among the indicator items. That is, how similar is the estimated covariance of the indicator variables (Σ_k) to the observed covariance in the sample data (S). The closer the values of the two matrices are to each other, the better the model is said to fit. As shown in Figure 25.4, the various measures designed to assess fit consist of absolute fit, incremental fit and parsimony fit indices. In absolute fit indices, each model is evaluated independently of other possible models. These indices directly measure

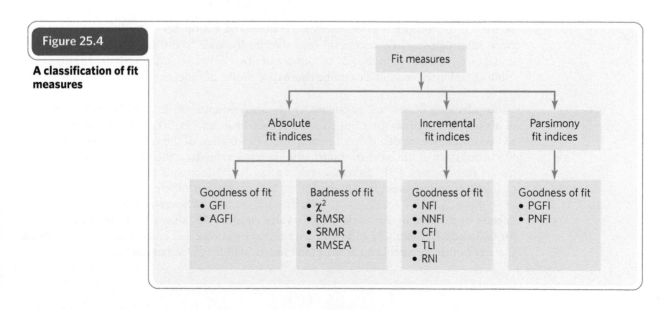

Figure 25.4

A classification of fit measures

how well the specified model reproduces the observed or sample data. Absolute fit indices may measure either goodness of fit or badness of fit. Goodness-of-fit indices indicate how well the specified model fits the observed or sample data, and so higher values of these measures are desirable. Measures that are commonly used are the goodness-of-fit-index (GFI) and the adjusted goodness-of-fit index (AGFI). On the other hand, badness-of-fit indices measure error or deviation in some form and so lower values on these indices are desirable. The commonly used badness-of-fit measures are the chi-square (χ^2), root mean square residual (RMSR), standardised root mean square residual (SRMR) and the root mean square error of approximation (RMSEA).

In contrast to the absolute fit indices, the incremental fit indices evaluate how well the specified model fits the sample data relative to some alternative model that is treated as a baseline model. The baseline model that is commonly used is the null model that is based on the assumption that the observed variables are uncorrelated. These are goodness-of-fit measures, and the commonly used incremental fit indices include the normed fit index (NFI), non-normed fit index (NNFI), comparative fit index (CFI), the Tucker Lewis index (TLI) and the relative non-centrality index (RNI).

The parsimony fit indices are designed to assess fit in relation to model complexity and are useful in evaluating competing models. These are goodness-of-fit measures and can be improved by a better fit or by a simpler, less complex model that estimates fewer parameters. These indices are based on the parsimony ratio that is calculated as the ratio of degrees of freedom used by the model to the total degrees of freedom available. The commonly used parsimony fit indices are the parsimony goodness-of-fit index (PGFI) and the parsimony normed fit index (PNFI). We discuss these indices briefly and provide guidelines for their use. Given its foundational nature, chi-square (χ^2) is discussed first, followed by other indices.[12]

Chi-square (χ^2). A chi-square test provides a statistical test of the difference in the covariance matrices such that $\chi^2 = (n-1)$(observed sample covariance matrix – estimated covariance matrix), where n is the sample size, or

$$\chi^2 = (n-1)\,(\mathbf{S} - \Sigma_k)$$

At specified degrees of freedom, since the critical value of the χ^2 distribution is known, the probability that the observed covariance is actually equal to the estimated covariance in a given population can be found. The smaller the probability ($p < 0.05$), the greater will be the chance that the two covariance matrices are not equal, similar to the χ^2 test discussed in Chapter 18. For SEM, the degrees of freedom (df) are determined by the following formula:

$$df = (1/2)[p(p+1)] - k$$

where p is the total number of observed variables and k is the number of estimated parameters. Although the chi-square is the only statistically based fit measure, its limitation is that it increases with sample size and the number of observed variables, introducing a bias in the model fit. Hence, we should examine alternative model fit indexes.

Other absolute fit indices: goodness of fit. The goodness-of-fit index (GFI) is a measure of absolute fit whereas the adjusted goodness-of-fit index (AGFI) accounts for the degrees of freedom in the model. If F_k is the minimum fit function of the estimated model and F_0 is the fit function of the baseline model with no free parameters, then GFI $= 1 - F_k/F_0$. As the model fit improves, F_k/F_0 decreases and as a result GFI increases. AGFI adjusts for degrees of freedom and is useful for comparing across models and different complexities. AGFI $= \{1 - [p(p+1)/2df](1 - \text{GFI})\}$ where p is the total number of observed variables and df is the degrees of freedom of the model. Higher values in the 0.90 range are considered acceptable for GFI and AGFI, but GFI and AGFI are affected by sample size and can be large for models that are poorly specified, and as such their use as fit indices is rather limited.

Other absolute fit indices: badness of fit. The notion of a residual was discussed earlier. The root mean square residual (RMSR) is the square root of the mean of these squared residuals. Thus, RMSR is an average residual covariance that is a function of the units used to measure the observed variables. Therefore it is problematic to compare RMSR across models unless standardisation is done. Standardised root mean residual (SRMR) is the standardised value of the root mean square residual and helps in comparing fit across models. Like RMSR, lower values of SRMR indicate better model fit, and values of 0.08 or less are desirable. Root mean square error of approximation (RMSEA) examines the difference between the actual and the predicted covariance, i.e. residual or, specifically, the square root of the mean of the squared residuals. RMSEA = $\sqrt{[(\chi^2/df - 1)/(n - 1)]}$, which adjusts the chi-square value by factoring in the degrees of freedom and the sample size. Lower RMSEA values indicate better model fit. An RMSEA value of $\leq$0.08 is considered conservative.

Incremental fit indices. Normed fit index (NFI) and comparative fit index (CFI) are also widely used model fit measures, and these represent incremental fit indices in that the specified model is compared with the null model in which the variables are assumed to be uncorrelated (i.e. the independence model). NFI is a ratio of the difference in the χ^2 value for the proposed model (χ^2_{prop}) and the null model (χ^2_{null}) divided by the χ^2 value for the null model (χ^2_{null}), i.e. NFI = $(\chi^2_{null} - \chi^2_{prop})/\chi^2_{null}$. As the χ^2 value for the proposed model approaches zero, NFI tends to be a perfect fit of 1. NFI does not reflect parsimony: the more parameters in the model, the larger the NFI, which is why NNFI is now preferred. NNFI = $(\chi^2_{null}/df_{null} - \chi^2_{prop}/df_{prop})/[(\chi^2_{null}/df_{null}) - 1]$ where df_{prop} and df_{null} are the degrees of freedom for the proposed and null models respectively. For both NFI and NNFI, values of $\geq$0.90 are considered acceptable.

The CFI is related to NFI and factors in degrees of freedom for model complexity. It is determined by the following formula: CFI = $1 - (\chi^2_{prop} - df_{prop})/(\chi^2_{null} - df_{null})$ where χ^2_{prop} and df_{prop} are the chi-square value and degrees of freedom for the theoretically based proposed model and χ^2_{null} and df_{null} are the same for the null model. CFI varies from 0 to 1, and values of 0.90 or greater are usually associated with good model fit. CFI is similar in meaning to NFI but penalises for sample size. The Tucker Lewis index (TLI) is conceptually similar to CFI, but is not normed and so the values can fall outside of the 0 to 1 range. Models with good fit have a TLI value that is close to 1. The relative non-centrality index (RNI) is another incremental fit index, and its values generally range between 0 and 1 with values that are 0.90 or larger indicating a good fit.

Parsimony fit indices. It should be emphasised that parsimony fit indices are not appropriate for evaluating the fit of a single model but are useful in comparing models of different complexities. The parsimony goodness-of-fit index (PGFI) adjusts the goodness-of-fit index by using the parsimony ratio that was defined earlier. The values of PGFI range between 0 and 1. A model with a higher PGFI is preferred based on fit and complexity. The parsimony normed fit index (PNFI) adjusts the normed fit index (NFI) by multiplication with the parsimony ratio. Like PGFI, higher values of PNFI also indicate better models in terms of fit and parsimony. Both PGFI and PNFI should be used only in a relative sense, i.e. in comparing models. PNFI is used to a greater extent as compared to PGFI.

Of the measures we have considered, CFI and RMSEA are among the measures least affected by sample size and quite popular in use. It is highly desirable that we use multiple (at least three) indices of different types. It is good practice always to report the χ^2 value with the associated degrees of freedom. In addition, use at least one absolute goodness-of-fit, one absolute badness-of-fit and one incremental fit measure. If models of different complexities are being compared, one parsimony fit index should also be considered.

Assess reliability and validity. The measurement accuracy, reliability, validity and general-isability considerations discussed for multi-item scales in Chapter 12 also apply to SEM. You are advised to review those concepts. Here we discuss the approaches to reliability, convergent validity and discriminant validity that are unique to SEM.

Reliability. Recall from Chapter 12 that an unreliable construct cannot be valid. So first we should assess the reliability of the constructs in the measurement model. As in Chapter 12, the coefficient alpha can be used to assess reliability. In addition, we compute composite reliability (CR), which is defined as the total amount of true score variance in relation to the total score variance. CR is computed as:

$$CR = \frac{\left(\sum_{i=1}^{p} \lambda_i\right)^2}{\left(\sum_{i=1}^{p} \lambda_1\right)^2 + \left(\sum_{i=1}^{p} \delta_i\right)}$$

where   CR = composite reliability
λ = completely standardised factor loading
δ = error variance
p = number of indicators or observed variables

Thus, CR corresponds to the conventional notion of reliability in classical test theory (see Chapter 12). As general guidelines, CRs of 0.7 or higher are considered good. Estimates between 0.6 and 0.7 may be considered acceptable if the estimates of the model validity are good.

Convergent validity. Recall from Chapter 12 that convergent validity measures the extent to which the scale correlates positively with other measures of the same construct. Hence the size of the factor loadings provides evidence of convergent validity. High factor loadings indicate that the observed variables converge on the same construct. At a minimum, all factor loadings should be statistically significant and higher than 0.5, ideally higher than 0.7. A loading of 0.7 or higher indicates that the construct is explaining 50% or more of the variation in the observed variable, since $(0.71)^2 = 0.5$. Sometimes a cut-off level of 0.6 is used.[13]

Another measure that is used to assess convergent validity is the average variance extracted (AVE), which is defined as the variance in the indicators or observed variables that is explained by the latent construct.[14] AVE is calculated in terms of the (completely) standardised loadings as

$$AVE = \frac{\sum_{i=1}^{p} \lambda_i^2}{\sum_{i=1}^{p} \lambda_1^2 + \sum_{i=1}^{p} \delta_i}$$

where   AVE = average variance extracted
λ = completely standardised factor loading
δ = error variance
p = number of indicators or observed variables

AVE varies from 0 to 1, and it represents the ratio of the total variance that is due to the latent variable. Using the logic presented earlier, an AVE of 0.5 or more indicates satisfactory convergent validity, as it means that the latent construct accounts for 50% or more of the variance in the observed variables, on average. If AVE is less than 0.5, the variance due to measurement error is larger than the variance captured by the construct, and the validity of the individual indicators as well as the construct is questionable. Note that AVE is a more conservative measure than CR. On the basis of CR alone, the researcher may conclude that the convergent validity of the construct is adequate, even though more than 50% of the variance is due to error. One should also interpret the standardised parameter estimates to ensure that they are meaningful and in accordance with theory.

Discriminant validity. In order to establish discriminant validity, we must show that the construct is distinct from other constructs and thus makes a unique contribution. First, individual observed variables should load on only one latent construct. Cross-loadings indicate lack of distinctiveness and present potential problems in establishing discriminant validity. In SEM, we typically assume that a set of observed variables represents only one underlying construct, and this concept is called unidimensionality. All cross-loadings are specified (i.e. fixed) to be zero.

One formal way to show distinctiveness is to set the correlation between any two constructs as equal to 1, i.e. we are specifying that observed variables measuring the two constructs might as well be represented by one construct. Evidence of discriminant validity is obtained if the fit of the two-construct model is significantly better than the fit of the one-construct model. However, this actually turns out to be a weak test as significant fit differences may be obtained even when the correlations between the two constructs are very high.

An alternative test of discriminant validity is based on the logic that a construct should explain its observed variables better than it explains any other construct. The test is conducted by showing that the average variance extracted is greater than the square of the correlations. Equivalently, discriminant validity is achieved if the square root of the average variance extracted is larger than the correlation coefficients.

Lack of validity: diagnosing problems

If the validity of the proposed measurement model is not satisfactory, then you can make use of the diagnostic information provided by CFA to make appropriate modifications. The diagnostic cues that can be used to make appropriate modifications include (1) the path estimate or loadings, (2) standardised residual, (3) modification indices, and (4) specification search.

The path estimates or loadings link each construct to its indicators or observed variables. You should examine the completely standardised loadings because standardisation removes the effect due to the scales of measurement. Different indicators may be measured using different scales, and this is taken into account via standardisation. Completely standard-

ised loadings that are not in the −1.0 to 1.0 range are infeasible and suggest problems that should be identified and investigated. A loading should be statistically significant. A non-significant loading suggests that the corresponding indicator should be dropped, unless there are strong theoretical reasons for retaining it. Furthermore, the loadings should be preferably above 0.7 or at least minimally greater than 0.5 when absolute values are compared. These guidelines were provided earlier. Significant but low loadings (less than 0.5) suggest that the corresponding indicators may still be candidates for deletion. The signs of the loadings should be in the direction hypothesised by theory, and the loadings should be meaningful from a theoretical viewpoint. It is also useful to evaluate the squared multiple correlations. A *squared multiple correlation* represents the extent to which the variance of an observed variable is explained by the associated latent construct.

Standardised residuals
Used as a diagnostic measure of model fit, these are residuals, each divided by its standard error.

As noted earlier, residuals refer to the differences between the observed covariances (i.e. the sample data) and the estimated covariance terms. A standardised residual is the residual divided by its standard error. The following guidelines are observed with respect to the absolute values of the standardised residuals. Absolute values of standardised residuals exceeding 4.0 are problematic, while those between 2.5 and 4.0 should also be examined carefully but may not suggest any changes to the model if no other problems are associated with the corresponding indicators or observed variables.

SEM programs also calculate a *modification index* for each possible relationship that is not freely estimated but is fixed. The index shows the improvement in the overall model χ^2 if that path was freely estimated. As a general guideline, the value of the index should be less than 4.0; the values of 4.0 or more indicate that the fit could be improved by freely estimating the relationship or path.

A specification search is an empirical approach that uses the model diagnostics and trial and error to find a better fitting model. It can be easily implemented using SEM software. In spite of this, the approach should be used with caution because there are problems associated with determining a better fitting model simply based on empirical data. We do not recommend this approach for the non-expert user.

Specification search
An empirical approach that uses the model diagnostics and trial and error to find a better fitting model.

It should be noted that all the adjustments, whether based on path estimates, standardised residuals, modification indices or specification searches, are against the intrinsic nature of CFA, which is a confirmatory technique. In fact, such adjustments are more in keeping with exploratory factor analysis (EFA). However, if the modifications are minor (e.g. deleting less than 10% of the observed variables), you may be able to proceed with the prescribed model and data after making the suggested changes. However, if the modifications are substantial then you must modify the measurement theory, specify a new measurement model and collect new data to test the new model.[15]

Specify the structural model

Once the validity of the measurement model has been established, you can proceed with the specification of the structural model. In moving from the measurement model to the structural model, the emphasis shifts from the relationships between latent constructs and the observed variables to the nature and magnitude of relationships between constructs. Thus, the measurement model is altered based on the relationships among the latent constructs. Because the measurement model is changed, the estimated covariance matrix based on the set of relationships examined will also change. However, the observed covariance matrix, based on the sample data, does not change as the same data are used to estimate the structural model. Thus in general, the fit statistics will also change, indicating that the fit of the structural model is different from the fit of the measurement model.

Figure 25.5 shows the structural model that is based on the measurement model of Figure 25.3. While the constructs C_1 and C_2 were correlated in Figure 25.3, there is now a dependence relationship, with C_2 being dependent on C_1. Note that the two-headed curved arrow in Figure 25.1 is now replaced with a one-headed straight arrow representing the path from C_1 to C_2. There are also some changes in the notations and symbols. The construct C_2 is now represented by η_1. This change helps us to distinguish an endogenous construct (C_2) from an exogenous construct (C_1). Also note that only the observed variables for the exogenous C_1 are represented by X (X_1 to X_3). On the other hand, the observed variables for the endogenous construct (C_2) are represented by Y (Y_1 to Y_3). The error variance terms for the

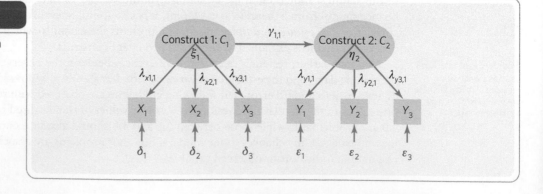

Figure 25.5

Path diagram of a simple structural model

Y variables are denoted by ε, rather than by δ. The loadings also reflect the endogenous and exogenous distinction. Loadings for the exogenous construct, as before, are still represented by λ_x. However, the loadings for the endogenous construct are represented by λ_y. The graphical representation of a structural model, such as in Figure 25.5, is called a *path diagram*. The relationships among the latent constructs are shown with one-headed straight arrows in the path diagram; fixed parameters, typically set at zero, are not shown. The structural parameters fall into two groups. Parameters representing relationships from exogenous constructs (ξ) to endogenous constructs (η) are denoted by the symbol γ (gamma), as shown in Figure 25.5. Parameters representing relationships from endogenous constructs to endogenous constructs are denoted by the symbol β (beta).

If the measurement model is identified, then the structural model is too, provided that it is recursive in that there are no feedback loops or dual dependencies and, in addition, there are no interaction terms. In such cases, generally the structural model is nested within the measurement model and contains fewer estimated parameters. A model is nested within another model if it has the same number of constructs and variables and can be derived from the other model by altering relationships, such as by adding or deleting relationships. Dual dependencies exist when C_1 and C_2 are mutually dependent on each other, and models containing such relationships are referred to as non-recursive.

In specifying the structural model, it is desirable also to estimate the factor loadings and the error variances along with the structural parameters. These standardised estimates from the structural model can then be compared with the corresponding estimates from the measurement model to identify any inconsistencies (differences larger than 0.05). This approach also allows us to use the measurement model fit as a basis for evaluating the fit of the structural model. An alternative approach that uses the estimates of factor loadings and error variances obtained in the measurement model as fixed parameters in the structural model is not recommended. The reason is that the change in fit between the measurement model and the structural model may be due to problems with the measurement theory instead of problems with the structural theory.

Assess structural model validity

Assessing the validity of the structural model involves (1) examining the fit, (2) comparing the proposed structural model with competing models, and (3) testing structural relationships and hypotheses.

Assessing fit. The fit of a structural model is examined along the same lines as that for the measurement model discussed earlier. As explained, in general a recursive structural model has fewer relationships than a measurement model from which it is derived. At most, the number of relationships in a structural model can equal those in a measurement model. This means that comparatively fewer parameters are estimated in the structural model. Therefore the value of χ^2 in a recursive structural model cannot be lower than that in the corresponding measurement model. In other words, a recursive structural model cannot have a better fit. Thus the fit of the measurement model provides an upper bound to the goodness of fit of a structural model. The closer the fit of a structural model is to the fit of a measurement model, the better. The other statistics and guidelines for assessing the fit of a structural model are similar to those discussed earlier for the measurement model and the same fit indices are used.

Comparison with competing models. In addition to having a structural model with a good fit, it is good practice to show that the proposed model has a better fit than competing models that might be considered as alternatives. A good fit does not prove the proposed theory or structural model best explains the sample data (covariance matrix). An alternative model may produce the same or even a better fit. Thus a good fit does not prove that the proposed structural model is the only true explanation. Our confidence in the proposed model can be enhanced by comparing it with competing models. The proposed model (M1) and the competing model (M2) can be compared in terms of differences in χ^2, incremental or parsimony fit indices (see Figure 25.4).

When the models are nested, the comparison can be done by assessing the chi-square difference statistic ($\Delta\chi^2$). From the value of χ^2 for the proposed model, M1 the χ^2 value for a lesser constrained model M2, is subtracted. For example, M2 can have additional paths compared with M1. The degrees of freedom for the χ^2 difference are also determined as the difference in the degrees of freedom for M1 and M2.[16] The equations involved may be represented as

$$\Delta\chi^2_{\Delta df} = \chi^2_{df(M1)} - \chi^2_{df(M2)}$$

and

$$\Delta df = df(M1) - df(M2)$$

The difference of two chi-square distribution values also has a chi-square distribution. Therefore, we can test whether the difference $\Delta\chi^2$ with Δdf degrees of freedom is statistically significant. This procedure can also be used to test the significance of the difference in the fits of the structural and measurement models. The structural model is more constrained than the measurement model and is nested within it. If the fit of the structural model is significantly and substantially worse than the fit of the measurement model, then the validity of the structural theory is questionable. On the other hand, if the fit of the structural model is not significantly worse than the fit of the measurement model, then there is evidence for the validity of the structural theory.

Testing hypothesised relationships. In SEM, theoretical relationships are generally transformed into hypotheses that can be empirically tested. The structural theory is considered to be valid to the extent that these hypotheses are supported in the SEM analysis. The estimated parameter for a hypothesised relationship should be statistically significant and have the correct sign. You should also examine the variance explained estimates for the endogenous constructs, and analysis that is similar to η^2 in analysis of variance (Chapter 19) or R^2 in multiple regression (Chapter 20). If SEM is being used to examine the nomological validity of a newly developed scale, then the hypotheses are replaced by known relationships that are empirically investigated to provide support for nomological validity.

Structural model diagnostics

The model diagnostics for the structural model are the same as for the measurement model. Thus, this examination is similar to that of the measurement model. Based on the model diagnostics, additional analysis may be conducted. For example, one or more additional paths may be specified that were not hypothesised by the original theory. However, it should be emphasised that any relationships that result based upon the modifications do not have theoretical support and should not be treated in the same way as the original relationships based on structural theory. The relationships based on modifications should be theoretically meaningful and should be validated by testing the modified model on new data.

Draw conclusions and make recommendations

If the assessment of the measurement model and the structural model indicates satisfactory validity, then we can arrive at conclusions and, if appropriate, make recommendations to decision-makers. The conclusions can be reached regarding the measurement of key constructs based on CFA. For example, it may be concluded that a newly developed scale has satisfactory reliability and validity and should be used in further research. Conclusions can be arrived at based on tests of hypotheses in the structural model. It may be concluded that relationships with significant and meaningful estimated structural parameters are supported.

The theoretical, managerial and decision-based implications of the relationships can be discussed. Appropriate recommendations to decision-makers may be made based upon what are perceived to be the managerial implications.[17]

Higher order CFA

The measurement model presented in Figure 25.3 is a first-order factor model. A first-order factor model is one in which the covariates between the observed variables (X) are explained by a single level or layer of latent constructs. In contrast, a higher order factor model contains two or more levels or layers of latent constructs. The most common higher order model is a second-order factor model in which there are two levels or layers. In such models, a second-order latent construct causes multiple first-order latent constructs, which in turn cause the observed variables. Thus, the first-order constructs now act as indicators or observed variables for the second-order factor. The differences between a first-order and a second-order measurement model are illustrated in Figure 25.6 and Figure 25.7. These figures describe the representation of a scale to measure Internet users' information privacy concern (IUIPC). IUIPC has three dimensions: namely, collection (COL), control (CON) and awareness (AWA), measured by four, three and three observed variables, respectively. Note that the covariances between the three latent constructs, COL, CON and AWA, are freely estimated in the first-order model, as shown by the two-headed curved arrows. On the other hand, the second-order model accounts for these covariances by specifying another higher order construct (IUIPC) that causes the first-order constructs (COL, CON and AWA).

When we move from the measurement model to the structural model, a structural relationship between information privacy concern and another latent construct such as trust (TRU)

Figure 25.6	
First-order model of IUIPC	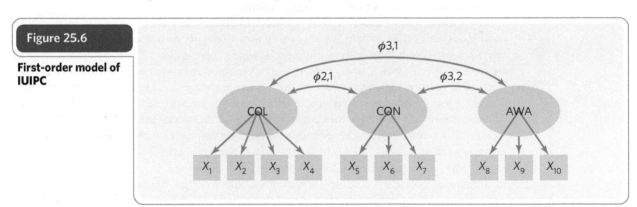

Figure 25.7	
Second-order model of IUIPC	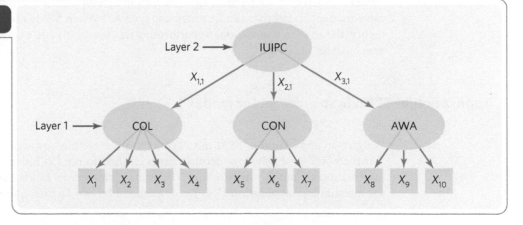

will be represented by multiple paths in a first-order model (COL→TRU, CON→TRU, AWA→TRU). However, in the second-order model it will be represented by a single path (IUIPC→TRU). Thus a second-order model assumes that all the first-order dimensions (COL, CON and AWA) will affect the other theoretically related latent constructs (e.g. TRU) in the same way. If this assumption is not reasonable, then the first-order factor model is preferred.

If there are four or more first-order constructs, a second-order model is more parsimonious as it uses fewer paths than a first-order model. However, it is not necessarily simpler because it involves a higher level of abstraction. We emphasise that the choice between a first-order and a second-order factor model should be made based upon theory.

Relationship of SEM to other multivariate techniques

SEM is a multivariate technique because there are multiple variables that are analysed simultaneously (see Chapter 17). Exogenous constructs are used to predict endogenous constructs. In this vein, SEM is a dependence technique (Chapter 17) that is similar to other multivariate dependence techniques such as multiple regression (Chapter 20). The equation for each endogenous construct can be written in a form similar to a multiple regression equation. The endogenous construct is the dependent variable and the constructs with arrows pointing to the endogenous construct are the independent variables. However, there are two major differences. One is that the dependent construct in one relationship may become the independent construct in another relationship. The other is that all of the equations are estimated simultaneously. Using the same reasoning, when categorical variables are used in SEM, one can see its similarity to MANOVA (Chapter 19). (See also Chapter 20 on the similarity of analysis of variance and covariance to regression.)

The measurement model in SEM is similar to factor analysis (Chapter 22) in that both techniques have variables with loadings on factors. Concepts such as correlations and covariances are also common to both techniques. However, there is also a major difference. In SEM we have to specify, based upon theory, which variables are associated with each construct. Thus SEM requires the specification of the measurement model. The loadings are estimated only for these specified relationships; all other loadings are assumed to be zero. The estimation then serves as a test of the measurement theory. In this sense then, SEM is a confirmatory technique. As noted earlier, the technique to estimate the measurement model is called confirmatory factor analysis (CFA). In contrast, factor analysis as discussed in Chapter 22 is an exploratory technique, often called *exploratory factor analysis* (*EFA*). EFA identifies underlying dimensions or factors that explain the correlations among a set of variables. Every variable has a loading on every factor extracted and these loadings are contained in the factor matrix (see Chapter 22). Thus EFA does not require specification; rather the underlying structure is revealed by the data. EFA results can be useful in developing theory that leads to a proposed measurement model that can be tested using CFA.[18] When SEM is used to test a structural theory, the analysis is analogous to performing factor analysis and a series of multiple regression analyses in one step.

Application of SEM: first-order factor model

We give an application of SEM in the context of the technology acceptance model (TAM). TAM is a well-established model that has been used to predict individuals' reactions to an information technology application.[19] In essence, this model holds that one's intention to use a technology application (INT) is determined by two factors, namely perceived usefulness (PU) and perceived ease of use (PE). Perceived usefulness refers to the degree to which the person finds it useful to use the technology application, whereas perceived ease of use is defined as the degree to which the person finds it easy to use the technology application. This theoretical framework was applied to explain university students' use of an educational portal in a certain university. To collect data, an online survey was administered to a sample of students. A total of 253 completed questionnaires was analysed on questions related to the use of a web portal on campus. In the following, we illustrate how the various steps involved in SEM presented in Figure 25.2 were carried out.

Define the individual constructs

In an attempt to assess measurement errors, each research latent construct was measured by multiple observed variables or items. The items were measured on seven-point scales anchored with 'strongly disagree' (1) and 'strongly agree' (2). Perceived usefulness was measured by three items. The items were 'Using this (website) increases my performance' (PU1), 'Using this (website) improves my productivity' (PU2) and 'Using this (website) enhances my effectiveness' (PU3). Perceived ease of use consisted of three items. The items were 'This (website) is easy to use' (PE1), 'It is easy to become skilful using this (Website)' (PE2) and 'Learning to operate this (website) is easy' (PE3). Intention to use was measured by the following three items: 'I plan to use this (website) in the next 3 months' (INT1), 'I predict that I would use this (website) in the next 3 months' (INT2) and 'I intend to use this (website) in the next 3 months' (INT3). Table 25.1 shows the means, standard deviations and correlations of the nine variables based on the collected data.

Table 25.1	TAM model: means, standard deviations and correlations										
			Correlations matrix								
	MF	SD	1	2	3	4	5	6	7	8	9
1 PU1	3.58	1.37	1								
2 PU2	3.58	1.37	0.900*	1							
3 PU3	3.58	1.36	0.886*	0.941*	1						
4 PE1	4.70	1.35	0.357*	0.403*	0.392*	1					
5 PE2	4.76	1.34	0.350*	0.374*	0.393*	0.845*	1				
6 PE3	4.79	1.32	0.340*	0.356*	0.348*	0.846*	0.926*	1			
7 INT1	3.72	2.10	0.520*	0.545*	0.532*	0.442*	0.419*	0.425*	1		
8 INT2	3.84	2.12	0.513*	0.537*	0.540*	0.456*	0.433*	0.432*	0.958*	1	
9 INT3	3.68	2.08	0.534*	0.557*	0.559*	0.461*	0.448*	0.437*	0.959*	0.950*	1

*$p < 0.5$. ME = means, SD = standard deviations.

Specify the measurement model

The estimates of structural relationships are likely to be biased unless the measurement instrument is reliable and valid. In this case, the measurement model is specified in such a way that the three factors are allowed to correlate with each other, and each of the three factors is associated with the designated three items but not with the other items. Figure 25.8 depicts the resulting measurement model. The result of data analysis produces model fit as well as various parameter estimates such as item loadings, item measurement errors and factor correlations.

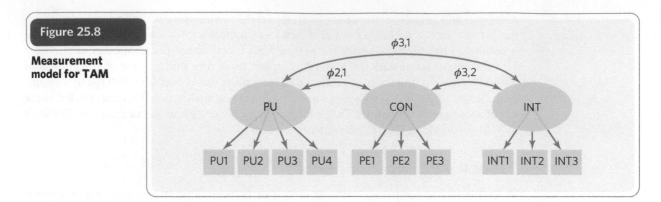

Figure 25.8

Measurement model for TAM

Assess measurement model reliability and validity

A three-factor measurement model was set up to validate the scales, and CFA was conducted to test the measurement model. The fit of the model was evaluated based on three different fit indices: comparative fit index (CFI), goodness-of-fit index (GFI) and root mean square error of approximation (RMSEA). The results of CFA indicated that the model fits the data quite well ($\chi^2 = 43.32$, $p < 0.01$, given that $df = 24$); specifically CFI was found to be 0.99, GFI was 0.96 and RMSEA was 0.057.

In addition to model–data fit, other psychometric properties of the scales such as composite reliability and validity were examined. As shown in Table 25.2, in terms of composite reliability (CR), the scales exceed the recommended cut-off value of 0.70; thus it is reasonable to conclude that the scales are reliable. In terms of AVE, all the values were greater than 0.50. Furthermore. Table 25.2 shows that each of the item loadings is greater than 0.80, which provides empirical support for the convergent validity of the scales.

The estimates of correlations and their standard deviations indicated that the scales are empirically distinct from each other. Formally, the square root of the average variance extracted is larger than the correlation coefficients, indicating discriminant validity of the scales. Overall, the measurement model was believed to be appropriate given the evidence of good model fit, reliability, convergent validity and discriminant validity.

Table 25.2   **TAM model: results of measurement model**

Constructs	Items	Item loadings	Item errors	CR	AVE
PU				0.97	0.91
	PU1	0.92***	0.15***		
	PU2	0.98***	0.05***		
	PU3	0.96***	0.07***		
PE				0.95	0.87
	PE1	0.88***	0.23***		
	PE2	0.96***	0.07***		
	PE3	0.96***	0.08***		
INT				0.98	0.95
	INT1	0.98***	0.03***		
	INT2	0.97***	0.05***		
	INT3	0.98***	0.05***		

***$p < 0.001$ (two tailed). CR = composite reliability; AVE = average variance extracted.

Specify the structural model

The structural model was specified based upon TAM theory, as shown in Figure 25.9.

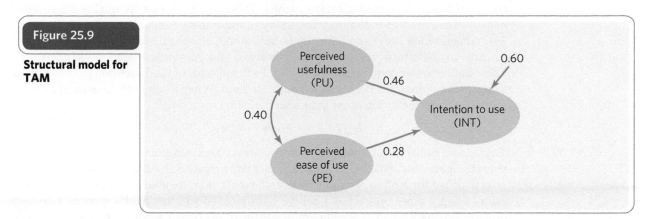

Figure 25.9

Structural model for TAM

Assess structural model validity

The results of data analysis are shown in Figure 25.9. First, as with the case of the measurement model, the proposed model was found to fit the data satisfactorily as the fit values were well within acceptable ranges ($\chi^2(24) = 43.32$, $p < 0.01$, CFI = 0.99, GFI = 0.96 and RMSEA = 0.057). According to TAM, perceived usefulness and perceived ease of use are the significant predictors of intention to use. As shown in Figure 25.9, perceived usefulness is significant in determining intention to use (path estimate = 0.46, $p < 0.001$). Similarly, perceived ease of use is found to have a significant effect on intention to use (path estimate = 0.28, $p < 0.001$). The squared multiple correlation (SMC) coefficient for intention to use is 0.40, which indicates that the two predictors, i.e. perceived usefulness and perceived ease of use, together explained 40% of the variance on intention to use.

Conclusions and recommendations

Overall, the results of TAM indicate that it is a reasonable representation of individuals' reactions to a web portal in a university setting. In order to increase the use of the portal by the students, this university should enhance the perceived usefulness and perceived ease of use of the website. Perceived usefulness could be increased by adding features such as checking email, weather, current events on the campus, schedule of classes, etc., that the students find useful and check frequently. Perceived ease of use could be enhanced by making the website easy to navigate.

Application of SEM: second-order factor model

We give an illustrative application of SEM in the context of personal banking services. The data were collected through face-to-face interviews. The sample size selected for this analysis was based upon 250 participants. The dataset used in this analysis can be downloaded from the website for this book. In the following, we illustrate how the various steps involved in SEM presented in Figure 25.2 were carried out.

Define the individual constructs

The purpose of this study was to predict bank patronage intent based upon service quality. The theory developed was based on past research in which 'service quality' was conceptualised as having five dimensions.[20] The theory postulated that service quality would influence service attitude and service satisfaction, and the latter two constructs would then influence patronage intent. Thus, in our dataset, we have eight constructs and 30 indicators with each construct having multiple indicator variables. These are the five service quality dimensions: namely, Tangibility (4 indicators), Reliability (4 indicators), Responsiveness (3 indicators), Assurance (4 indicators) and Empathy (4 indicators), and the three outcome constructs of Attitude (4 indicators), Satisfaction (4 indicators) and Patronage Intention (3 indicators). These indicators are contained in Table 25.3. Each indicator of the dimensions was measured using a nine-point scale. For example, indicator 1 was 'When it comes to modern equipment (tangibles), my perception of my bank's service performance' is:

Low 1__2__3__4__5__6__7__8__9 High

To measure global attitude, we used four indicators on a seven-point scale: favourable–unfavourable, good–bad, positive–negative and pleasant–unpleasant. All attitude indicators were reverse coded for analysis. To measure overall satisfaction, we used the following four indicators using a nine-point scale: 'I believe I am satisfied with my bank's services' (strongly disagree–strongly agree), 'Overall I am pleased with my bank's services' (strongly disagree–strongly agree), 'Using services from my bank is usually a satisfying experience' (strongly disagree–strongly agree), 'My feelings towards my bank's services can best be characterised as' (very dissatisfied–very satisfied). We used three indicators to measure patronage using a nine-point scale: 'The next time my friend needs the services of a bank I will recommend my bank' (strongly disagree–strongly agree), 'I have no regrets for having patronised my bank in the past' (strongly disagree–strongly agree), 'I will continue to patronise the services of my bank in the future' (strongly disagree–strongly agree).

Specify the measurement model

We first test the measurement model in order to validate the psychometric properties of our measures. In our example, because prior research has already established the reliability and validity of the five-component service quality construct, we test for the measurement properties in our sample using a confirmatory mode. In testing for the measurement model, we freely correlate the eight constructs and fix the factor loading of one indicator per construct to a value of unity. All measured indicators are allowed to load on only one construct each, and the error terms are not allowed to correlate with each other. The measurement model is described in Figure 25.10.

Assess measurement model reliability and validity

Our measurement model ($n = 250$) yields the following model fit results: χ^2 ($df = 377$) = 767.77; RMSEA = 0.064; SRMR = 0.041; NNFI = 0.94; and CFI = 0.95 (see Table 25.4). Notice that the program computes the degrees of freedom ($df = 377$) by using the formula $df = (1/2)[p(p + 1)] - k$, where p is the total number of observed variables and k is the number of estimated parameters. Since $p = 30$ and $k = 88$ (i.e., number of loadings (= 22), measurement errors (= 30), factor covariance (= 28) and variances (= 8) estimated by the program), $df = (1/2)[30(30 + 1)] - 88$, which equals 377. NNFI is computed using the formula NNFI $= (\chi^2_{null}/df_{null} - \chi^2_{prop}/df_{prop})/[(\chi^2_{null}/df_{null}) - 1]$, where df_{prop} and df_{null} are degrees of freedom for the proposed and the null models respectively. The null model (χ^2_{null}) equals 7780.15 with $df = 435$ and the proposed model (χ_{prop}) equals 767.77 with $df = 377$. NNFI = (7780.15/435

Table 25.3	Service quality model: psychometric properties of measurement model	
When it comes to...		*Loadings*
TANG1:	Modern equipment	0.71
TANG2:	Visual appeal of physical facilities	0.80
TANG3:	Neat professional appearance of employees	0.76
TANG4:	Visual appeal of materials associated with the service	0.72
REL1:	Keeping a promise by a certain time	0.79
REL2:	Performing service right the first time	0.83
REL3:	Providing service at the promised time	0.91
REL4:	Telling customers the exact time the service will be delivered	0.81
RESP1:	Giving prompt service to customers	0.73
RESP2:	Willingness to always help customers	0.89
RESP3:	Responding to customer requests despite being busy	0.81
ASSU1:	Employees instilling confidence in customers	0.81
ASSU2:	Customers' safety feelings in transactions (e.g. physical, financial, emotional, etc.)	0.71
ASSU3:	Consistent courtesy to customers	0.80
ASSU4:	Employees' knowledge to answer customer questions	0.86
EMP1:	Giving customers individual attention	0.80
EMP2:	Dealing with customers with care	0.84
EMP3:	Having customer's best interests at heart	0.87
EMP4:	Understanding specific needs of customers	0.87
Overall attitude towards your bank (items reverse coded)		
ATT1:	Favourable 1__2__3__4__5__6__7 Unfavourable	0.95
ATT2:	Good 1__2__3__4__5__6__7 Bad	0.95
ATT3:	Positive 1__2__3__4__5__6__7 Negative	0.95
ATT4:	Pleasant 1__2__3__4__5__6__7 Unpleasant	0.95
SAT1:	I believe I am satisfied with my bank's services	0.93
SAT2:	Overall I am pleased with my bank's services	0.93
SAT3:	Using services from my bank is usually a satisfying experience	0.88
SAT4:	My feelings towards my bank's services can best be characterised as	0.92
PAT1:	The next time my friend needs the services of a bank I will recommend my bank	0.88
PAT2:	I have no regrets of having patronised my bank in the past	0.89
PAT3:	I will continue to patronise the services of my bank in the future	0.88

$- 767.77/377)/[(7780.15/435) - 1]$, which equals 0.939 or approximately 0.94. CFI $= 1 - (\chi^2_{prop} - df_{prop})/(\chi^2_{null} - df_{null})$ computes to $1 - (767.77 - 377)/(7780.15 - 435)$, which equals 0.947 or approximately 0.95. Similarly for RMSEA, $\sqrt{[(\chi^2/df - 1)/(n - 1)]}$ can be computed as $\sqrt{[(767.77/377 - 1)/(250 - 1)]}$, which equals 0.064. Based on our previous discussion of model fit criteria, these fit indices collectively indicate that overall fit of the measurement model is acceptable and that the researcher needs now to test for reliability and validity.

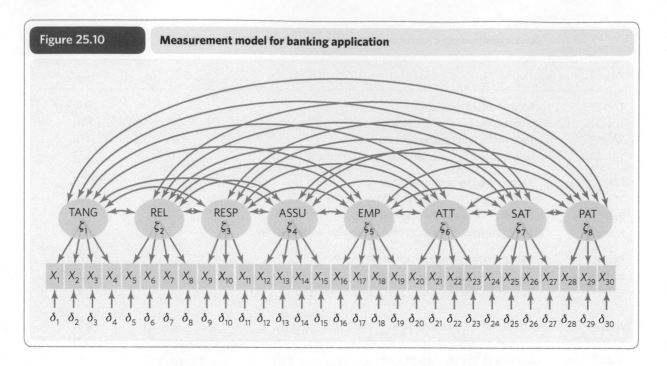

Figure 25.10   Measurement model for banking application

Table 25.4   Goodness-of-fit statistics (measurement model)

Degrees of freedom = 377
Minimum fit function chi-square = 767.77 (p = 0.0)
Chi-square for independence model with 435 degrees of freedom = 7780.15
Root mean square error of approximation (RMSEA) = 0.064
Standardised RMR = 0.041
Normed fit index (NFI) = 0.90
Non-normed fit index (NNFI) = 0.94
Comparative fit index (CFI) = 0.95

Reliability and validity tests. The main purpose of the measurement model is to assess and verify that the indicators or scale items used for each construct are both reliable and valid. We first conduct a test of reliability by examining the composite reliability. The factor loadings and the measurement error for all indicator variables are presented in Table 25.3. For example, the composite reliability for tangibility is $[(0.71 + 0.80 + 0.76 + 0.72)^2]/[(0.71 + 0.80 + 0.76 + 0.72)^2 + (0.49 + 0.36 + 0.42 + 0.48)]$, which equals 8.94/10.69 = 0.84. AVE reflects the overall variance in the indicators accounted for by the latent construct. For the tangibility dimension, AVE is $[(0.71^2 + 0.80^2 + 0.76^2 + 0.72^2)]/[(0.71^2 + 0.80^2 + 0.76^2 + 0.72^2) + (0.49 + 0.36 + 0.42 + 0.48)]$, which equals 2.24/3.99 = 0.56. Values of CR and AVE for each measurement are shown in Table 25.5. All constructs exceed the critical levels of 0.70 and 0.50 for CR and AVE respectively. This establishes the reliability and convergent validity of the measurement scales in our study.

Convergent validity is further established if all item loadings are equal to or above the recommended cut-off level of 0.70. In our sample, of a total of 30 items in the measurement model, 8 items had loadings ≥ 0.90, 16 items with loadings in the range ≥0.80 to <0.90, and 6 items with loadings in the range ≥0.70 to <0.80 (see Table 25.3). All the factor loadings were statistically significant at the $p < 0.05$ level. Thus the data in our study support convergent

Table 25.5	Measurement model: construct reliability, average variance extracted and correlation matrix

			Correlations matrix							
Construct	Construct reliability	Average variance extracted	1	2	3	4	5	6	7	8
1 TANG	0.84	0.56	0.75							
2 REL	0.90	0.70	0.77	0.84						
3 RESP	0.85	0.66	0.65	0.76	0.81					
4 ASSU	0.87	0.63	0.73	0.80	0.92	0.80				
5 EMP	0.91	0.71	0.69	0.75	0.85	0.90	0.85			
6 ATT	0.97	0.90	0.42	0.46	0.52	0.54	0.58	0.95		
7 SAT	0.85	0.83	0.53	0.56	0.66	0.67	0.69	0.72	0.91	
8 PAT	0.92	0.78	0.50	0.55	0.57	0.62	0.62	0.66	0.89	0.89

TANG=Tangibility, REL=Reliability, RESP=Responsiveness, ASSU=Assurance, EMP=Empathy, ATT=Attitude, SAT=Satisfaction, PAT=Patronage.

Value on the diagonal of the correlation matrix is the square root of AVE.

validity of the model. Discriminant validity is achieved if the square root of the AVE is larger than the correlation coefficients. In our study, we found all of the correlation estimates met the criterion except in 4 out of the 28 cases. Given that the five dimensions measure different aspects of service quality, some degree of intercorrelation can be expected. However, given the size of the correlation matrix (i.e. 28 estimates), some violations can occur through chance. The test for discriminant validity is shown in Table 25.5. Values on the diagonal of the correlation matrix represent the square root of the AVE. For example, to test for discriminant validity between tangibility and responsiveness, we compare the correlation between tangibility and responsiveness with their respective square root of the AVE. So, the square roots of the AVE for the tangible and responsiveness dimensions are 0.75 and 0.81, and both are greater than their correlation of 0.65. In summary and overall, the scale items were both reliable and valid for testing the structural model.

Specify the structural model

Based upon theoretical considerations, we hypothesised perceived service quality as a higher order construct consisting of five dimensions of tangibility (TANG), reliability (REL), responsiveness (RESP), assurance (ASSU) and empathy (EMP). Specifically we model service quality as a second-order model with first-order dimensions of TANG, REL, RESP, ASSU and EMP. In other words, these five dimensions are indicators of service quality and therefore the arrows flow out from service quality to the five dimensions (see Figure 25.11). On the right-hand side of Figure 25.11 we link second-order service quality with attitude towards service (ATT) and satisfaction with service (SAT). The latter two constructs are linked to patronage intention (PAT). The entire structural model (i.e. eight constructs) is tested simultaneously as shown in Figure 25.11. In testing for the structural model, we free the structural linkages and fix the factor loading of one indicator per construct to the value of unity. All measured items are allowed to load on only one construct each, and the error terms are not allowed to correlate with each other. We also fix the second-order loading of one dimension (i.e. tangibility) to unity for scaling purposes. While the measurement model tests for reliability and validity of the measures, the structural model tests for the structural relations in the model.

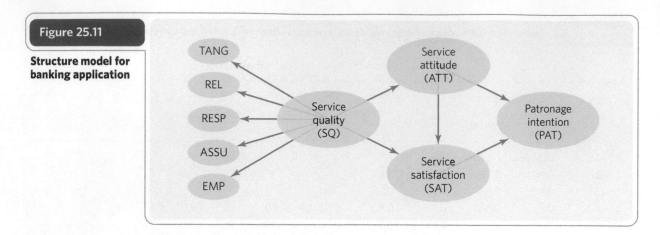

Figure 25.11

Structure model for banking application

Assess structural model validity

We estimated the structural model with the same sample ($n = 250$) yielding the following model fit results: $\chi^2(df = 396) = 817.16$; RMSEA = 0.065; SRMR = 0.096; NNFI = 0.94; and CFI = 0.94 (see Table 25.6). These fit indices were computed using the formulae given earlier. For example, CFI = $1 - (\chi^2_{prop} - df_{prop})/(\chi^2_{null} - df_{null})$ computes to $1 - (817.16 - 396)/(7780.15 - 435)$ which equals to 0.943 or approximately 0.94. Similarly RMSEA = $\sqrt{[(\chi^2/df - 1)/(n - 1)]}$ can be computed as $\sqrt{[(817.16/396 - 1)/(250 - 1)]}$ which equals 0.065. Both CFI and NNFI are ≥ 0.90 and RMSEA and SRMR are ≤ 0.08. Collectively these fit indices indicate that the structural model is acceptable. That is, the second-order perceived service quality model is robust and theoretically explains the constructs of attitude, satisfaction and patronage intention. The structural coefficients linking the five dimensions with second-order service quality (i.e. the second-order loadings) were all significant and in the expected direction. Table 25.7 contains the structural coefficients with corresponding t values. For example, the loading for tangibility is 0.82, which indicates that service quality explains 67% (= $(0.82)^2$) of the variance in tangibility. Similarly, the loading for reliability is 0.85, which indicates that service quality explains 72% (= $(0.85)^2$) of the variance in reliability. On the right-hand side of the figure, the coefficient for SQ→ATT is 0.60, for SQ→SAT is 0.45, for ATT→SAT is 0.47, for ATT→PAT is 0.03, and SAT→PAT is 0.88. All these links are significant at $p < 0.005$ except for ATT→PAT.

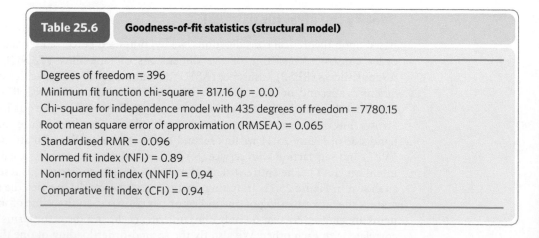

Table 25.6	Goodness-of-fit statistics (structural model)

Degrees of freedom = 396

Minimum fit function chi-square = 817.16 ($p = 0.0$)

Chi-square for independence model with 435 degrees of freedom = 7780.15

Root mean square error of approximation (RMSEA) = 0.065

Standardised RMR = 0.096

Normed fit index (NFI) = 0.89

Non-normed fit index (NNFI) = 0.94

Comparative fit index (CFI) = 0.94

Table 25.7	Structural model coefficients		
Dimensions of service quality		Second-order loading estimates	t values
TANG	γ_{11}	0.82	λ fixed to 1
REL	γ_{21}	0.85	13.15
RESP	γ_{31}	0.93	13.37
ASSU	γ_{41}	0.98	16.45
EMP	γ_{51}	0.93	15.18
Consequences of service quality		Structural coefficient estimates	
SQ→ATT	γ_{61}	0.60	10.25
SQ→SAT	γ_{71}	0.45	8.25
ATT→SAT	β_{76}	0.47	8.91
ATT→PAT	β_{86}	0.03	0.48
SAT→PAT	β_{87}	0.88	13.75

Draw conclusions and make recommendations

The magnitude and significance of the loading estimates indicate that all of the five dimensions of service quality are relevant in predicting service attitude and service satisfaction. Moreover, service quality has a significant impact on both service attitude and service satisfaction as the structural coefficients for these paths are significant. Service satisfaction, in turn, has a significant impact upon patronage intent. Service attitude does not directly impact upon patronage intent; rather it has only an indirect effect through service satisfaction.

If the sample was representative of the target population, we could cautiously suggest the following marketing implications to the management of a bank. All the dimensions of service quality are relevant and should be emphasised. Marketing campaigns should be crafted to enhance customers' perceptions of tangibility, reliability, responsiveness, assurance and empathy. The indicators for each service quality dimension suggest how that dimension should be affected by management action. Also, customer satisfaction with banking services is important in influencing patronage intent. Therefore the bank should conduct customer satisfaction surveys at regular intervals, e.g. quarterly. This will help the bank to monitor customer satisfaction and take appropriate actions as needed to ensure that a high level of satisfaction is maintained.

Path Analysis

Path analysis (PA) can be viewed as a special case of SEM. We could think of PA as SEM with only single indicators for each of the variables in the causal model. In other words, PA is SEM with a structural model, but no measurement model. Other terms used to refer to PA include *causal modelling, analysis of covariance structure* and *latent variable models*.[21] PA may also be viewed as an extension of the regression model. The PA model is depicted in a rectangle-and-arrow figure in which single-headed arrows indicate causation. A regression is done for each variable in the model as dependent on others, which the model indicates are causes. The regression weights estimated by the model are compared with the observed correlation matrix for the variables, and a goodness-of-fit statistic is calculated. PA calculates the strength of each relationship using only a correlation or covariance matrix as input. We illustrate PA with an example.

Illustrative example of PA

Suppose we observe the following correlation matrix between three variables Y_1, X_1 and X_2:

	X_1	X_2	Y_1
X_1	1		
X_2	0.40	1	
Y_1	0.50	0.60	1

The first step is to construct a path diagram, as in Figure 25.12. This is similar to that done in SEM for the structural model and should be specified by the researcher based on theory. Figure 25.12 portrays a simple model with two exogenous constructs X_1 and X_2, both causally related to the endogenous construct Y_1. The correlational path A is X_1 correlated with X_2. Path B is the effect of X_1 predicting Y_1, and path C shows the effect of X_2 predicting Y_1. The value for Y_1 can be modelled as:

$$Y_1 = b_1 X_1 + b_2 X_2$$

Note that this is similar to a regression equation. The direct and indirect paths in our model can now be identified:

Direct paths	Indirect paths
A = X_1 to X_2	AC = X_1 to Y_1 (via X_2)
B = X_1 to Y_1	AB = X_2 to Y_1 (via X_1)
C = X_2 to Y_1	

In PA, the simple or bivariate correlation between two variables is decomposed into the sum of the direct and indirect paths connecting these variables. In our illustrative example, the unique correlations among the three constructs can be shown to be composed of direct and indirect paths as follows:

$$\text{Corr}_{x_1 x_2} = A$$
$$\text{Corr}_{x_1 y_1} = B + AC$$
$$\text{Corr}_{x_2 y_1} = C + AB$$

The correlation of X_1 and X_2 is simply equal to A. The correlation of X_1 and Y_1 ($\text{Corr}_{x1,y1}$) can be represented by two paths: B and AC. B represents the direct path from X_1 to Y_1. AC is a compound path that follows the curved arrow from X_1 to X_2 and then to Y_1. Similarly, the correlation of X_2 and Y_1 can be shown to consist of two causal paths: C and AB. Given our observed correlation matrix, these equations can become

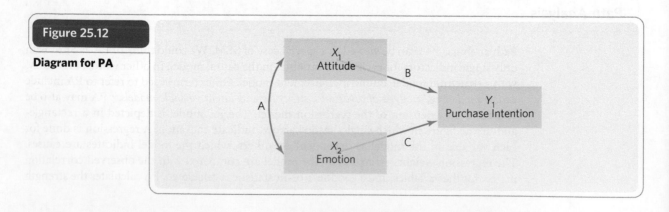

Figure 25.12

Diagram for PA

X_1 Attitude

X_2 Emotion

Y_1 Purchase Intention

A

B

C

$$0.40 = A$$
$$0.50 = B + AC$$
$$0.60 = C + AB$$
Substituting $A = 0.40$
$$0.50 = B + 0.40C$$
$$0.60 = C + 0.40B$$
Solving for B and C
$$B = 0.310$$
$$C = 0.476$$

The paths represent either correlational estimates or causal relationships between constructs and their interpretation is similar to that in SEM. SEM is used widely in marketing research as further illustrated in the following two examples. The first example illustrates an application of SEM in the context of international marketing research. The second example shows how SEM can be used in researching the relationships among values, ideology and ethical beliefs.

Real research | **The path to international success[22]**

A study sought to explain the internationalisation of professional service firms. The underlying theoretical framework was based upon attribution theory. The structural model posited that three causal constructs or factors (i.e. uniqueness of offering, financial resources and competitive pricing) influenced cognitive social consequences (i.e. expectations of success) and the resulting behavioural consequence (i.e. international success). The model is shown below. The data were obtained from a sample of 152 USA-based professional service firms via a postal survey. First, a measurement model was specified and estimated using confirmatory factor analysis. The results showed acceptable composite reliability and convergent and discriminant validity. Then, the structural model was estimated and found to be valid. The results of the structural model provided support for all the four hypotheses (H_1 to H_4), thereby providing support for the attribution theory framework. Several managerial implications were drawn. For example, the influence of cognitive psychological consequence on behavioural consequence means that managers who expect international success tend to be successful. Hence professional service firms wishing to make greater inroads into international markets may wish to search out and promote such managers.

Attribution model of internationalisation of professional service firms

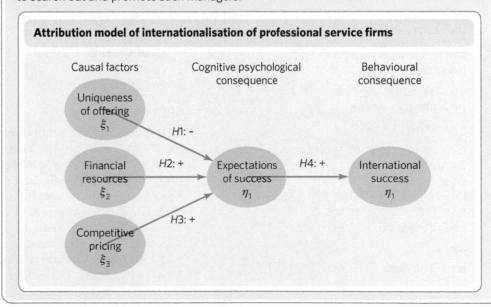

Personal values, ethical ideology and ethical beliefs[23]

The relationships among an individual's personal values, ethical ideology and ethical beliefs were investigated using structural equation modelling. The data were collected in an online survey based upon a final sample size of 609 participants. First, a measurement model was tested for key validity dimensions. Then the hypothesised causal relationships were examined in several path models. The results indicated that individual differences in values directly and indirectly (through idealism) influence the judgement of ethically questionable consumer practices. The findings not only contributed to the theoretical understanding of ethical decision making, but also had managerial implications. For example, understanding what underlies consumers' unethical attitudes and behaviour would enable retailers to influence appropriate behaviour positively by appealing to personal values. This could result in a reduction of unethical behaviours such as shoplifting.

SPSS and SAS Learning Editions

Several computer programs are available for SEM. The most widely used program is LISREL, an acronym for LInear Structural RELations. LISREL is a flexible program that can be used in a range of SEM applications normally encountered in marketing research. AMOS (Analysis of Moment Structures) is another user-friendly program that is available as an added module to SPSS. SAS offers the CALIS program.

Because LISREL is a popular program, we give detailed instructions for conducting SEM using this software for the first-order factor model application that we discussed. The data file can be downloaded from the website for this book.

LISREL

!CFA-Lisrel
Raw Data from File CH 22 TAM.PSF

Latent Variables: PU PE INT
Relationships:

PU→PU1 PU2 PU3
PE→PE1 PE2 PE3
INT→INT1 INT2 INT3

Method of estimation = Maximum Likelihood
Number of Decimals = 2
path diagram
Lisrel Output: SE TV MI EF FS RS SS SC AD = off
IT = 1300
End of Program

!SEM-Lisrel
Raw Data from File CH 22 TAM.PSF

Latent Variables: PU PE INT
Relationships:

PU1 = 1*PU
PU2 = PU
PU3 = PU

PE1 = 1*PE
PE2 = PE
PE3 = PE

INT1 = 1*INT
INT2 = INT
INT3 = INT
INT = PU PE

Method of Estimation = Maximum Likelihood

Number of Decimals = 2
path diagram
Lisrel Output: SE TV MI EF FS RS SS SC AD=off
IT =1300
End of Program

SPSS

AMOS provides you with powerful and easy-to-use SEM software. Using AMOS you specify, estimate, assess and present your model in an intuitive path diagram to show hypothesised relationships among variables. There are some distinctions to note when comparing the various SEM software packages. For example, AMOS varies from LISREL in how it approaches exogenous variables. LISREL (correctly) asks researchers to make a conceptual distinction between exogenous and endogenous variables prior to the testing of a model. AMOS simply treats any variables that do not have paths going to them as exogenous. As a result, LISREL by default allows all exogenous variables to covary freely with one another, while researchers using AMOS have to be proactive in establishing this set of relationships. We give detailed instructions for conducting SEM using AMOS for the first-order factor model application that we have discussed. The data file can be downloaded from the website for this book.

```
'CFA

Sub Main ()
Dim sem As New AmosEngine

sem.Standardized

sem.TextOutput

sem.BeginGroup "CH 22 TAM.sav"

sem.Structure "PU1 = PU + (1) E1"
sem.Structure "PU2 = PU + (1) E2"
sem.Structure "PU3 = PU + (1) E3"
sem.Structure "PE1 = PE + (1) E4"
sem.Structure "PE2 = PE + (1) E5"
sem.Structure "PE3 = PE + (1) E6"
sem.Structure "INT1 = INT + (1) E7"
sem.Structure "INT2 = INT + (1) E8"
sem.Structure "INT3 = INT + (1) E9"

sem.Structure "PU (1)"
sem.Structure "PE (1)"
sem.Structure "INT (1)"

sem.Structure "PU ↔ PE"
sem.Structure "PU ↔ INT"
sem.Structure "PE ↔ INT"

End Sub

SEM

Sub Main ()
Dim sem As New AmosEngine

sem.Standardized
sem.TextOutput

sem.BeginGroup "CH 22 TAM.sav"

sem.Structure "PU1 = (1)PU + (1) E1"
sem.Structure "PU2 = PU + (1) E2"
sem.Structure "PU3 = PU + (1) E3"
sem.Structure "PE1 = (1)PE + (1) E4"
sem.Structure "PE2 = PE + (1) E5"
```

```
sem.Structure "PE3 = PE + (1) E6"
sem.Structure "INT1 = (1)INT + (1) E7"
sem.Structure "INT2 = INT + (1) E8"
sem.Structure "INT3 = INT + (1) E9"

sem.Structure "INT = PU + PE + (1) ERR"
End Sub
```

SAS Learning Edition

The instructions given here and in all the data analysis chapters (17 to 25) will work with the SAS Learning Edition as well as with the SAS Enterprise Guide. SAS offers the CALIS procedure. We give detailed instructions for conducting SEM using the SAS Learning Edition for the first-order factor model application that we have discussed. The data file can be downloaded from the website for this book.

1 Select File>New>Code. (Note that SEM is not available as an SAS Learning Edition task and that SAS code needs to be submitted in order to run this analysis.)

2 Type the following SAS statements into the Code window and enter the physical location of the dataset in the libname statement:

```
Libname <INSERT LOCATION OF DATA>;
proc calis data = <INSERT DATASET NAME>
cov;
Lineqs
    PE1 = a1 f_PE + e1,
    PE2 = a2 f_PE + e2,
    PE3 = a3 f_PE + e3,
    PU1 = a4 f_PE + e4,
    PU2 = a5 f_PE + e5,
    PU3 = a6 f_PE + e6,
    INT1 = a7 f_PE + e7,
    INT2 = a8 f_PE + e8,
    INT3 = a9 f_PE + e9,

Std

f_PE f_PU f_INT = 3 * 1.,
e1-e9 = ev1-ev9;

Cov
f_ PE f_PU = phi1,
f_ PE f_INT = phi2,
f_ PU f_INT = phi3;

run;
```

3 Select Code>Run Code on Local.

Summary

Structural equation modelling (SEM) is a procedure for estimating a series of dependence relationships among a set of concepts or constructs represented by multiple measured variables and incorporated into an integrated model. SEM is mainly used as a confirmatory rather than exploratory technique.

It is very important that an SEM model be based on theory because all relationships must be specified before the SEM model can be estimated. A construct is an unobservable or latent variable that can be defined in conceptual terms but cannot be measured directly. Rather, a construct is measured approximately and indirectly by examining the consistency among multiple observed or measured variables. It is recognised that each construct be measured by using at least three observed variables. The steps involved in conducting SEM are (1) define the individual constructs, (2) specify the measurement model, (3) assess measurement model validity, (4) specify the structural model if the measurement model is valid, (5) assess structural model validity, and (6) draw conclusions and make recommendations if the structural model is valid.

SEM analyses covariance. Model fit is determined by comparing how closely the estimated covariance matrix, $\sum_k$, matches the observed covariance matrix S, i.e. the fit statistics are based on $|S - \sum_k|$. The various measures designed to assess fit consist of absolute fit, incremental fit and parsimony fit indices. In absolute fit indices, each model is evaluated independently of other possible models. In contrast to the absolute fit indices, the incremental fit indices evaluate how well the specified model fits the sample data relative to some alternative model that is treated as a baseline model. The baseline model that is commonly used is the null model that is based on the assumption that the observed variables are uncorrelated. The parsimony fit indices are designed to assess fit in relation to model complexity and are useful in evaluating competing models. These indices are based on the parsimony ratio that is calculated as the ratio of degrees of freedom used by the model to the total degrees of freedom available.

In assessing the validity of the measurement model, it is useful to examine composite reliability and convergent and discriminant validity. Composite reliability (CR) is defined as the total amount of true score variance in relation to the total score variance. High factor loadings indicate that the observed variables converge on the same construct. Another measure that is used to assess convergent validity is the average variance extracted (AVE), which is defined as the variance in the indicators or observed variables that is explained by the latent construct. Cross-loadings indicate lack of distinctiveness and present potential problems in establishing discriminant validity. Discriminant validity is established by showing that the average variance extracted is greater than the square of the correlations.

If the validity of the proposed measurement model is not satisfactory, then you can make use of the diagnostic information provided by confirmatory factor analysis to make appropriate modifications. The diagnostic cues that can be used to make appropriate modifications include (1) the path estimates of loadings, (2) standardised residual, (3) modification indices, and (4) specification search. If the modifications are substantial, then you must modify the measurement theory, specify a new measurement model and collect new data to test the new model.

Once the validity of the measurement model has been established, you can proceed with the specification of the structural model. In moving from the measurement model to the structural model, the emphasis shifts from the relationships between latent constructs and the observed variables to the nature and magnitude of the relationships between constructs. Assessing the validity of the structural model is similar to that for the measurement model and involves (1) examining the fit, (2) comparing the proposed structural model with competing models, and (3) testing structural relationships and hypotheses.

Questions

1 What characteristics distinguish SEM from other multivariate techniques?
2 What is the role of theory in SEM?
3 What is a measurement model? Why is it estimated?
4 How is model fit assessed in SEM?
5 What are the similarities and differences between an absolute and incremental fit index?
6 What are the similarities and differences between a parsimony and incremental fit index?
7 What is confirmatory factor analysis? How is it similar to and different from exploratory factor analysis?
8 How do you assess the validity of a measurement model?
9 How do you establish convergent and discriminant validity in an SEM framework?
10 What is average variance extracted? Why is it useful to calculate this statistic?
11 What is a second-order factor model? How is it different from a first-order factor model?
12 What is a structural theory and how is it different from measurement theory?
13 How do we determine whether the difference between two structural path coefficients is significant?
14 What is a recursive model? Why is this aspect relevant in SEM?
15 SEM is similar to what other multivariate techniques? How is it similar?

Exercises

1 As a research consultant to the Union of European Football Associations (UEFA), you are to develop a model that explains supporters' attendance at professional games. Evaluate literature, secondary data and intelligence sources to identify the factors that influence attendance at professional football games. Formulate a structural model and draw a path diagram.

2 As a research consultant for Google, you are to develop a model that explains consumers' patronage of an Internet portal. Evaluate literature, secondary data and intelligence sources to identify the factors that influence patronage of an Internet portal. Formulate a structural model and draw a path diagram. If you were a director of marketing at Google, how would you use the structural model in any design decisions?

3 Draw a path diagram with three exogenous constructs and one endogenous construct. The exogenous constructs are measured by 5, 4 and 3 observed variables or indicators. The endogenous construct is measured by four indicators. Two exogenous constructs are expected to be positively related and one negatively related to the endogenous construct. What are the degrees of freedom of the associated measurement model?

4 Compare and contrast the following SEM software: LISREL, AMOS and EQS. Which software is the most user-friendly? Which is the most useful? Why?

5 In a small group discuss the similarities and differences between EFA and CFA. Which is the more useful?

Notes

1. The help of Professor James Agarwal with the banking service application and Professor Sung Kim with the TAM application is gratefully acknowledged. The material presented in this chapter is drawn from several sources on SEM. Special mention is made of Bollen, K.A.,, *Structural Equation Modelling with Latent Variables* (New York: Wiley, 1989) and Hair, J.F., Black, W.C., Babin, B.J., Anderson, R.E. and Tatham, R.L., *Multivariate Data Analysis*, 6th edn (Upper Saddle River, NJ: Prentice Hall, 2006).

2. Truong, Y., 'Personal aspirations and the consumption of luxury goods', *International Journal of Market Research* 52 (5) (2010), 653–672.

3. Good sources for an introduction to SEM include: Harrington, D., *Confirmatory Factor Analysis* (New York: Oxford University Press, 2008); Kline, R.B., *Principles and Practice of Structural Equation Modelling*, 2nd edn (New York: Guilford Press, 2005); Arbuckle, J.L., *AMOS 6.0 User's Guide* (Chicago: SPSS, 2005); Bollen, K.A., *Structural Equations with Latent Variables* (New York: Wiley, 1989).

4. For a history of SEM, see Bielby, W.T. and Hauser, R.M., 'Structural equation models', *Annual Review of Sociology* 3 (1977), 137–161; Bollen, K.A., *Structural Equations with Latent Variables* (New York: Wiley, 1989); Epstein, R.J., *A History of Econometrics* (Amsterdam: Elsevier, 1987).

5. Berk, R.A., 'Causal inference for sociological data', in Smelser, N.J., ed., *Handbook of Sociology* (Newbury Park, CA: Sage, 1988).

6. Anderson, J.C. and Gerbing, D.W., 'Structural equation modelling in practice: a review and recommended two-step approach', *Psychological Bulletin* 103 (1988), 411–423.

7. Typically, we assume reflective measurement theory. This theory posits that latent constructs caused the observed variables, and the inability to explain fully the observed variables results in errors. Therefore the arrows are drawn from the latent constructs to the observed variables. An alternative approach that is sometimes used is formative measurement theory, where the observed variables cause the construct. Formative constructs are not considered latent. Reflective measurement theory is commonly used in marketing and the social sciences and hence the approach is adopted here.

8. For more discussion, see Cudek, R., 'Analysis of correlation matrices using covariance structure models', *Psychological Bulletin* 2 (1989), 317–327.

9. MLE is the most widely used estimation approach and is the default option in most SEM programs. However, alternative methods such as weighted least squares (WLS), generalised least squares (GLS) and asymptotically distribution free (ADF) are also available.

10. Hair, J.F., Black, W.C., Babib, B.J., Anderson, R.E. and Tatham, R.L., *Multivariate Data Analysis*, 6th edn (Upper Saddle River, NJ: Prentice Hall, 2006).

11. Harrington, D., *Confirmatory Factor Analysis* (New York: Oxford University Press, 2008); Jackson, D.L., 'Sample size and number of parameter estimates in maximum likelihood confirmatory factor analysis: a Monte Carlo investigation', *Structural Equation Modelling* 8 (2) (2001), 205–223; Kaplan, D., 'Statistical power in structural equation modelling', in Hoyle, R. (ed.), *Structural Equation Modelling: Concepts, Issues and Applications* (Thousand Oaks, CA: Sage, 1995), 100–117; Hu, L.T. and Bentler, P.M., 'Cutoff criteria for fit indexes in covariance structure analysis: conventional criteria versus new alternatives', *Structural Equation Modelling* 6 (1999), 1–55.

12. Hu, L. and Bentler, P.M., 'Fit indices in covariance structure modelling: sensitivity to underparameterized model misspecification', *Psychological Methods* 3 (4) (1998), 424–453; Hu, L.T. and Bentler, P.M., 'Cutoff criteria for fit indexes in covariance structure analysis: conventional criteria versus new alternatives', *Structural Equation Modelling* 6 (1999), 1–55; Marsh, H.W., Balla, J.R. and McDonald, R.P., 'Goodness of fit indexes in confirmatory factor analysis: the effect of sample size', *Psychological Bulletin* 103 (1988), 391–410; Marsh, H.W., Balla, J.R. and Hau, K., 'An evaluation of incremental fit indices: a clarification of mathematical and empirical properties', in Marcoulides, G.A. and Schumacker, R.E., (eds), *Advanced Structural Equation Modelling: Issues and Techniques* (Mahwah, NJ: Lawrence Erlbaum Associates, 1996), 315–353; Nevitt, J. and Hancock, G.R., 'Improving the root mean squared error of approximation for nonnormal conditions in structural equation modelling', *Journal of Experimental Education* 68 (2000), 251–268; Marsh, H.W. and Hau, K.T., 'Assessing goodness of fit: is parsimony always desirable?', *Journal of Experimental Education* 64 (1996), 364–390.

13. Chin, W.W., Gopal, A. and Salisbury, W.D., 'Advancing the theory of adaptive structuration: the development of a scale to measure faithfulness of appropriation', *Information Systems Research* 8 (4) (1997), 342–367.

14. Fornell, C. and Larcker, D.F., 'Evaluating structural equation models with unobservable variables and measurement error', *Journal of Marketing Research* 18 (February 1981), 39–50.

15. MacCallum, R.C., Roznowski, M. and Necowitz, L.B., 'Model modifications in covariance structure analysis: the problem of capitalization on chance', *Psychological Bulletin* 111 (1992), 490–504.

16. MacCallum, R.C., Browne, M.W. and Cai, L., 'Testing differences between nested covariance structure models: power analysis and null hypotheses', *Psychological Models* 11 (2006), 19–35.

17. Boomsma, A., 'Reporting analyses of covariate structures', *Structural Equation Modelling* 7 (2000), 461–483; McDonald, R.P. and Ho, M.-H., 'Principles and practice in reporting structural equation analyses', *Psychological Methods* 7 (2002), 64–82.

18. Brown, T.A., *Confirmatory Factor Analysis for Applied Research* (New York: Guilford Press, 2006); Hurley, A.E., Scandura, T.A., Schriesheim, C.A., Brannick, M.T., Seers, A., Vandenberg, R.J. and Williams, L.J. 'Exploratory and confirmatory factor analysis: guidelines, issues and alternatives', *Journal of Organizational Behavior* 18 (1997), 667–683.

19. Davis, F.D., Bagozzi, R.P. and Warshaw, P.R., 'User acceptance of computer technology: a comparison of two theoretical models', *Management Science* 35 (August 1989), 982–1003; Kim, S. and Malhotra, N.K.,

'A longitudinal model of continued IS use: an integrative view of four mechanisms underlying post-adoption phenomena', *Management Science* 51 (5) (May 2005), 741–755; Malhotra, N.K., Kim, S. and Patil, A., 'Common method variance in IS research: a comparison of alternative approaches and a reanalysis of past research', *Management Science* 52 (December 2006), 1865–1883.

20. Parasuraman, A., Zeithaml, V.A. and Berry, L.L., 'SERVQUAL: a multiple item scale for measuring consumer perceptions of service quality', *Journal of Retailing* 64 (1) (1988), 12–40.

21. Croon, M., *Methods for Correlational Research: Factor Analysis, Path Analysis and Structural Equation Modelling* (Harlow: Pearson, 2008); Bollen, K.A., 'Total, direct and indirect effects in structural equation models', in Clogg, C.C. (edn), *Sociological Methodology* (Washington, DC:

American Sociological Association, 1987), 37–69; Kelm, L., 'Path analysis', in Grimm, L.G. and Yarnold, P.R. (eds), *Reading and Understanding Multivariate Statistics* (Washington, DC: American Psychological Association, 2000), 65–97; Loehlin, J.C., *Latent Variable Models: An Introduction to Factor, Path and Structural Analysis*, 3rd edn (Mahwah, NJ: Lawrence Erlbaum Associates, 1998).

22. Cort, K.T., Griffith, D.A. and White, D.S., 'An attribution theory approach for understanding the internationalization of professional service firms', *International Marketing Review* 24 (1) (2007), 9–25.

23. Steenhaut, S. and van Kenhove, P., 'An empirical investigation of the relationships among a consumer's personal values, ethical ideology and ethical beliefs', *Journal of Business Ethics* 64 (2006), 137–155.

26 Report preparation and presentation

Managers should find reports easy to understand, be confident in the findings, and be clear about the action they should take, based on the researcher's approach, insight and integrity.

Objectives

After reading this chapter, you should be able to:

1 discuss the basic requirements of report preparation, including report format, report writing, graphs and tables;

2 discuss the nature of digital dashboards and how marketing research can be presented in the context of other key performance indicators (KPIs);

3 discuss the nature and scope of the oral presentation;

4 describe the approach to the marketing research report from the client's perspective;

5 explain the reason for follow-up with the client and describe the assistance that should be given to the client and the evaluation of the research project;

6 understand the report preparation and presentation process in international marketing research;

7 identify the ethical issues related to the interpretation and reporting of the research process and findings to the client and the use of these results by the client;

8 appreciate how digital developments are shaping the manner in which reports may be designed, delivered and experienced.

Overview

This chapter describes the importance of report preparation and presentation and outlines the process of producing written and oral presentations. We provide guidelines for report preparation, including report writing and preparing tables and graphs. Many reports are now presented in digital formats in manners that allow data to be interrogated. We discuss these developments in the context of describing the nature and use of digital dashboards. We discuss the nature and characteristics of successful oral research presentations. Research follow-up, including assisting the client and evaluating the research process, is described. The special considerations for report preparation and presentation in international marketing research are discussed, and relevant ethical issues are identified. The chapter concludes by examining how digital developments beyond dashboards can help in the design of more engaging reports for research users and decision-makers.

We begin with an example of how the BMW Group devised an innovative and engaging means to convey the findings of a large complex study. This is followed with an example that illustrates why the research team at Motorola have turned to digital dashboards to help convey consumer feedback to different levels of decision-makers. Companies and decision-makers may be swamped with data. The challenge that companies and decision-makers face is to find the meaning and insight in this data. These examples illustrate that the researcher has to go beyond just feeding research findings, to find a reporting format that is relevant, engaging and credible to decision-makers.

Real research ## Visualising future consumers[1]

A client approached BMW Group Designworks (**www.bmwgroup.com**) with the following brief:

> *Devise a method to transfer 2,000 pages of research content, communicating very new consumer environments in under an hour to 15,000 corporate knowledge workers.*

The research the group was asked to communicate represented a very large study on changes in consumer behaviour in the future. As part of the study, the group's researchers created text-based scenarios around personas from different age segments, and tested the communication impact on a small sample of the target audience. They designed four short films to act as 'visual management summaries', communicating the most important five to seven points for different future time frames. Another 40–50 supporting points per time frame were woven into dialogue or communicated visually in set, action sequences, costume design, or graphic effects. The four films were digitised and integrated into an interactive CD-ROM, acting as 'visual hooks' to get viewers engaged with the data. The CD-ROM contained the entire body of research for reference and was organised to parallel the structural aspects of the key points. The films were structured as interviews with consumers typical of an age and time frame. Set against black backgrounds for neutrality, the characters answered questions in a way that implied an off-screen narrator, delivering the audience observations on their behaviours and values. As the characters talked, their observations were shown in live action scenes, which were cut into the studio footage. When a key point was reached, it was punctuated either through sound (a narrated voice-over), visuals (graphic overlays) or pacing (shift in flow). The researchers used a variety of techniques to juxtapose the present and the future in these films. The work was tested iteratively during development to ensure the general approach and the specific techniques were creating the intended impact and increased retention. The researchers searched for techniques that had transferability, and tested these on sample members of development and marketing teams including engineers, general managers, researchers, designers and financial controllers.

Real research ## Motorola's use of dashboards to extend visibility and access to research[2]

The nature of Motorola's research context – many products, multiple countries, broad and diverse client group – has required thinking differently about how to keep management updated on progress on key metrics, and how to customise reporting and give decision-makers access to the information that is most relevant to them, anytime, from anywhere. Given this reality, Motorola's research team has turned to using a dashboard approach to communicate key metrics and consumer feedback on products. The dashboard approach has several advantages including broad reach, ability to customise, real-time reporting, increased visibility to available research, and providing decision-makers with the ability to view results at their leisure. Dashboards and web reporting put digestible and understandable decision-making knowledge right at the fingertips of the decision-makers who need it. All relevant key metrics can be included in a dashboard, and very detailed information, even raw data, can be part of the same web reporting system. Links to full research reports and contacts can be provided, in the event that the viewer would like more information on a particular outcome. Because of the hierarchical structure of the system, it is possible to define different access and information levels: (1) *Executive dash boards* – provide key performance metrics at a glance for top management; this level serves as an early warning system and a high-level summary. (2) *Operational dashboards* – targeted to those who want and need more detailed information, on different products, subgrouped in a variety of ways. They need the performance at multiple levels, not just an overall view, and the options to compare with other models or competition. (3) *Marketing research level* – for the researcher it provides the ability to do data analysis, cross-tabulations, links to simulation tools and access to tables/raw data.

Importance of the report and presentation

For the following reasons, the report and its presentation are important parts of the marketing research project:

1 They are the tangible products of the research effort. After the project is complete and management have made the decision, there is little documentary evidence of the project other than the written report. The report serves as a historical record of the project.

2 Management decisions are guided by the report and the presentation. If the first five steps in the project are carefully conducted but inadequate attention is paid to the sixth step, the value of the project to decision-makers will be greatly diminished.

3 The involvement of many decision-makers in a research project is limited to the written report and the oral presentation. These managers evaluate the quality of the entire project on the quality of the report and presentation.

4 Decision-makers' decision to undertake marketing research in the future or to use the particular research supplier again will be influenced by the perceived usefulness of the report and the presentation.

The above factors of importance seem self-evident, but many researchers fail to heed this advice. The following quote encapsulates the environment in which researchers have to engage decision-makers:

> *In today's ever more complex and fragmenting business environment one thing is clear. Everyone is time pressured, low attention spans are prevalent and if you have something to say, often you have to say it clearly and concisely. And just to make things even more difficult, real 'face time' with clients is at a premium and importantly the synopsis of a research study is most often widely distributed and communicated in a written form primarily by email and the dreaded PowerPoint.[3]*

There has long been criticism of how researchers fail to appreciate the needs of decision-makers and engage them in presenting reports. It has been argued that the barriers between researchers and decision-makers have grown due to the following factors:[4]

- *Overload.* Decision-makers can be overloaded with marketing research, which can mean large numbers of presentations and meetings every month. As well as marketing research, there is an increasing amount of other data that decision-makers have to deal with, including financial reports, information systems data, corporate news feeds and other intelligence sources.

- *Pace of work.* The pace of work has increased; this is driven in part by personal technology, adoption of other countries' working practices and also by increased competition. Distractions add to this pace with a 'BlackBerry culture', meaning that decision-makers get easily distracted with exacerbated short attention spans.

- *Quality.* Researchers making presentations of variable quality; sometimes they are too long (100-page presentations are still being produced), sometimes they are badly presented, sometimes they are not very easy to understand and lack a point of view and/or insight – and sometimes they are just plain boring.

Researchers need to appreciate the context and manner in which decision-makers use information. Based upon this appreciation, they need to address the quality of their written (be that digital or hard-copy) reports and their oral presentations. If decision-makers view researchers as responsible for poor-quality presentations that do not address their needs and/or engage them, the researchers' credibility can be seriously harmed.

Preparation and presentation process

To develop high-quality presentations, we begin by examining the report preparation and presentation process; this is illustrated in Figure 26.1. The process begins by interpreting the results of data analysis in light of the marketing research problem, approach, research design and fieldwork. Instead of merely summarising the quantitative and/or qualitative analyses, the researcher should present the findings in such a way that they can be used directly as input into decision making. Wherever appropriate, conclusions should be drawn and recommendations made. The researcher should aim to make the recommendations actionable. Before writing the report, the researcher should discuss the major findings, conclusions and recommendations with the key decision-makers. These discussions play a major role in ensuring that the report meets the decision-makers' needs and is ultimately accepted. These discussions should confirm specific dates for the delivery of the written report and other data.

The entire marketing research project should be summarised in a single written report or in several reports addressed to different readers. Generally, an oral presentation supplements the written documents. The client should be given an opportunity to read the report. After that, the researcher should take the necessary follow-up actions. The researcher should assist the client in understanding the report, help in interpretations of the findings that can affect their implementation, offer to undertake further research and reflect upon the research process to evaluate its overall worth.

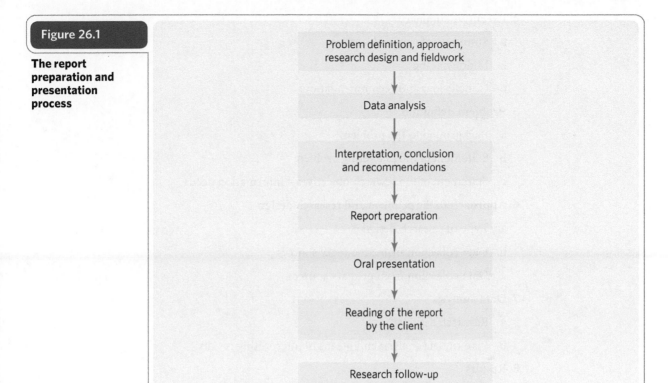

Figure 26.1

The report preparation and presentation process

Problem definition, approach, research design and fieldwork

↓

Data analysis

↓

Interpretation, conclusion and recommendations

↓

Report preparation

↓

Oral presentation

↓

Reading of the report by the client

↓

Research follow-up

Report preparation

Researchers differ in the way they prepare a research report. The personality, background, expertise and responsibility of the researcher, along with the decision-maker to whom the report is addressed, interact to give each report a unique character. Yet there are guidelines for formatting and writing reports and designing tables and graphs.[5]

Report format

Report formats are likely to vary with the researcher or the marketing research firm conducting the project, the client for whom the project is being conducted, and the nature of the project itself. Hence, the following is intended as a guide from which the researcher can develop a format for the research project at hand. Most research reports include the following elements:

1 **Submission letter**
2 **Title page**
3 **Table of contents**
   a Main sections
   b List of tables
   c List of graphs
   d List of appendices
   e List of exhibits

4 Executive summary

a   Summary of prime objectives

b   Major findings

c   Conclusions and recommendations

5 Problem definition

a   Background to the problem

b   Statement of the marketing problem

c   Statement of the research objectives – information needs

6 Approach to the problem and research design

a   Type of research design

b   Data collection from secondary sources

c   Data collection from primary sources

7 Data analysis

a   Research design

b   Plan of data analysis and means of interpreting results

8 Results

9 Conclusions and recommendations

10 Limitations and caveats

11 Appendices

a   Letter of authorisation

b   Questionnaire development and pretesting

c   Questionnaires, forms, interview guides

d   Sampling techniques, including error and confidence levels

e   Fieldwork

f   Lists including contact individuals and organisations.

This format closely follows the earlier steps of the marketing research process. The results may be presented in several chapters of the report. For example, in a national or international survey, data analysis may be conducted for the overall sample and then the data for each geographical region may be analysed separately. If so, the results from each analysis may be presented in a separate chapter.

Submission letter. A formal report generally contains a letter of submission that delivers the report to the client and summarises the researcher's overall experience with the project, without mentioning the findings. The letter should also identify the need for further action on the part of the client, such as implementation of the findings or further research that should be undertaken.

Title page. The title page should include the title of the report, information (name, address and telephone number) about the researcher or organisation conducting the research, the name of the client for whom the report was prepared, and the date of release. The title should encapsulate the nature of the project with a tone that is meaningful to the target decision-makers, not one of technical 'research-speak'.

Table of contents. The table of contents should list the topics covered and the appropriate page numbers. In most reports, only the major headings and subheadings are included. The table of contents is followed by a list of tables, a list of graphs, a list of appendices and a list of exhibits.

Executive summary. The executive summary is of vital importance in a report. In many instances this may be the only portion of the report that decision-makers read. The summary should concisely describe the problem, approach and research design that was adopted. A summary section should be devoted to the major results, conclusions and recommendations. The executive summary should be written after the rest of the report has been written.

Problem definition. The problem definition section of the report gives the background to the problem. This part summarises elements of the marketing and research problem diagnosis. Key elements of any discussions with decision-makers, industry experts and initial secondary data analyses are presented. Having set this context for the whole project, a clear statement of the marketing decision problem(s) and the marketing research problem(s) should be presented.

Approach to the problem and research design. The approach to the problem section should discuss the broad approach that was adopted in addressing the problem. This section should summarise the theoretical foundations that guided the research, any analytical models formulated, research questions, hypotheses and the factors that influenced the research design. The research design should specify the details of how the research was conducted, preferably with a graphical presentation of the stages undertaken, showing the relationships between stages. This should detail the methods undertaken in the data collection from secondary and primary sources. These topics should be presented in a non-technical, easy-to-understand manner. The technical details should be included in an appendix. This section of the report should justify the specific methods selected.

Data analysis. The section on data analysis, be it quantitative or qualitative, should describe the plan of data analysis and justify the data analysis strategy and techniques used. The techniques used for analysis should be described in simple, non-technical terms, with examples to guide the reader through the interpretations.

Results. The results section is normally the longest part of the report and may entail several chapters. It may be presented in any of the following ways:

1 *Forms of analysis.* For example, in a health care marketing survey of hospitals, the results were presented in four chapters. One chapter presented the overall results, another examined the differences between geographical regions, a third presented the differences between for-profit and non-profit hospitals, and a fourth presented the differences according to bed capacity. Often, results are presented not only at the aggregate level but also at the subgroup level (market segment, geographical area, etc.).

2 *Forms of data collection.* For example, a study may contain significant elements of secondary data collection and analyses, a series of focus group interviews and a survey. The results in such circumstances may be best presented by drawing conclusions from one method before moving on to another method. The conclusions derived from focus groups, for example, may need to be established to show the link to a sample design and questions used in a survey.

3 *Objectives.* There may be a series of research objectives whose fulfilment may incorporate a variety of data collection methods and levels of analysis. In these circumstances the results combine methods and levels of analyses to show connections and to develop and illustrate emerging issues.

The results should be organised in a coherent and logical way. Choosing whether to present by *forms of analysis*, *forms of data collection* or *objectives* helps to build that coherence and logic. The presentation of the results should be geared directly to the components of the marketing research problem and the information needs that were diagnosed in the initial research brief and proposal. The nature of the information needs and characteristics of the recipients of the report ultimately determine the best way to present results.

Conclusions and recommendations. Presenting a mere summary of the quantitative or qualitative findings is not enough for most marketing research users. The researcher should interpret the results in light of the problem being addressed to arrive at major conclusions. Based on the results and conclusions, the researcher may make recommendations to the decision-makers. Sometimes, researchers are not asked to make recommendations because they research only one area and do not understand the bigger picture at the client firm. The researcher may not have been fully involved in the diagnosis of the marketing and research problems, in which case the researcher's interpretations may not fit into the context that the decision-maker understands.

In any research project there are many approaches that can be taken to analyse the data. This can result in a potential overabundance of data (quantitative and/or qualitative), and distilling the 'meaning' from the data and presenting this in a clear report can result in much of the original meaning or richness being lost.[6] To maintain the meaning or richness, the researcher should strive to understand the nature of the decision-making process that is being supported. Only then can sound interpretations of the collected data be made. This is illustrated in the following example, where the main factor in selecting a research agency to work with is an understanding of the decision-making process that is being supported.

Real research	**French marketing research looks abroad**[7]

Mark Whiting, Research Director at Hennessy, was quite content with the support he got from French marketing research agencies. He pointed out that 99% of the cognac brand's business was conducted outside France, and he therefore could not expect to find everything he needs among French agencies. What drives his desire to work with a particular agency?

> *Above all, I'm looking to work with agencies who understand the business issues which concern us and who can make recommendations as to how to solve those issues, based on the research data that they have collected. This means searching near and far, so sometimes I find what I'm looking for in France, and sometimes I use agencies in the UK, the US and Asia.*

Limitations and caveats. All marketing research projects have limitations caused by time, budget and other organisational constraints. Furthermore, the research design adopted may be limited in terms of the various types of errors, and some of these may be serious enough to warrant discussion. This section should be written with great care and a balanced perspective. On the one hand, the researcher must make sure that decision-makers do not rely too heavily on the results or use them for unintended purposes, such as projecting them to unintended populations. On the other hand, this section should not erode management's confidence in the research or unduly minimise its importance.

Appendices. At the end of the report, documents can be compiled that may be used by different readers to help them to understand characteristics of the research project in more detail. These should include the letter of authorisation to conduct the research; this authorisation could include the agreed research proposal. Details that relate to individual techniques should be included relating to questionnaires, interview guides, sampling and fieldwork activities. The final part of the appendix should include lists of contacts, references used and further sources of reference.

Report writing

Readers. A report should be written for a specific reader or readers: namely, the decision-makers who will use the results. The report should take into account the readers' technical sophistication and interest in the project as well as the circumstances under which they will read the report and how they will use it.[8]

Technical jargon should be avoided unless the researcher is absolutely sure of the technical abilities and demands of the readers of a report. As expressed by one expert, 'The readers of your reports are busy people; and very few of them can balance a research report, a cup of coffee, and a dictionary at one time.'[9] Instead of technical terms such as maximum likelihood, heteroscedasticity and non-parametric, researchers should try to use descriptive explanations. If some technical terms cannot be avoided, definitions should be presented in a glossary or appendix. When it comes to marketing research, decision-makers would rather live with a problem they cannot solve than accept a solution they cannot understand. Often the researcher must cater to the needs of several audiences with different levels of technical sophistication and interest in the project. Such conflicting needs may be met by including different sections in the report for different readers or separate reports entirely.

Easy to follow. The report should be easy to follow.[10] It should be structured logically and written clearly. The material, particularly the body of the report, should be structured in a logical manner so that the reader can easily see the inherent connections and linkages. Headings should be used for different topics and subheadings for subtopics. A logical organisation also leads to a coherent report. Clarity can be enhanced by using well-constructed sentences that are short and to the point. The words used should express precisely what the researcher wants to communicate. Difficult words, slang and clichés should be avoided. An excellent check on the clarity of a report is to have two or three people who are unfamiliar with the project read it and offer critical comments. Several revisions of the report may be needed before the final document emerges.

Presentable and professional appearance. The look of a report is important. The report should be professionally reproduced with quality paper, typing and binding for hard copies, and with skilful graphic design for online reports. The typography should be varied. Variation in type size and skilful use of white space can greatly contribute to the appearance and readability of the report. However, a balance should be sought with styles of variation. Too much variation can lead to confusion; variation is only useful if it aids understanding.

Objective. Objectivity is a virtue that should guide report writing. Researchers can become so fascinated with their project that they overlook their 'objective' role. The report should accurately present the research design, results and conclusions of the project, without slanting the findings to conform to the expectations of management. Decision-makers are unlikely to receive with enthusiasm a report that reflects unfavourably on their judgement or actions. Yet the researcher must have the courage to present and defend the results objectively.

Reinforce text with tables and graphs. It is important to reinforce key information in the text with tables, graphs, pictures, maps and other visual devices. Visual aids can greatly facilitate communication and add to the clarity and impact of the report. Guidelines for tabular and graphical presentation are discussed later.

Reinforce tables and graphs with text. Conversely it is important to illustrate tables and graphs with verbatim quotes from questionnaires and interviews. Quotes can bring to life the meaning in tables and graphs and, used carefully, can make the reading of the report far more interesting than a solid body of statistics.

Conciseness. A report should be concise. Anything unnecessary should be omitted. If too much information is included, important points may be lost. Avoid lengthy discussions of common procedures. However, brevity should not be achieved at the expense of completeness.

Drawing together the above considerations in writing a good report can be challenging. There can be a delicate balance between keeping a report short and concise against superficiality and not addressing specific information needs of decision-makers. The following list should focus the mind of the report writer as it encapsulates typical mistakes that can make good research ineffective:[11]

- *The order in the report is based on the order of the questionnaire.* A report based on the order of questions in a questionnaire typically has no beginning or end and has to be completely rewritten by the buyer before it can be used by anybody else in the organisation.
- *The report does not discriminate between relevant subgroups but only shows totals.* The need to go back and ask for more, deeper analysis (sometimes for more money) can be a great factor of annoyance.
- *The report contains too much research jargon,* so that any reader outside of the profession can only guess at its meaning.
- *The report contains tables with too many figures.* In the end, there is only confusion. For researchers, the percentages derived from their data files have meaning, but not so for the reader.
- *The report does not distinguish between different audiences* in the organisation buying the research.
- *The vast majority of reports are still prepared and delivered on 'paper'* (including virtual paper like Word, PowerPoint or PDF documents). In a modern-day business environment, with its fast-pace decision making, research information on 'paper' can be too difficult to find and penetrate. Decision-makers need the right information at the right time and have no time to wait or to search through reports.

Guidelines for tables

Statistical tables are a vital part of the report and deserve special attention. We illustrate the guidelines for tables using data from a Racetrack study conducted by IFM Sports Marketing Surveys. Table 26.1 presents the findings from three questions. The rows in Table 26.1 show groupings of Formula One viewing habits. The columns in Table 26.1 present gender and age groupings of the participants.

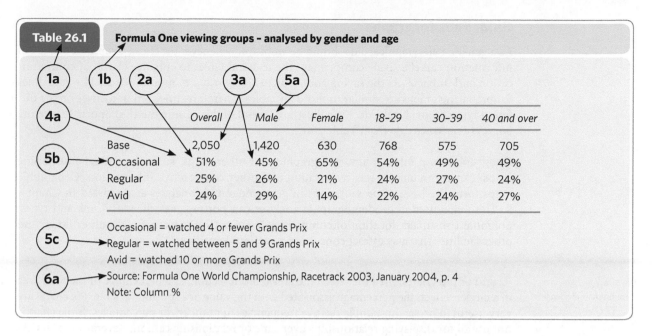

Table 26.1 Formula One viewing groups – analysed by gender and age

	Overall	Male	Female	18-29	30-39	40 and over
Base	2,050	1,420	630	768	575	705
Occasional	51%	45%	65%	54%	49%	49%
Regular	25%	26%	21%	24%	27%	24%
Avid	24%	29%	14%	22%	24%	27%

Occasional = watched 4 or fewer Grands Prix
Regular = watched between 5 and 9 Grands Prix
Avid = watched 10 or more Grands Prix

Source: Formula One World Championship, Racetrack 2003, January 2004, p. 4
Note: Column %

The numbers in parentheses in the following subsections refer to the numbered sections of the table.

Title and number. Every table should have a number (1a) and title (1b). The title should be brief yet clearly descriptive of the information provided. Arabic numbers are used to identify tables so that they can be referenced in the text.[12]

Arrangement of data items. The arrangement of data items in a table should emphasise the most significant aspect of the data. For example, when the data pertain to time, the items should be arranged by appropriate time period. When order of magnitude is most important, the data items should be arranged in that order (2a). If ease of locating items is critical, an alphabetical arrangement is most appropriate.

Basis of measurement. The basis or unit of measurement should be clearly stated (3a). In Table 26.1, the total sample size is shown and the subsample sizes of the different ways of classifying participants. The main body of data is shown in percentages. The % signs would normally be removed, with a note to tell the reader that the main body is based upon column percentages or row percentages, or percentages related to the total sample size.

Leaders, rulings and spaces. The reader's eye should be guided to be able to read across the table clearly. This can be achieved with ruled lines (4a), alternate shaded rows, or white spaces with dotted lines leading from the row headings to the data.

Explanations and comments: headings, stubs and footnotes. Explanations and comments clarifying the table can be provided in the form of captions, stubs and footnotes. Designations placed over the vertical columns are called headings (5a). Designations placed in the left-hand column are called stubs (5b). Information that cannot be incorporated in the table should be explained by footnotes (5c). Letters or symbols should be used for footnotes rather than numbers. The footnotes that are part of the original source should come after the main table, but before the source note.

Sources of the data. If the data contained in the table are secondary, the source of data should be cited (6a).

Guidelines for graphs

As a general rule, graphical aids should be employed whenever practical. Graphical display of information can effectively complement the text and tables to enhance clarity of communication and impact.[13] As the saying goes, a picture is worth a thousand words. The guidelines for preparing graphs are similar to those for tables. Therefore, this section focuses on the different types of graphical aids.[14] We illustrate several of these using the IFM Sports Marketing Surveys Racetrack data from Table 26.1.

Geographic and other maps. Geographic and other maps, such as product positioning maps, can communicate relative location and other comparative information. Geographic maps form the bases of presentations in geodemographic analyses as discussed in Chapter 5. The maps used in geodemographic analyses can portray customer locations and types, potential consumers, location of competitors, road networks to show consumer flows, and other facilities that may attract consumers to certain locations.

Pie chart

A round chart divided into sections.

Round or pie charts. In a pie chart, the area of each section, as a percentage of the total area of a circle, reflects the percentage associated with the value of a specific variable. Pie charts are very useful in presenting simple relative frequencies in numbers or percentages. A pie chart is not useful for displaying relationships over time or relationships among several variables. As a general guide, a pie chart should not contain more than seven sections.[15] Figure 26.2 shows the percentages of different forms of travel to work. Great care must be taken with 3D pie charts as the relative sizes of the pie segments can become distorted.

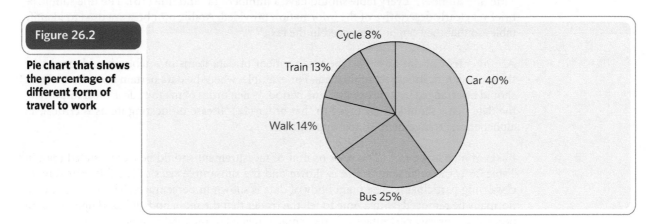

Figure 26.2

Pie chart that shows the percentage of different form of travel to work

Line chart

A chart that connects a series of data points using continuous lines.

Line charts. A line chart connects a series of data points using continuous lines. This is an attractive way of illustrating trends and changes over time. Several series can be compared on the same chart, and forecasts, interpolations and extrapolations can be shown. If several series are displayed simultaneously, each line should have a distinctive colour or form (see Figure 26.3).[16]

Bar chart

A chart that displays data in bars positioned horizontally or vertically.

Histogram

A vertical bar chart in which the height of the bar represents the relative or cumulative frequency of occurrence.

Histograms and bar charts. A bar chart displays data in various bars that may be positioned horizontally or vertically. Bar charts can be used to present absolute and relative magnitudes, differences and change. A histogram is a vertical bar chart in which the height of the bar represents the relative or cumulative frequency of occurrence of a specific variable (see Figure 26.4). Other variations on the basic bar chart include the stacked bar chart (Figure 26.5) and the 3D bar chart (Figure 26.6). Stacked and cluster bar charts can work well with a few data items presented, to represent differences qualitatively between groups. As noted with pie charts, 3D charts should be used with great caution as they can distort the message and confuse an audience. Most graphics packages have a great array of 3D options; however, there are few circumstances where they can be used to present data in a clear and unbiased manner.

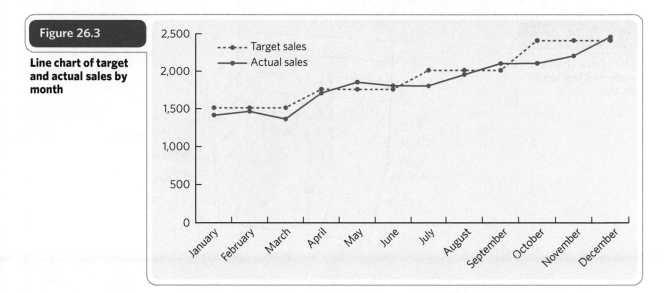

Figure 26.3

Line chart of target and actual sales by month

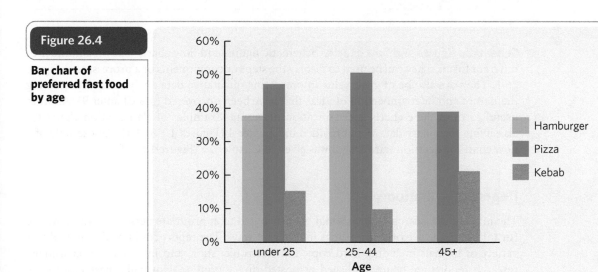

Figure 26.4

Bar chart of preferred fast food by age

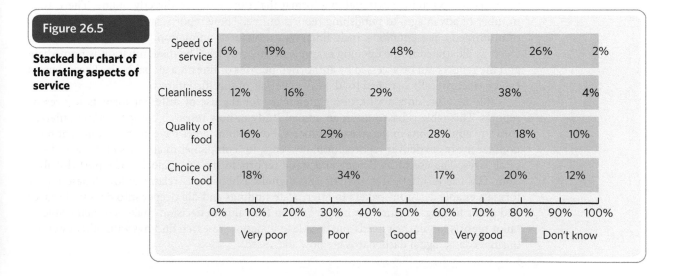

Figure 26.5

Stacked bar chart of the rating aspects of service

The 3D bar chart of preferred fast food by age

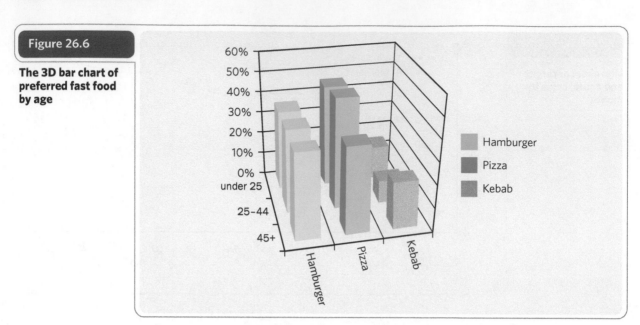

Schematic figures and flow charts. Schematic figures and flow charts take on a number of different forms. They can be used to display the steps or components of a process, as in Figure 26.1. They can also be of great value in presenting qualitative data analyses by representing the nature and interconnection of ideas that have been uncovered (see Chapter 9). Another useful form of these charts is classification diagrams. Examples of classification charts for classifying secondary data were provided in Chapter 4 (Figures 4.1 to 4.4). An example of a flow chart for questionnaire design was given in Chapter 13 (Figure 13.3).[17]

Report distribution

The marketing research report should be distributed to appropriate personnel who may use (or influence the use of) the findings in different ways. The report could be distributed in a variety of formats including hard copy and electronic, static and interactive. Increasingly, research reports are being published or posted directly online. Normally these reports are not located in publicly accessible areas but in locations that are protected by passwords or on intranets. The various presentation, word-processing and spreadsheet packages have the capacity to produce material in a format that can be posted directly online. There are a number of advantages to publishing reports online. These reports can incorporate all kinds of multimedia presentations, including graphs, pictures, animation, audio and full-motion video as illustrated in the opening example of this chapter. The dissemination is immediate and the reports can be accessed by authorised persons online on a global basis. These reports can be electronically searched to identify materials of specific interest.

Table 26.2 presents a rank order preference for the use of different formats to present reports. This table is based upon an annual study of how research companies use different software applications in the research process. PowerPoint slides have been the outright most popular means to deliver reports for many years, for companies in all parts of the world and of all sizes. The use of hard copy and static reports forms the majority of report distribution. The use of interactive analysis and digital dashboards is relatively low. These report formats enable decision-makers to interrogate findings and dig deeper into data to discover and tailor findings to suit their needs.[18] Given the value to decision-makers of being able to tailor reports to suit their needs and be able to juxtapose research findings with other essential business data, digital dashboards are now addressed.

Table 26.2	Percentage of projects using each mode of report distribution, 2010

Microsoft PowerPoint	53%
Acrobat PDF	21%
Microsoft Excel	20%
Microsoft Word	16%
Online static reports	16%
Interactive analysis	10%
Printed tables	8%
Digital dashboards	6%

Digital dashboards

The dashboard of a car, given its simplicity and broad familiarity, is a fitting visual metaphor for software that displays business performance. The purpose of a dashboard is to communicate a rich and often dense assortment of information in an instant. There should be no place for useless content and complexity which our eyes and brains must sort. To achieve data richness that is intuitive, what decision-makers see on a dashboard must be the result of thoughtful and skilful design, using graphics and displays specifically designed to work well on a dashboard.[19] It is appropriate and sometimes most effective to enhance dashboard displays with key charts, graphs or even tabular data and so the principles of clarity we presented earlier also apply in the context of dashboards.[20]

Building consumer profiles from website events

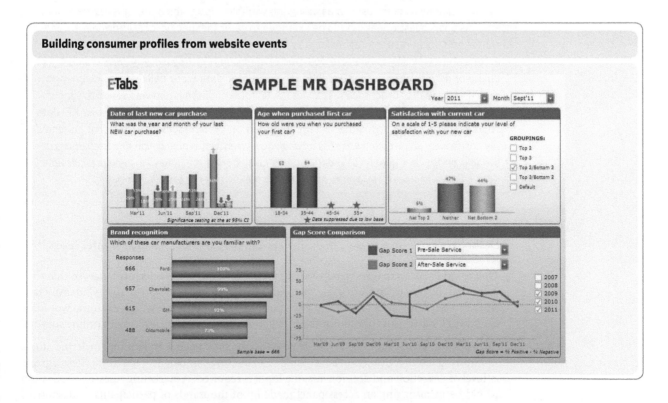

Digital dashboards have long been used within organisations to consolidate data from internal and external sources, such as operational, financial and marketing data. Such a consolidation delivers at-a-glance summaries presented in a highly visual and intuitive format. It can take valuable time to sift through masses of tabular data and graphical presentations to determine how a business is performing against key business metrics. It is easy to get caught up in the analysis and miss the bigger picture. Because their attention is directed to the most important information they should monitor, decision-makers can quickly identify problem areas and take corrective action. Immediacy is a crucial element in any successful dashboard since decision-makers can only take the right action when they have timely information.[21]

Dashboards provide a rapid and convenient way to assess quickly how a business is doing by observing critical business, marketing and consumer metrics.[22] Though sometimes difficult to capture and integrate, many business metrics can include findings from marketing research studies. The following example illustrates why and how Heineken uses a digital dashboard, and how marketing research data in the form of consumer performance indicators were integrated with other data sources.

Real research   **The worldwide Heineken brand dashboard**[23]

The Heineken Company has a strong decentralised organisation structure. Local markets are responsible for all their business activities including marketing research, within given rules and guidelines. Following a major reorganisation, Heineken developed a more fact-based management and measurement style. One of the key projects in this reorganisation was to develop a Heineken brand dashboard. In devising this dashboard Heineken decided that key performance indicators (KPIs) should indicate their brand performance in the areas of consumer performance (CPIs), sales/marketing performance (S&MPIs) and financial performance (FPIs). In developing CPIs, it faced a major challenge to ensure a uniform measuring model of over 80 markets across the world. For the CPIs a standard questionnaire was composed, measuring the variables upon which the CPIs were calculated. This basis questionnaire could be extended to cater for specific local information needs. Heineken's local research agencies had to adhere to a number of guidelines to achieve a consistency in: (1) *sample size and type of sampling*, (2) *frequency of measurement*, (3) *timing of data delivery*, (4) *deliverables* (all consumer data were delivered as cleaned raw data files instead of processed result files). A uniform coding system was set up to synchronise brands, markets and time, which were also common dimensions for the other KPI data sources. In technical terms the system consisted of: (1) *a presentation layer that presented the dashboards in a web browser*; (2) *an analytical layer, performing online KPI calculations depending on the user query*; (3) *a data storage layer storing the data and some pre-calculated KPIs*; (4) *a data processing layer to manage both the CPI and the S&MPI processing.*

Dashboards are typically used in businesses and in marketing research at three levels:[24]

1 *Operational.* For managers to be aware of short-term changes in performance, so that they can target resources appropriately to optimise performance and profitability, identify failures and work towards remedying any shortfall. A marketing research example would be for a CATI supervisor to monitor interviewers or to monitor progress with online surveys.

2 *Tactical.* For managers to be aware of activities such as resource planning, ordering stock, monitoring the effectiveness of advertising or marketing campaigns – activities where a greater level of discretion and decision-making input is required. A marketing research application would be in managing an access panel made up of thousands of participants. A dashboard

could be used in monitoring the performance of panellists; identifying 'underperforming' participants and identifying shortfalls in areas where recruitment needs to take place.

3 *Strategic.* Whereas the tactical or operational user's view of data is typically restricted on a need-to-have basis, the strategic user needs to be able to roam freely across all sources of data. There is a need for the strategic dashboard to be highly tailored to individual decision-makers' needs for data, with the ability to turn controls on and off and drill down into data. Senior strategic users will expect to find the numbers they are seeking with very few mouse clicks. They may have very sophisticated analytical requirements which may even mean creating custom reports from the raw data that make up the metrics.

Many decision-makers working at these three levels are using digital dashboards to view disparate data from across their businesses. Marketing researchers need to think how they may be able to fit their research findings and reports into such formats. This is particularly important at the strategic level, where senior decision-makers need to see the value of marketing research supporting major decisions. As indicated in Table 26.2, a number of companies now present marketing research findings using digital dashboards. The principal use of dashboards in marketing research has been in large-scale studies, primarily surveys that are administered in longitudinal studies and multiple cross-sectional research designs. The most common continuous applications that use dashboards lie in customer satisfaction monitoring, brand health, brand positioning studies and in mystery shopping. With software developments in marketing research this format may be used to deliver results from surveys and even qualitative studies. Digital dashboards offer great possibilities for ad hoc marketing research projects.

Oral presentation

The entire marketing research project should be presented to the management of the organisation that has commissioned the research (bearing in mind this may be in-house). This presentation will help decision-makers understand and accept the written report. Any preliminary questions that decision-makers may have can be addressed in the presentation. Because many executives form their first and lasting impressions about the project based on the oral presentation, its importance cannot be overemphasised.[25]

The key to an effective presentation is preparation. A written script or detailed outline should be prepared following the format of the written report. The presentation must be geared to the audience. This audience may physically be in the same room as the researcher(s) and/or they may be at remote locations through video-conferencing. Wherever the audience is located, the researcher should determine the backgrounds, interests and involvement of those in the project, as well as the extent to which they are likely to be affected by it. The presentation should be rehearsed several times before it is made. Visual aids such as tables and graphs should be displayed with a variety of media. Flip charts mounted on an easel enable the researcher to manipulate numbers or respond in a spontaneous manner. They are particularly useful in communicating answers to technical questions. Visual aids can also be drawn on the pages in advance, and the speaker flips through the pages during the presentation. Although not as flexible, magnetic boards and felt boards allow for rapid presentation of previously prepared material. Overhead and high-definition projectors can present simple charts as well as complex overlays produced by the successive additions of new images and even certain objects to the screen. The use of presentation packages such as PowerPoint are of obvious immense help as illustrated by their prominence in use in Table 26.2. However, the presenter must not lose sight of the message, must not just think that the audience have to be 'talked to' and must put every effort into engaging them. The value of 'performance' in presenting research findings is illustrated in the following example.

A cunning plan was formed . . .[26]

In presenting the findings of a study for the Swiss Bank UBS (**www.ubs.com**), Spring Research (**www.springresearch.co.uk**) delivered a one-day workshop which brought together over 30 stakeholders from Publicis Starcom (UBS's media partner) and UBS teams. This grouping brought together a broad mix of experience and creativity. Spring wanted to hold the session in a climate where people felt confident about themselves and could work well with one another. It picked a comfortable, relaxed hotel in Zurich that allowed freedom of movement. Spring arrived early to dress the room with insights, images and stories of individuals that took part in the research as it wanted the environment to act as a stimulus. All workshop participants were given an HNWI (High Net Worth Individual, the type of participant the research project had focused upon) in advance of the session and

asked to spend time thinking about this person's needs, wants and desires. The workshop began with objectives for the day and a quick introduction on the state of the market. Spring then asked the workshop participants to really get into the minds of the HNWIs. Each was asked to get into character and then form into teams of eight people. In their teams, each individual was asked to introduce themselves before being interviewed by a journalist from 'The Examiner' (a fake national newspaper) who was tasked with finding out as much as possible about them and their colleagues. Each team was then asked to put together a 'front page story' that would give the world the inside scoop on the audience's lives. Each team was then asked to present its story to the rest of the group. As well as the individual consumer profiles, the teams put together verbatim comments and six short films to bring to life individuals and key themes. There was some reluctance about role playing before the event, but for many it ended up being the most rewarding element as they really got into the minds of the people they wanted most to reach. The level of involvement generated through this approach ensured greater ownership and commitment to the outcomes of the research from UBS and Publicis Starcom and really helped introduce consumer insight directly into the 'bloodstream' of each organisation. It also enabled Spring to fast-track ideas as the right people were in attendance, so the session worked as an effective means of taking key decision-makers on a journey which led to consensus and an agreed forward direction which was able to be acted on immediately.

Research follow-up

After the presentation of research findings, decision-makers should be given time to read the report in detail. This means that there are two other tasks for the researchers after the oral presentation. The researcher should help the client understand and implement the findings and take follow-up action. Second, while it is still fresh in the researcher's mind, the entire marketing research project should be evaluated. The following example illustrates how these tasks are managed in the relationship between Motorola and the research company GfK.

Dedicated staffing at Motorola and GfK to ensure focus on the 'debrief'[27]

An approach to ensuring proper post-presentation follow-up and action planning is to 'staff' for it, i.e. build the action-planning function into the research organisation to foster and support the client. Motorola has built a follow-up capability into its research organisation by having a staff of 'consultants' whose primary responsibility is servicing its respective key client groups. These 'consultants' are not only responsible for following up and ensuring that results are properly understood and used, but also for synthesising research across studies. The result of this new structure for Motorola has been greater research mileage, impact, visibility, and more satisfied research users. It also off loads the research manager who must move back to the 'implementing' mode – next project, next country – from the often time-consuming, yet critical, follow-ups and post-presentation analysis. It has the effect of essentially splitting the project responsibilities, so that the same level of energy and effort that were placed on set up and execution are devoted to delivering the results and planning action steps. The same structure is mirrored at GfK, from the supplier side. The research teams of the different projects provide professional research execution in terms of planning and executing global research, as well as in preparing the final presentation. However, there is an additional insights team which consists of two functions: a 'consultant' responsible for analysis and insight generation; and a 'synergy' manager responsible for learning across all studies, in all stages of the process – from planning, to executing, to delivering the results. The insight team at GfK explores different sources to create valuable insight not only from one single project, but from all it knows about the specific topic under consideration. This team prepares the basis for actionable output. It understands what Motorola knows already, and where gaps exist. It also supports workshops and meetings with internal stakeholders, and prepares the results that address a special need of a certain audience. It also can support the Motorola consultants within the workshops and meetings to generate actions out of the findings, by applying workshop techniques and thus being a kind of 'process-enabler'.

Assisting the client

After the client has read the report in detail, several questions may arise. Parts of the report, particularly those dealing with technical matters, may not be understood and the researcher should provide the help needed. Sometimes the researcher helps implement the findings. Often, the client retains the researcher to help with the selection of a new product or advertising agency, development of a pricing policy, market segmentation or other marketing actions. An important reason for client follow-up is to discuss further research projects. For example, the researcher and decision-makers may agree to repeat the study after two years. Where possible, and as illustrated in the Motorola–GfK example, the researcher should also aim to make links between the findings of a project and other studies. By reviewing 'historical' findings in the context of current issues, project findings can be seen as more valid and decision-makers may increase their trust in the process.[28] Finally, the researcher should help the client firm make the information generated in the marketing research project a part of the firm's decision support system. Ad hoc marketing research should be seen as a significant component of an ongoing link and understanding of target consumers. A key element of researchers being able to assist marketing decision-makers is the level of trust that exists between the two parties. The nature of personal interaction between managers and researchers is very important in creating trust in the researcher and consequently in the results of the research. The quality of personal interaction affects managers' perceptions of the overall quality of the report itself. Trust between the decision-maker and the researcher has been found to influence the perceived quality of user–researcher interactions, the level of researcher involvement, the level of user commitment to the relationship and the level of market research utilisation.[29]

Evaluation of the research project

Although marketing research is scientific, which may seem to imply a rigid, systematic process, it clearly involves creativity, intuition and personal judgement. Hence, every marketing research project provides an opportunity for learning, and the researcher should critically evaluate the entire project to obtain new insights and knowledge. The key question to ask is: 'Could this project have been conducted more effectively or efficiently?' This question, of course, raises several more specific questions. Could the problem have been defined differently so as to enhance the value of the project to the client or reduce the costs? Could a different approach have yielded better results? Was the research design that was used the best? How about the method of data collection? Should an SMS survey have been used instead of an online survey? Was the sampling plan employed the most appropriate? Were the sources of possible design error correctly anticipated and kept under control, at least in a qualitative sense? If not, what changes could have been made? How could the selection, training and supervision of fieldworkers be altered to improve data collection? Was the data analysis strategy effective in yielding information useful for decision making? Were the conclusions and recommendations appropriate and useful to the client? Was the report adequately written and presented? Was the project completed within the time and budget allocated? If not, what went wrong? The insights gained from such an evaluation will benefit the researcher and the subsequent projects conducted.

International marketing research

The guidelines presented earlier in this chapter apply to international marketing research as well, although report preparation may be complicated by the need to prepare reports for decision-makers with distinctive organisational roles in different countries and in different languages. In such a case, the researcher should prepare different versions of the report, each geared to specific readers. The different reports should be comparable, although the formats may differ. The guidelines for oral presentation are also similar to those given earlier, with the added proviso that the presenter should be sensitive to cultural norms. For example, making jokes, which is frequently done in many countries, is not appropriate in all cultures (which may also include particular organisational cultures). In oral and even written reports, the potential impact of cultural variations in humour should be considered. The following example, based upon contemporary research into cultural variations in humour, illustrates what a challenge such a task may be. Whether you recognise any of the following characteristics or not, one must really know an audience well in order to make the right impact using humour.

Real research | Humour in magazine advertising in the USA, China and France[30]

Humour in China

In China, humour is perceived uniquely. In fact, the term *humour* – as it is known in the West – in Chinese is a neologism whose meaning had to be promoted by Western artists in the twentieth century. Yutang Lin, named the 'master of humour' in modern China, stated that humour in Chinese literature had been 'marginalized and unappreciated'. Studies indirectly support these claims. In China, individuals cherish a strong desire to gain and maintain harmony between persons; reciprocal relationships of respect and courtesy are appreciated. In this setting, humour can be perceived as an individualistic motivation that may put at risk the promotion of harmony and courtesy. Thus, to maintain group cohesion, humour is used in neutral or affiliative ways.

Humour in the USA

Humour in the USA is more culturally accepted than it is in China. Studies have shown that individuals with a good sense of humour were perceived as more attractive and that humour, in fact, may signal social adaptiveness. The use of humour in advertising increased in the USA since it was first used – a consequence of the need to attract more audience attention. Cultural differences may explain why humour is more accepted in the USA than in China. The former embraces individualistic values more than the latter, as the USA is identified as the most individualistic nation. Americans generally are less concerned with people and nature than the world average, and they value hedonism, achievement and social power at a higher degree than most countries, including China. Given that individualistic values guide the American culture, the preservation of group harmony, therefore, is less important, and several forms of humour become more acceptable. As humour is marginalised and unappreciated in China and socially accepted in the USA, the authors expected the percentage of humorous ads in the USA to be higher than in China.

Humour in France

The French value intellectual, hostile, aggressive and sarcastic types of humour (whereas the English tend to focus more on emotional, affectionate, gentle, kindly and genial types). Also, the French are more likely to use sexual themes and may employ messaging on occasions when the Americans and the British likely would not (e.g. at the dinner table with well-educated people). In terms of types of humour, the French have a better appreciation for puns than the Americans and the British – a finding that presumably reflects that culture's ongoing interest in language preservation. Furthermore, research has shown that the use of humour in France was more acceptable than in the USA, in part because France is as individualistic as the USA; thus, individuals are less concerned with the possibility that humour may threaten group harmony.

Most marketing decisions are made from facts and figures arising out of marketing research. But these figures and how they have been arrived at have to be credible to decision-makers. The subjective experience and gut feeling of managers could vary widely across countries, necessitating that different recommendations be made for implementing the research findings in different countries. This is particularly important when making innovative or creative recommendations such as in advertising campaigns.

Ethics in marketing research

Report preparation and presentation involves many issues relating to research integrity. These issues include defining the research problem to suit hidden agendas, ignoring pertinent data, compromising the research design, deliberately misusing statistics, falsifying figures, altering research results, misinterpreting the results with the objective of supporting a personal or corporate point of view, and withholding information.[31] A survey of 254 researchers found that 33% believed that the most difficult ethical problems they face encompass issues of research integrity. The researcher must address these issues when preparing the report and presenting the findings. The dissemination of research results to the client and other stakeholders, as may be appropriate, should be honest, accurate and complete.

The researcher should aim to be objective throughout the research process. Dilemmas may be faced in maintaining an objective stance and presenting unbiased findings, as illustrated in the following example.

Using video clips in reports[32]

The judicious use of video clips can help communicate findings very effectively and can boost engagement among the audience. However, videoing a focus group can often result in poor-quality clips: participants mumble, other people interrupt, and it can simply be difficult to hear. Even if a manned camera is used instead of a static camera, very often the operator cannot pan round to the relevant participant in time to catch the beginning of a quote. There are a number of ways around this problem – although some of the solutions raise issues about ethics. One solution that is sometimes used for focus groups is to film participants individually at the end of the group for two to three key questions. In some circumstances researchers ask them to repeat what they said earlier in the session so that it can be captured on camera. There may be some doubts about this in terms of whether it is 'proper' behaviour for a researcher; however, we would argue that as the participants are repeating something they have already said, this approach is acceptable, and enables the effective illustration of a finding that will help to engage its audience at the presentation. If producing video clips is the main focus of the project it can be most effective to screen participants so that we know how they will answer the questions before they are recruited! Again, this could be seen as unethical; however, if, for example, the objective is to illustrate the differences between two segments then this is an acceptable approach, on the proviso that robust research has already been carried out to identify and validate the segments.

Ethical challenges are also faced when research procedures and analyses do not reveal anything new or significant. For example, the discriminant function may not classify better than chance (Chapter 21). Ethical dilemmas can arise in these instances if the researcher nevertheless attempts to draw conclusions from such analyses. The researchers are being paid for their expert interpretation of data, and can nothing meaningful be said?

Like researchers, clients also have the responsibility for full and accurate disclosure of the research findings and are obligated to employ these findings honourably. For example, consumers can be negatively affected by a client who distorts the research findings to develop a biased advertising campaign that makes brand claims that have not been substantiated by marketing research. Ethical issues also arise when client firms, such as tobacco companies, use marketing research findings as a foundation to formulate questionable marketing campaigns.

Digital applications in marketing research

One of the main challenges of writing and making oral presentations of research reports lies in engaging clients, decision-makers and other users/influencers. Engagement means that these individuals will take the time and space to read, watch, listen to the intended message. It means they will appreciate the integrity of the researcher and their professionalism in conducting and delivering the research.

To achieve engagement, researchers have to compete against many other demands on the time and space of decision-makers, but at their disposal are a myriad of digital developments and creative means of communication. We have illustrated examples of digital developments in presenting findings through creative communications at BMW Group Designworks and Spring Research working with UBS. The following example illustrates the communications challenges faced by researchers with a complex and dispersed audience. It shows a balance of the distinctive skills of researchers and their views of the real insights in a study, matched with the communication skills of digital marketers.

| **Real research** | **Animated information graphics video – 'Meet Ryan and Maria'[33]** |

A digital marketing team undertook a study to support the development of a strategy for how the UK government should communicate online with young people aged 14 to 19. When the research was complete, the project presented several reporting challenges. Feedback to the client had to combine 11 overlapping work streams from a range of disciplines (qualitative, quantitative, ethnographic, secondary and academic). Furthermore, a diverse range of client audiences needed to be engaged, including: the commissioning client team which was spread across four locations; two layers of senior departmental colleagues; a government ministerial audience; and an additional audience of interested third parties. In addition to the geographical dispersion of the audiences it was anticipated that many would have little prior knowledge of the project. Another challenge was the time available to present findings; for example, in one case the researchers had a five-minute meeting slot in which to summarise six months of work. In responding to these challenges the researchers' aim was to tailor the information to meet the needs of each audience as clearly as possible. Video was considered at an early stage due to the likely need to describe the project to a number of other audiences over the course of the project's lifetime. The creative team produced a five-minute animated information graphics video called 'Meet Ryan and Maria', demonstrating how two digital natives navigate between the real and virtual worlds seamlessly, some of the places they go and the possible role that government could play in this journey. The video was complete with music, voice-over and a hand animation technique. It helped to communicate complex ideas persuasively in a short space of time and was produced in a range of formats which could be easily shared among client audiences.

As in the above example, the technology may be there and a good relationship between researchers and visual designers to make a big impact in report and presentation dynamics. However, those regularly on either side of the marketing research debrief know that the pressures of timetable and budget do not always allow for this. They know that quantitative-based presentations are not regularly given this kind of treatment, and that the balance of time between thinking and physically charting is often awry. There may be few chances to extend timetables, or to make budgets magically increase, so a change of mindset is required, to enable better use to be made of the time and money that are available.[34]

Given the ability to search electronically and tailor reports online, research findings are now becoming more 'pull' oriented, as opposed to the 'push' orientation of a printed report. The 'pull' orientation means that decision-makers and other research users can conduct analyses to suit their needs, sometimes working with raw data. Beyond the researcher's presentation of the focus and findings of a study, many interactive reporting formats enable users to create their own unique reports. Using database-driven technology and reporting software it is possible to have a completely interactive experience that allows data interrogation through the specification of questions, filters, cross-tabulations and even applied weighting.[35] The use of digital dashboards with their flexibility in terms of presenting both quantitative and qualitative data represents a major development in how research findings are presented and used. Examples of the use of dashboards at Motorola and Heineken presented earlier clearly illustrate a 'pull' orientation.

The 'push' orientation, i.e. the static report, is the most popular form of reporting, as detailed in Table 26.2. The interpretation that a researcher may generate will continue to be written, but can now be accessed as a result of a search, instigation of a link, or even just rolling the mouse pointer over an icon. The basic structure of a website, and the ease with which it is possible to navigate around a large amount of information, ensures that decision-makers can quickly find exactly what they want. It is also possible to have index areas constantly visible on the screen to ensure that areas of information contained within a single report, or indeed multiple reports, can be accessed quickly. With mobile technology, access can be such that, at any time and any place, the report readers can immerse themselves in the report in an environment and context that really suits them.

Examples of how marketing research reports online are making decision-makers' lives easier are:[36]

- Reporting and interrogating real-time data (not just from online interviews but from CATI and CAPI data).
- Creating automated report formats – as illustrated in the example below.
- Linking different research projects' reports together to create a more detailed overview.
- Building charts and tables by adding different elements (such as confidence limits and explanation of chart movements).
- Applying rules to the reporting to ensure the robustness of the presented results.
- Applying complex modelling calculations and processes to data as they are made available.

Though these benefits are clear, as illustrated in Table 26.2, the use of interactive and online marketing research reports is still primarily 'locked' into static presentations, and there is some way to go to realise these benefits.

Real research   ## Automated reporting for dental practices

Researchers are facing a dilemma: how to provide clients with powerful reporting with cost effective pricing? In developing their custom Patient Experience System for dental practitioners, Snap Surveys was faced with providing complex reporting for each of several thousand dental practices (**www.snapsurveys.com/dental**). Each client required an individual interpretation of the results of the survey of clients, an indication of how they performed when benchmarked against other dental practices, and an action plan based on the results of the survey. These requirements would normally be handled by an experienced research team, but with a resulting cost . . .

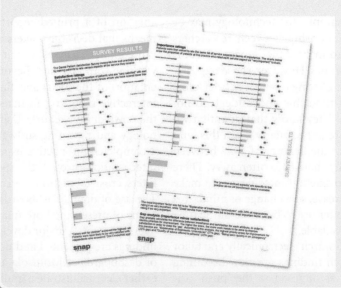

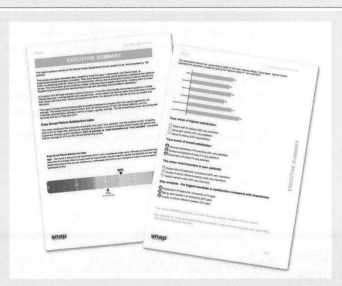

Snap Surveys developed a fully automated reporting system that was triggered at the completion of the survey and generated a custom report highlighting areas where the practice was performing well and where there was room for improvement. An executive summary was generated automatically together with an individual list of actions based on the performance of the individual dental practice. Results from the individual dental practice were then automatically benchmarked against national average results with practice results in green and benchmarked results in red.

Summary

Report preparation and presentation is the final step in the marketing research project. This process begins with interpretation of data analysis results and leads to conclusions and recommendations. Next, the formal report is written and an oral presentation made. After decision-makers have read the report, the researcher should conduct a follow-up, assisting management and undertaking a thorough evaluation of the marketing research project.

For the researcher, the oral presentation is usually considered the end of what could have been months of long hours, exhausting travel and intense data analysis, all in search of the valuable insights. The presentation is delivered and the researcher may see it is finally over, and time to move on to the next project. For the receiver of the research report, this may be just the beginning. The researcher may have delivered some provocative insights and may have considered every possible angle. Reports, however, can raise more questions, and decision-makers may want more details.[37] The researcher has to consider how to assist decision-makers to get the most out of reports and presentations. Researchers also have to learn from the experience of presenting their findings, in order to plan more creative, efficient and effective research in the future.

In international marketing research, report preparation may be complicated by the need to prepare reports for management in different countries and in different languages. Several ethical issues are pertinent, particularly those related to the interpretation and reporting of the research process and findings to the client and the use of these results by the client. Digital developments in marketing research are enabling reports and presentations to be delivered in far more engaging and relevant formats. With the use of mobile technology, this can mean that research users can access reports and presentations anywhere and at any time. The uses of digital dashboards in marketing research are facilitating new ways to present reports. Digital dashboards can enable research data to be interrogated and juxtaposed with performance data from across an organisation.

The final example presents a metaphor on the use of the guitar in supporting presentations. It is a final reminder that digital developments that facilitate professional presentations can never replace the creative skills of conveying the story and impact of a piece of research upon a decision-making situation.

Real research

My paradigm is the guitar[38]

Developments in modern technology have had a profound impact on the art of business presentation. There is no doubt that the standard of visualisation in presentations has improved immeasurably, but has the presentation itself? Technically good presentations are becoming commonplace, perhaps even predictable. Predictability precedes boredom.

Presenters spend too much time creating a slide show and not enough on their performance. Presenters have forgotten to plan their personal involvement and the involvement of their audience.

My paradigm is the guitar. The guitar represents a tool that supports presentation, but that can never do the performance for you. From my own experience as a guitarist, presentations and gigs have many parallels. You have to prepare diligently, and have a good plan for the progress of the performance. You should know your material. You must be able to excite the audience and get them involved. You must be able to improvise and respond to requests. You should have a good guitar, but the good guitar on its own won't carry the day. You will.

Questions

1　Describe the process of report preparation.
2　Why is the quality of report presentation vital to the success of a marketing research project?
3　Describe a commonly used format for writing marketing research reports.
4　Describe the following parts of a report: title page, table of contents, executive summary, problem definition, research design, data analysis, conclusions and recommendations.
5　Why is the 'limitations and caveats' section included in the report?
6　Discuss the importance of objectivity in writing a marketing research report.
7　Describe the guidelines for report writing.
8　How should the data items be arranged in a table?
9　What is a pie chart? For what type of information is it suitable? For what type of information is it not suitable?

10 Describe a line chart. What kind of information is commonly displayed using such charts?

11 What are the advantages and disadvantages of presenting data using 3D charts?

12 What is the purpose of an oral presentation? What guidelines should be followed in an oral presentation?

13 To what extent should researchers interpret the information they present in a report?

14 Describe the evaluation of a marketing research project in retrospect.

15 Graphically represent the consumer decision-making process described in the following paragraph:

> The consumer first becomes aware of the need. Then the consumer simultaneously searches for information from several sources: retailers, advertising, word of mouth, and independent publications. After that a criterion is developed for evaluating the available brands in the marketplace. Based on this evaluation, the most preferred brand is selected.

Exercises

1 Obtain a copy of an old marketing research report (many marketing research agencies or companies that have commissioned research will provide copies of old reports for educational purposes). Evaluate the ways in which you could improve the structure and style of presentation in this report.

2 Prepare an oral presentation of the report above, to be targeted at senior marketing managers. Deliver your presentation to a group of fellow students (role playing the managers) and ask them to critique the presentation.

3 Visit www.confirmit.com to evaluate the formats of reports used by this company. How does the format of the automated reports compare with the one in this book?

4 You are a researcher preparing a report for a high-tech firm on 'The demand potential for digital cameras in Europe'. Develop a format for your report. How is that format different from the one given in this book? Discuss the format and purposes of each section with your boss (role played by a student in your class).

5 In a small group discuss the following issues: 'Writing reports is an art. Presenting reports is an art. Reading reports is an art. It is all a matter of art.' And 'Writing a report that is concise and yet complete is virtually impossible as these two objectives are conflicting.'

Video case exercise: Burke Inc.

Burke describes how it communicates marketing research findings to its clients. What factors of success do you see in its approach to reporting? Are there any other factors not mentioned that you feel could create more successful reporting?

Notes

1. Bernstein, A., Robin, L. and Zych, M., 'The art of research narratives – impact through entertainment', ESOMAR, Annual Congress, London (September 2006).

2. Bendzko, A. and Ricketts, A., 'No more death by research debrief: innovative ways to convert insights into action', ESOMAR Annual Congress, Berlin (September 2007).

3. Saxton, G. and Davidson, A., 'The business of storytelling with qualitative research', Market Research Society, Annual Conference (2009).

4. Johnston, A., 'It's engagement, but is it research? Effectively engaging decision makers', ESOMAR, Qualitative Research, Istanbul (November 2008).

5. Few. S., *Show Me the Numbers: Designing Tables and Graphs to Enlighten* (Burlingame, CA: Analytics Press, 2004); Tufte, E.R., *Visual Explanations: Images and Quantities, Evidence and Narrative* (Cheshire, CT: Graphic, 1997); Fink, A., *How to Report on Surveys* (Thousand Oaks, CA: Sage, 1995).

6. Birks, D.F., 'Market research', in Baker, M.J. (ed.), *The Marketing Book*, 3rd edn (Oxford: Butterworth–Heinemann, 1994), 262.

7. Heeg, R., 'We have some catching up to do', *Research World* (November 2004), 6–7.

8. Keys, T. Jr, 'Report writing', *Internal Auditor* 53 (4) (August 1996), 65–66.

9. Anon., 'What you say', *Advertising Age* 79 (14) (April 2008), 4; Wolcott, H.F., *Writing up qualitative research*, 2nd edn (Thousand Oaks, CA: Sage, 2001); Britt, S.H., 'The writing of readable research reports', *Journal of Marketing Research* 8 (2) (May 1971), 265. See also Mort, S., *Professional Report Writing* (Brookfield, IL: Ashgate, 1995); Shair, D.I., 'Report writing', *HR Focus* 71 (2) (February 1994), 20.

10. Anon., 'New international aims for young readers with quick response codes in news stories', *Marketing Week* 31 (11) (March 2008), 13; Low, G.S., 'Factors affecting the use of information in the evaluation of marketing communications productivity', *Academy of Marketing Science Journal* 29 (1) (Winter 2001), 70–88; Boland, A., 'Got report-o-phobia? Follow these simple steps to get those ideas onto paper', *Chemical Engineering* 103 (3) (March 1996), 131–132.

11. van Meel, I. and Rietberg, J., 'Information à la carte – the need to select, prepare and present', ESOMAR, Congress, Montreux (September 2009).

12. Tanase, G., 'Real-life data mart processing', *Intelligent Enterprise* 5 (5) (8 March 2002), 22–24; Wilson, L.D., 'Are appraisal reports logical fallacies?', *Appraisal Journal* 64 (2) (April 1996), 129–133; Leach, J., 'Seven steps to better writing', *Planning* 59 (6) (June 1993), 26–27; Ehrenberg, A.S.C., 'The problem of numeracy', *American Statistician* 35 (May 1981), 67–71.

13. Wallgren, A., Wallgren, B., Persson, R., Jorner, U. and Haaland, J.A., *Graphing Statistics and Data* (Thousand Oaks, CA: Sage, 1996); Tufte, E.R., *Visual Display of Quantitative Information* (Cheshire, CT: Graphic, 1992).

14. Dean, J., 'High-powered charts and graphs', *Government Executive* 34 (1) (January 2002), 58; Kauder, N.B., 'Pictures worth a thousand words', *American Demographics* (Tools Supplement) (November/December 1996), 64–68.

15. Gutsche, A.M., 'Visuals make the case', *Marketing News* 35 (20) (24 September 2001), 21–22; Hinkin, S., 'Charting your course to effective information graphics', *Presentations* 9 (11) (November 1995), 28–32.

16. Lee, M., 'It's all in the charts', *Malaysian Business* (1 February 2002), 46; Chen, M.T., 'An innovative project report', *Cost Engineering* 38 (4) (April 1996), 41–45; Zelazny, G., *Say It with Charts*, 3rd edn (Homewood, IL: Business One Irwin, 1996).

17. Clarke III, I., Flaherty, T.B. and Yankey, M., 'Teaching the visual learner: the use of visual summaries in marketing education', *Journal of Marketing Education* 28 (3) (December 2006), 216–226; Anon., 'Flow chart', *B-to-B* 87 (4) (8 April 2002), 16; Johnson, S. and Regan, M., 'A new use for an old tool', *Quality Progress* 29 (11) (November 1996), 144; Parr, G.L., 'Pretty-darned-quick flowchart creation', *Quality* (August 1996), 62–63.

18. Macer, T. and Wilson, S., *GlobalPark Annual Market Research Software Survey 2010*, Seventh annual survey (meaning ltd, 2011).

19. Few, S., 'Dashboard design: taking a metaphor too far', *DM Review* 15 (3) (March 2007), 18.

20. Dagen, B., 'Dashboards and scorecards aid in performance management and monitoring', *Management Science* (September 2007), 23–27.

21. Dover, C., 'How dashboards can change your culture', *Strategic Finance* 86 (4) (October 2004), 42.

22. Dagen, B., 'Dashboards and scorecards aid in performance management and monitoring', *Management Science* (September 2007), 23–27.

23. Koornstra, S. and de Nooij, G.J., 'Monitoring brand health – the worldwide Heineken brand dashboard', ESOMAR, Annual Congress, Cannes (September 2005).

24. Macer, T. and Birks, D.F., 'Digital Dashboards: An enquiry among research buyers and research providers', *Consultancy Report* (April 2010).

25. Bendzko, A. and Ricketts, A., 'No more death by research debrief: innovative ways to convert insights into action', ESOMAR, Annual Congress, Berlin (September 2007); Desiderio, L., 'At the sales presentation: ask and listen', *ID* 38 (4) (April 2002), 55; McConnell, C.R., 'Speak up: the manager's guide to oral presentations', *Health Care Manager* 18 (3) (March 2000), 70–77; Verluyten, S.P., 'Business communication and intercultural communication in Europe: the state of the art', *Business Communication Quarterly* 60 (2) (June 1997), 135–143.

26. Hamburger, S. and Lawry, P., 'Storytelling with international millionaires – a creative approach to research', ESOMAR, Annual Congress, Montreal (September 2008).

27. Bendzko, A. and Ricketts, A., 'No more death by research debrief: innovative ways to convert insights into action', ESOMAR, Annual Congress, Berlin (September 2007).

28. Eshpeter, B., 'Communicating research findings: eight common pitfalls', *Imprints* (January 2004), 8–9.

29. Niven, A. and Imms, M., 'Connecting with clients: re-thinking the debrief', Market Research Society, Annual Conference (2006); Moorman, C., Deshpande, R. and Zaltman, G., 'Factors affecting trust in market research relationships', *Journal of Marketing* 57 (January 1993), 81–101; Deshpande, R. and Zaltman, G., 'Factors affecting the use of market research information: a path analysis', *Journal of Marketing Research* 19 (February 1982), 25.

30. Laroche, M., Nepomuceno, M.V., Huang, L. and Richard, M.-O., 'What's so funny? The use of humor in magazine advertising in the United States, China and France', *Journal of Advertising Research* 51 (2) (2011), 404–416.

31. Liebman, M., 'Beyond ethics: companies deal with legal attacks on marketing practices', *Medical Marketing and Media* 37 (2) (February 2002), 74–77; Giacobbe, R.W., 'A comparative analysis of ethical perceptions in marketing research: USA vs Canada', *Journal of Business Ethics* 27 (3) (October 2000), 229–245; Milton-Smith, J., 'Business ethics in Australia and New Zealand', *Journal of Business Ethics* 16 (14) (October 1997), 1485–1497; Chonko, L.B., *Ethical Decision Making in Marketing* (Thousand Oaks, CA: Sage, 1995).

32. Johnston, A., 'It's engagement, but is it research? Effectively engaging decision makers', ESOMAR, Qualitative Research, Istanbul (November 2008).

33. Shaw, S., 'Communicating creatively: from digital media to stains on the bedroom floor', Market Research Society, Annual Conference (2010).

34. Swan, N. and Cathcart, B., 'Tell the truth and shame the devil: how can the discipline of journalism improve insight and research?', Market Research Society, Annual Conference (2010).

35. Macer, T., 'On your marks, get set…', *Research in Business* (May 2006), 7–8: Macer, T., 'PowerPoint slammed as research results delivery device', *Research* (May 2006), 14.

36. Hummerston, A., 'Net reporting comes of age', *Research* (May 2000), 36.

37. Bendzko, A. and Ricketts, A., 'No more death by research debrief: innovative ways to convert insights into action', ESOMAR Annual Congress, Berlin (September 2007).

38. Willetts N.J., 'Going live', *Marketing Week* (13 November 1997), 47–48.

27 International marketing research

Stage 1

Problem definition

Stage 2

Research approach developed

Stage 3

Research design developed

Stage 4

Fieldwork or data collection

Stage 5

Data integrity and analysis

Stage 6

Report preparation and presentation

The global impact of social media and digital developments demands an international mindset from all marketing researchers.

Objectives

After reading this chapter, you should be able to:

1   develop a framework for conducting international marketing research;

2   explain in detail the marketing, governmental, legal, economic, structural, informational and technological, and socio-cultural environmental factors and how they have an impact upon international marketing research;

3   describe characteristics of the use of secondary data, qualitative techniques, online, telephone, face-to-face and postal survey methods in different countries;

4   discuss how to establish the equivalence of scales and measures, including construct, operational, scalar and linguistic equivalence;

5   describe the processes of back translation and parallel translation in translating a questionnaire into a different language;

6   discuss the ethical considerations in international marketing research;

7   appreciate how digital developments are shaping the manner in which international marketing research is planned and administered.

Overview

This chapter starts by evaluating the need for international marketing research. It then discusses the environment in which international marketing research is conducted, focusing on the marketing, governmental, legal, economic, structural, informational and technological, and socio-cultural environments.[2] Although illustrations of how the six steps of the marketing research process should be implemented in an international setting have been presented in earlier chapters, here we present additional details on secondary data, qualitative techniques, survey methods, scaling techniques and questionnaire translation. Relevant ethical issues in international marketing research are identified. The chapter concludes by examining how digital developments can help in the design and administration of international marketing research. We begin with two examples illustrating multinational studies in international marketing research. The first example illustrates how research is helping to reveal the nature and development of affluent consumers across Africa. The second example illustrates how an online survey enabled an understanding of consumer values across six nations.

Real research	**Brands and African middle classes[3]**

The first cross-market survey measuring the media habits, buying patterns and attitudes of Africa's most affluent people was launched in 2010 by global market research firm Synovate (**ems.synovate.nl**). EMS Africa showed the emergence of an aspiring, broad-minded and brand-conscious upper class in the strongest African markets. It provided data for international media owners and advertisers, who were looking to win new business in these important economies. EMS Africa tracked media usage, prosperity and influence across the top 15% of income earners in 12 cities across the key strategic African markets: Nigeria, South Africa, Kenya, Morocco and Cameroon. The survey measured consumption of nearly 50 TV channels, 80 print titles, 29 websites and 8 radio stations. It also monitored what affluent Africans own, what they intend to buy, and their attitudes to work, family, shopping and brands. EMS Africa found that 79% of affluent Africans preferred to buy well-known brands, 64% said they are usually among the first people to buy technologically innovative products, and 91% said they do not mind paying more for higher quality. International brands were increasingly spotting the opportunity. Hugo Boss has stores in Mauritius, Egypt, Morocco, Mozambique, South Africa and Tunisia. Spanish fashion retailer Mango has expanded into Algeria, Benin, Ivory Coast, Egypt, Ghana, Libya, Morocco, Nigeria, South Africa and Tunisia. Coca-Cola has said it plans to double its annual investment in Africa, focusing on non-carbonated water and juice-based drinks aimed at the middle classes. Nestlé too has spotted the potential to capture a rising market, expanding factories and distribution in East Africa.

| Real research | **A measure of global brands[4]** |

Research company Fresh Intelligence (**www.freshintelligence.com**) used cross-cultural communication theory (a combination of anthropology, sociology and psychology) to underpin a study of values across international markets. It developed a list of 22 values that described a wide range of attitudes towards personal and social well-being. The researchers worded values in such a way that they could be attributed both to a consumer personally and to a brand. The online survey was conducted with 3,000 participants over the age of 18, with 500 participants in each country (samples representative to each country by age, gender, regions; industry exclusions). The countries picked differed greatly in their history and current position in the world. All of them were large and very attractive markets. The researchers chose three developing and promising economies: Brazil, Russia, and China representing the BRIC block; and three developed prosperous countries: Canada, the USA and Australia. These countries had some core similarities and strong differences in their values. The researchers saw, for example, that feeling safe, secure and protected was among the top five values across all six countries, and it was the highest value in the USA, Canada and Russia. The most economically wealthy countries valued hard work the most: the USA, Canada and China. Three others, Russia, Brazil and Australia, seemed to put more value on the other side of work–life balance: only these countries had 'family' in their top three values; hard work was not a priority at all. Only China highly valued both hard work and family. All countries except for Brazil included being responsible, reliable and trustful in their top five values.

What is international marketing research?

The term 'international marketing research' can be used very broadly. It denotes research for true international products (international research), research carried out in a country other than the country of the research-commissioning organisation (overseas research), research conducted in all important countries where a company may have existing and/or potential consumers (multinational research), and research conducted in and across different cultures (cross-cultural research). The last category of cross-cultural research does not have to cross national boundaries. Many countries have a vast array of ethnic groups, giving the researcher many challenges in understanding consumers in these groups within their home country. The following example is a brief illustration of the array of problems faced by researchers working in India.

Real research	**Engaging with Indian consumers**[5]

The Indian consumer market is at once both a tremendous opportunity and a great challenge. Heading towards 2020, it has been argued that India will grow in economic stature from a 50 million 'middle class' to 600 million. Moving to higher levels of urbanisation, with the youngest median age population in the world, and an active workforce, the aggregate demand for consumer goods from this massive middle class will outstrip that of almost every other country in the world. What makes India different and often a puzzle is its sometimes surprising dissimilarity to other eastern countries, and its amazing diversity. With more than 5,000 towns and 600,000 villages spread across 28 states, India's people speak over 17 major languages and 844 dialects and practise eight religions.

The example above supports the contention that, in research approach, there is no difference between domestic and international marketing research. In other words, researchers have to adapt their techniques to their target participants, and the subtle cultural differences within a country offer the same challenges as the much more apparent differences over thousands of kilometres. The following example does not present an actual case but the opinions of the respected international researcher Mary Goodyear. Though these views stem from the early 1990s, they are still relevant in the contention that there is no difference between domestic and international research. She then goes on, however, to argue why international marketing research should be examined as a distinct subject area.

Real research	**The world over, a group is a group is a group**[6]

It has become the convention to talk about international research as if it were a discrete sector of the industry. Methodologically, in qualitative research at least, it is not really very different from what is done at home. A group is a group is a group. However, it is important to realise that international research is different: first, in terms of analysing the social and cultural dynamics of the society, how the overseas society is structured, how power is gained and expressed, the roles allotted to men and women, the interactions between different sectors of society and so on; and second, in the practical problems involved in organising the research.

The first point established in the above example is that many of the cultural and societal assumptions that we take for granted have to be examined. This we discussed when considering how researchers 'see' in Chapter 9. Without such an examination we have the potential to be naïve in the questions we pose, who we pose those questions to, and the manner in which we interpret the answers we generate. The second point reminds us of the features of the infrastructure that supports the research process, features that we may get used to and take for granted. For example, without the benefits of accurate sampling frames, accurate and up-to-date secondary data and reliable and widespread use of mobile devices, our research plans may be weak. Our whole approach to organising and conducting research in international markets has to reflect these physical conditions. The following example builds upon Mary Goodyear's notion that, the world over, a group is a group is a group. It illustrates that even if methodologically the focus group can be conducted in the same manner anywhere in the world, the cultural and societal assumptions and the infrastructure for conducting research have to be appraised.

| Real research | **Managing research among Saudi women[7]** |

What you find behind the veil is what you would find anywhere: outgoing women, shy women, women with a sense of humour, serious women – the entire spectrum of characters and temperaments is present among Saudi women. In a qualitative project (for a financial institution interested in managing the assets of Saudi women), some women stressed that their husbands should never know that they had a bank account or even that they had money or other assets. Hana Balaa, Director of TNS's Saudi Female Research Centre, found it fascinating to learn about this confident determination to maintain a level of independence, and to think about the marketing communication implications.

Focus group participants are selected through referrals and will be driven to the focus group by their driver, husband or son, as women were not allowed to drive in Saudi Arabia. Ten years ago it would have been impossible to conduct this type of focus group in Jeddah, Riyadh or the Kingdom's other major cities. But Saudi society is opening up, slowly, but steadily.

Overseas expansion has become more important for European companies due to increasing economic integration, the lowering of trade barriers and in some instances intensive competition in domestic markets. International markets such as the vast developing economies of Brazil, Russia, India and China offer huge prospective returns. As attractive as these markets may be, companies must realise that establishing or further developing relationships in these markets does not guarantee success. Understanding the nature, scope and dynamics of these markets is vital to realising the opportunities and presents a major challenge to researchers. This challenge also lies in overcoming the 'red tape' in countries that may well have laws and policies designed to protect their own businesses. Realising the opportunities and overcoming the challenges may mean, at one extreme, that researchers work with decision-makers in their own domestic markets, trying to coordinate research in distant lands. It may mean that client and research companies operate in multiple markets with indigenous marketing research operations and many complex working relationships. The nature and challenges of the relationships between a client and research agency working in multinational research projects are detailed in the following example.

| Real research | **Motorola and GfK: managing global research projects[8]** |

There has been an enormous increase in the number and variety of multi-country research projects linked to the trend of globalisation within multinational companies. Often, these projects can include up to 25 markets, e.g. to derive global segmentation, to support a global brand strategy, or to help develop global products. Global business and global research means complexity: international teams are responsible for the coordination of the business between the countries, and for global tasks like the development of a global brand strategy. Regional or local (country) teams are responsible for the 'go to market' tasks, like local marketing and sales support and local pricing strategies. Global and local teams need to work hand in hand; they need to concentrate on their respective tasks and responsibilities and need to define 'rules' for cooperation and collaboration. This is true for global research teams as well, on both sides: client and research agency. Consequently, global project teams include a global research team and local research teams for the client and agency side. The capability of coordinating research projects with global and local teams is a key success factor for globally active companies. For companies such as Motorola and GfK, global or multi-country research is more than simply repeating a study in several languages. It involves a sound knowledge of the research topic at a global level and a highly professional and well-crafted research approach. To apply this approach in different countries involves a deep understanding of the local markets and a cultural sensitivity to the specifications of those local markets. Multi-country research means being able to respect and learn from local business practices and cultures and adapt them into 'global thinking'. It should be a fruitful two-way process requiring much mutual understanding. At Motorola, it means that the global CMI (Consumer Market Insights) team, based in Chicago at Motorola's headquarters, makes sure that the selection of the markets, the selection of research designs and techniques, the timing of the research and the interaction between different research projects are consistent and complementary. It also means that there are regional and local CMI teams, making sure that the research is meaningful when applied in the country, and that it delivers what it is expected to deliver: insight at a global and local level. From an agency point of view, it means being able to offer a global network which provides global know-how, capabilities and skills, allied to local capacities, contacts, know-how and cultural sensitivities. At GfK, a global team based in the headquarters in Nuremberg makes sure that the research design and techniques, quality, interpretation and reporting are at a consistently high level, following general guidelines, and that clients get what they are used to from GfK in all local markets. Best practice requires linking the four involved teams: global Motorola, local Motorola, global GfK and local GfK. This linkage, and the balancing act of coordinating the four involved parties, is the art and science of multinational projects. In only this way can research deliver insights that can be assimilated globally and applied and acted on locally.

A framework for international marketing research

Conducting international marketing research can be much more complex than conducting domestic marketing research. Although the basic six-step framework for domestic marketing research is applicable, the environment prevailing in the countries, cultural units or international markets that are being researched influences the way the six steps of the marketing research process should be performed. Figure 27.1 presents a framework for conducting international marketing research.

The differences in the environments of countries, cultural units or overseas markets should be considered when conducting international marketing research. These differences may arise in the marketing, governmental, legal, economic, structural, informational and technological, and socio-cultural environments, as shown in Figure 27.1.

Marketing environment

The role of marketing in economic development varies in different countries. For example, many developing countries are frequently oriented towards production rather than marketing. Demand typically exceeds supply, and there is little concern about customer satisfaction, especially because the level of competition is low. In assessing the marketing environment, the researcher should consider the variety and assortment of products available, pricing policies, government control of media and the consumer attitudes towards advertising, the efficiency of the distribution system, the level of marketing effort undertaken, and the unsatisfied needs and behaviour of consumers. For example, surveys conducted in Europe usually

Figure 27.1

**A framework
for international
marketing research**

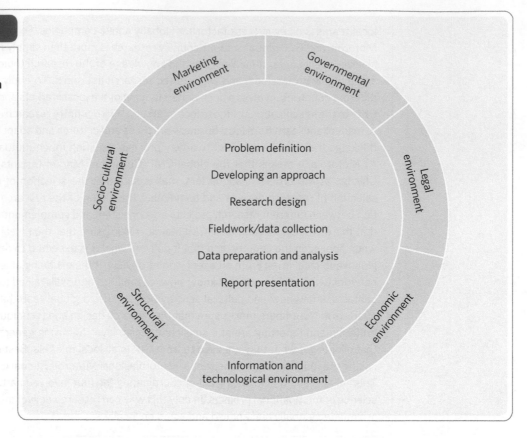

Marketing
environment

Governmental
environment

Socio-cultural
environment

Legal
environment

Problem definition

Developing an approach

Research design

Fieldwork/data collection

Data preparation and analysis

Report presentation

Structural
environment

Economic
environment

Information and
technological environment

involve questions on the variety and selection of merchandise. These questions would be inappropriate in some African countries, which are characterised by shortage economies. Likewise, questions about pricing may have to incorporate bargaining as an integral part of the exchange process. Questions about promotion should be modified as well. TV advertising, an extremely important promotion vehicle in Europe, is restricted or prohibited in many countries where TV stations are owned and operated by the government. Certain themes, words and illustrations used in Europe are taboo in some countries. This is illustrated in the following example which describes characteristics of research in the Middle East.

Real research   **Tackling the acquiescence bias among Arab participants[9]**

Among the numerous sources of measurement error, the ones that have the strongest influence on the quality of responses are 'acquiescence bias' and 'social desirability bias'. Acquiescence bias is a systematic bias caused by some participants tending to agree with whatever is presented to them. Such a bias may be caused by either participants or interviewers being overly friendly during interviews. Although the Arab culture is very diverse and kaleidoscopic from several perspectives, there are still some traits that make it suitable to be seen in a unified way. Extremity of acquiescence bias is one such facet. Politeness is at the core of interaction between Arabs. It is quite common to see an Arab express a heartfelt greeting to a total stranger. Such a gesture is just one of the various ways an Arab exhibits politeness. 'Being agreeable' is important too. In a business meeting, for instance, in response to a proposal or a viewpoint, it is unlikely that an Arab would evince outright disagreement in the very first instance. This is, in fact, analogous to the inability of an Arab participant to express a negative reaction in the context of a survey involving assessment of product concepts. An Arab would rather subtly suggest an alternative point of view or move the discussion to another topic than express dissent. In addition, being polite is in accord with being a good host. A guest at one's home is treated with deference and every attempt is made to please and serve the guest's needs. In surveys done in the Middle East, most interviews are done face to face at the participant's place of residence. In such a scenario, it is easy to see why a participant treats the interviewer as a guest, and exhibits behaviour that is seen as fitting for a good host. A negative response to a product concept would thus be seen as equivalent to being disagreeable and, hence, impolite. In effect, the participant would rather say that the concept is likely to be acceptable than say that it will not succeed.

Governmental environment

An additional relevant factor is the governmental environment. The type of government has a bearing on the emphasis on public policy, regulatory agencies, government incentives and penalties, and investment in government enterprises. Some governments, particularly in developing countries, do not encourage overseas competition. High tariff barriers create disincentives to the efficient use of marketing research approaches. Also, the role of government in setting market controls, developing infrastructure and acting as an entrepreneur should be carefully assessed. The role of government is also crucial in many developed countries, where government has traditionally worked with industry towards a common national industrial policy. At the tactical level, the government determines tax structures, tariffs and product safety rules and regulations, often imposing special rules and regulations on overseas multinationals and their marketing practices. In many countries, the government may be an important member of the distribution channel. The government purchases essential products on a large scale and then sells them to consumers, perhaps on a rationed basis.

Legal environment

The legal environment encompasses common law, overseas law, international law, transaction law, antitrust, bribery and taxes. From the standpoint of international marketing research, particularly salient are laws related to the elements of the marketing mix. Product laws include those dealing with product quality, packaging, warranty and after-sales service, patents, trademarks and copyright. Laws on pricing deal with price fixing, price discrimination, variable pricing, price controls and retail price maintenance. Distribution laws relate to exclusive territory arrangements, type of channels and cancellation of distributor or wholesaler agreements. Likewise, laws govern the type of promotional methods that can be employed. Although all countries have laws regulating marketing activities, some countries have only a few laws that are loosely enforced and others have many complicated laws that are strictly enforced. In many countries the legal channels are clogged and the settlement of court cases is prolonged. In addition, home-country laws may also apply while conducting business or marketing research in overseas countries.

Economic environment

Economic environmental characteristics include economic size (gross domestic product, or GDP); level, source and distribution of income; growth trends; and sectoral trends. A country's stage of economic development determines the size, the degree of modernisation and the standardisation of its markets. Consumer, industrial and commercial markets become more standardised and consumers' work, leisure and lifestyles become more homogenised by economic development and advances in technology.

Informational and technological environment

Elements of the informational and technological environment include information and communication systems, access to broadband, broadband speeds, the prevalence and use of mobile devices, the use of other electronic equipment, energy, production technology, science and invention. Advances in science and technology have had disproportionate impacts upon consumers across the globe. It would be a mistake to generalise about the impact of information and technology upon developing economies and upon particular rural consumers. The following example illustrates the progress made in developing economies in terms of information and technology. Understanding such progress in individual target communities is vital for international researchers.

Real research | **Moving straight to a mobile infrastructure[10]**

It is important not to oversimplify the term 'developing markets'. Developing markets should also not be treated as a single 'region'. There are many points of cultural, economic, social and technological difference in every country and even within some countries. While a piecemeal transport infrastructure in many developing countries can make travel challenging for researchers, particularly in rural areas, there is evidence that many developing countries are ahead of the developed world in implementing mobile communications infrastructure. This is particularly true in Africa, where more than 600 million people now have mobile phones. It is a mistake to assume that developed markets are simply behind the pace of change in marketing research, simply because they have not progressed from door-to-door, pen and paper interviewing (PAPI) to computer-assisted telephone interviewing (CATI) or online research. While face-to-face surveys will remain important in these markets, they will not be the only method of data collection. Cambodia, for example, has very limited fixed-line coverage for telecoms because of the dark years under the Khmer Rouge and subsequent Vietnamese occupation, but it has bypassed the development of fixed-line communications (now around 1 per 100 people) and moved straight to a mobile infrastructure (currently around 30 per 100 people). The situation is the same across Africa and many other developing countries, and signifies a different evolution in the development of technology that can be used for data capture in research, to that for developed countries. Mobile phones are embedded into the daily lives of people throughout the developing world. Research across seven sub-Saharan African countries revealed that 7 out of 10 people first experience the Internet via a mobile phone, and for 6 out of 10 people it remains the main mode of access.

Structural environment

Structural factors relate to transportation, communication, utilities and infrastructure. Personal contact with participants may be difficult for a variety of reasons in individual countries. Based on geography alone, national samples in China and Indonesia are really challenging. China is predominantly rural and Indonesia consists of several thousand islands. There are creative research designs that enable participants to be accessed in remote communities where travel and infrastructure make research expensive and time consuming. Such a design is illustrated in the following example.

Smart- and non-smartphones in developing markets[11]

In China, TNS (**www.tnsglobal.com**) and MobileMeasure (**www.mobile-measure.com**) successfully ran qualitative and quantitative projects in both urban and rural settings using non-smart Java-enabled phones. The TNS research team used MobileMeasure's TPV platform (a text, photo and video blogging application). This enabled it effectively to bring qualitative and quantitative research to life without actually having to absorb substantial additional travel and moderation costs, particularly when researching in multiple remote locations. TPV worked on both smart and non-smart (Java-enabled) phones, facilitating a far more representative sample and rising to the challenge of conducting cost-effective qualitative and quantitative research in 'lower tier' cities and towns and remote and out-of-the-way areas. Through its partnership with MobileMeasure, TNS was able to have research participants use their non-smart (Java-enabled) phones to blog text and upload photos and videos in real time, capturing the moment's behaviour instantly. The TNS moderators were provided with a data online dashboard. They were often located remotely in other parts of the country, but could monitor the live feeds coming in. Additionally they could comment, communicate and elicit responses from the group or individual participants' in real time or in a pre planned manner, all done in both real time and remotely. On average TNS recorded 20–25 text blogs per week, 18–25 photos per week and 3–5 videos per week per participant, highlighting the validity and robustness of this technique and its natural fit with participants' daily lives.

Socio-cultural environment

Socio-cultural factors include values, literacy, language, religion, communication patterns, and family and social institutions. Relevant values and attitudes towards progress, time, achievement, work, authority, wealth, scientific method, risk, innovation and change could be considered here. In India, as noted earlier, there are 17 major languages and more than 844 dialects. India is divided into linguistic states. The country can be described as a mini-Europe, each state like a separate country within Europe, with its own language and cultural peculiarities. A survey which even approaches national representation in scope will generally be printed in at least 12 languages.[12]

In many countries, increasing economic prosperity has had an impact upon family size, structures and relationships as illustrated in the following example.

Changes in Latin American families[13]

TNS (**www.tnsglobal.com**) conducted research in Argentina, Brazil, Chile, Guatemala and Mexico in order to understand cultural changes. Its research targeted mothers of children aged between 3 and 9 years and their children. TNS found strong evidence suggesting that Latino children were becoming more informed and sophisticated consumers at early ages, and have a growing influence on the family purchase decisions and habits, reflecting a major change in their relationship with their parents. TNS also recognised that children have a strong awareness and concern for environmental issues. Over the past few decades, Latin America has followed socio-demographic trends in developed countries: birth rates have declined, from an average of six children to two or three children per woman. The number of single mothers as well as divorces has increased by 30%, more couples are delaying the birth of their first child, the age of first marriage is rising, and not marrying is an available option for many. At the same time, women are increasingly participating in the labour market and/or are becoming head of households. As a result, the traditional Latin American family has undergone significant changes: families are smaller, in many cases with only one parent at home, and as there are fewer children to support, purchase power per child is higher. As mothers have less time to spend with their families, their patterns of consumption become progressively more 'compensatory', accepting more of children's demands.

Each country's environment is unique, so international marketing research must take into consideration the environmental characteristics of the countries or overseas markets involved. The following example illustrates how dangerous terms such as the 'Asian market' may be for international marketers.

Real research

Diversities in the ASEAN region[14]

Many marketing commentators evaluating prospects in Asia focus on the two countries with the biggest populations and economic growth rates, China and India. It is easy to miss other rich and dynamic economies in the ASEAN (Association of South-East Asian Nations) region: Indonesia, Malaysia, Thailand, Singapore, the Philippines and Vietnam, as well as a collection of smaller countries. This is one of the world's most dynamic subregions with a combined young, literate population of 575 million and an average GDP growth rate consistently above 6%. However, there is no South-East Asian mindset, it is a complex subregion. The region may be viewed as immensely diverse, from the social acceptance of power and wealth inequalities in Indonesia, through to the strict, risk-averse Thais and a clear gender disparity in the Philippines. An acute understanding of cultural, historical and political differences will pay dividends to anyone operating across these markets. Marketers should apply the 'one-size-fits-all' mentality with great caution. There are some common themes that bring together the people of the ASEAN region, one of them being a thirst for digital technology. Filipinos are among the most avid blog readers on the planet, second only to the South Koreans. Thais spend the longest time talking on the phone of any nation in Asia. The region does not yet have a digital lifestyle in the Western image. What we see in the ASEAN countries is people longing to connect with the outside world and finding a platform for self-expression.

For companies that wish to expand into large geographical regions, the challenges in the above example can cause problems. Should they invest in research into every country or even regions within countries, or will this be prohibitive in time and cost terms? If they cannot manage to research individual countries in a region, which countries should they focus upon? Researching from the security of a key market may miss subtleties that local researchers would be quick to pick up on. Another benefit of local researchers is that desk research and their knowledge can help to fill in many gaps. The ideal is to have a multi-country project, coordinated from one location with local suppliers building out individual country knowledge within a common framework. The research approach should ensure quality control and consistency, and it should lead to actionable and global strategic recommendations, with all local markets represented. Such a maxim is fine, provided that international researchers can demonstrate the potential returns from such an investment, which is inherently very difficult to achieve.

The extent to which companies may invest in research targeted at individual countries may be evaluated in terms of not only the potential returns and idiosyncrasies of that country, but also the complexities of implementing research techniques that will work well. To help understand the problems of implementing international marketing research, we provide additional details for implementing secondary data, qualitative techniques, survey methods, measurement and scaling techniques, and questionnaire translation.[15]

Secondary data

The topic of secondary data was covered in detail in Chapters 4 and 5. An example of a secondary data source of great use in international marketing research is presented in the following example.

Real research   **Roper Reports Worldwide[16]**

Each year since 1997, GfK Roper Consulting (**www.gfkamerica.com**) has conducted over 30,000 face-to-face surveys with consumers aged over 13 years, across the world's leading markets. It aims to be representative of the national populations in North America and Western Europe, and of the urban population in other countries. The Roper Reports Worldwide study does not cover all countries but 22 megacities (population over 10 million and listed in order of size): Tokyo, Seoul, Mexico City, New York City, Mumbai, Delhi, São Paulo, Los Angeles, Shanghai, Osaka, Cairo, Kolkata, Jakarta, Guangzhou, Buenos Aires, Beijing, London, Paris, Istanbul, Rio de Janeiro, Moscow and Bangkok. The study is founded upon key factors that drive consumer behaviour in general and in the megacity, namely: (1) *Personal values*: With the blurring of age and gender, marketers are putting more emphasis on understanding the personal values of their consumers. (2) *Geography*: While globalisation is making lifestyles more similar around the world, life and consumer priorities still differ from one different country to another. (3) *Lifestage/demographics*: While differences between consumers of different ages and genders are eroding, lifestage can play an important role in driving consumer needs and product choices. (4) *Lifestyles*: Personal values show us the things that people aspire to; it is also important to understand the lifestyles that people actually lead. The two are not the same. (5) *Attitudes and behaviour*: How consumers relate to a specific product category, in terms of attitudes and behaviours.

It is worth recalling where secondary data can support the research process, especially given some of the difficulties of conducting primary research in international markets. Secondary data can help to:

1 Diagnose the research problem.
2 Develop an approach to the problem.
3 Develop a sampling plan.
4 Formulate an appropriate research design (e.g. by identifying the key variables to measure or understand).
5 Answer certain research questions and test some hypotheses.
6 Interpret primary data with more insight.
7 Validate qualitative research findings.

Obtaining secondary data on international markets to gain support for the above is much simpler with the power of the Internet. Online resources can allow access to international markets which in the past may have required travel to the country and a great deal of time-consuming searching. Judicious use of online resources does not mean that the international researcher will automatically gain support in the above seven areas. There may still be little or no secondary data that relate to the issues we wish to research in an international market, especially when new product/market opportunities are being explored. For what data we can obtain, the principles of evaluating secondary data, as set out in Table 4.2, still apply. Conducting an evaluation of the nature, specifications, accuracy, currency and dependability may be far more difficult in international markets. The process and specifications of research conducted in international markets may not be explicit; one may need a deep understanding of conducting primary research in a country to understand why data have been collected in a particular manner. Language is also a major issue, not only in reading and interpreting data, but in the definitions used in measurements. Finally, secondary research from a target country may have been heavily influenced by political forces. The researcher may need to be aware of such influences in order to interpret and make use of the findings.

Another major development in the use of secondary data is in the development of geographic information systems. In the use of geodemographic classifications of consumers, systems already exist in many countries across the globe. The systems work well in defining consumers within each country and, as described in Chapter 5, can be used as a foundation to add transactional and survey data generated within an organisation operating within each country. The international research problem emerges from the means of comparing classifications across the different countries. This problem emerges from the different data sources that are used to build the classifications in each country. There are different types of data that may be accessible, different standards and definitions used in data collection, and different laws allowing the use, or not, of certain types of data. As discussed in Chapter 5, Experian (**www.experian.com**) has produced 'Mosaic Global' as an attempt to produce a consistent segmentation system that covers over 380 million households from all of the world's most prosperous economies including North America, Europe and Asia–Pacific. Using local data from 16 countries and clustering methods, Experian has identified 10 distinct types of residential neighbourhood, each with a distinctive set of values, motivations and consumer preferences, which can be found in each of the countries. Mosaic Global uses the data from the national Mosaic classification systems for the following countries: Australia, Austria, Belgium, Canada, Czech Republic, Denmark, Finland, France, Germany, Greece, Hong Kong, Ireland, Israel, Italy, Japan, the Netherlands, New Zealand, Norway, Romania, Singapore, Spain, Sweden, Switzerland, the UK and the USA. Geodemographic databases can give an excellent introduction to a particular country and can form a foundation upon which other data sources can be built. At present, comparing consumer types across borders is problematic.

Qualitative techniques

Chapter 6 discussed the differences between European and American researchers in their approach to focus groups. In general, an American approach can be seen as far more structured and tends to be a foundation for subsequent surveys, while the European approach tends to be more evolutionary and exploratory. The question of the perspective from which one plans and conducts qualitative research is not really important until other researchers or moderators from international markets become involved in the process. As well as the training and thinking of researchers who plan and administer focus groups, there can be cultural differences in how participants engage in the technique. The resultant output of focus groups across cultures in international markets may not match the expectations of the decision-maker who will be supported by the research. The following example makes huge generalisations about national differences, but it does illustrate the challenges that international researchers face in planning and administering focus groups across the globe, and especially in Japan.

<table>
<tr><td>**Real research**</td><td>**Do focus groups work in Japan?**[17]</td></tr>
</table>

While qualitative research in Japan is typically 'packaged' in the same language, discourse and approaches as in the West, what it tends to deliver is often little more than 'viewed quantitative'. The focus group so often works well in the USA, arguably because it is a technique developed there. Put eight Americans in a room and ask them what they think about something and their very cultural heritage demands that they have an individual point of view and a story to tell. While the British do not take things quite to the extremes their American cousins do, it is nevertheless a society that celebrates the individual and they soon learnt to *let it all hang out* just enough to make a focus group work. France is another culture where focus groups work well. This is a culture which places huge emphasis on education, and a vital part of every citizen's education is training in oral expression. If the French, British and Americans come 'hardwired' with a cultural heritage that gives them unspoken cues of how to behave in focus groups (with felicitous results), so do other cultures: the Irish, for whom the pub is still a focal point of communities and where openness and conversation are the cultural norm, tend to get along famously in focus groups, enjoying the opportunity to share points of view and rub along with some new friends. In contrast to other cultures, Japan, arguably, has no clear reference situation for the focus group. Japan, traditionally and still, celebrates not the forthcoming and emotionally literate individual. There is little of that tradition of oral, emphatic expression that one finds in France. Japanese research participants shown into a focus group suite with other strangers rarely feel any obligation to make small talk. Without the presence of a moderator to give some kind of guidance, their culturally engrained instincts tell them that this is a non-place with no rules. Thus it is by no means uncommon for participants to fall asleep while waiting for the group to begin. When it comes to the focus group activity itself, both moderator and participants find themselves, unless otherwise encouraged, bound by the rules of their culture. Thus the culture dictates that strangers talking to each other should adopt a certain register of language. What this means is that the *default* outcome for a focus group in Japan is of emotionally superficial responses, no real assertion of personal experiences or feelings, reticence and a tendency to consensus. This is not conducive to arriving at insight about consumer motivations or their interactions with brands.

Decision-makers often require global answers to develop global marketing campaigns, yet data are often single-market related and cannot be easily interpreted across various countries. Researchers can be wary of using varying methods across different countries and cultures. They recognise that more control in the design and implementation of research is needed and that many forms of bias can emerge when working across cultures. However, there are many examples of where qualitative research is practised to great effect, especially in understanding subtle cultural nuances. Semiotics is an example which as a qualitative and analytic approach was discussed in Chapter 9. Semiotics has and continues to play a key role in formulating communication strategies for global brands entering developing markets. This visually based technique plays a critical part in the development of cross-cultural communications. It helps brands to keep up with rapid and culturally revolutionary change, especially in countries such as Brazil, Russia, India and China. In developing markets this involves tracking richer and more nuanced patterns of cultural diversity. Individual developing markets live with and increasingly celebrate their own inner diversity (India, for example, being as internally diverse as Europe) while global diversity simultaneously sweeps in. For the international researcher, developing overseas markets has become ripe for semiotics to be disseminated and practised by local research experts.[18]

Another example of an increasing use of qualitative research in international marketing research is in the use of social media research techniques, especially the use of marketing research online communities. From around 2005 in the USA, Canada, the UK and other parts of Western Europe, and in other parts of the world including Australia and New Zealand, online research communities have flourished. The technique provides primarily qualitative consumer insight on development topics in products, services, brands and communications.[19] An online research community is a group of people who have been provided with an online environment in which to interact with each other (and the client and researcher) about topics related to a research interest. Typically, they are constructed in content management systems (e.g. Community Server), which provide functionality such as forums, blogging, polls, personal spaces, videos and email contact mechanisms. The reasons for setting them up are to: monitor key issues within a market; tap into leading-edge consumers/innovators within a market; have a group of consumers available throughout a development process; genuinely collaborate in a two-way direction with consumers; easily monitor issues in many markets around the globe; have a cost-effective way to research many issues. There have been some well-documented case studies of successful multinational communities but most are run completely in English. Running successful communities, in situations where multicultural effects are larger or in multiple languages, presents many challenges though there are companies and researchers developing such approaches.[20] The following example illustrates some of the challenges in administering online research communities for international marketing research.

Real research	**The global Marketing Research Online Community**[21]

The application of Marketing Research Online Communities (MROCs) around the world is still an emerging discipline but a number of key principles of their success are emerging. A natural assumption with a multi-country community is to segment it by language alone. This is both for pragmatic reasons where there is a direct cost when needing to translate, and because this is the most visible differentiator. However, because two countries share a language, it does not mean they will naturally share ideals, beliefs or cultural terms of reference. The social interactions between a brand or representatives of a brand are more important for the success of an MROC than the interactions between participants. Conversations flourish only if there is a two-way flow. Emphasising the fact that feedback will be given to the community and how its input will help shape decisions is the primary message that should be presented through the lifecycle of a community. One of the biggest challenges that practitioners and clients using MROCs face is the need to embrace this conversational stance. Typically MROCs are moderated every day, asking questions, posting discussions and probing answers. This moderation needs to cater to the specific needs of participants and be pitched in a way that is easily understood. The moderator has a role in policing, providing technical support and answering other queries. Moderation is challenging in many ways. Content must be clear and concise, broad to encourage debate, specific so as not to be ambiguous, but not leading. The number of questions on any one topic can be limited. Moderators need to be sensitive to misunderstanding from participants, and to clarify the meaning or context of questions. By understanding the specific online behaviour of the target audience a moderator can make the question interesting to the participants and remain in tune with the client's objectives. A good moderator will be able to act intuitively and reflect the needs of participants. The moderator becomes an interpreter in the widest sense of the word. While language is a start point, it is not the destination. Moderators must understand their community and preferably show similar behaviours to those they are talking to in the community. Moderators need to understand 'the way things work' online in that country. By understanding the background to any conversation the moderator is able to add a greater understanding to the research. The right moderator not only adds to the knowledge of a particular country, but will also add to the knowledge of the community, not just as a group but sometimes even as individuals. It is also important for a moderator to be culturally sensitive and in a position to understand and acknowledge that social norms and simple points of reference are different both between and sometimes within countries.

This example also illustrates the essence of qualitative research in terms of exploring through rewording, of adapting an interview until sense is made. In international marketing research this calls for linguistic skills and a cultural awareness matching native speakers in any target country. This may not be a solution that is feasible for all international research projects. Depending upon the array of countries to be researched, recruiting researchers with the relevant linguistic skills may not be possible, but it is the best alternative should local research companies not exist or be considered to be of poor quality. Good-quality local researchers should be sought out, because, even if researchers with the relevant linguistic abilities are available, there are other cultural nuances that can affect the trust, rapport and comfort of qualitative research participants. Often participants are unfamiliar with the process or simply do not trust the researcher.

In general, patience and sensitivity are required to overcome cultural problems in conducting qualitative research in international markets.[22] An excellent working relationship with a local research company can be absolutely vital to success and in many cultures can only be achieved by developing a personal relationship. Listening to the advice of local research companies will also enhance sensitivity to participants. Patience is expressed by a preparedness to lengthen the research schedule, extra care in translation, pretests of wording and tact, and respect for participants and local researchers. Whether shaped by European or American paradigms or even any emerging paradigm that underpins social media research, good qualitative research should be open and a learning process. This openness and learning should be shared among decision-makers, the researchers coordinating research activities and local researchers working in individual countries. All parties should clearly understand the premises for exploring particular issues, probing certain individuals and the bases for interpreting data. In qualitative international marketing research, where there may be confusion about the premises for the whole approach, there is a much greater need for openness between all parties involved.

Survey methods

The following sections discuss the major interviewing methods in light of the challenges of conducting research in overseas countries.[23]

Online surveys

The vast majority of survey research is conducted online. This pattern has generally occurred across the globe, with countries like Canada, Japan, the Netherlands and Germany leading the way with high proportions of their research spend being devoted to online surveys. The primary benefits of reducing costs and the time needed to generate results are clear. Online surveys are also able to reach participants in places and at times where they are spending significant parts of their lives.[24] When considering the relative cost per interview it must far and away be the largest single source of quantitative data in the world. Online research has distinct advantages in all applications including international research, overseas research, multinational research and cross-cultural research. However, there is a body of criticism of the approach and alternatives mooted that are based upon social media research methods.

Online access panels remain the predominant sampling source for online research projects. The key concern for the owners of online panels is to acquire and maintain a critical mass of members who are motivated to participate repeatedly in online surveys.[25] For researchers, however, as more projects come online questions have been asked about the rigour, reliability, generalisability and interchangeability of panel sources. The quality of online surveys has been criticised as clients and researchers try to improve response rates, create representative samples and identify weak participants. Online access panels are not random samples of any definable population and some researchers view them as convenience samples. The extent to which they are comparable with each other is dependent on the recruitment sources used. In classical sampling theory they suffer from frame errors, and sometimes very substantial ones.[26] As dominant as the online survey and access panel are, it has been argued that people active in social networks do not tend to become members of panels, and vice versa.[27] This means that using social media research methods is no better than access panels at gaining representative views of target participants. Mixing various online research methods (beyond well-documented mixed-mode surveys) could well be the future for international researchers as illustrated in the following example.

Real research | **Fusing contemporary research methods at Danone[28]**

Danone (**www.danone.com**) wanted to understand the use of water in daily life and highlight consumer expectations for water consumption in general. In order to investigate water consumption from different angles, a 'fusion research' design was implemented. Fusion research is a research design where multiple (contemporary) research methodologies are combined in order to study a certain research question from different angles. The divide between taking data from more traditional and new sources is analogous to the divide between a walled garden and a wild garden. In the 'walled garden' where everything is controlled, traditional survey research can be used among research communities with questions posed and answers received. In the 'wild garden' social media netnography among natural communities can be used to generate spontaneous private but anonymous conversations, with far fewer controls. Such a hybrid brought great benefits to the Danone study: using the social web for better, faster recruitment, employing better survey vocabulary, inspiring and insightful data, and a happier, more open, conversational style of discourse between researchers and participants.

Telephone surveys and CATI

In the 1990s, telephone surveys were the dominant mode of survey data collection in countries with extensive telephone coverage. For some years, telephone surveys have ran second to online surveys in terms of global research spend.[29] This move can be attributed to the strengths of online surveys but also to some of the weaknesses of traditional telephone surveys as the use of mobile devices has grown. The development of mobile communications and especially smartphones has meant a move away from the telephone coverage configuration that enabled traditional telephone surveys to be conducted. This has impacted upon national surveys and even more so on international surveys using the telephone. Although the type of phone access varies greatly from country to country, across Europe there have been significant developments in telephone arrangements: the percentage of households equipped with a fixed phone has fallen, while the percentage of households equipped with mobile phone access has risen. In addition, the percentage of mobile-only households has increased, while the percentage of households that have only fixed-phone access has decreased. In countries such as Finland, Italy, Portugal, Belgium and Slovenia, fixed-phone coverage has already been overtaken by mobile phone coverage. There seems to be a tendency to a widespread generalisation of the phenomenon to other countries. International researchers need to understand the distribution and use of phone types in any particular country where they plan a telephone survey. Mobile phone users are different from fixed-phone users. Mobile surveys offer the possibility of covering segments of the population that own only a mobile phone and they are therefore excluded from current fixed-phone surveys. However, mobile-phone-based surveys pose technical, cost and ethical issues that are distinct from those associated with fixed-phone surveys. Not all mobile phones are the same and we have used the convention of the term 'mobile device' to cover a great breadth of mobile communications. An example within this term is the use of the smartphone. Not all mobile phones are smartphones and the term itself has no single accepted definition. What is clear is that the number of people across the globe owning such devices is growing rapidly. Surveys are already being completed on smartphones though there may be great limitations in their consistent use within a country, never mind in international research, given the challenges of using techniques such as Flash technology.[30]

Demographic differences between fixed-phone and mobile phone users may become less prevalent as mobile phone dissemination increases globally and extends to specific subgroups. In general (and there are good individual examples that demonstrate the reverse), mobile phone samples tend to over-represent younger people and employed people in urban and thriving economies, and to under-represent people living in smaller households, those with lower educational levels and rural economies. As with online surveys on an international basis, researchers need to improve survey quality, such as using multiple-mode surveys or switching to new methods altogether. Mixed phone designs may be easier to deal with if there is evidence that conducting an interview over a fixed phone or over a mobile phone has no influence on how the participants come up with their answers.[31]

Street surveys

In the 1980s, street surveys replaced the telephone for the bulk of consumer research and replaced home surveys for advertising research. The context of the street, the mall or the shopping centre offered the advantages of easy access to large groups of relatively homogeneous populations and allowed researchers to explain, test and control complex material including visuals. Because of the presence of a trained interviewer, attitudes, opinions, beliefs, and secondary claims and meanings could be probed with additional open-ended and closed-ended questions. Since the late 1990s, the street survey has been replaced by the use of online surveys for a significant percentage of consumer and advertising studies.[32] However, in many countries with low Internet and telephone penetration or with comparatively low literacy rates, the street survey still offers the best and predominant means to conduct surveys. This should not imply that the technique is 'relegated' to use in developing economies. There are still many survey challenges, where the quota sample enables a large and well-structured sample, and where the street survey captures complex views 'of the moment'. This is illustrated in the following example of a multinational research project.

| Real research | ## Emotional tennis[33] |

Many brands invest in sports events, essentially to benefit from the visibility they offer. Emotions felt by spectators are crucial in the sponsorship relationship between brands and consumers. By comparing emotions felt by spectators during the French and Australian Open tennis tournaments, a study wished to assess how emotions shaped the preliminary step of sponsorship effectiveness: the appreciation of the event. The study focused on the French and Australian Opens. There was no doubt that these two events were marketed differently and attended by different people, but it was felt that the universality of the emotional phenomenon should elicit similar emotional responses. To test hypotheses and allow for comparisons, two identical data collections were held during the Roland Garros (French) 2008 (N_1 = 437) and the Australian Open 2009 (N_2 = 375) tournaments. Data were collected during the first five days of each event, using a street survey technique. Each construct was measured using previously validated multi-item scales after three independent judges had translated them from English to French. Their findings revealed that positive emotions were felt twice as intensely as negative emotions, meaning that spectators' emotional experience was globally positive at both events.

Provided that the environment of the street allows a survey to be conducted, the street survey is an excellent means to identify and interview individuals where there are poor or non-existent sampling frames. Given the congestion in many major international cities, the locations where interviews will be conducted have to be carefully selected. However, this does not differ from planning and conducting street surveys in 'home' markets. As with home and workplace surveys, the differences lie in the culture of approaching someone in the street and their willingness to divulge information to a stranger.

Home and workplace face-to-face surveys

Home and workplace face-to-face surveys require a large pool of qualified interviewers and are time consuming and costly. However, when one considers the quality of rapport that can be built up between the interviewer and participant, the amount of probing and the quality of audio-visual stimuli that can be used, there are clear benefits that can outweigh the costs. In many areas of business-to-business marketing research, the only means to contact certain managers may be through the face-to-face survey, held in their workplace. In many countries, this approach may be the only means to reach particular participants and/or the only context in which they feel relaxed, open and are willing to give truthful responses to questions. Given the costs and time needed to conduct such interviews, there has been a growth in the use of ethnography and observational techniques to supplement interviews. The following example illustrates how home surveys may be applied to a selected sub group of a sample. In this case, participants who had read direct mail from a charity were deemed worthy for investment in expensive home surveys in order to be able to question and probe in a manner that other survey methods could not achieve.

Real research   **Pretesting direct mail**[34]

Many organisations use direct mail; fundraisers are significant users and were the focus of a study to pretest a mail campaign in Australia. The specific research questions were: Could a pretest predict which fundraising campaign would evoke the best response in terms of donations? What measure(s) would identify the 'winner', in terms of donations? Decisions on the measures to be included were determined through a number of development phases including: exploratory interviews with 20 fundraisers and 15 donors; and six pilot studies involving over 400 participants testing a range of measures and approaches. The pilot studies were conducted using a variety of methods to check the relevance of advertising pretesting measures, and new measures were introduced to suit fundraising. Face-to-face and self-completion surveys were conducted and, in the final pilot, 20 participants rated their agreement/disagreement that each measure described the direct mail literature they were shown. The technique worked well, but those who had not read the literature sent to them felt the exercise was irrelevant. This led to a change in the research design to screen participants to ensure they had read the literature. Computer-assisted telephone interviews were conducted with 261 regular donors of the charity. Participants who claimed to have read the literature were invited for a home interview.

Postal surveys

Because of their low cost, postal surveys continue to be used in most developed countries where literacy is high and the postal system is well developed. At 4%, postal surveys globally constitute the lowest form of quantitative data collection. Sweden (15%), Finland (14%), Norway (14%) and Japan (14%) constitute the highest levels of postal surveys worldwide.[35] In many parts of Africa, Asia and South America, the use of postal surveys and postal panels is low because of illiteracy and the large proportion of the population living in rural areas. In a study of past, present and future marketing research techniques in China, researchers reported rare occasions when they had good results with postal surveys. Participants did not seem to have as much enthusiasm in responding to a postal survey and taking the trouble to post it back, especially when the survey was commercial in nature.[36] However, there are still many survey situations where sampling challenges can be properly addressed and where participants are happy to complete a hard-copy questionnaire in a time and space that suit their circumstances. Such an application is illustrated in the following example.

| Real research | **When do you measure a service encounter?[37]** |

With the growth of the services sector in most market economies, service quality measurement has grown in strategic importance. Attention to extraneous factors that may impact upon service quality evaluations has also grown. One such factor is the duration between the service encounter and the evaluation of that encounter. Evaluations of the service provided by a financial planning company were collected via a self-completion postal survey from customers of a specific provider. A total of 1,039 questionnaires were mailed out to all clients of the service provider, with 356 returned, providing a response rate of 34%. A comparison of the demographic characteristics of the sample and the target population revealed that these were very similar. The sample validation meant that the risk of potential non-response bias in the results was minimal. The instrument consisted of 29 scaled statements, where participants rated their financial planner. Recency of service experience was captured by the question 'When was the last time you had any interaction with your financial planning adviser?' This question was essential to evaluate the duration between the service encounter and the evaluation of that encounter.

Construct equivalence
A type of equivalence that deals with the question of whether the marketing constructs have the same meaning and significance in different countries.

Conceptual equivalence
A construct equivalence issue that deals with whether the interpretation of brands, products, consumer behaviour and the marketing effort are the same in different countries.

Postal surveys are, typically, more effective in b2b international marketing research (see Chapter 28), although it can be a major challenge to identify the appropriate participant within each firm and to personalise the address.

Measurement and scaling

Functional equivalence
A construct equivalence issue that deals specifically with whether a given concept or behaviour serves the same role or function in different countries.

Category equivalence
A construct equivalence issue that deals specifically with whether the categories in which brands, products and behaviour are grouped are the same in different countries.

In international marketing research, it is critical to establish the equivalence of scales and measures used to obtain data from different countries. As illustrated in Figure 27.2, this requires an examination of construct equivalence, operational equivalence, scalar equivalence and linguistic equivalence.[38]

Construct equivalence deals with the question of whether the marketing constructs (e.g. opinion leadership, variety seeking and brand loyalty) have the same meaning and significance in different countries. It focuses on the basic conceptual definition of the underlying construct. In many countries, the number of brands available in a given product category is limited. In some countries, the dominant brands have become generic labels symbolising the entire product category. Consequently, a different perspective on brand loyalty may have to be adopted in these countries.

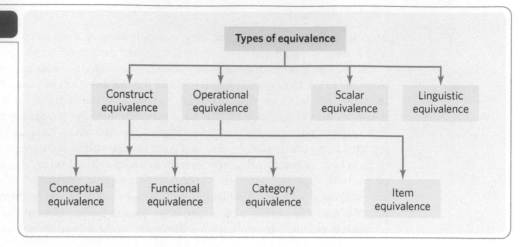

Figure 27.2

Scaling and measurement equivalence in international research

Operational equivalence
A type of equivalence that measures how theoretical constructs are operationalised in different countries to measure marketing variables.

Measurement equivalence
Deals with the comparability of responses to particular (sets of) items. Measurement equivalence includes configural (structural), metric (measurement unit) and scalar equivalence.

Configural equivalence
Concerns the relationships of measured items to the latent constructs and implies that the patterns of factor loadings should be the same across countries or cultural units.

Metric equivalence
Refers to the unit of measurement; the factor loading should be the same.

Scalar equivalence
The demonstration that two individuals from different countries with the same value on some variable will score at the same level on the same test. Also called metric equivalence.

Linguistic equivalence
The equivalence of both spoken and written language forms used in scales and questionnaires.

Construct equivalence comprises conceptual equivalence, functional equivalence and category equivalence. Conceptual equivalence deals with the interpretation of brands, products, consumer behaviour and marketing effort. For example, sales promotion techniques are an integral component of marketing effort throughout Europe. On the other hand, in countries with shortage economies, where the market is dominated by the sellers, consumers view sales with suspicion because they believe that the product being promoted is of poor quality. Functional equivalence examines whether a given concept or behaviour serves the same role or function in different countries. For example, in many developing countries, bicycles are predominantly a means of transportation rather than of recreation. Marketing research related to the use of bicycles in these countries must examine different motives, attitudes, behaviours and even different competing products than such research would in Europe. Category equivalence refers to the category in which stimuli such as products, brands and behaviours are grouped. In Europe, the category of the principal shopper may be defined as either the male or female head of household. This category may be inappropriate in countries where routine daily shopping is done by a domestic servant. Furthermore, the category 'household' itself varies across countries.

Operational equivalence concerns how theoretical constructs are operationalised to make measurements. In Europe, leisure may be operationalised as playing golf, tennis or other sports, watching TV, or basking in the sun for example. This operationalisation may not be relevant in countries where people do not play these sports or do not have round-the-clock TV transmission. Lying in the sun is generally not normal behaviour in countries with very hot climates.

Measurement equivalence deals with the comparability of responses to particular (sets of) items. Measurement equivalence includes configural (structural), metric (measurement unit) and scalar equivalence. Configural equivalence concerns the relationships of measured items to the latent constructs. Technically, configural equivalence implies that the patterns of factor loadings should be the same across countries or cultural units. Metric equivalence refers to the unit of measurement; the factor loading should be the same. Metric equivalence suggests that the survey instruments (questionnaires) are measuring the same constructs to the same extent in different countries or cultures.

Scalar equivalence refers to equivalence of both the unit of the unit of measurement and the constant in the equation between the construct and the items measuring the construct (the intercept). The distinction is important because for some purposes (e.g. comparing structural relationships across groups) both metric and scalar equivalence are needed. Finally, linguistic equivalence refers to both the spoken and the written language forms used in scales, questionnaires and interviewing. The scales and other verbal stimuli should be translated so that they are readily understood by participants in different countries and have equivalent meaning.[39]

Questionnaire translation

IFM Sports Marketing Surveys

Translation into eight languages[40]

Robert Kirby, who was the Telephone Research Director at Research Services Ltd and has many years' experience of pan-European telephone surveys, offers the following advice in coping with translation:

> *Translations require the most rigorous checking. In my experience it is not advisable to use someone from a home country who can speak the language fluently, because frequently a current idiomatic knowledge is required. A translation agency with no expertise could have the idiom but not the interviewing skills.*

His advice mirrors the practice in the Formula One Racetrack Project that has been illustrated in earlier chapters. The Racetrack questionnaire was translated from English into French, German, Italian, Japanese, Portuguese, Spanish and Chinese. The translation for the Racetrack Project was undertaken by its local agents (beyond the UK it has offices in Australia, Belgium, Brazil, France, Greece, Italy, Japan, Korea, Spain, Singapore, Turkey and the USA) in the target countries of the survey. These agents understood the idiom and the elicitation task required to connect with Formula One fans in their particular country.

Taking the people's temperature – right across Europe[41]

Eurobarometer measures public opinion across Europe on behalf of the European Commission. First published in 1974, it runs twice a year in spring and autumn, and now surveys some 25,000 participants in each wave. The objectives set by the EU for the Eurobarometer are threefold. First, to evaluate the activities of the EU and indicate how the public might welcome a particular proposition, e.g. nuclear  energy. Second, to measure how European public opinion has changed over a period of time. Third, to observe and anticipate public attitudes towards important events directly or indirectly linked to the development of the EU. One of the most challenging steps of the Eurobarometer is to ensure that question meaning is the same across all countries surveyed, taking into account specific national and cultural differences. For example, in France, the phrase 'mobile phone' is translated as 'téléphone mobile'. In French-speaking Belgium, that would mean 'wireless handset'. To address such issues, TNS always starts with a bilingual (English/French) version of the initial questionnaire. From this point, a meeting takes place to review the quality of the bilingual version to check whether the meaning of each question is clear for all countries. A final bilingual version of the questionnaire is then made available so that each country can carry out its translation into the local language(s). The translations are carried out, working from the final questionnaire by two different translators. After this, all questionnaires are back translated into English or French by external experts. Any differences between the back-translated version and the original are immediately identified and reviewed.

Back translation

A translation technique that translates a questionnaire from the base language by a translator whose native language is the one into which the questionnaire is being translated. This version is then retranslated back into the original language by someone whose native language is the base language. Translation errors can then be identified.

Parallel translation

A translation method in which a committee of translators, each of whom is fluent in at least two languages, discuss alternative versions of a questionnaire and make modifications until consensus is reached.

As in the above examples, questions may have to be translated for administration in different cultures. Frequent use is made of direct translation, in which a bilingual translator translates the questionnaire directly from a base language to the participant's language. If the translator is not fluent in both languages and is not familiar with both cultures, however, direct translation of certain words and phrases may be flawed. Procedures like back translation and parallel translation have been suggested to avoid these errors. In back translation, the questionnaire is translated from the base language by a bilingual speaker whose native language is the language into which the questionnaire is being translated. This version is then retranslated back into the original language by a bilingual whose native language is the initial or base language. Translation errors can then be identified. Several repeat translations and back translations may be necessary to develop equivalent questionnaires, and this process can be cumbersome and time consuming.[42]

An alternative procedure is parallel translation. A committee of translators, each of whom is fluent in at least two of the languages in which the questionnaire will be administered, discuss alternative versions of the questionnaire and make modifications until consensus is reached. In countries where several languages are spoken, the questionnaire should be translated into the language of each participant subgroup. It is important that any non-verbal stimuli (pictures and advertisements) also be translated using similar procedures. The following example underscores the importance of translation that does not impose the structure of a 'home country' from which the research is commissioned, in this case the UK.

Real research	The search for focus – brand values across Europe[43]

Land Rover wished to understand the values associated with its brand in Belgium, the UK, France, Germany, Italy, the Netherlands, Portugal and Spain. The project involved the use of CAPI and required the development of a questionnaire that could allow comparisons between the countries. The issue of questionnaire translation was a sensitive and pertinent one. What was crucial was that the translation was meaningful in all languages rather than forcing the English-language requirements into the local language. The translation was a difficult process and required an understanding of both the research process and the cultural context of the individual markets. It was the case that certain concepts that are expressive in English could not easily be translated into other languages. For instance, the word 'aspirational' does not easily translate into French, Spanish or Italian with the same meaning as in English. Consequently, in order to ensure comparability the translation process involved a series of iterative steps changing the master questionnaire to fit what was achievable overall in each market.

Ethics in marketing research

Ethical responsibilities for marketing research conducted internationally are very similar to those for research conducted domestically. In conducting marketing research across Europe (and indeed globally), ESOMAR produces codes of conduct that guide professional practice that protects the interests of all research stakeholders. In general, for each of the six stages of the marketing research design process, the same four stakeholders (client, researcher, participant and public) should act honourably and respect their responsibilities to one another. For individual countries, a key development in honourable practice lies in the development of professional associations. The ESOMAR website lists these associations should there be any specific operational and ethical concern related to conducting research in that country.

International research has become more commonplace and possible with the advent of digital and social media. The marketing and research opportunities are immense but, as consequence, new confidentiality and ethical concerns have emerged. Social networking, blogging, online communities and Web 2.0 technologies offer innovative ways of engaging participants, but introduce new privacy and legal issues for researchers to manage. These issues include identity theft, harassment, defamation of character and maintaining client confidentiality. At the same time, technological advances in computing power, mobile devices and storage media carry many benefits, but they too add risk that must be mitigated. Protecting participant privacy and client confidentiality has never been as challenging for researchers as it is in a digital world. Regulators and the public are quick to pounce when privacy breaches occur.[44] There are a number of institutions, both government and non-government (including professional research associations), that are attempting to support participants in protecting their privacy. This has and will continue to have a major impact on the way in which the researcher will be able to contact and engage with participants, as well as what type of information can be collected and shared with the business world.[45]

One of the biggest ethical challenges facing international researchers given the global impact of digital and social media lies in differentiating marketing research from other data gathering practices. In an ESOMAR conference dedicated to online panels, the challenges were encapsulated by Reg Baker, Chief Operating Officer, Market Strategies International (**www.marketstrategies.com**):

> The most sensitive issue of all to me is the fine line that divides research from marketing (in online communities). And this is not just a vague ethical issue. It's a legal issue that gets down to our ability to function as an industry. Europeans, in particular, are very sensitive to the problems that will rain down on our industry if the authorities discover that we're doing things that really are not any different than direct marketing. It strikes me that, throughout my career, marketing research was always tied to survey research. Now that link has been broken. There are fewer surveys and a lot more other things. Have we lost our standards to the IT geeks? The future is different than the past in ways we cannot imagine. We need to re-evaluate and possibly reinvent.[46]

Digital applications in marketing research

Digital developments in marketing research can be extensively used in all aspects of international research. These uses parallel those discussed around specific techniques in earlier chapters and hence will not be repeated here. Of particular note, however, are social media and online research developments that can be used to communicate with participants and marketing decision-makers anywhere in the world. The nature of that communication in its openness forms of expression and reach into distant communities has given a new dimension to international marketing research. For example, the online survey overcomes geographical boundaries and differences in postal systems to solicit responses from around the world. Research using mobile devices can facilitate engaging with specialist target groups that in the past may have been difficult or even impossible to reach. Online research can also enhance the quality of data supplied to participants, generating more meaningful and relevant responses. The environmental characteristics of international markets detailed in this chapter present a formidable research task, especially when first learning about a country. Providing that the researcher has strong critical facilities, the sheer mass of data available online can provide great insight into particular countries or cultures. Material can be accessed quickly and anywhere to help shape an understanding of the different environmental contexts of a target country. This is particularly relevant in tracking down secondary data sources that may not be available in the home country of a researcher. Many of the digital challenges facing international researchers' use of digital technology are encapsulated in the following quote. This was taken from a debate on the future of marketing research, held by a range of key decision-makers and researchers. The key point to note is the diversity of techniques and technologies that researchers will have at their disposal, that they will have to choose, integrate and apply in specific cultural conditions:[47]

Everyone accepts that there remains cultural and market development differences (such as the internet and mobile ownership) across geographies. Research has to be conducted in ways that are appropriate for the community, country or region. This is nothing new and is still the right way. In developing countries, where mobile use is high and internet penetration is low, it is now possible to conduct quantitative and qualitative mobile surveys with surprisingly powerful results. It is also increasingly common to create MROCs (marketing research online communities) or bulletin boards that bring customers from different parts of the world into virtual space. In the future, we will increasingly be forced to design research that combines multiple approaches. The list of tools that researchers now have at their disposal is growing exponentially; a Swiss Army knife is what we need when out in the bush – smart, sharp, robust and adaptable.

Summary

With the globalisation of markets, international marketing research is burgeoning rapidly. As well as the technical requirements of conducting successful marketing research as outlined in this text, the researcher has to cope with new cultures and languages in targeted international markets. Given the array of ethnic groups within most European countries, the challenges of understanding new cultures and languages can exist within a 'home' country.

The environment prevailing in the international markets being researched influences all six steps of the marketing research process. Important aspects of this environment include the marketing, governmental, legal, economic, structural, informational and technological, and socio-cultural environments.

In collecting data from different countries, it is desirable to use techniques with equivalent levels of reliability rather than the same method. Repeating identical techniques across borders may result in subtle cultural and linguistic differences being ignored, which may have a great effect upon the nature and quality of data that are generated. It is critical to establish the equivalence of scales and measures in terms of construct equivalence, operational equivalence, scalar equivalence and linguistic equivalence. Questionnaires used should be adapted to the specific cultural environment and should not be biased in favour of any one culture or language. Back translation and parallel translation are helpful in detecting translation errors.

The ethical concerns facing international researchers are similar in many ways to the issues confronting domestic researchers. International research has become more commonplace and possible with the advent of digital and social media. The marketing and research opportunities are immense but, as a consequence, new confidentiality and ethical concerns have emerged. Digital developments in marketing research can be extensively used in all aspects of international research. These developments are used to communicate with participants and marketing decision-makers anywhere in the world. They have brought an openness in forms of expression and reach into distant communities and have given a new dimension to international marketing research.

Questions

1 Evaluate the meaning of 'international' from the perspective of the researcher.

2 What characteristics distinguish international marketing research from domestic marketing research?

3 Describe the aspects of the environment of each country that should be taken into account in international marketing research.

4 Describe the importance of considering the marketing environment in conducting international marketing research.

5 What is meant by the structural environment? How do the variables comprising the structural environment influence international marketing research?

6 What is meant by the informational and technological environment? How do the variables comprising the informational and technological environment influence international marketing research?

7 What is meant by the socio-cultural environment? How do the variables comprising the socio-cultural environment influence international marketing research?

8 How should the researcher evaluate secondary data obtained from overseas countries?

9 Describe the factors that may influence the approach to qualitative techniques in different countries.

10 Select a country, using environmental characteristics to illustrate why CATI works particularly well as a survey technique.

11 Select a country, using environmental characteristics to illustrate why home surveys do not work particularly well as a survey technique.

12 Select a country, using environmental characteristics to illustrate why online surveys work particularly well as a survey technique.

13 How should the equivalence of scales and measures be established when the data are to be obtained from different countries or cultural units?

14 What problems are involved in the direct translation of a questionnaire into another language?

15 Briefly describe the procedures that may be adopted to ensure translation is correctly conducted in the development of a questionnaire.

Exercises

1 Obtain a copy of an old marketing research report that has been conducted in the country where you are studying (many marketing research agencies or companies that have commissioned research will provide copies of old reports for educational purposes). Evaluate how the research would have been conducted if the same project were conducted in Malaysia.

2 Compile data on the GDP, level of literacy and percentage of households with telephones for 20 different countries. Using a proprietary statistics package, run a regression analysis with GDP as the dependent variable and the other two variables as the independent variables. Interpret your results.

3 Visit the website of the Spanish fashion company Zara at **www.zara.com**. What can you learn about the company's international marketing efforts? Write a report on what you see as its main international marketing research challenges.

4 You are the Marketing Research Director of Unilever (**www.unilever.com**). What challenges do you see in researching markets for household products in the Far East? Prepare a report for the Unilever Board in Europe making the case for a higher investment in marketing research in this region.

5 In a small group discuss the following issues: 'Some marketing strategists have argued that a standardised marketing strategy should be adopted for all overseas markets. Does this imply that the research design and techniques should be standardised no matter where the research is being conducted?' and 'Given the huge cultural diversity that exists in many parts of Europe, should researchers have a mindset of "home" and "overseas" markets'?

Video case exercise: Nike

Given Nike's desire to operate globally, what internal marketing research challenges does it face in:

a Developing sponsorship partnerships?

b Understanding the culture of soccer?

Notes

1. Goodyear, M., Guest editorial – 'International Research and Marketing', *Journal of the Market Research Society* 38 (1) (January 1996), 1.

2. See de Jong, M.G., Steenkamp, J.-B. E.M., Fox, J.-P. and Baumgartner, H., 'Using item response theory to measure extreme response style in marketing research: a global investigation', *Journal of Marketing Research* 45 (1) (February 2008), 104–105; Denton, T., 'Indexes of validity and reliability for cross-societal measures', *Cross Cultural Research* 42 (2) (May 2008), 118; Ross, R.H., Broyles, S.A. and Leingpibul, T., 'Alternative measures of satisfaction in cross-cultural settings', *Journal of Product and Brand Management* 17 (2) (2008), 82; Malhotra, N.K., 'Cross-cultural marketing research in the twenty-first century', *International Marketing Review* 18 (3) (2001), 230–234; Douglas, S.P., 'Exploring new worlds: the challenge of global marketing', *Journal of Marketing* 65 (1) (January 2001), 103–107; Malhotra, N.K., Agarwal, J. and Peterson, M., 'Cross-cultural marketing research: methodological issues and guidelines', *International Marketing Review* 13 (5) (1996), 7–43.

3. Bowman, J., 'Targeting the lions – brands and Africa's new middle class', *Warc Exclusive* (February 2011).

4. Churkina, O. and Sandler, C., 'Glocalization – a measure of global brands: adaptation to local cultures', ESOMAR, Asia Pacific, Melbourne (2011).

5. Gupta, S. and Samanta, R., 'Of heads and hearts and cultures apart! How a billion minds consume communication', ESOMAR, Asia Pacific Conference, Singapore (April 2008).

6. Goodyear, M., 'The world over, a group is a group is a group', *ResearchPlus* (November 1992), 5.

7. Havermans, J., 'Connecting with Saudi women', *Research World* (August 2005), 16.

8. Landeck, F. and Jiu, P., 'Acting global and thinking local – Motorola post launch satisfaction', ESOMAR, Asia Pacific, Beijing (April 2009).

9. Joshi, A., Tamang, S. and Vashisthaz, H., 'You can't judge a book by its cover! A way to tackle the severe acquiescence bias among Arab participants', ESOMAR, Annual Congress, Montreal (September 2008).

10. Worthington, P., 'Research in developing markets: upwardly mobile', *Admap* (July/August 2010), 28–29.

11. Williams, N. and Fergusson, J., 'Bridging the digital divide in qualitative research in emerging markets: Smart Qual using Smart and non-Smart phones in developing markets', ESOMAR, Asia Pacific, Melbourne (2011).

12. Hutton, G., 'If you board the Asian bus, better mind your language', *ResearchPlus* (February 1996), 9.

13. Cilley, C., 'No Latin love – mixed views towards globalisation', ESOMAR, Latin American Conference, Mexico City (May 2008).

14. Young, M., 'Popularity of mobile and blogs is an untapped opportunity in ASEAN', *Admap, South East Asia Supplement* (February 2009), 6–7.

15. See Cho, H.J., Jin, B. and Cho, H., 'An examination of regional differences in China by socio-cultural factors', *International Journal of Market Research* 52 (5) (2010), 613–633; Craido, A.R. and Craido, J.R., 'International marketing research: opportunities and challenges in the 21st century', *Advances in International Marketing* 17 (2007), 1–13; James, D., 'Dark clouds should part for international marketers', *Marketing News* 36 (1) (7 January 2002), 9–10.

16. Chiarelli, N., 'Megacities as the new frontiers – a global consumer lifestyle study', ESOMAR, Annual Congress, Montreal (September 2008).

17. Parsons, J., 'Lipstick on a pig – getting the tastiest pork from Japanese qualitative research', ESOMAR, Asia Pacific, Beijing (April 2009).

18. Evans, M. and Shivakumar, H., 'Insight, cultural diversity, revolutionary change: joined up semantic thinking for developing markets', ESOMAR, Congress Odyssey, Athens (September 2010).

19. Cierpicki, S., Alexander, D., Alchin, S., Brunton, C. and Poynter, R., 'It works for us but does it work for them? How online research communities work for consumers invited to participate', ESOMAR, Online Research, Chicago (October 2009).

20. Comley, P., 'Online research communities – a user guide', *International Journal of Market Research* 50 (5) (2008), 679–694.

21. Child, P., Fleming, K., Shaw, K. and Skilbeck, T., 'Vive la difference: understanding, embracing and evolving MROCs globally', ESOMAR, Congress Odyssey, Athens (September 2010).

22. Zimmerman, A.S. and Szenberg, M., 'Implementing international qualitative research: techniques and obstacles', *Qualitative Market Research: An International Journal* 3 (3) (2000), 158–164.

23. Chisnall, P.M., 'International marketing research', *International Journal of Marketing Research* 49 (1) (2007), 133–135; Hsieh, M.-H., 'Measuring global brand equity using cross national survey data', *Journal of International Marketing* 12 (2) (2004), 28–57; Malhotra, N.K., 'Cross-cultural marketing research in the twenty-first century', *International Marketing Review* 18 (3) (2001), 230–234; Douglas, S.P., 'Exploring new worlds: the challenge of global marketing', *Journal of Marketing* 65 (1) (January 2001), 103–107.

24. ESOMAR, 'Global Market Research', ESOMAR Industry Report (2010), 29.

25. Brüggen, E., Wetzels, M., de Ruyter, K. and Schillewaert, N., 'Individual differences in motivation to participate in online panels: the effect on response rates and response quality perceptions', *International Journal of Market Research* 53 (3) (2011), 369–390.

26. de Jong, K., 'CSI Berlin: the strange case of the death of panels', ESOMAR, Online Research, Berlin (October 2010).

27. de Jong, K., 'Ready or not', in 'Global Market Research', ESOMAR Industry Report (2010), 30.

28. Baskin, M., 'Online research: now and next – peak panel, gamification and digividuals', *Warc Exclusive* (March 2011); De Ruyck, T., Verhaeghe, A. and Rogeaux, M., 'Exploring the world of water: fusing contemporary research methods', ESOMAR, Congress Odyssey, Athens (September 2010).

29. ESOMAR, 'Global Market Research', ESOMAR Industry Report (2010), 29.

30. de Jong, K., 'CSI Berlin: the strange case of the death of panels', ESOMAR, Online Research, Berlin (October 2010).

31. Vicente, P., Reis, E. and Santos, M., 'Using mobile phones for survey research: a comparison with fixed phones', *International Journal of Market Research* 51 (5) (2009), 613–634.

32. Maronick, T., 'Pitting the mall against the internet in advertising research completion: internet panels are more popular. Are they more effective?' *Journal of Advertising Research* 51 (1) (2011), 321–331.

33. Bal, C., 'Understanding sport-related emotions in sponsorship', *Admap* (November 2009), 45–47.

34. Faulkner, M. and Kennedy, R., 'A new tool for pre-testing direct mail', *International Journal of Market Research* 50 (4) (2008), 469–490.

35. ESOMAR, 'Global Market Research', ESOMAR Industry Report (2010), 103.

36. Fine, B., Ellis, R.S. and Xu, D., 'Research methodologies in China – past, present and future', ESOMAR, Asia Pacific, Beijing (April 2009).

37. Bogomolova, S., Romaniuk, J. and Sharp, A., 'Quantifying the extent of temporal decay in service quality ratings', *International Journal of Market Research* 51 (1) (2009), 71–91.

38. Giannakopoulou, C., Siomkos, G and Vassilikopoulou, A., 'The input of psychology in methodological considerations of cross cultural marketing research', *European Journal of Scientific Research* 20 (2) (April 2008), 249–254; Sharma, S. and Weathers, D., 'Assessing generalisability of scales used in cross-national research', *International Journal of Research in Marketing* 20 (3) (2003), 287–295; Baumgartner, H. and Steenkamp, J.-B. E.M., 'Response styles in marketing research: a cross-national investigation', *Journal of Marketing Research* 38 (2) (2001), 143–146; Myers, M.B., 'Academic insights: an application of multiple-group causal models in assessing cross cultural measurement equivalence', *Journal of International Marketing* 8 (4) (2000), 108–121; Malhotra, N.K., Agarwal, J. and Peterson, M., 'Cross-cultural marketing research: methodological issues and guidelines', *International Marketing Review* 13 (5) (1996), 7–43.

39. Denton, T., 'Indexes of validity and reliability for cross-sectional measures', *Cross-Cultural Research* 42 (2) (May 2008), 118; Wong, N., Rindfleisch, A., Burroughs, J.E., Steenkamp, J.-B.E.M. and Bearden, W.O., 'Do reverse-worded items confound measures in cross-cultural consumer research? The case of the material values scale', *Journal of Consumer Research* 30 (1) (2003), 72–91; Thorne, L., 'The sociocultural embeddedness of individuals' ethical reasoning in organisations (cross cultural ethics)', *Journal of Business Ethics* 35 (1) (January 2002), 1–13; McDonald, G., 'Cross-cultural

methodological issues in ethical research', *Journal of Business Ethics* 27 (1/2) (September 2000), 89–104.

40. Kirby, R., 'A pan-European view of the executive at lunch', *ResearchPlus* (October 1992), 7.

41. Whiteside, S., 'The international communications market: a summary of Ofcom research into global media brands', *Warc Exclusive* (December 2008); De Voogd, L. and Carballo, M., 'Taking the temperature', *Research* (January 2006), 38–39.

42. de Jong, M.G., Steenkamp, J.-B.E.M., Fox, J.-P. and Baumgartner, H., 'Using item response theory to measure extreme response style in marketing research: a global investigation', *Journal of Marketing Research* 45 (1) (February 2008), 104–105; Behling, O. and Law, K.S., *Translating Questionnaires and Other Research Instruments: Problems and Solutions* (Thousand Oaks, CA: Sage, 2000); Malhotra, N.K. and McCort, D., 'A cross-cultural comparison of behavioural intention models: theoretical consideration and an empirical investigation', *International Marketing Review* 18 (3) (2001), 235–269.

43. Bull, N. and Oxley, M., 'The search for focus – brand values across Europe', *Marketing and Research Today* (November 1996), 243.

44. Stark, D. 'From social engineering to social networking – privacy issues when conducting research in the web 2.0 world', ESOMAR, Congress, Montreux (September 2009).

45. Alioto, M.F., 'The researcher as Renaissance man: the creation of modern skill sets', ESOMAR, Annual Congress, Berlin (September 2007).

46. Precourt, G., 'ESOMAR Online-Panel panellists concur: market research still has a pulse', *Warc Exclusive* (November 2009).

47. Ibid.

28 Business-to-business (b2b) marketing research

Stage 1

Problem definition

Stage 2

Research approach developed

Stage 3

Research design developed

Stage 4

Fieldwork or data collection

Stage 5

Data integrity and analysis

Stage 6

Report preparation and presentation

The management of customer relationships is the core task of the b2b marketer. The researcher must help to unlock the nature and dynamism of these relationships.

Objectives

After reading this chapter, you should be able to:

1   explain what b2b marketing is;

2   describe the differences between b2b and consumer marketing;

3   explain the marketing research challenges that emerge from the differences between b2b and consumer marketing decision making;

4   understand how the concepts of networks and relationships underpin the distinctive challenges faced by b2b decision-makers;

5   understand what competitor intelligence is and how it may supplement or even take the place of marketing research for some businesses;

6   discuss the cultural challenges faced in conducting b2b marketing research in an international setting;

7   discuss the ethical considerations in b2b marketing research by comparing the challenges set in competitor intelligence with conventional marketing research;

8   appreciate how digital developments are shaping the manner in which b2b research is planned and administered.

Overview

This chapter starts by defining the nature of b2b marketing, presenting a definition that introduces the concept of 'relationships'. This is followed by a short introduction to the differences between b2b and consumer marketing. The evaluation of differences is crucial if one is to consider whether these have any impact upon the practice of b2b marketing research. The chapter then sets out the bases by which to evaluate the key challenges faced by b2b marketing decision-makers. These bases describe the importance of nurturing and developing relationships and the use of networks. From these bases, the key differences between b2b and consumer marketing are explained in more detail. There are five key areas of difference that are explored, followed in each case by the marketing research challenges these differences present. The 'threat' to conventional marketing research is then explored with a review of the nature and use of competitor intelligence. The challenges faced by b2b researchers in an international setting are then evaluated, discussing how language and cultural differences impact upon gaining access to businesses. This is followed by a discussion of the ethical issues raised in implementing competitive intelligence compared with conventional marketing research. The chapter concludes by examining how digital developments can help in the design and administration of b2b marketing research.

We begin with two examples illustrating how marketing research may be used in b2b marketing. The first example demonstrates the use of quantitative and qualitative techniques in an international setting. The case could well refer to any consumer marketing organisation, investing in the use of exhibitions and wishing to evaluate the worth of that investment. It basically illustrates that all the techniques that have been presented and discussed in this text can be used in a b2b context. It could also be used to support the argument that there is no difference between marketing research in b2b contexts compared with consumer marketing, as the case clearly shows that all techniques can be utilised. What it does not reveal are the many challenges facing b2b researchers when generating information in which b2b decision-makers will have confidence.

Fair's fair for Ericsson[1]

As the world's largest supplier of mobile systems and a leading player in fixed-line networks, Ericsson operates in more than 140 countries. It provides total solutions from systems and applications to services and core technology for mobile handsets. Its customers are network operators from around the world; indeed, the top 10 largest mobile operators are all customers of Ericsson. Telecoms companies like Ericsson recognise that trade shows play a crucial role in building the brand as well as providing showcases to demonstrate new products and technologies. They also provide the means to nurture and develop relationships by meeting and entertaining customers and other parties.

Ericsson has a clearly defined strategy for participation at trade shows and typically takes part in the 3GSM World Congress (France), CTIA (USA), CeBIT (Germany), CommunicAsia (Singapore) and ITU Telecom Asia (Hong Kong). Given the high levels of expenditure to participate and the importance of this communication channel, Ericsson determined that it needed to ensure that:

- the return on investment in a show could be measured;
- best practice guidelines were developed;
- the Ericsson brand was being communicated consistently.

In order to support the decisions involved in these areas, Ericsson used marketing research to provide feedback in five key areas:

- the 'quality' of visitors;
- the performance at an individual show;
- the impact on customer/employee relationships;
- the impact on the brand;
- the value of participation relative to other communication tools.

Working with the research company BPRI, Ericsson used an array of research techniques. Depending upon the nature of the target audience, CAPI, ethnography, telephone, web and self-completion surveys were used. The CAPI approach was used daily and enabled the company to capture findings from the previous day and to make changes to the visitor experience. For example, at the beginning of the 3GSM World Congress, some concern was expressed about the processes used for directing visitors to key Ericsson staff, as well as about the need for a more tailored approach. The daily briefings by the BPRI team highlighted these areas of concern and alternative solutions to these issues were implemented on the same day. Marked improvement was subsequently reflected in much higher scores for these aspects of performance.

The second example illustrates the breadth of decision-making areas that b2b research can support. In particular it highlights the how an understanding of competitor activities has such a prominent role in b2b research.

| **Competitor and consumer research at Hewlett-Packard[2]**

Hewlett-Packard (HP) was an innovator of 'Blades' server technology. Servers are behind-the-scenes workhorse engines that drive applications that are the backbone of electronic commerce. Although HP was a category innovator, its 'Competitor 1' had invested far more heavily in marketing and advertising than HP. This gave 'Competitor 1' an advantage in market share and a leadership position in how b2b consumers perceived them. 'Competitor 2', although not a category innovator, had built a strong overall brand image around low cost and ease of doing business and it was believed that these brand advantages had halo perceptions around all of its product offerings, including servers. HP wished to confirm quantitatively that its beliefs about competitive positioning were correct and launched a Blades survey of IT and business decision-makers. This survey has been repeated periodically to become a critical measurement and diagnostic tool in the Blades server category for HP. The research has helped it to: (1) assess the competitive landscape; (2) identify messaging that would differentiate and resonate with b2b consumers; (3) identify creative directions with the highest likelihood to succeed; (4) shape and refine creative communications campaigns; (5) diagnose in-market performance of HP and competitor Blades campaigns; (6) monitor HP progress in key consumer perception metrics.

There are many researchers who believe that b2b marketing research is quite distinctive from consumer marketing research. There is a professional group, the Business Intelligence Group (BIG) (**www.b2bresearch.org**), that was launched in 2001 to support the interests of individuals involved in b2b marketing research. We will progress by evaluating whether there are distinctive characteristics of b2b marketing decision making that may require a different approach to marketing research. To begin such an evaluation we continue by evaluating the nature of b2b marketing and what are contended to be the similarities and distinctions when compared with consumer marketing.

What is b2b marketing?

The term 'b2b marketing' is a relatively new one used to describe business marketing, industrial marketing or even organisational marketing. It is a simple acronym that was initially used to distinguish online business transactions, but is now used as the generic term for business marketing. In very simple terms b2b means businesses that sell products or services to other businesses, such as Intel selling processors to Dell or other computer manufacturers.

Such a simple term masks the challenges faced by b2b marketers. In the following definition, Dibb et al.[3] highlight the activities involved in the process of exchange between two parties. This definition presents little distinction between b2b marketing and the generic process of marketing, as discussed in Chapter 1:

> *Industrial [b2b] marketing concerns activities directed towards facilitating and expediting exchanges between industrial markets and industrial producers.*

In the second definition, Ford et al.[4] present a view of b2b marketing that goes beyond the more traditional marketing notions of exchange as presented above:

> *Business [b2b] marketing is the task of selecting, developing and managing customer relationships for the advantage of both customer and supplier, with regard to their respective skills, resources, technologies, strategies and objectives.*

In this definition the key element to emphasise is the task of managing customer relationships. This can be seen as a process that goes beyond the facilitating and expediting exchanges of goods, although it could be argued that the facilitation of exchanges could include the management of relationships. Nonetheless, Ford *et al.*'s emphasis upon the management of relationships forming the essence of b2b marketing could lead to the case that there are more differences than similarities between b2b marketing and consumer marketing.

The distinction between b2b and consumer marketing

There are many products and services which may be clearly identified as b2b transactions, such as electrical components used in the manufacture of earthmoving equipment. Other products and services, which at first glance may appear to be b2b transactions, may also be sold to consumer markets as illustrated in the following example of telecoms services.

Real research	BT's customer satisfaction programmes[5]

Telecoms company BT (**www.bt.com**) has long invested in measuring customer satisfaction and taking action to increase satisfaction. BT had three main current programmes that covered the overall satisfaction of domestic consumers, business (small and medium enterprises) and global business in separate (but linked) continuous programmes. In addition it conducted numerous event-driven customer satisfaction programmes which focused on satisfaction with a specific event, where surveys were conducted within a short time of the event's occurrence. There were many ways in which BT's continuous research programmes delivered value to BT. The cost of the research was in excess of £4 million per year, with additional budget spent on event-driven customer satisfaction surveys and ad hoc satisfaction work. The sample sizes and survey approaches were: domestic consumers 12,000+, by face-to-face, telephone and online survey methods; small and medium-sized enterprises 6,000+; and global businesses 3,000+ (interviews with business decision-makers in 1,000+ accounts), both by telephone and face-to-face survey methods.

Other more obvious examples of products and services which may be bought by both businesses and consumers include: cars, private health insurance, meals in restaurants, laptop computers and stationery equipment – the list could go on. The key factor that distinguishes b2b and consumer transactions has been argued as the *purpose for which products and services are sold.*[6] In b2b transactions, products are bought for resale or for the production of other goods, and services are bought to facilitate the resale and production of goods. In consumer transactions, products and services are generally bought for oneself, the household or as gifts. This distinction clearly does not rule out consumers reselling products, as any glance at the classified columns of newspapers for 'unwanted Christmas presents' or a search on eBay (**www.ebay.com**) would quickly reveal!

If there are different purposes for which goods and services are sold in the two sectors, the approaches to marketing them could differ quite significantly, the nature of target markets may be fundamentally different, and the marketing techniques that communicate and generate sales could differ. However, the underlying reason for such a difference may be simply that business consumers tend to be seen as rational buyers, while consumers tend to be seen as more intuitive and emotive. In examining the differences between business and consumer purchases, it is difficult to dispel the persistent images of professional committees deciding proactively on organisational purchases, and wilful or manipulated individual consumers engaging in semi-rational or impulsive buying behaviour.[7] Such images can be defended if one is circumspect in choosing examples to illustrate the argument, from either perspective. For example, if one were to contrast the buying decision for a train manufacturer selecting the supplier of braking mechanisms compared with a consumer buying chocolates, there would very different time frames and stages to the decision-making process. If one were to compare the differences between the two sectors in the decision to buy a Christmas hamper as a gift, the time frame and stages to the decision-making process may be very similar. The purposes behind the decision to buy a Christmas hamper may also be very similar. There are also many examples of consumer purchasing that may be very 'professional' in terms of knowledge of prices, quality, source reliability, product availability and product applications. Such 'professional' purchasing behaviour has been supported by the growth of price comparison sites, e.g. **www.moneysupermarket.com** or **www.uswitch.com**. There are clearly many grey areas between a notion of business purchasing equating to being rational and 'professional' and consumer purchasing equating to being emotive and impulsive.[8] The task of setting out clear differences is difficult given the breadth of products and services that are purchased by businesses and consumers and the great overlap in the nature and intention of the purchase. Many years ago, one of the foremost industrial marketing writers, Frederick Webster,[9] recognised that many of the differences may be only by degree, but that there are substantial differences:

> If we are to understand and intelligently attack industrial marketing problems, a number of substantial differences between industrial and consumer marketing must be recognized. While it may be true that these are often differences of degree rather than kind, the degrees of difference are substantial.

In examining the similarities and differences between b2b and consumer marketing, the strength of the argument lies in the examples chosen to make the case for the difference to be 'substantial'. These differences may not be absolutes; there may always be specialised b2b and consumer markets that can be used to counter-argue a point. The emphasis may be upon the propensity or tendency for b2b and consumer marketing problems to be different. The 'tendencies' for b2b purchases to develop distinctive characteristics do have implications for the b2b researcher. Before examining these implications, two factors at the heart of the defence for the distinction of b2b marketing need addressing, namely *relationships* and *networks*. These factors are founded in Ford *et al.*'s definition of business marketing and are the basis for the contention that there are fundamental differences between b2b and consumer marketing, and thus differences in the approaches and challenges faced by b2b and consumer researchers.

Bases for the distinction of b2b marketing research

Relationships

Ford *et al.* use the term 'relationship' to describe 'the pattern of interactions and mutual conditioning of behaviours over time, between a company and a customer, a supplier or other organisation'.[10] The time dimension of a relationship requires decision-makers to shift their emphasis away from each single discrete transaction towards tracking how things unfold in the relationship over time and changing them when appropriate. Relationships with business customers are likely to be complex. A business's relationships with its suppliers, development partners and financial institutions that constitute its network all depend upon its relationships with its customers and on solving their problems in those relationships. Ford *et al.* make the clear distinction between the growth of customer relationship management (CRM) systems and the stream of books and articles dealing with 'relationship marketing'. They contend that the idea that underpins most relationship marketing literature is that relationships are the creation of the marketing company. Such views do not help b2b marketers who have to cope with:

- The history of their relationship and the impact of those events upon how different individuals in separate businesses react to each other.

- Relationships that are not necessarily positive and coping with differences in aims and understanding that may result in conflict as well as cooperation.

- Both businesses interacting with each other, both attempting to manage the relationship in a way that they think appropriate.

The b2b relationship is not a relationship that is managed in a unilateral manner, i.e. a relationship that the marketer can 'drive'. CRM systems (as discussed in Chapter 5) that hold the details relating to every customer, that are typically used to ensure all interactions with the customer are consistent and knowledge driven, are typically 'unilateral'. Though CRM systems may measure and model characteristics of transactions that develop over time, they are electronic observations of measurable characteristics of those transactions. CRM systems are not a means to acquire a realistic understanding of the rich and qualitative complexities of continually developing b2b relationships.

In the context of understanding networks and relationships, the prime objective of researchers in business markets therefore is to establish and support an understanding of how successful relationships evolve and how networks operate. There is a need to understand how networks develop and how businesses and individuals in them relate to each other. By being able to recognise patterns of behaviour in the network, businesses should gain some guidance on how they should act and react. To develop such an understanding of patterns requires more than analysis in the traditional sense of gathering and interpreting the available data on patterns of sales and market shares. It means capitalising on the tacit knowledge inside the business and in other networked businesses. Tacit knowledge in this sense could mean, for example, understanding the psychological barriers that may exist in managers when presented to new offerings that evidently offer better monetary value than they get from their present suppliers. They may have worked with their present suppliers for many years and developed economically and socially together; what price would they pay to sever that relationship?

The network

Is has been argued that the transactions between a business supplier and its customers are not isolated events that are unrelated to each other.[11] Instead, each of the transactions takes place in a relationship and each is related to the previous experience of the companies and what they plan for the future. Business marketers have relationships with their suppliers and these relationships are vital if the marketer aims to build strong relationships with their customers. Each of their suppliers will have relationships with other suppliers and with their customers. All of these relationships are affected by the other ones and are intertwined in a network, and it is in this network that the b2b market operates. The distinctive element of seeing b2b marketing as a series of relationships in a network is that, if researchers wish to understand the behaviour of an individual company, then they have to understand its relationships with other companies. Businesses are not seen as free agents, able to develop and implement their strategy in isolation; each is dependent upon the other in order to act and react to the strategies of others. In other words, the basic assumption of network thinking is that 'no business is an island'.[12] Figure 28.1 illustrates a distribution network from the perspective of a large supplying company: IBM. The figure demonstrates the different ways that computers can reach customers in Italy.

In order to understand a network, a focal relationship is usually chosen. By choosing a particular relationship the network can be examined from that perspective. As soon as the focal relationship changes, a new set of relationships emerges. By examining a network carefully, b2b marketers can achieve a realistic and balanced understanding of their own position in the minds of customers and suppliers. It is very important to evaluate the network from different focal points because drawing the network from the perspective of just one business can lead it to believe that it is more important to others than it actually is. The existence of a network should not cloud the fact that the key task of b2b marketing is to manage each single relationship. It is through its relationships that a business learns and adapts to its surrounding network; that a business exploits and develops its own abilities and gains access to others; and it is also through relationships that a business can influence different businesses elsewhere in the network.

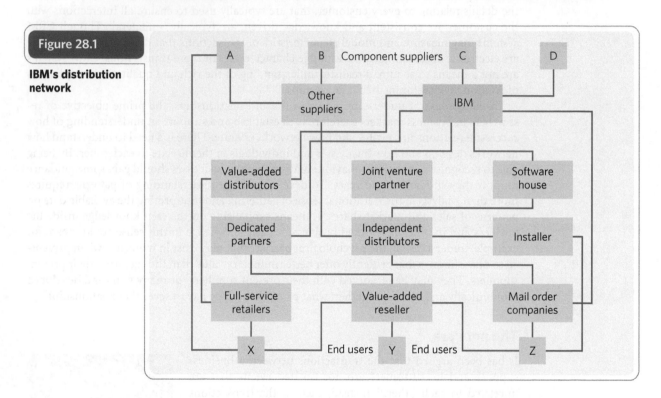

Figure 28.1

IBM's distribution network

Faced with such a challenge in understanding networks and relationships, b2b researchers have all the techniques as detailed and illustrated in this text at their disposal. Having the techniques available is one thing, implementing them is another. The challenge for b2b researchers is to adapt creatively and develop the techniques to overcome the obstacles in the b2b environment. In order to understand the challenge set for these researchers we now examine the implications they face from the differences between business and consumer purchases.

Implications of the differences between business and consumer purchases for researchers

The differences between b2b and consumer purchases have implications for the approach, research design and individual data gathering and analysis techniques that may be employed by researchers. We now examine the nature of the differences between business and consumer marketing and the challenges faced in applying marketing research techniques using the framework of arguments as presented by Ford *et al.*[13] As we work through the individual challenges you will also see how these challenges become interrelated. The five key differences are summarised in Figure 28.2 and then individually evaluated.

Figure 28.2	Key differences between b2b and consumer marketing	b2b marketing tends towards	Consumer marketing tends towards
Summary of differences between b2b and consumer marketing	1 Number of people involved in purchasing decision	High	Low
	2 Professionalism of those involved in the purchasing decision	More rational	More emotive
	3 Time taken to negotiate from decision to buy to actual purchase	Lengthy	Short
	4 Importance of individual consumer to supplier	High	Low
	5 Relationship development	Joint negotiation	Unilateral

Number of people involved in purchasing decision

The concept of the 'buying centre' is well established in business purchasing. Collective decisions are more typical of complex, expensive or controversial purchasing decisions in larger businesses, whereas routine decisions and/or decisions made by smaller organisations are typically made by individuals rather than by groups.[14] However, even in cases of decisions apparently made by an individual, there could still be many other roles of influence involved in the phases of the purchasing process before and after the actual decision itself.

Webster and Wind famously identified five buying 'roles' within the context of 'buying centres'.[15] We can illustrate these roles by using an example of a b2b scenario involving an FMCG business buying marketing research services:

1 *Users.* This may be a brand manager seeking marketing research support for the decisions faced in the launch of a new product.

2 *Influencers.* This may be a human resources director who has used a range of research organisations for staff surveys over the past two years.

3 *Buyers.* This may be a purchaser who is responsible for drawing up a research brief, contacting research organisations, gathering research proposals and managing the negotiation process.

4 *Deciders.* This may be the marketing director if the budget for the project exceeds a set amount.

5 *Gatekeepers.* This may be another brand manager who may be supportive or downright secretive and may help or hinder in feeding information and the interpretation of that information.

Further categories have been suggested such as those of:

6 *Initiator.*[16] This may be a more senior manager to the brand manager who recognises the decision problems faced by the brand manager/user and encourages that manager to purchase marketing research support or even champions the case for marketing research support.

7 *Analyst.*[17] This may be an individual who has the technical ability to evaluate critically the offerings and associated costs as presented in the proposals from competing research agencies.

8 *Spectator*. This may be the brand manager of a competing brand who may react in the way the brand manager/user desires. A feeling of 'sheer panic' may be introduced by the thought that the competition is employing a major ethnographic study to support the development of a new integrated communications strategy.

This example shows eight people involved in the decision. In some organisations, these roles may be performed by one person, in others there may be numerous influencers and gatekeepers, sometimes working in different managerial functions, hierarchical levels and geographic locations. The people in the 'buying centre' will have different needs because of their different responsibilities, so a buyer is likely to be more interested in price and contractual details than a user is. Behind these roles there are individuals who will have their own perceptions, expectations and objectives based on their personalities and backgrounds.[18] The researcher needs to help decision-makers measure and understand these individuals and their interrelationships.

Marketing research challenges. The main challenge of the number of people involved in a business purchase is one of sampling. In a team such as that illustrated above, who would be the target *element* when putting together a sampling plan? Even if there were sampling frames that listed the managerial roles of individuals in an organisation, it is highly improbable that they would be listed by their roles in a 'buying centre'. The views of the researcher Ruth McNeil illustrate this point.

Real research	**Open for business?**[19]

Sampling is becoming ever more demanding. Clients are requiring specialist samples, targeting particular people with particular job titles or skill sets. Such detailed specifications require the fieldwork company to know both where to find and how to access good lists. The absence of good, globally relevant sampling frames is still an issue. Given that SIC codes are rapidly becoming out of date, the increasingly specific demands for participant type mean that a b2b researcher's skill now lies as much in finding the right participant as in conducting and analysing a good interview.

The above example illustrates something of the 'detective' skills in tracking down the right participant for a survey or interview. Researchers building b2b samples via telephone typically recruit participants at their place of work, giving researchers some guarantee that participants are who they claim to be. As researchers have come to rely increasingly on online panels in b2b data collection, concerns about data quality have grown.[20] These concerns can be justified, because a growing literature provides evidence that within online panels, participant behaviours and response patterns have the potential to compromise data quality.[21] Even when researchers track down the right target participants, the challenge of getting them to respond in the manner desired can be great. This challenge is developed in the next difference between b2b and consumer purchases discussed below.

Professionalism of those involved in the purchasing decision

The concept of the professional buyer is well established in business purchasing. Businesses use professional buyers to make economically sound purchases that support their strategic and operational decisions. Such professionals establish auditable systems of purchasing to cope with relatively cheap and routine goods through to expensive, complex and risky one-off products and services such as the purchase of a new accounting information system in a multinational company. Purchasing professionals in essence aim to manage b2b transactions in a rational and economic manner. The following example briefly describes the nature and mission of the professional body that represents purchasing professionals.

The professional buyer – a Chartered Purchaser

The Chartered Institute of Purchasing and Supply (CIPS) is an international education and qualification body representing purchasing and supply chain professionals. CIPS exists to promote and develop high standards of professional skill, ability and integrity among all those engaged in purchasing and supply chain management. It is the largest organisation of its kind in Europe and a central reference point worldwide on matters relating to purchasing and supply chain management. Its Professional Code of Ethics is the model for the international code and the domestic codes of many countries. CIPS acts as a centre of excellence for the whole profession of purchasing and supply chain management.

A body of professionals with rational, economic and ethical practices and who are auditable in a business should make the research challenge of measuring their practices relatively easy when compared with emotive and fickle consumers. However, even assuming that it is the professional buyers who make the purchasing decision, one has to consider why they should divulge or share their practices with researchers.

Marketing research challenges. The first major challenge for researchers targeting professionals is *access*. Access can be described as working at two levels:

1 *Initial contact.* Getting to meet target participants in the first instance so that they understand the nature, purpose and benefits of taking part in an interview or completing a questionnaire.

2 *True feelings.* Assuming that a researcher has managed to persuade target participants to participate, are they able to access what they really feel or think about the research subject? How guarded or sensitive may the participants be in responding to the set questions and probes? Will they be responsive to research techniques that seek to uncover issues that are difficult to conceive and/or express?

The example on page 40 illustrated how increasingly difficult it is to gain access to chief executive officers, especially in a b2b context. It illustrated the despair faced by researchers when they are briefed to interview managers who the researchers know have been targeted in many other studies, and they realise the difficulty or impossibility of gaining access to them, at both levels of access described above. The views of the researcher Richard Field further illustrate this point.

Is nothing straightforward in b2b research?[22]

Organisational changes are making it increasingly difficult to complete business research. It is, for example, harder to contact business executives. Routes to them are less likely to be through a secretary or even a switchboard. Phone numbers are more likely to be direct, unlisted or routed through a central department or an automatic exchange that is immune to the persuasive interviewer. On a wider level, researchers have also had to contend with both the seemingly inexorable conglomeration of the business world and policy changes on compliance. Increasingly, corporate policy forbids interviews – even in corporations that need, and commission, research themselves. In areas where there is a restricted pool of potential participants, one cannot afford low strike rates. It does not just take longer to complete the quotas, one just runs out of contacts.

Beyond quantitative or qualitative interviewing, other techniques like ethnography are increasingly difficult to conduct through the challenges of gaining initial access. In b2b ethnography, business people may be reluctant to allow researchers into their office to shadow them, or to walk around with video cameras. Both processes are highly visible to colleagues and bosses in a way that in-depth interviews are not. While researchers can give participants incentives, for many the money given does not outweigh the inconvenience. In addition, the length of the working day and the need for work–life balance also mean that putting time aside for a lengthy research interview becomes almost impossible.[23]

The second level of access ('true feelings') also presents major challenges for the b2b researcher. The issue raised by professional purchasers at this level is whether they actually behave in a rational and economic manner and whether they understand or are willing to discuss any emotive or subjective reasons for their purchasing behaviour. The following quote illustrates that, although business purchasers may be professional and strive to be rational in economic terms, the reality is somewhat different:[24]

> … consider how an SME or Owner/Manager buys. They typically buy as an individual would, but in a quasi-corporate context. The rationalist approach is strictly limited. Even where it is applicable, good qualitative research also needs to cover the irrational, spontaneous and emotional response set. They don't stop being human beings just because they buy a suit and carry a briefcase.

The following example illustrates the techniques used by Insight Research Group to clarify the issues that may cloud rationalism in b2b purchases.

Real research | **A spoonful of research helps the medicine go down[25]**

The only difference between doctors and other consumers is that this is a classic b2b market, in which customers are not in themselves the end consumers. However, they still have a set of beliefs about the value of a brand for themselves and their patients. It is imperative therefore that researchers get beyond doctors' rational and logical outer shell. They need to find a robust way to underpin functional data with the kind of emotionally driven information that could be used to feed into differentiated pharmaceutical products. Having long known that doctors were adept at assuming and maintaining a professional, logical 'distance' in research, the Insight Research Group began looking at how this behaviour might affect the depth of the overall findings. The often thoughtful, cogent, technical and articulate responses from doctors were in themselves something of a barrier to getting at the more fundamental drivers and triggers for prescribing which were required to make really compelling campaigns. This led to the development of a research approach which placed a greater emphasis on non-direct questioning, increased observation and interpretation of materials, generated from purpose-designed exercises. In small workshops, doctors participated in group and individual work that helped to dismantle the 'doctor' behaviour and facilitate access to their deeper 'sensing' levels. At the analysis stage, the specific sorts of communication, imagery, language and even tone that would help the brand to trigger response at both rational and emotional levels became the focus.

It could be quite easily argued that such research approaches are commonplace in consumer marketing research; there is nothing distinctive in such an approach for b2b researchers. What makes it distinctive is the juxtaposition of the access issues discussed above, i.e. getting to interview professional purchasers in the first instance and, if access is gained, getting them to cooperate – with the implementation of qualitative techniques. The following example illustrates the difficulties and expense involved in making such approaches work.

Engineering the group discussion – the GlobalCash solution

Trying to bring together finance directors and cash managers from the largest companies in Europe to participate in focus groups could be viewed as an impossible task. The logistics of bringing together such senior managers, the rewards they may demand for attending such an event and the question of how much they would reveal to other managers and researchers in such a forum make the whole technique questionable. The solution demanded many months of planning, great expense to create an event that would draw managers together and the careful setting of a context that made managers relaxed enough to be open with their responses. Part of the incentive to complete a GlobalCash survey was an invitation to take part in a 'closed forum for participants'. This meant that a date was set to present findings from the survey exclusively to participants. The date and meeting place of The Management Centre in Brussels (a forum for 'serious' discussion of high quality) were established well in advance to allow managers the chance to put the date in their diaries. The day started with an initial session of presenting statistical findings to the whole group of managers who had participated in a previous survey. As questions were fielded in this forum, particular topics of interest were identified and focus groups (never named as focus groups but as 'workshops') were built around these topics. By mid-morning, groups of around 10 to 12 managers were together tackling a theme of importance to them. With a loose set of topics to develop into questions and probes, the format for a focus group was achieved.

The second major challenge of the people involved in a business purchase being professional is one of *interviewer credibility*. The subject of an interview may be technical in nature given the complexity of the product or service. This was discussed in Chapter 8 in the context of qualitative in-depth interviewing. The interviewer with credibility in the eyes of the participant would appreciate the significance of particular revelations, understand the language (even technical language and jargon in certain areas) and ultimately get the participant to open up, i.e. gain a greater level of access.

The nature of networks or relationships within an industry may have a level of complexity that could prove to be difficult for an interviewer to comprehend. These complexities may not present problems when a structured interview is being conducted. However, if there are open-ended questions or areas where probing is required, as would be necessary in any qualitative interview, the 'technical competence' of the interviewer will be revealed. If the interviewer has technical knowledge, probing can be much more meaningful to the participant, the process of building a rapport can be much stronger, and a richer and more revealing response may be obtained. In the GlobalCash example, the very precise technical nature of the subject and the seniority of the participants meant that interviewer credibility had to be tackled when the series of in-depth interviews was planned. The use of senior academics as supporting researchers from business schools in individual European countries helped in gaining access to key participants, and a local professor would be at hand to help with any language and cultural issues. The nature of the questions and probes was handled by a consultant with an international reputation in the field of cash management, who the participants respected, wanted to talk to and could relate to at their technical level. The consultant had knowledge of the banking techniques and, just as important, the nature of networks and relationships that operated in a highly competitive industry.

Time taken to negotiate from decision to buy to actual purchase

Given the complexity of a business customer's requirements, the importance or value of its purchase, the number of individuals involved in the purchase and the level of their knowledge, and the help and advice that negotiating suppliers can give, a business purchase can be a very lengthy process. The following example illustrates the time taken for what may seem to be a simple decision, i.e. to choose to work with a new bank.

Real research | **Interfering parents**

Hitachi Europe operated from offices in the UK and Germany. They managed transactions with wholesalers and retailers throughout Europe involving the euro and other currencies, e.g. Swiss francs and British pounds. They managed these transactions and the relationships with the parent company in Japan through a number of domestic and international banks. One of the key challenges that Hitachi Europe faced was trying to simplify the process of managing transactions and cutting down on the expense incurred in its thousands of transactions. The first route that it took was to purchase and implement a new accounting system, which in itself took three years from the moment of recognising the nature of the problem through to evaluating possible solutions, negotiations with alternative suppliers and on to buying and implementing the system through to changes in practices and training the staff. The second route was to concentrate the banking business by cutting down on the number of banks Hitachi Europe had accounts with and to develop a new business relationship with a bank that had the international expertise, compatible information systems and service support of the quality level it sought. For an organisation like Hitachi, choosing a new bank and setting up a new account was not like a consumer going into a bank branch or to a website and selecting a product from a range of standard products. The main obstacle to change faced by Hitachi Europe was the parent company's insistence that the European offices worked with certain Japanese banks. It is left to your imagination to appreciate the nature and intricacy of the networks and relationships between individuals working in Hitachi headquarters, regional offices, country offices, wholesalers, retailers and the banks that support their operations. Developing a new relationship between Hitachi Europe and a new bank, which would involve the demise of many established relationships, would involve much negotiation within Hitachi and between existing banks and the new bank. For Hitachi Europe, the process started at the time of choosing a new accounting system. Working with the new bank took another two years to complete, five years in all.

In this example, the compounding factors of the time taken from the moment when an issue is first raised, to final delivery, emerge from the numbers of individuals who may be involved in the negotiations and the fact that they are professionals expected to present clear cost/benefit analyses. Assuming then that researchers can identify who to talk to and gain access to them, what new challenges emerge given lengthy decision-making processes?

Marketing research challenges. The main challenge of the time taken to make a business purchase is one of *participant error*.

In Chapter 13 we discussed the errors caused when administering questionnaires through the inability of participants to remember events. Telescoping takes place when an individual telescopes or compresses time by remembering an event as occurring more recently than it actually occurred.[26] The ability to remember an event is influenced by (1) the event itself, (2) the time elapsed since the event, and (3) the presence or absence of things that would aid memory. We tend to remember events that are important or unusual or that occur frequently. Decision-makers that are part of a 'buying centre' are more likely to remember the negotiations, events and individuals associated with their most recent decisions. In the

Telescoping
A psychological phenomenon that takes place when an individual telescopes or compresses time by remembering an event as occurring more recently than it actually occurred.

Hitachi example, the time taken to conduct negotiations developed over five years. During that time, negotiations may unfold in different geographical locations, involving different business functions and types of decision-maker. The personnel involved may even change as decision-makers move on to other projects or other organisations. For the researcher this presents challenges in terms of accessing potential participants who were present through the process of negotiations. If such decision-makers can be accessed, the next challenge is to get them to remember key events and individuals. Questions that do not provide the participant with cues to the event, and that rely on unaided recall, can underestimate the actual occurrence and nature of an event.

In Chapter 3 we discussed the non-sampling errors termed 'response errors'. It was noted that a non-sampling error is likely to be more problematic than a sampling error. Its problematic nature emerges from the difficulties involved in identifying the error, measuring it and making changes in estimates. Response errors can be broken down into 'participant inability' and 'participant unwillingness':

- *Inability error* results from the participant's inability to provide accurate answers. Participants may provide inaccurate answers because language and logic used in a survey or questionnaire bear no relevance to their experiences, or the question format and content may be taking them into issues that are meaningless in their work context. Such an experience may result in participants suffering from fatigue, boredom and a general lack of engagement with the process of questioning. For example, in the GlobalCash example, imagine a participant being asked to respond to a series of Likert-scale items about the service quality of online technical support. Though the organisation may use such support, a professional buyer responding to the scales may see the overall issue of online technical support as being of very low priority in the context of all the issues involved in negotiating with a new bank. Could the researcher trust that the participant has thought through the measured issues carefully and is being honest?

- *Unwillingness error* arises from the participant's unwillingness to provide accurate information. Participants may intentionally misreport their answers because of a desire to provide socially acceptable answers, to avoid embarrassment or to please the interviewer. More especially in the b2b scenario, their answers have great commercial sensitivity and responding truthfully would reveal their commercial intellectual property. For example, to impress the interviewer participants may intentionally say that their business works with The Cooperative Bank in order to portray themselves as having relationships with organisations that profess a socially responsible agenda. They may not have any business with this bank, but would the interviewer be able to validate this response? As another example, the interviewer may pose questions about weaknesses in the services offered by a particular bank. The participants may consider this sensitive as the weaknesses may reveal flaws and, by implication, the individuals involved in these flaws in their own organisation. The participants may also question what may happen to their responses. If given directly to other banks in an unaggregated form, it would present all the elements required for another bank to make a sales pitch that may upset an established relationship.

Overcoming telescoping and participant errors raises fundamental questions about the techniques used to elicit information and the benefits and rewards given to participants. These types of error cannot be simply managed by larger samples as we will explore in the next subsection.

Importance of individual consumer to supplier

An example to illustrate this difference between b2b and consumer marketing is the extreme situation of dependence which can occur in commercial aviation, where there are only two main suppliers of airliners and only a few dozen major customers. In the following example, Cisco conducted research to support its market segmentation strategies. The outcome resulted in an analysis of and focus upon individual customers. This can occur in consumer marketing, but the depth of individual analyses and the resources allocated to important individual customers remain a distinctive b2b marketing challenge.

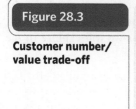

Real research

Cisco steps up[27]

The business information and networking company Cisco (**www.cisco.com**) believed that segmentation was not about creating a snapshot of the market and then communicating with or getting sales representative to concentrate on one or more of the segments. It saw segmentation as a means to understand the fundamental forces that determine buying behaviours, and building value propositions to individual businesses. From this perspective, Cisco created a Marketing Advanced Analytics team to develop data-driven insights to support its marketing decisions. The team was charged with building new segmentation models to identify previously unknown revenue opportunities and suggest strategies to capitalise on them. It built a data warehouse that integrated previously unconnected data from multiple sources such as: customer purchase history; marketing touch and response history; customer contact information; Harte-Hanks (**harte-hanks. com**) (direct marketing business) company data; Dunn & Bradstreet data; customer-reseller relationships; customer service contract status; customer technical support history; website visit history. The team evaluated the total addressable market value of each business and created an 'upside' metric, determined by the difference between the customer's total estimated purchasing power and the amount it had spent with Cisco. The team could roll those figures up to the country or regional level, to gauge where the best growth opportunities were. Its segmentation approach, which also includes propensity-to-buy scores, enabled Cisco to prioritise its marketing resources more effectively.

Not all b2b marketers have few target customers. A manufacturer selling photocopier paper could have potentially huge numbers of businesses to sell its wares to, from major multinationals through to home businesses. In consumer marketing, a manufacturer of bespoke shoes such as John Lobb (**www.johnlobb.com**) may retail at €3,000 a pair. John Lobb may have relatively small numbers of target consumers that are responsible for a significant proportion of its total sales.

In b2b and consumer marketing, examples can be found of businesses that have a few high-value customers and those that have huge numbers of customers with low-value transactions. In general, however, b2b marketers have a higher propensity to deal with fewer customers of high value when compared with consumer marketers. The comparison between the two is illustrated in Figure 28.3.

Figure 28.3

Customer number/ value trade-off

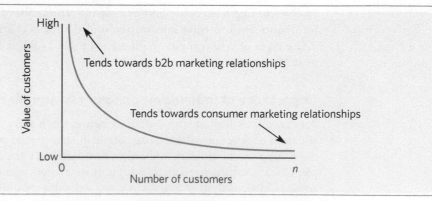

Size matters

Imagine yourself going on holiday and wanting to exchange your local currency for Australian dollars. All banks can help you make currency exchanges. The transaction is paid for through an exchange rate that is constantly changing and a commission fee. If you were a small business conducting transactions that involved a few currency exchanges per year, then you may have to pay the 'going rates' at your local bank or shop around for the best rates. However, for a company like Renault, imagine the variation in its profits depending upon the relative value of the euro to the US dollar and how much it costs for each currency transfer. Think of the currencies that Renault may have to deal in and the number of transactions and flows of funds. To Renault, the fluctuations in currency values and timing of cash

transfers are crucial factors that can make the difference between sound profits and a loss. Given the volume of its business and the size of its transactions, Renault would not pay the 'going rate' to a bank that you or a small business would. Renault would expect a cash-management banking service tailored specifically to its operations that may be radically different from the operations and expectations of BMW. The target markets in cash-management banking sought by major banks are those companies that operate internationally or even globally, dealing in huge sums and a variety of currencies. There may be millions of individual transactions to manage, huge networks of transactions across many countries or very high values to the transactions. When examining the nature of businesses that fulfil these requirements, there are relatively few compared with the total number of businesses, which is why the GlobalCash study, conducted on behalf of 15 of the largest pan-European banks, targeted just the largest 5,000 companies in Europe, a very small fraction of the total number of European businesses.

This example illustrates how the essence of relatively few consumers may be of high value – through careful target marketing. Some businesses may have a mass marketing strategy that aims to target a great breadth of business types; others may have to tailor their offerings specifically to suit the specific needs of quite distinctive businesses.

Marketing research challenges. The main challenge of each business customer being individually important to a supplier and responsible for a significant proportion of its total sales is one of coping with relatively few target consumers. As most quantitative marketing research techniques tend to assume large numbers of potential target consumers and survey participants, the challenge faced by b2b researchers is one of *sampling methods* and the subsequent *analyses that may be performed given sample selection*.

We have already presented the challenges of 'element' definition in a sampling plan, gaining access to participants (and the effect upon response rates) and response error. If we add on the challenge of conducting surveys when there are relatively few target participants, it is clear to see that the whole sampling process becomes very challenging.

In choosing a sampling method for a small target population, probability methods such as random and systematic sampling can be utilised. With simple random sampling it is often difficult to construct a sampling frame that will permit a simple random sample to be drawn. Simple random sampling may or may not result in a representative sample; this is the paradox faced when drawing a random sample – one does not know if it will be representative of a target population, only the probability that it will be, within margins of error. Although samples drawn will represent the population well on average, a given simple random sample may grossly misrepresent the target population. This is more likely if the size of the sample is small, as faced in many b2b surveys.

With systematic sampling, when the ordering of the sample elements is related to the characteristic of interest the technique increases the representativeness of the sample. If businesses within an industry are arranged in increasing order of annual sales, a systematic sample will include some small and some large firms. A simple random sample may be unrepresentative because it may contain, for example, only small firms or a disproportionate number of small firms. Choosing the right characteristics by which to order sample elements is crucial. With the wrong criteria, systematic sampling may decrease the representativeness of the sample. Thus, the power of systematic sampling lies in the accuracy of the sampling frame and the criteria used to order or arrange the sample elements.

With the time and cost factors of sourcing and building up-to-date and accurate sampling frames, with details of sample elements, many b2b researchers will favour administrative, i.e. timing and cost, criteria in preference to statistical criteria, and ultimately be forced to use non-probability sampling techniques. Non-probability sampling relies on the personal judgement of the researcher rather than on chance to select sample elements. The b2b researcher would aim to build the elements to include in a sample, rather than starting from a point of having an up-to-date and accurate sampling frame that resembles the target population. Building up the sample in this manner leads the b2b researcher commonly to use judgemental sampling and snowball sampling techniques (as discussed in Chapter 14). Samples created using these techniques may yield good estimates of the population characteristics, but they do not allow for objective evaluation of the precision of the sample results. Because there is no way of determining the probability of selecting any particular element for inclusion in the sample, the estimates obtained are not statistically projectable to the population.

The following example illustrates the challenges faced in accessing accurate sampling frames and how much time researchers could spend in building their own.

Non-probability sampling

Sampling techniques that do not use chance selection procedures but rather rely on the personal judgement of the researcher.

Real research	**Targeting business elites in India**[28]

In a study of the 'business elite' in India (senior executives living very comfortably, travelling widely, consuming luxury goods and services, and making important business purchases for their companies) many sampling challenges were faced. Though the number of participants surveyed was relatively high, researchers recognised that their work should be considered a pilot and that much more work was needed to generate a complete sampling frame. For their study, a systematic random sample was drawn from a 'cleaned-up' database of companies. In an initial telephone screening exercise, they targeted 1,714 companies and made successful contact with 859 of them (50.1%). They asked each of these companies: (1) who the most senior person in the company in that city was; (2) whether the company employed heads of a predefined list of other functions; and (3) what the contact details were for the most senior person and a randomly selected other function. Job functions were those core to the decision-making process and included: chief executive (most senior person); deputy chief executive/managing director (second most senior person); head of finance; head of international/domestic sales; head of marketing and communications; head of production management/operations; head of information technology. From the interviews they estimated that the universe of eligible business executives in qualifying companies across eight Indian cities totalled 106,307. This was based on the incidence, at each of the companies sampled, of a randomly generated list of job functions. They also pinpointed 1,499 executives they wanted to contact, of whom 600 (40%) agreed to be interviewed face to face.

Summary of sampling challenges. While the theory of sampling is the same for all types of markets whatever their nature, there are key differences between sampling in b2b and consumer markets. These may be summarised as:[29]

1 *Unit definition.* Is it the site (establishment), organisation, legal entity or some other business unit? Each definition offers different benefits and drawbacks, depending upon the research objectives. In consumer research only the individual or household has to be considered.

2 *Element definition.* In b2b research, an individual is interviewed as a representative of the business. We have to be sure to interview the right individual in each business, and be consistent across businesses. This can be complex as business titles and responsibilities vary widely across businesses of different sizes and sectors.

3 *Heterogeneity.* There is a lack of homogeneity in the business universe. There is much more variance between a small business and a large organisation than between any two consumers. There is also great variation between different types of small business.

4 *Sampling frames.* The available sampling frames of businesses and the nature of their detail that could allow stratification to vary considerably in accuracy and coverage.

5 *Public/private sector.* The public sector generally counts as business, though the usage and buying patterns are frequently very different from the private sector.

Relationship development

Salespeople, purchasing professionals and indeed anyone making decisions in a 'buying centre' do not just meet, negotiate a deal and move on to other things. Imagine a cement manufacturer wishing to buy a furnace that is expected to be part of its cement production process for over 20 years. There would be many meetings with staff from the cement company, the various competing furnace manufacturers and many potential suppliers of key components for the furnace. Even when the decision to buy from one particular supplier has been made, the interactions between technical, financial, production and legal staff could take place over many months or even years. The purchase could be the forerunner to servicing and repair contracts and the installation of similar equipment in other cement-making plants. In buying a new furnace, there could be a time when modifications need to be made. There are locations where local authorities allow cement manufacturers to burn old car tyres in their furnaces. Adding old tyres to a gas-fired furnace may require modifications to allow the tyres to be fed in, changes to the chimneys to get rid of different fumes and the lining of the furnace. All of these developments may again unfold over time, involving purchasing, technical, production, logistics, marketing and legal personnel. There may be components that need to be replaced frequently given the immense temperatures in the furnace. The delivery of these components may involve a repeat order which may need a simple telephone call or even be automatically generated without human intervention.

In all of these cases, the customer and supplier interact on the basis of their experiences of previous purchases between them, and given the nature of their expectations for future purchases. The interaction between a customer and supplier is a single episode in the relationship between them. Each episode is affected by the relationship of which it forms part and each interaction in turn affects the relationship itself.[30] Each interaction and each purchase or sale can only be understood in the context of that relationship, and ultimately within the network or businesses that enable the relationships to work.

Cross-sectional design
A type of research design involving the collection of information from any given sample of population elements only once.

Single cross-sectional design
A cross-sectional design in which one sample of participants is drawn from the target population and information is obtained from this sample once.

Multiple cross-sectional design
A cross-sectional design in which there are two or more samples of participants, and information from each sample is obtained only once.

Longitudinal design
A type of research design involving a fixed sample of population elements measured repeatedly. The sample remains the same over time, thus providing a series of pictures that, when viewed together, vividly illustrate the situation and the changes that are taking place.

Marketing research challenges. The main challenge of a b2b purchase or sale not being an isolated event is finding a research design that is appropriate to understanding complex networks and relationships. The cross-sectional study is the most frequently used descriptive design in marketing research. Cross-sectional designs involve the collection of information from any given sample of population elements only once. They may be either single cross-sectional or multiple cross-sectional designs. In single cross-sectional designs, only one sample of participants is drawn from the target population, and information is obtained from this sample only once. These designs are also called sample survey research designs. In multiple cross-sectional designs, there are two or more samples of participants, and information from each sample is obtained only once. In either variation of the design, much of the richness of the context of individual relationships and the network of relationships is lost. A more appropriate though more expensive and resource-intensive design is the longitudinal design. In longitudinal designs, a fixed sample (or samples) of population elements is measured repeatedly. A longitudinal design differs from a cross-sectional design in that the sample or samples remain the same over time. In other words, the same people are studied over time. In contrast to the typical cross-sectional design, which gives a snapshot of the variables of interest at a single point in time, a longitudinal study provides a series of 'pictures'. These 'pictures' give an in-depth view of the situation and the changes that take place over time.

A key feature of creating such 'pictures' of relationships and networks is the building of contextual material from sources such as sales data, customer data, secondary data statistics, intelligence through press and trade commentary that focuses upon particular markets or industries, and a vast resource of intelligence held within the employees of a business that may be seeking research support.[31] In the following example, the mobile phone company Orange has built what it terms a knowledge management system to help it create a 'picture' of relationships and networks.

Real research | **Knowledge management system at Orange[32]**

Mobile phone company Orange has invested in a knowledge management system and will add video to the online data stream. The driving force behind the move was to give decision-makers a self-serve interactive tool for all insights on marketing research and competitor intelligence. Their communications are now in one place and they are able to keep it updated regularly, sending out daily news bulletins and updates on recently completed projects with links to new information. Every week, they monitor who is using the information and exactly what they are looking for, what they download and how well the data are being used. That enabled them to focus on meeting those demands and ensure everything was relevant and usable.

There may be a lack of resources devoted to allowing b2b researchers to use longitudinal studies and develop knowledge management systems of the type favoured by Orange. Depending solely upon cross-sectional studies may not uncover the wider contextual issues that would allow detailed knowledge of relationships and networks. There could be a limitation on the way that b2b researchers view the value of contextual material. It has been argued that many b2b researchers demonstrate 'tunnel vision', which fails to recognise the wider business context of business findings.[33] Many researchers work comfortably within the standard research process of a brief, proposal, research setup, fieldwork, presentation and report. They continue to argue that 'desk research is a dying art and that the multitude of excellent Internet resources is sadly neglected'; many b2b researchers are consistently failing to put their research into a wider market or business context. Such a failing can affect the briefing/proposal stage as well as the analysis/reporting stage. This means that research findings are often set in a 'vacuum' without reference to the challenges faced by b2b marketers. The danger of this is that b2b marketing research is seen by decision-makers as a 'nice-to-know' or luxury item rather than a key part of the planning and decision-making process. Adding value by drawing on the various sources of market intelligence available reduces the risk of marketing research appearing irrelevant to decision-makers. It can also improve the research process so that decision-makers value the information provided.

The weaknesses of cross-sectional research designs, the resources required to perform longitudinal designs and the limitations of some b2b researchers to appreciate the wider context of their investigations may result in b2b decision-makers looking to other sources for decision support. Over recent years there has been a growth in the use and practice of competitor intelligence. Many organisations have developed competitor intelligence systems that allow them to have a relatively low-cost 'picture' of their environment, competitors and sometimes even their customers. Competitive intelligence uses many marketing research techniques and by using multiple sources aims to set a broad context to allow the b2b decision-makers to understand the networks in which they operate. The next section briefly explores the nature of competitor intelligence and its 'threat' to the nature and standards of conventional marketing research.

The growth of competitive intelligence

The research designs and techniques employed in competitive intelligence may in some respects differ from the structured methods of marketing research; in other respects there are many similarities. Over the past 20 years or so, those who professionally gather competitive intelligence have continued to refine research techniques and to distinguish their approach from industrial espionage. In general, the research design employed for competitive intelligence is exploratory, using primarily secondary data, intelligence sources and qualitative primary data.[34] Competitive intelligence has been defined as *a systematic process by which a firm gathers, analyses and disseminates information about its rivals*[35] or as *a process of researching a competitor's organisation, products, prices, financial performance, technology and strategy.*[36]

From these definitions we can see in 'systematic' and 'process' the continuous development of an understanding or knowledge of competitors. In the first definition we see the elements of managing data that replicate the marketing research process in terms of gathering, analysing and disseminating data. In the second definition we see the focus of data gathering in terms of products, prices, financial performance, technology and strategy. These are areas of measurement and understanding that go beyond the remit of marketing researchers.

While the nature of competitive intelligence has evolved there has been much confusion over what competitive intelligence is and what it is not. Competitive intelligence is not corporate espionage, stealing competitive documents or accessing competitors' computer files. Rather, the discipline is a structured approach to a different type of research which has evolved as an outgrowth of strategic planning and market research. The Society of Competitive Professionals (SCIP) was formed in 1986 to develop behavioural standards and a code of ethics.[37]

The most commonly used techniques in competitive intelligence are:

1 *Review of public records.* Monitoring secondary sources of information such as government records, commercial databases, media reports and news clippings, and company-produced literature, for potential threats and opportunities.

2 *Observational techniques.* Directly observing competitors' activities or facilities through overt surveillance is another way to acquire competitive data, though such practices may be viewed with suspicion. Likewise, learning about a competitor's capabilities, strengths and weaknesses through physical inspection of its products or actual use of its services is seen to be within the bounds of acceptable practice. Observers contribute to the gathering of 'informal' information concerning the market and business at different levels. Observers are not formal researchers but members of business departments, marketing specialists, technicians in engineering departments or plant-building departments. Employees in every department, including sales, purchasing and research and development, hear industry news well before it appears in a trade journal or in databases.[38] These observers and their contacts form key components of b2b relationships set in the context of networks.

3 *Face-to-face interviews.* Conversing with informed sources is beneficial when hard-to-find information about a competitor's strategies and intentions is used to fill critical gaps in secondary data and provide a more complete understanding of the competition.[39]

In the gathering and interpretation of 'public records', conducting face-to-face interviews and overt observations, competitive intelligence targets individuals from the following types of organisation:[40]

- Competitor companies
- Customers
- Suppliers
- Distributors
- Government organisations
- Trade associations
- Financial institutions.

Given the array of data sources, data gathering techniques, institutions and individuals that may be targeted (including consumers in some instances), and the array of employees that may be used to 'observe', competitive intelligence is clearly a 'broad-brush' approach. Competitive intelligence can offer the broad context and in many instances detail specific areas to b2b decision-makers that may be missing in conventional marketing research. Marketing research techniques may be more error free, less subjective and carried out with much stronger and more well-established codes of conduct when compared with competitive intelligence. However, for the b2b decision-makers needing to understand the long-term development of relationships and the dynamics of the network in which those relationships work, conventional views of marketing research may not offer the support they seek. They may forgo an amount of error, interpret subjective and biased views and even push the boundaries of ethical practice to gain support that is more attuned to the decisions they face. In the following example we see the views of in-house researchers from the Hong Kong Jockey Club and Hong Kong Disneyland. In-house researchers set out the expectations of researchers in being able to integrate a breadth of data sources that include competitive intelligence and marketing research.

| Real research | **The Expanded Market Intelligence Function**[41] |

With broader roles and responsibilities and widening research audiences, the expectations of in-house research professionals in monitoring the macro business environment and delivering market intelligence are becoming more significant. Researchers are expected to be more proactive in monitoring changes in the macro business environment (e.g. economy, policy, competition and tracking consumer/market trends). At the same time, they are also expected to analyse and evaluate the impact of these macro business environment changes upon the micro business initiatives (e.g. new product development, pricing, promotions, etc.). More analytics, insights and future outlooks are demanded from business leaders to help them better understand their customers, the marketplace and the overall business environment. Managing research projects has therefore become only part of the in-house researchers' daily responsibilities. The other larger part of their role includes understanding the macro business operating environment, monitoring market trends, conducting competitive analyses, answering business questions, identifying business opportunities and assessing potential risks. Given this wider job scope, the degree of business information required has also become broader. Information collected through conventional primary research channels alone no longer satisfies business requirements. Desk research, syndicated reports, news clipping, key performance indicators and customer behaviour data all contribute an important part of the business information that is frequently used by in-house researchers for business analysis.

This example illustrates that competitive intelligence should not be seen as a replacement or alternative to marketing research. The use of a breadth of data sources that includes competitive intelligence can increase the use and influence of marketing research. Without a systematic view of the relationship of marketing research and competitive intelligence, decision-makers may find themselves in the position illustrated in the following example.

| Real research | **Companies are awash with data**[42] |

A European fixed-line telecommunications company was being attacked by cable operators and was losing customers at a rate of 50,000 per month. This meant a huge loss of revenue, around €200 million per year. The cable operators offered cable TV and cheaper cable telephony. According to the company's competitive intelligence, the line rent could be between 25% and 43% less than that of the fixed-line company. There were significant savings for consumers on call charges too. The fixed-line company's response had been to introduce various price packages, but the brand continued to lose market share. Researchers were invited by the marketing director to help develop an alternative strategy to stop, or at least slow, the loss of customers. The researcher's first reaction was not to generate more research, it was to analyse and use the data already available. In this company there was a large marketing research library and also regular tracking, competitive intelligence and billing/sales data. The marketing research archive contained just under 2,900 reports. The reports were in hard copy only and were listed by title in a number of Excel files. 'Keyword' searching (e.g. any mention of cable, competitor, price, etc., as well as scanning the titles) reduced the total to 260 documents and reading summaries narrowed this further to 85, which were then analysed in detail. However, the eventual yield was small. Out of the 2,900 there was only one qualitative report that provided a clue as to how the cable threat might be contained. This report was several years old and long forgotten.

There still remain ethical issues to consider with competitive intelligence, which will be tackled later in the chapter.

International marketing research

It is clear from many examples throughout the book that b2b marketing research is practised in international settings. The challenges involved in conducting international research detailed in Chapter 27, i.e. adapting research techniques based upon different cultures and languages, simply add to the challenges of b2b marketing research detailed in this chapter. For many b2b companies new challenges in international marketing research lie in developing economies. The following example illustrates the challenges faced by the multinational company Dow Chemicals. It was facing major strategic and structural changes and used marketing research to underpin its new direction. The new market opportunities focused upon developing countries. Getting the research approach correct in these new environments and cultures would be key to the company's success.

Real research | Performance-driven marketing at Dow Chemicals[43]

The Dow Chemical Company (**www.dow.com**) is a leader in specialty chemicals delivering products and solutions to sectors such as electronics, water, energy and coatings. Dow developed a new company strategy, structure and culture in its Home and Personal Care Division. Generally, b2b companies have structures and cultures built around promoting their products and so the task of reshaping all aspects of Dow was huge, particularly for marketing directors who typically focus on sales alone. It involved first identifying the consumer companies who were leaders in the field and who would be Dow's key target customers. The second step was to explore and fully understand the problems that these companies had, by researching consumer behaviour, values and trends, and to look for the possibility of disruptive innovations. In other words, Dow had to understand the emotional and functional needs of its customers' consumers just as well as its customers did. The next step involved looking at geography, to identify areas and markets of growth. This revealed that growth was in markets that Dow was not in, principally developing countries. The final step was to reshape top management, which meant bringing in a large component of people with experience in consumer goods markets.

There are factors that make access and conducting b2b research easier in developing economies. Being able to access a great breadth of secondary data and intelligence across many industries and countries has become more commonplace. Globalisation in b2b as well as consumer industries is making marketing research interviews more familiar and acceptable. Online research technologies enable survey and focus group participants to be accessed in almost any country of the world. Social media research methods enable new forms of participant access and engagement to work. Technology developments enable far more centralisation of data collection and field operations alongside the more traditional options of using local subcontractors or partners.[44]

The global growth of online survey applications and the use of participant panels in consumer research have been mirrored in b2b contexts. In the following example, the researchers argue that the use of an online survey facilitated access to a most senior level in b2b organisations and a more open and revealing engagement with participants.

Feeling the pulse of global business leaders[45]

The potential for research targeted at b2b managers was demonstrated in an online survey conducted in 2009. The survey was carried out among 529 business decision-makers in Australia, Canada, France, Germany, Mexico, the UK and the USA. The online research panel and research company e-Rewards' (**www.e-rewards.com**) conducted the study. Among a cross-section of senior business decision-makers, 77% were managing directors, presidents, chief executive officers, chief operating officers, chairpersons, board members or owners and all were either the primary decision-maker or actively involved in making decisions for the company with a minimum of 100 people. A third were from companies employing more than 1,000 employees. As a result, participants had the capability to reveal intimate details about their companies. The survey confirmed that the effects of the recession have been felt globally, with at least two-thirds of senior decision-makers in each of the seven countries declaring that their companies had been adversely affected by the economic conditions. The actions taken by those companies affected by the recession were far reaching: from cutting spending on travel and entertainment, to reducing employment costs and bonuses. Most revealing, though, was the fact that decision-makers were prepared to reveal whether or not they had postponed or cancelled potential acquisitions. This subject was normally taboo, or at least politely avoided in marketing research.

As with all forms of research, there remain cultural differences in applying b2b marketing research which are worth debating. These are generalised observations but they give some sense of the need to appreciate cultural sensitivities when planning and implementing research:

- Telephone and web interviews with b2b participants can be very difficult to achieve in China. Managers are often unwilling to discuss important issues without the reassurance of face-to-face contact. On the other hand, face-to-face interviews, once started, can yield as much information and ideas as anywhere in the world, though it can be difficult to tie down participants to precise appointments in advance.
- b2b participants in other countries, including some Southern European countries where marketing research is less familiar, require more reassurance about confidentiality and security. Good websites that clearly establish the credentials and integrity of the research agency, the sponsoring client and the project are more likely to be required after initial contact by telephone (for a telephone or face-to-face survey). Once the interview is granted, excellent information can be provided.
- Telephone and self-completion questionnaires sometimes elicit less detailed and informative responses from Nordic (Denmark, Finland, Iceland, Norway, Sweden) participants than elsewhere. In this region b2b participants were more cautious, using formal ways to respond to unstructured questions, although this behaviour can be modified in the context of a face-to-face interview.[46]

This last observation was certainly the same experience as in the GlobalCash example detailed earlier in the chapter. The Nordic/Scandinavian participants were most cautious in responding to the more sensitive questions, with the Danes having the highest non-response levels to questions that referred to their experiences of specific banks.

With the spread of globalisation and increase of international trade, international b2b marketing research has similarly grown. The research industry has had to respond to the challenges set, with major agencies developing account or relationship teams that serve the worldwide operations of their customers.

Ethics in marketing research

In Chapter 1, we highlighted how ESOMAR distinguishes marketing research from other competitive forms of data gathering, primarily through the issue of the anonymity of participants. It stresses that in marketing research the identity of the provider of information is not disclosed. In b2b marketing research, the nature of the relationship between clients, researchers and participants has been undergoing a transformation in recent years. The change has been most evident in customer satisfaction research, where the research interview is tending now to be treated as an active component of customer relationship management. Rather than using aggregated research findings to guide process changes in customer-facing operations, clients are seeking to use the survey process as a tool for maintaining dialogue with individual customers. In response to this, customers are increasingly keen to lose their anonymity and have their responses passed on in an attributable form to appropriate people such as account management teams. Their motivation is that their responses will be used in a way that will improve the service or product they receive. Survey anonymity has to remain a fundamental right of any participant for both ethical and data validity reasons. However, the trend in b2b customer research is clearly towards participants choosing to forgo this.[47]

Another major ethical challenge facing b2b researchers lies in the growth of competitive intelligence. One of the major differences in competitive intelligence and traditional market research is the knowledge of the purpose of the study. Ethical marketing research should reveal the purpose of the study to the participants, and, sometimes, how the information will be used, especially when explaining why particularly sensitive questions are being asked. Competitive intelligence studies in contrast generally do not reveal the purpose of the study and how the

information will be used. Essentially, the competitive intelligence interviewers must develop a 'story' as to why they are calling the participants, e.g. they are interested in their products, they are conducting a general industry study, they are conducting a study as part of their degree or they are looking at specific issues within the industry (e.g. legislation or product safety). This may generate a response and some participants may be happy to cooperate. However, this would clearly be considered as unethical by traditional marketing research organisations.[48] Being duplicitous in gaining access to participants could potentially damage the reputation of legitimate researchers and ultimately damage response rates, making access continually more difficult.

For bona fide b2b researchers, it is usual to disclose the identity of their clients, i.e. who commissioned the research, either up front or in the course of an interview. This means that marketing research has to play an ambassadorial role. Researchers are not speaking for their clients, but are representing them in asking participants for their views. As a result the behaviour of researchers must be highly professional and care must be taken with client and participant reputation. The size of participant populations is often so small that treating participants with care is becoming more important and sometimes b2b researchers need to dissuade their clients from trying to cram more into ever-longer interviews. Although it is tempting to ask as much as possible in the one 'hit', this rebounds on researchers and their clients in the long run.[49] Look back to Chapter 15, where non-response issues were discussed, and re-examine the proposed means to improve response rates. Now consider how feasible it is to increase response rates with a small pool of participants who may be very irritated by the number of requests for interviews and the length of those interviews.

Digital applications in marketing research

Digital developments have created opportunities to engage with business participants in more convenient and less intrusive manners than other forms of data collection. With the growth of mobile device usage, research engagement can occur at a time and place that are convenient for the participant. However, researchers face challenges when researching business participants online, similar to the issues currently facing consumer online research. If researchers do not treat business participants with respect, if they are not engaged and rewarded fairly, they can be easily alienated. It has been argued that business participants should not be treated in the same way that many panel companies treat their consumer panellists. Measures should be taken to avoid the more common examples of poor practice, such as:[50] too many survey invitations … and reminders; too many 'screen outs' (establishing whether a participant has the qualities sought for a study), especially those that could have been avoided with adequate profiling information and sample selection protocols; long, dull and repetitive surveys; poorly designed and irrelevant surveys; a heavy reliance on prize draws, which typically do not deliver sustained engagement and loyalty. The following example illustrates the use of an online survey targeted at business participants. This survey required concentration and for participants to be fully engaged in the process. The academic researchers who crafted this study in a very specialised b2b market drew valuable lessons for the rollout of this study into other industries and countries.

Real research   **Relationship marketing in South African financial services[51]**

A study was conducted to identify the dimensions of relationship management that were perceived by managers as essential for the establishment and management of b2b relationships in the South African financial services industry. A national financial provider agreed to participate in the study and a sample of 75 relationship managers from this company were randomly selected as participants. The sample was representative of all the geographical areas served by the financial provider. A questionnaire was developed in which the participants had to indicate the importance of each of nine relationship dimensions, compared with each of all the other dimensions. The technique used a process of pairwise comparisons by participants between two variables at a time. An online survey approach was used to distribute the questionnaire. Each participant received an email with a direct link to a website where the questionnaire was hosted. This email was preceded by a letter (also by email) from top management in which the reasons for the study were explained and participants were encouraged to participate in the study. Two weeks after the initial questionnaire was sent to the participants, a follow-up reminder notice was sent to all 75 participants. In total, the participants were allowed four weeks to complete the questionnaire. The questionnaire was constructed in such a way that the participants could not continue with the next question unless an answer was provided for the previous question. This arrangement ensured that no non-usable questionnaires were received. To aid evaluation by the participants, a definition of each dimension (as defined in the literature) appeared next to each of the dimensions.

For some business participants, online surveys do not work well. Much depends upon the context of research engagement experienced by the participants and how comfortable they feel with a research approach. b2b is all about partnerships with other businesses, rather than selling to a consumer, so personal engagement can be vital and the relationship between the seller and the businessperson can often become a friendship, which can transcend the brand.[52] For the researcher this can mean looking for means to replicate the nurturing of a personal engagement. This is where social media research techniques are proving to be of great value in b2b research. Such techniques do not replace face-to-face engagement, which may not be feasible in many studies. They do, however, support the initial contact with participants, and the nurturing and growth of relationships. The following example illustrates how social media research techniques can be applied and work in a b2b context.

The guiding principle for b2b researchers embracing social media research techniques is that building credible relationships is paramount. Business people are more likely to be open, engaged and responsive if they are treated as equal partners and they can experience the benefits of participating in research. Digital developments should be seen as a tool to make them feel that they are and will be treated with respect.

Real research — Research 2.0 and b2b[53]

Research 2.0 has had a big impact upon consumer research practices and has been debated and presented in many forums. Much less discussion has taken place within the domain of b2b research. Many projects are in place and value is being delivered to b2b researchers through the use of social media research. The types of Research 2.0 that are happening within b2b include (1) blog mining, (2) blogging as a qualitative technique, (3) discussion forums and (4) online communities. For those businesses where buyers and suppliers are 'wired', an online community is almost a necessity. These online communities should be about much more than marketing research. Communities foster networks and relationships and as such should include design co-creation, marketing, sales information, and provide loyalty keys such as information, infotainment and possibly entertainment. An online community also has great potential as a research portal. The research conducted via this portal should be one of mutual respect, collaborative and interesting. The target should be to make an online community as large as possible, aiming to have 100% of customers and potential customers in it. Within the online community there could be one or more forums. Forums should have two elements, one driven by the agenda of the forum members, the other driven by the research/marketing agenda. Blogs should be used to explore the life of product users and of staff. Texting and tweeting can be used by users and staff to log key messages to their blogs, so that they can expand on them later.

Summary

This chapter was founded upon the key question of whether there are substantial differences between b2b and consumer marketing and thus differences in the approaches and challenges faced by b2b and consumer researchers. The two main bases of b2b marketing are the concepts of relationships and networks. In the context of understanding relationships and networks, the prime objective of researchers in business markets therefore is to support an understanding of how successful relationships evolve and how the network operates. The nature of relationships and networks underpins five key differences between b2b marketing and consumer marketing. These can be summarised as differences in: the number of people who may be involved in a b2b purchasing decision; the professionalism of those involved in the purchasing decision; the time taken to negotiate from decision to buy to actual purchase; the importance of individual consumers to a supplier; and b2b purchases or sales not being isolated events. These differences are the reason why there are distinctive differences in the approaches adopted and challenges faced by b2b and consumer researchers. The key challenges they face are in:

- Administering effective sampling plans with the associated problems of finding appropriate sampling techniques and the limitations of inference from the statistics that they may generate.
- Gaining access to key participants, in terms of getting to interview participants in the first instance and getting them to be open and honest. A key element of this access lies in how credible interviewers are perceived by business participants.
- Business participants actually remembering what has happened and why they or their organisation behaved as they did. The events may have taken a long time to unfold, involved numerous individuals and taken a great deal of time subsequently.
- Creating research designs that can measure or help to create an understanding of the dynamics of relationships and networks.

b2b researchers face further challenges from practitioners in competitor intelligence who have to work with decision-makers who may forgo an amount of error, interpret subjective and biased views, and even push the boundaries of ethical practice to gain support that is more attuned to the decisions they face. Competitive intelligence need not be a direct replacement for conventional marketing research; it can be a strong supplement that allows research findings to be understood in a more dynamic and broader context. Even though many of the techniques adopted in competitor research match those in marketing research and may be quite removed from notions of industrial espionage, there still remain clear ethical issues about such approaches.

b2b researchers tackle the challenges summarised above mostly in very creative ways, as illustrated in the examples throughout this chapter and indeed throughout this book. They do this so well that b2b researchers sometimes see themselves as superior to consumer researchers![54] With the spread of globalisation and increase of international trade, international b2b marketing research has similarly grown. The marketing research industry has had to respond to the challenges set, with major agencies developing account or relationship teams that serve the worldwide operations of their customers. Digital developments have enabled the management and control of international b2b marketing research to become far more cost effective. Social media research techniques are proving to be of great value in b2b research. Such techniques do not replace face-to-face engagement, which may not be feasible in many studies. They do, however, support the initial contact with participants, and the nurturing and growth of relationships. They can help to demonstrate the respect and integrity of researchers, a vital attribute in b2b marketing research.

Questions

1 Why is it important to ask the question 'Is b2b marketing research significantly different from consumer marketing research?'

2 What characteristics distinguish b2b marketing from consumer marketing?

3 From what focal point should a business network be analysed?

4 What challenges do b2b marketers face in managing relationships?

5 How do the concepts of business networks and relationships relate to each other?

6 What are the five major differences between b2b and consumer marketing?

7 Describe the sampling challenges that the b2b researcher faces.

8 What does 'access' mean in the context of b2b marketing research?

9 Evaluate the reasons why gaining access to key participants may be so difficult. Why may gaining access grow more difficult over time?

10 What is meant by 'interviewer credibility'? What may interviewers do to be seen as more credible in the eyes of target participants?

11 Describe the potential participant errors that may occur in b2b marketing research. What may be done to reduce these potential errors?

12 What is competitive intelligence? How does this definition differ from notions of 'conventional marketing research'?

13 What sampling frame challenges exist in international b2b marketing research?

14 To what extent do you think that competitor analysts have benefits to offer to potential participants in any interviews they conduct?

15 Describe the means by which the Web may improve the process of conducting b2b marketing research.

Exercises

1 Visit the website of Business Intelligence Group (BIG) (**www.b2bresearch. org**). Evaluate why it came into existence and present a case for why b2b researchers need a distinctive professional body to represent their interests.

2 You are the marketing research manager of a bank. Management have asked you to assess the demand potential for 'high-growth start-up businesses'. What sources of secondary data and intelligence would you consult? What kinds of information would you expect to obtain from each source? Ask a group of fellow students to play the role of management and explain to them the role of secondary data in this project.

3 You are a marketing manager for a company that manufactures adhesives for the construction industry. You wish to invest in an online focus group study of construction engineers and architects. Explain how you would identify and recruit such participants from across the globe. What incentive(s) would you offer potential participants?

4 A manufacturer would like to survey users to determine the demand potential for a new power press. The new press has a capacity of 500 tonnes and costs €400,000. It is used for forming products from lightweight and heavyweight steel and can be used by automobile, construction equipment and household appliance manufacturers.

    a Identify the population and sampling frame that could be used for this study.

    b Describe how simple random sampling could be used with your identified sampling frame.

    c Could a stratified sample be used? If so, how?

    d Could a cluster sample be used? If so, how?

    e Which sampling technique (it need not be random, stratified or cluster) would you recommend? Why?

5 In a small group discuss the following issues: 'What is the ideal educational background for someone seeking a career in competitive intelligence?' and 'There can never be any convergence in values between the professional bodies representing marketing research and competitive intelligence.'

Video case exercise: Eaton

1 What 'relationship' challenges does Eaton have to manage? How can marketing research help it to understand the nature and dynamics of relationships?

2 What 'network' challenges does Eaton have to manage? How can marketing research help it to understand the nature and dynamics of networks?

3 What would you see as being the main challenges faced by researchers working for Eaton?

Notes

1. Chilvers, V., 'Fair's fair at trade shows', *Research* (November 2003), 63.

2. Anon., 'Hewlett Packard – HP blades system servers positioning and share growth campaign', ARF Ogilvy Awards, Redefining Markets, Silver, Publicis West and Draft FCB (2008).

3. Dibb, S., Simkin, L., Pride, W.M. and Ferrell, O.C., *Marketing: Concepts and Strategies*, 4th edn (Boston: Houghton-Mifflin, 2000), 158.

4. David Ford conducts his work with a team of researchers in the IMP (International Marketing and Purchasing) Group. This group was founded in 1976 by researchers from five European countries. The group's 'interaction approach' is based on the importance for both researchers and managers of understanding the *interaction* between *active* buyers and sellers in continuing business relationships. Ford, D., *The Business Marketing Course: Managing in Complex Networks* (Chichester: Wiley, 2002), 6. See **www.impgroup.org**.

5. MacFarlane, P. and Wibberley, J., 'The ROI of customer satisfaction research – a case study proving its value', ESOMAR, Annual Congress, Montreal (September 2008).

6. Littler, D., 'Organizational marketing', in Baker, M.J. (ed.), *The Marketing Book*, 3rd edn (Oxford: Butterworth–Heinemann, 1994), 610.

7. Wilson, D.F., 'Why divide consumer and organizational buyer behaviour?', *European Journal of Marketing* 34 (7) (2000), 780–796.

8. McPhee, N., 'Is there a future for "real" qualitative market research interviewing in the digital age?', ESOMAR, Congress Odyssey, Athens (September 2010).

9. Webster, F.E. Jr, 'Management science in industrial marketing', *Journal of Marketing* 42 (January 1978), 22.

10. Ford, D., Gadde, L.E., Hakansson, H. and Snehota, I., *Managing Business Relationships*, 2nd edn (Chichester: Wiley, 2003), 38.

11. Ford, D., *The Business Marketing Course: Managing in Complex Networks* (Chichester: Wiley, 2002), 29.

12. Hakansson, H. and Snehota, I., 'No business is an island: the network concept of business strategy', *Scandinavian Journal of Management* 14 (3) (1990), 177–200.

13. Ford, D., *The Business Marketing Course: Managing in Complex Networks* (Chichester: Wiley, 2002), 3–6.

14. Spekman, R.E. and Stern, L.W., 'Environmental uncertainty and buying group structure: an empirical investigation', *Journal of Marketing* 43 (1979), 54–64.

15. Webster, F.E. Jr and Wind, Y., 'A general model of organizational buying behaviour', *Journal of Marketing* 36 (2) (1972), 12–19.

16. Pettit, R., 'The march toward quality: the ARF's quality enhancement process', *Journal of Advertising Research* 50 (2) (2010), 120–124; Bonoma, T.V., 'Major sales: who really does the buying?', *Harvard Business Review* 60 (3) (1982), 111–119.

17. Wilson, D.F., *Organizational Marketing* (London: Routledge, 1998).

18. Ford, D., *The Business Marketing Course: Managing in Complex Networks* (Chichester: Wiley, 2002), 79.

19. McNeil, R., 'Open for business', *Research* (May 2003), 3.

20. Harlow, B., 'Analytic implications of panel data quality – the role of panel recruitment', ESOMAR, Panel Research, Dublin (October 2008).

21. Downes-Le Guin, T., Mechling, J. and Baker, R., 'Great results from ambiguous sources – cleaning internet panel data', ESOMAR, Panel Research, Barcelona (November 2006).

22. Field, R., 'Open for business', *Research* (May 2003), 6.

23. Staig, J. and Tomlins, R., 'Technography/ethnography in the real world', ESOMAR, Qualitative Research, Istanbul (November 2008).

24. McPhee, N., 'Is there a future for "real" qualitative market research interviewing in the digital age?', ESOMAR, Congress Odyssey, Athens (September 2010).

25. Hamilton-Stent, S., 'A spoonful of research helps the medicine go down', *Research* (November 2003), 63.

26. Wilson, E.J. and Woodside, A.G., 'Respondent inaccuracy', *Journal of Advertising Research* 42 (5) (September/October 2002), 7–18; Menon, G., Raghubir, P and Schwarz, N., 'Behavioural frequency judgments: an accessibility–diagnosticity framework', *Journal of Consumer Research* 22 (2) (September 1995), 212–228; Cook, W.A., 'Telescoping and memory's other tricks', *Journal of Advertising Research* (February–March 1987), 5–8; Sudman, S., Finn, A. and Lannom, L., 'The use of bounded recall procedures in single interviews', *Public Opinion Quarterly* (Summer 1984), 520–524.

27. Anon., 'The B2B segmentation dilemma: insights stuck at marcom', *Marketing NPV* 4 (4) (2007).

28. Green, A., Heak, J. and Staplehurst, S., 'Measuring the business elites in India and China: a powerhouse methodology meets powerhouse economies', ESOMAR, Asia Pacific Conference, Singapore (April 2008).

29. Anon., 'Warc Exclusive – WARC Briefing: SMEs', (November 2010); Macfarlane, P., 'Structuring and measuring the size of business markets', *International Journal of Market Research* 44 (1) (2002).

30. Ford, D., Gadde, L.E., Hakansson, H. and Snehota, I., *Managing Business Relationships*, 2nd edn (Chichester: Wiley, 2003), 4.

31. Cummings, S., 'Secondary research: an essential part of the b2b toolkit', *Imprints* (May 2003), 30–31.

32. Allen, L., 'Get the most from your internal knowledge banks', *Admap* (October 2009), 42–43.

33. Bairfelt, S. and Wilkinson, T., 'Future proof', *Research* (May 2003), 13.

34. Page, A. and Lai, S., 'Understanding your competitors – completing the marketing intelligence jigsaw', ESOMAR, Asia Pacific Conference, Tokyo (March 2005); Le Meunier-FitzHugh, K. and Piercy, N., 'Integrating marketing intelligence sources – reconsidering the role of the salesforce', *International Journal of Market Research* 48 (6) (2006), 699–716; Stanat, R., 'The relationship between market research and competitive intelligence', ESOMAR, Power of Knowledge Congress, Berlin (September 1998).

35. Kahaner, L., *Competitive Intelligence: From Black Ops to Boardrooms. How Businesses Gather, Analyze, and Use Information to Succeed in a Global Marketplace* (New York: Simon & Schuster, 1996).

36. Stanat, R., 'The relationship between market research and competitive intelligence', ESOMAR, Power of Knowledge Congress, Berlin (September 1998).

37. van Hamersveld, M., 'What are we talking about? A short frame of reference', ESOMAR, Marketing & Competitive Intelligence, Geneva (March 1999).

38. Jakobiak, F., *ESOMAR Journal* (1999), **www.warc.com/fulltext/ESOMAR/13801.htm**, accessed 18 February 2005.

39. Lithwick, D., 'How to conduct a competitive intelligence phone interview', *Imprints* (December 2004), 15–16; Kassler, H.S., 'Mining the internet for competitive intelligence', *Online* (September/October 1997), 34–45.

40. Stanat, R., 'The relationship between market research and competitive intelligence', *ESOMAR Journal* (1998).

41. Kung, A. and Tse, G., 'The evolving role of in-house market research professionals – from "reactive" to "proactive"', ESOMAR, Asia Pacific, Beijing (April 2009).

42. Cowan, D., 'Forum – creating customer insight', *International Journal of Market Research* 50 (6) (2008), 719–729.

43. Lannon, J., 'Chief marketing officer conference report: Delivering high performance – foresight, insight and execution', *Warc Exclusive* (October 2010).

44. Connell, S., 'Travel broadens the mind – the case for international research', *International Journal of Market Research* 44 (1) (2002), 7.

45. Walton, M., 'Engaging business decision-makers online: what do they love and hate about online market research?', Market Research Society, Annual Conference (2010).

46. Connell, S., 'Travel broadens the mind – the case for international research', *International Journal of Market Research* 44 (1) (2002), 3–4.

47. Joseph, M., 'Loud and clear', *Research* (February 2005), 26–27.

48. Stanat, R., 'The relationship between market research and competitive intelligence', *ESOMAR Journal* (1998).

49. McNeil, R., 'Open for business', *Research* (May 2003), 3.

50. Walton, M., 'Engaging business decision-makers online: what do they love and hate about online market research?', Market Research Society, Annual Conference (2010).

51. Theron, E. and Terblanche, N.S., 'Dimensions of relationship marketing in business-to-business financial services', *International Journal of Market Research* 52 (3) (2010), 373–392.

52. Anon., 'Warc Exclusive – WARC Briefing: SMEs', (November 2010).

53. Poynter, R. and Lawrence, G., 'Insight 2.0: new media, new rules, new insight', ESOMAR, Annual Congress, Berlin (September 2007).

54. Britton, T., 'Superiority "devalues" b2b research', *Research* (21 May 2003), **http://www.research-live.com/news/ superiority-'devalues-b2b-research/3000259.article**, accessed 14 July 2011.

Appendix: Statistical tables

Table 1 **Simple random numbers**

Line/col.	(1)	(2)	(3)	(4)	(5)	(6)	(7)	(8)	(9)	(10)	(11)	(12)	(13)	(14)
1	10480	15011	01536	02011	81647	91646	69179	14194	62590	36207	20969	99570	91291	90700
2	22368	46573	25595	85393	30995	89198	27982	53402	93965	34095	52666	19174	39615	99505
3	24130	48390	22527	97265	76393	64809	15179	24830	49340	32081	30680	19655	63348	58629
4	42167	93093	06243	61680	07856	16376	39440	53537	71341	57004	00849	74917	97758	16379
5	37570	39975	81837	16656	06121	91782	60468	81305	49684	60072	14110	06927	01263	54613
6	77921	06907	11008	42751	27756	53498	18602	70659	90655	15053	21916	81825	44394	42880
7	99562	72905	56420	69994	98872	31016	71194	18738	44013	48840	63213	21069	10634	12952
8	96301	91977	05463	07972	18876	20922	94595	56869	69014	60045	18425	84903	42508	32307
9	89579	14342	63661	10281	17453	18103	57740	84378	25331	12568	58678	44947	05585	56941
10	85475	36857	53342	53988	53060	59533	38867	62300	08158	17983	16439	11458	18593	64952
11	28918	69578	88231	33276	70997	79936	56865	05859	90106	31595	01547	85590	91610	78188
12	63553	40961	48235	03427	49626	69445	18663	72695	52180	20847	12234	90511	33703	90322
13	09429	93969	52636	92737	88974	33488	36320	17617	30015	08272	84115	27156	30613	74952
14	10365	61129	87529	85689	48237	52267	67689	93394	01511	26358	85104	20285	29975	89868
15	07119	97336	71048	08178	77233	13916	47564	81056	97735	85977	29372	74461	28551	90707
16	51085	12765	51821	51259	77452	16308	60756	92144	49442	53900	70960	63990	75601	40719
17	02368	21382	52404	60268	89368	19885	55322	44819	01188	65255	64835	44919	05944	55157
18	01011	54092	33362	94904	31273	04146	18594	29852	71685	85030	51132	01915	92747	64951
19	52162	53916	46369	58586	23216	14513	83149	98736	23495	64350	94738	17752	35156	35749
20	07056	97628	33787	09998	42698	06691	76988	13602	51851	46104	88916	19509	25625	58104
21	48663	91245	85828	14346	09172	30163	90229	04734	59193	22178	30421	61666	99904	32812
22	54164	58492	22421	74103	47070	25306	76468	26384	58151	06646	21524	15227	96909	44592
23	32639	32363	05597	24200	13363	38005	94342	28728	35806	06912	17012	64161	18296	22851
24	29334	27001	87637	87308	58731	00256	45834	15398	46557	41135	10307	07684	36188	18510
25	02488	33062	28834	07351	19731	92420	60952	61280	50001	67658	32586	86679	50720	94953
26	81525	72295	04839	96423	24878	82651	66566	14778	76797	14780	13300	87074	79666	95725
27	29676	20591	68086	26432	46901	20849	89768	81536	86645	12659	92259	57102	80428	25280
28	00742	57392	39064	66432	84673	40027	32832	61362	98947	96067	64760	64584	96096	98253
29	05366	04213	25669	26422	44407	44048	37937	63904	45766	66134	75470	66520	34693	90449
30	91921	26418	64117	94305	26766	25940	39972	22209	71500	64568	91402	42416	07844	69618
31	00582	04711	87917	77341	42206	35126	74087	99547	81817	42607	43808	76655	62028	76630
32	00725	69884	62797	56170	86324	88072	76222	36086	84637	93161	76038	65855	77919	88006
33	69011	65795	95876	55293	18988	27354	26575	08625	40801	59920	29841	80150	12777	48501
34	25976	57948	29888	88604	67917	48708	18912	82271	65424	69774	33611	54262	85963	03547
35	09763	83473	73577	12908	30883	18317	28290	35797	05998	41688	34952	37888	38917	88050
36	91567	42595	27959	30134	04024	86385	29880	99730	55536	84855	29088	09250	79656	73211
37	17955	56349	90999	49127	20044	59931	06115	20542	18059	02008	73708	83517	36103	42791
38	46503	18584	18845	49618	02304	51038	20655	58727	28168	15475	56942	53389	20562	87338
39	92157	89634	94824	78171	84610	82834	09922	25417	44137	48413	25555	21246	35509	20468
40	14577	62765	35605	81263	39667	47358	56873	56307	61607	49518	89656	20103	77490	18062
41	98427	07523	33362	64270	01638	92477	66969	98420	04880	45585	46565	04102	46880	45709

Line/col.	(1)	(2)	(3)	(4)	(5)	(6)	(7)	(8)	(9)	(10)	(11)	(12)	(13)	(14)
42	34914	63976	88720	82765	34476	17032	87589	40836	32427	70002	70663	88863	77775	69348
43	70060	28277	39475	46473	23219	53416	94970	25832	69975	94884	19661	72828	00102	66794
44	53976	54914	06990	67245	68350	82948	11398	42878	80287	88267	47363	46634	06541	97809
45	76072	29515	40980	07391	58745	25774	22987	80059	39911	96189	41151	14222	60697	59583
46	90725	52210	83974	29992	65831	38857	50490	83765	55657	14361	31720	57375	56228	41546
47	64364	67412	33339	31926	14883	24413	59744	92351	97473	89286	35931	04110	23726	51900
48	08962	00358	31662	25388	61642	34072	81249	35648	56891	69352	48373	45578	78547	81788
49	95012	68379	93526	70765	10592	04542	76463	54328	02349	17247	28865	14777	62730	92277
50	15664	10493	20492	38301	91132	21999	59516	81652	27195	48223	46751	22923	32261	85653
51	16408	81899	04153	53381	79401	21438	83035	92350	36693	31238	59649	91754	72772	02338
52	18629	81953	05520	91962	04739	13092	97662	24822	94730	06496	35090	04822	86774	98289
53	73115	35101	47498	87637	99016	71060	88824	71013	18735	20286	23153	72924	35165	43040
54	57491	16703	23167	49323	45021	33132	12544	41035	80780	45393	44812	12515	98931	91202
55	30405	83946	23792	14422	15059	45799	22716	19792	09983	74353	68668	30429	70735	25499
56	16631	35006	85900	98275	32388	52390	16815	69293	82732	38480	73817	32523	41961	44437
57	96773	20206	42559	78985	05300	22164	24369	54224	35083	19687	11052	91491	60383	19746
58	38935	64202	14349	82674	66523	44133	00697	35552	35970	19124	63318	29686	03387	59846
59	31624	76384	17403	53363	44167	64486	64758	75366	76554	31601	12614	33072	60332	92325
60	78919	19474	23632	27889	47914	02584	37680	20801	72152	39339	34806	08930	85001	87820
61	03931	33309	57047	74211	63445	17361	62825	39908	05607	91284	68833	25570	38818	46920
62	74426	33278	43972	10119	89917	15665	52872	73823	73144	88662	88970	74492	51805	99378
63	09066	00903	20795	95452	92648	45454	69552	88815	16553	51125	79375	97596	16296	66092
64	42238	12426	87025	14267	20979	04508	64535	31355	86064	29472	47689	05974	52468	16834
65	16153	08002	26504	41744	81959	65642	74240	56302	00033	67107	77510	70625	28725	34191
66	21457	40742	29820	96783	29400	21840	15035	34537	33310	06116	95240	15957	16572	06004
67	21581	57802	02050	89728	17937	37621	47075	42080	97403	48626	68995	43805	33386	21597
68	55612	78095	83197	33732	05810	24813	86902	60397	16489	03264	88525	42786	05269	92532
69	44657	66999	99324	51281	84463	60563	79312	93454	68876	25471	93911	25650	12682	73572
70	91340	84979	46949	81973	37949	61023	43997	15263	80644	43942	89203	71795	99533	50501
71	91227	21199	31935	27022	84067	05462	35216	14486	29891	68607	41867	14951	91696	85065
72	50001	38140	66321	19924	72163	09538	12151	06878	91903	18749	34405	56087	82790	70925
73	65390	05224	72958	28609	81406	39147	25549	48542	42627	45233	57202	94617	23772	07896
74	27504	96131	83944	41575	10573	03619	64482	73923	36152	05184	94142	25299	94387	34925
75	37169	94851	39117	89632	00959	16487	65536	49071	39782	17095	02330	74301	00275	48280
76	11508	70225	51111	38351	19444	66499	71945	05422	13442	78675	84031	66938	93654	59894
77	37449	30362	06694	54690	04052	53115	62757	95348	78662	11163	81651	50245	34971	52974
78	46515	70331	85922	38329	57015	15765	97161	17869	45349	61796	66345	81073	49106	79860
79	30986	81223	42416	58353	21532	30502	32305	86482	05174	07901	54339	58861	74818	46942
80	63798	64995	46583	09785	44160	78128	83991	42865	92520	83531	80377	35909	81250	54238
81	82486	84846	99254	67632	43218	50076	21361	64816	51202	88124	41870	52689	51275	83556
82	21885	32906	92431	09060	64297	51674	64126	62570	26123	05155	59194	52799	28225	85762
83	60336	98782	07408	53458	13564	59089	26445	29789	85205	41001	12535	12133	14645	23541
84	43937	46891	24010	25560	86355	33941	25786	54990	71899	15475	95434	98227	21824	19535
85	97656	63175	89303	16275	07100	92063	21942	18611	47348	20203	18534	03862	78095	50136
86	03299	01221	05418	38982	55758	92237	26759	86367	21216	98442	08303	56613	91511	75928
87	79626	06486	03574	17668	07785	76020	79924	25651	83325	88428	85076	72811	22717	50585
88	85636	68335	47539	03129	65651	11977	02510	26113	99447	68645	34327	15152	55230	93448
89	18039	14367	61337	06177	12143	46609	32989	74014	64708	00533	35398	58408	13261	47908
90	08362	15656	60627	36478	65648	16764	53412	09013	07832	41574	17639	82163	60859	75567
91	79556	29068	04142	16268	15387	12856	66227	38358	22478	73373	88732	09443	82558	05250
92	92608	82674	27072	32534	17075	27698	98204	63863	11951	34648	88022	56148	34925	57031
93	23982	25835	40055	67006	12293	02753	14827	23235	35071	99704	37543	11601	35503	85171
94	09915	96306	05908	97901	28395	14186	00821	80703	70426	75647	76310	88717	37890	40129
95	59037	33300	26695	62247	69927	76123	50842	43834	86654	70959	79725	93872	28117	19233
96	42488	78077	69882	61657	34136	79180	97526	43092	04098	73571	80799	76536	71255	64239
97	46764	86273	63003	93017	31204	36692	40202	35275	57306	55543	53203	18098	47625	88684
98	03237	45430	55417	63282	90816	17349	88298	90183	36600	78406	06216	95787	42579	90730
99	86591	81482	52667	61582	14972	90053	89534	76036	49199	43716	97548	04379	46370	28672
100	38534	01715	94964	87288	65680	43772	39560	12918	80537	62738	19636	51132	25739	56947

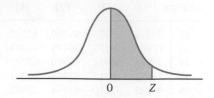

| Table 2 | Area under the normal curve |

Z	.00	.01	.02	.03	.04	.05	.06	.07	.08	.09
0.0	.0000	.0040	.0080	.0120	.0160	.0199	.0239	.0279	.0319	.0359
0.1	.0398	.0438	.0478	.0517	.0557	.0596	.0636	.0675	.0714	.0753
0.2	.0793	.0832	.0871	.0910	.0948	.0987	.1026	.1064	.1103	.1141
0.3	.1179	.1217	.1255	.1293	.1331	.1368	.1406	.1443	.1480	.1517
0.4	.1554	.1591	.1628	.1664	.1700	.1736	.1772	.1808	.1844	.1879
0.5	.1915	.1950	.1985	.2019	.2054	.2088	.2123	.2157	.2190	.2224
0.6	.2257	.2291	.2324	.2357	.2389	.2422	.2454	.2486	.2518	.2549
0.7	.2580	.2612	.2642	.2673	.2704	.2734	.2764	.2794	.2823	.2852
0.8	.2881	.2910	.2939	.2967	.2995	.3023	.3051	.3078	.3106	.3133
0.9	.3159	.3186	.3212	.3238	.3264	.3289	.3315	.3340	.3365	.3389
1.0	.3413	.3438	.3461	.3485	.3508	.3531	.3554	.3577	.3599	.3621
1.1	.3643	.3665	.3686	.3708	.3729	.3749	.3770	.3790	.3810	.3830
1.2	.3849	.3869	.3888	.3907	.3925	.3944	.3962	.3980	.3997	.4015
1.3	.4032	.4049	.4066	.4082	.4099	.4115	.4131	.4147	.4162	.4177
1.4	.4192	.4207	.4222	.4236	.4251	.4265	.4279	.4292	.4306	.4319
1.5	.4332	.4345	.4357	.4370	.4382	.4394	.4406	.4418	.4429	.4441
1.6	.4452	.4463	.4474	.4484	.4495	.4505	.4515	.4525	.4535	.4545
1.7	.4554	.4564	.4573	.4582	.4591	.4599	.4608	.4616	.4625	.4633
1.8	.4641	.4649	.4656	.4664	.4671	.4678	.4686	.4693	.4699	.4706
1.9	.4713	.4719	.4726	.4732	.4738	.4744	.4750	.4756	.4761	.4767
2.0	.4772	.4778	.4783	.4788	.4793	.4798	.4803	.4808	.4812	.4817
2.1	.4821	.4826	.4830	.4834	.4838	.4842	.4846	.4850	.4854	.4857
2.2	.4861	.4864	.4868	.4871	.4875	.4878	.4881	.4884	.4887	.4890
2.3	.4893	.4896	.4898	.4901	.4904	.4906	.4909	.4911	.4913	.4916
2.4	.4918	.4920	.4922	.4925	.4927	.4929	.4931	.4932	.4934	.4936
2.5	.4938	.4940	.4941	.4943	.4945	.4946	.4948	.4949	.4951	.4952
2.6	.4953	.4955	.4956	.4957	.4959	.4960	.4961	.4962	.4963	.4964
2.7	.4965	.4966	.4967	.4968	.4969	.4970	.4971	.4972	.4973	.4974
2.8	.4974	.4975	.4976	.4977	.4977	.4978	.4979	.4979	.4980	.4981
2.9	.4981	.4982	.4982	.4983	.4984	.4984	.4985	.4985	.4986	.4986
3.0	.49865	.49869	.49874	.49878	.49882	.49886	.49889	.49893	.49897	.49900
3.1	.49903	.49906	.49910	.49913	.49916	.49918	.49921	.49924	.49926	.49929
3.2	.49931	.49934	.49936	.49938	.49940	.49942	.49944	.49946	.49948	.49950
3.3	.49952	.49953	.49955	.49957	.49958	.49960	.49961	.49962	.49964	.49965
3.4	.49966	.49968	.49969	.49970	.49971	.49972	.49973	.49974	.49975	.49976
3.5	.49977	.49978	.49978	.49979	.49980	.49981	.49981	.49982	.49983	.49983
3.6	.49984	.49985	.49985	.49986	.49986	.49987	.49987	.49988	.49988	.49989
3.7	.49989	.49990	.49990	.49990	.49991	.49991	.49992	.49992	.49992	.49992
3.8	.49993	.49993	.49993	.49994	.49994	.49994	.49994	.49995	.49995	.49995
3.9	.49995	.49995	.49996	.49996	.49996	.49996	.49996	.49996	.49997	.49997

Each entry represents the area under the standard normal distribution from the mean to Z.

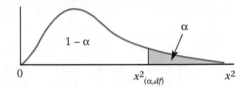

Table 3	Chi-square distribution

Degrees of freedom	Upper tail area (α)											
	.995	.99	.975	.95	.90	.75	.25	.10	.05	.025	.01	.005
1			0.001	0.004	0.016	0.102	1.323	2.706	3.841	5.024	6.635	7.879
2	0.010	0.020	0.051	0.103	0.211	0.575	2.773	4.605	5.991	7.378	9.210	10.597
3	0.072	0.115	0.216	0.352	0.584	1.213	4.108	6.251	7.815	9.348	11.345	12.838
4	0.207	0.297	0.484	0.711	1.064	1.923	5.385	7.779	9.488	11.143	13.277	14.860
5	0.412	0.554	0.831	1.145	1.610	2.675	6.626	9.236	11.071	12.833	15.086	16.750
6	0.676	0.872	1.237	1.635	2.204	3.455	7.841	10.645	12.592	14.449	16.812	18.548
7	0.989	1.239	1.690	2.167	2.833	4.255	9.037	12.017	14.067	16.013	18.475	20.278
8	1.344	1.646	2.180	2.733	3.490	5.071	10.219	13.362	15.507	17.535	20.090	21.955
9	1.735	2.088	2.700	3.325	4.168	5.899	11.389	14.684	16.919	19.023	21.666	23.589
10	2.156	2.558	3.247	3.940	4.865	6.737	12.549	15.987	18.307	20.483	23.209	25.188
11	2.603	3.053	3.816	4.575	5.578	7.584	13.701	17.275	19.675	21.920	24.725	26.757
12	3.074	3.571	4.404	5.226	6.304	8.438	14.845	18.549	21.026	23.337	26.217	28.299
13	3.565	4.107	5.009	5.892	7.042	9.299	15.984	19.812	22.362	24.736	27.688	29.819
14	4.075	4.660	5.629	6.571	7.790	10.165	17.117	21.064	23.685	26.119	29.141	31.319
15	4.601	5.229	6.262	7.261	8.547	11.037	18.245	22.307	24.996	27.488	30.578	32.801
16	5.142	5.812	6.908	7.962	9.312	11.912	19.369	23.542	26.296	28.845	32.000	34.267
17	5.697	6.408	7.564	8.672	10.085	12.792	20.489	24.769	27.587	30.191	33.409	35.718
18	6.265	7.015	8.231	9.390	10.865	13.675	21.605	25.989	28.869	31.526	34.805	37.156
19	6.844	7.633	8.907	10.117	11.651	14.562	22.718	27.204	30.144	32.852	36.191	38.582
20	7.434	8.260	9.591	10.851	12.443	15.452	23.828	28.412	31.410	34.170	37.566	39.997
21	8.034	8.897	10.283	11.591	13.240	16.344	24.935	29.615	32.671	35.479	38.932	41.401
22	8.643	9.542	10.982	12.338	14.042	17.240	26.039	30.813	33.924	36.781	40.289	42.796
23	9.260	10.196	11.689	13.091	14.848	18.137	27.141	32.007	35.172	38.076	41.638	44.181
24	9.886	10.856	12.401	13.848	15.659	19.037	28.241	33.196	36.415	39.364	42.980	45.559
25	10.520	11.524	13.120	14.611	16.473	19.939	29.339	34.382	37.652	40.646	44.314	46.928
26	11.160	12.198	13.844	15.379	17.292	20.843	30.435	35.563	38.885	41.923	45.642	48.290
27	11.808	12.879	14.573	16.151	18.114	21.749	31.528	36.741	40.113	43.194	46.963	49.645
28	12.461	13.565	15.308	16.928	18.939	22.657	32.620	37.916	41.337	44.461	48.278	50.993
29	13.121	14.257	16.047	17.708	19.768	23.567	33.711	39.087	42.557	45.722	49.588	52.336
30	13.787	14.954	16.791	18.493	20.599	24.478	34.800	40.256	43.773	46.979	50.892	53.672
31	14.458	15.655	17.539	19.281	21.434	25.390	35.887	41.422	44.985	48.232	52.191	55.003
32	15.134	16.362	18.291	20.072	22.271	26.304	36.973	42.585	46.194	49.480	53.486	56.328
33	15.815	17.074	19.047	20.867	23.110	27.219	38.058	43.745	47.400	50.725	54.776	57.648
34	16.501	17.789	19.806	21.664	23.952	28.136	39.141	44.903	48.602	51.966	56.061	58.964
35	17.192	18.509	20.569	22.465	24.797	29.054	40.223	46.059	49.802	53.203	57.342	60.275
36	17.887	19.233	21.336	23.269	25.643	29.973	41.304	47.212	50.998	54.437	58.619	61.581
37	18.586	19.960	22.106	24.075	26.492	30.893	42.383	48.363	52.192	55.668	59.892	62.883
38	19.289	20.691	22.878	24.884	27.343	31.815	43.462	49.513	53.384	56.896	61.162	64.181
39	19.996	21.426	23.654	25.695	28.196	32.737	44.539	50.660	54.572	58.120	62.428	65.476
40	20.707	22.164	24.433	26.509	29.051	33.660	45.616	51.805	55.758	59.342	63.691	66.766

Degrees of freedom	Upper tail areas (α)											
	.995	.99	.975	.95	.90	.75	.25	.10	.05	.025	.01	.005
41	21.421	22.906	25.215	27.326	29.907	34.585	46.692	52.949	56.942	60.561	64.950	68.053
42	22.138	23.650	25.999	28.144	30.765	35.510	47.766	54.090	58.124	61.777	66.206	69.336
43	22.859	24.398	26.785	28.965	31.625	36.436	48.840	55.230	59.304	62.990	67.459	70.616
44	23.584	25.148	27.575	29.787	32.487	37.363	49.913	56.369	60.481	64.201	68.710	71.893
45	24.311	25.901	28.366	30.612	33.350	38.291	50.985	57.505	61.656	65.410	69.957	73.166
46	25.041	26.657	29.160	31.439	34.215	39.220	52.056	58.641	62.830	66.617	71.201	74.437
47	25.775	27.416	29.956	32.268	35.081	40.149	53.127	59.774	64.001	67.821	72.443	75.704
48	26.511	28.177	30.755	33.098	35.949	41.079	54.196	60.907	65.171	69.023	73.683	76.969
49	27.249	28.941	31.555	33.930	36.818	42.010	55.265	62.038	66.339	70.222	74.919	78.231
50	27.991	29.707	32.357	34.764	37.689	42.942	56.334	63.167	67.505	71.420	76.154	79.490
51	28.735	30.475	33.162	35.600	38.560	43.874	57.401	64.295	68.669	72.616	77.386	80.747
52	29.481	31.246	33.968	36.437	39.433	44.808	58.468	65.422	69.832	73.810	78.616	82.001
53	30.230	32.018	34.776	37.276	40.308	45.741	59.534	66.548	70.993	75.002	79.843	83.253
54	30.981	32.793	35.586	38.116	41.183	46.676	60.600	67.673	72.153	76.192	81.069	84.502
55	31.735	33.570	36.398	38.958	42.060	47.610	61.665	68.796	73.311	77.380	82.292	85.749
56	32.490	34.350	37.212	39.801	42.937	48.546	62.729	69.919	74.468	78.567	83.513	86.994
57	33.248	35.131	38.027	40.646	43.816	49.482	63.793	71.040	75.624	79.752	84.733	88.236
58	34.008	35.913	38.844	41.492	44.696	50.419	64.857	72.160	76.778	80.936	85.950	89.477
59	34.770	36.698	39.662	42.339	45.577	51.356	65.919	73.279	77.931	82.117	87.166	90.715
60	35.534	37.485	40.482	43.188	46.459	52.294	66.981	74.397	79.082	83.298	88.379	91.952

For a particular number of degrees of freedom, each entry represents the critical value of χ^2 corresponding to a specified upper tail area, α.

For larger values of degrees of freedom (df), the expression $z = \sqrt{2\chi^2} - \sqrt{2(df) - 1}$ may be used and the resulting upper tail area can be obtained from the table of the standardised normal distribution.

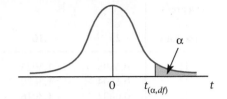

Table 4	**t distribution**

Degrees of freedom	Upper tail area					
	.25	.10	.05	.025	.01	.005
1	1.0000	3.0777	6.3138	12.7062	31.8207	63.6574
2	0.8165	1.8856	2.9200	4.3027	6.9646	9.9248
3	0.7649	1.6377	2.3534	3.1824	4.5407	5.8409
4	0.7407	1.5332	2.1318	2.7764	3.7469	4.6041
5	0.7267	1.4759	2.0150	2.5706	3.3649	4.0322
6	0.7176	1.4398	1.9432	2.4469	3.1427	3.7074
7	0.7111	1.4149	1.8946	2.3646	2.9980	3.4995
8	0.7064	1.3968	1.8595	2.3060	2.8965	3.3554
9	0.7027	1.3830	1.8331	2.2622	2.8214	3.2498
10	0.6998	1.3722	1.8125	2.2281	2.7638	3.1693
11	0.6974	1.3634	1.7959	2.2010	2.7181	3.1058
12	0.6955	1.3562	1.7823	2.1788	2.6810	3.0545
13	0.6938	1.3502	1.7709	2.1604	2.6503	3.0123
14	0.6924	1.3450	1.7613	2,1448	2.6245	2.9768
15	0.6912	1.3406	1.7531	2.1315	2.6025	2.9467
16	0.6901	1.3368	1.7459	2.1199	2.5835	2.9208
17	0.6892	1.3334	1.7396	2.1098	2.5669	2.8982
18	0.6884	1.3304	1.7341	2.1009	2.5524	2.8784
19	0.6876	1.3277	1.7291	2.0930	2.5395	2.8609
20	0.6870	1.3253	1.7247	2.0860	2.5280	2.8453
21	0.6864	1.3232	1.7207	2.0796	2.5177	2.8314
22	0.6858	1.3212	1.7171	2.0739	2.5083	2.8188
23	0.6853	1.3195	1.7139	2.0687	2.4999	2.8073
24	0.6848	1.3178	1.7109	2.0639	2.4922	2.7969
25	0.6844	1.3163	1.7081	2.0595	2.4851	2.7874
26	0.6840	1.3150	1.7056	2.0555	2.4786	2.7787
27	0.6837	1.3137	1.7033	2.0518	2.4727	2.7707
28	0.6834	1.3125	1.7011	2.0484	2.4671	2.7633
29	0.6830	1.3114	1.6991	2.0452	2.4620	2.7564
30	0.6828	1.3104	1.6973	2.0423	2.4573	2.7500
31	0.6825	1.3095	1.6955	2.0395	2.4528	2.7440
32	0.6822	1.3086	1.6939	2.0369	2.4487	2.7385
33	0.6820	1.3077	1.6924	2.0345	2.4448	2.7333
34	0.6818	1.3070	1.6909	2.0322	2.4411	2.7284
35	0.6816	1.3062	1.6896	2.0301	2.4377	2.7238
36	0.6814	1.3055	1.6883	2.0281	2.4345	2.7195
37	0.6812	1.3049	1.6871	2.0262	2.4314	2.7154
38	0.6810	1.3042	1.6860	2.0244	2.4286	2.7116
39	0.6808	1.3036	1.6849	2.0227	2.4258	2.7079
40	0.6807	1.3031	1.6839	2.0211	2.4233	2.7045

Degrees of freedom	Upper tail area					
	.25	.10	.05	.025	.01	.005
41	0.6805	1.3025	1.6829	2.0195	2.4208	2.7012
42	0.6804	1.3020	1.6820	2.0181	2.4185	2.6981
43	0.6802	1.3016	1.6811	2.0167	2.4163	2.6951
44	0.6801	1.3011	1.6802	2.0154	2.4141	2.6923
45	0.6800	1.3006	1.6794	2.0141	2.4121	2.6896
46	0.6799	1.3002	1.6787	2.0129	2.4102	2.6870
47	0.6797	1.2998	1.6779	2.0117	2.4083	2.6846
48	0.6796	1.2994	1.6772	2.0106	2.4066	2.6822
49	0.6795	1.2991	1.6766	2.0096	2.4049	2.6800
50	0.6794	1.2987	1.6759	2.0086	2.4033	2.6778
51	0.6793	1.2984	1.6753	2.0076	2.4017	2.6757
52	0.6792	1.2980	1.6747	2.0066	2.4002	2.6737
53	0.6791	1.2977	1.6741	2.0057	2.3988	2.6718
54	0.6791	1.2974	1.6736	2.0049	2.3974	2.6700
55	0.6790	1.2971	1.6730	2.0040	2.3961	2.6682
56	0.6789	1.2969	1.6725	2.0032	2.3948	2.6665
57	0.6788	1.2966	1.6720	2.0025	2.3936	2.6649
58	0.6787	1.2963	1.6716	2.0017	2.3924	2.6633
59	0.6787	1.2961	1.6711	2.0010	2.3912	2.6618
60	0.6786	1.2958	1.6706	2.0003	2.3901	2.6603
61	0.6785	1.2956	1.6702	1.9996	2.3890	2.6589
62	0.6785	1.2954	1.6698	1.9990	2.3880	2.6575
63	0.6784	1.2951	1.6694	1.9983	2.3870	2.6561
64	0.6783	1.2949	1.6690	1.9977	2.3860	2.6549
65	0.6783	1.2947	1.6686	1.9971	2.3851	2.6536
66	0.6782	1.2945	1.6683	1.9966	2.3842	2.6524
67	0.6782	1.2943	1.6679	1.9960	2.3833	2.6512
68	0.6781	1.2941	1.6676	1.9955	2.3824	2.6501
69	0.6781	1.2939	1.6672	1.9949	2.3816	2.6490
70	0.6780	1.2938	1.6669	1.9944	2.3808	2.6479
71	0.6780	1.2936	1.6666	1.9939	2.3800	2.6469
72	0.6779	1.2934	1.6663	1.9935	2.3793	2.6459
73	0.6779	1.2933	1.6660	1.9930	2.3785	2.6449
74	0.6778	1.2931	1.6657	1.9925	2.3778	2.6439
75	0.6778	1.2929	1.6654	1.9921	2.3771	2.6430
76	0.6777	1.2928	1.6652	1.9917	2.3764	2.6421
77	0.6777	1.2926	1.6649	1.9913	2.3758	2.6412
78	0.6776	1.2925	1.6646	1.9908	2.3751	2.6403
79	0.6776	1.2924	1.6644	1.9905	2.3745	2.6395
80	0.6776	1.2922	1.6641	1.9901	2.3739	2.6387
81	0.6775	1.2921	1.6639	1.9897	2.3733	2.6379
82	0.6775	1.2920	1.6636	1.9893	2.3727	2.6371
83	0.6775	1.2918	1.6634	1.9890	2.3721	2.6364
84	0.6774	1.2917	1.6632	1.9886	2.3716	2.6356
85	0.6774	1.2916	1.6630	1.9883	2.3710	2.6349
86	0.6774	1.2915	1.6628	1.9879	2.3705	2.6342
87	0.6773	1.2914	1.6626	1.9876	2.3700	2.6335
88	0.6773	1.2912	1.6624	1.9873	2.3695	2.6329
89	0.6773	1.2911	1.6622	1.9870	2.3690	2.6322
90	0.6772	1.2910	1.6620	1.9867	2.3685	2.6316
91	0.6772	1.2909	1.6618	1.9864	2.3680	2.6309
92	0.6772	1.2908	1.6616	1.9861	2.3676	2.6303
93	0.6771	1.2907	1.6614	1.9858	2.3671	2.6297
94	0.6771	1.2906	1.6612	1.9855	2.3667	2.6291

Degrees of freedom	Upper tail area					
	.25	.10	.05	.025	.01	.005
95	0.6771	1.2905	1.6611	1.9853	2.3662	2.6286
96	0.6771	1.2904	1.6609	1.9850	2.3658	2.6280
97	0.6770	1.2903	1.6607	1.9847	2.3654	2.6275
98	0.6770	1.2902	1.6606	1.9845	2.3650	2.6269
99	0.6770	1.2902	1.6604	1.9842	2.3646	2.6264
100	0.6770	1.2901	1.6602	1.9840	2.3642	2.6259
110	0.6767	1.2893	1.6588	1.9818	2.3607	2.6213
120	0.6765	1.2886	1.6577	1.9799	2.3578	2.6174
130	0.6764	1.2881	1.6567	1.9784	2.3554	2.6142
140	0.6762	1.2876	1.6558	1.9771	2.3533	2.6114
150	0.6761	1.2872	1.6551	1.9759	2.3515	2.6090
α	0.6745	1.2816	1.6449	1.9600	2.3263	2.5758

For a particular number of degrees of freedom, each entry represents the critical value of t corresponding to a specified upper tail area α.

α = .05

$F_{(\alpha, df_1, df_2)}$

Table 5   F distribution

Numerator df_1

Denominator df_2	1	2	3	4	5	6	7	8	9	10	12	15	20	24	30	40	60	120	∞
1	161.4	199.5	215.7	224.6	230.2	234.0	236.8	238.9	240.5	241.9	243.9	245.9	248.0	249.1	250.1	251.1	252.2	253.3	254.3
2	18.51	19.00	19.16	19.25	19.30	19.33	19.35	19.37	19.38	19.40	19.41	19.43	19.45	19.45	19.46	19.47	19.48	19.49	19.50
3	10.13	9.55	9.28	9.12	9.01	8.94	8.89	8.85	8.81	8.79	8.74	8.70	8.66	8.64	8.62	8.59	8.57	8.55	8.53
4	7.71	6.94	6.59	6.39	6.26	6.16	6.09	6.04	6.00	5.96	5.91	5.86	5.80	5.77	5.75	5.72	5.69	5.66	5.63
5	6.61	5.79	5.41	5.19	5.05	4.95	4.88	4.82	4.77	4.74	4.68	4.62	4.56	4.53	4.50	4.46	4.43	4.40	4.36
6	5.99	5.14	4.76	4.53	4.39	4.28	4.21	4.15	4.10	4.06	4.00	3.94	3.87	3.84	3.81	3.77	3.74	3.70	3.67
7	5.59	4.74	4.35	4.12	3.97	3.87	3.79	3.73	3.68	3.64	3.57	3.51	3.44	3.41	3.38	3.34	3.30	3.27	3.23
8	5.32	4.46	4.07	3.84	3.69	3.58	3.50	3.44	3.39	3.35	3.28	3.22	3.15	3.12	3.08	3.04	3.01	2.97	2.93
9	5.12	4.26	3.86	3.63	3.48	3.37	3.29	3.23	3.18	3.14	3.07	3.01	2.94	2.90	2.86	2.83	2.79	2.75	2.71
10	4.96	4.10	3.71	3.48	3.33	3.22	3.14	3.07	3.02	2.98	2.91	2.85	2.77	2.74	2.70	2.66	2.62	2.58	2.54
11	4.84	3.98	3.59	3.36	3.20	3.09	3.01	2.95	2.90	2.85	2.79	2.72	2.65	2.61	2.57	2.53	2.49	2.45	2.40
12	4.75	3.89	3.49	3.26	3.11	3.00	2.91	2.85	2.80	2.75	2.69	2.62	2.54	2.51	2.47	2.43	2.38	2.34	2.30
13	4.67	3.81	3.41	3.18	3.03	2.92	2.83	2.77	2.71	2.67	2.60	2.53	2.46	2.42	2.38	2.34	2.30	2.25	2.21
14	4.60	3.74	3.34	3.11	2.96	2.85	2.76	2.70	2.65	2.60	2.53	2.46	2.39	2.35	2.31	2.27	2.22	2.18	2.13
15	4.54	3.68	3.29	3.06	2.90	2.79	2.71	2.64	2.59	2.54	2.48	2.40	2.33	2.29	2.25	2.20	2.16	2.11	2.07
16	4.49	3.63	3.24	3.01	2.85	2.74	2.66	2.59	2.54	2.49	2.42	2.35	2.28	2.24	2.19	2.15	2.11	2.06	2.01
17	4.45	3.59	3.20	2.96	2.81	2.70	2.61	2.55	2.49	2.45	2.38	2.31	2.23	2.19	2.15	2.10	2.06	2.01	1.96
18	4.41	3.55	3.16	2.93	2.77	2.66	2.58	2.51	2.46	2.41	2.34	2.27	2.19	2.15	2.11	2.06	2.02	1.97	1.92
19	4.38	3.52	3.13	2.90	2.74	2.63	2.54	2.48	2.42	2.38	2.31	2.23	2.16	2.11	2.07	2.03	1.98	1.93	1.88
20	4.35	3.49	3.10	2.87	2.71	2.60	2.51	2.45	2.39	2.35	2.28	2.20	2.12	2.08	2.04	1.99	1.95	1.90	1.84
21	4.32	3.47	3.07	2.84	2.68	2.57	2.49	2.42	2.37	2.32	2.25	2.18	2.10	2.05	2.01	1.96	1.92	1.87	1.81
22	4.30	3.44	3.05	2.82	2.66	2.55	2.46	2.40	2.34	2.30	2.23	2.15	2.07	2.03	1.98	1.94	1.89	1.84	1.78
23	4.28	3.42	3.03	2.80	2.64	2.53	2.44	2.37	2.32	2.27	2.20	2.13	2.05	2.01	1.96	1.91	1.86	1.81	1.76
24	4.26	3.40	3.01	2.78	2.62	2.51	2.42	2.36	2.30	2.25	2.18	2.11	2.03	1.98	1.94	1.89	1.84	1.79	1.73
25	4.24	3.39	2.99	2.76	2.60	2.49	2.40	2.34	2.28	2.24	2.16	2.09	2.01	1.96	1.92	1.87	1.82	1.77	1.71
26	4.23	3.37	2.98	2.74	2.59	2.47	2.39	2.32	2.27	2.22	2.15	2.07	1.99	1.95	1.90	1.85	1.80	1.75	1.69
27	4.21	3.35	2.96	2.73	2.57	2.46	2.37	2.31	2.25	2.20	2.13	2.06	1.97	1.93	1.88	1.84	1.79	1.73	1.67
28	4.20	3.34	2.95	2.71	2.56	2.45	2.36	2.29	2.24	2.19	2.12	2.04	1.96	1.91	1.87	1.82	1.77	1.71	1.65
29	4.18	3.33	2.93	2.70	2.55	2.43	2.35	2.28	2.22	2.18	2.10	2.03	1.94	1.90	1.85	1.81	1.75	1.70	1.64
30	4.17	3.32	2.92	2.69	2.53	2.42	2.33	2.27	2.21	2.16	2.09	2.01	1.93	1.89	1.84	1.79	1.74	1.68	1.62
40	4.08	3.23	2.84	2.61	2.45	2.34	2.25	2.18	2.12	2.08	2.00	1.92	1.84	1.79	1.74	1.69	1.64	1.58	1.51
60	4.00	3.15	2.76	2.53	2.37	2.25	2.17	2.10	2.04	1.99	1.92	1.84	1.75	1.70	1.65	1.59	1.53	1.47	1.39
120	3.92	3.07	2.68	2.45	2.29	2.17	2.09	2.02	1.96	1.91	1.83	1.75	1.66	1.61	1.55	1.50	1.43	1.35	1.25
∞	3.84	3.00	2.60	2.37	2.21	2.10	2.01	1.94	1.88	1.83	1.75	1.67	1.57	1.52	1.46	1.39	1.32	1.22	1.00

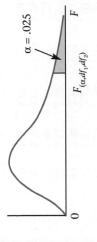

$\alpha = .025$

$F_{(\alpha,df_1,df_2)}$

Numerator df_1

Denominator df_2	1	2	3	4	5	6	7	8	9	10	12	15	20	24	30	40	60	120	∞
1	647.8	799.5	864.2	899.6	921.8	937.1	948.2	956.7	963.3	968.6	976.7	984.9	993.1	997.2	1001	1006	1010	1014	1018
2	38.51	39.00	39.17	39.25	39.30	39.33	39.36	39.37	39.39	39.40	39.41	39.43	39.45	39.46	39.46	39.47	39.48	39.49	39.50
3	17.44	16.04	15.44	15.10	14.88	14.73	14.62	14.54	14.47	14.42	14.34	14.25	14.17	14.12	14.08	14.04	13.99	13.95	13.90
4	12.22	10.65	9.98	9.60	9.36	9.20	9.07	8.98	8.90	8.84	8.75	8.66	8.56	8.51	8.46	8.41	8.36	8.31	8.26
5	10.01	8.43	7.76	7.39	7.15	6.98	6.85	6.76	6.68	6.62	6.52	6.43	6.33	6.28	6.23	6.18	6.12	6.07	6.02
6	8.81	7.26	6.60	6.23	5.99	5.82	5.70	5.60	5.52	5.46	5.37	5.27	5.17	5.12	5.07	5.01	4.96	4.90	4.85
7	8.07	6.54	5.89	5.52	5.29	5.12	4.99	4.90	4.82	4.76	4.67	4.57	4.47	4.42	4.36	4.31	4.25	4.20	4.14
8	7.57	6.06	5.42	5.05	4.82	4.65	4.53	4.43	4.36	4.30	4.20	4.10	4.00	3.95	3.89	3.84	3.78	3.73	3.67
9	7.21	5.71	5.08	4.72	4.48	4.32	4.20	4.10	4.03	3.96	3.87	3.77	3.67	3.61	3.56	3.51	3.45	3.39	3.33
10	6.94	5.46	4.83	4.47	4.24	4.07	3.95	3.85	3.78	3.72	3.62	3.52	3.42	3.37	3.31	3.26	3.20	3.14	3.08
11	6.72	5.26	4.63	4.28	4.04	3.88	3.76	3.66	3.59	3.53	3.43	3.33	3.23	3.17	3.12	3.06	3.00	2.94	2.88
12	6.55	5.10	4.47	4.12	3.89	3.73	3.61	3.51	3.44	3.37	3.28	3.18	3.07	3.02	2.96	2.91	2.85	2.79	2.72
13	6.41	4.97	4.35	4.00	3.77	3.60	3.48	3.39	3.31	3.25	3.15	3.05	2.95	2.89	2.84	2.78	2.72	2.66	2.60
14	6.30	4.86	4.24	3.89	3.66	3.50	3.38	3.29	3.21	3.15	3.05	2.95	2.84	2.79	2.73	2.67	2.61	2.55	2.49
15	6.20	4.77	4.15	3.80	3.58	3.41	3.29	3.20	3.12	3.06	2.96	2.86	2.76	2.70	2.64	2.59	2.52	2.46	2.40
16	6.12	4.69	4.08	3.73	3.50	3.34	3.22	3.12	3.05	2.99	2.89	2.79	2.68	2.63	2.57	2.51	2.45	2.38	2.32
17	6.04	4.62	4.01	3.66	3.44	3.28	3.16	3.06	2.98	2.92	2.82	2.72	2.62	2.56	2.50	2.44	2.38	2.32	2.25
18	5.98	4.56	3.95	3.61	3.38	3.22	3.10	3.01	2.93	2.87	2.77	2.67	2.56	2.50	2.44	2.38	2.32	2.26	2.19
19	5.92	4.51	3.90	3.56	3.33	3.17	3.05	2.96	2.88	2.82	2.72	2.62	2.51	2.45	2.39	2.33	2.27	2.20	2.13
20	5.87	4.46	3.86	3.51	3.29	3.13	3.01	2.91	2.84	2.77	2.68	2.57	2.46	2.41	2.35	2.29	2.22	2.16	2.09
21	5.83	4.42	3.82	3.48	3.25	3.09	2.97	2.87	2.80	2.73	2.64	2.53	2.42	2.37	2.31	2.25	2.18	2.11	2.04
22	5.79	4.38	3.78	3.44	3.22	3.05	2.93	2.84	2.76	2.70	2.60	2.50	2.39	2.33	2.27	2.21	2.14	2.08	2.00
23	5.75	4.35	3.75	3.41	3.18	3.02	2.90	2.81	2.73	2.67	2.57	2.47	2.36	2.30	2.24	2.18	2.11	2.04	1.97
24	5.72	4.32	3.72	3.38	3.15	2.99	2.87	2.78	2.70	2.64	2.54	2.44	2.33	2.27	2.21	2.15	2.08	2.01	1.94
25	5.69	4.29	3.69	3.35	3.13	2.97	2.85	2.75	2.68	2.61	2.51	2.41	2.30	2.24	2.18	2.12	2.05	1.98	1.91
26	5.66	4.27	3.67	3.33	3.10	2.94	2.82	2.73	2.65	2.59	2.49	2.39	2.28	2.22	2.16	2.09	2.03	1.95	1.88
27	5.63	4.24	3.65	3.31	3.08	2.92	2.80	2.71	2.63	2.57	2.47	2.36	2.25	2.19	2.13	2.07	2.00	1.93	1.85
28	5.61	4.22	3.63	3.29	3.06	2.90	2.78	2.69	2.61	2.55	2.45	2.34	2.23	2.17	2.11	2.05	1.98	1.91	1.83
29	5.59	4.20	3.61	3.27	3.04	2.88	2.76	2.67	2.59	2.53	2.43	2.32	2.21	2.15	2.09	2.03	1.96	1.89	1.81
30	5.57	4.18	3.59	3.25	3.03	2.87	2.75	2.65	2.57	2.51	2.41	2.31	2.20	2.14	2.07	2.01	1.94	1.87	1.79
40	5.42	4.05	3.46	3.13	2.90	2.74	2.62	2.53	2.45	2.39	2.29	2.18	2.07	2.01	1.94	1.88	1.80	1.72	1.64
60	5.29	3.93	3.34	3.01	2.79	2.63	2.51	2.41	2.33	2.27	2.17	2.06	1.94	1.88	1.82	1.74	1.67	1.58	1.48
120	5.15	3.80	3.23	2.89	2.67	2.52	2.39	2.30	2.22	2.16	2.05	1.94	1.82	1.76	1.69	1.61	1.53	1.43	1.31
∞	5.02	3.69	3.12	2.79	2.57	2.41	2.29	2.19	2.11	2.05	1.94	1.83	1.71	1.64	1.57	1.48	1.39	1.27	1.00

$\alpha = .01$

$F_{(\alpha, df_1, df_2)}$

Numerator df_1

Denominator df_2	1	2	3	4	5	6	7	8	9	10	12	15	20	24	30	40	60	120	∞
1	4052	4999.5	5403	5625	5764	5859	5928	5982	6022	6056	6106	6157	6209	6235	6261	6287	6313	6339	6366
2	98.50	99.00	99.17	99.25	99.30	99.33	99.36	99.37	99.39	99.40	99.42	99.43	99.45	99.46	99.47	99.47	99.48	99.49	99.50
3	34.12	30.82	29.46	28.71	28.24	27.91	27.67	27.49	27.35	27.23	27.05	26.87	26.69	26.60	26.50	26.41	26.32	26.22	26.13
4	21.20	18.00	16.69	15.98	15.52	15.21	14.98	14.80	14.66	14.55	14.37	14.20	14.02	13.93	13.84	13.75	13.65	13.56	13.46
5	16.26	13.27	12.06	11.39	10.97	10.67	10.46	10.29	10.16	10.05	9.89	9.72	9.55	9.47	9.38	9.29	9.20	9.11	9.02
6	13.75	10.92	9.78	9.15	8.75	8.47	8.26	8.10	7.98	7.87	7.72	7.56	7.40	7.31	7.23	7.14	7.06	6.97	6.88
7	12.25	9.55	8.45	7.85	7.46	7.19	6.99	6.84	6.72	6.62	6.47	6.31	6.16	6.07	5.99	5.91	5.82	5.74	5.65
8	11.26	8.65	7.59	7.01	6.63	6.37	6.18	6.03	5.91	5.81	5.67	5.52	5.36	5.28	5.20	5.12	5.03	4.95	4.86
9	10.56	8.02	6.99	6.42	6.06	5.80	5.61	5.47	5.35	5.26	5.11	4.96	4.81	4.73	4.65	4.57	4.48	4.40	4.31
10	10.04	7.56	6.55	5.99	5.64	5.39	5.20	5.06	4.94	4.85	4.71	4.56	4.41	4.33	4.25	4.17	4.08	4.00	3.91
11	9.65	7.21	6.22	5.67	5.32	5.07	4.89	4.74	4.63	4.54	4.40	4.25	4.10	4.02	3.94	3.86	3.78	3.69	3.60
12	9.33	6.93	5.95	5.41	5.06	4.82	4.64	4.50	4.39	4.30	4.16	4.01	3.86	3.78	3.70	3.62	3.54	3.45	3.36
13	9.07	6.70	5.74	5.21	4.86	4.62	4.44	4.30	4.19	4.10	3.96	3.82	3.66	3.59	3.51	3.43	3.34	3.25	3.17
14	8.86	6.51	5.56	5.04	4.69	4.46	4.28	4.14	4.03	3.94	3.80	3.66	3.51	3.43	3.35	3.27	3.18	3.09	3.00
15	8.68	6.36	5.42	4.89	4.56	4.32	4.14	4.00	3.89	3.80	3.67	3.52	3.37	3.29	3.21	3.13	3.05	2.96	2.87
16	8.53	6.23	5.29	4.77	4.44	4.20	4.03	3.89	3.78	3.69	3.55	3.41	3.26	3.18	3.10	3.02	2.93	2.84	2.75
17	8.40	6.11	5.18	4.67	4.34	4.10	3.93	3.79	3.68	3.59	3.46	3.31	3.16	3.08	3.00	2.92	2.83	2.75	2.65
18	8.29	6.01	5.09	4.58	4.25	4.01	3.84	3.71	3.60	3.51	3.37	3.23	3.08	3.00	2.92	2.84	2.75	2.66	2.57
19	8.18	5.93	5.01	4.50	4.17	3.94	3.77	3.63	3.52	3.43	3.30	3.15	3.00	2.92	2.84	2.76	2.67	2.58	2.49
20	8.10	5.85	4.94	4.43	4.10	3.87	3.70	3.56	3.46	3.37	3.23	3.09	2.94	2.86	2.78	2.69	2.61	2.52	2.42
21	8.02	5.78	4.87	4.37	4.04	3.81	3.64	3.51	3.40	3.31	3.17	3.03	2.88	2.80	2.72	2.64	2.55	2.46	2.36
22	7.95	5.72	4.82	4.31	3.99	3.76	3.59	3.45	3.35	3.26	3.12	2.98	2.83	2.75	2.67	2.58	2.50	2.40	2.31
23	7.88	5.66	4.76	4.26	3.94	3.71	3.54	3.41	3.30	3.21	3.07	2.93	2.78	2.70	2.62	2.54	2.45	2.35	2.26
24	7.82	5.61	4.72	4.22	3.90	3.67	3.50	3.36	3.26	3.17	3.03	2.89	2.74	2.66	2.58	2.49	2.40	2.31	2.21
25	7.77	5.57	4.68	4.18	3.85	3.63	3.46	3.32	3.22	3.13	2.99	2.85	2.70	2.62	2.54	2.45	2.36	2.27	2.17
26	7.72	5.53	4.64	4.14	3.82	3.59	3.42	3.29	3.18	3.09	2.96	2.81	2.66	2.58	2.50	2.42	2.33	2.23	2.13
27	7.68	5.49	4.60	4.11	3.78	3.56	3.39	3.26	3.15	3.06	2.93	2.78	2.63	2.55	2.47	2.38	2.29	2.20	2.10
28	7.64	5.45	4.57	4.07	3.75	3.53	3.36	3.23	3.12	3.03	2.90	2.75	2.60	2.52	2.44	2.35	2.26	2.17	2.06
29	7.60	5.42	4.54	4.04	3.73	3.50	3.33	3.20	3.09	3.00	2.87	2.73	2.57	2.49	2.41	2.33	2.23	2.14	2.03
30	7.56	5.39	4.51	4.02	3.70	3.47	3.30	3.17	3.07	2.98	2.84	2.70	2.55	2.47	2.39	2.30	2.21	2.11	2.01
40	7.31	5.18	4.31	3.83	3.51	3.29	3.12	2.99	2.89	2.80	2.66	2.52	2.37	2.29	2.20	2.11	2.02	1.92	1.80
60	7.08	4.98	4.13	3.65	3.34	3.12	2.95	2.82	2.72	2.63	2.50	2.35	2.20	2.12	2.03	1.94	1.84	1.73	1.60
120	6.85	4.79	3.95	3.48	3.17	2.96	2.79	2.66	2.56	2.47	2.34	2.19	2.03	1.95	1.86	1.76	1.66	1.53	1.38
∞	6.63	4.61	3.78	3.32	3.02	2.80	2.64	2.51	2.41	2.32	2.18	2.04	1.88	1.79	1.70	1.59	1.47	1.32	1.00

For a particular combination of numerator and denominator degrees of freedom, each entry represents the critical value of F corresponding to a specified upper tail area α.

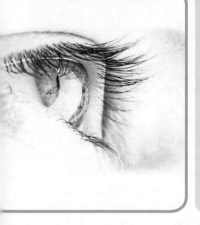

Glossary

A

A posteriori contrasts Contrasts made after conducting the analysis. These are generally multiple comparison tests.

A priori contrasts Contrasts determined before conducting the analysis, based on the researcher's theoretical framework.

Access panel A general 'pool' of individuals or households who have agreed to be available for surveys of widely varying types and topics.

Action research A team research process, facilitated by a professional researcher(s), linking with decision-makers and other stakeholders who together wish to improve particular situations.

Agglomerative clustering A hierarchical clustering procedure where each object starts out in a separate cluster. Clusters are formed by grouping objects into bigger and bigger clusters.

Alpha error (α) See Type I error.

Alternative hypothesis A statement that some difference or effect is expected. Accepting the alternative hypothesis will lead to changes in opinions or actions.

Alternative-forms reliability An approach for assessing reliability that requires two equivalent forms of the scale to be constructed and then the same participants to be measured at two different times.

Analysis of covariance (ANCOVA) An advanced ANOVA procedure in which the effects of one or more metric-scaled extraneous variables are removed from the dependent variable before conducting the ANOVA.

Analysis of variance (ANOVA) A statistical technique for examining the differences among means for two or more populations.

Analysis sample Part of the total sample used to check the results of the discriminant function.

Analytical model An explicit specification of a set of variables and their interrelationships designed to represent some real system or process in whole or in part.

Analytical services Companies that provide guidance in the development of research design.

Area sampling A common form of cluster sampling in which the clusters consist of geographical areas such as counties, housing tracts, blocks or other area descriptions.

Association techniques A type of projective technique in which participants are presented with a stimulus and are asked to respond with the first thing that comes to mind.

Asymmetric lambda A measure of the percentage improvement in predicting the value of the dependent variable given the value of the independent variable in contingency table analysis. Lambda also varies between 0 and 1.

Audit A data collection process derived from physical records or performing inventory analysis. Data are collected personally by the researcher, or by representatives of the researcher, and are based on counts usually of physical objects rather than people.

Average linkage A linkage method based on the average distance between all pairs of objects, where one member of the pair is from each of the clusters.

B

Back translation A translation technique that translates a questionnaire from the base language by a translator whose native language is the one into which the questionnaire is being translated. This version is then retranslated back into the original language by someone whose native language is the base language. Translation errors can then be identified.

Balanced scale A scale with an equal number of favourable and unfavourable categories.

Bar chart A chart that displays data in bars positioned horizontally or vertically.

Bayesian approach A selection method where the elements are selected sequentially. The Bayesian approach explicitly incorporates prior information about population parameters as well as the costs and probabilities associated with making wrong decisions.

Beta error (β) See Type II error.

Bibliographic databases Databases composed of citations to articles in journals, magazines, newspapers, marketing research studies, technical reports, government documents, and the like. They often provide summaries or abstracts of the material cited.

Binary logit model The binary logit model commonly deals with the issue of how likely an observation is to belong to each group. It estimates the probability of an observation belonging to a particular group.

Binominal test A goodness-of-fit statistical test for dichotomous variables. It tests the goodness of fit of the observed number of observations in each category to the number expected under a specified binominal distribution.

Bivariate regression A procedure for deriving a mathematical relationship, in the form of an equation, between a single metric-dependent variable and a single metric-independent variable.

Blog and buzz mining Provide the means to observe, track or initiate views in research communities, social networks and anywhere else that people post comments, visuals, music and other forms of art on the internet.

Branching question A question used to guide an interviewer (or participant) through a survey by directing the interviewer (or participant) to different spots on the questionnaire depending on the answers given.

Branded market research products Specialised data collection and analysis procedures developed to address specific types of marketing research problems.

Broad statement of the problem The initial statement of the marketing research problem that provides an appropriate perspective on the problem.

Buzz score Is based on the total number of people searching for specific subjects on web search engines.

C

Carryover effects Where the evaluation of a particular scaled item significantly affects the participant's judgement of subsequent scaled items.

Cartoon tests Cartoon characters are shown in a s pecific situation related to the problem. Participants are asked to indicate the dialogue that one cartoon character might make in response to the comment(s) of another character.

Case study A detailed study based upon the observation of the intrinsic details of individuals, groups of individuals and organisations.

Casewise deletion A method for handling missing responses in which cases or participant's with any missing responses are discarded from the analysis.

Category equivalence A construct equivalence issue that deals specifically with whether the categories in which brands, products and behaviour are grouped are the same in different countries.

Causal research A type of conclusive research where the major objective is to obtain evidence regarding cause-and-effect (causal) relationships.

Causality Causality applies when the occurrence of X increases the probability of the occurrence of Y.

Census A complete enumeration of the elements of a population or study objects.

Centroid method A variance method of hierarchical clustering in which the distance between two clusters is the distance between their centroids (means for all the variables).

Characteristic profile An aid to interpreting discriminant analysis results by describing each group in terms of the group means for the predictor variables.

Chi-square distribution A skewed distribution whose shape depends solely on the number of degrees of freedom. As the number of degrees of freedom increases, the chi-square distribution becomes more symmetrical.

Chi-square statistic The statistic used to test the statistical significance of the observed association in a cross-tabulation. It assists us in determining whether a systematic association exists between the two variables.

Classification information Socio-economic and demographic characteristics used to classify respondents.

Cluster sampling A two-step probability sampling technique where the target population is first divided into mutually exclusive and collectively exhaustive subpopulations called clusters, and then a random sample of clusters is selected based on a probability sampling technique such as SRS. For each selected cluster, either all the elements are included in the sample, or a sample of elements is drawn probabilistically.

Co-creation The practice of developing new designs including products or marketing communications through collaboration with consumers.

Codebook A book containing coding instructions and the necessary information about the questions and potential answers in a survey.

Coding Assigning a code to represent a specific response to a specific question along with the data record and column position that the code will occupy.

Coding and data entry services Companies whose primary service offering is their expertise in converting completed surveys or interviews into a usable database for conducting statistical analysis.

Coding data Breaking down qualitative data into discrete chunks and attaching a reference to those chunks of data.

Coding data in grounded theory A form of shorthand that distills events and meanings without losing their essential properties.

Coefficient alpha A measure of internal consistency reliability that is the average of all possible split-half coefficients resulting from different splittings of the scale items.

Coefficient of variation A useful expression in sampling theory for the standard deviation as a percentage of the mean.

Cohort analysis A multiple cross-sectional design consisting of surveys conducted at appropriate time intervals. The cohort refers to the group of participants who experience the same event within the same interval.

Common factor analysis An approach to factor analysis that estimates the factors based only on the common variance. Also called principal axis factoring.

Communality Communality is the variance of a measured variance that is explained by the construct on which it loads.

Comparative scales One of two types of scaling technique in which there is direct comparison of stimulus objects with one another.

Complete linkage A linkage method that is based on maximum distance of the farthest neighbour approach.

Completion rate The percentage of qualified participants who complete the interview. It enables researchers to take into account anticipated refusals by people who qualify.

Completion technique A projective technique that requires particpants to complete an incomplete stimulus situation.

Conceptual equivalence A construct equivalence issue that deals with whether the interpretation of brands, products, consumer behaviour and the marketing effort are the same in different countries.

Conceptual map A way to link the broad statement of the marketing decision problem to the marketing research problem.

Conclusive research A research design characterised by the measurement of clearly defined marketing phenomena.

Concomitant variation A condition for inferring causality that requires that the extent to which a cause, X, and an effect, Y, occur together or vary together is predicted by the hypothesis under consideration.

Concurrent validity A type of validity that is assessed when the data on the scale being evaluated and on the criterion variables are collected at the same time.

Confidence intervals The range into which the true population parameter will fall, assuming a given level of confidence.

Configural equivalence Concerns the relationships of measured items to the latent constructs and implies that the patterns of factor loadings should be the same across countries or cultural units.

Confounding variables Variables used to illustrate that extraneous variables can confound the results by influencing the dependent variable; synonymous with extraneous variables.

Conjoint analysis A technique that attempts to determine the relative importance consumers attach to salient attributes and the utilities they attach to the levels of attributes.

Conjoint analysis model The mathematical model expressing the fundamental relationship between attributes and utility in conjoint analysis.

Consistency checks A part of the data cleaning process that identifies data that are out of range, logically inconsistent or have extreme values. Data with values not defined by the coding scheme are inadmissible.

Constant sum scaling A comparative scaling technique in which respondents are required to allocate a constant sum of units such as points, euros, chits, stickers or chips among a set of stimulus objects with respect to some criterion.

Construct A specific type of concept that exists at a higher level of abstraction than do everyday concepts.

Construct equivalence A type of equivalence that deals with the question of whether the marketing constructs have the same meaning and significance in different countries.

Construct validity A type of validity that addresses the question of what construct or characteristic the scale is measuring. An attempt is made to answer theoretical questions of why a scale works and what deductions can be made concerning the theory underlying the scale.

Construction technique A projective technique in which participants are required to construct a response in the form of a story, dialogue or description.

Content analysis The objective, systematic and quantitative description of the manifest content of a communication.

Content validity A type of validity, sometimes called face validity, that consists of a subjective but systematic evaluation of the representativeness of the content of a scale for the measuring task at hand.

Contingency coefficient A measure of the strength of association in a table of any size.

Contingency table A cross-tabulation table. It contains a cell for every combination of categories of the two variables.

Continuous rating scale A measurement scale that has participants rate the objects by placing a mark at the appropriate position on a line that runs from one extreme of the criterion variable to the other. The form may vary considerably. Also called graphic rating scale.

Contrasts In ANOVA, a method of examining differences among two or more means of the treatment groups.

Contrived observation Observing behaviour in an artificial environment.

Controlled test market A test-marketing programme conducted by an outside research company in field experimentation. The research company guarantees distribution of the product in retail outlets that represent a predetermined percentage of the market.

Convenience sampling A non-probability sampling technique that attempts to obtain a sample of convenient elements. The selection of sampling units is left primarily to the interviewer.

Convergent validity A measure of construct validity that measures the extent to which the scale correlates positively with other measures of the same construct.

Cookie technology A group of letters and numbers stored in a web surfer's browser that identify the browser's computer.

Correspondence analysis An MDS technique for scaling qualitative data that scales the rows and columns of the input contingency table in corresponding units so that each can be displayed in the same low-dimensional space.

Covariance A systematic relationship between two variables in which a change in one implies a corresponding change in the other ($COVxy$).

Covariate A metric-independent variable used in ANCOVA.

Cramer's V A measure of the strength of association used in tables larger than 2×2.

Criterion validity A type of validity that examines whether the measurement scale performs as expected in relation to other selected variables as meaningful criteria.

Critical request The target behaviour being researched.

Cross-cultural analysis A type of across-countries analysis in which the data could be aggregated for each country and then aggregate statistics analysed.

Cross-sectional design A type of research design involving the collection of information from any given sample of population elements only once.

Cross-tabulation A statistical technique that describes two or more variables simultaneously and results in tables that reflect the joint distribution of two or more variables that have a limited number of categories or distinct values.

Cross-validation A test of validity that examines whether a model holds on comparable data not used in the original estimation.

Customer database A database that details characteristics of customers and prospects that can include names and addresses, geographic, demographic and buying behaviour data.

Customised services Companies that tailor research procedures to best meet the needs of each client.

D

Data assembly The gathering of data from a variety of disparate sources.

Data cleaning Thorough and extensive checks for consistency and treatment of missing responses.

Data display Involves summarising and presenting the structure that is seen in collected qualitative data.

Data reduction The organising and structuring of qualitative data.

Data verification Involves seeking alternative explanations of the interpretations of qualitative data, through other data sources.

Debriefing After a disguised experiment, informing participants subjects what the experiment was about and how the experimental manipulations were performed.

Decomposition of the total variation In one-way ANOVA, separation of the variation observed in the dependent variable into the variation due to the independent variables plus the variation due to error.

Deduction A form of reasoning in which a conclusion is validly inferred from some premises, and must be true if those premises are true.

Demand artefacts Responses given because the participants attempt to guess the purpose of the experiment and respond accordingly.

Dependence techniques Multivariate techniques appropriate when one or more of the variables can be identified as dependent variables and the remaining ones as independent variables.

Dependent variables Variables that measure the effect of the independent variables on the test units.

Derived approaches In MDS, attribute-based approaches to collecting perception data requiring participants to rate the stimuli on the identified attributes using semantic differential or Likert scales.

Description The unique labels or descriptors that are used to designate each value of the scale. All scales possess description.

Descriptive research A type of conclusive research that has as its major objective the description of something, usually market characteristics or functions.

Design control A method of controlling extraneous variables that involves using specific experimental designs.

Determinism A doctrine espousing that everything that happens is determined by a necessary chain of causation.

Dichotomous question A structured question with only two response alternatives, such as yes and no.

Direct approach A type of qualitative research in which the purposes of the project are disclosed to the participant or are obvious given the nature of the interview.

Direct method An approach to discriminant analysis that involves estimating the discriminant function so that all the predictors are included simultaneously.

Directory databases Databases that provide information on individuals, organisations and services.

Discriminant analysis A technique for analysing marketing research data when the criterion or dependent variable is categorical and the predictor or independent variables are interval in nature.

Discriminant analysis model The statistical model on which discriminant analysis is based.

Discriminant function The linear combination of independent variables developed by discriminant analysis that will best discriminate between the categories of the dependent variable.

Discriminant validity A type of construct validity that assesses the extent to which a measure does not correlate with other constructs from which it is supposed to differ.

Disordinal interaction The change in the rank order of the effects of one factor across the levels of another.

Distance The characteristic of distance means that absolute differences between the scale descriptors are known and may be expressed in units.

Divisive clustering A hierarchical clustering procedure where all objects start out in one giant cluster. Clusters are formed by dividing this cluster into smaller and smaller clusters.

Double-barrelled question A single question that attempts to cover two issues. Such questions can be confusing to participants and result in ambiguous responses.

Double cross-validation A special form of validation in which the sample is split into halves. One half serves as the estimation sample and the other as a validation sample. The roles of the estimation and validation halves are then reversed and the cross-validation process is repeated.

Dummy variables A respecification procedure using variables that take on only two values, usually 0 or 1.

E

Editing A review of the questionnaires with the objective of increasing accuracy and precision.

Elbow criterion A plot of stress versus dimensionality used in MDS. The point at which an elbow or a sharp bend occurs indicates an appropriate dimensionality.

Electronic observation An observational research strategy in which electronic devices, rather than human observers, record the phenomenon being observed.

Element An object that possesses the information sought by the researcher and about which inferences are to be made.

Empiricism A theory of knowledge. A broad category of the philosophy of science that locates the source of all knowledge in experience.

Estimated or predicted value The value $Y_i = a + b_x$, where a and b are, respectively, estimators of β_0 and β_1, the corresponding population parameters.

Ethnography A research approach based upon the observation of the customs, habits and differences between people in everyday situations.

Euclidean distance The square root of the sum of the squared differences in values for each variable.

Evolving research design A research design where particular research techniques are chosen as the researcher develops an understanding of the issues and respondents.

Experiment The process of manipulating one or more independent variables and measuring their effect on one or more dependent variables, while controlling for the extraneous variables.

Exploratory research A research design characterised by a flexible and evolving approach to understand marketing phenomena that are inherently difficult to measure.

Expressive technique A projective technique in which participants are presented with a verbal or visual situation and are asked to relate the feelings and attitudes of other people to the situation.

External analysis of preferences A method of configuring a spatial map such that the ideal points or vectors based on preference data are fitted in a spatial map derived from the perception data.

External data Data that originate outside the organisation.

External suppliers Outside marketing research companies hired to supply marketing research services.

External validity A determination of whether the cause-and-effect relationships found in the experiment can be generalised.

Extraneous variables Variables, other than dependent and independent variables, which may influence the results of an experiment.

Eye tracking equipment Instruments that record the gaze movements of the eye.

F

F distribution A frequency distribution that depends upon two sets of degrees of freedom: the degrees of freedom in the numerator and the degrees of freedom in the denominator.

F statistic The ratio of two sample variances.

F test A statistical test of the equality of the variances of two populations.

Factor An underlying dimension that explains the correlations among a set of variables.

Factor analysis A class of procedures primarily used for data reduction and summarisation.

Factor scores Composite scores estimated for each participant on the derived factors.

Factorial design A statistical experimental design used to measure the effects of two or more independent variables at various levels and to allow for interactions between variables.

Factors Categorical independent variables in ANOVA. The independent variables must all be categorical (non-metric) to use ANOVA.

Field environment An experimental location set in actual market conditions.

Field force Both the actual interviewers and the supervisors involved in data collection.

Field notes A log or diary of observations, events and reflections made by a researcher as a study is planned, implemented and analysed.

Field services Companies whose primary service is offering their expertise in collecting data for research projects.

Filter question An initial question in a questionnaire that screens potential participants to ensure they meet the requirements of the sample.

Fixed-response alternative questions Questions that require participants to choose from a set of predetermined answers.

Focus group A discussion conducted by a trained moderator among a small group of participants in an unstructured and natural manner.

Forced rating scale A rating scale that forces participants to express an opinion because a 'no opinion' or 'no knowledge' option is not provided.

Frequency distribution A mathematical distribution whose objective is to obtain a count of the number of responses associated with different values of one variable and to express these counts in percentage terms.

Friendship pair A technique used to interview children as two friends or classmates together.

Frugging The use of marketing research to deliberately disguise fundraising activities.

Full-service suppliers Companies that offer a full range of marketing research activities.

Full-text databases Databases that contain the complete text of secondary source documents comprising the database.

Functional equivalence A construct equivalence issue that deals specifically with whether a given concept or behaviour serves the same role or function in different countries.

Funnel approach A strategy for ordering questions in a questionnaire in which the sequence starts with the general questions, which are followed by progressively specific questions, to prevent specific questions from biasing general questions.

G

Galvanic skin response Changes in the electrical resistance of the skin that relate to a participant's affective state.

Gamma A test statistic that measures the association between two ordinal-level variables. It does not make an adjustment for ties.

Generalisability The degree to which a study based on a sample applies to the population as a whole.

Geodemographic classification This groups consumers together based on the types of neighbourhood in which they live. If a set of neighbourhoods are similar across a wide range of demographic measures, they may also offer similar potential across most products, brands, services and media.

Geodemographic information system (GIS) At a base level, a GIS matches geographic information with demographic information. This match allows subsequent data analyses to be presented on maps.

Graphic rating scale *See* Continuous rating scale.

Graphical models Analytical models that provide a visual picture of the relationships between variables.

Grounded theory A qualitative approach to generating theory through the systematic and simultaneous process of data collection and analysis.

H

Hierarchical clustering A clustering procedure characterised by the development of a hierarchy or treelike structure.

Histogram A vertical bar chart in which the height of the bar represents the relative or cumulative frequency of occurrence.

History Specific events that are external to the experiment but that occur at the same time as the experiment.

Hit ratio The percentage of cases correctly classified by discriminant analysis.

Hybrid conjoint analysis A form of conjoint analysis that can simplify the data collection task and estimate selected interactions as well as all main effects.

Hypothesis An unproven statement or proposition about a factor or phenomenon that is of interest to a researcher.

I

Identification information A type of information obtained in a questionnaire that includes name, address and phone number.

Implicit alternative An alternative that is not explicitly expressed.

Implicit assumptions An assumption that is not explicitly stated in a question.

Imputation A method to adjust for non-response by assigning the characteristic of interest to the non-participants based on the similarity of the variables available for both non-participants and participants.

Incidence rate Refers to the rate of occurrence or the percentage of persons eligible to participate in a study.

Independent samples The samples are independent if they are drawn randomly from different populations.

Independent variables Variables that are manipulated by the researcher and whose effects are measured and compared.

In-depth interview An unstructured, direct, personal interview in which a single participant is probed by an experienced interviewer to uncover underlying motivations, beliefs, attitudes and feelings on a topic.

Indirect approach A type of qualitative research in which the purposes of the project are disguised from the participants.

Induction A form of reasoning that usually involves the inference that an instance or repeated combination of events may be universally generalised.

Instrumentation An extraneous variable involving changes in the measuring instrument, in the observers, or in the scores themselves.

Interaction When assessing the relationship between two variables, an interaction occurs if the effect of X_1 depends on the level of X_2, and vice versa.

Interactive testing effect An effect in which a prior measurement affects the test unit's response to the independent variable.

Interdependence technique A multivariate statistical technique in which the whole set of interdependent relationships is examined.

Interdependence techniques Multivariate statistical techniques that attempt to group data based on underlying similarity and thus allow for interpretation of the data structures. No distinction is made as to which variables are dependent and which are independent.

Internal analysis of preferences A method of configuring a spatial map such that the spatial map represents both brands or stimuli and participant points or vectors and is derived solely from the preference data.

Internal consistency reliability An approach for assessing the internal consistency of a set of items, where several items are summed in order to form a total score for the scale.

Internal data Data available within the organisation for whom the research is being conducted.

Internal secondary data Data held within an organisation for some purpose other than a research problem at hand.

Internal validity A measure of accuracy of an experiment. It measures whether the manipulation of the independent variables, or treatments, actually caused the effects on the dependent variable(s).

Interquartile range The range of a distribution encompassing the middle 50% of the observations.

Interval scale A scale in which the numbers are used to rank objects such that numerically equal distances on the scale represent equal distances in the characteristic being measured.

Intra-cultural analysis Within-country analysis of international data.

Itemised rating scale A measurement scale having numbers or brief descriptions associated with each category. The categories are ordered in terms of scale position.

J

Judgemental sampling A form of convenience sampling in which the population elements are purposely selected based on the judgement of the researcher.

K

k-sample median test A non-parametric test used to examine differences among more than two groups when the dependent variable is measured on an ordinal scale.

Kolmogorov–Smirnov (K–S) one-sample test A one-sample non-parametric goodness-of-fit test that compares the cumulative distribution function for a variable with a specified distribution.

Kolmogorov–Smirnov (K–S) two-sample test Non-parametric test statistic that determines whether two distributions are the same. It takes into account any differences in the two distributions, including median, dispersion and skewness.

Kruskal–Wallis one-way ANOVA A non-metric ANOVA test that uses the rank value of each case, not merely its location relative to the median.

Kurtosis A measure of the relative peakedness of the curve defined by the frequency distribution.

L

Laboratory environment An artificial setting for experimentation in which the researcher constructs the desired conditions.

Laddering A technique for conducting in-depth interviews in which a line of questioning proceeds from product characteristics to user characteristics.

Latin square design A statistical design that allows for the statistical control of two non-interacting external variables in addition to the manipulation of the independent variable.

Leading question A question that gives the participant a clue as to what the answer should be.

Least squares procedure A technique for fitting a straight line into a scattergram by minimising the vertical distances of all the points from the line.

Level of significance The probability of making a Type I error.

Lifestyles Distinctive patterns of living described by the activities people engage in, the interests they have, and the opinions they hold of themselves and the world around them.

Likert scale A measurement scale with five response categories ranging from 'strongly disagree' to 'strongly agree' that requires participants to indicate a degree of agreement or disagreement with each of a series of statements related to the stimulus objects.

Limited-service suppliers Companies that specialise in one or a few phases of a marketing research project.

Line chart A chart that connects a series of data points using continuous lines.

Linguistic equivalence The equivalence of both spoken and written language forms used in scales and questionnaires.

Linkage methods Agglomerative methods of hierarchical clustering that cluster objects based on a computation of the distance between them.

Listening Listening involves the evaluation of naturally occurring conversations, behaviours and signals. This information that is elicited may or may not be guided, but it brings the voice of consumers' lives to brand.

Longitudinal design A type of research design involving a fixed sample of population elements measured repeatedly. The sample remains the same over time, thus providing a series of pictures that, when viewed together, vividly illustrate the situation and the changes that are taking place.

Loyalty card At face value, a sales promotion device used by supermarkets, pharmacists, department stores, petrol stations and even whole shopping centres and towns to encourage repeat purchases. For the marketing researcher, the loyalty card is a device that can link customer characteristics to actual product purchases.

M

Mahalanobis procedure A stepwise procedure used in discriminant analysis to maximise a generalised measure of the distance between the two closest groups.

Main testing effect An effect of testing occurring when a prior observation affects a later observation.

Mann–Whitney _U_ test A statistical test for a variable measured on an ordinal scale, comparing the differences in the location of two populations based on observations from two independent samples.

Market research reports and advisory services Companies which provide off-the-shelf reports as well as data and briefs on a range of markets, consumer types and issues.

Marketing decision problem The problem confronting the marketing decision-maker, which asks what the decision-maker has to do.

Marketing intelligence Qualified observations of events and developments in the marketing environment.

Marketing research A key element within the total field of marketing information. It links the consumer, customer and public to the marketer through information which is used to identify and define marketing opportunities and problems; to generate, refine and evaluate marketing actions; and to improve understanding of marketing as a process and of the ways in which specific marketing activities can be made more effective.

Marketing Research Online Community An invited group of consumers with a common focus on a particular brand. This group is brought together online to develop conversations and to react to set quantitative and qualitative tasks.

Marketing research problem A problem that entails determining what information is needed and how it can be obtained in the most feasible way.

Marketing research process A set of six steps which define the tasks to be accomplished in conducting a marketing research study. These include problem definition, developing an approach to the problem, research design formulation, fieldwork, data integrity and analysis, and report generation and presentation.

Matching A method of controlling extraneous variables that involves matching participants on a set of key background variables before assigning them to the treatment conditions.

Mathematical models Analytical models that explicitly describe the relationship between variables, usually in equation form.

Maturation An extraneous variable attributable to changes in the test units themselves that occur with the passage of time.

Mean The average; that value obtained by summing all elements in a set and dividing by the number of elements.

Measure of location A statistic that describes a location within a dataset. Measures of central tendency describe the centre of the distribution.

Measure of variability A statistic that indicates the distribution's dispersion.

Measurement The assignment of numbers or other symbols to characteristics of objects according to certain pre-specified rules.

Measurement error The variation in the information sought by the researcher and the information generated by the measurement process employed.

Measurement equivalence Deals with the comparability of responses to particular (sets of) items. Measurement equivalence includes configural (structural), metric (measurement unit) and scalar equivalence.

Media panels A data gathering technique composed of samples of participants whose TV viewing behaviour is automatically recorded by electronic devices, supplementing the purchase information recorded in a diary.

Median A measure of central tendency given as the value above which half of the values fall and below which half of the values fall.

Metric data Data that are interval or ratio in nature.

Metric equivalence See Scalar equivalence.

Metric MDS An MDS scaling method that assumes the input data are metric.

Metric scale A scale that is either interval or ratio in nature.

Missing responses Values of a variable that are unknown because the participants concerned provided ambiguous answers to the question or because their answers were not properly recorded.

Mode A measure of central tendency given as the value that occurs with the most frequency in a sample distribution.

Model fit Model fit is determined by comparing how closely the estimated covariance matrix Σk matches the observed (sample) covariance matrix $\mathbf{S}$, i.e. the fit statistics are based on $|\mathbf{S} - \Sigma k|$.

Model identification Model identification concerns whether there is enough information in the covariance matrix to enable us to estimate a set of structural equations.

Moderator An individual who conducts a focus group interview, by setting the purpose of the interview, questioning, probing and handling the process of discussion.

Monadic scale See Non-comparative scale.

Mood board A collage created in a focus group setting. Focus group participants are asked to snip words and pictures from magazines that they see as representing the values a particular brand is perceived to have. In some circumstances, collages can also be made up from audio- and videotapes.

Mortality An extraneous variable attributable to the loss of test units while the experiment is in progress.

Multicollinearity A state of high intercorrelations among independent variables.

Multidimensional scaling (MDS) A class of procedures for representing perceptions and preferences of participants spatially by means of a visual display.

Multi-item scale A multi-item scale consists of multiple items, where an item is a single question or statement to be evaluated.

Multiple comparison tests A posteriori contrasts that enable the researcher to construct generalised confidence intervals that can be used to make pairwise comparisons of all treatment means.

Multiple cross-sectional design A cross-sectional design in which there are two or more samples of participants, and information from each sample is obtained only once.

Multiple discriminant analysis Discriminant analysis technique where the criterion variable involves three or more categories.

Multiple regression A statistical technique that simultaneously develops a mathematical relationship between two or more independent variables and an interval-scaled dependent variable.

Multiple regression model An equation used to explain the results of multiple regression analysis.

Multiple time series design A time series design that includes another group of test units to serve as a control group.

Multiple η_2 The strength of the joint effect of two (or more) factors, or the overall effect.

Multivariate ANOVA (MANOVA) An ANOVA technique using two or more metric dependent variables.

Multivariate techniques Statistical techniques suitable for analysing data when there are two or more measurements on each element and the variables are analysed simultaneously. Multivariate techniques are concerned with the simultaneous relationships among two or more phenomena.

Mystery shopper An observer visiting providers of goods and services as if they were really a customer, and recording characteristics of the service delivery.

N

_n_-way analysis of variance An ANOVA model where two or more factors are involved.

Natural observation Observing behaviour as it takes place in the environment.

Netnography An adaptation of ethnography that analyses the free behaviour of individuals in online environments.

Neuromarketing The application of neuroscience in marketing, primarily to measure emotions through brain imaging.

Nominal scale A scale whose numbers serve only as labels or tags for identifying and classifying objects with a strict one-to-one correspondence between the numbers and the objects.

Nomological validity A type of validity that assesses the relationship between theoretical constructs. It seeks to confirm significant correlations between the constructs as predicted by a theory.

Non-comparative scale One of two types of scaling techniques in which each stimulus object is scaled independently of the other objects in the stimulus set. Also called monadic scale.

Non-hierarchical clustering A procedure that first assigns or determines a cluster centre and then groups all objects within a pre-specified threshold value from the centre.

Non-metric ANOVA An ANOVA technique for examining the difference in the central tendencies of more than two groups when the dependent variable is measured on an ordinal scale.

Non-metric correlation A correlation measure for two non-metric variables that relies on rankings to compute the correlation.

Non-metric data Data derived from a nominal or ordinal scale.

Non-metric MDS A type of MDS which assumes that the input data are ordinal.

Non-metric scale A scale that is either nominal or ordinal in nature.

Non-parametric tests Hypothesis testing procedures that assume that the variables are measured on a nominal or ordinal scale.

Non-probability sampling Sampling techniques that do not use chance selection procedures but rather rely on the personal judgement of the researcher.

Non-response bias Bias caused when actual participants differ from those who refuse to participate.

Non-response error A type of non-sampling error that occurs when some of the participants included in the sample do not respond. This error may be defined as the variation between the true mean value of the variable in the original sample and the true mean value in the net sample.

Non-sampling error An error that can be attributed to sources other than sampling and that can be random or non-random.

Null hypothesis A statement in which no difference or effect is expected. If the null hypothesis is not rejected, no changes will be made.

Numeric databases Databases containing numerical and statistical information that may be important sources of secondary data.

O

Objective evidence Perceived to be unbiased evidence, supported by empirical findings.

Oblique rotation Rotation of factors when the axes are not maintained at right angles.

Omega squared (ω^2) A measure indicating the proportion of the variation in the dependent variable that is related to a particular independent variable or factor.

Omnibus survey A distinctive form of survey that serves the needs of a syndicated group. The omnibus survey targets particular types of participants such as those in specific geographic locations, e.g. Luxembourg residents, or consumers of particular types of products, e.g. business air travellers. With that target group of participants, a core set of questions can be asked, with other questions added as syndicate members wish.

One-group pretest–post-test design A pre-experimental design in which a group of participants is measured twice.

One-shot case study A pre-experimental design in which a single group of participants is exposed to a treatment X, and then a single measurement of the dependent variable is taken.

One-tailed test A test of the null hypothesis where the alternative hypothesis is expressed directionally.

One-way analysis of variance An ANOVA technique in which there is only one factor.

Online community providers Build online research communities where researchers can employ a wide variety of quantitative and qualitative techniques to connect to consumers.

Online databases Databases that require a telecommunications network to access.

Online focus groups and streaming Provide platforms for running online focus groups and streaming the results.

Online services Companies which specialise in the use of the Internet to collect, analyse and distribute marketing research information.

Operational data Data generated about an organisation's customers, through day-to-day transactions.

Operational equivalence A type of equivalence that measures how theoretical constructs are operationalised in different countries to measure marketing variables.

Operationalised The derivation of measurable characteristics to encapsulate marketing phenomena, e.g. the concept of 'customer loyalty' can be operationalised through measurements such as frequency of repeat purchases or the number of years that a business relationship has existed.

Optimising partitioning method A non-hierarchical clustering method that allows for later reassignment of objects to clusters to optimise an overall criterion.

Order The relative sizes or positions of the descriptors. Order is denoted by descriptors such as greater than, less than and equal to.

Ordinal interaction An interaction where the rank order of the effects attributable to one factor does not change across the levels of the second factor.

Ordinal scale A ranking scale in which numbers are assigned to objects to indicate the relative extent to which some characteristic is possessed. Thus, it is possible to determine whether an object has more or less of a characteristic than some other object.

Origin The origin characteristic means that the scale has a unique or fixed beginning or true zero point.

Orthogonal rotation Rotation of factors in which the axes are maintained at right angles.

P

p value This is the probability of observing a value of the test statistic as extreme as, or more extreme than, the value actually observed, assuming that the null hypothesis is true.

Paired comparison scaling A comparative scaling technique in which a participant is presented with two objects at a time and asked to select one object in the pair according to some criterion. The data obtained are ordinal in nature.

Paired samples The samples are paired when the data for the two samples relate to the same group of participants.

Paired samples t test A test for differences in the means of paired samples.

Pairwise deletion A method for handling missing responses in which all cases or participants with any missing responses are not automatically discarded; rather, for each calculation, only the cases or participants with complete responses are considered.

Pan-cultural analysis Across-countries analysis in which the data for all participants from all the countries are pooled and analysed.

Panel A sample of participants who have agreed to provide information at specified intervals over an extended period.

Panel providers Provide access to consumer, b2b and specialist panels of participants alongside scripting and hosting surveys.

Paradigm A set of assumptions consisting of agreed-upon knowledge, criteria of judgement, problem fields and ways to consider them.

Parallel threshold method A non-hierarchical clustering method that specifies several cluster centres at once. All objects that are within a pre-specified threshold value from the centre are grouped together.

Parallel translation A translation method in which a committee of translators, each of whom is fluent in at least two languages, discuss alternative versions of a questionnaire and make modifications until consensus is reached.

Parametric tests Hypothesis testing procedures that assume that the variables of interest are measured on at least an interval scale.

Part correlation coefficient A measure of the correlation between Y and X when the linear effects of the other independent variables have been removed from X (but not from Y).

Partial correlation coefficient A measure of the association between two variables after controlling or adjusting for the effects of one or more additional variables.

Personal observation An observational research strategy in which human observers record the phenomenon being observed as it occurs.

Personification technique Participants are asked to imagine that the brand is a person and then describe characteristics of that person.

Phi coefficient (ϕ) A measure of the strength of association in the special case of a table with two rows and two columns (a 2×2 table).

Picture response technique A projective technique in which participants are shown a picture and are asked to tell a story describing it.

Pie chart A round chart divided into sections.

Pilot-testing Testing the questionnaire on a small sample of particpants for the purpose of improving the questionnaire by identifying and eliminating potential problems.

Population The aggregate of all the elements, sharing some common set of characteristics, that comprise the universe for the purpose of the marketing research problem.

Position bias See Order bias.

Positivism A philosophy of language and logic consistent with an empiricist philosophy of science.

Post-test-only control group design Experimental design in which the experimental group is exposed to the treatment but the control group is not and no pretest measure is taken.

Power of a statistical test The probability of rejecting the null hypothesis when it is in fact false and should be rejected.

Pre-coding In questionnaire design, assigning a code to every conceivable response before data collection.

Predictive validity A type of validity that is concerned with how well a scale can forecast a future criterion.

Pre-experimental designs Designs that do not control for extraneous factors by randomisation.

Pretest–post-test control group design An experimental design in which the experimental group is exposed to the treatment but the control group is not. Pretest and post-test measures are taken on both groups.

Primary data Data originated by the researcher specifically to address the research problem.

Principal axis factoring See Common factor analysis.

Principal components analysis An approach to factor analysis that considers the total variance in the data.

Probability proportionate to size (PPS) A selection method where the probability of selecting a sampling unit in a selected cluster varies inversely with the size of the cluster. Therefore, the size of all the resulting clusters is approximately equal.

Probability sampling A sampling procedure in which each element of the population has a fixed probabilistic chance of being selected for the sample.

Probing A motivational technique used when asking questions to induce the participants to enlarge on, clarify or explain their answers.

Problem audit A comparative examination of a marketing problem to understand its origin and nature.

Problem definition A broad statement of the general problem and identification of the specific components of the marketing research problem.

Problem identification research Research undertaken to help identify problems that are not necessarily apparent on the surface, yet exist or are likely to arise in the future.

Problem-solving research Research undertaken to help solve marketing problems.

Product moment correlation (r) A statistic summarising the strength of association between two metric variables.

Projective technique An unstructured and indirect form of questioning that encourages participants to project their underlying motivations, beliefs, attitudes or feelings regarding the issues of concern.

Psycho-galvanometer An instrument that measures a participant's galvanic skin response.

Psychographics Quantified profiles of individuals based upon lifestyle characteristics.

Pupilometer An instrument that measures changes in the eye pupil diameter.

Purchase panels A data gathering technique in which participant's record their purchases in a diary.

Q

Q-sort scaling A comparative scaling technique that uses a rank order procedure to sort objects based on similarity with respect to some criterion.

Quantitative observation The recording and counting of behavioural patterns of people, objects and events in a systematic manner to obtain information about the phenomenon of interest.

Quantitative research Research techniques that seek to quantify data and, typically, apply some form of statistical analysis.

Quasi-experimental designs Designs that apply part of the procedures of true experimentation yet lack full experimental control.

Questionnaire A structured technique for data collection consisting of a series of questions, written or verbal, that a participant's answers.

Quota sampling A non-probability sampling technique that is two-stage restricted judgemental sampling. The first stage consists of developing control categories or quotas of population elements. In the second stage, sample elements are selected based on convenience or judgement.

R

Random error An error that arises from random changes or differences in participants or measurement situations.

Random sampling error The error because the particular sample selected is an imperfect repesentation of the population of interest. It may be defined as the variation between the true mean value for the sample and the true mean value of the population.

Randomisation A method of controlling extraneous variables that involves randomly assigning test units to experimental groups by using random numbers. Treatment conditions are also randomly assigned to experimental groups.

Randomised block design A statistical design in which the test units are blocked on the basis of an external variable to ensure that the various experimental and control groups are matched closely on that variable.

Range The difference between the smallest and largest values of a distribution.

Rank order scaling A comparative scaling technique in which participants are presented with several objects simultaneously and asked to order or rank them according to some criterion.

Ratio scale The highest scale. This scale allows the researcher to identify or classify objects, rank order the objects, and compare intervals or differences. It is also meaningful to compute ratios of scale values.

Regression analysis A statistical procedure for analysing associative relationships between a metric-dependent variable and one or more independent variables.

Reliability The extent to which a scale produces consistent results if repeated measurements are made on the characteristic.

Repeated measures ANOVA An ANOVA technique used when participants are exposed to more than one treatment condition and repeated measurements are obtained.

Reporting Offers research companies reporting solutions that seek to engage clients in oral and electronic presentations beyond conventional reporting methods such as hard-copy reports and PowerPoint.

Research brief A document produced by the users of research findings or the buyers of a piece of marketing research. The brief is used to communicate the perceived requirements of a marketing research project.

Research design A framework or blueprint for conducting the marketing research project. It specifies the details of the procedures necessary for obtaining the information needed to structure or solve marketing research problems.

Research proposal The official layout of the planned marketing research activity.

Research questions Refined statements of the specific components of the problem.

Residual The difference between the observed value of Y_i and the value predicted by the regression equation $\hat{Y}_i$.

Response error A type of non-sampling error arising from participants who do respond but who give inaccurate answers or whose answers are mis-recorded or mis-analysed. It may be defined as a variation between the true mean value of the variable in the net sample and the observed mean value obtained in the market research project.

Response latency The amount of time it takes to respond to a question.

Response rate The percentage of the total attempted interviews that are completed.

Role playing Participants are asked to assume the behaviour of someone else.

Runs test A test of randomness for a dichotomous variable.

S

Sample A subgroup of the elements of the population selected for participation in the study.

Sample control The ability of the survey mode to reach the units specified in the sample effectively and efficiently.

Sample size The number of elements to be included in a study.

Sampling control An aspect of supervising that ensures that the interviewers strictly follow the sampling plan rather than select sampling units based on convenience or accessibility.

Sampling distribution The distribution of the values of a sample statistic computed for each possible sample that could be drawn from the target population under a specified sampling plan.

Sampling frame A representation of the elements of the target population that consists of a list or set of directions for identifying the target population.

Sampling unit An element, or a unit containing the element, that is available for selection at some stage of the sampling process.

Sampling with replacement A sampling technique in which an element can be included in the sample more than once.

Sampling without replacement A sampling technique in which an element cannot be included in the sample more than once.

Scalar equivalence The demonstration that two individuals from different countries with the same value on some variable will score at the same level on the same test. Also called metric equivalence.

Scale transformation A manipulation of scale values to ensure compatibility with other scales or otherwise to make the data suitable for analysis.

Scaling The generation of a continuum upon which measured objects are located.

Scanner data Data obtained by passing merchandise over a laser scanner that reads the UPC from the packages.

Scanner diary panels Scanner data where panel members are identified by an ID card, allowing information about each panel member's purchases to be stored with respect to the the individual shopper.

Scanner diary panels with cable TV The combination of a scanner diary panel with manipulations of the advertising that is being broadcast by cable TV companies.

Secondary data Data collected for some purpose other than the problem at hand.

Selection bias An extraneous variable attributable to the improper assignment of test units to treatment conditions.

Semantic differential A seven-point rating scale with end points associated with bipolar labels.

Semiotics The study of signs in the context of consumer experience.

Sentence completion A projective technique in which participants are presented with a number of incomplete sentences and are asked to complete them.

Sequential threshold method A non-hierarchical clustering method in which a cluster centre is selected and all objects within a pre-specified threshold value from the centre are grouped together.

Shadow team A small cross-functional boundary spanning group that learns everything about a competitive unit.

Sign test A non-parametric test for examining differences in the location of two populations, based on paired populations, that compares only the signs of the differences between pairs of variables without taking into account the magnitude of the differences.

Significance of the interaction effect A test of the significance of the interaction between two or more independent variables.

Significance of the main effect of each factor A test of the significance of the main effect for each individual factor.

Significance of the overall effect A test that some differences exist between some of the treatment groups.

Simple random sampling (SRS) A probability sampling technique in which each element has a known and equal probability of selection. Every element is selected independently of every other element, and the sample is drawn by a random procedure from a sampling frame.

Simulated test market A quasi-test market in which participants are preselected; they are then interviewed and observed on their purchases and attitudes towards the product.

Single cross-sectional design A cross-sectional design in which one sample of participants is drawn from the target population and information is obtained from this sample once.

Single linkage A linkage method based on minimum distance or the nearest neighbour rule.

Skewness A characteristic of a distribution that assesses its symmetry about the mean.

Snowball sampling A non-probability sampling technique in which an initial group of participants is selected randomly. Subsequent participants are selected based on the referrals or information provided by the initial participants. By obtaining referrals from referrals, this process may be carried out in waves.

Social desirability The tendency of respondents to give answers that may not be accurate but may be desirable from a social standpoint.

Software providers Provide software packages that create platforms to script, host and analyse surveys, or Software as a Service (SaaS) options.

Solomon four-group design An experimental design that explicitly controls for interactive testing effects, in addition to controlling for all the other extraneous variables.

Special-purpose databases Databases that contain information of a specific nature, e.g. data on a specialised industry.

Specific components of the problem The second part of the marketing research problem definition that focuses on the key aspects of the problem and provides clear guidelines on how to proceed further.

Specification search An empirical approach that uses the model diagnostics and trial and error to find a better fitting model.

Split-half reliability A form of internal consistency reliability in which the items constituting the scale are divided into two halves and the resulting half scores are correlated.

Standard deviation The square root of the variance.

Standard error The standard deviation of the sampling distribution of the mean or proportion.

Standard test market A test market in which the product is sold through regular distribution channels. For example, no special considerations are given to products simply because they are being test marketed.

Standardisation The process of correcting data to reduce them to the same scale by subtracting the sample mean and dividing by the standard deviation.

Standardised residuals Used as a diagnostic measure of model fit, these are residuals, each divided by its standard error.

Stapel scale A scale for measuring attitudes that consists of a single adjective in the middle of an even-numbered range of values.

Static group A pre-experimental design in which there are two groups: the experimental group (EG), which is exposed to the treatment, and the control group (CG). Measurements on both groups are made only after the treatment, and test units are not assigned at random.

Statistical control A method of controlling extraneous variables by measuring the extraneous variables and adjusting for their effects through statistical methods.

Statistical designs Designs that allow for the statistical control and analysis of external variables.

Statistical inference The process of generalising the sample results to a target population.

Statistical regression An extraneous variable that occurs when test units with extreme scores move closer to the average score during the course of the experiment.

Stepwise discriminant analysis Discriminant analysis in which the predictors are entered sequentially based on their ability to discriminate between the groups.

Stepwise regression A regression procedure in which the predictor variables enter or leave the regression equation one at a time.

Story completion A projective technique in which participants are provided with part of a story and are required to give the conclusion in their own words.

Stratified sampling A probability sampling technique that uses a two-step process to partition the population into subsequent subpopulations, or strata. Elements are selected from each stratum by a random procedure.

Structural equation modelling (SEM) Collection of statistical techniques including factor analysis and multiple regression. It allows the researcher to examine relationships between several continuous or discrete independent variables and several continuous or discrete dependant variables. The independent and dependent variables can be latent or measured variables.

Structured data collection Use of a formal questionnaire that presents questions in a prearranged order.

Structured observation Observation where the researcher clearly defines the behaviours to be observed and the techniques by which they will be measured.

Structured questions Questions that pre-specify the set of response alternatives and the response format. A structured question could be multiple-choice, dichotomous or a scale.

Substitution A procedure that substitutes for non-respondents other elements from the sampling frame who are expected to respond.

Sugging The use of marketing research to deliberately disguise a sales effort.

Surrogate variables A subset of original variables selected for use in subsequent analysis.

Survey method A structured questionnaire administered to a sample of a target population, designed to elicit specific information from participants.

Survey techniques Techniques based upon the use of structured questionnaires given to a sample of a population.

Surveys Interviews with a large number of people using a questionnaire.

Symmetric lambda The symmetric lambda does not make an assumption about which variable is dependent. It measures the overall improvement when prediction is done in both directions.

Syndicated services Companies that collect and sell common pools of data designed to serve information needs shared by a number of clients.

Syndicated sources (services) Information services offered by marketing research organisations that provide information from a common database to different firms that subscribe to their services.

Systematic error An error that affects the measurement in a constant way and represents stable factors that affect the observed score in the same way each time the measurement is made.

Systematic sampling A probability sampling technique in which the sample is chosen by selecting a random starting point and then picking every *i*th element in succession from the sampling frame.

T

***t* distribution** A symmetrical bell-shaped distribution that is useful for sample testing ($n < 30$). It is similar to the normal distribution in appearance.

***t* statistic** A statistic that assumes that the variable has a symmetric bell-shaped distribution, that the mean is known (or assumed to be known), and that the population variance is estimated from the sample.

***t* test** A univariate hypothesis test using the *t* distribution, which is used when the standard deviation is unknown and the sample size is small.

Target population The collection of elements or objects that possess the information sought by the researcher and about which inferences are to be made.

tau *b* A test statistic that measures the association between two ordinal-level variables. It makes an adjustment for ties and is the most appropriate when the table of variables is square.

tau *c* A test statistic that measures the association between two ordinal-level variables. It makes an adjustment for ties and is most appropriate when the table of variables is not square but a rectangle.

Telescoping A psychological phenomenon that takes place when an individual telescopes or compresses time by remembering an event as occurring more recently than it actually occurred.

Territorial map A tool for assessing discriminant analysis results by plotting the group membership of each case on a graph.

Test market A carefully selected part of the marketplace particularly suitable for test marketing.

Test marketing An application of a controlled experiment done in limited, but carefully selected, test markets. It involves a replication of the planned national marketing programme for a product in test markets.

Test statistic A measure of how close the sample has come to the null hypothesis. It often follows a well-known distribution, such as the normal, *t*, or chi-square distribution.

Test units Participants, organisations or other entities whose response to independent variables or treatments is being studied.

Testing effects Effects caused by the process of experimentation.

Test–retest reliability An approach for assessing reliability, in which respondents are administered identical sets of scale items at two different times, under as nearly equivalent conditions as possible.

Thematic maps Maps that solve marketing problems. They combine geography with demographic information and a company's sales data or other proprietary information and are generated by a computer.

Theoretical sampling Data gathering driven by concepts derived from evolving theory and based on the concept of 'making comparisons'.

Theory A conceptual scheme based on foundational statements, or axioms, that are assumed to be true.

Third-person technique A projective technique in which participants are presented with a verbal or visual situation and are asked to relate the beliefs and attitudes of a third person in that situation.

Time series design A quasi-experimental design that involves periodic measurements of the dependent variable for a group of participants. Then the treatment is administered by the researcher or occurs naturally. After the treatment, periodic measurements are continued to determine the treatment effect.

Topic guide A list of topics, questions and probes that are used by a moderator to help manage a focus group discussion.

Total error The variation between the true mean value in the population of the variable of interest and the observed mean value obtained in the marketing research project

Trace analysis An approach in which data collection is based on physical traces, or evidence, of past behaviour.

Transcripts 'Hard copies' of the questions and probes and the corresponding answers and responses in focus group or in-depth interviews.

Transitivity of preference An assumption made to convert paired comparison data with rank order data. It implies that if Brand A is preferred to Brand B, and Brand B is preferred to Brand C, then Brand A is preferred to Brand C.

Treatment In ANOVA, a particular combination of factor levels or categories.

Trend analysis A method of adjusting for non-response in which the researcher tries to discern a trend between early and late participants. This trend is projected to non-participants to estimate their characteristic of interest.

Triangulation A process that facilitates the validation of data through cross-verification from more than two sources.

True experimental designs Experimental designs distinguished by the fact that the researcher can randomly assign test units to experimental groups and also randomly assign treatments to experimental groups.

True score model A mathematical model that provides a framework for understanding the accuracy of measurement.

Two-group discriminant analysis Discriminant analysis technique where the criterion variable has two categories.

Two-sample median test Non-parametric test statistic that determines whether two groups are drawn from populations with the same median. This test is not as powerful as the Mann–Whitney U test.

Two-tailed test A test of the null hypothesis where the alternative hypothesis is not expressed directionally.

Type I error An error that occurs when the sample results lead to the rejection of a null hypothesis that is in fact true. Also known as alpha error (α).

Type II error An error that occurs when the sample results lead to acceptance of a null hypothesis that is in fact false. Also known as beta error (β).

U

Univariate techniques Statistical techniques appropriate for analysing data when there is a single measurement of each element in the sample, or, if there are several measurements on each element, when each variable is analysed in isolation.

Unstructured observation Observation that involves a researcher monitoring all relevant phenomena, without specifying the details in advance.

Unstructured questions Open-ended questions that participants answer in their own words.

V

Validation sample That part of the total sample used to check the results of the estimation sample.

Validity The extent to which a measurement represents characteristics that exist in the phenomenon under investigation.

Variable respecification The transformation of data to create new variables or the modification of existing variables so that they are more consistent with the objectives of the study.

Variance The mean squared deviation of all the values of the mean.

Variance method An agglomerative method of hierarchical clustering in which clusters are generated to minimise the within-cluster variance.

Varimax procedure An orthogonal method of factor rotation that minimises the number of variables with high loadings on a factor, thereby enhancing the interpretability of the factors.

Verbal models Analytical models that provide a written representation of the relationships between variables.

Verbal protocol A technique used to understand participants' cognitive responses or thought processes by having them think aloud while completing a task or making a decision.

Voice pitch analysis Measurement of emotional reactions through changes in the participant's voice.

Volume tracking data Scanner data that provide information on purchases by brand, size, price and flavour or formulation.

W

Ward's procedure A variance method in which the squared Euclidean distance to the cluster means is minimised.

Web analytics The process of collection, measurement and analysis of user activity on a website to understand and help achieve the intended objective of that website.

Weighting A statistical procedure that attempts to account for non-response by assigning differential weights to the data depending on the response rates.

Wilcoxon matched-pairs signed-ranks test A non-parametric test that analyses the differences between the paired observations, taking into account the magnitude of the differences.

Word association A projective technique in which participants are presented with a list of words, one at a time. After each word, they are asked to give the first word that comes to mind.

Z

z test A univariate hypothesis test using the standard normal distribution.

z value The number of standard errors a point is away from the mean.

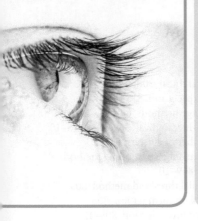

Subject Index

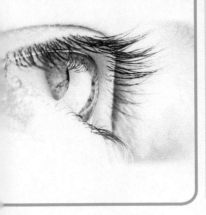

Name Index

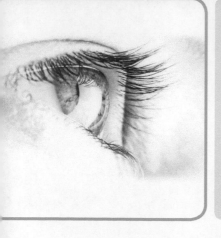

Company Index